Community Care Practice and the Law
Second Edition

Michael Mandelstam

Jessica Kingsley Publishers
London and Philadelphia

First edition published in 1995 by Jessica Kingsley Publishers.
This edition published in the United Kingdom in 1999 by

Jessica Kingsley Publishers Ltd,
116 Pentonville Road,
London N1 9JB, England

and

325 Chestnut Street,
Philadelphia
PA 19106, USA.

www.jkp.com

Second impression 1999
Third impression 2001

© Copyright 1999 Michael Mandelstam

Material from House of Commons Papers and Crown copyright
material reproduced with the permission of the Controller of Her Majesty's Stationary Office

Library of Congress Cataloging in Publication Data
Mandelstam, Michael, 1956 –
Community care practice and the law / Michael Mandelstam. -- 2nd ed.
p.cm. Includes bibliographical references and index.
ISBN 1 85302 647 6 (pbk. : alk. paper)
1. Public welfare -- Law and legislation -- Great Britain. 2. Social service-- Great Britain.
3. Community health services--Law and legislation--Great Britain. I. Title.
KD3299.M261998
344.41'0316--dc2198-37066
CIP

British Library Cataloguing in Publication Data
Mandelstam, Michael, 1956-
Community care practice and the law. - 2nd ed.
1. Public welfare – Law and legislation – Great Britain
2. Community health services – Law and legislation – Great
Britain 3. Social services – Great Britain
I. Title
344.4'1'0313

ISBN 1 85302 647 6

Printed and Bound in Great Britain by
Athenaeum Press, Gateshead, Tyne and Wear

CONTENTS

PART IV DISPUTES, LOCAL OMBUDSMAN INVESTIGATIONS AND LEGAL JUDGMENTS (DIGESTS OF CASES)

Acknowledgements

Community care is a large, complex and rapidly changing field. A significant difficulty in getting to grips with it is that information about what is going on (whether in law or practice) tends to be diverse, elusive and sometimes ill-reported. Thus my thanks are due to the many community care practitioners and managers, voluntary organisations, civil servants, lawyers, librarians and others, with whom I discuss matters during the course of my work generally – in the quest to hunt down the relevant information, without which this book would not have been possible. More specifically, Chapters 2 and 3 have benefited from the advice of my father, whilst as usual Jessica Kingsley and her staff have been immensely efficient, helpful and encouraging.

February 1999

Disclaimer

Every effort has been made to ensure that the information contained in this book is correct or at least represents a reasonable interpretation. None of the views I have expressed (as opposed to other people's views I have reported) represent those of any employer or contractor with whom I have been involved.

Not only is a book of this nature likely to contain errors, but the law is anyway subject to rapid change and to considerable uncertainty. Furthermore, particular situations and disputes possess their own unique set of circumstances and, whilst this book will provide detailed pointers, the reader should seek appropriate advice when attempting to solve particular problems, formulate legally sound policies, challenge decisions and so on.

PART I

OVERVIEW, UNDERLYING THEMES AND PRACTICAL CHECKLIST

CHAPTER I

INTRODUCTION

Coverage

1. How to use the book

2. Whom the book is for

3. Function

4. Scope

5. Sources

6. Approach

7. Changes from the first edition

1. HOW TO USE THE BOOK

This book can be used in different ways and at different levels. Chapter 2 summarises the community care system, which is dealt with chapter by chapter in the rest of the book. Chapter 3 picks out the underlying themes of community care, without which it is arguably impossible to understand how the system works. These two chapters provide a foundation; the reader is strongly recommended to look at both.

The practical checklist contained in Chapter 4 is intended to indicate the types of question which busy practitioners and managers need to ask – in order to test for the potential unlawfulness, of individual decisions, policies or criteria of eligibility. Cross referencing to the main text points to further detail if required.

Part II of the book deals with specific elements of community care in relation to local authority social services departments. A summary of *key points* introduces each chapter which is then divided into a series of numbered sections; each section in turn consists of a short *summary, extracts* from legislation and then *discussion*. The considerable detail contained in some of these chapters has not been included for the sake of it; it is the author's experience that local authority managers, staff and users of services find themselves enmired in just such detail and complexity.

Part III covers provision of services by the NHS and of home adaptations by housing authorities; though not legally defined as community care, such services are clearly essential to community care in its wider everyday meaning.

Part IV is introduced by Chapter 17 describing the various channels of redress and remedies available to people, ranging from the informal to judicial review in the law courts. Chapter 18 consists of a digest of local ombudsman investigations, to which the main text of the book makes full cross reference. However, they also stand alone in their own right and provide considerable insight into community care practice. Lastly, a digest of relevant legal cases is included in Chapter 19, to which, again, full cross reference is made from the main text. Like the ombudsman investigations, the legal cases stand in their own right as evidence and illustration of the disputes and problems that characterise community care.

2. WHOM THE BOOK IS FOR

The book has been written for a) the staff of local authority social services (and housing) departments, health authorities and NHS Trusts; b) voluntary and advice-giving organisations; c) interested users of services and carers; d) lawyers; e) academic staff and their students.

3. FUNCTION OF THE BOOK

The book brings together a wide range of information and analysis relating to community care practice and law. By including many practical examples and using non-legal language, the book attempts to bridge the gap between law and practice. Community care practice is – or at least should be – based on legislation, the decisions of the law courts and Department of Health guidance. It is important for all concerned to be aware of these sources. Neither service providers nor service users can understand fully what they are doing without being aware of relevant powers, duties, rights and remedies.

Few disputes reach the stage of formal legal proceedings, and few even get as far as social services complaints procedures or the local ombudsmen. Therefore, although the book aims to assist people involved in formal disputes, its predominant aim is to give useful information about legislation and guidance as a way of avoiding, not just solving, such disputes. For example, the statutory service manager who is well-informed is, hopefully, less likely to try to implement a legally dubious policy. Conversely, well-informed service users (or their representatives) are more likely to be able to challenge successfully, and perhaps informally, particular decisions or policies at the outset. Indeed, it appears that mainstream community care is ill understood not just by users of services but by the very local authority staff (including sometimes lawyers) who are responsible for community care services.

4. SCOPE OF THE BOOK

The book covers relevant social, health and housing services for various groups of vulnerable people including some elderly people, younger adults with disabilities (physical, sensory or learning), people with mental health needs, and people with drugs or alcohol problems.

'Community care services' as defined in legislation are provided by local authority social services departments. However, in the sense that community care is about caring for people in their own homes or in institutional accommodation, health and housing services are very much part of the picture. There are also practical reasons why all concerned need to know about the range of responsibilities across social, health and housing sectors. For example, a statutory authority might be planning services and demarcation of responsibilities between it and another authority (eg, between social services and the health service). It is clearly important that the authority is fully aware not only of its own legal powers and duties – but also those of the other authority. Conversely, for service users and their representatives or advisers, it is important to know the duties and responsibilities of different agencies; if one agency does not deliver a service, another might.

For reasons of space, the following have not been included in their own right, although references are made to them. They include children's services, state benefits including Social Fund payments, and the Independent Living Fund. In addition, the book does not apply to Scotland or Northern Ireland, where the legislation and guidance differ (but see eg, McKay, Patrick 1997 for Scotland; and Public Law Project 1995 for Northern Ireland). Generally speaking, Wales is covered for the most part in respect of the legislation, although the reader should be aware that the Welsh Office issues its own guidance.

5. SOURCES FOR THE BOOK

The book collates and analyses information from different types of material in order to try and give a rounded picture of community care practice and law. These include:

- Acts of Parliament;
- statutory instruments (regulations);
- directions and approvals made under Acts of Parliament;
- guidance (including policy guidance, practice guidance and Circular guidance);
- law court cases;
- Hansard (House of Commons and House of Lords questions, answers and debates);
- ombudsman (local and health service) investigations;
- registered homes tribunal decisions;
- reported practice (books and journal articles).

There is clearly a danger in blending law and practice, in case the two become muddled. The book takes care to distinguish them in the text. However, the two are so hopelessly entangled in reality, that dealing with one but not the other is, in the author's view, to give but an incomplete view of community care.

(N.B. References to Hansard are given by means of the following abbreviations: HCWA (House of Commons Written Answers), HCOA (House of Comons Oral Answers), HLD (House of Lords Debates), SC (Standing Committee, with the committee letter in brackets: eg, SC(C) is Standing Committee 'C'). References to registered homes tribunal decisions are given as RHT followed by the number).

6. APPROACH OF THE BOOK

The approach of the book is descriptive rather than prescriptive, and attempts to deal even-handedly with a number of controversial issues. The book does not make a judgement about whether community care is 'working' and does not attempt to provide statistics about who is getting (or not getting) appropriate services – or about how much genuine misery or hardship might be reasonably and practicably avoided.

The many examples in the book are intended to illustrate the problems individual authorities or service users can face; inevitably, these are often about things going wrong. However, in itself this is not *necessarily* a criticism of the system: even in the best of systems, things go wrong. That said, the book contains enough evidence to suggest that community care is in some disarray, and that the uncertainty and inconsistency within it are not merely on the periphery or fringes of the system, but are substantial problems (unless it were perversely contended that the system is designed to embrace precisely such uncertainty and inconsistency). This is clear, whether one considers the complex legislation, the piecemeal judgments of the law courts, the numerous investigations of the ombudsmen – or the significant numbers of people who are adversely affected by the variability, uncertainty and sometimes scarcity of service provision. Indeed, the Royal Commission on Long Term Care (1999), reporting at the end of February 1999 had this to say:

> 'The Commission conclude that doing nothing with respect to the current system is not an option. It is too complex and provides no clarity as to what people can expect. It too often causes people to move into residential care when this might not be the best outcome. Help is available to the poorest but the system leads to the impoverishment of people with moderate assets before they get any help. There is a degree of fear about the system which is of concern in a modern welfare state. It is riddled with inefficiencies. The time has come for it to be properly modernised'.

7. CHANGES FROM THE FIRST EDITION

The book has been substantially reworked from the first edition. Apart from a large number of judicial review cases heard since 1994, there is also new legislation, including the Community Care (Direct Payments) Act 1996 and the Carers (Recognition and Services) Act 1995. Brief mention is also made of the relevance to community care of the Disability Discrimination Act 1995, the Human Rights Act 1998 and the Manual Handling Operations Regulations 1992.

Other changes are as follows. First, two substantial digests of local ombudsman investigations and legal cases have been added in Part IV of the book – to which full cross reference is made from the main text. The author is not aware of such comprehensive digests having been published elsewhere. Second is the addition of a practical checklist as an aid to asking relevant questions about the lawfulness of local authority decisions, policies, and eligibility criteria (Chapter 3). Third, is the reorganisation of certain chapters to better reflect salient issues.

CHAPTER 2

OVERVIEW

This chapter provides a freestanding overview of community care, by summarising the content of this book. It will also provide a useful foundation for readers before they consider the much greater detail in the ensuing chapters.

UNDERLYING THEMES (Chapter 3)

Community care is about services and assistance for vulnerable groups in society, such as some elderly people, people with disabilities (physical, sensory or learning), people with mental health problems, and people with problems arising from the use of drugs or alcohol. Services are of many sorts, including residential or nursing home accommodation, practical assistance in the home, personal assistance, home help, respite care (breaks for people being cared for, or for their carers), holidays, daily living equipment, home adaptations, meals-on-wheels, day centres, recreational activities and so on. This is not to mention the equally wide range of NHS or housing services.

However, underlying community care are endemic uncertainties going to the very heart of the system, which sometimes leave both users and providers of services confused and unable respectively to obtain or provide an adequate level of consistent, equitable services. This chapter analyses these uncertainties and the context in which they flourish.

PRACTICAL CHECKLIST (Chapter 4)

This chapter sets out a rough checklist which indicates some of the relevant questions to be asked when decisions are made, and policies and criteria of eligibility are formulated and applied. It is intended to provide at least a starting point for assessing their potential lawfulness.

ACCESS TO COMMUNITY CARE ASSESSMENT (Chapter 5)

The community care system revolves around assessment. Assessment is the new element introduced by s.47 of the NHS and Community Care Act 1990. In fact, what are legally defined as 'community care services' had long been provided under pre-existing legislation, some of it dating from 1948 (see Chapter 8). It is the gateway through which people have to pass in order to obtain services. Therefore, access to assessment is of paramount importance, since without assessment, people get no services.

Local authorities have a legal duty to assess people who appear to them to be in possible need of community care services. Then they have a separate duty to decide what services they will actually provide. This means that assessing people's needs for services is not the same as saying that those services will be provided. There is a separate decision involved.

Authorities do not have to assess people on request – that is, they do not have to assess everybody who asks for an assessment except in the case of disabled people. However, the courts have stated that the threshold for eligibility for assessment is a low one and cannot be raised because a local authority is short of resources. Nevertheless, in practice some local authorities either do impose excessive restrictions on people's access to assessment or at least on the level of assessment available.

When applications or referrals are made to local authorities, the latter decide whether people qualify for assessment at all, what sort of 'priority' they are, the type of assessment they should get, and how quickly they should get it. For authorities, this initial 'screening' process is a powerful tool for controlling and channelling demand for services.

The local ombudsmen have investigated many cases where the priorities and resource problems of local authorities have led to long waits. Sometimes, the ombudsmen look unfavourably on long waiting times, even for people who are deemed to be 'low priority'; at other times they accept their inevitability. Much can depend on the facts of individual cases, although sometimes the ombudsmen apply rough guidelines. The law courts rarely pronounce on cases involving waiting times; if they do, then they will normally state that public bodies must carry out duties within a reasonable length of time. However, in one community care case, a court did find a breach of statutory duty, when a local authority, two years after assessment of a person, had still not decided what services to provide for her.

During assessment, local authorities have a duty, if they think people are disabled, to decide what home welfare services (under the Chronically Sick and Disabled Persons Act 1970) they require and to tell them about their rights under that legislation. It would seem that in practice people are seldom informed in this way, and that local authority staff themselves are seldom aware of this specific duty.

During assessment, local authorities also have a duty to invite health and/or housing authorities to participate, if it appears that people might have health or housing needs. Health and housing authorities are not under an explicit duty to accept such invitations, although clearly the purpose of the legislation cannot be to sanction wholesale refusal. Nevertheless the scale and speed of the participation of these other authorities will inevitably be influenced by their own priorities and available resources. Guidance states that local authorities must not make commitments about service provision on behalf of other authorities without agreeing the commitments with those authorities first.

Local authorities do not have a positive duty to identify all the people who might be in need of services and who therefore should be assessed. But they do have duties to find out how many disabled people there are locally and to keep a register of disabled people. However, this is not to say that local authorities can stick their heads in the sand and pretend not to notice the presence of individuals that are in need.

COMMUNITY CARE ASSESSMENT (Chapter 6)

Legislation states that assessment is about what community care services a person might be in need of. After that, authorities must decide which of those services, and to what level, they are actually going to provide (NHS and Community Care Act 1990,s.47).

Guidance from the Department of Health states that assessment should be 'needs-led'. This means in principle that service provision should be moulded to people's needs, rather than people's assessed needs moulded to whatever services happen to be available. When local authorities have completed assessments, they have a duty to decide whether people's identified needs for services 'call for' provision, or whether services are 'necessary'. They do not necessarily have a duty to provide all the services for which they have identified needs. For example, an authority might be able to state, quite lawfully, that ideally a person 'needs' a service, but say also that it is not necessary for the authority to provide it, because the person does not fall into a 'high risk' category. In which case, it might record 'unmet need' – in other words, need which it has identified but which it is not going to meet.

Of course the distinction between a person's assessed needs, and the needs for which a local authority will provide, can become confusing. One solution proposed by the Department of Health was that authorities should distinguish between recording people's 'needs' (for which they must provide) and people's 'preferences' or 'desires' (for which they do not have to provide). However, this proposal itself generated controversy.

Usually, local authorities identify needs and decide about services by formulating and applying eligibility criteria. Considerable uncertainty has surrounded the question of how far resources can lawfully inform the type and severity of these criteria. The law courts have provided an answer by stating that, when local authorities determine what they mean both by 'need' and whether services are 'necessary' or 'called for', resources may be taken into account. However, a) local authorities are not legally obliged to take account of resources; b) if they do, resources should not be *paramount*, since they must be balanced against people's needs; and c) criteria should not be so extreme that they lead to legally unreasonable decisions (although the courts may be reluctant to intervene on this ground).

Furthermore, having decided that it is necessary to meet a person's need (at least under some, if not all, community care legislation), a local authority must do so even if it is short of resources. Moreover, although this prevents arbitrary refusal or withdrawal of some services, any duty to make provision is diluted by the fact that local authorities are permitted to rework eligibility criteria in the light of new policies and reduced resources, to reassess existing users of services and accordingly to remove or reduce services. In addition, if an authority has identified more than one way of meeting a need, it can take into account resources when choosing a particular service option, so long as the need is still genuinely met.

Therefore, the courts have afforded local authorities considerable leeway in which to tailor services to available resources, and so to allow just enough people to qualify for services within budget. However, part of the ability to set criteria rationally in this way depends on local authorities' being well-informed about needs amongst the local population; but it is generally accepted that many authorities do not have good quality information of this type. Consequently, it is difficult to develop sensitive criteria which regulate the flow of demand precisely in line with resources. Yet once resources become stretched unpredictably, authorities are tempted to cut services in an arbitrary and ill-thought out manner; in turn this risks unlawfulness. For instance, the criteria might a) fail to represent a proper balancing act between resources and people's needs (see above); b) offend against the principle that authorities should not apply policies so rigidly that they 'fetter their discretion' and so fail to take account of (exceptional) individual needs; or c) be blatantly inconsistent with relevant legislation.

CARE PLANS (Chapter 7)

Following a decision about what services will be provided, various guidance (but not legislation) states that a *care plan* should be drawn up containing details about objectives, services, agencies involved, costs, needs which cannot be met, date of first review, and so on. The form and complexity of a care plan will vary greatly depending on the level and types of service involved. The law courts have held that a either a failure to follow, or at least to have proper regard to, this guidance, can amount to unlawfulness.

REVIEW AND REASSESSMENT (Chapter 7)

Guidance states that care plans should be regularly reviewed and people reassessed as appropriate. Clearly, if people's needs increase or decrease, then the level of services they receive might be varied. However, and rather confusingly, it is also possible for people's needs to remain the same, but for the level of services still to be varied. This can happen if an authority's policy and eligibility criteria alter, so that people no longer qualify for the same level of services, even though their own circumstances have not changed at all. Government guidance suggests that where this happens, people should at least be informed about what is happening, and be reassessed before services are altered or withdrawn. The requirement of individual reassessment has been explicitly confirmed by the law courts (in respect of some services, such as those provided under s.2 of the Chronically Sick and Disabled Persons Act 1970 – and probably applies in all cases).

CARERS (Chapter 8)

In certain circumstances, local authorities have a duty to assess, or at least to have regard to the ability of carers to provide, or to continue to provide, a substantial amount of care on a regular basis. In practice, the extent and thoroughness with which the needs of carers are taken into account varies. The purpose of the legislation covering carers relates not only to their welfare, but also to a saving of costs. This is because informal caring exists on a large scale and is of similarly high financial value – compared to what it would cost statutory services to provide the same amount of care.

ORDINARY RESIDENCE (Chapter 8)

Sometimes the existence of a duty on a local authority to provide community care services depends on where a person is 'ordinarily resident', or indeed on whether he or she is without ordinary residence altogether and is instead of 'no settled residence'. In the case of homeless people, or of people seeking residential or non-residential services in an area to which they have recently moved, the question of ordinary residence can sometimes cause delay in, or non-provision of, services.

This is despite the fact that guidance from the Department of Health emphasises that disputes between local authorities should not result in assessment and service provision being delayed.

LIFTING AND HANDLING (Chapter 8)

Health and safety at work legislation, in the form of regulations governing the lifting and handling of loads (including people), has far-reaching implications in community care for both care staff and users of services. The regulations are designed to minimise, and totally remove where reasonably practicable, the risk of injury to employees (and self-employed people) through manual handling.

DISABILITY DISCRIMINATION: GOODS AND SERVICES (Chapter 8)

Part of the Disability Discrimination Act 1995 makes unlawful discrimination against disabled people in relation to the provision of goods and services – including those supplied by public bodies such as local authorities. In particular, the availability, standards and terms of services for disabled people are covered – as is the making by providers of adjustments or changes to policies, practices, procedures and physical features. The eventual extent to which community care services will be affected by the Act is to some extent unknown; at present not all the relevant sections of the Act are in force, and few cases concerning goods and services (as opposed to employment matters) have to date been dealt with by the law courts.

HUMAN RIGHTS (Chapter 8)

The European Convention for the Protection of Human Rights and Fundamental Rights (ECHR) is due to be incorporated, via the Human Rights Act 1998, into the domestic law of the United Kingdom in the year 2000. The extent of the effect which it will eventually have on the availability, rationing and allocation of social and health care services is at present unknown.

NON-RESIDENTIAL COMMUNITY CARE SERVICES (Chapter 9)

Community care services are defined by legislation to include a range of non-residential services (such as personal care, day services, equipment and adaptations to people's homes). Such services are provided under a range of legislation for groups of people such as those with disabilities (physical, sensory or learning), some older people, people with a mental disorder, people with drugs or alcohol problems, people who are ill.

Central to community care is s.2 of the Chronically Sick and Disabled Persons Act 1970, under which services are arranged to enable people to remain in their own homes. The duty under the 1970 Act is a strong one towards individual disabled people, although a judgment by the House of Lords in *R v Gloucestershire CC, ex p Barry* is perceived to have undermined it significantly.

CHARGES FOR NON-RESIDENTIAL SERVICES (Chapter 10)

For non-residential services, local authorities can charge if they wish (although they do not have to) but only a) if the charge is a reasonable one, and b) to the extent that they are satisfied, following representations from any particular person being charged, that it is 'reasonably practicable' for him or her to pay it. Guidance states that people should not be charged for assessment, but otherwise central government has encouraged authorities to make more charges for services. In practice, this is what has happened.

The move towards increased charging illustrates the flexibility built into the community care system, since no change in legislation has been required and authorities have made more use of existing legal powers. If people do not pay the charges for the services they have been assessed as needing, it is thought that local authorities cannot legally withdraw services – at least those which they have a duty (as opposed to a power) to provide. But authorities do have the power to recover the money owed as a debt. One significant, and from the point of view of service users, worrying trend, is the re-defining of certain services as 'social' rather than 'health' care. For example, services such as bathing or respite care, previously provided free of charge by the NHS, might now be provided by social services departments for a charge.

RESIDENTIAL AND NURSING HOME ACCOMMODATION (Chapter 11)

Local authorities have in some circumstances a duty to make arrangements for the provision of residential and nursing home accommodation for people who because of age, illness, disability or other circumstances are in need of care and attention not otherwise available to them. When local authorities have found themselves short of money in relation to this duty, disputes have predictably arisen about when it arises and its extent – for instance, in relation to vulnerable older people in the north west of England or destitute asylum seekers in the south east.

SERVICES IN RESIDENTIAL AND NURSING HOMES (Chapter 11)

There has long been confusion about what services and equipment people should, or are likely to, receive in residential homes or nursing homes, and in particular who will provide and pay for them – the care home, the NHS, social services, the resident or relatives. Neither legislation nor guidance sheds much light; for example, the vagueness of Department of Health guidance on the provision of specialist nursing services in nursing homes, merely underlines the wide discretion of health authorities (HSG(95)8). For residents, their relatives and their advisers, uncertainty is fuelled by the absence of detailed agreements or contracts between resident and care home.

CHARGES FOR RESIDENTIAL AND NURSING HOME CARE (Chapter 12)

When local authorities place people in residential or nursing homes, they have a duty to assess them financially and charge (or not charge) according to the result of a legally prescribed means-test – although some local authorities have attempted to find loopholes in the rules so as either to evade or at least to defer their obligations. Depending on what sort of needs people have, and thus what sort of home they need to go to, local authorities set a 'usual cost' which represents a maximum amount they are prepared to pay in relation to different levels of need. If people are staying a short time (up to eight weeks) in residential care, local authorities have discretion how much to charge. They can apply the prescribed residential care means-test and charging system, or they can decide not to do so and charge much less. Practices vary.

JOINT WORKING (Chapter 13)

The delivery of 'seamless' services between agencies (eg, social services, health and housing services) is a major stated aim of community care policy (though not legislation). Seamless can be taken to mean non-fragmented. The importance of this aim is emphasised by guidance, precisely because of a long history of fragmented welfare services.

One of the difficulties in achieving seamless services is that a combination of imprecise legislation, rigid organisational structures and the complexity of people's needs can lead to gaps and overlaps between services. 'Grey' areas can result, which at worst lead to buck-passing or cost-shunting between agencies; that is, agencies will not take responsibility for certain types of provision, usually because of the costs involved. The result can be delay, and sometimes non-provision of certain services – as well as confusion amongst both service users and providers of services about who can or should provide what, and who is going to pay for it.

During 1998, central government was actively considering how to bring about better cooperation between local authorities and the NHS, and held out the possibility of legislative change in 1999.

INFORMATION AND PUBLICITY (Chapter 13)

Community care guidance (but not legislation) states that social services departments should make detailed information accessible to all potential users of community care services. Taken literally this is a difficult and probably over-ambitious task, though much hinges on what is meant by 'all' and by 'accessible'. Similarly, user empowerment, stated by guidance to be a function of information provision, does not necessarily follow simply from that provision. For instance, clear information about a defective and unclear system is possibly a contradiction in terms; and telling people about their ineligibility for services is of limited use. In addition, the effectiveness of information is anyway difficult to measure.

The Chronically Sick and Disabled Persons Act 1970 (s.1) has long imposed a duty to publish information generally about welfare services. How effectively local authorities have carried out these duties over the years is not evident, but a number of studies have pointed to general shortcomings.

PLANNING FOR COMMUNITY CARE (Chapter 13)

Local authorities have duties to consult about, and to publish, community care plans. They are likely to vary in form, clarity, detail and coverage, although government guidance does state what subjects should be covered. An essential ingredient is meant to be knowledge about the local needs of the population. This is because such knowledge is the basis for setting local priorities, allocating resources, and setting criteria of eligibility and need. However, it seems that good quality information about local needs is not easily available to local authorities. This threatens to undermine basic community care policy that services should be planned, carefully targeted and delivered within budget.

NATIONAL HEALTH SERVICE PROVISION (Chapter 14)

Local authorities have a duty to consult health authorities about community care plans and to ask them (ie, their staff) to participate in community care assessments. Basically, however, the duties of health authorities remain unchanged by community care legislation and are indeed not covered by it. This creates the anomaly that the essential and pivotal duty of community care, which is to assess people's needs, does not apply directly to health authorities and NHS Trusts.

As for provision of services by the NHS, health authorities have a general duty which includes the provision of medical and nursing services as well as the prevention of illness, care of people who are ill, and after-care for people who have been ill. The duty is a general one only (towards the local population, but not towards individuals) and extends only to providing services 'necessary to meet all reasonable requirements'. The effect is that the duty is far from absolute and is carried out within the resources which authorities have available and according to priorities which they set.

The law courts have generally denied relief to applicants complaining about the rationing or withholding of services, and have avoided the sort of close scrutiny they have brought to bear in some other welfare fields such as housing, education and to some extent community care. This discretion has been checked occasionally by the health service ombudsman, and by Department of Health guidance, of which blatant disregard might attract the censure of the courts. However, by and large, health authorities and NHS Trusts have had more to fear from public outcry than from serious legal challenge. Even so, the NHS sometimes loses cases because of inadequate consultation – and in 1997 and 1998 unexpectedly did lose at least three judicial review cases more directly related to the allocation of priorities and resources.

For patients, the situation is one of considerable uncertainty. Service provision can vary from authority to authority, which means that what services people get can depend on where they live. Even within the same authority, provision can be uneven from week to week and from month to month, depending on the resources and facilities available. For example, one person with particular needs might be admitted to an NHS bed one week. Two weeks later, a second person with the same needs could be denied a bed on the grounds that there is over-demand and that other people's needs are greater.

NHS CHARGES FOR SERVICES (Chapter 14)

The NHS does not have the same wide powers as social services to make charges. Certain items can be charged for if specified in legislation – for example, equipment and drugs prescribed by general practitioners, as well as certain items supplied in hospitals, such as wigs, surgical brassieres, and spinal supports. But everything else, both services and equipment, which is not so specified, must be provided free of charge. Legally, this would seem to be a straightforward situation, but in fact it is not. In practice, it appears that NHS Trusts continue to make legally dubious charges, mainly because of their confusion or ignorance about what the legislation actually permits. However, a little-appreciated irony is that, while health authorities and NHS Trusts cannot charge for most services and equipment, they do have the discretion simply not to provide them at all. For example, incontinence pads cannot be charged for; but a decision could be taken, on the basis of local priorities, not to provide them either to certain groups of people or to limit the quantity available per person. Similarly, it is unlawful to charge for nebulisers (respiratory equipment) for home loan, but not necessarily unlawful to ask instead that people obtain their own.

NHS CONTINUING CARE (Chapter 15)

A combination of vague legislation, lack of resources and deliberate policy has resulted in attempts by health authorities, especially over the last ten years, to shed services. In particular, there has been a significant reduction in the number of long-stay beds they are prepared to pay for, whether in hospital or elsewhere (eg, in nursing homes). Consequently, when there is no free health service bed available, people have to enter a private nursing home where they will have to pay for a bed (unless they have very little money to start with) until they have used up most of their savings.

For service users, it has been unclear when they will be judged to 'need' NHS care rather than private nursing home care. This is because even if they are acknowledged to be in clinical 'need', NHS care might still not follow since its provision might depend on local priorities and on available resources at a particular time. The extent to which health authorities and NHS Trusts will provide other continuing care services such as respite care, rehabilitation, palliative care, specialist equipment and other community health services, has also been in doubt.

Following a highly critical report by the health service ombudsman in 1994, about the continuing care policy of Leeds health authority, the Department of Health felt obliged in 1995 to issue guidance. It states that certain services must be provided, but gives little specific detail about levels at which they should be provided. However, in respect of continuing NHS inpatient care, it goes a little further by setting out vague criteria of eligibility – which in practice are likely to operate highly restrictively. The consequence is that the guidance appears to confirm that most people who require continuing care in nursing homes will not be paid for by the NHS: instead, social services departments will be responsible for means-testing and for arranging nursing home care.

In practice, not only will the content of criteria of eligibility vary locally, but also their comprehensibility, the extent to which they are publicised, and the consistency with which they are applied. The language used in the guidance is at times firm, but the circumstances in which it could be enforced by an individual in a judicial review case are probably limited. The health service ombudsman might offer a greater chance of success; he has made findings on several occasions against health authorities which had policies inconsistent with guidance – in respect not only of continuing inpatient care but also, for example, of the provision of incontinence pads in residential homes.

Overall, the guidance appears to be stating that, though armed with great discretion to set priorities and levels of services, health authorities should resist the temptation to jettison completely certain continuing care services.

DISCHARGE FROM HOSPITAL (Chapter 15)

Hospital discharge involves decisions about where, how, and with whom a person is going to live. Of particular importance is whether suitable and effective arrangements have been made and whether people's needs and wishes have been taken into account.

People's needs when leaving hospital can be complicated, requiring consideration of many factors including physical ability, mental ability and attitude, social and environmental factors and financial situation. There are sometimes many arrangements to make. Whether or not these are eventually made successfully would appear to depend on chance, since there are many variable factors which influence the outcome of discharge. This makes the discharge process unpredictable and yet one more uncertainty in community care.

Legislation does not mention hospital discharge, but in the face of evidence of unsatisfactory practice, central government guidance continues to emphasise the importance of improving practice; and the health service ombudsman regularly investigates cases concerning hospital discharge.

HOME ADAPTATIONS (Chapter 16)

Common sense would suggest that since the preferred aim of community care is to enable people to remain in their own homes, housing services would be particularly important. However, they are not for the most part defined legally as community care services.

It is beyond the scope of this book to examine housing law in detail, and so this chapter focuses on the provision of home adaptations – mentioned in community care policy guidance as one of the key elements in enabling people to remain in their own homes – and especially on disabled facilities grants. Although there are many examples of good practice, the local ombudsmen has consistently found, over many years, maladministration in the provision of adaptations, as well as general chaos caused by a lack of resources beyond the control of local authorities. Given that adaptations are indeed listed as a crucial element of community care in the policy guidance, it is unfortunate that they, and potential problems surrounding them, were not considered in detail by the Department of Health when community care policy was formulated and implemented.

DISPUTES AND THEIR REMEDIES (Chapter 17)

Disputes can arise in any welfare system, no matter how well run it is, when people are dissatisfied with the decisions or actions of public bodies such as local authorities and health authorities. As already explained, there are many uncertainties in the community care system, including the wording of legislation, the vagaries of guidance, the patchy decisions of the law courts and the variable practices of local authorities and health authorities.

These uncertainties can give rise to disputes; for example, over whether a person really 'needs' a service or not. When disputes arise, there are a number of remedies available ranging from the informal to judicial review hearings in the law courts. It is important for both users of services and local authorities to know not just what the remedies are, but when they can be used and – if there is a choice – which one is most appropriate. Remedies and rights are inter-dependent; but as already explained above, absolute or enforceable rights in community care are not easily found. This is reflected in the limitations affecting remedies available in relation to the allocation, rationing and provision of community care services. For instance, a) the in-house *complaints procedures* of local authorities are not always effective either in principle or practice; b) ultimately, local authorities have a discretion whether or not to follow the recommendations of the *local ombudsman*; c) the effect of *judicial review* on local authorities tends to be oblique and indirect; and d) private law actions, through which people sue for damages for *breach of statutory duty, negligence* or *breach of contract*, are of very limited application to challenging community care decision-making.

LOCAL OMBUDSMAN INVESTIGATIONS: DIGEST OF CASES (Chapter 18)

This chapter contains selected summaries of investigations by the local ombudsman. They illustrate potential unlawfulness, maladministration, bad professional practice (and by implication, lawfulness, good administration and good practice), the difficult decisions facing local authorities, and sometimes the sheer messiness and difficulty of assessing people's needs and providing services.

LEGAL JUDGMENTS: DIGEST OF CASES (Chapter 19)

This chapter contains selected summaries of cases heard in the law courts – mostly judicial review cases, but also some dealing with breach of statutory duty, negligence or breach of contract. The cases bring community care (and other) legislation to life, demonstrate considerable logic chopping, and show how hard it is sometimes for the courts to superimpose clear law on an unclear and contentious welfare system such as community care.

CHAPTER 3

UNDERLYING THEMES

Coverage

1. Uncertainties in community care
2. Rights and obligations
3. Identifying the purpose of community care
4. Allocation of scarce resources: rationing
5. Transparency of policy
6. Community care legislation
7. Guidance from the Department of Health
8. Guidance and the law courts
9. Judicial review: incursion into community care
10. Judicial review: overall effectiveness
11. Law and practice: the gap
12. Good administration and common sense: local ombudsmen
13. Good practice and law
14. Parliamentary debates and questions

KEY POINTS

This chapter identifies underlying themes to community care. These include the very considerable uncertainties present, the tension between people's needs and resources – and the function of legislation, guidance, the law courts and the local ombudsman.

1. UNCERTAINTIES IN COMMUNITY CARE

Community care is about services and assistance for vulnerable groups in society, such as some elderly people, people with disabilities (physical, sensory or learning), people with mental health problems, and people with problems arising from the use of drugs or alcohol. Services are of many sorts, including residential or nursing home accommodation, practical assistance in the home, personal assistance, home help, respite care (breaks for people being care for, or for their carers), holidays, daily living equipment, home adaptations, meals-on-wheels, day centres, recreational activities and so on. This is not to mention the equally wide range of NHS or housing services.

However, community care is rife with uncertainties affecting both law and practice. Indeed, they are so prevalent as to be an integral and essential part of the system. Perversely, it could even be argued that it is certainties, rather than uncertainties, which are chimerical and anomalous in this context. They are not merely theoretical in effect, since they bear upon people's access to assessment (Chapter 4), the nature of assessment itself (Chapter 5), decisions about services (Chapter 6), how long it takes to get agreed services (Chapter 6), the charges to be made for those services (Chapter 9), and the availability of NHS services (Chapters 13 and 14) and of home adaptations (Chapter 15). As a government White Paper has put it, people 'do not know what services are available, in what circumstances they might get them, or whether they will have to pay'. Nor are the implications of these uncertainties to be disregarded lightly, since 'social services are for all of us ... Any decent society must make provision for those who need support and are unable to look after themselves' (Secretary of State for Health 1998,pp.4,6).

It is also plain that these uncertainties multiply in number and degree when resources are short or local authorities come under pressure for other reasons (such as poor practice or financial inefficiency). Their function is to give the system some flexibility or 'give', and to allow authorities to regulate it according to their resources and priorities. They can be thought of as safety valves, discretionary elements, or variables with unpredictable values – and as a mechanism which allows authorities to ration services. When triggered, and as central government has conceded, they in turn allow the proliferation of problems, including a lack of protection for vulnerable people, poor co-ordination between services, a lack of clarity about what services are available, and inconsistency in provision both between local authorities and within a single authority (Secretary of State for Health 1998,pp.5–7).

The uncertainties emerge through the following legal or quasi-legal vehicles. First, Acts of Parliament set out statute law. They confer duties and powers on local authorities. Second, come regulations which are made under Acts of Parliament and are also classed as legislation, though only as 'secondary' legislation. Third, are directions and powers which are made under statute, but are not themselves regarded as legislation and do not go through Parliament. Nevertheless, the courts generally accept that they, too, confer duties and powers respectively. Fourth, comes guidance issued by the Department of Health. It is not law, but is legally relevant to greater or lesser extent, depending on whether it is of a stronger or weaker type (see below). Lastly, are the law courts which hear judicial review cases, with a view to deciding whether authorities are acting lawfully.

All of these form a rich medium within which, when necessary, uncertainties can flourish. For instance, within *legislation* are a) key undefined words (such as 'need'); b) duties which are qualified so that it is not clear in which circumstances they will be performed or what they actually entail; and c) powers which authorities can anyway choose not to exercise. *Guidance*, issued by the Department of Health and other government departments to supplement legislation, represents substantial uncertainty because of its indeterminate legal status and effect. In principle, it does not constitute law (which is to be found only in legislation and the decisions of the law courts). However, at one extreme the courts nevertheless identify legal obligations within guidance – while at the other, they view it as largely irrelevant. And lastly, the *law courts* interpret community care legislation (statute law) and add their own common law principles of good administrative law. Nevertheless, their decisions are made on a piecemeal basis, are dependent on which disputes happen to reach them in the first place, and are neither predictable nor consistent.

Therefore, the tempting belief, that law can be learned like multiplication tables and so yield certain answers, is false. It depends on the assumption that there is a series of right answers which exist in some objective form, waiting only to be uncovered by the correct judicial utterance. Yet such a notion was famously dismissed by a leading judge, Lord Reid, as a discredited fairy tale (see: Lee 1988,p.3). This is aptly illustrated in community care by the case of *R v Gloucestershire CC, ex p Barry*. It concerned whether disabled people's needs could be measured taking into account the resources of a local authority. Two judges in the High Court decided the main issue one way. On appeal, three judges in the Court of Appeal reached a 2–1 split decision which overruled the High Court. The Court of Appeal was then in turn overruled by the House of Lords, with five law lords arriving at a split 3–2 decision. If all this were not enough to dismiss the idea of pre-ordained answers, the House of Lords then even indicated in the later case of *R v East Sussex CC, ex p Tandy* some apparent regrets about the *Gloucestershire* decision, though without questioning its basic correctness.

The *Gloucestershire* case also shows that these uncertainties are not simply affecting the odd aggrieved individual. The case was brought originally by four individuals, but in fact stemmed from a reduction in home help services to as many as 1,500 people. Similarly, the case of *R v Sefton CC, ex p Help the Aged* concerned a policy applied by the local authority to more than just the two people referred to in that case – and was symptomatic also of what was going on in other authorities. The local ombudsmen, too, sometimes investigate policies that clearly affect hundreds if not thousands of people within a local authority, for example, in respect of long waits for disabled facilities grants or of the introduction of charges for non-residential services. In other words, the disputes affecting community care at present are not about peripheral matters.

The 1998 White Paper on social services declared that some of these uncertainties, such as grossly inconsistent and unpredictable eligibility criteria and charges for services, must cease. To this end the Department of Health would be issuing *Fair access to care* guidance, to which local authorities would be working by April 2001. The test of its success will be whether this guidance will genuinely clarify matters, or itself simply become one more uncertain variable in the equation.

2. RIGHTS AND OBLIGATIONS

It is at the points of uncertainty, referred to immediately above, that significant decisions are made and actions taken. It is at these points too, that disputes arise between service providers and users of services; for example, when a person's view of 'need' does not correspond with that of a local authority. A consequence of the 'give' in the system at these points is that local authorities have very considerable discretion to regulate the provision and level of services – and to resolve the tension between people's needs and available resources.

The existence of this tension has over the last few years led local authorities, users of services, voluntary organisations and lawyers to attempt to identify the existence of legal rights and corresponding obligations in community care. The answer has turned out to be that users of services have few absolute legal rights or entitlements. This is reflected not only in the often vague and qualified language of legislation and guidance, but also in the limitations of the various remedies open to people in case of dispute (since a right only exists insofar as, when necessary, it is practically enforceable).

3. IDENTIFYING THE PURPOSE OF COMMUNITY CARE

It follows too, from the uncertainties inherent in the system, that the very aim of community care is sometimes obscure.

On its face, community care is about assisting people with social care needs, and enabling them to remain living at home, as independently as possible for as long as possible, apparently on the assumption that this is what most people want. If this is its purpose – and a reading of the policy guidance (DH 1990) might suggest that this is a reasonable interpretation – then community care should be straightforward. However, this is by no means the case and the book attempts to chart a system sometimes characterised by extraordinary contortion and complexity.

It is clear that community care is of both actual, or at least potential, benefit to disadvantaged groups in society (Morris 1997b,p.45). Nevertheless, underlying such benefit for some, is the tension between people's needs and resources, already referred to, that denies it to others. To some extent, the apparently straightforward aim of community care, just alluded to above, seems at times to have evaporated and been replaced by constant anxiety about resources, cost-shunting between statutory services, ever-stricter eligibility criteria, waiting times for services, and attempts by local authorities to evade or at least reinterpret legal duties. The basic and often commonsense requirements of people in need remain but are sometimes lost sight of. For instance, the Chief Inspector of the Social Services Inspectorate has explained that personal family experience has opened her eyes to the weaknesses of the health and social care system more effectively than years of experience as a social worker (Ivory 1998). There are no doubt many relatives who might say the same thing. This is a simple reminder that the needs of people (patients, clients, users of services – however we choose to call them) are often glaringly obvious and straightforward when understood from their point of view. Nevertheless, it is curious if, as seems to be the case, it takes senior social workers and other care professionals, the experts in the field, so long to realise this. Indeed, one commentator (Walker 1994,p.11) suggests a dire picture for some people:

> 'It is not surprising that the current state of community care has been described as a nightmare, a term that I do not regard as melodramatic. This is certainly the correct term to describe the experiences of the many frail and vulnerable older people that are in limbo between the NHS and social services; it is also correct to describe in this way the situation of family carers, often old and frail themselves, being driven to the end of their endurance by the need to provide 24-hour care to a spouse or parent, especially if that person is suffering from depression, confusion or dementia'.

Apart from the inevitable tension, implicit in the new community care policy, between people's needs and limited resources, there were other respects in which the policy appeared to be launched without adequate preparation – in effect setting to sea with a leaking ship. To take but one example, equipment and home adaptations are mentioned most prominently in policy guidance – as a major plank of community care's preferred option – allowing people to remain in their own homes (DH 1990,para 3.24). Yet the overwhelming evidence has been that the system of equipment provision, and the provision of home adaptations (for which social services departments usually assess), have been subject to significant problems for many years. It is worth considering the details – as an example of a concrete problem, which vague statements at national level about good practice, do not automatically dispose of. Thus the following is about equipment, but an equivalent set of details could equally well be assembled about various other aspects of community care.

Example of problematic community care service: equipment (and home adaptations) provision. Provision of equipment by local authorities (and by the NHS) has long been fragmented, subject to excessive delays (both for assessment and provision), sometimes limited in range to the clear detriment of disabled people, or simply not available at all. This has been compounded by a considerable ignorance of what is available and through whom, not only on the part of users of services, but also staff and managers. In addition, occupational therapists, experts in assessing for daily living equipment and home adaptations, have sometimes been marginalised within the structure and management hierarchy of social services departments. This has been reflected even at national level, where the Social Services Inspectorate at the Department of Health has not included occupational therapists within its ranks. At local authority level, there have also been problems affecting the recruitment and retention of occupational therapists; because of the large volume of community care referrals made for occupational therapy assessment (for equipment and adaptations), this has resulted for many years in excessively long waiting lists in some areas (SSI 1994b,pp.9–11; also LGMB 1997). The detrimental consequences for people in need of assistance are only too apparent in the many reports of the local ombudsmen involving home adaptations and equipment. Such delays have also long prevented or delayed the satisfactory discharge of people from hospital back into their own homes – and continue to do so (SSI 1998b,p.41).

The evidence of significant deficiencies in provision has been consistent over a long period of time, quite apart from the investigations of the local ombudsmen. To give but a few of the many examples. Thirty years ago, the British Medical Association (1968,pp.8,25,35) found 'glaring defects' in equipment provision and such fragmented administration and split responsibilities that 'few people are aware of all that is available'. The Mair report (1972,p.25) found 'a majority of staff of the health service, including medical staff, have an inadequate knowledge of what aids can be supplied, where they can be obtained and what their limitations are'. In 1984, the Research Institute for Consumer Affairs (RICA 1984), reporting on disability equipment information, found haphazard referrals between agencies, fragmented information and ignorance of where to find it. The Coopers and Lybrand report of 1988 (para 3.7), commissioned by the Department of Health and Social Security, made similar findings about disability information in relation to service providers, disabled people and carers.

A 1988 King's Fund report (Beardshaw 1988,pp.27–28) found equipment 'the single most confused area of service provision for disabled people'. In 1992, a Department of Health 'guidance' document reported that it 'was very difficult to find a good all-round service' (DH 1992a ,p.1). The National Institute for Social Work Research Unit reported non-provision of equipment and adaptations as a prominent problem for elderly people discharged from hospital (Neill, Williams 1992,p.141). A research study of district nurses reported a confused and inefficient system of equipment provision with a scarcity of relevant and helpful information (Ross, Campbell 1992,p.1).

A joint strategy group was belatedly formed by the Department of Health in 1995 with a view to investigate 'the serious issue of lengthy waiting lists' for assessment and provision of equipment in local authorities (LASSL(97)27). In 1996, Age Concern England identified the numerous problems experienced by older people stuck on waiting lists (Salvage 1996). In the same year a detailed study revealed the complexity and sometimes ineffectiveness of the system of home adaptations – including excessive delays. A year later, another King's Fund report noted confusion, inconsistency and delay (Appleton, Leather 1997); and a SCOPE report in 1998 found similarly a lack of information, severe delays in provision, and unsuitable or even no equipment being provided (Marks 1998).

In 1998, the Department of Health commissioned a good practice guide on running equipment services, produced by the Disabled Living Centres Council. It, too, identified a serious of failures within equipment services, which was why better practice was so important (Winchcombe 1998). This guide was clearly welcome and much needed. Indeed, the foreword within the guide by the Under-Secretary of State for Health states that equipment a) is needed to maintain the independence and quality of life of many disabled and older people; b) is often a key element in discharge from hospital, in rehabilitation, in the community, in services for disabled children and in support for carers; and c) has never been high on the management agenda. Despite this foreword in the publication itself, the Department chose not to elevate the issue to one of policy and priority, and to offer the guide as a tool towards this. The Departmental Circulars that accompanied the guide belied the message in the foreword by a) being merely labelled 'good practice' rather than policy guidance; and b) using timid language – for example, it was (italics added) 'to be *hoped* that many managers will take this opportunity to review disability equipment services') (HSC 1998/200 and CI(98)20). The courts will scarcely detect a 'badge of mandatory requirement' (see *R v North Derbyshire HA, ex p Fisher*) in such words – compare terms such as *must* or *should* (in guidance such as HSG(95)8 on continuing care). The consequence will almost certainly be that hard-pressed senior managers with little or no interest in, or knowledge about, equipment, will do nothing. Yet it is such managers who are in the majority since, as the foreword to the guide points out, equipment is generally low on the management agenda. Thus, it would appear that the provision of equipment remains a low priority, despite its theoretical eminence in the community care policy guidance, and actual importance in practice. On any view, given the weight and persistence of the evidence, the failure to raise equipment as a policy issue of reasonable priority appears to be blameworthy.

4. ALLOCATION OF SCARCE RESOURCES: RATIONING

As already mentioned, it is a lack of resources that can so often activate the points of uncertainty within community care.

Allocation of resources (priority setting, rationing or whatever name is chosen) is highly sensitive, not new, but now highlighted by community care policy, guidance and the decisions of the law courts. The allocation of scarce resources is, of course, a thankless task whether planned and executed by central or local government – or even, at the other extreme, not planned at all but allowed to develop in haphazard fashion or by lottery. It not only involves 'tragic choices' but can also too easily bring opprobrium on rationing agents, such as government, whatever strategy or lack of strategy is adopted (Calabresi, Bobbitt 1978).

Nevertheless, scarce resources invite sometimes harsh decisions and the apportioning of blame. For example, users of services might blame 'front-line' professionals (such as social workers or occupational therapists), and the latter in turn their managers; those managers might in turn reproach their senior managers, who point the finger at the social services committee; it might in turn blame central government – and so on. Perhaps the recrimination comes full circle if a government, keen to reduce public spending, is voted in by electors who are apparently shy of paying tax, yet wish to enjoy high quality services: perhaps a case of 'won't pay must pay' (Economist 1998).

The shifting in April 1993 of financial responsibility for funding residential care and nursing home care from central government to local authorities meant that what had been an open-ended, demand-led, central government budget, would now be subject to finite resources at local level.

Together with a reduction in the number of NHS beds available for people with continuing health care needs, it was predictable that this would lead to problems and disputes – whether about residential care (eg, *R v Sefton MBC, ex p Help the Aged*) or non-residential services (*R* v Gloucestershire CC, ex p Barry). The diminishing of NHS continuing care, replaced by means-tested care in residential and nursing homes, has led to accusations that central government has abandoned the 'cradle-to-grave' philosophy of the welfare state and broken its promises to people who believed they would be cared for at no cost – with a policy which is unfair and favours the spendthrift over the thrifty (House of Commons Health Committee 1996,p.xxiv). People might feel cheated because they had been led to believe – whilst paying National Insurance contributions, and 'scrimping and saving' all their lives – that the State would care for them in their time of need, that they and their spouses would not be reduced to penury, and that their inheritance would be safeguarded for their children (Salvage 1995,p.3).

A Royal Commission on Long Term Care for the Elderly sat during 1998 with a brief to report on the future funding of long-term care for elderly people, both in their own homes and other settings. The Commission was in effect asked to look at a problem deferred from the 1980s when central government became anxious about the high cost of looking after people with long-term care needs in institutions (hospitals, residential or nursing homes). In advance of the Commission, the Joseph Rowntree Foundation's own inquiry into the funding of continuing care simply concluded that a) good quality health care should be free to all; b) all older people 'should have a clear entitlement to good quality continuing care – whether in their own homes or in a residential establishment – irrespective of their income or wealth'; c) however, those in work should contribute to a national care insurance scheme to pay for any long-term care costs they might face in old age (Barclay 1996,p.vi). The matter boils down to three main options: insurance, taxation or liquidation of personal assets (Grimley Evans 1995). Even so, the need to decrease rather than maintain or increase public welfare spending because the latter is not affordable has been contested; maintaining services for an ageing population would not take welfare spending above the proportion of national income expended in other European countries (Hills 1997,p.5).

Extra resources alone are not of course a universal nostrum for all community care ills. To take but one example, good practice in terms of informed planning and purchasing of services from independent providers might lead to more effective use of resources (Audit Commission, SSI 1998a,p.6). The scope for efficiency savings might be large – for instance, where a '30 per cent difference in unit costs for the same service between similar authorities in the same part of the country' is exposed (Secretary of State for Health 1998, p.7). But at the same time, to say that there is always room for cost-savings is to state no more than a truism applicable to all organisations and systems. Beyond a certain point a shortage of resources will impact inevitably not only on the provision of services to the public but also precisely on improving, planning and changing those very services – even within those authorities hitherto promoting good practice. Recognising that increased efficiency alone is not enough, the government confirmed in 1998 that over a three-year period, nearly £3 billion pounds in extra funding would be made available. But at the same time, some of the funding would be dependent on improved performance and be tied to a Social Services Modernisation Fund, which would act as a 'lever for modernisation' (Secretary of State for Health 1998, p.11).

When resources are not forthcoming because the financial policies of the moment (operated by local authorities though often stemming from central government), the effect on clear statutory duties laid down by Parliament, can be highly corrosive. The courts have accepted that resources cannot be conjured up out of thin air (eg, *R v Islington LBC, ex p Rixon*), but decided also that financial cuts must stop somewhere (*R v East Sussex CC, ex p Tandy*). In this last case, the House of Lords stated that when there is an absolute statutory duty imposed on an authority to do something, it must find the resources, even if it has to raid other budgets. It is not sufficient to claim that one budget in particular has been exhausted and therefore the statutory duty cannot be performed.

Whatever the perceptions and views about the meaning of lack of resources, one thing at least is clear; virtually all of the community care judicial review cases heard to date have focused on an apparent lack of resources to meet people's community care needs. This was predictable. Some ten years ago, the Griffiths (1988) report on community care emphatically denied that it represented a cost-cutting exercise, although it did concede a) that many local authorities felt that 'the Israelites faced with the requirement to make bricks without straw had a comparatively routine and possible task'; and b) that what could not 'be acceptable is to allow ambitious policies to be embarked upon on without the appropriate funds' (pp.iii,ix). The ensuing White Paper spoke of better use of tax-payer's money, but arguably did not confront sufficiently forcibly or transparently the inevitable conflict which would follow between people's needs and available resources (Secretaries of State 1989,p.5). Subsequent policy guidance (DH 1990) and practice guidance (SSI, SWSG 1991a) tended to camouflage in verbiage relating to good practice, though not totally to conceal, the issue of resources. The disparity between the stated policy and the policy actually pursued was highlighted in 1997 by one of the members (Lord Lloyd) of the House of Lords in *R v Gloucestershire CC, ex p Barry*. He confirmed the soundness of the warning (about appropriate funding) given in the Griffiths report nearly ten years before, when he stated that central government had indeed departed from its 'fine words' in its 1989 White Paper and simply failed to supply the resources required.

5. TRANSPARENCY OF POLICY

As already indicated immediately above, beyond the adequacy of funding, lies an arguably even more fundamental issue. This is whether central government was sufficiently forthright about the purpose and implications of the new community care policy at its inception. Some might contend that the overall presentation of the policy was far from candid and even intentionally misleading. A more charitable view would be that central government was simply unaware of the full implications of its policy, and that the inevitability of some of the problems is apparent in retrospect, but was not clear prospectively.

For instance, policy guidance states that the preferable option for each individual is to provide care in people's own homes where this 'would provide a better quality of life' than would entry into a residential or nursing home, and wherever it is 'feasible and sensible'. Certainly, it also refers to resource issues, such as the need for 'cost-effective' services and for difficult decisions sometimes having to be made (DH 1990,para 3.25). However, this language does not on its face appear to sanction the common practice of imposing stringent ceilings on the weekly cost of domiciliary care packages for older people (above which they have to enter residential or nursing home care) – or of making wholesale reductions in the availability of home help services. Thus, although resources are referred to, the policy guidance as a whole does not portray community care as an exercise in limiting expenditure on groups of vulnerable people. Why then the discrepancy between the policy guidance and ensuing practice?

The obvious way to limit expenditure on continuing health care and social care was to cut off the open-ended provision by central government of residential and nursing home care, and to reduce the number of long-stay beds within the NHS. If such a cessation and reduction coincided with people's wishes and needs, and with professional good practice, then so much the better. To these ends, government clearly hoped that providing assistance for people in their own homes would be the answer. However, when it transpired that this option might turn out to be the more expensive, then in 1995 the Department of Health involved itself in an important test case (*R v Lancashire CC, ex p RADAR*). It aligned itself in this case behind the cheaper residential or nursing home option, even though the woman involved was opposed to leaving her own home and was arguably the sort of person for whom community care at home was intended.

The original White Paper on community care stated that people should be enabled to remain in their own homes, wherever 'feasible and sensible' (Secretaries of State 1989,p.5), a phrase echoed in policy guidance (DH 1990,para 1.1). Towards the end of 1998, a new White Paper (Secretary of State for Health 1998) used the same word, 'feasible' in its stated national objective, namely 'to enable adults assessed as needing social care to live as safe, full and normal a life as possible, in their own home wherever feasible' (p.111). It also seemed to condemn the widespread of financial ceilings on weekly packages of care, above which people have to enter a care home (p.14). However, whether this will mark a genuine change in practice, so as to avoid the situation typified by the *Lancashire* case, will presumably depend simply on the availability of resources (see above section).

When guidance (eg, SSI, SWSG 1991a,p.54) refers to priorities, it does so in an orderly and rational way, suggestive of an outcome where people who really 'need' help will get it quickly, others will get it in good time, and that everything will work out in the end. Yet the financial pressures on community care from the start, meant that the measured language of guidance was always at risk of fraying on contact with reality – and that sanitised notions such as 'prioritisation' (awarded as part of an efficient 'customer service') would be a facade for rationing and deterring people from taking up services (Middleton 1997,p.19). All this is a) a salutary reminder that guidance from central government must sometimes be examined for euphemism; and b) is not in itself a criticism of a policy, but rather the manner of its presentation.

Thus, the point here is not simply whether the real, as opposed to the superficial, community care policy has been sensible or defensible, but about the lack of hard-nosed, public explanation. To the extent that there has been such a failure, then both care professionals and the general public are ill-informed. An example of this general unawareness is sometimes illustrated by outrage expressed in the media; for instance, in the *Basingstoke and North Hampshire Gazette* (24th July 1998) which contained a feature of several pages on community care. About withdrawal of home help services from a number of disabled people, the article referred to people's age, wheelchairs, polio, blindness, six heart attacks, dignity and anger – and to the response of the chairman of the social services committee that 'no one is going to die from cuts in cleaning'. This sort of news-worthy article and the indignation it stirs up might suggest that the scale of rationing implicit in government policy has outstripped the general public's awareness. Otherwise it would presumably be barely worth reporting. Yet not only is the general public ill-informed, but it is reported that care professionals within local authorities have themselves also been caught unawares by the nature of community care and its implications for their work (Hadley, Clough 1996).

It should be said that the government White Paper, *Modernising social services* (Secretary of State for Health 1998), has severely criticised the way in which community care is working. It will be welcomed by many receiving, or working within community care, insofar as it reflects appropriately their everyday experiences and concerns. However, like its predecessor dealing with community care nearly ten years before, *Community care in the next decade and beyond* (Secretaries of State 1989), it contains many fine words. The real question is whether eight years on, another law lord will find that these words in turn have been departed from, just as Lord Lloyd found in *R v Gloucestershire CC, ex p Barry* in relation to the 1989 White Paper.

6. COMMUNITY CARE LEGISLATION

Referred to above, is the intense scrutiny which has taken place of community care legislation and Department of Health guidance, in the search for rights and obligations. Irregular in look even at a distance, it is no surprise that on closer inspection both legislation and guidance reveal considerable ambiguity, a lack of cohesion and sometimes obvious flaws and contradictions. However, even if the legislation and guidance were to be clearer and more cohesive, it would still develop cracks if placed under undue pressure and scrutiny. A tenable view is that the shortcomings of community care legislation have been exaggerated because of the strain exerted on it by, ultimately, the consequences of government policy. To the extent that it has created, failed to deal with or even sufficiently acknowledged (see above) the problems affecting community care, then arguably it is government policy which has to be looked to for proper solutions – a general point made by Lord Lloyd in the key community case of *R v Gloucestershire CC, ex p Barry.*

Community care legislation as a whole is not easily understood, spread as it is across a number of different Acts of Parliament. For instance, s.47 of the NHS and Community Care Act 1990, for the main part, only puts in place a framework for assessment; it is not an Act which introduced a whole new and integrated system of services. To find the real 'community care services' other than assessment, one has to look back to a range of pre-existing pieces of legislation stretching back several decades to 1948. In addition, even once different pieces of legislation have been identified and their content understood, their compatibility with one another is not always evident. For instance, in cases such as *R v Gloucestershire CC, ex p Barry* and *R v Powys CC, ex p Hambidge*, attempts were made to clarify the relationship between s.47 of the NHS and Community Care Act 1990 and s.2 of the Chronically Sick and Disabled Persons Act 1970. The issues disputed in these cases were far from academic; hinging on the outcomes were very considerable implications in terms of services for disabled people and local authority finances.

The disparate nature of the community care statutes has predictably led to calls for new, integrated legislation written in language appropriate to society and its needs in the 1990s. It would, for instance, jettison terms such as 'substantial and permanent handicap' to be found in the National Assistance Act 1948. Community care legislation would be consolidated, much as the Children Act 1989 consolidated child care legislation. These calls have not so far been visibly heeded by central government, although it is possible that the Royal Commission (mentioned above), sitting during 1998, might herald the beginning of legislative reform. Nevertheless, as already mentioned, the shortcomings of existing legislation have only been exposed so glaringly because of the close attention it has received in the light of a series of judicial review cases brought over the last few years. And these disputes for the most part arise when local authorities, pleading lack of resources, withdraw or withhold services from people who need them. Thus, legislative reform might be a *necessary* element in producing an effective system of community care, but scarcely a *sufficient* one, since the issue of resources must also be dealt with. For instance, s.2 of the Chronically Sick and Disabled Persons Act 1970 survived for about 25 years with relatively little exposure in the law courts and for that reason might have been supposed to be relatively clear in its meaning. However, the case of *R v Gloucestershire CC, ex p Barry*, brought only because of resource problems in a harsh financial climate, has suddenly made it look distinctly equivocal.

Finally, individual pieces of legislation sometimes give little away. For instance, s.47 of the NHS and Community Care Act 1990, which forms the gateway of assessment through which people must pass to obtain any community care services at all, is notable for its brevity. It places a duty on local authorities to assess people who appear to be in need of community services and then to decide whether services are called for. Yet the Act is perfectly silent about what the terms *assessment, need, appearance* or *called for* mean or might look like in practice.

7. GUIDANCE FROM THE DEPARTMENT OF HEALTH

Beyond legislation, by way of supplement, lies the copious quantity of guidance issued by the Department of Health to local authorities and to the NHS. Indeed, the bareness of s.47 of the NHS and Community Care Act 1990 (see immediately above) is deliberate. During the Parliamentary passage of the Bill, the government repeatedly opposed amendments which would have given it rather more substance – on the grounds that such legislative detail would have placed local authorities in a bureaucratic straitjacket. Far better express what was wanted in guidance, and leave local authorities the freedom to get on with it.

Although there are advantages to the use of guidance over legislation, the drawbacks are potentially considerable because, as already mentioned, the legal status and effect of guidance are elusive. This can render guidance ineffective. For instance, a glance back to the debates in 1989 and 1990 on the NHS and Community Care Bill reveals that some of the amendments, so dismissively rejected by the government at the time, were about matters which have continued to be troublesome and are precisely those not resolved by guidance. These include hospital discharge procedures, care plans, giving of reasons for decisions, advocacy, incontinence services, assessment of carers, direct payments and so on. Indeed, the last two of these issues did finally trigger legislation: the Carers (Recognition and Services) Act 1995 and the Community Care (Direct Payments) Act 1996.

The following quotes from Parliament provide a flavour of the arguments *for and against* the use of guidance (the fourth example being a reminder that if guidance is not effective, nor necessarily is legislation):

Example 1: guidance and incontinence services 'We feel that it is important to have such a provision written into the [NHS and Community Care] Bill. I say that because when a Bill becomes an Act of Parliament people look upon it as legislation and they forget everything else. They forget about White Papers and Green Papers and also, with the hurly-burly and the rush which ensue, they forget about the circulars issued by the department' (Baroness Masham: HLD,24/4/1990,col.551).

Example 2: guidance and incontinence services. 'The Minister referred to government health notice 88/26 ... That circular is what the Government recommend. It is from that circular that the wording of the amendment [duty to provide a district-wide continence service] comes. It is what the Government want, but the Minister went on to say that district health authorities should be left to decide on their own priorities. The situation has continued to deteriorate since the health notice went out. That shows how ineffective notices without legislation can be ... There is therefore a need for an amendment such as this so that provision is guaranteed under legislation' (Baroness Masham: HLD,7/6/1990,col.1589).

Example 3: guidance and the Chronically Sick and Disabled Persons Act 1970. 'Apart from a couple of silly circulars they have sent to local authorities, the Government's excuse for inaction is that they do not wish to dictate to local authorities. They say that they respect local autonomy' (Jack Ashley: HCD,9.4.1973,col.1024).

Example 4: guidance, discharge from hospital and after-care under s.117 of the Mental Health Act 1983. Lord Mottistone demanded of Baroness Blatch: 'Is she telling us that effectively – and until we see it we cannot believe it – regulations and guidance will replace this part of the Bill? Does she not agree with me that it is very important to have in major legislation underpinning matter from which circulars can be developed rather than circulars, even if they are already in existence? Circulars can be changed at the drop of a hat because they do not even have to come before Parliament. The whole burden of my noble friend's remarks, as I saw it, was: "Oh yes, it is all in circulars". Does she not agree that that is a very inadequate reply? It is terrible that, after seeing my noble friend, this very important matter is being left to circulars, whether or not they are issued. I just do not like this'.

In reply: 'My Lords ... my noble friend has in a sense contradicted himself in his last remarks in that he has pointed to a matter which is enshrined in legislation and then said that that was not effective – that is section 117 of the Mental Health Act' (HLD,14/6/1990,col.492).

The dichotomy between legislation and guidance is longstanding, and there are various arguments for and against the greater use of the latter in the implementation of policy (eg, Baldwin 1995b, Ganz 1987). For instance, guidance can be written in ordinary and helpful language, be produced and disseminated more quickly than legislation and tends to give the relevant public bodies (eg local authorities) flexibility in how to implement policy. On the other hand, it is not placed before and considered by Parliament as is legislation; this means that important policy matters, seriously affecting people, can by-pass Parliamentary scrutiny altogether. Guidance might simply be badly written. And even if the language is clear, the obligations (if any) created might be indistinct. Matters are made worse if the dissemination of guidance is poor; for instance, it is only in the last three years that the Department of Health has been able to indicate annually which of its social care guidance published over the last thirty years or so is extant and which obsolete (see LASSL(96)10, LASSL(97)15, and the latest list, LASSL(98)14). It has also now placed the full text of recent guidance on the Internet – a most helpful step for those with access, given the past problems associated with both the identification and distribution of its guidance.

The general drawbacks and uncertainties of government guidance are nothing new; some fifty years ago, a court characterised it as 'four times cursed'. It a) did not go through Parliament; b) was unpublished and inaccessible by those affected; c) was a jumble of legal, administrative or directive provisions; and d) was not expressed in precise legal language. This was in contrast to legislation which was 'twice blessed' when it passed through both Houses of Parliament (*Patchett v Leathem*).

8. GUIDANCE AND THE LAW COURTS

If central government had originally hoped to use guidance as a non-statutory veil – in which to swathe community care and so conceal its problems, and behind which the law courts would not venture – then it must be disappointed. Faced with the sparse nature of s.47 of the NHS and Community Care Act 1990, the courts have not only shown themselves willing to scrutinise guidance, in order to understand the implications of the legislation – but also, for good measure, to identify its shortcomings, both general and specific.

Sometimes community care guidance is judged by the courts to be of the strong variety, because it is made under s.7 of the Local Authority Social Services Act 1970 (which states that local authorities have a duty 'to act under the general guidance of the Secretary of State') and it contains language of obligation. In such cases, they might simply rule that failure to follow it amounts to a breach of statutory duty (*R v North Yorkshire CC, ex p Hargreaves* about failing to take account of the preferences of a user). A court might search for a 'badge of mandatory requirement' (*R v North Derbyshire HA, ex p Fisher* about refusal by a health authority to provide beta-interferon treatment for a man with multiple sclerosis). If that badge is found, the court might rule that guidance can amount to a direction (see p.52), and thus is binding, even though the term 'direction' has not been used to label the document (*R v Secretary of State for Health, ex p Manchester Local Committee*).

A failure to have regard even to weaker guidance (ie, not made under s.7 of the 1970 Act), might also make a decision unlawful because a relevant factor (ie, the guidance) has not been taken into account (*R v Islington LBC, ex p Rixon* about a failure in care plan; see also *R v North Derbyshire HA, ex p Fisher*). In contrast, guidance expressed in vague terms, for example in the form of annual Circulars about NHS priorities (such as those listed in HSC(1998)159), generally give much less scope for legal challenge.

Alternative to pressing guidance into service to supplement legislation, the courts sometimes dismiss it with varying degrees of severity. In *R v Gloucestershire CC, ex p Barry*, Lord Clyde did not regard it as 'proper material for the construction of the critical provision' but still found it satisfactory that his view, arrived at independently of the guidance, nevertheless was consistent with it. In *R v Gloucestershire CC, ex p Royal Association for Disability and Rehabilitation*, the judge expressed his respect and sympathy (given the complexity of the legislation) to the authors of practice guidance (SSI/SWSG 1991a) but questioned, in places, its coherence and logic. And in *R v Wandsworth LBC, ex p Beckwith*, the House of Lords went further, again according its respect to the Department of Health, but concluding that the guidance in issue was simply wrong; the government department had in effect misunderstood its own legislation.

9. JUDICIAL REVIEW: INCURSION INTO COMMUNITY CARE

If the legislation is labyrinthine, and guidance intangible in meaning (and sometimes physically, when it is difficult to obtain), the position has been complicated further by a stream of judicial review decisions in the law courts. Thus, anyone wishing to understand community care law must not only grapple with the legislation and guidance, but try to make sense of these legal cases in terms of their application to everyday situations.

Judicial review is used to challenge the lawfulness of decisions of public bodies – such as local authorities, health authorities or NHS Trusts. The law courts examine actions and decisions of such bodies by employing flexibly and variably a wide range of concepts – which themselves both overlap and change over time, so making it difficult to predict exactly how they will be applied in future cases. Simplified, the concepts fall under headings such as *unreasonableness, illegality, legitimate expectation* (including *consultation*), *fettering of discretion, illegality,* taking account of *relevant factors* and disregarding irrelevant factors – and so on (see Chapter 4).

Through use of these concepts, the courts 'supervise' public bodies to ensure that they behave lawfully. If they do not, then the courts will tell them to take the disputed decision again, this time in a lawful manner. This means that the courts are in principle concerned more with how authorities reach their decisions than in what those decisions are (although this distinction sometimes blurs in practice). As central government has put it in guidance to civil servants, the judge is over the shoulder of a decision-maker, checking that he or she is acting 'fairly and not in an over-zealous or wrong-headed manner' (Treasury Solicitor's Department).

The judicial approach is therefore oblique, to ensure that the courts do not end up taking day-to-day decisions for authorities – either in terms of stepping into the shoes of professionals such as social workers or occupational therapists, or of making political decisions about the allocation of resources and making of priorities. The latter point has been clearly stated in respect of local authorities by the House of Lords in *R v East Sussex, ex p Tandy*, and of health authorities by the Court of Appeal in *R v Cambridge HA, ex p B*. In other words, the judges do not want to end up running the health service or community care, which Parliament has willed should be run respectively by statutory health authorities and local authorities – and not by the courts.

Since April 1993, there has been a steady flow of judicial review cases concerning community care. This is particularly notable since, as explained above, all the legislation covering community care services had long been in place before 1993, but had provoked relatively few legal challenges (but see *Wyatt v Hillingdon LBC, R v Ealing LBC, ex p Leaman*, and *R v Department of Health and Social Security, ex p Bruce* – all concerning the Chronically Sick and Disabled Persons Act 1970). There are no doubt a number of reasons for this change of pattern. First, a shortage of resources inevitably invites dispute. Second, central government, through the Citizen's Charter (Prime Minister 1991) initiative in general and local authority complaints procedures in particular, has encouraged people to complain about services. Although the complaints procedures are in part intended to keep people away from the law courts, it is inevitable that the more people are encouraged to complain, so the greater the proportion who might spill their grievances over into legal action.

Third, the complexity of the legislation, the morass of guidance and the contradictory elements of community care policy were always likely to provoke judicial intervention – or even, ultimately, new legislation (Schwehr 1997a; Clements 1996c). At times, in the light of such intervention, there has been criticism from some quarters that lawyers and law courts have inappropriately hijacked community care policy and shifted the focus away from central government and into the law courts. However, any such censure is ill-conceived, given that the policy is riddled with inconsistency and uncertainty (which features, if they were meant to be part of the policy, were not transparently explained at the outset). Besides which, it is one thing if judicial clarification is required for obscure matters, peripheral to a policy – but quite another if, from the beginning, it was foreseeable that the courts would have to resolve disputes at the very heart of the new system.

Fourth, judicial review of public bodies generally – whether at central or local government level – has been a growth industry in the legal world particularly over the last twenty years (Bridges *et al.* 1995a,p.1). The bringing of these cases has required not only grist to the legal mill in the form of users of services with grievances, but also lawyers and voluntary organisations to oil the wheels. For instance, the last mentioned help identify appropriate test cases and might themselves bring a judicial review case on behalf of one or more users of services. This has happened in relation to residential care (*R v Sefton LBC, ex p Help the Aged*), reassessment of people for home help services (*R v Gloucestershire CC, ex p Royal Association for Disability and Rehabilitation*) or community care assistance for asylum seekers (*R v Newham LBC, ex p Medical Foundation for the Care of Victims of Torture*). Indeed, it has been pointed out that the prevalence of judicial review cases brought in any one locality might be due not so much to the standard of decision-making by a local authority, but to the presence of, and links between, interested local lawyers and advice agencies (Mullen, Pick and Prosser 1996,pp.133–134).

That community care has found itself in the legal spotlight, is demonstrated not only by the string of judicial review cases but by a legal literature where none was before. To repeat, this is noteworthy, since most of the legislation had long been in place and, as already pointed out, there were problems before, as well as after, the implementation of community care in April 1993. Books on legal aspects of community care published to date include: Gordon (1993, and 2nd edition: Gordon and Mackintosh 1996), Meredith (1993, and 2nd edition: 1995), Public Law Project (1994) and (1995), Mandelstam with Schwehr (1995: ie, the first edition of this book), Clements (1996a), Richards (1996), Dimond (1997), McDonald (1997), Mandelstam (1998). To remedy the scattered, slow or perhaps even non-existent, reporting of community care cases in existing series of law reports, the Legal Action Group started in 1997 a new series, the *Community care law reports*. In the background, published in its present form for the first time in 1993 when it evolved from a more limited predecessor, is the *Encyclopaedia of social services and child care law* (Jones 1993a). This is a four volume, continually updated, looseleaf work which contains annotated legislation and guidance, and is relied upon heavily in the field for reference.

The aim of most of these publications has been to inform the unsuspecting legal, voluntary and academic sectors about community care law: with 'the recent blaze of the comet Hale-Bopp across our night skies it is timely to consider the little known legal galaxy that contains the community care statutes, which have also recently risen to prominence, igniting the judicial ether with a series of decisions' (Clements 1997). Of particular concern is the fact that some local authority legal departments, traditionally concentrating in the social services field on child care and mental health, appear to have been caught unawares by community care. Where this is the case, it has compromised their ability to assist local authority committees and officers to develop lawful and effective policies.

Lastly, one footnote to the flurry of legal activity is that nearly twenty years ago, the sponsor of the Chronically Sick and Disabled Persons Act 1970 had this to say during a debate about an ultimately unsuccessful amendment to the Act (which would have allowed resort to a county court to enforce service provision):

> 'As I have said on many occasions, my own concern over the years has been to argue not for litigation but for full implementation of the Act. I have never seen the judge as some kind of ayatollah of the disabled. Nor, in promoting the Act [CSDPA 1970], did I ever wish to create a new light industry for lawyers. What clause 1 of the Bill will do is to bring the law into line with what was always thought to be the effect of section 2 of the parent Act. I believe it will be helpful, but we should not expect too much from legal intervention' (Alfred Morris: HCD,2/2/1979,col.1922).

These words were prophetic; nearly twenty years later, their speaker was moved to write an article in *The Times* newspaper, heavily criticising the House of Lords for its decision in the case of *R v Gloucestershire CC, ex p Barry* (Morris 1997a).

10. JUDICIAL REVIEW: OVERALL EFFECTIVENESS

If the above explains the significant incursion of judicial review into community care law, the important question remains about how effective, overall, it has been. Its effectiveness can be tested in terms of a) whether the law has been objectively clarified; and b) the degree to which either local authorities, or users of services, have been significantly assisted.

First, judicial review deals with community care on a piecemeal basis only, so that for every one question aired in court, another is not – and for every one question answered, another might arise which remains unanswered until, perhaps, next time. Thus, while some particular questions have been answered – for instance, whether local authorities can take account of resources when assessing needs *R v Gloucestershire CC, ex p Barry*), make charges under s.2 of the Chronically Sick and Disabled Persons Act 1970 *R v Powys CC, ex p Hambidge*) or make cash payments to people being provided with accommodation under s.21 of the National Assistance Act 1948 *R v Secretary of State, ex p Hammersmith and Fulham LBC*) – many others have not. Furthermore, as explained below, not every issue decided legally translates easily into practice.

Second, honours are fairly even in terms of decisions in favour respectively of local authorities and service users. This situation both supports and refutes optimistic views (eg, Preston-Shoot 1996) about the extent of redress available for individuals through the law courts, in the context of community care. For instance, users of services have fared reasonably well in cases such as *R v Sefton LBC, ex p Help the Aged* about residential care, *R v Haringey LBC, ex p Norton* about assessment of different types of need, *R v North Yorkshire CC, ex p Hargreaves* about taking account of preferences of service users, *R v Staffordshire CC, ex p Farley* about withdrawal of night sitter services, *R v Islington LBC, ex p Rixon* about adequate care plans, *R v Sutton LBC, ex p Sutton* about delay in providing services, and *R v Westminster CC, ex p A* about the eligibility of asylum seekers for residential accommodation. Most recently, users of services won in two other cases: *R v North and East Devon HA, ex p*

Coughlan (closure of an NHS unit), and *R v Wigan MBC, ex p Tammadge* (local authority trying to back-track on a decision). In addition, as outlined below, many of the decisions of the law courts coincide with professional good practice. On the other hand, local authorities will have drawn succour, at least financial, from cases such as *R v Gloucestershire CC, ex p Barry* about withdrawing services and taking account of resources, *R v Powys CC, ex p Hambidge, Avon CC v Hooper, R v Somerset CC, ex p Harcombe* (all three cases about charging for services), and *R v Essex CC, ex p Bucke* about switching to cheaper services.

The case of *R v North Yorkshire CC, ex p Hargreaves (no.2)* sums up the ambiguous effect of judicial review. Having ruled that the local authority's policy about assistance with holidays for disabled people was unlawful, the judge then said that this did not necessarily mean that the applicant would get the assistance sought. This was because the local authority might reassess her needs but still come to the same conclusion as previously. In addition, the difficulty for voluntary organisations and other interested parties, which help to bring particular cases, is to know which ones to support. For instance, the key case of *R v Gloucestershire CC, ex p Barry* has arguably done users of services a distinct disservice by clarifying unfavourably (from their point of view at least) the implications of the legislation (Schwehr 1995).

Indeed, the law courts themselves recognise that judicial review is not always appropriate; for instance, there might be complex problems in meeting people's needs which are not amenable to judicial intervention *R v Islington LBC, ex p Rixon*). Similarly, the courts might simply state that investigation of facts (eg, behind a long delay in services), as opposed to an exploration of legal principle, is better carried out through a local authority's complaints procedure *R v Birmingham CC, ex p A*). More fundamentally, the supervisory, indirect approach to enforcing rights and obligations has already been explained above, as has the firm dislike expressed by the courts at being asked to intervene in respect of tragic choices, rationing and the allocation of priorities (see p.31). In this way, they avoid – in theory at least – advancing too far into areas of government policy, central or local, so as not to overstep the constitutional mark.

11. LAW AND PRACTICE: THE GAP

It would be tempting to accede to the following propositions: a) that local authority members and officers are as a matter of course always and fully aware of their legal obligations; b) that when local authority members and officers are aware of the law, then they always adhere to it; and c) that if the law were adhered to, then community care would run smoothly. Unfortunately, none of these propositions appears to be correct.

The first is undermined by the observation of the local ombudsman that a frequent cause of maladministration is that officers are not aware of their legal obligations (CLAE 1993,p.5).

The second proposition assumes that if local authorities and their staff were conversant with the law, then they would adhere to it. This proposition fails on a number of counts. Knowledge of the law might be located only in selective parts of a local authority (eg, the legal department) without reaching key managers of services. In addition, knowledge of the legislation or latest ruling in the courts is one thing, but converting it into local procedures, policies and guidelines is quite another; neatly delineated legal principle is not always easily superimposed on the rough edges of everyday practice. For instance, the *Gloucestershire* case established that local authorities should not apply eligibility criteria which are legally unreasonable, and that taking account of resources must be part of a balancing exercise involving people's needs. Yet the detailed ramifications of the case for local policies might be far less clear than might be supposed. For example, what constitutes unreasonableness, or a satisfactory balancing act? And even if the law does find its way successfully into policies and procedures, these might not be followed by staff, might be informally varied, or simply become out of date.

Indeed, case studies of how local authorities operate homelessness legislation have illustrated 'pervasive subversion of statutory requirements' and 'not infrequent disposition ... to sidestep legal restraints'. This means that 'administrative reality' might bear little resemblance to 'prescriptive legality' in local authorities, although a variety of motives might underlie this state of affairs (Loveland 1994). Judicial review certainly has the potential to perform an educative role and to set out principles and standards for local authorities to work to; but, disturbingly, it is unknown whether it has such an impact in practice – given the probably limited 'ability of juridical norms to infiltrate administrative cultures' (Richardson, Sunkin 1996).

The failure of the third proposition, just like the second, is a timely reminder that law simply does not provide all the answers. For instance, lawful practice on the part of a local authority does not necessarily mean that people will get all the services they need, and the courts sometimes recognise that it is for Parliament to solve fundamental problems such as lack of resources. Furthermore, the numerous examples given in this book of community care in action, including many local ombudsman investigations, suggest that at least some answers lie in good professional practice, organisation and administration. Indeed, users of services might suffer more from poor practice or maladministration than from unlawful decisions.

12. GOOD ADMINISTRATION AND COMMON SENSE: LOCAL OMBUDSMEN

The extraction of legal principle in judicial review cases sometimes can mean the discarding of untidy realities. In comparison, the local ombudsmen consider not only legal and administrative points, some of which overlap with the considerations of the law courts, but also the everyday, down-to-earth events and facts of a dispute. In this way, they provide a more detailed and richer, if less luminous, picture of community care than that achieved by the courts.

The local ombudsmen operate somewhere in the space between legal principle as explored by the courts and good practice as espoused by, for example, the Social Services Inspectorate at the Department of Health. They investigate maladministration and injustice perpetrated by local authorities. Their findings do not constitute part of 'the law', and their recommendations, though usually followed, are not legally binding.

At one extreme, they sometimes consider the same principles as the law courts – for instance, whether legislation has been explicitly breached, a policy has been applied too rigidly, or a decision made without taking account of relevant factors. Adverse findings in this respect are at least indicative of unlawful actions (ie, a court might have come to such a conclusion had it considered the case) and for that reason important. At the other extreme, the ombudsmen consider very basic administrative issues usually beneath the gaze of the law courts in judicial review – such as letters going astray in the post, whether a telephone call was made or a note of a meeting taken, staff not following up recommendations, or failure to let service users know what was going on. These do not represent matters of high legal principle but, as already mentioned above, they can affect service users just as adversely as unlawfulness.

Ombudsman investigations therefore reflect the fact that local authority staff and service users find themselves in the grip of unlike influences: on the one hand, complex legislation and abstract legal principle, on the other humdrum tasks. The investigations attempt to resolve difficulties arising by steering a middle path in terms of good administration, good professional practice and – what is perhaps often synonymous with both of these – common sense.

13. GOOD PRACTICE AND LAW

As explained immediately above, a glance through the local ombudsmen's axioms of good administration (CLAE 1993) quickly reveals their consonance with what both professionals and users of services are likely to equate with 'good practice'. Of further interest is that a number of the principles or interpretations enunciated by the courts in judicial review cases also equate with good practice.

For instance, rigid policies should be avoided and exceptional needs looked out for (*R v Ealing LBC, ex p Leaman; R v North Yorkshire CC, ex p Hargreaves (no.2); British Oxygen v Board of Trade*); screening procedures should not be restrictive (*R v Bristol CC, ex p Penfold*); assessment is useful in its own right (*R v Bristol CC, ex p Penfold*); people should not be kept waiting interminably for a decision about services (*R v Sutton LBC, ex p Tucker*); Department of Health guidance should be taken account of *R v Islington LBC, ex p Rixon*); people's preferences should be considered (*R v North Yorkshire CC, ex p Hargreavees*); people's needs should be viewed broadly (*R v Haringey LBC, ex p Norton*); people's needs should be assessed and reassessed individually and attentively (*R v Gloucestershire CC, ex p Mahfood* and *R v Gloucestershire CC, ex p RADAR*); needs should be distinguished from options for services (*R v Lancashire CC, ex p RADAR; R v Cornwall CC, ex p Goldsack; R v Kirklees MBC, ex p Daykin*); accurate letters should be written (*R v Bristol CC, ex p Bailey*) – and so on.

On a more abstract level, social work values, ethical and professional, can be found (at least in principle) in community care legislation: for example, 'normalisation' in the Chronically Sick and Disabled Persons Act 1970, or 'self-determination' in the Community Care (Direct Payments) Act 1996 (Preston-Shoot *et al.* 1998a). However, such terms do not occur explicitly and the array of specific duties and powers within community care might fail to amount to what social care professionals might recognise as clear 'social rights' (Preston-Shoot *et al.* 1998b).

14. PARLIAMENTARY DEBATES AND QUESTIONS

The book carries a number of quotes from Parliament, in relation to the passing of legislation (and to subsequent comments made about it).

First, the courts frequently refer, when reaching decisions, to what the intention of Parliament was, or must have been. In spite of this longstanding practice, it was, somewhat remarkably, only in November 1992 that a House of Lords ruling (*Pepper v Hart*) officially allowed the courts to consult (in certain circumstances) Hansard, the published record of Parliamentary proceedings. These circumstances are when a) 'legislation is ambiguous or obscure, or leads to an absurdity'; b) 'the material relied on consists of one or more statements by a minister or other promoter of the Bill together if necessary with such other parliamentary material as is necessary to understand such statements and their effect'; and c) 'the statements relied on are clear'. Even so, since this ruling, the courts do not necessarily refer to Hansard when they are speculating about what Parliament must have intended – even when legislation is troublesome in meaning. For instance, in *R v Gloucestershire CC, ex p Barry* the minority and the majority judges, in the split decision of the House of Lords, came to opposite conclusions regarding Parliament's intention about meeting disabled people's needs – without any reference to Hansard.

Second, the quotes are a reminder that legislation does not appear out of thin air but is debated and discussed in Parliament – sometimes in considerable and thoughtful depth, sometimes not. Either way, the quotes can be illuminating about the genesis of the legislation and surrounding policy (or, in the case of questions asked subsequently, about its ongoing operation).

CHAPTER 4

PRACTICAL CHECKLIST

Coverage

1. Law
2. Access to assessment
3. Assessment
4. Provision of services
5. Disputes and remedies

This chapter provides a rough checklist against which to begin to measure the *potential* lawfulness of the decisions, policies and criteria of eligibility of local authorities. Of course only the law courts can state what *actually* is lawful or not, but it is clearly useful if both local authorities and users of services (or their advisers or representatives) are aware of the types of question posed by the courts. In this way, there is a better chance that unlawful and disputed decisions will be avoided. The following list should therefore be viewed as at least a general starting point for some of these questions.

Indeed, the local ombudsmen have stated that one of the most common reasons for findings of maladministration is that local authority staff are unaware of their legal obligations (CLAE 1993,p.5). Therefore it follows from this that there are many local authority policies, criteria and decisions against which the proper questions are simply not being asked. One of the reasons for this would appear to be that relevant members and officers do not always inform themselves adequately about the implications of legislation and Department of Health guidance, or seek expert advice. That said, the complexity of community care legislation and the piecemeal procession of judicial review cases through the law courts does not make familiarity with the relevant law straightforward.

If any further reason were required for local authority staff to improve matters, it is that both the principles of administrative law as applied by the courts in judicial review, and good administration as encouraged by the ombudsmen, equate (on the whole) with what professionals would call good practice. Thus professionals have a dual incentive.

I. LAW

The logical starting point is legislation, since local authorities and their staff are creatures of statute; they exist only by virtue of legislation. Thus, in a straightforward sense, if decisions, policies and criteria are inconsistent with legislation, then the local authority will go wrong in law. At its simplest, this means that the relevant local authority members and officers should actually read the legislation carefully – something which apparently does not always occur. If they do not, then the policies they adopt might inadvertently and unlawfully put a line through the statutory wording of legislation (see eg, *R v London Borough of Ealing, ex parte Leaman*). For instance, the ombudsman might find that a local authority social services department is 'quite unclear' about the law in relation to disabled facilities grants (*Humberside CC 1996*), or legally incorrect in stating that it could only provide funding for registered residential accommodation (*Lancashire CC 1997*). A housing committee might approve policies, without receiving any advice as to whether they are consonant with the statutory framework in housing legislation (*Hertsmere BC 1995*).

The other place in which the law is located, is the decisions of the law courts. Similarly, local authorities need continually to be aware of and to adhere to these; but again it seems apparent that everyday practices in local authorities do not necessarily reflect judicial decisions. In addition, both local authorities and health authorities are awash with guidance issued by the Department of Health. Although guidance does not in itself constitute law, authorities must legally take account of, or have regard to, it – and, generally speaking, have good reasons if they choose not to follow it (see p.38). If they fail to do this, then the courts might strike down decisions, policies and criteria as unlawful. Once more, it would seem axiomatic that the relevant local authority staff should be aware of guidance and its content.

Law: legislation (Acts of Parliament)

Legislation places duties and powers on authorities. Duties are obligations, powers are generally 'take it or leave it'. There are two types of duty; specific duties towards individual people, and general target duties towards the local population.

Legislation: duties. It is crucial to identify duties in legislation, usually indicated by the word 'shall'. A duty is what an authority must do – as opposed to a power (associated with the word 'may') which enables, but does not oblige, the authority to do something.

Legislation: specific duties. The courts have chosen to distinguish specific duties aimed at individuals (often indicated by the term 'any person' in the legislation), and general duties. The former type of duty, regarded as easier to enforce in judicial review proceedings, is exemplified in s.2 of the Chronically Sick and Disabled Persons Act 1970 (and s.117 of the Mental Health Act 1983). It is thus no accident that the 1970 Act has been at the heart of a number of community cases heard in the courts.

Legislation: general duties. General duties might be in respect of people in general, rather than individuals in particular. For instance, those under ss.1 and 3 of the NHS Act 1977 cover provision of health services to the local population generally. Similarly, the duty to arrange welfare services under s.29 of the National Assistance Act 1948 is towards that group of people generally. Such duties are often regarded by the courts as less amenable to enforcement by an individual (see eg, *R v Inner London Education Authority, ex p Ali* an education case, commenting on the NHS Act 1977; *R v Gloucestershire CC, ex p Barry; R v Cornwall CC, ex p Goldsack; R v Islington LBC, ex p Rixon* – all three community care cases; *R v Bexley LBC, ex p B; Re T* – both child care cases; and *R v Ealing DHA, ex p Fox*, a mental health case). Nevertheless, depending on the context, it is possible that the courts might hold that even a generally expressed duty can only be made sense of if applied to individual circumstances (*Attorney General ex rel Tilley v London Borough of Wandsworth; or R v East Sussex CC, ex p Tandy*, an education case). Even when there is an absolute and specific duty, a question arises about how quickly it must be performed, and at what point a delay in performance amounts to a breach of statutory duty (see below).

Legislation: powers. It is important to identify powers in legislation, usually indicated by the word 'may'. A power is what an authority can do if it wants – as opposed to a duty (associated with the word 'shall') which obliges it to do something. For instance, local authorities have a power to make direct payments to users of community care services under the Community Care (Direct Payments) Act 1996, or to arrange services for older people under s.45 of the Health Services and Public Health Act 1968.

However, even in respect of powers, the courts have sometimes held that public bodies must not adhere to rigid policies which fetter their discretion by excluding the possibility of exceptions (eg, *R v Warwickshire CC, ex p Collymore* about education grants).

Law: judicial review in the law courts

In judicial review cases, the courts interpret legislation (statute law) and also add their own (common law) ideas about what lawful practice by public bodies should look like. The principles they apply include *unreasonableness* (taking leave of senses), *fettering of discretion* (rigid policies which cannot take account of exceptions), *illegality* (contravening legislation), taking account of *irrelevant factors* or failing to take account of relevant factors, people's *legitimate expectation* (eg, to consultation before a service is changed or a residential home closed) etc.

The following paragraphs summarise a few of the common law principles with which the courts test the lawfulness of decisions, policies and eligibility criteria. References to local ombudsman investigations are also included because, although the ombudsmen investigate maladministration rather than unlawfulness, they utilise some of the same principles as the law courts.

Judicial review (and ombudsman): consistency of local authority decisions. There is no explicit rule applied by the law courts in relation to the consistency of decisions made by local authorities, but arguably they do penalise inconsistency under other guises, such as irrelevance or irrationality (Steyn 1997).

Nevertheless, a number of factors appear almost to favour inconsistency in some circumstances. First, it can be argued that no two cases are exactly alike and that therefore there is no inconsistency anyway. Second is the obligation on local authorities to avoid fettering their discretion and to take account of exceptional cases; yet the line between doing this and being inconsistent may be very fine (*R v Ministry of Agriculture, ex p Hamble*).

Third, the courts accept that if local authorities were precluded from changing policies from time to time, their discretion would be fettered (eg, *Re Findlay*); but clearly, apparent inconsistency might be due to just such a change. Lastly, the courts sometimes simply accept that inconsistent decision-making is not necessarily unlawful, even when the same decision-maker reaches different conclusions about the very same person (eg, *R v Secretary of State for Education, ex p C*). The local ombudsman, too, might accept that even three different decisions (recommending three different types of home lift for a woman with multiple sclerosis) on the same facts is not maladministration (*Sheffield CC 1996*).

On the other hand, good administration demands that local authorities behave reasonably consistently and equitably rather than arbitrarily. For instance, variable standards or criteria for provision of services between different areas of the same local authority might be struck down by the law courts as unfair or irrational (*R v Tower Hamlets, ex p Ali*, a housing case). Inconsistency, without clear and unambiguous explanation, in the making of planning decisions might also be unlawful (*R v East Herts DC, ex p Beckman*).

Similarly, substantial discrepancies in waiting times for community care assessment, between areas of the same authority, might be deemed maladministration by the local ombudsman (*Hackney LBC 1992a, Newham LBC 1997b*). A failure to prioritise applications for home adaptations on a council-wide basis – and instead to depend on the fluctuating state of the repairs budget of local teams – was also maladministration (*Camden LBC 1993*); as was inconsistent decision-making that resulted in queue-jumping (*Lewisham LBC 1993*).

Judicial review (and ombudsman): consultation. Apart from duties laid down in legislation (eg, the duty to consult about community care plans in s.46 of the NHS and Community Care Act 1990), the courts might impose a common law duty of consultation to a reasonable standard when they judicially review local authorities or health authorities. For instance, they have been astute to the importance of consultation when residential homes or hospitals (or hospital units) are being closed (*R v Wandsworth LBC; ex p Beckwith (no.2); R v Devon CC, ex p Baker; R v North and East Devon HA, ex p Pow; R v NW Thames RHA; ex p Daniels; R v North and East Devon HA, ex p Coughlan*) or health authorities are considering new policies in relation to the registration of local nursing homes (*R v Kingston and Richmond HA, ex p Paxman*). The local ombudsman, too, criticised a local authority when it failed to keep residents and relatives – and indeed the home owner – informed about steps it was taking to deregister a residential home (*Hampshire CC 1996*).

On the other hand, in *R v Coventry CC, ex p CHOICE*, a local care home association claimed a right of consultation over a decision about the level of contractual payments; but the court ruled that in the circumstances there was no such right and, in any case, the scale of the consultation required would have been 'a quite unreasonable exercise'. See also: *Legitimate expectation* (below).

Judicial review (and ombudsman): fettering of discretion and exceptions to policies. Policies and criteria of eligibility must be able to take account of exceptions; otherwise the courts might rule that they are *fettering the discretion* of an authority.

An authority might fetter its discretion not only in respect of a *duty* (see eg, *R v North Yorkshire CC, ex p Hargreaves (no.2)* about holidays under the CSDPA 1970; *Attorney General ex rel Tilley v London Borough of Wandsworth* about child care) – but also a *power* (*British Oxygen v Board of Trade* about industrial grants; *R v Warwickshire CC, ex p Collymore* about education grants; *R v Bristol CC, ex p Bailey* about renovation grants). At an extreme, the very existence of a policy (even when hedged around with exceptions) has been held to be capable of fettering discretion. But on the other hand it can be argued that the application of priorities does not preclude individual consideration – because each person might still be matched up individually against the appropriate priority *R v Brent and Harrow HA, ex p Harrow LBC*, an NHS case about a child's eligibility for NHS therapies).

A policy which awarded housing medical points by household rather than by individual was illogical, rigid and inflexible, because it gave no consideration to the number of people in a dwelling (*R v Lambeth LBC, ex p Ashley*). The insertion of terms such as 'usually' or 'in exceptional cases' might help to save a policy from rigidity (*R v Gateshead MBC, ex p Lauder:* housing allocation). However, actually specifying the exceptions in a policy might (*R v Ministry of Agriculture, ex p Hamble* about fishing licences) or might not (*R v Southwark LBC, ex p Melak* about housing allocation) save an authority from unlawfully fettering its discretion; but in any event a term such as 'exceptional circumstances' refers to the unforeseen and there might be no requirement that it be further defined in the policy (*R v Buckinghamshire CC, ex p Sharma*). A local authority's caution in recommending stairlifts for people with multiple sclerosis did not necessarily amount to a blanket policy and consequent maladministration (*Sheffield CC 1996*).

The local ombudsman has commented that in his view the existence of a complaints procedure does not save a rigid policy from fettering the discretion of an authority (*Hertsmere BC 1995*). The strict application of a policy, penalising those in rent arrears in relation to housing allocation, was maladministration when the special needs of family with a severely disabled member were not taken into account (*Bristol CC 1998*). And the imposition of a financial ceiling on home care packages of community care services for older people was also maladministration – since the panel that met to consider exceptions apparently never made any (*Liverpool CC 1998b*).

Judicial review (and ombudsman): giving reasons. Community care legislation does not impose a duty on local authorities to give reasons, except at the final stage of the complaints procedure (see p.424), and the law courts will not necessarily impose a common law duty to do so. Nevertheless, a failure to give reasons is maladministration in the eyes of the local ombudsman (CLAE 1993,p.11).

However, there are some circumstances (ie, it depends on the context) in which the courts will anyway impose such a duty (for a summary, see *R v Ministry of Defence, ex p Murray,* a court martial case) – although in the community care context, it is unclear in what circumstances.

In any event, an absence of clear reasons given at the time of a decision a) might hinder a court (eg, in judicial review) at a later date from examining the decision; b) deprives the person involved of knowing what is going on; and c) does not force the decision-maker to concentrate his or her mind and to improve the quality of decision-making in disciplined fashion (see generally: Fordham 1998). For example, it has been suggested that well-communicated, clear reasons might in practice assist to improve the making of tragic choices in health care in cases such as *R v Cambridge HA, ex p B,* to explain them to patients and their families, and to improve the chances of a more informed debate in the media (Ham, Pickard 1998; on the media debate, see Entwhistle *et al.* 1996). Department of Health guidance on complaints also points out that giving people the reasons for, and background to, decisions is 'good practice as well as good sense' and might obviate confusion and resentment (SSI 1991b,p.4).

The courts are loath to allow local authorities to 'rewrite history' by adding reasons to a decision retrospectively (see eg, *R v Westminster, ex p Ermakov* and *R v Islington LBC, ex p Bibi,* both housing cases). However, they might sometimes be prepared to consider affidavits to this effect (eg, *R v Haringey, ex p Norton* concerning community care assessment), although will not automatically do so (ie, they will reserve the discretion not to), even if they are confident that the later material does genuinely represent the original reasons (*R v Northamptonshire CC, ex p W,* an education case).

Both service users and authorities should probably also be aware of the unimplemented s.3 of the Disabled Persons (Services, Consultation and Representation) Act 1986. Though not in force, it contains a detailed assessment procedure for disabled people approved by Parliament, and includes the giving of reasons for assessment decisions. The reader should also note that in contrast to community care legislation, the Housing Grants, Construction and Regeneration Act 1996 does impose a duty on local authorities to give reasons for adverse decisions in relation to housing grants, including disabled facilities grants (s.34).

Judicial review (and ombudsman): illegality. If a local authority makes a decision (typically based on a policy or criteria of eligibility) which contravenes legislation, the courts will strike it down as unlawful. Nevertheless, local authorities continue to adopt policies which fall into this trap, sometimes because they seem not to consider closely the wording of legislation before formulating the policy (eg, *R v Ealing LBC, ex p Leaman; R v North Yorkshire CC, ex p Hargreaves (no.2)* – both about holidays for disabled people). This principle can work to the advantage of users of services, but also against them, if a decision made in their favour is struck down because the local authority was not empowered to make it under the relevant legislation (eg, *Stretch v West Dorset; R v Ealing LBC, ex p Jennifer Lewis*).

Judicial review (and ombudsman): legitimate expectation. The courts sometimes recognise that if a public body has led people to believe that they will gain a certain benefit (if they meet certain conditions), then they have at least a right to some form of consultation (procedural expectation) if that benefit does not materialise, and occasionally to the benefit itself (substantive expectation).

In the community care context, the courts have made a stand on the matter of consultation in the context of closing residential homes (see above, p.49); and have confirmed that if people's services are being reduced or withdrawn, then they must at least be reassessed first. This is arguably one way of satisfying a person's legitimate expectation, at least in the procedural sense (*R v Gloucestershire CC, ex p Barry* – High Court stage). However, the courts will not always recognise a legitimate expectation to be consulted: see, for example, *R v Secretary of State for Health, ex p Alcohol Recovery Project; R v Cleveland CC, ex p Cleveland Care Homes Association*. Similarly, if a local authority warns a person from the outset that a service might be subject to some fluctuation, this too might in effect be a way of satisfying expectation (*R v Islington LBC, ex p McMillan*).

The right to a benefit itself (see eg, *R v Secretary of State for the Home Department, ex p Khan*, on immigration) has not generally been tried and tested in community care, and there would in any case be considerable problems in recognising legitimate expectation to any great extent. For instance, it would make it difficult for a local authority to alter its policies or eligibility criteria – because of the expectations both of existing users of services, and potential users of services who had expected to be treated on the basis of the old policy or criteria. (For disappointed expectations because of changes in policy, see *R v Secretary of State for the Home Department, ex p Hargreaves* about prisoner' home leave; *Re Findlay* about prisoners' parole; and *Hughes v Department of Health and Social Security* about the retirement age of civil servants).

Nevertheless, in a community care case about closure of residential care homes, the courts stated that the demands of fairness were likely to be higher in relation to people receiving an existing benefit than to people applying for a future benefit (*R v Devon CC, ex p Baker*). And in one ombudsman investigation, a woman had spent money on re-tiling, carpets and redecoration in her flat after the council said it would arrange an extension; the council then went back on its word. The ombudsman did not regard the undertaking to build the extension as binding, but did recommend compensation for the works the woman had undertaken in expectation (*Manchester CC 1994*).

However, in December 1998, the High Court in *R v North and East Devon Health Authority, ex p Coughlan* ruled a) that the consultation process over the proposed closure of an NHS unit had been inadequate; and also b) that an oral promise given by the health authority to a number of disabled patients in the unit, that it would be a home for life for them, could not be broken - unless the health authority established an overriding public interest. This judgment followed the principle set out in *R v Secretary of State, ex p Khan*, by going beyond identification of a procedural expectation (ie to consultation) to a substantive expectation (ie, retaining the actual benefit in question, namely the right to remain in that accommodation). In the NHS and community care context, this is potentially a landmark case - if it survives an appeal to the Court of Appeal.

Judicial review (and ombudsman): relevant factors. When reaching decisions, local authorities must take account of relevant, and ignore irrelevant, factors (*Associated Picture Houses v Wednesbury Corporation*). For instance, they should not introduce extraneous conditions to the statutory means test for renovation grants (*R v Sunderland CC, ex p Redezeus*) or to eligibility for disabled facilities grants (*Hackney LBC 1997b*: an ombudsman case).

Judicial review (and ombudsman): unreasonableness. Unreasonableness is defined in various ways by the law courts – for instance, it is a decision so unreasonable that no reasonable authority could have taken it (*Associated Picture Houses v Wednesbury*), outrageous in its defiance of logic or morals (*Council of Civil Service Unions v Minister for the Civil Service*) or represents a 'taking leave of senses' (*R v Haringey LBC, ex p Norton*). When wishing not to intervene, the law courts use these definitions to erect an impossibly high threshold to be crossed by local authorities, before they are deemed to be unreasonable (eg, *R v Haringey LBC, ex p Norton, R v East Sussex CC, ex p Tandy* in the Court of Appeal; *R v Department of Health and Social Security, ex p Bruce*).

Alternatively, when they do wish to interfere (and express 'judicial outrage', perhaps in place of more sophisticated, principled and articulate analysis: see Carnwath 1996) the courts lower the threshold and identify unreasonableness. This sometimes occurs even when local authorities (eg, *R v Cleveland CC, ex p Cleveland Care Homes Association* about care home contracts; *R v Staffordshire CC, ex p Farley* about night sitter services; *R v Tower Hamlets LBC, ex p Spencer* about housing allocation; *R v Wandsworth LBC, ex p M* about competent staff) – or even Secretaries of State (*R v Secretary of State for the Home Office, ex p Zakrocki* about immigration and community care) – have clearly not lost their senses. The courts have also stated that not to offer assistance to disabled people at severe physical risk would be unreasonable (*R v Gloucestershire CC, ex p Mahfood*); but that, although community care eligibility criteria must not be so strict as to be unreasonable (*R v Gloucestershire CC, ex p Barry*), nevertheless they will be very reluctant to intervene in such circumstances when resources are in issue (*R v East Sussex CC, ex p Tandy*).

Law: legislation (regulations)

Regulations (statutory instruments), known as secondary legislation, are made under primary legislation (ie, Acts of Parliament). For instance, the detailed procedures governing charges for residential accommodation are contained in regulations. Unlike Acts of Parliament, the courts can strike down regulations as unlawful (eg, *R v Secretary of State for Social Security, ex p Joint Council for the Welfare of Immigrants* about asylum seekers).

Law: directions

Directions are not contained in, but are made by the Secretary of State under, legislation, and impose duties on local authorities. However, the operation of legislation may depend on them; therefore awareness of their existence is important. For instance, they substantially govern the provision of residential and nursing home accommodation under s.21 of the National Assistance Act 1948, and of welfare services under s.29 of the same Act. As with regulations, the courts have the power to strike down directions – but unlike regulations, directions bypass Parliament when they are made.

Law: approvals

Approvals confer powers on local authorities and are not contained in, but are made by the Secretary of State under, legislation. However, the operation of legislation may depend on them, therefore awareness of their existence is important. For example, s.45 of the Health Services and Public Health Act 1968 is currently operative only via approvals, which give local authorities a power to arrange various community care services for older people (see p.213). Also some of the services arranged for disabled people under s.29 of the National Assistance Act 1948 are governed by approvals. Like regulations, approvals can be struck down by the courts as unlawful; but like directions, they bypass Parliament when they are made.

Law: guidance

Guidance is not law, but is sometimes referred to as quasi-legislation to indicate the no-man's land it occupies. There are two types in community care, 'stronger' and 'weaker'. Under s.7 of the Local Authority Social Services Act 1970, local authorities must act under the general guidance of the Secretary of State. Such guidance is of the stronger variety, for instance *Community care in the next decade and beyond: policy guidance* (DH 1990). Failure to follow it without good reason can amount to breach of duty (*R v North Yorkshire County Council, ex parte Hargreaves*). Weaker guidance such as the

Care management and assessment: practitioners' guide (SSI,SWSG 1991a) is not made under the 1970 Act but must still be had regard to. Substantial departure from it might suggest it has been overlooked; in which case a court might again find unlawfulness *(R v London Borough of Islington, ex parte Rixon, and R v London Borough of Sutton, ex parte Tucker).*

Law: standards of practice

Standards of practice in community care are set by local authorities themselves, and also at national level by the Social Services Inspectorate, part of the Department of Health, which applies them in its inspections of local authority services. Even the national standards do not in themselves impose legal obligations. However, the Inspectorate seeks 'to ensure that they are justifiable, sustainable and explainable. Their content is influenced by government policy, legislation, regulation, guidance, research findings and accepted good practice' (CI(96)23). It is clearly helpful for local authorities to know, of any set of standards, which individual standards purportedly relate to statutory obligations, and which represent merely desirable practice.

Nevertheless, unlike some of the standards published by the Social Services Inspectorate relating to children's services, and for whatever reasons, those dealing with community care refer little to relevant law. Compare, for instance, the extreme paucity of statutory reference in a volume of collated community care standards (SSI 1996h), with the relatively plentiful reference in two volumes of child care standards (SSI 1996f and 1996g). The reports of community-care related inspections predictably reflect this, drawing relatively little attention to the law, even when findings suggest practices which might be unlawful. Even so, some community care reports do make more reference (SSI 1998b) than others (SSI 1998f). Yet, it is of interest to note that a number of judicial rulings in community care have expressed principles which coincide with what those working in social services departments – such as social workers and occupational therapists – are likely to equate with good professional practice (see p.44).

Similarly, the Inspectorate's standards make no explicit reference to the local ombudsmen's axioms of good administration, despite an obvious and significant overlap.

Law: waiting times for assessment and services

Apart from identifying the circumstances in which they have a duty to do something, local authorities need to know how quickly they should perform a duty – before delay turns into breach of the duty and unlawfulness. Where no time limit is laid down in legislation, the courts might state that a duty must be performed within a reasonable time or without undue delay; and this will depend on all the circumstances of the case. Alternatively, the courts might be reluctant to deal at all with simple delay in judicial review proceedings.

To date, no pure waiting list cases have been heard in the community care field, although *R v Sutton LBC, ex p Tucker* involved an individual's two-year wait for community care services, which was a breach of statutory duty. In *R v Birmingham CC, ex p A*, the court would not become involved in a case solely about delay, because it hinged on investigation of facts rather than legal principle. During a wait, interim provision is acceptable, but should not go on for too long (*R v Sutton LBC, ex p Tucker*). In *Cross v Kirklees MBC* (about treatment by the local authority of an icy pavement – a breach of statutory duty case in private law, rather than a judicial review case), the Court of Appeal stated that sufficient measures should be taken in a reasonable time to comply with an absolute duty. The court in *R v Kirklees MBC, ex p Daykin* stated that, having accepted there was a duty to provide community care services, a local authority should get on with it as soon as 'reasonably practicable'. And, in *R v Lambeth, ex p A*, when a disabled child and his family needed rehousing, the Court of Appeal noted that nobody, no matter how great his needs, had an absolute right to be rehoused immediately.

The local ombudsman often decides about the reasonableness of waiting times on the facts of individual cases, although has recently suggested some rough guidelines for social services assessment of people who have applied for disabled facilities grants: two months for urgent, four months for serious, and six months for non-urgent cases (see p.96).

Law: resources

Unsurprisingly, resources have been at the heart of most, if not all, community cases heard in the law courts. The upshot has been that resources are relevant to determining people's needs and what services are to be provided.

It is accepted that local authorities have a general duty to be prudent in respect of expenditure (eg, *Bromley LBC v GLC; R v Brent LBC, ex p Connery*) and to ensure that expenditure has a statutory basis if it is not to be unlawful (*R v Ealing LBC, ex p Jennifer Lewis*). However, the crucial question has been the extent to which lack of resources can justify, legally, the dilution of statutory duties to provide community care services.

> **Resources: Gloucestershire case.** The case of *R v Gloucestershire CC, ex p Barry* controversially established that resources could be taken into account – as part of a balancing exercise with people's needs – under s.2 of the Chronically Sick and Disabled Persons Act 1970. It was held that resources were relevant when deciding a) about need, b) the necessity of meeting that need, c) the option chosen to meet the need. However, once need and necessity were established, a local authority could not refuse to meet the need on grounds of lack of resources; the money would have to be found from somewhere (see *R v East Sussex CC, ex p Tandy*).

> **Resources: retreat from the Gloucestershire case?** Although the 1997 *Gloucestershire* ruling stands, the law courts seem to have since had second thoughts about applying it to other cases. Perhaps they sense a loss of the middle passage they steer between protecting the individuals from the excesses of public bodies, understanding the difficulties facing public bodies, and not intruding on policies sanctioned by Parliament. There has been a retreat from the precipice reached in *Gloucestershire* – over which clear statutory duties might disappear (see above) – as is evident in subsequent cases such as *R v Bristol CC, ex p Penfold*, about eligibility for community care assessment; *R v East Sussex CC, ex p Tandy* about education at home for a child with myalgic encephalomyelitis; *R v Birmingham CC, ex p Mohammed* about disabled facilities grants; and *R v Social Fund Inspector, ex p Taylor* about assessment of need against a limited local Social Fund budget. Even in *R v Sefton MBC, ex p Help the Aged*, in which the Court of Appeal felt impelled (by the *Gloucestershire* case) to concede that resources were relevant to defining people's need for residential accommodation, it stated that they were only of *limited* relevance.

> **Resources: other contexts.** More generally, the effect of resources on service provision has been a recurrent theme in the local authority field. In another education case, a local authority decided to make charges for music tuition. The judge ruled that the charges were unlawful so long as the music remained part of the curriculum; however, had the authority withdrawn music from the curriculum in the face of scarce resources, the authority would not have been breaching its duty in making a reasonable decision that something would have to go (*R v Hereford and Worcester, ex p Jones*).

In *R v Secretary of State for Education and Science, ex p E*, the court concluded that local authorities were bound to meet all the special educational needs of a child; and in *R v Hillingdon LBC, ex p Queensmead*, held that resources could not affect the assessment of special educational needs. In *Staffordshire CC v J*, the court ruled that the Special Educational Needs Tribunal had been entitled to consider what efficient use of resources meant not just in the short-term but also in the long-term – for example, more expensive education for the child straightaway might have meant savings later on.

In another context, relying on the *Gloucestershire* case, the High Court ruled in *R v Norfolk CC, ex p Thorpe*, that a local authority could take account of resources in deciding whether it was necessary or desirable to maintain a footpath. And, in an earlier case about provision of local public transport for elderly and disabled people, the judge ruled that a county council could lawfully take resources into account, so long as it did not eliminate the service altogether (*R v Hertfordshire CCC, ex p Three Rivers DC*).

Within the NHS, challenges to the making of priorities, allocation of resources, and denial of treatment by health authorities have generally failed (eg, *R v Cambridge HA, ex p B; R v Secretary of State for Social Services, ex p Hincks; R v Central Birmingham HA, ex p Collier*).

Lastly, in a case from a somewhat different field, the High Court ruled that although the Secretary of State had discretion in how to measure the limits of an estuary (for the purposes of ascertaining the type and expense of sewage treatment required) – that discretion did not extend to taking into account financial matters when physical, geographical features were being determined (*R v Secretary of State for the Environment, ex p Kingston upon Hull CC*).

Law: policies and criteria of eligibility

The courts (and the ombudsmen) recognise that public bodies such as local authorities or health authorities might have to operate policies and criteria of eligibility, in order to deal fairly with the high demand for their services. Indeed, the absence – or unawareness on the part of staff – of policies, could well result in unlawful actions by local authorities and in potential detriment to users of services. It is true that in one child care case, the court stated that because each child must be approached individually, a policy was precluded – even one hedged around with exceptions (*Attorney General ex rel Tilley v Wandsworth LBC*). However, it has been pointed out in another context (prisons) that it is difficult to see how complex statutory duties can be fulfilled without a policy (*Re Findlay*).

Policies: formal. Policies and criteria should be formally adopted – for example, by the social services committee – as opposed to operated (or departed from) informally and orally by local groups of staff (eg, *R v Leeds CC, ex p Hendry* about taxi licences; see also the following three ombudsman investigations: *Dinefwr 1995* and *Merthyr Tydvil 1994*, about renovation grants, and *Westminster CC 1996* about home help). The ombudsman has criticised staff for adding their own informal criteria to an approved formal policy, since this could lead to inconsistency and queue-jumping, which is maladministration (*Lewisham LBC 1993*). Similarly, it was maladministration when a decision was made by a group of staff using the wrong criteria, which differed from those of a 'joint working group'; it was the latter that, according to the policy, should have been used (*Liverpool CC 1996/1997*). This sort of practice is in contrast to that envisaged by the House of Lords in *R v Gloucestershire CC, ex p Barry*, who assumed it would be the social services committee setting criteria at local level.

Policies: authorised staff. Policies should be followed and decisions not taken by staff unauthorised under a local authority's policy (eg, *R v Islington, ex p Aldabbagh*, housing; *R v Kirklees MBC, ex p Daykin*, stairlift provision); they should be coherent, recorded and backed up by criteria where appropriate (*Hertfordshire CC 1992*, an ombudsman investigation about 'topping up' grants for home adaptations).

Policies: absence of in practice. In practice, the existence of policies, guidelines and criteria might at least contribute to the safeguarding of users of services. Therefore, it was unimpressive that two years after a severely disabled young woman, known to statutory services for 19 years, died in circumstances of neglect, the local authority should still have no published policies, procedural statements or practice guides in relation to disabled people, who were still regarded as a low priority (SSI 1991a,p.2).

Law: procedures

Even if lawful and clear policies are in place, users of services might still suffer detriment because either adequate procedures are absent or staff are unaware of them. Such findings are not uncommon for the local ombudsman.

Procedures: examples. The local ombudsman might find that staff have not been given any clear, written guidance (*Hounslow LBC 1995*) – a failing which is maladministration (*Camden LBC 1993, Hackney LBC 1997c* both about home adaptations procedures). See also *Salford CC 1996* about a social worker's unawareness of her own authority's special fund for people with HIV/AIDS; *Tower Hamlets LBC 1992*, when decentralisation of services had outstripped the putting in place of new procedures; *Cornwall CC 1996* about exclusion of a service user from a day centre; and *Haringey LBC 1993*, when the local authority's stated complaints procedure was simply not put into practice.

Law: advice and information about

Even if sound and lawful policies and procedures (see above) are in place, they will be of little use if people do not find out about them. Indeed, if people are to obtain services under legislation which has been passed for their benefit, they clearly need to be told about the availability of those services and how to qualify. If this does not happen, they might go without. To this end, advice and information are obviously important – indeed, local authorities have explicit duties and powers to provide it under legislation such as s.1 of the Chronically Sick and Disabled Persons Act 1970, s.29 of the National Assistance Act 1948, and s.45 of the Health Services and Public Health Act 1968.

Advice and information: poor quality? Local authority staff give considerable amounts of advice and information both formally and informally. The ombudsmen have made findings of maladministration when poor advice is given to people about their entitlement to state benefits (*Devon CC 1996*), about local surveyor firms (*Cyngor Dosbarth Dwyfor 1994*), about eligibility for grants assistance (*Holderness BC 1995*), or to accommodation providers about registration and related matters of funding (*Lancashire CC 1997, Walsall MBC 1997*).

On the other hand, it might not be maladministration simply because a council officer gives an over-optimistic estimate of how long home adaptations will take to be completed (*Cumbria CC 1992*); or because an occupational therapist does not give 'absolutely clear' advice about submission of an application form for an adaptation (*Cumbria CC 1993*).

Advice and information: absence. It was maladministration when people were on waiting lists for assessment, but not told how long they are likely to have to wait (*Wirral MBC 1994c*); when a local authority failed to send a record of a meeting with a couple (applying for adaptations or alternative accommodation) and to outline the options available (*Barking and Dagenham LBC 1998*); when a recommendation was made by social services to the housing department but the person concerned was not told (*Durham CC 1993*); or when carers or relatives were not informed about what was happening to a person in a residential care home (*Dorset CC 1996, Lambeth LBC 1996*). A failure to inform of people of their right to a service, such as to disabled facilities grants, is also clearly maladministration (*Hackney LBC 1995, Humberside CC 1996*).

Advice and information: negligence? General informal advice is unlikely to give rise to liability in negligence (*Tidman v Reading BC*), but more specific advice might (*Lambert v West Devon BC; X v Bedfordshire CC; T v Surrey CC*). Nevertheless, the courts are sometimes wary of imposing liability in negligence when a local authority is performing a statutory function; and, as already pointed out, advice and information are contained within just such statutory functions.

Law: letter-writing

Local authorities are probably well advised to pay attention to letter-writing. At a time of increased scrutiny of local authority decisions, a carelessly written letter – which does not reflect what is in fact a perfectly lawful decision – might invite a legal challenge. Even if the challenge is not successful, it will waste everybody's time; and in any case, the local ombudsman might deem careless, misleading letters to be maladministration.

> **Effect of letters: examples.** A letter might be evidence in the eyes of the court that an authority was operating a strict policy and fettering its discretion (*R v Harrow LBC, ex p Carter; R v Gateshead MBC, ex p Lauder*); even if subsequently, it turns out that the letter was misleading and did not truly represent the authority's policy, which did in fact allow for flexibility in practice (*R v Bristol CC, ex p Bailey*). The local ombudsman might support a finding of maladministration – in terms of a breach of statutory duty in failing to assess a disabled person under the Disabled Persons (Services, Consultation and Representation) Act 1986 – with reference to a local authority letter which stated that the person did not appear to come within the 'service criteria' and so she would not receive a visit (*Sheffield CC 1995*). Conversely, a letter indicating that further consideration would be given to an application if requested, might be evidence that the authority had not 'shut its ears' and so not fettered its discretion (*R v Cumbria CC, ex p 'NAB'*).

Law: record-keeping

Generally speaking it is clearly poor practice for local authority staff not to keep proper records – both for the sake of the local authority if it is challenged and of the service user. Missing records might very well constitute maladministration in the eyes of the local ombudsman: for instance, in respect of applications for stairlifts (*Camden LBC 1993*), records of meetings (*Dorset CC 1996*), falls in a residential home (*Lambeth LBC 1996*) or a person's adoption file (*Birmingham CC 1993*). The absence of records makes it difficult for a person to pursue a complaint (*Wirral MBC 1993b*).

The consequences of poor record-keeping in the NHS context, but equally applicable to social services, are compromised patient care, loss of protection against negligence claims, and the devaluing of information used for contracting and audit (Audit Commission 1995a,p.15). Unsigned, undated, not easily readable – and inadequately distinguishing between fact, opinion and third party information – might all be criticisms of local authority social services records (SSI 1997d,p.13). Even individual teams within a local authority might keep records inconsistently in terms of style and content; and a lack of records might reflect a lack of arrangements for systematic monitoring of assessment and care management (SSI 1998d,p.33). In a national report, the Social Services Inspectorate found substantial shortcomings in local authority case records (SS1 1999), and has pointed out that effective record-keeping is not just 'an optional extra' (C1(99)1).

2. ACCESS TO ASSESSMENT

There are various strategies and practices in relation to screening people when they first come to the attention of local authorities. Not covered by legislation, screening is an ill-defined activity which can lapse easily into poor professional practice or unlawfulness.

Access to assessment: referral

There is no prescribed form of referral for community care services; people can refer themselves or be brought to the attention of a local authority by others. Between referral and assessment lies the crucial screening or reception stage (see below). It should be noted that the general duty to assess arises not when a person makes a request, but when it appears to the local authority that a person might be in need of community care services (but see below for the case of disabled people).

Access to assessment: screening and information gathering

Local authorities need to ensure that their screening procedures include adequate information gathering, if competent decisions are to be made about people's eligibility for assessment or the priority and level of assessment – or about the appropriateness of referring them to other services. This point would seem obvious; but local authorities sometimes fail on this score and incur findings of maladministration by the local ombudsmen (see p.83).

Access to assessment: appearance is only of possible need

The appearance required to trigger an assessment is only of potential, not actual or even likely, need (ie, assessment is for somebody who *may* be in need). The NHS and Community Care Act 1990, s.47(1)(a) states that:

> 'where it *appears* to a local authority that any person for whom they *may* provide or arrange for the provision of community care services *may be in need* of any such services, the authority (a) shall carry out an assessment of his needs for those services; and (b) having regard to the results of that assessment, shall then decide whether his needs call for the provision by them of any such services' (italics added).

Access to assessment: individual assessment

Assessment is of individuals; decisions about services cannot be made in blanket fashion (*R v Gloucestershire CC, ex p Mahfood*).

Access to assessment: making reasonable efforts to assess

Local authorities must make reasonable attempts to assess people who appear to be in potential need (*R v Gloucestershire CC, ex p RADAR*).

Access to assessment: duty even if only power to provide services

There is still a duty to assess people, even if it is clear from the outset that there is only a power (rather than a duty) to provide services for them (*R v Berkshire County Council, ex parte P*).

Access to assessment: low threshold and resources irrelevant

The threshold of eligibility for assessment should be low and resources cannot be taken account of in the setting of that threshold (*R v Bristol CC, ex p Penfold*).

Access to assessment: benefit in itself, even if no services

Assessment is a benefit in its own right, irrespective of whether any services are likely to be arranged (*R v Bristol City Council, ex parte Penfold*).

(Although in one children's case, the court indicated its realisation that the formalities of assessment can sometimes help only so far; the substantial issue was whether a service, in this case accommodation for a family, is actually available (*R v Lambeth, ex parte A*)).

Access to assessment: disabled people, request and decision

Disabled people are entitled to have a decision made about their needs for services under s.2 of the Chronically Sick and Disabled Persons Act 1970. To this effect, the Disabled Persons (Services, Consultation and Representation) Act 1986, s.4, states that:

> 'When requested to do so by (a) a disabled person ... or c) any person who provides care for him in the circumstances mentioned in section 8, a local authority shall decide whether the needs of the disabled person call for the provision by the authority of any services in accordance with section 2(1) of the 1970 Act (provision of welfare services)'.

Local authorities should not put their heads in the sand, waiting for exactly the right words, before being prepared to decide about a disabled person's needs for services under s.2 of the Chronically Sick and Disabled Persons Act 1970 (*R v London Borough of Bexley, ex parte B*).

Access to assessment: disabled people, request not necessary

If a person is already having a general community care assessment, then the decision about services under s.2 of the Chronically Sick Disabled Persons Act 1970 should be made automatically – and the person be told about their rights. This should happen without the person or carer having to make a request under the 1986 Act (see immediately above). The NHS and Community Care Act 1990, s.47(2) states that:

> 'If at any time during the assessment of the needs of any person under [the above subsection] it appears to a local authority that he is a disabled person, the authority (a) shall proceed to make such a decision as to the services he requires as is mentioned in section 4 of the Disabled Persons (Services, Consultation and Representation) Act 1986 *without his requesting them to do so* under that section; and (b) shall inform that they will be doing so and of his rights under that Act'. (The services mentioned in the 1986 Act are those services listed under s.2 of the Chronically Sick and Disabled Persons Act 1970).

Access to assessment: carers

Certain carers are entitled to an assessment in their own right. The Carers (Recognition and Services) Act 1995, s.1, states that when a local authority is carrying out an assessment under s.47 of the NHS and Community Care Act 1990 of the needs of a person ('the relevant person') for community care services and:

> 'an individual ("the carer") provides or intends to provide a substantial amount of care on a regular basis for the relevant person, the carer may request the local authority, before they make their decision as to whether the needs of the relevant person call for the provision of any services, to carry out an assessment of his ability to provide and continue to provide care for the relevant person; and if he make such a request, the local authority shall carry out such an assessment and shall take into account the results of that assessment in making that decision'.

Access to assessment: health and housing authorities

Local authorities have a duty to invite health or housing authorities to assist with a community care assessment if a person appears to have relevant needs (NHS and Community Care Act 1990, s.47).

Access to assessment: giving of information

Local authorities have a specific duty imposed on them to give information about relevant services to individual disabled people (already using the local authority's services). The Chronically Sick and Disabled Persons Act 1970 (s.1(2)(b)) states that:

> 'Every local authority … (b) shall ensure that any such person as aforesaid who uses any other service provided by the authority whether under any such arrangements [ie under s.29 of the National Assistance Act 1948] or not is informed of any other of those services which in the opinion of the authority is relevant to his needs and of any service provided by any other authority or organisation which in the opinion of the authority is so relevant and of which particulars are in the authority's possession'.

3. ASSESSMENT

Assessment is the gateway to the provision of community care services. It should, for example, be sensitive to individual needs, be needs-led (ie, distinguish needs from possible services), consider a wide range of different types of need (eg, social, recreational, leisure, not just physical), and take into account relevant factors and ignore irrelevant factors. Resources can be taken into account up to a point when people's needs are being assessed, and the necessity of services being decided.

Assessment: assessment of need, then decision about services

The legislation sets out a two-stage process which should be reflected in the policies and procedures of local authorities. The NHS and Community Care Act 1990, s.47(1)(a), states that:

> 'where it appears to a local authority that any person for whom they may provide or arrange for the provision of community care services may be in need of any such services, the authority (a) shall carry out an assessment of his needs for those services; and (b) having regard to the results of that assessment, shall then decide whether his needs call for the provision by them of any such services'.

Assessment: need for community care services

Assessment must consider various legislation in which community care services are found: part 3 of the National Assistance Act 1948, s.45 of the Health Services and Public Health Act 1968, s.2 of the Chronically Sick and Disabled Persons Act 1970, schedule 8 of the NHS Act 1977 and s.117 of the Mental Health Act 1983 (NHS and Community Care Act 1990, s.46).

Assessment: identifying when and by whom statutory decisions are made

Local authority staff should be able to identify at what point an assessment decision has been made under s.47 of the 1990 Act – and to be able to distinguish it from subsidiary information and recommendations provided through, for example, self-assessment forms, advocates, other professionals and so on. Failure to do this will result in confusion about whether the statutory duty of assessment (whether simple or complex) has been performed (eg, *R v Bristol CC, ex p Penfold; R v Kirklees MBC, ex p Daykin*), or about whether an absolute duty to provide services has arisen (*R v Wigan MBC, ex p Tammadge*).

Assessment: decision about whether it is necessary to meet needs under s.2 of the Chronically Sick and Disabled Persons Act 1970

In relation to disabled people, local authorities have to decide whether it is necessary to meet the needs of disabled people. The Chronically Sick and Disabled Persons Act 1970, s.2, states that:

'Where a local authority having functions under section 29 of the National Assistance Act 1948 are satis-fied in the case of any person to whom that section applies who is ordinarily resident in their area that it is necessary in order to meet the needs of that person for that authority to make arrangements for all or any of the following matters … then, subject to the provisions of section 7(1) of the Local Authority Social Ser-vices Act 1970 (which requires local authorities in the exercise of certain functions including functions un-der the said section 29, to act under the general guidance of the Secretary of State) it shall be the duty of that authority to make those arrangements in exercise of their functions under the said section 29'.

When setting eligibility criteria, against which to measure this necessity and need, local authorities may take account of resources (*R v Gloucestershire County Council, ex parte Barry; R v East Sussex County Council, ex parte Tandy*).

Assessment: breadth of need

Need has not just a physical, but also a social, recreational and leisure dimension. In *R v London Bor-ough of Haringey, ex parte Norton*, the court referred to the list of relevant services in s.2 of the Chronically Sick and Disabled Persons Act 1970, and to the notion of 'multi-faceted' need ex-pressed in practice guidance (SSI,SWSG 1991a,p.12).

Assessment: of preferences

Local authorities should take account of people's preferences (*R v North Yorkshire County Council, ex parte Hargreaves*). Sometimes a preference might amount to a need (*R v Avon County Council, ex parte M*). Department of Health guidance (DH 1990 and SSI/SWSG 1991a) emphasises the impor-tance of involving users and taking account of their preferences (see p.138). Subject to 'usual costs', local authorities also have a duty, under directions, to give people a choice of residential ac-commodation (see p.264).

Assessment: future needs

Local authorities should take account of people's imminent, not just their immediate, needs (*R v Bristol City Council, ex parte Penfold; R v Westminster City Council, ex parte A; R v Newham LBC, ex p Gorenkin*).

Assessment: recording unmet need

It is lawful to record unmet needs – ie, needs which the local authority is not going to meet even under s.2 of the Chronically Sick and Disabled Persons Act 1970 (*R v Gloucestershire County Coun-cil, ex parte Barry*). Guidance states that such needs should be recorded both in individual care plans, and within a local authority's planning processes and information (SSI,SWSG 1991a,p.67). Those local authorities that continue to instruct staff not to record unmet need individually would appear to be doing a distinct disservice to their clients, as well as worrying unnecessarily that to do so would be unlawful. Breaching the guidance in this respect might even be unlawful (*R v Islington LBC, ex p Rixon*).

Assessment: distinguishing needs from services

Legal, financial and practical implications flow from distinguishing need from options for services. For instance, need expressed as *24-hour care* might give two service options (care in a person's own home or care in a nursing home). But need expressed as *24-hour care in a person's own home*, leaves just that one option (*R v Lancashire CC, ex p RADAR*; for equivalent examples, see also *R v Kirklees MBC, ex p Daykin; R v Cornwall CC, ex p Goldsack*).

Assessment: simplicity or complexity

Assessments might be simple or complex (*R v Bristol CC, ex p Penfold; R v Kirklees MBC, ex p Good*). It is up to local authorities to attempt to ensure that the depth of assessment is adequate for the circumstances of each presenting individual. In other words simple assessment is not equivalent to inadequate assessment.

Assessment: carers' needs

The Carers (Recognition and Services) Act 1995, s.1, states that if the carer makes a request for assessment (see above), 'the local authority shall carry out such an assessment and shall take into account the results of that assessment in making that decision' (ie, the decision about services for the person being cared for).

Assessment: balancing exercise

If resources are taken into account when criteria of eligibility are set, they must be balanced against people's needs (*R v London Borough of Islington, ex parte McMillan; R v Essex County Council, ex parte Bucke*).

Assessment: disabled facilities grants

Resources are not relevant to the decision under the Housing Grants, Construction and Regeneration Act 1996 about whether proposed home adaptations for disabled people are 'necessary and appropriate' (*R v Birmingham City Council, ex parte Mohammed*)

4. PROVISION OF SERVICES

Provision of services: when an absolute duty arises

Following assessment, the degree of obligation arising to meet identified needs will depend under which legislation community care services come. For instance, if need and necessity are both established under s.2 of the Chronically Sick and Disabled Persons Act 1970, then there is an absolute duty to make arrangements which will meet that need (*R v Gloucestershire County Council, ex parte Barry*). The position is similar once need is established under s.21 of the National Assistance Act 1948 in respect of residential accommodation (see eg, *R v Sefton MBC, ex p Help the Aged*; and *R v Wigan MBC, ex p Tammadge*). This duty will persist even if the relevant budget has run out; it is up to the local authority, to find money from other budgets (*R v East Sussex CC, ex p Tandy*).

On the other hand, if services for older people under s.45 of the Health Services and Public Health Act 1968 are in question, only a power exists – ie, barely any obligation at all.

Provision of services: taking account of resources

Resources may be taken account of when deciding on which service option (if there is more than one) to provide, so long as the assessed need is still met (*R v Gloucestershire County Council, ex parte Barry; R v Lancashire County Council, ex parte RADAR*).

Provision of services: care plans

Care plans are not demanded by legislation, but are referred to in both policy guidance (DH 1990) and practice guidance (SSI/SWSG 1991a). Failure, in respect of care plans and their content, to follow the former type of guidance without good reason, and to have regard to the latter, is unlawful (*R v Islington LBC, ex p Rixon*).

Provision of services: delay

See above, p.53.

Provision of services: reassessment

People may be individually reassessed against reformulated eligibility criteria, and services might in consequence be reduced or withdrawn. However, if resources are taken into account when criteria are revised, then they must also be balanced against people's needs. Furthermore, criteria cannot be arbitrarily drawn and redrawn from day-to-day; for example, the House of Lords envisaged that they would be formally set by social services committees *(R v Gloucestershire CC, ex p Barry)*.

Provision of services: direct payments

The Community Care (Direct Payments) Act 1996 states that:

> 'Where ... a local authority has decided under s.47 of the NHS and Community Care Act 1990 (assessment by local authorities of needs for community care services) that the needs of a person call for the provision of any community care services, and (b) the person is of a description which is specified ... the authority may, if the person consents, make to him, in respect of his securing the provision of any of the services for which they have decided his needs call, a payment of such amount ... as they think fit'.

Direct payments cannot, at the time of writing, be made for the first time to older people (ie, aged 65 or over), although this situation is likely to change. Nor are they available for certain other categories of person (see p.229). Even for people who are eligible, only a power exists; but a blanket policy not to make payments might unlawfully fetter a local authority's discretion if exceptions were genuinely not considered.

Provision of services: charging for non-residential services

The Health and Social Services and Social Security Adjudications Act 1983, s.17, states that local authorities have the power to make reasonable charges (see *Avon CC v Hooper*) for community care services (excluding services under s.117 of the Mental Health Act 1983). But if a person:

> 'avails himself of a service ... and satisfies the authority providing the service that his means are insufficient for it to be reasonably practicable for him to pay for the service the amount which he would otherwise be obliged to pay for it, the authority shall not require him to pay more for it than it appears to them that it is reasonably practicable for him to pay'.

Charging for services under s.2 of the Chronically Sick and Disabled Persons Act 1970 is lawful *(R v Powys County Council, ex parte Hambidge 1998)*.

Provision of services: charging for residential services

Charging for residential or nursing home accommodation is governed by a statutory means-test under s.22 of the National Assistance Act 1948 and associated regulations.

5. DISPUTES AND REMEDIES

Disputes: complaints

Under the Local Authority Social Services Act 1970, s.7 (and associated directions), local authorities have a duty to operate complaints procedures:

> 'whereby a person, or anyone acting on his behalf, may make representations (including complaints) in relation to the authority's discharge of, or failure to discharge, any of their functions under this Act, or any of the enactments referred to in s.2(2) [other social services functions] of this Act, in respect of that person...'

> 'In relation to a particular local authority, an individual is a qualifying individual ... if (a) the authority have a power or a duty to provide, or to secure the provision of, a service for him; and (b) his need or possible need for such a service has (by whatever means) come to the attention of the authority'.

See Chapter 17 for details.

Disputes: local ombudsmen

The local ombudsmen investigate whether local authorities have behaved with maladministration causing injustice. Maladministration is understood broadly and covers good administrative practice (which tends to be consonant with good professional practice and basic common sense, as well as sometimes being indicative of unlawful practices).

Matters considered include breach of duty, fettering of discretion, wayward eligibility criteria, waiting times, poor communication between staff and between staff and clients, inadequate information, giving of reasons, operation of the complaints procedure and so on. Recommendations for substantial financial compensation are sometimes made, and adverse publicity is generated. Thus, local authorities do well to heed the concerns of the ombudsman, although they are not obliged to (see p.440).

Disputes: public law: judicial review

The basic workings of judicial review are explained elsewhere in this book (see p.445). Judicial review is a legal process by which the law courts supervise the doings of public bodies, including local authorities, health authorities and NHS Trusts. It has formed the main plank of challenges to community care decisions. Issues covered have included the relevance of resources to decisions about people's needs, the lawfulness of policies about eligibility for particular services, the closure of residential homes, the duty of assessment – and so on. The principles of good administrative law, as applied in judicial review, have already been summarised and illustrated above (p.48).

Disputes: private law: breach of statutory duty, negligence and contract

Private law proceedings (negligence, breach of statutory duty or contract), in which people seek damages, are of limited application to community care in relation to the challenging of decisions about assessment and provision of services.

Breach of statutory duty. Breach of statutory duty involves people seeking damages in private law from public bodies which have breached their duty in legislation. However, in the welfare field (compared, for example, to the health and safety at work field), the courts are most reluctant to award damages for such breach (see p.450). Nevertheless, as a matter both of good practice and of 'playing it safe' legally, authorities should clearly attempt to ensure that by their actions they do not breach their duties and thereby cause people detriment.

(Pursuing a remedy for breach of statutory duty in private law, should be distinguished from a judicial review application in public law based on breach of statutory duty).

Negligence. Negligence actions (ie, when people sue for damages: see p.450) – to be distinguished from judicial review applications – brought against local authority social services departments will only have a chance of succeeding if it can be shown that the action or decision in issue was a) 'operational' rather than connected with policy and resource issues, and b) was governed by a duty of care which was freestanding from the legislative framework and does not interfere with statutory functions. For instance, a long wait for assessment might be a policy issue. Conversely, the supply of a defective bed might be regarded as an operational matter that could give rise to a duty of care separate from the statutory function governing the decision to provide it (eg, *Wyatt v Hillingdon LBC*).

As far as the NHS is concerned, negligence is well-established in relation to clinical decision-making by health care staff, but less so where administrative duties are carried out directly under legislation (eg, *Clunis v Camden and Islington HA*).

Contract. Generally speaking, it appears that the private law of contract is of little application as between statutory agencies (such as local authorities and health authorities) and their clients or patients. It seems the courts are unlikely to identify contracts, enforceable in private law, in agreements to provide services, even when the client or patient is paying for them (see p.451).

PART II

COMMUNITY CARE ASSESSMENT AND SERVICE PROVISION

CHAPTER 5

ACCESS TO COMMUNITY CARE ASSESSMENT

Coverage

1. Duty to assess
2. Deciding about services for disabled people
3. Assessment on request of disabled people
4. Health and housing authorities in community care assessment
5. Initial screening for community care assessment
6. Priorities for community care assessment
7. Levels of community care assessment
8. Definition of disability
9. Waiting times for assessment
10. Identifying people in need

KEY POINTS

The NHS and Community Care Act 1990 makes assessment a duty and a service in its own right. Assessment itself is pivotal to the provision of community care services, including both residential and non-residential care services (see Chapters 9 and 11), and so access to it is crucial. A number of considerations control who will be assessed, when they will be assessed and what sort of assessment they will get.

The legislation states that a local authority has first to decide whether a person appears to be in possible need of community care services; if the answer is affirmative, there is a duty to assess, if negative, there is none. If, during the assessment, it appears to the authority that the person is disabled then the authority must specifically decide about what services are required under s.2 of the Chronically Sick and Disabled Persons Act 1970.

In order to determine who is eligible for an assessment, how quickly they should be assessed and what type of assessment they will get, local authorities normally operate screening procedures. Such screening is not legally prescribed, but in practice it acts as a powerful filter. This is particularly so because (within fairly wide limits) local authorities can create and apply their own definitions of terms such as 'need', 'priorities', 'levels' of assessment, 'urgency' – and so on. Thus, although only a 'pre-assessment' stage, screening can determine what happens to people, and is a tool used by authorities to regulate their responses to the demands made on them.

Screening is a somewhat shadowy area of activity and can give rise to some of the uncertainties identified in Chapter 3 of this book and consequently to disputes. The High Court reacted in one such dispute by stating that local authorities should set a low threshold for access to assessment, that in any case they could not take account of resources when setting that threshold – and that it was irrelevant that a person was unlikely to qualify for services, since assessment was of benefit in its own right (*R v Bristol CC, ex p Penfold*). The case also illustrated the fine line – and the significant legal implications falling either side of it – dividing what local authorities call screening and what they refer to as 'simple' or 'initial' assessment. The local ombudsmen too have emphasised the importance of adequate information-gathering by authorities at the screening stage, since otherwise they simply are not in a position to make competent judgements about need and priority for assessment.

All this suggests that authorities should think twice before denying assessment to people, even to those who are unlikely ultimately to qualify for services. Furthermore, local authorities sometimes appear to forget that because of the continued freestanding nature of the Disabled Persons (Services, Consultation and Representation) Act 1986, they anyway have a duty, on the request of a disabled person or carer, to make a decision about services under the Chronically Sick and Disabled Persons Act 1970; in other words, they cannot refuse disabled people an assessment.

Alternative to denying people assessment, local authorities sometimes make them wait a long time. The question often asked is at what point the carrying out of a duty slowly amounts to not carrying it out all and to unlawfulness? Failing timescales set out in legislation, both law courts and ombudsmen state that local authorities must carry out their duties within a reasonable time; and what is reasonable will depend on all the circumstances of the case (although the courts might anyway be reluctant to intervene if a dispute about delay involves a consideration of facts only, rather than points of law). This approach has both advantages and disadvantages; on the one hand, it allows for considerable flexibility in reacting to individual needs; on the other, it deprives all concerned of an easy rule of thumb.

Lastly, in order both to identify people who might require assessment and services and to plan services, local authorities in practice need to have information about a) the scale and type of the needs of the local population, and b) the identity of those people who require assessment and services. The NHS and Community Care Act 1990 is silent on these matters but s.29 of the National Assistance Act 1948 places a duty on local authorities to maintain registers of disabled people; and s.1 of the Chronically Sick and Disabled Persons Act 1970 imposes a duty on authorities to find out the number of disabled people in their area and what arrangements are required to meet their needs.

I. DUTY TO ASSESS

Assessment is a duty and service in its own right. It is the process around which the whole community care system ostensibly revolves. Legislation (s.47 of the NHS and Community Care Act 1990) states that if a person appears to be in need of community care services which a local social services authority has the power to provide, then there is a duty to assess that person. If a person does not appear to be in such need, then the authority will refuse to make the assessment. Therefore this does not amount to assessment on request. However, if a disabled person separately makes a request for assessment, the local authority cannot refuse to make a decision about the person's need for services under s.2 of the Chronically Sick and Disabled Persons Act 1970. This is because of the continued freestanding effect of s.4 of the Disabled Persons (Services, Consultation and Representation) Act 1986, irrespective of whether an authority has commenced an assessment under the 1990 Act.

It should be noted that local authorities are expressly empowered to provide services, prior to an assessment, for people they think are in urgent need.

EXTRACTS

Legislation (NHS and Community Care Act 1990, s.47) states that:

(duty to assess) where it appears to a local authority that any person for whom they may provide or arrange for the provision of community care services may be in need of any such services, the authority – (a) shall carry out an assessment of his needs for those services...'. (s.47(1)(a))

(urgent assessment) 'Nothing in this section shall prevent a local authority from temporarily providing or arranging for the provision of community care services for any person without carrying out a prior assessment of his needs in accordance with the preceding provisions of this section if, in the opinion of the authority, the condition of that person is such that he requires those services as a matter of urgency' (s.47(5)).

Policy guidance (DH 1990,para 3.34) states that where:

'an individual's care needs appear to fall entirely outside the responsibility of the local authority it will usually be sufficient to refer the person to the appropriate agency and to notify that agency accordingly. A record should be made of such referrals. Care should be taken that individuals are not repeatedly referred from one agency to another'.

DISCUSSION

Duty to assess: background

The duty to assess appears broad, since only an 'appearance' of possible need is required. The duty falls short however of 'assessment on request'. Circular guidance (CI(92)34) – now cancelled – stated that: 'authorities do not have a duty to assess on request, but only where they think that the person may be in need of services they provide' (para 5).

During the passage of the NHS and Community Care Bill, Baroness Blatch for the government resisted making 'assessment on request' a duty, since where 'the local authority deems that there is no case to take the assessment further, it may choose not to do so'. To impose a duty to assess on request would be to impose a 'wholly unrealistic burden' on local authorities. The amendment had been proposed by Lord Peston because, although the government had been arguing that the primacy of the individual lay behind the Bill, it was 'curious therefore that nothing is said about the rights of the individual' (HLD,10/5/1990,cols.1553–1554).

Yet a few weeks later, the government appeared to restore much of this burden by stating that the duty was 'virtually' assessment on request, since the clause 'requires any local authority to carry out an assessment of any person for whom it appears the authority might arrange community care services. The provision was intended to be as wide-ranging as possible and not to deny anybody making a request for an assessment the opportunity to have one' (Baroness Blatch: HLD,14/6/1990,col.519).

In the House of Commons, Virginia Bottomley had explained that some individuals might have only 'peripheral needs' but nevertheless have 'an unreasonable wish for an assessment', in which case a local authority 'must safeguard itself' by being able to refuse an assessment. However, she in effect anticipated what the law courts (*R v Bristol CC, ex p Penfold; R v Berkshire CC, ex p Parker*) would rule some years later when she could 'conceive of no circumstances in which a local authority that "may" provide an assessment would reasonably refuse such a request from an individual or carer'. She did not, however, appear to foresee that it would be the law courts doing the enforcing, since she instead referred optimistically (given that they have never been used) to use of her default powers (see p.433) in case of recalcitrant authorities (HCD,15/2/1990,col.1025).

The problem facing the government when it drafted the duty to assess was summed up as follows: 'It is impossible to oblige local authorities to take up every crackpot request. It is extremely difficult to draft a clause that lays an obligation on them to take up every reasonable request, but not every unreasonable request' (Andrew Rowe: HSC,15/2/1990,col.1028). A subsequent, unsuccessful amendment did attempt to take up the gauntlet: it would have imposed on local authorities a duty to determine, within 72 hours of receiving a request, whether a person was somebody 'for whom they may provide or arrange for the provision of any community care services' and 'whether that person's request for a determination and assessment is unreasonable, vexatious or obviously without foundation in any need for community care services' (Lord Allen: HLD,14/6/1990,cols.517–520).

Duty to assess: resources

In 1998, the High Court (*R v Bristol CC, ex p Penfold*) stated emphatically that a) authorities cannot take account of resources when deciding what they mean by need at the 'appearance of need' stage; b) the threshold for access to assessment should be low; and c) that it was irrelevant that a person was unlikely to qualify for services, since assessment is of benefit in its own right. This case underlined what had already been said by the High Court in *R v Berkshire, ex P* – and was in spite of the House of Lords ruling (*R v Gloucestershire CC, ex p Barry*) to the effect that when deciding about people's needs during an assessment, resources could be taken into account. Thus, although the meaning of the term 'need' at this pre-assessment stage is likely to vary between authorities, it cannot lawfully be varied with reference to resources.

Indeed, as the *Penfold* case showed and other evidence suggests, resources are in practice taken into account when hard-pressed local authorities regulate access to assessment. For example, individuals might frequently be 'told that they can't have an assessment because there is no money to pay for the services they might need' (NFHA 1993,p.12). At the outset of community care, the House of Commons Health Committee (1993,vol.1,p.xxi) reported its concern that assessment can be restricted by authorities: some 'local authorities have limited access to assessments so that only those with a certain level of need will be assessed. This is done through the application of criteria which assign individuals to particular categories depending on their level of need ... Very strict criteria could lead to an apparent very high level of success in meeting assessed needs, whereas if the criteria are broader and thus the gateway to assessment wider, it is less likely that the authority will appear to be meeting all the needs of those it assesses'.

Apart from the legal aspects clarified by cases such as *Penfold* and *Berkshire* (immediately above), there is in any case a vicious circle created if authorities set a restrictive definition of need. This is that before assessment has taken place, it is difficult to ascertain people's likely needs and the degree of risk to their welfare involved. Alternative to denying people assessments, local authorities might attempt to a) characterise the cursory approach of a few questions on the telephone as an assessment (p.83), or b) operate waiting lists for assessment (p.93).

Duty to assess: initiating assessment

The courts and the local ombudsman are likely to fault those local authorities who adopt deliberately passive approaches to initiating assessment.

For instance, in *R v Gloucestershire CC, ex p RADAR*, the High Court stated that the duty to reassess people for services could not be avoided simply by relying on people's failure to reply to a letter offering the reassessment. The local ombudsman (*Salford CC 1996*) found maladministration when a social worker left it to an enquirer with HIV (and already in possession from the council of an 'orange badge' for his car) to articulate his own needs and wishes and, when this did not happen, then closed the case; as did the occupational therapist when there was no response after she had called unannounced, found the man out and left a card. Staff explained that it was not normal to follow up any further because of long waiting lists for assessment. The local authority was found to have breached its statutory duty to assess a disabled person under the Disabled Persons (Services, Consultation and Representation) Act 1986 (see below). In *Sandwell MBC 1995*, the ombudsman noted that local authorities have a duty to assess needs and to respond to them quickly, given that disabled people are more dependent on council services than able-bodied people and that delay and inefficiency are not mere irritants for disabled people but 'afflict and blight' their quality of life.

The government also warned against too passive an approach, during the NHS and Community Care Bill's passage through Parliament, to the effect that an implication of the word 'appears' was that it 'says nothing about an individual having requested it [an assessment]. The referral or request can come from a number of sources', on which the authority should act (Virginia Bottomley: HCD,15/2/1990,col.1025).

Duty to assess: future need

The courts have ruled that 'need' is not to be unduly confined in its scope; for instance, it might include future need.

In *R v Mid-Glamorgan CC, ex p Miles*, a local authority refused to assess, on the grounds that the person did not need community care services but only had a possible need for services at an unspecified future time (ie, when he was out of prison). It concerned a prisoner who could not gain parole from the Parole Board without a prior assessment – but the local authority would not assess. This was clearly a vicious circle. Eventually, the parties came to an agreement before the hearing and with the court's approval that the authority should carry out the assessment. The effect of this was that the authority had to assess for possible future need as well as for present need (Clements 1994a).

In *R v Bristol CC, ex p Penfold*, the court stated that although s.21 of the National Assistance Act 1948 was couched in the present tense, nevertheless 'imminent events', such as eviction, 'must fall for consideration'. Similarly, in *R v Westminster, ex p A, and R v Newham LBC, ex p Gorenkin*, the courts referred to the need for local authorities to anticipate reasonably the point at which asylum seekers would become in need of care and attention under s.21 of 1948 Act. And the local ombudsman found maladministration when one of the reasons cited by a council for failing to assess a disabled school-leaver was that a full assessment could not be undertaken until the person was in the community – yet this very failure to assess properly meant that appropriately supported living was not arranged when he left school (*Knowsley MBC 1997*).

Duty to assess: which groups of people

Community care legislation does not contain an extensive list of specific groups of people for whom community care services should be available: for example, not mentioned are people with HIV/AIDS or with multiple sclerosis, or who are vulnerable due to domestic violence or physical and sexual abuse. (There are of course many more groups of people that could be mentioned).

The reason for this absence, given by the government during the NHS and Community Care Bill's Parliamentary passage, was that 'the policy objectives of the White Paper are to help to improve services to all vulnerable people ... We should be loath to write in the specific groups for which services shall be provided, because we are considering the overall, comprehensive range of services for those who need community care' (Virginia Bottomley: SC(E),13/2/1990,col.969). Nevertheless, this answer seems to neglect the fact that because certain groups of people are mentioned in community care legislation, it is inevitable that the omission of others will sometimes draw criticism. Groups referred to at present under the various community care statutes are people who are old, aged, handicapped, disabled, substantially and permanently handicapped, ill, blind, deaf, dumb, mentally disordered or mentally ill, nursing and expectant mothers, or dependent on drugs and alcohol. In addition, support grant for revenue expenditure on services for people with HIV/AIDS is available to local authorities under the Local Government Grants (Social Need) Act 1969 (see: LAC(98)9).

2. DECIDING ABOUT SERVICES FOR DISABLED PEOPLE

The duty in s.4 of the Disabled Persons (Services, Consultation and Representation) 1986 Act to 'assess on request' (see section immediately below, p.76) has been further strengthened by the NHS and Community Care Act 1990. If, under s.47(2) of the 1990 Act, local authorities are assessing people who appear to them to be disabled, then they have an automatic duty to decide, under s.4 of the 1986 Act, whether the person needs any of the services mentioned in s.2 of the Chronically Sick and Disabled Persons Act 1970. People do not have to make requests for this to happen.

Should a s.47 assessment not be underway for some reason and so the decision under the 1986 Act not be triggered, disabled people can still make a direct request under the 1986 Act (see section 3 below).

EXTRACTS

Legislation (NHS and Community Care Act 1990, s.47(2)) states:

'If at any time during the assessment of the needs of any person under subsection (1)(a) above it appears to a local authority that he is a disabled person, the authority

(a) shall proceed to make such a decision as to the services he requires as mentioned in s.4 of the Disabled Persons (Services, Consultation and Representation) Act 1986 without his requesting them to do so under that section; and

(b) shall inform him that they will be doing so and of his rights under that Act.'

Policy guidance (DH 1990,para 3.30) states:

'if at any time during their assessment, an individual is found to be a person to whom s.29 of the National Assistance Act 1948 applies, the authority must so inform them, advise them of their rights and make a decision as to their need for services, as required by s.4 of the Disabled Persons' (Services, Consultation and Representation) Act 1986'.

DISCUSSION

Deciding on services for disabled people: community care assessment

It is perhaps unclear from the legislation whether there are two separate assessments: one for community care (under s.47(1) of the 1990 Act), and one under 47(2) for services under the Chronically Sick and Disabled Persons Act 1970. Certainly, practice guidance (SSI,SWSG 1991a) does not suggest that there are separate assessments; it appears to be written on the assumption that a decision about services under the 1970 Act is a part, albeit special, of community care assessment generally.

Indeed, the wording of s.47(2) does not repeat the word 'assessment', but merely talks about a decision about services. On this basis it could even be argued that it does not relate at all to the general assessment process in s.47(1)(a) but only to the decision about what services are called for in s.47(1)(b). Even the 1986 Act itself, in freestanding operation, contains the words 'decide' and 'called for' as does s.47(1)(b). However, a difficulty with viewing the 1986 Act in this way is that it suggests that before the implementation of s.47 of the 1990 Act in April 1993, local authorities were deciding about people's needs for services under the 1986 Act without carrying out an assessment – a nonsensical proposition.

A further duty in s.47(2) obliges the local authority to inform the person what is going on and what rights he or she has under the 1986 Act. It would appear that this duty is commonly breached in practice, sometimes deliberately but often because local authority staff are a) unaware of the duty, and b) not always certain themselves of what legislation they are acting under. For instance, staff might not realise that services under s.2 of the Chronically Sick and Disabled Persons Act 1970 apply to older, as well as younger, disabled people (Davis, Ellis and Rummery 1997,p.15).

It is clear that central government did not intend that disabled people should be refused an assessment under s.47, which was seemingly designed to render unnecessary the request of a disabled person for a decision under the 1986 Act. However, in practice it is possible that a local authority will, at the s.47(1) stage, operate an overly restrictive or inadequate screening procedure, and so turn away a disabled person from an assessment. In challenging such practice, it can be pointed out a) that Department of Health guidance states that disabled people should not only be offered an assessment but that it should be a comprehensive one; and b) that, on a freestanding basis, a request under s.4 of the 1986 Act obliges the local authority to make a decision about services under the Chronically Sick and Disabled Persons Act 1970.

3. ASSESSMENT ON REQUEST OF DISABLED PEOPLE

The duty to provide or otherwise arrange for the provision of services under s.2 of the Chronically Sick and Disabled Persons Act 1970 is strengthened by s.4 of the Disabled Persons (Services, Consultation and Representation) Act 1986. If a disabled person or his or her carer asks the local authority for an assessment, the local authority has a duty to decide whether any of the services listed in s.2 are called for. As already explained above, this duty remains potentially freestanding from s.47 of the NHS and Community Care Act 1990.

EXTRACTS

Legislation (Disabled Persons (Services, Consultation and Representation) Act 1986, s.4) states:

> **(request for assessment)** 'When requested to do so by (a) a disabled person' or '(c) any person who provides care for him in the circumstances mentioned in s.8 [local authorities' taking account of carers' abilities], a local authority shall decide whether the needs of the disabled person call for the provision by the authority of any services in accordance with s.2(1) of the 1970 Act' (provision of welfare services). Disability in this context is governed by the definition contained in s.29 of the National Assistance Act 1948 (or, in the case of children, Part III of the Children Act 1989): see s.16 of the 1986 Act.
>
> **(having regard to the ability of a carer)** See p.168.

Circular guidance (LAC(87)6,para 3) states that:

> **(sealing of loophole)** s.4 of the 1986 Act is designed to close a possible loophole in s.2 of the 1970 Act, which:
>
> 'does not make it explicit whether a local authority has a duty to determine the needs of a disabled person … It was suggested in the course of debates in Parliament … that as the duty to "make arrangements" could be interpreted as applying only after the local authority are satisfied such arrangements are necessary in order to meet particular needs, local authorities might refuse to come to a view as to what those needs are as a means of avoiding the obligation to "make arrangements". It has never been the Government's view that s.2(1) should be interpreted in that way, and it is clear that this is shared by the vast majority of local authorities. However, it was agreed that the matter should be put beyond doubt'.

DISCUSSION

The duty in the 1986 Act ensures that authorities must – on request by a disabled person or his or her carer – decide whether the person's needs call for services under s.2 of the Chronically Sick and Disabled Persons Act 1970. It is true that the need to make this request is now redundant if an authority is already carrying out an assessment under s.47 of NHS and Community Care Act 1990 – because the duty to make this decision under the 1986 is automatically triggered. However, if an authority is not already undertaking an s.47 assessment – for whatever reason (eg, it has 'screened out' a disabled person), then s.4 of the 1986 Act continues to be effective in ensuring that a decision is made. The duty is clear and such as to lead to findings against local authorities who breach it.

Thus, the local ombudsman investigating almost a year's delay in assessing a person with multiple sclerosis, found maladministration in the 'failure by the Council to attempt even a partial assessment of the needs' of the applicant: 'when the Council were made aware of [her] disability they were under a duty to decide whether her needs called for their services. I do not believe this duty was fulfilled within a reasonable period' (*Northumberland CC 1989*). Similarly, when a local authority refused to visit a disabled woman, housebound except when using the electric wheelchair she had bought privately, the ombudsman found maladministration; it was in breach of its statutory duty under the 1986 Act (*Sheffield CC 1995*). The local ombudsman has also rejected lack of money, communication and administration problems as a reason for non-assessment under the 1986 Act and the Chronically Sick and Disabled Persons Act 1970 (eg, *Bolton MBC 1992*). Problems with this statutory duty of assessment are not new; in 1988, a woman had waited over six months for a full assessment following her request for it; before she received one she predictably had a fall and was admitted to hospital. The ombudsman found maladministration because of the 'unnecessary difficulty' in getting the assessment (*Powys CC 1990*).

The judge in *R v Bexley LBC, ex p B* pointed out that a request under s.4 of the 1986 Act is not a necessary pre-condition for receipt of services under s.2 of the Chronically Sick and Disabled Persons Act 1970; so if a person's needs are already within the view of the authority, it cannot refuse to consider provision under the 1970 Act simply because no formal request under the 1986 Act has been received.

Assessment on request of disabled people: loopholes

The government was sceptical in 1986 about the existence of a 'loophole' in s.2 of the Chronically Sick and Disabled Persons Act 1970, which apparently allowed authorities to fail to come to a decision about people's needs – in which case the duty to provide services would never arise. However, evidence was produced in Parliament of just such practices in the form of a letter from the chief executive of a local authority to a disabled person 'flatly denying' the existence of a duty to assess (Tom Clarke MP: HCD,4/7/1986,col.1324). It read as follows: 'there is nothing in the language of [s.2 of the Chronically Sick and Disabled Persons Act 1970] to suggest that the making of such an assessment on receipt of an application is mandatory on the council … If it were the intention of Parliament to impose upon the Council not only a duty to provide a service or services where the services had been determined but also a duty to determine whether such need exists, Section 2 would not have been worded in the way it is' (Baroness Masham: HLD,18/6/1986, col.979).

The passing of the 1986 Act apparently sealed this loophole but did not, if such was its intention, put an end to lengthy waiting lists for assessment, which in some areas continued to worsen and still afflict the community care system. Another gap, left open and thus duly explored by some local authorities, is that the duty to make a decision depends on the person being disabled; but the definition of disability under s.29 of the National Assistance Act 1948 is capable of at least some manipulation by local authorities (see p.91). Another chink was pointed to by the dissenting judge (Hirst LJ) at the Court of Appeal stage of *R v Gloucestershire CC, ex p Barry*. He suggested that the term 'call for' in s.4 of the 1986 Act (see extract above), found also in s.47(2) of the NHS and Community Care Act 1990, imported 'an element of discretion or value judgment' in the decision about whether needs call for services.

(N.B. Assessment of disabled school leavers. Not assessment on request, but related, is the separate duty under s.5 of the 1986 Act to assess disabled pupils or students leaving full time education. For pupils who have had a statement of special educational needs made when they were under the age of 14 years, the education authority must require the appropriate social services officer to give an opinion about whether the child is disabled either when it institutes the first annual review of the statement following the child's 14th birthday, or when a reassessment of the child's educational needs is made - whichever occurs earliest.

Education authorities, further education or higher education institutions, or the further education funding council (depending on circumstances) are obliged to notify in writing social services departments at least eight, but not not longer than twelve, months before a pupil with a statement of special educational needs, who has been assessed as disabled, will cease to receive full-time education. The social services department must then carry out an assessment 'of the needs of that person with respect to the provision by that authority of any statutory services in accordance with any of the welfare enactments' (namely s.2 of the Chronically Sick and Disabled Persons Act 1970, schedule 8 of the NHS Act 1977, Part 3 of the Children Act 1989). The assessment must be carried out within five months of the date of notification. If a disabled student has ceased to receive full-time education or will cease to do so within less than eight months, and no notification has been made to social services but should have been, then the education authority must notify in writing social services - who must then carry out the assessment as soon as reasonably practicable, and in any case within five months.

The evident intention that local authorities should thus anticipate and provide for the needs of disabled young people leaving school is not always realised in practice. For example, in one investigation, the local ombudsman found a failure to carry out such an assessment in 1990 when education authority funding was on the point of ceasing; that there was no planned budget to meet the person's needs at a resource centre (despite the fact that it had known about him since 1986); and that the authority did not carry out a proper assessment until 1993. This was maladministration (*East Sussex CC 1995a*). Similarly in another case, the council failed to carry out an adequate assessment of need and to draw up a proper care plan (*Knowsley MBC 1997*)).

4. HEALTH AND HOUSING AUTHORITIES IN COMMUNITY CARE ASSESSMENT

When a local authority is assessing a person for community care services and it thinks that he or she might need health or housing services, then it must notify the relevant health or housing authority (or both) and invite them to assist in the assessment. However, neither type of authority has a duty to accept the invitation. The fact that health and housing services are not defined legally as community care services under s.46 of the NHS and Community Care Act 1990 emphasises starkly the divided statutory functions which underpin community care.

EXTRACTS

Legislation (NHS and Community Care Act 1990,s.47(3)) states:

(community care assessment) 'If at any time during the assessment of the needs of any person under subsection (1)(a) above, it appears to a local authority':

(health service) '(a) that there may be a need for the provision to that person by such District Health Authority as may be determined in accordance with regulations of any services under the National Health Service Act 1977, or'

(housing authority) '(b) that there may be a need for the provision to him of any services which fall within the functions of a local housing authority (within the meaning of the Housing Act 1985) which is not the local authority carrying out the assessment';

(notification) 'the local authority shall notify that District Health Authority or local housing authority'

(invitation) 'and invite them to assist, to such extent as is reasonable in the circumstances, in the making of the assessment; and, in making their decision as to the provision of services needed for the person in question, the local authority shall take into account any services which are likely to be made available for him by that District Health Authority or local housing authority'.

Policy guidance (DH 1990, paras 3.32–3.33) states:

'the aim of assessment should be to ensure that all needs for care services are considered. Collaboration with health authorities and local housing authorities will therefore be of particular importance. Section 47(3) of the Act will require SSDs to bring apparent housing and health care needs to the attention of the appropriate authority and invite them to assist in the assessment. Arrangements for assessment and care management need to be addressed jointly by local agencies and roles and responsibilities agreed within those arrangements. As well as considering health and housing needs, staff from the local housing and health authorities may be able to offer expert advice on, and contribute to, the assessment of community care needs … All relevant agencies should be involved in the assessment process before commitments are made…'

DISCUSSION

The effectiveness of s.47 (3) of the 1990 Act is subject to a number of provisos. The first is whether the local authority is in the first place assessing a person who appears to be potentially in need of community care services (see above). The second is whether, during that assessment, it 'appears' (for a second time) to the local authority that there might be a 'need' for health or housing services. The third is whether a health or housing authority actually responds to the invitation to assist; and the fourth whether those authorities actually offer to provide any services. Last is the way in which the local authority takes account of what services might be available from either of those other two authorities.

Health and housing authorities in community care assessment: response to the invitation

The local authority makes an 'invitation' only. Health and housing authorities are not explicitly obliged by the legislation to accept it. Furthermore it is an invitation to assist in assessment only 'to such extent as is reasonable in the circumstances'. This appears to give considerable discretion to the invited authorities, in terms of whether they respond or on what scale and with what speed. It has been suggested (Gordon, Mackintosh 1996, p.36) that where a housing or health authority declines unreasonably to assist, a local authority could seek judicial review, claiming that it could not come to a decision.

The possible consequence of the lack of any sort of duty placed on health and housing authorities even to respond to the invitation to assess – let alone provide services – has been illustrated by *R v Northavon DC, ex p Smith*, in which the House of Lords declined to intervene when a district council refused to accede to a request from another council's social services department under the Children Act 1989. This ruling appears to give authorities considerable discretion in the child care context to refuse requests to assist, despite the legislative wording. How much more latitude for health and housing authorities in the community care context, given that the NHS and Community Care Act 1990 is silent both about compliance with the invitation and the provision of help (ie, services) by health and housing authorities. This contrasts with s.27 of the Children Act 1989 which at least states that an authority must comply with a request for help if it is 'compatible' with its own duties and obligations and does not 'unduly prejudice' the discharge of its functions.

Health and housing authorities in community care assessment: making the invitation

All this supposes that an invitation is actually issued. However, in practice this might depend on the ability of local authority staff to recognise relevant needs. In the past, Age Concern England has expressed its concern about the effectiveness of this part of the legislation. First, social services staff would need to be aware of relevant medical problems and how to respond to them and not, for example, assume that incontinence is just a fact of life, fail to identify depression, or misdiagnose confusion. If it was not aware in this way, it might simply fail to notify the health authority. Second, it might not be clear what happens in practice even when other agencies are informed about the problem: 'in fact, it then falls off the cliff, no one else has to do anything' (evidence to: House of Commons Health Committee 1993,vol.2,p.170).

Health and housing authorities in community care assessment: deciding about services

A local authority fails to adhere to the legislation (see extracts above) when it specifies in the care plan what services will be provided by other statutory agencies such as the NHS or housing authorities – but those other authorities then conduct their own 'secondary assessments' to establish whether the person really is eligible for service provision by them. As the Social Services Inspectorate pointed out, 'this runs counter to the principle that assessment is the responsibility of the care manager and that agencies need to have agreements on how to co-operate in delivering plans. It is also wasteful of scarce and expensive staff resources' (SSI 1997b,p.16).

5. INITIAL SCREENING FOR COMMUNITY CARE ASSESSMENT

'Screening' is a powerful, non-statutory (ie, not based on legislation) filter which can control the demand made upon the resources and services of local authorities. It determines what happens to people; for example, whether they are assessed at all, at what level and with what priority. It is often not apparent whether or not screening is meant formally to be part of statutory assessment or not. The legislation is of no assistance, since it does not define what assessment is; policy guidance has it both ways by envisaging screening as a) a non-statutory preliminary procedure, which leads to people either being turned away or being further assessed in depth; or b) statutory assessment in its own right, albeit at a simple level.

At one extreme, a decision might be made to refer a person to another agency because the apparent, possible need is nothing to do with social services. At the other, a person might be allocated a comprehensive community care assessment. Given the crucial role of such screening, some local authorities have trained staff specially for the role. Clearly, for screening to work, the information gathered must be of sufficient quality. However, for local authorities the difficulty is to find a middle way which balances their inability in practice (eg, because of demand exceeding resources) to visit promptly and assess properly everybody's potential needs – with their not turning people away on the basis of procedures (eg, cursory telephone conversations or perusal of letters of request or self-assessment forms) which, unless of high quality, can easily lapse into inadequacy.

EXTRACTS

Legislation is silent about the screening of people.

Policy guidance (DH 1990, para 3.20) refers to 'initial screening' as included in assessment arrangements:

> 'Assessment arrangements should normally include an initial screening process to determine the appropriate form of assessment. Some people may need advice and assistance which do not call for a formal assessment, others may require only a limited or specialist assessment of specific needs, others may have urgent needs which require an immediate response. Procedures should be sufficiently comprehensive and flexible to cope with all levels and types of need presented by different client groups'.

Practice guidance (SSI,SWSG 1991a,p.37) goes on to identify processes of information- gathering leading to assessment allocation decisions. Processes listed include:

- receive enquiries;
- give and gather information;
- encourage the full participation of the appropriate people;
- develop triggers for identifying other significant needs;
- designate responsibility for the allocation of the assessment response;
- set criteria for decision-making;
- identify levels of assessment;
- agree priorities for assessment allocation.

Practice guidance (SSI,SWSG 1991a,p.40) states that initial information gathering will include trigger questions aimed at identifying the following types of circumstance and associated risk and priority level:

- recent hospital discharge;
- recent move to independent living/change of accommodation;
- recent bereavement;
- living alone, experiencing loneliness and isolation;
- living on or below income support level;
- deteriorating health: eg, problems with continence, memory, falling;
- history of drug or alcohol abuse;
- carers' request for support;
- carer's or person's chronic loss of sleep;
- carer under stress (based on examples given in the practice guidance and in SSI,SIS 1991,p.10).

DISCUSSION

Initial screening: legally part of assessment?

Legislation is silent about what constitutes assessment (no directions have been given by the Secretary of State under s.47(4) of the NHS and Community Care Act 1990). Where no assessment for community services is judged to be needed, policy guidance (DH 1990, para 3.20) states that referral elsewhere will involve 'advice and assistance'. Practice guidance too refers to the 'information and advice' to be given in response to 'inappropriate enquiries' (SSI,SWSG 1991a, p.38). Policy guidance is ambivalent about whether screening is part of statutory assessment or not.

There is no clear picture of what assessment really is, since legislation defines neither the term itself nor any associated procedures. During the passage of the NHS and Community Care Bill the government tried to explain: 'a person presents himself to a social services department and asks what can be done for him. At that stage the social services department does not know whether he will turn out to need community care. Obviously further preliminary inquiries are needed to determine whether this is likely to be the case. If the person's needs turn out not to be for community care services then the preliminary inquiries may in fact amount to the assessment and this may be a perfectly reasonable way of dealing with the request' (HLD,10/5/1990,cols.1552–1553). The 'initial sift' would have a two-fold purpose: first, to identify those people who do not need a more 'detailed assessment' as well as those 'making unreasonable or vexatious' requests; and second, to decide on the 'most appropriate form of assessment' (Baroness Blatch: HLD,14/6/1990,col.519). This answer intimates that local authorities might decide retrospectively whether the screening process has amounted to a) a refusal to assess, b) a simple assessment or c) genuine screening in advance of a more formal assessment. This approach for people in the middle category might not only be highly unsatisfactory in some circumstances, but also introduce legal pitfalls. First, people might in practice be receiving assessments without even being aware of it; second, the statutory duty (under s.47(2) of the 1990 Act: see above) to inform disabled people during assessment about their particular rights is likely to breached; and third, the content of community care guidance is likely to be disregarded.

The risk that an ad hoc approach can result in unlawful decision-making was exposed in *R v Bristol CC, ex p Penfold*. The local authority was exposed as being prepared to characterise the same decision either as pre-assessment screening or as a simple assessment – depending on which option would be most legally expedient. The judge concluded that the authority had in fact failed to carry out an assessment, simple or otherwise, and so had breached its duty to assess under s.47(1) of the NHS and Community Care Act 1990; alternatively, if he was wrong about this, and the authority had in fact carried out an assessment, it had still acted unlawfully by failing to adhere to policy guidance and to explore need comprehensively, flexibly and fully. Thus, although the courts have recognised that assessments might be simple or complex, depending on circumstances (*Penfold* case, and *R v Kirklees MBC, ex p Good*), a simple assessment is not a byword for inadequate assessment.

Initial screening: practice

In practice it is possible that a few 'cursory' questions asked over the telephone might constitute an 'initial assessment' (Age Concern 1994b,pp.16–17). This is improved upon if it is followed up by telephone calls to other people such as informal carers, general practitioners, occupational therapists, community nurses – but even then, such further probing might be directed towards gathering information which will disqualify people from services. It is therefore possible that people are deemed to have received an assessment without having seen assessors face to face and without even knowing that they have had an assessment (Davis, Ellis and Rummery 1997,pp.25–26).

Administrative staff might see 'their task as to weed out enquiries which did not fit with their understanding of services available within the department. In taking referrals, they might record only such information as they think relevant to the range of specialist teams. Consequently, referrals for a "general assessment" might not be accepted but translated into a specific request' (Ellis 1993,p.17). Arguably, this means that assessment takes place already at the preliminary referral stage.

The importance of high quality initial screening and informed decision-making is underlined on the one hand by community care guidance about appropriate assessment responses (SSI,SWSG 1991a,p.37; and see CI(92)34, para 9); and, on the other, by recognition that in the past this has not always happened. For example, the provision of some services in the past has depended more on chance and haphazard referral patterns than on people's needs (SSI,DLF 1992,p.6). Authorities might train and appoint staff such as receptionists, customer service officers, information and access officers to handle enquiries and conduct initial screening (SSI,NHSE 1994a,p.18). Otherwise, the result might be entirely unsatisfactory, for instance, if written guidance for staff is 'non-existent or outdated. As a result, staff who were in contact with the general public were unclear about the care management and assessment process and could not advise potential service users and carers about their eligibility for services or how to apply for assessment' (SSI 1995b,p.4).

Symbolically, social services teams might be in inaccessible buildings and behind locked doors, visited by few disabled people (Davis, Ellis and Rummery 1997,p.27). Reception and screening procedures sometimes fail particular groups of people: for instance, the provision of interpreters for people with hearing impairment might be ill-organised, whilst local authority receptionists might have no, or very limited, signing skills and lack confidence in using text telephones (SSI 1997a,p.27). Furthermore, the giving of useful advice might be compromised if front-line staff view requests for it as yet more demands on their services, and are preoccupied with eligibility and risk rather than overall needs (Davis, Ellis and Rummery 1997,p.75).

Initial screening: adequate information

Screening ('trigger') questions themselves might be inadequate. Age Concern England (1993) expressed its concern: "'Can you get yourself out of bed; and can you make a cup of tea". If the answer to these is yes, they are told that social services cannot do anything for them. Is this really an assessment?' (p.11). Yet staff might be wary of over-reliance on written referral information, and feel that speech contact improves the quality of information; telephone conversations might sometimes be preferred (SSI,NHSME 1994b,p.8; see also SSI,NHSE 1994a,p.30). The situation will be exacerbated if, in addition to any general failings in screening procedures, staff have an inadequate understanding of the implications of particular types of disability – such as visual impairment – and so are unable to assess appropriately the level of risk present (Coles, Willetts and Winyard 1997,p.17). However, there might sometimes be little incentive for overworked staff to change things (Ellis 1993,p.18).

Local ombudsman investigations have exposed instances of inadequate referral information in relation to assessment and decisions about services under s.2 of the Chronically Sick and Disabled Persons Act 1970. For example, in one case an occupational therapist 'was unable to give the case its proper priority initially because she did not have the necessary information to help her make the decision' – although this was not maladministration because the therapist did all she could (*Liverpool CC 1992*). However, a two-year wait for assessment was maladministration; the council solicitor had suggested that the complainant was not 'substantially and permanently handicapped' and so not a priority, but another council officer conceded that the council could not say whether the man was substantially and permanently handicapped – precisely because he had not yet been assessed (*Wirral MBC 1993a*). Similarly self-defeating is the situation where a local authority states that it will offer an assessment to anybody scoring enough points on its priority scale, but in order for the score to be ascertained, an assessment is necessary (Baldwin 1995a,p.27).

In another investigation, the practice of identifying priority applications was described by staff as 'hit and miss', since the referral forms did not contain sufficient information to facilitate informed decisions about priority; the ombudsman found maladministration (*Bolton MBC 1992*). In a fourth case, a senior occupational therapist felt that a detailed telephone conversation was adequate by way of assessment and recommendation for adaptations; whereas the service user had felt unprepared since it was not a planned conversation, and the housing cooperative to whom the recommendations were made responded by saying that the Housing Corporation would be unlikely to award a grant on the basis of a telephone conversation. In fact, there appeared anyway to be some lack of clarity amongst staff about whether or not, as a matter of policy, telephone conversations were adequate (*Hackney LBC 1992a*). When another local authority gathered insufficient information at the referral stage for applications for disabled facilities grants, and did not seek additional information, problems inevitably arose. This led to possible unfairness and, in some cases, to applications being categorised as 'desirable' only, with the consequence that assessment was either delayed or never carried out even in the case of some people who were actually in substantial need (*Liverpool CC 1996/1997*). Similarly, a two year wait for an assessment for bathing adaptations was maladministration; the council's excuse that it had insufficient information to allocate a priority was rejected (*Wirral MBC 1993c*).

6. PRIORITIES FOR COMMUNITY CARE ASSESSMENT

In practice, local authorities do not have the staff and resources to assess all applicants immediately and in depth. Therefore they have to decide at, or immediately following the initial screening stage, how urgent people's needs probably are; how long they will have to wait for assessment; and what sort of assessment they will get. Legislation is silent about such matters, but practice guidance draws a sometimes confusing picture about how people's priority for assessment might be decided. It lists 'decision-making criteria'; priorities for assessment allocation; and factors to be taken account of when making those allocation priorities.

It is unsurprising that local authority screening systems are sometimes complex and ill-defined – giving rise to concerns about the basis on which priority criteria are drawn up, and whether the criteria are applied consistently and equitably. For example, the local government ombudsman has in the past found maladministration when priorities have been applied inconsistently; whilst the law courts will in principle wish to see consistent – rather than unpredictable and arbitrary – application of a policy, so long as exceptional cases can be considered (see p.49).

In practice, high priority is often accorded to those people deemed to be at *immediate physical risk*. The making of priorities sometimes leads to waiting lists, which have in some localities long been customary – especially, for example, in relation to assessment for equipment and home adaptations.

EXTRACTS

Legislation does not mention priorities for assessment.

Practice guidance (SSI,SWSG 1991a) states that the initial screening and information-gathering process is followed by 'allocation of the appropriate assessment response' (p.40). It lists three sets of criteria. It is not wholly clear how they relate to one another:

(decision-making criteria). Assessment allocation decisions 'should consistently apply the same criteria which should:

- reflect the policies and priorities set out in the published information on assessment practice;
- judge the urgency of the required response;
- take account of the assessment resources available in terms of the number of administrative, vocationally or professionally qualified staff relative to demand;
- weigh the options available to meet specific needs which will affect the level and complexity of the assessment required;
- use the assessment to make cost-effective use of the available resources' (pp.40–41).

(assessment allocation priorities). Most 'referrals for assessment will fall into four categories that can be related to the basic objectives of community care. There are those:

- for whom community living is no longer a possibility or who are at risk, for example, people with intensive care needs;
- reliant on others for survival, requiring help with, for example, feeding, toileting;
- reliant on others for support, requiring help with, for example, cleaning, shopping;
- whose functioning or morale is reduced, for example, as a consequence of depressive illness...

Most cases requiring statutory or crisis intervention are likely to fall in the first two categories. In each of the four categories, people may be rated as having a low, medium or high level of need' (p.43).

(factors to take into account when allocating assessment priorities) 'Any judgement of the appropriate assessment response and level of priority will have to take account of such factors as:

- severity or complexity of needs;
- degree of risk or vulnerability of user or carers;
- the level and duration of the projected resources required (whether immediately or in the future);
- the degree of stress experienced by user, carers or other agencies;
- the necessity of co-ordination with other care agencies, for example, about hospital discharge or housing transfer;
- the length of time already spent on a waiting list, for instance, a higher priority response should be triggered after a specified period on a waiting list' (pp.43–44).

DISCUSSION

Priorities for assessment: 'statutory or crisis intervention'

The silence of legislation about priorities is made up for by guidance. Practice guidance suggests that the first two of the four main categories of priority for allocation of assessment (see extracts above) are likely to require statutory or crisis intervention. The meaning attached to 'statutory' is unclear, since all community care functions, whether comprising duties or powers, are statutory. Nevertheless, the guidance seems to imply that people in the third and fourth categories are likely to be low priority, and so drop down the waiting list (or, as sometimes happens in practice, off it altogether). However, people can easily move from one category to another as their needs escalate or reduce, and there is anyway a question about the principles and policies on which priority criteria should be based. In addition, lack of information about people's needs (before they are assessed) can mean that people are wrongly given a low priority. In practice, 'fast-track' assessment might exist for 'emergency, high-risk cases, or cases involving people who misuse drugs or alcohol'. However, some other 'fast-track' applications, such as hospital discharge might be 'ways of introducing priorities into the system which do not necessarily relate to the intrinsic urgency of the case' (SSI,NHSME 1993,para 3.7).

Priorities for assessment: risk, safety and prevention

Risk and safety might seem to be rational and defensible priority criteria. Yet unfortunate consequences might follow for people with serious but not life-threatening, problems.

For example, there might be a five-month wait for a woman with a progressive illness and only able to mount and descend the stairs on her hands and knees; or for an older man smelling offensive because his son was unable to bath him (see Ellis 1993, p.17). Furthermore, the local ombudsman has pointed out that under s.2 of the Chronically Sick and Disabled Persons Act 1970, the law 'makes no distinction between the Council's duty to make an assessment in "urgent" and "non-urgent" cases. Any disabled person is entitled to request an assessment and to expect that the request is met within a reasonable time' (*Hackney LBC 1992a*). And referrals of visually impaired people, following certification of their impairment by a hospital, might in some authorities routinely be put 'at the bottom of the basket' in the absence of any additional information, despite the very considerable physical and emotional needs arising from loss of sight (Lovelock, Powell and Craggs 1995,p.29).

Indeed, a person, arguably in the third category (cleaning and shopping help: see extracts above) and therefore low priority, might not be able to continue 'community living' (a part of the first category) if that help ceases – and so immediately become higher priority and potentially a greater expense to the local authority. This raises the question of to what extent criteria should reflect a policy of prevention, not only with people's welfare in mind but also the prudent use of resources (eg, Alzheimer's Disease Society evidence to the House of Commons Health Committee 1993, vol.1,p.xxv).

Priorities for assessment: manipulation of priority criteria

One early report on community care (NFHA 1993) found that criteria could be manipulated in order to gain access to priority assessment. For example: 'One agency was emphasising aspects of the individual's mental health history when making a referral for assessment, rather than their homelessness. In a hostel for ex-offenders, funding was being agreed if the agency could prove that residents were additionally vulnerable in some way, through age, physical or mental illness for example. Callers felt they were being forced to play games with the local authority over criteria, but it had proved an effective approach' (p.13).

Priorities for assessment: complexity

The world of eligibility criteria can confuse staff as well as the general public (SSI,NHSME 1994b,p.8). For example, it might be difficult to distinguish between the different sets of criteria applied at various stages of the community care process: getting an assessment, type or level of assessment, speed of assessment response, priority of need, accessing resources (financial allocation), and particular services. Furthermore, false correlation between different types of eligibility can occur; for example, just because provision of a commode might be relatively 'simple' doesn't mean that it is not urgently required (SSI,NHSE 1994a,p.30).

Conversely, an over simple priority system under s.2 of the Chronically Sick and Disabled Persons Act 1970, which leaves on the waiting list for 12 months a disabled person with an urgent but complex need, is maladministration (*Rochdale MBC 1995*). And largely non-existent procedural and practice guidance gave the Social Services Inspectorate no confidence that people with multiple impairments would be given the appropriate priority and attention (SSI 1993a,p.17).

Priorities for assessment: professional judgement

As explained elsewhere (see pp.439 and 446), both the courts in judicial review cases and the local ombudsmen fight shy of direct attacks on the professional judgement of local authority staff. For example, the local ombudsmen will not find fault solely because there is some delay in assessment for home adaptations due to application of a priority policy; and generally will not criticise professional opinions even though recognising that they 'may differ on the assessment of individual needs' (*Newham LBC 1993a*). However, the ombudsmen might sometimes undermine apparently professional decisions by finding an administrative fault, such as a failure to consider obviously relevant factors.

For instance, it was maladministration when a decision about the priority of an elderly man, unsteady on his feet after four strokes, was taken on the basis of inadequate information. The ombudsman identified in particular the fact that a GP's medical certificate was given less weight than an incomplete occupational therapist's assessment which had been carried out over six months earlier. An assessment visit had been made by an officer who was neither professionally nor medically qualified. Other professionals involved, such as the district nurse, had not been contacted for information. A further communication by the GP that the applicant's condition had deteriorated was not investigated and therefore the decision not to raise his priority was made without evidence and in contravention of procedures (*Leicester CC 1992b*).

Priorities for assessment: fluctuation of priority and change of position on the waiting list

Waiting lists follow from the setting of priorities about speed of assessment; these are dealt with in detail below (see p.93). However, one particular issue is when the priority accorded to a particular individual fluctuates not because of his or her 'objective' circumstances, but because of changes in other people's circumstances and needs. Although this might seem unfair, it seems to follow logically from the existence of priority criteria. For example, in one case the local ombudsman noted that it could take eight months for a person with a lower priority rating to receive a visit. Altogether there were about eight or nine hundred people on the waiting list, but a person's position could change if new, urgent cases were added to the list, or if the needs of those already on the list either increased or decreased in urgency. The ombudsman did not criticise such a system of priorities (*Ealing LBC 1993*).

To avoid possible challenges when fluctuation of priority occurs, local authorities might be well-advised to keep people well-informed, and not to commit themselves absolutely to particular timescales. This might avoid accusations of maladministration because of lack of information (see p.100).

7. LEVELS OF COMMUNITY CARE ASSESSMENT

Legislation is silent about levels of assessment. However, community care practice guidance describes how, following a decision about urgency of assessment, a further decision should be made about the level of assessment which an individual is to receive. The guidance suggests six levels of assessment. In practice, it seems that local authorities adopt fewer levels, corresponding broadly to the type of staff required to do the assessment.

As already explained (p.74), the NHS and Community Care Act 1990 states that if, during an assessment, the local authority thinks a person is disabled then it must decide if he or she needs welfare services under s.2 of the Chronically Sick and Disabled Persons Act 1970. Community care guidance seems uncertain about the implications of this. It states that disabled people should be offered a comprehensive assessment; that many people in possible need of community care are disabled; but that comprehensive assessments should form only a minority of assessments because they are time-consuming and expensive. As a matter of common sense, local authorities have to strike the elusive balance between superficial assessment inadequate to uncover need and, at the other extreme, excessive assessment which is intrusive, generates need where there is none and is unjustifiably costly.

EXTRACTS

Legislation (NHS and Community Care Act 1990) is silent about assessment levels.

Policy guidance (DH 1990,para 3.20) states:

> **(flexible arrangements)** 'Assessment arrangements should normally include an initial screening process to determine the appropriate form of assessment. Some people may need advice and assistance which do not call for a formal assessment, others may require only a limited or specialist assessment of specific needs, others may have urgent needs which require an immediate response. Procedures should be sufficiently comprehensive and flexible to cope with all levels and types of need presented by different client groups'.

Practice guidance (SSI,SWSG 1991a) provides an illustrative model, consisting of six levels of assessment. Each level is illustrated in terms of the needs, services, agency and staff likely to be involved. The model is not prescriptive:

> 'Agencies will want to determine their own levels of assessment according to their policies, priorities and available personnel' (p.41). Assessment levels (with examples of service outcome) might be:
>
> - simple (bus pass, disabled car badge);
> - limited assessment (low-level domiciliary support);
> - multiple assessment (assistance with meals, chiropody, basic nursing);
> - specialist assessment: simple (simple disability equipment); complex (home adaptation);
> - complex assessment (speech therapy);
> - comprehensive assessment (family therapy, substitute care or intensive domiciliary support) (p.42).
>
> **(disabled people)** 'The type of assessment response will normally be related as closely as possible to the presenting need. However, there is one legally prescribed exception. Where a person appears to be "disabled" under the terms of the Disabled Persons (Services, Consultation and Representation) Act 1986, the

local authority is required to offer a comprehensive assessment, irrespective of the scale of need that is initially presented' (p.43).

Circular guidance (CI(92)34,para 9 now cancelled) stated:

'A full scale assessment of all needs should be offered to individuals appearing to be disabled, as prescribed by Section 47(2) of the NHS and CC Act'.

DISCUSSION

Levels of assessment: linking to criteria

That the simplicity or complexity of assessment will vary with individual circumstances is explained by the guidance and chimes also with the view of the law courts (*R v Bristol CC, ex p Penfold; R v Kirklees MBC, ex p Good*), the government in Parliament (Tim Yeo: HCWA,13/5/1993, col.567) and common sense.

Early community care monitoring (SSI,NHSME 1993) found that many authorities distinguished between simple and complex assessments, the basis for which might be unsatisfactory if it was not linked to 'fully worked-out eligibility criteria' (para 3.4). In other words, authorities might make, or at least be in danger of making, arbitrary and possibly inequitable decisions. There were 'instances in which a number of levels of priority of need were combined with a number of levels of complexity of assessment to produce systems which were almost impossible to work' (para 3.5). Indeed, the Social Services Inspectorate found that poor allocation procedures might result in some people not receiving a 'full comprehensive needs-led assessment appropriate to their circumstances' (SSI 1996d,p.13).

In practice, many authorities might operate no more than three levels of assessment based on the staff needed to carry them out: *simple* (administrative/auxiliary staff); *specialist* (auxiliary/qualified/specialist staff); *comprehensive* (qualified/multi-agency staff) (SSI,NHSME 1994b,p.9). Apparently similar terms such as 'comprehensive', 'full', or 'complex', are likely to mean different things from authority to authority. And even within the same authority, staff might be confused about the appropriate assessment response to make – for example, in relation to the referral of visually impaired people following certification of their medical condition by a hospital (Lovelock, Powell and Craggs 1995,pp.15,26).

There is a risk that staff will consequently fail to identify at what point statutory assessment decisions are made – ie, at what point the duty under s.47 of the NHS and Community Care Act 1990 is discharged (see eg, the confusion arising in *R v Kirklees MBC, ex p Daykin*). For instance, it appears that in some local authorities complex assessments are called 'community care assessments' and equated with the duty under s.47 – but that staff do not always appreciate that even simple assessments are likewise carried out under s.47 and are therefore of equal statutory significance.

Levels of assessment: disabled people

The legislation states that if a person is getting a community care assessment and it appears that he or she is disabled, then a decision must be taken about the need for services under the 1970 Act; and in any case the duty to make a decision on request about 1970 Act services remains (see above, p.76). The practice guidance states that disabled people must be offered a comprehensive assessment, and that the 'majority of adults who appear to have community care needs are affected by some form of disability'. This would appear to imply that there will be many comprehensive assessments. (SSI,SWSG 1991a,pp.43–44).

It is not obvious why the guidance states that comprehensive assessment for disabled people is a 'legally prescribed exception'. Comprehensive assessment is not referred to in legislation. Furthermore, the statement in the guidance (see immediately above) that such an offer must be made irrespective of the scale of need would seem to corrode the notion of a needs-based system of priorities and assessment levels. Indeed, early reports on community care found relatively high numbers of complex, comprehensive assessments, taking up excessive time and resources – caused by, for example, 'threshold criteria at too low a level' (SSI 1993b,p.9). Complex assessments were more numerous than had been anticipated, and were sometimes being given priority over simple assessments, 'leading to delays and possibly distortions' (SSI,NHSME 1993,para 3.5). Similarly, if comprehensive assessments were carried out (perhaps inappropriately) whenever more than one agency was involved, then complexity might be determined more by the type of service response than by the need of the individual person (SSI,NHSE 1994a,p.32).

Circular guidance pointed out that comprehensive assessments are 'both time consuming and expensive. They should be reserved for the minority of users with the most complex needs' (CI(92(34),para 9 now cancelled). The apparent inconsistency between the practice guidance and the Circular guidance can only be explained if many disabled people refuse the offer of a comprehensive assessment. This makes little sense, although from the point of view of speed, a simple assessment might have distinct advantages for service users. Alternatively, it is possible that an authority might define disability under s.29 of the National Assistance Act 1948 at a high threshold, thus 'reducing' the number of disabled people it is having to deal with. However, it should be noted that longstanding Circular guidance (LAC(93)10,appendix 4) on the definition of disability encourages a broadly inclusive and not a narrow, exclusive approach (see immediately below).

Whatever the Department of Health's real intention, the High Court, in *R v Gloucestershire CC, ex p RADAR*, expressed some puzzlement over the coherence of the practice guidance on this point. And the local ombudsman found maladministration in an investigation, because of the local authority's persistence with a series of 'single-service' assessments for a disabled person, instead of a comprehensive assessment (*Westminster CC 1996*).

8. DEFINITION OF DISABILITY

Provision of non-residential welfare services under the National Assistance Act 1948 (s.29) and the Chronically Sick and Disabled Persons Act 1970 (s.2) depend on people being disabled. Disability is defined in s.29 of the 1948 Act and refers to people who are blind, deaf, dumb, have a permanent and substantial handicap or have a mental disorder of any description. The definition is elaborated upon in longstanding guidance. The approach advocated by the guidance, and by the government during the passing of the NHS and Community Care Act 1990, appears to be a generally inclusive one, thus discouraging local authorities from setting narrow definitions of disability in order to exclude people from eligibility for services.

The 1948 definition (in its amended version) governs assessment and services under the a) NHS and Community Care 1990, s.47(2); b) Chronically Sick and Disabled Persons Act 1970; c)

Disabled Persons (Services, Consultation and Representation) Act 1986, s.4; and d) Housing Grants, Construction and Regeneration Act 1996 (grants for home adaptations, see p.400).

Nevertheless, though the Circular guidance does advise on the definition of disability, it explains that 'precise guidance' cannot be given. It is therefore for local authorities both to define what they mean by disability and also to decide whether particular individuals are in fact disabled under that definition.

EXTRACTS

Legislation (National Assistance Act 1948, s.29) states that it applies to people:

'aged eighteen or over who are blind, deaf or dumb, or who suffer from mental disorder of any description and other persons aged eighteen or over who are substantially and permanently handicapped by illness, injury or congenital deformity or such other disabilities as may be prescribed by the minister'.

Circular guidance (LAC(93)10,appendix 4) advises on eligibility under section 29. It states:

(eligibility) 'As indicated above, once it has been established that a person comes within the scope of section 29, the matter of registration in no way affects eligibility to receive help – in other words the material question in determining that eligibility is whether, for the purposes of section 29, the person is to be regarded as having a hearing, vision or speech impairment or is substantially and permanently handicapped by illness, injury or congenital deformity' (para 5).

(visual impairment) There are well established procedures for certification (by the NHS) of blindness or partial sight; but authorities should ensure that the effective date of registration coincides with that of certification (para 6).

(hearing impairment) 'There are no formal examination procedures for determining whether a person is deaf or hard of hearing for the purposes section 29, and there is no intention of introducing any new procedure in this respect' (para 7).

(general disability) 'It is convenient to continue to use the term "General Classes" to apply to those persons within the scope of section 29 whose primary handicap is neither visual nor auditory. It has not proved possible to give precise guidance on the interpretation of the phrase "substantially and permanently handicapped". However, as hitherto, authorities are asked to give a wide interpretation to the term "substantial", which the Department fully recognises must always take full account of individual circumstances. With regard to the term "permanent", authorities will also wish to interpret this sufficiently flexibly to ensure that they do not feel inhibited from giving help under section 29 in cases where they are uncertain of the likely duration of the condition' (para 8).

(categories of disability) Local authorities are asked by the guidance to keep registration data under three main headings:

- very severe handicap
- severe or appreciable handicap
- and other persons (for example, including people with a less severe heart or chest condition or with epilepsy (para 10).

The first two of these categories are themselves further explained.

(very severe handicap) Includes those who:

(1) 'need help going to or using the WC practically every night. In addition, most of those in this group need to be fed or dressed or, if they can feed and/or dress themselves, they need a lot of help during the day with washing and WC, or are incontinent';

(2) 'need help with the WC during the night but not quite so much help with feeding, washing, dressing, or, while not needing night-time help with the WC need a great deal of day-time help with feeding and/or washing and the WC';

(3) 'are permanently bedfast or confined to a chair and need help to get in and out, or are senile or mentally impaired, or are not able to care for themselves as far as normal everyday functions are concerned, but who do not need as much help' as the above two categories (annex 1 to appendix 4).

(severe or appreciable handicap) includes those who:

(4) 'either have difficulty doing everything, or find most things difficult and some impossible';

(5) 'find most things difficult, or three or four items difficult and some impossible';

(6) 'can do a fair amount for themselves but have difficulty with some items, or have to have help with or two minor items'.

DISCUSSION

Definition of disability: interpretation

The Circular guidance, dealing with general disability, asks local authorities to give a wide interpretation to the term 'substantial' and a flexible interpretation to 'permanent' – so, in the latter case not to deprive people of services. An inclusive approach to the definition is further confirmed by the categories listed immediately above, under which local authorities are asked to register disabled people. These categories cover both severe and less severe disabilities, so indicating that the term 'substantial' in section 29 does not necessarily equate with 'very severe' or even 'severe'.

During the Parliamentary passage of the National Assistance Bill, the government made clear that the words 'illness, injury or congenital deformity' covered both physical and mental illness (John Edwards: SC(C),22/1/1948,col.2560). Over 40 years later, when the NHS and Community Care Bill was before Parliament, the government explained that the definition of disability under section 29 of the National Assistance Act 1948 was 'cast in broad terms with the aim of being as inclusive as possible and related to a degree of severity rather than to a particular condition'. This made unnecessary the amendment being considered which would have extended the definition explicitly to people dependent on alcohol or drugs, people with HIV/AIDS, mental disorder including Alzheimer's Disease (Baroness Hooper: HLD,10/5/1990,cols1590–1591).

It appears that in practice some local authorities, faced with a demand for services under the Chronically Sick and Disabled Persons Act 1970 which they cannot afford, are tempted to restrict what they mean by disability. This might have the effect, for instance, of excluding certain groups of older people who – no longer classed as disabled and so ineligible for services under s.29 of the National Assistance Act 1948 and s.2 of the Chronically Sick and Disabled Persons Act 1970 – might at best qualify for services for 'aged' or 'old' people under either the weaker duty contained in schedule 8 of the NHS Act 1977 (see p.215) – or for services under the Health Services and Public Health Act 1968, but which an authority is under no duty to provide (see p.213). Alternatively, an authority might operate a very wide definition – for example, including even people who have had a hip operation and are substantially but not permanently disabled – but still restrict service provision by narrowly defining essential needs (RADAR 1997,pp.6–7).

In line with the Circular guidance, the identification by a local authority of a person as substantially and physically handicapped is in practice likely to be based on a medical model of disability, with all its shortcomings (see p.119), and to focus on physical limitation and degree of impairment, rather than on a social model (Clarkson 1997,p.4) and on potential ability.

Definition of disability: other definitions

In addition to the term 'substantial and permanent handicap' under s.29 of the 1948 Act, related terms also apply under other legislation. First, the term 'handicapped' is one of the conditions governing community care services arranged under schedule 8 of the NHS Act 1977 (see p.215). A question arising, for example, is whether this term (a condition for receipt of home help services or laundry facilities) is to be construed as including the whole class of so-called handicap (ie, both mild and substantial) – or only the mild. The correct construction is probably the former, inclusive one. However, it is not a theoretical issue; the answer will have an effect on the operation of the anti-duplication provision contained in s.29 of the 1948 Act in respect of schedule 8 of the 1977 Act (see p.325).

Second, 'disability' is one of the qualifying conditions for provision of residential or nursing home care under s.21 of the National Assistance Act 1948 (see p.253). Third, the term 'illness' is used in s.3 of the NHS Act 1977 in respect of health care and in schedule 8 in respect of certain community care services; it is defined in s.128 of the 1977 Act to include 'disability' requiring medical or dental treatment. Finally, the definition applied by the 1948 Act should be distinguished from the definition introduced by the Disability Discrimination Act 1995, although there are some similarities: see p.184.

9. WAITING TIMES FOR ASSESSMENT

Waiting lists for assessment, already referred to above have long been a problem for social services departments (especially in relation to daily living equipment and home adaptations). They continue to persist, at least for some services in some localities. What constitutes a reasonable response time, from time of referral to time of assessment, remains, of necessity, obscure and judicially undetermined – since what is reasonable will depend on all the circumstances of the case. Therefore, there is no general rule about how long a local authority can delay assessment, before that delay in effect becomes a refusal to assess and a breach of statutory duty under s.47 of the NHS and Community Care 1990 and/or under s.4 of the Disabled Persons (Services, Consultation and Representation) Act 1986. The courts might display reluctance to interfere with how quickly duties are being performed (see p.53).

Central government has urged authorities to set target response times; this is helpful for users. However, from the point of view of hard-pressed local authorities, they are well advised to qualify any such promises – so as to avoid possible challenges on the basis of people's 'legitimate expectation' (p.50).

The local government ombudsmen have investigated many cases of delay in assessment. The reports of their investigations give insight into the positions of both local authorities and service users. It is not easy to identify simple rules governing their decisions on waiting times, although the ombudsmen have suggested rough guidelines. Depending on the particular circumstances of the case, the ombudsmen might accept the explanations of local authorities that priority systems are necessary and waiting times inevitable. They will also take into account the efforts made by authorities to reduce the lists; for example, self-assessment clinics, staff recruitment and retention packages (to overcome staff shortages), and workload reorganisation. However, even then, they may invoke another aspect of maladministration, such as failure to let people know what is happening during the wait. (The Parliamentary ombudsman takes just the same sort of approach, distinguishing between avoidable and unavoidable delay, and looking for minimisation of the adverse effects of unavoidable delay: see McMurtrie 1997).

EXTRACTS

Legislation is silent about waiting times, and does not place a time limit within which assessment must be carried out (compare housing grant legislation: see p.400).

Circular guidance (LAC(94)24,para 18) about community care charters stated that charters should set standards which 'should be quantified wherever possible – eg, length of time for action'.

Circular guidance (CI(92)34, para 6, now cancelled) stated that readily understandable, published information should include:

'any standards against which the assessment arrangements will be measured, including the estimated length of time between referral and the completion of an assessment'.

Practice guidance states that as:

'a point of good practice, local authorities should publish their guidelines on timescales for responding to referrals. These guidelines should be monitored and adjusted to keep waiting lists for assessment to a minimum' (SSI,SWSG 1991a, p.41).

Framework document for community charters (DH 1994a,pp.14–15) refers to an entitlement to expect that assessments will be provided within a reasonable time, which might include specific standards for:

- time between initial contact and first response;
- time between that response and the start of assessment;
- time for completion of each type of assessment;
- time between completion of assessment and start of services;
- assessments in good time of people being discharged from hospital.

A standard suggested by the original consultation document (DH 1994b,para B2) – about the speed with which (when necessary) social services will refer people to the NHS or housing departments, and the speed with which the latter will respond – did not appear in the final document.

DISCUSSION

Waiting times for assessment: background

An unsuccessful amendment to the NHS and Community Care Bill attempted to ensure that authorities assess 'within a reasonable period of time'. The government responded that the need for assessments to be carried out 'without due delay is stressed in our guidance' (Baroness Blatch:

HLD,14/6/1990,col.520). Such an amendment would arguably have added nothing to what the law courts repeat from time to time, that public bodies should carry out their duties in a reasonable time (see eg, comment in *R v Kirklees MBC, ex p Daykin*). However, at the time of writing there have apparently been no community care cases in relation to waiting lists for assessment (but see *R v Sutton LBC, ex p Tucker* on delay in decision about what services to provide).

Community care guidance (immediately above) does not define unacceptable delay, but suggests that timescales should be set. However in practice, even if there are agreed response times, the definition of 'response' can vary between authorities, for example, running from the point of referral to assessment, to completion of assessment or to service delivery (SSI 1993c,p.7). Where response times are set, staff might struggle to meet them – although the general public will be none the wiser if policies on response times are not even published (SSI 1994a,p.15). A code of practice published on behalf of seven county councils discussed acceptable and unacceptable assessment delay under s.4 of the Disabled Persons (Services, Consultation and Representation) Act 1986. It comments about delays in assessment: 'There is no specific and absolute time limit regarding waiting list delays. Therefore the matter legally rests on a test of "reasonableness" … Waiting lists seem to be a fact of life for most social services departments. The Act is not clear when a delay in awaiting assessment becomes a refusal to assess. Professional advice is that a delay in excess of 6 months is unacceptable and that most Local Authorities should be working to a 3 month limit' (Devon SSD 1989,p.2). Nevertheless, publicising a three-month limit in the authority's community care charter is maladministration – if it is clear that there is no 'realistic prospect' of adhering to it (*Ealing LBC 1999*).

Waiting times for assessment: practice

Delay has characterised some local authority services for many years, meaning that people might have a long wait, especially those accorded 'low priority' and waiting for assessment in respect of equipment and home adaptations. For example, it has been reported that nearly 50 per cent of referrals of older people are for equipment (SSI 1991c,p.2; see also SSI,NHSE 1994a,p.22). About 23 per cent of total (all client groups) referrals to social services are directed toward occupational therapy services, which have over a considerable period fallen short of meeting the demands made on them (SSI 1994b,pp.9,37).

Following community care implementation in April 1993, there were reports of continuing problems involving equipment, adaptations, occupational therapists and waiting lists (SSI 1993d,p.13; SSI 1993e,p.16; SSI 1994c,p.18), the last of which stood sometimes at unacceptable levels (SSI 1994b,p.10). Later reporting continues to dwell on the same theme (eg, Salvage 1996), with the Department of Health very belatedly recognising by 1995 the 'serious issue of lengthy waiting lists' (LASSL(97)27,para 1; and see DH 1997d). The problem is not new (eg, SSI 1988a,p.3) and was entirely predictable before implementation of community care; indeed for many local authorities, it was simply business as usual. For example, reports prior to that date referred to periods of ten months between referral and allocation (and a further six months for service provision) (SSI 1991d,p.13); or any period between 11 days and over a year (SSI 1991e,p.11). The local ombudsmen's reports were (and are) also indicative of widespread problems, since in many cases the individual situations investigated have uncovered the plight of many other people.

For instance, waiting lists as large as 1500 people, and never less than 600, have sometimes been the subject of complaints to local authority councillors for a decade and more (*Lewisham LBC 1993*); and people, not necessarily exceptional cases, have waited nearer five than four years for assessment (*Hackney LBC 1992a*).

Waiting times for assessment: local ombudsmen's general approach

The ombudsmen consider the particular circumstances of each case, and so do not necessarily arrive at an easy rule of thumb of what constitutes a reasonable waiting time: it all depends. Nevertheless, faced with sometimes large numbers of complainants in a similar position, they have more recently considered what reasonable waiting times might look like. For instance, in relation to disabled facilities grants, they suggested in 1997 two months for urgent, four months for serious, and six months for non-urgent cases (*Liverpool CC 1996/1997*; see also *Sheffield 1997a* and *Sheffield 1997b*). Otherwise, the ombudsmen might work out in specific cases what a reasonable waiting time would have been, measure the excess and then assess the resulting injustice, if any (eg, *Wirral MBC 1992a*).

Waiting times for assessment: need for priorities

The making of policies and priorities might not only be accepted by the law courts (eg, *British Oxygen v Board of Trade*), but also even be required by the local ombudsman. For instance, where local authorities handle applications for disabled facilities grants by date order, the ombudsmen criticise them on the grounds that such a system cannot take account of differing levels of need or of exceptions (eg, *Leicester CC 1998*). And failure of an authority to award appropriate priority where it would have been possible to do so, meant that a stairlift was not installed before the applicant died and was maladministration (*Liverpool City CC 1996/1997*). Of course the existence of agreed priorities and waiting times for assessment are one thing, practice sometimes another. The ombudsmen might find maladministration where a joint social services/housing department assessment should, according to policy, have been made within seven days from receipt of referral – but instead took place six weeks later (*Camden LBC 1993*).

Waiting time for assessment: administrative inefficiency

Sometimes, simple administrative inefficiency – perhaps unconnected with resources, policies and priorities – is found by the local ombudsman. For example, when a request by a registered blind person (also at risk of falling and with a rare degenerative disease) for equipment was not passed to the sensory impairment team by an assistant director of social services, a nine month delay resulted (*Haringey LBC 1993*). In another case, the local ombudsman accepted that the failure to carry out a survey for over a year in relation to a disabled facilities grant was due to a huge increase in workload rather than maladministration, but the social services department was still at fault for failing to check matters with the housing department and to refer the case properly (*Barking and Dagenham LBC 1998*).

Waiting times for assessment: staff shortages

One reason pleaded by local authorities (under the Chronically Sick and Disabled Persons Act 1970,s.2 and Disabled Persons (Services, Consultation and Representation Act 1986,s.4) for delayed assessment has been a shortage of occupational therapists, experts in daily living assessments. The local ombudsman has investigated this issue on a number of occasions and is generally, but not always, unsympathetic to local authorities who use this excuse.

For instance, if authorities 'are unable to provide an assessment within a reasonable period of time, then they should look at other ways of providing the assessment' (*Wirral MBC 1993d*). The ombudsman might also look at how councils have attempted to carry out their duties under the Local Authority Social Services Act 1970,s.6 to ensure that there are 'adequate' staff to assist directors of social services 'in the exercise' of their functions. Maladministration might be found where problems have long since been reported to, and known by, the social services committee, and yet 'wider failure' in service delivery has continued, including a lack of monitoring and inadequate records of waiting lists (*Redbridge LBC 1993a, Redbridge LBC 1993b*). The minutes of social services committee meetings might provide useful evidence that s.6 of the 1970 Act has been breached, although the duty is usually regarded as one of 'imperfect obligation' and scarcely enforceable. The case of *R v Hereford and Worcester CC, ex p Chandler* was brought in relation to a breach of s.6(6) of the 1970 Act, given leave to proceed to a full judicial review hearing, but subsequently settled in favour of the applicant (Clements 1992).

On the other hand, if councils face 'particular resource and staffing difficulties' and have made attempts to remedy the situation, the ombudsmen might not find maladministration. For example, one council responded 'positively and creatively' to staff shortages, offered a recruitment and retention package, set up a special assessment clinic, and seconded health authority staff (*Lewisham LBC 1993*); whilst a five-month delay in assessment for a woman allocated a medium priority was not maladministration, given the priorities necessitated by the difficulty of recruiting and deploying occupational therapists (*Islington LBC 1995*)

Even so, in one case, a three month wait for assessment of a 19-year-old woman seriously ill with Asperger's Syndrome (a form of autism) – for attendance at a day centre – was found to be maladministration. She had been allocated to a particular officer on grounds of the latter's expertise (even though the officer had no experience of the relevant condition: autism). The officer was absent for a considerable period, but the case had not been reallocated. The ombudsman did not 'consider that staff shortages or a departmental reorganisation can ever justify a failure to respond to repeated requests of this seriousness for help' (*Sheffield CC 1994*). Similarly, a ten-month delay in assessing a woman unable to use her upstairs bathroom was maladministration. Shortage 'of money, communication and administration problems do not absolve the Council from their statutory duty' (*Bolton MBC 1992*).

Waiting times for assessment: professional exclusivity

The ombudsman will not necessarily defer to professional exclusivity. A failure to assess for 21 months was deemed maladministration; in the absence of professional occupational therapists, the council 'should have sought other means to ensure that people did not wait an acceptable length of time for an assessment'. When 'disabled people ask the Council for assistance in providing adaptations to their homes, they have the right to expect that assistance is provided with reasonable speed' (*Wirral MBC 1992c*; also *Middlesbrough BC 1996, Wirral MBC 1992a, Wirral MBC 1993d*).

Similarly, in another case the ombudsman stated that postponement of assessment for a year was not an option, and that an alternative channel for assessment should have been found (as the local authority had now done) if early use of occupational therapists was not possible – even though it would of course be ideal if professional advice were always to hand (*Sheffield CC 1989*).

In one authority, by the end of 1991, disability services were receiving 500 referrals per month and had over 1000 people awaiting assessment. Reorganisation and recruitment recommendations, made in a report to the social services committee, were thwarted shortly afterwards by a moratorium, imposed on financial grounds, on recruitment of non-qualified staff. Industrial action added to the three-year delay the complainant suffered. The ombudsman still found maladministration in that the local authority should have addressed both the resourcing problems and staffing levels long before (*Newham LBC 1993b*).

Waiting times for assessment: lower priority needs

Longer waiting times tend to be experienced by people deemed have needs of a 'lower priority'.

For example, in one local authority, the waiting times for the highest priority was some four months, but for people given priorities two and three, they were up to three years. A woman aged 86 applied for adaptations. She suffered from arthritis, asthma and sciatica and had fallen and broken her hip. She had not been able to use the bath for two of the three years she had spent awaiting assessment. The ombudsman's finding was maladministration, the delay being 'totally unacceptable' even though it was a 'relatively low priority' application. The assessment should have started within six months of the first approach to the local authority (*Redbridge LBC 1993a*).

The local ombudsman has stated that it is 'not acceptable that a client may wait up to two years for an assessment, whatever the outcome of that assessment'. This was maladministration, though she did commend the council for implementing a system of gathering information at an early stage so as to determine quickly whether it could assist the person (*Wirral MBC 1993c*). Even allowing for shortage of staff, and the fact that a person is not within the 'at risk' category, the local ombudsman might find that 'it cannot be acceptable for a client in need to face a two-year wait before their needs are even quantified' (*Wirral MBC 1992d*). Following a stroke, a man was discharged from hospital, awarded 'medium priority' and told that there would be a four-month wait for an assessment; his appalled wife had the bath removed and installed a shower and grab rails. The failure to assess in that time amounted to maladministration (*Barking and Dagenham LBC 1997*).

Waiting times for assessment: 'higher priority' people

Sometimes even people categorised as higher priority might have unacceptably long waits. In one case an elderly woman placed initially in the second-highest and then later in the highest category, had to wait 20 months for an assessment. This was 'totally unacceptable' according to the local ombudsman (*Redbridge LBC 1993b*). In another case, a woman regarded as high priority had also to wait 20 months; it had taken six months even to get as far as allocating her priority (*Hackney LBC 1997d*). It was maladministration when the clearing of a backlog of assessments for people with non-urgent needs affected adversely those with more urgent needs (*Wirral MBC 1993e*). And when a roofer became paralysed after a fall and was discharged from hospital, the local authority was at fault in taking ten weeks to produce a draft community care assessment, despite having information from the hospital (*Avon CC 1997*).

Waiting times for assessment: excessively long waits

Excessively long waits sometimes occur, such as four years and eight months in one case which was not exceptional in that authority; the ombudsman noted that a number of other people had been similarly affected (*Hackney LBC 1992a*). The severe criticism levelled at the local authority did not prevent it some years later from keeping the same woman waiting 20 months, when she requested a reassessment because of worn equipment and of additional needs in relation to looking after her two-year old son; the ombudsman found maladministration all over again (*Hackney LBC 1997a*).

Long waiting times can turn into never seeing people. In the first of the two cases referred to immediately above, the ombudsman found that the 'non-urgent' waiting lists had been closed indefinitely and believed that this might represent a failure of the council to discharge its statutory duty under s.2 of the Chronically Sick and Disabled Persons Act 1970 (*Hackney LBC 1992a*). The ombudsman might recognise the national problem of shortage of occupational therapists to carry out assessments, commend the practice of establishing priorities, but nevertheless find that 'it cannot be acceptable that those with the lowest priority may never be seen by an OT and thus never have their case considered' (*Wirral MBC 1992a*).

Waiting times for assessment: inconsistent application

About variations in waiting times between local authorities, the ombudsman can do nothing; however, there are sometimes discrepancies within the same local authority amounting to maladministration. For example, it could not be fair that an applicant should wait a few weeks for a renovation grant in one part of the borough, but for years in another (*Newham LBC 1997b*). In another finding of maladministration, one of the 'serious failures' was that a person who had waited four years and eight months for an assessment might have waited only five months had she lived a few hundred yards away in the same authority (*Hackney LBC 1992a*).

Another investigation found that a council had been misapplying its priority criteria: five people in a sample of 45 cases had been given priority incorrectly ahead of the particular complainant. The case illustrated the difficulties facing local authority staff such as occupational therapists. The reasons for the 'incorrect' decisions included 'soft-heartedness' in the case of a woman with asthma, emphysema and osteoarthritis who could just about manage indoor steps and stairs indoors. A second person 'had great difficulty getting up from a sitting position, and could not bathe without aids, was unable to get in and out of the bath, and lived alone'. Two sisters, aged 82 and 81, with various problems including Crohn's Disease, arthritis, osteoarthritis in spine, hips and knees were both unable to bathe. They should not have been given priority – but were given it, probably because of their joint needs and previous requests. Yet still, the misapplication of priority criteria amounted to maladministration (*Lewisham LBC 1993*).

Conversely, a six-month delay in assessment for home adaptations was not criticised, since the local authority had applied a system of priorities which took into account relevant factors and had fairly treated the complainant's priority as relatively low (*Ealing LBC 1993*). Similarly, a 15-month delay was not unreasonable in the circumstances, because the authority had adopted a policy of priority categories as they were entitled to (especially given particular staffing and resource problems) – and the complainant had been properly dealt with under that policy (*Lewisham LBC 1993*).

And a two-year wait might not draw the ombudsman's criticism if resources and staff restrictions mean that greater priority is given appropriately to those in greater need (*Wirral MBC 1994c*).

Waiting times for assessment: double queuing

The local ombudsmen are likely to disapprove of double-queuing; that is, where the administrative hoops of a local authority require that a person queues twice on the waiting list. For instance, when one man was originally classified as priority but then reclassified as high priority, he did not benefit as quickly as he should have because he was given a new 'start' date and so went to the end of the high priority list. This was maladministration (*Barking and Dagenham LBC 1998*) – as was the queuing twice when people applied for both a disabled facilities and a renovation grant (*Liverpool 1996/1997*) or for two occupational therapy assessments, the first for equipment, the second for adaptations (*Waltham Forest LBC 1994*).

Waiting times for assessment: giving information

The local ombudsman finds maladministration when local authorities give people inadequate information about waiting times – whether or not he or she faults the waiting time as well (eg, *Hackney LBC 1997c, Liverpool 1996/1997, Rotherham MBC 1995, Wirral MBC 1994c*).

10. IDENTIFYING PEOPLE IN NEED

The NHS and Community Care Act 1990 is silent about identifying the needs of the local population. However, policy guidance explains the importance of doing so. The Audit Commission makes the same point. Without adequate information about local needs, it becomes difficult if not impossible to plan and target, within budget, services for the people most in need, and to develop criteria of eligibility. Reports on community care have suggested that, for a number of reasons, local authorities have inadequate information about local population needs.

Nevertheless, there is an explicit statutory duty in s.1 of the Chronically Sick and Disabled Persons Act 1970 for local authorities to find out the numbers of disabled people in their area requiring services – although even this falls short of stipulating comprehensive identification of individuals.

EXTRACTS

Legislation (NHS and Community Care Act 1990) is silent about the needs of the local population.

Legislation (National Assistance Act 1948) creates a power for local authorities to maintain and compile 'classified registers' of disabled people to whom arrangements for welfare services under section 29(1) 'relate' (s.29(4)(g). Directions convert this power into a duty:

> 'The Secretary of State hereby directs local authorities to make the arrangements referred to in section 29(4)(g) of the Act (compiling and maintaining registers) in relation to persons who are ordinarily resident in their area' (*Secretary of State's Approvals and Directions under s.29(1) of the National Assistance Act 1948*: attached to LAC(93)10).

Legislation (Chronically Sick and Disabled Persons Act 1970,s.1(1)) states:

'It shall be the duty of every local authority having functions under section 29 of the National Assistance Act 1948 to inform themselves of the number of persons to whom that section applies within their area and of the need for the making by the authority of arrangements under that section for such persons'.

Circular guidance (LAC(93)10,appendix 4,paras 2–3) explains:

(registration under the 1948 Act) that the purpose of registration under the National Assistance Act 1948, s.29 is twofold. First, it is necessary for certain statutory purposes (eg, visually impaired people's benefits depend on registration). Second, registration is described as needed for planning and providing services. The form of the registers is not prescribed, and is left open. It is emphasised that provision of services under s.29 of the 1948 Act and s.2 of the Chronically Sick and Disabled Persons Act 1970 is not dependent on registration, and that people are entitled to request that they not be registered.

Circular guidance stated that:

(individual identification) the 'ultimate task' of local authorities was to identify 'everyone who both needs and wants a service'. This might only be achievable after various steps had been taken over time, such as sample surveys, the development of services, the creation and maintenance of lists of disabled people. Nevertheless 'comprehensive identification' was to be the eventual aim (DHSS 45/71,paras 11–12, now cancelled).

An earlier but still extant Circular is also cautious: 'It is not a requirement of the Section that authorities should attempt 100 per cent identification and registration of the handicapped. This would be a difficult, expensive and time consuming exercise, diverting excessive resources from effective work with those who are already known, involving a restrictive and artificial definition and likely to be counter-productive' (DHSS 12/70,para 5).

Policy guidance (DH 1990,para 4.32) makes it clear that information:

(community care generally) 'will be required for assessing the care needs of the resident population, to inform purchasing and to verify that contracts are being met in terms of both quality and quantity. SSDs will need to identify their information requirements and ensure that, where information is not available, they plan for its future provision'.

DISCUSSION

Identifying people in need: information

Identification of local needs is particularly significant for planning of services within limited budgets. For example, the Audit Commission (1993) commented on the lack of logic present when local authorities claim to have set eligibility criteria but not to have estimated local needs, since it is only upon the latter that the former can sensibly be based (pp.4–5). In addition to the requirements of policy guidance, good practice guidance on the assessment of population needs discusses and illustrates a wide range of methods which can be used to build up information about the local population (DH 1993).

Early reports about community care confirmed that local authorities needed more information about local needs and had problems in obtaining it (eg, SSI,NHSME 1994c,p.6; SSI,NHSE 1994d,p.11; Hardy, Wistow and Leedham 1994,p.40). The difficulty appears to be a continuing one, in terms of 'shaky knowledge' about needs, how current services are working, understanding costs and forecasting future activity and expenditure (Audit Commission, SSI 1998,p.6).

Problems of technology, information compatibility and confidentiality might exist, and some local authorities might focus on one group's needs at the expense of another's (eg, elderly people at the expense of younger adults with physical or sensory disabilities). Knowledge of the needs of minority ethnic groups might also be limited (DH 1994e,p.3). Furthermore, the gathering of information about local needs might be hampered by a) the reluctance of local authorities to record unmet needs and wishes because of misplaced legal anxiety; b) the inaccuracy of information (eg, recording a person as incontinent, whereas in fact the problem is due to forgetfulness, or to lack of directions in an institution); or c) the fact that information recorded in what are often crisis-led interventions focuses on limited, immediate needs and on too narrow a section of the population, so reducing its value to planners (Midgley, Munlo and Brown 1997,p.34).

Identifying people in need: 1948 and 1970 Acts

Local authorities are under a duty to keep registers of disabled people under s.29 of the National Assistance Act 1948. People do not need to be registered in order to receive services and can refuse registration. It is likely that, whatever their planning value, registers are in practice inadequate identification tools because it is difficult to keep them current and comprehensive. Indeed, it has been pointed out that people are more likely to be entered on the register (see above) after application and receipt of services rather than before. In which case, registers scarcely assist with identification at all (Topliss, Gould 1981,p.100).

Identifying people in need: duty to identify

In response to a 1988 Parliamentary question about the number of local authorities which had established the 'number and needs of people with disabilities' under the Chronically Sick and Disabled Persons Act 1970, the government replied: 'Local authorities have a clear duty under s.1 of the Act to inform themselves of the number of disabled people requiring services; to make arrangements for meeting any needs identified; and to provide information about relevant services. It is for local authorities to ensure that they fulfil these statutory duties' (Nicholas Scott: HCWA,11/7/1988,col.54).

Eighteen years before, the Chronically Sick and Disabled Persons Bill had originally included the words 'such steps as are reasonably practicable' as a qualification to the duty created by s.1 (see extracts above). The potentially vitiating effect of these words was recognised (see discussion: HCD,20/3/ 1970,col.876; HLD,30/4/1970,cols.1115–1123) and they were eventually removed in order to strengthen the duty (HCD,27/5/1970,cols.2004–2006). However, local authorities still have discretion, as central government has been quick to emphasise: 'Local authorities have a clear duty … to inform themselves of the number of disabled people in their areas and of their need for services. It is for individual authorities to determine how to fulfil this statutory duty' (Nicholas Scott: HCWA,18/7/1988,col.481). The government has stated that it has 'no power' to direct local authorities to implement the duty since the 'requirements to implement duties contained in s.1 are laid directly on local authorities by that section' (Hugh Rossi: HCWA,16/12/1982,col.241).

Identifying people in need: extent of duty

There seems to be no duty actually to identify individual people who might be in need of community care services.

The closest reference to a duty appears in s. 1 of the Chronically Sick and Disabled Persons Act 1970. However, it is generally accepted that, strictly interpreted, the duty extends only to finding out about the numbers of disabled people locally, rather than their identity. This can be seen by comparing the duty with its equivalent in the Northern Ireland version of the Act: the Chronically Sick and Disabled Persons (Northern Ireland) Act 1978. This contains additional words: 'The Department of Health and Social Services for Northern Ireland shall inform itself of the number of and, so *far as reasonably practicable, the identity of persons...*' (s. 1(1): italics added).

The later 1978 Act seems to acknowledge the loophole in the original 1970 Act; or at least, as Baroness Phillips (during the passage of the 1978 Bill) explained, it was making explicit what she had believed was always the intention of the 1970 Act: individual identification. The purpose was to 'ensure that the Department has a continuing duty to identify handicapped people, and that it cannot be content with, what one might term, a one-off operation' (HLD,19/7/1978,col.391). She did add, however, that even in the 1978 legislation there were 'too many words like "practicable" and "reasonable" in the Bill for some of us to be happy' (HLD,27/7/1978,col.984).

Therefore, the 1970 Act, contrasted with the 1978 Act, would seem to be about anonymous, rather than individual identification of disabled people. Indeed, even when the sponsor of the Chronically Sick and Disabled Persons Act 1970 became a Minister in the new Labour government of 1974, he did not give instructions to local authorities about individual identification (Topliss, Gould 1981,p.93). In 1983, two unsuccessful amendment bills attempted to bring the Chronically Sick and Disabled Persons Act 1970 into line with the Northern Ireland version. The government justified its resistance by referring to the expense of the frequent and extensive house-to-house surveys which would be required to establish the identity of every disabled person in the area (Tony Newton: HCWA,24/11/1983,col.281).

Identifying people in need: practice

It is not clear how extensively authorities have carried out their duties under s. 1. For example, one local authority reported during the 1990s that since 1970, 'there has not been a systematic study of the numbers and needs of people with physical disabilities ... This makes it very difficult to plan services which are responsive to need' (quoted in: Wistow, Leedham and Hardy 1993,p.17).

A Department of Health (SSI 1989a) report on services for deaf-blind people found that funding for this group of people was stifled because of an absence of 'useful data'. This seemed due to the ill-kept records of existing service users, together with the 'problems of defining the group, identifying all those who needed services and devising suitable ways to provide them' (p.15). The report concluded that 'many deaf-blind people themselves were probably not actually known' to local authorities (p.22). Local knowledge about, for example, the needs of disabled people from ethnic minority groups might be limited (SSI,NHSME 1994e,p.4).

Surveying local levels of need and disability can be difficult. For example, there are different views and definitions of need, including the difference between the social and individual models of disability/need, as well as cultural and conceptual barriers which hinder information-gathering

(Arnold *et al.* 1993,pp.8–13). The major, national disability survey carried out and published by the Office of Population Censuses and Surveys in the late 1980s opted for a method of asking people about their functional disabilities rather than their medical diagnoses (Martin, Meltzer and Elliot 1988,p.9).

Even by 1981, limitations to the practical usefulness of s.1 of the Chronically Sick and Disabled Persons Act were being exposed. For example, inquiries might even confuse matters and be afflicted by defective survey methodologies and by the problem of keeping information current. Thus, within 18 months of one survey, nearly a quarter of the people found to be disabled had undergone significant changes of circumstance (Topliss, Gould 1981,pp.94–97).

CHAPTER 6

COMMUNITY CARE ASSESSMENT

Coverage

1. Assessment as a service
2. Needs-led assessment
3. Determining need
4. Eligibility criteria and deciding about services
5. Resources and assessment
6. Needs and preferences

KEY POINTS

The concept of 'need' goes to the heart of community care assessment. If a person is not acknowledged by a local authority to have a need which calls for or necessitates provision, then he or she will not get any services. It is also a very uncertain concept, is essentially for each local authority to define, and is consequently an unpredictable element, varying from locality to locality.

The law courts have confirmed that, at the level of policy and criteria of eligibility, authorities can take account of the resources they have available when deciding what need is and whether it is necessary to meet it, and also when altering criteria from time to time. Consequently, people's assessed needs and the services they receive can fluctuate not just according to their own changing conditions and circumstances – but also as a result of the changing financial situation and policies of local authorities. This can lead to the application of more stringent tests of eligibility for both existing users and potential new users of services.

Eligibility criteria can cause confusion. For instance, if they are not based on relevant information about the needs of the local population, they might allow too many people to qualify for services and strain budgets to breaking point. Second, in some instances it is far from evident whether criteria are consistent with the legislation on which they are supposedly based. Third, their rigid application might result in an authority unlawfully fettering its discretion (see p.49). And fourth, they are sometimes misapplied by confused or ill-informed staff; for instance, criteria for service provision might be used to support a decision about a person's eligibility for assessment. This is certainly maladministration and could in some circumstances constitute unlawfulness (since, for example, criteria determining the necessity to provide services can legally be influenced by resources, but eligibility for assessment cannot be).

When assessing people's needs and deciding about services, a local authority is likely to distinguish 'preferences', 'desires' or 'wants' from needs. A further division is then likely between those needs which the authority agrees it will meet, and those which it will not ('unmet need'). A theme which has emerged from some of the judicial review cases in the law courts is the importance for both local authorities and service users about how need is identified and recorded in the assessment. Both financial and legal implications flow from the level of generality or specificity with which a person's need is expressed. For instance, need specified at a general level might leave open a number of options for service provision, some of which might be considerably cheaper and any one of which will meet identified need. The courts have confirmed that local authorities can take account of resources when deciding which option to choose.

Finally, it is noteworthy that a number of the rulings of the law courts about assessment have promulgated principles which coincide with what both users of services and social care professionals are likely to regard as good professional practice.

I. ASSESSMENT AS A SERVICE

As already explained in the previous chapter, community care assessment is a statutory duty and a service in its own right. Legislation states that a local authority must assess a person's needs for community care services if it appears to the authority that he or she may be in need of such services. Following the assessment, authorities then have a duty to decide which services are called for. The assessment, and decision about provision, are two separate duties. Legislation does not state what form assessment should take – this is left to what an authority might 'consider appropriate'.

EXTRACTS

Legislation: (NHS and Community Care Act 1990,s.47(1)) states:

> 'where it appears to a local authority that any person for whom they may provide or arrange for the provision of community care services may be in need of any such services, the authority – (a) shall carry out an assessment of his needs for those services; and (b) having regard to the results of that assessment, shall then decide whether his needs call for the provision by them of any such services'.

Policy guidance: (DH 1990,para 3.15) states that:

> 'assessment is a service in its own right and can be distinguished from the services that are arranged as a consequence'.

Directions: Under section 47(4) of the NHS and Community Care Act 1990, the Secretary of State has a power to make directions about:

> 'the manner in which an assessment under this section is to be carried out or the form it is to take but, subject to any such directions and to … [section 3 of the Disabled Persons (Services, Consultation and Representation) Act 1986: unimplemented] … it shall be carried out in such manner and take such form as the local authority consider appropriate'.

No such directions have been made.

DISCUSSION

Assessment as a service: background

The NHS and Community Care Act 1990 does not refer to how assessment should be carried out, nor has the Secretary of State's power been used to make directions specifying the form of assessment.

This lack of statutory detail is deliberate. During the passing of the NHS and Community Care Bill, the Secretary of State for Health, resisting an amendment to prescribe the form of assessment, referred to the 'cumbersome and time-consuming' assessment of special educational needs by education authorities, and indicated that similar formalities should be avoided in community care. She explained: 'The Government will not prescribe how local authorities should make the essential assessments. The challenge to local authorities will be to tackle that task within their resources'. Rule books were not the answer (Virginia Bottomley: SC(E),15/2/1990,col.1020). This means that the process of assessment, pivotal to the whole community care system, remains legally undefined: local authorities are apparently free to adopt their own approaches subject to their taking account of Department of Health guidance and following the decisions of the law courts.

Assessment as a service: for community care services

Community care assessment is about assessing people's needs for community care services. Community care services are defined in s.46 of the NHS and Community Care Act 1990 and are in fact covered by other, previously existing, pieces of legislation: the National Assistance Act 1948 (Part 3) and by extension s.2 of the Chronically Sick and Disabled Persons Act 1970, the NHS Act 1977 (schedule 8), the Health Services and Public Health Act 1968 (s.45) and the Mental Health Act 1983 (s.117).

This previous legislation contains a mixture of duties and powers governing the provision of a number of services which are described fully in Chapter 8. When local authorities have carried out an assessment under s.47 of the NHS and Community Care Act 1990, their decision about what services are 'called for' – having regard to the assessment – will be legally constrained by the degree of obligation imposed by the relevant piece of legislation. For instance, s.2 of the Chronically Sick and Disabled Persons Act 1970 imports a specific duty toward disabled people, s.29 of the National Assistance Act 1948 general duties and powers towards disabled people, and s.45 of the Health Services and Public Health Act 1968 powers only towards older but not disabled people (see p.213 for explanation of duties and powers).

Assessment as a service: challenging professional judgement

The professional judgement of staff such as social workers and occupational therapists is fundamental to assessment. The courts will fight shy of challenging professional judgments unless they are legally unreasonable. This is because judicial review is a form of supervision of public bodies such as local authorities, and the courts have neither the wish, nor the expertise, nor the mandate to step into the shoes of professionals and start running social services departments.

Likewise, the local ombudsmen will not generally challenge professional judgements (they are forbidden to do so by the Local Government Act 1974), unless they are 'utterly unreasonable' (*Leicester CC 1992a*). For instance, it was 'almost incomprehensible' that an occupational therapist decided not to recommend adaptations for a double amputee despite medical advice – a decision which led to the closing of the file and to the woman's being left in a house completely unadapted for her needs (*Gravesham BC 1987*). When an occupational therapist made basic errors in an assessment, such as describing a shower with a lip wrongly as 'walk-in' and failing to record these daily living activities that could not be observed during the visit, the ombudsman found maladministration because the assessment was so obviously flawed (*Barking and Dagenham LBC 1997*) – similarly, when an assessment recorded a curved staircase as straight (*Durham CC 1993*).

If a professional judgement is based on administrative flaws – and the line between the professional and the administrative can be a fine one – it is another matter. For example, in one case assessment had been made by an experienced and qualified officer. Her decision was in effect overruled by a manager on the grounds that the decision was not consistent with other comparable cases. The ombudsman found that there was no evidence supporting those grounds (which were anyway disputed by another officer) and that the overruling of the original decision was 'inconsistent' and constituted maladministration (*Leicester CC 1992b*). Similarly, when an occupational therapy manager failed to consult another occupational therapist (who knew about the particular circumstances of the applicant) before submitting recommendations, this was maladministration (*Liverpool CC 1996/1997*).

When a man was assessed for adaptations but no medical evidence was requested, no long-term prognosis sought and neither incontinence nor mobility problems were documented, the assessment was flawed (*Barnsley MBC 1998a*). An assessment was also inadequate because it failed to go into sufficient detail, introduced incorrect information and was carried out in an extremely subjective fashion; long-term prognosis was also ignored (*Barnsley MBC 1998b*).

Assessment as a service: professional judgement in context

Professional judgement does not occupy a vacuum. Not only is it tied closely to administrative issues, as illustrated immediately above, but it is also framed firmly by a local authority's policies and eligibility criteria.

For instance, when criticising the decision of a local authority to keep a disabled child waiting for new seating, the ombudsman focused not on the professional competence of staff, but on the application of eligibility criteria which were too simplistic (*Rochdale MBC 1995*). Illustrating the same principle, the judge in *R v Haringey LBC, ex p Norton* criticised the report of an independent occupational therapist, on the grounds that she could not know the background (eg, conflicting needs within the borough) to the authority's policies – a background which underlay the decision about needs and services in the particular case in question.

More controversially, guidance warns authorities about always taking at face value the recommendations of a person's own general practitioner, who 'may not be placed to act' as an assessor because of his or her personal relationship with the patient (DH 1990,para 3.48). If this is a suggestion that bias might creep into the recommendations of a person's general practitioner, then equally service users might perceive that their needs are being marginalised by a biased interviewer or professional assessor from the local authority, who is more concerned with the council's resources than with providing services.

For instance, in one local ombudsman investigation, the chair of a complaints review panel had concluded that a local authority's decision not to fund a residential placement for a young man with learning disabilities had been based solely on resources. In addition, the report on which the decision was based was found to be so offensive (and to contain inaccuracies) that the local authority offered to destroy it; it had in any case purported to sum up the person's needs, even though no proper assessment had been conducted. In such circumstances, it seems scarcely surprising that the man's mother thought the report had been 'cooked up' (*Kent CC 1998*). Nevertheless, the courts will generally be slow to intervene, recognising that it is for local authorities to decide how inquiries or assessments are to be handled (see *R v Tower Hamlets, ex p Khatum*, a homelessness case).

Assessment as a service: role of social care professionals

Hemmed in by restrictive policies, professional practitioners sometimes conclude that their integrity is being undermined.

For instance, a procedural, mechanistic and bureaucratic approach which follows guidelines closely, contrasts with a more traditional social work model which sees a relationship between social worker and client as a basis for the analysis and solving of problems. The former approach might also be associated with excessive prescription, the 'de-skilling' of social workers (eg, Davis, Ellis and Rummery 1997,p.12), and a substantial filling out of forms which comes to be a barrier between assessor and client. The tension between these different approaches can even mean that staff do not follow new procedures because they are adhering informally to traditional ways of working (Baldwin 1995a,pp.14–16,25; see also Singh 1995,p.19). However, community care assessments might now rarely be used for the professional social work practice of advocacy, promotion of self-determination, building of relationships, exploration of need, and response to particular individual and household circumstances (Davis, Ellis and Rummery 1997,p.27).

Assessors might find the procedural model conflicting not only with tradition, but simply with their wish to understand and to assist people; this might lead to their helping clients get around eligibility criteria which, on the face of it, they do not meet (Smale *et al.* 1993,p.21). For instance, a woman recovering from major surgery might require help with the housework, but the criteria rule out 'housework only' requests. To circumvent this restriction, the home care organiser persists by describing the woman's need as 'help with cooking'. This need then falls within the criteria and can thus be the vehicle for help with the housework – although the woman can actually manage cooking herself (Ellis 1993,p.37).

The concern about loss of professional integrity mirrors similar concerns expressed over the years in the field of special education, where the recording of only those needs of a child which can be met from resources (see eg, CLAE 1994,p.24; NAHA 1988b,p.8) can result in apparent conflicts between the professional standards of staff and their duties to their employer (Bhuttarcharji 1992). But perhaps the anxiety is in some circumstances misplaced; if a distinction is made in community care between professional judgement of need and subsequent decisions about eligibility for services, professional integrity would appear to be protected. This is especially so since the House of Lords confirmed in *R v Gloucestershire CC, ex p Barry* that it is quite legitimate to identify need which is not going to be met (RADAR 1997,p.7). Even so, professionals can be put in a difficult position when they are in the 'front line' dealing with people who may fail to perceive, and not be interested in, nuances of professional integrity but are more concerned about the services they have been denied. The situation is made worse if professionals are also having to put into practice a 'barrage of policy and operational guidance' riddled with inconsistencies (Davis, Ellis and Rummery 1997,p.11).

Despite all of this, expert professional opinion might sometimes be decisive. In one case, professional submissions which had been made to a complaints review panel confirmed the court in its view that the panel had made the right decision in favour of the applicant, and that the local authority had shown no grounds for its failure to act on the panel's recommendations (*R v Avon CC, ex parte M*). In addition, what the courts say might well coincide simply with what professionals consider to be good practice (see p.44).

Assessment as a service: components of assessment

The Audit Commission (1993) suggested about community care in general that 'providing services is not the only way of meeting needs' and that advice, guidance, information, counselling and sympathy are all components of assessment as a service in its own right. Providing these is one way of discharging local authority duties and 'this sort of advice could become an important way of meeting needs further down the needs pyramid, broadening the base (and the appeal) of local authority activities with services provided only in exceptional circumstances' (p.5). Such a statement, though clear on its face, is apt to confuse slightly, given that advice, guidance, information and counselling are all services in their own right (ie, not as part of assessment) under, for instance, s.29 of the National Assistance Act 1948 – in which case the distinction between assessment and services, made great play of in community care, blurs.

Assessment as a service: relevant factors and final decisions

Assessment of people's needs for services must take account of relevant factors; failure to do so will be maladministration in the eyes of the ombudsman and unlawful in the view of the courts (*Associated Provincial Picture Houses v Wednesbury Corporation*).

In community care, relevant factors include, for example, needs and resources (see eg, *R v Gloucestershire CC, ex p Barry*), Department of Health guidance (*R v Islington LBC, ex p Rixon*), the preferences of the person being assessed (*R v North Yorkshire CC, ex p Hargreaves*), and a broad range of needs (*R v Haringey LBC, ex p Norton*; and see the ombudsman investigation, *Tower Hamlets LBC 1993*, when information was not sought about the person's physical and mental health). In order to obtain all the relevant information, a range of sources might have to be consulted, including other health and social care professionals, voluntary organisation staff involved, carers and so on. For instance, it has been observed that the staff of voluntary organisations working with homeless people often feel that their input is ignored or under-valued, even though they might have substantial knowledge and experience of the client (O'Leary 1997,p.18). Such practice would suggest that relevant factors are not being taken into account, given that Department of Health guidance expressly recognises the expertise of the voluntary sector in respect of homeless people and people who are misusers of drugs or alcohol – and suggests that local authorities should consider utilising it (LAC(93)2,paras 16,27)

Relevant factors must ultimately be brought together by whoever is making the final statutory decision (ie, under s.47 of the 1990 Act) – whether individual front-line officers, managers, panels or committees (with sometimes colourful names such as the Star Chambers or Starlet Chambers mentioned in an ombudsman investigation: *Camden LBC 1993*). For instance, in *Durham CC 1993*, a housing sub-committee did not have all the relevant facts and the ombudsman found maladministration. In another case about adaptations, a report on which a committee based its decision had been prepared hurriedly and so was flawed because it lacked full information about costings, contained factual errors and did not explain why the applicant had objected to various options. To come to a decision on such 'uncertain evidence' was maladministration (*Sandwell MBC 1995*). And application of a home help policy, which prioritised shopping over cleaning – without taking account of the particular medical needs of a man who used a wheelchair, was an amputee and had double incontinence – was maladministration (*Westminster CC 1996*).

The courts have confirmed – what anyway would seem to be commonsense – that health and safety is a relevant factor to consider when deciding what services should be provided (*R v Cornwall CC, ex p Goldsack*). Even so, a local authority should not use health and safety as a factor to stall the making of a final decision. For instance, when problems arose because of a conflict between apparent need and safety standards, the local ombudsman could not tell the council what to do, but the latter still had to come to a proper decision and not let the matter drift. The family concerned had felt that the authority's refusal to provide a stairlift on grounds of safety was flimsy given the daily risk undergone by the carrying of one of its members up and down the stairs daily (*Islington LBC 1988*).

Assessment as a service: responsibility for statutory decisions

The final assessment decision made under s.47 of the NHS and Community Care Act 1990 is for the local authority to take: that is what the legislation says.

Local government legislation (Local Government Act 1972, s.101) allows local authorities to delegate functions to their own officers and committees; and community care legislation empowers authorities to employ as agents independent organisations to deliver community care services (see eg, National Assistance Act 1948, s.30, and the Health Services and Public Health Act 1968, s.45). However, nothing envisages that assessment decisions can in general be delegated; as it was put in a housing case, 'an authority should bear in mind that it is its function and no one else's to decide' (*R v Lambeth LBC, ex p Carroll*). Thus, whilst guidance anticipates that other people might be involved in the assessment, 'decisions to commit resources and ultimate responsibility for the assessment remains with' the local authority (LAC(93)2,para 17).

No order has been made in relation to community care under s.70 of the Deregulation and Contracting Out Act 1994, which does allow generally for the contracting out, by order, of local authority statutory functions. However, a health authority or NHS Trust could perform an assessment for a local authority under s.113 of the Local Government Act 1972 (see p.317) which allows for an agency arrangement – whereby the NHS could commit agreed amounts of local authority resources, although the latter would still retain ultimate statutory responsibility (see: DH 1995d,p.13).

Furthermore, even within a local authority, policy should make clear who is responsible for taking a particular (statutory) decision; for example, in *R v Kirklees LBC, ex p Daykin* the recommendations of a health authority occupational therapist and local authority 'advocate' did not amount to a decision under s.47 of the NHS and Community Care Act 1990 since they had no authority to make it (see also *R v Islington LBC, ex p Aldabbagh*).

2. NEEDS-LED ASSESSMENT

Both policy and practice guidance refer to 'needs-led' assessment, although the term is absent from legislation. The idea seems to be that local authorities should assess people's needs first, almost in the abstract, before considering what services they require and should be provided with. This principle of assessing people's 'real' needs fully, rather than solely in terms of available services ('service-led' assessment), is a model welcomed as a matter of good practice by many people. Nevertheless, as has become evident from several judicial review cases, it also carries significant financial and legal implications.

Practice guidance points out that such an approach requires local authorities to break with the past practice of service-led assessments. Nevertheless, it has been reported that social services staff are sometimes finding it difficult to assess without reference to services. Part of the difficulty is that insistence on a purist needs-led approach ignores the fact that a) financial and time pressures limit the amount of time local authority staff can spend on assessment; and b) some people know from the outset exactly what service or services they require. Furthermore, the legislation itself refers to assessment of need for services, not simply assessment of need in the abstract; and Department of Health guidance points out that assessment of need is not conducted in a vacuum.

EXTRACTS

Legislation: (NHS and Community Care Act 1990) describes the local authority's duty to assess as:

'an assessment of his needs for those services' (s.47(1(a)). It goes on: 'having regard to the results of that assessment, [it] shall then decide whether his needs call for the provision by them of any such services' (s.47(1)(b)).

Policy guidance: (DH 1990,para 3.15) states that the 'needs-led approach pre-supposes a progressive separation of assessment from service provision' and that:

'Assessment does not take place in a vacuum: account needs to be taken of the local authority's criteria for determining when services should be provided, the types of service they have decided to make available and the overall range of services provided by other agencies, including health authorities'.

Circular guidance: (CI (92)34,para 5 now cancelled) stated that 'the assessment of need and decisions about the services to be provided are separate stages in the process'.

Practice guidance: (SSI,SWSG 1991a) states that assessment should be:

'consistent with a needs-led, rather than a service-led, approach' (p.43). Also, 'the assessment of need will require a significant change in attitude and approach by most practitioners. They will have to make conscious efforts to treat the assessment of need as a separate exercise from consideration of the service response ... few practitioners currently make that distinction, nor are they encouraged to do so by the assessment procedures they are required to operate' (p.47).

'The needs should have been defined at the assessment stage but more detail may be required to specify the service requirements. The aim of the care planning stage is to target any intervention as precisely as possible on the identified needs' (p.62).

Practice guidance: (SSI,SWSG 1991b,p.43) also states that initial assessment response 'does not presuppose the service outcome'.

DISCUSSION

Needs-led assessment: breaking with past practice

The NHS and Community Care Act 1990, s.47(1), describes a twofold process. First, a person's 'needs for services' are assessed under s.47(1)(a); second, a decision is made about what services the local authority will provide under s.47(1)(b). Taking the needs-led approach in fulfilment of these two duties is viewed as breaking significantly with the past practice of service-led assessment. (Apart from the needs- and service-led approaches, assessments as a matter of practice might alternatively be demand-led when people get what they want, or budget-led when provision is linked to money and not need (SSI 1997a,p.21). However, neither of these two additional possibilities is explicitly mentioned or advocated in guidance).

The previous absence of such a need-led approach was confirmed by SSI research published in 1991 (SSI,SIS 1991,p.39). A Joseph Rowntree report (Ellis 1993,p.17) found the same pattern: 'administrative staff saw their task as to weed out enquiries which did not fit with their understanding of services available within the department. In taking referrals, they would record only such information as they thought "relevant" to the range of specialist teams. Consequently, referrals for a "general assessment" would not be accepted but translated into a specific request'.

Early reports on community care implementation suggested that in some areas, staff, users and carers were struggling with the needs-led approach (eg, SSI,NHSME 1994b,p.11; SSI 1994a,p.18); for example, where resources were limited and services had to be provided quickly (SSI 1994d,p.26). However, even some years later, limited service options might still lead to service-led assessments, and to a 'high throughput' of patients through hospital, with local authority staff offering little more than a (care home) placement service (SSI 1998b,pp.34–35).

The contrast between service- and needs-led assessment has been drawn in relation to people with a visual impairment. The former concentrates on how the person might fit into the normal range of services provided and might also be linked to restrictive screening at the pre-assessment stage. The latter involves a knowledgeable practitioner exploring and discussing the general impact of sight loss, achievement of autonomy, feelings, making the most of available vision, relearning everyday tasks, using special equipment, alternative methods of understanding the written word and employment (SSI 1998a,pp.5,17).

Needs-led assessment: duty to assess even if services are unlikely to be provided

Legally, needs-led assessment is dictated by law, to the extent that local authorities have a duty to assess people who appear to be in possible need of any community care service – even if the authority has only a power (rather than a duty) to provide it and is highly unlikely to do so. This has been confirmed specifically in *R v Berkshire CC, ex p P*, and in *R v Bristol CC, ex p Penfold*. Similarly, in an ombudsman investigation it was maladministration when a local authority came to a decision about not providing residential care for a man with learning disabilities, without having conducted an assessment of needs first and in contravention of its own policy (*Kent CC 1998*).

Needs-led assessment: generality or specificity of need

The generality or specificity with which need is identified and recorded goes to legal, financial and good practice issues, and has been rehearsed in the area of local authority education when need is determined for the purpose of statutory statements of children's special educational needs.

A straightforward interpretation of s.47(1) of the NHS and Community Care Act 1990 would be that the statutory duty to assess is the duty to *assess an individual's needs for services.* This is what the words say. The legislation goes on to state that the local authority must then decide which services actually to provide or arrange. Baroness Blatch explained during the Committee stage of the NHS and Community Care Bill: 'Assessment will identify needs for services. However, [the subsection] requires that, following assessment, local authorities must decide, having regard to the results of the assessment, whether there is a need for them to provide services. Therefore, the local authority is required to decide which of the needs it will meet taking account of duties under Section 2 of the Chronically Sick and Disabled Persons Act 1970. Apart from that, it is not obliged to meet all needs and will wish to take into account its priorities and resources' (HLD,10/5/1990, cols.1538–1539). Both the legislation and Baroness Blatch's statement seem to indicate distinctly that assessment will identify people's needs for services – but that not all those needs have to be met (although she did not appear to anticipate *R v Gloucestershire CC, ex p Barry* which established that this is the position even under s.2 of the CSPDA 1970).

In practice and at one extreme, assessment might be 'needs-led' to the extent that services are not mentioned in the assessment at all. It is only after the assessment is complete that its content is 'translated' via criteria of eligibility into a decision, under s.47(1)(b), about whether to provide services and, if so, what. In several judicial review cases, the law courts have assumed that local authorities will assess at a high level of generality, and have even intimated that the community care legislation is barely workable if this is not done (eg, *R v Cornwall CC, ex p Goldsack*).

Even so, there are commonsense limits to the generality of assessment. First, the legislation talks about assessment of 'needs for those services' – not just of 'needs'. Clearly, assessment cannot be in a total vacuum and must bear some relation to community care services, as stipulated by the wording of the legislation and confirmed by guidance (see extracts above). Further, if no mention of services – and criteria of eligibility for those services – is made even at the assessment (as opposed to the later care planning) stage, then it is difficult to see how users can participate fully as guidance states that they should (see p.138 below – and Keep, Clarkson 1994,p.27; SSI/NHSE 1994f,p.27; SSI 1994e,p.1). It has been suggested that it is legally 'unfair' to fail to tell the person not only about what services exist but also about the relevant eligibility criteria (Schwehr 1997b). For instance, local authorities might deliberately manipulate the expression of people's needs in order to limit what services are later specified in care plans – and not tell service users about possible services and how to access them. This might lubricate the administrative process, but scarcely accords with the spirit of Department Health guidance dealing with user participation.

Nevertheless, policy and practice guidance seems in places to suggest the removal altogether of reference to services. For example, policy guidance states: 'The needs-led approach pre-supposes a progressive separation of assessment from service provision' (DH 1990,para 3.15). Community care practice guidance gives an example of this. Assessment pro formas should 'focus the assessment on needs, without categorising those needs in terms of services'; although it then suggests, confusingly, that 'home care' (general) should be listed rather than 'domiciliary support' (specific) (SSI/SWSG 1991a,p.56). Yet both terms are surely general and virtually synonymous, and if they are not, it is the latter term which in fact bears the wider connotation. Indeed, 'practical assistance in the home', a service listed under s.2 of the Chronically Sick and Disabled Persons Act 1970, is already a broad term covering anything from basic housework to personal care. How non-specific, in this example, would the language of assessment need to be, in order to avoid words which will trigger a possible duty to provide such practical assistance?

Some commonsense examples of distinguishing need from service were given by the Court of Appeal (Swinton-Thomas L.J.) in *R v Gloucestershire CC, ex p Barry*. For instance, a need for cleaning and laundry could be met (in terms of services) by someone coming in to the home to use the washing machine or taking the laundry away; and likewise a need for a television set by either a new or a second-hand set. However, this last example demonstrates how confusing the need and service dichotomy can become – since television is specifically listed as a service in s.2 of the Chronically Sick and Disabled Persons Act 1970 (see p.197).

Needs-led assessment: legal implications

The way in which need is expressed in assessment brings with it legal, financial and good practice consequences. In practice and in law, by expressing need at a more general level, a local authority leaves itself open a greater choice of service options from which to meet that need.

The legal and financial implications of this have been underlined by the law courts; when deciding on which service option to provide, authorities are legally permitted to take account of resources, so long as the identified need is still met. For instance, if need is defined as '24-hour-a-day care' (as opposed to 24-hour-a-day care at home), then an authority has two service options rather than one: 24-hour care in the person's own home or 24-hour care in a nursing home (*R v Lancashire CC, ex p RADAR*; see also an ombudsman case, *Humberside CC 1995*, on a similar issue and the acceptability of the local authority's inability to provide 24-hour home support). If a person's needs are defined as need (in a day centre) for assistance with mobility, rather than walking assistance in particular – then the need can be met not only by walking assistance, but also, for example, by use of a wheelchair (*R v Cornwall CC, ex p Goldsack*). And if needs are defined as for getting in and out of premises, rather than more precisely as for a lift – then there are at least two service options: the lift, or a move to alternative accommodation (*R v Kirklees MBC, ex p Daykin*). Local authorities sometimes try to exploit this principle in order to reduce their obligations to provide expensive home adaptations – for instance, by suggesting that assessing need as 'general bathing' would leave open the option of offering transport to use nearby bathing facilities, rather than a bathroom with shower (*Middlesbrough BC 1996*).

In *Richardson v Solihull*, the Court of Appeal looked at the same type of issue in special education, finding that although an education authority could name a specific school in a statement of a child's special educational needs, it was not obliged to. But once a school was specifically named in a statement, an authority could not simply disregard this fact and maintain that the child should go to another school even if there were transport problems (*R v Havering LBC, ex p K*)

Along such lines, the Audit Commission explained to the House of Commons Health Committee (1993,vol.2) that if local authorities: 'say to people, "We have assessed you for home care, we think you qualify but we cannot provide it", then they are at risk of laying themselves open to being legally bound by that decision. If they assess people, people's mobility, their capability to undertake basic daily living tasks and so on and provide people with that sort of assessment and then say: "You may need help with some of these, our eligibility criteria are these, and therefore we can provide help with those but you still need help with other activities", then I think they sit on the right side of the law' (vol.2,p.8). Evidence to the same committee included reference to an SSI letter to directors of social services in London spelling out a similar message. It referred to the 'legal ambiguity as between the Chronically Sick and Disabled Persons Act 1970 which is service-led and the Disabled Persons Act 1986 and the NHS and Community Care Act 1990 which are needs-led ... It is this "service-led" definition of need which leads lawyers to be cautious. It reinforces the requirement to develop a "needs-led" language, which leaves open the selection of the appropriate level and type of service response' (vol.2,pp.44–45).

Even so, over-concentration on needs in the abstract can lead to apparent inconsistency with the words of s.47(1) of the NHS and Community Care 1990 ('assessment of his needs for those services'), as in the following example: '"We are assessing need and then offering services to relieve that need, but we are not assessing for services; hence we do not record need for services"' (AMA 1993,p.4).

Finance and law apart, a broad and wide-ranging assessment of need, followed by separate and creative identification of a range of service solutions might well conform to notions of good professional practice. Indeed, optimum solutions are not necessarily the most expensive. However, beset by shortage of resources, local authority staff might find it hard to separate good professional, from sharp financial and legal, practice.

3. DETERMINING NEED

The term 'need' is as elusive as it is legally important. It is crucial to the triggering of various duties in community care legislation. The judges in *R v Gloucestershire, ex p Barry* – though only narrowly, and following substantial disagreement – finally confirmed that in determining what is meant by need, local authorities may lawfully take account of resources. Legally significant consequences flow from the distinction made by local authorities, first between people's preferences and their needs – and, second, between need which will be met and need which will not ('unmet need'). However, the law courts have stipulated that local authorities should not overly restrict breadth of need (eg, it covers social, recreational, psychological needs, not just physical risk) and that it must be assessed on an individual basis.

EXTRACTS

Legislation: refers in several places to need, a key element in the triggering of certain duties; for example, assessment and services under s.47 of the NHS and Community Care Act 1990; the provision of residential accommodation under s.21 of the National Assistance Act 1948 (p.253); and the provision of welfare services for disabled people under s.2 of the Chronically Sick and Disabled Persons Act 1970 (p.197).

Practice guidance: (SSI/SWSG 1991a,pp.12–13) states that it uses the term need as:

(independence and quality of life): 'shorthand for the requirements of individuals to enable them to achieve, maintain or restore an acceptable level of social independence or quality of life, as defined by the particular care agency or authority'.

(dynamic concept): 'Need is a dynamic concept, the definition of which will vary over time in accordance with changes in national legislation, changes in local policy, the availability of resources, the patterns of local demand'.

(multi-faceted nature of need): 'Need is a multi-faceted concept which, for the purposes of this guidance, is sub-divided into six broad categories, each of which should be covered in a comprehensive assessment of need: personal care, health care, accommodation, finance, education/employment/leisure, transport/access'.

(individual nature of need): 'However, need is also a personal concept. No two individuals will perceive or define their needs in exactly the same way. Care management seeks to recognise the individuality of need by challenging practitioners to identify unique characteristics of each individual's needs and to develop individualised, rather than stereotyped, responses to those needs within the constraints of local policy and resources'.

Circular guidance: (DHSS 12/70,para 7)

'Criteria of need are matters for authorities to determine in the light of resources'.

DISCUSSION

Determining need: elasticity

The term 'need' is highly elastic, is used in a number of different ways and is capable of causing controversy, confusion and disagreement.

For instance, the implication of legislation such as s.2 of the Chronically Sick and Disabled Persons Act 1970 was always that local authorities would – up to a point – retain control over what is meant by need. In *R v Gloucestershire, ex p Barry* all five judges managed to agree on this point (Guthrie 1997), being of the opinion that it was for social services committees to formulate a yardstick against which to measure need (although there was disagreement about whether the yardstick applied should be determined by resources or by the civilised standards of society) – and that therefore what is meant by need might differ from area to area. So, a person deemed to be 'in need' in one local authority, might not be in need if he or she lives (perhaps only several hundred yards away) in another (although for the original intentions of the sponsor of the Chronically Sick and Disabled Persons Bill in relation to standardising provision for disabled people, see p.198). Practice guidance further explains that the meaning of need might vary in time even within one local authority (see extracts above). This suggests that a person deemed to be in need one year, might not be the next.

What the decision of the House of Lords in the *Gloucestershire* case spelt out was that in stretching or contracting the ambit of the word 'need', local authorities are permitted to take account of resources along with other relevant factors (see below, p.129). In fact, many local authorities have in practice very clearly always taken account of resources in setting criteria of need. What had changed in the last few years leading up to the *Gloucestershire* case was a matter of practice and degree rather than of legal principle: authorities simply had less money and so were setting tougher criteria. The reality that resources inevitably are – and have been – taken into account by local authorities was put simply and succinctly by the Court of Appeal (though its overall decision was later overruled by the House of Lords) in the education case of *R v East Sussex CC, ex p Tandy*. It recognised that where reassessment reduces the level of service provision, even the previous more generous level must likewise have been limited by resources – just less so.

Determining need: multi-faceted need (law)

Local authorities sometimes require no encouragement to limit the meaning of need, in order to reduce service provision. However, the law courts have shown themselves prepared to take a stand.

For instance, when a local authority reassessed a man with multiple sclerosis, it effectively dismissed his social, recreational and leisure needs, concentrating only on his physical needs. The judge referred to s.2 of the Chronically Sick and Disabled Persons Act 1970 and the range of services covered (see p.197), and to the Department of Health's guidance which states that need is multi-faceted and should be treated as such in assessment (*R v Haringey LBC, ex p Norton*). However, in practice such dismissal is probably not unusual: an SSI report on services for people with physical disabilities found that care plans rarely made reference to education and leisure activities (SSI 1996e,p.14).

In the earlier case of *R v Avon CC, ex p M*, a local authority's attempt to restrict the meaning of need failed; what it had claimed was the mere preference or whim of a person with learning disabilities, the judge accepted as a psychological need which the authority had a duty to meet. This case does not open the floodgates to anybody who says they have a fixed preference; the particular circumstances were that the expert opinion submitted (to the complaints review panel) had been to the effect that young adults with Down's Syndrome typically formed such an entrenched position.

Determining need: multi-faceted need (practice)

The shortcomings of assessments which focus merely on functional needs (d'Aboville 1995,p.27) ought to be self-evident to local authorities. To seek out dependence in terms solely of physical need and personal care, instead of looking at how people can achieve independence and personal autonomy, appears short-sighted and contrary to the aims of community care (Davis, Ellis and Rummery 1997,p.13): policy guidance refers to 'restoring and maintaining independence' (DH 1990,para 3.3).

That community care assessment should consider need broadly is no more than common sense, since it is obvious that independent living in the community makes no sense if issues such as appropriate housing, accessible transport and personal safety are not taken account of (Bewley, Glendinning 1994,p.36). It has been suggested that in practice it is a person's social situation which is the appropriate 'unit of assessment' (Smale *et al.* 1993,p.26). A failure to link home support services with policies on social regeneration can lead to older people marooned in their own homes, frightened of going out and not participating in daily, social life (Henwood 1998b,p.9). On this theme, disability organisations have identified seven basic needs: for information and counselling to assist choice, housing (suitable, accessible and well-located), equipment, personal assistance, transport, access to public places (eg, d'Aboville 1995,p.4). Similarly, for older people important issues identified include mobility, safe and accessible environments, transport, information, advice, advocacy (Harding 1997,pp.33–38).

For instance, assessment which concentrates only on obvious functional difficulties – rather than the emotional distress affecting people who have had a stroke following hospital discharge – might not identify the difficulties experienced in adjustment to new circumstances and to use of home care services or assistive equipment (Baldock, Ungerson 1994,pp.45–47). Also underlining the importance of assessing need in a broad sense, is the fact that older people's needs for assistance can be founded in loneliness, anxiety, a feeling of lowness, clinical depression (Pearson, Richardson 1994,p.3; SSI 1997c,p.13; Neill, Williams 1992,p.95) or simply fear – to the extent that it, rather than physical inability, can lead to a decision to enter residential care. The fear might be of loneliness, crime, physical falling, not recovering from illness, being a burden to others or of children for their parents (SSI 1994f,p.5). Of course, a range of other factors might also contribute to decisions about residential care: lack of choice and involvement in making a decision of what to do, living arrangements, increasing disability and impairment, lack of community services, stress on carers, inadequate arrangements following discharge from hospital, poor assessment and care management, lack of innovation and flexibility in services, professional and organisational concerns and vested interests (SSI 1994g,pp.52–55).

Thus, guidance (LAC(98)9, which states that eligibility criteria for people with HIV/AIDS should relate to assessment of need and not just HIV status, might in practice be double-edged. First, that people should not be stereotyped in terms of a medical condition and instead have their individual needs properly considered. Alternatively it might suggest that HIV status will not be an automatic passport to assistance. For instance, some local authorities might fail to take into account the future, but fast approaching and substantial, needs of a person with HIV, by doing little at an early stage – when the person is not yet deemed to be 'substantially and permanently handicapped' (see eg, *Salford CC 1996*, an ombudsman investigation with a similar element).

Determining need: models of disability

Broad conceptions of disability tend to support the notion that the needs of people in relation to their disability (as opposed to their medical condition) should be viewed as social, rather than medical, and are as much about identifying and changing barriers within society as identifying 'problems' with the individual (eg, Oliver 1990,pp.7–8; Nocon *et al.* 1995,p.6).

The one model identifies disability (as opposed to an impairment or an illness) as a problem created by society's failure, the other treats it as a wholly individual problem. From the latter follows the danger of treating disabled people as ill instead of treating their illnesses, and insistence on a detrimental notion of normality – for instance, trying to get or force disabled people to walk, even when it is not appropriate (Oliver 1996, chapters 3 and 7). Another way of looking at disability is simply to conclude that it is socially created insofar as it is a 'formal administrative category that determines the rights and privileges of a large number of people'; the category is determined by the 'distributive dilemma' in society about who is deserving of social aid and who is not; and it means, for example, that there is blindness and there is legal blindness (Stone 1984,p.27).

The arguments and literature on such issues are extensive, and taken to an extreme lose their force (eg, Oliver 1996, chapter 3; Low 1996). However, for the purposes of this book, there are at least two significant implications. First, and however one views the applicability of models of disability, it is obvious that if, as the courts have pointed out, social services committees define need (*R v Gloucestershire CC, ex p Barry*), then how they do so will affect fundamentally the identification, assessment and meeting of it. Second, different views about the nature of disability can lead to criticisms of professionals such as occupational therapists (working in the NHS or in local authorities), who sometimes stand accused of furthering their own professional ends rather than empowering disabled people (Abberley 1995). It would seem essential that if community care is to work to maximum effect within limited resources, that professionals and disability organisations should work together to learn from another and optimise provision. For example, some professionals should consider providing advice and services in a less prescriptive or patronising manner (French 1994); equally, it is arguable that professional eyes are more likely to be opened and practices changed through carefully considered persuasion than by overt antagonism.

Indeed, it has been pointed out that disabled people might have considerable difficulty achieving independence and control over their lives – for instance, if they feel 'isolated and on the edge of society' because of a) prejudiced attitudes caused by lack of understanding and knowledge; b) difficulty in obtaining equipment and home adaptations to move around in and outside their homes, and to use public transport; c) inadequate support in the community made worse by support from statutory services which is based frequently on the assumptions of service providers rather than on disabled people's needs; d) lack of control over how services are delivered leading to reduced autonomy; e) discrimination in health, social and leisure services; f) severely restricted employment opportunities; g) insufficient money to meet basic need; h) poor quality of life (Lamb, Layzell 1994, p.2).

Determining need: preventative services

In practice, the blunt approach of concentrating only on apparent physical risk – thus, for instance, prioritising personal care or shopping over housework – might substantially fail to identify individual needs. Such policies, entailing short term economies, are likely to prove costly to society in the longer term (Henwood 1998b,p.8) – ie, they are to the detriment of the individuals affected, local authorities, the NHS and the taxpayer (Secretary of State for Health 1998,p.14). Unsupported, people whose needs are deemed initially to be low priority can very quickly fall into those categories of people at risk – when they will be a much greater drain on the resources of local authorities (see eg, Age Concern Cheshire 1996,p.4).

This has contributed to the apparent decline of so-called preventative services, for example, where local authorities withdraw general home help services in favour of personal care, allow them to lapse into unreliability or charge for them (and thereby drive some users away). Excluded might be services, greatly appreciated by recipients, such as cleaning, ironing, washing, turning out cupboards, taking down curtains for cleaning, changing light bulbs (Collyer 1992), decorating – and home, garden and yard maintenance (Pearson, Richardson 1994,p.4). People might simply value talking as social contact, something staff might do even if it is not officially sanctioned (Neill, Williams 1992,p.103). Home help services might be withdrawn altogether, at least for people who do not have other physical or functional needs – although patterns of available services will vary from authority to authority (SSI 1996d, appendix C). Such withdrawal was occurring even before the implementation of community care in April 1993 (Alfred Morris: HCD,12/12/1991,col.1013), since when the situation has worsened.

Shortcomings are not hard to find. For instance, a policy which excludes housework in favour of shopping might not cater for the need of an amputee, with double incontinence and diabetes, for cleaning assistance in order to maintain hygiene and constitute maladministration in the view of the local ombudsman (*Westminster CC 1996*). Indeed, a clean house might anyway be highly significant for older women a) in maintaining their esteem and perception of being able to remain at home rather than seek institutional care, and b) in minimising the taking of risks, when carrying out such work themselves, which can result in accidents and falls (Clark, Dyer and Horwood 1998,p.25). For some people, living in dirt cannot be conducive to psychological and so, eventually, to physical well-being; nor the shame about an unkept garden which leads to loss of self-esteem (Beattie 1995,pp.6–8).

Nevertheless, in practice, the move toward personal care services at the expense of lower priority home help services is not without difficulty for local authorities. The problem of changing the strategy and resourcing of domiciliary services was recognised long ago because of the perceived difficulty of withdrawing services from long-established users (SSI 1988b,p.18). More recently, another report found local authorities still allocating very limited financial resources to large numbers of people, and thus spending only a limited amount of money on people with substantial needs (ACC,AMA 1995,p.31). One of the dilemmas facing local authorities is whether or not to reduce or withdraw services from existing users, in order to reflect a change in policy and thus a) to divert more resources to those with higher needs, and b) to make provision more equitable between existing users with low level needs and new applicants (already affected and excluded by the new policy). Legally at least, the case of *R v Gloucestershire CC, ex p Barry*, confirms that local authorities can, subject to certain provisos, withdraw or reduce services from existing users of services (see p.158).

Determining need: individual

The courts have emphasised that assessment and reassessment of need under s.47 of the NHS and Community Care Act 1990 must be based on the needs of individuals – just as the legislation states and guidance confirms at some length (see extracts above). Blanket decisions will not do – a point emphasised by the readiness of the courts to intervene if local authorities apply rigid policies and thereby fetter their discretion (p.49) or simply fail to assess on an individual basis, as spelt out in *R v Gloucestershire CC, ex p Mahfood* and *R v Gloucestershire CC, ex p RADAR*.

In *R v Avon CC, ex p M*, the judge referred to Circular guidance (LAC(92)15) which stated that services for people with learning disabilities 'should be planned on an individual basis'. In practice, this might mean that local authorities have to maximise, for instance, the use of recreation and leisure at day centres in order to enable people with learning disabilities to achieve personal development (SSI 1995j,p.2). And, if the long-term needs and aspirations of people with learning disabilities are not examined, care packages will be correspondingly limited in nature (Singh 1995,p.ii).

The identification of individual needs will also be hampered if the general assessment forms used by practitioners are not suitable for particular groups of people – such as those who are hard of hearing – but alternatives have not been developed (SSI 1997a,p.15). It has also been pointed out by the Audit Commission (1997a,p.34) that the fact that home care is provided so often in a standard form (eg, 40% of users receiving less than two hours a week, and 31% receiving one hour) might be suggestive that individual needs are not in fact driving provision.

4. ELIGIBILITY CRITERIA AND DECIDING ABOUT SERVICES

The NHS and Community Care Act 1990, s.47, lays down a two-stage process consisting of assessment for services and then a decision about what services will be provided by the local authority. It does not state how such a decision should be reached, but both practice and Circular guidance explain that priorities and criteria of eligibility should be applied. Local authorities have a discretion to set their own criteria for services, and the House of Lords in *R v Gloucestershire, ex p Barry* has confirmed that resources may be taken into account.

Eligibility criteria at this stage form one more hurdle which people have to get over in order to receive services, and which authorities can use to regulate provision in line with resources. Criteria are therefore a powerful tool; at the same time they form a potential trap for unwary authorities, and the lawfulness of their application might be susceptible to challenge on grounds of, for example, unreasonableness, rigidity, illegality or even inconsistency. There are also sometimes ways of manipulating the presentation of people's needs, so that they 'fit' particular criteria.

The formulation and application of eligibility criteria has been an uncertain art to say the least. Government has admitted in a White Paper that they are sometimes so 'broad or poorly framed that they help neither user nor staff'; that they vary between local authority areas; and that even within one area, there are 'different people getting different services according to what day it is and who they speak to' (Secretary of State for Health 1998,p.7).

EXTRACTS

Legislation: (NHS and Community Care Act 1990,s.47(1)(b)) states that the local authority,

> 'having regard to the results of that assessment, [it] shall then decide whether his needs call for the provision by them of any such services'.

Practice guidance: (SSI,SWSG 1991b,p.64) states that local authorities will probably wish to base the response to assessment on priority groups, such as those

> 'users with complex needs or those requiring significant levels of resources … Whatever groups are targeted, the criteria for selecting them should be understood by all staff, the other care agencies and by the public at large'.

Circular guidance: (CI(92)34 now cancelled) stated:

> **(discretion):** 'Authorities will still have considerable discretion, both with regard to their eligibility criteria for these services, and in respect of how assessed needs should best be met' (para 4).

> **(flexibility and relation to assessment)**: 'Authorities can be helped in this process by defining eligibility criteria ie a system of banding which assigns individuals to particular categories, depending on the extent of the difficulties they encounter in carrying out every day tasks and relating the level of response to the degree of such difficulties. Any "banding" should not, however, be rigidly applied, as account needs to be taken of individual circumstances. Such eligibility criteria should be phrased in terms of the factors identified in the assessment process' (para 14).

DISCUSSION

Eligibility criteria: management of resources

Eligibility criteria are envisaged by guidance as a tool for deciding whether a person is in sufficient need to qualify for services from the local authority. The idea behind such criteria seems to be that they will enable authorities to target their resources on those most in need without exceeding their budgets.

However, there are a number of difficulties involved in achieving even these limited aims. Formulation of criteria reflecting the levels of local needs depends on prior possession of adequate information about the needs of the local population; yet authorities might not possess this (see p.100). Without such information, criteria are unlikely to reflect local needs or to prevent assessed needs from outstripping the resources available. In other words, the criteria might let too many people through the gateway of assessment and put authorities in danger of attempting to provide more services than they can afford – anathema to the Audit Commission's view of what should be happening (1993,pp.4–5). If this occurs, there is in turn a risk that authorities might attempt to make hasty and ill-thought-out decisions in relation both to the setting of new eligibility criteria and to decisions in individual cases. This will increase their vulnerability to adverse findings by the law courts and local ombudsmen.

There is also doubt about the extent to which the application of eligibility criteria can aspire to an exact and simple 'science'; there is a contrary view that both professional and user input precludes the use of strict criteria, which can be interpreted variably even when highly specific (Kenny, Edwards and Stanton 1994,pp.11–12). Similarly, it might be an illusion to suppose that ticking boxes and simple arithmetic will allow 'an accommodation with individuals which best fits their aspirations and the resources that can be made available' (Middleton 1997,p.47).

Eligibility criteria: rationing

For obvious reasons, rationing is not a word used freely by local authorities. Nevertheless, eligibility criteria are in effect a rationing tool. An Audit Commission (1992,p.26) report referred to 'tough decisions on priorities and eligibility criteria' with local authority Members and senior managers having to 'take the decisions about rationing'. Candidly, a local community care plan might point out that whilst eligibility criteria are sometimes criticised as 'a backdoor route to rationing', rationing has, to an extent, 'always existed' (Kent County Council SSD 1993,para 1.4).

Eligibility criteria: how far can authorities legally go?

From the outset of community care, local authorities appeared to have ample discretion to set local eligibility criteria. Jack Ashley MP put it bluntly and with foresight during the passing of the 1990 Act in Parliament: 'this Bill will do nothing to avert future tragedies in community care or to raise the present inadequate levels of care. The provisions of the Bill give local authorities the right to assess on whatever criteria they choose – it is a charter for evasion' (HCD,7/12/1989,col.542).

The Department of Health had explained: 'The setting of eligibility criteria is a matter for each local authority in the light of local circumstances including the availability of resources. As in all things, authorities must act reasonably, and the setting of eligibility criteria cannot exempt them from meeting their statutory duties or exercising their discretion properly' (written evidence to the House of Commons Health Committee 1993,vol.2,p.44). Some of the guidance issued by the Department of Health refers optimistically to multi-faceted need, choice and participation, but also declares the necessity of establishing eligibility in terms of risk, self-care tasks, the needs of carers and 'other elements deemed necessary to a minimum quality of life, for example, social contact'

(SSI/SWSG 1991a,p.53). Risk and minimum quality of life do not immediately appear to equate with what is meant by independent living and choice.

The courts and local ombudsmen have since confirmed that authorities are free to set their own criteria of eligibility, subject to certain safeguards against excess. For instance, authorities should be conducting balancing exercises and weighing up resources against people's needs (*R v Gloucestershire CC, ex p Barry; R v Gloucestershire CC, ex p Mahfood; R v Essex CC, ex p Bucke; R v Islington LBC, ex p McMillan*). There are other safeguards; criteria should not be illegal by contradicting legislation (*R v Ealing LBC, ex p Leaman*), nor should they fetter an authority's discretion (*R v North Yorkshire, ex p Hargreaves (no.2)*; whilst the ombudsman found that a two-hour-per-week maximum to home help services might inhibit the 'proper assessment of each individual's needs' (*Tower Hamlets LBC 1994*). The House of Lords stated in *R v Gloucestershire CC, ex p Barry* that criteria should not result in legally unreasonable decisions (but see subsequent comments about this in *R v East Sussex CC, ex p Tandy*). Criteria should not be based on irrelevant factors – as occurred when one local authority decided to provide telephone equipment ('minicoms') only to deaf people who already had a telephone installed in their home. The ombudsman agreed with the complaining voluntary organisation that the prior existence of a telephone was irrelevant to the need for a minicom (*Wakefield MDC 1992*).

Nevertheless, all these safeguards might be of limited use in practice, because local authorities either deftly set strict but lawful criteria or simply pay little attention to the law. For instance, the courts might set a high threshold of unreasonableness, one of the supposed safeguards. In *R v Haringey LBC, ex p Norton*, the judge refused to intervene when a care package was reduced from 24 hours to five hours a day because he could not conclude that the authority had 'taken leave of its senses' (one of the tests for legal unreasonableness). In *R v DHSS, ex p Bruce* also, the court set out the daunting hurdles to be overcome in demonstrating unreasonableness. The statement by the court in *R v Gloucestershire CC, ex p Mahfood* that it would be legally unreasonable not to assist a disabled person at severe physical risk, should be weighed against the difficulties identified in *R v East Sussex CC, ex p Tandy* about deeming decisions to be unreasonable. The House of Lords in the *Tandy* case in turn supported its view by referring back to *R v Cambridge HA, ex p B*, in which the Court of Appeal had refused to interfere with a decision about lifesaving treatment in the NHS context. All this said, the threshold of unreasonableness is sometimes lowered; for instance, in *R v Staffordshire, ex p Farley*, it was suggested by the judge at an interim hearing that the removal of night sitter services from an elderly woman might well seem to be unreasonable because there was apparently no evidence on which the decision was based.

Eligibility criteria: national minimum standards

The Department of Health has hitherto avoided setting national standards governing criteria of eligibility, although a White Paper in late 1998 finally conceded that they should be drawn up in guidance called *Fair access to care* (Secretary of State for Health 1998,p.26).

For instance, in the past, asked about the 'acceptability of national minimum standards for care in the community', the government replied, that it 'is the responsibility of local authorities to manage the implementation of community care. We will continue to monitor progress closely and offer guidance and direction as is considered necessary' (HCWA,8/2/1994,col.188). Furthermore: 'It is most unlikely that the Secretary of State would wish to intervene in the setting of eligibility criteria. However, she does have powers generally and in cases of default, and she will therefore consider on their merits any cases in which it appears that an authority has manifestly failed to exercise its statutory functions without reasonable excuse' (statement to: House of Commons Health Committee 1993,vol.2,p.44).

The consequence has been that eligibility criteria have differed between local authorities; for instance, even if, on paper, a person with a certain set of needs might in principle qualify for provision in 80 per cent of local authorities, she might in practice live in an authority where she is deemed ineligible (ACC,AMA 1995,pp.18,23).

Eligibility criteria: consistent application in practice?

The task of applying eligibility criteria is commonly reported to give local authorities problems (SSI/NHSE 1994a,p.6) in terms of integrating them both with screening and assessment tasks and with criteria developed by the NHS in respect of continuing care (Challis *et al.* 1997,p.8).

Criteria might in practice be ill-defined, unclear to service users and interpreted variably by local authority staff. Alternatively for some groups of people – for instance, people with learning disabilities – there might simply be no eligibility criteria (SSI 1998d,p.33).

The danger alluded to by the Audit Commission (1993,p.4) is that if 'criteria are too vague they will produce arbitrary and variable results which will reduce equity and may not control expenditure if they are too tight they will limit creativity'. Nevertheless, a pragmatic view is that the 'initial fuzziness' of eligibility criteria could help rather than hinder authorities to achieve strategic policies which target people most in need (Jeffrey 1994). However, vagueness about how to apply criteria can lead to confusion when, for instance, they are developed to establish eligibility for services following assessment, but are instead used to determine allocation for assessment (Baldwin 1995a,p.23). Such practices are likely to be deemed by the local ombudsman as maladministration (eg, *Liverpool CC 1996/1997*) and could in some circumstances be deemed unlawful.

Anticipating just such muddles, an SSI letter to London Directors of Social Services pointed out that if assessment outcomes do not relate to published eligibility criteria, then local authorities could face charges of maladministration (see: House of Commons Health Committee 1993,vol.2,p.45). For instance, there might be a 'lack of a clear relationship between eligibility criteria and information collected in the assessment pro formas. In which case there would be little or no means of monitoring how, if at all, these criteria were being applied and with what degree of consistency' (SSI/NHSME 1994b, p.9). Adverse assessment decisions might be made on the basis of informal, orally communicated policies and eligibility criteria – which might not be available in documentary form. The consequence in such circumstances is that there is no 'formal means whereby clients, the public, new staff and elected members could be properly informed' (Keep, Clarkson 1994,p.33) and the ombudsman might identify maladministration (eg, *Lewisham LBC 1993*).

The potential problem is not new. A 1982 RADAR report about s.2 of the Chronically Sick and Disabled Persons Act 1970 gave an example of how one local authority, surveying its own home help service, found large disparities between different divisions within the authority. People in one division might receive up to twice the amount of services as people with the same level of disability in another (Cook, Mitchell 1982,p.22). It might be a simple case of policy and principle not being reflected in practice, when some clients who on paper meet eligibility criteria are in reality denied a service on grounds of non-eligibility (ACC,AMA 1995,p.19).

The courts have accepted that local authorities are legally able to change their policies and criteria of eligibility from time to time: see, for example, the *R v Gloucestershire CC, ex p Barry* and *R v North Yorkshire CC, ex p Hargreaves (no.2)* cases. But how often can they be changed? Community care plans are published annually and it is perhaps on this basis that it has been contended that eligibility criteria should not be altered in mid-year. However, one director of social services has pointed out that, whilst it is easy for ministers to say this: 'it seems only realistic to work out how many complex care packages and/or placements we can afford to buy, and then set up budget controls for this on a monthly or quarterly basis throughout the year ... In that way, practitioners will become involved in deciding who gets what, and when, if demand outstrips supply' (Jeffrey 1994).

Varying eligibility between areas of the same local authority might be maladministration for the local ombudsman (eg, *Hackney LBC 1992a; Newham LBC 1997b*) or even unfair or irrational in the eyes of the courts (*R v Tower Hamlets, ex p Ali*, a housing case). Similarly, the ombudsman found that the policy of imposing limits on the costs of home care packages for older people was discriminatory and unfair, when compared with the absence of such limits for people with mental health problems or with learning disabilities (*Liverpool CC 1998b*).

Eligibility criteria: rigidity

If criteria need to be consistent, nevertheless Circular guidance (extract above) states that the consequent 'banding' of priorities 'should not be rigidly applied' because individual circumstances must be taken account of. This is connected to the legal principle that authorities should not 'fetter their discretion' (see p.49) and is confusing to the extent that it appears to contradict the notion of consistency – there being a fine and sometimes imperceptible line between individual consideration and inconsistency (*R v Ministry of Agriculture, ex p Hamble*).

Nevertheless, despite the readiness of the law courts and the local ombudsman to intervene, authorities remain prone to snatching at blanket policies. This may be in the form of 'policy decisions to remove some sorts of service from the catalogue of need – the most notable being cleaning in the home' (House of Commons Health Committee 1993,vol.2,p.161). The Royal Association for Disability and Rehabilitation (RADAR) (Keep, Clarkson 1993,p.19) reported the withdrawal at a stroke by one local authority of telephone rental payments to 273 disabled people. Two particular complaints were made that this had been done without reassessment and where need for the service had not diminished. RADAR and the British Polio Fellowship challenged the legality of the decision, and the director of social services agreed to reassess all the people concerned and reinstate the service where necessary. RADAR reported that the service for all 273 people was reinstated. This incident anticipated some of the issues in *R v Gloucestershire CC, ex p Mahfood* concerning individual reassessment of users of services – in the face of the local authority's attempt at blanket removal or reduction of services to some 1,500 people.

If central government sometimes recognises the importance of the genuine exercise of discretion in individual cases, it sometimes mimics local authorities in forgetfulness. For instance, a Parliamentary ombudsman investigation noted (in passing) DHSS legal advice on this issue. A local authority had, because of financial pressures, withdrawn financial assistance for holidays for disabled people. The DHSS letter to the local authority stated that the s.2 duty 'placed an obligation on the local authority to assess the needs of all relevant persons for the service in question and sought an assurance that the Council were continuing to assess the needs of each individual and to take appropriate action where need was accepted' (PCA C.799/81). Conversely, over a decade later, it was pointed out that government ministers could blithely state in the House of Commons, 'without any suggestion of criticism, that some local authorities had now withdrawn cleaning-only home help services altogether. If so, then *ipso facto* such services are no longer available to any disabled person in their areas, irrespective of need and the requirements of the law' (Alfred Morris: HCD,12/12/1991,col.1013, and see Keep, Clarkson 1994,p.8).

Even so, legal considerations apart, common sense suggests that community care should not be operated on the basis of rigid policies, given the importance and variability of individual people's needs and circumstances. As one local community care plan realistically puts it: the 'use of eligibility criteria is not an exact science, so care managers and social workers must have some flexibility about how the criteria are interpreted and applied' (Kent County Council 1993,para 1.4). Indeed, one way of avoiding over-rigidity and fettering of discretion would be, for example, for assessors to ignore priority ratings and criteria which are clearly unsuitable for certain groups of people. For example, the priorities and criteria might be 'overly rigid, focusing on immediate or urgent needs rather than ongoing and changing needs' – and so be perceived to be inappropriate for people with learning disabilities (SSI/NHSE 1994f,p.25).

Eligibility criteria: financial ceilings

The imposition of financial ceilings on services for certain groups – such as older people – calls into question a) whether local authorities are genuinely taking account of the needs of individuals, and b) are in danger of applying unlawful, rigid policies. Authorities might attempt to save themselves from the latter by having special (appeal) procedures to consider exceptions, although this in turn takes the time and energy of care managers to argue the case (SSI 1997j,p.19).

For example, limits – equivalent to the net cost of a care home placement – might be placed on non-residential care packages for older people. The gross cost of a care home placement, per week might be up to £250 or £350 per week respectively. However, the net cost to a local authority will be considerably less – given that people will be contributing their pension and income support with residential allowance to the fees – perhaps as low as £100 a week in the case of an average residential home. This could in turn mean, in some authorities, a ceiling on non-residential services of £100 a week; furthermore in individual cases, where a person has capital of over £16,000, the cost to the local authority of residential care is nil, as it is if a person uses the benefits loophole (instead of support from the local authority) to fund the care (see p.294). All this, as has been frequently pointed out, creates a perverse incentive for authorities to arrange (or persuade people to make their own arrangements for) residential care rather than non-residential services (Harding 1997,p.25; RADAR 1997,p.7). This is particularly ironic given the longstanding recognition that some people have in the past been assessed – in terms of their actual needs – inappropriately as needing residential care (eg, SSI 1988c,p.1).

Limits on funding for older people can be compared to some supported living packages for people in other categories, such as younger severely disabled people, costing a minimum of £50,000 to £60,000 a year (SSI 1997k,p.36), or for people with learning disabilities or mental health problems on which ceilings might not be formally imposed (as illustrated in an ombudsman investigation: *Liverpool CC 1998b*). However, even for younger disabled people, such packages might in some areas be the exception rather than the rule (SSI 1996e,p.14), although such exceptions might still be more easily achieved than in the case of older people because of more loosely defined limits (Pettit 1997,p.1). The consequence of such ceilings is that existing service users might be afraid to acknowledge increasing needs for services, in case they are forced into residential care (SSI 1996e,p.14).

Local authorities might justify a ceiling on expenditure for home care packages by arguing a) that it is the consequence of a balancing exercise *(R v Gloucestershire CC, ex p Barry)*, and b) that most people's needs can equally be met in residential or nursing homes and that the courts have accepted that authorities can choose the cheaper of two options for meeting a need (*R v Lancashire CC, ex p RADAR*). However, they should still beware that the ceiling does not a) fetter their discretion by excluding the consideration of exceptions; or b) inhibit proper assessments and decisions about services called for by legislation (NHS and Community Care Act 1990,s.47). For instance, the local ombudsman has found maladministration where home care managers were imposing a limit of two hours of housework per week (*Tower Hamlets LBC 1994*), or where a weekly ceiling of £110 was imposed on home care packages for older people (*Liverpool CC 1998b*). On the other hand, when a local authority appeared to be limiting the care package for a 43-year-old man with multiple sclerosis to £240 per week, the court rejected the contention that this was perverse or irrational – although this decision was made in the light of further developments by the time the case was heard in court, namely an increase in the package to 45 hours per week at a cost of £280 (*R v Haringey LBC, ex p Norton (no.2)*).

Eligibility criteria: age-related policies

As already mentioned immediately above, local authorities might operate unequal financial ceilings and eligibility criteria between different groups of service users – even under the same piece of legislation. The nature of organisational structure and budget allocation is likely to encourage this process and result in more expensive care packages for younger adults than for older people (see eg, Age Concern England 1998a; Fitzgerald 1998,p.46).

Clearly, such practices are discriminatory and might be difficult to justify in common sense; for instance, why are the needs of a 64-year-old person with advanced Alzheimer's Disease any greater than those of a 66-year-old (65 being the usual watershed between services for younger disabled people and older people) (Harding 1997,p.24)? Since both would be categorised as disabled people under s.2 of the Chronically Sick and Disabled Persons Act 1970, the only logical justification would be that age can affect need by diminishing it (hence the justification of lesser provision). This of course is a nonsense, and leaves open only the explanation that age discrimination is involved.

However, whether a court would intervene, other than on grounds of a fettering of discretion (ie, if the policy were applied rigidly so as to exclude exceptions) is another matter. Perhaps it could be argued that age is a legally irrelevant factor; the Chronically Sick and Disabled Persons Act 1970 says nothing about preference being given to younger people. Moreover, the Secretary of State's approvals made in 1971, under the Health and Services and Public Health Act 1968, apply to older people who are not disabled and so are not covered by the 1970 Act – thus pointing back to the Chronically Sick and Disabled Persons Act 1970 for older, disabled people. Thus, it could be contended that if Parliament had wanted older, disabled people to have a second class service under the 1970 Act, it would have said so. As a Social Services Inspectorate report states, arbitrary division based upon chronological age 'is unlikely to be a helpful way of identifying individual need' – yet this is precisely what community care assessment under s.47 of the NHS and Community Care Act 1990 is meant to be about (SSI 1997m,p.19). Certainly, if it could be shown that a decision in relation to services for an older person was based substantially on the mistaken assumption (apparently held by some local authority staff) that s.2 of the 1970 Act applies *as a matter of law* only to people under the age of 65 years, then a court might well strike down the decision. In any event, such age discrimination is likely to constitute maladministration in the eyes of the local ombudsman (*Liverpool CC 1998b*)

Eligibility criteria: fitness for purpose

If eligibility criteria – at whatever stage they are used – are not designed and operated appropriately, they will in practice be unfit for their purpose and fail the people whose needs they are designed to categorise.

For instance, if social services, housing and the NHS do not collaborate over their criteria, then vulnerable people with low level but multiple needs might fall through the net. This is because each agency assesses them as low priority, not realising that, combined, these needs are not inconsiderable (DH 1994d,p.24). Guidance from the Department of Health warns that continuing care criteria must be agreed between the NHS and social services, so that people with HIV/AIDS have access to services (LAC(98)9,annex A,para 7). Local authorities 'should ensure that any criteria they may develop governing eligibility for assessment are sensitive to the circumstances of alcohol and drug misusers' (LAC(93)2,para 14). And the local ombudsman has found maladministration when a local authority's criteria were too simplistic and caused a disabled child to wait too long, given his level of need, for replacement equipment (*Rochdale MBC 1995*).

5. RESOURCES AND ASSESSMENT

Local authorities have to operate within limited resources and this inevitably affects provision of services. It is their unceasing search for a lawful formula for restricting expenditure which has led to the majority of community care cases in the law courts. These have established that to a significant extent, authorities can take account of resources when assessing people's needs and deciding about services. Broadly, the law as it stands at present appears to be as follows.

(1) Access to assessment: resources are irrelevant. As already explained (p.72), local authorities
    cannot take account of resources when deciding whether people appear to be in need of
    community care services – and thus whether they are entitled to an assessment.

(2) Assessing need: resources are relevant. When determining – through the application of criteria of eligibility – what constitutes assessed need, resources may be taken account of. It is also lawful to identify needs which will not be met (ie, 'unmet needs').

(3) Are services called for or necessary: resources are relevant. When deciding whether community care services are called for or are necessary, resources may also be taken into account.

(4) Meeting needs called for or necessary: resources are sometimes irrelevant. Fourth, once it is decided that a person is eligible for some (but apparently not all) community care services, then the local authority must provide them, irrespective of resources.

(5) Deciding on the type and level of services: resources are relevant. When deciding what type and level of services to provide, local authorities can take account of resources, so long as the option chosen meets the assessed need.

EXTRACTS

Legislation: The NHS and Community Care Act 1990, s.47(1) is silent about whether local authorities must provide services, once it has decided whether they are called for. All community care legislation is silent about the extent, if any, to which resources may be taken account of when local authorities determine people's needs and decide what services to provide.

Policy guidance: (DH 1990,paras 3.25,3.30) states:

> 'local authorities also have a responsibility to meet needs within the resources available and this will sometimes involve difficult decisions where it will be necessary to strike a balance between meeting the needs identified within available resources and meeting the care preferences of the individual … Once an individual's need for welfare services, specified in Section 2 of the Chronically Sick and Disabled Persons Act 1970, has been established, the authority must make the necessary arrangements to meet it'.

Practice guidance: states (SSI,SWSG 1991a,p.61):

> 'Wherever possible, the practitioner responsible for assessing needs should carry on to relate those needs to the available resources. This will help to ensure that assessment does not become a theoretical exercise but is firmly rooted in practical reality'.

Circular guidance: (CI(92)34 para 13 now cancelled) stated:

> 'An authority may take into account the resources available when deciding how to respond to an individual's assessment', but 'once the authority has indicated that a service should be provided to meet an individual's needs and the authority is under a legal obligation to provide it or arrange for its provision then the service must be provided. It will not be possible for an authority to use budgeting difficulties as a basis for refusing to provide the service'.

DISCUSSION

The driving force behind the community care reforms embodied in the NHS and Community Care Act 1990 was resources, as identified in the Griffiths (1988) report: namely an open-ended social security budget paying for residential and nursing home care. Therefore, a shifting of responsibility to local authorities was clearly not going to solve the lack of resources. As Baroness Seear put it when the NHS and Community Care Bill was progressing: 'Unless very adequate services of good quality are provided, we are heading for a disaster. I use that word deliberately. I can foresee a situation in which there are not adequate resources to back up those who are put back into society, the community' (HLD,3/4/1990,col.1374).

The tension between people's needs and resources was explored fundamentally in *R v Gloucestershire CC, ex p Barry*, in which the decision of the House of Lords is perceived to have undermined the working of s.2 of the Chronically Sick and Disabled Persons Act 1970. Nevertheless, the real problem, as one of the dissenting judges (Lord Lloyd) in the case put it, was that local authorities were in a 'truly impossible position' because of limited funds from central government and a legal inability to raise more local taxation. (Such a state of affairs leads, for instance, to a local authority's large expenditure on adaptations to help disabled people being a cause of both pride and concern: SSI/NHSME 1994e,p.21).

Resources and assessment: access to assessment

As explained in the previous chapter (p.72), local authorities cannot take account of resources when deciding whether people appear that they may be in need of community care services – and thus whether they are entitled to an assessment (*R v Bristol CC, ex p Penfold*).

Resources and assessment: deciding about need

The House of Lords in *R v Gloucestershire CC, ex p Barry* case said that resources were a surer yardstick against which to measure need under s.2 of the Chronically Sick and Disabled Persons Act 1970, than the 'values of a civilised society' – and could thus be taken into account along with various other factors. In addition, the Court of Appeal in *R v Sefton, ex p Help the Aged* grudgingly accepted, in the light of the *Gloucestershire* case, that there might be some limited scope for resources to affect the determination of whether a person is in need of care and attention (in residential accommodation) under s.21 of the National Assistance Act 1948. It would seem to follow that resources can be a factor in determining need under all community care legislation; although given the strength of the duty and sensitivity surrounding it, the courts might be reluctant to let local authorities play fast and loose with s.117 of the Mental Health Act 1983 (provision of after-care services: see p.218).

Resources and assessment: are services called for or necessary?

The House of Lords in the *Gloucestershire* case said that under s.2 of the Chronically Sick and Disabled Persons Act 1970, a local authority might have to match severity of need with the availability of resources; this meant that resources could be taken account of in deciding whether it was necessary for the authority to make arrangements to meet identified need (although see p.202 for more detail). (This can be contrasted with the field of special education; in *R v Secretary of State for Education, ex p E*, the local authority had to identify in a statement of special educational needs, all the educational needs of a child, list all the provision necessary to meet each and every one of those educational needs and then arrange that provision).

Of course if provision is made through alternative arrangements (eg, by another statutory body, a voluntary organisation, people themselves or by relatives), then clearly it will not be necessary for the local authority to make arrangements. In addition, however, the House of Lords in the *Gloucestershire* case also stated that local authorities could identify unmet needs (ie, needs which would simply not be met), even under s.2 of the Chronically Sick and Disabled Persons Act 1970, something previously not thought legally permissible (see eg, Department of Health guidance, extract above).

Decisions under s.21 of the National Assistance Act 1948 would appear to operate similarly, when a local authority has to decide a) whether a person is in need of care and attention which is b) not otherwise available to him or her. For instance, if a person has more than £16,000 and is capable physically and mentally of making their own arrangements, then the local authority might conclude that care and attention is otherwise available, and it then has no duty to make arrangements (see p.255).

Under s.117 of the Mental Health Act 1983, the local authority must provide after-care services for people to whom the section applies until it is satisfied that he or she no longer needs them. There is no intermediate stage of having to decide about necessity. However, under s.29 of the National Assistance Act 1948 (welfare services) 'there is no doubt that in the exercise of its powers', it is 'proper for a local authority to take into account the extent' of its available resources (*R v Gloucestershire CC, ex p Barry*). The same presumably goes for schedule 8 of the NHS Act 1977 (services for illness, home help, laundry, etc) and s.45 of the Health Services and Public Health Act 1968 (services for older people).

The courts have been forced to eke out from the legislation distinctions neither envisaged nor explained by the Department of Health. For instance, its guidance does not dwell on this separate stage of decision-making about the necessity of making arrangements. Similarly, various statements made in Parliament during the passage of the NHS and Community Care Bill omitted the distinction between need and necessity. For instance, Baroness Hooper, resisting an amendment to the Bill in the House of Lords, stated that apart from needs for day and domiciliary care local authorities would not 'be under a specific duty to meet all conceivable needs for community care across the board'. She explained that 'the aim of assessment should be to arrive at a decision on whether services should be provided by the local authority and in what form. Decisions must take account of what is available and affordable ... Where high priority needs are identified which cannot be met within the resources available, information flowing from the assessment process will need to feed back into the local authority's planning process so that a view can be taken about whether new provision is necessary'. It would not, she went on, be realistic to expand the type of specific duty, which local authorities had under s.2 of the Chronically Sick and Disabled Persons Act 1970, to all community care needs and services in general (HLD,10/5/1990, cols.1563–1564). This was reiterated: 'local authorities have a duty to provide for the domiciliary and day care needs of the disabled. They are a special case ... Local authorities will be expected to provide the services for which assessment calls' (Virginia Bottomley: Standing Committee E,15/2/1990, cols.1002–1026).

Resources and assessment: duty to provide services which are necessary or called for

Once eligibility for services has been established, then local authorities have a duty to make provision irrespective of the availability of resources – at least for services under s.2 of the Chronically Sick and Disabled Persons Act 1970 (*Gloucestershire case*), for residential accommodation under the National Assistance Act 1948 (*R v Sefton MBC, ex p Help the Aged*) and presumably for services under the Mental Health Act 1983, s.117 (despite the judge's comment about resources in *R v Ealing DHA, ex p Fox*).

For instance, where an authority had assessed the need for a stair lift under s.2 of the Chronically Sick and Disabled Persons Act 1970 but delayed ordering it for nearly two years, the ombudsman stated that 'insufficient financial resources is no justification for delay' (*Camden LBC 1993*). In practice, the existence of care plans and their possession by service users (see p.152), as well as detailed schedules relating to service delivery times, will clearly be of use in enforcing provision under this principle – as evidence of what has been agreed (Coombs 1998,p.28).

However, the comment made by the House of Lords in *R v Gloucestershire CC, ex p Barry* about the special nature of the 'express duty of performance' in s.2 of the Chronically Sick and Disabled Persons Act 1970, and the ruling in the *Sefton* case, both suggest that aside from these sections (in the 1970 and 1948 Acts, and presumably s.117 of the 1983 Act), there is no duty under the remaining community care legislation to make arrangements for provision of services even where it has been established (eg, by the application of eligibility criteria) that a person's needs call for them. However, this would bear the unacceptable implication that authorities could make almost arbitrary decisions, without reassessment of individual people's needs, to withdraw services already being received, or not to provide for the first time services previously agreed.

If this were indeed the case under some community care legislation (s.29 of the National Assistance Act 1948, schedule 8 of the NHS Act 1977 and s.45 of the Health Services and Public Health Act 1968) – then a nonsense would be made of Department of Health guidance which emphasises, for community care services generally, the importance of agreed and signed care plans, review and reassessment (SSI,SWSG 1991a). Alternatively, if this is not the case, and restrictions on arbitrary withdrawal apply to all community care services, then s.2 of the Chronically Sick and Disabled Persons Act 1970 occupies no special position and the House of Lords reasoning in the *Gloucestershire* case appears unclear.

Lastly, even where it has been agreed to meet the assessed needs, two further questions might arise about a) whether the proposed provision will actually meet the identified need; and b) whether the agreement is clear as to what actually is going to be provided. The field of special education provides comparable illustrations, although it should be borne in mind that the special education legislative framework is both different and more detailed than that of community care. First, in *Re L*, the congruence, in a child's statement of special educational needs (the equivalent of a community care assessment and care plan), between the list of needs and the list of provisions to meet those needs was considered. The Court of Appeal stated that there would have to a substantial mismatch between the two before it would consider intervening. Second, disputes sometimes arise over whether the precise amount of speech therapy to be provided to meet the communication needs of a child should be detailed in statements of special educational needs. In one case, the court would not make a declaration that, in general, statements ought to 'specify the number and length of weekly speech therapy sessions' – but in the particular case said that the authority ought to set out clearly what it was going to provide, so that the parents had material on which to decide whether to appeal or not (*R v Cumbria CC, ex p P*). Third, in *L v Clarke and Somerset CC*, the court held that the statutory duty under s.324 of the Education Act 1996, to list needs and specify corresponding provision, generally required a high degree of specificity, so as to leave no room for doubt as to what had been decided in an individual case.

Resources and assessment: options for type and level of service

When deciding to make arrangements to meet a person's needs, local authorities can take account of resources when choosing amongst several options for service provision, so long as the one chosen does genuinely meet the assessed need. This was recognised throughout the High Court, Court of Appeal and House of Lords stages of the *Gloucestershire* case and was not in dispute – and the same principle was acknowledged by the House of Lords in the comparable education case of *R v East Sussex CC, ex p Tandy*.

The principle was also decisive of the outcome in *R v Lancashire CC, ex p RADAR*, when it was ruled lawful for the local authority to choose the cheaper option of 24-hour care for a person in a nursing home rather than 24-hour care in her own home. In fact, this approach was generally accepted in practice long before the *Gloucestershire* and *Lancashire* cases. For example, many years earlier a Parliamentary ombudsman investigation had noted, in passing, that the DHSS had received legal advice to the effect that a 'local authority could not plead lack of money as a reason for not meeting need, but that they had discretion as to the means employed to meet it' (PCA C.12/K).

Local authorities have considerable flexibility by specifying need generally (see p.115), and by leaving themselves open a range of service options and thus the possibility of both generous or minimal, service provision (Midgley, Munlo and Brown 1997,p.28). As well, it means that even if eligibility criteria for services look similar between different local authorities, the type and level of services provided and the resources expended might differ significantly (ACC,AMA 1995,p.7). In practice, defensive practices could lead to staff who 'resist making fully explicit' how costlier options can be accessed. So, whilst equipment and adaptations are assessed for in relation to safety and functional loss, decision-making might also be 'partly governed by what people would accept'. For instance, in the case of older people it might be easier to 'get away' with recommending a commode or chemical toilet, even though a more expensive stairlift is usually more appropriate (Ellis 1993,p.21).

Resources and assessment: diluting statutory duties

Generally, resources must be legally taken account of by local authorities because of the general 'fiduciary duty' they owe to local council tax payers. For example, the House of Lords ruled in the early 1980s that the Greater London Council had such a duty in relation to its transport policy (*Bromley LBC v GLC*; see also *R v Brent LBC, ex p Gunning*). But the real question – epitomised by *R v Gloucestershire CC, ex p Barry*, but present in other cases as well (eg, *R v East Sussex CC, ex p Tandy*) – is whether clear statutory duties can be vitiated because a local authority pleads lack of resources.

In *R v Gloucestershire CC, ex p Barry*, the House of Lords denied that its decision meant that a statutory duty (under s.2 of the Chronically Sick and Disabled Persons Act) to provide services for disabled people had been collapsed into a power by allowing resources to be taken into account. However, in *R v East Sussex CC, ex p Tandy*, it appeared to say the exact opposite when it stated that allowing resources to determine suitable education for a child would precisely downgrade a duty to a power. It stated that the issue was not one of insufficient resources but of a 'preference for using money for other purposes'; and the local authority could not simply fail to provide the money necessary to perform its statutory duties.

However, in order to explain away the apparent contradiction contained in the *Gloucestershire* judgment, the House of Lords chose a contentious explanation. It claimed in *Tandy* that Parliament could never have intended that all the services listed in s.2 of the Chronically Sick and Disabled Persons Act should be subject to a strict statutory duty, since they could not give rise to need 'in any stringent sense of the word' and were not 'in any ordinary sense necessities'. Echoing the dissenting judge at the Court of Appeal stage in the *Gloucestershire* case, it mentioned in this connection radios, holidays and recreational activities – and concluded that this was the reason why the House of Lords in the *Gloucestershire* case allowed resources into the picture. The reasoning would appear open to question. First, such an explanation seems to imply that Parliament was unaware of what it was doing when it passed the Chronically Sick and Disabled Persons Act 1970, and not to reflect the language of s.2 which applies the duty equally and clearly to all the services listed. Second, a reading of Hansard when the CSDP Bill was being debated would have shown the importance attributed to items such as radio. Third, the court appeared not to realise that for some disabled people and their carers radio, recreation and holidays might be essential, not just luxuries. Fourth, it is unclear that the House of Lords in the *Gloucestershire* case was limiting the relevance of resources simply to a few non-essential services in s.2; elsewhere in the judgment it appeared to embrace all of the listed services (see p.201).

Resources and assessment: balancing exercise

In the *Gloucestershire* case, the House of Lords referred to a cost-benefit analysis which local authorities must perform when weighing people's needs against the resources available; the High Court also in the same case had, referred to a balancing exercise. Despite the criticism heaped on the House of Lords for its decision in this case, such sentiments about balancing exercises are nothing new. In 1970, Circular guidance (DHSS 12/70) about the Chronically Sick and Disabled Persons Act urged that 'criteria of need' would be developed locally in the light of resources but also stated: 'Its underlying purposes are to draw attention to the problems, varying with age and incapacity, of people who are handicapped by chronic sickness and disablement; to express concern that these problems should be more widely known and studied and to urge that when priorities are settled, full weight is given to finding solutions. While recognising the effect of constraints on resources, the Government are confident that local authorities will have these purposes in mind' (para 3).

The court in *R v Essex CC, ex p Bucke* considered what a balancing exercise might look like; when thirteen users were reassessed, with seven keeping a more expensive service, and six losing it, it decided that this was evidence of a balanced approach to weighing needs against resources – even though in one sense the whole exercise was resource-driven. For instance, in *R v Haringey LBC, ex p Norton (no.2)*, despite an apparent ceiling of £240 on the care package for a disabled man, which suggested that the exercise was resource-led, the judge thought the final care package offered to be reasonable and neither perverse nor irrational.

Alternatively, some local authorities undoubtedly make impromptu decisions about eligibility for services – not on the basis of balanced decision-making – but because the budget has suddenly run out. When challenged in such circumstances, authorities might attempt to put a different gloss on rationing decisions by explaining them retrospectively in terms of need rather than the reason given at the time to users: lack of resources. For the ombudsman, a confounding of resources with need is maladministration (eg, *Salford CC 1996*, concerning denial of a telephone under s.2 of the Chronically Sick and Disabled Persons Act 1970). It was also maladministration when the views of a hospital social worker and charge nurse were not fully considered and not balanced against the authority's financial resources, when a decision was made about provision of social work support for a man with mental health problems (*Tower Hamlets LBC 1993*).

Resources and assessment: good practice

It is obvious that a lack of resources will affect services adversely, but it is important to remember that adequate resources are only a necessary, rather than a sufficient condition, for good practice and high quality services.

The best solutions are not always the most expensive, as creative problem-solving by users and professionals can demonstrate; and there is evidence that the making of cash payments by local authorities to users of services not only enables people to live more independently but can work out more cheaply for authorities than if they were providing the services directly (see p.236). Also, small changes to services, not necessarily involving extra resources overall, might make large differences to people. For instance, a mobile bath scheme might circumvent the delay and difficulty in obtaining equipment and adaptations: a nine-month wait might be reduced to two. Similarly, the quality of services provided in a day centre might suddenly improve following a change of management and proper training (Henwood 1995,p.24).

Resources and assessment: identifying lack of resources

It is not always clear what 'lack of resources' really means. For example, in an ombudsman case where lack of resources was held to be no defence for delay in providing a stairlift, the ombudsman went on to explain that the authority should have 'instituted procedures to ensure that adaptation works were prioritised on a borough-wide basis. Instead it appears that whether a need was met depended on competing demands on the local repairs budget for a particular week' (*Camden LBC 1993*). In other words, the local repairs budget might have been short of money – but the whole borough was not. Similarly, in *R v Cornwall CC, ex p Goldsack*, the question arose, though was not pursued, over whether the lack of resources was at the level of the day centre involved or the county council as a whole.

More recent judicial comments in both the Court of Appeal and the House of Lords in *R v East Sussex CC, ex p Tandy*, make it clear that in order to fulfil statutory duties, local authorities must look across their range of functions and budgets and if necessary take money previously allocated to functions based on discretionary powers. For instance, they might locate extra money for education by cancelling a proposed leisure centre or football ground.

This statement in the *Tandy* case was made precisely in recognition of one of the effects of the House of Lords judgment in *R v Gloucestershire CC, ex p Barry*, which had made it easier for funds to flow away from, instead of towards, the statutory duty under s.2 of the Chronically Sick and Disabled Persons Act 1970. In Parliament, the *Gloucestershire* judgment was referred to as having made a hotch-potch and a witches' brew out of needs and resources; it would now be easier for local authorities to switch funds away from provision for disabled people to, for example, environmental conservation, since 'much more excitement is created by the threat to fell a beautiful tree than by the announcement of a cut in the supply of incontinence pads. As a paraplegic of thirty years' experience, I know that you cannot become more continent simply because the local authority is strapped for cash' (Baroness Darcy: HLD,9/7/1997,col.706).

Resources and assessment: taking account of the user's resources

The temptation for a local authority is to argue, for example, that if people have adequate resources – financial, physical and mental – then it is clearly not necessary for the authority to arrange services, because people can then make their own arrangements (albeit with advice from the local authority). In respect of residential accommodation, this argument was used by the High Court in *R v Sefton MBC, ex p Help the Aged*. Despite the Court of Appeal's overall reversal of the High Court judgment and the passing of the Community Care (Residential Accommodation) Act 1998, this argument was sound in principle and has survived, though only when a person's capital resources are over £16,000, in Department of Health guidance (LAC(98)19,para 10).

In similar vein, one of the minority judges in *R v Gloucestershire CC, ex p Barry* stated that if people could afford to buy their own non-residential services, it would not be necessary for the local authority to make arrangements under s.2 of the Chronically Sick and Disabled Persons Act 1970. The local ombudsman has also accepted that an individual's means might be relevant when the local authority decides whether to make arrangements for adaptations under s.2 of the 1970 Act (*Sheffield CC 1995*). And, when local authorities consider how to respond to a continuing duty to assist with home adaptations also under the 1970 Act, they sometimes base assistance on a hardship test (ie, a test of the applicant's resources) – a practice sanctioned by guidance (DoE 17/96,p.47). Likewise in another investigation, the ombudsman did 'not doubt, that in the prudent management of a limited budget the Council would wish to assess the claimants' resources' (*Hertfordshire CC 1992*).

6. NEEDS AND PREFERENCES

Local authorities have a duty under the NHS and Community Care Act 1990 to assess people's needs for services and then decide what services to provide. However policy guidance also states that they must take account of the preferences of users. This can lead to difficulty for practitioners, since there is a significant grey area within which it might be difficult to distinguish need from preference – both notions depending in part on a series of vague value judgements implicit in the local authority's policy, the approach of front-line practitioners and the wishes of service users.

In addition, community care practice guidance states quite explicitly that for various reasons, assessed needs for services might not always be met by local authorities. When this happens, any 'unmet needs' should be recorded so that improvements can be made in services. After this guidance was issued, concern apparently grew in central government that if such 'unmet need' related to mandatory services under s.2 of the Chronically Sick and Disabled Persons Act 1970, then local authorities could be challenged legally. This was largely because of the view, discussed above, that local authorities could not plead lack of resources in individual cases under that Act. However, the House of Lords in the *Gloucestershire* case expressly envisaged that *in some circumstances* unmet need can be recorded quite lawfully under s.2 of the 1970 Act. Nevertheless, as pointed out in chapter 2, law does not necessarily translate into practice either very quickly or at all; at the time of writing, some local authorities continue to outlaw the recording on an individual basis of unmet need.

Legislation itself is silent about preferences and increased choice for users, but these considerations are referred to in policy and practice guidance. Many authorities probably attempt to implement the spirit of this guidance, but a number of limiting factors remain. Differences of opinion are sometimes inevitable and final decisions about needs and services are, as the legislation clearly states and guidance reiterates, for local authorities to make; whilst advocacy, promoted by community care guidance, still lacks the statutory basis which the unimplemented s.3 of the Disabled Persons (Services, Consultation and Representation) Act 1986 would have supplied.

EXTRACTS

Legislation: is silent about the distinction between people's needs or preferences; for instance, s.47 of the NHS and Community Care Act 1990 refers only to needs, as does s.2 of the Chronically Sick and Disabled Persons Act 1970.

Policy guidance: (DH 1990) states that users and carers should:

> **(choice and participation):** be enabled 'to exercise genuine choice and participation in the assessment of their care needs' (para 3.18). Also, the 'individual service user and normally, with his or her agreement, any carers should be involved throughout the assessment and care management process. They should feel that the process is aimed at meeting their wishes. Where a user is unable to participate actively it is important that he or she should be helped to understand what is involved and the intended outcome' (para 3.16).

> **(availability to all potential users/carers and non-discrimination):** 'Assessment procedures must be readily accessible by all potential service users and their carers. Decisions on service provision must be, and be seen to be, non-discriminatory. Authorities will need to take positive steps so that people with communication difficulties arising from sensory impairment, mental incapacity or other disabilities can participate fully in the assessment process and in the determination of service provision. Authorities also need to ensure that assessment is accessible to people from black and minority ethnic backgrounds. They may wish to make information about assessment and services available in braille, on tape and in appropriate ethnic minority languages. Staff may need to be recruited from a range of racial or ethnic backgrounds' (para 3.21).

> **(cultural background):** 'Because of their cultural background, some users may need services of a special type or kind; service geared to the requirements of the majority may not always be appropriate' (para 3.22).

> **(interpreters):** 'Authorities should promote the involvement of people who can assist service users and carers during assessment, including interpreters, both to help with communication and to explain cultural needs' (para 3.23).

> **(preferences, resources and decisions):** 'The aim shall be to secure the most cost effective package of services that meets the user's care needs taking account of the user's and the carer's own preferences. Where supporting a user in a home of their own would provide a better a quality of life, this is to be preferred to admission to residential or nursing home care. However, local authorities also have a responsibility to meet immediate needs within the resources available and this will sometimes involve difficult decisions where it will be necessary to strike a balance between meeting the needs identified within available resources and meeting the care preferences of the individual' (para 3.25).

> 'The aim should be to secure the most cost-effective package of services that meet the user's care needs, taking account of the user's and carer's own preferences ... However, local authorities also have a responsibil-

ity to meet needs within the resources available and this will sometimes involve difficult decisions where it will be necessary to strike a balance between meeting the needs identified within available resources and meeting the care preferences of the individual' (para 3.25).

Practice guidance (SSI,SWSG 1991a) states:

(need defined ultimately by local authorities): 'Need is unlikely to be perceived and defined in the same way by users, their carers and any other care agencies involved. The practitioner must, therefore, aim for a degree of consensus but, so long as they are competent, the users' views should carry the most weight … Ultimately, however, having weighed the views of all parties, including his/her own observation, the assessing practitioner is responsible for defining the user's needs' (p.53).

(recording of unmet need): 'Having completed the care plan, the practitioner should identify any assessed need which it has not been possible to address and for what reason'. A care plan should contain 'any unmet needs with reasons – to be separately notified to the service planning system', for example:

- 'statutory obligations', for example, those included in the Disabled Persons (Services, Consultation and Representation) Act 1986;
- defined as entitlements under local policies, for example, failure to provide services within defined timescales;
- new needs, identified by assessing staff but falling outside current policies or criteria, for example, the emerging needs of those with HIV/AIDS' (pp.66–67).

(reasons for unmet need): There may be a number of reasons for unmet needs including lack of resources, irrelevant or unacceptable quality and type of service, conditions of service (p.67).

(advocacy): 'Users and carers should be given every assistance and opportunity to represent their own interests. Where it is clear, however, that a user or carer would benefit from independent advocacy, they should be given information about any schemes funded by the authority or run locally … it is consistent with aims of basing service provision on the needs and wishes of users that those who are unable to express their views, for example, those with severe learning disabilities or dementia or those who have been previously disadvantaged, for example, those from minority ethnic groups should, as a matter of priority, be supported in securing independent representation' (p.51).

(race and culture): 'Local authorities are positively encouraged to promote the development of local advocacy schemes within available resources, giving priority to individuals from previously disadvantaged groups, such as those from black and minority ethnic communities' (p.17). 'It is important that all assessment staff have a knowledge and understanding of racial and cultural diversity, and the impact of racism, as well as having access to specialist advice' (p.58). 'Wherever possible, users should be offered a genuine choice of service options, appropriate to their ethnic and cultural background' (p.63).

Circular guidance: stated (CI(92)34, now cancelled):

(unmet preferences): 'Procedures will be needed which enable assessment staff to identify when the care packages actually provided do not accord with the preferences of users, either in terms of type, quantity, quality, cost, availability or cultural acceptability. A useful distinction might be drawn between those preferences which can be met within existing criteria of eligibility and those which would require some revision of the current policy' (para 24).

(individual or 'aggregate' recording of unmet preferences): 'Authorities should consider whether such information for planning purposes is best provided on the basis of individual assessments or as aggregate returns in respect of each practitioner's total assessments. If individual feedback is recorded, it should be borne in mind that, even though it may not form part of the user's assessment or care plan, it might still be accessed by users, under the terms of the access to information legislation, if the data identifiably relates to them. Practitioners will, therefore, have to be sensitive to the need not to raise unrealistic expectations on the part of users and carers...' (para 25).

(statutory obligations): 'For their part, authorities will want to ensure that their actual service responses are in full compliance with their statutory obligations and that the identification of alternative responses does not imply any failure to meet these obligations...' (para 26).

DISCUSSION

Needs and preferences: differentiating

The importance of the distinction between needs and preferences, is that needs tend to trigger statutory duties but preferences do not. Thus, local authorities might seem to have an incentive a) to disregard, or not take too seriously, preferences, and b) to recategorise as preference what in more affluent times they might instead have labelled as need.

Indeed, statements from government ministers in Parliament can seem remote from the reality confronting service users and local authorities, in their respective attempts to gain services and save money. For instance: 'At the very heart of our community care reforms lies the principle that all decisions about services must reflect the individual needs and wishes of users of the services and anyone who helps to care for them' (Tim Yeo: HCOA,23/3/1993,col.747). More realistically, policy guidance differentiates between needs and preferences and does not mention 'unmet needs'. Nevertheless, a 1993 court case about provision of residential accommodation showed that there are limits to manipulation of the concepts of 'need' and 'preference'. The judge accepted the view – a 'crucial finding of fact' based on expert opinion – of the authority's complaints procedure review panel that the person had particular 'psychological needs' which were more than just preferences. This meant that the authority had a duty to meet the need (*R v Avon CC, ex p M*).

The case of *R v North Yorkshire CC, ex p Hargreaves*, too, illustrates that authorities ignore people's preferences at their peril. A social worker had failed to elicit the wishes of a woman with learning disabilities who was seeking respite care, instead speaking only to the brother. This failure rendered unlawful the authority's decision because it breached paragraphs 3.16 and 3.25 of community care policy guidance (DH 1990). The case probably reflects the practices of some local authorities who make insufficient attempts to obtain the views of people with learning disabilities, or at least to find out before the assessment the degree to which a person is likely to be able to participate (Singh 1995,p.24).

Another example of failing to take account of preferences led the local ombudsman to find maladministration when a) the local authority changed the home visiting arrangements of a woman with severe learning disabilities, b) her mother said she did not agree to this, but c) the council simply wrote back confirming the change in arrangements – without a promised discussion – and said that her complaints would be dealt with by a complaints review panel (*Manchester CC 1996a*). Conversely, after three assessments for a home lift had all arrived at different recommendations (vertical lift, straight stairlift and curved stairlift), the last satisfied the applicant; the ombudsman accepted the explanation that all the decisions were 'professionally and technically correct', but it was only the third which had sufficiently reflected the woman's personal feelings and circumstances (*Sheffield CC 1996*).

Yet, taking completely at face value people's expressed preference might in some circumstances not be in their interests at all. It is well recognised that some users of services, although in dire need of assistance, might deny this during an assessment – especially, for instance, homeless people who have mental health problems or who are dependent on drugs or alcohol (O'Leary 1997,p.16). It is sometimes claimed that assessing social workers might take the denial at face value, and ignore evidence to the contrary of any voluntary sector workers who are involved with such clients. This would be with a view to saving money, since it obviously costs nothing if no intervention is agreed. Arguably, such a situation would mean that the local authority assessors are behaving unlawfully by not assessing and recording what a person's *needs* are, taking account of *all* relevant factors (including, but not only, expressed preferences) and sources of information. The fact that the person would anyway refuse intervention and services is neither here nor there, since assessment is a service and benefit in its own right (*R v Bristol CC, ex p Penfold*). Indeed, a failure to record the potential needs, the views of the voluntary sector workers, and refusal of services might lay the social workers open to allegations of negligence, should harm subsequently befall the client (although see p.451 for negligence and social services).

Lastly, it is worth pointing out that the distinction between 'need' and 'preferences' was routinely made by local authorities long before the implementation of community care in April 1993. For instance, a Parliamentary ombudsman investigation in the 1980s noted in passing that a council was justifying non-provision of a telephone aid for a disabled person on the grounds that it was 'desirable', but not essential according to their assessment criteria (PCA C656/87).

Needs and preferences: recording unmet need

Alternative to dismissing needs as preferences is to record them as 'unmet' – in other words, needs which the authority has identified but is not going to meet. Guidance states that such unmet need should be both recorded in individual care plans and fed back into the planning process (SSI,SWSG 1991a,p.67); and the House of Lords in *R v Gloucestershire CC, ex p Barry* stated that it was lawful to identify unmet needs even under s.2 of the Chronically Sick and Disabled Persons Act 1970.

Nevertheless, reacting still to Department of Health guidance (CI(92)34), and not taking account of either the *Gloucestershire* ruling or the 1991 practice guidance, local authorities continue to avoid identifying and recording individual needs which cannot be met. For instance, euphemistic terminology, avoiding the term 'unmet need', might include 'issues/tasks causing problems', 'issues identified', 'could have been met in a more desirable or satisfactory manner' (AMA 1993,p.3), 'service shortfalls' (Neate 1994), 'service preference deficit' (SSI 1994a,p.27). The term 'unmet need' might be used but in aggregate (ie, anonymous) form (SSI 1994d,p.40).

Asked in Parliament to rescind the Circular (CI(92)34) which the questioner interpreted as saying that 'the extent of a person's needs should not be assessed unless those needs could be met', the government unhelpfully denied that any such guidance had been issued (Tim Yeo: HCWA,14/4/1993,col.613). It also stated casually (in apparent disregard of its own guidance which states that unmet need 'should' be recorded for planning purposes) it 'is a matter for the authority if, for the purposes of planning its services in the longer term, it wishes to keep some record of needs which it would be desirable to meet but which it is not necessary to meet immediately'

(Tim Yeo: HCOA,23/3/93,col.748). Similarly, an SSI letter to London directors of social services suggested use of the term '"unmet choice", possibly differentiating between choices that fall inside and outside the current eligibility criteria' (in: House of Commons Health Select Committee 1993,vol.2,p.45).

Service user files might have a 'confidential module' to record 'service gaps', or 'service deficiency/improvement forms' might be kept, inaccessible to users and used for 'aggregated' information. One authority would not produce care plans which 'spell out to clients that they have specific needs which we are not specifically addressing'. Another authority's care plans did 'not cover alternatives to those services offered or services which are not available to meet the assessed needs' (AMA 1993,p.3). Yet care plans omitting such information are in breach of the relevant guidance (SSI,SWSG 1991a,p.67) and on that account might in some circumstances be unlawful (eg, *R v Islington LBC, ex p Rixon*).

Even if a local authority is recording unmet need, the typical focus in assessment of physical and functional disability will result in people's social needs being neither met nor recorded as unmet need – thus reducing both the usefulness for planning of information about unmet need and the overall efficacy of the authority's community care policy (Clarkson 1997,p.9). Alternative to all of this, authorities might not record unmet needs for the more pragmatic reason that it is just more paperwork at a time when resources are short (Davis, Ellis and Rummery 1997,p.43).

Needs and preferences: self-assessment

High demand and waiting lists (eg,SSI 1988a,p.6) have led to the introduction of 'self-assessment' for some services; for example, where people need simple items of equipment which are deemed not to have safety or risk implications. Such developments were identified as good practice by an SSI/NHSME (1994e,p.iv) report.

Nevertheless, self-assessment would seem, in many cases at least, to be a misnomer – since, in the statutory sense, it is the local authority (ie, not the service user) which is empowered and obliged to carry out assessment and take the final decision about provision of services. Therefore, in principle a self-assessment form is merely relevant information which goes towards that final statutory decision. In practice, it can in some circumstances help people take greater control of the process of assessment and in effect become their own care managers (SSI, Arthritis Care 1996,p.8); on the other hand, some people might ignore self-assessment forms because they find it difficult and dispiriting to portray their own vulnerabilities (Coombs 1998,p.25).

In one case investigated by the local ombudsman, a system of self-assessment led to confusion and disappointed expectation. The council agreed to meet a person's self-assessed need by arranging home adaptations in the form of an extension, but then went back on its word by stating that its original willingness did not amount to acceptance of a duty, because the self-assessed need had indicated desirability rather than necessity under s.2 of the Chronically Sick and Disabled Persons Act 1970 (*Manchester CC 1994*).

Needs and preferences: choosing type and quality of service

The inability sometimes of people to choose what home help services (eg, cleaning rather than shopping) they receive has already been discussed (see p.120). More generally, it has been pointed out that people who use services want a) to be able to decide for themselves what would be most helpful; b) to have consistent reliable helpers who arrive on time, who are easy to get on with, and who respect people's autonomy and privacy. When one considers that such help sometimes involves personal, intimate care it is no surprise that people should wish to use the community care direct payments scheme (p.???) through which they can purchase their own services (Harding 1997,p.26).

Needs and preferences: advocacy and unimplemented legislation

Community care guidance refers to the importance of advocacy, particularly for potentially disadvantaged groups of people such as those with dementia or learning disabilities. It also recognises that a conflict of interest might render local authority staff unsuitable to take on an advocacy role (see above).

However, legislation (in force) is silent largely because statutory provisions in existence since 1986 concerning representation and advocacy for disabled people remain unimplemented in sections 1–3 of the Disabled Persons (Services, Consultation and Representation) Act 1986. Briefly, people would have the right to an authorised representative; the authorised representatives would themselves be given rights; and disabled people would have the right to make representations and have their views taken into account. They would also have the right to a written statement of a decision with an explanation, and to a review.

An attempt to introduce similar provisions into the NHS and Community Care Bill failed, on the grounds, explained by the Secretary of State for Health, 'that the assessment should be informal' and that local authorities should not be given an additional formal burden (Virginia Bottomley: Standing Committee E,15/2/1990,col.1061). In the House of Lords, the government explained that the first three sections of the 1986 Act were the most complex and potentially the most expensive of all the Act's provisions. Baroness Masham, in response, pointed to the logical consequence of non-implementation of those sections of the 1986 Act which after all had been accepted by Parliament four years previously. She queried 'how one undertakes an assessment without taking into consideration a person's views. It is most extraordinary. I cannot understand it. If a person has a view and can express himself and that view is not taken into consideration, he is being treated like an animal. When one assesses a pig or cow one cannot ask them, but with a human being one can' (HLD,10/5/1990,cols.1580–1584).

Needs and preferences: people from minority ethnic groups

Guidance (see extracts above) makes reference to minority ethnic groups and the importance of taking account of their needs. However, community care legislation is silent on the issue: compare s.22(5) of the Children Act 1989.

During the passage of the NHS and Community Care Bill, an amendment sought to make mandatory assessments which would 'take account of the needs of people of ethnic minority origin'. The Parliamentary Under-Secretary for Wales explained this was not necessary because both social services departments and health authorities 'should have full regard to the needs of ethnic minority and national interests'. They would 'live up to ... professional guidance because they will have helped to draw it up' (Ian Grist: HCD,15/2/1990,col.1042). Similarly, it would not be 'helpful to draw particular attention' to minority communities on the face of the legislation, but 'the need to take account of these factors will be stressed in our guidance, which can be reinforced by directions' (Baroness Blatch: HLD,14/6/1990,col.482; see also HLD,26/6/1990,cols 1375–1376). However, whilst legislation makes no mention of minority ethnic groups, guidance fills the gap, albeit in brief (see extracts above).

As a matter of practice, for example, caring tasks need to be arranged with matters in mind such as language, religious observances (including particular dates), diet, particular personal needs (eg, relating to skin, hair care, bathing customs), and other cultural requirements (CRE 1997,p.46). For instance, white people might not know how to look after Afro-style hair; and domiciliary services should be flexible to take account of fluctuating conditions (eg, sickle-cell anaemia or thalassaemia) and a festival such as Ramadan when Muslims fast during the day (Begum 1995,pp.24,28). An inability to find a Muslim carer to provide for an elderly Asian man, despite attempts to do so, and instead to recruit a Sikh, might cause problems (example cited in Butt, Mirza 1996). Guidelines for residential homes about death and funeral practices will be useful (SSI 1995k,p.35).

Where reception staff, in a multi-cultural area, are all white and have received no training about the needs of ethnic minority older people, then they have to rely on interpreters or other colleagues happening to be available to talk to a person whose first language is not English (SSI 1998f,p.38). If religion, culture, language and experience of racism need to be considered, so too should stereotypical assumptions be avoided since in any religion or culture there are varying degrees of orthodoxy (Begum 1995,p.19).

More generally, local authorities need to keep in mind the Race Relations Act 1976, in particular the provisions relating to non-discrimination in the provision of goods, facilities and services (s.20). Nevertheless in 1998 it was the Audit Commission's and Social Services Inspectorate's view that community care assessments were not experienced by those being assessed as 'taking proper account of people's ethnic, religious and cultural needs' (Audit Commission, SSI 1998,p.11).

Needs and preferences: participating in the assessment

If people do not have the opportunity of understanding what is going on, they will be unable to participate genuinely in community care assessment and decisions about services.

Anecdotal evidence might be that 'in many places users and carers still find the bureaucracy difficult to deal with and have problems understanding complex assessment processes' (SSI 1993d, Summary). Community care for younger disabled adults might include good practice involving independent advocacy services; but elsewhere the concept of advocacy might not feature in policy and practice documents (SSI/NHSME 1994e,p.14). An advocate might either enable a person's interests to be represented, or enable the person directly to represent his or her own interests. However, a distinction must be made as to whose interests are being advocated, the carer or the person being cared for (SSI 1996b,p.21).

Users and carers might find the process of assessment over-bureaucratic, especially, for example, where they have to sign seven times during an assessment. Yet they might still have no clear recollection of the choices offered them and completed assessments might bear all the hallmarks of prescribing particular services rather than recording agreed objectives (SSI/NHSME 1994b,pp.25–26). They might not realise that there is an assessment and care management system at all, either because they have not been told or because of forgetfulness; in fact, those, who through special knowledge are able to act as their own care managers, are likely to fare best (Baldock, Ungerson 1994,p.12; also Singh 1995,p.21). Staff might believe that people have participated in assessment, but users feel the opposite (Godfrey, Moore 1996,p.69; Davis, Ellis and Rummery 1997,p.52). Conversely, care managers might, rightly or wrongly, believe that people do not want to get 'involved beyond being given the service that will meet their needs' (Baldwin 1995a,p.13). And if people have insufficient information about possible solutions to their needs before assessment and a decision about services, then they will not be able to generate options for themselves (Midgley, Munlo and Brown 1997,p.26).

Needs and preferences: final decision and conflict

Ultimately, as the legislation (see eg, s.47(1) of the NHS and Community Care Act 1990) implies and guidance emphasises, it is for local authorities to make final decisions about need and services. Whilst final decisions still have to be taken lawfully, this clearly puts local authorities in a strong position in case of dispute.

There are obvious limits to choice: 'Users and carers also commented that the combination of tight eligibility criteria and charging policies were precluding the effective take-up of services by those in need and resulting in a continued over reliance on carers. It is difficult to see how Authorities can respond to this criticism given their need to ration resources' (SSI/NHSME 1994b,p.46). Similarly: 'Painful decisions have to be made and people will often not be able to have what they want, sometimes through lack of resources, sometimes because their needs conflict with others, sometimes through irretrievable loss of a person or personal capacity and often through some combination of all of these factors' (Smale *et al.* 1993,p.62). Even when people – for example, parents with learning difficulties – are represented by advocates, there is only so much the latter can achieve if there are few resources in the first place for them to mobilise (Booth, Booth 1998).

Despite the rational, cordial tone of the guidance, in practice there is a danger that people who are aware of their entitlements, express preferences or challenge the decisions of practitioners might, on that account, be stigmatised by staff as demanding, grabbing, fussy or manipulative (Ellis 1993,p.22). Alternatively, some local authority and NHS staff experience aggression from clients and patients when they make unfavourable decisions. The local ombudsman sometimes investigates conflicts of opinion and explains that simple disagreement is of course not in itself grounds for findings of maladministration (*Manchester CC 1993*).

Needs and preferences: clarity of definition

Need has been characterised generally as having no fixed quantity or definition, but as being 'a complicated mixture of social resources and individual striving, of public expectations and private imagination' (Stone 1985,p.19). Such is its elusiveness, that it has been suggested that 'hopes, wishes, aspirations, dreams and the barriers that prevent their realisation' might actually seem easier for practitioners to work with than need (Middleton 1997,p.19) – even though these are meant to be the opposite, or at least the complement, of the statutory trigger of need.

Needs and preferences: independence and control

If services are to be effective in terms both of assisting people and of cost, it would seem that they should attempt to promote the independence of people or at least their control over what is happening to them. Independence is likely to bring greater self-reliance and therefore a reduced burden on statutory services, and should not be interpreted narrowly. For instance, it could mean that a person exercises control over what is happening to him or her, even when heavily reliant on human or technical assistance. The following very different examples are illustrative:

Example 1: independence and control: In the case of people who have become impaired following an accident or from birth, independence might give the opportunity of a fulfilling life in terms both of work and on a personal level – and accordingly cost the state less in terms of social assistance. But if they are confined to an institution, or to inactivity at home by inadequate or inappropriate services, this chance will be denied. Moreover, it was the anger felt by disabled people who had been confined in residential institutions, but who then left to live independently in the community, that has led to the forming of campaigning organisations run by disabled people (Nocon *et al.* 1995,Chapter 2).

Example 2: independence and control: For an older person, mildly impaired through arthritis, a responsive home help service over which the person has some control may likewise allow him or her to remain independent. Home help staff – who are friendly and reliable and not prevented by a local authority's policy from doing what the person wants (eg, housework) – might make the difference between people feeling, physically and mentally, able to stay at home more cheaply (which is their preference) or considering, reluctantly, going into residential care which may be more expensive for everybody, both individual and the public purse.

Example 3: independence and control: Where people are impaired because they are dying of a terminal illness (eg cancer) at home over a longer or shorter period, what quality of life is left to them will be immeasurably enhanced if service providers give (and reinforce) relevant information, present choices about treatment and management clearly, and allow the person control, or at least even a feeling of control, over what is happening – even though the progress of the overall terminal condition cannot be halted. Indeed, the choices of treatment people make in such situations are not necessarily the most expensive (for instance, they may choose non-intervention at home, rather than expensive intervention in hospital).

The theme of independence and control is a pervasive one urged by number of individuals and organisations. For instance, the influential Wagner (1988) report concluded that moving into a residential establishment should be a 'positive choice', and that no one 'should be required to change their permanent accommodation in order to receive services which could be made available to them in their own home' (pp.114–115). It has been pointed out in a Counsel and Care publication, that rather than concentrate negatively on what people cannot do, a care manager can ask, not about the needs of the client, but about how his or her rights to a reasonable quality of life might be enhanced by the services offered (Smith 1994). A Help the Aged report states that the 'key to independence and inclusion for older people is to stay in control of their own lives – to be able to make their own choices, choose their own way of life, and access those services and facilities that enable them to do so on their own terms' (Harding 1997,p.39). For instance, on a very basic level, people might feel they are actually leading normal lives, simply by being able to choose when they get up and when they go to bed (SSI 1995b,p.10). In late 1998, a government White Paper emphasised that community care should be about promoting people's independence, including extra support for those with the ability to work. In particular, there should be a national objective, 'to ensure that people of working age who have been assessed as requiring community care services, are provided with these services in ways which take account of and, as far as possible, maximise their and their carers' capacity to take up, remain in or return to employment' (Secretary of State for Health 1998, pp.14,19,111).

If effective services are to be delivered, it would again seem obvious that they should be based on a knowledge of what people's needs are. It is equally clear that when it comes to daily living matters, the most important (though not the only) source for that knowledge is those people themselves. In order to achieve appropriately designed services, their planning and delivery should arguably be based on consultation with, joint working with, and delegation of management and service delivery to, users of services or their representative groups (Begum, Fletcher 1995,p.20).

CHAPTER 7

CARE PLANS, SERVICE PROVISION, REVIEW AND REASSESSMENT

Coverage

1. Recording and communication of assessment
2. Care plans
3. Service provision
4. Review and reassessment of people's needs

KEY POINTS

Legislation and guidance envisages that, following assessment, people will either be informed of a negative outcome or have a care plan drawn up specifying the nature and purpose of services to be arranged. Though not mentioned in legislation, it is clear from decisions of the law courts that inadequate care plans can amount in some circumstances to unlawfulness. Of course a care plan in itself puts services on paper only; the receiving of adequate services promptly is another matter which is sometimes investigated by the local ombudsman or even reviewed by the law courts.

Also set out in guidance is the expectation that people's needs and circumstances will be kept under review, so that reassessment can be carried out as appropriate. It states that reassessment and alteration of services might be required not just in the light of an individual service user's changing needs, but also of the local authority's changing policies, priorities and criteria of eligibility. This means that people might lose services, even if their needs have not lessened; objectionable to some, the law courts have confirmed that if local authorities pass through the right procedural and legal hoops, this is lawful.

I. RECORDING AND COMMUNICATION OF ASSESSMENT

Guidance states that the result of assessment should be communicated to users. This would in any case be good practice and failure to do so might also amount to maladministration.

EXTRACTS

Legislation is silent about the communication of assessment results.

Policy guidance (DH 1990, 3.56) states that:

> 'local authorities will need to have in place … arrangements for communicating the outcome of assessments and decisions on service provision to applicants and carers and those participating in the assessment process'.

Practice guidance (SS1,SWSG 1991a) states:

> **(recording of assessment and care plan)** 'All assessments are likely to be recorded on some kind of pro forma … A copy of the assessment of needs should normally be shared with the potential user, any representative of that user and all the people who have agreed to provide a service. Except where no intervention is deemed necessary, this record will normally be combined with a written care plan (the next stage of the management process) setting out how the needs are to be addressed…' (p.56).

> **(written or oral)** In the case of simple needs, guidance states that the outcome of the assessment and care planning process may be communicated on a 'verbal basis' (presumably oral is meant). However, if a continuing service has been offered, the outcome should 'normally be communicated in writing in the form of an individual care plan' (p.46).

DISCUSSION

Legislation does not refer at all to whether a copy of the assessment be given to users. However, guidance envisages that in some circumstances at least, written copies should be provided. Similarly, there is no statutory obligation to give reasons for an adverse decision (in which case there will be no care plan); and although the law courts are still evolving the scope of the common law duty to give reasons (see p.50), the local ombudsman states that giving reasons is good administration (CLAE 1993). As a matter of common sense, it will be difficult for people to decide whether to complain (itself a statutory right: see p.423) if they are not given reasons for adverse decisions. Also people quite naturally might wish to see what has been written about them, simply to check that there has been no misunderstanding (Age Concern England 1993,p.11).

Furthermore, having to provide copies of assessments for service users is likely in turn to have the beneficial effect of raising the standard of local authority record-keeping – and so avoid situations in court where a judge is unable to discern what the assessment concluded or whether it was ever completed (*R v Cornwall County Council, ex p Goldsack*).

2. CARE PLANS

Legislation is silent about care plans. Policy guidance states that care plans should follow assessments and lists, in order of preference, a number of types of care packages, from support for people in their own homes to institutional long-term care. Practice guidance states explicitly that users should receive copies of their care plans and goes on to list what their content should be. The courts have ruled in more than one case that failure – without good reason – to draw up a care plan approximating in form to that set out in the guidance, is unlawful. Despite this, there is evidence that in practice a significant number of service users do not receive care plans at all, let alone ones which conform to the guidance.

EXTRACTS

Legislation (NHS and Community Care Act 1990 (s.47(1)) states that after assessment of a person a local authority:

'having regard to the results of that assessment, shall then decide whether his needs call for the provision by them of any such services'.

Policy guidance (DH 1990) states that:

(**order of preference for services**) 'Once needs have been assessed, the services to be provided or arranged and the objectives of any intervention should be agreed in the form of a care plan. The objective of ensuring that service provision should, as far as possible, preserve or restore normal living implies the following order of preference in constructing care packages which may include health provision, both primary and specialist, housing provision and social services provision';

(**home support**) 'support for the user in his or her own home including day and domiciliary care, respite care, the provision of disability equipment and adaptations to accommodation as necessary';

(**alternative accommodation**) 'a move to more suitable accommodation, which might be sheltered or very sheltered housing, together with provision of social services support';

(**private household**) 'a move to another private household (ie, to live with relatives or friends or as part of an adult fostering scheme)';

(**institutional care**) 'residential care, nursing home care, long-stay care in hospital' (para 3.24).

(**informing people about result of assessment**) 'Service users and carers should be informed of the result of the assessment and of any services to be provided ... Where care needs are relatively straightforward the most appropriate way of conveying decisions can best be determined taking individual circumstances into account. A written statement will normally be needed if a continuing service is to be provided. Written statements should always be supplied on request' (para 3.27).

Practice guidance (SSI,SWSG 1991a) states that:

(**all users to have a care plan**) 'All users in receipt of a continuing service should have a care plan' (p.61) and a copy 'should be given to the user' (p.67).

(**elements of a care plan**) 'A care plan should contain the following: overall objectives; the specific objectives of users, carers, service providers; the criteria for measuring the achievement of these objectives; the services to be provided by which personnel/agency; the cost to the user and the contributing agencies; the other options considered; any point of difference between the user, carer, care planning practitioner or other agency; any unmet needs with reasons – to be separately notified to the service planning system; the named person(s) responsible for implementing, monitoring and reviewing the care plan; the date of the first planned review' (p.67).

(**legal force of a care plan**) 'The care plan does not have a legal standing as a contract but, to reinforce the sense of commitment, contributors (including the user) may be asked to signify their agreement by signing. With or without signatures, the expectation is that contributors will honour their commitments and the care plan will be the means of holding them to account. As such, a care plan may be used as evidence in the consideration of a complaint' (p.68).

DISCUSSION

Care plans: list of preferred community care options

Community care policy guidance lists the preferred options for care packages, and it is clear that residential care is some way down the list. On the face of it, it would therefore seem counter to this policy that local authorities should seek to place people in residential care when they do not want to go there, simply to save money (eg, *R v Lancashire CC, ex p RADAR*). It would also seem to contradict at least some government statements made during the passing of the NHS and Community Care Bill: 'When a local authority assesses a person as needing residential or nursing home care, by virtue of that assessment, it has concluded that it is not possible for the person to be supported in his own home' (Baroness Blatch: HLD,10/5/1990,col.1586).

The danger that the aim of independent living in the community would be undermined was recognised by an unsuccessful attempt to amend the duty of assessment in the NHS and Community Care Bill to: 'an assessment of his needs having regard first to his ability to live outside residential care'. Furthermore, so as to ensure that inappropriate residential placement did not persist, the local authority would be obliged a) to 'appoint a named social worker to be in charge of each case where assessment has shown need for institutional care or care in a residential nursing home'; and b) to 'explain in writing as part of the assessment why a residential placement is in the best interests of that person' (HCD,15/2/1990,col.1034).

Care plans: provision of not a statutory duty

Legislation does not refer to care plans. However, attempts were made, via amendment to the NHS and Community Care Bill, to impose a duty on a local authority to give a person 'in writing the outcome of his assessment and set out the services they intend to provide'. The government objected to such detail, but nevertheless conceded that it was 'an important part of good practice, and I have every reason to believe that once local authorities get the mechanism under way, they will ensure that those who are being assessed have their results in writing' (Virginia Bottomley: SC(E),15/2/1990,cols.1055–1058).

Rejecting the amendment at a later stage also, the government stated that it did not want 'to enshrine in legislation the particular means by which local authorities decide to communicate with clients'. For example, visits might be more appropriate than confusing or intimidating written communications, but it agreed that 'communicating the outcome of assessment is absolutely key to the mutual understanding of what can and cannot be provided' (Baroness Blatch: HLD,10/5/1990,col.1576).

In fact, Department of Health guidance dealing with this issue was later forthcoming in 1991 (SSI,SWSG 1991a); yet by 1997 it was still being reported that many service users and carers were not being given copies of care plans (SSI 1996d,p.14); perhaps unsurprising if care planning is anyway not distinguished from assessment (SSI 1995b,p.6). And it seems that even the very existence of care plans for people in residential care homes is rare (Redmayne 1995,p.19; SSI 1995k,p.38).

Care plans: scrutiny by the law courts

When scrutinising closely the actions and decisions of local authorities, the courts have been prepared to examine how closely authorities follow the guidance about care plans – and to declare that substantial divergence from it without good reasons is unlawful (see eg, *R v Islington LBC, ex p Rixon*, and *R v Sutton LBC, ex p Tucker*) – thereby going some way to mitigate the omission from legislation of reference to care plans. The court in the *Rixon* case also pointed out that 'a care plan is the means by which the local authority assembles the relevant information and applies it to the statutory ends, and hence affords good evidence to any inquirer of the due discharge of its statutory duties'.

In practice, reports have continued to suggest that service users do not receive care plans as envisaged by guidance (see eg, SSI 1994h,p.26; SSI/NHSE 1994g,p.38). For service users, the lack of an effective care plan might, for example, be part of the failure to enable a person to leave NHS premises (*R v Sutton LBC, ex p Tucker*) or hinder the arranging of suitable service provision for a severely disabled person (*R v Islington LBC, ex p Rixon*).

Deficiencies in care plans also surface in investigations of the local ombudsman. They might contribute to accidental death in a residential care unit (*Cleveland CC 1993*), compound difficulties in appropriately managing the care of a person in residential care (*Dorset CC 1996*), or hinder the success of independent living in a flat (which admittedly would probably have failed anyway) (*Hackney LBC 1992b*). In another investigation, practical support for a person with mental health problems would have been more effective if embedded in a 'properly thought out care plan' (*Tower Hamlets LBC 1993*). And receipt of the care plan enables a user to check what is happening with his services; it is maladministration not to receive a copy of the care plan (and of the assessment document) (*Tower Hamlets LBC 1994*).

3. SERVICE PROVISION

In order to cope with the demands made on them, local authorities might operate not only waiting times for assessment but also for the arranging of services; in addition, the standard and reliability of service provision might also be sometimes in question.

EXTRACTS

Legislation is mostly silent about the time and manner in which local authorities should carry out a duty to provide community care services (except see the Housing Grants, Construction and Regeneration Act 1996 for time limits on deciding applications for, and making payments of, disabled facilities grants: see p.400).

DISCUSSION

Waiting times for services are specified neither in legislation nor guidance. However, they represent one way in which local authorities attempt to reconcile finite resources with the demands made on them – not by refusing to perform duties but by doing so slowly. Their existence is nothing new; for example, a Parliamentary ombudsman investigation (PCA C.12/K) in the 1970s noted (in passing) the view of the DHSS that some local authorities were placing people on waiting lists after assessment under s.2 of the Chronically Sick and Disabled Persons Act 1970, simply because they were short of money. Both the courts and the local ombudsman generally say that local authorities should do their duty (ie, provide services) within a reasonable time (or without undue delay) and that in turn this will depend on the particular circumstances.

A more recent development is that waiting times now exist in some authorities for residential care, as well as for non-residential services – for instance, 85 very frail people in one authority might be waiting on the 'one in, one out' principle (Coombs 1998,p.44).

Service provision: waiting times, examples of judicial rulings

In the field of housing law, when there was a duty 'to secure that accommodation becomes available', the judge ruled that the duty was not necessarily to produce a house immediately – and that putting a person on a waiting list sufficed (*R v Brent LBC, ex p. Macwan 1994*). The housing law duty to, 'secure that accommodation becomes available', could be regarded as comparable to the Chronically Sick and Disabled Persons Act 1970 (s.2) duty, to 'make arrangements' for the provision of services.

Back in the community care field, the judge commented in *R v Kirklees LBC, ex p Daykin* (about provision of a stairlift) that having identified needs and what had to be done about them, it was the duty of the local authority to make arrangements as soon as reasonably practicable. In *R v Sutton LBC, ex p Tucker*, a two-year wait for a final care plan and provision of services was a breach of statutory duty under s.47 of the NHS and Community Care Act 1990; although the authority was entitled to make interim provision, this had gone on too long. Again in a different legal context (ie, a private law action for a breach of statutory duty), in *Cross v Kirklees MBC* (a highways case), an absolute duty to do something about an icy pavement was to be identified by sufficient measures taken within a reasonable time; this test was applied in *Goodes v East Sussex CC* and the local authority was found wanting.

Sometimes the courts are reluctant to intervene if a dispute about whether the period of delay is reasonable hinges on establishing certain facts rather than legal principle *R v Birmingham CC, ex p A* about a delay in a child care placement). Even if they do find an authority in breach of its duty because of delay, they might not make an order against it, if it is doing all it can in the circumstances (*R v Bristol Corporation, ex p Hendy* about housing accommodation). In *Cumbria Professional Care v Cumbria CC*, in respect of waiting lists for residential accommodation, the court repeated a point made in *R v Islington LBC, ex p Rixon* that even an equivocal statutory duty cannot conjure up resources where there are none.

Service provision: waiting times, interim provision

The theme of interim provision of services, during a wait for the final service to be provided (eg, home adaptations or a move of accommodation), is a recurring one. The housing case of *R v Brent LBC, ex p Macwan* is an example; the permissibility of interim provision, at least up to a point, was also referred to in *R v Sutton LBC, ex p Tucker*. Department of Health guidance states that suitable interim provision should be made to meet people's needs, in case of their having to wait to enter residential accommodation (LAC(98)19,para 11).

Investigations of the local ombudsman carry various examples; a local authority might provide a bath aid during a wait for alternative accommodation (*Barnsley MBC 1998a*); and provision of a commode by the social services department, while a person waits for a disabled facilities grant from the housing department, might seem to discharge the authority's duty under s.2 of the Chronically Sick and Disabled Persons Act 1970 (*Barnsley MBC 1998b*; see also *Liverpool CC 1996/1997, Tower Hamlets LBC 1997*).

Service provision: waiting times, examples of ombudsman findings

The local ombudsman is likely to consider the circumstances of each case in deciding what a reasonable waiting time should have been. For instance, in one investigation, the local authority claimed, in relation to s.2 of the Chronically Sick and Disabled Persons Act 1970, 'that although they may be under an obligation to provide a facility they do not consider that they have an obligation to provide the facility immediately. Thus, they argue some delay is acceptable'. The ombudsman stated that 'whether or not any particular delay is so excessive as to constitute maladministration will depend on the facts of the individual case' (*Wakefield MDC 1992*).

Thus, when a man with paraplegia (following an accident) was discharged home from hospital, it took the local authority 16 months to put a complete care package in place; this was too long (*Avon CC 1997*). A delay of two or three months in changing the meals-on-wheels for a person with special dietary needs and following a request from the man's general practitioner was maladministration (*Kensington and Chelsea RB 1992*). It was also maladministration when cleaning and laundry services promised for February did not materialise until late March for a man discharged from hospital after a stroke – and when there was a failure to place straightaway and mark as urgent an order for a gas fire with top controls, given that he was blacking out when bending down to use the existing controls (*Kirklees MBC 1993*). A delay in providing services of nine months, following the assessment of a young man who had just left school (and was later diagnosed as schizophrenic) was maladministration (*Liverpool CC 1997a*); as was a delay of 12 months in making arrangements for an alternative care package, after heavily supported independent living in a bungalow had failed (*Liverpool CC 1997b*). Even a ten-day wait for a visit to be made following the discharge of a man from hospital – when normally a visit would have been made next day – was blameworthy (*Sheffield CC 1996*).

Delay in payment of a housing (renovation) grant could not be justified by the absence of the 'one person' who could make it, even in the absence of an authorised deputy (*Kirklees MBC 1997*). And when a stairlift company was being slow in responding to the council's request that it assess and estimate the cost of installing a stairlift, the council should have been monitoring the situation and pursuing the company (*Liverpool 1996/1997*). Sometimes the ombudsman breaks down the stages of assessment and service provision and gives to each a reasonable time – which is then measured against what actually happened in a particular case. For instance, in establishing a blameworthy period of waiting (18 months), the ombudsman considered the time involved for each of the following: request for assessment, assessment, occupational therapist's report and request for costing, preliminary inspection and completion of grant enquiry form, stairlift estimate, test of resources, sending and return of application package, grant approval (*Liverpool CC 1996/1997*). Work arranged by the social services department to replace a bath with a shower, which took five months instead of only one, constituted maladministration (*Liverpool CC 1996/1997*).

Service provision: adequacy of services

It is likely that disputes about the adequacy of services which have been agreed will often be more appropriately resolved through complaints procedures or the local ombudsmen than through judicial review, since they will usually concern matters of fact rather than law.

In one case involving the provision of home help, the ombudsman found no evidence of staff 'fiddling' their timesheets or 'pulling flankers' and accepted that it might take a little time to establish regular visiting times (*Kensington and Chelsea RB 1992*). In a child care case, the ombudsman did not fault the professional judgement underlying the original priority and services to be given to a family, even though it later became clear that there were more serious problems and child protection issues. However, a break in the management and supervision of the case, when it was being referred between an area office and a specialist team was maladministration (*Nottinghamshire CC 1998*). Receipt of an irregular and erratic home help service for a total of thirteen months, with no reason given for the failure in service, was maladministration (*Westminster CC 1996*).

When a council had only one short-stay respite house available for women in the north of the city, the premises did not have bathing facilities on the ground floor, adaptations were still in progress 21 months after the property came into use, and reliance was placed on agency staff about whom 'concern' had been expressed by council officers, the ombudsman found that the facilities were 'unsatisfactory'; this was maladministration (*Manchester CC 1996b*). Similarly, the failure of a council to investigate day provision for a young, physically disabled man outside of its own area was maladministration, given the very limited facilities it had of its own (*Trafford MBC 1996*). It was also maladministration when a council did not take sufficient care in ensuring that a hotel was suitable for the needs of a woman with learning disabilities, whom it was assisting to arrange a holiday under s.2 of the Chronically Sick and Disabled Persons Act 1970 (*Buckinghamshire CC 1998*). And when a service user was excluded from a service because of disputes with fellow attenders at a day centre, the ombudsman stated that natural justice required that she be told a) the reasons, b) the duration of the exclusion, c) how she could re-enter the service, d) who would decide, and e) how to appeal (*Cornwall CC 1996*).

4. REVIEW AND REASSESSMENT OF PEOPLE'S NEEDS

Legislation does not refer to the review and reassessment of people's needs. However, guidance states that people's needs should be regularly reviewed. Clearly, if people's needs increase or decrease, then the level of services they receive might be varied.

However, and rather confusingly, the guidance states that it is also possible for people's own situation to remain the same, but for the level of services still to be varied. This can happen if an authority's policy and eligibility criteria alter, so that people no longer qualify for the same level of services, even though their own circumstances have not changed at all. The guidance suggests that where this happens, people should at least be informed about what is happening, and be reassessed before services are altered or withdrawn. It is no surprise that such decisions provoke disputes; however, the law courts have basically confirmed this position, outlining one or two safeguards for service users along the way.

When local authorities have not had such a financial incentive to carry out reviews and reassessments, they have in the past not reviewed people's needs adequately. This was recognised when community care was . . ิ ented; and remains a problem. The White Paper at the end of 1998 acknowledges as much, sตั.ng that forthcoming guidance (under the *Fair access to care* initiative) would set out the government's expectations. For instance, it states that when people begin to receive services, residential or non-residential, reviews should be conducted within three weeks, and thereafter at least annually, although frequency will depend on various factors. Reviews should 'wherever possible' be carried out face to face, and authorities should be explicit about who is to carry them out, what they consist of and how often they will happen (Secretary of State for Health 1998,p.19).

EXTRACTS

Legislation does not mention review or reassessment.

Policy guidance (DH 1990) states:

> **(regular reviews)** 'Care needs, for which services are being provided, should be reviewed at regular intervals. This review, especially where it relates to complex needs, should wherever possible, be undertaken by someone, such as a care manager, not involved in direct service provision, to preserve the needs-led approach. The projected timing of the first review should be stated in the original care plan. However, reviews may take place earlier if it is clear that community care needs have changed...' (para 3.51).

> **(purpose of review)** 'The purpose of the review is to establish whether the objectives, set in the original care plan, are being, or have been met and to increase, revise or withdraw services accordingly. Reviews should take account of any changes in need or service delivery policies...' (para 3.52).

Practice guidance (SSI,SWSG 1991a) states that:

> **(review purposes)** 'review fulfils a number of different purposes which are to:
> - review the achievement of care plan objectives;
> - examine the reasons for success or failure;
> - evaluate the quality and cost of the care provided;
> - reassess current needs;
> - reappraise eligibility for assistance;
> - revise the care plan objectives;
> - redefine the service requirements;
> - recalculate the cost;
> - notify quality assurance/service planning of any service deficiencies or unmet needs;
> - set the date for the next review;
> - record the findings of the review' (pp.84–85).

> **(policy review causing change in services to users)** Not only are people's 'needs subject to change but so are the policies of the authority or agency. The increasing emphasis on targeting will mean that reviews not only confirm or increase services, they will also sanction their reduction and withdrawal. Where the level of assistance is adjusted, the reasons for that change should be explained to the user or their representative' (p.85).

Circular guidance (CI(92)34 now cancelled) explained that:

> **(reassessment before adjustment of services)** 'care plans of all users should be subject to regular review. For frail people in the community, frequent reviews and adjustments of their care plans are likely to be needed. Before any changes in services are made for existing users, they should be re-assessed. In those cases, where assessments have been undertaken, particularly under section 2(1) of the CSDP Act 1970, authorities must satisfy themselves, before any reduction in service provision takes place that the user does not have a continuing need for it. So long as there is a continuing need, a service must be provided although, following review, it is possible that an assessed need might be met in a different way' (para 31).

(scope of review) Review will cover 'criteria of eligibility for services to take account of: new policy objectives; more efficient targeting of resources; newly available resources; changing volumes and types of assessed needs and user preferences; available resources' (para 28).

DISCUSSION

Review and reassessment: background

Reassessment and review are not mentioned in legislation, although a failed amendment to the 1990 Act would have ensured that explicit reference was made: 'Having carried out an assessment of a person's needs and provided him with that assessment in writing, the authority shall undertake a review of the assessment six weeks later and convey the results to him in writing. Subsequent reviews shall take place at intervals of not more than six months'. However, the government thought that this would be too mechanistic and that reviews should not be inflexibly enshrined in legislation but left for local authorities to decide on (Ian Grist: HCD,15/2/ 1990,cols. 1034–1038). For example, some people might need much more frequent review and amendment of services, others might require more modest support (Baroness Blatch: HLD,10/5/ 1990,col.1577).

Review and reassessment: safeguards

As the legislation stands, reassessment is simply assessment being carried out again under s.47 of the NHS and Community Care Act 1990; thus any considerations applying to assessment (see Chapters 5 and 6) apply to reassessment as well – including the safeguards of individual reassessment, eligibility criteria which reflect a balancing exercise involving needs and resources, and avoidance of unreasonable decisions (see *R v Gloucestershire, ex p Barry*: High Court and House of Lords hearings). The local ombudsman has argued on similar lines, finding, for instance, maladministration when psychotherapy was suddenly withdrawn from a person by the local authority – instead of being reduced in stages (*Brent LBC 1994*), or when the residential placement of a person with dementia was changed without reassessment (*Doncaster MBC 1997*).

Furthermore, it was established in *R v Gloucestershire CC, ex p RADAR*, that local authorities must go to some lengths to carry out individual reassessments. Sending a letter to existing users of services, and offering to reassess only if a reply was received, was held in the circumstances to be inadequate in relation to vulnerable people. This decision might have seemed surprising given the pressures on local authorities. Indeed, the cost of reassessment (in this case estimated at £200,000) might itself sometimes be a safeguard for service users against cuts in services (Schwehr 1995).

The requirements of individual reassessment were spelt out in the *Gloucestershire* case in relation only to services under s.2 of the Chronically Sick and Disabled Persons Act 1970. It might be thought, however, that such requirements apply to the provision of all other community care services as well, given that assessment is in the first place in respect of individual people (ie, the 'any person' referred to in s.47 of the NHS and Community Care Act 1990). Nevertheless, the ruling of the House of Lords in that case appeared to leave open the possibility of almost arbitrary withdrawal or interruption of services in relation to at least some community care services (see p.133).

Review and reassessment: withdrawal or reduction of services

Reassessment in the light of reduced resources and stricter policies predictably leads to disputes – when, for instance, authorities threaten to reduce or withdraw home help services for 1,500 people *R Gloucestershire CC, ex p Barry*), domiciliary services for people with learning disabilities *R v Essex CC, ex p Bucke*), a care package for a young man with multiple sclerosis (*R v Haringey LBC, ex p Norton*), night sitter services for an elderly, arthritic woman with a weak bladder (*R v Staffordshire CC, ex p Farley*) – and so on.

The ability to withdraw or reduce services in the light of reworked policies and eligibility criteria – sanctioned both by guidance (see extracts above) and by the House of Lords in the *Gloucestershire* case – marks an apparent departure from a previous view sometimes repeated by central government. For example, in 1991 Alfred Morris MP had sought to confirm that 'for provision of a telephone to be withdrawn is unlawful without diminution in the need in any particular disabled pensioner's case'. In reply, the government stated: 'The right hon. Gentleman has correctly interpreted the law on the responsibilities of local authorities...' (Ann Widdecombe: HCOA,24/6/1991,col.667). Whilst intuitively attractive, the practical flaw in this approach is of course that provision could become drastically inequitable within a locality, if existing service users continue to receive a quantity and quality of service denied (under a changed policy) to new applicants. Conversely of course, it might seem just as inequitable to remove services on which vulnerable people have come to rely.

Writ large in practice, a review of services in a local authority might consist of reassessment, for example, of 3,474 recipients of home care services according to new criteria, resulting in 14 per cent of people losing their services, 42 per cent suffering a reduction but 44 per cent enjoying an increase (Audit Commission 1997b,p.36). Similarly, a review might involve 600 people partially or wholly losing services, and 175 people gaining more services or at least experiencing no change (*Community Care 1998d*).

Although both guidance and the courts sanction the withdrawal of services subject to certain safeguards, nevertheless authorities sometimes attempt to justify such withdrawal by 'rewriting history'. For instance, in *R v Haringey LBC, ex p Norton*, the authority appeared to argue that the reduction in the care package following reassessment was not as drastic as it appeared – because the original care package had not really been 'needed', but merely reflected the authority's generosity at the time. The courts are likely to tolerate such attempts only up to a point; generally, they are hostile to the submission of such retrospective explanations (*R v Westminster CC, ex p Ermakov*).

Review and reassessment: difficulties in carrying out

The high profile of the reviewing process afforded in guidance is in contrast to past practice. Some local authority services have in the past been unable to conduct reviews adequately. Practice guidance acknowledges that reviewing 'has traditionally been afforded a low priority' (SSI,SWSG 1991a, p.83) and subject to delay where it has taken place. This might account for a continuing tendency to treat monitoring and review as 'rubber stamping exercises' (SSI/NHSME 1994b,p.34), or for concern at the workload implications of comprehensive review systems (SSI 1994a, p.31). For instance, only a minority of people receiving home support services might be routinely reviewed (SSI 1996d,p.5); the position might be similar for those who leave hospital, even though one function of the review would be to check that services actually are in place (SSI 1998b,p.44). Even so, as some of the community care judicial review cases have shown, it does appear that if the purpose of review and reassessment is to reduce services overall and save money, authorities are more likely to find the resources to reassess than they would do otherwise.

It is reported that even if multi-disciplinary assessment involving the NHS is carried out when people first go into nursing and residential homes, it seldom, or at least only unsystematically, takes place once people are in care homes (Health Advisory Service 1997,p.11). Local authorities sometimes simply close a case when a person is in continuing receipt of a non-residential service, until the case is opened afresh if a re-referral is ever received (SSI 1997j,p.22; SSI 1997b,p.19). This can add to the anxieties of users of services – for instance, when the local authority fails to recognise the recurring nature of an illness such as HIV/AIDS (SSI 1994e,p.3). Indeed, not only does regular review of services give the local authority information about the progress of people on whom it is spending substantial sums of money – but it is also gives people (eg, residents in homes) the opportunity of continuing involvement in decisions about their way of life (SSI 1995k,p.16).

Review and reassessment: continuity of provision between authorities

During the passing of the NHS and Community Care Bill, Lord Kilmarnock unsuccessfully proposed an amendment to cover the situation where a person changed ordinary residence: 'any existing assessment shall apply in whichever local authority the person becomes resident for a period of 28 days in default of a new assessment'. The government resisted the amendment because it would be burdensome on local authorities and cause 'automatic continuation of treatment' even if inappropriate. Nevertheless, Baroness Blatch recognised that 'continuity of provision is essential' and that 'urgent treatment could be invoked if the person required care as a matter of urgency' (HLD,25/6/1990,col.1379).

CHAPTER 8

ASPECTS OF ASSESSMENT AND SERVICE PROVISION

Coverage

1. Carers: Carers (Recognition and Services) Act 1995
2. Carers: Disabled Persons (Services, Consultation and Representation) Act 1986
3. Ordinary residence
4. Capacity, vulnerability, decisions and choice
5. Lifting and handling
6. Disability discrimination
7. Human rights

KEY POINTS

This chapter covers a number of specific factors relevant to assessment and actual provision of services. First, the importance of the role of carers and of taking account of their needs was recognised explicitly in the Disabled Persons (Services, Consultation and Representation) Act 1986, and more recently and emphatically in the Carers (Recognition and Services) Act 1995.

Second, sometimes giving rise to dispute, particularly when a local authority thinks that there is a risk of incurring avoidable substantial expenditure, is the question of where a person is 'ordinarily resident' and which authority has financial responsibility.

Third, are a number of questions about the degree to which people are able to exercise choice, to have an informed say about their care needs and solutions, to be represented adequately by somebody else – or at least to have decisions made in their best interests by other people. At one extreme such questions affect people without mental capacity to make decisions about themselves and their care. At the other extreme are people perfectly well aware of what is going on but deprived of choice because of the limiting nature of a local authority's practice through policy, lack of resources or accident. Somewhere in the middle are those who cannot make a choice because they have no information and those who, although not lacking mental capacity, are vulnerable – that is they are unable to take care of themselves or unable to protect themselves from significant harm or serious exploitation.

Fourth, attention is increasingly being given to the impact of a) 1992 health and safety regulations governing manual handling; b) the continued implementation of the Disability Discrimination Act 1995 in respect of the provision of goods and services; and c) the forthcoming incorporation of the European Convention for the Protection of Human Rights and Fundamental Freedoms (ECHR) into United Kingdom domestic law.

I. CARERS: CARERS (RECOGNITION AND SERVICES ACT) 1995

The Carers (Recognition and Services) Act 1995 places a duty on local authorities to assess, on request, carers who provide a substantial amount of care on a regular basis. In some situations where the 1995 Act does not apply, there is a duty to have regard to the needs of carers under the Disabled Persons (Services, Consultation and Representation) Act 1986 (see below).

(NB. In February 1999, central government published a new national strategy on carers, cutting across various aspects of welfare and employment. In relation to local authorities in particular, it includes not only details of a new special grant for services for carers, but also an intention to pass new legislation which would remedy the two following deficiencies in the 1995 Act. Currently, carers can only benefit from an assessment if the person being cared for agrees to an assessment. In addition, the 1995 Act does not empower local authorities to make direct provision for carers (Prime Minister 1999,pp.57-60)).

EXTRACTS

Legislation (Carers (Recognition and Services) Act 1995, s.1) states:

(community care assessment) Where 'a local authority carry out an assessment under section 47(1)(a) of the NHS and Community Care Act 1990 of the needs of a person ("the relevant person"), and'

(substantial, regular care) 'an individual ("the carer") provides or intends to provide a substantial amount of care on a regular basis for the relevant person'

(request for an assessment) 'the carer may request the local authority, before they make their decision as to whether the needs of the relevant person call for the provision of any services, to carry out an assessment of his ability to provide and to continue to provide care for the relevant person;'

(duty to assess) 'and if he makes such a request, the local authority shall carry out such an assessment and shall take into account the results of that assessment in making that decision'.

(children) Where 'a local authority assess the needs of a disabled child for the purposes of Part III of the Children Act 1989 or section 2 of the Chronically Sick and Disabled Persons Act 1970, and

- **(substantial, regular care)** 'an individual ("the carer") provides or intends to provide a substantial amount of care on a regular basis for the disabled child'
- **(request for an assessment)** 'the carer may request the local authority, before they make their decision as to whether the needs of the disabled child call for the provision of any services, to carry out an assessment of his ability to provide and to continue to provide care for the disabled child;'
- **(duty to assess)** 'and if he makes such a request, the local authority shall carry out such an assessment and shall take into account the results of that assessment in making that decision'.

(prohibitions) 'No request may be made' for an assessment 'by an individual who provides or will provide the care in question – (a) by virtue of a contract of employment or other contract with any person; or (b) as a volunteer for a voluntary organisation'.

Policy guidance (DH 1996a) states:

(services for the carer?) 'The Act links the results of a carer's assessment to the local authority's decision about services for the user. The aim is to encourage an approach which considers support already available from family, friends or neighbours, the type of assistance needed by the person being assessed and how and whether current arrangements for care can sustain the user in the community. Many of the services which assist carers are provided to the user' (para 9).

(meaning of substantial care on a regular basis – and eligibility criteria) The 'terms "regular" and "substantial" ... should be interpreted in their everyday sense since Parliament has not provided otherwise in the Act ... It will be for local authorities to form their own judgement about what amounts to "regular" and "substantial" and to make their views known ... Local authorities should ensure that any eligibility criteria (or other statements) which describe levels of need which they will meet under community care legislation also reflect their responsibilities under this Act' (paras 10–12).

(young carers or parents of disabled children) 'Where the carer is either under 18 or the parent of a disabled child, local authorities should consider whether the Children Act 1989 applies' (para 13).

(information) 'Local authorities should ensure that their published information about community care tells carers about their rights under this Act ... [and] ensure that it becomes part of routine assessment practice to inform any carer who appears to be eligible under this Act of their right to request an assessment' (paras 19–20).

(assessment) 'The focus of the carer's assessment for the purposes of this Act should be on the carer's ability to care and to continue caring. The assessment should take account of the carer's circumstances, their age, views and preferences, the amount of support available to them. It should not automatically assume a willingness by the carer to continue caring, or to continue providing the same level of support' (para 21).

DISCUSSION

Carers (1995 Act): background

The NHS and Community Care Act 1990 does not refer to carers. However, policy guidance about that Act does state that carers could request assessments; whilst the Disabled Persons (Services, Consultation and Representation) Act 1986 had already, some years before, placed a duty on local authorities to 'have regard' to carers when they were assessing people under welfare legislation. Nevertheless, in 1995 a private member's Bill became law in the form of the Carers (Recognition and Services) Act 1995.

This addition to community care legislation followed the very considerable concern expressed about the needs of carers – given their numbers (estimated at over six million), the immense value of their care (estimated at £30 billion a year), their vulnerability to stress and physical injury, and the fact that their needs can differ from and even conflict with those of the people they are caring for. It has been pointed out that caring for a disabled or chronically sick person is unlike shorter term caring because a) it is a long-term responsibility; b) for parents of a disabled child it may be difficult to look forward to the future because of the fewer opportunities disabled people might have to lead independent lives; c) carers might be affected by the discrimination routinely shown to disabled people (Lamb, Layzell 1995a, p.2).

The need to protect and assist carers, given the apparently preferred community care policy of encouraging non-institutional care (DH 1990,para 3.24), was clear long before the passing of the 1995 Act. Apart from s.8 of the 1986 Act, attempts had been made in 1990 to amend the NHS and Community Care Bill. Baroness Seear had pointed out that 'a so-called carer had a right not to care', that a carer's needs might be different but just as heavy as those of the person being cared for, that carers required legal protection of their rights – and that a failure to achieve this would mean that the 1990 Act would have 'positively evil results' (HLD,3/4/1990,col.1376). Nevertheless, the government, though accepting 'the spirit' of such an amendment which required the assessment of carers, did not feel that it was 'appropriate to put such a provision on the face of the Bill' (Baroness Hooper: HLD,10/5/1990,cols.1555–1562).

Consideration of and assistance for carers, effective or otherwise, is not just the province of social services, since the NHS has a full role to play. However, it appears that it does not always fulfill it – for instance, in terms of help with caring, meeting carers' needs so as to prevent both physical and mental harm befalling them, provision of information, properly organised hospital discharges which do not place an excessive burden on ill-informed and poorly supported carers – and so on (Henwood 1998a).

Carers (1995 Act): assessment

The sponsor of the 1995 Act stated in Parliament that he did not envisage 'a social worker visiting a home with a clipboard and ticking or crossing boxes in a bureaucratic manner. That would be almost worse than useless, and insulting to the carer. I envisage that the social worker will visit and have a discussion with the carer, in which the carer can explain the difficulties and the life that she leads, often doing so not in the presence of the person being cared for' (Malcolm Wicks: HCD, 21/4/1995, col.431).

A report from the Social Services Inspectorate approvingly refers to the following checklist; the carer's perception of the situation; tasks undertaken; social contacts and other commitments; emotional, mental and physical health; impact on sleep patterns; information about breaks from caring; support required (SSI 1995a,p.12). In addition to information being given about the right to an assessment, it will also be important that information be provided about the options and services available to meet needs – since otherwise the participation in assessments by carers, and the taking account of their preferences and views (stipulated by the policy guidance: above), will be limited (SSI 1995c,p.33).

Carers might need a separate assessment in some circumstances, when, for example, they have their own needs and even more so when those needs conflict with the needs of the person being cared for. As Malcolm Wicks, sponsor of the 1995 Act, put it in Parliament, 'although a caring relationship is based on affection and love, one cannot be too romantic about it. Just as, in the horrible jargon, the "user" – the person being cared for – should have a right to an assessment with the social worker at which the carer is not present, so there should be a right for the carer to be able to sit down with the social worker and explain the position' (HCD,21/4/1995,col.431).

Even before the 1995 Act, local authorities in practice sometimes provided separate community care assessments for carers whose separate needs sometimes do conflict with those of 'users' (SSI 1993b,p.20). On the other hand, it was reported that many carers might find it difficult to obtain separate assessments (Warner 1994,p.48).

Carers (1995 Act): failure to ask or ineligibility for assessment

The duty to assess under the 1995 Act depends at least on a request by the carer and on his/her eligibility – although there in nothing to stop local authorities carrying out such assessments as part of a general community care assessment under s.47 of the NHS and Community Care Act 1990 (see policy guidance extract below). However, there is other legislation relevant to carers which might apply even if the 1995 Act does not (see below).

People's ability to make a request clearly depends on their knowledge of their entitlement, and this will only come with information (CNA 1997a,p.23). Therefore, policy guidance (see extract above) points out that information should be published generally and also given to individual carers at the time of assessment of the person being cared for. In addition, a failure to inform people might be seen by the local ombudsmen as an effective denial of a statutory right and as maladministration (much as they have found maladministration when local authorities conceal from council tenants their right to apply for disabled facilities grants: see p.404).

Insistence by local authorities on an over-formal request (eg, requiring that the Act be mentioned in the request, as opposed to acting on a general request for assistance by a carer) before offering and carrying out an assessment might not only be regarded as poor practice but even be criticised by the law courts (see eg, *R v Bexley, ex p B*, in relation to a request for a decision under the Disabled Persons (Services, Consultation and Representation) Act 1986).

A commonsense and helpful approach by local authorities would seem to be all the more important given that people might not only be unaware of the 1995 Act but a) not know what an 'assessment' is either before or after it has been carried out (see eg, Dearden, Becker 1998,p.63; CNA 1997a,p.32); or b) not think of themselves as carers (Fiedler 1996,p.15). Local authorities should also ensure that a purported *policy* about giving people information about assessment is effective; for instance, their claims about such policies might diverge substantially from the findings of a national voluntary organisation about what actually goes on in *practice* (CNA 1997a,p.31). To make matters worse, not only might carers be unaware of – and so be unable to ask about – available services during the assessment, but also staff might be unaware of the full range of services available for carers and users, for example, carers' support groups. And even if assessment is successfully carried out and a care plan drawn up by the local authority, the carer might never get to see it (SSI 1998g,p.22).

Furthermore, practice guidance from the Social Services Inspectorate (SSI) states that in the case of young carers (ie, child carers) who provide regular and substantial care but who do not request an assessment, the care manager 'should still consider whether there is a need to assist or relieve the child either through the provision of community care services for the user or through the provision of services to promote the welfare of the child' (SSI 1996c,p.11).

Carers (1995 Act): substantial care on a regular basis

A pre-condition for assessment is that the carer be providing, or intending to provide, a substantial amount of care on a regular basis. Policy guidance leaves it up to local authorities to decide what this means (see extract above). Practice guidance from the Social Services Inspectorate suggests that questions about the following may indicate whether such care is being given: a) the type of tasks undertaken; b) the time spent in providing assistance; c) the degree of supervision required by the person being cared for; d) whether the carer's commitment is or will be a continuing one (SSI 1996c,p.2). The requirement that care be provided on a substantial and regular basis perhaps reflects the fact that although a commonly quoted figure is that there are six million carers, a better view might be that there are about 1.3 million carers heavily involved in caring activities (Parker 1992).

It has been suggested that taking account only of the time spent takes too narrow an approach in determining what is 'substantial', since 'the impact of providing care is different from carer to carer and what is substantial to one person may not be to another'; and that 'regular' does not necessarily connote 'frequent' (Clements, Ruan 1997,p.15). Practice guidance from the Social Services Inspectorate states that indicative of a 'heavily involved carer' might be a person who puts in long hours, performs a range of helping activities, provides both personal and physical assistance, cares for a person in the same household, cares for someone with a mental impairment and cares without help from anybody else (SSI 1996c,p.16).

Local authorities are faced with the dilemma of adopting generous criteria with attendant resource implications, or tighter criteria which might have the effect of reducing preventative, in favour of crisis, intervention; in which case the assistance might come too late and a person be left feeling, 'perhaps I did not get hysterical enough' (SSI 1995m,p.24). In practice, it appears that many local authorities base their criteria on a list, originally used by one particular local authority to determine whether to assess a carer separately and referred to in a report by the Social Services Inspectorate. These are: a) providing long hours of care (eg, 20 hours); b) no assistance from other people; c) living in the same household; d) carrying out physical tasks, personal care and a wide range of duties; e) over 75 or under 18 years old; f) ill or disabled; g) supporting someone with dementia, Alzheimer's disease, a severe mental health problem or learning disabilities (SSI 1995c,p.27). However, unclear in a survey of local authorities was the extent to whether eligibility was triggered by only a single criterion, or whether a combination of criteria was required (CNA 1997a,p.36). Furthermore, there was considerable disparity from authority to authority: some examples of how 'regular and substantial' were defined included a) entirely flexible depending on individual circumstances, b) eligibility for a comprehensive assessment by the person being cared for, c) receipt of Invalid Care Allowance (ie, a minimum of 35 hours per week of care being given), d) 10 hours a week including personal care, e) 14 hours a week, f) withdrawal of care would mean residential care home admission – and so on (p.37).

Nevertheless, if this is a general picture, some carers might still be told that they are not eligible for assessment because they are considered a low priority (despite providing 100 hours of care a week), the budget has run out, nothing can be done if the person being cared for is not terminally ill and does not live alone, there are not enough social workers – or the assessment is not worth the trouble since there is no duty to act on it (CNA 1997b,p.19).

Carers (1995 Act): young carers

A young carer has been defined by the Social Services Inspectorate as 'a child or young person who is carrying out significant caring tasks and assuming a level of responsibility for another person which would usually be taken by an adult. The term refers to children or young people under 18 years caring for adults (usually their parents) or occasionally siblings. It does not refer to young people under 18 years caring for their own children. Nor does the term refer to those children who accept a role appropriate to their age when taking an increasing responsibility for household tasks in homes with a disabled, sick or mentally ill parent' (CI(95)12). It has been suggested that children who are carers should automatically be assumed to be 'children in need', so that they could receive services in their own right under s.17 of the Children Act 1989, whilst the adults being cared for would receive services under s.47 of the NHS and Community Care Act 1990 (Dearden, Becker 1998).

Carers (1995 Act): caring tasks and useful services
Caring might typically revolve the following types of task: help with personal care (dressing, bathing etc), physical help (walking, getting out of bed, stairs etc), paperwork and finances, practical help (meals, shopping, housework etc), keeping company, taking the person out, keeping an eye on, help with medicines/dressings, care of siblings (SSI 1996c,p.15; Walker 1996,p.7).

Carers (1995) Act: duty to assess but not to provide for carers
It will be noted that the duty to assess carers does not include a subsequent duty to provide services for them; and this can lead to the sort of comment made in one judicial review case that simply making an assessment under the 1995 Act 'does not get anyone anywhere' (*R v Kirklees MBC, ex p Good*), or in another that a formal assessment will not necessarily help matters when everyone knows what is required, but it is simply not immediately available (*R v Lambeth LBC, ex p A*).

Nevertheless, in many cases, a service provided for the user will also serve the carer; for example, respite care (sitting services, residential care, day centre attendance, short breaks sometimes in the form of holidays etc), equipment and adaptations, resource centres, information, counselling and home support services. As the government put it during the passing of the 1995 Act, an 'integrated approach should enhance the carer's ability to provide care as well as the independence of the person whom they are looking after' (Baroness Cumberlege: HLD,17/5/1995,col.643).

An ultimately unsuccessful amendment to the NHS and Community Care Bill sought to ensure that authorities would consider 'the particular need for respite care if requested to do so by the person being assessed or by a person who has the responsibility of caring for the person being assessed'. The government responded that highlighting in the legislation one particular form of care would be unhelpful and could discourage innovation (HLD,14/6/1990,cols.520–522).

Carers (1995 Act): resources
As ever, the ability of local authorities to embrace duties positively and effectively hinges in part on the availability of resources; and it was pointed out during the passing of the Carers (Recognition and Services) Bill that 'if local authorities genuinely cannot afford to provide proper practical support, the carer may be little better off' (Baroness Jay: HLD,17/5/1995,col.640).

One example given in debate was of a 17-year-old woman who was 'still trying to finish her studies at the local college, but when she approached the social work department to ask whether her grandmother could have some rails in her bathroom, she was told that as she, the carer, was now present in the home, all her grandmother's home care would be withdrawn. The 17-year-old explained that, although she was helping in the evenings, she was out at college all day and could not provide support in the daytime. She was told that her grandmother was now low priority as she was no longer alone, and that going to college was her choice, which she could give up if it was too difficult. Her needs and right to study were entirely disregarded' (Malcolm Wicks: HCD,21/4/1995,cols.429–430).

On the issue of resources, Malcolm Wicks also suggested that a local authority which cuts social services spending but employs a play development officer and dance development officer, and spends £40,000 on keeping a public library open on Sunday afternoons had its priorities wrong – when one considered the needs of carers and those cared for (HCD,21/4/1995,col.438). Nevertheless, the government did not 'ring-fence' resources for the 1995 Act, although its message to social services departments was that it was 'not good enough' for the arrival of a carer to signal the withdrawal of services; authorities 'should not assume anything; they should check that carers can cope, and that support for the user ensures their ability to do so'. Otherwise 'they may find that they must take on the whole responsibility' (John Bowis: HCD,21/4/1995,col.465). Yet it has been precisely the harsh judgements by local authorities about who is at greatest risk that has led to increased burdens on carers when services are denied and withdrawn (Henwood 1995,p.14).

Carers (1995) Act: other legislation relevant to carers

In addition to the 1995 Act, there is other legislation relevant to carers.

First, a decision under s.47 of the NHS and Community Care Act 1990 about whether a person's needs call for community care services to be arranged can only sensibly be made at all by taking account of a person's home environment and social circumstances – including the existence and role of carers. Second, services provided ostensibly for the user might well be for the carer as well; for instance, a hoist loaned under s.2 of the Chronically Sick and Disabled Persons Act 1970 to enable the user to get in and out of bed or bath, will also save a carer's back. Third, carers might qualify in their own right for a community care assessment under s.47 of the NHS and Community Care Act 1990. Community care policy guidance states that: 'Most support for vulnerable people is provided by families, friends and neighbours. The assessment will need to take account of the support that is available from such carers ... The preferences of carers should be taken into account and their willingness to continue caring should not be assumed. Both service users and carers should therefore be consulted – separately, if either of them wishes – since their views may not coincide ... Carers who feel they need community care services in their own right can ask for a separate assessment. This could arise if the care plan of the person for whom they care does not, in their view, adequately address the carer's own needs' (DH 1990,paras 3.28–3.29).

Fourth, when making a decision under s.4 of the Disabled Persons' (Services, Consultation and Representation) Act 1986, local authorities have a duty to have regard to the carer's ability to continue caring (see below). There are various distinctions between the provisions of the 1986 Act and the 1995 Act (see below). The 1986 Act does not apply if an assessment is carried out under the 1995 Act. Fifth, the NHS Act 1977, schedule 8 refers to provision of home help and laundry facilities for 'households' (including carers), required because of the presence of somebody who is ill, lying-in, an expectant mother, aged or disabled (see p.215). Sixth, young carers might come under s.17 of the Children Act 1989 – which imposes a duty to promote and safeguard the welfare of 'children in need' – and so receive services and support in their own right (rather than as carers). Their parents might also qualify for provision under s.17 of the 1989 Act, since services to safeguard and promote the welfare of a child in need may be provided not only for the child, but for the family as a whole or any particular member of the family.

Finally, community care policy guidance states that local authorities can continue 'to use their powers in paragraph 2(1) of schedule 8 of the NHS Act 1977 [see p.216] supplemented by section 111 of the Local Government Act 1972 to provide or support services such as carer support groups and information. Such services should be available to all carers without requiring an assessment' (DH 1996a,para 5).

2. CARERS: DISABLED PERSONS (SERVICES, CONSULTATION AND REPRESENTATION) ACT 1986

Almost ten years before the advent of the Carers (Recognition and Services) Act 1995, the Disabled Persons (Services, Consultation and Representation) Act 1986 had placed a duty on local authorities to have regard to carers in certain circumstances. The 1986 Act is expressly disapplied if the 1995 Act applies (see s.1 of the 1995 Act).

EXTRACTS

Legislation (Disabled Persons (Services, Consultation and Representation) Act 1986 states that where:

> **(substantial care)** 'a disabled person is living at home and receiving a substantial amount of care on a regular basis from another person (who is not a person employed to provide such care by any body in the exercise of its functions under any enactment), and'

> **(assessment)** 'it falls to a local authority to decide whether the disabled person's needs call for the provision by them of any services for him under any of the welfare enactments' (ie, under s.4 of the 1986 Act)

> **(ability of carer)** 'the local authority shall, in deciding that question, have regard to the ability of that other person to continue to provide such care on a regular basis' (s.8).

> **(welfare enactments)** The welfare enactments referred to above are defined as the National Assistance Act 1948, s.29; the Chronically Sick and Disabled Persons Act 1970, s.2; the NHS Act 1977, Schedule 8; and Part 3 of the Children Act 1989 (s.16).

Circular guidance (LAC(87)6,para 6) states that although s.8 of the Disabled Persons (Services, Consultation and Representation) Act 1986:

> 'places no specific requirement on the local authority to provide services or support for the carer, authorities will no doubt continue as part of normal good practice to have regard to the possible need for such services and to the desirability of enabling the disabled person to continue living at home for as long as possible if this is what he or she wishes to do'.

DISCUSSION

Carers (1986 Act): 1986 and 1995 Acts compared

The various distinctions between the 1986 and 1995 Acts have been helpfully summarised (Clements, Ruan 1997,p.21) as follows.

First, under the 1986 Act no request by the carer is necessary. Second, under the 1986 Act the local authority must 'have regard' to the ability of the carer; whereas under the 1995 Act, it must carry out an assessment. Third, under the 1986 Act, employees of statutory services are excluded from the definition of 'carer' (but perhaps not employees of voluntary organisations and not volunteers). Under the 1995 Act, employees of voluntary organisations and volunteers are excluded. Fourth, the 1986 Act applies – at least on its face – only when a carer is already providing care; whereas the 1995 Act refers explicitly also to an intention to provide care. Fifth, the 1986 Act does not apply to community care services under s.117 of the Mental Health Act 1983 or to s.45 of the Health Services and Public Health Act 1968 – whereas the 1995 Act does. Lastly, the 1986 Act applies only when a disabled person is receiving care; but the 1995 Act applies to a person receiving (or going to receive) care who is disabled, ill, or elderly.

3. ORDINARY RESIDENCE

Some local authority obligations to provide community care services (both residential and non-residential) depend on whether a person is 'ordinarily resident' in the authority's area. If a person is not ordinarily resident, then the duties do not exist – or might be converted to powers; that is authorities can provide the services if they want to but don't have to (see p.48).

Local authorities have sometimes even argued that they have no obligation to assess a person who is not an ordinary resident of the area, because there could never be a duty (at least under some legislation) to make provision. However, the courts have confirmed that even where there is at most only a legal power to provide a service, authorities have a duty to assess if the conditions under s.47 of the NHS and Community Care Act 1990 are met (ie, there is an appearance of possible need for community care services).

Should a dispute arise about where a person really lives, Circular guidance makes it clear that assessment and service provision should anyway not be delayed or prevented. The decision about which of two authorities is responsible for arranging and paying for services should be made afterwards. In addition, directions state that if a person's need is urgent, a local authority cannot refuse to provide residential accommodation on grounds that the person is not 'ordinarily resident' in its area (see p.253).

If a person has housing needs and a housing authority becomes involved as well as the social services department, there is some scope for uncertainty because the social services and housing tests for 'ordinary residence' differ.

EXTRACTS

Legislation (National Assistance Act 1948,s.24) states in respect of the provision of residential accommodation under s.21 of the National Assistance Act 1948:

(relevant local authority) the local authority is empowered to provide residential accommodation is the authority in the area of which the person is ordinarily resident (s.24(1));

(people with no settled residence, or not ordinarily resident in the area but in urgent need) a local authority has a power to provide residential accommodation a) for people with no settled residence and b) for people ordinarily resident elsewhere but who are in urgent need of accommodation (s.24(3));

(people ordinarily resident in the area of another authority) a local authority has a power to provide residential accommodation for a person ordinarily resident in the area of another authority – with the consent of that authority (s.24(4));

(ordinary residence immediately before entry into residential accommodation) where a person is provided with residential accommodation, he or she is deemed to be ordinarily resident in the area in which he or she was ordinarily resident immediately before the residential accommodation was provided (s.24(5));

(NHS patients) an NHS patient is deemed to be ordinarily resident in the area he or she was living in immediately before entering hospital (s.24(6)).

These general provisions have to be read in the light of the specific directions and approvals made under s.21 of the National Assistance Act 1948 in respect of residential accommodation (see p.253).

DISCUSSION

Ordinary residence: community care legislation affected

Legislation which is affected by the ordinary residence condition comprises the National Assistance Act 1948 (s.21: provision of residential accommodation; and s.29: welfare services) and the Chronically Sick and Disabled Persons Act 1970 (s.2: welfare services).

For instance, what might be a duty towards an 'ordinary resident' might be a power (discretion) only towards a non-resident of the area: see directions and approvals made under ss.21 and 29 of the 1948 Act see pp.193 and 253) – whilst s.2 of the Chronically Sick and Disabled Persons Act 1970 extends only to ordinary residents, there not being even a power (under s.2) to provide those services to people who are not ordinarily resident.

Ordinary residence: meaning of 'ordinarily resident'

There is no statutory definition of 'ordinarily resident' and it is ultimately for the courts to decide what it means. Guidance states that the 'the term should be given its ordinary and natural meaning subject to any interpretation by the Courts. The concept of ordinary residence involves questions of fact and degree, and factors such as time, intention and continuity, each of which may be given different weight according to the context, have to be taken into account' (LAC(93)7,para 2). A number of court cases which have considered 'ordinary residence' are cited (paras 12,13): *R v Barnet LBC, ex p Shah* ('abode in a particular place or country which he had adopted voluntarily and for settled purposes as part of the regular order of his life for the time being, whether of short or long duration'); *Levene v IRC* ('residence in a place with some degree of continuity and apart from accidental or temporary absences'); and *R v Waltham Forest LBC, ex p Vale and R v Redbridge LBC ex p East Sussex CC 1992* (about people with learning difficulties making choices as to residence).

More recently, *R v Lambeth LBC, ex p Caddell* considered a dispute about responsibility under the Children Act 1989 for a young man who had reached 18 years old and had moved between authorities.

Ordinary residence: disputes affecting services

Uncertainty and disputes between authorities about ordinary residence sometimes arise. However, Circular guidance states that delay in assessment and service provision should not occur: 'If there is a dispute about the ordinary residence of a person in need of services it should be debated after the care assessment and any provision of service' (LAC(93)7,summary and para 3). However, this guidance might be of little help to the person concerned if there is no duty in issue (wherever ordinary residence is eventually located), since both authorities concerned might simply maintain that in any case they are not obliged to do anything.

Ordinary residence: homelessness and housing issues

Social services and housing authorities apply different tests to establish the 'ordinary residence' of homeless people. There is some concern that without good cooperation this could lead to confusion.

The test for 'local connection' in the context of homelessness legislation is to be found in s.199 of the Housing Act 1996 and covers normal residence (past or present), employment, family associations or special circumstances. Guidance states that when 'a person states that he has no settled residence or describes himself as NFA (no fixed abode) the social services authority where he presents himself should normally accept responsibility. For a person in urgent need, the social services authority of the moment cannot argue that the possible existence of a "local connection" elsewhere excuses it from the duty to assess and provide any necessary social services; decisions on where the responsibility for the funding of such services rests, based on ordinary residence, should be decided subsequently. Rules for determining responsibility under Housing Acts should not be used to identify ordinary residence for social purposes. Any outstanding ordinary residence questions should be clearly recorded in social services records at the time they arise. Failure to do this may prejudice subsequent consideration' (LAC(93)7,para 16).

It continues: '"Local connection" for housing purposes ... may be established by present or past settled residence in an area, by employment in that area, by family connections, or other special circumstances. Where the test of "local connection" results in the transfer of responsibility for securing accommodation to another housing authority, the social services authority will wish to consider where "ordinary residence" then rests. The homelessness legislation provides that, where a person has no local connection, the duties to provide accommodation rest with the housing authority to whom he first applies. Even if a housing authority suspects that a person may have a local connection elsewhere, this does not absolve it from an initial duty to provide temporary accommodation if the immediate circumstances require it, pending the transfer of responsibility to another housing authority' (para 17).

Ordinary residence: people in hospital, nursing homes, prison and similar establishments

Legislation states that people in hospital are to be regarded as ordinarily resident in the area (if any) they were ordinarily resident in before entering hospital (National Assistance Act 1948,s.24(6)).

Circular guidance suggests that local authorities 'could reasonably apply this approach when considering responsibility for people leaving prisons, resettlement units and other similar establishments without a permanent place to live who will require social services involvement at the time of their discharge. No case law exists however, and any dispute must be resolved in the light of the specific circumstances' (LAC(93)7, para 14).

Ordinary residence: resolution of disputes

Circular guidance refers to the fact that disputes about ordinary residence under Part III of the National Assistance Act are ultimately to be determined by the Secretary of State, as stated by s.32(3) of the 1948 Act. Disputes about ordinary residence could be in relation to responsibility for non-residential, as well as residential services. The guidance states that each case has to be considered on its own facts; that the Secretary of State's decision is final subject only to judicial review; that the question of establishing ordinary residence is essentially a legal one; and that authorities must have agreed provisional liability for service provision before the dispute is referred to the Secretary of State. The guidance describes the procedure to be followed by local authorities (paras LAC(93)7,paras 24–28).

When the National Assistance Bill was passed, the government foresaw that, although conditions as to ordinary residence did not revive the old law of settlement, nevertheless 'to some extent the problems of the old law of settlement cannot be avoided … Granted good will on the part of authorities nearly all cases will be amicably settled' but otherwise the Minister would determine any disputed case (John Edwards: SC(c),22/1/1948,col.2535).

Ordinary residence: after-care under Mental Health Act 1983

The Secretary of State's powers of dispute resolution under s.32 of the National Assistance Act 1948 do not apply to s.117 of the Mental Health Act 1983 (after-care for discharged patients) (LAC (93)7,para 24).

Ordinary residence: responsible health authority for giving consent to placements in nursing homes

Legislation (statutory instrument) governs how health authorities, responsible for giving consent for an individual to enter a nursing home, are to be identified by local authorities when seeking consent for nursing home placements under s.26 of the National Assistance Act 1948 (SI 1992/3182 as amended by SI 1993/582). The rules appear straightforward. In case of doubt the local authority should accept the address given by the person as the address at which he usually lives. If the person doesn't give such a usual address but gives instead his or her most recent address, then that address should be accepted. If the person gives neither a usual nor a most recent address, then the responsible health authority is identified simply by wherever the person is at the time.

Ordinary residence: responsible health authority for health care

The same basic method outlined immediately above is used also to identify the responsible health authority for providing health care (in general) to people (SI 1991/554; see also LAC(93)7,para 18); guidance from the NHSME (1993), due to be reissued in April 1999, provides more detail in relation to particular categories of patient.

Ordinary residence: responsible health authority for people in residential/nursing homes

Circular guidance states that if a person is placed permanently in residential accommodation outside the person's usual health authority, then responsibility transfers to the authority in whose area the home is situated. If the placement is temporary then the original DHA normally retain responsibility (LAC(93)7,para 20). This could mean then that whilst people's social services authority remains the same (ie, the original placing authority), their health authority does not.

However, additional guidance (NHSME 1993, due to be revised in April 1999) elaborates further, dealing amongst other things with a) jointly funded placements; b) total funding by a health authority; and c) rules about courses of treatment for people in residential or nursing home care who are undergoing a course of treatment.

First: 'There may be situations where a placement is jointly funded by the local authority and the DHA of usual residence. If this jointly funded placement is outside the district of usual residence, then the original DHA remains responsible for funding its proportion of the placement cost. However, the DHA responsible for health care costs not associated directly with the placement is the DHA where the `home' is situated ... The new DHA is immediately responsible for the health care needs of people moving into residential care or nursing homes (as it is for anybody else)...' (pp.11–12).

Second: 'If a placement is funded totally by the health authority, then for residence purposes it is regarded as equivalent to continuing in-patient care. It follows, therefore, that the district in which the patient was resident on the date of admission to in-patient care remains responsible' (p.12).

Third, if a person 'who is undergoing a course of treatment as an in-patient changes their home address during that course of treatment, they shall be treated as usually resident at the address at which they were usually resident when the course of treatment began until they cease to be an in-patient'. Similarly, where an out-patient changes home address 'during that course of treatment, they shall be treated as usually resident at the address at which they were usually resident when the course of treatment began until a trigger date is reached'. A trigger date is a) three months after the change of address; b) 1st April following the change of address; or c) the course of treatment is completed – whichever occurs first (p.15). (There are separate rules for GP fundholder patients, although the imminent demise of fundholding means that they will presumably not apply in the future).

4. CAPACITY, VULNERABILITY, DECISIONS AND CHOICE

At present, many relatives, carers and sometimes professionals find themselves handling the affairs of a person who no longer appears to be able to handle their own. The law governing such situations is complex and regarded by many as unsatisfactory. However, in summary the following are the practical possibilities.

Where a person still retains capacity, arrangements which can be made include third party mandates in respect of bank or building society accounts; putting accounts into joint names; having another person act as agent to collect social security benefits for the recipient. When capacity has been lost, a system of formal appointeeship exists whereby another person can be appointed by the Benefits Agency to receive social security benefits on behalf of the person who has lost capacity.

Other formal arrangements can entail a person acting with an enduring power of attorney; so called because it persists even when the donor of the powers is no longer able to manage his or her affairs. However, the power can only be created in the first place if, at the time the power is signed, the donor knows what is going on. Therefore if a person loses mental capacity before a power has been signed, it is too late to create one. In which case, it might be necessary for somebody to apply to the Court of Protection, which looks after and manages the affairs of people with a mental disorder, who can no longer do so themselves (Letts 1998).

However, it should be noted that both an enduring power of attorney and the Court of Protection are limited to dealing with financial and property affairs, but not personal and health care matters. This means that neither the informal nor formal options mentioned above sanction the making of decisions (by relatives, cares etc) about personal or health care matters on behalf of somebody else. It is vaguely assumed and hoped that such decisions are made in the person's best interests. However, this situation, without clear procedures or legal rules applying, can put both the person without capacity at risk of abuse – and well-intentioned carers or relatives who are making difficult decisions at risk of accusation of abuse. As far as local authorities are concerned, their power in the National Assistance Act 1948 to remove people from their homes in certain circumstances is regarded as both too limited and too blunt a tool.

All this has led to increasing concern about how decisions are made in relation to a) people who are deemed to lack mental capacity, and b) people who are vulnerable (ie, people who are at risk of potential harm or abuse of various types) and the degree to which decisions are made in their best interests. Consequently, a number of papers published by the Law Commission culminating in an overview paper (Law Commission 1995) have been followed by a government Green Paper, *Who decides*, consulting about possible legislation (Lord Chancellor 1997). Some of the concerns and possible solutions are roughly summarised below.

EXTRACTS
Not applicable.

DISCUSSION

Capacity, vulnerability: removal of people

Under s.47 of the National Assistance 1948, local authorities can by order of a magistrate remove to institutional care people who a) 'are suffering from grave chronic disease or, being aged, infirm or physically incapacitated, are living in insanitary conditions; and b) are unable to devote to themselves, and are not receiving from other persons, proper care and attention'. It must be necessary to remove the person either in his or her own best interests, or for prevention of injury to the health of, or serious nuisance to, other people. However, the person does not have to be mentally incapacitated or mentally disordered for s.47 to operate. Seven days notice is required – but this can be dispensed with under the National Assistance (Amendment) Act 1951.

This power has been criticised a) as limited because of the particular conditions stipulated, b) as at the same time draconian, and c) as relatively little used (perhaps about 200 times a year). Environmental health legislation enabling local authority intervention on other grounds includes the Environmental Protection Act 1990, ss.79–82 covering filthy or verminous premises or people; and the Public Health Act 1936, s.83 covering filthy or unwholesome premises, and s.36 fumigation (Law Commission 1993,pp.15–16).

Capacity, vulnerability: guardianship for people with learning disabilities

The use of guardianship under s.7 of the Mental Health Act 1983 cannot be used for many people with learning disabilities. This is because the definitions of mental impairment and severe mental impairment, either one a condition for guardianship, refer not only to significant or severe impairment of intelligence but also to 'abnormally aggressive or seriously irresponsible conduct'. This exclusion of many people with learning disabilities might have been unintentional and is thought not to be desirable, since guardianship could be a helpful way of enabling people to live in the community (eg, Law Commission 1993,p.19).

Capacity, vulnerability: determining mental capacity

The favoured common law test for mental capacity is the 'functional' approach, focusing on a particular decision and whether a person is capable of making it (ie, understanding its nature and implications) at the time. This contrasts with the 'status' or 'outcome' approach, which measures capacity according to the general mental health status or to the outcome of a decision respectively (Law Commission 1995,p.33).

The functional approach also emphasises the particular decision; a person might be able to make some decisions but not others, and incapacity in one type of situation does not necessarily imply incapacity in another. For instance, a person might be able to make decisions about day-to-day matters such as what to eat, but be unable to deal with a complex decision such as whether to enter a nursing home (Age Concern England 1994b,p.23).

Capacity, vulnerability: ability to communicate

The Law Commission proposed that people should not be regarded as unable to communicate decisions unless 'all practicable steps' have been taken; the government has queried how to define 'all practicable steps' (Law Commission 1995,p.40).

Capacity, vulnerability: people's best interests

It is widely agreed that decisions made on behalf of a person without mental capacity should be in that person's best interests. The Law Commission has proposed that these interests might be identified in relation to a) ascertainable past and present wishes and factors a person would have considered; b) the need to encourage the person to participate as fully as possible in decisions; c) the views of other people whom it is appropriate and practical to consult with about best interests; and d) achieving the purpose of an action or decision by means which least restrict the freedom of action of the person (Law Commission 1995,pp.44–45).

In practice, ascertaining a person's best interests or the appropriate people to make the decision might not be straightforward. For instance, in Re S the mistress of a man who had suffered a stroke and was unable to communicate clashed with his family about where the man should be cared for. And in R v Bournewood NHS Trust, ex p L, the House of Lords ruled (overturning the Court of Appeal's decision) that the common law doctrine of necessity justified a decision by the NHS Trust to admit informally (ie, bypassing the compulsory, statutory detention procedures) to hospital and there to treat, in his own best interests, a man unable to give consent to what was happening to him.

Capacity, vulnerability: protection of incapable person and carers

It has been suggested that a 'general authority' to act reasonably needs to be recognised legally to cover all the many actions and decisions made by carers, family members, care professionals, and so on, on behalf of people without capacity. At present, there is concern both that the people without capacity are at risk of some form of abuse (eg, financial, physical, psychological) and that equally carers might have no legal protection, since the basis on which they have been acting might not be legally recognised. This concern applies not only to informal carers, but also to local authority staff who might be assisting in the management of the finances of a service user (eg, who has dementia) without reference to the legal position and without any guidance from the local authority (SSI 1997b,p.23).

Such a general authority would make lawful the doing of 'anything for the personal welfare or health care of a person who is, or is reasonably believed to be, without capacity in relation to the matter in question if it is in all the circumstances reasonable for it to be done by the person who does it' (Law Commission 1995,pp.50–51).

Nevertheless, in practice, matters get complicated; for instance, when decisions about the funding of long-term care have to be taken, the person concerned is mentally frail and his or best interests compete with the concern of the rest of the family about their inheritance (Ashton 1995a). Financial abuse might involve large sums of money being signed over by elderly people; alternatively it might involve relatives as appointees for state benefits (see below) not handing over all the money or, for example, buying cheap clothes and a minimum of food so as to save some of the money for themselves. On the other hand, it has also been pointed out that financial abuse of elderly people without capacity is likely in the majority of cases to be due to the inadequacy of the present legal and administrative framework rather than to the fraudulent intent of carers and professionals. For instance, how does a social worker decide whether the family's opposition to a person entering a nursing home is based on fear of inheritance loss or on strong feelings about the suitability of nursing home care (Langan, Means 1995,pp.13,44–45). Even where there is abuse, it might be more helpful sometimes to see it not in terms of victim and perpetrator but 'taking place within the changing context of family or social relationships' (SSI 1992a,p.6).

People with an enduring power of attorney (see immediately below) might commit abuse, a possibility increased by the lack of supervision by the Court of Protection even in the case of registered powers of attorney (and only one in twenty enduring powers are thought to be registered). However, as already discussed, there might be difficulty in identifying what constitutes abuse and taking action to stop it. For instance, it has been asked whether it is in the donor's interests for the attorney, often a close relative, to be prosecuted for theft, or for civil proceedings to be undertaken in order to recover money which the attorney might anyway inherit. Similarly, the police might be reluctant to intervene if the attorney is a close family member because a) they regard it as a domestic problem better suited to civil than criminal justice, and b) it might be difficult to distinguish a criminal act from an act which goes merely beyond the scope of the enduring power of attorney. Solicitors in turn might be reluctant to do anything in case, having initially advised on the creation of the power of attorney, they are held responsible for the subsequent abuse (Lush 1998).

Capacity, vulnerability: enduring powers of attorney and Court of Protection

Currently, people can create an enduring power of attorney (EPA), by appointing a person to look after their property and financial affairs from the point when they lose mental capacity. It has been proposed that a continuing power of attorney (CPA) be available instead, which a) would cover personal and health care matters as well as property and finance, and b) would not preclude the donor still acting in situations where he or she was capable: ie, it need not be an 'all or nothing' power.

Similarly, when there is no enduring power of attorney and the Court of Protection (or Public Trust Office) steps in to deal with property and finance matters, it has been proposed that for the future financial, personal welfare and health care matters should all be covered (Law Commission 1995,part 7).

Capacity, vulnerability: people at risk and public law protection

The Law Commission identified that not only might people without mental capacity require public law protection from abuse and neglect, but also vulnerable people with capacity. For the purposes of public law protection, it defined a vulnerable person, with or without mental capacity, as 'any person of 16 or over who (1) is or may be in need of community care services by reason of mental or other disability, age or illness and who (2) is or may be unable to take care of himself or herself or unable to protect himself or herself against significant harm or exploitation' (Law Commission 1995,p.159).

It proposed that local authority social services departments should have an additional duty to investigate if they had reason to believe that a vulnerable person was suffering or likely to suffer harm or serious exploitation. In some circumstances, this might lead to applications for measures such as entry warrants, assessment orders, removal (from home) orders, temporary protection orders (Law Commission 1995,part 9). The government has expressed some reservations about these proposals (Lord Chancellor 1997, Chapter 8).

Capacity, vulnerability: appointeeship

There is concern about the system of appointeeship, where there is perceived lax control by the Department of Social Security about who acts as appointee to receive a person's state benefits – for instance, where an appointee is the proprietor of a residential or nursing home and collects on behalf of the resident (Law Commission 1995,pp.58–59).

Capacity, vulnerability: contracting for necessaries

At present, the common law ensures that if 'necessaries' (goods or services) are supplied to people without capacity, suppliers have a right to receive a reasonable price, whether or not they knew of a person's incapacity. Necessaries are basic necessities suitable to a person's condition in life and requirements at the time of supply. The Sale of Goods Act 1979 currently contains this rule in respect of goods; the Law Commission proposed that the rule be clarified for both goods and services in new legislation (Law Commission 1995,para 4.9).

Capacity, vulnerability: choice in practice

Even for a person not lacking mental capacity, or vulnerable in the sense used by the Law Commission, the ability of a person to make a decision about what is wanted does not, in community care, mean that he or she will get it. This is particularly so given not only an absence of appropriate services in some instances to meet people's needs, but also a lack of resources on the part of local authorities.

For instance, in *R v Lancashire CC, ex p RADAR*, the Court of Appeal ruled that in order to save money a local authority could insist that it would provide care for a woman via a nursing home rather than in her own home – although this was against her wishes. It has also been pointed out that an individual with money, whose care needs have not been properly assessed and who is vulnerable to the self-interest of others, might fare no worse than the person dependent on local authority funding, whose personal care needs have been assessed, but who is vulnerable to a lack of resources to meet them. The former is more likely to suffer financial abuse, but both types of person might have arrangements 'corrupted by financial restraints' (Ashton 1995b).

Hospitals sometimes discharge people prematurely, do not tell them that they have a right to a review of the decision, do not tell them about possible options once they have been discharged, and do not ensure that adequate home care arrangements are in place. In such circumstances, it is arguable that people are given little choice (SSI 1995k,p.12; Godfrey, Moore 1996,p.45). Indeed, many elderly people might perceive the decision that they enter a residential home as made, not by themselves, but by family or care workers (Smith 1994). Similarly, elderly people might be unable to choose which tasks a home help service should tackle, because a local authority's policy excludes what it considers to be non-essential tasks (eg, Collyer 1992; Clark, Dyer and Horwood 1998,p.21). So, a person's need for a downstairs bathroom might be considered, but not a preference for help with the garden (Midgley, Munlo and Brown 1997,p.22). Thus, rather than exercising meaningful choice, perhaps the best that some people can hope for is to know what is going on, rather than make informed decisions about what they want to do.

5. LIFTING AND HANDLING

Given the danger and level of back injuries suffered by carers, both professional and unprofessional, lifting and handling legal issues are of great significance to employers and staff in both the statutory and independent sectors, to self-employed care assistants and not least to those people being lifted and handled. These issues have been given a sharper edge by specific health and safety legislation in the form of the Manual Handling Operations Regulations 1992. The following paragraphs outline some of the issues, and refer to a number of legal judgments dealing with civil liability either under the Regulations or under the common law of negligence.

EXTRACTS

Legislation (SI 1992/2793) states that:

(avoidance of injury) 'Each employer shall

(a) so far as is reasonably practicable, avoid the need for his employees to undertake any manual handling operations at work which involve a risk of their being injured;

(b) where it is not reasonably practicable to avoid the need for his employees to undertake any manual handling at work which involve a risk of their being injured

    (i) make a suitable and sufficient assessment of all such manual handling operations to be undertaken by them, having regard to the factors which are specified ... and considering the questions which are specified...'

    (ii) take appropriate steps to reduce the risk of injury to those employees arising out of their undertaking any such manual handling operations to the lowest level reasonably practicable;

    (iii) take appropriate steps to provide any of those employees who are undertaking any such manual handling operations with general indications and, where it is reasonably practicable to do so, precise information on – (aa) the weight of each load, and (bb) the heaviest side of any load whose centre of gravity is not positioned centrally (r.4(1)).

(review of assessment) 'Any assessment such as is referred to in paragraph (1)(b)(i) of this regulation shall be reviewed by the employer who made it if:

(a) there is reason to suspect that it is no longer valid; or

(b) there has been a significant change in the manual handling operations to which it relates; and where as a result of any such review changes to an assessment are required, the relevant employer shall make them' (r.4(2)).

(employees) 'Each employee while at work shall make full and proper use of any system of work provided for his use by his employer in compliance with r.4(1)(b)(ii)' (r.5)'.

(self-employed) self-employed people are under the same obligations as employers (r.2).

(factors to which regard must be had)

(tasks) do they involve:

- holding or manipulating loads at distance from trunk,
- unsatisfactory bodily movement or posture, especially twisting the trunk, stooping, reaching upwards,
- excessive movement of loads, especially excessive lifting or lowering distances, excessive carrying distances,
- excessive pushing or pulling of loads,
- risk of sudden movement on loads,
- frequent or prolonged physical effort,
- insufficient rest or recovery periods,
- rate of work imposed by a process,

(loads) are they:

- heavy, bulky or unwieldy, difficult to grasp, unstable or with contents likely to shift
- sharp, hot or otherwise potentially damaging,

(working environment) are there:

- space constraints preventing good posture,
- uneven, slippery or unstable floors,
- variations in level of floors or work surfaces,
- extremes of temperature or humidity,
- conditions causing ventilation problems or gusts of wind,
- poor lighting conditions.

(individual capability) does the job:

- require unusual strength, height etc,
- create a hazard to those who might reasonably be considered to be pregnant or to have a health problem,
- require special information or training for its safe performance.

(other) is movement or posture hindered by personal protective equipment or by clothing (schedule 1).

DISCUSSION
Lifting and handling: training, equipment and guidance

The 1992 Regulations have considerable implications for practitioners such as nurses, physiotherapists, occupational therapists, personal care assistants, residential and nursing home staff – some of whom are at constant risk of serious back injury. The Regulations give a sharp edge to legal actions (including civil actions for damages) in respect of a type of injury to staff which is common. The implications are that employers such as NHS Trusts, local authorities and independent care agencies must provide their staff with a safe system of work, adequate training, with more lifting and handling equipment, and with guidance. In practice some employers are taking the new legislation seriously. For example, NHS Trusts now employ lifting and handling advisers and provide increased quantities of lifting equipment, setting aside sometimes tens of thousands of pounds per annum in order to implement a policy of 'minimal lifting' in, ideally, a 'no-lifting' culture (Snell 1995).

Lifting and handling: legal judgments and guidance

Although the Manual Handling Operations Regulations have lent a sharper edge to the question of lifting, moving and handling, the reader should be aware that the common law of negligence (as well as other health and safety legislation) anyway applied before the Regulations came into force – and indeed continues to do so. Nevertheless, there is considerable interest as to how the courts will apply the Regulations; a few judgments are now beginning to be reported.

For example, the courts have held that it was reasonably practicable under r.4(1)(b) (appropriate measures to reduce risk of injury to lowest level reasonably practicable) to put up written notices about the weight limitations to be applied to hospital laundry loads (*Anderson v Lothian Health Board*), or to supply a second person to assist with the hanging of 72lb doors in a block of flats (*Hawkes v Southwark LBC*). They have held that it was reasonably practicable simply to avoid the need for the manual handling of a laundry load (*Anderson v Lothian Health Board*) or of a bucket which was being filled in a sink (*Warren v Harlow DC*). Furthermore, the risk of injury covered by the Regulations is not necessarily restricted to the imposition of a load, but covers manual handling activities generally, including the risk of tripping (*Cullen v North Lanarkshire Council*). On the other hand, it has been held that an emergency situation in a hospital might not be reasonably practicably avoidable (under r.4(1)(a)), nor be capable of attracting the duty to carry out a risk assessment and to take appropriate measures to reduce the risk to the lowest level reasonably practicable (under r.4(1)(b): *Fraser v Glasgow Health Board*). It is not clear that this last judgment is quite what the Health and Safety Commission had in mind in its guidance, when it stated that in the context of the health service, risk assessment should 'cover predictable but non-routine situations, such as emergency evacuation of the building and patient falls' (HaSC 1998,p.15).

Alternatively, both local authorities and the NHS might be liable in negligence for the injuries sustained through moving and handling operations; for instance, when a local authority fails to train a foster carer how to handle a heavy and disabled child (*Beasley v Buckinghamshire CC*), or to give training to a social worker, who subsequently suffers a back injury lifting a client back into bed on a home visit (*Colclough v Staffordshire CC*) – or when a health authority (or health board in Scotland) fails to institute an effective system of tuition (*Dickson v Lothian Health Board*), provides inadequate or insufficiently clear instructions (*Fraser v Glasgow Health Board*), or approves a method of lifting which is unsafe and negligent (*Williams v Gwent HA*). On occasion, the courts exercise their discretion to allow injured staff to bring a case long after the normal limitation period (three years) for bringing a case has passed (*Coad v Cornwall and Isles of Scilly HA*). On the other hand, the courts will not always find (full) liability; for instance, it might be for a trained nurse to use her own judgement in certain situations as to what lifting technique to use, rather than for the health authority to warn her against the method of lifting that subsequently caused the injury (*Woolger v West Surrey and North East Hampshire HA*; see also an older case involving an ambulance worker, *Parkes v Smethwick Corporation*). Even where liability is imposed on an employer in respect of insufficient training, the court might find contributory negligence, for instance, where a nurse had been warned against heavy lifting (because of a previous back injury) and she had not arranged the patient's bed so as to optimise the lifting environment (*McCafferty v Datta*).

The Health and Safety Commission guidance sounds a warning to statutory services about the costs they face if they do not take steps to safeguard their staff in manual handling situations, by reporting a number of cases involving nurses and physiotherapists – and awarded damages ranging from £57,000 to £172,000 (HaSC 1998,pp.4–5). Local authorities should note that in the case of *Colclough v Staffordshire CC* involving a social worker, the court awarded damages in excess of £200,000 (see Zindani 1998,p.212). Indeed, it is reported by the Health and Safety Executive, generally, that more than 25 per cent of all accidents reported to enforcing authorities each year involve manual handling; and, specifically, that of injuries in the health and social work field, 54 per cent are caused by manual handling (HSE 1998,p.2).

Lifting and handling: 'no lifting'

Employers who claim that only a complete 'no lifting' policy conforms to the law would appear, on the face of it, to be overstating the effect of the Regulations – which refer to the avoidance of manual handling with a risk of injury, where 'reasonably practicable'. The Regulations do not totally prohibit manual handling; the question hinges on a) which tasks are considered to constitute a risk of injury, since if there is no risk the Regulations do not apply; and b) what manual handling with a risk of injury it is reasonably practicable to avoid. In addition, if such manual handling cannot be avoided, then the employer has a duty to take appropriate steps to reduce the risk of injury to employees to the `lowest level reasonably practicable'. Thus, there are two risk assessments; the first, to identify those manual handling operations carrying a risk of injury, is not explicitly referred to in the Regulations and would in fact be carried out under the Management of Health and Safety at Work Regulations 1992 (SI 1992/2051); the second, detailed in the Manual Handling Operations Regulations, covers an assessment of those identified operations, so as to take those appropriate steps. The test for 'reasonably practicable' is quite a strict one, but does not equate with 'physically possible'; and if the risk is a minimum one, and the measures required grossly disproportionate in terms of money, time or trouble, then the courts might find that those measures are not reasonably practicable (eg, *Edwards v National Coal Board*). The courts have stated that this traditional approach to the meaning of reasonably practicable does indeed apply to the Regulations (*Hawkes v Southwark LBC*), notwithstanding that they derive from the context of a European directive which does not mention the term and that some commentators believe that the term should on that account be treated more strictly (Zindani 1998,p.212). Nevertheless, in the *Southwark* case, applying the test, the court held that although the risk involved (of hanging doors in a block of flats) was slight, so too would have been the 'sacrifice' made by the local authority, in supplying a second man to assist the plaintiff with the job. It was thus liable.

Nevertheless, it has been pointed out that on closer scrutiny, a policy which implies that lifting should be avoided for nearly all patients might in fact be reasonably practicable in the legal sense. This conclusion is reached if one compares the cost to an organisation (relatively small as a percentage of its budget) of purchasing the requisite lifting and handling equipment (such as hoists) to preclude the need to lift – with the degree of risk and the costs, both direct and indirect, of sickness and injury arising from manual handling. It might even be 'that the cost of taking no action is disproportionate to the cost of establishing a safer handling policy' (Richmond 1997).

A policy which states that 'patients are never lifted manually' – as advocated by the Royal College of Nursing's *Introducing a safer handling policy,* covers 'lifting the whole, or a large part of the weight of a patient'. It does not preclude assistance being given to a patient or client or 'using pushing, pulling, upward or downward forces' – but 'this is only acceptable if forces are as low as is reasonably practicable'. There are circumstances in which manual lifting might be required, for example, in case of emergencies (although safe systems of work should cater for foreseeable, and therefore, most emergencies). Sometimes when a person is being assisted to stand, he or she will take some of his or her own weight; but if the person falls unexpectedly there is a risk of injury to those assisting. However, 'if a good assessment has been made and the carers position themselves properly or use suitable equipment, the risk to the carers is low'.

Furthermore, the policy goes on, if a person's 'needs are genuinely so complicated that there is a true conflict of interest, a formal risk assessment must be done with great care. When deciding what is reasonably practicable, the risk to the patient from how elements of care are given or withheld, and his needs, must be taken into account as well as the risk to the nurse. A balance must be found where one party's benefit does not significantly increase the other party's risk' (Tracy, Ruszala 1997).

Lifting and handling: complications in community care

In community care, conflicts sometimes arise between on the one hand people's needs, wants and welfare, and on the other manual handling policies and the welfare of carers or personal assistants. The following examples should be read with the above legal considerations in mind.

Adherence to the Regulations might prompt the NHS or the local authority to state that baths cannot be provided unless two staff are present. However, the rarity of two staff, and difficulties in transport to a local bathing centre, might mean that people become resigned to strip washes (Pearson, Richardson 1994,p.3). Rehabilitation therapists sometimes transfer people manually from bed to chair, in order to assist them regain physical function – because lifting via means of a hoist might not aid rehabilitation in such circumstances (although use of other equipment such as turning discs, transfer boards might both protect staff and serve rehabilitation purposes).

Sometimes use of hoists causes discomfort and is awkward and time-consuming (Grant 1995), and seems undignified to some people who would prefer to be lifted out of bed by their carers or helpers (SSI 1995e,p.41). Discomfort might be caused by use of inappropriate slings (Love 1996). The withdrawal of staff from providing walking support for a disabled woman at a day centre might be explained by the local authority as due to health and safety reasons, but by the woman's parents as more in the way of a resource-cutting exercise (*R v Cornwall CC, ex p Goldsack*).

The extent to which conflict of opinion can lead to unfortunate consequences was illustrated in a local ombudsman investigation, covering issues about whether manual handling of a particular patient would breach the regulations or not, the injury caused to the person by use of a hoist, differing risk assessments, suitable training, breakdown in the relationship between the person being lifted and care home staff, the withdrawal of personal care as a result, the reasons why the person maintained that women and not men should lift him, his ability to exercise a choice over who his carers should be – and so on (*Redbridge LBC 1998*).

If health and social care practitioners refuse to lift people in their own homes and suitable equipment is not available, informal carers are left to do the lifting – but they are not covered by the regulations, which apply to employers and employees, and to self-employed people. Good practice demands that in such circumstances carers should receive training or advice from health or social care professionals – something which might also protect authorities from liability in the common law of negligence should carers suffer injury and decide to sue (Clements 1996a,p.89). The potential problem for informal carers is certainly not merely peripheral; it has been reported that physical injury is common amongst carers (Henwood 1998a, p.25). Nevertheless, proving negligence liability would run up against various obstacles – such as establishing that the harm suffered was foreseeable, the applicable standard of care, and causation – as well as judicial wariness of opening the floodgates to new types of claim (Richmond 1997).

The Health and Safety Commission has illustrated the possible complexity of decision-making. An 83-year-old, mentally confused, abusive and aggressive woman was discharged home. Two community nurses visited, and were helping the woman out of bed when she lifted both her feet so as to increase the weight on the nurses. Both nurses experienced back pain. Continued visiting by the two nurses was ruled out and three alternatives considered: provision of a hoist, readmission to hospital, and provision of an adjustable height bed which the woman could get in and out of herself. The hoist was ruled out on safety grounds, since the woman might be uncooperative and thrash around; the family opposed readmission to hospital; so, after a delay, a suitable bed was provided (HSAC 1998,pp.41–42).

6. DISABILITY DISCRIMINATION: PROVISION OF GOODS AND SERVICES

The Disability Discrimination Act 1995 covers, amongst other things, discrimination against disabled people in the provision of goods and services – including provision by public bodies such as local authorities, health authorities and NHS Trusts. Some uncertainty remains over the extent of the impact which the Act will eventually have on local authorities, not only on matters such as public access to buildings and on the provision of appropriate information in a range of formats, but also on the delivery of services. At present the Act is in force in respect of providers who discriminate by not providing a service, or of the terms or standards on which it is offered. It is expected that in 1999, the duty to make reasonable adjustments to policies, practices and procedures will come into force; as will, in 2004, the duty to make adjustments to physical features.

Reasons for the uncertainty are several including a) the fact that some of the relevant parts of the Act are not yet in force; and b) it is not clear how the courts will interpret certain key terms, simply because there have, at the time of writing, been very few cases under the Act about the provision of goods and services. Furthermore, the legal channels allowed for enforcement of the Act have been perceived to be weak because they leave legal enforcement to the individual, who has to bring a county court case (or in some circumstances a judicial review case). However, in this last respect, a Disability Rights Commission is being created, the functions of which will include assisting individuals to secure their rights if a matter of legal principle were in issue (DfEE 1998,p.18; and see Disability Rights Commission Bill 1998).

EXTRACTS

Legislation (Disability Discrimination Act 1995) states that:

(definition of disability)

- **(basic definition)** physical or mental impairment which has a substantial and long-term adverse effect on the ability of a person to carry out normal day-to-day activities (s.1);
- **(mental impairment)** a mental impairment includes mental illness which must be a clinically recognised illness (schedule 1), but does not have the same meaning as in the Mental Health Act 1983 (s.68);
- **(long-term)** the impairment must have lasted at least 12 months; is likely to last at least 12 months; or likely to last for the rest of the person's life (schedule 1);
- **(recurrence)** if an impairment ceases to have a substantial, adverse effect on a person's ability to carry out normal day-to-day activities, it is to be deemed to continue to have that effect if it is likely to recur (schedule 1);
- **(normal day-to-day activities)** normal day-to-day activities cover mobility; manual dexterity; physical coordination; continence; ability to lift, carry or otherwise move everyday objects; speech, hearing or eyesight; memory or ability to concentrate, learn or understand; or perception of the risk of physical danger (schedule 1);
- **(substantial)** guidance states that substantial means more than minor or trivial in effect (DfEE 1996,p.4);
- **(effect of medical treatment, aids/equipment)** an impairment is still deemed to be such even if measures (including medical treatment, prostheses or other aids) treat or correct the impairment (except in the case of spectacles or contact lenses) (schedule 1);
- **(Disabled Persons (Employment) Act 1944)** certification of registration under the 1944 Act is evidence of disability (schedule 1);
- **(progressive conditions)** progressive conditions such as cancer, MS, muscular dystrophy, HIV are taken to have a substantial effect, even if at present there is only an impairment which has an effect (but not a substantial, adverse one) on the person's ability to carry out normal day-to-day activities (schedule 1);
- **(future disabilities)** future disabilities are not covered (except where a progressive condition has begun to manifest itself);
- **(past disabilities)** people who have had a disability in the past, but no longer have it, are covered (schedule 2);
- **(people deemed disabled in error)** are not covered;
- **(babies and young children)** if a child under six years old has an impairment which does not have an effect on normal day-to-day activities, the impairment will nevertheless be treated as having a substantial and long-term effect if it would normally have that effect on the ability of a child aged over six years (SI 1996/1455);
- **(severe disfigurement)** severe disfigurement is covered (schedule 1), but not tattoos or non-medical body-piercing (SI 1996/1455);
- **(addiction)** addiction to alcohol, nicotine or any other substance does not amount to an impairment – unless the addiction was originally the consequence of administration of medically prescribed drugs or treatment (SI 1996/1455);

- **(other exclusions)** also excluded are hayfever, tendency to start fires, tendency to steal, tendency to physical or sexual abuse, exhibitionism, voyeurism. However, hayfever can be taken into account if it aggravates the effect of another condition (SI 1996/1455).

(goods, facilities and services) Services include goods or facilities. A provider of services 'is concerned with the provision, in the United Kingdom, of services to the public or to a section of the public'. It is irrelevant whether the service is for payment or not. Examples of services include:

- access to and use of any place which the public are permitted to enter;
- access to and use of means of communication;
- access to and use of information services;
- accommodation in a hotel, boarding house, etc;
- facilities by way of banking or insurance for grants, loans, credit or finance;
- facilities for entertainment, recreation or refreshment;
- employment agency facilities under s.2 of the Employment and Training Act 1973;
- the services of any profession or trade, or any local or other public authority;
- but not education funded, secured or provided at educational establishments (s.19).

(discrimination in various ways) It is unlawful for a provider of services to discriminate against a disabled person:

- **(not providing a service)** 'in refusing to provide, or deliberately not providing, to the disabled person any service which he provides, or is prepared to provide, to members of the public';
- **(reasonable adjustments)** in failing in its duty to make reasonable adjustments 'in circumstances in which the effect of that failure is to make impossible or unreasonably difficult for the disabled person to make use of any such service' (operation dependent on the coming into force in 1999 and 2004 of the duties in s.21 of the Act to make reasonable adjustments: see below);
- **(standard of service)** 'in the standard of service which he provides to the disabled person or the manner in which he provides it to him';
- **(terms of service)** 'in the terms on which he provides a service to the disabled person' (s.19).

(discrimination: definition). Discrimination occurs 'for a reason which relates to the person's disability, he treats him less favourably than he treats or would treat others to whom that reason does not or would not apply' – and he cannot justify the treatment. There is also discrimination if the provider fails in its duty to make adjustments without justification (s.20).

(justification of treatment). Justification is only valid if 'in the opinion of the provider of services, one or more of the conditions [below] are satisfied'; and also 'it is reasonable, in all the circumstances of the case, for him to hold that opinion'. The conditions relate to:

- **(health and safety)** health and safety of any person being affected;
- **(incapacity)** incapacity of disabled person to enter an enforceable agreement (but not where another person is exercising a power of attorney or functions under Part 7 of the Mental Health Act 1983);
- **(non-provision and other members of the public)** refusing or deliberately not providing a service, because this would result in an inability to provide the service to members of the public;
- **(standard or terms of service: the disabled person and other members of the public)** in relation to standard or terms of service, the treatment is necessary in order to provide the service to the disabled person or other members of the public;
- **(greater cost)** in relation to the terms of service, 'the difference ... reflects the greater cost to the provider of services in providing the service to the disabled person' – but costs incurred under the duty to make reasonable adjustments cannot be counted here (s.20).

(adjustments to policy, practice, procedure). The duty to make adjustments (not yet in force) applies where a provider 'has a practice, policy or procedure which makes it impossible or unreasonably difficult for disabled persons to make use of a service which he provides, or is prepared to provide, to other members of the public, it is his duty to take such steps as it is reasonable, in all the circumstances of the case, for him to have to take in order to change that policy, practice or procedure so that it no longer has that effect' (s.21(1): due to come into force in October 1999).

(adjustments to physical features). 'Where a physical feature (for example, one arising from the design or construction of a building or the approach or access to premises) makes it impossible or unreasonably difficult for disabled persons to make use of such a service, it is the duty of the provider of that service to take such steps as it is reasonable, in all the circumstances of the case, for him to have to take in order to:

(1) remove the feature;

(2) alter it so it no longer has that effect;

(3) provide a reasonable means of avoiding the feature;

(4) provide a reasonable alternative method of making the service in question available to disabled persons' (points 1, 2, 3 due to come into force in 2004, but point 4 is due in force in October 1999).

(adjustments: auxiliary aids or services). If an auxiliary aid or service (eg, information on audio-tape or a sign language interpreter) would 'enable disabled persons to make use of a service which a provider of services provides, or is prepared to provide, to members of the public', or would 'facilitate the use by disabled persons of such a service' then: 'it is the duty of the provider of that service to take such steps as it is reasonable, in all the circumstances of the case, for him to have to take in order to provide that auxiliary aid or service' (s.21: due to come into force in October 1999).

(adjustments: expenditure limit). Providers of services are not obliged to exceed the prescribed maximum of expenditure (s.21: not yet in force).

(immunity and other legislation) 'Nothing in this Act makes unlawful any act done (a) in pursuance of any enactment; or (b) in pursuance of any instrument made by a Minister of the Crown under any enactment; or (c) to comply with any condition or requirement imposed by a Minister of the Crown (whether before or after the passing of this Act) by virtue of any enactment' (s.59).

(disposal and management of premises) It is unlawful to discriminate against disabled people in the disposal or management of premises (s.22); it is beyond the scope of this book to consider the relevant provisions in any detail here.

DISCUSSION

Disability discrimination: services covered

In so far as community care services are concerned, obvious aspects covered by the Act (see s.19 above) include a) physical access to buildings; b)the provision of information in different forms including tape, braille, large print, and so on; c) communication with disabled people, involving for example, use of specialist staff, training for other staff in communicating and using specialist equipment such as text telephones, installation of induction loops (for accessibility of information, see Gregory 1996).

In respect of such 'access' services, there is still uncertainty about the legal and financial implications of the Disability Discrimination Act (see eg, George 1996). Beyond them, however, lies perhaps even greater uncertainty about how the Act will affect actual provision of substantive services – for example, in terms of policies, eligibility criteria, methods of service delivery and charges. It is not at present clear what the answer is, since there is as yet no case law (for a couple of examples of goods and services cases, not involving local authorities, see *Blankley v Lyon* and *Rose v Bouchet*) – but for general examples, see the present code of practice (NDC 1996) and proposed replacement (NDC 1998). However, the following types of matter have been subject to speculation at least.

Permission was given to bring a judicial review case (*R v Barnet LBC, ex p Biggs*) in relation to a local authority's policy which barred from its housing list people wishing to leave residential or nursing homes in its area to live independently – but who had originally (as long as 25 years ago) been placed in those homes by another local authority (ie, where the people concerned had originally lived). It was claimed that this policy breached the Disability Discrimination Act because nearly all the people affected were disabled people. What a court would have decided is unknown, but the local authority changed its policy anyway (Clements 1998).

Leave was also given to bring a judicial review case on the grounds that charging people extra for non-residential services, simply because they are in receipt of attendance allowance or disability living allowance, is a breach of the Act (*R v Powys CC, ex p Hambidge (no.2)*: see *Community Care* 1998c). Some local authorities have stated that they might have to introduce charges for those groups of people who have previously received services free (eg, people with mental health problems or with learning disabilities) – because otherwise other groups of disabled people who are paying charges (eg, adults with physical disabilities) could claim that the Act is being breached. This is argued because, under the Act, discrimination against a disabled person is measured not only against treatment afforded to non-disabled people, but also to people with a different disability. The alternative, to abolish all charges, and therefore also achieve equal treatment, is not likely to be embraced by local authorities (eg, *Community Care* 1996). The questions that might be asked about possibly discriminatory local authority policies are endless. Consider a policy which states that people who can make their own way to a drop-in centre will be assessed immediately, but that those who are housebound will have to wait many months for an assessment. (For instance, is being housebound a disability, or is it associated closely with a particular type of disability, not characteristic of those who get to the drop-in centre, and which can therefore be cited as the reason for the less favourable treatment? Or is the policy, if it does constitute less favourable treatment, justifiable?). Similarly, some groups of disabled people (eg, those with a sensory impairment) might simply be afforded a lower priority by local authorities than other groups, and so receive a worse standard of service – even though no such lower priority is explicitly sanctioned by community care legislation. (Would this be discrimination, would there be a justification, or will there simply be immunity? See immediately below).

Disability discrimination: immunity under other legislation

To an extent, local authority policies and decisions will be immune from the Act under s.59, if they are made under other legislation (see extract above); the question is to what extent?

The equivalent issue has been tested under s.41 of the Race Relations Act 1976. In one case, an employment appeal tribunal held that immunity would not attach to a statutory body just because it was a statutory body, but only where it was carrying out a duty or statutory function – because otherwise statutory organisations would be given complete protection for grossly discriminatory acts (*General Medical Council v Goba*). Similarly, in *Hampson v DES*, the House of Lords held that, interpreted broadly, s.41 would give excessive immunity to public bodies; thus it should be treated narrowly and immunity only be given to performance of an express obligation, but not to administrative practice or discretion unprescribed by legislation.

7. HUMAN RIGHTS

Hitherto, people have had to take their grievances about alleged breaches of human rights by national governments (including public bodies), under the European Convention for the Protection of Human Rights and Fundamental Freedoms, to a) the European Commission on Human Rights for a decision about the admissibility of the complaint; and then b) perhaps ultimately to the European Court of Human Rights, if no prior settlement is reached between the Commission and the United Kingdom government. (Towards the end of 1998, the procedure for bringing a case changed: instead of first going to the Commission, application is now made direct to the court).

The United Kingdom is a signatory to the Convention and so in principle has in the past, following an adverse decision by the Court, introduced legislation to ensure that UK law conforms with the Convention. However, unless United Kingdom domestic legislation is ambiguous in meaning, then the courts in the United Kingdom have not enforced principles embodied in the Convention, even if the legislation in issue has been inconsistent with those principles (*R v Secretary of State for the Home Department, ex p Brind*). Nevertheless, following many years of argument that a basic set of rights should underlie United Kingdom law, the Human Rights Act 1998 is due to come into force in the year 2000. It establishes that, so far as possible, legislation must be interpreted by the courts in a manner compatible with the Convention; and that it is unlawful for public authorities to act in a way which is incompatible with it. The courts cannot strike down legislation they find to be incompatible, but can make a declaration of that incompatibility; the government then has a power (but not a duty) to amend the legislation as necessary and if there are compelling reasons to do so.

EXTRACTS

It is beyond the scope of this book to go into detail, but some of the articles, or parts of articles, of the Convention which might be relevant to community care and related services include the right:

- to life (article 2)
- not to be subjected to torture or degrading treatment or punishment (article 3)
- to liberty and security of the person (article 5)
- to a fair and public hearing by an independent and impartial tribunal in relation to a determination of civil rights (article 6)
- to respect for private and family life, home and correspondence (article 8)
- to an effective remedy even if the violation of a right has been committed by people acting in an official capacity (article 13 – although this article is not directly incorporated into the Human Rights Act 1998)

- that the Convention's rights and freedoms 'shall be secured without discrimination on any ground such as sex, race, colour, language, religion, political or other opinion, national or social origin, association with a national minority, property, birth or other status' (article 14). (Note: article 14 does not mention disability discrimination but the phrase 'any ground such as' suggests that it is implicit: Cooper, Vernon 1996,p.50).

DISCUSSION

The following are a few examples relevant to this book of application, or attempts at application, of the Convention.

The two child care cases heard in *X v Bedfordshire CC* were taken to the European Commission and ruled in 1998 to be admissible at least to be considered under the Convention. In the first (the neglected and abused five children), the articles under consideration were three and thirteen; in the second (mistaken identity of child abuser), articles six, eight and thirteen (Childright 1998).

In 1989, in *Gaskin v United Kingdom*, the European Court of Human Rights ruled that the United Kingdom was in breach of article 8 (right to respect for private and family life). A local authority had withheld personal information about the applicant's upbringing in foster care arranged by the authority. The court recognised the importance of confidentiality, and that the need for the consent of the contributor of personal information was not necessarily inconsistent with article 8. However, when consent was not forthcoming (either because it was withheld or there was simply no answer by the contributor to the request for consent), there should have been an 'independent authority' to take the final decision about whether to grant access. Therefore the procedures available in this situation were inadequate under article 8. This case turned on events prior to the Access to Personal Files Act 1987 and the regulations made under it (effective since 1989: see p.453). However, even since these came into force, there has still been no independent authority to make final decisions when consent is withheld. This means it is likely that the United Kingdom has remained in breach of the Convention, at least in the case of manual records (computerised records have been covered by the Data Protection Act 1984). This deficiency will be remedied by the Data Protection 1998 (see p.457).

Article 2 (right to life) was cited by the High Court in *R v Cambridge HA, ex p B*, when it asked the health authority to think again about its refusal to provide leukaemia treatment for a dying child; however, the Court of Appeal overturned the decision the same day, without making reference to article 2. Indeed, it seems that article 2 has not generally been explored in relation to a positive obligation to prevent death through lack of medical attention (Harris, Boyle and Warbrick 1995,p.40) by, for example, allocating adequate resources (O'Sullivan 1998). In a very different context, the principle under article 2 was also referred to in *R v Westminster CC, ex p A*, concerning the duty of local authorities towards destitute asylum seekers. The High Court equated a common law of humanity, referred to by the courts in 1803, with the modern-day fundamental right to human life and the Convention. The Court of Appeal this time upheld the High Court's decision, though again without referring to the Convention. In yet a further case, the Court of Appeal in *R v Secretary of State for the Home Office, ex p Joint Council for the Welfare of Immigrants* referred to human rights which were so basic, and part of domestic law, that it was unnecessary even to refer to the Convention (see also *R v Brent LBC, ex p D*).

It has also been suggested that closing long-term care accommodation and transferring older people to other settings (see eg, p.377), without adequate consultation, might also breach the right to life under article 2 (Steele 1998); or alternatively that article 3 (inhuman or degrading treatment) might apply to NHS patients who are left for hours on stretchers in corridors; who, wheelchair-bound, are left in the toilet with the door open whilst other patients are attended to (Dimond 1998,p.21); or who are denied palliative care on grounds of rationing (Wadham, Mountfield 1999,p.69).

In *R v North and East Devon HA, ex p Coughlan*, about a health authority breaking its promise to provide accommodation for life for a number of disabled people in a particular NHS unit, and instead closing the unit, the applicants eventually abandoned their argument under article 3. However, the judge ruled that article 8 (right to respect for private and family life and home) did apply and had been breached by the health authority – since none of the exceptions, that could have justified interference with that right, applied (namely interests of national security, public safety, economic well-being of the country, prevention of disorder or crime, protection of health or morals, protection of the rights and freedoms of others).

The Convention concentrates on civil and political rights and, unlike some other international conventions (eg, the United Nations Declaration of Human Rights) fails to deal explicitly with economic, social and cultural rights – such as the right to adequate medical care and social services (Knaffler 1998).

CHAPTER 9

NON-RESIDENTIAL COMMUNITY CARE SERVICES

Coverage

1. Welfare services for disabled people: National Assistance Act 1948,s.29
2. Welfare services for disabled people: Chronically Sick and Disabled Persons Act 1970,s.2
3. Information for disabled people: Chronically Sick and Disabled Persons Act 1970,s.1
4. Services for older people: Health Services and Public Health Act 1968,s.45
5. Home help and laundry facilities: NHS Act 1977, schedule 8
6. Services for illness and mental disorder: NHS Act 1977, schedule 8
7. Services for expectant or nursing mothers: NHS Act 1977, schedule 8
8. After-care and other mental health services
9. Drugs and alcohol
10. Direct payments to users of services

KEY POINTS

Community care services, of the non-residential variety, cover:

- *welfare services* under the National Assistance Act 1948, s.29 – and by extension under the Chronically Sick and Disabled Persons Act 1970, ss.1 and 2;
- *welfare services for older people* under the Health Service and public Health Act 1968, s.45;
- *home help, laundry facilities and services in relation to illness and mental disorder* under the NHS Act 1977, schedule 8;
- *after-care services* under the Mental Health Act 1983, s.117.

Provision is made also for the making of special grants by central government in relation to mental illness or to people dependent on drugs and alcohol under s.7E of the Local Authority Social Services Act 1970. In addition, flexibility in the delivery of services for some service users has been introduced by the Community Care (Direct Payments) Act 1996, in force since April 1997. This enables local authorities to make cash payments, so that people can then choose and buy their own services, so exercising more control of their own lives. Such payments remain dependent on an assessment of need and decision about the services required.

Non-residential community care spans a very wide variety of services including practical assistance in the home, personal assistance, home help, respite care (ie, breaks for a person being cared for or for a carer), daily living equipment, adaptations to the home, telephones, televisions, radios, assistance with travel, social work services, advice, support, information, facilities for rehabilitation, meals-on-wheels, lunch clubs, day centres, recreational activities, lectures, games, outings, visiting services, helping with sheltered housing – and so on.

In the past, providers of non-residential services have not been subject to registration and inspection: compare the registration and inspection of independent providers of residential or nursing homes. A White Paper in late 1998 announced that this would change, to the extent that registration and inspection requirements will in future apply to all providers of domiciliary care, whether statutory, private or voluntary. This will cover organisations providing 'personal social care to people living in their own homes'. Thus, services such as cleaning or gardening will not be covered (Secretary of State for Health 1998,p.70).

(NB. For reasons of space in this chapter, the Chronically Sick and Disabled Persons Act is in places abbreviated to CSDPA).

I. WELFARE SERVICES FOR DISABLED PEOPLE: NATIONAL ASSISTANCE ACT 1948,s.29

The National Assistance Act 1948, s.29 is the bedrock for provision of non-residential community care services for disabled people. Although the Chronically Sick and Disabled Persons Act 1970 is sometimes regarded as the main plank of provision for disabled people in the community, nevertheless it remains underpinned by the 1948 Act. This is despite the fact that the duties and powers to provide services in the 1948 Act are legally weaker than the duty imposed by the 1970 Act. The definition of disability contained in s.29 of the National Assistance Act 1948 governs also s.2 of the 1970 Act; and services under s.2 are arranged legally as part of a local authority's functions under s.29 of the 1948 Act (see below, p.197).

EXTRACTS

Legislation (National Assistance Act 1948,s.29): local authorities have both powers, and duties in respect of welfare services for people who are ordinarily resident in the local authority's area and who come within the statutory definition of disability:

> **(definition of disability)** people 'aged eighteen or over who are blind, deaf or dumb, or who suffer from mental disorder of any description and other persons aged eighteen or over who are substantially and permanently handicapped by illness, injury, or congenital deformity or such other disabilities as may be prescribed'.

> **(directions and approvals)** A 'local authority may, with the approval of the Secretary of State, and to such extent as he may direct in relation to persons ordinarily resident in the area of the local authority shall make arrangements for promoting the welfare of persons to whom this section applies…' (ie, disabled people as defined immediately above). The exercise of the powers and duties under s.29 is dependent on the *Secretary of State's approvals and directions under s.29(1) of the National Assistance Act 1948* (contained in Circular LAC(93)10).

(duties) In respect of disabled people who are ordinarily resident in the area, local authorities are directed, and so have a duty, to make arrangements:

- **(registers)** to compile and maintain registers of disabled people
- **(social work service, etc)** to provide a social work service and such advice and support as needed for people at home or elsewhere;
- **(rehabilitation, etc)** to provide, whether at centres or elsewhere, facilities for the social rehabilitation and adjustment to disability including assistance in overcoming limitations of mobility or communication;
- **(activities)** to provide, either at centres or elsewhere, facilities for occupational, social, cultural and recreational activities – and, where appropriate, payments to persons for work they have done.

(powers) By means of approval, the above duties are reduced to powers in the case of disabled people who are not ordinarily resident within an authority's area. In addition, other approvals create the following powers to make arrangements, irrespective of whether a person is ordinarily resident in the area of the authority:

- **(holiday homes)** to provide holiday homes;
- **(travel)** to provide free or subsidised travel for people who do not otherwise qualify for other travel concessions;
- **(accommodation)** to assist a person to find accommodation which will enable him or her to take advantage of arrangements made under section 29(1);
- **(wardens)** to contribute to the cost of employing a warden in warden-assisted housing, and to provide warden services in private housing.
- **(information)** to inform people to whom s.29 relates about services available under that section;
- **(instruction)** to give instruction to people at home or elsewhere in methods of overcoming effects of their disabilities;
- **(workshops)** to provide workshops where such people may engage in suitable work and for providing associated hostels;
- **(work)** to provide suitable work in people's own homes or otherwise, and to help people dispose of the produce of their work.

(prohibitions) There are two express prohibitions in s.29 of the 1948 Act. 'Nothing in the foregoing provisions of this section shall authorise or require…':

- **(payment of money)** 'the payment of money to persons to whom this section applies (except in relation to workshops and provision of suitable work)';
- **(non-duplication of services)** 'the provision of any accommodation or services required to be provided under the NHS Act 1977…'

DISCUSSION

National Assistance Act 1948, s.29: general duties

The courts have on more than one occasion characterised the duties imposed by s.29 of the National Assistance Act 1948 as being in the nature of general, 'target' duties towards the local relevant population – rather than duties towards individuals (for example, as found in s.2 of the Chronically Sick and Disabled Persons Act 1970). The former, general type of duty is taken to be less easily enforceable by an individual than the latter type, because it allows available resources to be more readily taken into account by local authorities when they decide whether to arrange services (eg, *R v Cornwall CC, ex p Goldsack; R v Gloucestershire CC, ex p Barry*).

National Assistance Act 1948, s.29: substantial and permanent handicap

The term 'substantial and permanent handicap' controls access to services under s.29 of the National Assistance Act 1948, s.2 of the Chronically Sick and Disabled Persons Act 1970, and disabled facilities grants under the Housing Grants, Construction and Regeneration Act 1996. More detailed definition of this term and its application is discussed elsewhere in this book (p.90).

National Assistance Act 1948, s.29: registers of disabled people

Local authorities have a duty to keep registers of disabled people: see p.100.

National Assistance Act 1948, s.29: social work service

Local authorities have a duty (in respect of people ordinarily resident in the area, and otherwise a power) to make arrangements for the provision of a social work service.

In one investigation relating to support and advice given to people entering or resident in nursing homes (before April 1993, when social services departments assumed responsibility for nursing home funding), the local ombudsman stated that a social work service should be available to 'all those living in their area', including residents of private nursing homes (*Buckingham CC 1992*). In another, the ombudsman found maladministration because, in considering whether to provide social work support, the authority had not balanced the views of relevant professionals against the resources it had available (*Tower Hamlets LBC 1993*).

As explained above, the courts accept that s.29 imposes at most only a general duty and thus is difficult to enforce in relation to individual rationing decisions. Nevertheless, if an individual were denied such a service because the authority had completely ceased provision for everybody, then he or she might have a more arguable case. It is clearly one thing to ration a service governed by a general duty, another to abandon it altogether. In practice the question sometimes arises as to whether a local authority breaches its duty by integrating social workers into 'care manager' roles, so that there is no longer a named social work service. However, were the courts to look at whether an authority was failing, in such circumstances, to provide a social work service at all for people in its area, they would presumably scrutinise not what the service was called but whether it was present in substance – whether under the banner of care management or any other name. Nevertheless, a preoccupation with meeting physical care needs only (eg, washing, dressing, toileting) might lead to care plans which omit social work support or counselling (SSI 1997c,p.18) and to doubts about the extent, if not the very existence, of a social work service.

The community care White Paper stated that it would not be appropriate for local authorities to make charges for social work support (Secretaries of State 1989,p.29).

National Assistance Act 1948, s.29: advice and support

The duty (in respect of people ordinarily resident in the area, and otherwise a power) to make arrangements to provide advice and support is clearly a very broad one – and for that very reason it is potentially all-inclusive but also difficult to pin down.

However, on more than one occasion the local ombudsman has found maladministration because of a failure on the part of local authority staff either to provide directly – or at least to ensure provision of (eg, by pointing people to other sources) – adequate advice about welfare benefits (eg, *Devon CC 1996, Stockton-on-Tees BC 1997, Wakefield MDC 1993*). And, in refusing to advocate on a person's behalf with a housing department and the Department of Social Security, the local authority had not reached a decision based on objective criteria which would balance the client's need against resources; this was maladministration (*Tower Hamlets LBC 1993*).

The community care White Paper stated that it would not be appropriate for local authorities to make charges for advice (Secretaries of State 1989,p.29).

National Assistance Act 1948, s.29: rehabilitation

The duty (in respect of people ordinarily resident in the area, and otherwise a power) to make arrangements for provision of facilities for social rehabilitation and adjustment to disability – including assistance in overcoming limitations of mobility or communication – sometimes comes as a surprise to local authority staff. Typically they assume that such matters as mobility or communication fall mainly within the remit of the NHS – for instance, provision of physiotherapy, walking aids, speech and language therapy, communication aids.

In *R v Cornwall CC, ex p Goldsack*, the judge concluded that the walking assistance being given to a young disabled woman at a day centre was being provided under s.29 of the 1948 Act (rather than under s.2 of the CSDPA 1970). On a more general point, the local ombudsman found that the provision of a support worker for 30 hours a week under the duty to arrange for social rehabilitation and adjustment to disability was reasonable – but the failure to set, work to, and record targets was maladministration (*Manchester CC 1993*).

National Assistance Act 1948, s.29: activities

There is a duty (in respect of people ordinarily resident in the area, and otherwise a power) to make arrangements for the provision of facilities – either at centres or elsewhere – for occupational, social, cultural and recreational activities and, where appropriate, payments to persons for work they have done. This duty will typically cover day centres and their activities – although the word 'elsewhere' gives a potentially wide scope to the duty.

National Assistance Act 1948, s.29: holiday homes

The power to make arrangements for the provision of 'holiday homes' is narrower than the equivalent duty in s.2 of the CSDPA 1970 which refers to facilitating the taking of a holiday at a holiday home *or elsewhere* (see p.198). However, although it is only a power, it does extend to people who are not ordinarily resident within the area of the authority – whereas the duty under s.2 of the 1970 Act does not.

National Assistance Act 1948, s.29: informing people about services

The power to inform people, to whom s.29 of the 1948 Act, applies about services available under section is overshadowed – at least for people ordinarily resident in the local authority's area – by the duty to provide information under s.1 of the CSDPA 1970 (see below, p.211).

National Assistance Act 1948, s.29: instruction to people at home or elsewhere in methods of overcoming effects of their disabilities

The power to give instruction to people at home or elsewhere in relation to overcoming their disability is clearly a wide one. One example in practice is when local authority staff show disabled people how to use equipment and adaptations and to deal with other daily living tasks. However instruction is not the same as education; in *R v Bradford MBC, ex p Parkinson*, the court held, in it its attempt to separate out the education and social services functions of the local authority, that instruction could not include a service which was 'purely educational'.

National Assistance Act 1948, s.29: prohibition of payments

The general prohibition on the making of cash payments to service users has long been criticised as unduly restricting the power of local authorities to give to disabled people more control over their own lives. Consequently, for some years, local authorities attempted to find ways around the prohibition by making payments to third parties to administer money on behalf of service users – and in April 1997, the Community Care (Direct Payments) Act 1996 came into force to alleviate the problem, at least for some groups of people: see p.229.

National Assistance Act 1948, s.29: non-duplication of services

A non-duplication provision (see extracts above) prevents a local authority from arranging a service under s.29 of the 1948 Act if there is a duty to provide that service under the NHS Act 1977.

There are two possible interpretations of this prohibition: that it refers a) only to a service which a *local authority* has a duty to provide under the 1977 Act (ie, under schedule 8); or b) to a service which either a *local authority or the NHS* has a duty to provide under the 1977 Act. The second interpretation is clearly very much wider than the first. Whichever is correct, and although the principle of non-duplication is sound, *in practice* there are considerable problems in making sense of such provisions (see p.325).

In *R v Islington, ex p McMillan*, it was claimed that the anti-duplication prohibition affecting s.29 of the 1948 Act must also affect s.2 of the CSDPA 1970, since the latter is regarded as an extension of s.29 of the 1948 Act. If so, it was argued, the fact that there was a general duty to provide home help under the NHS Act 1977 (schedule 8), meant that it could not be provided under s.2 of the CSPDA 1970 – even if a decision had been made not to provide it under the 1977 Act. The judge dismissed this argument, stating that what authorised provision of home help under s.2 of the CSDPA was s.2 of that Act – not s.29 of the 1948 Act (although, confusingly a subsequent Court of Appeal ruling in *R v Powys CC, ex p Hambidge* has – albeit on a different issue – confirmed that s.2 of the 1970 Act is firmly yoked to s.29 of the 1948 Act).

National Assistance 1948, s.29: employment of agents in making arrangements

In accordance with arrangements for welfare services under s.29, local authorities are empowered to employ as agents 'any voluntary organisation or any person carrying on, professionally or by way of trade or business, activities which consist of or include the provision of services for any of the persons to whom section 29 above applies, being an organisation or person appearing to the authority to be capable of providing the service to which the arrangements apply' (National Assistance Act 1948, s.30).

National Assistance Act 1948, s.29: residential accommodation

The House of Lords confirmed in *Vandyk v Oliver* (a rating valuation case) that s.29 could not authorise the arranging of residential accommodation.

2. WELFARE SERVICES FOR DISABLED PEOPLE: CHRONICALLY SICK AND DISABLED PERSONS ACT 1970,s.2

Services available under s.2 of the Chronically Sick and Disabled Persons Act (CSDPA) 1970 are central to community care objectives, since those services assist people to remain in their own homes (see p.33). They include practical help in the home, equipment and home adaptations, educational facilities, telephone and radio, holidays – and are available to any person a) whom the authority defines as disabled under s.29 of the National Assistance Act 1948; b) who is 'ordinarily resident' within the authority's area; and c) for whose needs the local authority is satisfied that it is necessary for it to make arrangements.

In summary, s.2 of the 1970 Act ostensibly places a strong duty on local authorities to make arrangements for specific services for individual disabled people. Unsurprisingly, therefore, it has featured in important community care cases including *R v Gloucestershire CC ex p Barry*, *R v Islington LBC ex p Rixon, and R v Haringey LBC ex p Norton*. The *Gloucestershire* case has provoked considerable controversy and significant criticism, in so far as it is perceived to have undermined the strength and effectiveness of s.2. The case establishes a) that resources may be taken into account when establishing, against eligibility criteria, people's needs and whether it is necessary to meet them – but resources must not be the sole factor determining the nature of the eligibility criteria, which must reflect a balancing of needs and resources; b) that once both need and necessity have been identified, then the authority has an absolute duty to meet the need irrespective of resources; c) the local authority can determine how to meet that need, and take account of resources when deciding which service option to arrange; d) it is open to the local authority at a later date to reassess need and necessity against revised eligibility criteria.

EXTRACTS
Legislation (CSDPA 1970, s.2) states:

> **(need, necessity, satisfaction)** 'Where a local authority having functions under section 29 of the National Assistance Act 1948 are satisfied in the case of any person to whom that section applies who is ordinarily resident in their area that it is necessary in order to meet the needs of that person for that authority to make arrangements for all or any of the following matters, namely' –
>
> - **(practical assistance)** '(a) the provision of practical assistance for that person in his home';
> - **(wireless, television, recreation)** '(b) the provision for that person of, or assistance to that person in obtaining, wireless, television, library or similar recreational facilities';
> - **(lectures, games, outings, education)** '(c)the provision for that person of lectures, games, outings or other recreational facilities outside his home or assistance to that person in taking advantage of educational facilities available to him';
> - **(travel)** '(d) the provision for that person of facilities for, or assistance in, travelling to and from his home for the purpose of participating in any services provided under arrangements made by the authority under the said section 29 or, with the approval of the authority, in any services provided otherwise than as aforesaid which are similar to services which could be provided under such arrangements';
> - **(adaptations and equipment)** '(e) the provision of assistance for that person in arranging for the carrying out of any works of adaptation in his home or the provision of any additional facilities designed to secure his greater safety, comfort or convenience';

- **(holidays)** '(f) facilitating the taking of holidays by that person, whether at holiday homes or otherwise and whether provided under arrangements made by the authority or otherwise';
- **(meals)** '(g) the provision of meals for that person whether in his home or elsewhere';
- **(telephone and telephone equipment)** '(h) the provision for that person of, or assistance to that person, in obtaining, a telephone and any special equipment necessary to enable him to use a telephone',
- **(duty to make arrangements under s.29 of the 1948 Act)** 'then subject to the provisions of section 7(1) of the Local Authority Social Services Act 1970 (which requires local authorities in the exercise of certain functions, including functions under the said section 29, to act under the general guidance of the Secretary of State) it shall be the duty of that authority to make those arrangements in exercise of their functions under the said section 29'.

DISCUSSION

CSDPA 1970, s.2: background

The following paragraphs give the background to the Chronically Sick and Disabled Persons Act 1970, in order to put the recent focus on the Act (eg, in *R v Gloucestershire CC, ex p Barry* into context); they consider its purpose, past effectiveness and consistency of application.

CSDPA background: purpose. The Chronically Sick and Disabled Persons Act 1970 was introduced into Parliament as a Private Member's Bill by Alfred Morris MP – who later pointed out that before the coming of the 1970 Act, the needs of disabled people were sometimes never debated in entire Parliaments (for instance there was not one debate from 1959 to 1964: HCD,17/1/86,col.1356). Moving the second reading of the Bill in December 1969, he stated that the intention was 'to increase the welfare, improve the status and enhance the dignity of the chronically sick and of disabled persons' (HCD,5/12/1969,col.1851). More specifically, what was to become s.2 meant that 'provisions for the disabled which are now permissive would be mandatory upon local authorities. The whole Clause is intended to standardise local provision on the basis of the best existing practice' (HCD,5/12/1969,col.1856).

The Earl of Longford, moving the second reading of the Bill in the House of Lords, stated generally of the Bill: 'We are going a long way to establish the mandatory instead of the permissive principle. No longer will the disabled have to go round cap in hand, hoping for largesse from well-meaning individuals or bodies. The benefits will belong to them as a matter of law – in every way a healthier relationship' (HLD,9/4/1970,col.241). In the past, a 'very disturbing gap' had been perceived between those 'better' and those 'sluggish' authorities in respect of provision for disabled people under s.29 of the National Assistance Act 1948 (Alfred Morris: SC(E),4/2/1970,col.153). For instance, typical of the need for change was that a local authority might spend more on its illuminations for a seaside resort than on its disabled citizens (Alfred Morris: HCD,5/12/1969,col.1857).

The central importance of s.2 of the CSDPA 1970 to community care seems obvious, since it deals precisely in those welfare services which enable people to remain living in their own homes. This is referred to by policy guidance as the preferred aim of community care and achievable through 'support for the user in his or her own home including day and domiciliary care, respite care, the provision of disability equipment and adaptations to accommodation as necessary' (DH 1990, para 3.24). As the Earl of Longford put it 20 years before, the purpose of s.2 was to ensure 'that the disabled should, wherever possible, be enabled to earn their own living, and in any case to live in their own homes' (HLD,9/4/1970,col.242).

CSDPA background: effectiveness. It is recognised that s.2 of the CSDPA 1970 has greatly improved services for disabled people, since it imposed a specific duty in relation to individuals. This was in contrast to the more general duty under s.29 of the National Assistance Act 1948 which, before 1970, had allowed via approved 'schemes' some authorities to make adequate provision for disabled people, but done little to force others to do so. However, the operation of s.2 of the Act since 1970 has not been without problems – which long preceded the much-criticised judicial ruling in *R v Gloucestershire CC, ex p Barry* that local authorities could take account of resources when determining people's needs and the necessity of meeting those needs. So, between 1971–1972 and 1981–1982, there was a substantial increase in provision for disabled people; but some authorities still 'dragged their feet' (Darnborough, Kincade 1995,p.31).

Criticisms in Parliament have been persistent over a long period, such as these in 1991: 'Is the Minister ... aware that, like myself, each weekend many hon. Members meet many chronically sick and disabled constituents who are not receiving adequate services to enable them to lead a reasonable and respectable life?' (Mr Lofthouse: HCOA,3/12/1991,col.137). Similarly: 'how many local authorities had reduced or removed services in cases where there was no diminution of need? How does the Minister react to the case ... in which home help provision was withdrawn from an elderly couple, both of whom are severely and progressively disabled' (Alfred Morris: HCOA,3/12/1991,col.138).

In 1985, Alfred Morris MP asked: 'Is the Minister aware of the increasing concern among local authority leaders, not least the Conservative leader of Hillingdon, that in obeying the law on rates they are being forced to break the law passed by this House to help the disabled and their families?' (HCOA,16/4/1985, col.122). And in 1984, he expressed concern about the perceived failure of Liverpool City Council to provide telephones for those assessed to be in need of them (HCWA,19/1/1984, col.313; see also HCWA,22/3/1982,col.257 on the same subject). In 1973, it was claimed that nearly 'three years after the Act was passed, some authorities are carrying out their duty in a praiseworthy manner, but too many are unfortunately lagging behind, apparently either not knowing of their duties under Sections 1 and 2 or doing far too little to carry out those duties' (David Weitzman: HCD,9/4/1973,col.1057). About two-thirds of local authorities were 'good' and one-third 'bad' (Alfred Morris: HCD,9/4/1979, col.1067).

CSDPA background: enforcement. By 1979, ultimately fruitless attempts were being made, following the decision in *Wyatt v Hillingon LBC*, to amend the Act to enable a person to enforce the provision of services under s.2 through the county court – once an authority had accepted that it was necessary to meet the person's need (Chronically Sick and Disabled Persons (Amendment) Bill 1979). The aim was to put a stop to waiting lists (Edwin Wainwright: HCD,2/2/1979,cols.1897–1930) – although such amendment would not have covered, nearly 20 years later, the issue dealt with in *R v Gloucestershire CC, ex p Barry* concerning the manipulation of need and necessity before the waiting list stage is ever reached. Indeed, following the *Gloucestershire* judgment in 1997, another amending Bill was introduced, unsuccessfully, to ensure that an authority would 'have no regard to the resources available' when satisfying itself about need and necessity (Chronically Sick and Disabled Persons (Amendment) Bill 1997).

CSDPA background: consistency in application of the Act. Widely varying levels of service from authority to authority might seem to conflict with the intention of the sponsor (Alfred Morris MP) of the CSDPA 1970 who wished to standardise provision nationally (see above).

Indeed in 1983, when asked about 'any proposals for ensuring the attainment of nationally determined standards by local authorities in implementing' the CSDPA, the government replied that implementation 'is the responsibility of local authorities, which are best placed to judge the provision necessary to meet the needs of disabled people in their particular area' (Tony Newton: HCWA,26/7/1983,col.410).

The government further explained why it was opposed to standards for the CSDPA 1970: 'detailed guidance prepared by a Government Department, however well-intentioned, would not be an adequate substitute for on-the-spot decisions by the authorities that are closest to the needs of the individual and the services which exist in his area. More important, there is always a risk that minimum standards – in practice that is all that we could sensibly talk about – would be treated in some cases as maximum standards and would inhibit some of the developments we would wish to see. They would restrict rather than enlarge the scope for flexibility and innovation ... However, to acknowledge that local authorities are the best judges of local needs is not to absolve them of their statutory duties under the Act' (Tony Newton: HCD,10/6/1985,col.651) (But see now proposals for standards in community care, as outlined in a recent White Paper: Secretary of State for Health 1998).

CSDPA 1970, s.2: functions under s.29 of the National Assistance Act 1948

The reference in s.2 of the Act to the exercising of functions under s.29 of the National Assistance Act 1948 has given rise to dispute in the law courts. This is not just theoretical dispute, since it has focused on, for instance, a) whether CSDPA services are legally 'community care services' under s.46 of the NHS and Community Care Act 1990; and b) whether local authorities are empowered to charge for CSDPA services under s.17 of the Health and Services and Social Security Adjudications Act 1983. The problem is that s.2 of the CSDPA 1970 is listed in neither of these two Acts at the relevant place; and if s.2 were to be regarded as 'freestanding' and not embraced by s.29 of the National Assistance Act 1948, then services under s.2 could be neither community care services nor capable of being charged for. In fact, the Court of Appeal ruled in 1998 that s.2 of the CSDPA is not freestanding (*R v Powys CC, ex p Hambidge* about charges). This confirmed the High Court ruling in the same case, another Court of Appeal judgment of nearly twenty years before (*Wyatt v Hillingdon LBC*) and the view of the Secretary of State that the CSDPA 'relates to local authority functions under s.29 of the National Assistance Act 1948, and it is therefore already covered by the definition of community care services in the Bill' (Virginia Bottomley: SC(E),13/2/ 1990,col.969). In any case, the House of Lords had already found that s.2 was 'clearly embodied in the whole of the community care regime' (*R v Gloucestershire CC, ex p Barry*).

CSDPA 1970, s.2: disabled people

The fact that the authority must be exercising functions under s.29 of the 1948 Act means that only disabled people (including people with a mental disorder) are eligible for services under s.2 of the CSDPA.

CSDPA 1970, s.2: satisfaction of the local authority

The term 'satisfied' is usually considered to be a subjective term – in other words, it is for the authority to decide whether it is satisfied, rather than for the courts to say whether the authority should have been satisfied. The courts will be wary of intervening when statutory terms leave much to the subjective judgement of local authorities (see eg, *X v Bedfordshire CC*), although they do sometimes intervene (*Secretary of State v Tameside MBC*).

CSDPA 1970, s.2: any person

This phrase has been interpreted by the courts to indicate the existence of a specific duty towards an individual disabled person which is more susceptible to enforcement than a general, 'target' duty such as is found in s.29 of the National Assistance Act 1948 (see eg, *R v Gloucestershire CC, ex p Barry*, and also p.47).

CSDPA 1970, s.2: *ordinarily resident*

Eligibility is restricted to people who are ordinarily resident (see p.169) within the area of the authority.

CSDPA 1970, s.2: *necessary*

The local authority has to decide whether in order to meet a person's needs it is necessary for it to make arrangements.

Therefore, the duty to make arrangements is not triggered simply by identification of need, but by a further stage involving a decision about necessity. This has been confirmed by the courts. In *R v Gloucestershire CC ex p Barry*, the majority judges in the House of Lords held that local authorities may take account of resources when deciding this. The author of the CSDPA 1970, during its Parliamentary passage, also explained that the section required a local authority to provide services 'when it is satisfied that these services are necessary in a particular case' (Alfred Morris: HCD,4/2/1970,col.152). There might be various circumstances in which it is not necessary for a local authority to meet a need.

(1) *Unmet needs.* A local authority might state that not every need is regarded as a priority, and that there are certain needs which will remain 'unmet' – an option confirmed in the *Gloucestershire* case.

(2) *Some services more necessary than others?* There is possibly some uncertainty as to the exact implications of the *Gloucestershire* judgment in respect of necessity. Either it supports the proposition that resources may be taken account of in respect of all the services listed in s.2, when the authority decides whether it is necessary to make arrangements. Or the judgment might suggest that Lord Clyde, who gave the relevant opinion on this point, did not intend that resources could be taken account of in respect of all the services listed, but only in respect of some. Referring to the extensive service list, he stated a) that it was unlikely that Parliament intended that *all* of them might be provided regardless of cost, and b) that it was not necessary to hold that resources would always be an element in determining necessity, but simply that for the purposes of the present case they could be.

This theme was elaborated on in the comments made by the House of Lords in *R v East Sussex CC, ex p Tandy*, when it referred to the difficulty of regarding a radio, holiday or recreational activity as being necessities under s.2 of the CSDPA 1970 – seeming to imply that other services might normally be a necessity. In *R v Birmingham CC, ex p Mohammed*, the High Court continued along the same path, stating that adaptations to the home (carried out by means of disabled facilities grants under the Housing Grants, Construction and Regeneration Act 1996) were necessities, unlike *some* of the services contained in s.2 of the CSDPA 1970: thus resources could not come into account. But this would suggest that adaptations listed in s.2 would likewise constitute a necessity, just as they do under the 1996 Act.

The problem with this second, alternative explanation of how to measure necessity – namely that resources can be taken account of only in respect of certain services under s.2 – is that the services being withdrawn in the *Gloucestershire* case were cleaning and laundry, which come under 'practical assistance in the home', surely one of the more obviously 'necessary' services. Furthermore, Lord Nicholls in the *Gloucestershire* case by no means restricted his comments to non-essential services, finding that relative cost and relative benefit would have to be weighed up in relation to daily home care, installing a ground floor lavatory or widening doorways for wheelchair access.

A third option would be to suggest that the *Gloucestershire* judgment might allow the question to reduce in each individual case as to whether it was necessary to provide s.2 service for the particular person, *whatever the service*. For instance, one can envisage circumstances in which a holiday is essential (one of the services mentioned in the *Tandy* case as non-essential); but also a situation in which cleaning (which comes under practical assistance, as a seemingly essential s.2 service) is not. The court in *R v Islington LBC, ex p McMillan* concluded this when pointing out that provision of meals was more important than cleaning; interruption to the latter, but not to the former, might be acceptable. Yet even this comparison might falter in individual cases, as the local ombudsman pointed out when a local authority prioritised food-shopping services over cleaning services, but failed to consider a person's special medical need for hygiene in the home (*Westminster CC 1996*).

(3) *Alternative arrangements*. It is obvious in some circumstances that it is not necessary for the local authority to make arrangements, perhaps when somebody else is going to do so: a relative might offer to buy a piece of equipment, or a disabled facilities grant might be available under housing legislation.

(4) *Resources of disabled person*. It might be that the resources of applicants are a relevant factor when local authorities determine whether it is necessary for them to make arrangements – for instance, whether people are able (financially, physically and mentally) to make their own arrangements (see p.137).

CSDPA 1970, s.2: need

The case of *R v Gloucestershire CC, ex p Barry* established that when assessing disabled people's needs under s.2 of the CSPDA, resources may be taken into account – for example, when setting the criteria of eligibility with which to identify and measure need. Nevertheless, at the same time, the court stated that decisions based on such criteria should show that some sort of cost-benefit analysis has been carried out. The High Court in the same case *(R v Gloucestershire, ex p Mahfood)* put it another way, stating that a balancing exercise must be carried out, weighing up people's needs against the resources available. How the court might analyse whether a balancing exercise has been performed is illustrated in *R v Essex CC, ex p Bucke*.

The *Gloucestershire* ruling has provoked adverse comment, with the Law Lords being accused of undermining both the rights of disabled people and the will of Parliament. Put more graphically and emotively in *The Times* by the sponsor of the CSDPA 1970, the decision was 'perverse' (Morris 1997a). Lord Ashley, speaking to his fellow peers in the House of Lords, attacked it as creating 'an Alice in Wonderland world where, with resources affecting assessment of need, it becomes theoretically possible for a paraplegic to have no needs – and you cannot get more bizarre than that! … The ruling takes us back 30 years to the days when the problems of disabled people were hidden behind net curtains' (Lord Ashley: HLD,9/7/1997,col.701).

In fact, local authorities have always taken resources into account when deciding about provision under the CSDPA 1970; *the only difference now is in degree (ie, there are relatively fewer resources) rather than principle*. Arguably the *Gloucestershire* case was not about the meaning of need at all, but about the lack of resources. The final pronouncement of the House of Lords that once need and necessity have both been identified, then an absolute duty arises, is more or less what was understood over the preceding twenty five years – as was the elasticity of the term 'need' in the light of resources. For instance, in 1970, Circular guidance stated: 'Criteria of need are matters for the authorities to determine in the light of resources' (DHSS 12/70,para 7). As early as 1973, it was recognised that local authorities were in practice varying what they meant by need and necessity – for instance, whether people really needed a telephone (Jack Ashley: HCD,9/4/1973,col.1024).

In 1975, Barbara Castle explained: 'Of course "need" is an imprecise concept and local authorities have discretion in determining that need. Parliament did not attempt to define that precisely, so that there is and must be an area of discretion of which local authorities will take advantage in dealing with the conflict between what they desire to do and the resources they have available' (HCOA,5/8/1975,col.220).

In 1984 Margaret Thatcher joined the fray by explaining that whilst there certainly was a statutory duty to meet need at one level, there was actually discretion at another: 'I seem to remember that in that Act there is a good deal of discretion as to how it is applied. It is not absolutely mandatory. Any questions arising from the case … would not be for me but would be a matter for the courts to decide' (HCOA,13/12/1984,col.1206). This answer provoked protest and had to be explained by the Prime Minister at a later date: 'Where a local authority is satisfied of an individual disabled person's need for one of the services listed in s.2 of the Act, it has a duty to make arrangements to meet that need. In that sense this part of the Act is certainly mandatory. However, it is for the local authority itself to assess need and to determine how it should best be met. To that extent there is also an element of discretion. You can rest assured that it was not my intention in any way to question the statutory duties imposed by the Act on local authorities, nor to indicate any change in the advice given by successive Ministers for the Disabled on this point' (Margaret Thatcher: HCWA,31/1/1985,col.294).

Likewise, a Parliamentary ombudsman investigation in the 1970s remarked that legal advice to the DHSS at the time was that whilst lack of resources might be no excuse for failing to meet assessed individual need, nevertheless 'a local authority could exercise some discretion in fixing the standard by which the need is to be determined' (PCA C.12/K). Thus the accuracy of the two following contentions in 1997 in Parliament is doubtful, resting as they do on the premiss that the Circular, DHSS 12/70 (stating that criteria of need could be determined in the light of resources), had largely been ignored by local authorities. First: 'The Government referred to a circular. Circulars do not matter all that much. They are advisory, they offer guidance etc. But the law is the law; and local authorities should have observed the law. In fact, most did' (Lord Ashley: HLD,9/7/1997,col.715). Second: 'The day before the judgment on 20th March those needs were met by the local authority, as they have been met for nearly 27 years. Therefore, there can be no question of extra new costs if the Bill [to reverse the judgment] before the House is passed. We simply revert to the position as everyone has known and understood it for all those years' (Lord Ashley: HLD,9/7/1997,col.703).

These statements do not acknowledge a) that local authorities have always explored 'escape routes' from their obligations when short of money; b) that they do so more vigorously and sometimes deviously when they have less money than usual; c) that the increasing restriction of services by local authorities in the last few years is new not in principle but in degree; and d) that it is precisely because such behaviour has been common that an example, not an exception, such as *R v Gloucestershire CC, ex p Barry*, reached the courts. Even before the 20th March 1997, when the Court of Appeal's ruling – that resources could not be taken into account, that assessed needs had to be met and that there could be no 'unmet need' under s.2 of the CSDPA 1970 – still stood, local authorities were busy finding ways of limiting provision. For instance, they were reducing access to assessment, discouraging people from articulating needs and wishes, and rarely recording needs which could not be met (Midgley, Munlo and Brown 1997,p.6). As the local authority associations put it in 1995, social services 'will always need to find a mechanism for reconciling infinite need with finite resources' (ACC,AMA 1995,p.38). Indeed, following the Court of Appeal judgment, a Department of Health letter to the Association of County Councils hinted discreetly at how local authorities might attempt to limit provision, by referring a) to the eligibility condition of disability; b) to needs as being 'basic or essential requirements'; and c) to the taking of account of resources in the decision about how to meet a need (DH 1996c).

The *Gloucestershire* case also confirmed that services can be removed without a diminution of need, but simply because policies and eligibility of criteria have changed. Yet ironically this was not apparently always the view of government; for instance, in 1991, asked whether it was legally permissible that a telephone be withdrawn without a lessening of need, the government answered that it was not (Ann Widdecombe: HCOA,24/6/1991,col.667). This was despite an answer given nine years earlier when the government accepted that it was legitimate for local authorities to look 'more carefully' at whether individuals really needed telephones under the CSDPA (Hugh Rossi: HCOA,15/6/1982,col.718).

CSDPA 1970, s.2: needs, preferences and service options

The word 'need' is a necessary condition for the triggering of the duty under s.2; hence the longstanding distinction made by local authorities between need and 'preference' (see p.140). Furthermore, the degree of specificity or generality with which a local authority identifies and expresses need, will in part determine the range of service options available for meeting the need (see p.113).

CSDPA 1970, s.2: shall

Once a local authority has accepted that it is necessary for it to make arrangements to meet a person's needs, then the legislation states that it must make those arrangements.

The House of Lords in the *Gloucestershire* case confirmed that at this stage a local authority has an absolute duty to make the arrangements, irrespective of its resources. However, if there are several options by which to meet the need, the local authority may take account of resources, so long as the identified need is still met (see *Gloucestershire* case at all three stages). Nevertheless, arguing exhaustion of a particular budget will not assist a local authority in evading this absolute duty; in such circumstances it will have to raid another budget (*R v East Sussex CC, ex p Tandy*).

This merely repeats what had been generally understood for many years. For instance, 1970 Circular guidance stated quite clearly that if local authorities are 'satisfied that an individual is in need ... they are to make arrangements which are appropriate to his or her case' (DHSS 12/70,para 7). In 1975, Barbara Castle emphasised: 'I repeat that, once a local authority accepts that need exists in respect of one of the services listed in s.2, it is incumbent on it, I am advised, to make arrangements to meet that need' – although she did add that 'it may be difficult sometimes in present circumstances to balance the discharge of the duty with due exercise of financial restraint' (HCOA,5/8/1975,col.218). And some years later, as a Minister for Social Security, Alfred Morris (the sponsor of the 1970 Act) stated that 'when a local authority has identified and accepted a need, it shall be the duty of the authority to meet that need' (HCD,2/2/1979,col.1923). It should be noted however, that these statements fail to recognise the separate decision required (and highlighted in *R v Gloucestershire CC, ex p Barry*), when the local authority decides whether it is satisfied that it is necessary actually to meet identified need.

CSDPA 1970, s.2: make arrangements

The term 'make arrangements' does not entail that the authority make direct provision under s.2, since the National Assistance Act 1948 (s.30) authorises the employment by local authorities of agents to deliver services. When a local authority chooses neither to make direct provision nor to make a direct payment nor to employ another as agent to do so – but to give advice instead – it would probably be doing so under s.1 of the CSDPA 1970 (provision of information) or under s.29 of the National Assistance Act 1948 (duty to provide advice and support). This is because the person would be going on to make his or own arrangements for services, rather than have them made by the authority.

CSDPA 1970, s.2: all or any of the services

This emphasises that the duty to make arrangements, when the local authority is satisfied that it is necessary to meet the needs, applies to any one or all of the services listed. It is perhaps unfortunate that the House of Lords found in *R v Gloucestershire CC, ex p Barry* that not all the services listed in s.2 of the CSDPA 1970 were 'essential'. This notion was carried over into *R v East Sussex CC, ex p Tandy* and contributed to the distinction made between that case and the *Gloucestershire* case: radio, recreation and holidays were mentioned.

What the judges apparently failed to appreciate was that for disabled people confined to their homes, and with carers at breaking point, something like a holiday might be far from non-essential, but be more in the way of a necessary break. Indeed, it could be maintained that the judicial relegation of certain items in the s.2 list undermines the apparently clear intention of Parliament to give all the services on the list equal statutory weight in the Act. Yet the House of Lords stated, in both the *Gloucestershire* and *East Sussex* cases, that Parliament could not have intended this, despite the statutory language and without having consulted the Parliamentary debates of the time. In contrast, the judge in *R v Haringey LBC, ex p Norton* did appreciate the importance of assessing the social, recreational and leisure – not just the physical – needs of a young man with multiple sclerosis.

CSDPA 1970, s.2: practical assistance in the home

In principle, practical assistance in the home can cover a range of services from general household tasks to personal care: for instance heavy household (gardening, window cleaning, decorating, repairs, lighting fires), housework (cleaning, laundry, cooking meals), tasks outside the home (shopping, collecting a pension), personal tasks (getting in and out of bed, moving about, dressing, toileting, washing, teeth and denture care, bathing, nail cutting, taking medicines (Age Concern England 1992,p.13). It might also cover lifting things, checking spectacles and hearing aids, foot care, catheter and stoma care, care of pressure areas, exercises, preparing meals, errands, care of pets and guide dogs, budgeting and record-keeping, reading, letter-writing, telephone calls (SSI 1996d,p.21).

In practice, many local authorities now concentrate increasingly on providing personal care services to people at higher physical risk, rather than basic household tasks for those at lower risk.

This has been criticised on the grounds that denying people such preventative services simply causes or accelerates their entry into the higher risk category, and not only induces misery but is a short-sighted use of resources (see p.120).

Practical assistance in the home has been an issue in a number of community care cases; for instance, *R v Gloucestershire CC, ex p Barry, R v Islington LBC, ex p McMillan, R v Staffordshire CC, ex p Farley* (even though night sitter services, disputed in this last case, are actually mentioned by name in schedule 8 of the NHS Act 1977).

CSDPA 1970, s.2: wireless, television, library or similar recreational facilities

The Department of Health has issued no guidance on the provision of radio or television. However, in Northern Ireland, following the passing of the Chronically Sick and Disabled Persons (Northern Ireland) Act 1978, the Department of Health and Social Services (DHSS) in the province gave guidance on the provision of televisions by health and social services boards (HSSBs). The person had to be housebound and living alone, or confined to a room which meant that a television was needed in that particular room. As well as providing the sets, the licence fees of eligible applicants could also be paid (HSS(PH)5/79). The Northern Ireland DHSS also issued guidance stating that HSSBs should provide batteries free of charge for people who had radio sets provided by the British Wireless Fund for the Blind (HSS(OS5A)4/76).

In 1971, an apparent example of a local authority's deciding that it was not necessary to provide a radio was given in Parliament: a severely disabled man, using an environmental control system with an interface for a radio, wished to take an educational degree and required a radio. The local authority refused because he already had one; so he had, but he could not operate it because he was completely paralysed (Lewis Carter-Jones: HCD,21/5/1971,col.1667). Yet radio was amongst the services deemed inessential by the House of Lords in *R v East Sussex CC, ex p Tandy*: see p.201).

Television was not included in the original CSDP Bill but was added by amendment. The proposer explained that television was one 'way of overcoming that sense of complete isolation which is one of the most important problems facing the disabled' (John Golding: HCD,20/3/1970, col.884). The government accepted the amendment as a clarification, a 'spelling out more clearly of the reality of modern mass media', since it was conscious of the importance that television could have for disabled people (Dr Dunwoody: HCD,20/3/970,col.885).

CSDPA 1970, s.2: lectures, games, outings or similar recreational facilities

The High Court ruled against the local authority in *R v Haringey LBC, ex p Norton*, because when undertaking a reassessment, it had failed to consider the man's social, recreational or leisure needs – despite their being clearly spelt out in s.2 of the CSDPA 1970 and in the Department of Health's notion of need as a multi-faceted concept (SSI,SWSG 1991a,p.12).

In contrast to those judicial members of the House of Lords hearing the cases of *R v Gloucestershire, ex p Barry and R v East Sussex CC, ex p Tandy*, another member of the House did in 1970 recognise the importance of recreational facilities during the passage of the CSDP Bill: 'One of the difficulties that besets disabled people is that of getting out of the main stream of life, into a bit of a backwater. I know this from my own experience' (Viscount Ingleby: HLD,9/4/ 1970,col.281).

CSDPA 1970, s.2: educational facilities

Taking advantage of educational facilities, under s.2 of the CSDPA 1970, was held in *R v Bradford MBC, ex p Parkinson* not to include actually making arrangements for the provision of education – but merely to take advantage of what was already potentially available. This was in line with the government's understanding of the amendment to the CSDP Bill in 1970, introducing the word 'educational' so as not to 'confuse the relationship with educational services. We are not talking about educational services in the narrower sense' (Dr John Dunwoody: HCD,20/3/1970,col.885). Likewise, in the same case, the court also stated that the power under s.29 of the National Assistance Act 1948 to give instruction to disabled people in their own homes (see p.195) could not be read into the duty regarding educational facilities in s.2(1)(b) of the 1970 Act.

However, notwithstanding this, the duty could still apply in some circumstances in relation to transport – and also for equipment which people might require in order to pursue an educational course. For instance, in 1992, the government stated in Parliament that such assistance under this part of s.2 'might, in appropriate cases, include the funding by the local authority of personal care required to enable the student in question to pursue his or her studies' (Tim Yeo: HCWA,8/12/1992,col.642). Local authorities might also reflect on whether access to educational facilities could include arranging for the provision of equipment such as a powered wheelchair. Thus, it might be needed by a disabled child to move around a school with long corridors and a large playground, and to get to the shops and library outside the school. In this not atypical situation, the local NHS wheelchair service might decline to assist (see Aldersea 1996,part 2,p.11).

Conversely, the court stated in *G v Wakefield MDC* that in considering special educational provision, an education authority had no power to request (under s.322 of the Education Act 1996) that a local authority social services authority arrange respite care – because the need for such a service fell outside the sphere of special education, and such a request under s.322 had precisely to be in connection with special education functions.

CSDPA 1970, s.2: assistance for that person in arranging for the carrying out of any works of adaptation

The duty to make arrangements in relation to home adaptations is qualified by a lengthy chain of wording: 'making arrangements for the provision of assistance for that person in arranging the carrying out of adaptations'. This suggests to some local authorities that direct provision is not contemplated.

The local ombudsman has stated in this context that 'the Chronically Sick and Disabled Persons At 1970 does not place a statutory obligation on the council to make a financial contribution' (*Hertfordshire CC 1992*), and has not necessarily disagreed with authorities who claim that advice and assistance might suffice in place of direct provision (*Wirral MBC 1992d*).

The correct view is that in some circumstances an arms-length approach might legitimately be taken, but if the need cannot be met in any other way then the local authority is probably committed to some form of direct arrangement (always assuming that the applicant has surmounted both the need and necessity tests: see above). This is expressly contemplated by Circular guidance on home adaptations (see DoE 17/96,p.191 and see p.402 of this book).

CSDPA 1970, s.2: additional facilities

The meaning of additional facilities is slightly uncertain and has not been examined by the courts in this context.

It might be viewed as signifying a) any extra item needed (and therefore an extra cost) on account of the person's disability; or b) an item, likewise needed because of the person's disability, but which is a specialist disability item. (A related issue of interpretation, about extra costs incurred because of disability, arose in *R v North Yorkshire CC, ex p Hargreaves (no.2)*, concerning holidays under s.2 of the CSDPA 1970).

The practical consequences of the two different interpretations are as follows. Under the first, authorities could provide both ordinary equipment (not designed specially for disability or frailty) such as electric tin openers, footstools, jar openers, non-slip bath mats, portable heaters, security locks or systems – as well as specially designed equipment such as hoists – so long as they are needed because of the person's disability. Under the second, authorities could only provide specialist equipment.

The second interpretation would be a restrictive one. There are also practical problems with it, because clearly it depends on distinguishing specialist, disability equipment from ordinary equipment. Yet disputes in the field of VAT have shown that this distinction can be difficult to make, in those circumstances when zero-rating depends on equipment having been designed solely for disabled people. For instance, in one case involving overbed tables, a VAT Tribunal decided that though of particular value to disabled people, they were also useful to all sorts of other hospital patients as well; therefore zero-rating could not apply (*Princess Louise Scottish Hospital v C and E*).

On the other hand, the first interpretation might make local authorities anxious about 'opening the floodgates', being asked to furnish disabled people's homes from 'top to bottom', and having to relieve poverty by meeting the costs of everyday items. However, this might be a mistaken notion, since eligibility would still be dependent on need and necessity arising from the person's disability. Local authorities are anyway fearful of floodgates even in relation to specialist disability equipment: in one investigation, the ombudsman was not convinced that the local authority had 'no responsibility' in relation to the provision of electric wheelchairs for indoor and outdoor use, even though their provision is normally regarded as the responsibility of the NHS (*North Yorkshire CC 1993*).

CSDPA 1970, s.2: safety, comfort or convenience

The legislation does not state that the three terms – safety, comfort and convenience – form an order of priorities, and it is something of an irony that some local authorities concentrate only on 'safety' – given that this word was only added by amendment during the Parliamentary passage of the CSDP Bill: it did not appear in the original.

The proposer of the amendment to add the word 'safety' explained that 'distinctions between comfort and convenience will, in practice, often be blurred, and similarly there will be areas of overlap between considerations of convenience and of safety. However ... in practice safety will often be a dominant or even the first consideration ... It is worth considering that according to individual circumstances ... adaptations and facilities ... which might be construed as convenient when somebody else is in the house, can become matters of safety at such times as when the disabled person is alone. I have in mind such items as hand and guard rails, types of heating appliances, cooking stoves and even floor coverings' (Lord Gray: HLD,30/4/1970,cols.1152–1153).

Nevertheless, some local authority policies state that provision will not – or at least not normally be made – in respect of comfort and convenience. For instance, a policy might refer to a lower priority category as: 'needs unlikely to be met (clients who require assistance and support to fulfil potential role in society – including advice on leisure time activities, employment preparation; clients whose quality of life could be improved to "care, comfort and convenience" standards – eg. adaptations to allow access to hobby areas)' (Mandelstam 1993, p.40). Such policies might in some circumstances lead an authority into unlawfulness in terms of either fettering its discretion (making no exceptions) or simply acting illegally (ie, having a policy inconsistent on its face with the legislation). Consider the case of *R v Haringey LBC, ex p Norton*, in which the authority behaved unlawfully by neglecting to assess properly a person's social, recreational and leisure needs under s.2 of the CSDPA – despite the inclusion of terms such as 'recreational facilities' in s.2. Similarly in *R v Ealing LBC, ex p Leaman*, the local authority adopted a rigid policy about holidays which effectively struck out two words from s.2(1)(f) of the 1970 Act – comparable to a policy which strikes out 'comfort or convenience' from s.2(1)(e). Indeed, the local ombudsman has referred not only to the potential danger, but also to the 'extreme discomfort' and the 'inconvenient' accommodation, in which a disabled woman had to live – whilst waiting four years and eight months for the simple aids that eventually made such a difference to her life (*Hackney LBC 1992a*). On the other hand, an authority might maintain that its priorities or criteria conform, albeit strictly, to the statutory wording by referring to safety in terms of 'personal danger' and to convenience as the absence of 'serious inconvenience' (*Sheffield CC 1995*, an ombudsman investigation).

CSDPA 1970, s.2: greater (safety, comfort or convenience)

In principle, the comparative word 'greater' could be treated a) negatively, in the sense that a person's safety, comfort or convenience might be increased without necessarily attaining to a desired plateau; or b) more positively in the sense that even if somebody has already a particular level of safety, comfort or convenience, it is capable of being improved upon. The word has not been interpreted in this context by the law courts.

CSDPA 1970, s.2: holidays

The provision of holidays has been examined in two court cases in particular. In *R v Ealing LBC, ex p Leaman*, the local authority had – in order to save money – adopted a blanket policy of only providing assistance with holidays which it had arranged itself. The judge found this blanket policy to be 'quite wrong', since the legislation expressly contemplates that authorities might assist with holidays 'otherwise arranged'. In *R v North Yorkshire CC, ex p Hargreaves (no.2)*, the local authority argued that its role under s.2 of the CSDPA 1970 was not to relieve poverty, and that it would only assist with the extra costs of a disabled person's holiday arising because of disability – in other words, not with the ordinary travel and hotel expenses which everybody has to pay when they go on holiday. It also argued that the term 'facilitate' precluded it from paying for the full cost. The judge found that the policy fettered the local authority's discretion and was not consistent with the wording of the legislation.

Assistance with holidays can, therefore, come in various forms; even, as became clear in one ombudsman investigation (*North Yorkshire CC 1993*), retrospective payment of petrol money to a service user (although, made before the Community Care (Direct Payments) Act 1996, there might be some doubt about the legality of such a payment: see p.196).

Holidays were amongst the services deemed to be inessential by the House of Lords in *R v East Sussex CC, ex p Tandy* (see p.201) in its comments on *R v Gloucestershire CC, ex p Barry* – apparently not appreciating their importance, as even a government Minister did in 1992, when he referred to them as a 'vital part' of everyday life, which should be enjoyed by disabled people just as by everybody else (Keep, Clarkson 1993,p.18, citing Nicholas Scott, MP).

CSDPA 1970, s.2: telephones and related equipment

The Department of Health has issued no guidance on the provision of telephones. However, in 1971, the Association of County Councils (ACC) and Association of Metropolitan Authorities (AMA) – now both part of the Local Government Association (LGA) – issued a joint Circular (note: not a government Circular). In summary, people would qualify if, in the view of an authority, they lived alone, or were frequently alone – or lived with a person who was unable, or could not be relied on, to deal with an emergency or maintain necessary outside contacts. *In addition* to this, the person either a) would have a need to get in touch with a doctor, other health worker or helper and would be in danger or at risk without a telephone; or b) be unable to leave the dwelling in normal weather without assistance or have seriously restricted mobility – and need a telephone to avoid isolation. Also, there should be *no* friend or neighbours willing and able to help (ACC, AMA 1971). Guidance on telephones was issued in Scotland and Northern Ireland and contained similar criteria to the AMA/ACC guidance (SW7/1972; HSS(OS5A)5/78).

Local authorities attempt from time to time to limit the provision of telephones and related equipment – for instance, withdrawing at a stoke, without reassessment, telephone rental payments from 273 disabled people, before being pressurised to restore them (Keep, Clarkson 1993,p.19). Such restrictions have to be seen in the light of the fact that for older people, telephone might be seen as a basic survival need – together with warmth, adequate income and good health care (Age Concern England 1994b,p.40).

For instance, in one case a local authority was restricting provision of minicoms (telephone equipment for deaf or hearing-impaired people) to people who already had a telephone; the local ombudsman agreed with the British Deaf Association that this criterion was a legally irrelevant consideration (*Wakefield MDC 1992*). The Social Services Inspectorate has pointed out in an inspection report the inappropriateness of applying the general eligibility criteria for telephone provision based on mobility and health, to the provision of text telephones for deaf people. It 'is important to make a distinction between providing a phone – which would be no more necessary for a deaf person than a hearing person – and enabling deaf people to have equal access to the telephone system so they can do normal things, such as ring their child's school'. It also suggested that the provision of a text telephone might be covered not only under s.2(1)(h) of the 1970 Act, but also under s.2(1)(e) which refers to facilities for greater, safety or convenience (SSI 1997a,p.21).

Many years before, the discretion exercised by local authorities in determining the need and necessity for telephones was attacked in the claim that there were some directors of social services, 'backed by niggardly, backward and indolent councils, saying that telephones are not really necessary or vital for the disabled, and recommending flashing lights or sirens, or even, in some cases, whistles. Imagine a meeting of severely disabled people ... with the director of social services saying "If you are in trouble do not call for the ambulance or your doctor –just turn your house into a lighthouse or a police car and hope that some passer-by will either see or hear you, and come in and help. If no one does, that is bad luck on you". That kind of thing is not good enough. It is outrageous that the Government are permitting this shocking variation in provision for the disabled' (Jack Ashley: HCD,9/4/1973,col.1024).

The different notions of what might constitute need for a telephone permeated Parliament and gave rise to the identification of pre-electronic man. In 1972, one MP was 'depressed to hear the Secretary of State being somewhat sceptical about the value, other than the social value, of a telephone. All of us have become aware in talking to our constituents of the extent to which the telephone is now regarded as a general facility to which people are far more accustomed than they were a few years ago. To dismiss it and say that its provision in this context is not appropriate or it may have little value apart from its social use is harmful in two ways. Firstly, because those local authorities which are dragging their feet ... will be discouraged, and, second, because it betrays in the Minister an attitude which one can only describe as "pre-electronic man"' (Phillip Whitehead: HCD,21/2/1972,cols.996–997).

As Baroness Masham had pointed out in her maiden speech during the passing of the Bill through Parliament, a 'telephone is a lifeline in times of trouble, eliminating isolation and alleviating loneliness' (HLD,9/4/1970,col.274). Even by 1971, the value and cost benefit of loudspeaking (ie, hands-free) telephones provided under the CSDPA 1970 was being alluded to in Parliament; although too often, when medical doctors recommended their supply to disabled people, they would be greeted with the answer of 'not enough money' (Dr Tom Stuttaford and Lewis Carter-Jones: HCD,21/5/1971,cols.1733–1734).

Finally, the word 'telephone' was only added into the CSDP Bill during its Parliamentary passage and was not present in the original Bill, which referred only to specialist equipment to use the telephone. As a supporter of the amendment pointed out, 'the first essential is to have a telephone, not to have equipment to help one to use it' (Baroness Brooke: HLD,30/4/1970,col.1156).

3. INFORMATION FOR DISABLED PEOPLE: CHRONICALLY SICK AND DISABLED PERSONS ACT 1970,s.1

Local authorities have a specific duty under s.1 of the CSDPA 1970 to existing service users about other services which the authority thinks relevant and which it knows about. This is a strong duty which a local authority has towards individual people; it is not just a general duty. Failure to provide this information might give clear grounds for challenge, although even this duty is qualified since it depends on the authority's opinion about other relevant services and on its having particulars of those other services.

Nevertheless, the local ombudsman does sometimes find maladministration in relation to the giving of information by local authorities in specific instances – for example, poor advice about social security benefits, or unclear information about disabled facilities grants.

EXTRACTS

Legislation (CSDPA 1970,s.1(2)(b)) as amended by the Disabled Persons (Services, Consultation and Representation) Act 1986, s.9) states:

'Every local authority…

(b) shall ensure that any such person as aforesaid who uses any other service provided by the authority whether under any such arrangements or not is informed of any other of those services which in the opinion of the authority is relevant to his needs and of any service provided by any other authority or organisation which in the opinion of the authority is so relevant and of which particulars are in the authority's possession'.

DISCUSSION

A 'relevant' service is left to the opinion of the authority, but Baroness Masham explained, supporting the passing of the Disabled Persons (Services Consultation and Representation) Bill which amended s.1 of the 1970 Act: 'The list of what may be included is endless, but would obviously include all the activities of voluntary organisations, transport schemes, leisure opportunities, and I hope also education and employment opportunities. Basic information on benefits should be included as well as all the personal services provided by the Council and the NHS' (HLD,14/5/1986,col.1227).

The original CSDP Bill, in one of its forms, actually listed particular services and benefits about which people should be informed, including aids and appliances, domestic help and financial benefits. These specific references failed to reach the statute book. Further amendment was proposed to include 'information to cover all relevant aids and appliances available from the local authority or the National Health Service'. This was opposed by the government for a number of reasons. First, it did not want to place duties on social services 'to provide public information in a meaningful manner about medical services'. Second, there were dangers in giving information to disabled people if it put them in a position to demand or at least request services, thus undermining the role of professional workers (compare this sentiment with more recent ideas about service users as 'consumers' with 'rights'). Third, the amendment assumed that 'the respective authorities and medical staffs are insufficiently informed about each other's services to be fully helpful to patients or clients'. If this was the case, the situation should be looked into at a later date when the new social services departments were well-established (Dr John Dunwoody: HCD,20/3/1970, cols.876–881).

Section 1 of the CSDPA 1970 sharpens up the general duty to give advice and support under s.29 of the 1948 Act, by making it a specific duty towards individual users of services. The local ombudsman has on occasion considered provision of information under s.1, finding maladministration when inaccurate advice is given, for example, about entitlement to state benefits (*East Sussex CC 1995a*), or when a social services authority fails to discuss the possibility of home adaptations (available through a housing authority) with a disabled person (*Leicester CC 1992b*). However, in *North Yorkshire CC 1993*, there was no maladministration in respect of information provision. First the complainant had been given a range of leaflets in response to his request for information. Then, following a complaint the man had made, a council officer visited him to go through the relevant legislation and to leave copies with him.

4. SERVICES FOR OLDER PEOPLE: HEALTH SERVICES AND PUBLIC HEALTH ACT 1968, s.45

Under s.45 of the Health Services and Public Health Act 1968, local authorities have the power to make arrangements to provide non-residential community care services for older people who are not classed as disabled – and thus do not qualify for services under s.29 of the National Assistance Act 1948 and under s.2 of the Chronically Sick and Disabled Persons Act 1970. The services listed by approval made under s.45 read similarly to those listed under s.2 of the CSDPA 1970.

EXTRACTS

Legislation states (Health Services and Public Health Act 1968, s.45) that:

(welfare of old people) local authorities 'may with approval of the Secretary of State, and to such extent as he may direct shall, make arrangements for promoting the welfare of old people'.

(prohibition on cash payment) Local authorities are prohibited from making payments to old people, unless it is remuneration for suitable work in accordance with arrangements made under s.45.

(anti-duplication provision) Local authorities must not make available any accommodation or services 'required to be provided under the National Health Service Act 1977'.

Approvals (in Circular, DHSS 19/71) give local authorities the power to make arrangements 'for any of the following purposes to meet the needs of the elderly':

(meals and recreation) '(a) to provide meals and recreation in the home and elsewhere';

(information about services) '(b) to inform the elderly of services available to them and to identify elderly people in need of services';

(travel) '(c) to provide facilities or assistance in travelling to and from the home for the purpose of participating in services provided by the authority or similar services';

(boarding) '(d) to assist in finding suitable households for boarding elderly persons';

(visiting, advice, social work support) '(e) to provide visiting and advisory services and social work support';

(practical assistance, adaptations, equipment) '(f) to provide practical assistance in the home, including assistance in the carrying out of works of adaptation or the provision of any additional facilities designed to secure greater safety, comfort or convenience';

(warden-assisted housing) (g) 'to contribute to the cost of employing a warden on welfare functions in warden assisted housing schemes';

(wardens for private housing) (h) 'to provide warden services for occupiers of private housing'.

Guidance (DHSS 19/71) states:

(elderly but not disabled: preventative services) 'the purpose of section 45 is to enable authorities to make other approved arrangements for services to the elderly who are not substantially and permanently handicapped, and thus to promote the welfare of the elderly generally and so far as possible prevent or postpone personal or social deterioration or breakdown' (para 2).

(development of services) 'The Secretary of State nevertheless recognises that there are limitations ... The present shortages of staff, and the limited knowledge of the total needs of the elderly and how best to meet them, make it in his view both impracticable and undesirable for all authorities to seek to provide from the outset all possible services for all the elderly. It appears to him that it will be necessary ... to lay down priorities both of recipients and of services, and to proceed by way of experiment and in stages to provide services of various kinds. But ... authorities should have the wide powers of section 45 available to them so that they will be in a position over the whole social services field to re-plan their services, to re-deploy their resources, and to develop both so far as they are able' (para 3).

(priorities) 'Home-help, including laundry services and other aids to independent living, should probably be high on any priority list ... So should social visiting organised and coordinated by the local authority but largely undertaken by voluntary workers or others after suitable preparatory training. Many of the elderly who are mobile or who can be transported will require social centres providing meals and opportunities for occupation as well as companionship and recreation. For the housebound and the frail elderly meals-on-wheels will also need to be developed' (para 10).

DISCUSSION

Services for older people, 1968 Act: background

During the passing of the 1968 Act in Parliament, the government explained that s.45 of the Act would 'in time, come to affect considerable numbers of elderly people' and would fill the gap where no provision was being made 'for the common case in old age of considerable, but still not substantial, handicap arising similarly from the infirmity of old age'.

Furthermore, whilst adequate powers for prevention were present in the NHS Act 1946 (now the NHS Act 1977), there were no powers enabling preventative social welfare measures to be taken (except for meals and recreation). The 1968 Act would remedy this. The government also recognised the importance of home adaptations, equipment, small personal services, special housing services – and visiting services which would be not just to advise and give practical help, but also to make and keep contact and 'fill the void of loneliness which afflicts so many elderly people on their own' (Mr Robinson: HCD,7/12/1967,cols.1688–1689).

It was envisaged that practical assistance in the home might include obvious 'care' services and also tasks such as gardening and decorating (Baroness Phillips: HLD,23/4/1968,col.560). But when pressed in the House of Commons about whether it would specify provision of services such as gardening (given, for instance, that some tenancy agreements could be terminated if the garden was not kept up), decoration, collecting pensions and getting library books, the government replied that local authorities were democratically elected bodies and 'should be allowed, within reasonable limits, to get on with the job' (Mr Robinson: HCD,20/2/1968,cols.413–420).

Services for older people, 1968 Act: prevention

The perceived reduction in practice of home help for older people with needs deemed to be lower priority – in favour of personal care services for those at greater immediate risk – goes precisely against the reference to preventative services in the guidance on s.45 of the 1968 Act.

Services for older people, 1968 Act: power only

This part of the 1968 Act is somewhat of a poor relation to s.2 of the CSDPA 1970, not because of any lesser potential importance, but because the approvals made under it create only powers – to which local authorities might adopt a 'take-it or leave-it' approach. For local authorities with few resources, s.45 of the 1968 Act is therefore likely to present itself as a soft option. They might be tempted even to recategorise some elderly frail people previously regarded as disabled, and to refer to them now as 'older' but not 'disabled' people – so that they come under the 1968 Act powers instead of the duty under s.2 of the 1970 Act (although see p.90 for defining disability).

It is just possible that if, in developing its community care policies and services, a local authority could be shown not even to have taken account of the approvals and guidance in respect of s.45, then a case might be arguable in the law courts. Local authorities should at least have regard to guidance (*R v Islington LBC, ex p Rixon, R v North Yorkshire CC, ex p Hargreaves, R v North Derbyshire HA, ex p Fisher*); and even in respect of powers, should beware of fettering their discretion (eg, *R v Bristol CC, ex p Bailey; British Oxygen v Board of Trade*).

Services for older people, 1968 Act: ordinary residence

Exercise of the powers is not restricted to those elderly people ordinarily resident in the area of a local authority.

Services for older people, 1968 Act: employment of agents in making arrangements

For the purposes of arrangements for welfare services under s.45 of the 1968 Act, local authorities are empowered to employ as agents 'any voluntary organisation or any person carrying on, professionally or by way of trade or business, activities which consist of or include the provision of services for old people, being an organisation or person appearing to the authority to be capable of providing the service to which the arrangements apply' (National Assistance Act 1948, s.30).

Services for older people, 1968 Act: anti-duplication provision

See p.325.

5. HOME HELP AND LAUNDRY FACILITIES: NHS ACT 1977, schedule 8

Local authorities have a duty to provide or arrange home help and a power to provide or arrange laundry facilities in relation to households with somebody who is ill, lying-in, an expectant mother, aged or disabled.

EXTRACTS

Legislation (NHS Act 1977, schedule 8).

> 'It is the duty of every local authority to provide on such a scale as is adequate for the needs of their area, or to arrange for the provision on such a scale as is so adequate, of home help for households where such help is required owing to the presence of ... a person who is suffering from illness, lying-in, an expectant mother, aged, handicapped as a result of having suffered from illness or by congenital deformity ... and every such authority has power to provide or arrange for the provision of laundry facilities for households for which home help is being, or can be, provided...'.

DISCUSSION

The duty to provide or arrange home help – to be complied with on a scale adequate for the area – is likely to be regarded by the courts as a general, target duty, as opposed to a specific individual one – and not easy to enforce by an individual (see p.47). Nevertheless, how the courts might deal with the phrase 'scale as is adequate for the needs of their area' is possibly unclear. Home help is capable of covering a range of tasks (see p.120).

In contrast to s.2 of the CSDPA 1970 and s.29 of the National Assistance Act 1948, eligibility is not restricted or qualified in relation to people who are ordinarily resident within the area of the local authority. Provision is expressed to be for the household, not for any particular person, and this part of schedule 8 seems not to be restricted to adults. Illness is defined as including 'mental disorder within the meaning of the Mental Health Act 1983 and any injury or disability requiring medical or dental treatment or nursing' (NHS Act 1977, s.128). The term 'aged' is not defined nor the term 'handicapped', other than that illness or congenital deformity must be the cause. There is no apparent express prohibition on the making of cash payments to people in respect of home help and laundry facilities – compare such a prohibition for other services under schedule 8 (below) – but it is not clear that the courts would rule that it was lawful, given their reasoning in *R v Secretary of State for Health, ex p Hammersmith and Fulham LBC* in relation to charges under the National Assistance Act 1948.

When this provision was originally passed in Parliament (it started life in the Health Services and Public Health Act 1968), it was lamented that the provision of a laundry service was not mandatory like the home help provision, 'because the problem of soiled bed linen is probably the most common single factor which results in old folk having to be unnecessarily admitted to hospital' (Dr Dunwoody: HCD,7/12/1967,col.1767). In practice, laundry facilities might include not only ordinary laundry arrangements, but also, for example, the provision of washing machines (eg, where there is a special need caused by heavy incontinence, or a person with AIDS).

By way of an anti-duplication measure (contained in NHS Act 1977, s.21), provision is subject to s.3(1)(e) of the NHS Act 1977 (ie, provision of services, expressed in similar language, by the NHS). Also, by virtue of a provision in s.29 of the National Assistance Act 1948, any service which is required to be provided under schedule 8 of the NHS Act 1977 cannot be provided under s.29 (see p.193, and for comment on anti-duplication, p.325). There is also a question about how the word 'handicapped' in schedule 8 compares to the term 'substantial and permanent handicap' in s.29 (see p.93).

6. SERVICES FOR ILLNESS AND MENTAL DISORDER: NHS ACT 1977, schedule 8

These services relate a) to the prevention of illness, the care of people who are ill, the after-care of people who have been ill – including specific duties towards people with a mental disorder; and b) to provision of home help and laundry facilities for people who are ill, 'handicapped', 'aged', lying-in or expectant mothers.

EXTRACTS

Legislation (NHS Act 1977,schedule 8,para 2) states that:

> **(illness: prevention, care, after-care)** Local authorities have a duty so far as directed – and the power so far as approved – by the Secretary of State, to make arrangements for the prevention of illness, the care of people who are ill, and the after-care of people who have been ill (NHS Act 1977,schedule 8,para 2). Directions and approvals have been issued: see below.

> **(prohibition on cash payments)** Cash payments to users of services are forbidden except in relation to remuneration for those users working in accordance with arrangements made under paragraph 2 of schedule 8.

Directions (*Secretary of State's Approvals and Directions under paragraphs 1 and 2 of schedule 8 to the NHS Act 1977*, attached to LAC(93)10) give local authorities certain duties for the purpose of preventing mental disorder, and in relation to people who are – or have been – suffering from mental disorder. These duties are to make arrangements:

(centres) for the provision of centres (including training centres and day centres) for the training or occupation of such people;

(approved social workers) for the appointment of sufficient approved social workers;

(guardianship functions) for the exercise of their functions towards people received into guardianship under Part 2 or 3 of the Mental Health Act 1983;

(social work services for mental disorder) for the provision of social work and related services a) to help in the identification, diagnosis, assessment and social treatment of mental disorder and b) to provide social work support and other domiciliary and care services to people living in their homes or elsewhere.

Approvals (*Secretary of State's Approvals and Directions under paragraphs 1 and 2 of schedule 8 to the NHS Act 1977*, attached to LAC(93)10) give local authorities the power to make arrangements generally. In particular they have the power to make arrangements for the provision:

(centres and occupation) of centres or other facilities for training or keeping people suitably occupied, to equip and maintain such centres, and for the provision for those people of ancillary or supplemental services;

(meals) of meals at centres and at other facilities, and meals-on-wheels for housebound people (not already provided for under s.45 of the Health Services and Public Health Act 1968, or schedule 9 of the HASSASSA 1983);

(remuneration for work) for the remuneration of people engaged in suitable work at centres or at other facilities;

(advice and support) for the provision of social services (including advice and support) in order to prevent the impairment of physical or mental health of adults in families where such impairment is likely, or to prevent the break-up of such families, or for assisting in their rehabilitation;

(night sitter services) night sitter services;

(recuperative holidays) recuperative holidays;

(social and recreational activities) facilities for social and recreational activities;

(alcohol- and drug-dependence) services specifically for alcoholic or drug-dependent people.

(use of other bodies) In making arrangements, local authorities may use services facilities made available by another authority, voluntary body or person – but in making such arrangements, the authority 'shall have regard to the importance of services being provided as near to a person's home as is practicable'.

DISCUSSION

By way of an anti-duplication measure (contained in NHS Act 1977, s.21), provision is 'subject to' s.3(1)(e) of the NHS Act 1977 (ie, to provision of services, described in the same language, by the NHS: see p.345). Also, by virtue of a provision in s.29 of the National Assistance Act 1948, any service which is required to be provided under schedule 8 of the NHS Act 1977 cannot be provided under s.29 of the 1948 Act (see pp.193 and 325).

7. SERVICES FOR EXPECTANT OR NURSING MOTHERS: NHS ACT 1977, schedule 8

Local authorities have the power to make arrangements for the care of expectant and nursing mothers.

EXTRACTS

Legislation (NHS Act 1977, schedule 8) states that local authorities have a duty so far as directed – and the power so far as approved – by the Secretary of State, to make arrangements for the care of expectant and nursing mothers (other than residential accommodation). Approval for such provision has been issued under cover of Circular LAC(93)10: *Secretary of State's Approvals and Directions under paragraphs 1 and 2 of schedule 8 to the NHS Act 1977.*

DISCUSSION

By way of an anti-duplication (see p.325) measure, provision is subject to s.3(1)(d) of the NHS Act 1977 where services provided by the NHS are described in the same language (NHS Act 1977,s.21). Also, under s.29 of the National Assistance Act 1948, any service which is required to be provided under schedule 8 of the NHS Act 1977 cannot be provided under s.29 of the National Assistance Act 1948 (see p.193).

8. AFTER-CARE AND OTHER MENTAL HEALTH SERVICES

The basis for services for people with mental health needs in the community includes the following:

(1) provision of after-care services by social services and the NHS under s.117 of the 1983 Act (see below);

(2) the (non-statutory) care programme approach, described and advocated in guidance, and intended to be jointly delivered by the NHS and local authorities but resting mostly on the former (see below);

(3) the funding of mental health services through the mental illness specific grant – and other special grants (see below);

(4) the general duties in relation to after-care imposed on health authorities by s.3 of the NHS Act 1977 (see p.345);

(5) the general community care assessment and care management system operated by local authorities (Chapters 5, 6 and 7);

(6) services provided by local authority social services departments for people with a mental disorder under s.2 of the Chronically Sick and Disabled Persons Act 1970 (and s.29 of the National Assistance Act 1948) (see pp.192 and 197)

(7) services provided by local authority social services departments for people with a mental disorder under schedule 8 of the NHS Act 1977 (see p.217).

The above provisions should be seen in the light of the widespread recognition that moving people with mental health needs from long-stay institutions into the community must – if it is to work – be accompanied by effective community services, properly organised, resourced (eg, Mental Health Foundation 1994,p.7; Audit Commission 1994,p.70) and coordinated (Secretary of State for Health 1997a,p.30; DH 1995b). Against a background of public disquiet, based on a small but well-publicised number of violent and sometimes fatal incidents, the government stated (not uncontroversially: see Woodman 1999) at the end of 1998 that care in the community had failed and that policy and legislative change was required (DH 1998d).

Department of Health guidance has stated that the main responsibilities of local authority social services departments for mentally ill people in the community are as follows: a) agreement with the health authority about a general community care plan for the local population; b) assessment of people in need; c) design, implementation and monitoring of individual care packages; d) provision of social work support; e) making arrangements for a range of personal social services; f) registration and inspection of residential care homes; g) liaison with health authorities implementing the care programme approach; h) employment of sufficient approved social workers to provide an assessment and emergency service seven days a week; i) provision of after-care services jointly with health authorities under s.117 of the Mental Health Act 1983; j) publication of policies and arrangements for guardianship under the 1983 Act (DH 1995b,p.31).

(1) After-care services: Mental Health Act 1983, s.117

Health authorities and social services have a legal duty to provide for certain patients (under the Mental Health Act 1983) after-care services under s.117 of the Mental Health Act 1983. The duty has been characterised judicially as a strong one towards individuals and to be distinguished from the more general duty to provide after-care under s.3 of the NHS Act 1977. Superimposed on it is the power of health authorities to make supervision orders in relation to after-care under s.117 for a limited group of patients who pose a substantial risk to their own safety or that of other people.

EXTRACTS

Legislation (Mental Health Act 1983) states that social services and health authorities have a duty to provide after-care for people detained under the Act under s.3 (people admitted for treatment), s.37 (convicted offenders with hospital or guardianship orders), or s.47 and s.48 (prisoners – serving a sentence, on remand, civil prisoners, people detained under the Immigration Act 1971 – for whom a transfer direction has been made):

> **(after-care)** 'It shall be the duty of the District Health Authority and of the local social services authority to provide, in co-operation with voluntary agencies, after-care services for any person to whom this section applies until such time as the District Health Authority and the local social services authority are satisfied that the person concerned is no longer in need of such services' (s.117).

In certain circumstances supervision orders may be made; the two extracts below are but a small part of the new procedures set out in the amended 1983 Act in ss.25A to 25J.

> **(supervision orders)** If a patient is 'liable to be detained in a hospital in pursuance of an application for admission for treatment', and 'has attained the age of 16 years ... an application may be made for him to be supervised after he leaves hospital ... with a view to securing that he receives the after-care services provided for him under section 117' (s.25A).

> **(application for supervision order)** An application for a supervision order 'may be made in respect of a patient only on the grounds that he

(a) he is suffering from mental disorder, being mental illness, severe mental impairment, psychopathic disorder or mental impairment;

(b) there would be a substantial risk of serious harm to the health or safety of the patient or the safety of other persons or of the patient being seriously exploited, if he were not to receive the after-care services to be provided for him under section 117 below after he leaves hospital;

(c) his being subject to after-care under supervision is likely to help to secure that he receives the after-care services to be so provided' (s.25A).

Code of practice (DH,WO 1993: made under s.118 of the Mental Health Act 1983) states that in establishing a care plan for after-care, a number of professionals should be involved in the discussion. These are the person's 'responsible medical officer', a hospital nurse involved in caring for the person, a social worker specialising in mental health work, the person's GP, a community psychiatric nurse, a voluntary organisation representative (where appropriate and available), the person (if he wishes) or a nominated relative or other representative. The issues to be considered should be:

(patient's wishes and needs) 'the patient's own wishes and needs';

(other views) 'the views of any relevant relative, friend or supporter of the patient';

(agreement) 'the need for agreement with an appropriate representative at the receiving health authority if it is to be different from that of the discharging authority';

(other agencies) 'the possible involvement of other agencies, eg. probation, voluntary organisations';

(care plan) 'the establishing of a care plan, based on proper assessment and clearly identified needs, in which the following issues must be considered and planned so far as resources permit: day care arrangements, appropriate accommodation, out-patient treatment, counselling, personal support, assistance in welfare rights, assistance in managing finances, and, if necessary, in claiming benefits';

(key worker) 'the appointment of a key worker from either of the statutory agencies to monitor the care plan's implementation, liaise and co-ordinate where necessary and report to the senior officer in their agency any problems that arise which cannot be resolved through normal discussion';

(unmet need) 'the identification of any unmet need' (pp.106–108).

In addition, a timescale for implementation should be agreed; people with specific responsibilities should be identified; changes to the plan must be fully discussed; the plan should be recorded in writing; and the plan should be regularly reviewed – this is the responsibility of the key worker. Responsibility for ensuring the whole procedure is followed lies with the 'senior officer' responsible for s.117 in the key worker's agency (DH,WO 1993, pp.107–108).

Code of practice (DH,WO 1996,para 5) states:

(revolving door patients) 'Supervised discharge is intended for patients whose care needs to be specially supervised in the community because of risk to themselves or others. This applies particularly to "revolving door" patients who have shown a pattern of relapse after discharge from hospital'.

Circular guidance (HSG(94)5):

(supervision registers) 'requires' that all mental health care provider units set up supervision registers to identify and provide information about patients at significant risk of self-neglect, suicide or committing serious violence towards others (annex A,para 9).

DISCUSSION

After-care services: strength of duty

In *R v Ealing LBC ex p Fox*, the judge interpreted s.117 of the Mental Health Act as placing a strong duty (towards individuals) on health authorities and local authorities – contrasting it with the less specific duty in relation to after-care owed by the health authority under s.3 of the NHS Act 1977 (see p.345). By the same token, it would seem that the duty placed by s.117 on local authority social services departments is likewise a stronger duty (towards individuals) than their general duty to provide after-care for mentally disordered people under schedule 8 of the NHS Act 1977 (see p.217).

Even so, it should be noted that although the judge emphasised the strength of the s.117 duty, he also seemed deliberately to exclude from the ambit of his judgment the situation where authorities plead lack of resources for non-performance of duty. Given some similarity between s.117 and s.2 of the CSDPA 1970 (eg, both carry the words 'satisfied' and 'need'), health authorities and local authorities might be tempted to argue lack of resources on the basis of *R v Gloucestershire CC ex p Barry* (which dealt with s.2). However, they should bear in mind a) that the *Gloucestershire* case still identified an absolute duty (irrespective of resources) once need and necessity had been established; b) the courts have since apparently retreated in other contexts from their stance in the *Gloucestershire* case (see eg, *R v East Sussex CC, ex p Tandy* about education, and *R v Birmingham CC, ex p Mohammed* about disabled facilities grants); c) initial eligibility for s.117 services is more formal and objective than for services under s.2 of the CSDPA. And given the obvious sensitivity about community care for people with a serious mental disorder, the courts might be reluctant to allow dilution of the s.117 duty by arguments about lack of resources.

After-care services: decision to provide

The local ombudsman has pointed out that local authorities cannot simply arbitrarily – or by asking irrelevant questions – decide not to, or to cease to, provide s.117 after-care services. Nor can they casually recategorise services being provided under s.117 as suddenly coming under other community care legislation, with a view to imposing financial charges (which are barred under s.117). Furthermore, the after-care duty is imposed jointly on both health authorities and local authorities; therefore a local authority would be acting erroneously if it were to base its decision solely on a medical decision, since it must make its own reasoned decision as a social services authority (*Clwyd CC 1997*, an ombudsman investigation). Such decisions to cease after-care services are likely to become all the more problematic if staff are without clear written guidance about discharge of people from s.117 services (*Hounslow LBC 1995*, another ombudsman investigation).

After-care services: supervision orders

A small number of people with mental health problems leaving hospital constitute a risk either to themselves or to other people. This state of affairs led to the Mental Health (Patients in the Community) Act 1995 which amended the Mental Health Act 1983 and gives health authorities the power to make supervision orders in respect of certain patients who qualify for after-care services under s.117. (Unimplemented still is s.7 of the Disabled Persons (Services Consultation and Representation) Act 1986, which would impose statutory obligations on both health and social services authorities to secure assessments of people with mental disorder who have been in hospital for six months or more – before they leave hospital).

In 1996, a government report into homicides and suicides by mentally ill people summarised some of the key problems it found: failures of communication between professionals, lack of clarity about care plans, lack of time for face-to-face contact with patients, need for additional staff training, poor compliance with treatment by the sample group, insufficient use of legal powers to supervise at-risk patients (Steering Committee of the Confidential Inquiry into Homicides and Suicides by Mentally Ill People 1996,p.8).

An earlier report into the killing of Jonathan Zito by Christopher Clunis found a 'catalogue of failure and missed opportunity' on the part of a number of people and agencies. It expressed its concern that 'doctors, nurses and social workers who are primarily responsible for providing this aftercare may not fully understand that the principles underlying s.117 and Care Programme Approach are the same'. Of s.117, the report stated: 'We consider that this is a vital provision to ensure effective care in the community. Its impact should not be diminished by any other provisions for care in the community' (Ritchie 1994,pp.105–111). Notwithstanding such failure, the Court of Appeal refused a claim for damages brought by Christopher Clunis for breach of statutory duty and for negligence; it characterised the duties under s.117 as administrative rather than clinical and as not giving rise to a common law duty of care (*Clunis v Camden and Islington HA*).

After-care services: code of practice

The Code itself explains that it 'imposes no additional duties on statutory authorities'. Instead it provides 'guidance', although there is no legal duty of compliance, 'failure to follow the Code could be referred to in evidence in legal proceedings' (DH,WO 1993,p.1).

(2) Care programme approach

The 'care programme approach' (CPA) is non-statutory – it is not embodied in legislation – but has been described and advocated by guidance. The CPA approach to after-care applies to people with a mental illness (including dementia) who are referred to the specialist psychiatric services. Subsequent guidance has suggested that the CPA should apply where relevant to the after-care of all mentally disordered patients. Thus the scope of the CPA is obviously wider than the duty to provide after-care services under s.117 of the 1983 Act.

EXTRACTS

Circular guidance (HC(90)23/LASSL(90)11):

(**implementation**) 'requires' health authorities 'to implement the care programme approach ... for people with a mental illness, including dementia, whatever its cause, referred to the specialist psychiatric services...' (p.1);

(**social services**) 'asks social services authorities to collaborate with health authorities in introducing this approach and, as resources allow, to continue to expand social care services to patients being treated in the community' (p.1);

(**resources**) 'Health authorities are expected to meet any health service costs arising from the introduction of more systematic procedures from existing resources. Introducing the care programme approach places no new requirements to provide services on either health or social services authorities ... Health authorities will judge what resources they make available for such services. Social services authorities will make similar decisions but will have available specially targeted resources through the new specific grant' (p.2).

The guidance (Annex) outlines the main components of this approach. This is to 'ensure that in future patients treated in the community receive the health and social care they need'. Key elements involved are:

(assessment and review of health care) 'systematic arrangements for assessing the health care needs of patients who could, potentially, be treated in the community, and for regularly reviewing the health care needs of those being treatment [sic] in the community';

(assessment and review of social care) 'systematic arrangements, agreed with appropriate social services authorities, for assessing and regularly reviewing what social care such patients need to give them the opportunity of benefiting from treatment in the community';

(provision of services) 'effective systems for ensuring that agreed health, and where necessary, social care services are provided to those patients who can be treated in the community'.

(patient involvement) 'It is important that proper opportunities are provided for patients themselves to take part in discussions about their proposed care programmes, so that they have the chance to discuss different treatment possibilities and agree the programme to be implemented'.

Circular guidance (HSG(94)27) states:

(hospital discharge) that patients should only be discharged when they are ready to leave hospital, that any risk to the public or patients themselves should be minimal and managed effectively, and that they should receive the required support and supervision (p. 1).

Full account must be taken of a) whether there is continuing serious risk even if there is adequate medication, care and supervision in the community; b) whether there is a need for therapy, supervision, sanctuary or security requires continuing inpatient treatment; c) whether the person could be cared for safely and effectively in the community, if required in staffed or supported accommodation (para 1).

The guidance emphasises that no patient 'should be discharged from hospital unless and until those taking the decision are satisfied that he or she can live safely in the community, and that proper treatment, supervision, support and care available' (para 2).

(care programme approach) The key elements of the approach are systematic assessment, a care plan, a key worker and regular review (para 10).

(care plan) The patient and professionals involved should be aware of the contents of the care plan and understand the first review date, information in relation to violence, name of the key worker and how that person and other service providers can be contacted, action to be taken in case of a failure to attend for treatment or to meet other requirements (para 11).

(discharge and continuing care in the community). Practices associated with the CPA are sometimes relevant not just to mentally ill people but also to some other people with personality disorders or with learning disabilities (paras 20–21).

The Circular gives guidance on risk assessments (paras 23–32), and generally emphasises the importance of clear and explicit contracts which should lead at least to a mental health information system (including supervision register), adequately trained staff with suitable management and supervision arrangements, suicide audits, and agreed procedures in case of murder or assault by a patient (para 40).

DISCUSSION

The 1990 guidance (see above) 'asks' social services departments to collaborate with health authorities, and 'requires' health authorities to implement the care programme approach. In practice this has not been straightforward; in 1994 the Social Services Inspectorate was reporting that the CPA had been implemented belatedly (SSI 1994j,p.26) or not at all (SSI 1994k,p.19); the Audit Commission (1994,p.40) found the same.

There has also been confusion over the relationship between the care programme approach, general community care assessment/care planning, and after-care provision under s.117 of the Mental Health Act 1983 (SSI,NHSME 1994h,pp.46–48; North, Ritchie and Ward 1993,p.101). Questions are sometimes raised about how the CPA is applied locally in terms, for example, of whether eligibility criteria are explicit, comprehensible and agreed – as well as how inclusively or restrictively they are applied in screening systems (SSI,NHSME 1994h,p.41). Further guidance from the Department of Health (DH 1995a,pp.52–59) tries to explain by urging that health authorities and local authorities should ensure that CPA and care management are coordinated and integrated, since they are based on the same principles: in other words, assessment of need, followed by agreed care plan, followed by implementation, monitoring and review of the care plan.

It appears that one particular consequence of the confused relationship between the CPA and care planning has been that the CPA has not been used generally for older people with mental health problems or dementia (SSI 1997j,p.21; SSI 1997b,p.15).

(3) Mental illness specific grant

Specific grant is available for local authorities in relation to the development of mental health services.

EXTRACTS

Legislation (Local Authority Social Services Act 1970,s.7E) states:

> **(specific grant)** 'The Secretary of State may, with the approval of the Treasury, make grants out of money provided by Parliament towards any expenses of local authorities incurred ... in connection with the exercise of their social services functions in relation to persons suffering from mental illness'.

Guidance (LAC(98)7,para 12) sets out the standard conditions governing eligibility for the grant which should be used to fund services which:

(1) 'contribute to the health and social care needs of people whose mental illness, including dementia, is so severe that they have been accepted for treatment by the specialist psychiatric services and therefore subject to the Care Programme Approach';

(2) 'are aimed at bringing in touch with the specialist psychiatric services people in the community not currently in touch with those services but whose needs are so severe that it is clear that they would benefit from those services, for example, those among the homeless population whose seriously impaired social functioning is a consequence of mental illness'.

DISCUSSION
Mental illness specific grant (MISG)

The grant has been distributed annually since 1991/92 to supplement general spending on social care for mentally ill people in the community. It supports the care programme approach, supervision registers and supervision orders.

Grant might in practice be spent on projects involving, for instance, residential care, hostels, adult placements, housing (including rehabilitation), community mental health teams, resource centres, social workers, employment schemes, respite services, night-sitting services, support for carers (eg, for people with dementia), advocacy, advice, friendship, drop-in centres, development workers, training, emergency/out-of-hours services, minority/ethnic services, crisis intervention, information systems, volunteer coordinators, occupational therapy, recreation and leisure services, evening and weekend activities, day care, services for homeless people with mental health problems (SSI 1992b,p.17; SSI 1993f,p.33).

Mental illness specific grants: Partnership Fund

One element of the MISG is the Mental Health Social Care Partnership Fund, announced in 1998 for projects based on multi-agency assessment of need and dealing with one or more of the following priorities: employment or meaningful occupation, 24-hour crisis services, dual diagnosis, prevention of severe mental health problems. It is designed to improve the social care of mentally ill people (including those with dementia) requiring specialist psychiatric care and supports the care programme approach, supervision registers and supervision orders. In addition, projects should aim at putting people with severe needs in touch with specialist psychiatric services, and aim at preventing the onset or avoidable recurrence of severe mental illness in vulnerable people (LAC(98)16, LAC(98)7).

Mentally ill people: supplementary credit approvals

Other financial assistance (not under the specific grant provisions but under s.54 of the Local Government and Housing Act 1989) was made available for the year 1998/99 in the form of 'supplementary credit approvals' for the development of capital facilities for the social care of mentally ill people. This assistance could cover, for example, building, purchase, renovation of premises; equipment for employment and activity schemes; purchase of a minibus (LAC(98)10).

9. DRUGS AND ALCOHOL

Community care delivered by social services departments is intended to cover all groups of people potentially in need of such services – including people dependent on drugs and alcohol. In practice, it is recognised that this group of people has often been neglected by local authorities.

EXTRACTS
Legislation states:

(specific grant) 'The Secretary of State may, with the approval of the Treasury, make grants out of money provided by Parliament towards any expenses of local authorities incurred … in making payments, in accordance with directions given by the Secretary of State to voluntary organisations which provide care and services for persons who are, have been, or are likely to become dependent upon alcohol or drugs' (Local Authority Social Services Act 1970,s.7E).

(approval for services) Explicit approval (ie, power) is given to local authorities to provide services for people dependent on alcohol or drugs – either residential (Approval under s.21 of the National Assistance Act 1948) or non-residential services (NHS Act 1977, schedule 8): see pp.254 and 217.

Directions (*Payments to Voluntary Organisations (Alcohol or Drugs Misusers) Directions 1990*, contained within DH 1990 and LAC (98)17) state that:

(specific grant) local authorities receiving the specific grant must make payments to voluntary organisations 'for any of the following purposes:

(a) to provide or assist in the provision of new or additional residential places for alcohol or drugs misusers where the local authority are satisfied that new or additional places are necessary in order to meet the existing or future needs of their area;

(b) to provide non-residential facilities for alcohol or drugs misusers where the authority are satisfied that such facilities will increase the effectiveness of the residential facilities in their area for alcohol or drugs misusers;

(c) to provide financial assistance for the running of the existing residential facilities for alcohol or drugs misusers;

(d) to provide or assist the training of any staff of voluntary organisations providing care and services for alcohol or drugs misusers;

(e) to refurbish or assist the refurbishment of existing residential facilities for alcohol or drugs misusers.

(f) to provide non-residential care and services for drug or alcohol misusers, including rehabilitation, assessment, counselling and social support;

g) to prepare plans for delivering in the area of the local authority, with the involvement of other agencies, care and services to drug or alcohol misusers with additional needs, in particular those who suffer from mental illness'.

Guidance is issued in relation to procedures surrounding the giving of the specific grant: see, LAC(98(6), LAC(98)17, LAC(99)3 and LAC(99)4.

Guidance states:

(priority) 'The Government attaches a high priority to tackling the problems associated with the misuse of alcohol and drugs, and expects LAs to attach a high priority to alcohol and drug misusers within community care' (LAC(93)2,para 1).

(special circumstances) Misusers of alcohol and drugs present a particular challenge. Since they might 'present to LAs' with other problems, assessment procedures must be capable of identifying alcohol or drug misuse. Also, they might have complex needs, move between areas frequently, have no settled residence, self-refer to agencies in areas in which they are not resident, avoid contact with statutory services, require services several times before they bring the misuse under control, behave unpredictably, and require rapid responses if serious deterioration is to be avoided (LAC(93)2,paras 12–13).

(suitability of eligibility criteria) Local authorities 'should ensure that any criteria they may develop governing eligibility for assessment are sensitive to the circumstances of alcohol and drug misusers' – and, for example, do not exclude from assessment people with no settled residence, on the basis of a minimum residence requirement (LAC(93)2,para 14).

(contracting out assessment) There is expertise in the independent sector and local authorities should consider involving that sector in the assessment process. However, a) 'in these circumstances, LAs will need to ensure that the specialist agency is aware of other potential needs for which LAs have responsibilities'; b) residential placements will normally require a comprehensive assessment; and c) 'decisions to commit resources and ultimate responsibility for the assessment remains with' the local authority (LAC(93)2,paras 16–17).

(out-of-area placements) Generally, local authorities, within certain financial bounds, must attempt to give people a choice of residential accommodation. There might be 'therapeutic benefit in referring people to a residential area away from the area in which they are experiencing their alcohol and drug problems ... LAs should ensure that resources can be identified for out of area placements' (LAC(93)2,para 23).

(probation service) Some clients of the Probation Service who misuse drugs or alcohol might require residential or non-residential care; local authorities 'should liaise with probation services to ensure that these needs can be considered within community care arrangements' (LAC(93)2,para 25).

(purchasing services for drug misusers) Local authorities and health authorities 'should ensure that the following key principles inform purchasing of treatment and care services for drug misusers:

- practical co-operation and, wherever possible, long term partnership between all the agencies involved in drug misuse service purchasing and provision, including DATs' (drug action teams);
- a user-centred approach, which gives drug misusers information about treatments and support and the best affordable choice of effective treatments and support for their particular needs;
- an evidence-based approach to purchasing, underpinned by monitoring of costs and outcomes' (LAC(97)9,para 9).

(rights of the individual drug misuser) Guidance states that drug misusers 'have the same rights as any other people requiring help from health or social services'. It refers to standards outlined by a national task force, whose report was published by the Department of Health (DH 1997c) and issued with LAC(97)9 and HSG(97)14. These should 'ensure that individual clients have:

- the right to an assessment of individual needs within a specified number of working days;
- the right of access to specialised services within a specified time;
- the right to respect for privacy, dignity and confidentiality, and an explanation of circumstances in which information will be divulged to others;
- the right to access to a complaints procedure;
- the right to full information about treatment options and informed involvement in making decisions on treatment;
- the right, in appropriate circumstances, to be referred for a second consultant opinion;
- the right to an individual care and treatment plan' (DH 1997c,pp.23,89).

DISCUSSION

Drugs and alcohol: services

Services provided for people with drug or alcohol problems – requiring social services in some way (eg, providing alone, jointly with the NHS or via a voluntary organisation) – might include residential/non-residential detoxification or rehabilitation; domiciliary services; chemical dependency teams; community drugs or alcohol teams; counselling, information and support; self-help networks; therapeutic communities; alternative therapies such as acupuncture clinics – and so on (see eg, SCODA 1997; DH 1996b,Chapter 5).

Drugs or alcohol: policy and practice

The above extracts from guidance suggest that central government regards services for misusers of alcohol and drugs – especially the latter – as a high priority. Indeed, it has published also a 1995 White Paper, *Tackling drugs together* (Lord President 1995), the report of a task force on drug treatment services (DH 1996b), and a book of guidance arising from the Task Force's work (DH 1997c). However, it should be noted, in relation to community care at least, that the specific references to alcohol and drug misuse are in terms of powers rather than duties – with the inevitable consequences which seem to follow when local authorities are short of money (see p.31). Thus, local practice might diverge considerably from national policy. In 1991, the Social Services Inspectorate commented that the input of local authorities to drug misuse services was 'relatively limited' and that most 'had no written policies or strategies of their own to guide their work in this area' (SSI 1991g,p.2).

In 1995, a national overview report from SSI exposed a number of flaws. For instance, the priorities set out in LAC(93)2 were met in only one of the five local authorities inspected; the relationship with the Probation Service was on the verge of breakdown in two of the authorities; there were no examples of formal arrangements to involve the independent sector in assessment arrangements. Assessments were resource-led, not based on need, and reactive (thus precluding outreach and preventative work). Care plans based on assessments of need did not exist – and choices and service options were not explored. Joint planning groups frequently lacked purpose and direction, as well as omitting key groups such as the police, Probation Service and housing departments. In addition, the few services available consisted basically of residential detoxification or rehabilitation centres (but even these might be scarce or not within an authority's area) and of some counselling. Day care provision was mostly absent, domiciliary services little used and community-based detoxification 'under-developed and often not available'. Provision was mostly in the form of chemical dependency teams (CDTs) or of community drugs or alcohol teams; however, these were mainly NHS-led and social workers played an ill-defined role (SSI 1995f).

10. DIRECT PAYMENTS TO USERS OF SERVICES

In April 1997, the Community Care (Direct Payments) Act 1996 came into force empowering local authorities to make direct cash payment to certain categories of users of community care services – namely disabled people under the age of 65 years at the date of application. They are not therefore, at the time of writing, available for older people. However, a government White Paper in late 1998 announced that the age limit will be removed (Secretary of State for Health 1998,p.18).

EXTRACTS

Legislation (Community Care (Direct Payments) Act 1996) states:

> **(making a payment)** If an authority has decided under s.47 of the NHS and Community Care Act 1990 that the needs of a person call for the provision of any community care services, then – if that person 'is of a description which is specified … by regulations … the authority may, if the person consents, make to him, in respect of his securing the provision of any of the services for which they have decided his needs call, a payment of such amount as … they think fit' (s.1(1)).

> **(taking account of the means of the user)** If an authority makes a payment at a level below its estimate of the reasonable cost of providing the service – and the 'payee satisfies the authority that his means are in-

sufficient for it to be reasonably practicable for him to make up the difference ... the authority shall so adjust the payment to him ... as to avoid there being a greater difference than that which appears to them to be reasonably practicable for him to make up'. However, for services provided under s.117 of the Mental Health Act 1983, local authorities are prohibited anyway from paying less than their estimate of the reasonable cost of provision (s.1).

(This mirrors provisions under s.17 of the Health and Social Services and Social Security Adjudications Act 1983, under which local authorities make charges for non-residential services: see p.237).

(repayment of the money) The local authority can insist that money be repaid if it has not been used to secure provision of the service in respect of which it has been paid, or if any properly imposed condition of payment has not been adhered to (s.1).

(continuing responsibility of the local authority) When it makes a payment, the local authority 'shall not be under an obligation to the payee with respect to the provision under the relevant community care enactment of the service to which the payment relates as long as they are satisfied that the need which calls for the provision of the service will be met by virtue of the payee's own arrangements' (s.2).

Legislation (regulations: SI 1997/734) state:

(people eligible for payment) Payments may only be made to a person a) to whom s.29 of the National Assistance Act 1948 applies and b) 'who appears to the authority to be capable of managing a direct payment by himself or with assistance'. However, excluded from eligibility are the following groups of people:

- people aged 65 or over unless payment was first made before that age;
- people who – through a probation, combination order or release licence – are required to submit to treatment for mental disorder, or for drug or alcohol dependency;
- people who are placed under guardianship in relation to an application made under s.7 of the Mental Health Act 1983 or an order made under s.37 of the same Act;
- people who are absent from hospital under s.17 of the Mental Health Act 1983;
- people who are subject to after-care under supervision under s.25A of the Mental Health Act 1983;
- people who are subject to conditions in relation to restriction orders under s.42(2) or 73(4) of the Mental Health Act 1983;
- people who are subject to a supervision and treatment order in relation to the Criminal Procedure (Insanity and Unfitness to Plead) Act 1991 (r.2).

(people from whom services cannot be obtained for payment: list of relatives) Direct payments cannot be used to obtain services from the following categories of people, living in the same household as the payee, in return for providing services: spouse or person living with payee as spouse; parent or parent-in-law; son or daughter; son-in-law or daughter-in-law; stepson or stepdaughter; brother or sister; aunt or uncle; grandparent; or the spouse – or person who lives as spouse – of any of these (r.3).

(residential accommodation) Payments cannot be made for the provision of residential accommodation for any period of more than four weeks within any twelve month period. However, within the twelve-month period, if periods of residential accommodation of less than four weeks each are separated from one another by a period of not less than four weeks – then they are not added together to exceed the overall four weeks allowed (r.4).

Policy guidance (DH 1997b) states:

(control by user) Carers or other third parties may receive and handle the money, but it is the user who 'must remain in control of the arrangements, and remains accountable for the way in which the direct payments are used ... Direct payments are intended to facilitate independent living, not to switch from dependence on the local authority to dependence on a third party' (paras 10,23).

(information/publicity) 'As with all local authority services, information about direct payments should be made readily available and accessible' (para 18).

(assessment) 'Authorities should ensure that, if they are considering offering direct payments, they build time into the assessment process for both their own assessment as to whether direct payments are appropriate, and the user's consideration'.

(blanket policies) 'Local authorities have the discretion to refuse direct payments to anyone who they judge would not be able to manage them, but should avoid making blanket assumptions that whole groups of people will necessarily be unable to do so' (para 22).

(explanation of responsibilities) 'Local authorities should explain what is involved as fully as they can ... In particular, authorities should draw people's attention to the fact that any contract they make for the provision of services will involve legal responsibilities, and that if the person contracts directly with an individual they may be regarded as an employer' (para 29).

(what payment is spent on) 'Local authorities should make clear to people, before they start to receive payments, what the money may or may not be spent on ... It is up to the local authority to decide how much flexibility to allow people, but it will wish to bear in mind that the aim of the policy is to give people more choice and control over the services they are assessed as needing' (para 33).

(people from whom services cannot be obtained for payment) In addition to the prohibition concerning close relatives in the same household contained in regulations (see above), 'local authorities should not allow people to use direct payments to secure services from a close relative living elsewhere or from someone else living in the same household ... The restriction applies where the relationship between the two people is primarily personal rather than contractual ... A local authority may decide that an exception to this general rule is justified'.

On the other hand, authorities 'should not set a condition that someone who receives direct payments may only use certain providers' (paras 35,36).

(cost effectiveness) 'A local authority should not make direct payments unless they are at least as cost-effective as the services which it would otherwise arrange' (para 39).

(amount of payment) 'The Act requires local authorities to make direct payments at a rate, which taken with any financial contribution from the person ... is equal to the authority's estimate of the reasonable cost of his or securing the provision of the service concerned ... This means direct payments must be sufficient to enable the recipient legally to secure a service of a standard which the local authority considers adequate to fulfil the needs for which the payment is made' (para 40).

(disputes) If the user thinks the payment should be greater than the local authority thinks reasonable, 'the local authority is under no obligation to increase the amount ... The authority may decide to increase the amount nevertheless ... if it is satisfied that the benefits of doing so outweigh the costs and that it is still cost-effective in comparison with services arranged by the local authority'. Where resolution is not possible, the user should be told about the complaints procedure (para 41).

(repayment) 'It is up to the local authority to decide when it is appropriate to seek recovery, but local authorities should bear in mind that this power is intended to enable them to recover money which has been diverted from the purpose for which it was intended, or which has simply not been spent at all. It is not intended to be used to penalise honest mistakes' (para 52).

(discontinuation of payments) 'Either the authority or the individual may decide at any time that they no longer wish to continue with direct payments. However, the authority should not automatically assume when problems arise that the solution is to discontinue direct payments. If the local authority does decide to withdraw direct payments then it will need to arrange the relevant services instead, unless the withdrawal was following a reassessment after which the authority concluded that the services were no longer appropriate...

Authorities should set a minimum period of notice which will normally be given before direct payments are discontinued, and include it in the information to be provided to people who are considering direct payments' (paras 54–55).

Practice guidance (DH 1997b) states:

(amount of payment: assessing costs to be incurred) 'In deciding on the level of a direct payment, local authorities will need to discuss with the user the arrangements that he or she is planning to make and the costs that may be associated with this (eg National Insurance, sick pay, maternity pay, employers's liability insurance, public liability insurance, VAT)' (para 28).

(equipment) 'It is up to the local authority to decide whether to make direct payments to allow people to purchase equipment. If they do so, they will need to bear in mind the specialist expertise that may be needed to ensure that equipment purchased is safe and appropriate, and the question of whether making a direct payment is a cost-effective way of purchasing such equipment. Authorities would also need to clarify, with the user, the ownership of any equipment, and where responsibility lies for its ongoing care and maintenance. For these reasons the Department considers that direct payments are unlikely to be appropriate for purchasing complex and expensive pieces of equipment, although they may well make sense for smaller, less specialised items' (para 6).

DISCUSSION

Direct payments: purpose

The 1996 Act was passed with the avowed intention of giving service users greater choice and control over their own lives, so as to 'put the people who need community care services in the driving seat and allow them to make important decisions about how their needs are met. We are adding dignity, independence and choice to care and support...' (John Bowis: HCD,6/3/1996,col.372: moving the 2nd reading of the Bill in the House of Commons). At the 2nd reading in the House of Lords, Baroness Cumberlege had said that 'at the heart of community care is the aim of supporting and sustaining individuals within the community rather than encouraging people to withdraw from it. It is driven by a commitment to respond to the individual's to lead as normal a life as possible. Direct payments are a natural progression in community care towards that goal, giving users more control and more choice' (HLD,7/12/1995,col.1050).

The issue of direct payments is therefore 'part of a wider debate about autonomy and disability rights' and the ability of disabled people to live independently and not be subordinate and subject to the control of other people (Kestenbaum 1996,p.4). It is true that the making of such payments still depends on the local authority first coming to a formal decision about what a person's needs are and what services are required. However, it is clear that depending on how – in terms of generality or specificity (see p.113) – an assessment and care plan describes needs and services, service users will have a greater or lesser amount of flexibility in how they choose to meet those needs (eg, Hasler, Zarb and Campbell 1998,p.6).

Direct payments: background

The passing of the 1996 Act reversed a longstanding policy of not making payments direct to users of services, embodied in the prohibitions (still) contained in s.29 of the National Assistance Act 1948, s.45 of the Health Service and Public Health Act 1968, and schedule 8 of the NHS Act 1977.

Unsuccessful attempts were made to amend the law in order to make such payments possible: for example, the Disabled Persons (Services) Bill 1992, presented by Andrew Rowe MP; and a failed amendment to the NHS and Community Care Bill (HLD,10/5/1990,col.1589). During the passage of the latter, the government explained that it had 'concluded that it is not possible to find a formula to enable payments to be simple and unbureaucratic for local authorities and recipient clients, on the one hand, and which, on the other, can prevent expenditure from running out of control' (Baroness Hooper: HLD,25/6/1990,col.1390). Even so, some months earlier, the Secretary of State for Health had admitted the logic to payments in some circumstances and had held out some hope of a government amendment to the Bill – though nothing ever came of this (Virginia Bottomley: SC(E),22/2/1990,cols.1229–1230).

Prior to 1996, the Independent Living Fund (ILF) scheme had provided a precedent for giving cash assistance, by means of grant, to severely disabled people, so that they could purchase their own care services. (Current eligibility for ILF assistance is as follows. A person must a) at the time of application be between the ages of 16 and 65; b) receive the highest care component of disability living allowance and be able to live in the community for at least six months; c) have savings of less than £8,000 and income insufficient to cover care needs; and d) be assessed by the local authority as being at risk of entering residential care or as being capable of leaving it to live in the community, and receive at least £200 worth of services per week from the local authority (net of charges made), and be assessed as requiring additional care up to a maximum of £300 a week: ILF 1997).

In addition, also before the passing of the 1996 Act, local authorities sometimes circumvented the statutory prohibitions – for instance, by making cash payments to an intermediary, voluntary organisation (see: House of Commons Health Committee 1993,vol.2, p.10), or placing the money in an independent trust (p.100) which would hold the money on behalf of service users. Such schemes are known as third-party arrangements. One such scheme 'topped up' the difference between a person's personal assistance needs and his or her financial resources (having claimed maximum benefits available) (Fiedler 1988,p.42). Another gave people control of a budget by cheque book, without any cash flowing from authority to user but effectively giving the user power to purchase services (Wiggin, Carpenter 1994). The legality of these schemes has sometimes been doubted, although the Department of Health has generally turned a blind eye. By 1996, some sixty local authorities were operating such schemes and the government confirmed that the Community Care (Direct Payments) Bill was not intended to affect such schemes one way or another (John Bowis: HCD,6/3/1996,col.380). The Act would therefore not threaten third-party arrangements for people who would not qualify for direct payments either because of their age or because they were deemed by the local authority to be unable to manage the payments. Some authorities are therefore continuing to use a third-party scheme for older people (Hasler, Zarb and Campbell 1998,p.7).

It has been pointed out that direct payments might in fact work out more cheaply for local authorities than direct provision of services. For instance, various evaluations of the use of ILF payments have concluded that when disabled people have arranged and purchased their own services, they have done it (up to 30%) more cheaply than statutory services would have, because a) they have taken on most of the administrative tasks themselves, and b) they have used cheaper sources of assistance such as friends or relatives – or, for instance, might have trained a personal assistant for bowel management instead of relying on an expensive, qualified nurse (Kestenbaum 1996,p.22).

Direct payments: restrictions on categories of recipient

The major restriction that direct payments can only first be received by people under the age of 65 years, was severely criticised both during the passing of the Bill in Parliament and since. Although the government stated at the time of the Bill's passage that it would review the working of the Act, it failed to produce convincing arguments in Parliament as to why this restriction should be imposed – especially since the power (as opposed to a duty) to make payments anyway gives local authorities ample discretion as to whom they make payments. Given such discretion, the government arguments against allowing wider scope were somewhat unconvincing and were confined to terms such as 'unripe time', 'running before walking' (Baroness Hollis: HLD,20/2/1996,col.1046), 'pace' or 'manageable scale' (John Bowis: HCD,6/3/1996,col.375).

Whether a potential recipient can manage (albeit with assistance) is another restriction imposed by regulations. In fact, it can be seen as a protection to service users to ensure that it is they who are controlling what is happening, and that payments are not used to reinforce dependency (Hasler, Zarb and Campbell 1998,p.5).

In late 1998, the government announced that it would be removing the age limitation, so making direct payments available to older people as well (Secretary of State for Health 1998,p.18).

Direct payments: power and not duty

It should be emphasised that the Act gives local authorities only a power and not a duty to make direct payments. This of course gives rise to the fear that for financial reasons, a local authority might choose not to make payments.

Aware of the essential weakness of such a power in relation to those local authorities unwilling to make direct payments, the following amendment was tabled but withdrawn during the Bill's Parliamentary passage: 'An authority shall not unreasonably refuse a disabled person access to direct payments' (Baroness Hollis: HLD,12/2/1996,col.429). The government opposed this, stating that even as the Bill stood, local authorities should not make 'whimsical decisions' and would have to 'exercise their discretion reasonably'. A local authority would, in the case of 'someone' (ie, for each person) who wanted to receive such a payment, have to take account of the person's wishes and ability to benefit from the payment. However, at the same time, local authorities had to have discretion 'to base their decisions on the wider interests of the local population – for instance, taxpayers and other service users – and not just on the interests of the particular individual concerned' (Baroness Cumberlege: HLD,12/2/1996,col.431).

Such statements merely spell out the implications of s.1 of the Act which gives a local authority the discretion to decide whether or not to make payments in individual cases; thus any blanket policies not to make such payments to anybody, or to particular groups of people (otherwise eligible) might run the risk of being unlawful on the grounds of fettering of discretion (see p.49). Even so, following the coming into force of the Act in April 1997, the setting up of systems and procedures to administer direct payments has taken longer in some authorities than in others. For instance, it was reported in October 1997 that 52 per cent of authorities were not making payments either under the Act or under any other scheme (eg, third party arrangements: see above), while two per cent had apparently made decisions not to make payments at all (Zarb *et al.* 1997,p.2). At the beginning of 1998, it was estimated that about one thousand people were participating in schemes in about 31 local authorities. Conscious of this slow start, the government has stated that it might consider making the availability of payments mandatory in all local authorities (Secretary of State for Health 1998,p.18).

As part of their discretion to make decisions about direct payments, local authorities have the power to nominate some of an individual's needs as eligible for direct payment, but to exclude others (see guidance: DH 1997b,para 6); it is therefore not a question of all or nothing.

Direct payments: financial circumstances of users

The Act gives local authorities the power to pay less then their estimate of the reasonable cost of obtaining the relevant services – on the basis that people will contribute the rest from their own means. This is equivalent to the power that authorities have to make charges under s.17 of the Health and Social Services and Social Security Adjudications Act 1983 for directly provided services. However (also comparable to the 1983 Act), if a person satisfies the authority that it is not reasonably practicable for him or her to make that contribution, then the authority has a duty to make up the difference.

In its original form, the term 'reasonably practicable' was absent; instead the test would have been to 'have regard to his financial circumstances', which could be regarded as harsher than considering whether it is 'reasonably practicable' for a person to pay (see eg, HLD,12/2/1996, cols.432–435).

Direct payments: deductions and making payments

A CIFPA (1998) document considers how local authorities should arrange the collection of contributions when a mixture of services is in place, some provided directly and charged for, others arranged through direct payments. It warns authorities against deducting all contributions from the direct payment, since this might significantly reduce the amount of the direct payment and destroy the whole basis of the scheme (presumably it might be unlawful as well, since the relevant legislation – the 1983 (see p.237) and 1996 Acts – consists of quite distinct provisions dealing with charges and direct payments respectively). Similarly it questions both the practicality and legality of making the direct payments gross and then collecting the total contributions (ie, charges for the direct services and deductions for the direct payments) all in one. It also advises that where 'disaggregation' is not possible – ie, identifying how much contribution attaches to each service component – then authorities should allocate contributions between direct payments and direct services proportional to the respective total costs of the services (CIPFA 1998,p.23).

It is recommended that local authority and service user sign an agreement covering the operation of a separate cheque account into which the payments are made, the timing of payments, financial record-keeping, the meeting of statutory employment requirements (eg, public liability), audit arrangements, and recovery of unused or misused money (CIPFA 1998,p.25).

Direct payments: recovery of money

Policy guidance points out that the power to recover money should cover misuse or non-use of money, but not the making of honest mistakes. There might also be legitimate reasons why a surplus builds up (eg, for quarterly payments of employees' PAYE) (DH 1997b,para 52). Examples given by CIPFA (1998,p.30) of situations justifying recovery include those where payments intended for personal care are used on home adaptations, services are obtained at a reduced price, or there are unspent direct payments following the death of a recipient. The guidance cautions that local authorities should take into account hardship in deciding whether to seek repayment (DH 1997b,para 52). Failure to repay could lead to debt recovery proceedings.

Direct payments: effect on social security benefits

The government gave a firm commitment that social security regulations would be amended when necessary to ensure that direct payments would not be counted as income for the purpose of assessment of benefit entitlement – something which would disadvantage recipients of payments compared with recipients of services direct from the local authority (Baroness Cumberlege: HLD,15/1/1996,col.399).

Direct payments: elements

Elements of direct payments, which have to be identified and costed, might include wages in relation to basic or specialised care, varied payments for unsocial hours and overtime, employer's national insurance contributions, employer's liability insurance, sick pay, holiday pay, training time, emergency cover, travel costs in some circumstances (eg, where higher costs are incurred in rural areas) (Hasler, Zarb and Campbell 1998,pp.9–10).

Direct payments: support and advice

Policy guidance states that people receiving direct payments should be given explanation of what is involved (see extracts above). The most effective way in practice of ensuring good outcomes for both users and authorities might be to set up a support scheme operated by an organisation run by disabled people, which can offer the appropriate information, advice, training and peer support (Hasler, Zarb and Campbell 1998,p.4). Practice guidance echoes this, pointing out the advantages of independent advice provided by people who themselves have experience of managing direct payments (DH 1997b,para 33).

In particular, advice and support might be required for five main areas: identification and selection of service providers, financial and administrative assistance, employment matters, dealing with emergencies, and the transition from receiving services directly to receiving direct payments. For instance, VAT will not apply where a person is employed directly by the recipient of the direct payment, nor where a service is purchased from a supplier who is not registered for VAT because its turnover is below the threshold which makes registration obligatory or is a charity providing care in the home on a 'not-for-profit basis'. In other circumstances it might apply and neither the service users nor the local authority will be able to reclaim it (CIPFA 1998,pp.10,19).

Direct payments: cost-effectiveness

It has been suggested that when local authorities examine the cost-effectiveness of services as demanded by guidance (see above), they should remember to consider both cost and effectiveness. For instance, a direct comparison between the cost of residential care and supported living in the community might be not appropriate because these options are not equivalent in effectiveness. In addition, local authorities should bear in mind the 'free' administration which users of payments might be contributing, and which would otherwise have to be paid for if services were being directly provided by the authorities (Hasler, Zarb and Campbell 1998,p.12).

Policy guidance states that the full costs of direct services and direct payments should be compared, including administrative costs and other overheads (DH 1997b,para 39).

Direct payments: monitoring

In practice local authorities need to balance the requirement of public probity and accountability against imposing an unreasonable burden on service users to demonstrate that the money is being spent appropriately (CIPFA 1998,p.3).

CHAPTER 10

CHARGES FOR WELFARE (NON-RESIDENTIAL) SERVICES

Coverage

1. Charges for welfare (non-residential) services

KEY POINTS

Local authorities have a power, but not a duty, to make charges for non-residential care services. That is, legally, they can charge if they want but they don't have to. Nevertheless, Department of Health guidance encourages local authorities to charge, and this is what local authorities appear to be doing increasingly – although the community White Paper and other guidance has made clear that assessment itself cannot be charged for. Guidance states also that financial assessment should take place separately from assessment of need.

A charge can only be made if it is considered reasonable by an authority. But if a person is able to satisfy the local authority that it is not reasonably practicable for him or her to pay the assessed charge, the local authority must reduce it accordingly. The local ombudsman has investigated charging procedures and set out requirements of fairness for service users. The Court of Appeal has in one case considered the implications of the terms reasonable and reasonably practicable, and in another confirmed that it is lawful to make charges under s.2 of the Chronically Sick and Disabled Persons Act 1970.

Approaches to charging vary widely in practice from authority to authority. The legislation is bare as is formal guidance; the advice note issued by the Department of Health 'for the Social Services Inspectorate' is of somewhat indeterminate status. However, towards the end of 1998, a government White Paper acknowledged that the widely varying practices in charging were yet one more obstacle to fair and consistent access to services, and this was 'unacceptable'. Guidance would be produced to improve the situation as part of a *Fair access to care* initiative (Secretary of State for Health 1998,p.27).

EXTRACTS

Legislation (Health and Social Services and Social Security Adjudications Act 1983,s.17: shortened to HASSASSA) states that local authorities, in relation to a service:

(reasonableness of charge) 'may recover such charge (if any) for it as they consider reasonable'.

(reasonably practictable to pay charge) If a person 'satisfies the authority providing the service that his means are insufficient for it to be reasonably practicable for him to pay for the service the amount which he would otherwise be obliged to pay for it, the authority shall not require him to pay more for it than it appears to them that it is reasonably practicable for him to pay.'

(recovery of charges) 'Any charge under this section may, without prejudice to any other method of recovery, be recovered as a civil debt.'

(services covered) There is a power to charge for services under:

- s.29 of the National Assistance Act 1948 (welfare arrangements for disabled people);
- s.45 of the Health Services and Public Health Act 1968 (welfare of old people);
- schedule 8 of the NHS Act 1977 (prevention of illness and care and after-care and home help and laundry facilities);
- schedule 9 (Part 2,para 1) of the HASSASSA 1983 (meals and recreation for old people provided by district councils),

but not under s.117 of the Mental Health Act 1983.

Community Care White Paper (Secretaries of State 1989) states:

(charges for some services) 'If a user represents that they cannot afford to pay the charge the local authority are statutorily required to reduce the charge to such amount (if any) as appears reasonable to them. The Government proposes to preserve these arrangements, which will apply equally to services provided through other agencies. This provision permits charging for home help, home care, meals provision and day care services' (p.29).

(no charges for other services) 'Local authorities also provide other services for which it would not be appropriate to charge including social work support, occupational therapy, advice and assessment of client needs. These services, including assessments under the new arrangements [ie, community care] ... will continue to be provided free of charge' (p.29).

Policy guidance states:

(expectation of charging) 'It is expected that local authorities will institute arrangements so that users of services of all types pay what they can reasonably afford towards their costs' (DH 1990, p.29).

(timing of assessment of ability to pay) 'But the provision of services, whether or not the local authority is under a statutory duty to make provision, should not be related to the ability of the user or their families to meet the costs, and delegated budgeting systems should take this into account. The assessment of financial means should, therefore, follow the assessment of need and decisions about service provision' (DH 1990,para 3.31).

Circular guidance (LAC(94)1) states:

(encouragement to make charges) 'The Government's view, confirmed in the Community Care White Paper "Caring for People" of 1989 and in the subsequent policy guidance, has consistently been that users who can pay for such services should be expected to do so taking account of their ability to pay. The White Paper and Policy Guidance also make it clear that ability to pay should not influence decisions on the services to be provided, and the assessment of financial means should therefore follow the care assessment.'

(accountability to local and national taxpayers) 'Authorities are locally accountable for making sensible and constructive use of the discretionary powers they have, in order to prevent avoidable burdens falling on council and national taxpayers. Authorities are reminded that the standard spending assessment formula for domiciliary care for elderly people does not take account of the level of income from charges actually received by each authority. This means that any authority which recovers less revenue than its discretionary powers allow is placing an extra burden on the local population or is foregoing resources which could be used to the benefit of the service' (paras 17–18).

Advice note for use by the Social Services Inspectorate

An advice note (SSI 1994m) is referred to extensively below and represents the only detailed 'guidance' by the Department of Health. However, as its title indicates, it is not formal guidance (eg, it is not explicitly issued under s.7 of the Local Authority Social Services Act 1970) – and was apparently not even aimed directly at local authorities, but rather at the Social Services Inspectorate (although the Inspectorate has never dedicated an inspection to charging systems). The note is commonly regarded as a backdoor contrivance, saving the Department of Health at that time from issuing formal, well-publicised and controversial guidance on a sensitive issue.

DISCUSSION

Charging for welfare services: background

The power in s.17 of the 1983 Act (see extracts above), to make charges for various welfare services, drew together previously scattered powers to make charges – under schedule 8 of the NHS Act 1977 (power to make reasonable charges) and s.29 of the National Assistance Act 1948 (power to make charges having regard to the cost of the service). Though the 1983 Bill was criticised during its passage for raising the spectre of means-testing, the government argued that by emphasising whether it was reasonably practicable for a person to pay a charge in relation to his or means, rather than the cost of the service, users would be protected from paying charges they could not afford (Lord Trefgarne: HLD,13/12/1982,col.378).

Charging for welfare services: relevant legislation covered

In the list of legislation referred to in s.17 of the 1983 Act, covering services for which charges may be made, s.2 of the Chronically Sick and Disabled Persons Act 1970 is absent. Nevertheless, it has long been assumed that charges for s.2 services can be made because, as the SSI advice note explains, they 'are arranged by local authorities in exercise of their functions under s.29 of the 1948 Act' (SSI 1994m,p.1) – and s.29 of the National Assistance 1948 Act is of course listed in s.17 of the 1983 Act. Even prior to the 1983 Act, it was assumed that charges under the 1970 Act were covered by s.29(5) (since repealed) of the National Assistance Act 1948 which gave authorities the power to make charges for welfare services under s.29 (Lord Trefgarne: HLD,13/12/ 1982,col.375). This assumption was upheld in the case of *R v Powys CC, ex p Hambidge*, in which the Court of Appeal declined to recognise the 1970 Act as sufficiently freestanding to move it out of the shadow of s.29 of the 1948 Act and away from charges for welfare services made under that section.

Of the services defined as community care services by s.46 of the NHS and Community Care 1990, only services (for after-care) under s.117 of the Mental Health Act 1983 are not covered by this power to make charges. However, charges can be made for non-residential services arranged for people with a mental disorder under schedule 8 of the NHS Act 1977 – and for older people under s.45 of the Health Services and Public Health Act 1968. It is therefore imperative that local authorities are clear about which legislation services are being provided under – since otherwise confusion will arise about the legality of any charges made.

For example, there is some uncertainty about the extent of the exclusion under s.117 of the Mental Health Act 1983. First, the Department of Health has given an opinion that residential accommodation for people who come within s.117 cannot be charged for. At issue is whether the accommodation is provided under that section or under s.21 of the National Assistance Act 1948, in which case it could be charged for (see Clements 1996a,p.235). The code of practice for the Mental Health Act 1983 certainly envisages that accommodation is one of the after-care services to be provided under s.117 (DH,WO 1993,p.108 – and see p.220 of this book); and this seemed to be accepted in *Clunis v Camden and Islington HA LBC*. The local ombudsman in Wales has answered the question by finding not only that accommodation can be provided under s.117 of the Mental Health Act 1983, but that where a person's condition warrants it, it must be. Furthermore, the local authority cannot arbitrarily – ie, without a change in the person's needs and in the accommodation – switch the statutory basis on which the accommodation is provided, from s.117 to s.21 (and thus try to make charges) (*Clwyd CC 1997*).

The same point has arisen in respect of non-residential services; namely whether, for people coming under s.117, at least some services could be provided under other community care legislation and thus be charged for (*R v Ealing LBC, ex p Olensu*: at the time of writing, permission had been given to bring this case but it had not yet been heard). In addition, central government stated in a White Paper that it would not be appropriate to charge for certain services, including social work support, occupational therapy, advice and assessment of client needs (Secretaries of State 1989,p.29). Practice guidance states that local authorities 'cannot charge for care management and assessment' (SSI,SWSG 1991a,p.64); and the SSI (1994m) advice note repeats that authorities 'are not empowered to charge for providing advice about the availability of services or for assessment, including assessments of community care needs' (p.2).

The White Paper and guidance notwithstanding, there appears in any case to be no legal power to charge for assessment under s.47 of the NHS and Community Care Act 1990, since this Act is not referred to by s.17 of the 1983 Act. Conversely, on the basis of the legislation alone, there appears to be no legal obstacle to making charges for advice or social work support arranged under s.29 of the National Assistance Act 1948.

Charging for welfare services: power to make charges

The Circular guidance (see above extract) does not state that authorities *must* make charges, since the legislation imposes no such duty. However, the guidance does seem to carry a veiled threat by referring to the accountability of local authorities to local taxpayers. This is suggestive of the 'fiduciary duty' owed by local authorities to taxpayers – much as the House of Lords found that the GLC had such a duty when implementing its transport policy (*Bromley LBC v GLC*). A fiduciary duty is basically a duty of good faith to use people's money wisely.

The approach of the guidance sits a little uneasily with the supposed 'discretion' which local authorities are meant to have in deciding for themselves whether or not to impose charges. However, given a shortage of resources in relation to demand, local authorities might anyway need little encouragement to make charges – especially since the calculation of financial allocations from central government apparently assumes that authorities will raise certain amounts of money in charges (ACC,AMA 1996,p.7; Harvey, Robertson 1995,p.5). This leaves authorities in a situation where they are 'blamed for heartlessness if they put charges up, and blamed for profligacy if they do not' (Thomas 1994,p.38).

Nevertheless by the same token, sound financial administration means that local authorities should assess properly the costs of operating a charging system. As the SSI advice note states 'authorities will want to have regard to the costs of administering the arrangements … The operating costs of a very complex system of financial assessment may reduce the net benefit of the charges collected' (SSI 1994m,para 7). Elements to be considered might include staff time for assessment, monitoring, payment, debt recovery, review (but not for preparing the policy in the first place); accommodation for staff and client records; information technology; and office equipment (NCC 1995,p.33).

Charging for welfare services: reasonable charges

The SSI (1994m) advice note states that local authorities have discretion to decide what a 'reasonable' charge is. However, it is 'the Government's view, in setting charges (whether flat rate or on a scale) authorities should take account both of the full cost of providing the service and within that of what recipients can reasonably be expected to pay' (p.3). However, the 1983 Act does not confer general revenue-raising powers.

The note suggests that capital, managerial and other overheads directly connected with provision can be taken into account, but not costs associated with the purchasing function or operation of the scheme of charging itself. It says also that 'authorities should perhaps consider the likely range of financial circumstances and ability to pay of the generality of users of the service as a group, although they will always have to be able to allow for exceptions to be made in individual circumstances' (p.3).

Yet it is precisely in 'deciding what charges are "reasonable" that the unresolved political problem rests' (Balloch 1994,p.25) – especially in relation to the assessment as income of state benefits received by service users. Furthermore, the SSI advice note has been criticised a) for failing to acknowledge the difficulties involved in disaggregating and identifying costs, and b) because charging the full cost could result in a very high price being charged. It has been suggested that a policy based on reasonable charges should take account of, apart from the cost of the service, the income profile of potential users generally, and the wider anti-poverty strategy of the local authority (AMA,LGIU 1994,pp.5,43). Indeed, it has been suggested that charging people on income support might be unlawful, since it is meant to represent the minimum on which people can live (MENCAP 1999, p.7).

In *Avon CC v Hooper*, the Court of Appeal emphasised that the flexibility of the 'overriding criterion of reasonableness' enabled the local authority to make charges retrospectively (ie, when the resources of service users have increased long after services had been provided). The reasonableness of such conduct on the part of the authority had to be assessed at the time of the conduct and with regard to all the relevant circumstances. Nevertheless, the local ombudsman has questioned the reasonableness of a charging policy when the council a) failed to give careful thought as to how much a person receiving income support could be expected to pay; and b) adopted a threshold, above which charges would be automatically exempted, of weekly expenses exceeding income by £10 – a criterion which was 'quite arbitrary' and not well thought out (*Essex CC 1991*).

Charging for welfare services: reasonably practicable

The legislation states that if a person satisfies the authority that it is not reasonably practicable for him or her to pay a charge, the authority should only charge what appears to be reasonably practicable for the person to pay. Thus it is for the service user to convince the local authority that he or she cannot afford a charge; in *Avon CC v Hooper*, the Court of Appeal stated that it was for the service user to 'discharge his burden of persuasion' by showing that he or she had insufficient means to pay.

One question arising is whether the onus to precipitate the financial assessment or review lies with the authority or the service user. It has been suggested that the statutory language means that authorities should in some cases instigate a review, even if it has not been formally requested – for instance, in those cases where low income makes it apparent that the person might be unable to afford the charge. And even if there is a burden on the user to make the request, then a duty must lie with the authority to inform all users about the possibility of waiver or reduction of the charge (AMA,LGIU 1994,p.25) – something which authorities sometimes fail to do (Harvey, Robertson 1995,p.12). The opportunity to seek a review of the charge might be particularly important when initial financial assessments routinely fail to take account of specific outgoings related to a person's disability and situation (Baldwin, Lunt 1996,p.77); and when assessment forms actively encourage people to pay the full charge without explaining about the possibility and advantages of a financial assessment (NCC 1995,p.107).

The local ombudsman has pointed out that for people to be able to exercise their statutory right to satisfy the authority that they cannot afford charges, a) they must be informed that the local authority has the discretion to waive charges, and b) a proper appeals procedure must exist in order to assess people's cases (*Greenwich LBC 1993*). In another investigation, the ombudsman stated that essential to the appeals procedure was a) the application of clear and thought-out criteria; b) accurate and sufficient information on which decisions were based; c) information about how to challenge the outcome of the appeal; d) clear reasons explaining decisions. In particular, criteria should have been relevant – for example, they should have related to ability to pay (as demanded by s.17 of the 1983 Act) and not to a reassessment of needs – and been applied consistently. The information on which appeal decisions were based should have been of good and consistent quality (*Essex CC 1991*). The local ombudsman here set out high standards, relating to a level of fairness and individual consideration, which might be administratively difficult for local authorities to achieve within reasonable time and expense, given the numbers of people involved. This should therefore be borne in mind when reviews of charging policies are undertaken (Schwehr 1997b). For instance, in this particular case, a total of 23,000 people were receiving home help (though not all were appealing), and an appeal board sometimes considered 200 or more appeals in one sitting.

Charging for welfare services: means

The Court of Appeal in *Avon CC v Hooper* said that the word 'means' in s.17 of the 1983 Act meant financial resources including a person's realisable 'assets, sources of income, liabilities and expenses'. This would suggest taking account of different types of means, as well as expenses; both considerations are pertinent given the question marks over a) whether property can be taken into account in assessing means for non-residential services (as it is for residential services); and b) the degree to which the extra expenses attributable to disability should be taken into account (see below).

Charging for welfare services: having a policy on means-testing

The local ombudsman has found maladministration when a local authority has failed to have a) 'a properly recorded policy on financial assessment'; b) 'a statement of the criteria for the basis of assessing financial resources and need'; and c) 'advice and explanation of this together with information on what information must be submitted' for the assessment. In this particular ombudsman investigation, part of the problem had arisen because the local authority refused to disregard charitable pledges obtained by the applicants for adaptations for their daughter. The applicants claimed that such assessment was inconsistent with the purpose of the pledges which were designed to bridge the shortfall between the authority's contribution and the actual cost of the works. The ombudsman did not fault the authority for wanting to practice 'prudent' budget management, but for the lack of policy and criteria for such practice, and of advice and explanation (*Hertfordshire CC 1992*). More generally, policies on charging and means-testing should be based on relevant criteria – as the ombudsman pointed out in the Essex investigation (*Essex CC 1991*).

Charging for welfare services: financial assessment

Policy guidance (see above) states that the assessment of people's ability to pay should follow the assessment and decision about services. The SSI advice note states that information about charges should be given to people 'at the same time that they are given written information about the care assessment process and the available services'. This is so that people will not commit themselves to particular care plans without knowing what they might have to pay (SSI 1994m,p.9). Note should be taken also of *Avon CC v Hooper* in which the Court of Appeal accepted that in some circumstances, a retrospective charge may be made.

Yet some local authority assessment forms might be designed to combine assessment of need and finances, so that the duty to assess could in effect become also 'a power to ration services at the point of assessment according to the means of the person' (Age Concern England evidence to: House of Commons Health Service Committee 1993,vol.2,p.142). In practice, local authorities might first assess financially and simply deny an assessment of need to people on the basis of their savings or income (Age Concern England 1994b,p.25; Balloch, Robertson 1995,p.5); this is, on its face, simply unlawful.

A potential, practical drawback to separating the two types of assessment is that people's expectations can be raised unrealistically. There is also concern that where financial assessment is prolonged after service provision has commenced, actual charges calculated subsequently might exceed estimates. The general quality of financial advice given by local authority staff might point to the need for local authorities to utilise specialist financial assessors (SSI,NHSME 1994b,p.26). This, in turn, can complicate the whole process of financial assessment; especially since assessors have to balance the collection of sufficient information against the seeking of excessive detail which is both unnecessary and intrusive. Good advice about other state benefits might be relevant in order for people to maximise their income (ACC,AMA 1996,p.15); but local authorities then

have to weigh up the costs of funding additional welfare rights posts against the additional revenue expected from higher charges (Baldwin, Lunt 1996,p.46). Likewise, a refined means-test
which takes account not of only income, but also outgoings and a range of individual circumstances, is likely to be expensive to administer and to rely on the use of discretion in addition to the
more straightforward income-related rules (eg, AMA,LGIU 1991,p.28).

Charging for services: assessment of family carers or spouses

SSI advice states that local authorities are legally empowered to charge only service users and
should therefore be assessing only those people's ability to pay. This means that family members
should not be required to pay charges unless they are managing the resources of service users; nor
should family members' own resources be taken into account (SSI 1994m,para 19). It goes on to
say that authorities 'may in individual cases, wish to consider whether a client has sufficient reliable access to resources beyond those held in his/her own name for them to be part of his/her
means for the purposes of Section 17(3). The most likely instances of this kind will arise in relation
to married or unmarried couples' (SSI 1994b,para 19). This is viewed as confused and controversial (eg, Clements 1996a,p.241) because of doubt about whether it is consistent with the legislation which refers only to the service recipient's 'means'. (Compare Department of Health guidance
on obtaining financial details about a spouse or partner when local authorities are assessing a person for residential or nursing home care: see p.302).

Various reports indicate that local authorities vary considerably in their practices, and whilst
there might be a grey area – as outlined by the SSI advice note – some authorities would seem to be
overstepping the mark, or at least failing to explain why they are gathering additional information
(eg, it might be for the purpose of establishing entitlement to other state benefits). For instance,
'some authorities appear to be mirroring the social security system by routinely asking for information about the partner's income and capital, regardless of whether the couple are married, het-
erosexual or homosexual, and without any explanation of why or what the information will used
for. A few authorities actually ask for details of the income of everyone in the household, sometimes stating that this will be used for benefits checks' (NCC 1995,p.70).

Charging for services: taking account of extra disability costs

SSI (1994m) advice states that authorities should 'have regard' not only to the income of service
users but also to their overall financial circumstances. This means that they should take account in
particular of additional expenditure 'incurred because of the user's disability or frailty' (para 21).

This reiterates the gist of long-standing Circular guidance on charges made for services under
s.2 of the Chronically Sick and Disabled Persons Act 1970: 'wherever clients of an authority are
required to make a payment for a service or facility (or are entitled to claim a rebate from their expenditure) and the authority in exercising its discretion in such matters takes account of the cash
resources and requirements of such a person, authorities are invited to take into consideration any
claim by a chronically sick and disabled person that he does, by reason of disability, incur abnormal
expenditure and to make sure that clients know this and that they will do so. This is not to imply
any diminution of the statutory powers of discretion of authorities to determine charges or waive
them...' (DHSS 12/70,para 40).

The Disablement Income Group, in an illuminating study (including interviews with disabled people, and examination of expert witness reports in connection with personal injury claims), leaves little doubt as to the wide range of extra everyday costs incurred by disabled people for equipment and adaptations as well as services (Kestenbaum 1997). The latter typically include services in the home relating to odd jobs or gardening, pharmacy items, laundry, clothes, bedding, diet/food, heating, transport, telephone calls, and so on (NCC 1995,p.58). A range of items, seen as luxuries by non-disabled people, might be necessities for disabled people and entail considerable cost: for instance, microwave ovens, washing machines, freezers and kitchen gadgets (Thompson, Lavery and Curtis 1990,p.27). Other examples include taking the car to be washed because of inability to do it oneself, and buying smaller packets because of inability to handle larger, cheaper packets (SSI,Arthritis Care 1996,p.10). Furthermore, the imposition of charges by local authorities (and of means-testing by the Independent Living Fund) can act as disincentives to disabled people who, having found work, find their earnings swallowed up by charges (Kestenbaum, Cava 1998,pp.23–30).

An unsuccessful amendment to the 1983 Act (via the NHS and Community Bill), that a local authority should 'take into account any extra costs attributable to any disability of that person', failed. The government countered that this was anyway implicit in s.17 of the 1983 Act: 'local authorities should have regard to the amount the user pays for these and any other expenses arising from his or her disability in deciding what it is reasonable to expect someone to pay' (Lord Henley: HLD,14/6/1990,cols.465–466). In 1988, the government stated that it was considering whether to issue guidance about the disregarding of payments from the Independent Living Fund (ILF) when charges are assessed (Nicholas Scott: HCWA,30/6/1988,col.343); six years later the SSI (1994m) advice note stated that when a person was receiving a grant from the ILF, the local authority could 'levy its usual charges', but 'should not take into account payments from the Fund' (para 24).

Charging for welfare services: taking account of state benefits

Some would say that the corollary of taking account of the extra costs of disability would preclude local authorities assessing as income, the amounts received by disabled or frail people in the form of state benefits. However, the SSI (1994m,para 13) advice note recommends otherwise, opining that there should not be 'automatic exemption' from charges simply because people receive benefits such as income support, attendance allowance, invalidity benefit (now incapacity benefit), housing benefit, severe disablement allowance, disability living allowance, disability working allowance or payments from the Social Fund (para 13). Instead, authorities should assess the level of any charges in relation to individual financial circumstances. The mobility component of disability living allowance must by law (Social Security Contributions and Benefits Act 1992, s.73) be disregarded.

This view appears flatly to contradict the government's position, stated during the 1983 Act's Parliamentary passage, that its 'advice to local authorities has always been that we would prefer them not to charge people on supplementary benefit for most of the range of services, including home helps ... That remains our advice, which I am happy to confirm on behalf of the Government. We hope that local authorities will, as steadily as circumstances allow, move towards the elimination of charges to those on supplementary benefit' (Kenneth Clarke: HCD,11/5/1983, col.880) Similarly, in the House of Lords, the government was 'in complete sympathy with the principle of not charging those who are living at supplementary benefit or who would suffer real hardship if they were required to pay charges' (Lord Trefgarne: HLD,1/2/1983,col.770). The issue persisted during the 1980s, highlighted for example, by such charging in the Prime Minister's own constituency (Alfred Morris MP, HCD,17/1/1986,col.1359). Concern extends also to people whose income hovers just above income support levels and who on that account might have to pay charges; a poverty trap can be created, making them even worse off than those people receiving income support who might be exempted from paying (AMA,LGIU 1994,p.35).

The wish of government to allow local authorities ample discretion to decide about charges is nothing new or recent; in 1948, it stated during the passage of the National Assistance Bill that the power to charge disabled people under s.29 (a power since moved to s.17 of the 1983 Act) should be exercised 'reasonably' but with the 'fullest discretion' by local authorities. And in answer to the point that, if local authorities did not charge able-bodied people for use of community recreational facilities such as golf and tennis, it was surely not equitable to charge disabled people, the government replied that it would be quite permissible to charge people for going to a club – perhaps 2d. a week (John Edwards: SC(C), 22/1/1948,cols.2569–2575).

Charging for welfare services: home help and attendance allowance

During the passing of the NHS and Community Care Bill, the government resisted the specific disregarding of attendance allowance in the financial assessment. Lord Henley stated that if the 'home help' included personal care, then attendance allowance could be taken into account quite appropriately, but not in relation to ordinary domestic help, for which attendance allowance was not intended. This was despite the argument of Lord Carter that disabled people should enjoy a level playing field and that it was wrong to proceed on the basis that 'those who can pay should pay, even if they are disabled' (HLD,14/6/1990,cols.466–467). This statement followed discussion of an old 1971 Circular (DHSS 53/71) which had stated explicitly that local authorities should disregard attendance allowance when assessing charges for home help.

The issue becomes considerably more pointed when local authorities decrease the provision of ordinary home help services and increase that of personal care. However, the rationale for this distinction between home help and personal care might anyway be misconceived. It is argued that attendance allowance and disability allowance do not necessarily represent the amount a person is going to spend on care, but are instead an indicator of disability and are given towards the extra costs faced by a disabled person who can choose how to use the allowances (see eg, discussion in Kestenbaum 1997,pp.12–13; AMA,LGIU 1994,p.35; Age Concern England 1992,p.9).

For example, a woman might be charged £20.00 per month for a home-help who provided two hours service and be expected to use her attendance allowance to pay this. However she was using the allowance on other things – an orthopaedic bed and chair, a bed-settee for nights when she could not get up the stairs to bed, and a motorised scooter to get to the nearest village (evidence to the House of Commons Health Committee (1993,vol.2,p.156). Similarly, people receiving attendance allowance might, because of their health, be spending it on items such as gardening, decorating, window cleaning, transport (eg, taxi to dentist) – which, however, local authorities fail to take into account. In general, local authorities might as a matter of policy not take into account a range of other outgoings – for instance in respect of holidays, hairdressing, special diet, private medical care and aids and adaptations. Although able to seek a review, people might be discouraged from doing so at the outset by the authority's policy (NCC 1995,pp.55,130).

Charging for welfare services: taking account of capital, savings and property

Some local authorities appear to be applying some of the financial assessment rules for residential accommodation to non-residential services – for instance, by taking account of capital, savings and property. Such policies have been criticised because they fail to take account of the expensive – and sometimes unexpected – items and services required by disabled people living at home, and of their need to preserve independence and maintain their family's standard of living (Bennett 1996,p.29; AMA,LGIU 1994,p.39). It also appears to be unclear whether a local authority can lawfully take account of a person's home (eg, by placing a legal charge against it in respect of assessed charges) in relation to non-residential services. It has been pointed that no other statutory means-test permits this *while the person is still living in the home*, and that such practices would be a 'fundamental and retrograde step' (NCC 1995,p.64).

Charging for welfare services: people who refuse to pay

There is nothing in legislation to suggest that authorities can withdraw, or refuse to provide, services solely on the grounds that a person will not pay. The generally accepted legal view seems to be that if an authority has a duty to provide a service, then non-payment of a charge cannot justify withdrawal of the service – since a duty (to provide a service) cannot be overridden by a mere power (to make a charge). However, the information provided by local authorities might not make this clear, staff might themselves be unaware of the legal position and of their own authority's policy (which might itself be unclear), and sometimes services might in practice be withdrawn from service users who have refused to pay (eg, Baldwin, Lunt 1996,p.80). Nevertheless, the SSI advice note states that services should not be withdrawn because of non-payment (SSI 1994m,para 26).

Instead, the legislation empowers authorities to recover charges as a civil debt through the magistrates courts; alternatively, a county court could be used. The problem for local authorities lies in deciding in what circumstances to pursue such debts, especially given the sensitivity and potentially adverse publicity surrounding the legal pursuit of disabled, elderly or vulnerable people. This makes it all the more important for authorities to have clear guidelines about debts (AMA,LGIU 1991,p.35).

In deciding whether to recommend pursuit of a debt, practitioners might be faced with difficult decisions. For instance, they might react in various ways when faced with a man with learning disabilities who owes money to the local authority, has recently won several thousand pounds through a lottery, but who refuses to reduce the debt. Some practitioners might inform the finance department and urge that the debt be pursued for the sake of equity (ie, having regard to other users of services). Also in the name of equity, they might even suggest that, since services cannot legally be withdrawn on non-payment (see above), they should instead be withdrawn by means of a reassessment and a downward adjustment of assessed need and service provision. Others might wish to preserve confidentiality and not pass on the information; others still might decide to keep quiet because to do otherwise would be 'snitching' and taking away the luck that had come the client's way (Bradley, Manthorpe 1997,pp.70–73).

Nevertheless, faced with potential loss of significant sums of money, a local authority might announce its intention to pursue non-payers – for instance, when about seventy people with learning disabilities have not paid charges and owe a total of over £70,000 between them (Valios 1998).

Charging for welfare services: local approaches

Local authorities have been encouraged to charge for services and there is evidence over the last few years that this is now happening and at higher rates (see eg, Harvey, Robertson 1995; Thomas 1994,p.22; Balloch 1993; AMA,LGIU 1994; AMA,LGIU 1991) such that few authorities have been able to retain policies of not charging for home care (*Community Care* 1998a). Even so, the amount of income received by way of charges, as a proportion of the cost of services provided varies widely from 4 to 28 per cent (Audit Commission,SSI 1998a,p.25).

The imposition or raising of charges might come as a shock to users of services; for instance, a rise of over 200 per cent for assistance with the daily needs might be experienced by an 82-year-old disabled and housebound woman – from £9.50 per week to £28.45, though this was later reduced on appeal (Age Concern England 1993,p.16). Local authorities might decide to raise simultaneously their charges for a number of essential services, thus causing sizeable increases for some people (AMA,LGIU 1991,p.7).

In practice, local authorities operate different charging systems – for example, no charge; flat rate (eg, by service or by unit of service); or differential charges (hinging on concessions which might relate to people's income or to the policy preferences of an authority, or both) (AMA,LGIU 1991,p.11). Within differential charges, there might be a) a standard charge with exemptions; b) banded charges based on means, on means and cost of the service, or on level of service received; or c) variable charges based on a percentage of a user's net disposable income (Harvey, Robertson 1995,p.9). Local authorities might continue to work out separate charges for each service provided, or alternatively make one overall, combined charge for a package of different services being used by one person (eg, Baldwin, Lunt 1996,p.32).

Flat rate charges run the risk of being unlawful if they are high (and therefore not reasonable), applied inflexibly and fail to take account of whether it is reasonably practicable for individual users to pay them. Even so, it has been pointed out that a flat-rate, low charge for meals might be acceptable, since even income support recipients have to buy food. Furthermore, flat-rate charges set at a genuinely low level might be advantageous for those on low incomes, since differential charges can leave disabled people in employment little better off than if they were receiving income support (Bennett 1996,p.21).

Charging for welfare services: collecting charges

There is a wide variety of methods for collecting charges, including cash, direct debit, standing order, bank giro/girobank, credit card, cheque, stamp card system, swipe card system, Post Office vouchers, and collection via independent providers (ACC,AMA 1996,pp.38–40. On the last option, the SSI advice note (1994m,para 8) warns that 'it should be clear to the user that any collecting of charges is being done on behalf of the Authority and any revenue is remitted to the

Authority'. In one investigation, the local ombudsman approved the revision of payment procedures, so that people did not have to pay postage charges in making their payments (instead they could pay via Girobank at post offices, and they were sent pre-paid envelopes) (*Greenwich LBC 1993*).

A separate issue which sometimes arises is that local authorities expect service users to pay even when services are not received – for example, when monthly statements are generated by computer and sent out before information about cancelled visits has been received and taken account of (Coombs 1998,p.43).

Charging for welfare services: equity

Authorities might find difficulty in achieving equity in charging even within their own boundaries. In the past, some authorities have waived the charges for some people (eg, people with learning disabilities), but raised them for others (eg, people from a different authority or people with physical disabilities). On the other hand, one authority doing so introduced day centre charges so as to remove the inequity of people at home paying for services but those at day centres not doing so (Balloch 1993,pp.7–10). The SSI advice note recognises that the full cost of a service might vary from area to area within one authority because different providers are being used (there might presumably be other reasons as well); in such circumstances, it is 'for the authority to decide whether the charges to individuals should reflect these cost differences or whether to have one notional charge for all recipients' (SSI 1994m,para 6).

Charging for welfare services: a rationing tool

It is often claimed that the imposition or raising of charges acts as a rationing device; even when it does not, it is likely a) to impose hardship on some of the people who continue to receive services and b) to affect the relationship between service users and professionals. Existing service users might not request reassessments or more services – even if their needs have increased – for fear of having to pay higher charges (variously: Baldwin, Lunt 1996,p.69; Age Concern England 1992,p.16; Chetwynd, Ritchie 1996,pp.39,63).

For instance, the Alzheimer's Disease Society has adverted to the practice of 'charging for home care which goes against the preventative nature of community care by discouraging users in the early stages where a small amount of home help, cleaning help, shopping help, would enable them to go on staying at home. Those pensioners on low incomes faced with a home care of £6 an hour will just say: "I can't afford that, that is such a chunk out of my pension I'll do without it", and the likelihood is they will need health care sooner rather than later if that is the case' (House of Commons Health Committee 1993,vol.2,p.178). Another example is of the woman who attended a day centre run by a local charity, where she had a bath (which she could not have at home) and her husband had a break from caring of a few hours. The charity then entered into a contract with social services, which involved the imposition of charges of £3.00 an hour up to a maximum of £14 per week. The couple could not afford this and so the wife would have to stop attending the centre (Lamb, Layzell 1995b,p.52).

Charging for welfare services: Local Government Act 1972, s.111

Some local authorities attempt to make use of another statutory route for making charges, namely s.111 of the Local Government Act 1972. This enables authorities to do things to facilitate, or which are conducive or incidental to, the discharge of any of their functions. However, in *McCarthy v Richmond LBC*, the House of Lords sounded a clear warning against use of this section by local authorities to make charges for services.

Charging for welfare services: health care or social care

Because health services are generally free of charge, there are significant financial implications for service providers and users, depending on how services are defined. For example, respite care previously provided free by the NHS, might now have to be paid for by users and their relatives if arranged by local authorities in residential or nursing homes. This can impose a severe financial burden (Alzheimer's Disease Society 1993,p.9).

Health authorities might perceive an imbalance insofar as they are not empowered legally to charge for services, but local authorities are. This might 'impose an additional and unscheduled burden on the health authority' (RCN, Spastics Society 1992,para 8.1) and provide an incentive for health authorities not to provide some services (for blurred boundaries between health and social care: see p.322).

The House of Commons Health Committee (1993) took evidence of concerns that due to the community care changes, a number of health services provided hitherto free of charge were in fact being re-defined as 'social care' services for which charges may be made. There was a view that 'a fundamental right of the individual to free health care from the NHS is being eroded with little public awareness of the implications of the new policies' (vol.2,p.144). For example, if a person who has had a stroke is cared for at home by services purchased by a GP, then those services will be free. If provided by social services, the person could be liable to contributions (vol.2,p.74). Another specific example given was when a service such as bathing, delivered free by a nurse, is re-defined as social care. There might be 'substitution of an inexperienced home carer for a nurse to bathe her mother, who had frequently collapsed and needed medication during the bathing process. The older woman was charged at the £5.88 hourly rate for a 20-minute bath, which had formerly been provided free by the National Health Service'. Such redefinitions can result in people being unable to pay and services consequently being withdrawn (vol.2,pp.143,156).

Apart from the inequity arising when one person is charged and another is not for a similar service, a legal difficulty affects the charging for services which are arranged jointly by social services and health authorities (Balloch 1994,p.25) – since the latter cannot legally make charges for most services (see p.353). A more recent House of Commons Health Committee report (1998, p.xxii) returned to the issue of social services charging policies and the shift of some health care to social care – highlighting the confusion, anomalies, inconsistencies and barriers to joint working.

RESIDENTIAL AND NURSING HOME ACCOMMODATION

Coverage

1. Making arrangements for the provision of residential and nursing home care

2. Making arrangements with the independent sector for residential and nursing home care

3. Ordinary residence (see Chapter 7)

4. People in residential or nursing home accommodation before April 1993

5. Making charges for residential and nursing home accommodation (see Chapter 11)

6. Choice of accommodation

7. Services for residents

8. Extra services provided by local authorities

9. NHS services in residential care and nursing homes

10. Registration and inspection of residential care homes

11. Services and facilities provided by residential care homes

12. Registration and inspection of nursing homes

13. Services and facilities provided by nursing homes

KEY POINTS

Care homes as part of community care. As already explained in Chapter 3, community care policy ostensibly favours care in people's own homes rather than institutional homes. However, residential and nursing home care remain the most suitable option for some people. In addition, there are financial incentives for local authorities to fund such care when it is cheaper than the alternative of arranging services in people's own homes. The case of *R v Lancashire CC, ex p RADAR* confirms the notion that community care is not simply about enabling people to remain in their own homes. This is reflected by the widespread practice of applying financial ceilings on packages of home care services for older people – although this practice appears not to be condoned in a White Paper issued at the end of 1998 (Secretary of State for Health 1998, p.14).

Duty to arrange residential accommodation. Local authorities have both duties and powers to arrange residential accommodation (with or without nursing care), either in their own residential homes or in independent sector homes, for people who – because of age, illness, disability or other circumstances – are in need of care and attention which is not otherwise available to them. With certain provisos, local authorities are also obliged to give people a choice of residential accommodation. At the time of writing, a High Court judgment has cast some doubt on whether it is lawful for local authorities to purchase the nursing care element of nursing home accommodation. Depending on the outcome of the appeal being made, the implications are considerable (*R v North and East Devon HA, ex p Coughlan*).

The case of *R v Sefton MBC, ex p Help the Aged* in the Court of Appeal has illustrated the financial difficulties some local authorities experience in performing this duty – much as *R v Gloucestershire CC, ex p Barry* did in relation to the provision of non-residential services. However, a batch of other cases involving asylum seekers have also been heard, resulting in close analysis of the wording of s.21 of the National Assistance Act 1948. These have demonstrated its breadth in terms both of whom it can legally benefit and of different types of accommodation (which need not necessarily include personal care and board).

Services within homes. This chapter also outlines responsibilities for the provision of services, equipment and facilities in residential and nursing homes. It does not attempt to cover the whole of the statutory regime governing the operation of such homes. However, service provision is a particularly important issue for a number of reasons, including a) the fear that people might be 'warehoused' and forgotten in care homes; b) the danger of reduced access to basic NHS and other services; and c) uncertainty about who should pay for various services – for instance, the home as part of the fees it charges, the NHS or the resident.

(*N.B. Reform of registration and inspection of care homes.* It should be noted that substantial reform of the registration and inspection system for both residential homes and nursing homes was announced in a White Paper at the end of 1998. Basically, new legislation will replace local authorities and health authorities in their registration and inspection capacities, with independent statutory bodies at regional level, called Commissions for Care Standards. Regulations and national standards of care will be brought together so as to apply both residential and nursing homes (differing only to reflect nursing care).

Local authority residential homes will be subject to registration and inspection, something to which they have not previously been subject to under the Registered Homes Act 1984. Registered small homes, that is homes with less than four adult residents, will no longer be exempt from inspection. The Commissions for Care Standards will also regulate domiciliary care agencies; this is also a new departure (Secretary of State for Health 1998, Chapter 4).

I. MAKING ARRANGEMENTS FOR THE PROVISION OF RESIDENTIAL AND NURSING HOME CARE

The National Assistance Act 1948 (together with directions and approvals made under it) places both duties and powers on local authorities to make arrangements for providing residential and nursing home accommodation for people aged 18 years or over – who because of age, illness, disability or any other circumstances are in need of care and attention not otherwise available to them. Whether, under these directions and approvals, an authority has a duty or power in the case of any particular person can depend on, for example, where the person lives (or is 'ordinarily resident': see p.169), the urgency of his or her need, and whether he or she suffers from a mental disorder.

EXTRACTS

Legislation (National Assistance Act 1948) states that:

(make arrangements) 'a local authority may with the approval of the Secretary of State, and to such extent as he may direct shall, make arrangements for providing –

(a) residential accommodation for persons aged 18 or over who by reason of age, illness, disability or any other circumstances are in need of care and attention which is not otherwise available to them; and

(aa) residential accommodation for expectant and nursing mothers who are in need of care and attention which is not otherwise available to them' (National Assistance Act 1948, s.21(1)(a)).

(welfare of residents and different types of accommodation) 'In making any such arrangements a local authority shall have regard to the welfare of all persons for whom accommodation is provided, and in particular to the need for providing accommodation of different descriptions of such persons as are mentioned' (s.21(2)).

(care and attention: disregarding capital) 'In determining ... whether care and attention are otherwise available to a person, a local authority shall disregard so much of the person's capital as does not exceed the capital limit for the purposes of section 22 of this Act' (s.21(2A) as inserted by the Community Care (Residential Accommodation) Act 1998).

At the same time as this Act was passed in 1998, regulations (SI 1992/2977) were amended, making it quite clear that the rules governing the assessment of a resident's assets and what contribution he or she should make, apply both to residents in accommodation and prospective residents (SI 1998/1730).

Directions and approvals: the operation of s.21 hinges on the *Secretary of State's Approvals and Directions under section 21(1) of the National Assistance Act 1948*: see: LAC(93)10, appendix 1,para 2).

(ordinary residence and urgency) In relation to s.21(1)(a) of the 1948 Act (above), the Secretary of State has directed local authorities to make arrangements for people 'who are ordinarily resident in their area and other persons who are in urgent need' of them.

(no settled residence, or resident elsewhere) In addition, approval has been given to 'the making by local authorities of arrangements ... in relation to persons with no settled residence and, to such extent as the authority may consider desirable, in relation to persons who are ordinarily resident in the area of another local authority with the consent of that other authority' (and see s.24 of the National Assistance Act 1948).

(urgency) In addition, it is directed that 'local authorities make arrangements ... to provide temporary accommodation for persons who are in urgent need thereof in circumstances where the need for that accommodation could not reasonably have been foreseen'.

(mental disorder) In addition, local authorities are directed to make arrangements 'in relation to persons who are or who have been suffering from mental disorder, or ... for the purposes of the prevention of mental disorder'. Also, approval is given to authorities to make arrangements in relation to mentally disordered people or for the prevention of mental disorder, for those 'who are ordinarily resident in the area of another local authority but who following discharge from hospital have become resident in the authority's area'.

(illness) In addition, approval is given to authorities to make arrangements for accommodation to meet the needs of people for ... '(a) the prevention of illness, (b) the care of those suffering from illness; and (c) the aftercare of those so suffering'.

(drugs and alcohol) In addition, approval is given to the making of arrangements by local authorities 'specifically for persons who are alcoholic or drug-dependent'.

(expectant and nursing mothers) Approval is given to the making of arrangements for this group under s.21(1)(b) of the 1948 Act.

Guidance (LAC(98)19) states:

(duty to assess even those people who have resources over the capital limit and are able to make their own arrangements) 'Local authorities are under a legal duty under the NHS and Community Care Act 1990 to assess the care needs of anyone who, in the authority's view, may be in need of community care services. It is the Department's view that the law does not allow authorities to refuse to undertake an assessment of care needs for anyone on the grounds of the person's financial resources, eg, because they have capital in excess of the capital limit for residential accommodation. Even if someone may be able to pay the full cost of any services, or make their own arrangements independently … they should be advised about what type of care they require, and informed about what services are available' (para 8).

(resources over the capital limit and whether care and attention is otherwise available) 'It is the Department's view that having capital in excess of the upper limit of £16,000 does not in itself constitute adequate access to alternative care and attention. Local authorities will wish to consider the position of those who have capital in excess of the upper limit of £16,000 and must satisfy themselves that the individual is able to make their own arrangements, or has others who are willing and able to make arrangements for them, for appropriate care. Where there is a suitable advocate or representative (in most cases a relative), it is the Department's view that local authorities should provide guidance and advice on the availability and appropriate level of services to meet the individual's needs. Where there is no identifiable advocate or representative to act on the individual's behalf it must be the responsibility of the LA to make the arrangements and to contract for the person's care' (para 10).

(delaying provision) 'Once a LA has determined that care and attention are not otherwise available and that they will make arrangements for residential accommodation, they should do so without undue delay. Where it is foreseen that there will be a delay the authority should ensure that suitable arrangements are in place to meet the needs of the individual and of their carer if appropriate' (para 11).

(taking over arrangements for a self-funding resident) 'Similarly, where a self-funder in a care/nursing home has capital that has reduced to the £16,000 upper capital limit it is the Department's view [that] as soon as reasonably practicable, the local authority should undertake an assessment and, if necessary, step in to take over arrangements so as to ensure the resident is not forced to use up capital below £16,000' (para 11).

(ending arrangements for a person who becomes self-funding) 'It is the Department's view that if an authority is to end a contract and make the person "self funding" they should satisfy themselves that the person is able to manage their own affairs or has someone who can take over the arrangements on their behalf. Where the person is unable to manage their own affairs or has no one to act on their behalf it would be for the authority to continue to manage the contract and the person should remain a Part III placement. If the person is capable or has someone to act on their behalf for them, then if the authority decides to terminate its involvement, they must inform the resident or representative in writing, explaining why. A person placed in a residential care home directly managed by a local authority cannot become a self funder by entering into a private contract with the care home manager, as in an independent sector home. They remain under contract under the National Assistance Act 1948 as a full payer' (para 12).

DISCUSSION

Residential accommodation: age, illness, disability

The NHS and Community Care Act 1990 amended s.21 of the National Assistance Act 1948 and substituted the terms 'illness' and 'disability' for 'infirmity'. This change both updated the terminology and marked a widening of scope, necessary because of the repeal under schedule 8 of powers to provide accommodation for less dependent people, and the extension of local authority responsibilities to arrangements for nursing home care. It was this very broadening which meant that the government resisted an amendment to the NHS and Community Care Bill which would have specifically mentioned also mental disorder and dependency on drugs or alcohol. It maintained that being 'specific in one direction usually implies some restriction in another' and that s.21 was to be 'wide and comprehensive in its coverage of all clients for whom social care may be necessary' (Baroness Blatch: HLD,8/5/1990,cols.1273).

None of the three terms, age, illness or disability is defined in relation to s.21.

Residential accommodation: any other circumstances

In *R v Westminster CC, ex p A*, the Court of Appeal ruled, upholding a decision of the High Court in relation to asylum seekers, that the term 'any other circumstances' did not necessarily have to be of a kind with age, illness or disability (the other conditions for assistance). However, the court also stated that even if it were wrong and it did have to be of a kind with these other terms, it was clear that the circumstances of the asylum seekers – without food and accommodation, inability to speak the language, ignorance of Britain, and stress – could result in illness or disability, thus establishing potential eligibility through these terms rather than 'any other circumstances'. Likewise a similar term, 'other special reason', in housing legislation and concerning people's vulnerability and priority, was held to be capable of covering asylum seekers *(R v Kensington and Chelsea RLBC, ex p Kihara)*.

Nevertheless, the Court of Appeal in the *Westminster* case did qualify what the High Court had stated in the same case by emphasising that the Act was not a safety net provision for just anyone who was short of money or accommodation. This conclusion is consistent with the original explanation of the phrase 'any other circumstances', when the National Assistance Bill was going through Parliament. It was precisely to cover the 'difficult or marginal case' which did not concern age or infirmity (ie, the original criteria in the section), but when the absence of such a power might 'run us into trouble'. However, there was no intention 'to place indefinite responsibility on local authorities' (John Edwards: SC(C),21/1/1948,col.2498)

Residential accommodation: care and attention otherwise available

In *R v Sefton MBC, ex p Help the Aged*, the High Court accepted that if people a) were in need of attention, b) had over £1,500 of resources of their own, and c) were able (physically, mentally and financially) to make their own arrangements for residential care – then care and attention was 'otherwise available' and the local authority had no duty to arrange it. The Court of Appeal reversed this judgment, stating that once a person's resources had gone below £16,000 (the current capital limit for assessing residents' liability to contribute to their accommodation costs: see p.303), then the authority had to regard care and attention as not being otherwise available and had therefore to make arrangements for accommodation.

Subsequently, the Community Care (Residential Accommodation) Act 1998 was passed to confirm this ruling and make clear that capital equal to or less than the capital limit must be disregarded when determining whether care and attention is otherwise available to a person. However, accompanying guidance goes further by pointing out that simply because people do have more than the capital limit does not *necessarily* mean that they are not in need of care and attention not otherwise available to them – because they might be unable to make their own arrangements and have no suitable advocate or representative (eg, a relative) to make the arrangements for them (LAC(98(19),para 10). This would seem to reflect the import of the original summary (in a House of Commons command paper) of the National Assistance Bill published in 1947. This explained that residential accommodation would be 'available to all those in need of it irrespective of their means. The Local Authority will thus cease to be merely a reliever of destitution and will become the provider of comfortable accommodation, with care and attention, for those who, owing to age or infirmity, cannot wholly look after themselves' (Ministry of Health 1947,para 23).

In *R v Newham LBC, ex p Gorenkin*, a case concerning asylum seekers, the High Court stated that the fact that a person still had accommodation of some sort did not preclude the local authority from arranging for residential accommodation – since a person starving in a garret and destitute might reach the point where he needed care and attention, despite still having a roof over his head. In contrast, the High Court ruled in *R v Newham LBC, ex p Plastin* that it was not perverse of the local authority to have decided that the applicant was not in need of care and attention. He was 51 years old and thus of working age, had worked as a ship's captain and cook, was under no physical or mental disability (except a need for dental treatment which he could obtain on the NHS) – and s.21 of the Act was not a safety net for anybody short of money or accommodation. However, to the extent that an illegal immigrant with advanced HIV/AIDS was not fit to travel, and could not therefore return to Brazil to receive care there, he could be eligible for assistance under s.21 because care and attention would not be otherwise available – even though public policy would normally exclude an illegal entrant or overstayer from benefiting from his or her own wrongdoing (*R v Brent LBC, ex p D*). Conversely, a person who was in this country because he had served a lawful prison sentence for drugs offences, whose deportation order was ineffective – since Sweden (which had originally granted him political asylum) would not permit him to re-enter – and who was cooperating fully with the United Kingdom authorities, was not, as a matter of public policy, to be excluded from assistance under s.21 of the 1948 Act (*R v Lambeth LBC, ex p Sarhangi*).

Guidance points out that (in the Department of Health's view) just because people do have more than the capital limit and *are able* to make their own arrangements – and therefore care and attention is otherwise available – does not mean that local authorities can refuse both to assess, and then to advise and inform them about what they require and what services are available (LAC(98)19,para 8). Even so, there is evidence not only that some local authorities in practice refuse to assess and to assist, but that staff might continue such practices even after the policy sanctioning them has officially been discontinued (Wright 1997,pp.4,7).

Residential accommodation: waiting times

Some local authorities apparently try to defer incurring financial responsibility by putting people on a waiting list for residential accommodation – and then not reimbursing them for the resources they have spent during the waiting time before residential accommodation is eventually arranged (Age Concern England 1998d,pp.15–16). The guidance (above) states that once a need is recognised, arrangements should be made without 'undue delay'; this is a vague term. Were the courts to consider what a reasonable delay was – and they might be reluctant to become involved (see p.53) – it is possible they might apply a reasonably stringent test given what is at stake for elderly, vulnerable people.

Residential accommodation: different types

The law courts have emphasised the broad nature of accommodation which local authorities are empowered to arrange, from nursing homes and residential accommodation with full personal care, to bed-and-breakfast accommodation (*R v Newham LBC, ex p Medical Foundation for the Care of Victims of Torture*) and even ordinary housing in some circumstances *R v Bristol CC, ex p Penfold*). However, they have also pointed out in (*R v Wandsworth LBC, ex p Beckwith* that local authorities are not obliged to manage directly any residential homes at all, despite the Department of Health's view at one time to the contrary (LAC(93)10,para 4).

Residential accommodation: cash payments

The High Court ruled in *R v Secretary of State for Health, ex p Hammersmith LBC* that s.21 did not enable a local authority to make cash payments. It had wanted to do this because the most convenient and cost-effective way of assisting asylum seekers was to provide them with bed-and-breakfast accommodation – and then to give them cash to buy breakfast and other items such as toiletries. The court stated that s.21 did not allow the making of such payments. The Court of Appeal subsequently upheld this decision.

Residential accommodation: closing local authority care homes

In the drive to save money and move to independent sector provision, many local authorities have closed numbers of their residential homes. When they do this, the courts have insisted that adequate consultation should take place, even though legislation is silent on the matter (*R v Devon CC, ex p Baker; R v Wandsworth LBC, ex p Beckwith (no.2)*).

Residential accommodation: ordinary residence or urgent need

Directions (see above) state that local authorities have a duty to make arrangements for the provision of residential accommodation under s.21 of the National Assistance Act 1948 for people who are ordinarily resident in their area, and for 'other people who are in urgent need' of it. Other people in this context presumably covers both those ordinarily resident elsewhere as well as those with no settled residence (see below).

In addition, local authorities are also directed to make arrangements under s.21 for the provision of 'temporary accommodation' where there is an urgent need for it which could not 'reasonably have been foreseen'. It was this direction, together with the approval (see extracts above) in relation to the prevention of illness, that was held by the Court of Appeal, in *R v Westminster CC, ex p A*, to apply to asylum seekers.

And in *R v Brent LBC, ex p D*, it was accepted that illegal immigrants would normally be deprived of eligibility for assistance, because they should not benefit from their own wrongdoing. However, where there was a risk of serious damage to their health or of loss of life if they were to travel (back to their own country for care), then they would be eligible for assistance (subject to normal assessment).

Residential accommodation: mental disorder

Local authorities are directed to make arrangements in relation to persons who are or who have been suffering from mental disorder, or for the purposes of the prevention of mental disorder. In addition, approval is given to authorities to make arrangements in relation to mentally disordered people – or for the prevention of mental disorder – for those 'who are ordinarily resident in the area of another local authority but who following discharge from hospital have become resident in the authority's area'.

Residential accommodation: drug and alcohol misusers

Circular guidance stresses the importance of 'rapid assessment procedures for drug and alcohol misusers' whose needs might be so urgent that they will need immediate residential care; and that those who have no 'settled residence' should not be denied assessment because they have not been long enough in a particular locality to qualify (LAC(93)2,paras 14,21).

Residential accommodation: no settled residence

Local authorities are given, by s.24(3) of the 1948 Act, the power to provide residential accommodation for people with no settled residence (in any authority), and this power is reiterated in the directions (see above). However, in cases of urgent need or mental disorder this might become a duty (see above).

On the face of it, this would seem to mean that no duty arises in the case of people with no settled residence and without 'urgent' needs, and that local authorities could interminably avoid financial responsibility. A suggested practical solution is that a person with no settled residence could be deemed ordinarily resident in the place where or she is actually living, or even wherever the night before was spent (Clements 1996a,p.74). However, while this makes practical sense, a) it is not clear that this solution is sanctioned by the legislation, directions and approvals; and b) it might mean that nobody can ever be of no settled residence, which is not what the legislation envisages. However, guidance does state that if 'a person states that he has no settled residence or describes himself as NFA (no fixed abode) the social services authority where he presents himself should normally accept responsibility. For a person in urgent need, the social services authority of the moment cannot argue that the possible existence of a "local connection" elsewhere excuses it from the duty to assess and provide any necessary social services' (LAC(93)7,para 16).

In terms of assessment, guidance suggests that vulnerable people who are homeless might require urgent responses: for example, because of frailty, physical disability or mental disorder of any description. It goes on to state local authorities 'will be aware that there are a wide variety of agencies which specialise in providing residential care for homeless people. As with specialist alcohol and drug providers, these agencies may be in a position to assist in assessment procedures' (LAC(93)2,para 27).

Residential accommodation: provision for people ordinarily resident elsewhere

Legislation states that a local authority can provide residential accommodation, to such extent as it considers desirable, for people ordinarily resident in another authority if they have the consent of the other authority (in which the person is ordinarily resident) (NAA 1948,s.24(4); see also directions above).

Residential accommodation: placements in another area

Relying on s.24(5) of the 1948 Act (see p.170), guidance states that a person 'will not as a general rule become ordinarily resident in the other local authority's area' if he or she is placed by one authority in the other authority's area.

The other authority should be informed of the placement by the original authority, which 'should also ensure that satisfactory arrangements are made before placement for any necessary support services, such as day care, and for periodic reviews, and that there are clear agreements about the financing for all aspects of the individual's care'. Conversely, 'no host authority should alter the accommodation or services provided for that person to a significant degree without consulting in advance the responsible local authority' (LAC(93)7,paras 7–8).

However, although a person placed in a home in the area of another authority remains the responsibility of the original placing authority, if 'by private arrangement, the person moves he may, depending on the specific circumstances, become ordinarily resident in the area of the local authority where he has chosen to live' (LAC(93)7,para 8). For instance, in one local ombudsman investigation, the Secretary of State, in resolving a dispute about ordinary residence in such a situation, stated that if the person remained in the care home he would remain the responsibility of the original placing authority, but if he moved into the community into his own home, then he would become ordinarily resident in the area, and therefore the responsibility, of the second authority (*Redbridge LBC 1998*).

Residential accommodation: ordinary residence and privately arranged placement in another area

Guidance states that if a person moves into residential accommodation situated in another area without any social services involvement, then he or she will 'usually' become ordinarily resident within that new area. This would seem to follow from s.24(5) of the 1948 Act. Any subsequent need for social services should be sought in the new area (LAC(93)7,para 10). In practice, people sometimes move into the area of another local authority in anticipation of a need for residential care, if there is a waiting list in their own. When they then actually require it, dispute might arise about which local authority is responsible.

A Department of Health letter to Age Concern England reiterated that the Department's view was that if the person has moved 'voluntarily into the area of another authority with a settled intention to live in that authority's area then this would suggest that they become ordinarily resident in the new authority's area from the time of the move' – and thus the 'new' authority would be responsible for making arrangements for residential accommodation. The letter also gave an opinion about the situation in which an authority makes a 'cross-boundary placement' by placing (and taking financial responsibility for) a person, who is waiting to sell his or her house, in a residential home in the area of another authority. When the proceeds of the sale are available and the authority is reimbursed, it might (though not necessarily) then cease to make arrangements because the person's capital now exceeds £16,000 (see p.255). When the resources (ie, the sale proceeds) drop below £16,000, and the person again requires assistance under the National Assistance Act 1948, then 'almost certainly' he or she has become ordinarily resident in the area of the new authority (DH 1998c).

However, any cessation of arrangements made by the original local authority would have to be made quite clear to the resident, as stated both by guidance (LAC(98)19,para 12) and the High Court's decision in *R v Sefton LBC, ex p Help the Aged*. In that case, the judge failed to find evidence of termination of involvement of the local authority with the resident, even though his assets had at one stage risen above £16,000 during his stay in the residential home (this part of the High Court's decision was not overturned by the Court of Appeal).

Residential accommodation: asylum seekers

Unexpectedly, the provision of residential accommodation for a certain category of asylum seeker (ie, those who do not apply for asylum immediately at place of entry to the United Kingdom) has become a significant legal, financial and practical issue for some local authorities.

The immediate background was that in 1996, regulations (SI 1996/30) were introduced to deny this group of asylum seekers access to income-related benefits including income support and housing benefit. The courts struck down these regulations as unlawful, given rights implicit in the Asylum and Immigration Appeals Act 1993 (*R v Secretary of State, ex parte Joint Council for the Welfare of Immigrants*). The government reacted by quickly amending the Asylum and Immigration Act 1996, so as to restore the effect of the regulations. Consequently, asylum seekers were deprived of accommodation, funds, benefits, permission to work (for at least six months), friends, contacts, and so on.

The last resort then became s.21 of the National Assistance Act 1948 and the duty to arrange residential accommodation in certain circumstances for those in urgent need of it. Faced with unexpected expenditure, the affected local authorities resisted and fought several issues in the courts, including whether s.21 was relevant at all to asylum seekers *(R v Westminster CC, ex p A*: it was), whether cash payments could be made to those being provided with residential accommodation (*R v Secretary of State for Health, ex p Hammersmith and Fulham LBC*: they could not), whether food vouchers could be given under s.21 even if residential accommodation was not being provided *(R v Newham LBC, ex p Gorenkin*: they could not), whether accommodation alone – without food, laundry and other facilities for personal hygiene – could be provided *(R v Newham LBC, ex p Medical Foundation for the Care of Victims of Torture*: it could), or whether choice could be exercised in relation to where the accommodation was arranged (*R v Westminster CC, ex p P*: the question was not answered).

The consequence of all this is the 'past misery, present muddle' described by the Medical Foundation for the Care of Victims of Torture (1997) in its report, which illustrates an almost bewildering variety of arrangements made by local authorities in London, involving, for instance: bed-and-breakfast accommodation, hostels, food parcels, toiletry parcels, food vouchers for supermarkets, food vouchers for Halal butcher shops, vouchers for travel or clothing, travel cards (so that people can collect the vouchers), luncheon vouchers, meal centres to which people walk (because for example, it is not clear if it is lawful to pay public transport fares), packed lunches, delivery of frozen meals, volunteers who take the asylum seekers to a supermarket, shopping services, small sums towards gas and electricity. The legality of some of the arrangements is in doubt; although where children are involved, the position is clearer because s.17 of the Children Act 1989 allows the making of cash payments, 'in exceptional circumstances' to families with children in need.

The Department of Health makes available to local authorities support, by way of a special grant, towards expenditure incurred in relation to asylum seekers under s.21 of the National Assistance Act 1948 – up to a maximum of £140 per asylum seeker. Only 'relevant expenditure' qualifies for support. This might include 'a) the provision of accommodation and board, or accommodation only with meals or food provided separately (either in the form of groceries where cooking facilities are available or by other means, eg, meals on wheels); b) administration costs together with any social services assessment costs; c) the costs involved in commissioning premises to be used to accommodate asylum seekers' – up to a maximum of £10 for each person supported in such premises.

However, excluded are 'a) the provision of services not covered by the National Assistance Act; b) the provision of accommodation under section 21(1)(a) ... for adults who are in need of accommodation for reasons other than non-entitlement to social security benefits and housing assistance; c) the provision of cash payments to individual asylum seekers for which there is no provision in section 21 of the National Assistance Act. Authorities should be aware that giving vouchers with a cash value equates to giving cash. Section 21 would however allow for arrangements to be made with a provider (eg, a supermarket chain) to enable asylum seekers to obtain by pre-arrangement food and other necessities not provided in their accommodation'.

In order to identify relevant expenditure and whether a person has been excluded from benefits, local authorities have to contact the Immigration and Nationality Directorate for sight of relevant documentation, such as a standard acknowledgement letter (SAL for short) (LAC(98)5). A separate special grant is available for the support of asylum seeking families with children – who might become children in need under s.17 of the Children Act 1989, when benefits are withheld from their parents (LAC(98)3).

In July 1998, legislative change was proposed such as to remove from local authorities the duty to provide assistance for 'healthy and able bodied asylum seekers' under the National Assistance Act 1948. Instead it proposed a national support scheme for all asylum seekers, to be created, operated and funded by the Home Office (Home Office 1998,pp.39–40). In February 1999, the consequent Asylum and Immigration Bill was published, containing clauses which would prohibit, in relation to people subject to immigration control (as defined by the Bill and including asylum seekers), the provision by local authorities of assistance under a) s.21 of the National Assistance Act 1948 if the need for care and attention has arisen solely because of destitution or because of the physical effects of destitution; b) under s.45 of the Health Services and Public Health Act 1968, except for any categories of people prescribed under regulations; c) under schedule 8 of NHS Act 1977, except for any categories of people prescribed under regulations; d) under ss.161 (housing allocation) and s.185 (homelessness) of the Housing Act 1996, except for any categories of people prescribed by regulations (clauses 96–97). However, local authorities would be empowered to provide support in accordance with arrangements by the Secretary of State (ie, the Home Office) (clause 80).

2. MAKING ARRANGEMENTS WITH THE INDEPENDENT SECTOR FOR RESIDENTIAL AND NURSING HOME CARE

Residential care accommodation may be provided either directly by the local authority or by its making arrangements with the independent sector. In the case of the independent sector, any residential accommodation providing both board and personal care or nursing care must be registered under the Registered Homes Act 1984. However, it is clear from the wording of the National Assistance Act, from court cases and from guidance, that local authorities are empowered to arrange accommodation of widely varying types, not necessarily entailing personal care or board.

In the case of nursing home accommodation, local authorities make arrangements with the independent sector, but require the consent of the appropriate health authority before placing a person, except temporarily in case of urgency. Nursing homes must be registered under the Registered Homes Act 1984.

EXTRACTS

Legislation states that:

(**arrangements with independent sector**) 'arrangements under section 21 of this Act may include arrangements made with a voluntary organisation or with any other person who is not a local authority' (National Assistance Act 1948, s.26).

(**residential care homes**) If board and personal care are provided for 'persons in need of personal care by reason of old age, disablement, past or present dependence on alcohol or drugs, or past or present mental disorder', then the home must be a registered residential care home under Part 1 of the Registered Homes Act 1984 (unless it is a certain type of 'small home' (see p.276) or managed or provided by an exempt body – which is 'an authority or body constituted by an Act of Parliament or Royal Charter') (National Assistance Act 1948, s.26(1A)).

(**nursing home accommodation**) 'Arrangements made with any voluntary organisation or other person ... must, if they are for the provision of residential accommodation where nursing care is provided' – be in respect of premises registered as a nursing home under the Registered Homes Act 1984, unless they are not required to be because they are maintained or controlled by an exempt body (National Assistance Act 1948, s.26(1B)).

(**health authority consent for nursing home accommodation**) In respect of residential accommodation with nursing care (ie, nursing homes), no 'such arrangements ... may be made by an authority for the accommodation of any person without the consent of such health authority as may be determined in accordance with regulations ... [This] does not apply to the making by an authority of temporary arrangements for the accommodation of any person as a matter of urgency; but, as soon as practicable after any such temporary arrangements have been made, the authority shall seek the consent required' (National Assistance Act 1948, s.26).

DISCUSSION

During the passage of the NHS and Community Care Bill, the government stated that if health authorities were to place people in nursing homes directly, without seeking the consent of the local authority, then the latter would be under no obligation to pay for the placement – at least until it had carried out an assessment of its own and agreed that nursing home care was in fact required (Baroness Hooper: HLD,8/5/1990, cols.1285–1287). Of course health authorities are themselves free to place, and pay for, people in nursing homes as NHS patients.

3. ORDINARY RESIDENCE

The 'ordinary residence' of a person may affect whether a local authority has a potential duty or only a power, in relation to him or her, to make arrangements for residential or nursing home care: see p.169.

4. PEOPLE IN RESIDENTIAL OR NURSING HOME ACCOMMODATION BEFORE APRIL 1993

Generally speaking local authorities are unable to make arrangements straightforwardly for people who have 'preserved rights' – in other words, those who were already being supported by the Department of Social Security in residential or nursing homes on or before 31st March 1993. However, there are a number of exceptions to this rule.

EXTRACTS

Legislation states that:

(prohibition on making arrangements for residents with 'preserved rights') Local authorities are prohibited from making arrangements for residential or nursing home accommodation for people who were already living in such accommodation before 1st April 1993 – subject to various exceptions (National Assistance Act 1948, s.26A). Regulations extend this prohibition also to small residential homes (ie providing both board and personal care for less than four people) and to Abbeyfield homes (SI 1993/477,r.2).

(exceptions in relation to prohibition) There are certain exceptions to the prohibition contained in s.26A of the National Assistance Act 1948.

In summary, the prohibition does not extend to people already being provided on 31st March 1993 with accommodation by the local authority (under the National Assistance Act 1948 or NHS Act 1977, schedule 8), or to people who after that date lose their preserved rights because of absence from the care home (SI 1993/477,rr.4–5).

In addition, local authorities may continue to support financially (ie, provide extra payments or 'top up') certain residents with preserved rights in residential or nursing homes who are (or were when the topping up began) under pension age – and to continue the support once pension age is reached. If the person is evicted, not allowed to return to the accommodation or has been served with notice to quit – then the local authority can step in to make arrangements for accommodation, but not in premises owned or managed by the same person who owned or managed the previous home – unless the home has closed (SI 1993/477,rr.6–7; and LAC(93)6,paras 15–17).

For people in residential accommodation over pension age faced with eviction etc, local authorities are also enabled to provide financial support under the same conditions (ie, not in the same home or in another home under same management or ownership – unless the home has closed). If a local authority places a person with preserved rights in a residential home in this manner, it has the power subsequently to place the person in a nursing home. However, for those already in nursing homes, over pension age and still with preserved rights but who now face eviction etc, the local authority is legally barred from making arrangements for the provision of alternative nursing home accommodation (SI 1993/477,rr.8,9; and LAC(93)6,paras 22–28).

DISCUSSION

People in residential or nursing home accommodation before April 1993: eviction from nursing homes

A health authority has the power to fund a person being evicted or otherwise having to leave a nursing home, on the grounds that the person is eligible for NHS-inpatient care (whether provided in a nursing home or hospital).

This power will be particularly relevant in the case of people evicted from a nursing home who are over pension age, because the legislation prevents local authorities from stepping in (see extracts above). However, the guidance points out that although 'the NHS has a responsibility to assess the health needs of the residents and to offer appropriate services within the resources available', nevertheless 'the level of service offered is a matter for the local health authority determination, taken in the light of local needs and priorities'. Somewhat dubiously, the Department of Health justifies this situation by explaining that apart from the possible help from the health authority, finding alternative accommodation is up to 'the resident or their relatives, with help from the home owner. This is because the patient will have arrived at the home as a result of their private arrangements in the first place'. In addition, the local authority will be able to provide 'advice and guidance' (LAC(93)6,paras 26–29).

5. MAKING CHARGES FOR RESIDENTIAL AND NURSING HOME ACCOMMODATION

See Chapter 12.

6. CHOICE OF ACCOMMODATION

Directions have been made about choice of residential or nursing home. Basically, people can allow the local authority to choose for them, can themselves choose from a preferred list (if there is such a list) or can choose any accommodation which the authority deems is suitable for their needs.

There are however restrictions which confine choice to some extent: for example, the varying level of home fees which different local authorities are prepared to meet for different categories of need, the availability of suitable local accommodation, and the willingness of local authorities to fund accommodation outside of their area.

EXTRACTS

Directions (*Choice of Accommodation Directions 1992*: in LAC(92)27 and in LAC(93)18 and issued under s.7A of the LASSA 1970) state that:

> **(duty to grant choice)** Following a community care assessment which identifies a need for residential or nursing home care under the NAA 1948 (s.21), a local authority, subject to the provisos below, 'shall ... make arrangements for accommodation pursuant to section 21 for that person at the place of his choice within England and Wales ... if he has indicated that he wishes to be accommodated' there.
>
> **(provisos)** A 'local authority shall only be required to make or continue to make arrangements for a person to be accommodated in his preferred accommodation if':
>
> **(needs):** '(a) the preferred accommodation appears to the authority to be suitable in relation to his needs as assessed by them';

(usual level of cost) '(b) the cost of making arrangements for him at his preferred accommodation would not require the authority to pay more than they would usually expect to pay having regard to his assessed needs';

(availability) '(c) the preferred accommodation is available';

(terms and conditions) '(d) the persons in charge of the preferred accommodation provide it subject to the authority's usual terms and conditions...'

(third party contributions). The directions also make it clear that authorities have a duty to place people in preferred more expensive accommodation if a third party is prepared to pay the difference between the actual cost and what the local authority usually pays.

Circular guidance elaborates (LAC(92)27):

(presumption of choice) 'As with all service provision, there should be a general presumption in favour of people being able to exercise choice over the service they receive. The limitations on authorities' legal obligation to provide preferred accommodation set out in the direction are not intended to deny people reasonable freedom of choice, but simply to ensure that authorities are able to fulfil their obligations for the quality of service provided and for value for money...'

(justification for not granting choice) 'Where for any reason an authority decides not to arrange a place for someone in their preferred accommodation it must have a clear and reasonable justification for that decision which relates to the criteria of the direction' (para 7).

(inability to express a preference) There 'will be cases in which prospective residents are unable to express a preference for themselves. It would be reasonable to expect authorities to act on the preferences expressed by their carers in the same way that they would on the resident's own wishes, unless exceptionally that would be against the best interests of the resident' (para 13).

(placement in another area) 'Costs will vary around the country. There may be circumstances where an authority might judge the need to move to another part of the country to be an integral part of an individual's assessed needs (eg, to be near a relative) and therefore one of the factors to be considered in determining what the authority would usually expect to pay' (para 7.6).

(third parties) Even if there is an agreement whereby a third party is meeting the extra costs of the accommodation, it is the local authority – in case of breakdown of the agreement – that remains liable to pay the full cost of the accommodation, whether it is the resident or third party who has failed to pay (para 11.4).

DISCUSSION

Choice: residential care outside the local authority's area

It is reported that in practice some local authorities restrict choice by operating policies which rule out residential care support outside of their own area. Where accommodation suitable to a person's needs is not available within the area, or where the cost of a home outside of the area is within the usual cost limit (taking account of varying costs in different parts of the country), then such a policy would appear to be inconsistent with the directions and guidance.

Such policies can certainly act to people's detriment; for instance, people with visual or hearing impairment might be denied access to specialist homes (House of Commons Health Committee 1993,vol.2,p.227). Indeed, during the passage through Parliament of the National Assistance Bill, the government explained that one of the ways in which a local authority might have to provide different types of accommodation was by arranging accommodation outside its area, since 'it may not be possible to provide in his own home district the kind of care and attention which is needed by the individual' (John Edwards: HCD,SC(C),21/1/1948,cols.2507–2508). More generally, restrictive policies will hinder residents being near their family and run counter to the Department of Health guidance (see extract above).

Choice: costs paid by local authority

This is covered in Chapter 12 on finance and charging.

Choice: difference between a person's choice, usual cost and needs

The case of *R v Avon CC, ex p M* demonstrated the difference between 'choice' and 'need' in the context of residential accommodation. The judge accepted the views of experts and the conclusion of the local authority's own complaints review panel that the entrenched preference of a young man with Down's Syndrome amounted to a psychological need. This prevented the authority from referring to its usual cost level as the reason for excluding the man' choice – since usual cost is meant to be a limiting factor on people's preferences but not on their assessed needs.

In *R v Westminster CC, ex parte P,* the Court of Appeal avoided ruling on whether asylum seekers had a right to exercise their entitlement to choice of accommodation (ie, so that they could remain in London instead of being sent to the south coast instead). The court stated that the dispute a) was suitable for referral to the Secretary of State with a view to exercise of the default powers (see p.433); and b) was primarily factual (as to whether or not there was alternative accommodation in London) and was a matter which could not be resolved one way or another by legally deciding about the existence and nature of the duty imposed by the directions on the local authority.

Choice: exercise of

Some local authorities reportedly deny people choice of home because of their block purchasing arrangements in relation to their own, council-run homes, and insistence that the beds in those homes must be filled first. For example, staff might tell prospective residents that they can either wait six months or more for a placement in the private home of their choice or enter a council-run home immediately – even though use of private homes rather than its own homes is cheaper for the council (Wright 1997,p.11).

Where a person is discharged to a care home from hospital in a crisis situation and thus not afforded a choice, an SSI report suggests that 'the resident should be offered the choice of staying in the home or moving to another when the crisis has passed' (SSI 1995k,p.13).

Choice: cross-border placements

The original *Choice of Accommodation Directions* (in LAC(92)27) issued in 1992 contained an error by referring to the placing of people in homes anywhere in the United Kingdom. However, s.26 of the National Assistance Act 1948 in fact restricts placement to homes in England and Wales because both residential accommodation providing board and personal care, and nursing home accommodation, must be registered under the Registered Homes Act 1984 (which applies to England and Wales only). Therefore an amendment was made to the directions in 1993, limiting the choice to England and Wales. However accompanying guidance (LAC(93)18) further clarified the position.

First, a local authority in England and Wales is empowered under s.21 of the National Assistance Act 1948 to arrange with a Scottish local authority for the latter to place a person (ordinarily resident in England or Wales) in a residential home run by that Scottish authority (see s.33 of the 1948 Act defining a 'local authority').

Second, the Social Work (Scotland) Act 1968 anyway does not prevent Scottish local authorities from themselves directly placing people who are ordinarily resident in their area in residential homes outside Scotland.

Third, a Scottish local authority has the discretion to place a person, ordinarily resident in England and Wales, in an independent home (residential or nursing) in Scotland. The contract would be between the home and the Scottish local authority; however, guidance states that 'the two authorities should agree an appropriate financial arrangement so that the Scottish authority can recover the cost of making the arrangements (net of the charges it makes directly on the resident) from the English authority' (LAC(93)18,para 7).

Fourth, the power of a Scottish local authority to recover from another local authority the financial cost of making arrangements for a person ordinarily resident elsewhere (in Scotland, England or Wales) is contained in s.86 of the Social Work (Scotland) Act 1968; and the equivalent power of recovery for English and Welsh authorities is in s.32 of the National Assistance Act 1948.

Fifth, Scottish local authorities are limited by s.13 of the 1968 Act to placing people in nursing homes which are registered under the 1968 Act – which applies only to Scotland. However, guidance states that English local authorities have a discretion, by arrangement with Scottish authorities, to place people ordinarily resident in Scotland in nursing homes in England – and to come to an arrangement as to recovery of cost (LAC(93)18,para 10; see also Scottish Office Circular, SWSG 6/94).

Sixth, both sets of guidance, English and Scottish, make it clear that the Secretary of State expects full cooperation between authorities (LAC(93)18, SWSG 6/94).

Lastly, the guidance states that it is 'currently not possible for English authorities to pay for residential care in Northern Ireland for one of its [sic] residents, nor for Health and Social Services Boards in Northern Ireland to pay for residential accommodation arranged by English authorities' (LAC(93)18,para 11).

Choice: detailed agreements about services and facilities

It has been pointed out that, given the amount of money involved in paying the weekly rate of residential and nursing home charges, there should be clear and detailed agreements between resident and home owner. However, it appears that this has not been the case, whether for residents paying for themselves, or those being supported by local authorities (Office of Fair Trading 1998,p.21). One of the consequences of an absence of clear, detailed agreements is that residents will not know what services are meant to be included within the basic fee and which will be charged extra for. The Office of Fair Trading found that only one brochure in 155 supplied by care homes gave information about extra charges for instance, for hairdressing, outings or chiropody. Other services, over which uncertainty typically hangs, include provision of television sets, toiletries, dry cleaning, optician services, occupational therapy, and daily or weekly activities (Office of Fair Trading

1998,p.19; see also discussion of personal expenses allowance in care homes on p.297 of this book).

Home life, a code of practice for residential care, recommended in 1984 (as did its companion volume, *A better home life* in 1996) that residents be given a clear, written statement about the terms and conditions of residence – including, for instance, the fees, services and personal items covered – or not covered – by the fees, procedure for increasing the fees, policy on pets, procedure for termination of the agreement, registration details of the home, complaints, procedure on death of the resident, insurance cover (CPA 1984,p.20; CPA 1996,p.18). Going a step further, the Continuing Care Conference has produced a framework contract between resident and residential care provider covering a range of such matters and designed to form the basis of a legal contract (CCF 1995).

However, it might not be necessary to have a formal contract, which could put off potential residents; instead a brochure can list the normal terms and conditions, and a simple letter or form be used to record variations negotiated with a particular resident. In addition, the existence of a contract might not only help service users; for instance, when a family has agreed to ensure that fees or a 'top up' amount are paid, the home proprietor might suffer if it is unclear whom he or she should sue for the arrears (Ashton 1995b) – although, in the case of accommodation arranged by the local authority, it is the authority which remains ultimately responsible (LAC(92)27,para 11.4).

Nevertheless, it should be realised that when a local authority arranges accommodation then, even if the person is paying a substantial amount towards his or her care, there is unlikely to be a contract enforceable in private law between the resident and the care home, or indeed between the resident and the local authority (see p.452).

Choice: single rooms

In evidence to the House of Commons Health Committee (1993) the Department of Health stated: 'If the client believes that a single room is an over-riding consideration as far as he/she is concerned, then I think it is clear from the statutory direction that they have a right to choose a home which provides the facilities they need'. Nevertheless, in the same context the Department maintained also that the direction on choice 'does not specifically enable a person to choose a single room if that is what they prefer' (vol.2,p.40). Age Concern England pointed out that choice of room type would be subject to the limits on the local authority's usual costs (vol.1,p.xiii).

7. SERVICES FOR RESIDENTS

Local authorities have duties in relation to arrangements for board and other services in residential accommodation, except where they are deemed unnecessary.

EXTRACTS

Legislation (National Assistance Act 1948) states that:

> **(board and other services)** 'References … to accommodation … shall be construed as references to accommodation … including references to board and other services, amenities and requisites provided in connection with the accommodation except where in the opinion of the authority managing the premises their provision is unnecessary' (s.21(5)).

(transport and other services) 'a local authority may (a) provide in such cases as they may consider appropriate, for the conveyance of persons to and from premises in which accommodation is provided for them under this Part of the Act; (b) make arrangements for the provision on the premises in which the accommodation is being provided of such other services as appear to the authority to be required' (s.21(7)).

(non-duplication) 'nothing in this section shall authorise or require a local authority to make any provision authorised or required to be made (whether by that or any other authority) by or under any enactment not contained in this Part of this Act or required to be provided under the National Health Service Act 1977' (s.21(8)).

Directions (*Secretary of State's Approvals and Directions under section 21(1) of the National Assistance Act 1948*: see: LAC(93)10, appendix 1,para 4) state that local authorities must:

'make arrangements in relation to persons provided with accommodation under s.21(1) of the Act for all or any of the following purposes':

(welfare) 'for the welfare of all persons for whom accommodation is provided';

(hygiene) 'for the supervision of hygiene of the accommodation so provided';

(health services, etc) 'to enable persons for whom accommodation is provided to obtain:

(i) medical attention,

(ii) nursing attention during illnesses of a kind which are ordinarily nursed at home, and

(iii) the benefit of any services provided by the National Health Service of which they may from time to time be in need,

but nothing in this paragraph shall require a local authority to make any provision authorised or required to be provided under the National Health Service Act 1977';

(board, amenities, etc) 'for the provision of board and such other services, amenities and requisites provided in connection with the accommodation, except where in the opinion of the authority managing the premises their provision is unnecessary';

(reviewing arrangements) 'to review regularly the provision made under the arrangements and to make such improvements as the authority considers necessary'.

Approvals (*Secretary of State's Approvals and Directions under section 21(1) of the National Assistance Act 1948*: see: LAC(93)10, appendix 1,para 5) state that:

(transport) local authorities may make arrangements 'to provide, in such cases as the authority consider appropriate, for the conveyance of persons to and from premises in which accommodation is provided under Part III of the Act' (see LAC(93)10).

Guidance (LAC(92)24,annex,para 2) states:

'Local authority contracts for independent sector residential care should not include provision of any service which it is the responsibility of the NHS to provide'.

DISCUSSION

Services in residential accommodation: board, welfare, amenities

In *R v Newham LBC, ex p Medical Foundation for the Care of Victims of Torture*, the council claimed that in arranging accommodation for asylum seekers under ss.21 and 26 of the 1948 Act, it could offer accommodation only if it included a package of services such as food, laundry and personal hy-

giene facilities. Because, it argued, there was no such accommodation in Newham, it would therefore have to offer accommodation to asylum seekers in Eastbourne. The court ruled that the effect
of ss.21(5) (above) and s.26(1A) was that residential accommodation without board and personal
care could in some circumstances be offered.

However, the reverse situation of providing food without accommodation under s.21 has been
held to be unlawful. In *R v Newham LBC, ex p Gorenkin* (also concerning asylum seekers), the High
Court ruled that because the need for care and attention was a condition for arranging residential
accommodation, a local authority was not empowered under s.21 to provide food (vouchers) alone
without accommodation.

The local ombudsman in one investigation considered the welfare arrangements, hygiene and
medical attention provided in a council hostel, finding serious failures relating to, for example,
sleep interruption, theft, missing lavatory seats, lost laundry, failure to observe a resident's pain and
need for dental treatment – and a failure to provide the required medication for epilepsy on several
occasions (*Manchester CC 1993*).

The government explained during the passing through Parliament of the National Assistance
Bill that the 'dominant factor must be that of welfare, and if local authorities carry out their obligations in that respect properly they will always take into account the wishes of the people for whom
they are providing' (John Edwards: HCD,SC(C),21/1/1948,col.2508).

Services in residential accommodation: non-duplication

Local authorities have a duty to provide various services in their own residential homes as far as
they think necessary, but should not duplicate services which either they can or must provide under other legislation or which the NHS is under a duty or has the power to provide (see p.325 on
anti-duplication measures).

8. EXTRA SERVICES PROVIDED BY LOCAL AUTHORITIES

Local authorities might arrange non-residential services for people living in residential homes,
whether these are run by authorities themselves or by independent providers. Clearly care must be
taken to distinguish between services which should be provided as part of the home's services, and
those non-residential services which are extra and an authority might consider charging for (and
which under the anti-duplication measure in s.21(8), dealt with immediately above, it would anyway not be empowered to arrange under s.21 of the 1948 Act).

EXTRACTS
Legislation: charges for non-residential services are made under the Health and Social Services
and Social Security Adjudications Act 1983, s.17 (see Chapter 10).
Guidance states that:

> 'Residents should not be charged extra for day time activities which have been negotiated as part of the res-
> idential care package, as the cost of these services would already be included in the standard charge agreed
> by the LA for that package. Where a separate package of services has been arranged by the LA for a resident
> then the LA can consider whether to charge the resident extra for these services (using the discretionary
> charging powers for non-residential services). As the resident may only have their PEA any disregarded in-
> come available, the amount charged (if any) is likely to be minimal' (CRAG 1993, para 1.024A).

DISCUSSION

Local authorities can provide additional non-residential services for residents of homes – and could consider making discretionary charges for these, although the guidance suggests they would be minimal. For instance, although residential homes have a duty to provide adaptations and facilities to make the home suitable for disabled people, residents might also require particular items for their personal use. Thus, Circular guidance (LAC(86)6) explained that local social services authorities are not precluded 'from supplying individual aids such as walking frames and dressing aids to residents in private and voluntary homes provided such items are supplied individually for their personal use and on the same basis as for other people living in the community' (para 11).

9. NHS SERVICES IN RESIDENTIAL CARE AND NURSING HOMES

Legislation places general duties on health authorities to provide health services to the population. There is apparently nothing in the legislation to exclude people in residential and nursing homes from receiving these services. However, in the case of nursing homes, Department of Health guidance has stated that basic nursing services to individual residents should be provided by the nursing home and not by the NHS. As far as residential homes go, the guidance states that residents should have the same rights to NHS services as people still living in their own homes. However, the helpfulness of this statement relies of course on the assumption that people in their own homes are receiving adequate services.

It should be noted that the guidance (extracted immediately below), to the effect that local authorities should be responsible for purchasing the general nursing care element of nursing home accommodation, is hard to reconcile with the judgment of the High Court in late 1998 that both specialist and general nursing care are the sole responsibility of the NHS – and that nursing is health care and can never be social care (*R v North and East Devon HA, ex p Coughlan*). Clearly, if this judgment is upheld on appeal, the financial and organisational implications would appear to be considerable.

EXTRACTS

Legislation (NHS Act 1977, s.3) places general duties on the Secretary of State to provide medical and nursing services, and care for people who are, or have been, ill.

Circular guidance (HSG(92)50) states that:

> **(nursing homes: responsibilities of statutory services)** 'When ... a local authority [social services] places a person in a nursing home after a joint HA/LA assessment, the local authority is responsible for purchasing services to meet the general nursing care needs of that person, including':

> **(nursing homes: NHS incontinence and nursing supplies)** 'the cost of incontinence services (eg laundry) and those incontinence and nursing supplies which are not available on NHS prescription'.

> **(nursing homes: NHS physiotherapy, chiropody, speech and language therapy)** 'Health authorities will be responsible for purchasing, within the resources available and in line with their priorities, physiotherapy, chiropody and speech and language and therapy, with the appropriate equipment'.

(nursing homes: NHS specialist nursing advice) 'and the provision of specialist nursing advice, eg incontinence advice and stoma care, for those people placed in nursing homes by local authorities with the consent of a DHA…' (annex,para 3).

(nursing homes: NHS resources and priorities) 'The extent to which community health services can be provided is a matter for health authorities' judgement taking account of the resources available and competing priorities. In securing such services, health authorities will also need to consider the medium to long term resource implications given that the number of people placed in nursing homes by local authorities will increase in future years. Changes in overall levels of provision should be discussed first with the local authority concerned' (Annex, paras 3,10).

(nursing homes: NHS, normal, dignified life and prevention) 'Health authorities are reminded of the role which the services they are responsible for providing can play in helping people to live as normal and dignified a life as possible and in preventing a resident's health deteriorating to the point where admission to higher levels of continuing care or acute inpatient care is necessary' (HSG(92)50,annex,para 8).

(residential care: NHS community health services) 'It will continue to be the responsibility of the NHS to provide where necessary community health services to residents of LA and independent residential care homes on the same basis as to people in their own homes. These services include the provision of district nursing and other specialist nursing services (eg, incontinence advice) as well as provision, where necessary, of incontinence and nursing aids, physiotherapy, speech and language therapy and chiropody. Where such services are provided they must be free of charge to people in independent sector residential care homes as well as to residents of local authority Part III homes' (Annex,para 2).

Circular guidance (LAC(92)24) states:

(nursing homes: specification in contracts of nursing services) 'Local authorities are asked … to ensure that the nursing home care that is funded by them includes the provision of all general nursing care services (including incontinence services and aids but not specialist incontinence advice). Their contracts with the independent sector must ensure that general nursing care services are fully provided' (para 2).

(nursing homes: no contracting for NHS services) 'Local authority contracts for independent sector residential care should not include provision of any service which it is the responsibility of the NHS to provide' (annex,para 2).

(residential and nursing homes: occupational therapy services) 'Responsibility for the provision of occupational therapy services varies around the country. Health and local authorities often provide such services for different groups and purposes. They need to discuss and agree at local level appropriate arrangements for occupational therapy services for residents of residential care and local authority controlled nursing home places' (annex,para 6).

Circular guidance (HSG(95)8,pp.16–17) states:

(nursing homes: NHS specialist services and equipment) 'Some people who will be appropriately placed by social services in nursing homes, as their permanent home, may still require some regular access to specialist medical, nursing or other community health services. This will also apply to people who have arranged and are funding their own care. This may include occasional continuing specialist medical advice or treatment, specialist palliative care, specialist nursing care such as continence advice, stoma care or diabetic advice or community health services such as physiotherapy, speech and language therapy and chiropody. It should also include specialist medical or nursing equipment (for instance specialist feeding equipment) not available on prescription and normally only available through hospitals. It would not cover basic equipment such as incontinence supplies which should be included in the basic price charged by the home to the local authority or the person'.

(residential homes: NHS specialist services) 'Such services should also be available on the same basis for people in residential homes or in their own homes' (HSG(95)8,pp.16–17).

DISCUSSION
NHS services in nursing homes: basic nursing and incontinence services

Basic nursing services and incontinence supplies should, according to guidance, normally be provided for individual residents by the home and paid for by the home (where they are not available on NHS prescription through the GP). The cost to the home of these services should therefore be included in the home's fees, whether paid by social security, by social services, by a health authority (which has placed a person in a home as an NHS patient), or by people paying for themselves.

This has been a consistent theme found in guidance (HSG(92)50 and HSG(95)8) and statements by government: 'Our guidance to health authorities is that support services such as ... incontinence materials fall within the care that nursing homes could reasonably be expected to provide for their patients. Health authorities may provide support services to nursing home patients at their discretion' (Tim Yeo: HCWA,22/5/1992,col.303). This in turn conformed to much earlier 1974 guidance (HRC(74)16) stating that health authorities 'should not therefore provide' home nursing aids and equipment ... and laundry services for incontinent people 'direct to patients in nursing homes'. (Although it has been pointed out that under income generation powers in s.7 of the Medicines Act 1988, health authorities can supply nursing homes with incontinence (or other nursing) materials generally (but not to individuals) for an element of profit (Stephen Dorrell: HCWA, 5/2/1991, col.96)).

NHS services in nursing homes: paramedical services

Guidance states that health authorities are responsible for the provision in nursing homes of services such as physiotherapy, chiropody, speech and language therapy. However, it refers to the provision of services within available resources, thus leaving authorities with a considerable discretion to determine the level of service to be provided. Past confusion has been illustrated by a) the policies of some health authorities not to provide services in nursing homes; and b) guidance which originally stated that chiropody services could not be provided by health authorities for people in private nursing homes by health authorities (HRC(74)16, only to be corrected four year later by subsequent guidance: HC(78)16).

Guidance is otherwise substantially silent about therapy services, but Tim Yeo answered in 1992: 'Our guidance to health authorities is that support services such as physiotherapy ... fall within the care that nursing homes could reasonably be expected to provide for their patients. Health authorities may provide support services to nursing home patients at their discretion' (HCWA,22/5/1992,col.303). However, in practice people in private nursing homes are likely to be accorded a low priority by health authorities – for instance, they might be losing access to physiotherapy and occupational therapy services even faster than their peers who are still in their own homes (Counsel and Care 1998,p.43). It might be a matter of chance whether people receive NHS therapy services (eg, CSP 1993,p.2); in some areas there might even be no physiotherapy service provided in residential homes, nursing homes or people's own homes (Clark 1998,p.27).

Similarly, a study of chiropody services to private nursing homes in London found a variable picture of a) the NHS providing services to all, some or no residents, and b) DSS-supported residents sometimes having their treatment provided by the home within the fees paid, but private residents paying in full (Collyer, Hanson-Khan 1989,p.5).

In 1989, Kenneth Clarke confirmed the variable picture: 'In my experience, people who are living in private residential and nursing homes are not deprived of all rights to NHS ancillary care, but I agree that the practice varies widely from place to place' (HCD,12/7/1989,col.980). In fact this statement is itself a little unclear. It uses the word 'ancillary' which in the Registered Homes Act is differentiated from 'professional'. One would not normally class NHS therapists and chiropodists providing services to nursing homes as ancillary workers. In addition, it is a very loose reference to 'rights', since a) rights under the NHS are anyway difficult to identify (see p.345), and b) if they could be identified a person surely cannot be deprived of the rights themselves, but only the exercise of them.

NHS services in nursing homes: specialist medical and nursing support: eligibility criteria

The guidance (HSG(95)8 on continuing care refers specifically to specialist medical and nursing support (including equipment) being provided by the NHS for people in nursing homes, as well as in residential homes and in their own homes. On top of the general confusion over provision of NHS services to people in nursing homes, a further layer has now been added in terms of what is meant by 'specialist'.

Some health authorities define specialist services in detail, others only generally. Some point out that the meaning of 'specialist nursing' might vary depending on the situation; thus, all nursing homes would be expected to provide basic nursing care, but nursing homes registered to provide specialist care (eg, for elderly mentally ill people) would be expected to provide, as a basic service, specialist nursing (eg, adequate mental health nursing).

The provision of specialist equipment in nursing homes has become more important because of reduction of NHS continuing care beds in hospitals. Thus health authorities attempt to develop policies about what items nursing homes should be providing within their fees, and which the authorities should provide for residents. For instance, nursing homes might shoulder responsibility generally for items such as hoists, commodes and bathing equipment as part of registration requirements – whilst a health authority might accept responsibility (for individual patients) such as specialised mattresses, feeding equipment, syringe drivers, aspirators, special wheelchairs, feeding equipment, suction machines, ventilators – and so on. As usual, too 'little detail means that ambiguity remains, while too much detail may produce a constraining and legalistic style of document' – but it appears that many authorities are making progress in defining responsibilities (Henwood 1996,p.29).

The existence of Department of Health guidance does not mean that local health authorities and NHS Trusts will necessarily follow it. For instance, in one investigation the health service ombudsman found that the family of a woman – who had had a stroke, was unable to swallow, had to use a gastric tube for eating and drinking and had entered a nursing home – was required to pay for the specialist feeding equipment required. This came to £25 a week on top of the weekly fee of £375. The health authority accepted that even where it was not funding the nursing home accommodation, it had a responsibility, in the light of the guidance (HSG(95)8), to meet the costs of this equipment (*North Worcestershire HA 1996*).

NHS services in residential homes

The statement in the guidance (HSG(92)50) that people in residential homes have the same rights to provision as people in their own homes is not necessarily helpful in a practical way. This is because community health services both for people in their own homes and for those in residential homes are subject to local priorities and resource allocation. People in residential homes might often be regarded as lower priority because less at risk, since they are not living alone.

> **Example: community nursing services (health service ombudsman).** For example, one health service ombudsman investigation found that although there was no local policy to withhold community nursing services from people in private residential homes, nevertheless they 'would normally be considered a lower priority than … a patient in his own home'. A letter written by the area nursing officer and referred to in the report is instructive about the fears within some health authorities (even though the letter was found subsequently to be erroneous). It stated that given over-demand, 'to extend the service to private homes would be creating a "precedent service" they had no means of supporting'. The investigation accepted that 'assessment of priorities has to be made' (W.360/77–78).

The guidance makes clear that basic incontinence supplies should not be provided by the NHS to residents of nursing homes but should be available to people in residential homes on the same basis as they are to people still living in their own homes. This of course begs the question of what level of provision is being made to people in their own homes, but may nevertheless still be a lever for residents of homes who are losing access to NHS provision, when people in their own homes are not. The health service ombudsman investigated one such situation:

> **Example: incontinence pads.** The health authority had been dilatory in replying to the owner of a residential home who wanted reimbursement for the cost of incontinence pads for residents over a two-year period – on the grounds that they had been treated unfairly compared to people in their own homes. Apart from finding repeated delays and failures on the part of authority to respond, the ombudsman found that the authority's policy of funding incontinence supplies for some but not all people in residential homes contravened the Department of Health guidance (HSG(92)50: see extracts above).
>
> The ombudsman also referred to a reply from the Parliamentary Under-Secretary of State for Health to an MP further explaining that once a health authority had decided its overall level of provision, "'continence materials/aids should be made available to people in residential care homes using the same criteria as for people living in their own homes'". In fact the authority had been supplying incontinence materials to people in residential homes only if they were doubly incontinent or had dementia, but applied broader criteria to people still living in their own homes.
>
> The authority was right to think that the guidance allowed it 'discretion to decide on services according to resources', but wrong to suppose that 'the requirement for consistency between services to persons at home and to those in residential homes was secondary to considerations of resources' – given the Department of Health guidance and the letter. The authority agreed to reimburse the home owner (*East Norfolk HA 1997*).

In turn, there might be resentment by nursing home owners over what they consider to be discrimination in favour of residential homes in relation to the supply of incontinence pads, since the guidance does not envisage the provision of pads by health authorities to nursing home residents.

In practice, some nursing homes might carry the cost themselves but others will pass it on to residents (Clark 1998,p.29).

The issue of access to NHS services is not new. An SSI (1988) report (issued with HN(89)7) on health care in local authority residential homes, found that the specific guidance set out in *Residential homes for the elderly, arrangements for health care: a memorandum of guidance* (published in 1977 and reproduced in the 1988 report) had been patchily implemented. The extent of implementation 'varied from home to home, even between individual homes within the same local authority'. Therapy and nursing services were amongst those services in need of improvement. This variability appears to continue within the new community care system, operative since April 1993. For instance, incontinence services might be funded in a very limited way and might or might not be included in the contract price paid by local authorities. Similarly, paramedical services (eg, physiotherapy, occupational therapy and chiropody) might be limited, absent altogether or charged privately to residents; and there was no clear understanding about entitlement to services. Meanwhile, health authorities were claiming that they had not been given the additional funding they needed (SSI 1993d,p.13; see also for such matters SSI/NHSME 1994e,p.21; SSI 1995k,pp.45–46; Wright 1998; Counsel and Care 1998,p.43 and 1992,p.19; Clark 1998,p.27).

10. REGISTRATION AND INSPECTION OF RESIDENTIAL CARE HOMES

It is beyond the scope of this book to set out the detailed registration and inspection requirements in relation to nursing and residential homes (which are anyway due to change: see Secretary of State for Health 1998,Chapter 4). The following contains only brief extracts; full legal explanation can be found in specialist books (Jones 1993b, Ridout 1998).

EXTRACTS

Legislation states that:

> **(registration of residential care homes)** Registration as a residential care home is required 'in respect of any establishment which provides or is intended to provide, whether for reward or not, residential accommodation with both board and personal care for persons in need of personal care by reason of old age, disablement, past or present dependence on alcohol or drugs, or past or present mental disorder' (Registered Homes Act 1984, s.1(1)).

> **(small homes)** A small home 'provides or is intended to provide residential accommodation with both board and personal care for fewer than 4 persons, excluding persons carrying on or intending to carry on the home or employed or intended to be employed there and their relatives'.
>
> Guidance explains that the definition covers, for example, adult placement and respite care schemes which provide both board and personal care – for those in need of personal care as outlined in s.1(1) above (LAC(92)10,para 15). Small homes in which the residents consist only of the people running the home, their employees or their relatives are not obliged to register. Otherwise, such homes must be registered, but they are subject to a 'lighter touch' of regulation – for example, the frequency of inspection (twice a year) normally stipulated does not apply (SI 1984/1345,r.18). Guidance explains that local authorities 'are not expected to check routinely on compliance with [many of the provisions of] Regulation 10 [see below] or on any other requirements about the situation in the home...' (LAC(92)10,annex A,para 3). Some of those requirements are anyway reduced for small homes (SI 1984/1345,r.10(1A)).

(refusal of registration) Registration can be refused to an applicant on the grounds '(a) that he or any other person concerned or intended to be concerned in carrying on the home is not a fit person to be concerned in carrying on a residential care home; (b) that for reasons connected with their situation, construction, state of repair, accommodation, staffing or equipment, the premises used or intended to be used for the purposes of the home, or any other premises used or intended to be used in connection with it, are not fit to be used; or (c) that the way in which it is intended to carry on the home is such as not to provide services or facilities reasonably required' (Registered Homes Act 1984,s.9(1)).

In the case of small homes, the only one of the above grounds on which registration can be refused is that concerning fitness of the person to carry on the home (Registered Homes Act 1984,s.9(2)).

(cancellation of registration). Registration can be cancelled for the following reasons; any of the grounds in respect of refusal of initial registration (see immediately above), non-payment of the annual fee, a conviction for an offence under the Act, or non-compliance with a condition imposed on the home and currently in force (Registered Homes Act 1984,s.10).

In the case of small homes, an additional ground for cancellation is failure to submit an annual return in accordance with the statutory requirements (s.10). Guidance explains in relation to small homes that while 'the adequacy of accommodation, staffing, services and facilities are not grounds in themselves for the refusal of registration and cannot therefore automatically form the basis of de-registration it may prove possible to demonstrate that failures in such areas are indicative that the person running the home is not fit to do so' (LAC(92)10,para 2).

(inspection of homes) Persons authorised by either the Secretary of State or by the registration (ie, the local) authority have the power to enter and inspect residential homes (Registered Homes Act 1984,s.17). Homes must be inspected at least twice in every 12 months (SI 1984/1345,r.18).

(welfare of residents) Legislation states that the 'person registered shall arrange for the home to be conducted so as to make proper provision for the welfare, care and, where appropriate, treatment and supervision of all residents'.

In reaching 'any decision relating to a resident the person registered shall give first consideration to the need to safeguard and promote the welfare of the resident and shall, so far as practicable, ascertain the wishes and feelings of the resident and give due consideration to them as is reasonable having regard to the resident's age and understanding'.

Every home 'shall be maintained on the basis of good personal and professional relationships between the person registered and persons employed at the home and the residents' (SI 1984/1345, r.9).

DISCUSSION

Residential care homes: personal care

Personal care is defined as 'care which includes assistance with bodily functions where such assistance is required'; therefore, as confirmed by *Harrison v Cornwall CC*, personal care does not necessarily include assistance with bodily functions.

Residential care homes: contracting and registration

Since local authorities have become responsible from April 1993 for purchasing residential care from the independent sector, they act as both registration authority and contracting body for residential care (and contracting body for nursing home care). This sometimes gives rise to disputes. Thus, in *R v Cleveland CC, ex p Cleveland Care Homes Association*, the High Court ruled that the local authority had failed unreasonably to consult the local care homes about new contractual terms.

However, both in that case, and in *R v Newcastle upon Tyne, ex p Dixon*, the court found that authorities were entitled to specify contractual terms which go beyond the statutory requirements of the Registered Homes Act 1984. In two other cases, local care home associations were unsuccessful in challenging the local authority about its policies in relation to purchasing care from the independent sector (*Cumbria Professional Care v Cumbria CC*; and *R v Coventry CC, ex p CHOICE*). And in *R v Cleveland CC, ex p Ward*, the court found that the local authority was not acting beyond its powers or unreasonably by requiring that a nursing home owner supply full company, as opposed to abbreviated, company accounts.

The local ombudsman has pointed out that the relationship between local authorities and private care homes goes beyond the purely commercial and that councils are expected to provide advice and support; he referred, for instance, to *Building partnerships for success* (DH 1995b) which talks of local authorities 'working together' with independent providers (*Lancashire CC 1997*). However, disputes might arise precisely about just what is a commercial matter; for example, at an extreme, over the disposal of the bodies of dead residents in independent sector homes, when the local authority refused to make funeral arrangements and referred to live residents as 'income-producing raw material' and dead residents as 'waste' (*Castle Morpeth BC 1998*).

The question of what residential homes are expected to provide within the basic fee is helped if detailed contracts are drawn up between the home and whoever is paying the fees – specifying in detail which services are provided within the basic fees and which not. Of course local authorities also need to check that contractual terms are being met. For instance, in one investigation the ombudsman found maladministration when a council failed to ensure that a resident received the care it was paying extra for, even though the home was in a different part of the country (thus making monitoring by the funding authority more difficult): ultimately the local authority remained responsible for the failure (*Redbridge LBC 1998*).

Residential care homes: welfare of residents

The regulations contain what might be called a 'policy statement' relating to the general welfare and interests of residents; thus a conflict between residents' welfare and the home's profit, should be resolved in favour of the former (Ashton 1995a).

Residential care homes: Registered Homes Tribunals

Disputes between home proprietors and registration and inspection authorities (local authorities in the case of residential homes and health authorities in the case of nursing homes) are heard before registered homes tribunals. A number of these cases are summarised in this chapter – particularly in relation to the provision of facilities and services. They give insight into the issues and disputes which can arise in residential and nursing homes – and into the factors to be taken into account when solutions are sought. The decisions of the tribunals sometimes demonstrate also the number and disparity of factors which have to be taken into account when judging whether services are adequate. The decisions are not necessarily predictable and often seem to depend on the particular facts and circumstances of each case.

Residential care homes: inspection

Local authority inspection units have a duty to inspect independently run residential homes in their area at least twice a year (SI 1984/1345,r.18); however, guidance states that they should also inspect the authority's own residential homes as well (DH 1990,para 5.13). The establishment of inspection units themselves is stipulated by the *Inspection Units Directions 1994* (attached to LAC(94)16).

In addition, the Social Services Inspectorate (SSI) inspects from time to time samples of local authority residential homes (as well as a whole range of non-residential services) under s.48 of the NHS and Community Care Act 1990, with a view to ensuring that standards are kept up. The Inspectorate does not provide a direct method of redress for individuals, but its inspectors do interview service users and can be instrumental in resolving problems. In extreme circumstances, an adverse SSI report to the Secretary of State could result in a formal inquiry being instituted (see p.437).

Considerable debate has preceded the reforms to registration and inspection proposed in a White Paper (Secretary of State for Health 1998,Chapter 4). This has included questions about scope, consistency, even-handedness, effectiveness, clarity, costs (and fee levels, setting and application of standards, distinguishing legal requirements from good practice, relationship of residential and nursing home inspection, organisation of inspection and so on (eg, Burgner 1996,pp.4–10; Day, Klein and Redmayne 1996; Counsel and Care 1995; Raynes 1997,p.24).

11. SERVICES AND FACILITIES PROVIDED BY RESIDENTIAL CARE HOMES

Adequate services and facilities in residential homes are demanded by legislation. Residential care homes in the independent sector are subject to the Registered Homes Act 1984 and associated regulations. The legislation requires, for example, that the premises be fit, and certain services and facilities be provided. Residential homes are both registered and inspected by local authorities. Appeals go to registered homes tribunals which have interpreted some of the requirements placed on homes.

Summaries of tribunal cases are included below and provide a selective insight into the some of the issues and disputes which can arise in residential homes and into the range of factors and particular circumstances to be taken into account when solutions are sought.

Legislation states:

(independent sector homes: premises and services and facilities) An applicant for registration might be refused, for example, if the premises are not fit to be used because of 'their situation, construction, state of repair, accommodation, staffing, or equipment'. Similarly, an application may be refused because 'the way in which it is intended to carry on the home is such as not to provide services or facilities reasonably required' (Registered Homes Act 1984,s.9).

(independent sector residential homes: list of services and facilities) A number of services and facilities must be provided, 'having regard to the size of the home and the number, age, sex and condition of residents.' The list includes:

- employment of enough suitably qualified and competent staff, 'adequate for the well being of residents';
- reasonable accommodation and space;

- adequate and suitable furniture, bedding, curtains and where necessary equipment and screens;
- adequate washing facilities and lavatories;
- making of adaptations and providing facilities necessary for physically disabled people;
- adequate light, heating and ventilation;
- keeping of all parts of the home in good repair, clean and reasonably decorated;
- adequate fire and accident precautions;
- sufficient and suitable kitchen and eating equipment;
- 'suitable, varied and properly prepared wholesome and nutritious food in adequate quantities'
- satisfactory hygiene in the home;
- regular laundry service and provision for residents to do their own laundry so far as 'reasonable and practicable in the circumstances';
- arrangements for residents to see GPs and dentists;
- arrangements concerning handling, keeping, recording, disposal of drugs;
- arrangements for residents' training, occupation, recreation;
- safe place for residents' valuables to be kept;
- connection of the home to a public telephone service, and so far as 'reasonable and practicable in the circumstances, make arrangements for residents to communicate with others in private by post or telephone' (SI 1984/1345, r.10).

DISCUSSION

Services and facilities provided by residential care homes: general

Apart from the increasing focus on people's access to residential and nursing home care – and who pays for it – there has been also enduring concern about the standards of care and services available to people in residential homes. It is beyond the scope of this book to consider the details of this concern (except for the tribunal cases selected below) which covers all those matters relevant to daily life – for example, access to health services, activities, advice, autonomy, clothing, complaints, dignity, domestic routines, finances, furniture, laundry, social work support, staff selection – and so on.

However, such matters are covered in publications such as *A positive choice* (Wagner 1988), *Home life* (CPA 1984), *A better home life* (CPA 1996), *Homes are for living in* (SSI 1989b). These stress the importance not only of how homes cater physically for residents, but also for intellectual, emotional and social needs (eg, CPA 1984,p.15). Thus, for example, local authority inspection units which have developed and refined their methods will take account not just of the physical and practical, but also quality of life (SSI 1996a,p.3).

Services and facilities provided by residential care homes: registered homes tribunal decisions

The following is a selective sample of decisions of registered homes tribunals. Those chosen concentrate on services and facilities, as opposed to the many other issues dealt with by tribunals, including violence, cruelty, dishonesty, poor record-keeping and staff inadequacies. The references 'RHT' refer to the number of the registered homes tribunal decision; copies of decisions are available from the Department of Health.

Residential homes: welfare principle. A number of deficiencies in the running of a home led a tribunal to the conclusion that there was a fundamental breach of r.9 of the regulations – namely that the home should be conducted so as to make proper provision for the welfare, care, treatment (if appropriate) and supervision of residents'. For example, not all fire doors were fitted with self-closing devices, The requirements for the safe handling and recording of drugs were not observed, nor for a public telephone. The home was in poor structural repair. The standard of cleanliness had deteriorated, as had the standard of cooking and the amount of money available to buy food (RHT 239).

In another case, it was not in the interests of the welfare of residents that the home owners should have inappropriately involved residents in their appeal to the tribunal 'by putting them to the great stress and anxiety of writing statements and letters' (RHT 239). In another, the independence and freedom of a resident was restricted when she was kept in the lounge against her will, had cot sides put on her bed and her sticks removed so as to restrict her movement – despite the tribunal's recognition that people have to be protected against self-injury and a doctor's support for this regime (RHT 269).

Residential homes: situation of the premises. A residential home situated in a village was found unsuitable on the basis of its situation: because the residents 'would be unduly restricted in their independence and ability to move freely outside the house'. This was mainly because of the 'unlevel nature of the site' and poor access to the shop and Post Office (RHT 5).

However, in another case, the Tribunal found in favour of a home despite a number of apparent disadvantages: for example, the area around the home was too small to allow active recreation; the parking facilities could on occasion prove inadequate; and the steepness of the hill posed some risk to unaccompanied wheelchair users. Against these however, was the fact that there was nearby a large public car park, a bus route, an area of grassland. The home's own vehicle was available for use and had a parking space alongside the home. Perhaps the home might take care in the future not to accept, as far as possible, wheelchair users (RHT 83).

Where residents would not be able to maintain independence and become part of the community because of the home's distance from amenities and inadequate transport facilities, the Tribunal found the home not suitable. The fact that many of the residents might not want to go out 'fails to appreciate a fundamental characteristic of independence': namely independence of choice. This was to be measured not in 'quantitative terms, that is, how many residents of care homes can go out, but in qualitative terms, that is, are they able to enjoy and be part of the local community if they wish to?' The Tribunal referred to 'Home Life' which states that the location and surrounding environment need to be 'suited to the stated aims of the establishment, and at the same time provide a setting which enables the home to blend into the neighbourhood. The accessibility of local facilities, community health services and public transport should be considered fully prior to registration' (RHT 145).

Residential homes: management of residents and quality of life. An authoritarian approach by a home owner included insistence on set times for getting up and going to bed, on doing exercises before breakfast, and on compelling people to eat and drink against their will. The owner lost her appeal against being deemed an unfit person (RHT 9).

One example which resulted in loss of registration included regimentation (meal-times), staff distancing themselves from residents, little stimulation, lino in bedrooms (indicating acceptance, instead of prevention, of incontinence), no regular opportunities to go out to the shops, no concern about residents' individuality, autonomy and control of their own finances (RHT 15).

A system to be avoided in residential homes is 'warehousing': 'keeping the residents clean, warm and fed and sitting them in front of the TV'. In this particular case, this was not present in its worst form. However, good care practice 'does not require a home to be run like an over hearty holiday camp but it does require that residents be treated as individuals and helped to follow their individual interests'. The Tribunal was left 'with the impression of a good hospital geriatric ward but not a good residential home' (RHT 147). In one case, under a heading of 'management of residents', a number of observations were made which contributed to the home losing its appeal. They included regimentation, lack of privacy, no screening, overcrowding, few personal possessions, no telephone for residents able to use one, and restraint (eg, being bound with a cord) (RHT 23).

In another case, there was an 'unacceptable degree of regimentation of residents who were not allowed in their bedrooms during the daytime unless they were sick, were subjected to rigid dressing, undressing, toileting and meal time routines and had little autonomy or opportunity to live as individuals' (RHT 69).

It is 'faulty running' of a home where a resident 'was not toileted with sufficient regularity, leading to incontinence problems, the removal of her underwear, catheterisation and an entirely unnecessary dispute about who should do her personal laundry'. Similarly, the tying of residents to commodes was 'destructive of' comfort and dignity' (RHT 53).

In another case, the dignity of residents was not respected: for example, two ladies were accorded no privacy at bath-time; another 'enfeebled old lady' was left on the lavatory for many hours (RHT 58).

The installation of electronic listening devices, ostensibly to monitor one member of staff, was used, on the balance of probabilities, to record resident and staff conversations. The Tribunal found that 'use of equipment of this nature is regarded as being a very serious breach of the right to privacy of staff and residents' (RHT 195).

Residential homes: arrangement of residents. A home lost its appeal, given that there was, for example, insufficient understanding of mentally handicapped people, shouting, threats, excessive obsession with routine and hygiene leading to over-regimentation, and set and rigid ideas (RHT 45).

Another appeal was lost for reasons including the fact that the home was 'permeated by the stench of urine, the general attitude was of poor care, residents were wearing unlaundered or dirty clothing and some residents were apparently wearing no clothing below the waist other than a blanket. An honest, accurate and damning indictment' (RHT 34).

Residential homes: sufficient qualified and competent staff (SI 1984/1345,r.10). The registered homes tribunals frequently investigate this matter. However, as the regulations state, what is adequate depends on the size of the home and the number and type of residents. As a result, there are many variables involved and this book cannot cover the decisions in sufficient depth. However, relevant factors include night cover, the effectiveness and organisation of rota systems, competence etc.

Staff shortages, or inappropriate staff, can lead to direct lack of care. For instance, in one case, this meant that it was difficult to keep one resident dry (eg, helping her on to the commode, changing sheets, and showering). For instance, the showering was sometimes undertaken with the help of a cleaner or with only one care assistant. There were 25 incidents recorded of this resident in wet clothes. More generally, there were 'numerous occasions when untrained domestic staff were performing care tasks, including bathing and showering of residents' (RHT 269).

Residential homes: reasonable accommodation and space (SI 1984/1345,r.10). The code of practice, *Home life*, states that single rooms are normally preferable, and that if more than two people share a room then there must be special reasons. However, depending on (perhaps exceptional) circumstances a three-bedded room might be acceptable. However, this does not mean that the Tribunals enforce the guidance to the letter; for example, where a 'Council's decision [against the home] was taken on the matter of principle alone without as full a consideration of all the circumstances as there might have been. This is not a case, in our view, for the rigid application of a rule of thumb'. The home won its appeal (RHT 10).

In another similar case, the tribunal found that the council had not acted with sufficient 'circumspection and flexibility' when demanding a reduction in the number of residents in a home with three-bedded rooms. The tribunal found that two of the three-bedded rooms could continue to be so used (RHT 16).

On the other hand, for example, a three-bedded room with shared wardrobe, beds close together, one armchair and a commode and no screening failed to provide privacy and dignity. The home lost its appeal (RHT 12). Where three-bedded rooms were used by two permanent residents and periodically by a third short-term (respite care) resident, the tribunal found that despite the general high standards of care this practice was potentially disruptive to the residents. The home was given about six months to phase out the three-bedded rooms (RHT 25).

Where a home appealed against the phasing out of three-bedded room within five years, the Tribunal found in favour of the local authority which 'has both the right and the duty to seek to implement those standards set out in the Code of Practice, standards which strive to attain "the good rather than … the acceptable". The dignity of residents must be preserved and maintained. Fundamental to dignity is the right to privacy and true privacy may only be attained in single rooms'. For example, in one of the rooms 'privacy for one resident was invaded each time the other residents entered to reach their own beds. Attempts had been made to use cupboards as room dividers but the essential lack of privacy remained, the only effect achieved being a tiny claustrophobic area with poor lighting' (RHT 71).

The following observations were generally accepted by the Tribunal as evidence of inadequate efforts to provide suitable accommodation: lack of privacy, absence of personal space, three beds in a room with 18" gaps between them, passageway passing through a bedroom, and no lift, which meant that residents were marooned (RHT 23).

Home Life states that though single rooms are preferable, there are a number of factors to consider when determining the ratio of double to single rooms in a home. For example, standard of care provided, size and nature of rooms, degree of privacy provided in them, and the amount of other public space provided for residents. In finding in favour of a home's appeal against a reduction of the number of double rooms, the Tribunal took into account size, attractiveness (which would be spoiled by division), difficulty of division, and the generous provision of public space for residents (RHT 52).

In another case, illustrating generally the tension between applying policies consistently but not rigidly, the Tribunal stated that if: 'a registration authority formulate rigid guidelines, particularly concerning matters such as occupancy and space, it must nevertheless take account of the totality of each situation presented and be ready to apply them flexibly in an appropriate case. Such an approach was visualised in paragraph 9 of Local Authority Circular (86)6 [ie, LAC (86)6] by the statement: "Decisions on the size and occupancy of bedrooms will need to take account not only of the design and construction of the premises but also of the levels of dependency of prospective residents and their likely needs for privacy and care". We appreciate the conflicting considerations often faced by a registration authority; on the one hand it is expected positively and confidently to apply its policies without suspicion of weakness or favouritism, but on the other hand it has to do so in a sensible way that takes account of the circumstances of each individual case, and therefore may appear to be discriminatory' (RHT 99).

Where a home was appealing against the decision restricting it to 11 single and 3 double rooms, instead of 10 single rooms and 4 double rooms, the Tribunal found for the home – and against the local authority. The Tribunal acknowledged that the question of double rooms most obviously revolved around privacy and the provision of a 'homely, non-institutional atmosphere'. However, other factors relevant to residents' welfare might include 'the character of an attractive building; the danger of a proprietor being tempted or even obliged to reduce the benefits available to residents in order to survive financially; the maintenance of such good relations and mutual respect between the proprietor and the registration authority and its officers that they can work in partnership for the benefit of residents; and no doubt a number of other factors that may be relevant in particular cases'. The local authority, having adopted a policy of a certain ration of single to double rooms 'must not slavishly apply that ratio in every case' (RHT 56).

In another instance, the Tribunal stated that in the case of the particular home '(and for the avoidance of doubt we make it clear that we are not laying down any principles of general application), it would not be inappropriate to have two double rooms in order to accommodate residents who wanted to share (eg, sisters, spouses, very old friends), or were prepared to share…' This decision was based on the fact that the criteria for shared rooms 'should first and foremost be the choice of the residents themselves'; and despite the fact that 'even a most respectable and responsible home owner, financially motivated to keep all available beds filled, could unintentionally or even deliberately persuade an elderly person to agree to share, in circumstances where the resident's consent was not entirely voluntary' (RHT 106).

However, where a home opposed limitations to the number of residents permitted and made a 'head-on attack' against single rooms, stating that its philosophy was that 'sharing improves human morale', the Tribunal had no difficulty referring to *Home life* and finding against the home. It stated that 'a single room is a very valuable asset in a residential care home because it gives a resident that private territory and opportunity for privacy which is so necessary for most people' (RHT 57).

The Tribunal considered in one case two narrow, single rooms which both fell below the minimum size prescribed by the local authority. Both residents were happy in the rooms. One, which the Tribunal approved (though not unanimously) contained all the furniture recommended in *Home life* but looked like the inside of a caravan because it was fitted so closely. The other room was disapproved of unanimously: it was not suitable for occupation by an elderly resident. For example, there was no room for a bedside table; and there were great difficulties in transferring a resident from wheelchair to bed (RHT 112).

Residential homes: kitchen/dining area. A kitchen area used for staff should not be available to residents as well and it was 'not desirable to have dining accommodation for the residents in the kitchen area where food had been prepared and cooked' (RHT 19).

Residential homes: sufficient number of baths, water closets, etc. Unacceptable is a home where there was no ground floor bathroom and the male toilet facilities consisted only of urinals (RHT 46).

Residential homes: adequate and suitable furniture. Where residents had to keep their clothes in lockers outside the bedrooms, but there was space in the bedrooms for wardrobes, the tribunal dismissed the home's appeal and stated that wardrobes should be installed in all the bedrooms. Thus residents would be enabled to 'at least have some say in what they wear, even though some may not be capable of exercising a rational choice' (RHT 30).

Residential homes: adaptations and provision of facilities necessary for physically disabled people. A home lost its appeal for a number of reasons including the small size and lack of facilities in the bathrooms (eg, no handles on bath or on wall); a staircase was too narrow to enable two people to assist anybody who needed assistance; it would be difficult for residents using a zimmer frame or wheelchair to use a WC without leaving the door open (RHT 36). A lack of free-standing baths and extra handgrips or handrails to help infirm residents was not acceptable (RHT 46).

The lack of a lift in a home with ambulant residents might not be fatal to registration, but in the particular circumstances the lack of a lift contributed 'to the restricted and depressing life offered to the residents' (RHT 53).

A home wished to bring its basement into use as a dining area. The Tribunal considered whether the staircase was suitable. It found that the staircase could not be safely used. This was because it was narrow and steep, made narrower by the existence of a handrail. Without a chair lift 'the problem of getting an old and or infirm person up and down the staircase is self evident. Twelve residents would use the staircase twice a day in order to take lunch and tea'. Yet a chair lift would have caused other problems. For example, the door at the top of stairs would have to remain off its hinges: yet a condition of registration was that the door remain locked. Further, the chair lift would have had to travel some way along the ground floor in order for people to get on and off. This would have caused congestion. The home lost its appeal (RHT 90).

An unsuitable staircase might be a principal reason for refusal of registration. The Tribunal concurred with the decision of the local authority, pointing out that the staircase 'is steep and the treads are too narrow even for a reasonably agile person to use without care. It is difficult to come down safely without turning one's feet at an angle to the stair and exercising some caution. The obstruction of the entrance to [the] lounge by the protrusion of [1.5] steps makes access to that room, both from the stairway and the hall difficult and hazardous for elderly and infirm persons' (RHT 104).

Commodes are sometimes inappropriately denied to people in an attempt to get them to use the lavatories whenever possible; they might be forced to use zimmer frames in the attempt to do this and but suffer falls (RHT 268).

Residential homes: food. Though not in itself sufficient grounds to cancel registration, the cooking of food in one home and transporting of it to another was stated by the Tribunal to be 'undesirable practice' (RHT 208).

Residential homes: adequate heating. A county council's guidelines, interpreting the regulations, stated that 'a full central heating system which maintains adequate heating levels to all parts of the home must be provided'. The temperature should have been 68' F in living accommodation and bedrooms during the day; and in all night-time accommodation at night. Inspectors had found lower temperatures and other witnesses stated that they often felt cold. It seemed that the heating system was deliberately programmed and sometimes switched off in order, probably, to save money. This was one of the grounds on which registration had been cancelled and the Tribunal found that the proprietors indeed failed in their duty under regulation 10(1)(f) (RHT 58).

In another case the tribunal, in dismissing an appeal of the home owner's, found 'a complete lack of understanding of the frailty and vulnerability' of the residents – two of whom, aged 76 and 78 in second-floor rooms with sash windows, were without heating over Christmas and New Year (RHT 256).

Residential homes: adequate fire and accident precautions. Locks on front doors preventing the escape of residents in case of fire were found not acceptable and had remained without being remedied for nearly nine years (RHT 15).

In one case, a home's application to increase its number of residents was rejected for a number of reasons. These included failure to carry out requirements covering regular tests to (and certificates for) the electrical system, emergency lighting, fire alarm system, gas installation, audibility of alarm, and lift. In addition there was failure to fire-proof basement ceilings, to link the emergency lighting and alarm systems, to provide window guards, to propose how hot water should be regulated, to renew the heating system and to provide a lavatory for food-handlers (RHT 217).

Residential homes: hygiene. Unacceptable was a sluice consisting of a large kitchen sink situated adjacent to a vestibule with a potato peeler and a deep freeze; and where the same room contained washing machines and a tumble drier (RHT 46). Amongst a number of shortcomings posing a risk to the health and/or welfare of residents in one home was the fact that clothes, bed linen and the clothing of incontinent residents were not laundered separately. As a result all clothing smelled of urine (RHT 129).

Residential homes: arrangements concerning handling, keeping, recording, disposal of drugs. Observations leading to a home losing its appeal included, for example, non-existent or inadequate medical records, incomplete medical cards, tablet bottles re-used so date on the bottle was incorrect, tablets/medicines not corresponding to record cards, bottles inadequately labelled or unreadable, out of date eye drops not disposed of (RHT 23).

Residential homes: public telephone. In one tribunal case, there was a payphone; but this had been installed in order to prevent abuses by staff of the owner's phone. However, the consequence was that, to the detriment of residents, staff could not make urgent phone calls unless they had the right money to hand. This contributed to the tribunal's finding that the home owner possessed 'little understanding of the importance of the delivery and continuity of care' (RHT 239).

12. REGISTRATION AND INSPECTION OF NURSING CARE HOMES

Health authorities have delegated responsibility for the registration and inspection of nursing homes. The following contains only brief extracts; full legal explanation can be found in specialist books (Jones 1993b, Ridout 1998). However, substantial reform of the registration and inspection system has been outlined in a White Paper (Secretary of State for Health 1998,Chapter 4).

EXTRACTS
Legislation states that:

> **(meaning of nursing home)** A nursing home is 'any premises used or intended to be used, for the reception of, and the provision of nursing for, persons from suffering from any sickness, injury or infirmity'. It is also 'any premises used, or intended to be used, for the reception of pregnant women, or of women immediately after childbirth…'
>
> Otherwise it is other premises not covered by the above but 'used or intended to be used for the provision of all or any of the following services': surgical procedures under anaesthesia, pregnancy termination, endoscopy, haemodialysis or peritoneal dialysis, treatment by specially controlled techniques (Registered Homes Act 1984, s.21).

> **(registration of nursing homes)** Any person who 'carries on' a nursing home must be registered (Registered Homes Act 1984,s.23).

> **(refusal of registration)** Registration, which is delegated by the Secretary of State to health authorities, can be refused on grounds:

>> **(fit person)** 'that the applicant, or any person, employed or proposed to be employed by the applicant at the home, is not a fit person (whether by reason of age or otherwise) to carry on or be employed…'; or

>> **(situation, construction, etc)** 'that, for reasons connected with situation, construction, state of repair, accommodation, staffing or equipment, the home is not, or any premises used in connection with the home are not, fit to be used for such a home, or any other premises used or intended to be used in connection with it, are not fit to be used'; or

>> **(impropriety, etc)** 'that the home is, or any premises used in connection with it are, used, or proposed to be used, for purposes which are in any way improper or undesirable in the case of such a home…'; or

>> **(registered practitioner)** 'that the home is not, or will not be, in the charge of a person who is either a registered medical practitioner or a qualified nurse or, in the case of a maternity home, a registered midwife'; or

>> **(sufficient qualified nurses)** there must be such number of qualified nurses (or midwives) as is specified by the registering health authority (Registered Homes Act 1984,s.25).

> **(cancellation of registration).** Registration can be cancelled on any of the grounds in respect of refusal of registration (see immediately above), non-payment of the annual fee on or before the due date, a conviction for an offence under the Act or regulations made under it, non-compliance with a condition imposed on the home and currently in force (Registered Homes Act 1984,s.28).

> **(inspection of nursing homes)** Health authorities have the power – delegated from the Secretary of State – to inspect nursing homes (SI 1984/1587,r.10).

13. SERVICES AND FACILITIES PROVIDED BY NURSING HOMES

Private nursing home owners are subject to the Registered Homes Act 1984 and associated regulations which together state that the owner must be a fit person, the premises be fit, and certain services and facilities be provided.

Under the 1984 Act, homes are both registered and inspected by health authorities. Appeals go to registered homes tribunals which have interpreted some of the requirements placed on homes. Below are a number of summaries of tribunal cases, relating mostly to the provision of services and facilities. The cases are instructive in giving insight into the issues and disputes which can arise in nursing homes – and into the range of factors to be taken into account when solutions are sought. Thus, these decisions are not necessarily predictable and sometimes depend on the particular facts and circumstances of each case.

The interpretation that a home owner places on the legislation affects how much additional health service support is needed – or how much extra residents or their relatives have to pay. Regulations state that the home must provide adequate professional staff, medical and nursing equipment. This legislative requirement appears to cover a diversity of practice: for example, whether or not homes provide, within the fees, incontinence pads to the right quantity and quality is likely to vary from home to home. Much would seem to depend on what the contracts specify and how they are monitored and enforced.

Though having no direct statutory force, a guide commended by the Department of Health was produced in 1984 by the National Association of Health Authorities (NAHA 1984) (now the NHS Confederation) on the registration and inspection of nursing homes. Commended by the Department of Health and Social Security (now the Department of Health) in guidance (HC(84)21), it has been used by health authorities widely in their capacity as registration and inspection authorities. It recommends what facilities and services would represent good practice; and the Registered Homes Tribunals make reference to the guidelines when investigating cases. A supplement was later published (NAHA 1988a).

EXTRACTS

Legislation states that a number of services and facilities must be provided, 'having regard to the size of the home and the number, age, sex and condition of the patients'. The list includes:
- adequate professional, technical, ancillary and other staff;
- adequate accommodation for each patient;
- adequate furniture, bedding, curtains and where necessary adequate screens and floor covering;
- adequate medical, surgical and nursing equipment and ... treatment facilities;
- adequate wash basins and baths supplying hot and cold water and adequate water closets and sluicing facilities;
- adequate light, heating and ventilation;
- keeping of all parts of the home in good repair, clean and reasonably decorated;
- adequate fire and accident precautions;
- adequate food, kitchen and eating equipment, food preparation and storage facilities;
- adequate laundry facilities;
- adequate arrangements for disposal of used medical and nursing materials;

- adequate arrangements for patients to see GPs and dentists;
- adequate arrangements concerning handling, keeping, recording, disposal of drugs;
- adequate arrangements to prevent infection;
- adequate arrangements for residents' training, occupation, recreation;
- adequate facilities to receive visitors in private;
- connect the home to a public telephone service (SI 1984/1578, r.12).

DISCUSSION

The following includes a selective sample of decisions of registered nursing home tribunals. Those chosen concentrate on services and facilities, as opposed to the many other issues dealt with by tribunals, including violence, cruelty, dishonesty, poor record-keeping and staff inadequacies.

Nursing homes: adequate qualified and competent staff. Registered homes tribunals frequently investigate this matter. However, as the regulations state, what is adequate depends on the size of the home and the number, age, sex and condition of the residents. As a result, there are many variables involved and this book cannot cover the decisions in sufficient depth. Because of the variables involved, the NAHA (1984) guidelines do not list staffing ratios but do list a number of factors to be taken into account (pp.25,65–66).

In practice, from the point of view of what private nursing homes provide within their basic services, there are different possibilities in practice. Some homes might provide such services within the fee; in others, people or their relatives have to pay extra for such services. For example, a home might provide, within its fees, a) no physiotherapy at all, b) general physiotherapy classes (eg, an exercise class once a week for interested residents) only, or c) include physiotherapy for individual residents as part of the service it provides within the fees.

Nursing homes: adequate nursing equipment. In practice, provision of, for example, incontinence materials in nursing homes is likely to vary from home to home, both in quality and in how the materials have been paid for. It seems that some homes have provided a better service within their fees than others; but sometimes residents and relatives have to pay extra. It is not necessarily a question of whether, for example, incontinence pads are provided at all; but whether the appropriate types are provided and in sufficient quantities.

Nursing homes: nursing care. A lack of care was evident in the documented evidence that a person who died of multiple, infected pressure sores, was constantly sliding down in his chair towards the end of his life – with the inevitable friction, discomfort and skin and tissue damage. Another resident was left in her chair all day, was dehydrated, and wearing unsuitable footwear. When her teeth fell out, she was not consulted about their replacement. Her body was left exposed in a public and degrading way, and a urine bag left on her bed prevented adequate bladder drainage. There was no evidence of aseptic techniques being used.

A third resident had, within one month of entering the home, suffered severe weight loss, become incontinent and suffered reduced mobility. When admitted to hospital she had a fungal infection, ragged nails, a bleeding encrusted mouth, and untreated head lice. A fourth – who had suffered a stroke, was paralysed down the left side of her body, had diabetes and hypertension, and was physically very frail – had had her bed placed by a radiator. Despite instructions that she be turned every two hours, the evidence suggested that this did not happen on the night she was severely burned (RHT 272).

Nursing homes: adequate bedding for incontinence. In one appeal before a tribunal, the home owner was appealing against an order sought from, and made by, a magistrate's court, cancelling the registration of the home on grounds of serious risk to the life, health or well-being of the patients in the home (under s.30 of the Registered Homes Act 1984). Amongst various findings, the health authority inspectors reported that one 'patient had been put to bed in net knickers filled with cut up incontinence sheets and gamgee, despite the ready availability of usual incontinence pads. Several patients were lying on plastic sheeting and found to have inflamed skin consistent with the early onset of low grade pressure sores ... in six of the nine bedrooms, patients were sleeping directly on plastic sheets, despite the fact that a full and adequate supply of cotton sheets was available nearby'. Even the home owner agreed that such practices were dangerous; the tribunal agreed (RHT 255).

Nursing homes: lifts. Where, given their average age, residents have difficulty negotiating steep and narrow stairs between floors, then although 'some of the residents were satisfied to remain in their own area ... the provision of a lift might enable some residents to lead a fuller life, and association with others'. The Tribunal implied that this would have been desirable although did not explicitly refer to this when finding against the home owner (RHT 8). In another case where the home lost its appeal, the absence of a lift meant that top-floor residents were 'virtually isolated there indefinitely' (RHT 29).

Nursing homes: accommodation/privacy. A tribunal found that the local health authority's approach to approving only exceptionally rooms with more than two beds was based on *Home life* which applied to residential homes (but not nursing homes). This was the wrong approach. Instead the authority should have considered 'all the facts and circumstances' in deciding whether proper facilities were provided in the relevant bedrooms. The tribunal found the accommodation satisfactory (RHT 27).

In one case a health authority opposing use of a double room was insisting on 100 square feet per person. This was both greater than NAHA's guidelines which suggested 86 square feet, and apparently more stringent than most other authorities' requirements. The Tribunal stated that even the lower figure should not be taken as an absolute minimum, since the Tribunal was inclined to agree with the opinion 'that a purpose-built room may be regarded as having the same special attribute as a less well-designed room up to 30 sq. ft. larger simply by reason that the doors and windows and other fittings are sensibly positioned'. Thus the particular room in question, though not conforming even to the NAHA guidelines had a 'special attribute that is quite sufficient in all the circumstances' (RHT 61).

Use of a four-bedded room was accepted by the Tribunal in the particular circumstances of one case. The Tribunal was satisfied that the room was not used in connection with maximum occupancy in (and therefore maximum income from) the home. It was used as a nursing station for seriously ill patients and was more in the nature of a hospice ward than a sick bay. The Tribunal inspected the room and found it attractive and of a light and tranquil atmosphere which would not be distressing to patients. Patients, relatives and sometimes the patients' doctors would be consulted before a move into this room (RHT 207).

Nursing homes: second-floor accommodation. A tribunal did not agree with the local health authority that only exceptionally could second floor accommodation be provided. NAHA guidelines did not state this and none of the residents on the second floor had substantial difficulty using the stairs. The Tribunal had 'regard to the lack of disapproval in NAHA guidelines, to the fact that we were referred to no other authority which had adopted a similar approach to that of the respondent, to the lack of any expert evidence of any detrimental effect on patients generally from occupying second floor accommodation'; and it took into account the views of its own expert members.

The authority needed to 'look with great care at the use of such accommodation to ensure that there were adequate means for patients to move between floors, that the fire safety precautions were adequate and that patients could be properly cared for on a second floor'. For example, the stairway was not ideal because it was rather narrow and the chair lift did not reach the last few steps. However, 'the evidence was that the patients with rooms on the second floor were all ambulant and had not experienced any substantial difficulty in negotiating the stairway'. There were always staff to attend to people when using the stairs and chair lift and there was no evidence that the care of the patients was affected adversely through being on the second floor. However, the Tribunal did order that a condition of registration should be that only ambulant patients occupy the second floor (RHT 27).

In another case the Tribunal ruled that the second floor could only be occupied by people who were ambulant, and not dependent on wheelchairs or walking aids, and not mentally confused. The staircase between the first and second floors needed handrails on both sides. There was a lift but the stairs needed to be useable in case of failure of the lift; and there was evidence that some people would not use the lift anyway (RHT 60).

Nursing homes: bedroom/day/dining space. Where a health authority refused registration of an additional bed because of the day/dining space involved, the tribunal noted a lack of clarity arising from NAHA's guidelines which talked about space per ambulant patient, not space per bed. For example, the fact that somebody was not ambulant did not mean they could not use the day/dining space. In this specific case, the tribunal allowed the home's appeal, but noted that different considerations would apply in other cases (RHT 28).

A Tribunal found in favour of a home which was proposing to use a particular room as a communal sitting room, despite the fact that it failed to conform in size to either NAHA's or the health authority's guidelines. The Tribunal felt that 'a separate dining room, and 25 sq. ft. of space in a communal room for each of the patients, is not necessary – and even the lack of a separate staff room we regard as unimportant in all the circumstances. We do not doubt that nowadays the number of ambulant patients is seen to be decreasing so that a requirement that "one or more sitting rooms must be provided to give 25 sq ft of space for all patients" within the home would appear to merit some reconsideration' (RHT 61).

However, in another case a Tribunal held that the lounge should be big enough to accommodate all the residents whether or not all of them used it: for example, in the future, a greater proportion of the residents might be ambulant. In addition, if one took into account a main and busy thoroughfare through the day space (dining room and lounge), the amount of space fell below the NAHA guidelines (RHT 124). Similarly, where a home had day space 'barely appropriate' for 14 patients, the Tribunal was not prepared to consider an increase in the number of patients. It was 'no answer to say that many of the patients are/will be bedridden and will not choose to use the day room'. Indeed, there was no lift, 'and so patients would have to be mobile, or be carried, to negotiate the stairs to reach the day room, and they would not be inclined to do this (or to ask nurses to assist them downstairs) if they are aware that the room is already overcrowded. So it is no answer that the room is not used by all'. The Tribunal was prepared to accept that day space could be 'scattered'; but in the particular case, the suggested areas of entrance hall and upstairs landing were not appropriate for reasons such as obstruction, hazard of being near the top of a staircase and so on (RHT 175).

In one home, the space required for bed sitting rooms was achieved by the use of folding beds. The Tribunal noted the weighty objections in principle against their use but approved them in the particular case, whilst emphasising that they were not setting a precedent. Reasons for their acceptability in the particular circumstances were that it was easy for a nurse to move a chair a foot or two in order to fold or unfold the bed; the beds could be lowered in a matter of seconds; nearly all the patients would anyway have to call a nurse for assistance whether moving from a chair to any type of bed, folding or not; the beds were easily height adjustable; though ripple mattresses could not be used with them, sheep skins were satisfactory for pressure sore prevention; the rooms were made more pleasant to sit in with the beds folded away (RHT 75).

A room which is adequate in size for an ambulant resident might become inadequate, once lifting techniques, wheelchair use or hoist use are necessary for a less able resident (RHT 271).

Nursing homes: kitchen, food and eating facilities. A tribunal found a number of below-standard features of nursing home kitchen, including damp, flaking paintwork, cracked and uneven floor looking dirty, lack of crockery storage space, rusty refrigerator and old-looking freezer. In addition, dry food was being stored near damp ground and near domestic cleaning materials (RHT 124).

Nursing homes: heating. A tribunal found a proprietor an unfit person because, despite warnings that the home was too cold, he maintained it at a 'totally unacceptable temperature', knew that the boiler was old and unreliable and should be repaired or replaced. Secondary, compensatory, heating was not provided. Patients were bathed in unacceptably cool water which was not only uncomfortable for the patients but could have increased risk of hypothermia. Sometimes the temperature during the day was verging on an unacceptable condition of work for staff; and at night there was no heating (RHT 187).

Where heating and lighting to a home is put at risk because of failure of the home to discharge its financial responsibilities (eg, to the electricity and gas boards), the home is seriously failing to maintain standards of care. Patients are put seriously at risk thereby (RHT 138).

Nursing homes: washing facilities and lavatories. A health authority's apparent reliance on *Home life* (applying to residential homes) for the proportion of lavatories to residents (1 to 4) was not reasonable. For example, where residents were dependent upon staff assistance to get to the lavatory, a high proportion of lavatories would be superfluous. There would be enough staff to justify the proportion. The home's appeal was allowed (RHT 27).

Nursing homes: laundry facilities. It is unacceptable for sluices (for soiled linen) to be in close proximity to laundry facilities because of the danger of cross-infection. The home lost its appeal (RHT 8). In another case where the home also lost its appeal the tribunal noted as serious the absence of proper sluicing facilities on either floor in a home where heavily dependent patients and soiled linen had to be dealt with (RHT 29).

A sluice in a bathroom/lavatory with a paper towel dispenser over it was not acceptable. There is a danger of cross-infection if a sluice is situated in a bathroom or lavatory; it should not be made of ceramic; it should not be sited and provided with paper towels so as to invite people to wash their hands in it (RHT 75).

Nursing homes: cleanliness and hygiene. A tribunal pointed out that patients 'in a nursing home are even more vulnerable than the residents of a residential care home. Matters such as cleanliness and hygiene are of vital importance, and those suffering from sickness, injury or infirmity require the best possible care. It is therefore reasonable to expect even higher standards of a nursing home than of a residential home' (RHT 223).

CHAPTER 12

CHARGES FOR RESIDENTIAL AND NURSING HOME ACCOMMODATION

Coverage

1. Status of residents
2. Making charges
3. Personal expenses allowance
4. Temporary residents
5. Less dependent residents
6. Assessment of couples
7. Assessment of capital
8. Assessment of property
9. Assessment of income
10. Responsibility for payment
11. Pursuing third parties
12. Placing a charge on land/property
13. Insolvency proceedings
14. Information for the resident
15. Social security benefits and residential accommodation
16. Personal financial issues

KEY POINTS

Charging people for residential or nursing home accommodation arranged by local authorities is determined by a statutory means-test (this is in contrast to non-residential services: see Chapter 10). The rules are detailed and complicated; the following represents an outline only. Reference should be made to the full, original sources of legislation and guidance, to expert advice or to specialist publications. The application of these rules sometimes proves controversial when people's savings or homes have to be used to pay for residential or nursing home accommodation – or when assets, which have previously been made a gift of to somebody else (eg, another family member), are nevertheless taken account of in the means-test.

Note: The extracts in the following chapter are drawn in the main from the National Assistance Act 1948, the National Assistance (Assessment of Resources) Regulations 1992, and the Charging for Residential Accommodation Guide (CRAG 1993), a looseleaf, regularly updated manual of guidance available free of charge from the Department of Health. The Regulations frequently cross-refer to, and rely on, the *Income Support (General) Regulations 1987* (SI 1987/1967; however, CRAG helpfully summarises the effects of the cross-referencing.

Other sources of information include, for example, the Child Poverty Action Group's *National Welfare Benefits Handbook* (1998–1999 edition), or the *Disability Rights Handbook* (1998–1999 edition) published by the Disability Alliance. Age Concern England produces a series of very helpful factsheets.

I. STATUS OF RESIDENTS

There are several different classes of resident in residential and nursing accommodation, distinguished by the financial arrangements made for their care.

EXTRACTS

Legislation: reference is made to legislation in the following discussion.

DISCUSSION

Status of residents: people with preserved rights (from before April)

People who were living in a home before April 1st 1993, and were supported by the Department of Social Security (DSS), have 'preserved rights' and continue to be supported from central social security funds. Legislation prevents local authorities from providing 'topping up' funding (ie, in addition to the social security funding), except in the case of people under pension age (see p.263).

Discrepancies have arisen between these residents (ie, those in accommodation before April 1993) and those supported by local authorities since that date under community care legislation (eg, Laing 1998; ACO 1996; Age Concern England 1994a). For example, if a local authority sets its contribution level higher than that of the DSS, homes in the area might raise their fees to the higher level (Age Concern 1994a,p.8). It was reported that by May 1995, some 70,000 – half of all 'preserved rights' residents – faced a shortfall between the fees payable and the Income Support available (ACO 1996,p.1). This leaves DSS-supported residents and their relatives with that shortfall to make up, or possibly face eviction. If local authorities then act to help those in residential homes, people have to move to another home – they cannot receive local authority assistance in the home in which they have been living up to that point. However, local authorities are anyway not empowered to assist people with preserved rights who are in nursing homes and over pension age. (The converse situation might also arise, when the level of fees paid by the local authority lags behind the annual rate of increase paid by the Department of Social Security – as occurred in *R v Coventry CC, ex p CHOICE*).

Status of residents: people supported by local authorities

People who have entered a home after 31st March 1993, and require at least some public support, come under the new system; local authority social services departments assess their needs and finances and arrange accommodation and financial support as appropriate. This chapter is mainly concerned with this type of provision.

Status of residents: NHS inpatients

People who are placed (whether before or after March 31st 1993) contractually in nursing homes by the health service retain the status of NHS patients and their care is paid for by the NHS. They are not entitled to the higher rate of income support available to qualifying residents in independent care homes.

Just as local authorities sometimes seek to shift financial responsibility for supporting people in residential accommodation on to central government (see below), so too does the NHS. For example, in August 1993, the Court of Appeal in *White and Others v Chief Adjudication Officer* made a ruling affecting the funding of people leaving long stay hospitals. A health authority had contracted for a dual registered (nursing/residential) home to accommodate former long-stay hospital patients. The assumption was that the former patients, now residents, could claim higher rates of income support which would be paid to the nursing home, complementing the health authority's contribution.

However, the court ruled that the home fell under the definition of 'hospital or similar institution' (NHS Act 1977,s.128). This meant that the residents were ineligible for income support. Even if nursing was not a dominant purpose, the home could still be defined as a hospital or similar institution, since it had agreed to maintain nurses amongst its permanent and resident staff. If the nursing requirement had been minimal then the home might not have been deemed to be a hospital.

The point this case seems to illustrate is that either people are NHS patients or they are not (in this context). If they are, then the NHS has to pay all the costs; if they are not, then the authority does not have the power to pay any part of their nursing home costs, even if it wanted to. The Department of Health issued advice in 1990 to health authorities and NHS Trusts (EL(90)MB/45 – now superseded by HSG(95)45). This is to the effect that if patients are being discharged to homes where they claim higher rates of income support, then the NHS can at most make *non-contractual* payments in relation to such homes, under the Health Service and Public Health Act 1968 (s.64: grant-making) or under the NHS Act 1977 (s.28A: contributions towards expenditure of other bodies). As the guidance explains, a s.64 grant is 'based on statute and not contract'. However, payments made under s.23 of the NHS Act 1977 are contractual and for NHS care; thus residents are deemed to be NHS inpatients, cannot be charged and cannot claim the higher rates of income support (annex,paras 4.1 – 4.6). For 'joint finance' arrangements, see p.315.

Status of resident: social security support (since April 1993)

A fourth category exists apparently because of a legal loophole. From April 1st 1993, the community care system was intended to terminate the system of social security support for people in residential and nursing homes (except for those with preserved rights: see above). Wrongly, it was thought that for people in independent homes, attendance allowance or disability living allowance (care component) would cease after four weeks. In fact people can still enter a home supported by social security, and therefore 'by-pass' the new system of social services assessment and placement. For example, a single person over 65 might be able to claim income support (including pensioner, higher pension premium or sometimes severe disability premium) with attendance allowance or disability living allowance.

That disputes should arise is no surprise, since some local authorities, short of resources, encourage people to obtain funding for residential accommodation precisely through social security benefits (Wright 1997,p.5). Apart from thereby not having to go on to a waiting list for a placement arranged by the local authority, a potential advantage for residents of choosing this route is that if they are trying to sell a house, the Department of Social Security disregards it (at least for a reasonable period) in the financial assessment of the person's capital – and so does not claim back any benefit paid (unlike a local authority in the same circumstances). Another reason for using this route arises when a local authority assesses that a person does not need residential care, but nevertheless the person wishes to enter a home.

However, disadvantages are as follows. First, central government could at any time decide to close the loophole. Second, the money payable through benefits might not be sufficient to meet the home's fees – either at the outset, or if they are subsequently increased. Whereas, if a local authority has arranged a placement, it remains contractually responsible for paying the fees. Third, if a property is not sold within a reasonable time, then even the Department of Social Security will eventually take account of its value. Fourth, when their savings fall below £16,000, people might then ask a local authority for assistance; but a) the authority might not be prepared to assist in relation to the home the person is in, and b) it might not necessarily consider that they are in need of residential care at all. Fifth, if somebody is not already in receipt of attendance allowance or disability living allowance, the qualifying period (except for terminal illness) for the benefits is six months for people aged over 65 years. Lastly, by going down the social security benefits route, the resident will not have a social worker assigned them to consider their changing needs (based on: Age Concern England 1997,p.4; and Age Concern Cheshire 1997,pp.8–9).

In this connection, concern has been expressed that inappropriate or incorrect advice is sometimes given by local authority staff about very important matters such as people selling their homes (Age Concern England 1994b,p.25). Furthermore, if local authorities advise people to use the benefits loophole without even fully assessing them they are depriving themselves of information about a those people's assets. Yet such information might indicate a) on any future application of assistance by the person, that assets had not been improperly disposed of; and b) possible future financial demands on the local authority. In addition, when a person has a property which could be disposed of, a failure to assess and to consider individual circumstances means that the local authority is depriving itself of the possibility of exercising its power to arrange accommodation for the person, to place a charge on the property and to recoup the amount owing when the property is finally sold (Age Concern Cheshire 1997,p.6). Local authorities do not have an incentive to do this because, if they are short of money, they do not want to lay out more than they have to – and they cannot add interest to the amount of the charge placed on the property unless the person dies (see p.309). However, the consequence is that people are then forced to make their own arrangements, such as taking out disadvantageous commercial loans to tide them over until the property is sold (Age Concern England 1998d,p.19; and see eg, *Community Care* 1999).

Status of residents: people who fund themselves

Some people pay the whole costs of their residential or nursing care from their own resources, and so have nothing to do with either the old or new systems of publicly supported care – unless or until their money runs out. It has been reported that 60 per cent of self-funding residents are charged more than local authority-funded residents. The consequence of this could be that residents who have been paid for by the local authority, whilst they are selling their home, suddenly find the fee increased – once the home has been sold, the local authority reimbursed and they have become self-funding. Such a state of affairs would suggest that self-funding residents are in effect subsidising residents paid for by local authorities (Laing 1998,p.21).

2. MAKING CHARGES FOR RESIDENTIAL AND NURSING HOME ACCOMMODATION

In contrast to the power (but not duty) that local authorities have to make charges for non-residential community care services, they have a duty in respect of residential services to apply a statutory means-test and make charges accordingly.

EXTRACTS

Legislation states that:

> **(accommodation provided directly by the authority: standard, full-rate charge)** 'where a person is provided with accommodation under this Part of this Act the local authority providing the accommodation shall recover from him the amount of the payment which he is liable to make … the payment which a person is liable to make for any such accommodation shall be in accordance with a standard rate fixed for that accommodation by the authority managing the premises in which it is provided and that standard rate shall represent the full cost to the authority of providing that accommodation' (National Assistance Act 1948, s.22);

> **(arrangements made with the independent sector for provision according to agreed rate)** 'any arrangements … shall provide for the making by the local authority to the other party … of payments in respect of the accommodation at such rates as may be determined by or under the arrangements and … the local authority shall recover from each person for whom accommodation is provided under the arrangements the amount of the refund which he is liable to make' (National Assistance Act 1948, s.26). Guidance states that the amount payable will be 'the gross cost to the local authority of providing or purchasing the accommodation' CRAG 1993, para 1.007);

> **(reduction or waiving of charges)** Local authorities are under a duty to make charges, but they also have a duty to reduce the amount payable if (a) in the case of local authority accommodation, a person 'satisfies the local authority that he is unable to pay therefore at the standard rate'; or (b) in the case of accommodation arranged with the independent sector, he 'satisfies the local authority that he is unable to make a refund at the full rate determined' (National Assistance Act 1948, ss.22(3) and 26(3));

> **(statutory means-test)** local authorities must assess people's liability to charges through a statutory test of resources contained in regulations (National Assistance Act 1948, s.22(5); the test of resources is set out in SI 1992/2977).

DISCUSSION

Making charges: standard rate

The local authority must set a standard rate up to which it will pay for people who cannot afford to pay themselves. The rate should represent the full cost to the local authority of providing the accommodation. Costs will vary depending on the type of care involved and the locality (but see p.264 for the extent to which this is consistent with people's choice of accommodation).

Guidance states that authorities should not set 'an arbitrary ceiling on the amount they are willing to contribute towards residential care and require third parties routinely to make up the difference. If challenged an authority would need to be able to demonstrate that its usual cost was sufficient to allow it to provide people with the level of service they could reasonably expect did the possibility of third party contributions not exist' (LAC(92)27,para 10).

3. PERSONAL EXPENSES ALLOWANCE

When deciding what a person can afford to pay, local authorities are under a duty to assume that the person will require a certain amount of money each week for his or her personal requirements. The amount is determined by regulations, but the local authority has a discretion to vary it in special circumstances. The amount allowed for is known as the personal expenses allowance (PEA).

EXTRACTS

Legislation states that:

> 'In assessing ... a person's ability to pay, a local authority shall assume that he will need for his personal requirements such sum per week as may be prescribed by the Minister, or such other sum as in special circumstances the authority may consider appropriate'. Regulations currently set the current standard amount at £14.45 (SI 1998/498).

Guidance states that:

> **(purpose of allowance)** the allowance is 'intended to enable residents to have money to spend as they wish, for example, on stationery, personal toiletries, treats and small presents for friends and relatives' (CRAG 1993,para 5.001).

> **(use of allowance)** in the Department of Health's view, the PEA cannot be used to contribute to fees which are not wholly covered by the local authority's contribution: the 'National Assistance Act requires authorities to leave all residents with their PEA. Authorities may not therefore take these amounts into account even for "more expensive accommodation" and they should not enter into agreements which involve the use of PEA' (LAC(94)1, para 13).

Guidance states that the amount of the personal expenses allowance might be varied in the following circumstances:

> **(nursing mothers)** 'it may be necessary for local authorities to vary the amount ... to reflect the needs of the infant' (CRAG 1993,para 1.011);

> **(less-dependent resident)** a person might not come under the less-dependent resident rules (see below) because he or she is living in registered or local authority residential accommodation with board – but nevertheless needs 'to retain more of his income in order to help him lead a more independent life' (CRAG 1993,para 5.005);

(income support receipt for other person) a person temporarily in residential accommodation might be receiving income support which includes an amount for a partner still at home (CRAG 1993,para 5.005);

(unmarried couple: income) where a person in residential accommodation is the main recipient of the couple's income (eg, an occupational pension), the authority could increase the personal expenses allowance, so as to allow more income for the person remaining at home. However authorities should beware that this increased income to the person at home could have an adverse effect on any benefits he or she is receiving (CRAG 1993,para 5.005).

DISCUSSION

Personal expenses allowance: adequacy of and misuse

It is clearly arguable that an item covered by the personal expenses allowance (PEA), such as 'personal toiletries', should not include basic toiletries which the home should be providing within the agreed fees. Nevertheless, there is concern that people's allowance is in practice eroded by 'extras' charged by the home (eg, physiotherapy, incontinence pads provided for people in nursing homes, or private laundry charges). In principle, people could be protected from such extra healthcare costs if local authorities were to specify what was expected in the contracts they draw up with nursing and residential homes – a protection not enjoyed by residents with preserved rights (see above) under the old funding system (Age Concern England 1994a,p.7). In practice, such protection will clearly depend on the clarity, detail and monitoring of contracts.

Despite the Department of Health's guidance (above) to the contrary, there is concern that homes routinely charge residents a little more than the local authority's contribution: the PEA being used to bridge the gap (Age Concern England 1993,p.19). Similarly, the equivalent allowance for residents with 'preserved rights' (see p.293) might be used to bridge the increasing gap between the fees charged and income support available. Residents might not be aware even that there should be a personal expenses allowance (if, for example, the amount is automatically included in the home's fees) – and thus, for instance, homes might charge extra money for items such as birthday cakes for residents (ACO 1996,p.7). Furthermore, even ordinary needs which the allowance might normally be expected to cover, might be increased by the nature of residential care; for instance, expenditure on underwear or nightclothes might rise because of vigorous washing procedures in a home (Wright 1998).

Blatant misuse of personal expenses allowances is sometimes reported. For instance, it has been suggested that home owners sometimes retain the allowances paid for individuals, and then pool them to spend collectively on the residents of the home. This means that individual residents not only lose control of their money, but there might not even be an itemised account of how it has been spent (Office of Fair Trading 1998,p.26). And, in a registered homes tribunal case, it became clear that when the manager of the home was short of money, as she always was (because she was not allowed an adequate float), she would resort to using the personal expenses allowances of residents in order to buy food (RHT decision no.273).

Quite apart from improper erosion of the allowance by one means or another, a thorough study – providing a salutary reminder of a 'modest-but-adequate' living standard which residents reasonably require – concluded that the allowance should anyway be nearer £40 than £14. It considered the recurrent cost of items including personal food (fruit, biscuits, tea/coffee, sugar, milk, soft drinks), alcohol (eg, glass of sherry to give a visitor), clothing, personal care (eg, plasters, cough mixture, aspirin, hairbrush, shampoo, bath oil, sponge bag, walking stick, watch, small mirror, household goods (eg, furniture, linen, electrical appliances, crockery, batteries, shoe brushes), household services (eg, postage, telephone call, footwear repair, dry cleaning), leisure goods (eg, television, radio, newspapers, magazines, books, games, knitting, embroidery), leisure services (eg, cinema, keep-fit classes, dancing, social club), transport (eg, dentist, optician, hairdresser, shopping, cinema, dancing, keep fit classes) (Parker 1997).

Personal expenses allowance: discretion to vary

Local authorities have a discretion to vary the level of the allowance 'in special circumstances'. The discretion might enable a resident to hand over some of his or her income to a partner or spouse remaining at home. This might benefit the person at home who, for instance, does not qualify for Income Support but has a low income; but it might not be to the advantage of someone receiving means-tested benefits, which might be reduced in the light of the extra money being given by the resident (Age Concern England 1998f,p.7).

When the National Assistance Bill passed through Parliament, the government explained that the 'intention was to leave the maximum discretion' with local authorities. This was in answer to a question of whether local authorities therefore had the power not only to allow a higher sum but also a lower one; the answer presumably allows for both (John Edwards: SC(C),21/1/1948, cols.2527–2528).

4. TEMPORARY RESIDENTS

When people stay no more than eight weeks in accommodation, the local authority has a discretion to limit what it charges; in other words, it is not obliged to follow the statutory means-test in these circumstances. This gives local authorities considerable discretion in charging for respite care or short-term breaks. Beyond eight weeks the local authority is obliged to apply the statutory charging procedure, subject to a few special rules if people's stay is not expected to exceed 52 weeks, and they are therefore classed as temporary residents.

EXCERPTS

Legislation states that:

> **(eight week periods of residence)** 'Where they think fit, an authority managing premises in which accommodation is provided for a person shall have power on each occasion when they provide accommodation for him, irrespective of his means, to limit to such amount as appears to them reasonable for him to pay the payments required from him for his accommodation during a period commencing when they begin to provide the accommodation for him and ending not more than eight weeks after that' (National Assistance Act 1948, s.22(5A)).

> **(definition of temporary resident: likely stay of no more than 52 weeks)** A temporary resident's stay is 'unlikely to exceed 52 weeks' or 'in exceptional circumstances, unlikely substantially to exceed that period' (SI 1992/2977,r.2). Guidance explains that if a stay which was thought to be permanent turns out to be temporary, it would be 'unreasonable' for the authority to continue to apply the permanent residence rules to the resident. Conversely, if what was expected originally to be a temporary stay turns out to be per-

manent, the permanent residence rules should only be applied from the date of this realisation, not from the outset (CRAG 1993 paras 3.004–4A).

(temporary residence: disregarding the resident's own home) In assessing a temporary resident's resources, the local authority must disregard the value of the person's own home (only one dwelling) if he or she is a) 'taking reasonable steps to dispose of the dwelling in order that he may acquire another dwelling which he intends to occupy as his home' – or b) 'he intends to return to occupy that dwelling as his home; and the dwelling to which he intends to return is still available to him' (SI 1992/2977,schedule 4, para 1);

(temporary residence: disregarding income support (housing costs element) and housing benefit) If a person is receiving income support which includes an element for housing costs, then the local authority must disregard that element in assessing the person's income. Housing benefit should be disregarded if received for the home address (SI 1992/2977,schedule 3,paras 3,26).

(temporary residence: disregarding home commitments) Income support and housing benefit might not meet the costs of continuing home commitments, in which case the authority should disregard an amount which it considers reasonable. Such commitments might include fixed heating charges; water rates; mortgage payments, rent or service charges not covered by income support of housing benefit; insurance premiums.

Where neither income support nor housing benefit is being received, the local authority should disregard a reasonable amount in connection with home commitments, such as interest charges (on hire purchase agreement to buy the dwelling (eg, a caravan), repair or improvement loans); mortgage payments, ground rent or other rental relating to a long tenancy; service charges; insurance premiums; standard fuel charges; water rates; payments relating to co-ownership schemes, or tenancy agreement or licence of a Crown tenant (SI 1992/2977,schedule 3,para 27, and guidance: CRAG 1993 paras 3.011–12).

(disregarding attendance allowance and disability living allowance) Both attendance allowance and the care component of disability living allowance should be ignored – although both would anyway be withdrawn after four weeks if financial support is available from the local authority (SI 1992/2977,schedule 3,para 6, and CRAG 1993,para 3.014).

DISCUSSION

Temporary residents: change in status

Without clear guidelines and communication, confusion can attend the question of when a resident's status changes from temporary to permanent – as illustrated in an investigation by the local ombudsman (*Humberside CC 1992*).

Temporary residents: respite care

Short breaks (eg, a period of several weeks) in hospital, residential or nursing homes, are known as respite care. Such arrangements for a person cared for is often to give carers a break from caring. When arranged by local authorities (as opposed to the NHS), it can be charged for. If the normal full rate is charged, this can be a very considerable burden on families. However, local authorities have a discretion not to apply the normal statutory means-test but to charge less. As a result, it seems that some authorities do not conduct a means test and instead charge a much lower flat weekly rate (Balloch 1993,p.6). The result can be enormous variation: for example, an Age Concern Scotland survey of Scottish local authorities found charges ranging from £43.45 to £322.00 per week (Thomas 1994,p.18).

5. LESS DEPENDENT RESIDENTS

For people classed as less-dependent residents, authorities are explicitly given the option of not applying the normal charging rules.

EXCERPTS

Legislation states that:

(**disapplying the usual rules**) 'In assessing a less dependent resident's ability to pay for his accommodation, a local authority need not apply [the usual rules] … if they consider it reasonable in the circumstances not to do so' (SI 1992/2977,r.5).

(**definition of less-dependence**) A less dependent resident lives in premises which a) are not registered under the Registered Homes Act 1984, or b) though owned or managed by the local authority, do not provide board.

Board means 'at least some cooked or prepared meals which are both cooked or prepared, by a person other than the resident or a member of his family, and consumed at those premises or in associated premises, if the cost of those meals is accounted for as part of the standard rate for the accommodation at those premises' (SI 1992/2977,r.2).

Guidance (CRAG 1993,paras 2.007,2.010) states that:

'It is recognised that the normal charging rules would not be appropriate for "less dependent" residents because they will usually need to be left with more than the standard personal expenses allowance if they are to live as independently as possible …

It is for the local authority to decide how much of the resident's resources to ignore in working out his or her liability to pay. But factors include necessary commitments (eg, food, fuel, clothing), the extent to which he should be encouraged to take on expenditure commitments, and the importance of an incentive (eg, disregarding his earnings may encourage him to get a job).

Less dependent residents: examples

Examples from community care judicial review cases concerning accommodation for less dependent residents include *R v Bristol CC, ex p Penfold* in relation to arrangements for the provision of 'normal' housing; and *R v Newham LBC, ex p Medical Foundation for the Care of Victims of Torture*, in respect of 'ordinary' or 'bare' accommodation for asylum seekers.

6. ASSESSMENT OF COUPLES

Legislation does not authorise the financial assessment of the joint resources of a couple; and even though spouses have a duty to maintain one another, local authorities are not empowered to apply the statutory means-test under regulations (SI 1992/2977) to ascertain the liability of the spouse of a resident.

EXTRACTS

Legislation states:

(**liability of spouses**) 'For the purposes of this Act … (a) a man shall be liable to maintain his wife and his children, and (b) a woman shall be liable to maintain her husband and her children' (National Assistance Act 1948,s.42).

(rules about payments) Certain rules for assessing 'liable relative payments' (ie, made under s.42 of the 1948 Act) are set out in regulations, governing treatment of either 'periodical' (made at regular intervals) or non-periodical payments (SI 1992/2977,rr.29–34).

Guidance (CRAG 1993) states:

(no joint assessment) Under the National Assistance Act 1948, the local authority may not assess the joint resources of a couple. Each person entering residential care should be assessed individually – although the liability of a married person to maintain their spouse should be taken into account. Thus, in order to be excluded from local authority support because of the level of capital owned, a resident would need to have £16,000 in his or own right, not £16,000 jointly held (paras 4.001,4.003).

(unmarried couples) Liability to maintain under the 1948 Act applies only to husband and wife, and not to unmarried couples (para 11.002).

(assessing a spouse's liability) 'Where it appears to be appropriate to pursue liability, LAs may ask a spouse to refund part or all of the authority's expenditure in providing residential accommodation for his/her husband or wife. LAs should note that this does not mean that an authority can demand that a spouse provide details of his/her resources. LAs should not use assessment forms for the resident which require information about the means of the spouse. LAs should use tact in explaining to residents and spouses the legal liability to maintain and point out that the extent of the liability is best considered in the light of the spouses' resources ... if it is worth pursuing the spouse for maintenance, consider in each case what would be "appropriate" for the spouse to pay ...

This will involve discussion and negotiation with the spouse, and will be determined to a large extent by his/her financial circumstances in relation to his/her expenditure and normal standard of living. In the Department's view, it would not be appropriate, for example, to necessarily expect spouses to reduce their resources to Income Support levels ...

Ultimately, only the courts can decide what is an "appropriate" amount ... the LA should therefore consider whether the amount being sought would be similar to that decided by the courts' (paras 11.005–6).

DISCUSSION

Assessment of couples: liability of spouse

For residents, spouses and local authorities alike, the position is somewhat obscure – since on the one hand, legislation states that spouses do have a liability, but on the other, guidance warns that local authorities cannot demand and force a spouse to provide financial details. Yet somehow, the local authority still has to come to a view of what it might be reasonable for the spouse to contribute. In case of disagreement, the courts would have to be resorted to; but it is not clear what a court might consider to be appropriate in any particular set of circumstances (Age Concern England 1998f,p.10).

In practice, despite the clear statement in guidance that local authorities should not be making joint assessments of spouses, they nevertheless sometimes do so (NCC 1995,p.75). It also appears that individual social workers take very different approaches – ranging from discouraging any full declaration of savings to fully encouraging such disclosure (Wright 1998).

7. ASSESSMENT OF CAPITAL

Resources are assessed in terms of both capital and income. If a resident individually has more than £16,000, then he or she will automatically pay the whole amount due and receive no financial support from the local authority. This means that there is then no call to assess income. Between £10,000 and £16,000, the capital over the figure of £10,000 is taken to produce a (totally unrealistic) weekly tariff income of £1 for every £250. Capital of up to £10,000 is totally disregarded.

Capital includes buildings, land, national savings certificates, premium bonds, stocks and shares, capital held by the Court of Protection or a receiver it has appointed, building society accounts, bank accounts, SAYE schemes, trust funds, Co-operative share accounts, Unit Trusts (CRAG 1993,para 6.002). Income from capital is generally treated as capital (not income), except in the case of certain disregarded capital.

Depending on type, the rules provide for capital to be wholly or partly disregarded or taken into account in full. In addition, residents are sometimes assessed as owning 'notional capital' – for example, where they have disposed of capital in order to reduce or avoid the charges they have to pay.

EXTRACTS

Legislation (and guidance) states:

(more than £16,000) 'No resident shall be assessed as unable to pay for his accommodation at the standard rate if his capital … exceeds £16,000' (SI 1992/2977,r.20).

(between £10,000 and £16,000) 'Where a resident's capital … exceeds £10,000 it shall be treated as equivalent to a weekly income of £1 for each complete £250 in excess of £10,000 but not exceeding £16,000' (SI 1992/2977,r.28).

(valuation of capital) Apart from National Saving Certificates, capital has either a current market or surrender (whichever is highest), less 10 per cent sale expenses and any encumbrances (ie, debts) (SI 1992/2977,r.23).

(jointly held capital) 'Where a resident and one or more other persons are beneficially entitled in possession to any capital asset except any interest in land – (a) they shall be treated as if each of them were entitled in possession to an equal share of the whole beneficial interest in that asset; and (b) that asset shall be treated as if it were actual capital' (SI 1992/2977,r.27).

(notional capital) In some circumstances, a resident may be assessed as possessing capital – even though not actually in possession of it. This is called notional capital and might be capital a) of which the resident has deprived himself or herself in order to decrease the amount payable for the accommodation (see immediately below); b) which would be payable if he or she applied for it (but not a discretionary trust, capital held in trust following payment for personal injury, or a loan which could be raised against capital – eg, the home); or c) which is paid to a third party for the resident (SI 1992/2977,r.25 and CRAG 1993 6.049–6.053).

(deprivation of capital) 'A resident may be treated as possessing actual capital of which he has deprived himself for the purpose of decreasing the amount that he may be liable to pay for his accommodation' (SI 1992/2977,r.25).

Guidance states that avoiding the charge 'need not be the resident's main motive but it must be a significant one'. Furthermore, it would not be reasonable for the authority to identify such deprivation of income if the resident was, at the time of the disposal, 'fit and healthy and could not have foreseen the need for a move to residential accommodation'. The authority can attempt to recover the assessed charge owing from either the resident as normal – or, if the resident cannot pay, then in some circumstances from the third party to whom the asset was transferred (see below) (CRAG 1993,paras 6.064– 6.067).

(diminishing notional capital rule) If notional capital is taken into account, it must be regarded by the local authority as reduced each week by the difference between the (greater) amount the resident has been assessed to pay because of the notional capital, and the (lesser) amount he or she would have paid but for the notional capital (SI 1992/2977,r.26).

(disregarded capital) Certain capital is disregarded indefinitely including property (in some circumstances: see below), surrender value of life insurance policies and annuities, payments in kind from charities, personal possessions (unless bought to reduce the accommodation charge payable), payments from the MacFarlane Trust, the Fund (payments for non-haemophiliacs infected with HIV) or Independent Living Fund, funds held in trust or administered by a court (eg, Court of Protection) following payment for personal injury, Social Fund payments etc.

Other capital is disregarded for up to 26 weeks or more, including the assets of a business owned or part-owned by the resident in which he or she intends to work again; money acquired for replacement of the home or repairs to it – or premises which the resident intends to occupy but to which essential repairs or alterations are needed; premises for which the resident has commenced legal proceedings to obtain possession; the proceeds of the sale of a former home which are to be used to buy another home; money deposited with a housing association and to be used to buy another home; or a grant obtained under housing legislation to buy a home or to repair it, so as to make it habitable.

Still other capital is disregarded for 52 weeks, for example: arrears or compensation in relation to non-payment of a range of state benefits; payments or refunds in relation to the NHS (dental treatment, spectacles and travelling expenses), free milk, vitamins or prison visits.

The assets of a business – owned or part-owned by the resident who is no longer a self-employed worker in it – must be disregarded for a 'reasonable period', so that the resident can dispose of the business assets (SI 1992/2977,schedule 4 and CRAG 1993,section 6).

DISCUSSION

Assessment of capital: rules

For people in need of residential or nursing home accommodation not otherwise available to them (see p.255), local authorities must carry out a financial assessment, the nature of which is determined by legislation and guidance. One rule is that once a person's capital sinks below £16,000, then he or she may be eligible for financial assistance – whereas, above that level, a local authority is precluded from financially contributing to accommodation (though not from making arrangements for the accommodation: see p.256).

Assessment of capital: deprivation of capital

The rules concerning deprivation of capital and the holding of notional capital (see extracts above) are crucial to the potential ability of local authorities to enforce payment of the charges which they have assessed residents should pay. Thus, before any enforcement (see below) is undertaken, a decision has to be taken that deprivation of assets has actually taken place.

However, this decision, and the corollary of informing the local authority finance department, is not always straightforward in practice. For instance, social care practitioners might differ on how to regard disposals of assets by a client; some might be sympathetic to gifts within the family, others simply dismiss them as wilful 'asset stripping'. They might be more sympathetic in relation to gifts of tangible goods – such as a car given by mother to daughter, which might be seen as practically benefiting them both – rather than money. Yet dilemmas might arise even in the case of money; for example, when a daughter reveals that she placed a gift of money from a parent (now in residential accommodation) into a private pension following her divorce and loss of financial security – but the assessing practitioner has likewise just been given money by his own parents to put into his own, inadequate private pension. The practitioner might consider preserving confidentiality on this matter and not report it to his manager or to the finance department; but this might breach his or her own contractual duty as employee (Bradley, Manthorpe 1997,pp.27–44). Practitioners might find it difficult to prove an intent to defraud, and to establish the intention either of relatives or the donor – for example, when a daughter explains that her mother had given her £4,000 because the latter had always wanted her to have the money (Langan, Means 1995,p.44).

In *Yule v South Lanarkshire Council*, the petitioner claimed that the power to take account of notional capital conferred by r.25 of SI 1992/2977 was limited to disposals of assets only up to six months before entry into residential accommodation – a limit deriving from s.21 of the Health and Social Services and Social Security Adjudications Act 1983. However, the court confirmed what had been widely supposed to be the case, that there was no such time limit (the limit of six months applying only when an authority wishes to make liable a third party, to whom assets had been transferred).

8. ASSESSMENT OF PROPERTY

In some circumstances, a resident's property might be disregarded in the assessment of assets, but otherwise it is fully taken account of.

Legislation (and guidance) states that:

(temporary residents) The value of one dwelling of a temporary resident will be disregarded (see above).

(occupation of own home by other people) The value of the resident's home should be disregarded if it is occupied, whether wholly or partly, a) by the resident's partner or former partner (except in case of divorce or estrangement); b) by a relative or member of the family who is at least 60 years old, is under 16 years old and is liable to be maintained by the resident, or is incapacitated – ie, somebody for whom the resident is treated as responsible (SI 1992/2977,schedule 4,para 2, and CRAG para 7.003).

If anybody else is living in the home, local authorities have a discretion to disregard the property, if they 'consider it would be reasonable' (SI 1992/2977,schedule 4,para 18). Guidance suggests that it might be reasonable 'where it is the sole residence of someone who has given up their own home in order to care for the resident, or someone who is an elderly companion of the resident particularly if they have given up their own home'. However, it would be for the authority to decide on a review of any such discretion – for example, when the carer has died or moved out (CRAG, paras 7.007–8).

(intention to occupy) If the resident has acquired a home which he intends to occupy, then it should be disregarded for up to 26 weeks or a longer period if reasonable (SI 1992/2977,schedule 4,para 18, and CRAG 1993, 7.006).

(joint ownership and willing buyer) In the case of land, 'the resident's share shall be valued at an amount equal to the price which his interest in possession would realise if it were sold to a willing buyer (taking into account the likely effect on that price of any incumbrance secured on the whole beneficial interest), less 10 per cent and the amount of any incumbrance secured solely on the resident's share of the whole beneficial interest' (SI 1992/2977,r.27).

DISCUSSION

In *R v Somerset CC, ex p Harcombe*, the local authority exercised its discretion not to disregard the value of the property in a situation where the son of a woman in residential care was occupying her home.

The value of property might only have a nominal value if a co-owner is still living in it, since in reality there will be no market for it: ie, there will be no willing buyer to purchase the resident's interest. In some circumstances the value could therefore be nil (CRAG 1993,para 7.014), since the value hinges on the current, actual market value, and not the value of the resident's share in the whole beneficial interest (*Chief Adjudication Officer v Palfrey*).

There is evidence of people sometimes being given wrong advice by a local authority; for instance, when it tells the son of a resident that he could be taken to court and forced to sell the property he jointly owned with his mother (Age Concern England 1994b,p.25).

9. ASSESSMENT OF INCOME

A payment of income (other than earnings: see below) is generally distinguished from capital on the basis that it is made in relation to a period and is part of a series (regular or irregular) of payments (CRAG 1993,paras 8.001–2). As with capital, income might be wholly or partly disregarded, or taken fully into account. Residents may also be assessed as having notional income if, for example, they have deprived themselves of income in order to reduce the charge payable.

EXTRACTS

Legislation (and guidance) states that income shall be taken into account (r.15).

> **(notional income)** A resident may be treated by the local authority as having notional income, even though he or she does not actually receive it – if it is income a) paid by a third party as a contribution towards the cost of the accommodation; b) which would be available on application; c) due but not yet paid; or d) which the resident has deprived himself or herself 'for the purpose of decreasing the amount that he may be liable to pay for his accommodation' (SI 1992/2977,r.17, and CRAG 1993,paras 8.059–70A).
>
> Guidance states that there 'may have been more than one purpose of the disposal of income only one of which is to avoid a charge, or a lower charge. This may not be the resident's main motive but it must be a significant one'. The authority can then attempt to recover the assessed charge owing from either the resident as normal – or, if the resident cannot pay, from the third party to whom the asset was transferred (see below) (CRAG 1993,paras 8.077–82).
>
> **(earnings)** Earnings consist of payment or profit from employment including, for example, bonus or commission, payment in lieu of notice, holiday pay, payment by way of retainer, expenses payments not 'wholly, exclusively and necessarily incurred in the performance' of employment duties, payments by the employer to an employee who is unable to work through illness or confinement. Various rules govern how earnings are assessed as income (SI 1992/2977, rr.9–20, and CRAG 1993, section 9).

Guidance (referring to the regulations) states:

> **(income fully taken account of)** The following are taken into account in full: most social security benefits, annuity income, child support maintenance payments (if the child is accommodated with the resident under Part 3 of the 1948 Act – ie, mother and baby unit), *ex gratia* incapacity allowances from the Home Office, income from certain disregarded capital (eg, from property or business assets which have been dis-

regarded), insurance policy income, income from certain sub-lets, occupational pensions, income tax refunds, payments made by third parties, trust income, war orphan pension (CRAG 1993,para 8.005).

(income partly disregarded) Partly disregarded (£10 per week) are payments made under German or Austrian law to victims of National Socialist persecution, war disablement pension, war widow's pension and civilian war-injury pension. In addition, various amounts are disregarded from occupational pensions, personal pensions and retirement annuity contract payments; some charitable payments; annuity income from a home income plan; sub-letting income; insurance policies for mortgage protection; income from certain disregarded capital (eg, disregarded might be the element of the income representing mortgage repayments, council tax or water rates). (CRAG 1993,paras 8.021–37, and SI 1992/2977,schedule 3).

(income fully disregarded) Fully disregarded are income support for the home commitments of temporary residents (see above); some charitable and voluntary payments; child support maintenance and child benefit payments (unless the child is living with the resident in accommodation: ie, mother and baby unit); Christmas bonus associated with various benefits including retirement pension; payments from the Macfarlane Trust, Independent Living Fund, Eileen Trust and the Fund, council tax benefit, disability living allowance (mobility component), mobility supplement for war pensioners; dependency increases associated with some benefits; gallantry awards; income in kind or frozen abroad; social fund payments; some payments made to trainees; special payments to war widows; work expenses paid by employer, expenses payments for voluntary workers (CRAG 1993,paras 8.038–56, and SI 1992/2977,schedule 3).

10. RESPONSIBILITY FOR PAYMENT

The ultimate responsibility for paying an independent provider of accommodation is the local authority as a party to the contract – although the resident can make payment direct if this is agreed by the authority, the provider and the resident. Where this is agreed, but the resident fails at some point to make the required payment, the local authority is obliged to pay the shortfall to the provider. Similarly, if by agreement a third party is making up the difference between the cost of the home, and the contribution of the local authority and the resident, it is the local authority which remains contractually responsible for the full amount in case of default.

EXCERPTS

Legislation and guidance (National Assistance Act 1948, s.26(3A) and CRAG 1993, 1.024): the local authority retains ultimate responsibility for ensuring that an independent provider receives the payment due – even where the resident is, by arrangement, paying the home directly. **Circular guidance** (LAC(92)27) states that:

(local authority responsible) local authorities are responsible for the full cost of accommodation. This includes the situation where the accommodation is more expensive than usual and a third party makes up the extra cost. Thus the authority 'must contract to pay the accommodation's fees in full' (para 11.1).

(basic or extra payment direct to home) The liability of the local authority remains, even where an agreement has been made (under NAA 1948,s.26(3A)) for either the basic contribution, or extra costs, to be paid direct by the resident to the provider of the accommodation – and where the resident or third party then defaults on payment. The guidance states also that local authorities 'should assure themselves' that third parties will be able to keep up payments, which should represent the difference between the actual cost of the accommodation and what the authority would normally pay. The calculation should be on gross costs (paras 11.1–11.7).

(change in fees) The guidance explains that a home's fees and the local authority's usual amount of contribution might change. But they might not change at the same rate. Thus, authorities should tell residents and third parties 'that there cannot be a guarantee that any increases in the accommodation's fees will automatically be shared evenly between the authority and the third party should the particular accommodation's fees rise more quickly than the costs the authority would usually expect to pay for similar people' (para 11.8).

(no reliance on third party payments) Local authorities should not 'set an arbitrary ceiling on the amount they are willing to contribute towards residential care and require third parties to routinely make up the difference. If challenged an authority would need to be able to demonstrate that its usual cost was sufficient to allow it to provide people with the level of service they could reasonably expect did the possibility of contributions not exist' (para 10).

DISCUSSION

It is thought that in practice, the use of third party payments can lead to 'widely varying levels of contributions from relatives' (Health Committee 1993,vol.1,p.xxiv). An SSI report (1993d, Summary) found evidence that some authorities were setting too low a 'usual cost', so that most placements in those areas were achieved only by third party contributions: for example, extra payment by relatives. The Department of Health has confirmed that, whilst third party payments are permissible, extra payment by the resident from his or her own resources is not permitted – despite 1992 guidance which stated the opposite (LAC(98)8,para 6, replacing the apparently incorrect para 11.14 in LAC(92)27).

I I. PURSUING THIRD PARTIES

Under the Health and Social Services and Social Security Adjudications Act 1983, local authorities are empowered to pursue money owing to them from a third party to whom the resident transferred assets (see p.312) not more than six months before entry into residential accommodation, with a view to avoiding charges for the accommodation.

EXCERPTS

Legislation (Health and Social Services and Social Security Adjudications Act 1983,s.21) states that:

(assets transferred to third parties) If (a) a person 'avails himself of Part III accommodation; and (b) that person knowingly and with the intention of avoiding charges for the accommodation –

(i)   has transferred any asset to which this section applies to some other person or persons not more than six months before the date on which begins to reside in such accommodation; or

(ii) transfers any such asset to some other person or persons while residing in the accommodation; and

(c) either –

(i)   the consideration for the transfer is less than the value of the asset; or

(ii) there is no consideration for the transfer,

the person or persons to whom the asset is transferred by the person availing himself of the accommodation shall be liable to pay to the local authority providing the accommodation or arranging for its provision the difference between the amount assessed as due to be paid for the accommodation by the person avail-ing himself of it and the amount which the local authority receive from him for it'.

Guidance (CRAG 1993,annex D,para 2.1) states:

'In order for Section 21 [of the 1983 Act] to apply the LA must have decided that the resident has trans-ferred an asset to someone else with the intention of avoiding charges for accommodation. The transfer must have taken place no more than six months before admission to residential accommodation (or six months before resuming occupation in the case of a resident who has been absent from such accommoda-tion). Also, the resident must either have received no consideration for the transfer or any consideration must have been less than the value of the asset'.

In addition, the six-month rule is only triggered where the local authority has assessed the person as need-ing residential accommodation under Part III of the 1948 Act, and has arranged a placement. The rule does not apply if the resident is self-funding in an independent sector home, has not been assessed, and has not had their placement arranged by the local authority. Even if these conditions are met, the rule only applies to assets which would have been taken into account when assessing the charge.

DISCUSSION

A local authority is empowered to take into account assets transferred to a third party within the six months prior to the date when the resident began to live in residential or nursing home accom-modation. However, in order to do this, the authority must have decided that the transfer of assets was with the intention (see discussion of purpose and motive for deprivation of assets: p.304) that local authority charges for accommodation be avoided. The transfer must also have been either for no consideration or for consideration at an under value. The authority could then hold the third party liable to pay the difference between what the resident is actually paying, and what he or she has been assessed to pay.

12. PLACING A CHARGE ON LAND/PROPERTY

If a resident fails to pay assessed charges for accommodation, the local authority is empowered to place a charge on any land or property in which the resident has a beneficial interest. The legisla-tion states that such a charge will only bear interest from the day after the resident dies.

EXTRACTS

Legislation (Health and Social Services and Social Security Adjudications Act 1983) states:

(charge on land) 'where a person who avails himself of Part III accommodation provided by a local au-thority in England, Wales or Scotland –

(a) fails to pay any sum assessed as due to be paid by him for the accommodation; and

(b) has a beneficial interest in land in England and Wales,

the local authority may create a charge in their favour on his interest in the land' (s.22).

(interest on charge) 'Any sum charged on or secured over an interest in land ... shall bear interest from the day after that on which the person for whom the local authority provided the accommodation dies ... The rate of interest shall be such reasonable rate as the Secretary of State may direct or, if no such direction is given, as the local authority may determine' (s.24).

Guidance (CRAG 1993,Annex D,paras 3–4.1) states:

> **(charging interest under other legislation)** The Department of Health believes that because a specific power to create a charge is contained in the 1983 Act, local authorities cannot decide instead to use other general powers contained in s.111 of the Local Government Act 1972 in order to be able to charge interest during the person's lifetime.

DISCUSSION

The discretion to place a charge on a person's property can be used when, for example, a resident is waiting to sell his or her house which has been taken into account in the financial assessment. Unless the property is of low value (eg, less than £16,000), then the person will have been assessed as having to pay the whole cost of the accommodation – but, prior to sale, might be unable to pay anything. In this case, the local authority may place a legal charge on the property, to be determined when the property is sold (at which point the person might also become self-funding until his or her capital has been used up). No interest can accrue unless the person dies, and the Department of Health has warned local authorities that in its view it is not lawful for them to attempt to justify the imposition of interest by using alternative legislation to place the charge. However, there is some concern that local authorities are anyway refusing to place charges on properties, sometimes to people's detriment (see p.295).

13. INSOLVENCY PROCEEDINGS

If local authorities attempt to enforce charges, but the person being pursued has no money, they clearly have a problem. However, they might consider utilising provisions under the Insolvency Act 1986 to enable them to recover assets which are owing – for example, which the resident transferred previously to somebody else.

First, they might take steps (under ss.339–341 of the 1986 Act) to have the resident declared bankrupt, in which case any of the resident's transactions made at an undervalue in the past two years can be set aside (or in the last five years, in the unlikely event that the resident was already insolvent at the time of such a transaction). However, pursuing the debt in this way involves complicated proceedings. Second (under ss.423–425), a gift, no matter how long ago it was made, can be set aside if the court is convinced that the purpose (not necessarily the sole or even the dominant, but at least a substantial, purpose) of the gift was to place the assets beyond the reach of a possible creditor or otherwise prejudice a creditor's interests (ie, to avoid paying residential care charges). It would be for the local authority to establish the purpose of the gift, and although correspondence and file notes between solicitor and client are normally covered by legal professional privilege or confidentiality – there are some circumstances in which a court might order disclosure (based on: Ashton 1995d; Law Society 1995,p.6).

14. INFORMATION FOR THE RESIDENT

Guidance states that residents must be given clear information, usually in writing, about financial assessment.

EXTRACTS

Guidance (CRAG 1993,para 1.015) states that:

> local authorities must ensure that 'the resident is given a clear explanation, usually in writing, of how the assessment of his ability to pay has been carried out. This should explain the usual weekly assessed charge. They should also inform the resident of the reasons why the charge may fluctuate, particularly where a new resident's charge may vary in the first few weeks of admission' – for example, because of particular benefit paydays or the withdrawal of benefits at a certain point.

DISCUSSION

Not applicable.

15. SOCIAL SECURITY BENEFITS AND RESIDENTIAL ACCOMMODATION

Detailed rules govern the availability of a range of social security benefits in residential and nursing home accommodation. The following covers a few basic issues.

EXTRACTS

Guidance states:

> **(disability living allowance (care component), attendance allowance)**. In relation to people placed by local authorities since 1st April 1993, these allowances are not available in accommodation provided directly by the local authority, except for the first four weeks (if already being paid). They are however available in independent sector homes, so long as no financial support is received from the local authority and the resident is not entitled to income support or housing benefit (CRAG 1993, annex E).

> **(income support, housing benefit)** Residents of accommodation managed or provided directly by a local authority are eligible for income support only up to the level of basis State Retirement Pension – unless the accommodation does not include board, in which case normal income support and housing benefit are claimable.
>
> Residents of registered, independent sector homes are entitled to normal income support and a residential allowance – but not to housing benefit. However, if the home is not registered then both Income Support (but no residential allowance) and housing benefit can be claimed (CRAG 1993,annex E).

> **(residential allowance element of income support)** The residential allowance element of Income Support (see immediately above) is available to residents even where assistance with bodily functions is not part of the assistance provided in the accommodation. This means that groups of people such as those with learning disabilities or dependency on drugs or alcohol are not excluded (LAC(98)8,para 7).

DISCUSSION

A number of anomalies affect rules about social security benefits in relation to residential care. First, levels of income support available to residents of local authority homes and independent homes differ, being substantially higher in the latter (because of the special residential allowance).

Second, pending sale of a person's home, a local authority might meet the charges for residential accommodation. However, when the property is sold, the local authority is reimbursed up to the full cost of the charges it has met, and the person then subsequently becomes self-financing – until his or her capital again falls below £16,000. In such circumstances, the person effectually is self-financing from the outset, once the reimbursement has been made. However, he or she is entitled to attendance allowance or disability living allowance only for the first four weeks – and then again only after the property has been sold, the local authority has been reimbursed, and the local authority has ceased to provide assistance. But it is not available for the interim period (DSS 1998). However, although local authorities cannot disregard the value of a property whilst it is being sold, the Department of Social Security does so when it is assessing income support payable to residents – ie, it does not claim it back after the sale (see above p.305).

Third, a loophole in the law means that people who have made their own arrangements for care home accommodation since 1st April 1993 may be eligible for attendance allowance or disability living allowance even if they receive income support: see eg, Disability Alliance 1998,p.187)

16. PERSONAL FINANCIAL ISSUES

Possible or actual need for residential or nursing home accommodation raises various financial issues for people and their families including how to raise capital on their own home, making gifts and transferring assets to avoid possible charges.

EXTRACTS

Not applicable.

DISCUSSION

Personal financial issues: raising capital on a home

A problem faced by some older people is that they have a low income, but live in a relatively valuable property. There are now various options for exploiting the value of the property, whilst allowing the older person to continue living in it. These are, in summary, *home income plans* which entail the owner mortgaging the property for part of its value, and using the proceeds to buy an annuity which provides an income); and *home reversion schemes* which means selling all or part of the home and living in it as a tenant – on death, the provider receives the value of the part of the home sold. There are also various types of loan including ordinary, interest-only and, 'roll-up' (all of the above are explained and evaluated in: Hinton 1997; see also Wilkinson 1997 and Age Concern England 1998e, which emphasise the importance of obtaining advice).

Personal financial issues: making gifts of assets and property

Fearful that they will in effect be forced by local authorities to sell their home in order to pay residential or nursing home fees, some people contemplate making a gift of their home – for example, to close family – so as to put the property out of the reach of the local authority. Recommended by some – for example, in books such as *Residential care: don't let them grab the house* (Heritage 1996) – nevertheless others have pointed out a range of complications, and it is clear that expert advice should be sought by those considering gifts of property or other assets.

The Law Society (1995) has produced brief guidelines on the subject. In summary, these set out the possible benefits of gifts – such as the saving of inheritance tax and of probate fees, and so on; the securing of the family's inheritance because the home does not need to be sold to pay for the residential or nursing home fees; and the fact that the home is not taken into account in means-testing for any other benefits or services. Against this is the following. First, the value of a gifted home might still be taken into account (under various powers given to local authorities in relation to deprivation of assets or under insolvency proceedings. Second, although capital gains tax might not apply on transfer (the owner-occupier rule), there is no 'uplift' to the market value

market value on the eventual death of the resident. Third, people may never require residential or nursing home care, in which case the various risks might outweigh the benefits of the gift. Fourth, if people do need nursing or residential care, but are unhappy with the basic care offered by the local authority (eg, a shared room), they would no longer have the assets to decide to pay for their own care – and so be dependent on relatives for 'topping up' the local authority payments. Fifth, the relatives involved might fail to keep their side of the bargain, deliberately or otherwise. For instance, they might not top up residential care, attempt to move the person into residential or nursing home care prematurely in order to sell or move into the house, themselves die without having made proper provision for the person, or run into financial difficulties and be unable to support the person. The home might be lost due to bankruptcy, divorce or death of the relatives and the person end up homeless. An inheritance tax liability could arise for the person if a relative dies – or the relatives themselves could lose entitlement to certain benefits or services by obtaining an interest in, or owning, a property in which they are not living. When arrangements fail, the considerable complications which can arise have been illustrated in the law courts in cases such as *Cheese v Thomas* and *Baker v Baker* (Martin 1994).

CHAPTER 13

JOINT WORKING, INFORMATION AND PLANNING

Coverage

1. Joint working
2. General information provision
3. Community care planning

KEY POINTS

Joint working and grey areas of provision. Community care legislation places duties on local authorities to consult with other agencies. Both policy and practice guidance also stress the importance of collaboration between agencies, so that service users receive a 'seamless' service. Indeed, the need for collaboration has long been recognised.

Some services occupy 'grey' areas of uncertain responsibility – for example, disability equipment and home adaptations, laundry services, washing, dressing, bathing, lifting, mobility rehabilitation, respite care, long-term nursing care – where it might be unclear whether a service will be provided by the NHS, the local authority social services department or the local authority housing department. At best, grey areas mean that statutory authorities can deliver services flexibly – in such a way that by local agreement or by one-off decisions, they are able to meet people's needs without resorting to destructive 'boundary' disputes about who should be proving what. At worst, they afford excuses to authorities to 'pass the buck' when resources are scarce. Although this might apparently benefit – at least in the short term – the agency which jettisons an unwanted and expensive service, it does of course tend to increase pressure on other agencies, whether statutory or voluntary – quite apart from the detriment suffered by users of services. Service provision for individuals can be delayed, and where, for example, health care is re-defined as social care, what was a free (health) service might suddenly be subject to means-testing and charges by social services.

Information. Information provision is an important issue for users whose needs do not always fall neatly into one statutory service or another but into several. Comprehensive information about different services benefits all concerned: service users, carers and their advisers, as well as providers of services. Thus, voluntary organisations or lawyers would be giving poor advice to people if they were aware of only half the picture. Similarly, service providers can scarcely plan services generally, or make individual care plans, if they are unaware of what services are available and where.

The NHS and Community Care Act 1990 is silent on the provision of information about community care assessment and services, apart from duties to publicise community care plans (s.46) and complaints procedures (amending s.7 of the Local Authority Social Services Act 1970). This omission is made up for by guidance. However, s.1 of the Chronically Sick and Disabled Persons Act 1970 (CSDPA) does place an explicit duty on local authorities to provide information about welfare services for disabled people.

Policy guidance encourages local authorities to publish information about sensitive issues, such as criteria of eligibility which determine who gets a service and who does not. In the past, many local authorities have tended not to publish these criteria; and even if they do, the question remains of how much detail to include.

Planning. Various duties are imposed on local authorities in relation to the drawing up, and consulting about, community care plans.

I. JOINT WORKING

The NHS and Community Care Act 1990 places duties on local social services departments both to consult with other agencies about community care plans and to invite health and housing authorities to participate in individual community care assessments where appropriate. Both policy and practice guidance refers to the importance of a 'seamless' service, to avoid the service fragmentation of the past.

Indeed, a glance at the contents list of a recent House of Commons Health Committee (1998) report on the relationship between social services is instructive: confusion, duplication, fragmentation, lack of information, restricted access to services, fragmented assessments of need, delays in provision of services and equipment, uncoordinated hospital discharges, fragmented ombudsman service, lack of clarity of role and responsibilities, financial barriers, different charging policies, legal barriers, different priorities, lack of geographical coterminosity, different cultures, differences in democratic accountability.

Although central government is proposing further legislative measures to promote joint working (DH 1998b), an array of statutory provision already exists consisting of both powers and duties. This is outlined in the extracts immediately below (see also Parker, Gordon 1998; CVS Consultants and Prince Evans Solicitors 1995) – as are a number of recent initiatives, all of which have implications for joint working, including joint investment plans, health improvment programmes, health action zones, primary care groups, pooled budgets, lead commissioning and transfer of functions between health and social services.

EXTRACTS
Legislation and guidance:

1. NHS Act 1977, s.23: health authority payments to other bodies for providing NHS services.
Section 23 of the NHS Act 1977 enables health authorities to arrange with 'any person or body' – for example, local authorities, nursing homes, voluntary organisations – to 'provide, or assist in providing, any service' under the NHS Act 1977.

This could include the making of payments to the relevant person or body. However, any services provided through such arrangements made by a health authority, are still to be regarded as NHS services. By way of example, Circular guidance makes clear that if such arrangements are used for the provision of nursing home care in an independent nursing home, then the service must be provided free of charge as stipulated by s.1 of the NHS Act 1977. Even 'topping up' by a health authority, to meet the shortfall between a person's entitlement to benefits and the fees of the home, would be unlawful (HSG(95)45,para 3.2). This follows from the case of *White v Chief Adjudication Officer.*

Because the services contracted for under s.23 remain NHS services, they cannot be charged for even though they are actually provided by a non-NHS body.

2. NHS Act 1977, s.28A: health authority payments to other bodies. Section 28A of the NHS Act 1977 enables health authorities to make payments to local social services authorities, local housing authorities, local education authorities, housing associations, voluntary organisations and various other bodies – towards expenditure incurred by any of those bodies in connection with their own functions. A local authority might use the payment in turn to purchase the relevant service from statutory, voluntary or other independent providers; alternatively, in the case of a service to be provided by a voluntary organisation, the health authority may make the payment direct to that organisation (s.28A(9)). However, any payments cannot be made for the provision of health services by any of these bodies – since the payments must be made towards expenditure incurred by those bodies in connection with their own functions.

A health authority may make a s.28A payment if it 'thinks fit' (s.28A), but a) it must be satisfied that the 'payment is likely to secure a more effective use of public funds than the deployment of an equivalent amount on the provision of services under s.3(1) of the Act' (Direction 2(2), HSG(92)43); b) the payment must be recommended by the joint consultative committee (under s.22 of the NHS Act 1977); c) any payment must be in accordance with the directions made by the Secretary of State (which are attached to HSG(92)43); and d) a health authority cannot delegate (eg to an NHS Trust) the power to make such payments (HSG(92)43,para 4.3).

Further detailed rules about the making of such payments is given in Circular guidance HSG(92)43 and the attached directions. A later direction (attached to LASSL(98)2) specifies that for the year 1998/99, 30 per cent of allocated joint finance should be spent on services for people with a mental illness.

(Payments can be used for both residential and non-residential community care services – for example, 'dowry payments' (typically to fund the discharge of patients from NHS long-term care), accommodation provided by housing associations or voluntary organisations, home adaptations, and so on. Unlike contracted services under s.23, services provided by another body using s.28A money could in some circumstances be charged for).

3. Health Services and Public Health Act 1968: grants. A health authority has delegated authority to make a grant (but not a loan) under s.64 of the Health Services and Public Health Act 1968 to a voluntary organisation whose activities involve the provision of a service similar to a service which 'must or may' be provided by the NHS. Such grants cannot be made to local authorities or to for-profit independent providers, and are made on a statutory, not a contractual basis – for the latter, s.23 should be used (HSG(95)45,para 4.6).

Similarly, local authorities have the power to give a grant or a loan to voluntary organisations whose activities involve the provision of a service similar to a service which 'must or may' be secured by a local authority (Health Services and Public Health Act 1968,s.65).

4. NHS Act 1977, s.28(3): local authority staff available to health authority. A local authority has a duty to make available to the local health authority the services of staff employed in connection with its social services functions 'so far as is reasonably necessary and practicable to enable Health Authorities and Special Health Authorities and NHS Trusts to discharge their functions under this Act [ie the the NHS Act 1977] and the National Health Services and Community Care Act 1990' (NHS Act 1977,s.28(3)).

5. NHS Act 1977,s.26(3): NHS services and facilities available to local authorities. Health authorities must make available services and facilities 'so far as is reasonably necessary and practicable to enable local authorities to discharge their functions relating to social services, education and public health'.

6. Mental Health Act 1983,s.117: after-care services. Joint duty to provide after-care services for certain patients (see p.218).

7. Local Authorities (Goods and Services) Act 1970. Local authorities have the power to make agreements for the supply of goods and services with specified public bodies including other local authorities and health authorities (see NHS Act 1977,s.28(1)).

8. Local Government Act 1972, s.113: agreements involving staff. 'Without any prejudice to any power exercisable apart from this section, a local authority may enter into an agreement with a health authority, special authority or NHS Trust (a) for the placing at the disposal of the health authority, special authority or NHS Trust for the purposes of their functions, on such terms as may be provided by the agreement, of the services of officers employed by the local authority; (b) for the placing at the disposal of the local authority for the purposes of their functions, on such terms as may be provided by the agreement, of the services of officers employed by the health authority, special authority or NHS Trust' (s.113(1A)).

'An officer whose services are placed at the disposal of a local authority in pursuance of subsection (1A) of this section shall be treated as an officer of the authority for the purposes of any enactment relating to the discharge of local authorities' functions' (s.113(3)).

This last paragraph allows a social services authority to delegate its functions to an NHS officer – but not a health authority or NHS Trust to delegate its functions to a social services officer.

9. Local Government Act 1972, s.101: delegation of local authority functions. Local authorities have the power to delegate functions to their own officers and committees – but not to anybody else. The Deregulation and Contracting Out Act 1994 would allow contracting out of functions if the Secretary of State were to make an order to that effect. No such orders have been made in relation to community care (but see s.113(1A) of the Local Government Act 1972, immediately above).

10. Children Act 1989, s.27: help. If it appears to a local authority that another authority can help in the exercise of its functions under Part 3 of the Children Act 1989 (in relation to children in need, disabled children, children looked after, other members of the family), it 'may' request help from that authority.

'An authority whose help is so requested shall comply with the request if it is compatible with their own statutory or other duties and obligations and does not unduly prejudice the discharge of any of their functions'. This applies to any other local (social services) authority, housing authority, education authority or health authority.

Every local social services authority 'shall assist any local education authority with the provision of any services for any child within the local authority's area who has special educational needs'.

11. Housing Act 1996,s.213: homelessness. If a local housing authority requests either another housing authority, new town corporation, registered social landlord, housing action trust – or a social services authority – to assist it in discharging its homelessness functions, then the authority or body requested 'shall cooperate in rendering such assistance in the discharge of the functions to which the request relates as is reasonable in the circumstances'.

12. Housing Act 1996,s.170: allocation of housing. 'Where a local authority so request, a registered social landlord shall cooperate to such extent as is reasonable in the circumstances in offering accommodation to people with priority on the authority's housing register'.

13. NHS and Community Care Act 1990, s.47(3): assessment. If it appears to the local authority that there may be a need for NHS or housing services, it must notify the health or housing authority and invite them to assist in the assessment to such extent as is reasonable in the circumstances. In coming to a decision about services, the local authority must take into account any services likely to be made available by the health or housing authority (see p.78).

14. NHS Act 1977, s.22: general cooperation. In the exercise of their respective functions, health authorities and local authorities 'shall cooperate with one another in order to secure and advance the health and welfare of the people of England and Wales'.

15. Anti duplication measures. Local authorities may not provide a) under s.29 of the National Assistance Act 1948 what is required to be provided under the NHS Act 1977; b) under s.45 of the Health Service and Public Health Act 1968 what is authorised or required to be provided under the NHS Act 1977; c) under s.21 of the National Assistance Act 1948 what is authorised or required to be provided under the NHS Act 1977.

16. Pooled budgets, lead commissioning, transfer of functions. In September 1998, the Department of Health issued a discussion document on joint working which put forward, in particular, three proposals which it would support with new legislation.

Pooled budgets. At present, the creation of multi-disciplinary, multi-agency teams resulted in integration of practitioners, but budgetary and administrative arrangements had to remain separate. New legislation would allow a health authority or primary care trust to delegate functions and finance to the pool – although such pooled budgets would 'still not absolve health and social services authorities from their statutory responsibilities for service delivery but provide a new way to discharge them'. A joint strategic plan would be required, based on joint investment plans (DH 1998b,pp.20–22).

Lead commissioning. This would involve one authority (health or social services) taking the lead on commissioning services for a particular client or patient group. One authority would delegate its functions and transfer funding to the other, leading to a single budget, and a holistic and better coordinated approach to care. The delegating authority would retain accountability for its functions, and so would need to be confident that the full range of delegated functions was being carried out satisfactorily (DH 1998b,p.26).

Integrated provision. This could be brought about by legislation which would allow NHS and primary care trusts to provide some social care services (currently only possible through use of income generation powers, which bring with them certain restrictions); and allow 'social services inhouse providers to provide a range of community health services (for example, chiropody or physiotherapy)'. To 'ensure probity, contestibility and best value for money this flexibility would be subject to indentifaction' in health improvement programmes and joint investment plans (see below) (DH 1998b,p.28).

17. Health action zones (HAZs). Bids can be made for funding for health action zones – which will provide a framework for the NHS, local authorities and other partners to tackle the causes of ill health and to reduce health inequalities. The effectivenes, efficiency and responsiveness of services should be increased by addressing various matters including 'intermediate care and rehabilitation', the 'balance between primary and community care and specialist services', joint working between health and local government – and so on (EL(97)65).

18. Joint investment plans (JIPs). As part of continuing care and community care services for vulnerable people, health authorities and local authorities have been asked to work together to agree local joint investment plans, drawing from existing purchasing and community care plans. Such plans will include joint analysis of local population needs, current resources and investment and agree service outcomes – and identify gaps in the provision of services and both present and future commissioning priorities (EL(97)62).

19. Health improvement programmes (HImPs). Health authorities must prepare local health improvement programmes in collaboration with primary care groups, NHS Trusts and local authorities – including the completion of joint investment plans (see above). One of the overall aims is to 'bring together the local NHS with local authorities and others, including the voluntary sector, to set the strategic framework for improving health, tackling inequalities, and developing faster, more convenient services of a consistently high standard'.

In relation to local authorities, the guidance goes on to explain that 'this represents an opportunity to engage in health improvement in its broadest sense – complementing their proposed new duty to promote the economic, social and environmental wellbeing of their areas and their proposed community planning responsibilities. This will engage the local authority corporately, since action on the determination of health will span the range of local authority responsibilities: for example, housing, transport, education, environment, leisure' (HSC 1998/167).

20. Primary care groups (PCGs). Primary care groups, a new development in the NHS (created by Directions by the Secretary of State as to the establisment of primary care groups: see HSC 1998/230), led primarily by general practitioners and community nurses have, overall, the role of improving the health of the community, developing primary and community health services, and commissioning secondary care services. Amongst various functions, they should build relationships with local authority social services departments to allow the development of joint commissioning (through joint investment plans) and integrated provision of services as appropriate (HSC 1998/228,pp.3–6).

Their health improvement role might include, for example, focusing on those in greatest need (eg, working with local authorities and other agencies to help people with drug and alchohol problems), working with the local housing authority to reduce falls for elderly people, making services more responsive for vulnerable groups such as elderly people and so on) (HSC 1998/228,p.9).

Primary care group boards should include a social services officer – although if a group covers more than one local authority, there can apparently be only one officer and the authorities would have to agree which will supply the officer (LAC(98)21,para 21).

Policy guidance (DH 1990) refers to the importance of a 'seamless' service (para 2.3) and collaboration between agencies (para 3.32):

'At an early stage they should draw up joint resource inventories and analyses of need which enable them to reach agreement on the key issues of "who does what", for whom, when, at what cost and who pays' (DH 1990, para 2.11). 'Care should be taken that individuals are not repeatedly referred from one agency to another' (para 3.34).

Practice guidance (SSI,SWSG 1991b) states that:

(seamless service) 'providing a seamless service to users and carers, is one of the fundamental objectives of the NHS and Community Care Act 1990'. Agreements between agencies should include statements about the responsibilities of each agency. It goes on to list not only health and housing authorities in general amongst collaborating agencies, but specifically: general practitioners, community nurses, therapists – as well as employment, leisure, criminal justice, independent sector and advocacy services (pp.81–99).

(grey areas) contains 'indicative advice' on the 'division between health and social care'. Significantly, many of the items listed fall into the category of being 'either' health or social care. For example, disability equipment, incontinence laundry, washing, dressing, bathing, lifting, mobility rehabilitation, medicine application, learning disability behavioural management, mental health promotion and rehabilitation, drug/alcohol misuse counselling and HIV/AIDS rehabilitation (p.86).

Circular guidance (EL(93)18,para 17) stated that:

(avoidance of delay for service users) 'provision of proper care should not be delayed pending resolution of a dispute over responsibilities ... recourse to formal dispute arrangements should be regarded as a rare and serious event. The aim should be to ensure that disputes are resolved at the lowest possible level'.

(continuing care) 'In implementing the new community care arrangements health and local authorities have been required to make agreements for hospital discharge. These agreements should continue to form the basis for local collaboration ... Where either health or local authorities are proposing a significant change in the pattern of services which will impact on the resources of other agencies for providing care, they must seek the agreement of the other agency' (HSG(95)8,p.12).

DISCUSSION

Joint working: background

The exhortation of central government that different statutory agencies should work together has an almost timeless quality about it.

For instance, 1971 Circular guidance about services for elderly people could have been written yesterday: 'In practical terms the ability to provide a wide range of services in the domiciliary field will require the closest cooperation between those who are responsible for the various elements that make up the community health and social services ... no individual service or group of services can be considered in isolation and planning of overall improvements will require the fullest consultation and exchange of views and information between those closely concerned with services for the elderly...' (DHSS 19/71,para 7). Similarly, a 1981 White Paper on *Growing older* talked of the need for public authorities to work together to achieve effective collaboration and reduce the overlapping and duplication of services (Secretaries of State 1981,para 9.14).

The fact that the same message is repeated year after year suggests that its effect in the real world is sometimes limited. The Court of Appeal recently commented that government guidance to local authorities to deliver a 'seamless service' was the 'sort of prose which comes easily to ministerial advisers at department headquarters' but fares badly when confronted with the reality facing local authorities (*R v Lambeth, ex p A*). Perhaps realising this, a 1997 government White Paper referred to possible legislative change in order to bring about better cooperation between agencies (Secretary of State 1997b,p.79). This was followed in September 1998 by a consultation paper which suggested that the solution for joint working between social services lies in genuinely pooled budgets, lead commissioning or integrated provision (the last of these options could involve some social care services coming under the NHS, and some health care services under social services). Legislative change will be required to bring about these changes, although it is not envisaged that any new powers will be enabling rather than mandatory (DH 1998b,pp.19,28).

Solutions to enable joint working typically refer to matters such as clarifying relationships, building trust, developing understanding, recognising mutual compatibility, developing resources (Arblaster *et al.* 1998), partnership, sharing, cooperation, collaboration, coordination, networks (Means *et al.* 1997). Undoubtedly representing common sense, alone they indicate what joint working consists of, though not necessarily how to achieve it.

Joint working: joint finance

The extracts above summarise various legislation and guidance in relation to joint working and joint finance.

In practice, joint finance has in the past been used for both residential and non-residential community care services: for example, community and primary care centres run by both health and social care staff, resettling people from long stay hospitals (including 'dowry' payments), installing central heating to prevent people having to go into residential care, on local 'care and repair' schemes, joint night-sitting services, quick-response respite care via a voluntary organisation (DH 1995d,Chapter 6).

Joint working: passing the buck and cost-shunting

Examples from the law courts illustrate how cost-shunting occurs, sometimes between local agencies (eg, between local authorities and health authorities), sometimes between local and central government. On a general level, the introduction of mainstream community care in April 1993 represented a massive cost-shunting exercise, by transferring responsibility for financing residential and nursing home accommodation from an open-ended central government budget to finite local authority budgets. More specifically, cases such as *Chief Adjudication Officer v Quinn* and *Steane v Chief Adjudication Officer* represent the fallout – central government and local government arguing about financial responsibility for certain classes of resident. In a slightly different context, the case of *R v Swansea City and County Council, ex p Littler* was about whether housing benefit could be used to pay for certain counselling or other support services. The court decided they could not – with the inevitable implication (subject to a government review) that the financial burden for such services would inevitably fall elsewhere (see generally, Richards 1997). Another illustration of cost-shunting is afforded by the local authority which launches a 'benefits take-up campaign' to enable service users in its area to claim up to £3 million in central government benefits previously unclaimed – some of which it will reclaim for itself when it implements its own new policy on charging those very same people for non-residential services (*Community Care* 1998b). Housing cases sometimes illustrate how people are batted to and fro between authorities like a shuttlecock *(R v Harrow LBC, ex p Carter)*. And in *R v Northavon DC, ex p Smith*, when a housing authority had refused to assist with housing a family – having been asked for assistance by the social services authority under s.27 of the Children Act 1989 – the House of Lords declined to interfere, stating that judicial review was not the way to obtain cooperation between authorities.

Though not directly in the domain of adult community care, special education cases sometimes illustrate shifting responsibilities between local authorities and the NHS – consider for example, disputes about occupational therapy, physiotherapy and speech and language therapy (eg, the linked cases: *R v Brent and Harrow HA, ex p Harrow LBC; R v Harrow LBC, ex p M*) or about speech and language therapy alone (*R v Lancashire CC, ex p M; R v Oxfordshire CC, ex p W*). Social services and housing departments might not communicate well across authorities to the extent that the lo-cal ombudsman finds a 'sorry tale of confusion' (*Durham CC 1993*).

Typically, authorities might not look too closely at whether legislation empowers them to pro-vide a particular service when there is no problem with funding it; however, when funds run low, the legal basis for a service might suddenly, though belatedly, be questioned, when an authority wishes to cease provision – for example, as occurred in a local ombudsman investigation about provision and withdrawal of psychotherapy by a social services department (*Brent LBC 1994*).

Joint working: fragmentation of services

Fragmented service provision has long been recognised. For example, community care practice guidance states: 'In 1986, the Audit Commission report *Making a reality of community care* showed that, while there had been some progress in developing co-operation between community care agencies, much remained to be done. Services were still experienced by users as fragmented, unco-ordinated and wasteful in their use of resources' (SSI,SWSG 1991b,p.81).

Obstacles consisting of different priorities, organisational styles and cultures can lead to differ-ent agencies holding 'uncomplimentary opinions of each other and a reluctance to work coopera-tively' (Audit Commission 1992,p.2). Strained relations, misunderstandings, hostility (SSI/NHSE 1994j,p.25) or antipathy (Audit Commission,SSI 1998b,p.9). The range of services needed by dis-abled people might lead to formidable organisational problems, with the overall fragmentation of such services leading predictably to gaps and overlaps (NAHAT 1991b,p.125; NAO 1992,p.2). Early reporting on community care had pointed out that the 'old problems' of divided responsibil-ities could threaten the new system (SSI/NHSME 1994k,p.27).

Even when a person is receiving a high level of services, they might be organised in a frag-mented fashion: for instance, 17 home care visits each week involving seven different home care workers, four district nurses visiting twice daily, and three different day care settings (SSI 1996d,p.17).

Joint working: demarcation of responsibilities

Community care practice guidance (SSI,SWSG 1991b) states that to achieve clear agreements, a 'considerable amount of negotiation may be required' (p.84). The guidance declines to 'define a rigid demarcation between health and social care; the interface between the two is for local discus-sion and agreement'. It warns against 'sterile debates or rigid demarcation' (p.85).

Audit Commission evidence to the House of Commons Health Committee (1993,vol.1,p.xvii) pointed out that even if the boundaries of health and social care could be agreed in principle, 'funding arrangements between authorities do not always match those agreements'. One reason for this is the existence of 'perverse incentives'. For example, since April 1993, residential and nursing home care is contracted for by social services, with people paying more or less of a contri-bution depending on their means. But nursing services for people in their own homes are provided by the NHS and must be free of charge (NHS Act 1977,s.1). Thus 'there is a disincentive for the health authorities to see people placed in the community' (vol.2,p.7) (or indeed to provide NHS inpatient care – since health authorities are prohibited by law from charging for either community or acute services: see p.353).

A specific example given to the Committee involved 'a young woman, a teenager, with multiple handicaps. The health authority are saying ... that this person has very great care needs, but does not have medical needs and therefore it is the social services' responsibility; the social services are saying this person needs round the clock nursing care. For 14 months this child has been in an assessment bed, blocking it for everybody else because neither side will say it is their responsibility' (vol.2,p.39).

The advice in practice guidance (see extract above) about the division between health and social care was itself based on another study (NAHAT 1991a), which referred to a 'swathe of "grey area"' (p.14). The introduction noted that in the 'widest sense, health and social care are difficult to differentiate. The nurse who enters the client's home to treat a leg ulcer is performing health care; but by her or his personal contact with the client, is also conducting an important social function. Equally, many aspects of social care, (if not all) such as house and personal cleanliness, poverty (possibly because of non claiming of benefits), or social life (reduction of stress) have important health or ill health sequelae' (p.5). Some might say that in this large grey area, the difference between health and social care can be detected only in terms of finance: NHS services are generally free of charge, whereas social care is not (Clark 1998,p.40).

Typically, bathing has fallen into the grey area between health and social care – sometimes resulting in non-provision. For instance, a person's mother with mental health problems and who is incontinent might be deemed not to need a medical bath, but be told that social services does not provide a bathing service; her son would then have to find private help. A woman who has had a stroke might be unable bath herself; she is sometimes incontinent, her husband is unable to help her but she is not considered to need a medical bath. As a result she cannot have a bath at all (Age Concern England (1994b,p.41). Local authorities might sometimes simply state that bathing is not their responsibility (*Kirklees MBC 1993*). A case cited by the Carers' National Association further illustrates the point. A woman had a district nurse coming in to bath her husband who had Parkinson's Disease. When the nurse ceased to visit, social services provided a care attendant who was, however, instructed not to carry out 'any intimate personal tasks'. The problem was resolved only because the care attendant ignored the instruction (House of Commons Health Committee (1993),vol.2,p.168). Moreover, it might not just be service users who become confused about the definition of what constitutes a medical as opposed to a social bath; so too might professionals, with the consequence that district nurses take different approaches and might be labelled 'soft' or 'hard' depending on how strictly they apply eligibility criteria (Griffiths 1998).

Changes to bathing (and other) services have brought with them a variety of problems including the way in which those changes are managed, the imposition of charges by social services, the feelings of clients about home carers (as opposed to nurses) providing intimate personal care, and concern that home carers will not detect early signs of deterioration in a person's condition (Henwood 1994,p.15). For instance, responsibility for assisting with catheter and stoma care, both highly personal matters, might fall between personal care and nursing care (SSI 1996d,p.8). Reaction rather than anticipation by social services departments of changes in NHS services, might lead to confusion and uncertainty about where services are coming from (if anywhere) and indicate the financial reluctance of social services to take on yet more responsibility (Collyer, Hanson-Kahn 1990,p.8).

The Department of Health has summed up the situation by conceding that: 'All too often when people have complex needs spanning both health and social care, good quality services are sacrificed for sterile arguments about boundaries. When this happens people, often the most vulnerable in our society – the frail elderly, the mentally ill – and those who care for them find themselves in no man's land between health and social services. This is not what people want or need. It places the needs of the organisation above the needs of the people they are there to serve. It is poor organisation, poor practice, poor use of taxpayers' money – it is unacceptable' (DH 1998b,p.3).

Joint working: pooling of finances

The pooling of resources from different statutory agencies, to the extent that 'the origin of that money in terms of its respective authorities is virtually lost', might begin to overcome some of the problems. The money can be used to meet immediate individual needs: debate about whether it was health or social need can take place later. Joint 'contingency' funds are another possibility (Henwood 1994,p.30).

However, even given local 'joint working and shared values', it has been recognised 'that if finances are very, very difficult there might be a temptation for the various parties to retreat, as it were, into their financial corners' (evidence to the House of Commons Health Committee 1993,vol.2,p.60) – hence the warning of Circular guidance in the past against 'unilateral withdrawal' (EL(93)18). For example, attempts have been made over the years to rationalise disability equipment provision by creating joint health and social services stores. Such stores are regarded as generally representative of good practice (DH 1992a,p.9), but they do not necessarily overcome all the problems since budget contributions might remain distinct and subject to dispute.

Even when there is every incentive genuinely to pool resources and 'jointly commission' services, awkward questions might arise including the legal status of the money and the danger of entering into agreements which are ultra vires – ie, unlawful. For example: 'How much should each authority put in the pool? Who is to be held accountable for it? What is the role of democratically elected councillors – is the money being removed from democratic control? What are the limits of legality of such schemes? Local authorities cannot purchase health care – but can pooled budgets be used to purchase health care? How are disputes to be resolved?' (House of Commons Health Committee 1993,vol.1,pp.xxxviii–xxxix. Also: vol.2,p.2).

With such problems in mind, the Department of Health proposed (September 1998) new legislation to enable pooled money genuinely to lose its original NHS or social services identity, and to remove legal obstacles to the exercising by the NHS and by local authority social services departments, of each other's statutory functions (DH 1998b,p.21).

Joint working: within the same statutory authority

Much of the debate around joint working focuses on cooperation between different statutory authorities – for example, between a health authority and a local authority, or between two local authorities.

When legislation is drafted and approved it is normally assumed to be on the basis that a local authority cannot consult with itself (although for conflicting conclusions on this principle, see *G v*

Wakefield MDC and *R v Tower Hamlets, ex p B*). So, for example, the Housing Grants, Construction and Regeneration Act 1996 (s.24) stipulates consultation only between housing and social services authorities where they are different authorities. The assumption is that departments within the same authority should anyway be working closely. However, such an assumption is far from always warranted as the local ombudsman sometimes finds when identifying maladministration (*Camden LBC 1993*). Indeed, failures might occur at a very basic level; for instance, when a message from a social worker to a housing officer is never received and service provision is delayed (*Rotherham MBC 1995*); or when a bathroom adaptation falls victim for 16 months to 'complete breakdown' of communication between social services and housing departments, instead of being resolved in a matter of days (*Wirral MBC 1993e*). In another investigation, one group of council officers trying to help a family with its housing problems, but being 'rendered helpless' by another group following its own set of policies, contributed to an 'appalling catalogue of neglect' by a council (*Bristol CC 1998*). And a failure in liaison between occupational therapist and technical officer, resulting in recommendations being left off the schedule of works, was maladministration (*Liverpool CC 1996/1997*).

Within the same department of a local authority, joint working might be less than adequate. For instance, it has long been recognised that occupational therapists in some social services departments operate to greater or lesser extent in isolation from social workers (eg, SSI 1993a,p.19). Alternatively, communication between the social services departments of two different authorities might be poor – for instance, where social workers from one local authority are assessing hospital patients for discharge back into the area of another authority (Joule 1994,p.20). Even where a local authority decides to combine its social services and housing departments, in order to avoid the 'territorialism' of senior staff which can adversely affect the public, the potential benefits do not flow automatically (SSI 1997h,p.1).

Joint working and grey areas: anti-duplication

Certain 'anti-duplication' provisions appear in community care legislation. For example, a local authority is prohibited from providing under s.29 of the National Assistance Act 1948 what is 'required' to be provided under the NHS Act 1977 – or from providing under s.21(8) of the National Assistance Act 1948 and under s.45 of the Health Services and Public Health Act 1968 what is 'authorised or required' to be provided under the NHS Act 1977. (Similarly, for example, there are anti-duplication measures in the Social Fund rules in respect of medical items (because they will be provided by the NHS); and items provided by local authorities are also excluded from consideration for Social Fund community care grants).

There is a lack of clarity about the implications of these provisions; for instance, do the prohibitions under the National Assistance Act 1948 refer only to what local social services authorities might provide under the NHS Act 1977 (a narrow interpretation), or also to what health authorities and NHS Trusts might provide (a much broader interpretation and, in the author's view, the correct one)?

Such anti-duplication provisions clearly have a commonsense basis but can in practice raise awkward problems. Take, for instance, incontinence pads. It is clear that the NHS is at least empowered and – in a general sense at least (see p.345) – obliged to provide them. But when consideration is given as to whether there is a requirement to provide, should the question be asked in principle, or with regard to local practice? Given the wide discretion possessed by health authorities, and disparities in policies and provision from locality to locality (and even in the same locality over time), this might be a difficult question to answer. For instance, in relation to a particular person in need, does the local health authority a) provide pads generally to certain classes of patient; and b) will it provide them for this person at this time?

In *R v Social Fund Inspector, ex p Connick*, the local health authority did supply pads generally – but the particular applicant did not qualify in practice, because she failed to meet the eligibility criteria of terminal illness or regular, double incontinence. The High Court found a way around the difficulty, by ruling that incontinence pads were not necessarily medical items and that therefore the Social Fund was not precluded, in certain circumstances, from assisting. On the same basis, the Social Fund sometimes helps with electric wheelchairs (normally the statutory responsibility of the NHS) (IRS 1995,pp.73–77). Also suggestive of fluid statutory boundaries was the local ombudsman's doubt in one investigation, about whether the local authority social services department simply had no responsibility for the provision of electric wheelchairs under s.2 of the Chronically Sick and Disabled Persons Act 1970 (*North Yorkshire CC 1993*).

In *R v Islington MBC, ex p McMillan*, the unsatisfactory nature (even on the narrow interpretation) of the exclusion in s.29 of the National Assistance Act 1948 was demonstrated when the local authority argued that because it had a general duty to provide home help under the NHS Act 1977 (schedule 8) it could not provide it under s.2 of the CSDPA 1970 (which comes under the umbrella of s.29 of the 1948 Act) and so no duty arose under the 1970 Act – even though it was not actually providing the home help under the 1977 Act. The court found a way out of this highly negative argument, but in a manner not entirely consonant with a later Court of Appeal decision about the relationship between the 1948 and 1970 Acts *R v Powys CC, ex p Hambidge*).

2. GENERAL INFORMATION PROVISION

For obvious reasons, the provision of information is crucial if people are to be able sensibly to request assessments and service provision, and to choose or suggest themselves what might be of most assistance. The provision of a reasonable quality of information would appear to be requisite if people are to participate in their assessments and drawing up of care plans.

EXTRACTS

Legislation (NHS and Community Care Act 1990) is silent about community care information provision (other than in relation to community care plans and complaints procedures).

Legislation (Chronically Sick and Disabled Persons Act 1970,s.1) states:

'Every ... local authority ... shall cause to be published from time to time at such times and in such manner as they consider appropriate general information as to the services provided under arrangements made by the authority under the said s.29 [of the National Assistance Act 1948] which are for the time being available in their area'.

Policy guidance (DH 1990) states that:

(**accessible to all service users**) local authorities 'will need to have in place published information accessible to all potential service users and carers, including those with any communication difficulty or difference in language or culture, setting out the types of community care services available, the criteria for provision of services, the assessment procedures to agree needs and ways of addressing them and the standards by which the care management system (including assessment) will be measured' (para 3.56).

(choice and participation) local authorities 'should publish readily accessible information about their care services' so as to 'enable users and carers to exercise genuine choice and participate in the assessment of their care needs and in the making of the arrangements for meeting these needs' (para 3.18).

(eligibility criteria) Published information should include 'the authority's criteria for determining when services should be provided and the assessment procedures' (para 3.18).

(other service providers) Information should be 'compiled in consultation with health and housing authorities and other service providers. The information should cover residential care homes, nursing homes and other community care facilities' (para 3.18).

Practice guidance states that:

(empowerment) 'empowering users and carers, enabling them not only to make choices about the services they receive but also to be more in control of the process through which they gain access to services' (SSI,SWSG 1991a,p.31).

(increased demand for services) 'Because information is seen as one of the most effective ways of empowering users and carers, agencies should give this aspect of their work a high priority. It is recognised that this will generate increased demand but it is preferable that services should be allocated on the basis of known need rather than being rationed on the basis of public ignorance. This does mean, however, that the information should frame realistic expectations in the minds of potential users and spell out the priorities which will govern the response they receive' (SSI,SWSG 1991b,p.42).

(what can and cannot be provided) Local authorities should explain to people 'what your department can and cannot provide' (SSI 1991f,p.10).

(targeting) 'Above all, any information strategy should be targeted on those most likely to require the services, particularly those in need who do not tend to seek help' (SSI,SWSG 1991b,p.42);

(reaching users and carers) 'It is the responsibility of the practitioner to ensure that this published information reaches potential users and carers who are considering seeking assistance' (SSI,SWSG 1991a,p.31).

(different forms of information) 'This information should be presented in a readily accessible form that takes account of potential users who have:

- a language other than English;
- a different cultural background;
- a sensory impairment;
- a communication difficulty (illiteracy or learning disability).

Subject to the availability of resources and departmental priorities, experimentation with media other than the written word, for example, videos or audio cassettes should be encouraged' (SSI,SWSG 1991a,p.32).

(staff: where to find information) 'The information strategy should also address the needs of staff. There is no substitute for an informed workforce able to relate information to needs and provide the right amount of information, in the right way, at the right time. It may not be feasible for all staff to be regularly updated but they should all know where they can obtain the information they need' (SSI,SWSG 1991b,p.42).

(staff: in-depth knowledge) 'The priority requirement for assessment staff will be an in-depth under-standing of the needs associated with particular user groups and a knowledge of the range of services and community resources available to meet those needs' (SSI,SWSG 1991b,p.45).

(staff: at all levels) 'Staff at all levels require this information if they are to give a good quality service to people' (SSI 1991f,p.10); whilst reception staff 'must know the types of services available, how they are ac-cessed and the likely response times for assessment' (SSI,SWSG 1991a, p.37).

Circular guidance (EL(93)22) stated:

(staff: NHS) Health authority managers 'should satisfy themselves' that health service staff know about community care policy and objectives; and that staff, particularly medical and nursing, are told about local community care arrangements. It stated also that staff directly involved in community care should be fully briefed and appropriately trained, and that health service managers should work closely with local authori-ties in planning communications.

Circular guidance (DHSS 45/71 now presumed cancelled) explained what the nature of such publicity (under the Chronically Sick and Disabled Persons Act 1970) might be:

(CSDPA 1970: encouragement to people) 'The authority's publicity must be designed to encourage handicapped people themselves to come forward and seek services and hence facilitate the gradual build-ing up of comprehensive lists of people needing help. Authorities should try to ensure that their publicity reaches those most in need of help and encourage them to seek it. To achieve this there is a need for public-ity of a variety of kinds from a wide range of sources' (para 21).

(CSDPA 1970: media and methods) 'Authorities will, for example, need the cooperation of local news-papers and radio stations in making their services known and in supplementing their own leaflets and printed guides. They will also have in mind the help voluntary agencies can give in publicising services. Some authorities already avail themselves of the arrangement whereby local offices of the DHSS will en-close publicity material of this kind with notices of the award of retirement pensions. General practitioners will also be able to help here particularly as local authority staff are increasingly working in association with practices ... Chemists may also be able to assist...' (para 21).

DISCUSSION

General information: extent of duty to provide

There are a number of uncertainties surrounding information provision: for example, taking the words of the policy guidance literally, it seems a very ambitious task to make information accessi-ble to 'all' potential users. Furthermore, even if it is accessible to all, it does not follow necessarily that information *alone* empowers people; for instance, it is difficult to produce reliable and effective information describing an unreliable and unpredictable system. In addition, the empowerment that comes from being told about why one is excluded from services is likely to be limited.

General information: legal benefit

Exactly what benefits generally published (as opposed to individually-given) information confers on particular individuals in legal terms is difficult to say. For example, information might give a chance to people to decide whether they want or need services; a chance to decide whether they will approach an authority; and a chance that they will actually qualify and might eventually re-ceive (an unknown type and quantity of service). The benefits of such generally published infor-mation might be difficult for the courts to measure, especially in terms of any remedies. Except in extreme circumstances, possibly where it could be shown that an authority provided no publicity at all, it would probably be difficult to challenge an authority about how it performs this duty.

Furthermore, where legislation imposes a general duty to make available or to publish information without further specification, it might be difficult to show that the form in which it has been published is legally inadequate (*R v Bradford MCB, ex p Sikander Ali*).

General information: welfare services for disabled people

Local authorities have a duty under the Chronically Sick and Disabled Persons Act 1970 (s.1) to publish information about welfare services for disabled people. Given that many potential users of community care services are likely to be disabled, this duty to provide information about welfare services would appear central to community care. Yet, despite the longstanding nature of the duty, information has not always been available (Adams 1996,p.40). As a result, disabled people, for example, might not benefit from services and suffer difficulties or hardship (see eg, NAO 1992,p.2).

General information: effectiveness

Producing effective information provision about community care might be a substantial task. Thus, 'an authority can provide good readable and accessible material and yet this can have very little beneficial impact on users and carers'; and 'the users and carers we spoke to were not more empowered as a result of information provision; the majority did not understand how the system has changed and what this means for them' (KPMG 1993,pp.8,15). Similarly, leaflets translated into a number of different community languages might be of little use if they are not based on efforts by a local authority to establish the most effective way of communicating with ethnic minority older people (SSI 1998f,p.343).

In any case information does not necessarily deliver choice for all: for example, for people who are not capable of choice, such as mentally ill people or people with learning difficulties (Roberts, Steele and Moore 1991, p.123). Where service users do not receive information about assessments either before or during assessment visits (SSI 1994a,p.12), then clearly choice and 'user empowerment' are likely to be impaired.

Guidance states that the question that practitioners should ask themselves is: 'does the information give the public a clear understanding of their entitlements to service provision?' (SSI,SWSG 1991a,p.9,35). Other SSI (1991f) practice guidance declares in its title the necessity for clarity: *Getting the message across*. Local authorities should: 'ensure that people have information that is straightforward, relevant, accurate and sufficient so that they can make informed choices' (p.11). It reminds authorities that jargon needs to be avoided and gives (p.20) examples of words which it found were misunderstood by service users. These included (mistaken meaning in brackets) advocacy (was associated with going to court), agencies (second hand clothes shops), allocation process (being offered re-housing), common (cheap and nasty), criteria (unknown to most), eligibility (good marriage catch), equitable manner (unknown to most), format (for wiping feet at the front door), gender (unknown to most), maintain (confused with divorce maintenance settlements), networks (unknown to most), sensitive (tender and sore), voluntary agencies (people with no experience, volunteers).

Jargon, allied with brevity, can make for poor information; whilst out-of-date or undated information is unhelpful (see variously Berry 1990,pp.5,18; KPMG 1993,pp.27–29; Steele *et al.* 1993,part 3,p.44).

General information: expectations, eligibility, publicity

Eligibility (who can get services – and who can't) is a sensitive issue. The existence of clear information might result in rationing openly by need; its absence in rationing covertly by ignorance (see eg, Steele *et al.* 1993,Part 1,p.12; KPMG 1993,p.39; Berry 1990,p.18). Practitioners might 'feel that no good purpose is served by informing a client about services for which that particular client would not be eligible' (Roberts, Steele and Moore 1991,p.123).

Sometimes criteria might not exist; in which case they cannot be published. For example, a Royal Association for Disability and Rehabilitation project (Keep, Clarkson 1993) on the CSDPA 1970 reported a request made in May 1992, assessed within a few days but finally turned down in August. Eligibility criteria for 1992/1993 were neither published nor otherwise known to the applicant or assessor (p.25). Similarly, a local ombudsman investigation, about provision of holidays for disabled people under the CSDPA 1970, found no criteria determining how the £800 budget was to be allocated (*North Yorkshire CC 1993*). Alternatively, information might simply omit reference to eligibility criteria, charging policies (SSI 1996d,p.3; SSI 1996e,p.10) or waiting times (Adams 1996,p.40).

Detailed statements of eligibility might create a straitjacket, preventing local authorities from considering special individual needs or taking account of resources during the year – and not be read by service users (Steele *et al.* 1993,Part.3,p.42). On the other hand, broad statements might be meaningless. For example: "'MEDIUM NEED. For people whose assessed needs falls within High and Medium eligibility, although NOT qualifying because by law the council has discretion, we will seek to provide a level of service depending on whether we have sufficient money available (having regard to High Need)'" (quoted in: Keep, Clarkson 1993,p.8).

A leaflet might contain details of services available but omit reference to the limited provision imposed by lack of resources; priorities and criteria of eligibility might not be explained. Resource constraints sometimes deny services even to people who are supposedly eligible, according to published information, to receive those services; and information about such non-provision even for eligible people is not made public. The potential therefore exists for publicity to generate 'false expectations' about available services (KPMG 1993,p.33).

In the past, some local authorities have been concerned that publicity can create excessive demands on services, although there are conflicting views about whether this invariably occurs. For example, one local authority might publicise its intensive community-based services only for the service to be saturated within nine months and the publicity withdrawn. In a second authority on the other hand, an area team might advertise itself 'aggressively' through leaflets, videos in post offices and the local press. It might not be overwhelmed with 'unrealistic or inappropriate demands' and conclude that people 'self select' and do not approach social services except as a last resort (SSI,SIS 1991,p.20).

Typically, information published by local authorities will set out *its interpretation* (eg, in terms of eligibility criteria) of duties contained in legislation; so that people are not necessarily informed directly about their rights (Age Concern England 1994b,p.32) – such as they are, in community care law.

General information: dissemination for potential users

Taken literally, the statement in policy guidance about information being accessible to 'all potential users and carers' is over-ambitious, though much depends on how local authorities interpret the terms 'accessible' and 'all'. Reaching potential users might be an onerous task.

Early reports on community care suggested, for example, the 'marginal impact' of information (KPMG 1993,p.46) and that many carers had not received assessments simply because they didn't know about assessments (Warner 1994,p.48). One local authority had produced a leaflet describing services, and distributed it to a range of people and public places: yet still many other people interviewed had not seen it and stocks were not available for continuous use by voluntary organisations (SSI 1994c,p.13). Similarly, a local authority might produce information for people with HIV/AIDS, which does not reach its intended target unless it is appropriately distributed – for example, in commonly-used hospital clinics both within and without the authority's area (SSI/NHSE 1994d,p.6). Even if leaflets are helpful in themselves, their impact will be limited if only 22 per cent of service users have seen them (SSI 1996d,p.3); or if comprehensive A-Z booklets of services are unknown not only to service users and carers, but also to social services staff (SSI 1995b,p.21). More generally, if there is no strategy, resources are likely to be wasted; but consultation with service users about the purpose and targeting of information is likely to improve its quality and take-up; whilst review systems, quality control and checks will also help (SSI 1998e,pp.4,26).

People might not 'tend to seek help' for a variety of reasons including attitudes and unwillingness to seek information, low perception of needs, loneliness and depression, antipathy toward social services, language barriers, disability (physical, sensory, mental) and so on (eg, Tinker, McCreadie and Salvage 1993,p.5; Steele et al. 1993,Part 2,p.18). People might fear loss of service if they 'make a fuss' about getting information (KPMG 1993,p.11). Conversely, it might be that existing service users are offered less information than potential users (Berry 1990, p.9). Certainly, the Audit Commission and SSI (1998a,p.10) report that even in better-performing councils only one third of people had information about social services before they started using them.

General information: dissemination for particular groups

The policy guidance (above) uses the language of obligation ('should' and 'will need to have') on the need to reach 'all potential users and carers'.

The courts have stated that 'where an English statute says information is to be provided, that information need only be provided in English' (R v Governors of Small Heath School, ex p. Birmingham City Council 1989 – referred to in R v Birmingham City Council, ex p. Kaur 1990). However, although the NHS and Community Care Act 1990 is silent on this point, guidance states that local authorities should take account of different languages and cultures.

In practice, it seems that the existence and quality of information for minority ethnic groups is likely to vary. A 1990 report found that social services information in minority languages was less well designed than the equivalent information in English (Berry 1990,pp.11,18). By 1993, a study (KPMG 1993) for the Department of Health reported that 'information was generally available in a variety of media pertaining to the ethnic and disability mix of the population' (p.37). Yet an SSI (1993g) complaints procedure inspection report suggested, as a result of its findings, that local authorities should 'show adherence to the principles of the Race Relations Act 1976 and other equal opportunities legislation' (p.17). Another Department of Health monitoring exercise reported on 'a dearth of appropriate, user-friendly and culturally sensitive information about community care policies, procedures and service options' (DH 1994e,p.8). Four years later, many older black people were still not obtaining information and knew nothing about available services (SSI 1998f,p.9). However, translation of written information can be expensive and creates an expectation that enquiries be answered orally in a particular language (see eg, KPMG 1993,p.38; Steele *et al.* 1993,Pt.3,p.39), which in turn means that staff need to know when it is appropriate to use an interpreter (SSI 1998f,p.10).

The practice guidance also suggests tentatively that authorities might wish to experiment with other media. It is arguable that without such experimentation, information will in some areas simply not be available – even potentially – to 'all' possible users and carers. However, in relation to people with sensory disabilities, there is evidence that practice has not always been effective. An SSI (1989a,p.15) report on services for people both deaf and blind was 'concerned to find so little information about services in suitable formats – such as in braille, large print or on tape. They were thus deprived of information readily available to sighted and hearing people'. Another SSI (1990) report found that despite the existence of procedures and systems for information, most social services departments failed to provide information in braille or large print (and information in other languages was scarce). The conclusion drawn was discouraging, although it was reported that social services departments were attempting to rectify the situation (pp.3,24–25). One particular example given by SSI is that of a woman, hard of hearing from birth, who at the age of 40 finally received a flashing door bell from social services; prior to this she had not seen any information about what was available, but now said that the provision of this simple item of equipment had changed her life (SSI 1997a,p.37).

Generally, people with multiple impairments (SSI 1993a,p.15), learning disabilities (Singh 1995,p.10) or older people with dementia (SSI 1997b,p.13) might all be poorly served with information.

General information: staff

Practice guidance explains the importance of well-informed staff. There is evidence from past studies suggesting that staff working in statutory services are sometimes ill-informed about the needs of, for example, disabled and elderly people. Sometimes staff might also be poor information providers, because they give inappropriate, selective or obsolete information; they do not see themselves as 'information providers'; they are ill-informed; or they simply withhold information (eg, variously Garden 1990,p.33; Tinker, McCreadie and Salvage 1993,p.5; Keep, Clarkson 1994,p.32).

For example, an SSI inspection of services for people with multiple impairments found that specialist staff within social services departments might provide only limited (specialist) information to users and carers. This contributed to the 'pigeon-holing' of users and was part of a widespread 'serious lack of information and communication between workers in the same department'.

This in turn contributed to a lack of multi-disciplinary contribution and to partial assessments carried out from a limited perspective (SSI 1993a,pp.17–18).

3. COMMUNITY CARE PLANNING

Planning features prominently in community care legislation and guidance and a number of duties apply to consultation about the publishing of plans. Community care plans vary in approach and quality from authority to authority making comparisons difficult; overall there must also be some doubt as to how helpfully, accurately and comprehensively plans determine practice locally, and reflect legislation and guidance.

EXTRACTS

Legislation (NHS and Community Care Act 1990,s.46(2)) states:

(duty to publish plan) 'Each local authority ... shall ... prepare and publish a plan for the provision of community care services in their area ... shall keep the plan prepared by them ... and any further plans prepared by them under this section under review; and ... shall, at such intervals as the Secretary of State may direct, prepare and publish modifications to the current plan, or if the case requires, a new plan' (s.46(1)).

(health authorities) Local authorities must consult '(a) any District Health Authority the whole or any part of whose locality lies within the area of the local authority; (b) any Family Health Services Authority the whole or any part of whose locality lies within the area of the local authority';

(housing authorities) '(c) in so far as any proposed plan, review or modifications of a plan may affect or be affected by the provision or availability of housing and the local authority is not itself a local housing authority, within the meaning of the Housing Act 1985, every such local housing authority whose area is within the area of the local authority';

(voluntary organisations: community care services) '(d) such voluntary organisations as appear to the authority to represent the interests of persons who use or are likely to use any community care services within the area of the authority or the interests of private carers who, within that area, provide care to persons, for whom, in the exercise of their social services functions, the local authority have a power or duty to provide a service.'

(voluntary organisations: housing) '(e) such voluntary housing agencies and other bodies as appear to the local authority to provide housing or community care services in their area; and'

(other persons) '(f) such other persons as the Secretary of State may direct'.

Directions (*Community Care Plans (Consultation) Directions 1993*: attached to LAC(93)4) state that:

(consultation with independent sector) 'Each local authority shall in carrying out any of their functions under section 46(1) of the National Health Service and Community Care Act 1990 (community care plans) consult any representative organisation (including any incorporated or unincorporated body of persons) which represents providers in the authority's area with whom the authority may arrange to provide community care services as defined in s.46 of the National Health Service and Community Care Act ... where that organisation notifies the local authority in writing of their wish to be consulted in respect of the authority's community care plans'.

Directions (*Community Care Plans Directions 1991*; attached to LAC(91)6) state that local authorities:

(frequency of publication) 'shall ... prepare and publish modifications to the current plan, or if the case requires, a new plan at intervals of not more than one year'.

Policy guidance (DH 1990) states:

(content of plans) 'In their plans SSDs should identify:

(assessment)

- 'the care needs of the local population taking into account factors such as age distribution, problems associated with living in inner city areas or rural areas, special needs of ethnic minority communities, the number of homeless or transient people likely to require care;
- how the care needs of individuals approaching them for assistance will be assessed;
- how service needs identified following the introduction of systematic assessment will be incorporated into the planning process'.

(services)

- 'the client groups for whom they intend to arrange services...;
- how priorities for arranging services are determined;
- how they intend to offer practical help, such as respite care, to carers;
- how they intend to develop domiciliary services.'

(quality)

- 'the steps they are taking to ensure quality in providing and purchasing services...;
- how they intend to monitor the quality of services they have purchased or provided;
- the setting-up and role of inspection units...;
- the setting-up and role complaints procedures...'

(consumer choice)

- 'how they intend to increase consumer choice;
- how they intend to stimulate the development of a mixed economy of care'.

(resources)

- 'the resource implications, both financial and human of planned future developments;
- how they intend to improve the cost effectiveness of services;
- their personnel and training strategy for meeting both short and longer term developments'.

(consultation)

- 'how they intend to consult on plans with DHAs, FHSAs, housing authorities, voluntary organisations representing service users, voluntary organisations representing carers, voluntary housing agencies and other bodies providing or community care services (as required by s.46(2) of the Act)'.

(publishing information)

- 'what arrangements they intend to make to inform service users and their carers about services...; – how and when they intend to publish CCPs in the following year' (para 2.25).

(groups of people covered by plans) 'groupings should show evidence of a balanced consideration of the needs of such groups as dependent elderly people, those with disabilities whether of a learning, physical or sensory nature and those whose needs for social care may be intermittent such as those affected by HIV/AIDS or women suffering domestic violence. Plans should include services for people with multiple and low incidence disabilities and will be required to include services for mentally ill people (including those with dementia), and those who misuse drugs and/or alcohol' (para 2.25).

(languages and media) 'in future all LAs will be required to publish CCPs annually. All CCPs should in future be available to the local population, presented in a form which is readily understandable. Authorities may wish to consider producing straightforward summaries of detailed statistical and financial planning documents. In order to ensure public accessibility authorities may wish to make plans available in languages relevant to the local population, in braille and on tape' (DH 1990,para 2.18).

Circular guidance (LAC(93)4 issued with the above directions on consultation states that the first direction is:

(consultation with independent sector) 'intended to ensure that there is full and proper consultation between local authorities and independent sector providers on community care plans'. Independent sector/providers includes private and voluntary providers of services. The requirement is that 'authorities must consult with representatives of independent sector providers of community care services in the authority's area' (para 11). This includes 'representatives of day and domiciliary service providers as well as providers of residential and nursing home care' (para 12).

(discretion) 'The nature and style of consultation will be a matter for each authority to decide. The basic principles, however, are clear':

(proposals) 'views must be invited on proposals, not the final document; those being consulted will not only need to be made aware of the proposals but be able to comment on proposed changes in service patterns;'

(reasonable time) 'reasonable time must be allowed for those consulted to formulate and give their view; views must be taken into consideration;'

(meetings) 'it may be sufficient to hold meetings or, where appropriate, place community care plan proposals on the agenda of a regular forum but care needs to be taken that those who need to be consulted are properly informed' (para 23).

DISCUSSION

Community care planning: content

Local authorities have a duty to prepare and publish community care plans. They must publish either modifications or new plans at least every year. Legislation does not specify what information these plans must contain, but policy guidance states what they 'should' contain. The guidance lists a number of headings including assessment (including assessment of the needs of the local population), services, consumer choice, quality, resources, consultation, and publishing information.

The list of items to be covered by a community care plan is considerable, some being easier to deal with than others. For instance, details of future resourcing for community care might be difficult to spell out if there is uncertainty about the level of central funding (Hardy, Wistow and Leedham 1994,p.47). The informativeness of plans can vary. In listing services, a well-structured plan might include a range of services for misusers of alcohol and drugs as well as plans for new services. On the other hand, many plans might not refer at all to services for these groups or do so only vaguely, using words such as 'prevention', 'rehabilitation', and 'support' without further detail (O'Brien,Wurr 1993,pp.1,25). Content also needs to be eligible; for instance, small print might make parts of plans unreadable by partially sighted people (Coombs 1998,p.16).

It has been pointed out that independent living for disabled people depends on many circumstances outside of 'community care services', such as appropriate housing, personal safety and accessible transport and buildings. Planning should ideally take account of these (Bewley, Glendinning 1994,p.36).

Community care planning: particular groups of people (background)

Legislation is silent about which specific groups of people should be covered by community care plans. Policy guidance, though declaring a non-prescriptive approach, nevertheless names some groups of people to whose needs 'balanced consideration' should be given. It then names some other groups of people, for whom services 'should' be included in plans.

Concern has been expressed that certain groups of people are at risk of being treated, inappropriately, as low priority. For example, during the Committee stage of the NHS and Community Care Bill in the House of Lords, eventually unsuccessful amendments proposed more specific duties in relation to community care plans. One such amendment concerned people with disabilities of low incidence. The government (Baroness Blatch) argued that even without the amendment, community care plans anyway would have to be 'comprehensive of the totality of need which the local authority has to address and the totality of the service provision it aims to provide within the resources available to it' (HLD,10/5/1990,col.1513). In fact the substance of this amendment eventually did find its way into policy guidance (see above).

Similarly, an amendment requiring plans to consider 'the religious persuasion, racial origin and cultural and linguistic background' of communities was not adopted. The government stated 'that the need to take account of these factors will be stressed in our guidance, which can be reinforced by directions' (Baroness Blatch: HLD,14/6/1990,cols.480–482). More recently, Alfred Morris suggested placing duties on social services 'to draw up a specific policy for meeting the needs of young people and adults with multiple disabilities, under the responsibility of a named officer, and to include this within community care plans'. Tim Yeo replied that plans were expected 'to set out how the authority intends to meet the needs of the whole of its population, including disabled people' (HCWA,25/5/1993,col.506).

Community care planning: particular groups of people (practice)

A survey of community care plans (Hardy, Wistow and Leedham 1994) analysed 'client group' coverage: 96 per cent of plans dealt specifically with elderly people, people with mental health problems, people with learning disabilities, physically and sensorially impaired people. Other groups were less well covered, ranging from drugs/alcohol misusers (80%) to travellers (4%).

One of the reasons for attempts to amend community care legislation and policy is the recognition that in the past certain groups of people have been accorded inappropriately low priority. For example, SSI (1991a) inspected services for people with multiple impairment in Gloucestershire following the death of a person with such impairment. Two years after her death, none of the agencies (social services, health authority, voluntary agency) had 'published policies, procedural statements and practice guides in relation to disabled people' (p.2). Another report suggested that minority ethnic communities might be neither contributing enough to planning, nor receiving services appropriate for disabled people. Local authorities needed better knowledge of the local population and the particular needs of disabled people from these communities (SSI,NHSME 1994e,p.24).

Policy documents and plans alone do not ensure services of quality for particular groups of people. For example, even when an SSI (1988e) inspection of services for people with a visual impairment did find relevant policy documents, they were inadequate (and many authorities anyway had no such documents). It found that such documents might take 'only a partial view of a department's responsibility for people with a visual handicap' (p.13). Conversely, absence of, for example, rural issues from a community care plan doesn't necessarily mean the local authority isn't in reality planning for those issues; although generally 'community care planning for rural areas has been of no more than marginal concern for the majority of authorities' (Gould 1994,p.95).

There was evidence, from the first community care plans, that some groups were particularly likely to be excluded from community care planning, or subsumed under broader headings (with attendant lack of detail and relevance): for example, ethnic minority groups, people with sensory impairments, people from rural communities, and people with learning difficulties (Bewley, Glendinning 1994,pp.25–26). Action plans for mental health might have existed but failed to be underpinned by a 'framework of principles specific to mental health' (SSI,NHSME 1994h,p.23). This trend seems to continue, for instance, in relation to people with sensory impairment (Lovelock, Powell and Craggs 1995,p.12; SSI 1997a,p.44; Davis 1998,p.11).

A survey of coverage by community care plans of services for alcohol and drugs misusers pointed beyond simple presence or absence of such services in plans. For example, because of their low status, these services might not be covered in their own right and instead be absorbed into sections of the plan dealing with mental distress or HIV/AIDS (O'Brien,Wurr 1993,p.1).

Community care planning: consultation

Legislation places duties on local authorities to consult with health authorities, housing authorities and voluntary organisations when preparing community care plans. These duties have been augmented by directions about consultation with the 'independent' (private and voluntary) sectors. Non co-terminous boundaries between different authorities can sometimes pose considerable difficulties for consultation.

Community care planning: housing

The NHS and Community Care Act 1990 (s.46) places a duty on the social services authority to consult with the local housing authority, if they are not one and the same authority. This duty does not therefore apply to unified authorities (ie responsible for both housing and social services functions).

However, this does not mean that departments within the same authority should not collaborate. Circular guidance clarifies the point: 'where social services and housing authorities are part of a unified authority ... discussions should take place between the respective departments' (DoE 10/92). During the passing of the NHS and Community Care Bill, there was some confusion about this. An amendment referring to consultation in unified authorities failed because it was deemed 'defective and unacceptable as it requires a local authority which is a housing authority to consult itself' (HLD,28/6/1990,cols.1754–1756).

Community care planning: consultation with users of services

Legislation imposes a duty to consult with voluntary organisations representing users of services, but there is of course nothing to stop a) local authorities consulting with service users direct as well – for instance by sending out 6,000 questionnaires to older people (Hunter 1998); or b) groups of service users submitting views before they are invited to (Coombs 1998,p.19).

Furthermore, consultation need not be restricted to prospective issues; it can include user-led evaluation and monitoring in order better to identify whether finite public resources are being used effectively (Morris 1995,p.35). Evaluation, genuinely led by service users, is likely to lead to improvements in services and to benefit both users and providers (Fletcher 1995).

Community care plans: consultation with specific groups

Legislation does not prescribe consultation with specific groups of people or their representatives.

An unsuccessful amendment to the NHS and Community Care Bill attempted to create duties to consult (and to create consultation procedures) with specific groups. These included users, carers, voluntary organisations providing community care services and representing the interests of users or providing advocacy services, bodies representing the interests of ethnic minorities, and housing associations. Virginia Bottomley, resisting the amendment, explained that whilst the government wanted to 'ensure practical, effective community care plans, taking all aspects into account', it did not wish 'to write on the face of the Bill precise mechanisms for consultation and to state precisely which groups should be considered'. This was for fear of creating a straightjacket, rather than a framework, for community care plans. Instead, guidance would allow flexibility, innovation and diversity and would be reinforced by Social Services Inspectorate monitoring and if necessary by Secretary of State Directions (SC(E),13/2/1990,cols 919–936).

Community care plans: adequacy of consultation

Health and housing authorities could legally challenge the failure of local authorities to consult, since legislation states that those authorities must be consulted locally. Local authorities also have a duty to consult with independent sector organisations who notify an authority in writing that they wish to be consulted. Although the Department of Health's guidance covers the nature of consultation, the courts sometimes impose, or superimpose, their own standards about what consultation should consist of (eg, *R v Devon CC, ex p Baker, R v Secretary of State for Social Services, ex p AMA; R v Wandsworth LBC, ex p Beckwith (no.2); R v North and East Devon HA, ex p Pow*).

Community care planning: different languages and media

Policy guidance states that local authorities must publish community care plans annually and should make them available in understandable form to the local population. In order to ensure public access to plans, the guidance suggests that the plans could be made available in other languages and in tape and braille form.

The guidance uses the language of obligation ('should in future be available') with the language of discretion about the form of plans: local authorities 'may wish to make plans available in languages relevant to the local population, in braille and on tape'. However, one report of a survey of community care plans commented that in 'a real sense, unless Plans are produced in such formats they remain unavailable to certain sections of the community' (Wistow, Leedham and Hardy 1993,p.8).

Terms such as 'available', 'understandable', 'public access' are rather vague when applied to information provision and difficult to measure. It has been suggested that local authorities need to think about, amongst other things, accessibility in terms of how many documents make up the plan; what 'level' the plans are written at; whom they are aimed at; and for what purpose. Community care plans sometimes comprise one or more documents, each containing a different level of information. Thus, one county, a single social services authority divided into five social services area teams, might have five separate 'distinctively different' community care plans (Wistow, Leedham and Hardy 1993,p.5).

Again, a local authority might have a plan which summarises a number of other planning documents also publicly available. This means that a full understanding might depend on reading all the documents. Other variations might include three updates of the plan in a single year; one three-year plan with annual updates; two multi-volume editions with separate documents for a specialist service (eg, mental health); two separate plans where the social services area covers two health authorities. On the one hand, a single document serving all purposes might be too ambitious; on the other, there is a question about the accessibility of information which itself has to be explained by other information (SSI,NHSME 1994h,p.21).

Jargon, technical language, layout and small print can be additional hindrances to accessibility (SSI,NHSME 1994h,pp.20–21). Plans might be aimed at the 'general public', all those who have a 'stake in community care', a 'wide audience' (from government down to users and carers), or a 'primary target' of major service providers in the area (Wistow, Leedham and Hardy 1993,pp.5,8–9). Authorities might have to consider that a community care plan may be fulfilling different purposes, for example, public information/accountability as opposed to business plan.

Community care planning: miscellaneous

Local authorities have various other duties in respect of community care plans. Under directions, they must publish details about their proposals for purchasing non-residential services from independent sector providers (*Community Care Plans (Independent) Sector Non-Residential Care Direction 1994*: attached to LAC(94)12). They must also publish details about how they propose to consult (*Community Care Consultation Directions 1993*: attached to LAC(93)4). Circular guidance goes on to state that the aim is to make consultation open and effective, and that it is helpful to clarify consultation methods and timetable at an early stage (LAC(93)4). Further guidance issued in 1995 dealt with a number of issues surrounding the formulation and publication of community care plans including their purpose, audience, consistency with local community care charters, strategic planning, collaborative working and consultation (LAC(95)19).

PART III

HEALTH SERVICES
AND HOME ADAPTATIONS

CHAPTER 14

NATIONAL HEALTH SERVICE PROVISION

Coverage

1. NHS provision generally
2. Community care assessment and the NHS
3. Charges for NHS services

KEY POINTS

This chapter covers provision by the NHS in general; the next considers particular 'continuing care' services.

The provision of NHS services introduces considerable additional uncertainty into the system of community care. This is so for a number of reasons. Health services, though recognised by guidance as in practice essential to care in the community, are nevertheless not legally defined as 'community care services'. Instead, they are provided under different legislation, and health authorities do not even have an explicit duty to participate in the pivotal process of the community care system – assessment (see p.79). Furthermore, a person cannot generally lay claim as of legal right to any particular NHS service at any particular time at any particular place. Services can vary greatly from place to place, and even in the same place at different times.

The law governing financial charges for NHS services and equipment is relatively straightforward and comprised of clear rules; however, this does not prevent misunderstanding and ignorance of the legislation giving rise to unlawful charges being made within the NHS.

1. NHS PROVISION GENERALLY

The statutory duties of health authorities remain basically unchanged by community care legislation. This means that the provision of many health services relevant to community care is governed by general duties placed on the Secretary of State (and transferred to health authorities) to provide a comprehensive health service, and to provide services and facilities so far as 'necessary to meet all reasonable requirements'.

The NHS Act 1977 applies this broad duty to the provision of hospital and other accommodation, medical, nursing, dental and ambulance services – and to the prevention of illness, care of people who are ill and after-care services. The Act does not mention particular medical or nursing specialisms, nor the therapy services which in principle are so important for community care and for enabling people to remain in their own homes.

These health service duties are towards the population generally and so are often viewed as 'weaker' duties (see eg, the comment about s.1 of the 1977 Act in *R v Inner London Education Authority, ex p Ali*) – compared with the stronger duties towards individuals to be found in some community care legislation (see p.47). Accordingly, health authorities appear to have very broad discretion to make priorities and allocate resources locally. Such is this discretion, that the general duty to provide services under s.3 of the NHS Act 1977 is sometimes seen, in respect of any particular service, to be in effect a power only. Specific services tend to vary in level from authority to authority; and particular services might not exist at all in some places.

The law courts appear to have confirmed this discretion as has, though not so unwaveringly, the health service ombudsman. The courts are most reluctant to intervene in cases concerning rationing of services – for instance, hole-in-the-heart operations, leukaemia treatment, infertility treatment and orthopaedic treatment. Therefore, just as in the case of social services but even more so, NHS local policies and practices can vary significantly and be subject to the same unpredictable elements of priorities, resource allocation, and definitions of what constitutes 'need'. Even so, the courts do occasionally rule against health authorities in judicial review cases about rationing; for instance, when authorities fail to consult over local hospital closures, to have regard to Department of Health guidance about providing a particular type of treatment, or to keep explicit promises in certain circumstances.

In contrast to their reluctance to judicially review decisions related to policies, priorities and resources – the courts frequently make findings of negligence against the NHS in relation to professional carelessness. However, even in negligence cases, the courts might shy away from imposing liability in certain circumstances – for example, when policies, priorities and statutory arrangements are concerned and it is not in the public interest to impose it.

Usually, the health service ombudsman likewise gives room to health authorities to make priorities and ration services. Nevertheless, in one notable investigation he faulted a health authority's continuing care policy as a breach of statutory duty. And he is quite ready to criticise, where warranted, a range of actions and decisions involving matters such as hospital discharge, giving information to patients, communications between staff, keeping of records. He investigates maladministration, failure in a service, and failure to provide a service which there is a duty to provide – and can scrutinise clinical as well as administrative matters.

Overall, it seems that, most of the time, health authorities have little to fear legally from their rationing decisions; bad publicity and public opinion are sometimes a greater threat.

EXTRACTS

Legislation (NHS Act 1977) states that:

> **(provision necessary to meet all reasonable requirements)** 'It is the Secretary of State's duty to provide throughout England and Wales, to such extent as he considers necessary to meet all reasonable requirements' a number of services including:

- medical, dental, nursing and ambulance services (s.3(1)(c));
- 'hospital accommodation' and 'other accommodation for the purpose of any service provided under the Act' (s.3(1)(a-b);
- 'such facilities for the prevention of illness, the care of persons suffering from illness and the after-care of persons who have suffered from illness as he considers are appropriate as part of the health service' (s.3(1)(e)).

(comprehensive health service): Section 1 of the NHS Act 1977 places on the Secretary of State 'a duty to continue the promotion in England and Wales of a comprehensive health service designed to secure improvement (a) in the physical and mental health of the people of those countries, and (b) in the prevention of, diagnosis and treatment of illness, and for that purpose to provide or secure the effective provision of services in accordance with this Act'.

Legislation (regulations: SI 1996/708) made under the NHS Act 1977 transfer the Secretary of State's functions under s.3 to health authorities.

Community care policy guidance states that the 'statutory responsibilities of health authorities to meet health care needs are unchanged...' (DH 1990,para 3.36).

DISCUSSION

NHS provision generally: discretion about services

The NHS Act 1977 (s.3) does not list specific services which 'must' be provided. 'Medical' and 'nursing' services are referred to, but these are of course very broad terms covering a range of services and specialisms. Therapy and other paramedical services (chiropody), so important for community care, are not mentioned at all.

Services provided under s.3 only have to be provided if they are 'necessary to meet all reasonable requirements'. This appears to mean that health authorities can set priorities and allocate resources locally, thus exercising wide discretion in deciding levels of service and sometimes even the very existence of particular services. The effect of this discretion appears to be that although services as a whole are covered by the general duties to provide health services, the level (or even provision at all) of any one service is not mandatory, so long as its level (or even non-provision) is justifiable in terms of local priorities and resources.

The wide discretion of health authorities has been confirmed by both the courts and the health service ombudsman: see below for examples. The implication of this is, according to one commentator (Brazier 1992), an 'absence of any right to health care'. Indeed: 'it has the effect of encouraging overstretched health authorities to withdraw services if resources are stretched rather than to struggle on doing their best. For while patients have no right to demand care, once a patient is admitted to a clinic or hospital a duty of care to him arises. If, owing to lack of resources, he suffers some injury resulting from lack of care, he may have a right to compensation from the authority. It will often be "legally safer" to close an underfunded casualty unit rather than seek to keep going with weary overworked staff' (p.23).

Even so, some limits are occasionally placed on the freedom of health authorities to do as they please. For instance, in 1994 the health service ombudsman effectively challenged the limits to the discretion of health authorities, at least in the context of long-term continuing NHS care (the Leeds case: see below). And in 1997, the failure of a health authority to have regard to guidance about the treatment with beta-interferon of people with multiple sclerosis, led to a finding of unlawfulness by the High Court. Indeed, the court did not deny that the health authority could take account of resources, but was not prepared to allow the authority to argue its way out of the challenge simply by using the blanket argument of lack of resources. This was because funds were not unavailable, but the authority had simply refused to allocate them (*R v North Derbyshire HA, ex p Fisher*).

NHS provision generally: illustrative legal judgments

The courts have confirmed the wide discretion of health authorities to make priorities, allocate resources accordingly and to ration services. Rationing, after all, has long been a fact of NHS life – for example, the restriction of early renal dialysis treatment to potential wage-earners (RCP 1995,p.9). More generally, although attention is given in the Press to reports of publicly declared rationing policies (eg, concerning tattoo-removal or infertility treatment), there has been a glaring lack of national, mainstream publicity for the informal, longstanding and endemic rationing of some of the less glamorous health services – such as provision of incontinence pads, chiropody, speech and language therapy and communication aids to name but a few.

In *R v Secretary of State for Social Services, ex p Hincks*, about long waits for orthopaedic treatment, Lord Denning in the Court of Appeal felt impelled to imply additional words into s.3 of the NHS Act 1977. The provision of services was to be made by the Secretary of State 'to such extent as he considers necessary to meet all reasonable requirements *such as can be provided within the resources available*' (added italics indicate the extra words). More recently, the Court of Appeal held that a health authority was not obliged to provide potentially lifesaving treatment for a 10-year-old child with leukaemia (*R v Cambridge HA, ex p B*). Similarly, in another two cases involving the postponement of heart operations on a child and on a baby, the Court of Appeal would not intervene and expressed its great reluctance to interfere with the allocation of resources by health authorities *(R v Central Birmingham HA, ex p Collier; R v Central Birmingham HA, ex p Walker)*. A court might otherwise find itself ordering priority for the patient in question, ahead of other patients about whose situation the court knows nothing (*Re J*). And in *R v Sheffield HA, ex p Seale*, the High Court was not prepared to hold as unlawful the application of an age-related rationing rule to infertility treatment – even though, in an ideal world, the judge conceded, a clinical decision on a case-by-case by basis would be preferable. In fact it was later pointed out that, in this particular case, the treatment might also have had the additional effect of curing the endometriosis suffered by the woman (Elliston, Britton 1994). If this was an added complexity to the *Sheffield* case, the *Cambridge* case was about far more than a simple question of resources, and involved resources, clinically unproven treatment, divided clinical opinion, a protesting father, ethical dilemmas, and the rights of children to give consent to treatment (Ham, Pickard 1998,pp.ix–x)

It has been suggested that total non-provision of a service might be subject to successful judicial review in relation to ss.1 and 3 of the 1977 Act (Dimond 1994). However, it is by no means clear what might be meant by total non-provision; would it be, for example, non-provision of nursing services overall (as mentioned in s.3), more specifically of a general specialism such as community nursing, or even more specifically of a particular service such as that provided by a continence adviser.

Even so, cases sometimes succeed; apart from *R v North Derbyshire HA, ex p Fisher*, mentioned already, decisions about the closure of services might be deemed flawed because of a lack of consultation (*R v NW Thames RHA, ex p Daniels* and *R v North and East Devon HA, ex p Pow*) – although such judicial rulings might typically only delay (while proper consultation takes place) procedurally the evil day rather than substantially avert such closure. Nevertheless, more recently at the end of 1998 the same judge (Mr. Justice Hidden) ruled unexpectedly against health authorities in two cases. The first was in relation to plans to close an NHS unit and the fact that the health authority had broken an explicit promise made to the disabled people living in it (*R v North and East Devon HA, ex p Coughlan*). The second involved a health authority's decision not to fund sex-change operations requested by three trans-sexuals. The policy was held to be unlawful, apparently (the case is unreported at the time of writing) because it interfered with the duty in s.3 of the NHS Act 1977 to provide treatment for the prevention of illness and the care of people who are ill (*R v North West Lancashire HA, ex p G, A and D*).

NHS provision generally: statements in the House of Commons

In reply to questions about people's rights to health services under the NHS, central government sometimes gives answers which are less than helpful. For instance, asked about apparent discrimination against older people (see eg, Hunt 1994) by 'refusal to provide, or withdrawal of treatment', the government replied: 'It is the duty of all health authorities to ensure that people of all ages have access to acute care and that specialist care is available to those who suffer with chronic conditions due to the ageing process' (Brian Mawhinney: HCWA,19/4/1994,col.474).

This answer appears only to re-state the general duty to provide health services and does not even acknowledge, let alone spell out, the implications for individuals of local priorities and rationing. It also does not explain that access to services according to clinical need can mean that a person with a lesser clinical need will go without if, at the time (eg, that day, week or month), there happen to be other people with a greater clinical need and therefore with a greater claim on limited NHS facilities.

There are in any case some rationing policies which in practice are not based on clinical factors. For instance, the Royal College of Physicians summarises the biological and financial considerations concerning older people's access to acute services: 'it is difficult to set any age (whether 65,75 or 82 years) as a cut-off point for defining services on biological grounds, though local circumstances and resource constraints may provide a rationale for such an arrangement' (RCP 1994,p.5). Likewise, Age Concern England has pointed out that if priorities are meant to be based on clinical needs, then those which are not, violate the Patient's Charter (DH 1995c,p.5) which states that every citizen has a right to receive health care precisely on the basis of clinical need. For example, there is evidence that coronary care units operate age-related admissions and thrombolysis treatment (reducing blood clots) policies – yet it is argued that there is no scientific evidence which supports the logic of such an approach. If this is so, then people are being denied treatment not on the basis of their clinical needs but on the accident of their age, whether it be cardiac rehabilitation, drugs (Whelan 1998) or physiotherapy (Age Concern England 1994b,p.34). In the absence of legislation covering age discrimination (compare sex, race and disability), this problem remains one of policy and is more likely to be solved – or not solved – according to the

climate of professional, political and public opinion, rather than by the law courts or the ombudsman.

NHS provision generally: meaning of clinical judgement

The suspicion that health authorities cloak financial decisions in clinical garments is sometimes
exposed by both the law courts and the health service ombudsman. When the latter investigated
the non-provision of crutches for a patient leaving hospital, he found maladministration because
the decision not to provide was not clinical but administrative, made as it was by a technician and
founded on a shortage of crutches (WW.3/79–80). On the other hand, in *R v North Derbyshire HA,
ex p Fisher*, the judge straightforwardly accepted as a fact of life that 'a clinician has to have regard
to many factors, including the resources available for that treatment and the needs of and likely
benefit to that patient, as compared with other patients who are likely to be suitable for that treatment during the financial year'.

Age Concern England (1991) has questioned exactly what the term 'clinical judgement'
means, since it can apparently be an exercise in resource management: 'Is it solely clinical judgement when a patient is judged as having a need for continuous nursing care, but when the consultant is prevented from offering suitable care because the health authority does not have this
provision, and has a policy not to make such provision? This could arguably be seen as a matter of
health authority policy, and not *solely* a matter of clinical judgement. In effect, this appears to be a
way of saying, "If the services are not available, there cannot be a clinical need". This could be seen
as a distortion of the concept of clinical judgement' (p.6). Conversely, the distinction between people who pay privately for nursing care and those who remain NHS patients has not always been
based on differences in clinical need. Instead, the distinction might arise because those who remain NHS patients, together with relatives, have become aware of their 'rights' to NHS services
and so have refused to pay for nursing home care (Henwood 1994,p.36).

In fact, clinical judgements need not be distorted. So long as such judgements acknowledge
people's need for care, they do not lose their integrity if a separate decision is then made about priority. However, a conflation of 'clinical need' with 'priority for NHS care' blurs matters, when they
should be kept quite separate. An example, would be where therapists working in elderly care hospital wards, under increasing workloads, set priorities for their patients which they would not have
set a year a two ago. They might have a dilemma of whether to write in patients' notes that 'rehabilitation is needed but that it cannot be supplied' – or whether to collapse this two-stage judgement
into one and record only that 'no rehabilitation is needed'. It is arguable that in the latter case, integrity of judgement has been lost.

Even if integrity is not lost sight of in the face of hard decisions about priorities, equity might
be. For instance, one person might be given an NHS bed one month, but another with similar
needs fail to get one the next because other people are judged to be a *higher clinical priority*.

NHS provision generally: blanket criteria of eligibility

A key question revolves around the extent to which health authorities can lawfully apply priority
categories, limiting eligibility for certain services and treatments to particular groups of people.

At one extreme, the alternative to priorities is to assess clinically every individual who might
need a service, and only then decide whether in fact that individual commands a sufficiently high

priority. This extreme alternative would seem effectively to preclude the creation by policy of priority groups, and scarcely seems practical, given limited time and resources within the NHS (see comment made in *R v Sheffield HA, ex p Seale* – but compare *Attorney General ex rel Tilley v Wandsworth LBC* in the child care field). The answer is that health authorities and NHS Trusts need, practically, to make priorities and policies. The law courts accept these might amount to rules – so long as room is left for considering exceptions (*British Oxygen v Board of Trade*) and authorities are thus not fettering their discretion (a question asked but not answered in *R v North Derbyshire HA, ex p Fisher*). Indeed, it was pointed out that the existence of priority criteria determining the provision of occupational therapy, and speech and language therapy, does not preclude individual consideration, since each child is still assessed individually against these criteria (*R v Brent and Harrow HA, ex p Harrow LBC*).

In practice, priority groups have been a relatively uncontroversial fact of life for years. For example, health authorities have long targeted chiropody services at four priority groups of people, and, in some authorities, only these groups of people are likely to receive services. Such a policy reflects government guidance given as long ago as 1974 which stated that: 'In general treatment should continue to be restricted to the existing priority groups' (HRC(74(33). Even at the National Health Service's inception, it was recognised that there would be temporary exceptions to 'comprehensiveness' of service: 'A full dental service for the whole population, for instance, including regular conservative treatment, is unquestionably a proper aim in any whole health service and must be so regarded. But there are not at present, and will not be for some years, enough dentists in the country to provide it. Until the supply can be increased, attention will have to be concentrated on priority needs' (Ministry of Health, Department of Health for Scotland 1944,p.9).

NHS provision generally: equity

An even broader question to be asked is to what extent health authorities' local exercise of discretion threatens the principle of an equitable, national health service. Certainly, one of the purposes behind the creation of the health service was to remedy the uneven distribution of, and access to, health services which existed before the war (Ministry of Health, Department of Health for Scotland 1944, pp.6–7). Yet, it has been pointed out that the 'central issue is the lack of coordination of the different funding arrangements both within and across health and social services. For example, funds for hospital and community health services, general practitioners, prescribed drugs, and personal social services are determined largely in isolation from one another. The scope for agencies to abdicate responsibility and for inequities to flourish is much greater than is commonly supposed' (Judge, Mays 1994).

It has also been suggested that since the boundary between health and social care is becoming more blurred, questions of equity (an explicit 'guiding principle' of health care legislation in the NHS Act 1946, but not of social care legislation in the National Assistance Act 1948) are increasingly spilling over into the area of social care (Challis, Henwood 1994). The question of equity is important but not one easily tackled in individual remedies. For example, the courts might refer to the importance of questions about levels of resources and facilities in the health service – but state that such questions are for Parliament and not the courts (*R v Central Birmingham HA, ex p Walker*). Even the health service ombudsman, who has explored, further than the courts, the limits of health authority discretion, has explained that he cannot 'conduct a more general review into variations in the level of service provided by different health authorities within the NHS' (W.707/85–86).

Nevertheless, whilst the courts and the ombudsmen are relatively powerless, and government continues to dodge matters by referring to local priorities and resources, individuals will draw scant consolation. For instance, children with cystic fibrosis receive new drug treatment in one area but not in another (Cystic Fibrosis Trust 1997,p.7). Thus, the extent to which the first key principle listed in the 1997 NHS White Paper heralds genuine change, remains to be seen. It states that the NHS should be a 'genuinely national service', with patients getting 'fair access to consistently high quality, prompt and accessible services right across the country' (Secretary of State for Health 1997b,p.11).

NHS provision generally: levels of rationing

There appear to be different levels of policy-making and priority-setting in the NHS. National and publicised priorities (eg,in HSC(98)159) might be one thing; but specific, sometimes ill-considered and arbitrary decisions another.

For instance, an NHS Trust manager might realise that a particular budget is running out and hastily decide to reduce or withdraw suddenly the provision of incontinence pads to people in residential homes. It is possible that such decisions might be slightly more susceptible to legal challenge, particularly if there is to hand relevant guidance from the Department of Health which can be used in support (as there was in *R v North Derbyshire HA, ex p Fisher*). In one instance, a health authority in 1992 retreated from its plans simply to cease providing incontinence people in residential homes with incontinence pads. Instead it agreed to reassess all the residents involved individually before making a decision (Wyatt 1992). A Department of Health Circular had warned authorities, when changing or withdrawing the supply of incontinence aids, not to do so until an 'assured alternative' is in place and not to expose vulnerable people to anxiety (EL(91)28).

2. COMMUNITY CARE ASSESSMENT AND THE NHS

There are a wide range of health services particularly relevant to community care.

EXTRACTS

Legislation states that when a local authority is assessing a person for community care services and it thinks there is a need for health or housing services, then it must notify health or housing (or both) and invite them to assist in the assessment (see p.78).

Legislation (regulations, SI 1992/635) concerning general practitioners' terms of service state that general practitioners are obliged to offer an annual consultation (including a home visit) to patients on their list who are at least 75 years old (schedule 2,para 16). The GP has to assess and record a number of matters including sensory functions; mobility; physical condition including incontinence; social environment; use of medicines. In addition, general practitioners have a specific contractual duty, under their terms of service, to give advice, 'as appropriate, to enable patients to avail themselves of services provided by a local social services authority' (schedule 2,para 12).

Policy guidance (on community care: DH 1990) refers frequently to various health service practitioners: for example to community nursing services and the:

(community nursing services) 'possibilities for supporting users with nursing care needs through community nursing services whether in their own homes, or in residential care homes, or in sheltered or very sheltered housing' (para 3.37).

(general practitioners) It 'is expected that, as a matter of good practice, GPs will wish to make a full contribution to assessment. It is part of the GP's terms of service to give advice to enable patients to avail themselves of services provided by a local authority' (para 3.47).

(personal relationship between GP and patient) 'Where advice is needed by the local authority in the course of assessment, this should be obtained from the GP orally (eg by telephone) as far as possible. A record should be kept of the advice given. In addition to the information that only the patient's own GP can provide, local authorities may, on occasion, also require a clinical examination or an interpretation of the medical report provided by the GP. Local authorities should, therefore, be aware that GPs have a personal duty to and a relationship with their patients, and may not be best placed to act in addition as an assessor on the authority's behalf. In such circumstances, local authorities may wish other practitioners to act in this capacity' (para 3.48).

Practice guidance refers to the potentially important roles of practice nurses, district nurses, health care assistants, occupational therapy, physiotherapy, speech therapy, psychology, chiropody, and therapists for both hearing and visual impairment (SSI,SWSG 1991b, pp.87– 89).

DISCUSSION

Community care assessment and the NHS: general practitioners

The terms of service for general practitioners summarised above are particularly relevant to community care since elderly people and particularly those who are least 75 years old are the 'biggest users of community care services'. There has long been evidence that many doctors, including general practitioners, could be better informed about rehabilitation and disability. It has also been observed that general practitioners tend to base their assessments on a medical, rather than a social or educational, model – reflecting their training and work priorities. This makes it likely that general practitioners will generally play a supportive, rather than a lead role, in community care assessments (Leedham, Wistow 1992,pp.10,15).

The British Medical Association has stated that it would be improper for GPs to carry out community care assessments for their own patients and where GPs do contribute to community care assessments, they should not be doing so against the local authority's eligibility for services (House of Commons Health Committee 1993,vol.2,pp.71,190). In any case, Department of Health policy guidance (above) suggests that the personal relationship between general practitioner and patient might render such assessment inappropriate.

Community care assessment and the NHS: list of goods and services

Fundholding general practitioners have been able, via a *List of goods and services*, to purchase additional items for their patients. The list of goods and services has been made under s.15(7)(b) of the NHS and Community Care Act 1990 and r.20 of SI 1993/567, and includes a range of services and equipment.

Services have included, for instance, outpatient services (such as orthodontic services and orthoptic services); community nursing services (such as health visiting, district nursing); mental health services (such as counselling, services for people with learning disabilities, referrals to all members of mental health care teams). Equipment includes three main categories: orthodontic equipment, orthopaedic footwear and, thirdly, therapy and home care equipment. This last category covers breast prostheses, cervical collars, communication equipment, continence equipment, hoists, nebulisers, special beds and mattresses, suction equipment, syringe drivers and walking aids. The list is almost certainly not intended to be exhaustive as to what can be included, although it contains a number of definite exclusions: hearing aids, prostheses (except breast prostheses), wheelchairs, environmental control equipment, and any equipment costing more than £6,000. Wigs, fabric supports and elastic hosiery (for all of which there are NHS prescription charges) are also excluded (HSG(97)22).

It should be noted that GP fundholders are due to be subsumed under the recently formed NHS primary care groups during 1999 (Secretary of State for Health 1997b,p.79; see also LAC(98)21 and HSC 1999/019 on transitional issues).

Community care assessment: other NHS services

Various health service specialisms are particularly relevant to community care. Medical specialisms include, for example, neurology, rehabilitation, elderly care, rheumatology, urology, otology, ophthalmology, ear-nose-throat (ENT), orthopaedics, diabetes, specialist psychiatric services. Nursing specialisms include, for example, stoma care, continence care, community nursing, health visiting, practice nurses (based in GP surgeries). Therapy specialisms include occupational therapy, physiotherapy, speech and language therapy, hearing therapy. Chiropody too is an important 'paramedical' service. The level, organisation and, in some cases, the existence of these services varies from place to place.

One of the difficulties faced by some disabled people is that they might need to be in contact with a whole range of NHS staff; if there is inadequate coordination, assistance can become fragmented. For instance, people with multiple sclerosis might, at various times, deal with a consultant neurologist, continence service, consultant urologist, sexual counsellor, wheelchair and seating clinic, physiotherapist, occupational therapist, pain control staff, clinical psychologist, low vision service, rehabilitation engineer, psychiatrist, speech therapist, information services – not to mention services from non-NHS sources such as social services and housing authorities (BSRM 1993,p.43).

3. CHARGES FOR NHS SERVICES

Health services and equipment provided by the NHS, unless otherwise specified, are by default free of charge. Despite this relatively clear position, misunderstandings and illegal charges do sometimes occur.

Specified charges cover equipment and drugs prescribed by general practitioners; dental services and appliances; spectacles and contact lenses; and elastic hosiery, wigs, abdominal or spinal supports and surgical brassieres. There are distinctions to be made depending on the status of a patient, since charges do not apply at all to NHS inpatients. There are also exemptions from, or reductions in, payment depending on factors such as the age, condition and financial status of patients. In addition, separate rules govern charges for private patients and overseas patients.

Although health authorities do not have the same wide powers to charge as social services authorities, they do, ironically, have a wide discretion not to provide services at all. For example, though a health authority cannot charge for incontinence pads, it can choose not to supply, or at least to ration, them: for example, in the case of people who are 'in need' but are not defined as a priority. Sometimes confusion arises as to whether NHS patients have had to pay for NHS services or equipment (which would be unlawful) or been asked to purchase them privately (which would be lawful).

EXTRACTS

Legislation (NHS Act s.1(2)) states that NHS services:

'shall be free of charge except so far as the making and recovery of charges is expressly provided for by or under any enactment, whenever passed'.

Circular guidance (EL(91)129) stated:

'Section 1 of the NHS Act 1977 requires that NHS services provided under the Act to NHS patients must be free of charge, except where the making and recovery of charges is expressly provided for by legislation. Later legislation, including the NHS and Community Care Act 1990, does not alter this position. Nor does it enable partial charges to be made to health service patients ... Health service managers should ensure that the statutory requirements are observed at all times. Before any charges are made the legality of the position must be established'.

Circular guidance (EL(92)20) stated that:

'services and equipment must not be charged for except where the legislation expressly indicates that a charge should be made. In all other cases, where an authority (taking account of resources, needs and clinical priorities locally) decides that a piece of equipment should be provided as part of NHS treatment, it should be provided free of charge. This applies whether the equipment is supplied on a permanent basis or on loan. It is also the responsibility of the health authority to check and maintain NHS equipment where necessary, and this should also be free'.

DISCUSSION

Charges for NHS services: free by default

NHS services are free by default: in other words, unless otherwise specified. Legislation does provide for the making of regulations to charge for drugs and appliances (NHS Act 1977,s.77), for private patients (NHS Act 1977,s.58), and for overseas patients – that is, people who are not ordinarily resident within the United Kingdom (NHS Act 1977,s.121). But otherwise, the NHS has no broad discretion, in contrast to local authority social services departments, to make charges.

Charges for NHS services: illegal charges

The law about NHS charges might seem clear, but this does not stop confusion sometimes affecting managers, staff and patients in practice. In 1992, it was reported that one NHS Trust had been charging people a £10 fee towards the provision of surgical footwear. If correct, this would have been unlawful; it appeared that the Trust's financial controller had simply been unaware of the law, and that up to 500 people and £10,000 might have been involved (*Therapy Weekly* 1992).

Similarly, a health service ombudsman investigation found that a health authority had tried to make unlawful charges for chiropody appliances supplied to a 13-year-old girl. The attempted justification by the authority referred to local financial constraints; but such constraints could not permit either a health authority or NHS Trust to breach their statutory duties. Furthermore, Circular guidance had made clear that services, new or existing, should be planned within resources. Thus, the health authority could at its discretion decide to continue or discontinue altogether the bio-mechanics service; what they could not do was make unlawful charges for it. There were possibly twenty patients involved in such charging: the health authority was urged to investigate all twenty (W.226/91–92). Some NHS Trusts request deposits for the loan of equipment; for instance one 'asked for a deposit ranging from £5.00 to £40.00; the NHS Trust said that this was "voluntary" but notices were said to be unclear on the matter and in very small print' (Clark 1998,p.29). If a deposit were to be regarded as a charge, then it would be unlawful.

Charges for NHS services: items which can be charged for

Items which can be charged for include a) drugs and appliances prescribed by general practitioners as well as some other items prescribed at a hospital, namely elastic hosiery, surgical/abdominal supports, wigs and surgical brassieres (SI 1989/419 as amended, made under the NHS Act 1977); b) spectacles, contact lenses (SI 1989/396 as amended, made under the NHS Act 1977); and c) dental appliances (SI 1989/394 as amended, made under the NHS Act 1977).

Charges for NHS services: exemptions

Depending on factors such as age, disability, illness or financial status, people might be exempt from some or all payment for the above-mentioned equipment which can be charged for under the NHS Act 1977. NHS inpatients are anyway exempt.

Charges for NHS services: repair/replacement charges

If there is a defect in an appliance 'as supplied', then NHS patients cannot be charged for replacement or repair (NHS Act 1977,schedule 12,para 1). If, however, the need for repair or replacement is due to an act or omission of the patient, then in principle a charge can be made (NHS Act 1977,s.82 and SI 1974/284).

Charges for NHS services: power to charge where no clinical need?

In the past, some health authorities seem to have assumed that where there is no clinical need, charges might be made in some cases even though not expressly authorised by legislation.

For instance, some years ago, the health service ombudsman (possibly without considering the underlying legality of the practice) found that a hospital occupational therapy department was justified in charging for a pick-up stick. The person's social services department, whose responsibility it really was, would eventually have provided one free, but the patient didn't want to wait; so the hospital OT charged a small amount (W.340/80–81).

In similar circumstances, it seems that many hospital therapy departments have in the past sold equipment (which would not normally be provided by the NHS) on a not-for-profit basis. The advice given by the Department of Health is that such activities are probably not lawful, but that ways around the problem might be for a hospital shop (eg, run by the 'friends' of the hospital) to stock and to sell the equipment. In this way money would not pass into hospital therapy departments. Department of Health correspondence stated: 'We see no objection to the purchase of equipment being regarded as an option for some people. This could be through retail outlets or voluntary organisations and there would be clear advantages if some of these could be located on NHS premises. The only objection is to the NHS selling equipment' (DH 1992b).

This advice was given in the aftermath of heated Parliamentary debate about charges in the NHS for items such as nebulisers (see below). As a result hospital occupational therapy departments have had to reconsider their practices, although enforcement of the law might not benefit people in the particular context of therapy departments. This is because patients might have to, or prefer to, buy items in hospital for a number of reasons including their likely failure to meet social services criteria; desire for new rather than secondhand equipment (eg, raised toilet seats) from social services; or better quality equipment (eg, padded rather than a hard bathboard) (NWTROTAG 1993).

Charges for NHS services: income generation schemes

It is arguable that under s.7 of the Health and Medicines Act 1988 (covering income generation), hospital occupational therapy departments actually do have the power to sell equipment (see immediately above). This would have to be on 'the appropriate commercial basis' (s.7(2)) and must not 'to a significant extent interfere' with the performance of duties to provide NHS services under the 1977 Act (s.7(8)).

The *latter condition* might appear to be fulfilled if the equipment were to be sold to meet social, rather than clinical, needs – in other words, those needs not normally within the NHS remit. Some support for this point of view might be gathered from Department of Health guidance on income generation. It explains how free hospital transport must be given to people with 'medical' needs – but not necessarily to people with 'social' needs only. For example, 'patients who, in the opinion of a clinician, do not have a medical need for transport but who have no suitable public transport and no recourse to private transport of their own or assistance from a relative or friend (ie, the need is a "social" rather than a medical one) may under s.7 be charged for provision of transport' (DH 1989b,para 45). However, the *former condition*, referring to an appropriate commercial basis, presumably might not be met if a scheme – such as the sale of equipment for social need – were to be run on a not-for-profit basis.

The Department of Health's advice (above) to refer people instead to retail outlets or a charity shop on hospital premises seems a sensible solution but also carries a danger of abuse. For example, a health authority might define a 'need' or a priority so high, or provide such unattractive (and cheaper) models of a particular type of equipment – such as orthopaedic footwear – that people no longer qualify or wish for NHS provision and are then referred to a shop on the hospital premises (see eg, Tomkin 1991).

Charges for NHS services: asking people to buy their own

The NHS does not have the power to charge for services or equipment (except those specified by legislation). However, ironically, it does have the power not to provide services or equipment at all either on the grounds that there is no clinical need, or that the person is in need, but it is a low priority need which cannot be met.

A Circular (EL(92)20) issued to health authorities in March 1992 explained: 'Where authorities do not provide equipment, a consultant may advise a patient that such equipment could be used on an optional basis if the patient wishes. In such cases, the health authority has no responsibility for supplying or maintaining the equipment, and the patient should make their own arrangements to obtain it … Any patients who have erroneously been required to pay for equipment which should have been provided free should be appropriately recompensed' (paras 3–4).

Confusion sometimes arises, as shown by 1991 exchanges in the House of Commons over NHS charges and in particular the provision of nebulisers (oxygen breathing equipment) and incontinence pads. The Secretary of State for Health made it quite clear that 'NHS patients cannot be charged and will not be charged' (HCD,21/10/1991,col.662). Accusations had been made that some health authorities had been charging patients for equipment. If true, then the health authorities would have been breaking the law. However, if they had simply said that they (the authorities) could not provide the equipment and that the patients should buy it themselves, then (all other things being equal) the authorities would have been acting lawfully. There was considerable confusion at the time as to what had in fact occurred in particular cases. (A Bill was introduced at the time by Rhodri Morgan to 'clarify the law': the NHS (Supply of Medical Equipment) Bill 1991. It did not progress).

The health service ombudsman has investigated a case where the complainant had bought a transcutaneous nerve stimulator (TNS) for the relief of pain and wanted reimbursement from the hospital. The ombudsman accepted the hospital's explanation that normally it could not loan its own stock of TNS machines on a semi-permanent basis because of demand and a finite budget. One of the hospital staff explained that there was a point at which people 'had to look after themselves', since if they attended the hospital indefinitely, the system would grind to a halt. It transpired however that a long-term loan might have been possible from elsewhere, but that the hospital had not given a proper explanation of the possibilities; the ombudsman therefore found fault with the lack of information given to the complainant (W.263/83–84).

Charges for NHS services: inpatient or outpatient status

NHS inpatients receive all services and equipment provided for their treatment free of charge (NHS Act 1977, schedule 12). This is the case, whether they are inpatients on NHS premises or on other premises (though still paid for by the NHS) such as a nursing home. Circular guidance has stated the importance of ensuring that patients on other premises are not persuaded to pay for extra services they do not need; and that there is 'no disparity between the clinical care and services provided to NHS patients and the hospital or nursing home's own private patients' (HC(81)1, annex,para 6).

NHS outpatients, on the other hand, are liable to pay charges – subject to the usual exemptions or reductions (see above).

Charges for NHS services: transfer from private to NHS treatment

This area of service provision sometimes confuses. Prior to 1986, as the health service ombudsman discovered, there was a lack of clarity about the procedures for such transfer and specifically about whether patients had to go through the usual NHS admission procedures, 'all over again' when transferring from private to NHS treatment (eg, W.194/78–79).

Guidance from the Department of Health and Social Security (as it was then: DHSS 1986) confirmed that though a person is free to change between private and NHS treatment, there are conditions. Dual status is not possible 'for the treatment of one condition during a single visit to a health service hospital' (para 22). However, a private inpatient could change status if, for example, after admission for a minor condition, 'a different, more serious complaint' is found (para 23). However, if a person does change status, then there must be 'an assessment of the patient's clinical priority for treatment as a NHS patient' so that he or she gains 'no advantage over other NHS patients' (paras 24–25).

Charges for NHS services: private treatment because of anxiety over waiting

The health service ombudsman has in the past explained that sometimes 'patients write to me alleging that they have had to pay for private care out of anxiety after a long time on a NHS waiting list' (Health Service Commissioner 1990,p.8). One such case (W.533/87–88) occurred when a consultant persuaded a man awaiting an urgent operation to go to a private clinic. In fact the man would have been transferred to the appropriate NHS hospital on the same day had he not moved into private care. The consultant had not found this out, and the man and his family did not know this. The family was reimbursed by the health authority.

Charges for NHS services: private patient charges in NHS hospitals

Misunderstandings sometimes arise over payment of private patient charges. Guidance states that (under the NHS Act 1977,ss.65–66) patients should give written undertakings to pay the charges prior to treatment. This applies both to private in- and outpatients. They must be warned also that if they stay longer than anticipated, then the charges will be higher than estimated; and that treatment which continues after April 1st in any year might be subject to a higher rate of charges from that date (DHSS 1986,paras 50–54).

Equipment provided as part of the treatment should be covered by the fixed daily charge which has been agreed to: 'supplementary charges must not be made for implants, aids and appliances, even if an appliance has been fitted after discharge, provided they have been prescribed for somebody while he was a private resident patient as part of the treatment for the medical condition for which he was admitted' (DHSS 1986,paras 83–84).

Charges for NHS services: oxygen equipment

For longer term use, oxygen cylinders are prescribed by general practitioners and attract a standard prescription charge. Oxygen concentrators, prescribed for people who need oxygen for long periods of the day, are prescribed in England mainly by general practitioners. There are no prescription charges for oxygen concentrators (see eg, HSG(92)10).

Charges for NHS services: ordinary residence and overseas visitors

Regulations (SI 1989/306) provide for charges to be made by the NHS for treating overseas visitors – except when exemptions apply, for instance, to people with communicable diseases or from countries with which the United Kingdom has reciprocal health agreements. A person is deemed to be an overseas visitor if he or she is not 'ordinarily resident' in the United Kingdom. Guidance from the Department of Health (DH 1991), *NHS charges to overseas visitors: manual for NHS staff*, a) draws on the definition of ordinary residence set out in *R v Barnet LBC, ex p Shah*; b) points out that the facts of each individual case will have to be considered; c) states that a person who is intending to remain for less than six months should not usually be regarded as ordinarily resident; d) states that somebody coming to take up permanent residence in the United Kingdom is immediately ex-

immediately exempt from charges; e) states that a person who has already, at the time of treatment, been in the United Kingdom for at least twelve months is exempt; and f) states that refugees who have been accepted as such, or people who have applied to take refuge in the United Kingdom, are exempt. There are also a number of other detailed rules.

CHAPTER 15

NHS CONTINUING CARE AND OTHER SERVICES

Coverage

1. Continuing care generally
2. NHS inpatient beds
3. Hospital discharge
4. NHS services: selected list of examples

KEY POINTS

Legislation is conspicuously silent about NHS responsibilities for continuing care. However in 1995, following a well-publicised health service ombudsman investigation into a health authority's policy on continuing inpatient care, the Department of Health felt impelled to issue guidance (HSG(95)8: *NHS responsibilities for meeting continuing health care needs*, which replaced previous guidance (HC(89)5 and its accompanying booklet (DH 1989a)).

The guidance covers not only the availability of NHS continuing care beds, but other continuing care services as well. It refers specifically to the following services: specialist medical and nursing assessment, rehabilitation and recovery, palliative health care, continuing inpatient care under specialist supervision in a hospital or nursing home, respite health care, specialist health care support nursing homes or residential homes, community health services in residential homes or in people's own homes, primary health care, specialist transport services. It also deals at some length with the process of hospital discharge, including a review procedure which is available to challenge discharge decisions in terms of whether eligibility criteria and procedures have been correctly followed and applied (though not as to the *content* of any such criteria).

The guidance was welcomed as an attempt to achieve some consistency across the country and to stem the loss of NHS continuing care services. In practice, much still hinges on the formulation, coherence, publicising and actual application in individual cases of the eligibility criteria. Indeed, whilst many calls had been made previously for such national guidance and criteria, there has since been criticism that the guidance does not go sufficiently far. This is because it still leaves health authorities and NHS Trusts with considerable local discretion as to what – or what not – to provide in terms of balance, type and level of service. First, it remains for local health authorities to determine their own criteria of eligibility of need for continuing NHS care. This invites considerable local variation in policy and practice, as well as disputes about what terms such as 'complex or multiple health care needs' really mean. Second, as the guidance generally makes clear throughout, any NHS responsibilities are subject to 'available resources'. Thus, authorities can alter their criteria from time to time. Even in the case of failure to provide for individuals who apparently meet the criteria, authorities could – on the basis of decided court cases (see previous chapter) – in some circumstances probably argue lack of resources. Third, as a former Secretary of State of Health herself pointed out (Bottomley 1994), no 'set of guidelines is likely to make less sensitive the dividing line' between health and social care. Fourth, the guidance is of little help in making clear to individuals whether they will receive a particular service at the particular time they need it; whether it be, for instance, the advice of a continence adviser, incontinence pads, palliative care or speech and language therapy.

On the other hand, breach of the guidance might in some circumstances form the basis of a judicial review case because although it is not law, it does contain a liberal sprinkling of words such as 'must', 'will need', 'should', 'will'. For example, it might be possible to show, as occurred in the case of *R v North Derbyshire HA, ex p Fisher* (about drug treatment for multiple sclerosis) that a health authority has adopted a policy in substantial disregard, without good reason, of Department of Health guidance. Or, a health authority's continuing care policy might simply be outwith HSG(95)8 and on that account be unlawful (*R v North and East Devon HA, ex p Coughlan*).

In late 1998, a government White Paper recognised that matters were still unsatisfactory. Apart from the need for compatibility between social services and NHS criteria, it stated that a *Long-term care charter* will be introduced, setting out at national level what services people can expect (Secretary of State for Health 1998, p.32).

This chapter also refers briefly and *selectively* to some other specific NHS services which are either relevant to community care, or illustrate how NHS provision works.

I. CONTINUING CARE GENERALLY

See immediately above for summary.

EXTRACTS

Legislation is silent about continuing care. It refers merely to medical services, nursing services, accommodation; to care and after-care of people who, or have been, ill; and to prevention of illness (NHS Act 1977,s.3: see p.345).

Community care White Paper (Secretaries of State 1989,para 4.19) states:

> (community health services) The 'aim of health authorities should be to ensure that community health services are available to enable people to live in their own homes for as long as possible'.

Guidance states (HSG(95)8, replacing the previous guidance HC(89)5):

> (NHS role and collaboration) 'The arrangement and funding of services to meet continuing physical and mental health care needs are an integral part of the responsibilities of the NHS ... Both the NHS and local authorities have responsibilities for arranging and funding services to meet people's needs for continuing care. Collaboration is crucial to ensuring the effective and integrated delivery of care' (p.3).

(range of services) The guidance states that health authorities and GP fundholders 'must' arrange and fund the following services: specialist medical and nursing assessment, rehabilitation and recovery, palliative health care, continuing inpatient care under specialist supervision in a hospital or nursing home, respite health care, specialist health care support in nursing homes or residential homes, community health services in residential homes or in people's own homes, primary health care, specialist transport services (p.6).

(within available resources) 'As for all other areas of NHS care, health authorities and GP fundholders will need to set priorities for continuing health care within the total resources available to them. While the balance, type and precise level of services may vary between different parts of the country in the light of local circumstances and needs, there are a number of key conditions which all health authorities and GP fundholders must be able to cover in their local arrangements' (p.6).

(key condition: population needs) 'Health authorities, in collaboration with GPs, are expected to base purchasing decisions on a full assessment of the needs of their population, fully discussed and, if possible, jointly agreed with local authorities. This should be reflected in policies for continuing care which should cover trends in demography, morbidity, clinical practice, and other factors which are likely to impact on the need for continuing health care' (p.14).

(key condition: balance of services and priorities) 'Health authorities must ensure, within the total resources available to them, that they purchase a full range of services to meet the needs of their population for continuing health care. They can however determine, in consultation with local authorities, the balance and type of services they purchase locally, in the light of local circumstances' (p.14).

(particular services) Particular services covered by the continuing care guidance are dealt with under their individual headings later in this chapter. They are community health services; continuing care beds; palliative health care; rehabilitation; respite health care, specialist support in nursing homes, residential homes and the community; specialist transport.

(agreement between health authorities and local authorities) 'In implementing the new community care arrangements health and local authorities have been required to make agreements for hospital discharge. These agreements should continue to form the basis for local collaboration ... Where either health or local authorities are proposing a significant change in the pattern of services which will impact on the resources of other agencies for providing care, they must seek the agreement of the other agency' (p.12).

DISCUSSION

Continuing care generally: lack of clarity

The problem of responsibility for continuing care is most likely to affect elderly people, but might also affect others, such as those with head injuries, severe learning disabilities or with requirements for convalescent or terminal care (Henwood 1994,p.15). The 1989 community care White Paper stated that health authorities would have duties to provide long-term, continuing care on the NHS for people who needed it. Yet despite these apparently clear statements, long-term care remains a politically, financially and practically difficult problem (see eg, Laing 1993). Concern about the decline in NHS beds for continuing care has been expressed during the 1990s (eg, Alzheimer's Disease Society 1993; Age Concern England 1995; House of Commons Health Committee 1995,p.xi) – though it should not be forgotten that even prior to this, standards of care for long stay NHS patients had given cause for concern (eg, Age Concern England 1990).

Unfortunately, the position on the ground for individual patients, as to what sort of services they are likely to get, has been left distinctly hazy. For example, in March 1994 it was stated in Parliament that: 'patients who require specialist medical and nursing supervision will continue to be the responsibility of the NHS. This means the NHS will continue to be responsible for providing assessment and rehabilitation facilities, and for retaining long-stay facilities for those whose medical needs or patterns of behaviour would be difficult to manage in a community-based setting' (Mr Stewart: HCWA,9/3/1994,col.268). Or, more simply and uninformatively, 'the provision of continuing care for those who need it for reasons of ill health remains the responsibility of the national health service' (John Bowis: HCWA,3/3/1994,col.855).

The guidance issued the following year (HSG(95)8) went some way to setting out a national framework of core continuing care services and criteria of eligibility – and to determining just how far health authorities can go in reducing continuing care beds and services. However, authorities and NHS Trusts are left with very considerable room for manoeuvre in how they choose to fill out – or not – some of the vague terms in the guidance. In addition, given the chaotic arrangements sometimes surrounding people's admission, treatment and hospital discharge, there must be considerable doubt about a) how criteria and policies are sometimes applied in practice in respect of individual patients, and b) whether patients are given adequate information about local policies (and about, for example, the review procedure available to challenge hospital discharge decisions: see below, p.374).

If guidance fails to resolve effectively the question of people's rights to NHS care, then the issue languishes with local management rather than national policy (Marks 1994,p.9). Indeed, the answers given by central government – that detailed, mandatory central criteria would usurp local medical judgment – are far from convincing, since even local criteria affecting a sizeable population will have the same effect (Price 1996,p.10). The House of Commons Health Committee (1995) pointed out that if its expert witnesses had difficulty understanding the eligibility criteria, then the general public had little chance of doing so – at least without illustrative cases being provided and widely disseminated. Nevertheless, the government was adamant that it would not be appropriate to give examples of inclusions and exclusions, and would not even be drawn on the hypothetical example of a person on a drip, with double incontinence, confined to bed 24 hours a day and requiring substantial care (p.xix).

Continuing care generally: eligibility criteria

As the 1995 guidance HSG(95)8 recognised, continuing care is about far more than NHS inpatient beds; and if diversity and innovation is to be achieved, then clear criteria are required for a whole range of community health services (Vellenoweth 1996).

It has been pointed out that concentration on criteria set by the NHS disadvantages local authority social services departments, and that the latter should respond by defining their own criteria for social need and care, 'rather than merely agreeing to accept responsibility for patients rejected by the NHS' (Clements 1996b). Even were this imbalance redressed, it could simply result in more people falling between the twin stools of NHS and social services criteria – as already sometimes happens, for instance, in relation to bathing, personal care, and equipment provision. Furthermore, the scope of social care is inherently more difficult to limit than health care; at the same time, provision of NHS health care is harder for individual people to enforce than social care provided by local authorities.

Perhaps recognising the potential for continuing lack of clarity, the monitoring of local policies and criteria based on the continuing care 1995 guidance resulted in further guidance being issued in 1996 which referred to best practice. This was identified as including clearly drafted and signposted criteria, strong involvement of front-line staff, clear and unrestrictive definitions of key terms, clarity about the application of criteria, clear operational protocols, criteria tested in case studies – and clear, comprehensible presentation for both staff and public (EL(96)8,para 14). Additional guidance dwelt on the same theme and noted that a) some criteria were too general to promote consistent and open decision-making, and that a balance between clarity and rigidity was required; and b) clarification of health and social services responsibilities, too rigidly applied, reduced the scope for flexibility in meeting people's overall needs (EL(96)89,p.4). Yet in 1998, SSI reported that nearly half of the authorities it had inspected had not achieved joint agreements, and community care and continuing care policies proceeded as two separate policies (SSI 1998b,p.53).

In practice, some health authorities might develop eligibility criteria which are generic to a number of services, others which are specific to particular continuing care services. The question is 'whether generic criteria address adequately the differing clinical conditions of particular client groups; if not, what particular differences might need to be addressed, and whether a separate set of criteria for each client group is likely to clarify eligibility criteria or introduce unnecessary complexity' (Henwood 1996,p.iii). Conveying eligibility criteria to members of the public is not helped if they are not publicised widely, clearly and comprehensibly. For instance, on the clarity issue, the definition of a service (eg, rehabilitation) might be an important element to include within criteria, but alone does not explain the eligibility test.

Continuing care generally: legal effect of Circular guidance

In the absence of detailed NHS legislation, continuing care guidance has to be looked to instead; however, the legal force of guidance is often unclear (see p.38).

On the one hand, it might be argued that because some of the language in HSG(95)8 appears mandatory, it is possible that the courts might find that health authorities are obliged to follow some of it – even though it is not itself legislation. Thus, in *R v North and East Devon HA, ex p Coughlan*, the health authority's continuing care eligibility criteria were unlawful because they were outwith the guidance as was the lack of multi-disciplinary assessment. At an extreme, they might even regard the language of guidance as constituting directions, which are accepted as legally binding (*R v Secretary of State for Health, ex p Manchester Local Medical Committee*).

The health service ombudsman has sometimes considered the effect of guidance on hospital discharge. In one investigation, he stated: 'that is not to say that the Health Authority were entitled … to consider what is said in circular HC(89)5 as merely guidelines which they were free not to implement'. This was in rejection of the view of a deputy manager which was that 'the advice in that circular was no more than guidelines and that, while the Health Authority would do their best to follow them, the booklet … used "should" and not "must", when referring to not transferring a patient who was unwilling to move and be responsible for the home's charges' (*Bromley HA 1994*).

However, even if it is accepted that the current guidance (HSG(95)8) does impose binding obligations – at least to some extent – on authorities, it might be difficult always to pinpoint them. For instance, of the previous guidance the ombudsman conceded that it was 'capable of different interpretations' and obscured by an 'unfortunate lack of clarity' (Health Service Commissioner 1994,p.5). In the case of the present guidance, a challenge concerning the level of services provided and in respect of a particular individual patient's failure to obtain a service at a particular time might be hard to press home'.

2. NHS INPATIENT BEDS

Of crucial importance to many people and their relatives, and to the finances of health authorities and NHS Trusts, is to know when patients are either permitted to (continue to) occupy an NHS bed (whether in a hospital or elsewhere) – and when they are not. To this end, the Department of Health has set out national criteria, albeit at a general level, in guidance; while the health service ombudsman has struggled in some of his investigations – through a legal, political and (for patients) distressing quagmire – to identify and disentangle relevant factors and considerations. Extracts from Department of Health guidance and advice are quoted at some length immediately below a) because of the absence of detailed legislation; and b) to illustrate the sometimes confusing explanation put forward.

Legislation does not explicitly refer to continuing inpatient care, although it does refer to caring for people who are ill and to after-care (NHS Act 1977,s.3.

Policy guidance (DH 1990) listing what the objectives of individual care should be in order of preference, places last 'long-stay care in hospital' (para 3.24). However, there:

> **(NHS beds: general availability)** 'will always be some people who cannot be supported in their own homes. Where such people require continuous care for reasons of ill-health, it will remain the responsibility of health authorities to provide for this. Examples here might include mentally ill people who require specialised residential health provision; as, indeed, may some people with mental or physical handicaps. Some frail elderly people may require continuous health care, traditionally provided in long-stay hospital wards ... Health authorities will need to ensure that their plans allow for the provision of continuous residential health care for those highly dependent people who need them, but that people should not be placed in this type of care unnecessarily. Whether this requires an increase or a reduction in the level of continuous health provided through the NHS will depend very much on local circumstances...' (paras 4.19–4.21).

Circular guidance (HSG(95)8,pp.15–16) states:

> **(adequate level of inpatient care)** 'All health authorities and GP Fundholders should arrange and fund an adequate level of service to meet the needs of people who because of the nature, complexity or intensity of their health care needs will require continuing inpatient care arranged and funded by the NHS in a hospital or in a nursing home ... The NHS is responsible for arranging and funding continuing inpatient care, on a short or long term basis, for people':
>
> > **(need and supervision)** 'where the complexity or intensity of their medical, nursing care or other clinical care or the need for frequent not easily predictable interventions requires the regular (in the majority of cases this might be weekly or more frequent) supervision of a consultant, specialist nurse or other NHS member of the multi-disciplinary team';

(specialist NHS staff) 'who require routinely the use of specialist health care equipment or treatments which require the supervision of specialist NHS staff';

(changing condition) 'who have a rapidly degenerating or unstable condition which means that they will require specialist medical or nursing supervision'.

(likely to die) In addition, people 'who have finished acute treatment or inpatient palliative care in a hospital or hospice, but whose prognosis is that they are likely to die in the very near future should be able to choose to remain in NHS funded accommodation, or where practicable and after an appropriate and sensitive assessment of their needs, to return home with the appropriate support'.

Circular guidance (HSG(95)8,pp.8–10) also states, partly repetitively:

(need and specialist supervision) The consultant, in consultation with the multi-disciplinary team, will decide whether inpatient care is required because the patient needs 'ongoing and regular specialist clinical supervision (in the majority of cases this might be weekly or more frequent) on account of':

(needs) 'the complexity or intensity of their medical, nursing or other clinical needs';

(interventions) 'the need for frequent not easily predictable interventions';

(terminal illness) 'or because after acute treatment or inpatient palliative care in hospital or hospice his or her prognosis is such that he or she is likely to die in the very near future and discharge from NHS care would be inappropriate';

(rehabilitation) 'the patient needs a period of rehabilitation or recovery arranged and funded by the NHS to prepare for discharge arrangements breaking down';

(appropriate discharge) 'the patient can be appropriately discharged from NHS inpatient care with:

- either a place in a nursing home or residential care home … arranged and funded by social services or by the patient or his or her family;
- or a package of social and health care support to allow the patient to return to his or her own home or to alternatively arranged accommodation'.

(refusal to go to residential or nursing home) If assessed as not requiring continuing NHS inpatient care, patients 'do not have the right to occupy indefinitely an NHS bed'. If other options are rejected, 'it may be necessary for the hospital, in consultation with the health authority, social services department and where necessary [the] housing authority, to implement discharge to the patient's home or alternative accommodation, with a package of health and social care within the options and resources available'.

Minister of State for Social Security and the Disabled: a letter to the health service ombudsman (quoted in investigation W.194/89–90) stated:

(clinical, not financial, decision to discharge) 'Decisions about the discharge of people from hospital are for the consultant in charge of the patient's care to make and must be made on clinical grounds. Financial considerations should not enter into the decision.'

(NHS bears cost wherever care provided) 'Where it is decided that a patient requires continuing in-patient medical or nursing care, it falls to the NHS to supply it at no cost to the patient. The on-going care can be provided either by the patient remaining in an NHS hospital bed or for example by transfer to a private nursing home under contractual arrangements, with the NHS meeting the full cost and retaining the ultimate responsibility for the patient's care.'

(discretionary level of care) 'It is of course for individual health authorities to decide the level of contractual arrangements. In making such decisions a variety of factors is to be taken into account; cost is an important factor but it is not the overriding consideration.'

(inability to pay for nursing home fees) 'In the last analysis, where a person in a home can no longer meet his fees but still requires nursing home or residential home care it will fall to the NHS or local authority as appropriate to provide that care if it is not otherwise available to the person'.

NHS Management Executive advice. The health service ombudsman obtained further advice from the NHS Management Executive (quoted in W.194/89–90). Basically, it confirmed that the duty to meet the clinical needs of people is qualified by the resources available.

(problems) 'There are, undoubtedly, real problems in the area which you are examining but it is difficult to be prescriptive about particular local circumstances. The position set out in the [Minister's] letter [see immediately above] is quite correct…'

(professional judgement about NHS care) 'If in a doctor's professional judgement a patient needs NHS care, then there is a duty upon the health service to provide it without charge (except for items where there is a specific power of charging)…'

(three care options) 'this can be done by providing community nursing care to the patient's own home, by providing in-patient care or by a contractual arrangement with an independent sector home (ie, paid in full by the health authority)…'

(discretionary level of service) 'The level of service provided overall is a matter for individual health authorities in the light of local circumstances and priorities'.

NHS Management Executive advice: further detail provided to the health service ombudsman (quoted in W.194/89–90) was as follows:

(no general duty even if a person is in need) 'There is no general duty on a health authority to provide inpatient medical or nursing care to every person who needs it. Legal precedents have established that the Secretary of State's duty under Section 3 of the [NHS] Act is qualified by an understanding that he should do so "within the resources available"';

(clinical priority) In 'any particular case the provision of such care may be deferred so that cases may be dealt with, in order of clinical priority, within the resources available'.

(non-provision of in-patient care to somebody in need) 'consideration of clinical priority may mean that a particular patient may never be provided with in-patient nursing care'.

(option 1: directly provided NHS care) There were three options open to a health authority. First, 'to provide an NHS in-patient bed in the hospital or other suitable NHS premises (if beds were available)';

(option 2: NHS care elsewhere) Second, 'to purchase a bed for their patient in a private hospital or home (if resources extended to this category of patient)';

(option 3: no NHS care) Third, 'to advise … that their resources did not extend to [either of the above two options] and the alternatives were that [the person] should be cared for at home, with some NHS services provided by the DHA or GP and such social services as could be provided by the Local Authority; [or] that [the person] should apply for a place privately in a private nursing home to which the NHS could not contribute.'

DISCUSSION

If the priority of individual patients is determined by the 'clinical judgement' of doctors, then it can sometimes become difficult to distinguish clinical decision-making from decisions made on the basis of available resources (see p.348). Despite the general criteria for continuing NHS care set out by the Circular guidance (HSG(95)8), people's eligibility remains unclear – since not only will criteria vary from one locality to another, but open to doubt must be a) the extent to which locally set criteria conform to the spirit of the guidance, and b) if they do, whether they are applied consistently, or even referred to, when decisions are made in respect of individual patients.

The guidance sets out in effect national criteria to determine eligibility for continuing care beds – but how the criteria are fleshed out locally and applied in individual cases leaves health authorities and NHS Trusts with very considerable discretion. It is also clear that the short-lived attempts of a few years ago to avoid the emergence of a distinction between 'continuous NHS nursing care' and 'continuous nursing care' – and to claim that all nursing care is simply a health matter and the province of the NHS whether in an acute unit or elsewhere (eg, Age Concern England 1991,p.8; NCC 1994,p.5) – have long since been overtaken by events. Nevertheless, in late 1998 the High Court apparently turned back the clock by stating that both general and specialist nursing are the sole responsibility of the NHS (*R v North and East Devon HA, ex p Coughlan* – although the case is being appealed).

Consequent upon the health service ombudsman's Leeds investigation (see p.371), the guidance was designed to reduce the flow away from the NHS of continuing care beds and to safeguard future patients.

NHS inpatient beds: complexity, intensity and interventions

Guidance states that eligibility for continuing inpatient care depends on a need for ongoing, regular specialist supervision on account of the complexity or intensity of nursing care or a continuing need for frequent, not easily unpredictable intervention.

These terms are not easily capable of precise definition and health authorities are undoubtedly left with discretion as to how to interpret them in different situations. However, guidance issued in 1996 does point out to health authorities that the complexity, intensity and unpredictability of conditions are alternative, *sufficient* conditions – not *necessary* conditions which all have to be met. The guidance criticises the fact that in practice, some criteria 'place too much emphasis on the need for people to meet multiple criteria to qualify for NHS funded care' (EL(96)8,section C).

NHS inpatient beds: death in the very near future

Guidance (HSG(95)8 states that people 'likely to die in the very near future' are eligible to remain in NHS-funded accommodation. This phrase does not equate with either what is meant by terminal illness or by the need for palliative care (see p.389). For instance, other guidance issued in 1993 states that terminally ill people 'are those with an active and progressive disease for which curative treatment is not possible or not appropriate, and whose death can reasonably be expected within 12 months' (EL(93)14,annex A,para 4).

Nevertheless, further guidance issued in 1996 sounded a warning to those health authorities operating very short time limits in relation to people who would shortly die. It explained that the purpose of the 1995 guidance (HSG(95)8) was to give people likely to die in the very near future

'the choice of being cared for in NHS funded accommodation. The crucial objective here is to ensure sensitive discharge practice for this group of patients while recognising that clinical prognosis in many cases will be imprecise ... Very short time limits (for instance of the order of a couple of
weeks) are not appropriate and any time limits should be applied flexibly in the light of individual
circumstances' (EL(96)8,section C).

Nevertheless, in practice, health authorities sometimes operate explicit, short time limits ranging from two to six weeks, with eligibility in relation to longer periods of survival regarded as 'exceptional'. Other authorities might not set absolute timescales and claim that they operate flexibly
in what are, after all, highly sensitive and distressing situations. But the flexible interpretation invited by such a lack of timescales, can also result in highly restrictive decisions in practice – for instance, where an authority identifies eligibility with the 'imminence' of death (Henwood
1996,pp.30–33).

NHS inpatient beds: refusal to leave hospital

Guidance states that a patient cannot be forced into a residential or nursing home, but at the same
time does not have a right to occupy a hospital bed if he or she is judged clinically not to need it. It
suggests that a home care package or alternative accommodation should be explored instead
'within the options and resources available' (HSG(95)8,p.10). This is consonant with a statement
made in Parliament in 1992 that: 'nobody should be discharged into a private sector establishment
against his or her will, unless the full costs are to be met from public funds. If a contribution is required, the agreement of the individual will be needed' (Tim Yeo: HCD,1/7/1992,col.874).

However, a home care package might not be possible in, for example, the following circumstances: when home care is clearly unsuitable (eg, person with dementia), discharge is not possible
(intravenous feeding or double incontinence), home care is possible but only after rehabilitation or
convalescence, or the carer is unable or unwilling to continue caring (NCC 1994,p.9). In such circumstances, if a person refuses to leave the hospital even after losing a review of the discharge decision (see p.374), the position is unclear. In principle, the patient might become a trespasser and be
subject to removal by the hospital authorities; in practice, NHS Trusts and health authorities
would face a political minefield if they were to attempt forcibly to remove patients. Isolated incidents will not worry health authorities and NHS Trusts; a minor 'epidemic' of people refusing to
leave a single hospital might.

Equally, guidance warns emphatically that where there is disagreement between the NHS and
social services department about responsibility for continuing care of a person, 'under no circumstances should the patient be put at risk or used as a pawn, for example, through coerced discharge
home' (SSI,SWSG 1991b,p.92).

In one health service ombudsman investigation, a woman had wanted the NHS to fund the
nursing home care of her husband who had Alzheimer's disease. The health authority was prepared to provide the health care element of his care, but the local authority would arrange the accommodation and meet the level of costs for which it would be liable in the light of its statutory
test of resources (see Chapter 12). However, the woman refused a financial assessment, without
which the local authority could not arrange the care. The health authority acknowledged it could
not force the husband into a nursing home, but at the same time clinical advice prevented his dis-

charge to his own home. He was cared for in a community hospital and funded by the health authority; the ombudsman found that the health authority had acted reasonably (*Oxfordshire HA 1996*).

NHS inpatient beds: advice to the health service ombudsman

The uncertainty facing patients has been illustrated by several health service ombudsman investigations which, although made before the new guidance (HSG(95)8 was issued, expose the apparent lack of straightforward entitlement to service.

For instance, seeking advice from the Department of Health, the ombudsman has elicited statements which declare basically that there is a duty to provide care for those who clinically need it – which, however, does not apply in all cases because authorities can always take resources into account at both policy level and in individual cases (see extracts above). The position would appear to be that authorities cannot adopt rigid policies which deny continuing care to people with complex and specialist needs. However, even a policy to provide care for such people might, in individual cases, be subject to available resources and non-provision be legally defensible on those grounds – at least in some circumstances.

Advice given to the health service ombudsman in the past (W.194/89–90) by the Department of Health contained two apparently contradictory statements. First, if 'in a doctor's professional judgement a patient needs NHS care, then there is a duty upon the health service to provide it without charge'. Second, there 'is no general duty on a health authority to provide inpatient medical or nursing care to every person who needs it. Legal precedents have established that the Secretary of State's duty under Section 3 of the [NHS] Act is qualified by an understanding that he should do so "within the resources available"'.

However, there is not in fact a contradiction, since there is a difference between saying that a person has a 'clinical need' and that a person has a 'clinical need for which this health authority is going to provide NHS care'. The second need does not necessarily follow from the first, since the second is only determined after priorities have been taken into account.

The health service ombudsman has tried to explain this. He stated in his annual report (for 1990–1991) that 'finite resources and other priorities can limit the help that is provided' (Health Service Commissioner 1991,p.5). In another investigation (*Bromley HA 1994*), he puts it another way, stating that he does 'not dissent from the view of the Department [of Health] that health authorities do not have an inalienable duty to provide hospital care for a person who is judged not to need it'. However, even this statement by the ombudsman seems to illustrate the confusion, because the Department of Health's view is not just that there is no duty to provide care for somebody who *does not* need it; but also that there is no absolute duty to provide care even for somebody who *does*.

Nevertheless, the ombudsman went on to state in his annual report for 1993–1994, that whilst this 'inalienable duty' might not exist for authorities, that was 'not the same as maintaining that they can reasonably choose not to provide full-time continuing nursing care under the NHS in every case where acute care in hospital is no longer needed' (Health Service Commissioner 1994,p.5). The ombudsman appeared to be cautioning health authorities not to adopt rigid policies which excluded, as a matter of course, the provision of continuing nursing care to all people who might need it; this general warning found specific expression in his criticism of Leeds health authority's policy on continuing care for people with a neurological condition (*Leeds HA 1994*). It is something of an irony that although this investigation precipitated the issuing of the guidance on continuing care (HSG(95)8), a patient in this condition could in practice still be at risk of exclusion from NHS inpatient care – even since the guidance was published – in those areas where health authorities insist that multiple criteria be satisfied (see above, p.367).

NHS inpatient beds: health service ombudsman investigations

Since the *Leeds* investigation, the ombudsman has continued to investigate policies about continuing inpatient care, remarking in 1996 that clear failures such as in the *Leeds* case were rare but that nevertheless a) some authorities did not have clear, written eligibility criteria, thus making it difficult for both complainant and ombudsman; and b) where criteria did exist they were often complex and restrictive (Health Service Commissioner 1996b,p.iii).

The following are examples of ombudsman investigations over a number of years. The variable outcomes reflect the difficulty facing the ombudsman and health authorities in balancing scarce resources with the needs of vulnerable patients and their relatives. The *Leeds* investigation suggests that the health authority had, in the view of the ombudsman, lost its sense of balance.

In summary, it was a failure in service not to provide a bed for a person with an emergency medical condition (example 1 below), severe head injuries (example 4) or severe neurological condition (example 5); but not such a failure when, because of limited resources, people with recognised clinical needs nevertheless were denied beds (examples 2 and 3). In a further case involving the same health authority, the ombudsman found that its continuing care policy amounted to a failure in service (the same finding as in the *Leeds* case); it agreed to change it (example 6). Further investigations have involved a health authority simply failing to reply to a solicitor's letter about a person's eligibility for continuing care (example 7); an unreasonable, apparent policy of not funding any continuing care beds (example 8); and failure to have written eligibility criteria (example 9).

Example 1: NHS inpatient care, clinical medical emergency (ombudsman). The health service ombudsman concluded that the health authority had a duty to provide care for a person with an emergency medical condition.

The person could not be found an NHS bed in either of the two local hospitals. Instead she was admitted to a private nursing home for which she had to pay. The ombudsman's opinion was that 'a health authority has a duty to provide accommodation when a patient from one of their districts needs admission to hospital immediately as an emergency. The Authority's failure to provide a hospital bed for the mother when she required one in a medical emergency amounted to a failure in a service which they had a duty to provide; I must therefore criticise them for this' (W.111/75–76).

The ombudsman reached this conclusion despite the fact that the authority was aware of the problem and was faced with a large population of elderly people who were 'blocking beds' – which meant that the number of beds available for medical emergencies had been reduced. In addition, there were staff shortages. An alternative solution of increasing the number of NHS beds by increased contracting with private nursing homes had not been adopted because it was deemed lower priority than other needs for resources within the authority.

Examples 2 and 3: NHS inpatient care, lower priority and non-provision (ombudsman). In contrast to the above case, the health service ombudsman investigated two cases in which he seemed to accept that a patient's clinical priority could be determined at least in part by the availability of resources at the particular time in question.

He investigated the case of a person denied admission to hospital for eight months after his GP had requested he be admitted because his wife felt she could no longer manage caring for him. He was suffering from a chronic, debilitating condition. The ombudsman did not uphold the complaint. The consultant concerned had assessed that the person did not need frequent medical intervention and so did not need '24-hour hospital care'.

He stated that 'where demand exceeds available resources there may be some whose clinical priority is such that their needs cannot be met under the NHS. I find that the decision by the DHA about the allocation of resources for the care of the chronic sick was a discretionary matter, and I cannot question such a decision unless I find evidence of maladministration in the way in which the decision was made...'. The ombudsman reached this conclusion despite the fact that health authorities had 'a duty to provide some level of care for persons such as the complainant's husband, who are judged to need long-term nursing care' (W.599/89–90).

In another case of non-admission to an NHS bed for a person with cerebral atrophy, the ombudsman found that health authorities 'have a duty to provide some level of care for persons such as the father, who are judged to need long-term nursing care. However, where – as in this case – demand exceeds available resources there may be some whose clinical priority is such that their needs cannot be met under the NHS'. The decision determining the lower priority was made by a consultant 'in the exercise of clinical judgement', even though the 'need for long-term nursing care had been established'. The ombudsman accepted the validity of this (W.194/89–90).

Examples 4 and 5: NHS inpatient care, nursing care (ombudsman). Two other cases ended in findings against health authorities. In the first case, a woman with severe head injuries had been in a neuro-surgical unit. A decision was made to discharge her to a private nursing home where she would have to pay the fees. The health authority's position was that it 'had finite resources and had to have regard to their responsibility for all patients and to consider what category of care was most appropriate for the particular needs of a patient who was recovering from head injuries ... not all such patients were, under the provisions of the [NHS] Act, the responsibility of the DHA ... the complainant's mother's needs [were] primarily for social care with clinical support ... the Act did not ... impose a responsibility upon health authorities for all head-injured people who no longer required in-patient medical care.'

The ombudsman retorted, given the severe incapacity of the person and the consultant's view that she was 'likely to need sustained nursing care for the rest of her life', that it seemed to him 'incontrovertible, therefore, in the light of the level of continuing care the complainant's mother will require and the chief executive's advice that the DHA had a duty to continue to provide the care ... required at no cost to her or her family' (W.478/89–90).

In the second investigation, well-publicised at the beginning of 1994 (*Leeds HA 1994*), the health service ombudsman investigated how a health authority had exercised its discretion to set priorities. It had decided not to provide directly, or pay for elsewhere (eg, a nursing home), continuing care for people with neurological conditions: the health authority neuro-surgical contract did not refer to institutional care at all. The person discharged was doubly incontinent, could not eat or drink without assistance, could not communicate – and had a kidney tumour, cataracts in both eyes and occasional epileptic fits. There was no dispute that when he was discharged he did not need active medical treatment but did need 'substantial nursing care'. The health authority defended its position with reference to resources, priorities and national policy (which was being followed by other health authorities).

The ombudsman found a failure in service. He cited s.3 of the NHS Act 1977 at the beginning of the report, including s.3(1)(e) which refers to 'after-care'. His findings read: 'This patient was a highly dependent patient in hospital under a contract made with the Infirmary by Leeds Health Authority; and yet, when he no longer needed care in an acute ward but manifestly still needed what the National Health Service is there to provide, they regarded themselves as having no scope for continuing to discharge their responsibilities to him because their policy was to make no provision for continuing care. The policy also had the effect of excluding an option whereby he might have the cost of his continuing care met by the NHS. In my opinion the failure to make available long-term care within the NHS for this patient was unreasonable and constitutes a failure in the service provided by the Health Authority. I uphold the complaint'.

The ombudsman recommended that the health authority reimburse nursing home costs already incurred by the man's wife and meet future costs; and also that it should review its 'provision of services for the likes of this man in view of the apparent gap in service available for this particular group of patients' (*Leeds HA 1994*).

Example 6: NHS inpatient care, highly dependent patient, failure in provision (ombudsman). A 55-year old man had had a stroke; following a hospital stay, he was discharged to a private nursing home where the health authority declined to fund his care, even though he was highly dependent. The authority had, at that time, a policy of not contracting at all for private nursing home beds, even though it conceded that its own 24 long-stay beds were inadequate to meet the need for continuing inpatient care. This meant that younger, highly dependent patients not requiring NHS hospital inpatient treatment were excluded from NHS funding. The regional health authority commented that if people such as the complainant's husband did not qualify for care, then who would? The ombudsman agreed and found a 'failure to provide a service which it is that authority's function to provide' (*North Worcestershire HA 1995*).

Example 7: NHS inpatient care, eligibility and failure to reply to solicitors (ombudsman). The health authority simply could not organise, over a period of two years, a response to a solicitor acting on behalf of two sons who were asking the authority to accept responsibility for their mother's nursing home care. The authority had passed the matter on to its solicitors, but they were unable, despite repeated requests, to obtain the information from the authority necessary to reply to the sons' solicitor. This was clearly a failure; the authority apologised, offered £3,090 compensation to cover the sons' legal fees and agreed to reply properly to the sons's request (*Gwent HA 1998*).

Example 8: NHS inpatient care, no continuing care beds (ombudsman). A policy of funding no continuing care beds either in hospitals or nursing homes was 'unreasonable' and meant that even highly dependent patients, such as the complainant's mother, were not even given the chance to be considered for NHS-funded continuing health care. This was unfair and warranted an *ex gratia* payment (*Avon HA 1996*).

Example 9: NHS inpatient care, lack of written eligibility criteria (ombudsman). The ombudsman could not say whether a man aged 91 – who was registered blind, was deaf, had difficulty in walking and had been admitted to hospital following a fall – might have been considered eligible for continuing NHS inpatient care had his family received information in writing. However, he criticised the health authority for not having written eligibility criteria (*Buckinghamshire HA 1996*).

3. HOSPITAL DISCHARGE

People's needs when leaving hospital can be complicated, involving physical ability, mental ability and attitude, social and environmental factors at home – and so on. Whether or not optimum arrangements are eventually achieved would appear sometimes to depend on chance, since there are many variables which influence the outcome of discharge. This makes the discharge process unpredictable and yet one more potential uncertainty in the community care process.

Legislation does not refer explicitly to hospital discharge. Yet hospital discharge is a crucial element of community care, involving decisions about where, how and with whom people are going to live. Against a background of evidence that practices sometimes fail to meet the basic needs of patients, the Department of Health continues to emphasise the importance of good practice. Guidance seeks to ensure that people do not leave hospital before adequate arrangements have been made for them, and before those arrangements have been understood and agreed by patients and their carers.

The process of hospital discharge has long been the subject of practical difficulties, and is now closely related to the criteria of eligibility which health authorities apply to determine who should receive continuing care beds (see above, p.364). The health service ombudsman regularly investigates complaints about hospital discharge procedures and covers matters such as inadequate consultation, decisions based on inadequate information, and failure to follow Department of Health guidance.

EXTRACTS

Legislation does not refer explicitly to hospital discharge.

Community care policy guidance (DH 1990) states that hospital discharge practices should ensure continuity of health and social care for people, and that people should not have to leave hospital until suitable arrangements have been agreed with themselves and their carers:

> **(continuity of health and social care):** 'health authorities, in conjunction with local authorities, are responsible for designating staff to develop, implement and monitor individual discharge plans. To ensure the continuity of health and social care the local authority and NHS staff working in the community and GPs should be given adequate notice of discharge to enable them to assess and provide for any community care needs, especially where residential or nursing home care may be a possible choice. Local housing authorities may also need to be involved' (para 3.42).

> **(decision-making: social services responsibilities):** 'Health authorities should bear in mind that responsibility for assessing and meeting needs for community social services (including nursing home care where the user is expected to contribute to the cost) rests with the SSDs. Subject to any arrangements agreed between authorities, local authorities should not be expected to endorse decisions about an individual's care needs, or ways of meeting them, taken by health authorities in advance of a recognised community care assessment' (para 3.43).

> **(consumer choice):** 'Subject always to consumer choice, patients should not leave hospital until the supply of at least essential community care services has been agreed with them, their carers and all the authorities concerned. Patients who have lost their homes should not be expected to leave hospital until suitable accommodation has been arranged. In such cases early liaison with the local housing authority is essential' (para 3.44).

Circular guidance (HSG(95)8) states:

> **(hospital consultants)** 'All consultants (or in some community hospitals, GPs) are responsible for the medical care of their patients. They are responsible, in consultation with other key staff working with them, especially nurses, for deciding when a patient no longer needs acute care. The large majority of people, after a stay in hospital, will be able to return their own homes' (p.8).

(multi-disciplinary assessment) 'Decisions about the discharge of these patients from NHS care and on how their continuing care needs might best be met should be taken following an appropriate multi-disciplinary assessment of the patient's needs' (p.8).

(views of patient, family and carers) 'The assessment should also take account of the views and wishes of the patient, his or her family and any carer' (p.8).

(package of social or health care support) A patient can be appropriately discharged either to a residential or nursing home – or with 'a package of social and health care support to allow the patient to return to his or her own home or to alternatively arranged accommodation' (p.9).

(information) 'Patients and their families and carers should be kept fully informed about how procedures for hospital discharge and assessment work and should receive the relevant information (in writing and in other formats appropriate to their needs) they require to make decisions'. This will include in particular information about continuing care options and written details of 'likely cost to the patient of any option which he or she is asked to consider' (p.9).

(review of discharge decisions). Patients and their family have the 'right' to ask the health authority to review the decision which has been made about eligibility for continuing inpatient care. The health authority should respond promptly and respond to the request within two weeks.

The key features of the review arrangements are a panel having a) an independent chairman, b) no 'legal status' and being advisory in nature; c) a representative of the health authority and local authority; and d) a key task of checking whether the authority's eligibility criteria have been correctly applied. The panel would seek appropriate professional advice from staff – and consider evidence from the patient and his family or carers. Rights to refer a complaint to the NHS complaints procedures or to the health service ombudsman are unchanged (pp.11–12).

Further guidance on the review process was issued in HSG(95)39. This emphasises various matters including a) that the review procedure is open to all NHS inpatients whether in a hospital or elsewhere (eg, hospice or nursing home; b) that the scope of the procedure is to check that discharge procedures have been followed and eligibility criteria properly and consistently applied; c) that the procedure is not appropriate to challenge the content (as opposed to the application) of the criteria, the type and location of NHS-funded continuing inpatient care, the content of any alternative care package offered, or treatment or other aspect of the hospital stay; d) that the procedure is not for resolving disputes between health authorities and local authorities about funding responsibilities.

Circular guidance (EL(94)8) expressed concern about hospital discharge: 'health authorities should be clear that their hospital providers have explicit and comprehensive procedures to ensure that there are no organisational delays to prevent patients being discharged from hospital when they are ready to go home' (EL(94)8,paras 1,4).

Department of Health discharge workbook. In 1994, continuing concern led to a 'hospital discharge workbook' being issued by the Department of Health (DH 1994c). It was to promote good practice and presents a series of checklists aimed at different 'stakeholders'.

The Patient's Charter states that before people are discharged from hospital, arrangements will be agreed with agencies such as community nursing services and social services departments (DH 1995c,p.18).

Framework for community care charters (DH 1994b,p.15, incorporating LAC(94)24) includes reference to hospital discharge standards which should ensure 'that:

- no-one will be discharged until it is clinically appropriate;
- the NHS will be responsible for securing continuing care for all people whose clinical needs fall within published eligibility criteria;
- no-one will be discharged from hospital until appropriate arrangements have been put in place for their subsequent care;
- these arrangements will begin as soon as the patient is discharged;
- patients and – unless patients object – their carers, will be fully informed and involved, will be given sufficient time and information to make decisions, and will be told how to seek a review of any decisions made'.

DISCUSSION

Hospital discharge: past practice

A 1994 King's Fund report referred to the 'consistency of research findings, stretching back over at least twenty years, which document the breakdown of routine discharge procedures'. It exposed a number of tensions 'between professional groups, between health and local authorities and between national guidance and local possibilities' (Marks 1994,p.6). Furthermore, any satisfaction expressed by patients to some studies or inspections of services should 'be seen in the context of significant frailty and vulnerability' (SSI 1995g,p.29).

Difficulties might include conflicts between staff over assessments, poorly understood eligibility criteria, lengthy procedures, discharge of people to nursing homes who would have previously remained in hospital beds (and who then die very soon afterwards), decision-making responsibilities – and so on (Henwood 1994,p.17).

Despite the apparent longstanding failure of hospital discharge processes, opportunities to inject statutory force were lost during the passage of the NHS and Community Care Bill. One amendment sought to make mandatory the assessment of people leaving hospital (before the person left hospital or at least within 14 days of discharge), the specifying of services needed and the appointment of a person to ensure that people's assessed needs were met. The government objected to the amendment as a 'blunt instrument', the aims of which could be better achieved by a mixture of legislation and guidance (Baroness Blatch: HLD, 10/5/1990, col.1539). Similarly, fixed times for assessment procedures could 'very often become a maximum amount of time and create inflexibility'. Instead, what should happen is that 'assessment will take as long as is necessary' (Baroness Hooper: HLD,14/6/1990,col.492).

In retrospect this was a highly unconvincing strategy on the part of central government. Not only did guidance (HC(89)5) on hospital discharge have to be withdrawn in 1995, just two years after the implementation of community care, but hospital discharge continues to be a serious problem even following the issue of new guidance (HSG(95)8). Furthermore, good practice documents such as the Department Health workbook (DH 1994c) are well received, yet the necessity of setting down lists of such obvious points – none particularly novel – is a depressing reminder of the continuing problems.

Hospital discharge: local authority criteria of eligibility

A single hospital, attempting to arrange discharges efficiently, consistently and equitably, might be faced with the considerable difficulty of having people from 'four counties, each of which is going to have its own different and separate criteria of eligibility for assessment and service provision' (Age Concern England's evidence to: House of Commons Health Committee 1993, vol.2,p.168). Ward staff might be confused 'by a variety of documentation, different eligibility criteria and delays in decision making and subsequent discharge. In one hospital there were three hospital teams from different Local Authorities, each with different systems and procedures' (SSI,NHSME 1994k,p.28). The confusion of staff over various sets of eligibility criteria might not be the result of inadequate training but simply 'reflect the turmoil or disagreement that existed in some areas between the health and social services agencies' (SSI 1998b,p.49).

Hospital discharge: delayed or premature

Tardiness in the provision of services for people going home can delay discharge: for example, waits for equipment and home adaptations are frequently cited as problems (eg, SSI 1998c,p.27; Age Concern London 1995). Even the need for simple items of equipment such as commodes can delay discharge for several days; special beds might be delivered only once a week; and assessment by community OTs could take several months. Equipment budgets might be under increasing pressure, which in turn increases the likelihood of demarcation disputes (SSI,NHSME 1994k,p.25). The term 'bed-blocking', covering a variety of circumstances, is never far from the hospital discharge and community care agenda (eg, LGA 1996).

On the whole, it seems that good practice is more likely to be found in specialist elderly care units or wards than in general medical or acute units (Health Advisory Service 1997,p.11; Henwood 1994,p.14; EL(96)89,p.6); in the latter, people might fail to get a proper community care assessment at all (Midgley, Munlo and Brown 1997,p.34). Discharge procedures 'are often poorly organised' with 'frequent delays in arranging transport and take-home medicines as well as longer delays because of the need to organise domiciliary support. Discharges are sometimes also delayed because residential or nursing home places cannot be easily be found' (Audit Commission 1992,p.1).

Alternatively, people are sometimes discharged too soon. They might not be prepared physically or psychologically if they are informed about the discharge at short notice, might not cope well (eg, they might be unable to leave the house, be in pain or have bladder and bowel problems), and sometimes not receive services for the first two weeks after discharge (Worth 1994). Notwithstanding such obvious problems, hospital consultants and other staff might pre-judge the outcome of assessments and attempt to discharge patients 'precipitously and against social work advice' (SSI 1995g,pp.12,18; also Joule 1994,p.20), thus truncating a proper recovery and rehabilitation period (SSI 1995h,p.18) and casting doubt at least on the application, or even the existence, of appropriate eligibility criteria. Therapists might find themselves involved in discharge facilitation rather than rehabilitation, able only to consider basic safety, rather than lifestyle and qualify of life (Clark, Dyer and Horwood 1996,pp.56–60).

Hospital discharge: transfer of frail older NHS patients to other long stay settings

The transfer of patients in NHS long-stay settings sometimes gives rise to concern when people's welfare is put at risk. For instance, the health service ombudsman reported adversely on one such incident:

Example: transfer against consultant's advice (ombudsman). In 1996, the health service ombudsman published an investigation in which an elderly man with dementia was transferred from a hospital, in which he had been a patient for four years, to a private nursing home. He died 17 days after the transfer which was a) opposed by the man's consultant but approved, in her absence, by a colleague who was aware of the consultant's opposition but believed there was no alternative; and b) as a result of a planned closure of the ward which had been brought forward by 21 months – a change of plan approved at a health authority meeting which had not been open to the public.

The ombudsman doubted whether the second consultant's acquiescence in the discharge amounted to sufficient authority to sanction the discharge and was particularly concerned that, given the first consultant's opinion, the second consultant made no entry on the clinical records. The NHS Trust did not comply with Department of Health discharge guidance (then HC(89)5) and drew the ombudsman's strong criticism, although he recognised that Winchester Health Authority's decision to speed up the closure gave the Trust little time to consult and make practical arrangements.

The ombudsman found it 'totally undemocratic that a public body should have considered it justifiable to discuss a policy matter of such importance to patients and their families at a meeting closed to the general public', and criticised the authority's calling the meeting informal. He concluded by stating that the circumstances of the complaint 'should serve as a grim warning to any health authority or trust planning the discharge of patients from hospital or elsewhere' (*North and Mid-Hampshire HA 1996*).

A House of Commons Select Committee looked further into the above case and a) criticised the closed meeting, believing that its description as informal was such as to, 'despite all the trappings (and consequences) of a formal meeting, suggest some sleight of hand and an attempt to rush through a decision without the inconveniences of public scrutiny and possible controversy'; c) could not criticise 'strongly enough this brazen attempt to ignore the expert advice of the responsible clinician who had known the patient for six years' and whose advice was 'inconvenient to the relevant managers'; and d) the responsible members and officers of the health authority 'should be ashamed of what took place' and should have their suitability to be in positions of responsibility reviewed by the Secretary of State (House of Commons Select Committee on Public Administration 1997,p.v).

In the light of such incidents, the Department of Health issued guidance on the subject (HSC 1998/048). It contains language which the courts might deem to be of some legal force – for instance, words such as 'should' and the phrase 'what to do' followed by a list (as opposed to phrases such as 'may like to consider doing') of what should be done. The guidance covers consultation, a project plan, the needs of the individual and their relatives or carers, the process of transfer and role to be played by staff in the new setting, and follow-up and monitoring. In particular, a care plan for each patient should be drawn up, be subject to regular review before the transfer, involve consultation with relatives and carers, and include the patient's preferences in terms of diet, eating habits, bathing arrangements and idiosyncrasies. There should be a checklist of actions and tasks for each patient before and after the transfer. Information should be provided for patients, relatives and carers. Crucially, because a move can seriously threaten 'physical, psychological and social well-being', it is 'very important, therefore, to be aware of the risks, to handle the process sensitively and to be prepared to delay or halt a transfer if necessary' (para 21). The requirement in the guidance, that a risk assessment be coordinated, was not adhered to in *R v North and East Devon HA, ex p Coughlan*; this failure formed part of the finding of unlawfulness in that case.

Hospital discharge: lack of information

Provision of information for people leaving hospital is not always sufficiently full. For example, an SSI inspection found examples of good practice but that 'overall, information available to people in hospital was sketchy and relied on previous experience or word of mouth'. Over 66 per cent of users and carers interviewed had not received 'any information either written or verbal describing what they could expect from [hospital social services], their priorities or how to gain access to services'. This jeopardised equitable access to services by patients – although the inspection overall found users well-satisfied with the services provided (SSI 1993h,p.10). Nevertheless, some years later, another inspection reported, without going into detail, that most users and carers were being kept informed about what was happening and what was planned; and half of the local authorities reinforced oral with written information (SSI 1998b,p.47).

There has long been concern that people are 'forced' to leave hospital to return to their own home – or enter a private nursing home – by being subjected to pressure and not given adequate information about the options open to them. Such concern was expressed to the House of Commons Health Committee (1993,vol.1,p.xiv) by the Alzheimer's Disease Society: 'It is quite clear that the relatives – and I am quite sure the older people themselves – are not aware of their rights and are not being made aware of their right to insist on staying where they are or continuing to receive an NHS funded bed, and they are often being very vigorously encouraged to seek a placement in an independent nursing home'. If a bed is blocked: 'the pressure from managers and doctors to get that person into a nursing home is immense and the person's wishes may also be blocked. They may go into a home which is too far from their family or on the wrong bus route' (1993,vol.2,p.15). The health service ombudsman noted in his 1994 annual report that in his experience Department of Health guidance 'is not adequately known or observed. In some instances patients or their relatives have simply not been properly told about the financial implications of discharge to a private nursing home' (Health Service Commissioner 1994,p.5). For example:

Example 1: information on discharge (ombudsman). When a woman left hospital to stay in a residential home for three weeks, the ombudsman found a) a conflict of evidence about how the arrangements had been organised, and b) an absence of any 'useful contemporary records' about what had happened. He concluded that the family had not been told about the possible costs involved in entering residential care – and was concerned that four years after national guidance (HC(89)5) had emphasised the importance of discharge procedures, there were 'no proper written procedures'. Instead, 'staff relied on custom and practice not easily communicated – if at all – to new staff'.

The health authority added insult to injury by stating that after she had been made aware of the cost, the woman could have moved elsewhere; it was 'lacking in humanity and unreasonable to expect that a woman of 89 years, recovering from a fall, should endure another move, which would have been needed only because the authority had not originally arranged her discharge properly'. The ombudsman recommended that the NHS Trust and health authority agree discharge procedures for the accident and emergency department and reimburse the woman for the costs of the stay in the residential home (*East Norfolk HA 1996*).

Example 2: information on discharge (ombudsman). A woman who had had a stroke and was unable to swallow had to be fed by a gastric tube. Initially her family wished her to return home and considerable effort was made to give them information about costs involved. However, when the family then changed their mind and considered a nursing home, they were told neither clearly nor in writing that they would have to pay the fees. (In addition, its continuing care criteria had anyway contradicted Department of Health guidance (HSG(95)8). The NHS Trust agreed to revise its procedures to ensure that families were fully informed in future about responsibility for nursing home fees, and also agreed to reimburse the family for expenses incurred (*North Worcestershire HA 1996*).

Examples 3 and 4: information on discharge (ombudsman). A complaint was not upheld because, although the NHS Trust was at fault for not providing the information about the nursing home fees, the local authority social services department remedied this omission and in any case the person concerned had not been entitled to NHS support (*Plymouth Hospitals NHS Trust 1997*). Similarly, where national guidance (HC(89)5) had not been followed because a woman discharged to a nursing home had not been informed in writing whether the NHS would meet the costs of the care – injustice or hardship was not caused because it was clear that from an early stage the woman was anyway aware of the position (*South Devon Healthcare Trust 1997*).

Example 5: information on discharge (ombudsman). A woman who had fallen and fractured her leg was discharged to a private residential home where she stayed for about a month and faced a bill of over £900. The ombudsman found that she had not been given information by the hospital about the fees and that therefore the NHS Trust 'did not carry out their responsibilities to the woman under the terms of the circular' – ie HC(89)5 (W.524/92–93).

Example 6: information on discharge (ombudsman). In the Leeds investigation, already mentioned, the ombudsman made a finding of duress, despite the fact that the wife of a brain-damaged person had apparently accepted the decision about discharge: 'Since it was made clear that continuing occupation of an acute bed was not clinically appropriate, the complainant was left in the difficult position of choosing between refusing to accept his discharge or meeting the [private nursing] home's charges. None of the hospital staff was aware of – nor did Infirmary policy apparently provide for – the requirement in the guidance [see above] to set out in writing, before discharge to a nursing home, who would pay the fees. I criticise this significant omission. The complainant was not given that information. I therefore regard her as having been placed under duress through that failure to inform her of all the relevant considerations ... Although she acquiesced in the need for her to pay the nursing home fees, in my opinion that was inequitable in the circumstances. I recommend that Leeds Health Authority remind their providers of the need to follow the Department of Health's guidance on discharge procedures' (*Leeds HA 1994*).

Example 7: information on discharge (ombudsman). A woman had suffered strokes in hospital, but her daughter was told that her mother did not meet the NHS eligibility criteria for continuing inpatient care. She was not informed in writing about the financial consequences of nursing home care. The health authority's system relied on social services to inform people about the financial implications of nursing home care. Yet hospital staff neglected to refer people in need of nursing home care to social services for a financial assessment, if they believed that those patients would be ineligible for financial assistance. Furthermore, a joint assessment form was not completed and social services, the community liaison nurse and the woman's daughter were not involved in the assessment. The daughter was denied an opportunity to explore other options, a proper discussion and advice. This was maladministration. The health authority agreed to make a payment to the daughter (*East Kent HA 1996*).

Example 8: information on discharge (ombudsman). A man was being discharged from hospital following a stroke. His wife was told that although he needed 24-hour nursing care, he would have to go into a nursing home. She was referred to a charitable home which received funding from the health authority and provided advice and help in relation to nursing home placement – but only for people receiving income support. The complainant was on this account not eligible and so received no advice about the costs of nursing home care or possible alternatives. The health authority had no long-term care beds of its own for elderly people at all, but its grant to the charitable body meant that it was in effect paying some of the cost of nursing home care for some patients. The ombudsman could not comment on the legality of such an arrangement, given the rules about 'topping up' (see p.294), but did find that it was 'no substitute for a proper mechanism for determining eligibility for NHS funding for continuing health care, regardless of the financial means of the patient' (*North Cheshire HA 1996*).

The effectiveness of the 1995 guidance on continuing care relies on people's being made aware of the local eligibility criteria and of their right to a review of the discharge decision. Yet not only will patients from hospital to hospital have uneven access to a varying quality of information (NCC 1997,chapter 4), but even staff might be unaware of criteria. For instance, NHS staff might not know about changes to social services criteria (SSI 1997f,p.25), or might not have a clear understanding of how even their own NHS criteria operate (Henwood 1996,p.40).

Hospital discharge: social services assessment

Records which fail to show the views of patients and carers, to identify need and to show that alternative options to residential care have been considered (SSI 1995g,p.22) – might be evidence that in fact such matters have not been discussed at all not only under s.47 of the NHS and Community Care Act 1990, but also in relation to the stipulation of policy guidance (DH 1990,para 3.25) that people's preferences be taken account of (*R v North Yorkshire CC, ex p Hargreaves,* and see p.138).

There might be 'inadequate collation and transfer of assessment and care planning information … which would enable a proper response to … social, emotional and spiritual needs' – whilst assessment and care planning records might barely refer to eligibility criteria, thus making it difficult to establish the basis for decisions (SSI 1995g,pp.25–26). Lack of integration between NHS assessment for continuing care and local authority community care assessments might affect the coherence of overall assessment (EL(96)89,para 6). Even when a judicial review ruling *(R v Sutton, ex p Tucker)* creates a climate 'over-concentrated on the legal aspects of care', a local authority might apparently still fail to base its care plans on written assessments of need (SSI 1997g,p.24), despite the fact that care plans were one focus of the ruling.

Some local authorities might take a pragmatic approach by filtering out referrals of patients unlikely to be eligible for services – for example, if they require only house cleaning or shopping. This is despite the fact that their own policies state that most people are eligible for an assessment, and that the courts have confirmed the duty to assess even when services are unlikely to be provided (*R v Bristol CC, ex p Penfold*). Similarly, hospital staff might simply fail to refer for social services assessment patients whose resources are such that they will not qualify for financial assistance in paying for residential or nursing home care (NCC 1997,p.34); or if there is an informal carer available and no need for support has been indicated (Godfrey, Moore 1996,p.30). Alternatively, following assessment and recommendations by a multi-disciplinary team about after-care services, a social services 'area panel' might question and undermine the apparent outcome of such assessments, without necessarily having the requisite clinical expertise (SSI 1997f,pp.16–23,SSI 1997g,p.19). In order to identify legally what is happening here (eg, in relation to assessment and a decision about services under s.47 of the NHS and Community Care Act 1990), it would be important to identify at what point the statutory decision under s.47 (as opposed to non-statutory recommendations: see eg, *R v Kirklees, ex p Daykin,* see also *R v Wigan MBC, ex p Tammadge* for pinpointing the decision) is actually being made – and whether legally relevant factors have been taken into account.

Assessment for hospital discharge can easily become a negative and sometimes patronising affair, conducted in terms of ability to make a cup of tea, and viewed by patients a) as a 'test' of ability and readiness to leave rather than a positive consideration of future needs; and b) as outside of their control (Godfrey, Moore 1996,pp.iv,34). Inadequate assessment can lead to all manner of problems: for example, when a person is discharged with no prior home visit because her hospital bed was needed; the local authority and housing association argue about who will fund the adaptations she requires; two weeks later she is in pain, depressed, unable to reach her kitchen cupboards, barely able to operate the sink taps, reaching over the cooker rings to the controls at the back – and trying to use her bed which was too high and armchair which was too low (Neill, Williams 1992,p.82).

Hospital discharge: treatment in hospital

In practice, successful discharge from hospital – based on proper assessment, information and planning – does not depend only on the actual physical discharge but also on the standard of care and service which has gone before. Thus, when hospital staff are 'overstretched', and elderly patients are neglected (physically or mentally) and deprived of information, rehabilitation and effective assessment, the omens are bad (eg, Age Concern London 1995).

Conversely for example, when people have had hip operations, rehabilitation and independence are promoted by a good ward environment in terms of the beds, chairs and tables being at an appropriate height; non-slip floors; hand rails; good lighting; sign-posting of doorways, exits, toilets, bathrooms; easy access to spectacles, hearing aids, walking aids and personal possessions. Effective practice might then demand that a properly supported early discharge scheme with home-based rehabilitation should follow, which might cost less than continued inpatient care and be more effective (Audit Commission 1995b,p.38). Conversely, confusion and discontinuity consequent on being shunted around different wards depending on bed availability (Godfrey, Moore 1996,p.iii) is highly undesirable.

The treatment of older people in hospitals is also reported to be inadequate in a number of very basic respects. For instance, on admission to accident and emergency, they might have to wait unacceptably long and be uncomfortable due to a lack of food and drink, and a lack of appropriate chairs, beds or trolleys. There might be deficiencies in respect of the physical fabric of wards, the availability of basic supplies of linen and technical equipment, a shortage of appropriate nursing and therapy staff, the availability and quality of food and drink, the help given by staff in relation to eating and drinking and to ensuring that people obtain adequate nutrition, personal hygiene and dressing – and so on (Health Advisory Service 1998,pp.i–ii). The Secretary of State made it clear this state of affairs 'is unacceptable' (HSC 1998/220). One example (not from the report) of what can happen, involving not only inadequate care but sheer absurdity is as follows:

Example: neglect of older person in hospital. A 93-year old woman, recovering from a heart attack, is offered 'high-tech' heart surgery (an offer which she immediately dismisses as irrelevant to her wishes and needs) – but at the same time is denied the opportunity for two weeks to have something as basic as a bath or hair wash. In addition she is given a drug which renders her apparently incontinent (but in fact just vulnerable to sudden urges); this is put down to 'age'. When relatives protest, the nursing staff agree to ask for another drug to be prescribed to counter the effects of the first drug. A few days later, this seems to have had no effect; relatives discover that the nurses have forgotten to give the second drug, even though it had been prescribed. The woman's dignity, morale and will to fight an infection she has picked up in hospital are completely sapped. During her stay, there is nothing to do on the ward, so she stays in bed, is not encouraged to exercise and receives no physiotherapy or occupational therapy. Out of the blue, she is then assessed by an occupational therapist, who does not want to let her return home, because she is 'unsteady' on her feet. However the therapist does not take account of the fact that anyone who has been in bed for two weeks is unsteady on their feet. Furthermore, she takes no account of the woman's independence (up to the heart attack), because a) she does not ask her about her lifestyle, and b) she carries out the assessment without having consulted the woman's hospital notes.

Hospital discharge: lack of communication

Although there is ample scope for discharge to go wrong because of inadequate communication between staff, patients and relatives, nevertheless simple misunderstandings between staff and a patient's carer will not necessarily lead to adverse findings by the health service ombudsman (example 3 below).

However, genuine misunderstanding can be contrasted with the maladministration inherent in a failure a) to fill in forms and pass on correct information to the GP, district nursing service and social services (W.421/88–89); b) to consult adequately with other agencies about the home arrangements to be in place (examples 1 and 2); c) to ensure that a person is discharged into a satisfactory environment (example 4); d) to keep adequate physiotherapy records, to communicate with the patient about her physiotherapy, and to assess her for equipment and adaptations before sending her home (*Redbridge Health Care NHS Trust 1997*).

Closely related are decisions taken on the basis of inadequate information, which might also result in adverse findings by the health service ombudsman. For instance, nursing notes might not reflect a change in the patient's normal condition/pattern and so the discharge decision would be based on inadequate information (example 5). Discharge arrangements might not be altered to reflect a deterioration in the patient's condition and so be made on the basis of 'insufficient thought' (example 6). Poor record-keeping and communication between staff might be compounded by a failure to take account of the GP's letter containing vital information (example 7). Hospital staff might themselves not know what is going on – for instance, mistakenly believing that a person was going to a nursing home when it fact it was a residential home, and be unable to correct the mistake because of a poor working relationship with social services staff (*James Paget Hospital NHS Trust 1998*).

Example 1: communication (ombudsman). Investigating the hospital discharge of a woman with Huntingdon's Chorea, the ombudsman found fault with a consultant who had 'made his proposal to send the patient home before he had consulted sufficiently with the social services department and voluntary organisations to ascertain whether they were in a position to provide the cover and assistance the patient required. I am in no doubt that the assurances which the consultant gave the complainant were faulty and I uphold this complaint'. The community organisations in question could not in fact deliver what the consultant had stated would be possible (W.40/84–85).

Example 2: communication (ombudsman). A hospital consultant had assured a woman's husband that if his wife was discharged from hospital, both home adaptations and home care would be available from social services or voluntary agencies. The health service ombudsman found in fact that the consultant had not consulted others sufficiently 'to ascertain whether they were in a position to provide the cover and assistance the patient required' (W.113/84–85).

Example 3: communication (ombudsman). The ombudsman will not uphold a complaint simply because genuine misunderstandings arise. A carer's mistaken belief is not enough: for example, where she believed that her mother would not be discharged but given a rehabilitation bed whilst she (the carer) was unable, following an operation, to cope. However, when, in the same case, the carer first knew about the discharge through a telephone call telling her that her mother was already on her way home, there had clearly been a breakdown in communication. No hospital 'key worker' had been identified. The ombudsman also found more broadly that discharge policy and procedures were not fully operational and unknown to some staff. This latter aspect of the complaint was upheld, and the health authority set about reinforcing its policy (W.254/88–89).

Example 4: communication (ombudsman). Even before the powers of the health service ombudsman were increased from April 1996 to cover clinical aspects of complaints, he would sometimes accept that hospital discharge was a clinical decision which he could not challenge, but nevertheless find fault with surrounding or underlying factors.

For example, in one case the decision was made 'solely in consequence of the exercise of … clinical judgement and therefore I may not question it. But having reached that clinical decision the HA and their staff had a duty to satisfy themselves that the environment in which she would be placed was suitable in the light of her prevailing medical condition and particularly her physical limitations'. This they did not do: 'I consider that in several respects the HA failed in that duty. The [house officer] wanted an [occupational therapist] to review the patient's condition but failed to ask an OT do so. All the medical and ward nursing staff considered that the patient required substantial support from the social services department but none, it appears to me, had an accurate understanding of the extent of the support which was planned. Furthermore their actions implied that once the [social worker] had been alerted to their intention to discharge her, the patient's welfare was not their concern unless readmission to hospital became necessary …

I regard this as a dangerous misconception. The hospital staff had a duty to ensure that the implementation of their decision to discharge the patient would result in her being placed in an environment which they knew to be satisfactory; in my opinion it is not sufficient for them to hope that the outcome would be satisfactory and to offer re-admission to hospital should it prove not to be. For these reasons I consider that the administrative arrangements for the patient's discharges were unsatisfactory…' (W.420/83–84).

Example 5: communication (ombudsman). The ombudsman criticised a nurse's decision because she failed to take account of all 'relevant factors'. The decision had been based on the pattern of the person's previous admissions for chemotherapy and overnight stays. But this particular admission had been under different circumstances which had not been recorded in the nursing notes. So discharge decisions were made without full and up-to-date information (W.286/86–87).

Example 6: communication (ombudsman). The ombudsman criticised staff for not arranging the necessary district nursing support for a discharged 68-year-old woman. The criticism arose because although a district nurse visit had been arranged, the arrangement had been made before the person's condition deteriorated. By the time of discharge, she was suffering severe abdominal pain, had been scalded and had fallen on the morning of discharge. The discharge arrangements had not taken account of the changed circumstances and had been made with 'insufficient thought'. She had been discharged to her home without, according to the complainant, the necessary equipment including wheelchair, commode or toilet seat extension, and oxygen equipment.

The ombudsman could not (at the time) legally question the clinical decision of the consultant that the oxygen equipment was in fact not needed. But the ombudsman found that the need for a commode had been assessed at least a week earlier, even before her condition had deteriorated. Thus, 'arrangements should have been made for both a commode and a toilet seat extension to be available when the patient was discharged. The failure to do so indicates that insufficient thought was given to the immediate problems the patient and her husband were likely to face on her discharge and accordingly I uphold this aspect of the complaint' (W.24 and W.56/84–85).

Example 7: communication (ombudsman). A woman had complained that she was unable to cope with the twice-daily bathing needs of her husband who had been discharged from hospital. The ombudsman found that he could not question the surgeon's clinical decision about discharge (at the time he was legally precluded from doing so). However, he did find that inadequate 'consideration was given to the consequences and in particular to the domestic circumstances'. The clinicians had overlooked 'vital' information from the GP that the woman could not cope. Misunderstandings between the sister concerned about the discharge and the registrar 'cast considerable doubt on the effectiveness of the registrar's communications'. There was little evidence of a multi-disciplinary approach to the discharge (as recommended by Department of Health guidance), and no system of recording discharge arrangements on patient records. The complaint was upheld (SW.82/86–87).

Hospital discharge: local policy documents and standards

The failure of health authorities or NHS Trusts to adhere to their own local policies and standards of service might result in a finding of maladministration by the health service ombudsman. For example, in one case where a woman was discharged to a nursing home without being advised about the fees she would have to pay, the ombudsman found that the staff did not 'adhere fully to what was required of them under the local policy standard'. The standard had been signed by the sister in charge of the relevant department and concerned consultation about, and recording of, arrangements for discharge (*Royal Cornwall Hospitals NHS Trust 1994*).

4. NHS SERVICES: SELECTED LIST OF EXAMPLES

Given below are listed examples of specific NHS services.

EXTRACTS
Not applicable.

DISCUSSION
The following examples of NHS services are illustrated variously with reference to, for example, cases in the law courts, health service ombudsman investigations, Department of Health guidance.

Blind or partially-sighted people (certification, registration). Circular guidance, referring to the certification and assessment arrangements (involving hospitals and social services) for visually impaired people, carries recommendations (quoted from a DH working group report) including a) effective management responsibility within social services; b) individual people should be assigned a specified member of staff (preferably at 'first line' management level); c) a full time worker to give advice and reassurance should be assigned to eye hospitals or large ophthalmic out-patients departments where there are sufficient numbers of patients to justify such a full-time worker; d) people certified as blind or partially sighted should be contacted quickly to discuss their needs for services and to make a comprehensive assessment; and e) the first priority of local agencies should be co-ordination at system and case levels (HN(90)5).

Over the years, evidence has continued to suggest that the system of certification of blindness or partial sight by the NHS followed by registration by social services departments fails a significant number of people, when the latter give referrals a low priority and fail to undertake visits and assessment promptly (eg, Bruce, McKennell and Walker 1991,p.273; SSI 1988e,p.20). While most authorities might fail to monitor and set targets for contacting newly certificated people and keep people waiting a year for first contact, some might do much better – for instance, contacting 97 per cent of people within two weeks and commencing assessments within four weeks for 60 per cent (SSI 1998a,p.36).

Chiropody (priority groups). Chiropody services have long been subject to considerable demand and to explicit priorities sanctioned by central government (HRC(74)33 para 11), by whom the inadequacy and variability of services has also been acknowledged (HRC(74)33,para 11; HC(77)9, para 1) along with the importance of foot care for elderly people (NHSE 1994,p.8). Indeed, the NHS was originally without a proper chiropody service, until the government in 1959 reluctantly agreed to begin implementing its promise made in 1956 about development of the service (Webster 1996,p.120). The priority groups have generally been four (although detailed practices, and availability to other people, might vary locally): older people, disabled people, expectant mothers and school children.

Evidence does not suggest that matters are necessarily improving with time, for reasons such as the following: a) even older people (one of the priority groups) might lose chiropody services because of revised eligibility criteria (eg, limiting services to people over 75 years old); b) longer waiting times for appointments (eg, up to a year despite a national standard of 13 weeks); c) insufficient numbers of mobile units; d) non-provision of toe-nail cutting by over 33 per cent of chiropody units (even though uncut toe nails are the most common cause of discomfort and mobility problems for older people); and e) a large increase in patient numbers coupled with reduction in budgets (Salvage 1998,p.4).

Some twenty years ago, the health service ombudsman (W.68/77–78) considered the use of a means test in relation to chiropody services. He found the authority's policy vindicated and quoted a DHSS letter to the authority: 'We know that many [authorities] do not have the manpower or other resources to provide a satisfactory service for even the elderly and have therefore decided to introduce their own criteria for determining priority amongst this and other groups ... decisions as to level of provision rest with individual [authorities] and if your [authority] considers that a "means" type test is the best way of determining priority amongst those seeking treatment that is entirely a matter for the authority...'. One suspects that, given the sensitive nature of NHS rationing, such policies would, if publicised, generate nowadays lively debate.

Contact lenses (fluctuating clinical needs for). The health service ombudsman investigated a complaint about the following. A man was assessed as having a clinical need for contact lenses at one hospital; then assessed as not having a clinical need for them at a second; and finally, whether or not he had a clinical need, was denied treatment at a third hospital which, on account of limited resources, would take no new contact lens patients anyway.

The ombudsman explained that although he could investigate individual health authorities, he had no power to 'conduct a more general review into variations in the level of service provided by different health authorities within the NHS'. Similarly, he had no jurisdiction (at that time) to question the clinical assessment made by the second hospital. The third hospital had decided to provide only ophthalmic services which could not be obtained elsewhere through the 'general ophthalmic services'. This decision arose from a review of services, and the ombudsman found no maladministration in the reaching of the decision (W.707/85–86).

Crutches (refusal to provide). A health service ombudsman investigation into refusal to provide crutches to a person leaving hospital found that the decision was not a clinical one, made by a medical doctor, but administrative and made by a technician. The technician had varied the policy on provision of crutches according to stock levels. Thus, 'he sometimes had to refuse crutches to patients for whom they ought to have been provided and would have been, had stock levels permitted'. The ombudsman's view was that 'it was unreasonable to have withheld crutches from the complainant for any reason other than a medical one' (WW.3/79–80).

Communication equipment (uncertain provision). Local priorities and resource allocation can affect the funding of equipment. So, for example, Circular guidance suggests that when people with communication difficulties are assessed at communication aids centres: 'referrals should be routed to a consultant associated with the Centre concerned by the patient's consultant … when a patient is referred to a Centre the health authority of the referring consultant will be expected to provide the aids that may be recommended by the Centre. It will be the responsibility of the patient's own consultant to prescribe such aids…' (HN(84)12,para 5).

Despite this guidance, the provision of communication aids has remained confused and patchy. Practices vary widely, with provision unpredictably spread between the health service, social services and the voluntary sector. Sometimes in the past, special assessment centres have preferred not to see people unless funding for equipment required was guaranteed (Mandelstam 1997,pp.480–482).

Community health services (as continuing care). Guidance states that community health services are a 'crucial part of the provision of continuing care for people at home or in residential care'. Policies should reflect changes in the number of people at home requiring care at home, changes in acute sector practices and changes in the local pattern of residential or nursing home care. Health authorities should 'take account of the need for any resource shifts to community and primary care services as a result of any planned changes in the pattern of services' (HSG(95)8,p.17): see also p.272.

In practice, policies and criteria for community health services might be 'weakly developed' and not get beyond describing what services are in principle available – and thus fall short of explaining eligibility. Some authorities argue that this is deliberate and that such services will be delivered where it is appropriate. However, the lack not only of criteria but even of a general policy about how community health services relate to provision of NHS health care generally, might suggest a lack of coherence in overall policy (Henwood 1996,p.25).

The advent of community care almost certainly increased the demands on community nursing services (eg, SSI 1993j,p.13; SSI 1993b,p.18). Yet even before April 1993, there was evidence that community nursing services might be inadequate to meet the needs of, for example, physically disabled people aged 16–64 (SSI 1988a,p.14), or unable for various reasons to deliver effective equipment services (Ross, Campbell 1992,p.92). For instance, one health service ombudsman investigation into the quantity (as opposed to the quality) of home nursing care for a 91-year-old woman following hospital discharge, accepted the community nurse's policy. This was that 'requests for her patients were assessed against the needs of other patients and the resources available and priorities were determined. These decisions stemmed from the exercise of professional judgement which I may not question' (this was before the ombudsman's legal powers were extended to cover clinical decision-making) (SW.28/84–85).

Haemophilia. Circular guidance (HSG(93)30) 'reminds NHS purchasers of the considerations they will need to take into account in order to secure continuity of access to comprehensive treatment and care' for people with haemophilia.

Considerations listed are a) 'variability and severity of the haemophiliac condition'; b) 'complexity of the condition which may require a diverse and complex range of services. Given the nature of the condition, the amount of treatment required by individual patients will be unpredictable'; c) 'expertise in treatment of haemophilia patients is not uniformly available across the country'; d) 'the need for ease of access of blood products to support home treatment programmes'; e) 'the prevalence of HIV, which is a significant problem in this group of patients, and the need for treatment and counselling for HIV infected haemophilia patients'; f) sophisticated treatment to be available through the planning and contracting processes.

Hearing aids (delay in provision, non-provision). The health service ombudsman (W.371/83–84) investigated an 18-month wait for provision of a hearing aid. He concluded that the delay was caused 'as a direct result of insufficient resources being available. But the allocation of resources within the HA was, and continues to be, a matter to be decided by them, and I have found no evidence of maladministration which would entitle me to criticise the respective priorities given by the HA to the competing demands for competing finance'.

Beyond a standard range of hearing aids, local health service discretion has affected the provision (or non-provision) of, for example, commercial hearing aids, health service batteries or maintenance for privately purchased hearing aids. In one case of non-provision of a commercial hearing aid and of batteries for a commercial aid, the Parliamentary ombudsman investigated – and accepted – the Welsh Office's explanation. This was that 'the resources available for the extension of Health Services are limited, and the case for development in each field of care and treatment has to be weighed carefully with other pressing demands' (PCA 5/915/78). Another Parliamentary ombudsman investigation about non-provision of NHS batteries for a privately bought hearing aid concluded that non-provision was justified 'because there are no powers in the NHS Acts to do this' (PCA 5/325/77). In fact, it does seem that in practice NHS provision, at local discretion, does sometimes cover NHS batteries for private hearing aids and that there is nothing unlawful about this.

Hole-in-the-heart operations (postponement). The courts have declined to intervene on grounds of illegality or unreasonableness when operations were postponed for babies or children with a hole in the heart: *R v Central Birmingham HA, ex p Walker,* and *R v Central Birmingham Health Authority, ex p. Collier.*

Incontinence services (rationing). The Department of Health has repeatedly stressed, in relation to incontinence supplies, that health authorities have the power to make priorities locally. All too often, looking to exercise such power, it appears that authorities and NHS Trusts view incontinence services, pads and other supplies as an 'easy target' when they wish to save money.

For example, in 1990 the government conceded that it had 'received a number of representations about the supply of incontinence pads to private nursing and residential homes. The free provision of incontinence pads does not extend to people living in private nursing homes; the same legislation provides that district health authorities may provide incontinence materials and other nursing aids to people in their own homes and at their discretion to residents of local authority residential homes. The extent to which this discretion is exercised varies from place to place and information about these decisions is not held centrally' (Stephen Dorrell: HCWA,22/11/1990,col.32).

One specific example quoted in 1990 was of a health authority's consultation document, proposing to withdraw 'free incontinence aids' from 400–500 people living in independent sector residential homes, though still continuing to advise home owners and sell supplies to them at cost price (Stephen Dorrell: HCWA,20/12/1990,cols.347–8). The Department of Health itself has acknowledged over a period that there have been 'wide variations in the level of services to people with incontinence' (Stephen Dorrell: HCWA,4/3/1991,col.22). Four years previously, the restriction of services in some areas had led to considerable concern about the situation and a request being made by the Department to health authorities for information about their practices (D(87)45). Even ten years before that, in 1977, the Department had written to nursing officers, having in mind 'positive action' even in the economic circumstances of the time. Although 'every effort should be directed towards maintaining continence, there are inevitably those whose control is so impaired as to make it necessary to meet as comprehensively as possible their need for the aids and equipment which will help to overcome this handicap' (CNO(SNC)(77)1). Yet one particular instance which found its way into the law courts does not suggest that all health authorities attempt comprehensively to meet needs when setting their eligibility criteria. In *R v Social Fund Inspector, ex p Connick*, the applicant sought help from the Social Fund for incontinence pads, because she was unable to meet her local health authority's strict eligibility for NHS provision: double incontinence or terminal illness.

Such was the growing level of public concern that the Department of Health stated in guidance: 'In particular, should any changes be proposed, it is obviously important that vulnerable patients or clients should not be exposed to anxiety, and that where for example a change in the supply of incontinence aids is proposed, there should be an assured alternative in place before action is put in train' (EL(91)28). Quite what that alternative might be is not explained. More recently, the shortage of resources apparently affecting NHS provision of incontinence equipment and materials has been highlighted by a dispute about tax avoidance – in particular about whether a) incontinence pads can be zero-rated when supplied by statutory services to individual service users (SI 1997/2744, and see Customs and Excise 1997); and b) if so, any extra resources would be provided to offset the cost to the NHS of VAT payable on incontinence supplies (Pollock 1998,p.7).

In 1990, Baroness Masham of Ilton attempted, unsuccessfully, to amend the NHS and Community Care Bill passing through Parliament: 'In carrying out its primary functions a District Health Authority shall provide a district wide incontinence service and shall identify a continence advisor and a consultant to take a special interest in incontinence'. In reply, Baroness Blatch for the government reaffirmed health authorities' discretion: 'in this as in other areas of health care provision district health authorities should be left free to determine the pattern and level of service in their districts in the light of local needs and circumstances' (HLD,24/4/1990,cols.546–550). A subsequent reply on the same subject referred to the fact that health authorities 'must determine what is an appropriate and affordable level of service at any given time'. And a vague undertaking to 'look again at strengthening the guidance' (Baroness Blatch: HLD,7/6/1990,col.1593) has, eight years later, so far come to nothing.

Baroness Masham also reminded Members of the House of Lords about the realities of rationing: 'The general public who are healthy and well have no idea that at such a basic level people who are incontinent are having many problems. They are having to buy pads or have them rationed or cut off. The mother of a spastic daughter who cannot speak and is doubly incontinent, living in a Cheshire Home, was told that she would have to pay for her daughter's incontinence pads as the Cheshire Home has nursing home status. The mother has to choose between supplying her daughter with pads or giving her a holiday. She cannot afford to do both. Other people have been told that they cannot have the pads which are the most suitable for them. If this goes on there will be an increase in pressure sores and all sorts of problems costing the health service millions of pounds. In addition to this, there are difficulties for carers who may find dealing with other people's urine and faeces none too pleasant. If people do not have adequate pads, life will become unbearable' (HLD,3/4/1990,col.1342).

The Department of Health has made gestures towards better continence services and attempted to promote better practice (Sanderson 1991), but has not taken a firm enough policy line with health authorities – despite admitting that substantial financial savings could be made if more emphasis were to be placed on relieving incontinence (House of Commons Public Accounts Committee 1993,para.38). In May 1998, against continuing concern about under-funding and gaps in services, and underlined by the confusion about VAT (Pollock 1998), the Department announced a policy review with the intention that the NHS should provide a 'modern continence service that lets people have access to high quality, prompt and readily available assistance' (Continence Foundation 1998,p.1).

Infertility treatment (rationing by age-related policy). In October 1994, the High Court refused to condemn a health authority's policy which denied fertility treatment to women aged over 35 year old; it was not for the court to challenge the cut-off point adopted by the authority when it was faced with budgetary restrictions *R v Sheffield HA, ex p Seale*).

Learning disabilities (special, individually based provision). Circular guidance (HSG(92)42) makes clear that people with learning disabilities (mental handicap) have the same rights of access to NHS services as everyone else, although they might need assistance to use services. It states that health service contracts should refer specifically to provision for such people and if necessary to special provision where needs cannot be met through the normal range of health services.

The guidance goes on to list examples of special provision which might be needed, including alternative dental services, specialist mental health provision, 'long term residential care in a health setting', and 'transitional responsibility for people in mental handicap hospitals'. It states that full use should be made of 'arrangements for joint finance, dowry payments and the powers available under section 28A of the NHS Act 1977'. (Other guidance (LAC(92)15), aimed at social services departments, stresses the importance of individual assessment of people with learning disabilities – a point picked up by the High Court in *R v Avon CC, ex p M*).

Multiple sclerosis. Following the issue of guidance (EL(95)97) to health authorities about introducing beta-interferon treatment for patients with multiple sclerosis, a health authority had in effect operated a blanket ban on such treatment. In *R v North Derbyshire HA, ex p Fisher*, the High Court found that the authority had failed even to have regard to the guidance and so had behaved unlawfully.

NHS Unit for disabled people. Having given a promise of lifelong accommodation (a specialist residential unit) to a number of severely disabled people, a health authority could not lawfully break that promise unless it could show that there was an overriding public interest at stake – something it failed to do in this particular case (*R v North and East Devon HA, ex p Coughlan*).

Nursing home provision. For services for nursing home residents: see p.271.

Orthopaedic treatment (waiting, non-provision). In *R v Secretary of State for Social Services, ex p Hincks*, the Court of Appeal considered the plight of people who had been waiting a considerable time for orthopaedic treatment in relation to the duties contained in ss.1 and 3 of the NHS Act 1977. It concluded that provision under s.3 was inevitably subject to available resources.

In like manner, a health service ombudsman investigation of a wait for a knee operation accepted that 'the backlog of patients for orthopaedic surgery was outside the control of the Authority and they were unable to give a reliable estimate of when the complainant could expect to have her operation'. The authority was waiting for the opening of an upgraded operating theatre and was also short of anaesthetists. The priority accorded to the complainant was a clinical decision which the ombudsman could not (then) question. However, a letter (quoted by the ombudsman) from the Minister of State for Health illustrated how concepts such as 'need' and 'priority' are elastic in such circumstances: 'Priority is given to the most urgent cases but there is now a high proportion of patients on the waiting lists who must be regarded as urgent from the point of view of the degree of pain and disability they are suffering'. Therefore, not everybody with urgent needs would also be given priority (W.224/78–79).

Palliative care. Guidance states that, closely working with the voluntary sector, the NHS 'retains responsibility for arranging and funding palliative health care' including: a) inpatient care in an NHS hospital, in a hospice or in a nursing home; b) specialist palliative health care for people already in nursing homes; c) 'palliative health care support to people in their own homes or in residential care' (HSG(95)8,p.15).

Later guidance states that for NHS inpatient palliative care, 'application of time limits will be inappropriate' (EL(96)8,section C). Thus, stringent criteria for palliative care applied in practice by the NHS, and which lay down strict time limits for eligibility – such as death being expected in two weeks, or two months (National Council for Hospice and Specialist Palliative Care Services 1996) – would appear to be inconsistent with the guidance.

Guidance refers to a definition of specialist palliative care produced by the National Association of Health Authorities and Trusts (now the NHS Confederation) as 'active total care when disease is not responsive to curative treatment. Palliative care neither hastens nor postpones death; provides relief from pain and other distressing symptoms; integrates the psychological and spiritual aspects of care; offers a support system to help the family cope during the patient's illness and in bereavement' (EL(94)14,annex A,para 7).

The 1995 guidance (HSG(95)8) differentiates palliative care for NHS inpatients and people in their own homes, from specialist palliative care for non-NHS inpatients in nursing homes – yet how the two should be distinguished in practice is far from clear (House of Commons Health Committee 1995,p.xxi). Yet further guidance states that *palliative care* 'encompasses the spectrum of care, ranging from the palliative approach to care which aims to promote both physical and psycho-social well being, and should be practised in all disciplines and regardless of whether or not death is expected, through to specialist palliative care' (HSC 1998/115,para iii).

However, *specialist palliative* care 'is the active total care of patients with progressive, far advanced disease and limited prognosis, and their families, by a multi-professional team who have undergone recognised specialist training. It provides physical, psychological, social and spiritual support, and will involve practitioners with a broad mix of skills, including medical and nursing care, social work, pastoral/spiritual care, physiotherapy, occupational therapy, pharmacy and related specialties. Specialist palliative care is provided ... in a variety of settings – inpatient, day care, home care – and also directly through advice to other professionals, patients and their carers ... Inpatient specialist palliative care should include respite care provision' (EL(96)85,annex A).

Physical or sensory disabilities. Circular guidance about people with physical or sensory disabilities (HN(88)26) stated that authorities should 'consider': '*effective assessment and referral systems*, co-ordination and collaboration both within and between health authorities; and with outside agencies, statutory and voluntary'. It went on to draw attention to various needs of different groups of disabled people including a) the *rehabilitation needs* of people with brain injury, stroke, progressive neurological diseases, spinal injury, epilepsy; b) *disability equipment*: need to ensure adequacy of service; c) *disabled young people* moving from child to adult health services: need for appropriate planning; d) *treatment of disabled people* for conditions unconnected with their disability: need for staff awareness; e) *personal relationships, sexuality and family planning*: need for advice and guidance; f) *availability of therapy services* to people in the community; g) *low vision aid service* for blind and partially-sighted people: need for access (travelling) particularly for elderly people; h) *hearing aid* centres, audiological rehabilitation services, and psychiatric services for deaf people; i) *people who are both deaf and blind*: need to bear in mind dual disability; j) *the need for district wide continence services*, including continence adviser, identified consultant and physiotherapist, adequate supply of incontinence aids and reasonable access to a urodynamic clinic; k) *physically, sensorily and multiply disabled people who also have learning difficulties* (mental handicap); and l) *counselling* for people with chronic, fatal conditions.

The sheer meekness of the request that authorities should 'consider' such matters indicates that the Department of Health was not setting out a firm policy. This was pointed out during an attempted amendment to the NHS and Community Care Bill in relation to incontinence services: 'The Minister referred to government health notice 88/26 ... That circular is what the Government recommend. It is from that circular that the wording of the amendment [duty to provide a district-wide continence service] comes. It is what the Government want, but the Minister went on to say that district health authorities should be left to decide on their own priorities. The situation has continued to deteriorate since the health notice went out. That shows how ineffective notices without legislation can be ... There is therefore a need for an amendment such as this so that provision is guaranteed under legislation' (Baroness Masham: HLD, 7/6/1990, col.1589).

See: *Rehabilitation* heading, below.

Pressure sores. Circular guidance (EL(94)3) pointed to the 'largely avoidable' but high prevalence of pressure sores: and their costs in terms of treatment and litigation. The Department of Health guidance document, *Pressure sores: a key quality indicator* (DH 1994a), was 'commended' to health service managers.

The health service ombudsman sometimes investigates complaints involving the incidence of pressure sores. Even before his powers were extended to include complaints about clinical treatment, he sometimes found fault with the administrative arrangements which framed the treatment – for example, the lack of foresight in relation to travel arrangements to protect adequately 'those with pressure sores or recently healed sores' (SW.28/84–85). Nevertheless, pressure sores can develop quickly, for example, within a couple of hours, and may be the result of vulnerable skin tissue developing over a longer period beforehand. Thus, it may not be easy to decide when or where lack of care, if any, contributed to a sore. However, when nursing records and care plan documents are incomplete, thus making such a judgement impossible, the ombudsman might uphold a complaint anyway (W.547/92–93).

Rehabilitation and recovery (continuing care eligibility). Guidance states that health authorities and GP fundholders 'must take full account of the need for services to promote the most effective recovery and rehabilitation of patients after acute treatment so as to maximise the chances of successful implementation of long term care plans. This is particularly important for older people who may need a longer period to reach their full potential for recovery and to regain confidence. Local policies should guard against the risk of premature discharge in terms of poorer experiences for patients and increased levels of readmissions ... Health authorities should agree with local authorities the need for any additional social or educational support which may be required as part of an agreed package of care' (HSG(95)8,pp.14–15).

In practice, eligibility criteria for rehabilitation set by health authorities might state that patients should be able to benefit from the service; distinguish criteria for rehabilitation from those set for recovery; or sometimes attach restrictive time limits within which goals must be reached (for instance, two weeks or six weeks). Alternatively they duck the issue by drawing up criteria for extra-contractual funding only, stating that otherwise rehabilitation will be provided through existing, routine contracts – but then fail to indicate exactly what services and eligibility are actually included routinely (Henwood 1996,p.19). Such generalities are likely to be of little value to individual patients who wish to know what services they are likely to get at any particular time in relation to their specific needs.

The availability of rehabilitation services varies across the country depending on local priorities. This has led to the lack of a clear picture of what is available and to gaps and shortages in services – a situation pointed out for many years (eg, Nocon, Baldwin 1998; House of Commons Public Accounts Committee 1993,p.xi; NAO 1992,p.3; Edwards, Warren 1990; Beardshaw 1988; RCP 1986; Tunbridge 1972). There has long been concern that despite increased emphasis in principle on rehabilitation services, wide disparities in levels of services are found. For example, physiotherapists are key rehabilitation workers, yet comparing two adjacent London health authorities there might be (relative to the local population) nearly three to four times as many physiotherapists in one authority as in the other (House of Commons Public Accounts Committee 1993,p.11). Aside from reduced rehabilitation in hospital due to the pressure to discharge people as quickly as possible, the lack of community-based rehabilitation services can mean that people enter residential or nursing home care when, with rehabilitation, they could instead regain independence and return to their own homes (Clark 1998,pp.26,32).

In the past, the NHS Management Executive's view of such variation was that it might be due to differing local needs and arrangements and that it would not set national targets, even broad ones (House of Commons Public Accounts Committee 1993,p.12). In similar, non-committal vein, the government stated in 1992 that health authorities 'fund rehabilitation services out of their general allocations and existing guidance sets out the range of services we would typically expect to see'. Though mentioned in an appendix of the Green Paper on the Health of the Nation, rehabilitation did not survive as a 'key area' into the White Paper because of 'insufficient knowledge about appropriate performance targets' (Tim Yeo: HCWA,16/7/1992,col.900). And, in answer to a question about the need for the active rehabilitation of people before going home from hospital, the government replied in 1993 that a 'wide range of rehabilitation facilities exists within the national health service and local social services authorities. Decisions about rehabilitation services are for the professional judgement of those concerned with the individual case' (Tim Yeo: HCWA,16/2/1993,col.160).

The tune has changed; for instance, 1996 guidance conceded that 'a significant number of people admitted to nursing home and residential care homes on a long term care basis might be inappropriately placed'. It went on to highlight the importance of considered and specialist – rather than premature – assessment, of rehabilitation schemes, of better identification and protection of rehabilitation services in the contracting process, and of social services in partnership with the NHS, 'developing a more therapeutic approach to long term care' (EL(96)89,pp.8–10). Rehabilitation was also listed amongst priority services for 1996 to 1998 (EL(96)109), 1998 to 1999 (EL(97)39) and 1999–2002 (HSC(98)159; whilst yet further guidance, *Better services for vulnerable people*, referred to the expectation that by the financial year 1999/2000 health and local authorities will have a) agreed a framework for multi-disciplinary assessment of older people, and b) implemented a plan for the development of recuperation and rehabilitation services for older people (EL(97)62). This was followed up with a directory of good practice, recognising the importance of occupational therapy, physiotherapy and speech and language therapy skills in rehabilitation (NHSE 1998). And at the end of 1998, on a grander stage, the government reiterated in a White Paper that a lack of rehabilitation and recuperation services was resulting in the avoidable, inappropriate and permanent institutionalisation of people in residential or nursing homes (Secretary of State for Health 1998,p.15).

Residential care services. For services for people in residential care: see p.271.

Respite care. Guidance states that all health authorities and GP fundholders 'must arrange and fund an adequate level' of respite care, in particular for: people who have complex or intense health care needs, people 'who during a period of respite care require or could benefit from active rehabilitation', or people 'who are receiving a package of palliative care in their own homes but where they or their carer need a period of respite care' (HSG(95)8,p.16).

Further guidance issued towards the end of 1996 noted that eligibility criteria sometimes operate too restrictively in relation to respite care (EL(96)89). In practice, some health authorities develop criteria which concentrate on the distinction between NHS care and social services care (for instance, the former is indicated when the respite care cannot be provided by non-clinically trained staff). They might also indicate that only a 'few people' will require NHS-funded respite care – for instance, those who are 'very ill' or have 'very complex health needs' normally requiring NHS inpatient care – or that it can only be provided for people who also require visits from specialist or district nurses at least four times a week on a long-term basis. It is not clear that such restrictive criteria fit easily into the three *alternative* conditions set out in the guidance (Henwood 1996,pp.20–23).

Sex-change operations. The High Court ruled that a health authority's policy, that denied sex-change operations to three transsexuals, was unlawful apparently because the policy interfered with its duty under s.3 of the NHS Act 1977 to provide treatment for preventing illness and caring for people suffering from illness (*R v North West Lancashire Health Authority, ex p G, A and D*).

Specialist or intensive medical and nursing support in nursing homes, residential homes or people's own homes – including specialist equipment. See p.271.

Specialist transport. Guidance states that health authorities and GP fundholders should make arrangements for ambulance and other specialist NHS transport, including (based on patients' needs) a) transport to and from hospital; b) transport for emergency admissions to residential or nursing home care; c) non-emergency transport for people (in nursing homes, residential homes or in their own homes) to and from health care facilities (HSG(95)8,p.17).

People sometimes have to wait hours when leaving hospital – with detrimental consequences. For instance, when a woman (frail and arthritic) sat in a chair all day waiting for the ambulance to take her home to the care of her husband (himself an amputee), she did not get home till 6pm. By that time, she had stiffened up so much from the sitting, that he could not get her to bed. They sat up all night in chairs (Neill, Williams 1992,p.80).

Speech and language therapy services. The discretion invested in health authorities leads to some caution in Parliamentary answers to questions about the obligations on health authorities to provide speech therapy services. For example, the Secretary of State for Health replied in 1991: 'It is the responsibility of health authorities to assess the health needs of their local population and to obtain appropriate services for them, including speech and language therapy services. We encourage the NHS to deploy qualified speech and language therapists as effectively and efficiently as possible...' (Virginia Bottomley: HCWA,3/12/1991,col.116). This type of statement appears to leave all to local discretion and prohibits neither a low level of service provision, nor possibly even non-provision.

Speech and language therapy has often been a bone of contention between the NHS and local education authorities in relation to children with special educational needs; the cases confirm the absence of an absolute obligation on the NHS to make provision (eg, *R v Lancashire CC, ex p M; R v Oxfordshire CC, ex p W; R v Brent and Harrow HA, ex p Harrow LBC*). The health service ombudsman reached a similar conclusion an investigation. It was about allegedly delayed and intermittent speech therapy provided by a health authority to a two-and-a-half-year-old child with severe communication difficulties. The ombudsman accepted the health authority's position. This was that, although the speech therapy service was understaffed and underfunded by national and regional norms, the health authority was well aware of, and concerned about, the situation. The 'HA have to balance the needs of the STS against other services and I am aware, from other investigations, of the problems health authorities face in deciding between competing demands. The HA is vested with the discretion to decide how to allocate its resources ... and the legislation which governs my work does not permit me to question such a decision unless I find evidence of maladministration in the way it was reached' (W.783/85–86).

Wheelchairs: waiting times. The wheelchair service has suffered criticisms of various kinds for many years (eg, McColl 1986; Aldersea 1996; House of Commons Committee of Public Accounts 1993,p.10). Recent changes have involved provision for the first time of outdoor/indoor electric wheelchairs (HSG(96)34) and of a voucher scheme, whereby people can add their own money to the cost the NHS is prepared to meet for a particular chair (HSG(96)53 and HSC 1998/004). In the face of evidence that some health authorities have done little to implement the voucher scheme (Oliveck 1998), despite the guidance that they should do so, it is possible that a judicial review case might be arguable against an authority if it could be shown that it had totally disregarded the guidance (see eg, *R v North Derbyshire HA, ex p Fisher*).

CHAPTER 16

HOME ADAPTATIONS

Coverage

1. Housing and community care generally
2. Home adaptations generally
3. Housing authority power to adapt its own stock
4. Home adaptations: disabled facilities grants
5. Home repair assistance

KEY POINTS

Housing would seem, according to common sense, to be a very important part of community care, since it is the stated policy aim of community care that people remain in their own (as opposed to institutional) homes where possible. But if the home is not suitable, cannot be made suitable or a suitable alternative is not found – this will clearly not be possible. However, housing services are not for the most part defined legally as 'community care services' and housing authorities do not even have an explicit duty to accept invitations to participate in community care assessments.

This chapter concentrates in particular on the provision of home adaptations through disabled facilities grants and home repair assistance, as well through the duty of social services departments under the Chronically Sick and Disabled Persons Act 1970. There are of course other housing functions of local authorities which have a very significant impact on community care – such as homelessness, council housing allocation, sheltered or supported housing, and housing benefit. However, it is beyond the scope of this book to deal with these. Adaptations to the home are re- ferred to in policy guidance from the Department of Health as one of the means of achieving the preferred aim of community care, namely enabling people to remain in their own homes. Further- more, both housing and social services legislation applies to the provision of adaptations, and co- operation between housing and social services is required legally as well as practically. Yet when community care was implemented, central government failed to acknowledge and respond prop- erly to the plentiful evidence of a long history of delays affecting adaptations. This would suggest a culpable oversight.

(N.B. For reasons of space, the term disabled facilities grant is sometimes shortened to DFG in this chapter).

1. HOUSING AND COMMUNITY CARE GENERALLY

Housing matters are in the main excluded from community care legislation.

EXTRACTS

Legislation (NHS and Community Care Act 1990) does not define housing services as 'community care services' (s.46). However, when a local social services authority is assessing a person for community care services and it thinks there is a need for housing services, then it must notify the local housing authority and invite it to assist in the assessment (s.47: see p.78).

The duty does not apply where the local authority is both a social services and a housing authority: in other words, metropolitan or unitary authorities. This is because there is an apparent assumption that different departments within one local authority anyway consult each other and work closely and because an authority cannot logically consult itself.

Circular guidance (DoE 10/92) states: 'Adequate housing has a major role to play in community care and is often the key to independent living' (para 1). The Circular goes on to discuss a number of areas of work in which housing authorities might be involved in relation to community care. These include a) community care planning; b) community care assessments; c) local housing strategies (within the Housing Investment Programme), involving cooperation with housing associations, and considering, for example, the closure of long stay hospitals and the 're-provision of services on a comprehensive local basis', and special needs housing; d) provision for homeless people; and e) home adaptations.

Guidance (DH,DoE 1997) states that its aim is 'to provide a framework to help housing, social services and health authorities to establish joint strategies for housing and community care so that at a strategic level, the necessary coordination between housing, social services and health is achieved'. The following 36 pages outline how these agencies should be working together.

DISCUSSION

It is generally accepted that the importance of housing in community care was inadequately reflected in community care legislation (Arnold *et al.* 1993). However, various guidance from central government now emphasises the importance of housing issues. Clearly, in attempting to meet the needs of local people, local authorities might need to consider not just community care legislation – but also other legislation covering, for example, the allocation of council housing, homelessness, sheltered housing and housing benefit. Indeed some court cases (eg, *R v Bristol CC, ex p Penfold; R v Tower Hamlets, ex p Bradford; R v Lambeth LBC, ex p A*) have shown how a local authority might have to assess a person's or family's needs under different pieces of legislation, which cut across housing and social services functions. For example, the Housing Act 1996 (homelessness and allocation), the Housing Grants, Construction and Regeneration Act 1996 (disabled facilities grants), Children Act 1989,s.17 (services for welfare of child in need might relate to housing), Chronically Sick and Disabled Persons Act 1970, s.2 (home adaptations), Carers (Recognition and Services) Act 1990.

One point being increasingly made is that flexibility between agencies and budgets is required if people's needs are to be met effectively (eg, Audit Commission 1998,p.75; Watson 1997,p.4). Ideally, money needs to follow the individual rather than administrative and legal boundaries. For instance, it is sometimes clear that a preferable and cheaper solution for both disabled occupant and the local authority would be for the person to move to alternative accommodation, rather than have expensive adaptations carried out. However, the money which would have been used on the adaptation is not available to assist with such a move (Pieda 1996,p.62). And if £2,000 cannot be found from an adaptations budget to alter a person's bathroom and enable him or her to stay at home (even if only, for example, for a year), then £12,000 might have to be found for that year from the residential care budget (Appleton, Leather 1998,p.60). Similarly, a woman with arthritis might be assessed as requiring residential care because she is at risk on the stairs – yet one possible alternative might be a stairlift costing £1,100 (Age Concern England 1998b,pp.3,6).

The existence of legal boundaries which impose limitations on service provision sometimes leads to the law courts. For instance, a dispute arose about what welfare services could be provided by wardens in sheltered council housing and paid for out of the housing revenue account (see: *R v London Borough of Ealing, ex p. Jennifer Lewis* heard in 1992, which led to the subsequent insertion of s.11A in the Housing Act 1985 via the Leasehold Reform, Housing and Urban Development Act 1993). This resolved the matter in relation to a number of services although excluded others; for example, community alarms were now clearly covered, whereas assistance with personal mobility, appearance or hygiene was excluded (SI 1994/42). However, legal doubt remains about the provision – or at least charging for – community alarms for people in the private sector (Audit Commission 1998,p.65).

Similarly, there is increased use of what has become known as 'floating support' – which can be defined as aimed at sustaining a tenancy, might be in the form of personal care, counselling or domestic help, is discontinued when no longer required, might be variously funded and is tied to the individual person and not the accommodation (Douglas, Macdonald and Taylor 1998,p.11). For instance, such support might sometimes obviate the need for people to move into residential or sheltered accommodation and prove to be a cost-effective alternative (Age Concern England 1998b,pp.9,16). This approach is part of a move not to tie personal assistance to physical buildings and not to create 'special needs' housing which segregates disabled people (Macfarlane, Laurie 1996; Simons, Ward 1997,p.3).

It has frequently been pointed out that if houses were better designed they would as a matter of course remain suitable for disabled people and significantly reduce the need to seek expensive adaptations or alternative accommodation. 'Lifetime Homes' are often cited; they include, for instance, convenient parking space; wide, level, gently sloping approach paths; covered and illuminated entrance with no steps; handrails where steps are unavoidable; wide front door and ample space in hall; ground floor WC with basin; ground-floor living room with possible bed space; easy-to-use doors, windows and switches; safe and convenient bathroom; kitchen with units designed for safety; walls in bathroom and WC suitable for handrails; ceilings suitable for hoists; stairs with suitable handrails (possibly on both sides) (based on Joseph Rowntree Foundation literature).

In March 1998, it was announced that Part M of the Building Regulations 1991, which had previously stipulated that new public buildings be accessible to disabled people, would be extended to new domestic dwellings from mid-1999 and would cover a number of the features listed immediately above (DETR 1998). The revised *Approved Document M* was duly published in late 1998 (DETR,WO 1998).

2. HOME ADAPTATIONS GENERALLY

Guidance recognises that home adaptations are important in enabling people to remain in their own homes. Home adaptations are of many types and include, for example, facilities such as handrails and fixed support frames, ramps, special bath or shower units, raised plug sockets, automatic garage doors, emergency call systems, accessible rooms, downstairs extensions, widened doorways, fixed hoists.

EXTRACTS

Legislation: see the following sections of this chapter.

Community care policy guidance includes 'adaptations' as one of the means of achieving the prime objective of community care: 'support for the user in his or her own home' (DH 1990, para 3.24).

Circular guidance (DoE 10/92) states:

(adaptations, improvements, repairs): 'Housing needs may include adaptations, repairs or improvements to allow people to stay in their existing home. In most cases this package of services will be based on a person's existing home, but in some cases it may mean alternative accommodation ... Referral procedures will need to be developed and agreed locally. Both housing and social services authorities should adopt joint arrangements to deal with assessments and should consider the need to nominate particular officers to be responsible for listing and agreeing the possible housing options' (paras 9–10).

(assessment, resources, needs and entitlements) 'Both community care planning and individual assessment and care management must take account of all the costs involved, including housing and other accommodation costs, and of the resources available to the various parties, and of the other claims on such resources. In no case should the resources of any authority be committed without the agreement of that authority. The ideal solution for an individual or group of individuals, based on a systematic assessment of needs, may not be achievable either immediately or in the near future, but it should inform the planning process. Community care in itself creates no new category of entitlement to housing, and housing needs which are identified by community care planning and individual assessments should be considered alongside existing processes and local priorities' (para 15).

DISCUSSION

Home adaptations can be provided through a number of different channels, including housing authorities' general powers and duties towards their own housing stock; disabled facilities grants (DFGs); home repair assistance (for elderly people receiving benefits); social services departments under s.2 of the Chronically Sick and Disabled Persons Act 1970 or s.45 of the Health Services and Public Health Act 1968; and housing associations (either from revenue or through a grant from the Housing Corporation).

Even if a housing authority funds the adaptation, a social services often carries out the assessment. In the case of an application for a disabled facilities grant, a housing authority anyway normally consults social services and in some cases has a duty to do so. Where social services a) assesses both the need for a home adaptation and that it is necessary that the need be met under s.2 of the Chronically Sick and Disabled Persons Act 1970; b) the housing authority does not provide (adequate) assistance; and c) the need cannot be met in any other way – then a continuing duty remains on the social services department to make arrangements to ensure that the need is met.

The carrying out of home adaptations can be a lengthy, complicated and disruptive process, sometimes made worse because of poor practice on the part of social services and housing authorities. As a result, delay in home adaptations features prominently in local ombudsman investigations and findings of maladministration. (A number of summaries of ombudsman investigations are included in this chapter.)

Statistics for the types of main adaptation approved through the disabled facilities grants system are as follows: stairlifts 28 per cent, shower and toilet 14 per cent, level access shower 14 per cent, central heating 12 per cent, removal of bath 10 per cent, ramps/access 7 per cent, shower over bath 7 per cent, bathroom alteration 6 per cent, ground-floor bath/shower 5 per cent, bed/bathroom extension 5 per cent, ground floor toilet 5 per cent, hand rails 4 per cent, floor drainage shower 3 per cent, kitchen alterations 3 per cent, adaptations in relation to wheelchair use 3 per cent, widened/altered doorways 2 per cent, through-floor lift 2 per cent, miscellaneous 9 per cent (Pieda 1996,p.42).

3. HOUSING AUTHORITY POWER TO ADAPT ITS OWN STOCK

Housing authorities have considerable scope to carry out adaptations to their own housing stock at no cost to disabled or older (non-disabled) people, by avoiding the more formal process of application and means-testing associated with disabled facilities grants (see below); however, the local ombudsman has on several occasions reprimanded authorities for not allowing council tenants to apply for disabled facilities grants (see below).

EXTRACTS

Legislation (Housing Act 1985) gives housing authorities the power to 'alter, enlarge, repair or improve', as well as to 'fit, furnish and supply a house provided by them under this Part with all requisite furniture, fittings and conveniences' (ss. 9–10).

Under s.8, authorities have a duty to consider housing needs in the district; and whilst discharging this duty, they are obliged to 'have regard to the special needs of chronically sick or disabled persons' (Chronically Sick and Disabled Persons Act 1970,s.3).

DISCUSSION

Not applicable.

4. HOME ADAPTATIONS: DISABLED FACILITIES GRANTS (DFGs)

Disabled facilities grants are part of the renovation grant system introduced by the Local Government and Housing Act 1989, but now to be found (from December 1996) in the Housing Grants, Construction and Regeneration Act 1996. Although the 1996 Act removed mandatory renovation grants from the picture, mandatory disabled facilities grants survived.

Housing authorities have a duty to approve applications for a disabled occupant (including a child) if certain conditions are met. Social services authorities must be consulted about whether the proposed works are necessary and appropriate. If a housing authority accepts that the adaptation is needed for certain daily living (mainly access) purposes prescribed in legislation, then it must approve the application. If the adaptation is needed for other purposes (prescribed as accommodation, welfare or employment), the housing authority has the power, but not duty, to approve the application.

After approval of an application, the amount of the grant is determined by a means-test and it can vary from 0 per cent to 100 per cent (up to a normal maximum of £20,000 – £24,000 in Wales) of the total cost of the adaptation. Therefore, approval of an application does not automatically trigger financial assistance.

(N.B. Referred to below is guidance issued in December 1996 by the Department of Environment on disabled facilities grants and home repair assistance, which are governed from that date by the Housing Grants, Construction and Regeneration Act 1996 (DoE 17/96).

This guidance explains that the previous guidance, DoE 10/90 (issued jointly with the Department of Health) is now obsolete. However, the new guidance (DoE 17/96) was not jointly issued, and the Department of Health has not issued any new guidance of its own. Thus, in a further Circular, DoE 4/98, it is explained that DoE 10/90 had been withdrawn in respect of the Department of Environment but not the Department of Health. This has led to the unfortunate situation that the provision of DFGs is now covered by two different Circulars – the earlier of which does not take account of the changes in the 1996 Act (for instance in respect of grants for baths and showers, and for the disabled occupant's safety in the home). A further consequence appears to have been that the new Department of Environment guidance has taken time to come to the attention of social services departments, since it was not drawn to their attention by the Department of Health (which takes responsibility for social services communications). This situation is unfortunate and a poor example of joint working between government departments).

EXTRACTS

Legislation (Housing Grants, Construction and Regeneration Act 1996). Housing authorities have a duty in some circumstances, and a power in others, to approve applications for disabled facilities grants – subject to various other qualifying conditions. The duty is towards each individual applicant.

(mandatory grants: access to/use of dwelling) Approval must be given (other things being equal) to a DFG application for the purpose of facilitating access by the disabled occupant:

(a) to and from the dwelling;

(b) to a room used as the principal family room;

(c) to, or providing for the disabled occupant, a room used or usable for sleeping;

(d) to, or providing for the disabled occupant, a room in which there is a lavatory – or facilitating its use by the disabled occupant;

(e) to, or providing for the disabled occupant, a room in which there is a bath or a shower (or both) – or facilitating its use by the disabled occupant;

(f) to, or providing for the disabled occupant, a room in which there is a wash-hand basin – or facilitating its use by the disabled occupant (s.23).

Other purposes are:

(g) making the dwelling or building safe for the disabled occupant and other persons residing with him;

(h) facilitating the preparation and cooking of food by the disabled occupant;

(i)   improving any heating system in the dwelling to meet the needs of the disabled occupant or – if there is no existing heating system or an existing system is unsuitable for use by the disabled occupant – providing a heating system suitable to meet his needs;

(j)   facilitating the use by the disabled occupant of a source of power, light or heat by altering the position of one or more means of access to, or control of, that source – or by providing additional means of control; and

(k)   facilitating access and movement by the disabled occupant around the dwelling in order to enable him to care for a person who normally resides in the dwelling and needs such care (s.23).

(discretionary grants) Disabled facilities grants which do not come under the above purposes may – but do not have to be – awarded for making the dwelling suitable for the accommodation, welfare or employment of the disabled occupant (s.23).

(owner and tenant certificates) Applications by tenants for disabled facilities grants must be accompanied by a tenant's certificate, making clear that the disabled occupant will live in the dwelling as his or her only or main residence. An owner's certificate from the current landlord to the same effect will normally be required as well as the tenant's certificate (ie, to confirm both the occupancy position and the landlord's permission). When it is an owner who is making the application, then an owner's certificate is required. Certificates must declare that the disabled occupant will live in the dwelling as his only or main residence throughout the grant condition period – or for as long as his health or other relevant circumstances permit (ss.21–22).

(necessary and appropriate, reasonable and practicable) A grant cannot be awarded unless the housing authority is satisfied that the 'relevant works are necessary and appropriate to meet the needs of the disabled occupant'. If the housing authority is not itself also a social services authority, then it is under an obligation to consult the latter about this (s.24).

In addition, the housing authority must be satisfied that 'it is reasonable and practicable to carry out the relevant works having regard to the age and condition of the dwelling or building'. In deciding this, the authority must at least take into account whether the dwelling is fit for human habitation.

(The definition of fitness for habitation is that a dwelling is structurally stable; free from serious disrepair; free from dampness prejudicial to the health of the occupants; has adequate provision for lighting, heating and ventilation; has satisfactory facilities for preparing and cooking food, including a sink with satisfactory supply of hot and cold water; has a suitably located water closet for exclusive use of the applicants; has a suitably located fixed bath or shower and wash-hand basin of which each has a satisfactory supply of hot and cold water and is for the exclusive use of the occupants: Housing Act 1985, s.604 as amended by the Local Government and Housing Act 1989,schedule 9,para 83).

(disabled occupant) Disabled facilities grants are available only for disabled occupants – defined as somebody who is either registered or registerable under s.29 of the National Assistance Act 1948, schedule 2 of the Children Act 1989 – or a) has a substantial impairment of sight, hearing or speech; b) 'has a mental disorder or impairment of any kind'; or c) 'is physically substantially disabled by illness, injury, impairment present since birth or otherwise' (s.100).

(giving reasons and time limits) Reasons must be given if applications for grants are refused, and applications must be approved or refused within six months from the date of application. If approved, payment must be made no longer than 12 months from the original date of application (ss.34,36).

(works already commenced or completed) A housing authority 'shall not approve an application for a grant if the relevant works have been begun before the application is approved ... Where the relevant works have been begun but have not been completed, the authority may approve the application for a grant if they are satisfied that there were good reasons for beginning the works before the application was approved ... a local housing authority shall not approve an application for a grant if the relevant works have been completed'. Exceptions to these rules relate to fitness requirements and repair notices (s.29).

Legislation. Even if an application for a DFG is approved, the housing department then has a duty to conduct a means-test, the result of which might mean that the cost of the works up to a maximum of £20,000 in England (and £24,000, under otherwise equivalent regulations, in Wales) is met fully, partially, or not at all. Thus, the formal approval of a grant application does not necessarily mean that full – or indeed any – grant will be forthcoming. Conversely, authorities do have the power – where the cost of the adaptation exceeds the maximum amount (£20,000) – to pay a further amount of money to increase the value of the grant beyond the maximum (SI 1996/2888).

In outline, the test of resources a) resembles the housing benefit test; b) assesses income of the applicant of other household members who are 'relevant persons' – in other words, a spouse or partner of the disabled occupant or the parents of a disabled occupant under 18 years old; c) includes a number of premiums calculated to assist particular groups of people; d) disregards altogether some types of income (listed in detail), including an applicant's (or spouse's or partner's) income support; e) disregards savings up to £5000 (SI 1996/2890 as amended).

Legislation. Various regulations govern different aspects of disabled facilities grants including: SI 1996/2888 *Disabled Facilities Grants and Home Repair Assistance (Maximum Amounts) Order 1996*, SI 1996/2889 *Housing Renewal Grants (Services and Charges) Order*, SI 1996/2890 *Housing Renewal Grants Regulations 1996*), SI 1996/2891 *Housing Renewal Grants (Prescribed Forms and Particulars) Regulations*. Preliminary or ancillary services and charges may be included within disabled facilities grants, including surveys, advice, assistance in completing forms, considerations of tenders etc, as well as services of occupational therapists (but not assessment) (SI 1996/2889).

Guidance (DoE 17/96):

(necessary and appropriate: consultation) Even where the relevant social services and housing departments are within the same authority, the former should be consulted by the latter (even though the statutory obligation to consult does not apply in this situation) (p.196).

(necessary and appropriate: care plans and meeting needs) Guidance states that the necessity and appropriateness of an adaptation concern a) whether it is needed to enable a care plan to be implemented and the person to remain in their own home and living as independently as possible; b) whether it will meet the person's assessed needs (physical and medical); and c) the distinction between the person's real needs, and 'what is desirable' and 'possibly legitimate aspirations' (p.198).

(necessary and appropriate: carers) 'In determining the needs of the disabled person consideration should be given to the particular household group in which the disabled occupant resides so that any adaptations being contemplated do not cause strain on the household which may lead to breakdown of the present care arrangements' (p.198).

(necessary and appropriate: independence of disabled occupant) 'DFGs are designed to give disabled people a degree of independence in the home. Consideration therefore needs to be given to the impact of adaptations on the level of care given to the disabled person and whether those tasks will be reduced or eased. Adaptation works would not have achieved their objective within a care package if the disabled person does not gain an acceptable degree of independence, where possible, or, where the disabled person remains dependent upon the care of others, where the adaptation does not significantly ease the burden of the carer' (p.199).

(necessary and appropriate: disagreement between housing and social services) If 'both the social services and housing authorities collaborate effectively it should be a rare occurrence where a housing authority determines not to approve particular adaptations recommended by a social services authority' (p.191).

(reasonable and practicable: fitness for habitation) 'Where, on inspection of a property in connection with a DFG application, it is found to be unfit to the extent that it would clearly be unreasonable and impractical to proceed with the proposed adaptations, the housing authority should, in consultation with the social services authority, consider alternative solutions in deciding the most appropriate course of action' – for example, seeking a renovation grant first, considering a reduced level of adaptations which would meet both the person's needs and considerations of practicality, or considering alternative accommodation (p.199).

(reasonable and practicable: age and condition of property) The following are issues 'which commonly arise in the processing of grant applications:

(a) the architectural and structural characteristics of the dwelling may render certain types of adaptation inappropriate;

(b) the practicalities of carrying out adaptations to smaller properties with narrow doorways, halls and passages which might make wheelchair use in and around the dwelling difficult'

(c) conservation considerations and planning constraints may prevent certain types of adaptation being carried out;

(d) the practicalities of carrying out adaptations to older properties with difficult or limited access eg steep flights of steps making access for wheelchair use difficult and therefore making continued occupation of the dwelling open to question;

(e) the impact on other occupants of proposed works which will reduce or limit the existing facilities or amenities in the dwelling' (p.199).

(continuing duty on social services department) Even where an application has been made to a housing department for a DFG, social services departments might still be called on to assist where a) 'the assessed needs of a disabled person exceed the scope for provision by the housing authority under section 23 of the 1996 Act; and b) where an applicant for a DFG has difficulty in meeting his assessed contribution determined by the means test and seeks financial assistance from the authority'.

In such circumstances, 'where the social services authority determine that the need has been established, it remains their duty to assist even where the local housing authority either refuse or are unable to approve the application' (p.191).

(mandatory grant: safety of dwelling) The legislation provides for making the dwelling safe 'for the disabled person and other persons residing with him'. For example, 'provision of lighting where safety is an issue or for adaptations designed to minimise the risk of danger where a disabled person has behavioural problems … For those with learning difficulties, an enhanced alarm system … in connection with the use of cooking facilities or works to provide means of escape from fire … specialised lighting, toughened or shatterproof glass … installation of guards around certain facilities such as fires or radiators … reinforcement of floors, walls or ceilings … cladding of exposed surfaces and corners to prevent self-injury' (p.193).

(mandatory grant: sleeping room) 'provision of a room usable for sleeping … should therefore only be undertaken if the housing authority are satisfied that the adaptation of an existing room in the dwelling (upstairs or downstairs) or the access to that room is unsuitable in the particular circumstances. Where the disabled occupant shares a bedroom with another person, mandatory grant may be given to provide a room of sufficient size so that the normal sleeping arrangements can be maintained' (pp.193–194).

(**mandatory grant: bathroom**) The provisions 'relating to the provision of a lavatory and washing, bathing and showering facilities have been separated to clarify that a disabled person should have access to a wash-hand basin, a WC and a shower or bath (or if more appropriate, both a shower and a bath)'. Therefore, the legislation provides that 'mandatory grant should be given to provide a disabled person with each of these facilities, and facilitating their use' (p.194).

(**mandatory grant: food, preparation and cooking**) The legislation 'covers a wide range of works to enable a disabled person to cater independently. Eligible works include the rearrangement or enlargement of a kitchen to ease manoeuvrability of a wheelchair and specially modified or designed storage units, gas, electricity and plumbing installations to enable the disabled person to use these facilities independently … Where most of the cooking and preparation of meals is done by another household member, it would not normally be appropriate to carry out full adaptations to the kitchen. However, it might be appropriate that certain adaptations be carried out to enable the disabled person to perform certain functions in the kitchen, such as preparing light meals or hot drinks' (p.194).

(**mandatory grant: heating, lighting, power**) 'People with limited mobility who remain in one room for long periods usually need more warmth in the dwelling than able-bodied people … Where there is no heating system or where the existing heating arrangements are unsuitable to meet his needs, a heating system may be provided. A DFG should not be given to adapt or install heating in rooms which are not normally in use by the disabled person. The installation of central heating to the dwelling should only be considered where the well-being and mobility of the disabled person would otherwise be adversely affected'.

The legislation also provides for 'works to enable a disabled person to have full use of heating, lighting and power controls in the dwelling. Such work includes the relocation of power points to make them more accessible, the provision of suitably adapted controls where a disabled person has difficulty in using normal types of controls and the installation of additional controls' (p.194).

(**mandatory grant: caring for somebody else**) Provision can be made where the disabled person is looking after somebody else who 'need not be disabled' (p.194).

(**mandatory grant: sight and hearing impairment**) It is the Secretary of State's view that the mandatory grant provisions 'enable authorities to give help for the full range of adaptations to cover all the circumstances which may arise. These provisions enable authorities to provide mandatory grant to meet the adaptation needs of disabled people whose needs are less obvious, such as those with sight or hearing impairment. For instance, partially sighted people may require an enhanced form of lighting of a particular kind in the dwelling to enable them to carry out every day tasks and activities in the home' (p.194).

(**mandatory grant: degeneration**) 'Where an applicant's prognosis implies that degeneration in the short term will occur, then this should be taken into account when considering the eligible works' (p.195).

(**discretionary grant: accommodation**) For example, extending or enlarging the dwelling 'which is already suitable for the disabled occupant in all other respects'. It would not include works 'of direct benefit only to other household members' (p.195).

(**discretionary grant: welfare**) For example, 'a safe play area for a disabled child or where certain works of adaptation are required to provide for a disabled occupant to receive specialised care or medical treatment in their own home for which the disabled person is responsible for meeting the costs of the work' (p.195).

(discretionary grant: employment) For example, so the disabled occupant can work from home (p.195).

(successive grant applications) Guidance recognises that for disabled people with degenerative conditions, more than one application might be made over time; the legislation imposes no express restriction on successive applications. Any previously assessed contribution will be taken account of in a new application; this is why it is worthwhile for applicants to follow an application through to completion even when they receive 'nil grant' because their contribution equals or exceeds the cost of the works. This contribution will then be taken account of in any future application within five or ten years (depending on whether the applicant is tenant or owner).

(recovery of equipment) The Housing Grants, Construction and Regeneration Act 1996, s.52, allows local authorities to impose additional conditions on grants – subject to consent from the Secretary of State. One such consent allows local authorities to recover special equipment such as stairlifts when it is no longer needed – although they should consider carefully the condition of recovery to be imposed, if the applicant has made a substantial contribution to the equipment.

In addition, where an applicant makes a 'significant contribution to the cost of the adaptations an authority should consider carefully any proposed conditions. In practice social services are best placed to recover the equipment so that it can be reassigned to another person in need of such equipment. Where it is clear that the equipment will not be reused because of age or condition a local authority may decide to waive their right to recovery' (DoE 17/96,p.201: and *Housing Renewal Grants (Additional Conditions) (England) General Consent 1996*, set out on p.259 of the guidance).

DISCUSSION

Disabled facilities grants: council tenants

Disabled facilities grants are available to private sector, council and housing association tenants (as well as owners). Yet, notwithstanding the legislation, and the emphasis by Circular guidance that it is 'open to Council tenants themselves to initiate adaptation works to their homes by applying for disabled facilities grants' (DoE 17/96,p.192), some councils apparently deny this option to their tenants. Alternatively, it is reported that some councils might in practice refuse, as a matter of policy, to provide as landlord the owner's certificate (of future intended letting to the tenant) which is required to accompany the tenant's application and certificate. This of course is an odd situation, given that both the landlord and the local authority considering the grant application are one and the same since the statutory proviso that a local authority can waive the requirement of an owner's certificate to accompany the tenant's – if it is 'unreasonable in the circumstances to require it' – might apply. Apart from the owner's certificate, a landlord's consent is also required generally for the carrying out of an adaptation. Without this, a grant cannot be given (DoE 17/96,p.164); but there is no explicit reference in the Act to overall consent reasonably having to be given.

The local ombudsman has found maladministration when local councils fail to inform their own tenants of their right to apply for DFGs (eg, *Hackney LBC 1995, Humberside CC 1996*) or are not even sure themselves about what the position is (*Durham CC 1993, Bristol CC 1998*). It is an important issue of public interest, because even if the council has an alternative scheme for its own tenants, people must not be denied their statutory entitlement to apply for DFGs (*Hackney LBC 1995*).

Disabled facilities grants: housing association tenants

Housing association tenants are eligible to apply for disabled facilities grants, although it appears that some local authorities adopt policies which preclude such applications. However, as with council tenants (immediately above), this would appear to be denying housing association tenants their statutory right.

Nevertheless, there are sometimes other options for housing association tenants; for works over £500 a grant might be available from the Housing Corporation under the Housing Act 1996, s.18, which gives a power to make grants. Alternatively, under that amount, a housing association might pay for works out of its own revenue. In some areas difficulties appear to arise when all concerned indulge in buck-passing and funding is forthcoming from neither the Housing Corporation, nor the housing association, nor local authority (housing or social services). More recently, against a backdrop of falling funding for adaptations (Appleton,Leather 1998,p.30), the Housing Corporation has adopted a policy in 1998 of not awarding grants to housing associations which have capital saved of £500,000 or more.

Disabled facilities grants: information about system

The local ombudsman has found maladministration, when an authority failed to give 'sufficiently clear' information to a grant applicant. The person misunderstood the costs involved and incurred unexpected debts – for a lavatory and shower for his wife who had Huntington's Chorea (see eg, *Pendle BC 1994*). The giving of incorrect advice to a woman that she was too young (under 60 years old) to qualify for a renovation grant also amounted to maladministration (*Holderness BC 1995*), as did failing to tell a person about delay (*North Yorkshire CC 1993*).

Disabled facilities grants: limited resources for adaptations

Some disabled facilities grants are mandatory: that is, once certain conditions are satisfied, housing authorities must approve grant applications and, depending on people's means, give financial assistance. Unlike renovation grants – which lost their mandatory element when the statutory basis transferred from the Local Government and Housing Act 1989 to the Housing Grants, Construction and Regeneration Act 1996 – disabled facilities grants remain mandatory and demand-led. This has led to concern that renovation grants will further suffer, as authorities divert money towards DFGs, and therefore undermine their strategic approach to improving poor housing conditions (Pieda 1996,p.iii).

Alternatively, in order to avoid incurring obligations which they cannot afford, housing authorities might, for example, limit publicity about DFGs, give people preliminary enquiry forms rather than proper application forms (thus prolonging the whole process) or maintain long waiting lists once the annual budget is spent (Heywood 1994,p.75). This might be in addition to restricting discretionary disabled facilities grants: about 98 per cent of grants awarded are mandatory (Pieda 1996,p.43).

The local ombudsman has set out various steps necessary in relation to applications for housing grants, including making known the details of priority systems to enquirers and applicants in a consistent and uniform way (eg, by leaflet or information sheet), and treating requests for information with 'helpful and meaningful responses' (*Merthyr Tydvil 1994*). So, it is maladministration if an authority fails to keep adequate records of information given to enquirers, and to explain clearly a) the priorities, b) the difference between initial enquiry and formal application, c) the necessity of a council survey, and d) the importance of not starting works before grant approval (*Newham LBC 1997b*).

The local ombudsman has disapproved of systems in which applicants are treated solely in date order, because this prevents priority being given to those in greater need (*Liverpool CC 1996/1997*) – but has accepted that local authorities should adopt priorities and that this means people will have to queue (*Newham LBC 1997b, Wakefield MBC 1996*). Furthermore, giving priority for grants (renovation and disabled facilities) to certain groups such as disabled people or those with houses with dangerous structures is not a fettering of discretion when room is left to consider exceptional cases. However, if waiting lists are uneven in different areas of the authority and priority criteria are applied inconsistently, this is maladministration (*Newham LBC 1997b*); whilst a three-year wait for an inspection visit for a renovation grant was simply too long (*Sandwell MBC 1997*).

Sometimes, housing and social services departments apparently collude in strategies of delay – for instance, by asking the latter to suspend assessment visits, thereby creating waiting lists and taking the pressure off the housing grants budget. However, such an approach might in turn lead to the social services department's failing to assess within a reasonable time and to a finding of maladministration by the local ombudsman (eg, *Bolton MBC 1992*).

When a council claimed that it could not process an application for a renovation grant because the woman had not submitted a certificate of owner occupation, the ombudsman found that technically this was correct. However, the situation had come about because the council had deliberately withheld the documents necessary for the woman to complete her application; this was maladministration (*Manchester CC 1998*). Simply putting on hold a recommendation received from the social services department – so that the adaptations were not ready almost two years after referral – was maladministration (*North Yorkshire CC 1993*).

Although the local ombudsmen have in the past been critical of delay in processing grants, they have also recognised the difficulties facing councils who have to operate a demand-led system of DFGs with insufficient resources. Thus, lack of resources leading to a failure to comply with housing grants legislation might not in itself necessarily be maladministration (*Cyngor Dosbarth Dwyfor 1994*). The ombudsmen might not be 'critical of councils which have, in effect, introduced a rationing system for limiting the number of applications they approve provided that the system has been designed fairly and operates fairly, and provided that the council concerned has done what can reasonably be expected to secure the resources needed to meet its responsibilities in this area' (CLAE 1994,p.24). However, failure to publish criteria about priority and to tell enquirers about them is maladministration, as is adopting a policy about priority without being able to produce a record of its formal adoption (*Dinefwr BC 1995*).

Overall, it is thought that about 35 per cent of applicants either drop out before their application is approved or are refused. The main reason is a) ineligibility because the works are not regarded as necessary or their income is likely to disqualify them from grant aid, or b) they are council tenants in an area where the local authority adapts its own stock outside the DFG scheme (Pieda 1996,p.i).

Disabled facilities grants: statutory timescale for dealing with applications

The local ombudsman may find maladministration where the statutory timescale (six months: see above) for approving an application is not complied with.

Guidance has stated that when local authorities operate a preliminary enquiry system, 'it should not be used to prevent potential applicants from submitting formal applications where it is their wish and it should at all times be made clear that no commitments about the availability and the amount of grant can be given until a formal application has been submitted' (DoE 17/96,p.160). Thus, preventing people from submitting formal applications or not telling that they have a right to do so is maladministration (eg, *Walsall MBC 1996*).

Whilst breach of the timescale is maladministration (*Newham LBC 1993*), nevertheless the ombudsmen might accept that councils get into financial difficulty because of increased demand for grants; if a complainant has not suffered injustice 'above and beyond' others in the same position, they might not recommend any remedy or compensation (*Middlesbrough BC 1996*; also *Newham LBC 1997b*) – other than that the council should get on and do all it can to eliminate delays for complainants who were still waiting (*Sheffield CC 1997b*).

Although an application must be dealt with in six months, the legislation now makes provision for a delay in payment of up to 12 months from the date of the original, formal application. This provision is designed to alleviate the burden where there is a 'particularly heavy caseload of applications involving works which attract mandatory grant'. However, the guidance goes on to say that the 'power should be used sparingly and not where it would cause hardship or suffering to an applicant whose adaptation needs have been assessed as urgent, for example where a disabled person will be leaving hospital or residential care to return home or move into a new dwelling' (DoE 17/96,p.200).

Disabled facilities grants: necessary and appropriate

Both social services departments when consulted, and housing departments when making the final decision, about the necessity and appropriateness of proposed works should also ensure that they do not take resources into account in the process. Resources were in 1998 emphatically rejected as a relevant factor by the High Court in *R v Birmingham CC, ex p Mohammed*. Quite apart from resources, social services departments also need to ensure that when they are consulted about necessity and appropriateness they do not adopt overly restrictive criteria inconsistent with the legislation – and housing departments should be alive to such practices.

For instance, in one ombudsman case the social services department was placing a narrow construction on the legislation and guidance about the circumstances in which it would recommend heating improvements as necessary and appropriate; the local ombudsman found maladministration (*Hackney LBC 1997b*). It is unsurprising that the investigation should have involved central heating; assessment and decisions about when it should be provided have long been debated in local authorities (Heywood 1996,p.101) – as well as within Housing Corporation regional offices when considering applications for grants for disabled housing association tenants (Appleton,Leather 1998,p.27). In another investigation, given the problems the housing department was having, the social services department suggested that baths at a day centre rather than a shower were the solution in apparent misunderstanding of the law (*Humberside CC 1996*).

Another major area of contention concerns recommendations for baths or showers. The Housing Grants, Construction and Regeneration Act 1996 and associated guidance make it quite clear that disabled occupants should have access to a bath or shower or both – in addition to access to a wash-hand basin. In fact the wording was slightly altered from its previous incarnation in the Local Government and Housing Act 1989 to make this absolutely plain. Nevertheless, because they award bathing needs a very low priority under s.2 of the Chronically Sick and Disabled Persons Act 1970, social services departments are tending to apply the same low priority when asked about the necessity and appropriateness of a DFG (Heywood 1996,p.133). Thereby, they are unduly restricting the provisions of the 1996 Act by applying to it eligibility criteria developed under completely different legislation (ie, the 1970 Act). Yet the two Acts must not be confused, even though they contain similar words such as 'necessary' (*R v Birmingham CC, ex p Mohammed*). If the wrong criteria are applied, authorities will be vulnerable to challenges made either through the local ombudsman or even the courts. The situation is not helped by the fact that the Department of Health has not issued guidance to social services departments about the new Act and the revised statutory wording (see p.399).

Disabled facilities grants: reasonable and practicable

A change in the legislation now means that when approving a disabled facilities grant, it is no longer mandatory that the dwelling be fit for human habitation even on completion of the works. However, the housing authority must still take account of this question and so has a discretion either to insist on, or to waive, the fitness for habitation criterion.

In relation to the age and condition of the property generally, housing authorities have to consider various factors, such as the following: a) architectural and structural characteristics; b) practicality of adaptations in smaller dwellings with narrow doors, halls and passages (eg, with wheelchair use in mind) – or in older dwellings with difficult or limited access (eg, steep flights of steps); c) conservation and planning considerations; d) impact on other occupants (DoE 17/96,p.199).

The High Court has ruled that resources may legitimately be taken into account when a local housing authority considers whether it is reasonable and practicable to carry out works of adaptation – for example, in relation to a dilapidated dwelling or one that is not fit for human habitation (*R v Birmingham CC, ex p Mohammed*). The local ombudsman too has acknowledged that the availability of alternative accommodation might obviate the duty to arrange adaptations under the 1970 Act, since 'there must be limits on what it is practicable and reasonable to provide and at some point an alternative to providing adaptations may be a fair response' (*Manchester CC 1994*).

Disabled facilities grants: discretionary

Local authorities have the power to award disabled facilities grants for the purposes of welfare, accommodation or employment. These are catch-all categories to cover anything that does not qualify for a mandatory grant. In practice, few discretionary grants are given – amounting to about 2 per cent of all disabled facilities grants approved (Pieda 1996,p.43). However, local authorities should beware of having a rigid policy on their use – since even in the case of a power, a court might consider, as it did in *R v Bristol CC, ex p Bailey* (about discretionary renovation grants), whether the authority's discretion is being fettered by not considering exceptions (see p.49).

The courts sometimes state that duties should take precedence over powers, and services under the latter (ie, discretionary services) should be sacrificed to enable duties to be performed (eg, *R v East Sussex, ex p Tandy* in the House of Lords). Nonetheless, the local ombudsman has not considered it maladministration for a council to continue to approve discretionary disabled facilities grants, at a time when it was breaching statutory timescales for mandatory grants (*Middlesbrough BC 1996/1997*).

Disabled facilities grants: limit to grant

The limit which a local authority can pay for a disabled facilities (and general renovation) grant is £20,000 in England and £24,000 in Wales. This sum is less than the previous limit of £50,000 placed on such grants – and a far cry from their originally unlimited nature – under the Local Government and Housing Act 1989. Amidst concern over the 'demand-led' system of provision of renovation grants generally, disabled facilities grants have survived as mandatory although subject to this reduced limit.

However, housing authorities do now have the power to make payment over £20,000 – in other words, to add a discretionary addition to the mandatory amount (SI 1996/2888). A report prepared for the Department of Environment recommends that this power should be exercised fully since 'it is important to recognise that there is a contradiction in the notion of setting a limit on mandatory grants, when it is a requirement that only works that are deemed necessary and appropriate should be mandatory' (Pieda 1996,p.73).

Within these limits, the housing authority will make a grant payment following the statutory means-test (above: SI 1996/2890), although people might sometimes be assessed for nil grant (a process worth going through in case a future application is made: see above, p.404). The means-test is frequently criticised since it is basically an income test and fails to take account, for instance, of outgoings such as the extra costs incurred by a person because of disability or mortgage payments. Nevertheless, local authorities should not introduce legally extraneous (ie, not envisaged in the statutory scheme) conditions to the means-test (see eg, *R v Sunderland CC, ex p Redezeus*).

Disabled facilities grants: recovery of equipment

If an adaptation includes specialised equipment, such as a stairlift, the housing authority is empowered to impose a special condition – such that the equipment can be recovered by the authority when it is no longer required (see extracts above). This is clearly designed to allow authorities to make best use of resources.

Disabled facilities grants: adaptations begun or completed before grant approval

Local housing authorities have a discretion to approve grants for works already begun, but not for works completed (except if certain fitness requirements apply): see above. Therefore, retrospective payments can become a vexed issue if applicants have got on with adaptations themselves. For instance, in one investigation, the ombudsman concluded that the council had failed to warn clearly that works should not be started before a grant is approved – but the applicant was also to blame because he had not read the booklet from the Department of Environment (*Gateshead MBC 1995*).

However, if as a consequence of maladministration (eg, delay in assessment by social services), a person has carried out adaptations in advance of any grant approval, the local ombudsman will sometimes recommend that a retrospective payment be made, equivalent to the grant the person would have received in the absence of the maladministration (*North Tyneside MBC 1994, Sheffield CC 1989, Northumberland CC 1989*).

Disabled facilities grants: continuing duty on social services

Central government guidance envisages that in some instances a continuing duty will fall on social services to arrange adaptations (see extracts from DoE 17/96 above), in the absence of (sufficient) assistance from housing authorities in the form of disabled facilities grants. This has been maintained also in Parliament when the Department of Environment stated that social services has 'responsibilities under the 1970 Act to provide financial assistance in cases where a disabled person will otherwise face hardship in meeting their share of the cost of adaptations' (Mr Baldry: HCWA,28/10/1992,col.670). This has given rise to financial anxieties within social services departments, in case they are obliged to make provision they cannot afford (eg, Pieda 1996,p.55).

For instance, the anxiety might be well-founded, if a court were to question a local authority social services department's decision that although an adaptation is 'necessary' under the Housing Grants, Construction and Regeneration Act 1996, it is not necessary under the Chronically Sick and Disabled Persons Act 1970. Indeed, guidance explains that 'necessary and appropriate' refers in part to whether the adaptations will assist with the carrying out of a care plan (which is formulated by social services and might often involve s.2 of the Chronically Sick and Disabled Persons Act). Therefore, it is not clear how sustainable in practice the distinction between the word 'necessary' in the two Acts really is.

However, in partial answer, the courts have held that there is indeed a difference between the import of the term 'necessary' in each of the Acts. The *Gloucestershire* case established that resources may be taken into account (at least for some services) when deciding whether arrangements under s.2 of the Chronically Sick and Disabled Persons Act 1970 are necessary. But the court in *R v Birmingham CC, ex p Mohammed* decided the opposite, namely that resources were irrelevant to the necessity and appropriateness of adaptations under the Housing Grants, Construction and Regeneration Act 1996. It supported this conclusion in part by referring to the list of arrangements in s.2 picked out as non-essential by the House of Lords in *(R v East Sussex CC, ex p Tandy)*; adaptations were not on the list.

Some local authorities might try to avoid expensive legal obligations by identifying two or three options under the Chronically Sick and Disabled Persons Act 1970, any one of which would be 'necessary' to meet the need; if an adequate DFG is forthcoming (eg, for a downstairs extension), all well and good. If not, then the authority might argue that under s.2 of the 1970 Act, it can meet the need via one of the other options (eg, a strip wash or commode in the living room). This would be on the grounds that the law courts have ruled that local authorities can take account of resources when deciding how to meet the assessed need (*R v Gloucestershire CC, ex p Barry; R v Lancashire CC, ex p RADAR*).

In practice, some social services departments might simply apply restrictive criteria when deciding what is necessary and appropriate, not only to safeguard their own budgets but also that of the housing department which is finding it cannot afford to meet the demand for DFGs. Where both departments are in the same local authority, they might work closely together in this respect

(Pieda 1996,p.61). However, they should be careful nevertheless that they do not breach their legal obligations when introducing restrictions of this nature (see p.50). Similarly, when authorities adopt a policy of never 'topping up' – in other words, never considering providing assistance additional to the DFG (ACC *et al.* 1996,p.20) – they might run the risk in some situations of acting unlawfully by fettering their discretion.

Disabled facilities grants: continuing duty on social services (local ombudsman)

The local ombudsman has investigated a number of cases which include reference to such a continuing duty resting on social services. For example, maladministration was found, when having identified a need for a downstairs extension, social services failed to act for 20 months – after the housing authority had offered a grant which the applicant family could not accept because it could not afford the contribution. The 'Council appear to have ignored the fact that their statutory responsibility to provide assistance did not come to an end with the offer of a grant [by the housing authority]' (*Salford CC 1993*). The duty might be to make full provision, or simply to make interim provision such as a commode (*Barnsley MBC 1998b*), until a grant is forthcoming (see eg, *Liverpool CC 1996/1997c*, also *Tower Hamlets LBC 1997*).

Some social services departments appear to draw a veil over any continuing involvement, not even telling the person what its recommendation is and lacking a system of responding if the housing department does not act on that recommendation (*Durham CC 1993*). Closing files prematurely also attempts to avoid continuing duties, but is maladministration (*Durham CC 1993, Gravesham BC 1987*). Alternatively, the social services department, when confronted with the continuing duty, might simply try to disown its original assessment of need (*Dyfed CC 1996*). In one investigation, the ombudsman found that the housing authority imposed a moratorium on expenditure having discovered half way through the financial year that finance was 'tighter than anticipated'. The need for a stairlift identified by social services therefore remained unacted upon for a long period. Social services in turn did not act (as it might have, given the continuing duty potentially incurred if the housing department fails to meet the need: see above). The ombudsman found maladministration which had caused a two-year wait (*Camden LBC 1993*).

The local ombudsman has also stated that when a housing authority 'is not immediately able to provide the necessary funding, the Council must meet the costs of making provision under the terms of the Chronically Sick and Disabled Persons Act by other means in its capacity as Social Services Authority' (*Wirral MBC 1992d*). It was maladministration when a council took two years to agree to provide an interest free loan as part of its 'continuing duty', following the inability of a person to meet the contribution which had been assessed by the housing authority (*Wirral MBC 1994b*). Again, the ombudsman has doubted a council's initial view (later reversed) that once it had assessed the need for a disabled facilities grant, it had done its duty under s.2 of the Chronically Sick and Disabled Persons Act. What it failed to do in this particular case was to establish whether the applicants could actually afford their contribution to the adaptations themselves, and if not, possibly offer an interest free loan (*Wirral MBC 1994d*).

Disabled facilities grants and other home adaptations: complexity

The arrangement of home adaptations can be a chaotic process involving, for example, social services, the housing department, planning department, means-tests, builders, surveyors, architects

(Pieda 1996,p.63). Add the sometimes complex needs of the disabled person, the characteristics of the dwelling (see eg, Statham, Korczak and Monaghan 1988), a shortage of resources and a legislative and administrative maze – and it is inevitable that difficulty, inconvenience, misunderstandings and delay sometimes occur (for a comprehensive overview of the whole system – its composite nature, problems, and good and bad practices – see Heywood 1994 and 1996). Delay in assessment and then provision is a long-established feature of the adaptations system (eg, Salvage 1996). Given this background, the local ombudsman is frequently called on to investigate; the following gives a flavour.

Example 1: disabled facilities grants and other adaptations, no maladministration (ombudsman). An 18-month wait for major adaptations following assessment, including design and construction taking a year, was deemed by the local ombudsman not to be 'unreasonable delay' (*Ealing LBC 1993*). The ombudsman did not criticise a council for failing to predict construction, foundation and drainage problems; nor the council's inability to get work finished quicker by a contractor (*Cumbria CC 1992*). Similarly, the council was not at fault when delay occurred because of disagreement between the person and council officers, the seeking of advice by the applicant from a doctor, and an indication by the applicant, without good cause, that she wished for no further help because of the delays. In addition, it was not the council's responsibility that the person had bought a home which was difficult to modify (*Wirral MBC 1993f*). And when an initial financial assessment was incorrect but was followed quickly by the formal assessment which correctly worked out the applicant's potential contribution, there was no evidence that the applicants were substantially misled (*Wirral MBC 1994b*).

The fact that a lift obtained through a disabled facilities grant broke down 16 times, the door was defective, it marked the wall when in use and turned out to be too small, was not in the circumstances maladministration, though the ombudsman had some sympathy for the complainants. However, in the same case, the amending of the original recommendation for a shower to a smaller model (because of cost) meant that the shower was too small for the shower chair used by the disabled person; in addition the shower leaked and the water temperature varied too quickly. The failure to ensure provision of a satisfactory shower was maladministration (*Leeds CC 1995*).

Example 2: disabled facilities grants and other adaptations, delay generally (ombudsman). The fact that a complex system requires considerable communication and cooperation between different departments and agencies does not mean that the local ombudsman will overlook administrative deficiencies. For instance, a 19-month period between application and final assessment was maladministration, including as it did insufficient record keeping, possible lost papers and the applicant's consequent uncertainty throughout the period about what was going on (*Wirral MBC 1994a*). A four-year wait for home adaptations, made up of a series of delays, was 'entirely unacceptable' (*Gravesham BC 1987*).

A considerable lapse of time caused by obtaining medical opinion, drawing up plans and getting planning permission might be reasonable in the eyes of the ombudsman. However, once all this was done, a delay in approving and submitting plans was maladministration; as was inadequate monitoring by the council of a contractor whose defects caused further delay (*Wirral MBC 1992b*). Workload might explain part of the delay in installing a shower, but the fact that an order marked urgent did not appear to have received the appropriate priority was maladministration (*Islington LBC 1988*). The monitoring of work and paying of builders can lead to misuse of public money and maladministration on a number of counts if proper procedures are not followed (*Newham London LBC 1997a*).

Whether or not delay itself is reasonable, failure to notify people about what is going on might be found by the local ombudsman to be maladministration. For example, a borough council's 'failure to notify [the applicant] formally of the decision to delay the work and then its failure to notify him formally of its schedule for carrying out the work … was maladministration'. Similarly, in the same case, the failure to notify the applicant about the fluctuations in the authority's views of what the applicant's needs really were was maladministration (*North Yorkshire CC 1993*). In another case, the authority's policy was to raise an order (for a stairlift) within seven working days of an assessment visit; in practice, this did not happen for 22 months and was maladministration (*Camden LBC 1993*).

Example 3: disabled facilities grants and other adaptations, joint working within and between authorities (local ombudsman). While there are many examples of effective arrangements between social services and housing departments, lapses also occur leading sometimes to findings of maladministration. For instance, things can go wrong in relation to different councils (*Durham CC 1993*), or even where social services and housing are different departments in the same council (*Camden LBC 1993*); and a breakdown in communication can result in nothing happening for months on end (*Leicester CC 1992d*).

Opportunities missed to progress works when finance was available and despite pressure from the hospital, the lack of finance when the application was submitted, a priority request not being progressed, availability of funding not checked, and misunderstanding between an occupational therapist and surveyors all constituted maladministration (*Tower Hamlets LBC 1992*). Allowing a disagreement, between the social services and housing departments about central heating for a man with AIDS, to drag on for over a year was maladministration; as was the concern about resources and about setting an unwanted precedent, which meant that genuine technical problems in installing the heating were identified only belatedly (*Tower Hamlets LBC 1997*). Delay caused by the seeking of medical advice will not be faulted; but subsequent failure to visit for three months, and a further three-month delay in approving a revised plan might be (*Wirral MBC 1992b*).

Problems of correspondence in a large organisation did not make it 'right that a Council should rely on a service user to follow up delays caused by non-arrival of internal mail. It should not be beyond the capability of the Council to devise a system of keeping track of applications such as this' (*Liverpool CC 1992*). Thus, communication failure between a social worker and housing officer meant that a message was never received and led to a two month delay; this was maladministration (*Rotherham MBC 1995*). Where attempts by senior officers to discuss delay with their opposite numbers in social services failed, 'officers in both departments should have taken responsibility to ensure such discussions took place'. Not to do so was maladministration (*Newham LBC 1993b*). Inadequate co-ordination between departments leading to delay in the meeting of assessed needs for equipment or adaptations was not acceptable; the council should 'exercise proper management to ensure that no unreasonable delays occur before those needs are met' (*Wirral MBC 1992d*).

In another case, the local ombudsman found a scheme to alter a bathroom 'characterised by a complete breakdown of communications between departments. Once it became clear that there had been confusion over the extent of the scheme … it should have been a matter of days to rectify the situation. Instead, a further 16 months passed before a fresh order was raised…'. And the eight-month delay between the approval and the placing of an order for an adaptation was regarded as not unusual and with 'apparent equanimity' by the council. All this was maladministration (*Wirral MBC 1993e*). Lack of 'effective liaison' between social services and housing authority, resulting in delay for adaptations, was maladministration (*Camden LBC 1993*); the same fault might result in an occupational therapist's recommendations being omitted from a schedule of works drawn up by a technical officer – or in a 'catalogue of disasters and duplicated work' as well as the disappearance of an application in the architect's department (*Liverpool City CC 1996/1997*). A wait of seven and a half months between receipt of instructions from social services and the housing department's sending of a preliminary form to the applicants was also maladministration (*Wirral MBC 1994b*).

In yet another investigation, the 'process of establishing what needs were to be met, the drawing up of plans, the obtaining of grant aid, and the granting of planning permission involved three different departments of the Council (and two separate sections of one of those departments). If such a process is to work properly, then different parts of the Council must work together more effectively than happened in this case. The failure of officers to co-ordinate their activities led to the submission and processing of an unacceptable planning application and consequent delay. The Council's failure to co-ordinate their activities was maladministration' (*Salford CC 1993*). Failure to provide clear information to clarify the exact works involved and the amount of contribution required of an applicant is maladministration (*Nottinghamshire CC 1998*).

Examples 4: disabled facilities grants, responsibility of users (local ombudsman). It is the responsibility of grant applicants to obtain estimates, choose surveyors, choose contractors etc, a point made by the local ombudsman when people complain after things have gone wrong (eg, *Hounslow LBC 1994*). The council's role has been described by the local ombudsman as being about monitoring of adaptations proceeding by way of grant to ensure that public money is spent wisely and building regulations adhered to; its inspections are therefore to protect the public revenue and not grant recipients. It is the latter's responsibility to ensure that works are carried out to a high standard (*Newham LBC 1995*). However, if a council is offering its own agency services to facilitate the adaptation, then it clearly takes on more responsibility (*Leicester CC 1992a, Leicester CC 1995*); but in any case it should at least make clear to people the responsibilities they are taking on in relation to a grant (*Hounslow LBC 1994*).

5. HOME REPAIR ASSISTANCE

For more minor works, home repair assistance is available in the form of grant or materials for works of repair, improvement or adaptation. However, authorities are not under a duty to provide this. They may if they wish (but even in respect of such a power, they should be aware of fettering their discretion by not taking account of exceptions: see p.49). Because home repair assistance is discretionary, its availability varies around the country. Where it is available, the local authority often operates the scheme through housing improvement agencies. The scheme is designed to be quick and easy to use compared to the disabled facilities grant system.

Various conditions have to be met, although if the works are to enable an elderly, infirm or disabled person to be cared for, then some are relaxed – for example, the condition that the applicant be receiving state benefits, or that he or she live in the dwelling as his only or main residence. Although the applicant must be over 18 years old, the works need not be directly for his or her benefit – and so could be applied for in respect of infirm or disabled children. The maximum amount of assistance available in respect of one dwelling is £2,000 per application and a total of £4,000 over a period of three years (Housing Grants, Reconstruction and Regeneration Act 1996, s.76–80, and SI 1996/2888).

EXTRACTS

Legislation (Housing Grants, Construction and Regeneration Act 1996) states:

> **(power to give assistance)** 'A local housing authority may on application being made to them, give assistance under this Chapter ("home repair assistance") in the form of a grant or the provision of materials for the carrying out of works of repair, improvement or adaptation to a dwelling' (s.76).

(general eligibility) The applicant must

- be aged 18 or over;
- live in the dwelling as his or her only or main residence (this condition is met if the application is to enable an elderly, disabled or infirm person – who lives or proposes to live in the dwelling as his or her only or main residence – to be cared for);
- be an owner or tenant;
- have a duty or power to carry out the works;
- be in receipt of income support, family credit, housing benefit, council tax benefit or disability working allowance (this whole condition is waived if the applicant is elderly, disabled or infirm, or if the application is for works to enable such a person to be cared for) (s.77).

Landlords and council tenants are not eligible for assistance (s.77).

(mobile homes and houseboats) Subject to various conditions, assistance is available for mobile homes and houseboats. The residency condition (three years before application in relation to occupation – and mooring location for a houseboat, or protected site (Mobile Homes Act 1983) for a mobile home) is met if the works are to enable an elderly, disabled or infirm person – who lives or proposes to live there as his or her only or main residence – to be cared for (s.78). From 1st January 1999, the availability of home repair assistance has been extended to occupiers of mobile homes on local authority sites for gypsies – and to people who either own, or are tenants of, the land on which their mobile homes are stationed (S1 1998/2998).

(assistance available) The maximum amount of assistance available in respect of one dwelling is £2,000 per application and a total of £4,000 over a period of three years (SI 1996/2888).

Guidance (DoE 17/96) states:

(adaptations) 'Adaptations can take many different forms and serve equally as many purposes. The Secretary of State expects local authorities to use their judgement and foresight when awarding home repair assistance for this purpose. Where the application is in respect of a piece of equipment and the use of the disabled facilities grant is not appropriate, an authority should have regard to the duties placed on the local social services by the Chronically Sick and Disabled Persons Act 1970. Nevertheless, authorities may award grants for this purpose, if they choose to. Where an applicant's prognosis implies that degeneration in the short term will occur, then eligible works should allow for this' (p.187).

(crime prevention) 'Authorities may wish to make home repair assistance available to the elderly, infirm or disabled applicants for the purpose of improving their home security through such works that may include: the provision and installation of improved door lock (both internal and external), window locks and where appropriate an optical enhanced intercom system' (p.187).

(home improvement agencies) 'Agencies are often well placed to advise authorities on the potential scope of work and on priorities, as well as assisting in securing grant targeting and take up. For this reason the Secretary of State sees local authorities using agencies both in shaping policy and delivering grant and other assistance...' (p.188).

Home repair assistance: prevalence

Home repair assistance was introduced by the Housing Grants, Construction and Regeneration Act 1996, replacing and exceeding in scope the previous system of minor works assistance. Whereas the 'staying put' and 'elderly resident adaptation' elements of minor works assistance were restricted to people at least 60 years old, the new scheme has no such age limitations. Not only can the applicant be as young as 18 years old, but an application could be made, for example, in respect of a disabled child.

Like its predecessor, home repair assistance is designed to complement mainstream grants and to be used flexibly and with discretion by authorities to support their overall private sector renewal strategy; guidance states that authorities 'should consider making full use' of it, particularly 'where small but essential works to a property, including a mobile home, will enable the applicant to remain living there or to enable an elderly or disabled person to move into a household to be cared for' (DoE 17/96,p.49).

Minor works assistance, similarly discretionary, was employed variably and usefully (Macintosh, Leather 1993; Macintosh, Leather and McCafferty 1993; Randall 1995) by local authorities in England; in 1996 it was reported that, for example, 75 per cent of authorities used the 'staying put' element to help elderly people remain in their own homes (Pieda 1996,p.51). The assistance was often operated on behalf of housing authorities by home improvement agencies, an arrangement which Circular guidance encourages for home repair assistance as well (DoE 17/96,p.188).

Indeed the usefulness of small scale, flexible assistance is further underlined by local 'handy person' schemes for elderly people on low incomes – run by organisations funded usually from social services or charitable sources. Carrying out minor repairs, mostly costing less than £150 per job (eg, repair of doors, windows, gutters, roofs, plumbing, electrical work, lock-fitting, security chains), these schemes might provide assistance more sensitively and responsively than formal applications for minor adaptations and result in beneficial effects on health, safety and well-being (Appleton 1996).

PART IV

DISPUTES, LOCAL OMBUDSMAN INVESTIGATIONS AND LEGAL JUDGMENTS (DIGESTS OF CASES)

CHAPTER 17

DISPUTES AND THEIR REMEDIES

Coverage

1. Councillors, MPs and newspapers
2. Local authority monitoring officers
3. District auditors
4. Social services complaints procedures
5. Secretary of State's default powers (social services)
6. Secretary of State's general and specific and general directions
7. Secretary of State's inquiries
8. Local ombudsman
9. NHS complaints procedure
10. Health service ombudsman
11. Secretary of State's default powers (NHS)
12. Charters
13. Judicial review
14. Breach of statutory duty, negligence and contract
15. Access to personal information

KEY POINTS

This chapter covers what are often called remedies – in other words, the courses of action which people can follow when trying to pursue and resolve disputes. These range from the informal at one extreme to, at the other, judicial review proceedings and actions for negligence which sometimes go on appeal to the House of Lords. The following sections summarise and explain these remedies, and include some observations on their relative advantages and disadvantages.

Social services complaints procedures. The complaints procedure of a social services department is intended to cover most grievances of community care service users. Directions impose time limits within which local authorities must respond to and resolve formal complaints, and where there is continuing disagreement, the dispute can be referred to review panels. The time limits apply only to formal complaints; thus there is scope for delay until a complaint is acknowledged to be formal.

419

Review panels are able to investigate not just the way in which local authorities have reached decisions in terms of procedure and legality, but also the merits of decisions in relation to professional judgment. To the extent that complaints procedures embrace this wide approach, as opposed to a narrow procedural one (ie, asking only if staff followed procedures), issues can be explored more widely than by the courts or the local ombudsmen who are generally restricted to questioning the *way* in which authorities decide things, rather than *what* they actually decide. The complaints procedure will therefore be the most suitable channel for the majority of disputes relating to social services – assuming that it operates to a reasonable standard.

Secretary of State's default powers. The Secretary of State has powers to declare both social services departments and health authorities 'in default' of their duties. In the case of social services, the default would not be declared if the authority had a 'reasonable excuse' for not complying with its duty. In fact no authority has ever been declared to be in default, although the Department of Health does make informal enquiries into possible 'default' cases. However, even these informal enquiries can take a long time. Judges sometimes refer to these powers when explaining why they will not intervene in a dispute, stating that this procedure, rather than a court case, is the appropriate avenue of redress. But the fact that the default powers have apparently never been used might suggest that the remedy exists more in theory than practice.

Local government ombudsmen. The local ombudsmen investigate maladministration in local authorities and can recommend remedies, including financial compensation, where people have suffered injustice. Although local authorities are not legally obliged to comply with recommendations, they receive worse publicity (than they are already getting for the original maladministration) when they do not.

In common with judicial review by the courts, the local ombudsmen investigate in principle the way in which authorities act and make decisions rather than what those decisions and actions ultimately are. Indeed they are barred from questioning professional judgements directly. Nevertheless, under cover of maladministration, the ombudsman seems to operate far more freely than the courts and investigates in detail all manner of acts and decisions. For this reason (and for reasons of time, effort and potential expense), service users are probably well-advised to use, where possible, the local ombudsman rather than the courts.

The local ombudsmen (there are several) have for many years investigated a number of issues relevant to community care: for example, waiting lists, the application of priorities and criteria of eligibility, communication between local authority departments and so on. The cases give considerable insight into the sorts of situation and difficulty which give rise to disputes in the first place.

NHS complaints. The NHS offers a unified complaints procedure; beyond this the health service ombudsman can investigate health authorities and NHS Trusts in relation to maladministration, failure within a service and failure to provide a service (which there is a duty to provide). The clinical judgement of staff can also be questioned.

Judicial review (public law). Judicial review in the law courts is what is known as a 'public law' remedy and is used to challenge the decisions and actions of public bodies. It is generally not used to obtain damages, but instead the law courts supervise public bodies to ensure that they are acting according to legislation and to common law principles which define good administration (in a legal sense) by public bodies. Judicial review has formed the main legal plank for challenging community care decisions.

Negligence, breach of statutory duty and contract (private law). In community care, private law claims in which people seek damages for harm suffered – either in a claim for negligence or for breach of statutory duty – are more problematic. They will have little chance of success if the alleged negligent action is linked closely with issues of policy, resources or statutory functions under legislation – since the law courts are likely, in those circumstances, to refuse even to consider imposing liability on local authorities and their staff. The awarding of damages for breach of community care legislation seems highly unlikely; whilst the law of contract is generally of no application beween statutory services and their clients or patients.

Personal information. In order to obtain services or to challenge decisions, people sometimes need to see the personal information which is held about them by a local authority. Currently, people have a qualified right of access to such information held by social services under the Access to Personal Files Act 1987 for manual records and the Data Protection Act 1984 for computerised records. The Data Protection Act 1998 will replace both of these Acts when it comes into force.

I. COUNCILLORS, MPs and NEWSPAPERS

Informal channels for seeking a remedy – for instance, provision or restoration of a service – might include gently querying the actions and decisions of local authority staff without pursuing a formal 'complaint', complaining to a local councillor or MP or contacting the local newspaper or radio. Such channels will in some circumstances be effective. For instance, MPs and local councillors might take up the cases of constituents not on compelling legal grounds but simply for benevolent or compassionate reasons. It is not unknown for a councillor to approve social services priority criteria in committee one month, but the next month to oppose them when a constituent falls victim to them.

Some disputes might be defused earlier still, because well-informed service users or their representatives effectively challenge decisions; or, alternatively, because well-informed authorities know they are on firm legal ground and can demonstrate that from the outset. Resolving disputes informally is often the preferable option; neither service user nor authority wishes to incur the time, trouble, stress and expense of engaging in a dispute. The possible souring of future relations between authority and user is also a significant consideration in practice.

Such has been the confusion about some aspects of community care legislation and guidance, that it might sometimes be possible to worry an authority even if, in fact, it is not clear whether it is doing anything legally dubious. For instance, local authority staff can be quite disconcerted when a local voluntary organisation 'waves' legislation or guidance from the Department of Health in front of them, and points out that they are following an ostensibly unlawful policy. A local authority might change its mind either because of legal anxiety (whether or not well-founded), concern about the costs of litigation or simply because it wishes to avoid bad publicity.

2. LOCAL AUTHORITY MONITORING OFFICERS

Local authority monitoring officers (each authority is obliged to have one) have a duty to report on actual or possible contraventions by the local authority of legislation or codes of practice made under legislation. The duty is also to report on actual or possible maladministration or injustice caused by the authority. The monitoring officer might be a useful avenue of approach for service users and their advisers, when questioning local authority policies: 'if it at any time appears to him that any proposal, decision or omission … constitutes, has given rise to or is likely to or would give rise to … a contravention of any enactment of rule of law of any code of practice made or approved by or under any enactment; or … any such maladministration or injustice…'

The proposal, act or omission – and the actual contravention – might be by the authority; by any committee, sub-committee or officer of the authority; or by any joint committee on which the authority is represented (Local Government and Housing Act 1989,s.5).

3. DISTRICT AUDITORS

Indirect redress might be had by complaining to the district auditor. For instance, where a local authority was paying an independent provider for a (level of) day services which the complainant stated were not in practice being provided, such a complaint led to the council stating that it would investigate and attempt to recover some money from the provider (*Liverpool CC 1998a*).

4. SOCIAL SERVICES COMPLAINTS PROCEDURES

Under the Local Authority Social Services Act 1970, regulations and directions have been made which place duties on local authorities to establish, operate and publicise complaints procedures in relation to social services functions. A person (or a representative) can complain only if the person is a 'qualifying' individual – that is the local authority must, or could, provide (or secure the provision of) services for the person. The local authority must also be aware of the person's need, or possible need, for services.

The complaints procedure is probably – in principle at least – suitable for most grievances and, because of the statutory time limits which apply to formal complaints, is not meant to be protracted. There is an appeal procedure within the complaints system involving review panels, which seem to have fairly wide powers to examine not only whether an authority has adhered to policy and procedure, but also factual decisions which it has reached.

The complaints procedure is not, however, generally suitable for people who are seeking financial compensation – although some local authorities provide it on occasion, either on their own initiative or at the prompting of the local ombudsman. Furthermore, the law courts have pointed out that the complaints procedure might be unsuitable for resolving matters of law – whilst if research has correctly found that over 50 per cent of complaints are about the rationing of resources (Simons 1995,p.40), then arguably the complaints procedure will be impotent in effecting remedies. Another potential weakness in the system is that a) the independent person required to sit on a review panel can be outvoted by other (council) officers on the panel; and b) local authorities are not obliged to follow a panel's recommendations (though they should have good reasons for not doing so).

More simply perhaps, a drawback of reliance on complaints procedures to ensure a good quality of decision-making is simply that a) people do not want to be in the spotlight or upset those providing services; and b) it is stressful, exhausting and demanding to complain, unless the complainant is a 'persevering, single-handed warrior, who thrives on skirmishes with public authorities'. These are not the characteristics of vulnerable, 'inarticulate and meek' (in the words of one social services officer) people (Coombs 1998, p.48).

Summary of procedure. The complaints procedure consists of three main stages: *informal, formal* and *review.* Local authorities must try to solve the matter informally. If this is not possible, they must send or give the person an explanation of the procedure and ask the person to submit the complaint in writing. The local authority must then respond to the complaint within 28 days or alternatively explain why this is not possible – and then, in any case, respond within three months.

The local authority must send its decision in writing to the complainant, normally (if different) the person on whose behalf the complaint has been made, and anybody else it thinks has sufficient interest. If the complainant is not satisfied and he or she writes to this effect within 28 days, then the local authority has to appoint a review panel (which must contain an independent person). The panel must meet within 28 days, and then within 24 hours send its written recommendations to the local authority, the complainant, the person on whose behalf the complaint has been made (if appropriate) and anybody else the local authority thinks has sufficient interest. The local authority must then decide what it is going to do and write to the same people as above within 28 days. The panel must also make a written record of the reasons for its recommendations.

Local authorities have a duty to publicise their complaints procedure in a way 'they consider appropriate'. The basic duty, but not the way in which it is carried out, is stipulated in legislation; guidance provides further detail.

EXTRACTS

Legislation (Local Authority Social Services Act 1970, s.7B) states:

(establishment of procedure) 'the Secretary of State may by order require local authorities to establish a procedure whereby a person, or anyone acting on his behalf, may make representations (including complaints) in relation to the authority's discharge of, or failure to discharge, any of their functions under this Act, or any of the enactments referred to in s.2(2) [other social services functions] of this Act, in respect of that person…'

(eligibility of complainants) 'In relation to a particular local authority, an individual is a qualifying individual … if (a) the authority have a power or a duty to provide, or to secure the provision of, a service for him; and (b) his need or possible need for such a service has (by whatever means) come to the attention of the authority'

(directions) 'A local authority shall comply with any directions given by the Secretary of State as to the procedure to be adopted in considering representations made … and as to the taking of such action as may be necessary in consequence of such representations…'

(publicity) 'Local authorities shall give such publicity to any procedure established pursuant to this section as they consider appropriate'.

Regulations (SI 1990/2244) state that local authorities must establish a representation/complaints procedure.

Directions (*Complaints Procedure Directions 1990*: in DH 1990, appendix C) include the following statements:

(coordination) 'The local authority shall appoint one of their officers to assist the authority in the co-ordination of all aspects of their consideration of the representations'.

(knowledge of procedures) 'The local authority shall ensure that all members or officers involved in the handling of representations … are familiar with the procedures'.

(informal stage) 'Where a local authority receives representations from a complainant they shall attempt to resolve the matter informally'.

(formal stage) 'If the matter cannot be resolved to the satisfaction of the complainant, the local authority shall give or send to him an explanation of the procedure set out in these Directions and ask him to submit a written representation if he wishes to proceed'.

(assistance and guidance) 'The local authority shall offer assistance and guidance to the complainant on the use of this procedure, or give advice on where he may obtain it'.

(28-day response) 'The local authority shall consider the representations and formulate a response within 28 days of their receipt, or if this is not possible, explain to the complainant within that period why it is not possible and tell him when he can expect a response, which shall in any event be within 3 calendar months of receipt of the representations'.

(withdrawal of complaint) 'The representation may be withdrawn at any stage by the complainant…'.

(notification in writing of result) The local authority must notify in writing the 'result of their consideration' to the complainant; the person on whose behalf the representation was made unless the local authority thinks that the person would not understand it or would be distressed; anyone else it considers has sufficient interest.

(review stage) 'If the complainant informs the authority in writing within 28 days of the date on which the notification … is sent to him that he is dissatisfied with that result and wishes the matter to be referred to a panel for review, the local authority shall appoint a panel (including any independent person) to consider the matter which the local authority shall refer to it'.

(review panel meeting) 'The panel shall meet within 28 days of the receipt of the complainant's request for review by the local authority to consider the matter together with any oral or written submissions as the complainant or the local authority wish the panel to consider'.

(review panel decision) The panel 'shall decide on its recommendations and record them in writing within 24 hours of the end of the meeting' and 'send written copies of their recommendations' to the local authority, the complainant, (if appropriate) the person on whose behalf the complaint was made, and any other person the authority considers has sufficient interest.

(panel's reasons) 'The panel shall record the reasons for their recommendations in writing';

(local authority's response) 'The local authority shall consider what action they ought to take, and notify in writing the persons specified [immediately above] of the local authority's decision and of their reasons for taking that decision and of any action which they have taken or propose to take within 28 days of the date of the panel's recommendation'.

(independent person) '"independent person" … means a person who is neither a member nor an officer of that authority, nor, where the local authority have delegated any of its social services functions to any organisation, a person who is a member of or employed by that organisation, nor the spouse of any such person'.

Policy guidance (DH 1990) states:

(easy to use) complaints procedures should be 'uncomplicated, accessible to those who might wish to use them and understood by all members of staff'; and be kept clearly separate from grievance procedures and disciplinary procedures (paras 6.12,6.14).

(purpose) The intention is 'to allow access to a statutory procedure to anyone who is likely to want to make representations, including complaints about the actions, decisions or apparent failings of a SSD; and to allow any other person to act on behalf of the individual concerned' (para 6.5).

(exclusion from procedure) 'The procedure excludes only those for whom the authority has no power or duty to provide a service. Complaints of a general nature which are not concerned with an individual case are also likely to fall outside the statutory definition, as are anonymous complaints. It will be open to authorities at their discretion to deal with a complaint not covered by Section 7B under the standard procedure' (para 6.5).

(publicity) The duty to publicise might be met by (para 6.26):

(leaflets). These should 'explain the procedure in straightforward terms and should include a reference to the role of the Commissioner for Local Administration (the Ombudsman) and to the separate leaflet "Complaint about the Council?". The leaflet should give the name, address and telephone number of the designated officer or of the person responsible for oversight of the procedure, and of organisations to whom those individuals might turn for advice. It should be made widely available. Where necessary, authorities will need to make available versions of their leaflet in ethnic minority languages in braille'.

(notices) 'These should be displayed in the authority's offices. They should also be supplied – with leaflets – to agencies offering independent advice'.

(visual/oral presentations) 'Authorities may wish to discuss with voluntary organisations and other local groups how information about the complaints procedure should be made available to those with sensory handicaps, the housebound and those whose first language is not English or who do not speak English'.

Practice guidance (SSI 1991b) states:

(staff awareness) 'It is recommended that managers are given responsibility to ensure that their staff are fully conversant with the procedures and have the opportunity to discuss them in staff meetings and supervision interviews' (para 2.11).

(informal stage) 'The fact that this stage is not "formal" does not mean that it is "casual". It may well be necessary to involve someone who is not connected with the immediate problem to help resolve it' (para 4.3).

(anonymous complaints) 'It is recommended that authorities should develop appropriate practices on anonymous complaints, particularly those which concern vulnerable groups and communicate these to appropriate managers' (para 4.41).

(financial compensation) 'It is most important to find out what the complainant expects to get out of the system as a result of the complaint. Experience suggests that most people want an apology and an assurance that policy or procedures will change so that the "same thing" cannot happen again to them or anyone else. Financial compensation is generally not the objective. When procedures do change as a result of a complaint, it is of course good practice to tell the complainant and this is usually greatly valued' (para 4.47).

DISCUSSION

Complaints procedure: access

The complaints procedure is in principle accessible to a broad class of people, since complaints can be made about any social services functions by people who need, or have only a possible need, of services. Thus, an authority cannot exclude people at random: for instance, by denying them access to the third stage of the complaints procedure, the review panel, on the grounds that it had received legal advice that its actions were sound and would not be overturned (Keep, Clarkson 1994,p.40).

Complaints procedure: ineligibility

However, somebody denied a community care assessment altogether, because the authority thinks that he or she is not someone it 'may' provide services for, might not be eligible to use the procedure. For instance, Baroness Blatch for the government explained during the passing of the NHS and Community Care Bill that if the authority judges that a person 'is not a person for whom they may provide community care services' and, as a result, declines to carry out an assessment, then the procedure could not be used. Instead it would be 'a matter of law' to be decided by the court: a complaints procedure would not be appropriate. On a practical level, availability of the procedure to such people could pave the way for vexatious applicants who would waste authorities' time. However, she also pointed out that people could instead resort to local councillors, members of the social service committee or, in the case of maladministration, the local ombudsman (HLD,25/6/1990,cols.1396–1397).

In practice, local authorities might produce guidance on complaints which they will not handle; for example, where a legal action is proceeding or pending. However, attempts to define other categories such as vexatious or unreasonable complaints – though an important policy issue (SSI 1996j,p.21) – should be made cautiously in case they are 'seen as an attempt to limit access to the complaints procedure' on grounds which might be difficult to substantiate (SSI 1996k,p.19).

Complaints procedure: which one

It is always not clear which complaints procedure of the local authority to use: a) the one for community care; b) the one for children under s.26 of the Children Act 1989 – which can be used not only by children but by parents, others with parental responsibility, local authority foster parents and other people considered to have sufficient interest; or c) a non-statutory complaints procedure for other complaints and operated, for example, by the chief executive of the local authority. However, the local ombudsman has pointed out that a failure to identify which is the appropriate procedure is maladministration (*Manchester CC 1995*); and in any case, even in the case of a non-statutory scheme for those complaints falling outside the statutory procedures, there should be proper systems in place in order to avoid scandalous and shocking failures (*Durham CC 1998*).

Complaints procedure: practical access

Practical access to a complaints procedure is clearly important, given the reluctance of many people to complain, the state of upset they might be in, and sometimes their fear (whether or not justified) of some sort of retribution from the staff they might still be relying on (Simons 1995,p.34).

Local authorities are under an express legal obligation to publicise the complaints procedure; yet in practice many service users might not receive written information (SSI 1996m,p.18), especially, as the ombudsman found, if a local authority simply has no written information available (*Trafford MBC 1997*). A local authority, offering no information or publicity at all, would be approaching the point at which it might breach its statutory duty to publicise the complaints procedure, as it considers 'appropriate' (see extract above) – since appropriateness presumably goes to the manner and type of, not to the very existence, of publicity.

It has also been pointed out that a free phone number for complaints at the end of which is an answer-phone might be unsatisfactory – since complainants might find it impersonal and be discouraged (SSI 1994n,pp.25–26). Appreciating the importance of first contact, SSI produced 'ideas for a practice booklet for clerks, receptionists and telephonists' in relation to complaints (SSI 1991g).

Complaints procedure: local authority appeals procedures

A complaints procedure differs from a formal appeal procedure. In recognition of this, an amendment was tabled during the passage of the NHS and Community Care Bill to the effect that a formal appeals procedure should exist for people who were dissatisfied with the local authority's assessment. However, the government resisted this, stating that although an appeals system might be more effective than the complaints procedure, it would 'not be helpful for local authorities to embark upon a cumbersome, bureaucratic system of appeals at this time, when they already have many new proposals on their agenda' (Virginia Bottomley: SC(E),15/2/1990,cols.1055–1059).

Nevertheless, in respect of particular services or procedures, local authorities sometimes do choose to set up a separate appeals procedure – for example, in relation to charging for home help and personal care (eg, SSI 1996n,p.31; and see the ombudsman investigation: *Essex CC 1991*).

Complaints procedure: no formal judicial appeal procedure

Policy guidance explains that when disagreement arises over service provision, the representation/complaints procedure is the channel for contesting the decision. There is no formal judicial procedure by way of appeal, although neither the local ombudsman, nor judicial review (which is a *supervisory* rather than *appeal* process) are precluded. The guidance explains that a 'formal judicial appeal procedure would be foreign to such arrangements and it would not be appropriate to introduce one' (DH 1990,para 3.54).

Complaints procedure: recording informal and formal complaints

Informal (unlike formal) complaints do not necessarily have to be made in writing (see directions above), but because they are 'informal' and possibly because of definitional problems, they might be less than thoroughly recorded and monitored (eg, SSI 1994o,pp.17,41).

For example, in one authority there was a policy of not recording complaints made in residential care or day care settings unless they were referred to the manager. The point of this was to avoid recording 'minor grumbles', but it appeared to contradict the authority's own procedural guidelines and reduced protection for vulnerable people (SSI 1994p,p.25). Few of an authority's staff might be 'clear about what constituted the definition of informal complaint and … frequently gave examples of "expressions of concern" and "complaints" which had been handled locally by them but which were not recorded'. To have done so would have caused a major increase in administration; besides which, many users and carers might not want minor concerns recorded (SSI 1996o,p.19).

Given the imprecision and inconsistency with which staff might use terms such as 'complaints' and 'recording', the Social Services Inspectorate has recommended that local authorities 'examine what information they wish to collect about service users' expressions of satisfaction and dissatisfaction, make it clear to all staff, and devise efficient systems for the collection and evaluation of information' (SSI 1994q,p.51). Yet the difference between suggestions, comments, expressions of dissatisfaction and complaints might in practice remain undefined (SSI 1996m,p.27).

The local ombudsman might find maladministration if formal complaints are not recorded; for example, when an authority could not produce documentary evidence that a complaint had been thoroughly investigated and had failed to send 'a full, written response' following the investigation. This finding was made despite the 'enormous staffing problems' (caused by an industrial dispute) in the local authority's neighbourhood office at the time (*Islington LBC 1994*).

Complaints procedure: prescribed time limits for response

There has been evidence that local authorities sometimes find it difficult to meet the response times, prescribed by directions (see extracts above) of 28 days or, failing this, three months (SSI 1993k,p.30). For example, formal investigations might take longer than three months, and 28 days might be regarded as an almost impossible timescale. In 1994, it was reported that up to 80 per cent of cases might be unresolved after four months (SSI 1994n,p.34); in 1996 that 54 per cent were not completed within the three-month limit (SSI 1996m,pp.8–9). Informal complaints might be solved more quickly, and in practice fifteen days might be a reasonable time scale for these (SSI 1993g,pp.36–37). In fact, the time limits imposed by the directions do not apply to informal complaints.

To avoid challenges and, for example, possible findings of maladministration by the local ombudsman, authorities should provide clear information about procedures at the informal stage. For service users, one way around possible delay is to ignore the informal stage and begin with the formal stage: policy guidance states that it is possible to do this (DH 1990,para 6.30).

One local ombudsman investigation found admirable aims in one complaints procedure – but serious flaws in practice. The maladministration was based on a number of criticisms. The complaints coordinator apparently made no real attempt to analyse the contents of a letter of complaint. The council did not respond to the complaint within 28 days as the law demanded – nor did it explain in writing to the complainant why it could not respond in that time. No 'substantive reply' to the complaint had been forthcoming from the council after 16 months. There was a question of whether the staff involved had sufficient training to 'distance themselves from the personal, and to identify the very real, issues' with which the complainant was concerned (*Haringey LBC 1993*). Delay is compounded if, despite making a special request for the complaint to be handled quickly, the complainant dies before the outcome is known (*Salford CC 1996*).

Complaints procedure: investigations

When an investigation is carried out, its findings clearly need to be communicated properly to the complainant. Yet sometimes responses fail both to deal with all the issues complained of and to inform the complainant of further options if he or she remains dissatisfied; and might concentrate unduly on pacification, rather than on giving a detailed account of the investigation (SSI 1996n, p.23).

Investigations should not only be independent but also seen to be so; for instance in one case the ombudsman had no reason to doubt the 'integrity and professionalism' of the investigating officer; but to the complainants, the officer, who worked within the same directorate of the council involved in the complaint, did not appear to be independent – whilst the ombudsman, too, stated that in fact she may not have been independent (*Manchester CC 1996b*). In another case (involving a complaint under a non-statutory complaints procedure), the council asked an officer to carry out an initial investigation into the actions of another officer – despite the fact that the two officers were in conflict. As the ombudsman put it, this beggared belief. A highly critical report emerged without the second officer having had the opportunity to put her point of view. Nothing was then done about the complaint until the two officers had left the council; this was 'shocking' to the ombudsman (*Durham CC 1998*). Clearly, if an investigation is to be effective, the officer responsible should fully understand her role and have been given guidance and support (*Salford CC 1996*).

The local ombudsman has also pointed out that the purpose of a complaint is 'first and foremost' to scrutinise a local authority's actions; therefore the focus of an investigation on the complainant's own background and history was maladministration (*Cornwall CC 1996*).

Complaints procedure: adequacy of response

Reports on local authority complaints procedures and investigations of the local ombudsman both show that complaints procedures falter when staff are unfamiliar with them and lack adequate training. The problem might be very basic; for instance, the Social Services Inspectorate (SSI) reported in 1996 that in over half of the local authorities inspected, 'staff interviewed were unclear about the different stages of the complaints procedures' (SSI 1996m,p.18).

For instance, staff might not 'understand that if a member of the public made a complaint to them they should note the information and refer to a manager, not expect the complainant to do so' (SSI 1994s,p.15). They might be incorrectly labelling a complaint as formal but then dealing with it as informal (SSI 1994r,p.20); this reflects wider confusion about the handling of informal complaints (see above). For most staff in an authority, training and awareness about complaints issues might be 'patchy, reflecting the lack of an explicit and monitored training strategy, as well as resource and time pressures on staff' (SSI 1996o,p.18). The local authority's written information about complaints might confuse its own staff – for example, by alluding to more stages in the procedure than actually exist (SSI 1996p,p.25).

Alternatively, local authorities might, in SSI's view of good practice, almost err too far the other way by involving the authority's most senior officer in the line management structure; whilst this had the positive effect of ensuring accountability and adding weight to the procedure, it also, negatively, meant that 'considerable senior management resources' were taken up in pursuing a relatively small number of complicated and longstanding complaints (SSI 1996p,p.19). An authority might also fail its staff if it omits suitably to inform them about the progress of complaints, even though it is otherwise successfully informing the complainants (SSI 1996m,p.46).

The local ombudsman sometimes criticises responses to complaints, for instance, in terms of gathering facts and evidence, recording meetings, acknowledging fault, conveying decisions, making written responses and taking an objective approach which enables staff to deal with difficult complainants (see eg, *Haringey LBC 1997, Islington LBC 1994, Liverpool CC 1997b*). 'Gross maladministration' and 'entirely unacceptable' local authority practices might be identified, such as ten months' delay in resolution, chasing up letters it had already received a response to, not informing complainants of their right to a review panel hearing, disingenuousness in blaming the complainant for not requesting a review panel in writing (when it was the authority which had not explained matters in writing and had not replied to correspondence) (*Liverpool CC 1997a*).

Similarly, sending responses which do not address what a complainant has written, and inappropriately concluding that the complainant was satisfied are maladministration; and councils should beware not to filter out informally complaints, thus preventing them from proceeding (*Liverpool 1998a, Manchester CC 1993*). Making a conscious decision not to offer the option of a complaints review panel is maladministration (*Manchester CC 1996b*). Serious concerns (and maladministration) arose when there was confusion about which stage of the complaints procedure was being followed; the complaint was being handled informally but the complainant had wanted it formally dealt with; there was no thorough investigation; 'presenting problems' were focused on to the exclusion of underlying issues; relevant case records were not examined and key people not interviewed; timescales were not adhered to and the complainant not informed about progress; and a letter sent at the end of investigation neither enclosed the relevant report nor indicated the next step of the procedure (*Newham LBC 1996*).

A council should be able to distinguish between a second complaint about how the original complaint has been handled and an appeal against the outcome of the original complaint (*Sandwell MBC 1995*). Gathering information (about alleged physical abuse) from council officers but not seeking the views of other people who had known the person concerned, and not gathering medical evidence, was maladministration (*Wakefield MDC 1997*). Cursory rather than specific response by means of a standard letter is also maladministration; likewise a letter, referring to the incidence of cancellation of home help services, unsupported by the compilation of any figures (*Westminster CC 1996*).

It might be maladministration to refuse to carry out particular home adaptations, simply because the applicant involved is complaining and threatening litigation in relation to other adaptations already installed; but on the other hand, delay caused by the person's unreasonable demands on the council, the personalising of the dispute and failure to take up the council's offer of using an independent advocate, was not the fault of the council (*Waltham Forest LBC 1993*).

Complaints procedure: giving reasons

The directions (see extracts above) state that the review panel must give reasons, as must the local authority when responding to the panel's recommendations. A failure of either to give those reasons in *R v Cornwall CC, ex p Goldsack* meant that the applicant was denied what she was entitled to; the court made a declaration that they should have been supplied.

However, at the earlier, formal, stage of the procedure it is only the 'result' which has to be communicated; it does not follow therefore that reasons legally have to be given (Schwehr 1997b).

However, if reasons are in practice not forthcoming even at that earlier stage, it is not clear how a complainant can judge whether to proceed further; and although the courts do not necessarily impose a common law duty to give reasons in all contexts (see p.50), the local ombudsmen take the giving of reasons to be an axiom of good administration (CLAE 1993).

Complaints procedure: independence of person on review panel

The directions (see above) state that a local authority member or officer – as well as a person who is a member of or employed by an organisation to which social services functions have been delegated – cannot be the independent person on the review panel. It has been suggested that the courts might not view this as an exhaustive definition of independence and might be prepared to extend it in some circumstances to, for instance, health authority employees (Schwehr 1997b) – for example, who are involved in joint working with the local authority social services department. In practice, an independent person might typically have knowledge of social work and, for instance, be working within social work education or the legal profession, or be a retired social worker (SSI 1996p,p.30).

The normal pattern in practice is for one independent chairman to sit with two members of the social services committee. However, there are variations. Sometimes two independent members might sit with a local authority member who is not on that committee. But if the director of social services is one of the panel members, then this interferes with the usual arrangement of submitting the panel's recommendations to him or her (SSI 1996m,p.32). The Social Services Inspectorate has recommended that an authority should 'stipulate clearly exemptions from eligibility to act as an independent person' (SSI 1994t,p.29). Indeed, drawing on people formerly employed in social services invites the obvious danger that 'the panel could be perceived by complainants as being compromised in its impartiality' (SSI 1996k,p.28).

Complaints procedure: review panel procedures

In addition to what the directions (above) say, policy guidance expands on the procedure to be followed by a review panel. It states that people appointed should, if possible, have relevant experience of the subject matter of the complaint. The guidance stresses the need for informality and states that if a complainant is accompanied by somebody (who might also speak for them at the meeting) that person should not be a barrister or a solicitor acting in a professional capacity. The complainant or accompanying person should be given the opportunity to make an oral submission before the authority (DH 1990, p.71). Given the vulnerable state which a complainant might be in when – often reluctantly and with misgivings – 'taking on' statutory services, it is easy to see why that formality might have the effect of 'crushing' complainants who come alone to panel proceedings (SSI 1996q,p.52), and putting them at 'serious disadvantage' (SSI 1996m,p.33).

The courts might say that sometimes professional representation is permissible if, for example, legal complexity is involved or the local authority is legally represented (Gordon, Mackintosh 1996,p.72) – despite what the guidance says. Conversely, it will scarcely seem fair to complainants if the authority employs a member of its legal department as 'clerk to the panel' (SSI 1996j,p.31). Indeed, the local ombudsman included in a finding of maladministration, the observation that he found it 'hard to see how a solicitor employed by the Council could be seen as an "unbiased observer" and consider[ed] the way in which he joined at the outset in the in camera deliberations of the Panel to be unwise at the very least' (*Cleveland CC 1993*).

Complaints procedure: scope of the review panel

There is sometimes uncertainty about the legitimate scope of the review panel's deliberations. Some panels do consider the actual merits of decisions, while others concentrate only on whether procedures have been followed. An example of the broader approached occurred in *R v Wigan MBC, ex p Tammadge*, when the complaints review panel found that the social services department had discharged its functions in relation to the complainant's application for services – but went on nevertheless to recommend that the department consider providing precisely those services it had hitherto denied.

An SSI inspection report comments that panels: 'should be concerned primarily with considering whether the action or decision being complained about was appropriate and whether it is still appropriate. Considering only whether the procedures have been followed correctly seems not to accord with the intention of the DH guidance' (SSI 1993g,p.29). However, restrictions in practice on how review panels operate, might result in the barring complaints about 'policy', scrutiny of procedural matters only, the exclusion of lawyers, and the exclusion of complaints by mentally disordered people compulsorily detained under the Mental Health Act (Simons 1995,p.28). For instance, when, because of a change in policy and eligibility criteria, people have been excluded from services previously received and wish to complain, they might be told that they cannot use the normal complaints procedure because it is a funding issue at stake (Wright 1997,p.6).

Complaints procedure: outcome of review panel recommendations

Although an independent person is a safeguard to the operation of review panels, his or her view is not necessarily decisive and might be overruled (Simons 1995,p.44).

Even in case of unanimity within the panel, the directions (see above) do not oblige local authorities to follow panel recommendations and in practice they sometimes decline. In response, the courts have with varying force suggested that local authorities should follow the recommendations. In *R v Avon CC, ex p M*, the judge stated that it was unlawful to disregard the review panel's findings without a good reason. In *R v Islington LBC, ex p Rixon*, the court stated that the greater the departure from the review panel's recommendations, the greater the need for 'cogent articulated reasons'. Slightly milder was the statement of the court in *R v North Yorkshire CC, ex p Hargreaves* that there was no general rule that local authorities must follow the recommendations of a review panel – but that in some circumstances, it might be unlawful not to do so without a good reason. The local ombudsman has found maladministration where the local authority failed to produce, as requested by the review panel, a detailed report within a year (*Hounslow LBC 1995*).

Conversely, a review panel's findings might be flawed on their face and lead to findings of maladministration by the ombudsman – for instance, because of deficient evidence considered by the panel or apparent misinterpretation of a coroner's report (*Cleveland CC 1993*). Or a panel might fail to evaluate a claim for compensation and to make adequate recommendations back to the council despite being ideally placed to do so (*Warwickshire CC 1997*). Similarly, it was not maladministration when the local authority refused to follow a panel's recommendation about arranging a residential placement for a man with learning disabilities. This was because no assessment of the man's needs had been carried out, although this failure to assess was maladministration in its own right (*Kent CC 1998*). And, when a local authority was prepared to follow its review panel's recommendations for compensation after poor advice about state benefits had been given, the ombudsman criticised the panel for taking into account an immaterial factor when coming to its decision about the level of compensation (*East Sussex CC 1995a*).

The fact that, apart from the independent member of a panel, the other two members of the panel are likely to be from the local authority, might give rise to allegations that the system is unfair, since the latter can dominate, and indeed, overrule the independent person. However, in *R v Kingston upon Thames, ex p T*, the court disagreed and did not believe that professionals who sat on children's complaints procedure panels would be biased; and in *R v Mid-Glamorgan CC, ex p B* (a special education case), the court declined to identify bias, finding that the proceedings had given rise to an 'impression', but not a 'real danger' of bias – despite the language of council members and an intemperate, hostile outburst from one of them.

Finally, the fate of recommendations might be subject to perverse twists – for instance, a) when the local authority appears to accept them but then nothing happens, or b) when the opposite occurs: the complaint appears to have been rejected, but the authority – perhaps by way of giving in without any public display of contrition – then proceeds to implement the changes the complainant wanted (Simons 1995,p.55).

Complaints procedure: remedies

Guidance states that financial compensation is not generally the objective of the complaints procedure; nevertheless, some authorities pay it and may be told that they should do by the local ombudsman – for instance, when the latter considers that an apology (*Avon CC 1997*), or the amount of financial compensation already offered by an authority (*Dorset CC 1996*), is simply inadequate.

5. SECRETARY OF STATE'S DEFAULT POWERS (SOCIAL SERVICES)

If a local authority fails, unreasonably, to carry out any of its social services duties, the Secretary of State can declare that the local authority is 'in default', and direct it to perform its duty. Such a direction can be enforced by the High Court. In some circumstances, the courts use the existence of the powers to argue that Parliament did not intend that people should resort to the courts for a remedy to their grievances. However, the usefulness to service users of this judicial approach is in some doubt, given that the default powers have apparently never been used. Even so, the Department of Health does make preliminary enquiries with a view to using the powers; and these can be assumed, at least sometimes, to exert pressure on authorities and to effect informal solutions.

EXTRACTS

Legislation (Local Authority Social Services Act 1970,s.7D) states:

(declaration of default) 'If the Secretary of State is satisfied that any local authority have failed, without reasonable excuse, to comply with any of their duties which are social services functions (other than a duty imposed by or under the Children Act 1989), he may make an order declaring that authority to be in default with respect to the duty in question'.

(directions) The order can 'contain such directions for the purpose of ensuring that the duty is complied with within such period as may be specified in the order as appear to the Secretary of State to be necessary.'

(High Court enforcement) The direction 'shall, on the application of the Secretary of State, be enforceable by mandamus.'

DISCUSSION

Default powers: background

The current default powers replaced those formerly available under s.36 of the National Assistance Act 1948 which had never been used. Jack Ashley had observed in 1979 that the powers of the Secretary of State were so sweeping that they were unlikely to be used since he 'can only suspend the operation of the social services department of the local authority concerned'. Thus, were he to intervene, 'he may end up by running a large part of the country's social services'. Given the Secretary of State's reluctance therefore to use the default powers, 'the individual disabled person can be ignored with impunity by a reactionary local council...' (HCD,2/2/1979,col.1909).

Section 7D, of the Local Authority Social Services Act 1970, differs from the old s.36 in that a) it does not refer explicitly to the ultimate sanction (if a local authority did not comply with a Secretary of State direction) in s.36 of the taking over by the Secretary of State of the functions of the local authority; b) it covers all social services duties (excluding children's services); whereas s.36 only covered the National Assistance Act 1948 – although s.7D only refers to duties, whereas s.36 referred to functions (ie powers and duties); and c) it explicitly makes provision for a direction under s.7D to be enforced by the High Court.

Default powers: use of

During the passing of the NHS and Community Care Bill, the Under-Secretary of State for Health explained that normally there would be various stages to pass through before the default powers were used: 'It is likely that there would have been earlier stages before reaching the legislative procedure on default – that is, perhaps a social services inspectorate investigation, a specific direction or even an inquiry. I share my hon. Friend's concern about not wanting to prolong an abuse or error. I assure my hon. Friend that the Department of Health will act with all speed in cases brought to its attention of clear abuse or when the general principles of the Act or the general directions given by the Secretary of State are clearly not being complied with. We do not want years of delay...' (Mr Freeman: SC(E),20/2/1990,col.1091).

The reference to 'all speed' apparently flies in the face of the slow approach taken in the past to use of the default powers. Moreover, the default powers have apparently never been used, although the Department of Health makes numbers of preliminary enquiries and might even complete some investigations without taking any further action. For instance, between 1978 and 1986, 54 cases were referred to the Secretary of State in relation to alleged default under s.2 of the Chronically Sick and Disabled Persons Act 1970. This contrasted with one case only, between 1982 and 1986, referred under the National Assistance Act 1948 (Tony Newton: HCWA,23/7/1986,cols.306–307). Not every referral results in an enquiry, and clearly not every enquiry triggers use of the default powers; for example, between 1979 and 1985, 33 sets of enquiries were made, but no default action was 'necessary or appropriate' (Tony Newton: HCWA,23/7/1985,col.534).

Asked in 1987 about the use of the default powers (under section 36 of the NAA 1948), John Major quoted Mr Justice Simon Brown in *R v Department of Health and Social Security, ex p Bruce*: "'So far as that Ministerial power is concerned it is, in my judgement, perfectly clear that the Minister could not properly intervene so as to declare the authority to be in default unless the authority had manifestly failed in the discharge of any of their functions in such a way that no reasonable Minister could take a different view: putting it a different way, had conducted themselves in a way which could only be regarded as a failure on the part of the authority to perform the duty'". In defence of the length of time that investigations could take, the Prime Minister also explained that the 'main problem is that the more complicated cases necessarily involve a considerable amount of detailed work by officials as well as correspondence, which can be protracted, with the other parties concerned' (HCWA,14/5/1987,col.354). For instance, of six cases under investigation in 1987, three had been under way for seven months, and the other three for 16, 17 and 31 months respectively (John Major: HCWA,6/4/1987,cols.100–101). Investigations undertaken between 1979 and 1986 took an average of five months to complete (Tony Newton: HCWA,9/7/1986, col.170).

The judge in the *Bruce* case had also rejected the notion that the Secretary of State could exercise the default powers so as to act as a 'factual review body'. Intervention would only arise 'where the local authority have either misdirected themselves in some particular way or formed a wholly untenable and irrational view of the facts'. Referring to the case of *Secretary of State for Education and Science v Tameside MBC*, he stated that 'the Secretary of State's power only arose in the same situation in which this court's power of intervention would arise'. Although the new default powers differ from the old, the judicial statement in the *Bruce* case is probably still a relevant guide.

Despite non-use of the powers, this does not stop the law courts sometimes ruling that the powers are the appropriate remedy rather than judicial intervention (eg, *Wyatt v Hillingon LBC* about provision of home help and a bed; *Southwark LBC v Williams* about, homeless people – both concerning the old powers). More recently in 1998, in *R v Westminster CC, ex p P* concerning provision of residential accommodation for asylum seekers under s.21 of the National Assistance Act 1948, the court found that it would be more convenient, expeditious and effective to use the default powers rather than judicial review, especially since the real dispute was apparently about facts (whether or not there was available accommodation in London) rather than law. However, equally, the courts might explain why judicial review is the more appropriate remedy – for instance, when the issue is one of law in a developing field (*R v Devon CC, ex p Baker*).

Default powers: ombudsman investigations

Notwithstanding excuses from central government about the causes of delay, the Parliamentary ombudsman might still criticise the sometimes slow response from the Department of Health. For example:

Example 1: delay in decision about the default powers (ombudsman). The British Deaf Association (BDA) complained of unreasonable delay in the response of the Department of Health and Social Security (DHSS, as it was then) to a claim that a borough council was in breach of its duty to supply a Vistel (deaf communicating terminal) telephone aid under the Chronically Sick and Disabled Persons Act 1970. The dispute was about whether the council was using blanket criteria precluding the supply of a telephone aid for any disabled person who did not meet the criteria for telephone provision.

Overall, the BDA had to wait over three years before the Department gave its decision. This was 'appalling delay for which they merit the strongest criticism'. The particular faults included a delay of six weeks between the completion of the Department's information gathering and its approach to solicitors; an inexcusable delay, overcome only by a reminder from the BDA, of eight months when no progress was made; another delay of two months in obtaining legal advice; and pressing the council for a response only after the complainant's MP had written to the Department. Even after this, it took nearly six months for this action to bear fruit. The ombudsman felt bound to say that 'the Department's papers in the case suggested prolonged periods not so much of deliberation as of inattention'.

The Department's explanation referred to such matters as a) the difficulties staff had in dealing with applications because legal uncertainty about what to do had not previously been clarified, given that the default powers had never been used; b) the distraction of a court case about the default powers *(R v Department of Health and Social Security, ex p Bruce)* and of the passage through Parliament of the Disabled Persons (Services, Consultation and Representation) Bill which demanded priority; and c) changes to key staff in a section of the Department which was under considerable pressure.

The ombudsman accepted the apologies of the Department and assurances about the future handling of such applications as an appropriate response by the Department to his investigation and findings (PCA C.656/87).

Example 2: delay in decision about the default powers (ombudsman). In another Parliamentary ombudsman investigation, concerning the provision of holidays by a local authority under the Chronically Sick and Disabled Persons Act 1970, the DHSS was again faulted. It took over a year to respond to the Royal Association for Disability and Rehabilitation's application that the default powers be used. In particular, it took over a month even to contact the local authority concerned, and took several months to consider the reply and to prepare a response.

The Department considered that the duties imposed in relation to the default powers were cumbersome and time-consuming; and that local authorities were likely to be helpful in such cases if they were given time to change – rather than if the Department adopted a confrontational approach. However, the ombudsman pointed out that whilst it was not for him to determine the Department's priorities or how it should use its limited staffing resources, nevertheless he was surprised at the delay, in the light of a Ministerial assurance in the House of Commons that the investigation would be handled rapidly. Thus the Department's standard of service fell short of what the complainant was entitled to expect; there was no absolute failure to act, but 'their action was slow'. However, even had progress been quicker, the outcome for the complainant was unlikely to have been markedly different: the local authority had now recognised its obligation to assist disabled people with holidays occasionally (PCA C.799/81).

Default powers: relationship to directions and inquiries

The Under-Secretary of State for Health explained, during the passing of the NHS and Community Care Bill, the possible sequence of use of the powers under s.7A (general and specific directions), s.7C (inquiries) and s.7D (default powers) of the Local Authority Social Services Act 1970. The sequence could be: 'general directions [7A] provided, in the sense of drawing up care plans and assessment, perhaps an inquiry [7C] if there is a problem, perhaps a specific direction [7A] to correct the errors discovered in an inquiry, and then perhaps a default order [7D]...' He added that the 'new powers would complete the circle. In the past, the Secretary of State may have known of abuse, but could not act. He had no powers to set up an inquiry, to issue specific directions or to go to the courts in cases of default' (SC(E),20/2/1990,cols.1088–1091).

6. SECRETARY OF STATE'S GENERAL AND SPECIFIC DIRECTIONS

The Secretary of State has the power to make both specific and general directions, see p.52.

EXTRACTS

Legislation (Local Authority Social Services Act 1970, s.7A) states that 'every local authority shall exercise their social services functions in accordance with such directions as may be given to them under this section by the Secretary of State'. The directions must be in writing and 'may be given to a particular authority, or to authorities of a particular class, or to authorities generally'.

DISCUSSION

The Notes on Clauses (DH,SHHD,WO 1989,p.68), accompanying the NHS and Community Care Bill, stated that: 'Generally, it is intended that this power be used infrequently and only to the extent necessary to safeguard the interests of users of services and their carers'. The Under-Secretary of State for Health explained during the passage of Bill that 'the specific directions break new ground because the Secretary of State for Health does not have the specific power at the moment to make directions concerning a home, for example…'. He went on to explain further that specific directions 'would be used in relation to the balance of care provision. If a local authority falls down in its duty as a result of either dogma or sheer inefficiency and abuse, the Secretary of State would have the power to intervene'.

There was concern that central government might use both general and specific directions to prejudice the activities of local authorities 'in providing local authority residential accommodation'. But the government pointed out that directions 'cannot upset the purpose of primary legislation and therefore the principles … which call for mixed care for the elderly in local authority residential accommodation and, in the independent sector, voluntary and private accommodation' (Roger Freeman: SC(E),20/2/1990,cols.1086–1089).

In a recent local ombudsman investigation concerning a dispute between two local authorities about where a person was ordinarily resident, the Secretary of State was asked not only to resolve the dispute under s.32(3) of the National Assistance Act 1948, but also to make a specific direction as to which authority should provide what service. The Department of Health appeared to be somewhat surprised by the request for a specific direction; it had never previously been asked for one and had no established procedure. In the event, it first of all appeared to do nothing; when it did reply after a further request, it stated that it would be improper for the Secretary of State to direct that a council arrange a service which it considered inappropriate. This was because a) there was no evidence that the judgement of either of the two local authorities involved was unreasonable, and b) it was natural and proper that professional judgement should differ (*Redbridge LBC 1998*).

7. SECRETARY OF STATE'S INQUIRIES

The Secretary of State has the power to institute inquiries in relation to the social services functions of a local authority.

EXTRACTS

Legislation (Local Authority Social Services Act 1970, s.7C) states that the Secretary of State can 'cause an inquiry to be held in any case, where on representations made to him or otherwise, he considers it advisable to do so in connection with the exercise by any local authority of any of their social services functions' (other than children's services). The Local Government Act 1972 (s.250(2)–(5)) applies to such inquiries.

DISCUSSION

The Notes on Clauses (DH,SHHD,WO 1989,p.68) state that the clause enables 'the person appointed to hold an inquiry to compel the attendance of witness [sic] and to take evidence on oath and enable the Secretary of State to make orders as to the payment of costs'.

An unsuccessful amendment to the NHS and Community Care Bill would have placed a duty on the Secretary of State to hold an inquiry when 'requested to do so by an organisation of or for disabled people which alleges that a local authority has failed to fulfil their duties to provide community care services'. Predictably, this was dismissed by Baroness Blatch for the government as 'wholly unrealistic' and 'cast in far too wide and general terms'. Instead, people or organisations were anyway free to draw the Secretary of State's attention to the failure of local authorities to do their duties; and if the allegations were sufficiently serious, an inquiry would be held. Nevertheless, Lord Ennals retorted: 'Anyone has a right to ask for an inquiry, but that does not mean anything. Anyone may write to anyone: a cat may look at a queen' (HLD,14/5/1990,cols.97–100).

8. LOCAL OMBUDSMAN

The following represents a brief summary of the function of the local ombudsman. Of particular significance for this book is that local ombudsman investigations explore widely aspects of local authority provision of social services and housing services.

For example, the local ombudsmen have considered the use of priorities, refusal to assess, length of waiting lists and closure of waiting lists, inconsistent application of eligibility criteria, provision of adequate information, communication within and between local authority departments, poor handling of complaints and so on. The Commission for Local Administration (the office of the local ombudsman) has published a useful guide containing 42 axioms of good administrative practice (CLAE 1993).

The local ombudsmen appear to make thorough and – within their remit of investigating maladministration and injustice suffered – wide-ranging investigations. In common with judicial review by the courts, the local ombudsmen investigate the way in which authorities act and make decisions rather than what those decisions and actions are. This is because they are legally barred from directly questioning the professional judgements of local authority staff. Nevertheless, they might do so indirectly, by faulting, for instance, the use of inadequate information or poor communication between staff – either of which might preclude the very possibility of a sound professional judgement. More generally, it has been suggested that the ombudsmen are able to base their investigations on 'equity' (ie, general fairness or 'natural' justice) rather than law – in a way which the courts are sometimes unable to (see eg, Williams, Goriely 1994).

The ombudsmen can investigate in response not just to the complaint of an individual person, but also of an appropriate organisation: for example, a local advice agency might make representations on behalf of a number of people affected by a common problem. They can also call for and examine information about other service users in a similar situation to that of the complainant. The ombudsmen frequently recommend financial compensation, sometimes substantial, as well as changes to policies and procedures. Although authorities are not obliged to follow the recommendations, they are likely to incur bad publicity if they do not. Generally speaking (in about 95 per cent of cases), the findings and recommendations of the ombudsmen are followed.

Normally, the local ombudsmen will not investigate unless complainants have exhausted the local authority's internal complaints procedure first. However, clearly where that procedure itself is unsatisfactory, the ombudsmen might take up complaints which have been made precisely about the complaints procedure. Indeed, not only have the local ombudsmen been critical in a number of investigations of local authority complaints procedures, but have also published their own guidance on devising complaints systems in local authorities (CLAE 1992).

EXTRACTS
Legislation (Local Government Act 1974,s.26) states:

(last resort) Before complaining to the ombudsman, the council must be given an opportunity to deal with the complaint first. If the complainant is not satisfied then he or she can contact the ombudsman in writing.

(exclusions) The ombudsman cannot investigate a matter:

(time limits) which occurred more than twelve months before the complaint is made unless the ombudsman accepts that there is a good reason for this.

(legal remedy) which has already been referred to a court, a tribunal or government minister, or could be referred (unless the ombudsman accepts that it would be unreasonable to expect the complainant to do this).

(general effect) which affects all or most of the inhabitants of a local authority's area: for example, a waste of public money.

(other matters) concerning personnel, investigation or prevention of crime, school and college internal affairs, some contractual or commercial matters (but land transactions can be investigated).

(complainant) The complaint can be made by the person directly affected or by a person (or organisation) on his or her behalf.

DISCUSSION
The local government ombudsman (formally known as the Commissioner for Local Administration – in fact there are three in England – function under the Local Government Act 1974 as amended by the Local Government and Housing Act 1989. The ombudsman can investigate maladministration in, amongst others, district, borough, city or county councils.

Local ombudsmen: maladministration
In principle maladministration alone is not generally for the courts to investigate because bad administration is not necessarily unlawful (*R v Inland Revenue, ex p Self Employed and Small Businesses*) and likewise the ombudsman, in principle at least, does not investigate matters which could be referred to a court of law. On the other hand, some of the issues considered by the local ombudsman relate to statutory duties or to the same legal principles applied by the courts in judicial review

cases (such as fettering of discretion: ie, not taking account of exceptions). Thus some findings of maladministration might at least be indicative of unlawful actions (ie, a court might find them to be so, were a judicial review case to have been brought). Maladministration is not defined in legislation and the ombudsmen have themselves developed the meaning of the term and published a useful guide (CLAE 1993). The 42 axioms listed include, for example, the following considerations:

- understanding by staff of relevant legislation and council policies;
- communication of policies to service users;
- adherence to, and consistent application of, policies;
- provision of adequate and accurate information;
- giving of proper consideration to the views of relevant parties;
- carrying out of sufficient investigation to establish relevant facts;
- seeking of appropriate advice;
- giving of reasons for adverse decisions;
- ensuring that decisions and actions are taken within a reasonable time;
- compiling and keeping adequate records;
- avoidance of misleading statements;
- give undertakings or promises carefully and discharge responsibilities which follow.

Advantages of using the ombudsmen have been identified as including the fact that the service is free, investigations are conducted in private, complainants are not cross-examined by local authority lawyers, the ombudsmen have access to council documents, the procedure is simple and not legalistic, maladministration is wider than illegality, defects in procedures are cured for the future, and the internal workings of councils are exposed (Pook 1998).

Local ombudsmen: outcome of investigations

Few referrals to the local ombudsmen result in findings of maladministration. It seems that only 3–4 per cent of complaints become formal; and only 3 per cent of these result in findings of maladministration. However, of the 16 per cent settled locally without formal reports being issued, many might concern maladministration about which reports probably would have been issued (Thomas 1994).

When maladministration has caused injustice, the ombudsmen can recommend unlimited financial compensation and any other lawful remedy. Compensation can be considerable; for instance, in two recent investigations concerning assessment and provision of a residential placement for a person with learning disabilities (*Kent CC 1998*), and rehousing of a family with a severely disabled son (*Bristol CC 1998*), sums respectively of £15,000 and £20,000 were recommended. In another investigation, extreme stress, caused by a rigid ceiling imposed by the council on the cost of home care packages and suffered by the daughter of a woman with severe disabilities and high needs, warranted £10,000 in compensation (*Liverpool CC 1998b*). The local ombudsmen also frequently recommend changes to local policies and procedures to ensure that other people do not experience the same maladministration in future.

Local authorities are empowered, though not obliged, to follow recommendations (including payment of compensation), although they are under a duty at least to consider them. If a council refuses to follow the ombudsman's recommendations, even after a second report, it can be forced to publish an agreed statement in a local newspaper at its own expense (Local Government Act 1974,s.31). Although councils usually follow recommendations, this is not always the case; for instance, during the year 1997/1998, one of the ombudsmen had to issue seven further reports (four in respect of one authority) and required the publication of three statements (CLAE 1998,p.9).

Unlike the Commissioner for Complaints in Northern Ireland, (under the Commissioner for Complaints Act (Northern Ireland) 1969), local ombudsmen in England, Wales and Scotland do not have a power to refer cases on to a court of law.

9. NHS COMPLAINTS PROCEDURE

The NHS complaints procedures were overhauled and simplified with effect from April 1996. Previously they had been characterised as fragmented, confusing and complicated. Past problems included unhelpful procedural differences relating to clinical and non-clinical complaints, limits on the jurisdiction of the health service ombudsman, lack of information about procedures and delays in handling complaints and appeals (NCC 1993; Consumers' Association 1993; ACHCEW 1993).

In the light of such criticisms, the Wilson (1994) report, *Being Heard* recommended a unified complaints procedure. This was duly implemented in April 1996 by means of directions made under the NHS Act 1977 and the Hospital Complaints Procedure Act 1995, and by regulations concerning family health services. At the same time, the powers of the health service ombudsman were extended by an amendment to the Health Service Commissioners Act 1993. In March 1996, substantial guidance on the new system was issued (NHSE 1996).

The procedure covers complaints against NHS Trusts, health authorities and NHS family health services practitioners (GPs, pharmacists, dentists, opticians). Essentially, informal local resolution should be attempted, before the setting up of an independent review panel. If both procedures fail to resolve a dispute, resort can be had to the health service ombudsman (see below). In outline the new system is described by the guidance (NHSE 1996) as follows:

(1) **Establishing complaints procedures.** NHS Trusts and health authorities must establish a written complaints procedure; family health service practitioners will also be obliged to operate procedures approved by the health authority.

Complaints procedures must be publicised. NHS Trusts and health authorities must have a designated complaints manager who is not an employee to act as convener for independent reviews (see below). Complainants can include current or former patients or their representatives. Complaints must be made within 6 months of the relevant incident, although this limit can be waived in some circumstances. If negligence is probably at issue, the complaints procedure should not be abandoned unless the complainant has instigated formal legal action; it should not be assumed that just because the complainant's initial communication is via a solicitor that legal action is imminent.

(2) **Local resolution of complaints.** NHS Trusts and health authorities must have a clear local resolution (ie informal) procedure – as must family health services practitioners in their practice-based complaints procedures. Attempts should be made to complete full investigation and resolution of complaints within 20 days in the case of NHS Trusts and health authorities, and 10 days in the case of family health services practitioners.

(3) Independent review panels. Complainants, if dissatisfied with the local resolution process, can request the setting up of an independent review panel. The convener must decide whether to set up such a panel on the basis of a signed statement by the complainant. If the convener decides not to set up the panel, the complainant can ask the convener to reconsider – or instead refer the complaint to the health service ombudsman.

Independent review panels must consist of three members, including a lay chairman, a convener or alternative, and a purchaser (eg a health authority non-executive or GP fundholder) in the case of NHS Trusts, or independent person in the case of health authorities. If the complaint is about clinical matters, two independent clinical assessors will advise the panel. The panel must be given access to relevant records, including clinical ones. The complainant can be accompanied by another person but not by somebody legally qualified acting in a legal capacity. The panel has no executive authority over any actions by the NHS Trust, health authority or family health services practitioner. The panel's final report must be sent to various people including the complainant.

Dissatisfied complainants can approach the health service ombudsman. Time limits to be achieved by panels, from notice of setting up of the panel to final letter on action to be taken on the panels's findings, are six months for NHS Trusts and health authorities, and three months for family health services complaints.

EXTRACTS AND DISCUSSION
Not applicable.

10. HEALTH SERVICE OMBUDSMAN

The health service ombudsman investigates injustice or hardship caused to a patient through failure in service, failure to provide a service which there is a duty to provide, or maladministration. This gives the ombudsman broad powers of investigation. The ombudsman's investigations sometimes expose important legal and policy issues: for example, a number of recent cases have examined the provision of long-term, continuing care by health authorities.

The health service ombudsman has been able since April 1996 to investigate clinical, as well as administrative, aspects, of decisions – and also complaints against GPs, dentists, pharmacists or opticians providing NHS services. Normally, although he can decide otherwise, the ombudsman cannot investigate incidents which happened more than a year ago, or complaints for which there are alternative remedies.

EXTRACTS
Legislation (Health Service Commissioners Act 1993):

(remit) provides for the health service ombudsman to investigate complaints about the sustaining of 'injustice or hardship in consequence of':

- failure in a service;
- failure to provide a service for which there is a duty to provide;
- maladministration (in the absence of maladministration, the ombudsman has no power to question the merits of decisions taken within the discretion of the decision-maker) (s.3).

(exclusions) The ombudsman cannot investigate a number of matters including those where:

- there is or has been an alternative remedy available unless the ombudsman 'is satisfied that in the particular circumstances it is not reasonable to expect that person to resort or have resorted to it';

- there is or has been a formal inquiry under the NHS Act 1977,s.84;
- staff/personnel matters;
- the complaint is made more than a year after the event/matters complained about – unless the ombudsman thinks it is reasonable still to accept the complaint (ss.4–9).

(complainant) Complaints can be made by individuals or a suitable body (whether or not incorporated) representing patients (s.8).

(bringing the complaint) The complaint must be in writing and must first of all have been made to the relevant health service body, which must have been given a 'reasonable opportunity' to investigate and respond to the complaint (s.9).

DISCUSSION

Health service ombudsman: maladministration

Maladministration has been described by the ombudsman's office as covering, non-exhaustively, 'bias, neglect, inattention, delay, incompetence, ineptitude, perversity, turpitude, arbitrariness'. In addition is:

- 'rudeness,
- unwillingness to treat the complainant as a person with rights;
- refusal to answer reasonable questions;
- neglecting to inform a complainant on request of his or her rights or entitlement;
- knowingly giving advice which is misleading or inadequate;
- ignoring valid advice or overruling considerations which would produce an uncomfortable result for the overruler;
- offering no redress or manifestly disproportionate redress;
- showing bias whether because of colour, sex or any other grounds;
- omission to notify those who thereby lose a right of appeal;
- refusal to inform adequately of the right of appeal;
- faulty procedures;
- failure by management to monitor compliance with adequate procedures;
- cavalier disregard of guidance which is intended to be followed in the interest of equitable treatment of those who use a service;
- partiality; and
- failure to mitigate the effects of rigid adherence to the letter of the law where that produces manifestly inequitable treatment' (Health Service Commissioner 1996a,p.13).

Health service ombudsman: remedies

Legislation does not lay down formal remedies, although the health service ombudsman can make recommendations. The ombudsman will send a report of the findings to the complainant and the NHS. If the complaint, or at least part of it, is upheld the ombudsman seeks a remedy – this could include getting a decision changed, or a repayment of unnecessary costs incurred by patients or their families. Otherwise, the ombudsman does not recommend financial damages. The ombudsman might also recommend that changes are made to procedures so that the same problem does not recur for other people (Health Service Commissioner 1996a,p.7).

Health service ombudsman: clinical judgement

From April 1996, the statutory prohibition on the ombudsman from investigating clinical aspects of complaints was removed. Special assessors are used by the ombudsman to investigate such matters, who will use the civil law test of the 'balance of probabilities' in reaching conclusions about causation. The ombudsman has noted that a) many complaints which appear to be related to clinical matters are in fact about administrative lapses such as breakdown in communications or failure to follow proper procedure; but b) where clinical judgement is in question, the test for maladministration is not appropriate (Health Service Commissioner 1996a,pp.3,10).

11. SECRETARY OF STATE'S DEFAULT POWERS (NHS)

Under s.85 of the NHS Act 1977, the Secretary of State can declare health authorities or NHS Trusts to be in default of their duty. This would be where 'they have failed to carry out any functions conferred or imposed on them by or under this Act, or have in carrying out those functions failed to comply with any regulations or directions relating to those functions'. It seems that no default order has ever been issued.

EXTRACTS AND DISCUSSION
Not applicable.

12. CHARTERS

For the NHS, a national Patient's Charter (DH 1995c) exists; there is also a special charter for mental health services (DH 1997a and EL(97)1). In community care, there is no national charter, but local authorities base their local charters on a national framework suggested by the Department of Health (LAC(94)24 and DH 1994a). In practice, local community care charters vary enormously from the bare to the detailed; overall, their practical effect is probably minimal. It is expected that a national *Long-term care charter* will be issued in 1999 to give people a clearer idea of what services and support to expect (Secretary of State for Health 1998,p.32).

The Patient's Charter refers to various rights, guarantees, standards, targets, performance levels, and expectations (DH 1995c; HSG(92)36). Nevertheless, the 'rights' are not straightforward legal rights (except where they happen to coincide with rights under existing legislation: for instance, access to records under the Access to Health Records Act 1990). Instead, if people wish to complain under the Charter, they should write to the chief executive or general manager (rather than the complaints officer) of the hospital. If complainants remain dissatisfied they can ask the health service ombudsman to investigate.

For instance, elements of the charter include a) right to receive health care on the basis of clinical need; b) right to get emergency treatment at any time; c) right to have clear explanations of treatment; d) access to records (under the Access to Health Records Act 1990); e) expectation, before leaving hospital, that a decision be made about how continuing needs will be met – the hospital 'will agree arrangements with agencies such as community nursing services and local authority social services departments' (DH 1995c). It should be noted that it might be difficult for an individual patient to enforce legally any of these except the one concerning access to records.

On the one hand, charters offer in principle a simple, direct and cheap route to obtaining apologies and redress from health authorities. On the other hand, they do not replace other remedies such as complaints procedures or legal action. This means that complainants still have to resort to these other remedies if they do not get satisfaction through charters. Seen in this light, an informal charter complaints process could in some circumstances become yet one more obstacle to obtaining a legal remedy (for a summary of these issues, see Williams, Goriely 1994). Indeed, it has been stated of charters generally that the 'precise status of these documents is difficult to ascertain. Formally they are of no legal effect, being merely aspirational, but they could be characterised as customer service documents or customer guarantees.' (Barron, Scott 1992).

Certainly, it seems that in community care, nobody has bothered to refer to local community care charters in court cases. Nevertheless, the ombudsmen might take note. For instance, the health service ombudsman has criticised a Scottish health board when its own charter did not conform to the Patient's Charter for Scotland (SW.81/92–93); and the local ombudsman found maladministration when a community care charter contained misleading timescales for assessment (*Ealing LBC 1999*).

EXTRACTS AND DISCUSSION
Not applicable.

13. PUBLIC LAW: JUDICIAL REVIEW

The law courts supervise the decisions and actions of public bodies by means of judicial review, a *public law* (as opposed to *private law,* for which see next section) process. In the community care field, judicial review cases have proliferated in the last few years; this means that in order to understand community care law, a knowledge of both legislation and judicial review decisions is required. The law courts employ an array of conceptual tools, which can be categorised under the following three umbrella terms: *unreasonableness, unfairness* and *illegality* – although there are many others (Fordham 1997).

Judicial review is not generally about people's direct rights to service, but about ensuring that authorities make decisions in a lawful manner. The courts do not wish to step into the shoes of professionals – such as social workers or occupational therapists – and question the merits of decisions; thus, there is room for professionals to make poor decisions without triggering judicial intervention; in other words, a bad decision is not necessarily an unlawful one (eg, *R v Haringey LBC, ex p Norton* about community care assessment). The courts take a hands-off approach; if an authority is found to have made an unlawful decision, the court does not generally order services to be provided but tells the authority to take the decision again – this time in a lawful manner. The authority might still reach the same conclusion as it did before, but this time around it will do so on the 'right' grounds (eg, *R v North Yorkshire CC, ex p Hargreaves (no.2)* about holidays for disabled people).

Judicial review is a complicated area of law and is by no means cheap, efficient and quick (Bridges *et al.* 1995b). However, in the community care field, it remains the main ground of legal challenge to local authorities. This chapter sets out its basic features; its effectiveness has already been outlined in Chapter 2.

EXTRACTS
Not applicable.

DISCUSSION

The particular impact of judicial review on community care has already been considered in Chapter 3 (p.41), and the principles applied by the law courts – such as unreasonableness, illegality, fettering of discretion – illustrated in Chapter 4 (p.48).

Judicial review: what can be challenged

In the context of community care, judicial review can be used to challenge aspects of, for example, assessment procedures, care plans, charging procedures, complaints procedures consultation procedures, criteria of eligibility, policies, priorities – and so on.

Judicial review: supervisory approach

It is important to remember judicial review is, in principle at least, about ensuring that local authorities have acted within the law, rather than about the merits of decisions.

For example, the courts are not so much interested in whether a particular person has or has not received community care services – but whether the local authority has arrived at its decision lawfully. If an authority has made an unlawful decision, the court orders it to go away and retake it – this time in a lawful manner. Therefore, in *R v Gloucestershire CC, ex p Barry*, the High Court ruled that the local authority's decision to withdraw services under s.2 of the CSDPA 1970 was unlawful, because the reassessment process was flawed. The High Court did not step into the shoes of the authority and decide who should or who should not have services. It ruled instead that this was still for the authority to decide – but this time by lawful means. On the other hand, sometimes the implications of an adverse ruling give a local authority little room for manoeuvre – and the court will actually order provision of a service in some circumstances (*R v Wigan MBC, ex p Tammadge*).

Judicial review: function

There are several other general points to make about judicial review.

First, when cases go to a full hearing (see below), the decisions of the courts set precedents for the future and have ramifications far beyond the particular applicant or applicants in the case. However, precedents can be sidestepped by, for instance, 'distinguishing' a later from a previously decided case, and so avoiding the precedent set by the earlier case. This occurred in *R v East Sussex CC, ex p Tandy* (about resources in education decisions) in which the House of Lords 'explained away' their earlier decision in *R v Gloucestershire CC, ex p Barry* (resources in community care), in order to come to the opposite conclusion in the later case.

Second, even the threat of judicial review might be effective in resolving a dispute. For instance, if leave (permission) to proceed to a full hearing is given by a judge, then the authority against whom the case is being brought will be aware that the case is an arguable one and might be tempted to settle the dispute before it goes further. Authorities might wish to avoid a) adverse publicity, b) high legal costs, and c) the danger of losing the case and the setting of an unwanted, expensive precedent (which might apply to many other service users in a similar position to the applicant). Third, judicial review might be used by voluntary organisations and others to highlight matters of public interest. Fourth, a local authority does not necessarily learn from judicial review cases which have been brought generally, and might react only when it is itself involved, and sometimes not even then (see p.43).

Judicial review: expense

Judicial review is a specialised legal procedure and, without legal aid, can be expensive. For example, a case settled following the obtaining of a barrister's opinion or at the 'leave' stage (see immediately below) might cost £1,000 or less. Following a High Court hearing this might rise to thousand of pounds – while tens of thousands of pounds might be involved if the case goes further to the Court of Appeal or beyond (Bridges *et al.* 1995a,p.49). Of course who pays these costs often depends on the outcome of the case and whether an applicant is legally aided.

Judicial review: leave or permission of the Court

Unlike private law actions (for example, for negligence), judicial review cannot be pursued without the 'leave' (permission) of the High Court (Supreme Court Act 1981,s.31, and Rules of the Supreme Court, Order 53, rule 3). When leave has been given, the case can proceed to a full hearing in the High Court. Appeal can be made (with permission) from the High Court to the Court of Appeal, and thence to the House of Lords.

Judicial review: time limits for bringing the case

An application for judicial review must be brought promptly and in any event within three months from the date when the grounds of action arose; the court can extend this time limit if there are good reasons why the case has been brought later (Supreme Court Act 1981,s.31, and Rules of the Supreme Court, Order 53, rule 4). This means that even within the three-month limit, it is open to a court to deny leave on grounds that the application has not been made promptly.

Because of this time limit and the possible requirement that alternative remedies (such as the complaints procedure) be used first, an application for judicial review could be made but then adjourned until the outcome of a complaint brought under the local authority's complaints procedure is known. If this were not done, then it might be too late to make the application.

Judicial review: length of process

Judicial review can take up to 18 months to come to court – unless urgency is pleaded and the case is expedited, in which case it might not take more than a few weeks. Similarly, an appeal might be heard quickly in certain circumstances, as occurred in *R v Cambridge HA, ex p B* when the High Court and Court of Appeal sat on the same day.

However, if a case is going to take a long time to come to court, an *interim injunction* ('interim relief') is sometimes possible. This might be in a sufficiently serious case where the court could order that services be provided until the dispute is finally heard and resolved (see eg, *R v Staffordshire CC, ex p Farley* involving the temporary restoration of night sitter services). This might be one argument for using the judicial review system directly in some circumstances, rather than going through the complaints procedure which can in practice, despite statutory time limits, be drawn out.

Judicial review: standing and the status of the applicant

The applicant must have a 'sufficient interest' in the case (Supreme Court Act 1981,s.31, and Rules of the Supreme Court, Order 53, rule 3). This is known as having 'locus standi' or 'standing'. For example, service users themselves or carers affected by a decision clearly have such an interest. However, sometimes established advisory organisations, representing particular groups of people, will also be recognised by courts (see eg, *R v Sefton MBC, ex p Help the Aged; R v Gloucestershire CC, ex p RADAR; R v Newham LBC, ex p Medical Foundation for the Care of Victims of Torture*).

Judicial review: alternative remedies instead

If the courts believe that there are appropriate 'alternative remedies' then they might insist that those remedies be used first, before judicial review can be applied for. The obvious alternative remedies in the community care field are the social services complaints procedure, and the powers of the Secretary of State to declare authorities in default of their duties. However, there are sometimes reasons why the courts might not insist on these two remedies being 'exhausted' first.

As far as the community care complaints procedure goes, service users could argue that a hearing before a panel of non-lawyers without legal representation is inadequate to deal with questions of law. For instance, in *R v Sutton LBC, ex p Tucker* (delay in community care services), the court ruled that it would not have been 'convenient, expeditious or effective' for the applicant to argue points of law before a non-qualified body (ie, the complaints review panel).

Indeed, where there is a question of law in a developing field, the courts will state that it is for them, and not for the local authority or Secretary of State, to decide it (*R v Devon CC, ex p Baker* about residential home closure). On the other hand, absent questions of law and the complaints procedure might be more appropriate (*R v Lambeth LBC, ex p A* about rehousing for child and family; and *R v Birmingham CC, ex p A* about delay in providing a placement for a child). In *R v Kingston upon Thames, ex p T* (a child care case), the court saw the complaints procedure as more effective and quicker than judicial review. And, in *R v Westminster CC, ex p P*, an asylum seeker case, the default powers of the Secretary of State were regarded as more appropriate than judicial review. Moreover, some of the community care disputes which have reached the law courts have involved complex problems, which might simply not be amenable to judicial resolution, since they are 'beyond the competence of courts of law' *(R v Islington LBC, ex p Rixon)*.

Judicial review: full disclosure of facts

The applicant must make a full disclosure of all relevant facts. Not to do so could jeopardise an applicant's case *(R v Leeds City Council, ex p. Hendry 1993*, a taxi licensing case).

Judicial review: remedies and court orders

The court can make the following types of order in judicial review, which have the effect of:

- overturning a decision and ordering the authority to take the decision again (*certiorari*: eg, quashing a decision not to provide services and then ordering the authority to decide again);
- obliging an authority to take a positive action (*mandamus*: eg, to undertake a community care assessment);
- an *injunction*: similar to mandamus, but in its interim form (ie, until the full hearing and resolution of the dispute) it obliges an authority not to do something (eg, not withdrawing services);
- forbidding an authority from doing something inconsistent with its legal powers (*prohibition*);
- making a statement about rights, remedies and the general legal position of the parties (*declaration*: eg, about whether a person is 'ordinarily resident').

Judicial review: discretion not to award a remedy

The court does not have to award a remedy at all, even if the claimant has 'won' the judicial review case in principle.

For example, in one case the court made a declaration (ie, an acknowledgement of what should have happened) that the government should have consulted properly with a local authority association about proposed housing benefit regulations – but by the time court heard the case, it was impracticable and pointless to consider striking down the regulations *(R v Secretary of State, ex p AMA)*. Similarly, a judge found himself unable to do more than suggest a declaration that the authority was 'quite wrong' when he found that a local authority had not acted in accordance with the law (the CSDPA 1970) when it had refused (nearly two years previously) to consider assisting a person with a holiday *(R v Ealing LBC, ex p Leaman)*. And if an authority is doing all it can, a court might not make an order even if a duty is being clearly breached *(R v Bristol Corporation, ex p Hendy* about housing; *R v Inner London Education Authority, ex p Ali* about education); or if the delay was not 'reprehensible' *(R v Gloucestershire CC, ex p P* about special education).

14. PRIVATE LAW: BREACH OF STATUTORY DUTY, NEGLIGENCE AND CONTRACT

Private law actions for damages on the ground of *negligence, breach of statutory duty* or *breach of contract* are private law remedies and must be distinguished from public law judicial review proceedings.

The common law of negligence is well established in the health care field in relation to clinical decisions, but less so in the social care field – while damages for breach of statutory duty are extremely difficult to win in either field. In addition, a third possible private law remedy, namely an action for breach of *contract*, appears generally not to be available to individual users of social services or the NHS (except in the case of private patients). The reason for this is that, because the provision of such services is governed by statute, legally enforceable contracts between statutory agencies and service users are precluded.

Private law: potential advantages of private law remedies

The existence of private law remedies is, or would be significant (if they were more commonly available), because there are a number of differences between private and public law procedures. First, in private law, the claimant does not, at the outset, have to gain the permission of a judge to pursue the case. Second, the court can in private law actually make a final decision about the matter in dispute, whereas judicial review often involves authorities themselves retaking a decision about services. Third, when a claimant wins a case, the judge in private law cases must normally grant a remedy of some sort; whereas in public law cases, the judge does not have to do this. Furthermore, a remedy in private law, but not usually in public law, can be in the form of financial compensation (damages). Lastly, in private law involving claims for negligence or breach of statutory duty, the claimant must have suffered some sort of harm: physical, psychological (in some circumstances only), property or financial (in limited circumstances only). For instance, if there is no harm, then a negligence case has nothing to bite on. However, in judicial review, such harm does not have to be shown – although the applicant still has to show that he, she or it (in the case of an organisation) has sufficient interest in the case.

Private law: breach of statutory duty

An action for breach of statutory duty requires identification of definite, potentially enforceable, individual rights. Such rights are difficult to identify in welfare legislation for a number of reasons – and private law actions in this field (compared, for example, to the health and safety at work field where they are well established: eg manual handling, see p.178) do not seem, at present, to be generally viable.

In the social welfare field, cases such as *Cocks v Thanet DC*, and *R v Northavon DC, ex p Palmer* (both housing cases) gave some encouragement to users of services, insofar as they appeared to state that damages might be available for breach of a duty arising from an *executive* function as opposed to a *decision-making* function. The courts explained that decision-making (eg, deciding about somebody's eligibility for services) was a public law function which could not give rise to damages; whereas breach of any duty which arose after the decision-making was finished (eg, actually to get on and provide the service) gave rise to private law rights and obligations which could result in liability for damages.

However, more recent cases have further refined the test for liability and imposed additional obstacles – such as a burden on the claimant to show a) that the legislation was designed to protect a specific class of people and also to confer a right to sue for damages; b) clear statutory language to this effect; and c) that there were no alternative remedies (such as an appeal to the Secretary of State). See, for instance, *X v Bedfordshire CC* about child care and education; *O'Rourke v Camden LBC* about housing, but which also cited approvingly *Wyatt v Hillingdon LBC* in relation to s.2 of the Chronically Sick and Disabled Persons Act 1970; *T v Surrey CC* about child care; and *Clunis v Camden and Islington HA* about the provision of after-care under s.117 of the Mental Health Act 1983. In the light of these cases, the speculation of the judge in *R v Bexley LBC, ex p B*, that damages might be possible for breach of the absolute duty to arrange services (once need and necessity have been established) under s.2 of the 1970 Act, is of probably little significance. However, it should be noted that in *Dennis Rye Pension Fund v Sheffield City Council*, the Court of Appeal did rule that non-payment of a mandatory housing grant could give rise to private law rights – which would allow for a private law action to recover the amount of the unpaid grant.

Private law: negligence

The bringing of a claim for negligence does not depend on locating rights in legislation, but lies in the common law. Negligence actions involve, basically, showing that there was a duty of care owed, breach of that duty, and causation of harm. Another way of putting this requires a consideration of a) what damage or harm has occurred; b) whether it is actionable at law; and c) whether it was caused by the act or omission of the defendant (*Barrett v Enfield BC*).

Negligence actions are well-established in the health care field when health care professionals act in a clinically careless manner. However, the courts might stop short of imposing liability if the duty of care is essentially administrative rather than clinical in nature and arises directly from the statute (*Clunis v Camden and Islington HA*: in this case from s.117 of the Mental Health Act 1983, concerning the provision of after-care services). Even so, the Court of Appeal has recently ruled that the failure (administrative in nature) to send an ambulance promptly in response to a 999 call could give rise to liability in negligence (*Kent v Griffiths*).

In the social care field, the position is not straightforward, and in certain circumstances the courts have conferred immunity from negligence actions on local authorities and social workers – particularly in the child care field. Generally speaking, this immunity is based on the fact that a common law duty of care will not arise where decisions or actions are related to issues of *resources or policy* – or where the decision or action is operational (ie, not related to resources or policy: see immediately below) but nevertheless stems from *statutory functions* (ie, in the legislation).

This exclusion test still leaves open the possibility of liability arising for *purely operational* actions or decisions existing independently of statutory functions. But even in this situation, the courts might state that it is not 'just and reasonable' to impose liability. Reasons for this might be that the statutory system is complex and involves a range of agencies; the difficult nature of the work involved; the danger of legal liability pushing authorities into defensive practices and encouraging hopeless, vexatious and costly actions; and the existence of other remedies, such as complaints procedures and the local ombudsman.

This approach was spelt out in *X v Bedfordshire CC*, a child care case in which the local authorities concerned were alleged to have made very poor decisions with serious consequences for those affected. Other cases which have followed this approach include *Barrett v Enfield BC* (about the effect of foster placements) and *H v Norfolk CC* (about alleged physical and sexual abuse by foster father). An older case *Wyatt v Hillingdon LBC*, about provision of home help and a bed under s.2 of the Chronically Sick and Disabled Persons Act 1970, referred to the fact that there was no duty of care freestanding from the legislation.

However, sometimes the courts do concede that an action or decision complained of is purely operational and that liability is not precluded, assuming it is proved on the balance of probabilities according to the ordinary rules of negligence. This is on the basis that in such cases, a common law duty arises separately from any statutory functions involved. For instance, *T(A Minor)* concerned a negligent statement about a childminder, the *Vicar of Writtle v Essex CC* the failure of a social worker to warn about the fire-raising tendencies of a child in the care of the local authority, and *W v Essex CC* the failure to warn a foster family that the fostered child was a sexual abuser. And in *Wyatt v Hillingdon LBC*, the court envisaged that liability in negligence might arise in relation to the supply of a defective bed, or if a person was physically dropped and injured. Local authorities might also be found liable for failing to train staff such as social workers (*Colclough v Staffordshire CC*) or quasi-employees such as paid foster carers (*Beasley v Buckinghamshire CC*) in manual handling techniques – which failure results in injury.

In the local authority education field, too, the courts have been prepared to consider negligence liability for clearly operational lapses and also less clearcut matters (see eg, *X v Bedfordshire CC; Phelps v Hillingdon LBC*). In similar vein, in the environmental health field, a local authority was held liable when an environmental health officer gave poor advice which was based neither on the relevant legislation nor the authority's policy of differentiating legal and non-legally enforceable requirements (*Welton v North Cornwall DC*).

Private law: contract

Legally, it is commonly supposed that when health care and social care is provided by the NHS or local authorities to users of services, there is no legal contract created between provider and user (except eg, in the case of private patients receiving treatment from the NHS). On the other hand, given the emphasis in community care on individual care plans, which sometimes bear the language of agreement and are signed by all parties, users of services and local authority staff sometimes imagine that enforceable contracts are being created. There are two particular aspects of statutory provision that may mean there is no contract: first and foremost the exclusion of contract by the statutory framework and obligations; second, a rule called *privity of contract*, whereby a third party (eg, a user of services) cannot enforce a contract between two other parties (eg, a local authority and independent provider), even if the contract is of the benefit of the third party.

First, the courts generally hold that the existence of statutory arrangements preclude the free negotiation and bargaining that are meant to be the hallmarks of a genuine contract. In this case, there will be no contract between the user of a statutory service and a statutory provider. This might be so even when money changes hands – as in a case concerning an NHS prescription charge, when the House of Lords stated that the transaction was governed by statutory obligations and not by contract (*Pfizer Corporation v Ministry of Health*). The same principle was even applied in respect of a very different type of public service altogether, when a court found that the relationship between a poultry farmer and a public utility company (an electricity board), was non-contractual. The farmer had lost a certain quantity of the poultry he was rearing because of fluctuations in the power supply and had wanted to sue for damages in contract (*Willmore v South Eastern Electricity Board*; see similarly *Norweb PLC v Dixon*). The Royal Commission on Civil Liability for Personal Injury also assumed that no contract exists between the NHS doctor and patient (Pearson 1978,para 1313); whilst community care guidance makes the same point that care plans, despite signatures on them which might suggest some sort of binding agreement have no 'legal standing as a contract' (SSI,SWSG 1991a,p.68).

However, the courts have on occasion identified enforceable contracts, in spite of a statutory framework. For example an agreement between a local authority and foster parents was held by the High Court as capable of being contractual; although the Court of Appeal reversed this, referring to one of the electricity cases and pointing out that the statutory arrangements precluded free negotiation which was essential for the existence of a contract (*W v Essex CC*). In another case, the payments made by a local authority to independent care home owners were held to be contractual, even though ultimately the arrangements, of which the payments were part, stemmed from statutory obligations in s.26 of the National Assistance Act 1948 *(R v Coventry CC, ex p CHOICE)*. Both these examples involve agreements with service providers rather than users of services.

Nevertheless, if it is generally correct that there is indeed no legal contract between users of services and statutory providers, then there is an odd outcome. People who are buying services or care (whether residential or non-residential) *privately* will have a legally enforceable contract with the independent provider. But when arrangements have been made *by a local authority*, whether for services provided directly by the authority or via an independent provider, the service user would seem not have a contract with the authority – even if they are paying the same amount of money as those people who have independently arranged services. This would be according to the rule in *Pfizer Corporation v Ministry of Health*. (It is open to speculation whether the courts might in some circumstances choose to modify the rule. For instance, is it possible that they might recognise an element of free negotiation (an essential part of the contractual process) in the arranging of residential accommodation by a local authority, insofar as people are meant to be given, within certain limits, a choice of residential accommodation? See p.???)

A second separate obstacle to the identification and enforcing of contracts by users of services arises in relation to independent providers. This is the rule in English law called privity of contract. This means that a third party (here the service user) cannot enforce a contract by two other parties (the local authority and the independent provider), even if it has been made for his or her benefit. Reform of this rule has been proposed (Law Commission 1996); and see Contracts (Rights of Third Parties) Bill 1999.

In the light of this rule, a person would have to rely on the local authority to enforce its contract with an independent provider, rather than to do so himself or herself. In an attempt apparently to circumvent this rule, some local authorities arrange for the drawing up of *three-way agreements* (or tripartite contracts) involving service users which set out clearly exactly what services an individual should be receiving (Office of Fair Trading 1998,p.21). The suggestion is that such contracts will create privity of contract between all three parties: local authority, independent service provider *and* service user. In order for this to work, 'consideration' would need to have been given by the service user towards the service provider. It has been claimed, rather speculatively and possibly erroneously that consideration could be identified, for example, by a) the payment made to the local authority; b) obligations established on the part of the service user, such as allowing access to domiciliary care staff, insuring premises, allowing care assistants to use domestic facilities; or c) acceptance or choice of a particular provider (AMA,ACC,ADSS 1995, pp.101–103).

Lastly, even where the courts would not accept the existence of an enforceable contract between service user and provider, there is still much that can be done to improve the lot of users of services. Full participation in three-way agreements (eg, AMA,ACC,ADSS 1994,p.8) is more likely to lead to the inclusion of appropriately detailed terms and conditions, and clarity amongst all concerned about the services to be provided. And, if enforcement is required, then an alert local authority will anyway pursue its contract with the provider (eg, if the latter is not supplying the specialist individual care it is being paid for: see ombudsman investigation, *Redbridge LBC 1998*). The service user can pursue a complaint either directly against the provider or indirectly via the local authority (in which latter case the local ombudsman could also be resorted to), or both. Of course, a local authority could in any case choose to act as if there were a legally enforceable contract with the service user, even if there is not one. For instance, it might draw up what it calls a 'service support contract' between itself and a person with profound learning disabilities and no verbal communication. Under this agreement, the person would be reimbursed part of the charge she has paid if specified services were not delivered (Morris 1997b,p.13).

15. ACCESS TO PERSONAL INFORMATION

Legislation gives people the right to access personal information about themselves. In the case of social services manual records, this has consisted of the Access to Personal Files Act 1987 and the Access to Personal Files (Social Services) Regulations 1989 – and, in the case of computerised records, the Data Protection Act 1984. However, the Data Protection Act 1998, covering both manual and computerised personal records, is now posed to repeal both the 1984 and 1989 Acts. At the time of writing, specific regulations in relation to social work are expected in the first half of 1999.

In respect of the NHS and independent sector healthcare, the Access to Health Records Act 1990 applies to manual records. This is similar to the legislation covering social services but is not covered in this book.

EXTRACTS

Legislation (Access to Personal Files Act 1987) states that:

(basic duty to give access to personal information) Subject to various provisions and qualifications, 'any authority keeping records containing personal information which is accessible personal information for the purposes of this Act shall have such obligations as regards access to, and the accuracy of, that information as are imposed by the regulators' (s.1).

(data protection legislation) The Act does not apply if the Data Protection Act 1984 applies (Access to Personal Files Act 1987, s.1) – ie, if automated records are in issue. That Act, together with SI 1987/1904, covers access to personal information held by local authorities under their social services functions; it prevents access if serious harm would be caused to the subject's, or anybody else's, physical or mental health. The distinction between legislation covering social services manual and automated records will disappear, once the Data Protection Act 1998 is properly in force.

(meaning of personal information) Personal information 'relates to a living individual who can be identified from that information (or from that and other information in the possession of the authority keeping the record) including any expression of opinion about the individual but not any indication of the intentions of the authority with respect to that individual' (s.2).

(information recorded prior to 1st April 1989) Information is not regarded as accessible prior to the date of commencement of relevant regulations made under the Act – 'except to the extent that access to it is required to make intelligible information recorded on or after the date' (s.2). Under the Data Protection 1998, individuals will have a right of access to personal information held manually by social services (in what the Act calls an 'accessible record' and including, typically, a person's file) without such a time restriction – and probably from the summer of 1999.

Legislation (regulations: SI 1989/206) state:

(specific obligation on social services authorities to inform people and give access) Subject to various provisos and exceptions, an authority has a duty '(a) to inform any individual whether the accessible personal information held by them includes personal information of which that individual is the subject, and (b) to give that individual access to any personal information of which he is the subject' (SI 1989/206,r.2).

The Data Protection Act 1998 provides, in addition this basic right to information, that the person has a right to have communicated to him or her a description of the personal data held, the purposes for which the data are being processed, the recipients or classes of recipients to whom the data may be disclosed, and information available to the data controller about the sources of the data (s.7).

(giving access and/or supplying a copy) Apart from supplying a copy straightaway, a local authority can comply with the duty by giving an individual access to the information in some other way. But if, in addition, the person then asks for a copy of it, the authority is obliged to supply the copy (r.2).

(jargon etc) If the information supplied 'is expressed in terms which are not intelligible without explanation', it must be 'accompanied by an explanation of those terms' (r.2).

(request with adequate details, and payment) The duty only arises if an individual makes a request and furnishes payment (£10). However, authorities are not under a duty to comply unless the request contains 'such information as they may reasonably require in order to satisfy themselves as to the identity of the person making the request and to locate the information which he seeks' (rr.3,4).

(rule about information relating to another individual) Another individual might be able to be identified from the information requested. If so, then within 14 days of the request, the local authority 'shall in writing inform that other individual of the request and that the accessible personal information contains information relating to him and ask that other individual whether he consents to the information relating to him being disclosed to the person making the request'.

If consent is not given, the authority is not obliged to disclose the information if the identity of the other individual 'would be likely to be disclosed to or deduced' by the person obtaining (or other person likely to obtain) access to the information – either from the information alone or combined with other information likely to be held by the person(s) gaining access. The information might either relate to the other individual or reveal him or her as a source of the information.

However, the duty will still apply if the person whose identity is likely to be disclosed or deduced is or was employed (or paid for reward) in connection with social services functions – and 'the information relates to him or he supplied the information in his official capacity, or as the case may be, in connection with the provision of that service' (rr.5,9).

(The Data Protection Act 1998 makes additional provision in relation to the question of consent: see discussion below).

(compliance with request within 40 days) The local authority must comply with a request within 40 days – either from receipt of the request, from when any further information is acquired, or from when consent is received (r.6).

(state of the information) The information to which access is given should be as it was at the time of the request – except it may take account of any amendment or deletion which would have been made 'regardless of the receipt of the request' (r.6).

(rule about information supplied by a health professional) The information requested may relate to the physical or mental health of the individual and have been supplied by a health professional. If so, the authority must inform either the employing health authority or NHS Trust, or other health care professional about the request. The authority is then relieved of its obligation to disclose if, within 40 days, the authority, trust or professional replies stating that either

(a) disclosure 'would be likely to cause serious harm to the physical or mental health of the individual who is the subject of the information or any other person'; or

(b) disclosure would be likely to reveal the identity of somebody else to whom the information relates, or who is a source of the information (unless this person is a health professional involved in the individual's care and the information relates to him or her (or was supplied by him or her) in a professional capacity (r.9).

(rule about social services functions and likely harm) Disclosure might mean that 'the carrying out of the social services functions of the local social services authority would be likely to be prejudiced by reason of the fact that serious harm to the physical or mental health or emotional condition of the individual who is the subject of the information or any other person would be likely to be caused'. If so the authority is relieved of the duty to disclose (r.9).

(partial disclosure) If an authority is not obliged to disclose the full information requested because of the various rules above (relating to other individuals, health professionals, social services functions and harm), nevertheless it is still under a duty to supply 'so much of the information sought by the request as can be supplied without causing such serious harm, or enabling the identity of another individual to be disclosed or deduced, whether by the omission of names or other particulars or otherwise' (rr.8,9).

(other exceptions) There are various exceptions to which the duty does not apply. These include information held by the local authority in connection with:

(a) for prevention or detection of crime, where disclosure would prejudice these matters;

(b) proceedings under the Magistrates Courts (Children and Young Persons) Rules 1988;

(c) restrictions on information disclosure in the Adoption Act 1976, Education (Special Educational Needs) Regulations 1983, Adoption Agency Regulations 1983, Adoption Rules 1984, Magistrates Courts (Adoption Rules) 1984.

(d) legal professional privilege (r.9).

(rectifying information) The individual 'may by notice in writing require the local social services authority holding the information to rectify or erase the information which he regards as inaccurate'. The local authority is not obliged to do anything about such a request unless it receives sufficient information to locate the information, and specific detail about the inaccuracy and how it should be rectified or erased.

If the authority is satisfied about the inaccuracy, then it has a duty to rectify or erase. If it is not satisfied, then it must add to the information a written note to the effect that the individual regards the information as inaccurate. The individual must then be given access (including a copy if required) to the amended information or the written note (r.10).

(review) If the individual is aggrieved by the authority's decision, he or she can within 28 days of being notified of that decision, request a review by a committee – consisting of three members of the authority (not more than one of whom may be a member of the Social Services Committee). The individual has the right to make representations (oral if he or she wishes) to the members of the committee (r.11).

DISCUSSION

Personal information: consent of contributors and review

In 1989, the European Court of Human Rights held in *Gaskin v United Kingdom* that the right to personal social services information, dependent as it was at the time on the consent of contributors to the information and with no independent review procedure, breached article 8 (right to respect for private and family life, home and correspondence) of the European Convention on Human Rights (see p.188). The case was not about the Access to Personal Files Act 1987 which did not apply in the circumstances; however, it is thought that limitations to the 1987 Act and the 1989 regulations have continued to put the United Kingdom in potential breach of the Convention. This will be remedied by the Data Protection Act 1998 (see below).

Personal information: information about other people

The right of access to personal information does not entitle a particular user to information about how other service users have been treated. Their consent would be needed, and probably each of them would have to make a separate application. Therefore, from the point of view of service users and their advisers, there is a need to pool local knowledge so that radically dissimilar decisions can be identified in similar cases. Such information might be useful, for example, in challenging an authority's assessment that somebody is not 'in need' and in bringing some objectivity to the concept of need. From the point of view of local authorities, they should be able to argue that no two cases are ever exactly the same because individuals' circumstances vary greatly, even where people's conditions or disabilities are apparently similar.

This rule means that even close relatives of a deceased service user do not have a right of access to his her personal information, and although local authorities might sometimes accede to such requests they will not always do so (see eg, the ombudsman investigation, *Lambeth LBC 1996*).

Data Protection Act 1998 and consent of third party

The Data Protection Act 1998 will apply to both automated and manual records. Rights of access to social services manual records, holding personal health or social work information (ie typically people's personal records), will be broadly similar to those existing at present. However, there are additional rights.

For instance, when disclosure of personal information requires the consent of a third party (see extracts above) and that consent is not forthcoming, the present 1987 Act and 1989 regulations (see extracts above) are silent about the process to be undertaken by the holder of the information. At most a person's redress is by way of a review committee of the local authority. This was the defect identified in the *Gaskin* case heard in the European Court of Human Rights, which pointed to the lack of an independent review.

In contrast, the Data Protection Act 1998 will oblige the local authority (the data controller) nevertheless to make disclosure if 'it is reasonable in all the circumstances to comply with the request without the consent'. In coming to this decision, the data controller will have to pay regard in particular to a) the duty of confidentiality to the third party; b) the steps being taken to obtain consent from that third party; c) whether the third party is capable of giving consent; d) an express refusal of consent by the third party (s.7). If the person requesting the information remains dissatisfied, he or she can request the Data Commissioner to carry out an independent 'assessment', which could cover the question of disclosure (s.42). Beyond this, the person could seek a court order (s.7).

The particular part of the Act (s.7) covering manual records, and containing people's personal social work and health information (what the Act calls *accessible records*) – and covering access to such information by individuals – is expected to apply from the summer of 1999. In addition, there will not be a retrospective time limit for access to these records, as there is (April 1989, except in limited circumstances) under the present regulations. See generally guidelines from the Data Protection Registrar (1998) and the Department of Health's initial guidance (LASSL(98)16.

Personal information: council meetings

In order to explore possible grounds of complaint or challenge to a decision, an individual might need other information beyond the personal – for example, about general council policy, perhaps with a view to finding out how other people have been treated in a similar situation.

The public has a right to attend local authority meetings (with some exceptions) including social services committee meetings. However, access is denied if 'confidential information' is at issue, either information supplied by a government department where disclosure to the public is forbidden, or information disclosure of which is prevented by legislation or a court order. In addition, councils have the power to deny access in relation to 'exempt information', which includes (amongst various items) information about applicants or recipients of services, and about legal proceedings. Access to agendas, reports and background documents must be given three days before a meeting, but items can be excluded if they relate to parts of the meeting which will not be open to the public (Local Government Act 1972,s.100A, schedule 12A).

Personal information: confidentiality

Hand in hand with access to personal information goes confidentiality. In summary, the position in respect of social services, described in Department of Health guidance (LAC(88)17), is as follows.

First, if the subject of information consents to disclosure then there is no problem. Second, health professionals pass on information on the assumption that the information will only be used for the particular purpose underlying disclosure; that it will not be passed on to anybody to whom disclosure is not essential for that purpose; and that the information will not be passed on further to a third party without the consent of the health professional. Thus, health authorities and health professionals 'should continue to be able to share personal health information about those in their care with social workers and others in social services authorities' (paras 10–12).

Third, personal information (including health information not derived from a health professional) in relation to social services functions should be treated as confidential and cannot be disclosed without the consent of the subject unless a) it is for social work purposes; b) it comes into a category of exceptional cases in which the law or public interest overrides confidentiality; or c) exceptionally, the need to avoid serious harm to others requires that consideration be given to breaching confidentiality (paras 15–17).

In practice, local authorities might not have a formal policy about confidentiality and staff might be unaware of the relevant legislation and its relevance to their work (SSI 1997d,p.19). Situations involving confidentiality issues can range in practice, for example, from older people with mental health problems demanding extreme confidentiality to situations in which 'everybody knows everything'. For people with HIV/AIDS, policy and good practice on confidentiality in relation to receptionists is particularly important (SSI 1994e,p.3). Even when policies on confidentiality do exist, problems might arise – for instance, the reluctance of specialist staff to share information with mainstream staff who are left to guess about the status of some service users. This can result in confidentiality lapsing into secrecy and even to the non-keeping of records, when this is requested by the service user; in turn this could in some circumstances work against the best interests of the user (SSI 1994e,pp.59–64). It has been suggested that what is required is a middle ground on which carers, both paid and unpaid, know enough about day-to-day issues to enable them to carry out their responsibilities (SSI 1997j,p.21).

CHAPTER 18

LOCAL OMBUDSMAN INVESTIGATIONS: DIGEST OF CASES

The functions of the local ombudsman have been explained previously (p.438). The following represent a selection of cases in summary, all of which are referred to at some point in the main text of this book.

(N.B. the provisions of the Local Government and Housing Act 1989, insofar as they covered disabled facilities grants, were superseded (with relatively minor changes only) in December 1996 by those within the Housing Grants, Construction and Regeneration Act 1996. The 1989 Act itself introduced disabled facilities grants and renovation grants, which replaced their predecessors, under the Housing Act 1985, namely improvement and intermediate grants – which themselves were previously found in the Housing Act 1974).

Avon County Council 1997 (95/B/5144). *Hospital discharge: delayed assessment*
Working as a roofer, a man fell 25 feet through a roof sustaining a number of injuries which left him paraplegic. Before discharge from hospital, the local authority responded quickly with home visits and discussion, but the occupational therapist then became ill and responsibility was not properly taken over.

Hospital discharge. The hospital gave the local authority one month's notice of discharge as well as carrying out its own community care assessment of the man's needs – which included bowel care, an alarm system and respite support for his wife. However, the local authority felt it had to make its own assessment; the ombudsman understood this but considered that the ten week delay in producing a draft community care assessment – given the information already to hand – amounted to maladministration.

Ramp to aviary. As well as requiring ramped access to the front entrance to the home, the man also requested a ramp access to his aviary – which would have had the effect of increasing the area in which he was mobile by 100 per cent. Having said that it would consider providing him with this ramp, the authority took five months to do the measurements and another two months to provide it. Although the authority's normal policy was to provide a ramp to one entrance of a dwelling only, the ombudsman considered that nevertheless, given the man's specific needs, this delay was maladministration.

Delay in overall care package. Overall, it took 16 months for a complete care package to be in place; this was 'an unreasonably long delay' and was also maladministration.

Complaints review panel. The man's wife had used the authority's complaints procedure; the review panel had pointed to shortcomings in the care plan, delay, and lack of communication between social workers and occupational therapists – and had recommended that procedures be reviewed. The authority wrote a letter of apology. She remained unsatisfied about the authority's response and so had gone to the ombudsman. By this time, the relationship between man and wife had broken down completely; he had entered residential care, following a request from his social worker – who had stated that he needed constant supervision due to memory loss, poor concentration, loss of balance and physical care needs. The ombudsman was pleased that the authority was now overhauling its community care procedures. However, he pointed out that it should use its complaints procedure to remedy injustice – and in cases such as this one, an apology was inadequate. He recommended payment of £2,750 to the wife.

Barking and Dagenham London Borough Council 1997 (94/A/4229). *Hospital discharge: delayed assessments*
A man had a severe stroke which resulted in some paralysis and immobility down his right side. In November 1993 he was discharged from hospital. Next October he was readmitted and had his right leg amputated. He and his wife complained about the delay by the local authority in providing bathroom and toilet aids from October 1993 and a lift from the following November 1994.

First hospital assessment and care plan. On discharge in November 1993, a hospital occupational therapist had carried out a home assessment and provided (from the social services store) chair raisers, raised toilet seat and bath board (which she fitted). She recommended also that social services provide a free-standing toilet frame and bath seat. A week after he was discharged, a social services care manager carried out an assessment, drew up a care plan which was given to, and signed by, man and wife. This delay of one week was not unreasonable, especially since the authority had not been informed in advance.

Delay in first occupational therapy assessment. The care manager also asked for an occupational therapist to visit to advise about grab rails to assist with transfers between bath and toilet. Because of a backlog for 'medium priority' cases, this would take four months. The wife found that bathing became a 'nightmare'; she could not lift her husband in and out of the bath and his confidence and dignity were damaged. Consequently, without telling the council, at a cost of over £3,500, they had the bath removed and replaced by a shower, and had a grab rail installed. The failure to supply the grab rails and free-standing toilet frame amounted to maladministration, as did the failure to carry out the recommended occupational therapy assessment; but the ombudsman did not hold the council liable for the cost of the shower because the couple had acted without consulting the council only two months after the care manager had requested an occupational therapy assessment.

Second hospital assessment. Following amputation of the leg, a second home assessment was carried out by a hospital occupational therapist at the end of October 1994. She identified the need for a stairlift, front and rear ramps and a chemical commode. The wife was loath to have her husband come home to what she considered an unsuitable environment, but agreed because a) her husband was becoming depressed in hospital, and b) she assumed that aids and adaptations would be supplied quickly.

Delay and flaw in second occupational therapy assessment. The local authority blamed the hospital for discharging the man before a full package of care had been agreed – even though it conceded that major works cannot generally be undertaken before discharge has taken place. The occupational therapy team manager carried out a reassessment of the case in November 1994 and awarded it high priority; in February 1995, a multi-agency community care assessment was carried out by an independent occupational therapist under contract to the council. However, the man was confined to his upstairs bedroom, so that the therapist was unable to observe transfers to toilet and shower (which were downstairs). Consequently, the therapist's report was flawed; she recommended only that a curved stairlift be provided, described the shower wrongly as 'walk-in' (it had a lip) and did not record those activities which she had been unable to observe. The ombudsman found that although the three-month delay in this February assessment was not maladministration, the assessment itself was incomplete and a reassessment should have been carried out after the installation of the lift.

Recommendations. In summary, the ombudsman recommended that a further community care assessment be carried out, a payment of £500 for distress and inconvenience, and consideration by the council of establishing targets, monitoring and remedial action in relation to occupational therapy assessments.

Barking and Dagenham London Borough Council 1998 (97/A/0337). *Delay in assessment for home adaptations; Chronically Sick and Disabled Persons Act 1970,s.2*

The complainant claimed that the council had delayed unreasonably in meeting the need for home adaptations and day care for her husband who was disabled. They lived in a council house with bedrooms, bathroom and WC upstairs. The husband had chronic arthritis and Steele Richardson Syndrome, a progressive form of Parkinson's disease.

Priority allocation and date given to application. In September 1993, they requested a ground-floor toilet, so that he could remain downstairs permanently. A care worker visited, noted that he did not want a commode and warned that there might be a delay of six to eight weeks in assessment. The husband was classified as medium priority, despite having had several falls, slipped in the bath and trouble getting up the stairs. In September 1994, he was given high priority (but was probably given a new date – ie, September 1994, rather than October 1993 – which meant he went to the end of the high priority waiting list). Both the failure initially to allocate a high priority, and then to stick to the original date of application (after the priority had been raised) was maladministration. Had this not occurred, the need for adaptations would probably have been considered before a huge influx of work in May 1995.

Assessment and further delay because of workload. By March 1995 the man had fallen backwards down the stairs on several occasions – at which point his wife visited the council office. In May 1995, he was assessed by an occupational therapist from an external agency used by the council to clear the backlog of cases. Adaptations were recommended but a survey of the property did not take place until June 1996; though this was distressing, the ombudsman accepted on balance that this was because of a huge increase in workload rather than maladministration. However, in October 1995 when an extension was first mentioned, no check was made by social services with the housing department to see whether the house was on its list for future adaptations; referral did not take place until February 1997. This was maladministration.

Failure to record meeting. There was then a conflict of evidence about what took place at a meeting in September 1996. The council maintained that the couple were asked to consider moving into housing association accommodation, but that they had refused. The couple denied that this option was ever mentioned. However, the council did not write to the couple after the meeting to give them a record of what had occurred and an outline of the options. This was maladministration. The ombudsman stated that had they received a clear explanation, they would have accepted the housing association option immediately, as they did in fact at a later date in February 1997. At the meeting, the council officers had explained that neither social services nor the housing department had the money to carry out the adaptations.

The ombudsman concluded that the principal injustice lay in the prioritising of the occupational therapy assessment; absent this, and it was likely that the shower and toilet would have been installed before the husband's condition had deteriorated. The ombudsman accepted that by July 1996, this deterioration meant that the council considered that conversion of a cupboard downstairs was no longer a suitable option – but this did not remove the injustice, since the husband had been denied a downstairs toilet and shower for several years. This had caused 'a great deal of distress, worry and inconvenience. The demands made on [the wife] have been enormous and I can only guess at the embarrassment and frustration' of the husband. (For example, by 1996, the wife was usually alone with her husband all day, having to get him up, dress him, and help him on the stairs. His prostate problems meant that she needed to help him up and down more often – and when he fell, he often pulled her down with him).

Recommendations. The ombudsman recommended that £3,000 compensation be paid in recognition of the suffering caused, and an apology be given to the son-in-law to whom the council had not explained its complaints procedure in terms of how to make a formal complaint.

Barnsley Metropolitan Borough Council 1998a (97/C/0433). *Inadequate assessment for adaptations; failure to inform of disabled facilities grant; Chronically Sick and Disabled Persons Act 1970,s.2.*

The complainant was born with cerebral palsy, was partially paralysed and so had impaired mobility; he had more recently developed serious bowel problems, resulting sometimes in incontinence. He lived with his adult son and wife. His previous home had been adapted by the council, but he then moved because it did not have a toilet on the ground floor; this need had become increasingly pressing. His move was against the advice of the housing department, and he and his wife had signed a statement acknowledging that they were moving into a property in some ways unsuitable and which was unlikely to be adapted by the council's housing department.

Request for shower; interim provision of bath aid; rehousing option. Having moved, the man requested a shower to replace the bath upstairs and an additional handrail on the stairs. Following assessment, a 'panel meeting' was held and the shower request was refused – although the need for a ground-floor shower was acknowledged as well as a handrail. Some weeks later, an officer visited and decided that the shower was after all impractical; another panel meeting then recommended that the family move to more suitable accommodation. In the meantime, a bath aid was provided; this was viewed as meeting his immediate needs, whilst rehousing would be the longer term solution. However, the man could not get up the stairs. He complained a few months later about this decision to rehouse him instead of to carry out adaptations.

As to the possibility of a stairlift, a council officer stated that it was not necessarily good use of resources, since alone it rarely solved all the problems and other adaptations would often be required; thus rehousing would be cheaper. Yet the council conceded that had the man applied for a disabled facilities grant, adaptations rather than rehousing would have been the primary consideration; however, it did not tell him of his right to apply for such a grant.

Inadequate assessment. The ombudsman found maladministration and injustice. The evidence pointed to an inadequate assessment, since no medical evidence had been requested, neither the incontinence nor mobility problems on the stairs had been documented, and no long term prognosis had been sought. Without such information, the ombudsman could not 'see that his needs can have been assessed adequately'.

Decision not workable. Furthermore, the panel's failure to ensure promptly that its decisions (ie, in respect of the shower) were workable was also maladministration, resulting in confusion, raised expectations and delay. Had its assessment been adequate 'it could reasonably have taken into account the needs of its disabled tenant and avoided any further duty under the Chronically Sick and Disabled Persons Act to provide adaptations by agreeing to offer alternative accommodation. I would, however, expect a proper consideration of meeting the costs of moving house'.

In addition, had an assessment of his needs for a disabled facilities grant been carried out, he might well have qualified for financial assistance (eg, in relation to access to the bedroom and to bathing facilities). The failure to tell him about his right to apply was maladministration, though the extent of the injustice done would depend on the outcome of a proper assessment.

Recommendations. The ombudsman recommended that a full assessment now be carried out – including consideration of whether the man's wish to remain in his current accommodation was justified (eg, in relation to caring and support network). He should also be given information about applying for a disabled facilities grant; and in any case, the council should pay £500 in respect of the delays, missed opportunity and the man's time and trouble in pursuing the complaint. The ombudsman was pleased that the council was reviewing its procedures.

Barnsley Metropolitan Borough Council 1998b (97/C/1096). *Inadequate assessment; home adaptations (toilet and shower); failure to inform of disabled facilities grant; Chronically Sick and Disabled Persons Act 1970,s.2*

The complainant lived with her adult daughter in a three-bedroom council house. She was born with deformed feet, used crutches and had rheumatoid- and osteo-arthritis which affected her hips and arms in particular. The drugs she took meant that she needed very frequent access to the toilet. She had a shower over her bath, but by early 1996 could no longer use this; she also had difficulties with the stairs. She washed either by visiting relatives who had a walk-in shower or by strip-washing in her bathroom. She requested a ground-floor toilet and that her bath be replaced by a walk-in shower.

Assessment. The social services officer who visited stated that the woman had explained that she had recently looked after a friend until she had died; he happened to know who this person had been, and his view was that if the woman was able to provide that sort of care, then she did not need a ground-floor toilet. He also recorded on the assessment form that the woman's daughter was not employed; this was incorrect. He noted the difficulty with the stairs and the problems of access to the toilet, bathroom and bedroom. However, he did not go into the bathroom, did not test the extent of the woman's bathing difficulties, did not comment on whether she needed help transferring in out of the bath/shower, did not record her arthritis or the effect of the drugs, and did not request any medical evidence. There was no mention of long-term prognosis. The officer stated that he used common sense when carrying out assessments and used as a yardstick his elderly relative who after three operations could still use the bath. The council commented that he had twelve years' experience of assessing disabled people.

Commode recommended. A panel meeting was then held. It concluded that her needs could be met by a commode and so refused the request for a downstairs toilet; it also refused the shower. The council explained that commodes were satisfactory where able-bodied people either lived with the disabled person or were frequent visitors – because they could empty and clean the commode bucket. The woman complained. Another officer visited; he suggested that the woman try a bath board, but she could not use it because she could not get her legs over the side of the bath. He concluded that the long-term solution was a two-bedroom bungalow; in the meantime, a commode and strip washing would meet her needs. Further panel meetings confirmed this.

Rehousing option. A housing appeals sub-committee further considered the case, and decided that although it would be practicable to install a water closet downstairs, there was not enough space to provide a shower. This would mean eventual provision of a stairlift to get to the existing bathroom; rehousing therefore remained the sensible option. Throughout, the woman was not told of her right to apply for a disabled facilities grant, nor had a commode been loaned.

Subjective assessment. The ombudsman found maladministration and injustice. The initial assessment 'failed to go into sufficient detail, imported incorrect information and was carried out in an extremely subjective fashion without proper reference to medical evidence. There is no indication that the Council has any well-founded knowledge of the long term prognosis ... and yet a view has been taken that her condition will deteriorate'. Furthermore, if the assessment had been adequate, the council could have fulfilled its duty under the Chronically Sick and Disabled Persons Act by providing a commode (as an interim measure) and avoided further duties under that Act by offering alternative accommodation (though taking account of the costs of a move). But, had the woman been informed of her right to apply for a disabled facilities grant, the situation might have been different, and she might have received a grant for access to toilet and bathing facilities. This was a missed opportunity.

Recommendations. The ombudsman recommended that a full assessment now be carried out – including consideration of whether the woman's wish to remain in her current accommodation was justified (eg, in relation to caring and support network). She should also be given information about applying for a disabled facilities grant; in any case, the council should pay £500 in respect of the delays, missed opportunity and the woman's time and trouble in pursuing the complaint. The ombudsman was pleased that the council was reviewing its procedures.

Birmingham City Council 1993 (91/B/1262). *Loss of adoption file*
The failure in administrative arrangements for the transfer of adoption files (which resulted in loss of the complainant's person's file) and subsequent inadequate action and attempts to find the file, amounted to

maladministration. Compensation of £1,000 (and £200 for time and trouble on the complaint) was recommended.

Bolton Metropolitan Borough Council 1992 (92/C/0670). *Bathroom adaptation in housing association property; disabled facilities grants; Chronically Sick and Disabled Persons Act 1970, s.2*

A housing association tenant suffered from a mild form of spina bifida, weakness and wasting of the left leg and ankle, osteo-arthritis, chronic disc degeneration causing neck pain, and problems with balance. She could not use the upstairs bathroom; downstairs she had a wash basin, but the result was that she had not had a bath or shower for three years.

Delay in assessment. Having applied for a disabled facilities grant for a downstairs bathroom, it took about 10 months for an assessment to be carried out. When it finally was, and a recommendation made, the housing association replied that there would be no problem funding it (though eventually a stairlift was decided on). This rendered irrelevant the local authority housing department's strategy, in the face of shortage of resources, of asking social services to suspend visits and create a waiting list for assessments – so that hopes would not be raised, only for applicants to find payment delayed.

Low priority of bathing needs. In addition, the wait had been caused by the fact that social services regarded a need for bathing facilities as not a priority, since the lack of them was not 'life-threatening'. The average wait was a year; at the time 549 people were waiting, 111 of whom were priority cases.

Priority evaluation 'hit and miss'. However, the social services assessment officer involved conceded that priority assessments were 'hit and miss', since the application forms contained inadequate information on which to make informed decisions about priority.

Applicant seen out of turn. The particular applicant had been seen sooner because the assessment officer was spending so much time dealing with the woman's enquiries, that an assessment visit, made out of turn, would save time.

Conclusion and recommendations. The ombudsman concluded that waits of a year for assessment amounted to maladministration and could not be justified by shortage of money, communication and administration problems. The woman had waited longer than was reasonable in order to bath or shower. Furthermore, the basis for evaluating priority was inadequate and also amounted to maladministration. She said the council needed to establish a proper method for determining priority, and should pay the woman £250 in respect of the delay and of her time and trouble in pursuing the complaint.

Brent London Borough Council 1994 (93/A/0523). *Provision of psychotherapy by social services*

The local authority had, from 1987, been making up the difference between the charges of a residential therapeutic community home and the DHSS (as it was then) funding available – for a woman with mental health needs. When the placement came to an end, the authority agreed to fund psycho-therapy sessions for the woman. The dispute arose around the authority's subsequent attempt to stop such funding, and its rather belated attempt to suggest that such provision was health, rather than social, care – and so was properly an NHS responsibility.

Proper review and assessment before withdrawal of service. The ombudsman concluded that whatever view the authority took in hindsight, it had obligations to the woman. Although it was entitled to reduce or stop the funding, it had to take into account the woman's needs as well, not focus solely on an overspent budget, and to make the 'promised assessment' of the benefit and value of the therapy. Had a proper review been carried out, the authority might have decided to stop the payments earlier than it did. However, the failure to carry out proper review and assessment meant that the authority made a sudden decision to withdraw without giving adequate notice.

Psycho-therapy: health or social care need. Once the director of social services had decided that these were health rather than social care needs, no approach was made to the health authority about alternative sources of funding.

Conclusion. All this was maladministration causing injustice. The ombudsman recommended that the council pay the woman a) the amount she owed to the psychotherapist for the sessions in 1993 which had not yet been paid for; b) travel expenses; and c) £1,250 for distress caused and for the time and trouble in pursuing the complaint with both ombudsman and council.

Bristol City Council 1998 *(96/B/4035 and 96/B/4143). Family with severely disabled son; severe needs; appalling catalogue of neglect*

The complainants were council tenants and the parents of a teenage boy who required twenty-four hour care. He had cerebral palsy, microcephaly, developmental delays, spastic quadriplegia, chest problems, was unable to walk or talk and used a wheelchair. His parents had always carried him up and down the stairs, but as he grew older, bigger and heavier this became increasingly difficult.

Fettering of discretion. In the light of this, the family's need for rehousing was 'severe and going to worsen' as the son got older; yet the council gave inadequate consideration to these exceptional needs when applying its policy of not arranging a move in case of rent arrears. This was a fettering of discretion and maladministration. In addition, the lumping together of rent and housing benefit when considering the amount of rent in arrears was unlawful under housing benefit legislation; therefore the council's failure to differentiate rent arrears from overpayment of housing benefit was maladministration.

Disabled facilities grants: no information given. The parents were told several times that the council did not have the money to fund adaptations but were not told about disabled facilities grants; in fact some of the council's officers were not even sure whether council tenants were entitled to such grants (which they clearly were); this was maladministration.

Appalling neglect. The ombudsman found that this amounted to an 'appalling catalogue of neglect by the Council. It seems to me to have disregarded its obligations to this family trying to cope with the needs of one of its members who is suffering from severe disability. To whom should such a family turn if not to the Council, especially when, as in this case, the Council is also its landlord? Yet at every approach the family has been spurned. They have been the victim of a too-rigid adherence to policy; they have suffered from poor communication between social services and housing officers which has meant that those officers who were attempting to help were rendered helpless by other officers presumably responding to their own priorities; they have been told that a lack of resources has meant they cannot be helped with aids and adaptations yet officers have failed to point them in the direction of other resources within the Council's control'.

Recommendations. This was 'very substantial' injustice; the ombudsman did not conclude that the father's heart attack 'derived specifically' from the council's maladministration, 'but the toll on [the family's] health and well-being must have been enormous'. He recommended that the council apologise, make an ex gratia payment of £20,000 (but in such a way that benefit entitlement was not affected), review its arrangements for dealing with the housing needs of disabled people, and ensure that its housing officers were adequately trained.

Buckinghamshire County Council 1992 (90/B/1340). *Advice; support; social work service for people in nursing homes*

A case concerning support by social services for a nursing home resident (before April 1993 and thus before social services departments had assumed responsibility for arranging and funding nursing home care). The complainant was the only child of a man in his seventies who had suffered a stroke and whose mental state was deteriorating. He had abused her as a child and been violent towards her mother – but she still wished to ensure that he was in a nursing home near her, so that she could ensure that he received satisfactory care.

Contact with succession of duty social workers. Initially she contacted a duty social worker who suggested she contact a few private nursing homes. She did so, on the understanding that her father would receive income support, although she was still concerned about a potential shortfall once her father's savings had been used up. She contacted a second duty social worker, worried about the delay in the income support claim, the fees, a missing pension book and the staff at the home. A third social worker contacted the Department of Social Security (DSS) and gave the woman the telephone numbers of charities – so she could get advice about an increase in income support. However, she did not mention to the woman the existence of the 'terminal illness limit' payable by the DSS. A fourth duty social worker suggested the woman contact SSAFA (ex-service-men's charity) for financial help (which was not forthcoming) and her father's general practitioner in case the health authority had a place in a long-stay hospital (also not forthcoming). However, no arrangement was made for social services to follow up the father's case. Again terminal illness limit had not been mentioned.

A fifth duty social worker advised that the woman should contact the DSS and the matron of the nursing home. The woman felt she was being shunted from pillar to post; she now wrote to the nursing home terminating any contractual agreement – and wrote to the DSS and the council, saying she was leaving her father in their hands, because he had no more funds. Age Concern advised that the nursing home might turn her father out and send him home to her by taxi; in which case, she should refuse to accept him and send the taxi to the local hospital instead. Neither the council nor the DSS replied. The health authority said there were no hospital beds available. The case was finally allocated to a social worker for elderly people – who initially had not wanted to deal with the case because the father was in a nursing (as opposed to a residential) home. Further confusion arose over the issue of appointeeship in relation to the DSS benefits.

Social work service for nursing home residents. The ombudsman found maladministration: 'councils have the responsibility to ensure that suitable care is provided for elderly people who need it. If they do not provide it themselves they should provide an efficient service in finding suitable accommodation and establishing that sufficient funding is available to pay for it … impression given by the Council officers throughout their dealings with the complainant that the Council wished to shift the responsibility to another organisation … The Council in offering a social work service should ensure that this is readily available to all those living in their area. They should not discriminate against residents of private nursing homes … The Council ought to have checked with DSS what level of benefit [the father] was receiving and then advised the complainant correctly … The Council gave the complainant incorrect information'. (The ombudsman did not refer to it, but a social work service would be provided under s.29 of the National Assistance Act 1948: see p.193 of this book).

Recommendations. The ombudsman concluded that the council should review its procedures and ensure that 'those responsible for dealing with such enquiries should receive regular training in benefits available to the elderly, and related matters such as appointeeship'.

Buckinghamshire County Council 1998 (97/B/0876). *Holidays; arrangements; s.2 of the Chronically Sick and Disabled Persons Act 1970*
A local authority was assisting an older woman with learning disabilities to take a holiday under s.2 of the Chronically Sick and Disabled Persons Act 1970. She arrived at the hotel, but such serious problems arose in relation to her behaviour that the hotel owners drove her home again that same evening (a distance of 115 miles). The council complained to the local tourist information centre and the English Tourist Board, and wanted the money for the holiday refunded by the hotel both to itself and to the woman. However, the hotel owners consulted a solicitor and themselves demanded an apology and compensation.

The council knew from a recent previous holiday that the woman required a more specialised caring environment than previously and so should have given 'careful consideration' to this holiday. Instead, the ombudsman concluded – from the 'total absence' of records about how a hotel was identified and about the taking up of references – that the 'proper degree of care' in arranging the holiday had not been exercised. The hotel owners had not been given the 'full and accurate information' about the needs of the woman to which they had been entitled. This was all maladministration, as was the precipitate complaint to the tourist organisations before the hotel owners had had the opportunity to put their case. The hotel owners had kept the holiday money which covered their transport costs and some of the solicitor's fee; in addition, the ombudsman recommended that the council pay £250 to them for their anxiety, sense of grievance, and time and trouble in pursuing the complaint.

Camden London Borough Council 1993 (91/A/1481). *Assessment and provision of stairlift; delay; Chronically Sick and Disabled Persons Act 1970,s.2*

A woman who was a council tenant requested a special chair. An occupational therapist visited in March 1990 to assess for this request and for other potential needs. The woman walked with Fischer sticks, had limited knee movement and very limited strength and movement in her hands. The living room and kitchen were on the first floor – and on the second were the bedroom, bathroom and WC. The occupational therapist suggested the installation of a stairlift between the first and second floors.

Long delay between assessment and placing of order. The occupational therapist first approached the housing department in April 1990. A joint visit which should have been made within seven days was not made for six weeks. The specification required by the procedure was never supplied; and an order which should have been placed within 14 days took 22 months – even though the installation was not complex and required only removal of a radiator and confirmation that the bannisters did not need altering. Adaptations for disabled council tenants had been paid for out of the repairs budget; in October 1991, the council imposed a moratorium on expenditure because the financial position was worse than had been anticipated. Thus ordering of the lift was put off and contributed to the overall delay.

Star and Starlet chambers. In this financial difficulty, decisions on whether works could be approved were taken by a central 'Star Chamber' (for works over £10,000) or by a 'Starlet Chamber' at district level (under £10,000).

Ineffective liaison, missing records, insufficient resources. There was no effective liaison between departments, crucial records were missing and the council could not explain the delays. Under s.2 of the Chronically Sick and Disabled Persons Act 1970, insufficient resources were no justification for delay. Indeed, once 'the Council became aware of their financial position they should have instituted procedures to ensure that adaptation works were prioritised on a boroughwide basis. Instead it appears that whether a need was met depended on competing demands on the local repairs budget for a particular week. I cannot therefore be certain that people with similar needs were dealt with in a similar way'. The overall wait was nearly two years between the assessment visit and placing of the order, during which time the woman's condition worsened.

Worsening condition of woman during wait. The woman took water tablets to reduce swelling, but this meant that she had to go to the WC several times a day. Her hand and elbow suffered from gripping the stair rail. Her knees got worse. Her husband had to push her up the stairs from behind. She had to go down the stairs backwards, stop halfway up, and stay upstairs once there because it was too painful to come down. She took a lot of pain killers and wore hand splints to protect her joints (which the occupational therapist explained would not recover their function once lost). She got depressed about all of this.

Staff's unfamiliarity with procedures and inconsistent adoption. It also became apparent that some key staff had never been aware of the council's written procedures for adaptations, and that the procedures were not adopted uniformly by different housing area teams.

Conclusions and recommendations. The delays, non-following of procedure, ignorance about procedures, lack of liaison, missing records – all amounted to maladministration. The ombudsman recommended that the council pay £1,000 to the couple and review procedures, so that in future it could act on a corporate basis and ensure that priority would be dealt with on a boroughwide basis, rather than be dependent on state of the local repairs budget in any particular week.

Castle Morpeth Borough Council 1998 (97/C/4412). *Resident of home; responsibility for arranging and paying for funeral*

The manager of a nursing and residential home complained that the council unreasonably refused to pay the funeral expenses of people within its area who died without means – and specifically it had refused to do this for a particular resident who died at the home after 57 years in hospital and residential care, and had no relations and very little money.

Notwithstanding its apparent duty under s.46 of the Public Health (Control of Diseases) Act 1984, the council maintained that private care homes should take responsibility for funerals if there was nobody else to do it. It further referred to a duty it supposed fell on the home under the Environmental Protection Act 1990 (s.33), which deals with the disposal of 'controlled waste'; it stated that 'from a commercial viewpoint residents of a home are its income-producing raw material. Ergo, from a purely commercial point of view, deceased residents may then be regarded as being the waste produced by their business'.

The ombudsman believed the council had misunderstood both pieces of legislation and that it was 'far-fetched, not to say insulting, to regard deceased residents as a waste by-product of a business'. The refusal to accept responsibility for the funeral was maladministration; the ombudsman recommended that the home owner be reimbursed the cost of the funeral and be paid an additional £250 for her time and trouble in bringing the complaint.

Cleveland County Council 1993 (92/C/1042). *Death of woman with learning disabilities in residential unit; care plan; complaints procedure*

The case concerned a woman in her thirties who, the coroner found, died accidentally by drowning (perhaps following an epileptic fit or cardiac arrhythmia) in the bath at a six-person residential care unit run by the council.

Lack of formal decisions about abilities. The woman had an 'Individual Programme Plan', but the ombudsman criticised the fact that it still contained an objective about learning certain skills – despite the fact that the officer with responsibility for the 'Goal Plan', designed to achieve such an objective, said that the woman was not capable of learning those skills. The absence of a formal decision to relax the requirement about these skills was maladministration. More specifically: 'No formal decision was ever taken that Anne had reached a stage where she could safely be left to bath alone. I can understand staff's concern to maximise her privacy and independence. Such concerns needed to be balanced against the needs of safety. It may be that, had a proper assessment been made, a decision could have been properly reached that Anne was able to bath alone but this is not what had happened and no such decision was conveyed to [the parents]'.

This, together with a temporarily reduced staffing level, was maladministration, although the ombudsman – in line with the findings of the coroner – did not conclude that it had resulted in the woman's death. However, the staffing level was a factor which delayed discovery of what had happened.

Complaints procedure. The parents also complained about the way in which the complaints procedure had operated. The review panel had considered a report produced by an officer, but the report was deficient in relevant information (about the Goal Plan). The review panel recorded that the coroner had stated that death did not result from lack of care; the ombudsman saw no such statement in the coroner's report. A number of officers from the council's legal department were present at the review panel meeting; the ombudsman could not see how a solicitor employed by the council could be present as an 'unbiased observer' and found that 'the way he joined at the outset in the in camera deliberations of the Panel to be unwise at the very least'. This, too, was maladministration.

Conclusion and recommendations. The ombudsman concluded that there was maladministration in the way in which the woman was cared for, but that this did not cause death; and also in the operation of the complaints procedure. The injustice suffered by the parents would be resolved by a review by the council of its procedures (to prevent a similar occurrence), and a payment to the parents for their extra distress caused by the maladministration – and for their time and trouble in making the complaint.

Clwyd County Council 1997 (now Conwy County Borough Council: 97/0177 and 97/0755). *After-care services; Mental Health Act 1983,s.117; whether accommodation can be charged for*

A woman was originally detained in hospital under s.2 of the Mental Health Act 1983. She was then discharged home with after-care services under s.117 of the 1983 Act – for which, under s.17 of the Health and Social Services and Social Security Adjudications Act 1983, there was no power to charge.

Transition from s.117 after-care services to ordinary services. The care arrangements broke down and she was readmitted to another hospital, before being placed in a residential care home for elderly people. The placement was 'disastrous' and lasted one night only, after which she was readmitted to the second hospital. She was then placed in a care home for elderly people with mental health problems. The council charged her for this accommodation, although it subsequently conceded that up to the end of February 1996, it should not have done so – because the accommodation was being provided under s.117. However, the council continued to maintain that after that date (February 1996) the accommodation was no longer being provided under s.117 but under s.21 of the National Assistance Act 1948 – in which case it could be charged for. A decision was made by the local authority to register a caution against the woman's property in respect of the money owing.

Asking irrelevant questions: maladministration. The council argued that, because by that date she had settled in the home and there was no possibility of her returning to her own home, she no longer needed monitoring under s.117. In which case, s.21 applied, since she could be regarded as being in normal residential care. The ombudsman found these to be immaterial considerations; not only did the woman remain during this time in the specialist home for elderly, mentally infirm people, but the council itself assessed her in early 1997 as being extremely paranoid, hallucinating and having worsening dementia. The council also conceded that its original contention, that the decision to cease s.117 services was a medical decision alone, was misguided – since the s.117 duty is imposed jointly on the health authority and the local authority. It had therefore to come to its own decision in its capacity as a social services authority – something which it had failed to do.

Thus, if 'the two local authorities had asked themselves the relevant question, they would have had to conclude that she was in need of specialist care provided at a home for the elderly mentally infirm rather than accommodation at a residential home'. The failure to do this was maladministration; as was the failure to deal with the daughter's persistent complaints, to consult with the daughter about the discharge under s.117 (as should have happened under the code of practice on the 1983 Act: DH,WO 1983,p.108), to inform her about the charge on the property, and to reply promptly and fully to correspondence.

Recommendations. The ombudsman recommended a) that the council confirm that it was continuing to provide for the woman after-care services under s.117; b) that it would continue to do so until it was satisfied that it was no longer necessary; c) that it would consult the daughter and seek her views before deciding to discontinue s.117 services; d) that it should confirm that it would not seek to recover the charges so far made; and e) that it should pay the daughter's solicitor's costs and a further £500 for distress and inconvenience.

Cornwall County Council 1996 (95/B/0166). *Exclusion of person from day centre for people with mental health needs; procedures; handling of complaint*

The case concerned the exclusion of a person from a day centre, following disputes between her and other attenders about the way the centre was run. (At monthly meetings, increasingly more decisions were being taken by users of the centre – one of the complainant's objections concerned this development).

The ombudsman stated that if people were excluded from a service on which they rely, then 'natural justice' required that they be told promptly a) why, b) the duration of the exclusion, c) what action was planned to facilitate re-entry, d) who would decide about re-entry, and e) how to appeal. Yet none of these requirements was fulfilled.

Managers had not been given clear guidance on how to manage or record difficult events – foreseeable at such centres – and this was maladministration. Also maladministration was the focus on the complainant's background and history in the investigation report produced in response to her complaint, because the 'purpose of a complaint is, first and foremost, to scrutinise the actions of the Council'.

Cumbria County Council 1992 (90/C/2438). *Estimate of time an adaptation would take*
The complainant was a woman who lived with her daughter who suffered from muscular dystrophy. Adaptations – to be funded by the district council with a contribution from the county council – would extend the cottage at the rear, convert the mother's studio into a study-bedroom and bathroom for her daughter, and include a new studio to be built in the back garden.

The adaptations took some nine months longer than the estimate given by the council. The woman complained that as a result her daughter's needs were not met and her own work had been set back several months. The delay had been caused by ground conditions and drainage, problems with the neighbour, alterations to the proposals and failings of the building contractor.

The ombudsman found that the time estimate given by the council certainly turned out to be over-optimistic – but was not so unrealistic as to amount to maladministration. She did not blame the council for failing to predict the problems with the foundations and drainage; the mother and daughter themselves introduced amendments as the work progressed; and terminating the contract of the contractor might have only caused yet more delay. The complaint was not upheld.

Cumbria County Council 1993 (91/C/2345). *Change of home adaptations grant system: consequences of failure to submit full and complete application*
The case concerned an application for a home adaptation by a disabled person – caught in the transition between the old improvement grant system under the Housing Act 1985 and the disabled facilities grant system introduced by the Local Government and Housing Act 1989.

In order to qualify for a grant under the old system (under which the applicant would have had to make over £1,000 less in contribution), a full and complete application had to be submitted by a certain date. In fact, the application was lacking the application form itself, the certificate of owner occupation, the certificate of interest in land, and approval under the Building Regulations. Furthermore, the work shown on the drawings differed from that which had previously been agreed in principle.

The ombudsman decided that the occupational therapist's advice might not have made 'absolutely clear' that the full and complete application had to be submitted by a certain date. However, she was not prepared to find maladministration, because the occupational therapist had 'provided correct advice earlier and had urged action ... because of the deadline. [The applicant] herself cannot escape significant responsibility for not realising the position.'

Cyngor Dosbarth Dwyfor 1994 (93/465 in: *Local Government Review Reports,* 18 March 1995,pp.207–220). *Breach of statutory duty in respect of a renovation grant*
An investigation about approval of a mandatory renovation grant under the Local Government and Housing Act 1989.

Breach of duty and resources. The local authority conceded that it had breached its statutory duty by failing to process applications within six months, as stipulated by the legislation. Instead, processing only took place when the finance was in place to meet the commitment resulting from approval of an application. The ombudsman concluded that failure to comply with the legislation in such circumstances – ie, lack of funding – did not constitute maladministration.

Giving information about local firms. However, the 'informal and casual' way in which the council gave the applicants the names of three firms of surveyors – and then contacted those firms about the applicants' grant enquiry – was 'unsatisfactory and vulnerable to abuse'. This was maladministration, since: 'It is a matter for the council whether it gives grant inquirers information and advice on the availability of professional help from local firms, but if it does so, such advice should be in writing, and a comprehensive list of firms should be provided so that the choice of firm is clearly a matter for the inquirer, and he is left in no doubt that he is free to choose any firm he wishes to appoint'.

Devon County Council 1996 (94/B/2128). *Poor advice and information from social services about entitlement to social security benefits*

A woman gave up work to look after her mother who was terminally ill. She complained that the council delayed in submitting a claim for attendance allowance on her behalf and in making an appeal about backdating. It transpired that the specialist social worker involved was unaware that entitlement to the allowance ran from the date the claim was received, that it could not be backdated and that appeals for a review of a decision had to be made within three months.

This prompted the ombudsman to find that: 'I can understand the difficulties faced by social workers trying to ensure that clients claim the benefits to which they are entitled. But the Council should either provide adequate training to enable social workers properly to advise clients about the benefits system ... or it should instruct its social workers to advise their clients that they can obtain assistance ... from [Benefits] Agency offices, from the Citizens Advice Bureaux or other voluntary agencies. The Council says that social workers assist in making benefit claims only as a complementary service to other help they provide for their clients. I believe the Council should provide clear guidelines to their social workers on the extent of the assistance they are expected to provide...'.

Recommendations. Finding maladministration and injustice in relation to the delay in submission of the claim for the allowance, the ombudsman recommended an ex gratia payment of £583 representing a two-month period of loss – and £250 for the time and trouble of pursuing the complaint.

(The ombudsman made no reference to social services legislation but, assuming that the mother was disabled, the giving of information could come under the duty contained in s.1 of the Chronically Sick and Disabled Persons Act 1970 or the duty to provide advice and support under s.29 of the National Assistance Act 1948).

Dinefwr Borough Council 1995 (94/0772 in: *Local Government Review Reports,* 20 April 1996, pp.312–320). *Renovation grants: status of enquiries and breach of duty*

Faced with a demand for grants (under the Local Government and Housing Act 1989) which far outstripped available finance, the local ombudsman analysed the reactions of the local authority.

Delay: breach of duty. First, he found that it had not complied with the six-month limit for determining an application – and that this breach had been compounded by the failure for over three-and-a-half years to assess whether the home was unfit and would qualify for grant aid.

No record of adoption of policy. Second, the authority could not produce a record of the formal adoption of its 'date-order policy' – nor of a policy allowing the suspension of assessment visits. This compounded the maladministration.

Publication of criteria for priority. Third, once criteria of need for prioritising enquiries had been adopted, they should have been published and enquirers told about them. Failure to do so was maladministration, since knowledge of them was essential if enquirers were to furnish relevant information in support of their applications.

Information about difference between enquiry and full application. Fourth, enquirers should be told of the difference between an enquiry and a full application (the latter of which triggered the statutory six-month duty).

Statutory reports on breach of duty and options. Lastly, if the council could not fulfil its statutory duty because of lack of resources, the chief finance officer and monitoring officer should have considered whether to submit statutory reports to the council on the position and outline possible options.

Doncaster Metropolitan Borough Council 1997 (95/C/4390). *Move from one residential care home to another: lack of reassessment; National Assistance Act 1948,s.21*

The case concerned a woman with dementia and a family dispute amongst her three children. Unhappy with the care their mother was receiving at a home within the Doncaster area, the brother and one sister suggested their mother move down to a residential home in the south-west of England. The other sister objected, but the council agreed to fund the placement.

Change of placement without reassessment. The following year, the other sister contacted the council and alleged that her sister was not visiting frequently and that her mother was unhappy. The council agreed to arrange for the mother's return to a council-owned home in Doncaster. It was maladministration to take this decision without the reassessment which was 'clearly desirable and mandated by the Council's own policy' – and without at least some attempt at verifying the sister's claims. The sister collected her mother from the home in the south-west without explaining her intention of removing her permanently, but the council did not inform the brother and other sister. This was maladministration also.

(The council's policy had stated that a) residents had a right to ask for a move to another home, and that the officer in charge of the home should ask the appropriate care manager for a reassessment; b) similarly if a resident was considered to be inappropriately placed, the care manager should be asked for a reassessment; and c) the care manager would ensure that the appropriate level of reassessment took place and that the care plan was adjusted accordingly).

Recommendations. The ombudsman recommended that the brother and sister receive £100 each for stress, time and trouble.

Dorset County Council 1996 (94/B/0821). *Man with mental health needs, residential care; powers of attorney; complaint; National Assistance Act 1948,s.21; NHS and Community Care Act 1990,s.47; CI(92)34*

A complicated case about the care received by a man with schizophrenia, an under-active thyroid gland and an alcohol problem. As a consequence of not taking his thyroid medication, he suffered a stroke and was left dysphasic, thus limiting his speech, reading and writing ability. He could sign his own name and apparently understand what was said to him. He had lived with his parents; before they had died, his sister living close by had cared for her parents and her brother on a daily basis. He then went into a residential home run by the council. The sister complained about the way in which council officers had dealt with her brother. The ombudsman summed up as follows.

Keeping the carer informed. The council did not keep the sister, as main carer, informed of the arrangements for her brother's care – for instance, that his medication was running out, the changing of his general practitioner, handling and use of money (for which the council could not produce records showing what arrangements had been in place), about benefits payable by the Department of Social Security (DSS), and the granting of an enduring power of attorney (EPOA) to a solicitor. The reason for this was apparently that staff believed that the sister did not have her brother's interests at heart – yet the ombudsman saw no evidence supporting this view. As a result of this maladministration, the brother signed the EPOA and incurred legal expenses (initially £1,591.88, on the basis of £100 per hour and £10.50 per letter or telephone conversation) as a result.

Enduring power of attorney and solicitor's costs. In addition, the council failed to assess how the solicitor's costs would be met by the brother and should not have given the solicitor unaccompanied access him. The ombudsman was particularly concerned that a meeting (about EPOA) arranged by council officers, the brother and the solicitor at the residential home went on so long, that the brother missed an appointment with his general practitioner. This was despite the fact that the brother was feeling down and had contemplated self-harm. There were also failures in record-keeping (eg, no care plan drawn up on entry to the residential home, no record of the meeting with the sister when she complained about the handling of her brother's affairs, non-recording of 'off-the-record' comment by the solicitor – which he denied ever having made – that he would not act for the sister in respect of the EPOA). There was also a failure to let the sister know about DSS grant assistance (for decorating the brother's home) at the relevant time.

Complaints procedure. A thorough investigation – praised by the ombudsman – was carried out. The review panel then recommended a further apology, the payment of £500 and meeting of the legal costs incurred by the brother. The council's complaints officer queried with the director of social services whether the £500 would be adequate, and warned that the sister was likely to go back to the ombudsman. In the event, the council paid the £500, but not the legal costs. The ombudsman criticised the council for its handling of the informal and formal stages of the complaint and then for unreasonably not following the review panel's recommendations.

Recommendations. The ombudsman recommended that, in addition to the £500, the council pay £1,440 to cover the solicitor's bill, £60 to cover the 'taxing' by the court of the same bill, £1,200 to cover the amount that probably would have been available by way of DSS grant for cleaning and decoration, and £300 additional compensation. It should also carry out a thorough review of its procedures. The council complied, and the ombudsman discontinued the investigation.

Durham County Council 1998 (96/C/4083). *Registered carers; breaking down of placement; handling of complaint; Local Authority Social Services Act 1970,s.7B; Children Act 1989,s.26; non-statutory complaints procedure*
The complainants, man and wife, were registered carers on the council's family placement scheme, which aimed to match carers with people leaving institutional care or whose family could not longer care for them. The investigation concerned the placement, in succession, of three women with learning disabilities. The complaint particularly centred around the termination by the council of the third placement – because of doubts about the suitability of the complainants.

Termination of placement: flawed grounds. The ombudsman found as follows, severely criticising the council. The termination took place following discussion with community nurses who had furnished information which was factually incorrect and appeared to consist of gossip and hearsay. For instance, both of the first two women placed had had problems with incontinence prior to their placement – yet the complainants were blamed for it.

Furthermore, the council did not insist that the nurses put their concerns in writing and that these then be put to the complainants. Instead rumour was allowed to circulate. The relevant council officer should have reported her concerns to the family placement panel, instead of deciding herself that the complainants were suitable only as respite, rather than long-term, carers. The panel had approved them initially, and thus it was for the panel to decide otherwise. The ombudsman also criticised a line manager for not ensuring that a clash of personalities between two members of staff did not affect the public.

Complaints procedure. The council's statutory complaints procedures (children or adults) did not cover the family placement scheme. The ombudsman said that the handling of the complaint by the council was 'nothing short of scandalous. Officer G does not appear to have had even a passing acquaintance with the Council's Representation Procedure. That he asked Officer F to carry out the initial investigation, knowing the views Officers B and F held about each other, beggars belief. The report prepared by Officer F was highly critical of Officer B who was given no opportunity to put her side of events. The report cannot consequently be held to be fair and balanced. No system to follow up the complaint was in place. It is hardly surprising that [the complainants] felt they were being deliberately excluded … To leave the complaint until Officers B and F had left the Council is shocking. Even after they had left, nothing was done until [the complainants] complained to me'.

Recommendations. The ombudsman recommended a payment of £2,000 in compensation, improvement of the council's systems for assessment and support of carers, and the putting in place of proper systems for dealing with those complaints which did not fall within the scope of the statutory complaints procedures.

Durham City Council 1993 *(and Durham County Council: 92/C/2753 and 92/C/2754). Stairlift; 'sorry tale' of confusion between councils; closure of case; unawareness of legal rights of council tenants; Chronically Sick and Disabled Persons Act 1970, s.2; disabled facilities grants*

A couple applied for adaptations to their council home, in particular for a stairlift. The husband had arthritis and was registered disabled. The wife had restricted mobility and following a hospital stay was confined to her bedroom; she could only get down the stairs in a sitting position.

Initial assessment and recommendation. A request for assistance was first made in March 1990 when the wife was due to come home from hospital. A full assessment was carried out by two county council officers within a week. At the end of an April an occupational therapy assistant visited and recommended that an occupational therapist visit to assess for a stairlift. In July, the occupational therapist visited and recommended that the county council ask the city council to install a stairlift. The occupational therapist's report wrongly recorded the stairs as straight (this was maladministration). The recommendation for an adaptation was approved by a senior occupational therapist, information obtained from the wife's doctor, and a letter of recommendation sent to the city council in September.

Closure of the case with no follow-up. At this point, the county council closed the case, since it was not normal practice to follow up recommendations – although this was contrary to its official procedure, which stated that a follow-up visit should be made when adaptations were completed. The council's procedure stated that clients should always be advised of what recommendations had been made; this did not happen until a year later (October 1991). Both of these omissions were maladministration. The ombudsman was also concerned that the county council appeared to have no system for responding when the city council decides not to act on a recommendation. (The ombudsman was presumably thinking of a possible 'continuing duty' on the council under s.2 of the Chronically Sick and Disabled Persons Act 1970: see p.410 of this book).

City council's inaction and refusal to proceed. Confusion followed in which it was unclear whether the work had been cancelled by the city council because of the high cost, and whether the couple would be rehoused instead (they had been on a waiting list since 1984 – an offer was now made but refused because of the wife's illness). The couple were not contacted either before or after the initial decision not to proceed by the city council; indeed at no stage did the city council write to them: this was maladministration (since had they known what was happening they could have done something about the inaction and confusion). When the application was revived in 1991, it was misfiled. The county council failed to respond to a request from the city council for further assessment information: this was maladministration.

Committee's decision flawed. Decisions continued to be deferred. In June 1992, the housing sub-committee of the district council was informed that rehousing had been refused and resolved to take no further action. However, it had not been made aware of the reason for the refusal and had no information from the county council about whether rehousing was appropriate to the wife's needs. Therefore, the committee was not in possession of all the relevant facts and failed to give proper consideration to the application: this was maladministration. The husband's niece asked the county council to reassess her uncle, informed the city council that he wished to appeal against the sub-committee's decision and advised her uncle and aunt to apply for a disabled facilities grant. (The city council was unsure whether council tenants could apply for such grants: the ombudsman was concerned about this, given that the legislation is clear that council tenants have the right to apply for them). In September 1992, her aunt died.

Sorry tale of confusion. The ombudsman summed up as follows. It had been a 'sorry tale of confusion within and between the two councils'. Consequently, the wife had been 'denied an adaptation that would have made the last two years of her life easier for herself' and for her husband. She recommended a total of £1,400 in compensation to be paid to the husband – and that the two councils should review their procedures and improve liaison.

Dyfed County Council 1996 (95/0227). *Application for adaptation; loss of control of assessment process; disabled facilities grants; Chronically Sick and Disabled Persons Act 1970,s.2*

Following treatment for cancer, a woman living alone had difficulties in managing at home. Supported by Macmillan nurses to some extent, she needed more help and wished to have an additional room in which a carer could stay overnight.

Purported assessment. The social services department purportedly assessed her and made a recommendation to the district council that such an adaptation/extension was necessary and appropriate, and so qualified for a disabled facilities grant. The district council refused to provide one, explaining that the proposed adaptation did not come under the mandatory category of grant, but only under the discretionary; and the council had a policy of not awarding discretionary grants.

Continuing duty on social services? Relying on Welsh Office guidance (Welsh Office Circular 16/90) which stated that in such circumstances (ie, rejection by the district council of a social services recommendation) the social services department had a continuing duty to meet the person's needs – the woman asked the social services department for help. In the course of refusing, the department disowned its previous recommendation to the district council.

Delegation of original assessment. It transpired that, at the relevant time, the occupational therapy assistant originally involved had no substantial support or supervision from a qualified occupational therapist; and the possibility of using NHS therapists had been rejected on grounds of cost. As a consequence, and unknown at the time to the director of social services, the original assessment had been delegated to another organisation altogether (a home improvement agency) – and the recommendation, made without the use of qualified staff (eg, therapists), had been forwarded as the council's own and without question by the social services department to the district council.

Taking out of loan. During this process, and whilst other work was being carried out on her house (by means of a renovation grant from the district council), the roof was removed. Realising that for an extra £5,500 the extra room she needed could be added in the attic, the applicant borrowed the money, expecting that since social services had recommended the room, she would (one way or another) eventually receive the grant money for it. She never did.

No assessment carried out. The ombudsman found that at no time had the disabled facilities grant been promised – and so he would not immediately recommend reimbursement of the £5,500. However, he did recommend that the social services department assess whether the adaptation was required under the Chronically Sick and Disabled Persons Act 1970 – and, if so, to reimburse her the full cost. He pointed out that social services had throughout failed to assess the woman's needs properly, and recommended that the county council anyway make a payment to her of £500.

Ealing London Borough Council 1993 (91/A/3466). *Family with disabled son: move to new home, delay in adaptations; Chronically Sick and Disabled Persons Act 1970,s.2*

A family had lived in council property which had twice been adapted to provide a downstairs bathroom and bedroom. However, the family was keen to move because of alleged harassment from a neighbour, including insults to the son. Counter-allegations had been made. The council eventually agreed that the only realistic option was to find alternative accommodation – although it would mean that further adaptations would be needed. A new house was found, but the adaptations – downstairs bathroom and bedroom – took eighteen months to complete. The complaint was about this delay.

Home circumstances during the wait. During this time, the son (about 10 years old and incontinent) could not manage the stairs and slept in the downstairs living room. He had to be bathed and changed and regularly; his father helped or carried him upstairs, although sometimes he could manage to crawl himself. His mother had a bad back and could not carry him. During this time his toilet training was interrupted. His father had a heart attack which he blamed on the stress of the delays and on carrying his son a lot.

Analysing the delay. Following assessment, the works themselves took a year which – given that they were major – did not amount to unreasonable delay in the eyes of the ombudsman. The main delay was the six month wait for assessment by an occupational therapist. The council operated a priority system, with those clients at risk, terminally ill or living on their own being given high priority and receiving a visit almost immediately. Lower priority clients might have had to wait eight months. The family's priority was initially not increased because the son was sleeping downstairs, in a safe environment and using nappies (obviating the need for a downstairs lavatory). The priority was subsequently upgraded by the occupational therapist when she decided that there was a risk of accident because of the way in which her mother had to support her son on the stairs.

Conclusion. The ombudsman found, not upholding the complaint: 'In the circumstances I do not criticise the Council for not visiting sooner. They applied a system of priorities which took into account the sort of factors which might be important when such time scales were involved. Within this system John's priority was relatively low. I have considered whether the … application should have been given priority because of the reason for the transfer, but in my view this would have been unfair to other residents awaiting adaptations'.

Ealing London Borough Council 1999 *(97/A/4069). Assessment for community care services; misleading information in the community care charter about assessment times; Chronically Sick and Disabled Persons Act 1970, s.2; Disabled Persons (Services, Consultation and Representation Act 1986,s.4; NHS and Community and Community Care Act 1990,s.47*
The complainant had cerebral palsy, suffered from pain and fatigue, and required care and special equipment in order to manage daily living activities – as well as services to enable her to continue her work as a teacher. She applied for community care services in December 1996, but did not receive an assessment until April 1998. She was not informed about how long she would have to wait, nor about the criteria used to determine priorities for assessment. In addition, the local authority's community care charter contained clearly misleading information on timescales for assessment. The charter stated that even people in the lowest priority category would be seen within three months; failing this, the charter went on, people would be given a full explanation and told how long they would have to wait.

Despite recognising the difficulties caused by a national shortage of occupational therapists, the ombudsman concluded that the wait was unreasonably long, amounted to maladministration and caused injustice. He recommended that the council write to the complainant telling her about the improvements it was making to assessment and service provision, and pay £750 compensation. In respect of the charter, the ombudsman stated that there had been 'no realistic prospect that the assessment would be done within that time, as the Council would have known when it drafted the Charter if it had heeded the advice of the staff concerned'. This, too, was maladministration.

East Sussex County Council 1992 (91/A/0586). *Residential care funding; National Assistance Act 1948,s.21; NHS Act 1977, schedule 8*
An investigation concerning a council's refusal to 'top-up' the charges payable by a person with epilepsy, who was resident in a centre run by a voluntary organisation. (This was prior to the changes to arrangements for residential and nursing home care introduced in April 1993 by the NHS and Community Care Act 1990).

In conclusion, the ombudsman found maladministration since there a) were no proper procedures for ensuring that placement requests were assessed against clear criteria throughout the social services department; b) were no attempts made at first hand to establish the woman's needs, circumstances and wishes; c) was a delay of six months during an internal debate about the response to the Centre's request for funding; and d) was no attempt to help the Centre or the woman to plan for her future. He also expressed concern at the apparent inability of the NHS and social services to work adequately together in relation to people in the community with complex medical and social problems.

He recommended the adoption of clear procedures and criteria, a full assessment of the woman, and a payment of at least £500 to the Centre for its time and trouble in pursuing the complaint.

East Sussex County Council 1995a (93 / A / 3738). *Provision of benefits advice under the Chronically Sick and Disabled Persons Act 1970, s.1*

The complainants, man and wife, claimed that social services gave them incorrect advice about the wife's entitlement to benefits when she was registered as partially sighted. In 1989, at the time, the council's rehabilitation officer for the visually impaired (ROVI) visited and recorded requests for mobility training, catalogues, kitchen and bathroom equipment. No reference was made to benefits.

Eligibility for benefits and complaint. Three years later, the husband was reading a magazine article which referred to both severe disablement allowance and disability living allowance. They applied and the wife received these benefits. They then complained to the council which set up an investigation. The subsequent report noted that officers might not have been aware of their responsibilities under s.1 of the Chronically Sick and Disabled Persons Act 1970 (which had been extended by s.9 of the Disabled Persons (Services, Consultation and Representation Act 1986), and indeed no policy or guidance had been issued until October 1989. A copy of the report was not sent to the couple, but they received a letter from an area officer who said there was some uncertainty and that he could not conclude whether the complaint was justified. The complainants now requested a complaints review panel.

Review panel. The panel accepted the wife's version of events, and recommended that the council review its guidelines. It suggested a payment of £750 – although the amount of lost benefit was estimated at nearly £5,000. One of the reasons for this was the panel felt that it was inappropriate for social services to reimburse money which it was not responsible for issuing. The ombudsman said that this was not a material factor and should not have been taken into account by the panel.

Inaccurate advice. The ombudsman concluded that inaccurate advice had been given. This was maladministration which had caused injustice; consequently, the council should reimburse the wife £4,220 (the benefit owing less the £750 already paid), 8 per cent interest on that sum, and £250 for time and trouble in pursuing the complaint. He praised the council for the positive way in which it had responded to the general issues raised by the case in relation to the presentation and availability of information for visually impaired people in the area.

East Sussex County Council 1995b (92 / A / 2085). *Disabled young man; transition from school to the community; failures in assessment; Disabled Persons (Services, Consultation and Representation) Act 1986; Chronically Sick and Disabled Persons Act 1970, s.2*

The case concerned a young man with multiple disabilities: profoundly deaf, partially sighted, able to communicate in sign language and by using a computer. From the age of 16 on (statutory school-leaving age), the education authority considered whether he should continue to remain at a specialist residential boarding school. When he was 19 in 1990, it decided that it would cease funding, but that social services might wish to support him for a further period at the school.

Social services unprepared. Records from 1990 showed that social services had no planned budget for the man, that a newly formed resource centre could not meet his needs and that he should be given priority for assessment. No assessment took place, and some months later in January 1991, the man began attending the resource centre – even though it was recognised from the start that it was not able to meet his needs and that staff could not communicate with him. By 1993, he was still attending the centre, was also attending a local college of further education, and had been assessed by a national deaf association (in February 1993). Social services finally completed its overall assessment by August 1993.

No assessment of need, no planning ahead or budgetary provision, unreasonable delay. The ombudsman found various failings including a) no assessment of need in 1990 as promised; b) despite the council's knowing about the person since 1986, there had been no planning ahead and budgetary provision made; c) the placement at the resource centre went ahead despite the unhappiness amongst both its own staff and the mother – and without it being made clear to the mother whether there were any alternatives; d) a proper assessment had not taken place until 1993 (when the man's own views were first specifically sought) and this was unreasonable delay. This was all maladministration which caused distress, anxiety and trouble to both mother and son; the ombudsman recommended that £1,000 and £2,000 be paid respectively to them.

Essex County Council 1991 (90/A/2675 and others). *Setting up of charging system and appeals procedure; Health and Social Services and Social Security Adjudications Act 1983, s.17*
The investigation concerned the making of charges for home help services. The report concluded that the arrangements made fell short of the basic standards of an appeals system and summarised what the features of a good system would be. These would entail a) 'clearly thought out and relevant criteria'; b) accurate and sufficient information being available to those adjudicating in an appeal so that they can reach a proper decision in line with the criteria; c) that people appealing should be aware of any rights to challenge the outcome of the appeal; and d) clear reasons being given for the outcome of the appeal so that an appellant could judge whether to persist.

Reasonably practicable payment. The ombudsman found that the failure to give careful thought as to how much someone on Income Support 'could reasonably be expected to pay' seemed to be a failure to follow s.17 of the 1983 Act which refers to charges being 'reasonable'.

Arbitrary financial threshold. The threshold adopted by the council (namely whether a person's outgoings amounted to £10 more than income), which determined whether charges would be waived automatically, was found to be 'quite arbitrary'. The council was unable to justify the figure and the ombudsman had 'no confidence' that this criterion had been 'well thought out'.

Use of irrelevant criteria. In addition to financial assessments, 'social reports' (about the degree of risk consequent upon withdrawal of service) were considered by the appeals committee when considering possible reduction of the charges. The ombudsman found that there were apparently no written criteria used: rather decisions were left to the discretion of members of the committee. The ombudsman found that 'the "at risk" criteria introduced a consideration of need which does not seem to me to have been relevant to the task in hand. The clients who had appealed against the charges had all been assessed as needing the service under the terms of the 1977 Act. It was quite inappropriate for the Appeals Group to consider the question of need when deciding on ability to meet the charge, because it introduced factors which had nothing to do with a client's ability to pay'.

Variable quality of information on which appeals were decided and other matters. The ombudsman also criticised the following aspects of the appeal procedure. The information available to the committee in the 'social reports' was of variable quality and was sometimes incomplete and inaccurate. This meant there was a risk of some people having an unfair advantage in the appeals proceedings. People were not informed that they could re-appeal. The appeals seemed to be determined inconsistently. The earlier sets of appeals resulted in a greater proportion of charges being waived or reduced than did later appeals. There seemed no reason for this, other than that at the earlier stage there were fewer appeals being considered. The appeals committee gave no reasons for its decisions: 'Had Members used clear and objective criteria which were more closely related to clients' ability to pay, as referred to in the 1983 Act, it would have been much easier to provide a client with a clear reason for the decision, which the client could have challenged if this appeared to be based on accurate information'.

Recommendations. The remedy for the injustice was for the council to review its procedures.

Gateshead Metropolitan Borough Council 1995 (93/C/3807). *Renovation grants; incorrect allocation of points; consequences and compensation; work started prematurely; adequacy of information*
A council officer failed to record that a house had no adequate water supply. This failure led to an allocation of 60 'waiting' points too few. Had the correct amount of points been allocated, the applicant would have received an inspection visit before he decided to get on with the work himself. He now wanted the council to pay for the work carried out prior to the delayed inspection (after which he would have had the opportunity to obtain a renovation grant from the council).

The ombudsman concluded that this was maladministration; as was the council's failure to warn applicants clearly and consistently that their eligibility for grant aid is endangered if they start works before formal approval is given. However, she also pointed out that the applicant contributed to his own loss because he had failed to read a copy of a booklet from the Department of Environment, and because he had not contacted the council to check whether, once his number of points had been corrected, he would receive an early inspection visit. She therefore recommended that the council should pay 25 per cent of the grant he would have received.

Gravesham Borough Council 1987 *(and Kent County Council: 194/A/86). Adaptations; delay; incomprehensible decision by occupational therapist; housing grants for adaptations; Chronically Sick and Disabled Persons Act 1970,s.2*
The case concerned a request for various home adaptations (covered then under the Housing Acts 1974 and 1980) following the applicant's loss of both legs and other injuries after a road accident. A tortuous list of events set out by the ombudsman was summed up as follows.

Four years delay. It took four years, between 1983 and 1987, to provide the woman with a ground floor WC, shower and ramp to the front door. Even then, the ramp was not entirely satisfactory and the shower room needed further works. This was 'entirely unacceptable'. The county council area occupational therapist's decision in 1983 not to support the application for adaptations was 'almost incomprehensible', given the existence of medical advice that the woman would remain wheelchair bound – since the shower and ramp eventually provided were precisely with a wheelchair in mind. Nor could the ombudsman understand how the county council could close its file on the case, 'leaving Mrs Davies in a house completely unadapted for her needs, in particular with no bathing facilities which she could use at the time'.

Series of delays. There was a series of delays on the part of the county council: four months between a request to reactivate the application and an assessment; two-and-a-half months for the first architectural technician to visit following referral, and then four months to produce preliminary plans; three months between first and second site visits; seven months for the second architectural technician to produce revised plans after he had taken over the case; several months for details of the plans to be completed. In addition, there was confusion amongst occupational therapy staff as to the council's policy on use of a private architect rather than the property services department of the council. The ombudsman found no immutable policy on this issue, and yet the woman had been advised that it was out of the question (her former employer was an architect, and in the ombudsman's view would have been 'most unlikely' to take as long as the council).

Recommendations. All this was maladministration by the county council which caused extensive discomfort, inconvenience and frustration; a 'substantial' financial payment was recommended; the ombudsman hoped that changes in hand would improve the system and prevent similar problems in future. The ombudsman found no maladministration in the actions of the borough council.

Greenwich London Borough Council 1993 *(91/A/3782). Charging system for non-residential services; Health and Social Services and Social Security Adjudications Act 1983,s.17*
This was an investigation into the introduction of a charging system for non-residential services, discontinued because the authority took all reasonable steps to deal with the problems which had been exposed. The ombudsman made the following points:

(a) payment procedures had now been revised so that people did not have to pay postage charges in making their payments (instead they could pay via Girobank at post offices, and they were sent pre-paid envelopes)

(b) not all people had been informed that the authority had the discretion to reduce or waive charges (this needed to be remedied);

(c) no appeals procedure had been provided (this needed to be remedied;

(d) the authority had confirmed its commitment to leaflets, forms and letters about charges needed to be available in different languages;

(e) the authority had stated that it did not 'withdraw the service from any client as a result of the charging policy, or of a client's refusal to pay';

(f) the authority went to some lengths (including checking of records, advertisements in the local press) to identify people who might have suffered from the way in which charging was introduced – and to invite them to have a reassessment.

Hackney London Borough Council 1992a (91/A/0482). *Delay in assessment (56 months); closure of waiting lists; Chronically Sick and Disabled Persons Act 1970,s.2*

A complaint about how the occupational therapy service responded to a request for assessment for equipment and adaptations was made. This was against a background of problems for the service in the borough – for example, in 1987, the social services committee had considered a report entitled *Crisis in and management of the occupational therapy service.*

Closure of waiting list, long delays. By the end of 1988, another report had showed waiting lists of over 1,205 people. Efforts were made to recruit and retain occupational therapy staff and various initiatives were undertaken (eg, self-assessment at the Disability Resource Centre, drop-in centre assessments, telephone assessments). However, there had been difficulties; telephone assessments were regarded as unsatisfactory, because people might have 'inappropriate' ideas about what equipment they needed; and assessment of the home environment was necessary to meet needs cost-effectively.

There were also concerns that if people assessed themselves, took away bath equipment from the resource centre, installed it wrongly and had an accident – they would sue the council. The council operated through area teams and ran two types of waiting list: urgent, and non-urgent. In August 1988, the non-urgent waiting list had been closed in all four areas. However, a review of waiting lists had helped the situation; for instance, some people had died, moved out of the borough or recovered from a temporary disability. In addition, the updated information enabled people's priority to be reconsidered; some of the information received at initial referral had been 'scant'. In April 1991, social services committee had agreed to centralise the occupational therapy service in the cause of 'economics of scale, more effective mutual support, more equitable and standardised service delivery and more effective recruitment and retention of staff'.

Serious spinal injury and disabilities, and request for assessment in 1987. The particular complainant had suffered a serious spinal injury causing permanent disc damage; this resulted in considerable pain for her when standing, sitting, walking. She had to spend most of her time lying down. She found it difficult to use the WC, take baths, put on socks and shoes. She could not stand at the sink because of its inconvenient height, could not lift a full kettle, and could not operate the security locks on the doors and windows of the flat. In January 1987, her general practitioner wrote to the council asking that she be assessed for equipment, explaining that she had a lumbar disc injury and mobility problems. She was added to the non-urgent waiting list, but no acknowledgement or information (eg, about waiting times or criteria of eligibility) was sent to her. In addition, she was not told to get in touch with the council if her condition changed during the wait. A senior occupational therapist explained to the ombudsman that at that time, no specific officer in the area team had responsibility for new referrals – and the area offices used a variety of standard letters, with no common practice across teams.

Checking on position on waiting list. In January 1989, the woman wrote to the area office asking about an Orange Badge for her partner's car and for more information about the occupational therapy service; there was apparently no reply. She said she also rang the office twice each year to check the position on the waiting list. She then received a waiting list review form (see above) after the deadline for its return; she completed it including the comment 'can't sit, bend or walk far'. She was retained on the non-urgent waiting list. In November 1990, the housing co-operative which owned her flat wrote to the occupational therapy service, explaining that it was not prepared to carry out adaptations without an occupational therapy assessment first. It was concerned that she could not use any of the sinks in the flat and that her life would be endangered in case of fire, because of her inability to get out of the basement back door.

Telephone assessment and recommendations. The woman rang the senior occupational therapist 'in sheer desperation' to enquire about the waiting time; to her surprise they had a detailed discussion about the adaptations. On the basis of this, – which the occupational therapist felt was adequate to identify what was required (even though the woman, unprepared, felt she had omitted to raise certain important issues) – the occupational therapist wrote to the housing cooperative recommending alternative locks for the basement door and windows, raising of the handbasin, lever taps in basins/sinks, and repositioning of front door locks. The housing co-operative responded by saying that the Housing Corporation would be unlikely to make a grant on the basis of a telephone conversation. However, the occupational therapist said that such applications had been made successfully in the past on a similar basis.

Full assessment in 1991. In May 1991, the woman complained to the ombudsman. In October 1991, an occupational therapist visited to carry out a full assessment. At the end of October, the woman received a raised toilet seat and adjustable toilet frame, a perching stool, a jug-kettle tipper, long-handled shoe horn, dressing stick, and long-handled brush and pan. In November, the occupational therapist wrote to the housing co-operative recommending: alteration of front and rear steps, raising of electrical sockets, replacement of taps in kitchen and bathroom, raising of wash-hand basin, drop-down rails in bathroom and bedroom, investigation of alternative security grilles, stair handrails, and alternative locks for the front door.

Conclusion. The ombudsman referred to 'serious shortcomings' in relation to the complainant as well as a 'wider failure' in the delivery of occupational therapy services, since other people had suffered as a result of the crisis in the service. The woman had waited 56 months for an assessment; this was 'completely unacceptable'. In addition, she had not been advised about the likely long delay; when she rang in November 1990 nobody checked whether her circumstances had changed; and she was not told about the importance of notifying the area office if her condition did deteriorate. More generally, the 'gross disparities' between the area teams were never remedied; the social services committee had been aware of the crisis since December 1987, but did not consider reorganisation until April 1991; reports presented to the committee contained insufficient information about length of waiting time and numbers of people waiting.

Finally, he was concerned about closure of the non-urgent waiting list: 'the law makes no distinction between the Council's duty to make an assessment in "urgent" and "non-urgent" cases. Any disabled person is entitled to request an assessment and to expect that the request is met within a reasonable time. In my opinion the Council may be failing to discharge their duties under the Chronically Sick and Disabled Persons Act 1970, and I am concerned that they did not seek legal advice on this matter before the lists were closed ... The majority of the service users are elderly people suffering from severe disabilities who may not be able to make repeated enquiries to find out whether the list has been reopened in their area. Many of these people may not approach the Social Services Department a second time for assistance, and may continue to live in conditions of extreme discomfort and potential danger...'.

These serious failures were maladministration causing 'considerable injustice' to the complainant – who should have been dealt with in about twelve months. She 'thus lived in accommodation which was inconvenient and potentially unsafe, and her quality of life was seriously impaired for far longer than was justifiable. The fact that the simple aids eventually provided made such a tremendous difference to her life is as good an indication as any of the extent to which she suffered as a result of the Council's previous delays'.

Recommendations. The ombudsman recommended compensation of £1,875; that priority be given to centralisation of the service; that regular reports be presented to the social services committee; and that the legal position as to closure of the non-urgent waiting lists be immediately clarified (and, subject to that advice, they be reopened).

Hackney London Borough Council 1992b (90/A/3447). *Residential accommodation: suitable placement of younger disabled adult; National Assistance Act 1948,s.21*

This case concerned the council's attempt to place suitably a woman in her twenties suffering from severe epilepsy, learning difficulties, and considerable behavioural problems. Her fits at night led to urinary incontinence, and parts of her brain were degenerating.

Placements: flat, hostel. First, the council offered her a flat with a substantial care package to enable her to live independently; however, she had to give this up when she became depressed and suicidal. Her mother pointed out that she had been alone in the flat from 6pm every evening when the care attendant left (although a boyfriend had visited). Funding was then agreed for a placement with a local housing association for people with learning disabilities; but staff could not cope with her reluctance to accept support and her increasingly violent behaviour. She then moved to a hostel for people with learning disabilities (under s.21 of the National Assistance Act 1948). Things went badly; there were staff shortages, misunderstanding over whether her boyfriend could stay the night, and unwillingness to cooperate with staff and violence. At one point, the mother complained about a black eye which her daughter had sustained; there was no record of any action taken on the complaint. Finally, a suitable placement was found at a privately run establishment in Wales.

Conclusion. The ombudsman did not underestimate the difficulties facing the care staff. He also thought it possible that the mother might have had 'unrealistic expectations' about the amount of help which could have been given in the circumstances. Nevertheless, there were serious shortcomings. The care package in the flat had not been fully in place when she moved in. The placement at the hostel had been insufficiently monitored. The hostel had been 'chronically understaffed', thus precluding adequate training or proper evaluation of the woman's needs. There was poor communication between staff which led to inefficiency in organising benefits from the DSS. There was a clear breach of statutory duty in failing to investigate the serious complaint made by the mother. All this was maladministration.

Injustice and recommendations. The injustice caused by the inadequate care package in the flat was minimal, because the placement would probably have failed anyway; however, the ill-prepared move to the hostel caused greater injustice (eg, arrangements over the boyfriend). Shortcomings in physical care caused more worry and distress to the mother than the woman herself, although she suffered because staff were not equipped to channel her aggression. The mother had been left out of pocket by the inefficiencies and poor communication.

The ombudsman recommended a payment of £1,000 to the mother, expecting that she would use it for her daughter's benefit – as well as other money she was out of pocket for. In addition, the council a) should pay for counselling for the mother, if she wished it; b) investigate the complaint about the black eye; and c) ensure that there were sufficient hostel staff to provide an adequate service – and that they were trained so that residents could be cared for with 'sympathy and understanding of their individual needs'.

Hackney London Borough Council 1995 (93/A/3690). *Central heating: application by council tenant HIV positive; Chronically Sick and Disabled Persons Act 1970,s.1; disabled facilities grants*

The case concerned the application for central heating by a council tenant who had been diagnosed in 1988 as HIV positive and was receiving income support.

Original request. In August 1991, the Hackney Energy Audit Project wrote to the estate manager pointing out that the underfloor heating for the block in which the man lived had been defective since 1976, leaving tenants to heat their flats by using peak-rate electricity. The letter requested that affordable heating be installed for him and included supporting letters from the hospital and from an occupational therapist. The estate officer replied that there was no programme to fund central heating in individual cases, and that the man should apply for a transfer. However, the man did not wish to do this because of his network of friends and possible carers in the area.

Disabled facilities grant application. In June 1992, the man applied for both a renovation and disabled facilities grant; he was sent information, but this did not explain that there was a special procedure for council tenants. First he sent in a preliminary enquiry form (which he kept a copy of but which was not found on the council files). Then he sent in a full grant application form with tenant's certificate and estimates for the works, with a covering letter in which he asked that these be added to the form already sent. Again he kept a copy; again they were missing from the council files. In July, he submitted a new set. In August, another of the forms had gone missing; the man had to send it in again. During this time, the man was also complaining through solicitors about disrepair and lack of heating – and later conducted, successfully, statutory nuisance proceedings against the council.

Social services funding. By the end of 1992, the housing department had not agreed to fund the heating, so in December social services agreed to do so from its own budget. After some uncertainty about whether storage heaters should be installed rather than central heating (pending refurbishment of the whole estate), the heating was installed together with an electric shower in June 1993 at a cost of £3,393.60 – though without thermostatic radiator valves. The man complained that radiators in two of the bedrooms were too small; the contractors confirmed that this was so and replaced them in February 1994.

Failure to inform of right to apply for disabled facilities grant, and excessive delay. The ombudsman congratulated the council on offering its own tenants a procedure which is often better than the statutory procedure for disabled facilities grants. However, applicants should still have been given the choice between the two procedures; and if the council's own procedure is to be used, then it should 'be followed smoothly and without delay'. Neither of these things happened. Eventually, following confusion amongst council officers, the man had been told that he could not apply for a disabled facilities grant; his case was dealt with under the council's own procedure without his agreement being obtained. Furthermore, it took seven months for funding to be agreed and five months for the heating to be installed; this was 'too long' and was maladministration.

The injustice was that, had the council not made mistakes, the heating would have been installed by June 1992 rather than June 1993. In addition, the heating system installed was not what the man wanted (and which he could have specified if a disabled facilities grant had been awarded): there were no thermostatic valves, the water tank was wrongly positioned and the pipework not boxed in. The ombudsman recommended that the council check the heating against 'design temperatures', replace the valves, pay the man £700 compensation in respect of the delay, time and trouble – and review its procedures to enable council tenants to apply for disabled facilities grants, as is their statutory right. This last was an important issue of public interest: 'When a statutory entitlement exists and a Council considers that an alternative, non-statutory scheme would be preferable, the Council should publicise and explain both in an even-handed way and should leave the choice between the two schemes to the individual beneficiaries'.

Hackney London Borough Council 1997a (96/A/3762). *Delay in assessment for equipment and home adaptations; Chronically Sick and Disabled Persons Act 1970,s.2*
The background to this investigation was something of a crisis affecting occupational therapy services in the borough. A previous ombudsman's report (published in 1992: 91/A/0482) had found gross disparities between area teams of occupational therapists, excessively long waiting times and closure of non-urgent waiting lists. By December 1993, there were some 923 cases awaiting assessment, and by March 1994, the average waiting time was 17 months. A 1996 report then compared – unfavourably – the operation of the borough's occupational therapy service to other local authorities in respect of, for example, waiting lists, staffing levels, new referrals per month, average size of caseload, allocation of cases per month, closure of cases per month, lack of criteria of eligibility for service and policy on referral to other agencies, and speed of prioritisation of new referrals.

Disabled woman with new needs, deteriorating equipment and young baby. The complainant lived with her partner and three-year old son in a maisonette on the ground floor and basement of Victorian terraced house owned by a housing cooperative. She had a serious accident in 1985 which caused permanent damage to the discs in her back and considerable pain when she was standing, sitting or walking. Consequently she spent a lot of time lying down. She had difficulty climbing the stairs, bending and lifting objects. In 1991, the council provided various equipment. In November 1995, she wrote to the occupational therapy service saying that some of the equipment previously supplied had deteriorated and her needs had changed since 1991. In particular, she said she needed a replacement toilet frame, a more suitable shower cubicle, equipment and adaptations to help her look after her son (who was then 18 months old) and information and an assessment so she could care for her baby independently.

Allocation of case. In response, a replacement toilet frame was ordered (and soon delivered) and a self-assessment form sent, though with no accompanying information about waiting times for assessment, priority criteria or the duty service. The woman received no acknowledgement or confirmation that she had been placed on the waiting list; the occupational therapy manager said this was an omission – a view shared by the College of Occupational Therapists (which had been consulted by the ombudsman). It appeared from the records that it took six months (until June 1996) for the application to be placed on the high priority waiting list – even though the applicant was told in February 1996 that she had been placed on the list in November 1995.

Emergency-limited assessment. The applicant was becoming increasingly concerned because by mid-1996 she could not help her son (now 30 months old) on the stairs down to the basement (where the toilet was). A duty occupational therapist made an emergency visit and recommended stair handrails but said she could not – on a duty visit – assess other areas of need. Thus she did not consider the woman's inability to lift her son on to the toilet (the woman subsequently paid somebody from the housing cooperative £40 to install a makeshift arrangement). A full assessment was not completed until September 1997.

Conclusion. The ombudsman concluded as follows: occupational therapists 'provide an important but insufficiently recognised contribution to the quality of life of very many people who, without the advice and help of the occupational therapy service, would find living at home impossible or, at least, much more difficult. Delay in providing that help and advice must, therefore, be a matter for serious concern'. He commended the council for introducing independent occupational therapists to clear the backlog; however, it was not 'fair or reasonable' for a service user, regarded by the council as having a high priority, to wait for over 20 months for a full assessment of her needs as a carer for a child, as well as her own needs. This was maladministration, as was the six-month delay in allocating priority, the lack of information sent about waiting times, and the apparently broken promise (on the telephone) of the duty occupational therapist in March 1996 to review the case.

Recommendations. The ombudsman recommended £750 compensation and that a report (to be sent to him and the complainant) should be put to the social services committee in April 1998 about the action being taken in relation to the occupational therapy service (eg, exploring options with the Red Cross, district nurses, council home workers, drop-in assessment centre) and how it was performing.

Hackney London Borough Council 1997b (96/A/3072). *Home adaptations; social services eligibility criteria in relation to applications for central heating; disabled facilities grants; Chronically Sick and Disabled Persons Act 1970, s.2*
The complainants were council tenants living with their three teenage children in a five-storey mid-terraced Victorian property. Some years ago, they paid for central heating but the private contractor did not complete the work and disappeared with their money. The wife was registered disabled and suffered from generalised arthritis and back problems which severely restricted her mobility. A stroke had left her husband partially paralysed. They requested central heating and complained that the council had not dealt with the request fairly.

Occupational therapy service assessment for heating. Until the end of 1996, the housing department had not referred applicants for heating to social services occupational therapists for assessment and recommendation about whether a disabled facilities grant was 'necessary and appropriate'. Instead it would rely on a letter from the applicant's general practitioner or hospital consultant; however, it was then recognised that this appeared not to comply with the statutory requirement (originally in the Local Government and Housing Act 1989).

When new legislation (Housing Grants, Construction and Regeneration Act 1996) covering disabled facilities grants came into force at the end of 1996, the practice was therefore changed. Also, there had been concern that evidence supplied by doctors often appeared subjective. The social services occupational therapy service considered that it could only provide assessments for heating if the need arose from a severe functional loss or if there was a risk of injury: ie, risk of burning because of the dysfunction, or inability to control the existing heating where the person lived alone (or was frequently left alone for eg, four hours or more). The occupational therapy service did not consider that it should assess when poor housing conditions (eg, damp and cold) affected people with a medical condition.

1994 assessment: failure to obtain medical evidence. In 1994, when an application was made, neither the occupational therapy service nor the housing department considered whether it would be appropriate to fund central heating, even though an occupational therapist at the time noted that the cold in the house exacerbated the woman's arthritis. The occupational therapist agreed to seek further information from the general practitioner; this did not happen. This was maladministration.

1996 assessment: criteria for assessment too narrow. In 1996, when nothing had happened still, the couple complained and involved the ombudsman. In May 1997, an occupational therapist visited, recording again that the arthritis was exacerbated by cold and that three of the central heating radiators were not operational. The woman could just about operate the controls of the gas fire in the living room, but relied on her children to operate the electric fire in the bedroom. The occupational therapy service manager concluded that the height of the electric fire socket should be raised, but that it would not be appropriate for additional heating to be funded from the adaptations budget.

Conclusion. The ombudsman understood that the council did not have the resources to fund central heating throughout its housing stock. Nevertheless, it did 'have a duty to consider a request from one of its tenants for installation of central heating on medical grounds and to reach a decision'. After consulting with the Department of Environment, Transport and the Regions, he concluded that the criteria used by the occupational therapy service for assessing heating requests amounted to maladministration because they: 'placed a narrow construction on legislation and guidance about the circumstances in which grants might be awarded for heating improvements ... I can understand the difficulty for the occupational therapy service; its concern is with functional loss. But if that service is not able to advise on applicants with medical need, the Council should have some other mechanism which can'.

The ombudsman decided that in 1994, the couple probably would have received central heating (or been offered a transfer) if the medical evidence had been considered; likewise in 1996, if the request had been considered properly. He recommended £1,500 in compensation, and welcomed the intention of the occupational therapy service to review its criteria.

Hackney London Borough Council 1997c (96/A/0743). *Assessment for home adaptations; delay; lack of information; staff unaware of procedures; disabled facilities grants; Chronically Sick and Disabled Persons Act 1970,s.2*
The complainant acted on behalf of her mother (who had since died), who had requested an occupational therapy assessment for the provision of adaptations. The background in respect of the state of the occupational therapy service was as described above (Hackney LBC 1997a).

The mother was 64 years old at the time, received income support and disability allowance, lived in a two-storey Victorian council house with her three adult children, suffered from diabetes and renal problems, had impaired mobility following a stroke, had urinary incontinence which necessitated frequent use of the WC, but had difficulty climbing the stairs to get to the WC.

Lack of information about waiting times. In February 1995 the mother had been assessed at home and had stair rails installed and a commode provided. She had not wanted a stairlift at the time, and expressed herself satisfied. The council closed the case without telling her. Although the daughter protested to the ombudsman that she was unhappy about this, he did not find this to be maladministration. In October 1995, the daughter wrote to the occupational therapy service on her mother's behalf asking for a ground-floor WC to be provided urgently. Treated as a new referral, the case was placed on the high priority waiting list. This was not maladministration; however, it was maladministration not to send to the mother the standard letter and information for service users, and not to tell her about the waiting times and the priority that she had been allocated. This resulted in 'avoidable frustration and trouble' for mother and daughter, and was compounded by the failure of the council to keep the mother informed about an application she had made for a disabled facilities grant.

Nine-month wait. The daughter complained in May 1996 about the wait for assessment, and her mother's case was reclassified in error as now coming within the urgent category. However, the error worked to her advantage because she was now assessed in July 1996 rather than having to wait substantially longer (the average waiting time being 17 months).

The ombudsman decided that a nine-month wait for assessment was not maladministration: 'I realise that a wait of nine months for an assessment must seem far too long … But … there is a national shortage of occupational therapists; the demand on Hackney's Occupational Therapy Service is particularly high; and the Council is making efforts to find ways to reduce the waiting time taken for assessments. On balance, therefore, I have concluded that the delay between October 1995 and July 1996 in beginning the assessment does not amount to maladministration. This is in no way to brush aside the undoubted inconvenience, embarrassment and distress the delay must have caused…'.

Muddle and confusion. Following assessment, the ombudsman found that the occupational therapy service made reasonable progress in dealing with the case to progress the adaptation. However, the delay up to February 1997 when the mother died and a decision about funding had still not been made, was due to the 'muddle and confusion' in the relevant neighbourhood housing office, which the occupational therapy service had persistently tried to contact and meet. Not only had the office often not replied, but it became clear that the estate manager and team leader were not aware of either the procedure or their responsibilities for dealing with adaptations.

Conclusion. The ombudsman concluded that the muddle and delay caused maladministration insofar as the mother and family were not kept informed about progress; this added to their frustration. However, even if the muddle and delay had not occurred, the adaptations would probably not have been completed before the mother died – given how long they usually take.

Recommendations. The ombudsman recommended £250 be paid to the daughter for frustration and avoidable trouble; he commended her (and the mother) for wishing to see improvements, so that other people would not have the same problems; all this provided further support for the recommended action in relation to the occupational therapy service (see above: Hackney LBC 1997a). Lastly, the ombudsman was concerned that some housing department staff were unaware of their own procedure for dealing with disabled facilities grant applications from council tenants; this needed to be remedied.

Haringey London Borough Council 1993 (92/A/3725). *Provision of equipment for a blind man; failure of complaints procedure; Chronically Sick and Disabled Persons Act 1970,s.2*
The complainant, registered blind, had previously complained to the ombudsman: in 1989 about getting a rate rebate, and in 1990 about a white stick and bath mat (eg, over the non-supply of which he claimed £17,500 compensation when he slipped in the bath and lost a tooth), and about an alleged false statement to the Press by the leader of the council. The ombudsman recommended that the council apologise for the delay in supplying the equipment and offer £150 compensation (which the man refused).

Further request for equipment and delay. In January 1992, the man had requested from the council a wristwatch with large figures, a talking clock and a telephone with large numbers. The request was not passed on to the sensory impairment team, even after a reminder from the man. The delay of nine months made the man so angry that he refused to accept delivery of the aids unless accompanied by a letter of apology. The ombudsman found that the delay was maladministration causing injustice.

Seriously flawed handling of complaint. The man also complained about the way in which the council had handled his complaint. The ombudsman accepted that the man might not have been easy for staff to deal with and that his letters could be abusive. However, there was 'no evidence of a proper attempt to gather the facts, to record meetings, to acknowledge fault or to convey any decision'. In addition, 'social services staff should have sufficient training to distance themselves from the personal, and to identify the very real, issues'.

The complaints coordinator had produced a 'crude summary' which showed no real attempt to analyse the letter of complaint. At a meeting held in July, an opportunity was lost to clarify the complaint, make an accurate record and investigate the complaint properly. The council did not explain why it could not fulfil its statutory responsibility and respond to the complaint within 28 days. The responsible officer for the investigation was suspended; and the assistant director to whom responsibility passed was one of the officers complained of. This illustrated 'why good practice dictates that complaints should not be handled by those who have been significantly involved in the matters being complained of'. The briefing note provided for the leader of the council contained several inaccuracies which were passed on to the man – making him so annoyed that he refused to accept the delivery of the equipment. After sixteen months, the man had received no 'substantive' response from the council to the complaint.

Conclusion. All this was maladministration, causing injustice by making the man feel he was being victimised as a disabled person, increasing feelings of grievance and powerlessness, and affecting his ability to cope with the 'distressing symptoms of his illness'. The ombudsman recommended that a senior officer with no connection to the previous complaints be appointed to investigate properly a total of 14 allegations; that £500 compensation be paid; and that the council should consider why its stated procedure for complaints was not turned into practice. The procedures appeared 'seriously flawed: 'There seems to be no officer of sufficient seniority to run the complaints system and to ensure that complaints are dealt with, not only within the statutory times, but with sufficient commitment. A good complaints procedure should allow for an impartial investigation and for acknowledgement of mistakes. Officers also need training to develop the necessary skills to interact with difficult clients in order to help them express their complaints with clarity'.

The council should review its complaints for procedure and organise staff training, so that its good stated intentions could become practice.

Hertfordshire County Council 1992 (90/B/1676). *Home adaptations; improvement grants; misunderstanding; policy on assessment of hardship; Chronically Sick and Disabled Persons Act 1970, s.2*
The case concerned an application, by the parents of a child with cerebral palsy, for adaptations to the home – including conversion of an existing playroom, used by all the children of the family into a bedroom, and an extension to replace the existing playroom with a new playroom and training room for the child. The county council recommended to the district council that a grant be given for the conversion but not the extension (home adaptation grants were at the time, early 1989, covered by the Housing Act 1985).

Assistance from charity taken into account in assessment of means by council. The parents received a grant covering 90 per cent of the cost of the conversion; they then sought help from both social services and charities to fund the rest of the work including the extension. When the social services department made an offer of assistance, the parents objected to the fact that this offer took account of money donated by charities. The council claimed that government policy suggested that it should take account of the parent's financial capacity, whilst the ombudsman accepted that 'the Chronically Sick and Disabled Persons Act 1970 does not place a direct statutory obligation on the Council to make a financial contribution. Indeed, I do not doubt that in the prudent management of a limited budget the Council would wish to assess the claimants' resources'.

Lack of policy on topping up grants and assessing means. However, the ombudsman was concerned about the 'apparent lack of a coherent policy on such applications, the lack of any practical guidelines and the lack of any advice' to the parents. No policy was recorded, no statement of the criteria to be applied existed, and no advice, explanation and information had been given. This was maladministration and warranted compensation of £5,000 – the equivalent of the donations taken into account by the council – and an additional £250 in respect of the parents' expenses in pursuing the complaint.

Hertsmere Borough Council 1995 (92/B/2299). *Housing allocation; fettering of discretion despite complaints procedure; failure to consider the statutory framework*
A housing allocation case under the Housing Act 1985 (the relevant provisions are now in the Housing Act 1996), illustrating a fettering of a local authority's discretion in relation to its policy on medical priority, homelessness and removal from the transfer list because of arrears of rent. The council argued that people could use the complaints procedure or complain to a councillor, which meant that it was not fettering its discretion. The ombudsman stated that, in his view, 'such incidental mechanisms are no substitute for a proper decision-making process' and that the council had 'abdicated its responsibility for considering the circumstances of individual applicants'.

Amongst various other criticisms, the ombudsman could find no evidence that members of the housing committee had been advised as to whether their policies satisfied the council's statutory duties under housing legislation. No legal advice was given, nor the legal framework cited in the background papers; thus the council had failed to consider relevant information.

Holderness Borough Council 1994 (92/C/3402). *Renovation grant; effect of wrong advice*
The complainant claimed that he had received incorrect advice from the council about eligibility for a renovation grant (under, at that time, the Local Government and Housing Act 1989). Consequently, he carried out the work without a grant having been approved and with no financial assistance. His wife stated that she rang the council to ask about grants but was told that she would not qualify unless she was over 60 years old; also that this was confirmed when she rang later on to check that this was correct advice. The council had no record of the calls, but denied that such inaccurate advice would have been given.

On the 'balance of probabilities', the ombudsman decided that incorrect advice had been given and that this was maladministration. Injustice would arise if the complainants would have received a grant because the house was unfit; from the evidence, they would have done so. Therefore, the council now needed to establish what grant would have been payable and to pay an equivalent for the works already carried out and any others which would have been eligible. As compensation for the delay in bringing the house up to standard, and for the time and trouble involved with the complaint, an additional payment of £500 should be made.

Further report (June 1995). The council took issue with the ombudsman's findings, claiming that it had no power to make a retrospective grant (under s.108 of the 1989 Act), and that there was insufficient evidence that wrong advice had been given. However, the ombudsman explained that it was her responsibility to come to the view she had adopted. Furthermore, she did not dispute the lack of power to pay a retrospective grant; that is why she recommended a sum 'equivalent' to what the grant would have been – as a payment authorised under the Local Government Act 1974 (s.31).

Hounslow London Borough Council 1994 (92/A/2493). *Renovation grants; responsibilities of applicant*
A renovation grant case (under the then relevant legislation, the Local Government and Housing Act 1989), in which various things had gone wrong, including unforeseen work which was needed, connected work on a neighbour's dwelling, problems with the two contractors, stage payments and the council's delay in considering revision of the amount of grant approval (and failure to consider special circumstances where work was already in progress).

Amongst various points made, the ombudsman stated that the award of a grant does not remove 'an owner's responsibility for work to her home'. It was for her to provide estimates and to choose a contractor; but the council had not made this clear. It was 'imperative that councils do not allow the clear boundaries which should exist in the relationship between council, contractors and grant applicants to become blurred'. This was maladministration.

Hounslow London Borough Council 1995 (93/A/3007). *After-care under s.117 of the Mental Health Act 1983; failure to respond to complaints review panel's request*

The case concerned after-care for a man with schizophrenia under s.117 of the Mental Health Act 1983. He had been discharged from a hostel for people with mental health problems, because he had been smoking marijuana. (About a year later he fell to his death from a tower block). The parents claimed that the council had not dealt properly with the discharge.

Discharge from hostel: maladministration. The ombudsman concluded as follows. As the council accepted and its procedure stipulated, the events leading to the discharge were grounds for an emergency review, but not an immediate discharge. However, staff had been given no clear, written guidance. The discharge amounted to maladministration. Even though a number of professionals queried the discharge decision, the council gave no consideration to what had happened until the parents made a complaint.

Complaints review panel. The complaints review panel had expressly requested that a detailed report – on the implementation of recommendations made during investigation of the complaint – be made within a year. This did not happen and was further maladministration, since it further distressed the parents who had been expecting a copy of the report.

Inadequate guidance for staff. The ombudsman was further concerned that the council had still not offered adequate procedural guidance to staff; for instance, existing policy made no reference to the requirements of s.117 of the 1983 Act.

Recommendations. The ombudsman recommended that the authority should issue further guidance; furnish a report to the review panel and send copies to the ombudsman and the parents; and pay £500 to the parents for their distress, time and trouble.

Humberside County Council 1992 (91/C/0774). *Residential care; informing relative of change of status of resident; financial implications; National Assistance Act 1948, s.22; assessment of charges*

The son of a woman in residential care complained that the council did not tell him at the relevant time that his mother's status in the residential home had changed from temporary to permanent, and that therefore increased charges applied (eg, the value of her house would now be taken into account in deciding what she should contribute to her accommodation). Consequently, he claimed, he had delayed sale of her house and therefore a) lost interest on over £35,000 over a period of some seven months; and b) incurred both standing charges for that period in connection with the house, and travelling expenses from his home in the south of England to clean and maintain the interior of the house.

Review meeting. Particularly in contention was the outcome of a review meeting on 11th September 1989, at which the mother's senile dementia and future was discussed. A psychiatric assessment was completed later in the month. The council claimed that the mother's status changed from temporary to permanent at that meeting – although the minutes of the meeting did not record a change of status, and a doctor's view was recorded that a long-stay hospital bed might be possible. The son was not sent a copy of the minutes and did not accept that a change of status had occurred. Although by that time he accepted that his mother could not have gone back to her own home, he did not want to make a decision about selling her house until it was essential – ie, when he was informed by the council about imposition of higher charges.

Charges made for short-stay resident. On 1st November, the council wrote to the mother (care of her son) confirming the charge made for her as a short-stay resident of £38.55 per week. On 26th November, the son took four items of his mother's bedroom furniture from her house to her room at the residential home. The council claimed that this was evidence that the son had accepted that his mother was now a permanent resident; the son claimed that it simply represented his concern for her welfare, since the furniture in his mother's room at the care home was old and dilapidated.

On 16th July 1990, the son was informed in writing that his mother's status had changed the previous November (on the 26th), that the charge per week had been £181.13, and that there were accumulated arrears to be paid amounting to £9,121. The son protested; the director of social services replied that it was clear that the status actually changed in September 1989, but that he would accept 26th November as the date.

Change to permanent residency without formal notification. The ombudsman concluded that the status of the mother changed on 11th September 1989, but that no formal notification took place until 6th June 1990. This was maladministration and he recommended that the council pay the son the lost interest of about £3,300 – less the amount (£1,725)which the council undercharged him for the period 11th September to 26th November – and also £250 for the son's time and trouble in complaining. Furthermore it should 'also issue clear guidelines to staff about the criteria for deciding when such changes in status occur and how clients and/or their relatives should be informed of such changes. They should also prepare information sheets about this and the charging procedure which can be given to clients and relatives before such charges become due'.

Humberside County Council 1995 (94/C/1027). *Limits to council's home support; application to Independent Living Fund; NHS and Community Care Act 1990,s.47*

A mother complained that the council had not made adequate provision to enable the family to care for her 35-year old son. He had some physical disabilities from birth, and used to live independently in a ground-floor flat. Recently he had become profoundly disabled and tetraplegic, and required 24-hour supervision a day.

Discharge: care plan for 24-hour care. The son was admitted to hospital in December 1993. In February 1994, a meeting was held to decide how he could go home. He wanted to return to the flat. The son and the family decided that the family and one of his friends would be the main carers; but they identified a gap between 1pm and 6pm every weekday afternoon. The care coordinator advised that provision of this level of care would be difficult, but the family was adamant. In March, a discharge meeting was held; it had become clear that the friend could not help. Nevertheless, the plan proceeded, and a community care assessment was completed on 19th March, indicating the need for 24-hour care wherever the man ended up living. The care plan set out the tasks falling to the district nursing service, the council and the family.

Independent Living Fund. The care coordinator applied to the Independent Living Fund (ILF) for additional financial help, but at this time the man had not applied for the higher rate care component of disability living allowance – and thus would not meet all the ILF's criteria. The council conceded that at this point nobody had advised the family about benefits, nor checked on what benefits he was already receiving. This meant that the Fund's acceptance of the man's eligibility was delayed. Meanwhile the team of family carers diminished, and the council was unable to provide the extra help required. The son then had to go into respite care. He returned home two months later; soon after help from the ILF was agreed. His mother had taken out a loan of £3,000 to supplement the care the council had been providing – though of most of this she received back from the Fund).

Inability to provide 24-hour home support; delay in applying to ILF. The ombudsman did not criticise the inability of the council to provide 24-hour support at home – since it could have fulfilled its duties by providing such support in a nursing home, though the man would never have considered this. However, the delay in approval of the application to the ILF was maladministration, because the council had failed to make the necessary enquiries about the man's circumstances at an early stage. Had they been made, then both the period in respite care and the amount of the loan would have been reduced. The ombudsman recommended a) compensation of £300 and £500 to son and mother; and b) that staff avoid in the future such causes of delay when making applications to the ILF.

Humberside County Council 1996 (and *East Yorkshire Borough Council*: 94/C/2151 and 2783). *Home adaptations; disabled facilities grants; right to apply for; borough and county council; Housing Act 1985,s.8; Chronically Sick and Disabled Persons Act 1970,ss.2 and 3*

This was a complaint about alleged inadequate advice and assistance to secure the installation of a level access shower to replace the bath. Shortly before the ombudsman's report was issued, the complainant died. He was

77 years old, a council tenant, had two artificial hips, two artificial knees, an acute arthritic condition and his right shoe built up.

Policy on new tenancies. The man had obtained the tenancy in April 1993 through the National Mobility Scheme which enable tenants to move to a different part of the country. In July 1993, he requested that the borough council replace the bath with a shower and install ramps and handrails to assist access to and from the home. The council refused on the grounds that he had knowingly moved into the property – but that if the council had been aware of his needs at the time of transfer, then his application might have been successful (under s.8 of the Housing Act 1985).

Borough council's refusal to help and reluctance to offer disabled facilities grant. The borough council subsequently agreed to install a ramp but not a shower, stating that the county council should be approached in relation to the problem with the bath. However, a friend enquired about a disabled facilities grant from the borough council, but got little help from a grants officer to whom she spoke, and was not given a grant application form. The council's practice, in relation to disabled facilities grant applications from its own tenants, was to consider first whether it would fund works from its housing revenue account.

Allocation of tenancy letter. The man appealed, explaining that he had moved in order to receive regular help from his close family and so avoid going into residential care. He also pointed out that the tenancy allocation letter he received had given him (a sick, disabled pensioner) three days within to which to accept the tenancy – meaning he would in that time have to travel 200 miles, view the property, judge what adaptations would be required and discuss the situation with the council. Clearly unable to do this, he had relied on a friend's telephone description of the accommodation and decided to accept the offer.

Disabled facilities grant application. The council still refused but did now say that this did not affect his possible application for a disabled facilities grant; but for this he would require support from social services (within the county council). He finally obtained information about disabled facilities grants – after writing to the Secretary of State for Social Services – and made an application; the borough council finally agreed a mandatory grant for the shower in September 1994. The ombudsman concluded that maladministration had occurred, because the man had always been entitled to a disabled facilities grant and should have been advised to that effect. Furthermore, the 'circumstances of his move or of the Council's finances were quite irrelevant'.

County council's misunderstanding of the law. The ombudsman considered, too, the actions of the county council. After an occupational therapist had assessed, the council explained to the man the housing department's policy on new tenancies and that it would be unlikely to fund the shower; and suggested that he have baths at the day hospital (though this was in fact no longer possible: in the interim, the man made his own arrangements with help from his general practitioner for bathing assistance from the district nursing service).

The ombudsman found that the county council wrongly believed that it had recommended that the borough council take action, and that it appeared 'to have had regard to a policy which seeks to impose restrictions on assistance to which he was entitled by law'. Indeed it seemed that the county council was 'quite unclear' about the borough council's legal duty. All this was maladministration.

Recommendations. The ombudsman recommended that each council pay £150 each compensation.

Islington London Borough Council 1988 (88/A/303). *Shower and stairlift; Chronically Sick and Disabled Persons Act 1970, s.2*

The complainant was the mother of a man with motor neurone disease; she complained that the council had unreasonably a) delayed in providing a shower, and b) refused to provide a stairlift. The man had three children aged between 11 and 15 years; his wife had recently had heart surgery.

Range of options identified. The original assessment by an occupational therapist in July 1986 identified a number of options: transfer of accommodation, conversion of the basement, two internal stairlifts, through-floor lift, external shaft lift, level access shower unit. The shower and internal stairlifts were the options preferred by the family. In addition, a number of minor adaptations were installed quickly: entry phone, cordless telephone and stair rail.

Unacceptable delay in installing shower. The shower took 18 months to install; part of the delay had been because of the workload on the surveyors within the council. However, the order had been marked urgent and did not appear to have received corresponding priority. This was maladministration.

Conflict between a person's needs and safety policy. As to one of the stairlifts, the council stated that without an increase in the depth of the first floor landing, it would not achieve the recommended clearance (with safety in mind) at the top of the stairs as recommended in the council's *Design guide for people with disabilities.* However, any such alteration would have involved setting back the man's bedroom wall; this was not acceptable to the family because of the fear of dust and draughts during the works – since colds or respiratory illness could be extremely dangerous for people with motor neurone disease. Further options were considered but agreement could not be reached; for example, another type of stairlift with a swivel chair was considered, but the occupational therapy team leader expressed concern because the chair would block the staircase and constitute a risk for other members of the family. Differences of opinion persisted on the safety ground – between the architects' department (which was prepared to proceed) and the building works department which was not. In the meantime, the man had offered to sign any disclaimer (in case of accident) which the council felt was appropriate. This offer was not taken up. The family felt that the council's preoccupation with safety was somewhat 'hollow', since it appeared to disregard completely the daily risks to the family, when the children and elderly mother carried the man up and down the stairs.

Family's perception of situation and danger. The ombudsman pointed out that the family was in an unfortunate situation, both man and wife had serious health problems – and his mother, though in better health, was 76 years old. In the circumstances, it was inappropriate for 'others to quarrel with the family's perception of the situation' – ie, rejecting the idea of setting the bedroom wall back. Furthermore, the man faced 'very real danger' every day; the family had tried to cope with the situation as far as possible without calling on social services; and the man had offered to sign a disclaimer.

Conclusion. The ombudsman found these arguments 'compelling' and could not 'understand that the importance of the design brief must outweigh them all'. In the light of the council's policy of enabling people to remain at home, it needed 'to give very careful consideration to those cases where another aspect of their policy contradicts this'. The ombudsman did not believe that the council had thought through adequately the consequences of such a clash; and that it should 'put all the facts to Members who will then be in a position to come to a proper reasoned decision' as soon as possible.

Islington London Borough Council 1994 (92/A/4104). *Adequacy of advice and support from duty social worker for person with mental health needs*

The complainant was the mother of man in his twenties with schizophrenia who had apparently made a suicide attempt about a week after they had both visited the social services neighbourhood office. She claimed that the duty social worker had offered no advice and been unsympathetic – and that the council had subsequently not dealt properly with her complaint.

The ombudsman noted that the account of what took place at the office were 'conflicting and irreconcilable'. However, overall, he could find no evidence of maladministration – and was not prepared to find a direct correlation between the son's state of mind on the day of the visit and his state of mind a few days later. As to the subsequent complaint made to social services, the ombudsman noted that there was no documentary evidence that the complaint had been thoroughly investigated, and that the mother had not received a written response. This was maladministration, despite the fact that, due to industrial action, the office was barely offering even a skeleton service. This constituted injustice; she had been denied a full answer to her concerns and her right to take the complaint further. This led to additional frustration at a difficult time for the complainant; the ombudsman recommended a remedy of £250 and that the council should ensure that formal complaints were properly dealt with in future and in compliance with statutory duties.

Islington London Borough Council 1995 (94/A/2369). *Priority for assessment for equipment and adaptations; disabled facilities grants; renovation grants*

A woman complained about the way in which her application for a disabled facilities grant was handled. Registered disabled, she had arthritis and a spinal lump which caused pain and limited mobility, and found the stairs difficult to manage and usually slept downstairs. She was the leaseholder of a modern, two-storey maisonette.

In 1994, her heating and hot water system broke down; in March of that year she went to the council's neighbourhood office but was told that it could not help because she was not a council tenant. The Cypriot Association subsequently wrote to the council on behalf of the woman, to the effect that she wished to apply for a repairs and renovation grant. The environmental health officer found that the property was not unfit in the statutory sense and so would not qualify for a renovation grant. However, he suggested that she apply for a disabled facilities grant to pay for necessary adaptations. She was then referred to the occupational therapy department in August 1994, awarded a 'medium priority' which would mean a wait of about five months. In October she confirmed she wished to proceed with the disabled facilities grant application. In January the occupational therapist visited, found the heating and hot water already repaired (the woman had obtained a grant from the Social Fund), but assessed for various aids and adaptations and the need for a bathroom on the ground floor. The grant was approved in June 1995.

Conclusion. The ombudsman acknowledged the difficulties the council had in recruiting and deploying occupational therapists, and that it had to make 'judgements and prioritise on the basis of need'. In the particular circumstances, therefore, the time taken was not unreasonable so as to constitute maladministration.

Kensington and Chelsea Royal Borough 1992 (90/A/2232). *Home help and meals-on-wheels; appropriateness and reliability; Chronically Sick and Disabled Persons Act 1970,s.2; NHS Act 1977, schedule 8; National Assistance Act 1948,s.29*

The complainant suffered from Minieres disease which affected his balance and hearing, and involved unpredictable attacks lasting up to 72 hours during which he had to lie down. He could not cook because his grip was too weak; could not shave, bathe or get in and out of his bed without assistance; could not make his bed; and use of a vacuum cleaner could precipitate an attack.

Responding to the complaint about shortcomings in the home help service, the ombudsman accepted that it might take a little time to establish a regular visiting time – and that 'it would be unrealistic to expect home helps to arrive at exactly the same time at a client's home each week'. The man had complained about the amount of time the home helps stayed and about the quality of the service; he also claimed that they were 'pulling flankers' in terms of 'fiddling' their time sheets. The ombudsman found this complaint unsubstantiated by the evidence, not least because the complainant had in fact signed the time sheet on each visit and had not complained at the time.

The ombudsman criticised the period of two or three months which it took the council to respond to the request from the man's general practitioner and to change the type of meal he received – this was important because of his medical condition. He required meals for people controlling diabetes by diet (copper coded), rather than by insulin (red coded). Despite the request, red coded meals continued to be delivered for some time. This was maladministration, caused injustice and warranted a compensation payment of £150.

Kent County Council 1998 (97/A/1305). *Residential placement; person with learning disabilities; eligibility criteria; assessment: NHS and Community Care Act 1990,s.47; complaint handling*

A woman complained about the way in which the council dealt with requests for assistance for her son who had moderate learning disabilities caused by brain damage at birth. He had been in residential care since he was nine years old, then had gone at the age of 14 to a therapeutic learning centre where the placement was paid for first by the education and then by the social services department. When the placement was due to come to an end, the mother looked elsewhere; she withdrew her son from the centre and he took up a trial placement at a residential home.

No assessment of need. However, there was then considerable disagreement between the council and the mother as to exactly what her son's needs were and what sort of services he required. The council now stated that a residential placement was not necessary and wanted to assess the son at its own assessment centre. However, during a visit there he did not feel at ease and refused to go back because he felt unsafe. The council also gave the mother inaccurate information about the son's entitlement to 'preserved rights' support for residential care (the council offered subsequently to pay the equivalent of what the son would have received by way of preserved rights support had he taken up a residential placement in time).

Flawed report at review panel hearing. After complaining to the council, the complaints procedure review panel considered a report which stated that the son did not meet the eligibility criteria for residential care, but was instead entitled to day services, general support, advice, information and services provided by voluntary organisations. The mother felt that the report had been 'cooked up' because of the council's financial problem, was offensive and full of inaccuracies. Though signed by a particular officer, it had in fact been prepared jointly with his line manager and another officer. The council later offered to destroy the report in the light of its inadequacies.

The panel's chairwoman told the ombudsman that in her view the council's decision and supporting paperwork had been based 'solely on the fact that it did not want to pay for residential care'. She had expected to see a detailed assessment report of the son's needs, and reference to risk factors, growth and development – and a psychological assessment. This was all absent. The panel upheld the complaint, but the council rejected its recommendations, saying that an assessment at its centre needed to be carried out first. An independent assessment was finally carried out which concluded that a residential placement was called for.

Failure to follow own policy on assessment. The son was without a placement for nearly two years, primarily because of the council's maladministration. It was the council's policy to apply eligibility criteria after an assessment of need but before a decision about affordability; yet this policy had not been followed. Furthermore, the note of a meeting – at which the council had claimed that it had been agreed that the son should stay at the original therapeutic centre until an assessment had been completed – 'was so inadequate as to amount to maladministration in itself'. The council had failed to make clear its position.

Compensation: £15,000. Whilst not all the delay was attributable to the council's actions, most of it was; the ombudsman recommended compensation of £15,000.

Kirklees Metropolitan Council 1993 (90/C/1911). *Hospital discharge; arrangements at home; Chronically Sick and Disabled Persons Act 1970, s.2; NHS Act 1977, schedule 8*
The complainant was the aunt of a man who had been admitted to hospital in January 1990, having had a stroke; discharged in February, he was readmitted to hospital on May 9th, discharged nine days later, readmitted three days later and died on 21st May. The complaint concerned assessment of needs, arrangements for practical assistance in the home (bathing and laundry), arrangements for aids and adaptations, meals, liaison with carers.

Assessment. The ombudsman did not find maladministration in relation to the assessment of need concerning diet, mobility, frequency of blackouts, isolation and the effect of the stroke on the man's intellect.

Bathing. The council had stated that bathing was not its responsibility but the health authority's. The ombudsman found no maladministration; there was no evidence that the man had requested such assistance from the council. However, he was 'doubtful if the Council can always safely assume that they have no responsibilities'. As to cleaning and laundry, the council had promised in February that help would be provided every fortnight; but it did not commence until late March. This was maladministration and caused injustice in the form of some distress.

Gas fire controls. Even though an assessment had identified the need at the end of January for a gas fire with top controls – the man could not operate the low controls and was subject to blackouts if he tried – there was a delay of 10 weeks, because the order was neither placed straightaway nor marked as urgent. This maladministration caused injustice since, as a result, the man probably had more blackouts than he would otherwise have done.

Bath seat and board. A bath board and bath seat had also been identified as needed; these were not supplied, apparently because the social worker involved did not inform the relevant NHS physiotherapist who would have issued the equipment on behalf of the council. However, the social worker pointed out that even if she had done so, the physiotherapist could not have issued the equipment, because the man was not a patient in her department. This was also maladministration, although there was no injustice caused – because, as the man's aunt pointed out, he could not have used them unassisted anyway!

Assistance with meals. The ombudsman found maladministration in the failure of the council to provide the promised three visits a week from home care assistants to help the man prepare meals. This was maladministration, but not deemed to have caused significant injustice since it appeared that the man was able and willing to make simple meals himself, often refused assistance and did not seem to complain at the time. The ombudsman found no maladministration in relation to the meals-on-wheels that were provided; he accepted that the food might have been unsuitable (ie, the man could not swallow ordinary solid food), but there was no evidence that the man pointed this out – despite the many opportunities he had to do so.

Communication. Although a senior officer investigating the aunt's initial complaint had written a letter conceding that better communication with the family would have helped, the ombudsman found no maladministration in relation to the council's liaison with the family carers.

Kirklees Metropolitan Council 1997 (94/C/3349). *Renovation grants; authorisation of payments; staff absence*
This case concerned, amongst various matters, the delay in payment of a renovation grant, despite a promise (which the ombudsman concluded was probably made by the council) about prompt payment. This was caused by the absence of the 'one person' who could authorise payment; the ombudsman found this to be maladministration, since he could not 'accept that the absence of one officer is an adequate reason to delay the processing of grants, even in the absence of an authorised deputy'.

Knowsley Metropolitan Borough Council 1997 (95/C4681). *Person leaving school; assessment and care plan; National Assistance Act 1948,s.29; Chronically Sick and Disabled Persons Act 1970,s.2; NHS and Community Care Act 1990,s.47; Disabled Persons (Services, Consultation and Representation) Act 1986*
A 19-year old man with learning disabilities had attended a residential school outside Knowsley; in August 1993, the school wrote to the social services department inviting an officer to attend in March 1994 the last annual review of the man's statement of special educational needs. It was expected that he would spend the 1994 summer holidays at home with his parents and then move into local accommodation in September.

Despite the council's assurance that an 'appropriately supported living arrangement' would be in place by the time he left school, this did not happen. Apart from one attempt in May 1994 consisting of shared accommodation (the man realised he did not wish to share with the particular man in question), accommodation was not available until November 1995, and there was no evidence that priority had been given to resolving the situation. The council had failed to carry out an adequate assessment of need and to draw up a proper a care plan (the council had maintained that a full assessment could not be completed until the man was back in the community).

Consequently, the mother had suffered great emotional and physical strain which had affected the relationship with her son. Feeling unable to accept interim provision in the form of domiciliary support or a hostel, she had given up her job and incurred financial loss. The ombudsman commended the council for reviewing its arrangements for transition from school to adult services, and recommended it pay £500 in compensation for anxiety, stress and trouble – but not for her financial loss (since it was her decision to reject the temporary solution of hostel accommodation or domiciliary support).

Lambeth London Borough Council 1996 (94/A/3636). *Care in residential home; access to personal information; National Assistance Act 1948,s.21; Registered Homes Act 1984; Access to Personal Files Act 1987*
A woman complained about the care her mother received in a residential care home run by the council, claiming that it had led to her mother's deteriorating physical health and death. Her mother had been assessed as in need of help with climbing steps, getting in and out of the bath, washing hands and face, and dressing. She had been diagnosed as suffering from an under-functioning thyroid gland and congestive cardiac failure. There were four main complaints.

Giving of tranquilliser by residential social worker. The ombudsman concluded that it was not maladministration when the residential social workers exercised their professional judgement in giving the mother a dose of tranquillisers on Christmas day – despite the general practitioner's advice that it should not be given if the mother was drowsy, and she had in fact slept a lot the day before. However, it was maladministration not to inform the daughter of this; for instance, the daughter might then not have been so anxious about her mother's subsequent immobility and lethargy.

Recording of falls. The mother had fallen three times on Boxing Day; two of the falls were not recorded on accident forms until two days later, one was never recorded, and a doctor was not called. This was maladministration.

Complaint: withholding of investigating officer's report. When the daughter's complaint was investigated, the report of the investigating officer was withheld from her (although everyone else at the review panel hearing had one) – because the council was aware of the possibility of a negligence action. The ombudsman stated that the clear thrust of the Social Services Inspectorate's guidance on complaints was that such reports should be made available to the complainant in the absence of any special reasons; that 'further authoritative guidance from the Department of Health' was called for; but that in the circumstances, it was not unreasonable to refuse to disclose the report.

Access to mother's files. The council had changed its mind about giving the daughter access to her mother's files, arguing that the legislation (Access to Personal Files Act 1987 and Access to Personal Files (Social Services) Regulations 1989) gave only the subject of a file an entitlement to access it (unless, for example there was a power of attorney). The ombudsman did not find fault with this decision, nor the time which it took to take it (about two months from when it had first said it would allow disclosure).

Recommendations. The maladministration identified caused injustice to the mother and daughter, making the daughter's hurt worse in the last few weeks of her mother's life. Although money could not relieve the distress, a payment of £500 in compensation was warranted given the serious failings and additional distress caused. However, it was clear that the council had learnt from the case and made improvements in its residential homes.

Lancashire County Council 1997 (96/C/3213). *Support for people with mental health problems; erroneous advice by council about registration of accommodation; National Assistance Act 1948,ss.21,26; Registered Homes Act 1984*
The complainants, man and wife, had bought a property and decided to house people with mental health problems. A number of tenants were referred from social services; they required more care than the owners had foreseen and so the latter applied in November 1992 to social services for advice about additional funding. They were advised that this would only be possible of they registered the property as a residential care home.

An officer from the local authority's inspection unit visited the home in March 1993 and recognised the growing care element (eg, managing money, helping tenants keep hospital appointments); in April it was suggested to the couple that the council might 'top up' social security benefits, but only if the home was registered. In September 1993 the owners made an application; in February 1994, they paid the fees; but in June they were told that the scheme could not be registered because it did not include 'board' as referred to in the legislation. The owners pointed out that this was deliberate, since the idea of the scheme was for residents to live independently. The fees were refunded; instead the council agreed to pay for domiciliary care but not the accommodation costs.

Conclusion. The complainants claimed that as a consequence they lost funding of some £45,000 and had spent £2,000 in legal costs. The council maintained that this was simply a trading loss for which it should not be held liable. The ombudsman concluded that the 'complainants were running a business. However, it appears to me that the relationship between them and the Council goes beyond the purely commercial. The Government guidance I have cited [*Building Partnerships for Success*, DH 1995; and LAC(88)15] indicates a clear expectation that councils will work in partnership with carers, including those in the private sector. The Council is expected to provide advice and to be supportive of those providing care for people for whom the Council has responsibility'.

The council had claimed that it was not 'placing' tenants in the scheme, but 'facilitating' their residence. The ombudsman considered this distinction to be 'semantic rather than significant' and that the council were in fact making arrangements for 'care in the community'. Furthermore, the council's advice that funding could be provided only if the accommodation was registered was legally incorrect. She believed that had the council responded appropriately, funding for the care element would have been arranged by April 1993 instead of September 1994; this had caused injustice. The ombudsman recommended that the council reimburse the amount it would have paid had the funding commenced at that earlier date. In addition, it should pay the complainants £500 for their time, trouble and expense.

Leeds City Council 1995 (93/C/2475). *Assessment and decisions about home adaptations; disabled facilities grants; Chronically Sick and Disabled Persons Act 1970, s.2*
A man had an accident in 1990 which left him more or less paralysed from the neck down; in March 1991 he left hospital to return home. In January 1991, an occupational therapist recommended various adaptations including a ramp at the side of the house, a lift from the living room to the bedroom, a specially designed bath and doors which could be opened when approached by an electric wheelchair. In February, the application for a disabled facilities grant was made and in July it was approved; all but about £1000 of the grant (of over £26,000) had been paid by March 1994.

Ramp. The complainants (the man and his wife) felt that a delay of 13 months to build the permanent ramp was too long; for instance, in January 1992, the wife had slipped whilst pushing her husband down the temporary ramp and he suffered facial and shoulder injuries. They also could not understand why the council was reluctant to approve a wider ramp and platform than it had originally suggested – although it did eventually agree to the wider version. The ombudsman did not find maladministration, since when recommending the narrower version, the officer concerned had taken account of the relevant design standards.

Lift. In November 1990, a quote for a lift had been obtained; however, in accordance with the fire officer's recommendations, it would have required an enclosure on the first floor. Since this was not acceptable to the complainants, they decided to wait a few months until a new model was available which would not require such an enclosure. This lift was fitted in November 1991. It broke down 16 times, the door was defective, it left a mark on the wall when in use, and turned out to be too small – the man's feet stuck out. The lift was replaced with a larger model. The ombudsman found no injustice, although he did have some sympathy for the complainants.

Bath and shower. The bath was installed in May 1991. For a year, the man was unable to use it because of dressings for a skin infection on his feet. In August 1992, it became clear that though he could use the bath to wash, he could not get the water high enough so as to feel it – so he requested a shower. At first, the response from an environmental health officer to the occupational therapist was that there were no grounds for removing the bath 'an extremely expensive facility'. The wife then wrote, explaining that the bath was unsuitable because a) her husband had acne on his back and she could not pull him forward enough to wash his back; b) he fitted so tightly into it, she could not wash his whole body; c) the annual service charge (£58) was expensive; and d) a shower would be simpler and easier to use.

Eventually, after medical advice had been sought, a request for a shower was approved. However, when a quote was obtained (including a water storage tank), the council explained that it was too expensive and that a smaller shower base would have to be provided and there would be no storage tank. The complainants were asked to 'sign a disclaimer in case [the man] suffered a spasm while using the shower. The effect of such a form would mean that the Council would not be responsible for any accident while using the shower'.

The shower was fitted in July 1993; however, the length of the shower chair which the man had to use was now greater than the length of the shower base – which was not the size the occupational therapist had originally recommended. The complainants explained that they could not reduce the length of the shower chair by altering the foot supports – because the man's feet would slip off the end. In addition, water was leaking into the next room and the water temperature varied too quickly because of the absence of an independent water supply.

The ombudsman found the failure to ensure that a satisfactory shower was forthcoming was maladministration. She recommended payment of £100 in compensation and that the council should make 'immediate efforts' to ensure that the shower was large enough and that the other bathroom problems were resolved.

Doors. Electronic doors were fitted in 1991; the complainants pointed out that they were unsuitable because they would slam shut in a dangerous manner for anybody else behind. The occupational therapist then wrote to the company which had installed them claiming that the fitting had damaged the door frames, the kitchen door did not close properly, the man could not operate the opening system, and the doors were too heavy to push open.

In March 1992, the council said to the complainants that it would not approve grant payment because the installation was not complete and was possibly dangerous. The company said it would remove the installation, but the man refused because of his fear that it would not make good the door frames and doors. The company threatened legal action, and removed the installation in June 1992; the complainants spent £285 to repair the door frames and to rehang the original doors (£50 compensation was paid by the company). The ombudsman found no maladministration and that any outstanding compensation for the door frames and rehanging was a legal matter between the complainants and the company.

Leicester City Council 1992a *(and Leicestershire County Council: 91/B/2154 and 91/B/2155). Council's home improvement agency service; disabled facilities grants*
A case concerning both a renovation and a disabled facilities grant – and the City Council's home improvement agency, the purpose of which was to provide a 'trouble-free' service so that clients (particularly elderly or disabled people) could deal with the procedures involved with grant works. The applicants were a couple in their eighties; he had undergone major surgery in 1990, had restricted mobility and used a wheelchair. They applied in 1990 and the application was approved in April 1991; because they were using the council's home improvement agency, they were eligible for a lump sum payment and removal and storage costs during the work.

Removal and storage of household contents. The removals company did not take everything into storage nor provide a packing service as had been agreed in its contract with the council. The council's 'failure to ensure compliance with these major requirements of the contract is maladministration'. The agency was aware of the shortcomings and should have insisted that everything be taken into storage; instead the relevant officer made a judgement that the remaining items were of little value and could be stored in an outhouse. This, too, was maladministration. It was further maladministration when the officer took no steps to remove those items from the outhouse when a water pipe burst and caused a great deal of damage to carpets, bedding, clothing and paintings.

Delay in notifying completion. The works were completed in July 1991, but the Practical Completion and Final certificates were not sent until November 1991 and then not to the address where the man (his wife had since died) was staying; he did not find out the work was complete until December. The sending of the certificates three months late was maladministration.

Further assessment. By then, the man required further assessment and adaptations in the light of the death of his wife (who had been in comparatively good health). There had apparently been a breakdown in communication between city and county councils; the former had been waiting for the latter to notify it that the vertical lift was working; the latter for the former to notify it that the home was fit to live in. Months went by without the applicants' being informed of what was happening; this was maladministration, although the ombudsman was not prepared to conclude that the failings of the two councils led to the death of the wife.

Recommendations. The ombudsman recommended that an apology be given by the city council; substantial compensation be paid for damage to possessions (less the ex gratia payment of £1,000) already made by the city council; substantial compensation be paid in respect of the delay in notification of completion; and compensation be paid to Mr. Carter's niece with whom the husband had stayed 13 months longer than anticipated. As to the county council, it should apologise for the delay in organising a further assessment (once the wife had died) – and both city and county councils should review their liaison arrangements to avoid a repetition of such events.

Leicester City Council 1992b *(and Leicestershire County Council:* 91/B/0254 and 91/B/0380). *Home adaptations; priority allocated on insufficient information; Chronically Sick and Disabled Persons Act 1970,s.1*
This case concerned an application for a home improvement grant in respect of the grandfather of the family, who had had four strokes up to November 1988. The grandson complained that his grandfather was now not entitled to grant assistance as he would have been had the application been dealt with before July 1990 (when the grant system changed); and that his grandfather was still living in unsuitable accommodation three years after he had first completed a grant enquiry form.

Delay: enquiry forms. The ombudsman first of all considered delay. The first enquiry form the city council denied receipt of; the ombudsman thought it probably was sent to the council but 'lost subsequently'. However, he found that the county council had a statutory duty (under s.1 of the Chronically Sick and Disabled Persons Act 1970) to discuss adaptations (hence an occupational therapist had visited) – but that the discussion was apparently not recorded or acted upon by either council. This was maladministration.

The grandson submitted two more general enquiry forms; both of these did get on to the city council's files. However, the first was apparently never sent to the county council; if it had been, the grandfather would have got on to the waiting list 11 weeks earlier – this was maladministration and caused injustice because the grandson would 'never know' whether his grandfather might have had a grant approved under the old grant system.

Priority based on insufficient information. The county council placed the grandfather on its waiting list for assessment in 'category B, priority III'. However, this decision was flawed since it was taken on the basis of inadequate information because a medical certificate from the grandfather's general practitioner was given less weight than an incomplete assessment carried out by an occupational therapist six months previously. In addition, the officer who made the decision was neither professionally or medically qualified, and professionals such as the district nurse who were involved with the grandfather had not been contacted. All this meant that a decision was taken on the basis of insufficient, up-to-date information and was maladministration. Similarly, at a later stage after the general practitioner had contacted the county council about the grandfather's deteriorating condition and requested an urgent visit, the council did nothing to investigate this claim and decided not to change the grandfather's position on the waiting list. This was maladministration.

Finally, the ombudsman identified maladministration when a qualified, experienced officer was overruled by her team leader on the grounds that her recommendation would have been inconsistent with other comparable cases. Yet there was no evidence to back this claim up.

Recommendations. The ombudsman recommended an apology and that the county council should make an ex gratia payment to the grandson for the cost of the works for which the grandfather would have been eligible had grant approval taken place under the old scheme.

Leicester City Council 1995 (94/B/2813). *Council's home improvement agency service; disabled facilities grants*
A case concerning a disabled facilities grant in which the council provided a home improvement agency service to assist grant recipients with the procedures involved – for example, arranging for a builder to do the work, and regular inspections. The grant recipient had multiple sclerosis and was a wheelchair user.

The ombudsman found maladministration on several grounds. First, the council, through its home improvement agency, had 'failed to maintain a consistent, planned cycle of visits to supervise the contract and to ensure that existing problems were recorded on file'. Second, after a breakdown in the relationship between the man and the builder, arbitration was resorted to; the council advised the builder, but not the man, to appoint a surveyor to verify the extent of the completed work. Third, the council had failed to ensure that the works 'were carried out to a proper standard', with the result that there was dampness in the lounge and shower, and rainwater penetration. The ombudsman recommended that the council consider giving clients of the home improvement agency a document which 'explains the terms of the contract with the builder in plain English', reduce the man's contribution to the adaptations by one third, and pay him £500 as a contribution towards the remedial work still required.

Leicester City Council 1998 (97/C/3498). *Queuing for disabled facilities grants; flaws in date order*
The complainant had been in a serious road traffic accident and had enquired about a disabled facilities grant; however nine months later he was still in a queue for assessment – and the council was unable to say when the application would be formalised. The ombudsman found maladministration because as the man was not properly advised of his rights to make a formal application (in which case statutory time limits would start to run). Also consideration in date order of enquiries for disabled facilities grants was 'insufficiently sophisticated' to assess priority between cases, allowed 'no scope for giving weight to the individual circumstances of potential applicants or considering them as an exception', and was thus maladministration.

The ombudsman recommended compensation of £1,000 for a six month delay caused by the maladministration and a further £250 for the man's time and trouble in pursuing the complaint.

Lewisham London Borough Council 1993 (92/A/1693). *Delay in assessment for shower; long wait; queue-jumping; informal criteria; Chronically Sick and Disabled Persons Act 1970,s.2; Disabled Persons (Services, Consultation and Representation) Act 1986; Local Authority Social Services Act 1970*
This case concerned a complaint by a housing association tenant that the council failed to deal adequately with her request for a shower. She was in her late thirties and a work accident had caused permanent spinal damage; she could not move her head to right or left, lift her arm above waist level, use her right arm or hand to support herself, or endure without pain jolts or bumps to her right side. She had been advised by doctors that she would never work again, and unassisted daily activities such as shopping, cooking or housework were restricted or impossible.

Bathing presented particular difficulties: 'Her husband must help her step into the bath tub, and then lower her into the water, which is a problem because she is heavy. He must then wash one side of her at a time, wash and rinse her hair, and lift her out of the bath afterwards and towel her dry. The process is painful for her, leaves her exhausted, covers the bathroom floor in splashed water, and has resulted in several falls causing her bruising and further pain. It also exhausts her husband, who is diabetic and prone to fainting or even coma when tired. She says she is concerned that he might be taken seriously ill while she is in the bath, in which circumstances she would be unable to get out to assist him'.

Referral and waiting time. In April 1992, a social worker at a district office helped the woman complete a referral form. It was sent to the occupational therapy service, which put it into neither priority category – mainly because bathing was considered to be a low priority. In June, the woman contacted the district office and was told that she could expect to wait 17 or 18 months for an assessment. She complained to the local ombudsman who in turn wrote to the council's Chief Executive requesting that the complaint go through the council's internal complaints procedure. The Chief Executive wrote a letter to the woman, explaining the priority system and stating: "'Regrettably bathing is not considered a high priority unless the person is incontinent or has to bathe for medical reasons eg, certain skin conditions'".

In the meantime the woman had found out that funding for the shower would be available without delay from the housing association – subject to a recommendation from a council occupational therapist.

Background of long waiting lists. The ombudsman considered the background; for a number of years the council had been attempting to reduce its waiting list, since complaints had been constant. He was 'pleased' to note that the council had 'responded positively and creatively' with, for example, a recruitment and retention package for staff, an assessment clinic, secondment of a health authority occupational therapist. The waiting list, standing at over 1,000 people, had begun to fall; in the circumstances, after 'careful consideration', he concluded that a 15-month wait was not maladministration.

Queue-jumping and informal criteria. However, having looked at a sample of 45 other cases, the ombudsman was 'very concerned' that five of these had been given priority incorrectly ahead of the complainant. Even though the reasons for this were understandable – for example, soft-heartedness for somebody 'living on borrowed time' – this was maladministration which caused a slight injustice in the form of a small delay in assessment. The ombudsman recommended a payment of £250, and was pleased that a system of 'double-checking priority allocations had been introduced'. However, he was concerned that occupational therapy staff were not only working to priority categories set out in formal policy but also to criteria which were 'not standardised between senior occupational therapists or made explicit in any policy document'. Although he fully understood the practical reasons for this, he considered that where possible such informal arrangements should be incorporated into formal procedures, 'so that all are clear about how scarce resources are to be used in a demand-led service'.

Liverpool City Council 1992 (91/C/0121). *Loss of internal memorandum; tracking mail; application for home adaptations; Chronically Sick and Disabled Persons Act 1970,s.2; disabled facilities grants*

The case concerned assessment for home adaptations. Initially, the application was not given proper priority because the occupational therapist did not have the necessary information; however, this was not maladministration. Once the priority was identified the occupational therapist tried to get the application processed as quickly as possible. However, a report sent to the grants section never arrived; and the council had no system for checking the safe delivery of internal mail; this caused the application to get caught up in the national changeover of grants system and to be delayed for over a year.

The ombudsman understood 'the difficulty of keeping track of correspondence within a large organisation', but it could not be 'right that a Council should rely on a service user to follow up delays caused by non-arrival of internal mail. It should not be beyond the capability of the Council to devise a system of keeping track of applications such as this'. This was maladministration, warranting £450 compensation (£30 for each of the 15 months' delay).

Liverpool City Council 1996/1997 (a number of separate reports: see below). *Disabled facilities grants; Chronically Sick and Disabled Persons Act 1970,s.2*
A. General points (Liverpool City Council reports)
A number of detailed investigations have been reported in relation to the administration of the disabled facilities grants system within Liverpool City Council. Each report first deals with the system generally and then goes on to look at the facts of individual complaints. On the general issues, the ombudsman concluded in these reports as follows.

Insufficient information at referral stage. Details obtained on initial referral to social services were often insufficient, and there was a failure to seek additional information. This led to problems and possible unfairness between applicants when priority for assessment was being allocated. Furthermore, when there was little or no information, a referral would be categorised as 'desirable' and assessment either delayed or never carried out – even though some of those referrals concerned people in 'great need'. This was maladministration.

Timescales for assessment. Some people had not been assessed by social services within a reasonable time, and some urgent cases had been assessed more tardily than less urgent ones. The ombudsman suggested that it would be unreasonable not to assess to the following timescales: two months for urgent cases, four months for serious cases and six months for non-urgent cases.

Variation between areas. The waiting times for assessment by social services varied between areas. This was maladministration causing injustice to those who had to wait longer owing solely to their location.

Failure to inform about waiting times. Uncertainty and distress were caused because the council did not inform people how long they would have to wait for assessment by social services.

Double queuing. People applying for both a mandatory renovation grant and a disabled facilities grant had to queue twice. This was inequitable; the ombudsman stated that the date on which an enquiry was first made about one grant should be the effective start date of the enquiry as a whole.

Informing disabled facilities grant enquirers about renovation grants. The council was failing properly to inform people applying for disabled facilities grants that they might first require a renovation grant to bring the dwelling up to the fitness standard.

Lack of a priority system for grant applications. The ombudsman criticised the grant processing system for having lacked a priority system, for failure in publicity about the priority system (when one was adopted), and the system's inability to enable an assessment of priority at an early stage of enquiry.

Tenants of private landlords. It was maladministration for the council to take 15 months in setting up a system to deal with disabled facilities grant enquiries from tenants of private landlords.

Duty under s.2 of the Chronically Sick and Disabled Persons Act 1970. There was a failure by the council: 'adequately to carry out its duty to arrange for works of adaptation or to provide any additional facilities that are necessary to meet the assessed needs of a person with disabilities. The law states needs must be met within a reasonable time and that fulfilment of the duty is not dependent on the availability of finance. Nor has the council carried out all assessments, regardless of the scale of need initially presented, within a reasonable time. In some cases it has failed to assess. This is maladministration'.

Social services monitoring of progress of disabled facilities grant application. It was maladministration a) for social services to fail to monitor the progress of disabled facilities grant requests and check that the identified need was being met, and b) 'to consider whether provision, or part provision, of a facility could more rapidly be provided in some other way'.

B. Selected individual points (Liverpool City Council reports)

Social services' duty, and failure to consult (95/C/0867). When priority for a disabled facilities grant application was not awarded, the social services department should have considered whether it could have supplied and funded an electric hoist as a minor work. It was maladministration by the occupational therapy manager not to consult another occupational therapist before the case was considered by the 'Joint Working Officers' Group', since that occupational therapist would have 'given strong support' to the application the grounds that the person's health would deteriorate – one of the criteria employed by the group for awarding priority.

Clock starting to tick (93/C/1485). In passing, it was noted the problem of whether the 'clock starts ticking' for enquirers for disabled facilities grants from the date of referral or from the date of assessment. At the time, it started from the latter – but given the different lengths of waiting time between different areas of the local authority, this could be inequitable.

Pursuing delay and a liaison failure (92/C/2848). When a stairlift company has been requested to assess the feasibility of installing a stairlift, the local authority should monitor and pursue the company in case of delay on its part. And when an occupational therapist and technical officer visited the applicant, the former drew up a written list of recommendations; however, the latter failed to include all of these in the schedule of works, due to a failure of liaison. This caused confusion and a further six months' delay, and was maladministration.

Assessment delay and administrative failures (94/C/0805). A council tenant had suffered several strokes,, could not use the stairlift, slept downstairs and used a commode and wheelchair. He was cared for by his wife; she had angina and diabetes; he needed a 'push-in' shower. As an urgent case, he should have been assessed in two months; instead it took 16; this was maladministration. The application then 'disappeared' due to problems in the city architects' department at the time; subsequently there were apparently 'a catalogue of disasters and duplicated work' and a lack of liaison between the social services department and the grants section of the council. During such delay, the social services department should have given earlier and proper consideration to funding the works itself. The ombudsman considered that it took 33 months longer to carry out the work than it should have done and recommended £1,500 in compensation.

Loss of application forms and reasonable timescales (92/C/1165). The application forms in this case were probably lost either at or in the transfer to an area housing office, and it was apparently due only to the efforts of the applicant that any further progress was made, since the social services department did not follow up its referrals and recommendations. The ombudsman set out a detailed list of each stage of the grant application process and gave each a 'reasonable' timescale, before estimating how much delay was blameworthy (in this instance 18 months). The list was as follows; request for assessment/assessment carried out (four months), occupational therapy report and request for costing (one month), preliminary inspection and grant enquiry form completed (one month), estimate for stairlift (one month), test of resources completed (two months), application package sent (one month), application package returned (one month), grant approved (six months).

Failure to award priority (93/C/1173). Following assessment and the obtaining of a quotation for a stairlift in March, priority was not awarded for some eight months (in November) for a man with angina and a severe chest complaint, who gasped for breath and often had to be carried, was losing his sight – and whose health was too poor to undergo a prostate operation which he needed. Had priority been requested in March or April, the case would have been put in May and priority awarded; the stairlift could then have been installed three months before the man's death. That it was not amounted to maladministration and injustice.

Confusion and delay over social services role (93/C/4112). There was delay in relation to an application for a disabled facilities grant for a shower for a man who had had a massive stroke (leaving him partly paralysed, unable to use the bath and with a speech defect). Nevertheless, the social services department took no action despite queries being raised on four occasions. There was then confusion within the social services department about funding the work from its own budget. When the work was commenced it took five months to replace a bath with a shower, instead of the one month considered reasonable by the ombudsman. All this was maladministration; compensation of £1,000 was recommended.

Applying the wrong criteria (94/C/1902). The criteria cited by the council as justifying the non-awarding of priority were those used by the occupational therapists, and not the stated criteria of the Joint Working Officers' Group which were officially meant to be the criteria used. This was maladministration, although no injustice resulted since the woman would not have met even the correct criteria).

Delay in administrative procedures, and lack of priority system (95/C/0859). There was a four month delay between an assessment and the passing of the occupational therapist's report to the grants section; but such an administrative procedure should have taken only one month. This was maladministration causing injustice, since without a priority system, grant approvals were awarded in date order. It was also maladministration that, at the time of the application, the council had no proper priority system – nor during the period of delay were the applicants informed that the council had formed a 'Priority Committee'. Overall there was a blameworthy delay of two years, warranting a total of £1,060 compensation.

Liverpool City Council 1997a (96/C/0581). *Assessment; leaving school; Disabled Persons (Services, Consultation and Representation) Act 1986,s.5; Chronically Sick and Disabled Persons Act 1970,s.2; NHS and Community Care Act 1990*
This was a complaint about the assessment and arrangements for a young man leaving school, who was initially thought to have mild learning disabilities and a stress-related physical condition, and was later diagnosed as schizophrenic.

Failure to assess before leaving school. First, it was maladministration for the council not to assess him before he left school – as it was required to do under s.5 of the Disabled Persons (Consultation and Representation) Act 1986. However, it was not an injustice, because the ombudsman considered that, at this time, it was most unlikely that the person would have been assessed as disabled – in which case there would have been no automatic involvement of social services.

Further assessment issues. Second, following a community care assessment (two years after he had left school), nothing done was for nine months. This was 'too long'; the man had 'to wait longer for remedial help in overcoming his reclusiveness and … his family had to go longer than was necessary without practical support'. This was maladministration. Third, it was also maladministration for the council not to have given the parents a copy of the assessment report when requested – even though no injustice flowed from this because the services, which a written report would have recommended, were in fact obtained. Fourth, a delay in allocating the case to an officer following transfer to another team led to inadequate provision for seven months; this was maladministration. Fifth, it was maladministration when a particular officer failed to keep appointments with the father, or to tell him sooner about problems with the appointments; this led to the father taking time off work unnecessarily.

Handling of complaint. Two complaints were made; the first in September 1995 about the level of care, the second in October about the care provided in a mental health hostel. The father contacted the ombudsman in January 1996, who in turn wrote to the council. The director of social services then wrote to the father outlining the services being provided but not referring to the second complaint or to the right to a complaints review panel. The ombudsman asked the council to respond again and to deal with these matters; the council sent a second letter which covered some of the issues concerning the mental health hostel, but still failed to mention the review panel. The ombudsman asked the council to convene a review panel, pointing out that it appeared to be in breach of its duty.

The father received a letter in February asking him to contact the complaints section. He did so by telephone, saying that he would like his solicitor present at the panel hearing; this conversation was never formally recorded. In March, he received another letter, asking him for a response to the February letter and saying that if no reply was forthcoming by the end of March, it would be assumed that he did not wish to pursue the complaint. The parents never received a letter explaining why their complaints could not be dealt with in 28 days and indicating how long they would take; and a review panel was never convened.

Gross maladministration. The ombudsman found 'gross maladministration' in the handling of the complaint. The time taken was 'entirely unacceptable' (eg, by July 1996, nothing had been resolved). The council should not have been chasing up letters it had already received a response to. It was only because of the ombudsman's involvement that the father was ever informed about his right to have a review panel convened. Furthermore, although the council pointed out, rightly, that a request for a review panel is required in writing, it was 'disingenuous of the council to imply blame on the complainants when it failed to fulfil undertakings to put matters in writing and failed to respond to correspondence'.

Recommendations. The ombudsman recommended payment to the young man of £1,000 for the lack of service over a period, and to the parents of £500 for their time and trouble in going to the ombudsman and for the problems they had experienced with the social services complaints procedure. She also recommended that the council review its complaints procedure.

Liverpool City Council 1997b (96/C/1256). *Care package and handling of complaint; NHS and Community Care Act 1990,s.47; Chronically Sick and Disabled Persons Act 1970,s.2*

Solicitors acting for a man's grandmother, complained that he had not received adequate care and that she had not been supported properly as a carer. The grandson was 25 years old and severely disabled as a result of cerebral palsy; his mother had multiple sclerosis and was wheelchair-bound.

Domiciliary support from care agency. The council had arranged for him to move to a newly built and adapted bungalow, where he would receive domiciliary support for seven days a week. The contract for this was awarded to a care agency. Various complaints were made about the care provided including the standard of care generally as well as financial and security lapses and violence by a carer. The ombudsman however was satisfied that the council a) had no reason initially to doubt the care agency's ability to provide satisfactory care, and b) had adequate monitoring procedures through regular meetings and contact with the man and his family. However, after the man had left the bungalow, it took over a year for the council to make alternative arrangements (ie, to put a new care package in place) so as to enable him to return to live in the community. This was maladministration.

Handling of the complaint. The ombudsman concluded that the council did not deal 'properly, adequately or promptly' to the complaints made by the grandmother or her solicitors. For instance, its belated responses did not deal with all the issues set out in the complaint. When the council sent a reply to her MP, it did not send her a copy, even though she was the complainant. When her solicitors complained, the council still did not reply promptly, even after the ombudsman's intervention. This was maladministration causing injustice; the grandmother did not receive a full response to her letter of complaint for almost a year.

Recommendations. The ombudsman recommended £500 compensation for the grandmother for the time, trouble and stress involved with the complaint and looking after her grandson; and that the council review its complaints procedure.

Liverpool City Council 1998a (96/C/4284). *Incidents at day centre; handling of complaints; Chronically Sick and Disabled Persons Act 1970,s.2; NHS and Community Care Act 1990,s.47*

The complainant was the mother of an autistic man who attended a day centre run by a voluntary organisation but paid for (including transport) by the council. She became concerned over various incidents, including her son a) returning from the centre with injuries to the top of his legs (commensurate with a badly fitting climbing harness); b) drinking river water and being sick; c) stripping in public; d) opening the doors of the moving minibus in which he was being transported; e) going to a park and a carer's home to watch television when he should have been participating in a one-to-one care programme.

Complaint to district auditor about inappropriate use of money. The mother complained to the district auditor that the council was paying for a service which the centre was not delivering; in response to the auditor's enquiry, the council said it would try to recover money from the centre. Additionally, the Health and Safety Executive had become involved in respect of opening the doors of the minibus; such an incident had occurred more than once and the Executive threatened enforcement in case of recurrence. The ombudsman acknowledged that, unlike the case of residential care provided by the independent sector, the council had no powers of inspection or registration in relation to day services – and so at most could rely only on the contractual arrangements to monitor and enforce standards. The ombudsman stated that he intended to raise this anomaly with the Secretary of State.

Flawed handling of complaint. The mother went on to complain formally to the council. The ombudsman found maladministration in the Council's response. Despite saying she was dissatisfied with the response, the council sent her a letter saying that it understood she was in fact satisfied. The ombudsman pointed out that her complaint had been about the quality of care and the fact that the relevant officer 'was unable to obtain any more detail from her than that is no justification for sending a letter to her saying she had indicated she was satisfied'.

A subsequent letter from the mother explained that she had withdrawn the complaint following pressure from the officer involved; the council failed to respond to this letter, but should have given her the opportunity to take the complaint further. This would have allowed appointment of an independent person who might have resolved matters. Furthermore, the fact that the mother had agreed to a long-term care plan to remove her son from the centre was no justification for the council's failure to investigate the complaints – it was clear to everybody that he would remain at the centre for some time to come.

Filtering of complaints. The ombudsman recommended by way of remedy that the complaint be progressed by means of an independent investigator and that the council pay the mother £750 for her time and trouble and for its failure in pursuing the complaint. She further voiced her concern that 'the reason that few complaints proceed to review by a panel may be because there is an informal filtering process which is preventing complaints from proceeding. Complainants ... may be deterred ... because they have difficulty in articulating in detail their dissatisfaction'. The council should therefore review its procedures to ensure that this did not happen.

Liverpool City Council 1998b (96/C/4315) *Care package for severely disabled elderly woman; ceiling on cost; panel to consider exceptions; fettering of discretion; Chronically Sick and Disabled Persons Act 1970,s.2; Carers (Recognition and Services) Act 1990; NHS and Community Care Act 1990,s.47*
The council operated a ceiling of £110 per week on care packages available to elderly people, which was meant to reflect the average cost to the council of paying for an older person in residential care; however there was no budgetary limit for people with learning disabilities or mental health problems. It claimed that the ceiling was not rigid and that possible exceptions to it could be considered by a 'Caring for People' panel. Nevertheless, a senior social services manager explained to the ombudsman that the financial limits imposed by the panel were an 'officer practice' and not formal council policy approved by the social services committee. The council later reviewed and revised the policy (after the ombudsman became involved), accepting that the £110 standard ceiling for care in the person's own home did not reflect the cost of nursing home care which would be £190 per week. It eventually provided a home care package for the woman costing £406.63 weekly.

Special needs of severely disabled woman. The complainant, who cared for her mother, had had a long struggle to ensure that adequate support was given by the council to her and her family. The mother was blind and deaf, had diabetes, arthritis, hypertension and a heart problem, and was incontinent and depressed. She had become increasingly confused and had a loss of short-term memory. Her mobility was very restricted and she communicated by hand-signing. The daughter explained a) that given that her mother had 'no quality of life' but just existence, her going into a nursing home would mean that she would lose love, affection and understanding and that she could not abandon her mother in that way; and b) that her mother's needs were exceptional since she required constant one-to-one attention day and night including constant reassurance and stimulation, changing, frequent strip washing (particularly important because of bowel and kidney problems), safety measures (she would crawl around the floor like a baby) – and so on.

NHS continuing care criteria. During the drawn-out process of attempting to put adequate care in place, but hindered by the self-imposed financial ceiling, the council asked the health authority whether it could offer overnight hospital stays two or three nights a week; the authority stated that the mother did not fit its continuing care criteria.

Conclusions. The financial ceiling originally applied by the council to home care packages for older people constituted maladministration because it fettered the discretion of the council – and there was no evidence to suggest that the Caring for People panel ever admitted exceptions to the policy, even though it supposedly had the discretion to do so. Both the daughter and her MP were consistently told that the limit existed. Furthermore, the ceiling was unfair since it discriminated against elderly people in comparison with people with a mental illness or learning disabilities.

In addition, there was maladministration in how the council dealt with the daughter's complaint. First, she was never advised of a timescale for the handling of the complaint, nor did it seem that she had been advised in writing of her right to request a review panel hearing. Given the stress she was under, it was not good enough that she simply be told over the telephone about this right. Furthermore, the council appeared to believe, erroneously, that the referral of a complaint to the ombudsman precluded completion of its own procedure (ie, by the convening of a review panel); this put it in breach of the *Complaints Procedures Directions* (see p.423). Indeed, a review panel would have been able to expose shortcomings in the provision of services and in the complaints procedure – just as the ombudsman's investigation had done.

Remedy. Although the council had now put in place a package of care costing over £400 a week, having changed its policy and removed the ceiling of £110, nevertheless the previous restrictions meant that services had been 'lost' to the extent of £30,000 in value. Those services could not be replaced, but the ombudsman recommended that the council should a) pay £10,000 in compensation for the 'extreme stress' the daughter suffered; b) apologise in relation to the handling of the complaint; and c) ensure that the issues raised in relation to the complaint were addressed as part of improving its complaints procedure.

Manchester City Council 1992 (91/C/0553). *Hospital discharge; person with learning disabilities; National Assistance Act 1948, s.21; disagreement with parents*
The complainants were the parents of a 43-year old man with learning disabilities and epilepsy. The son lived in a hospital for 27 years until 1991, at which time he moved into a house owned by a housing association with support staff provided by the council.

The parents believed that he would be safer in hospital or in an institutional setting; they were consulted about the planned resettlement but withdrew from the process in the light of their opposition to it. However, the ombudsman concluded that it was not maladministration simply because 'those involved chose an option other than that favoured' by the parents; nor did one incident when the parents found the son helpless in a chair following a fit lend support to the parents' fears about the quality of care being provided. And although the parents had a preferred alternative, the ombudsman did not see fit to question the council's decision; the fact of disagreement did not imply maladministration.

Manchester City Council 1993 (90/C//2147). *Residential accommodation for man with learning disabilities; suitability and adequacy of care; National Assistance Act 1948, ss.21,29*
The complainants were the parents of a young man suffering from severe brain damage and epilepsy; he had a mental age of two years and needed a great deal of care. He had been placed, under s.21 of the National Assistance Act 1948, at one of the council's hostels – a residential unit for mentally handicapped children, which the council eventually closed (in favour of people with learning disabilities living in ordinary housing). The ombudsman concluded as follows, referring closely to the 1948 Act and associated guidance.

Suitable accommodation? The hostel was not an ideal placement but, had it been properly managed, then it would not have been unsuitable. The ombudsman noted that the authority had a duty under s.21 to make arrangements for the provision of accommodation and regularly to review the provision and make improvements considered necessary.

Welfare arrangements and hygiene. Under s.21, the authority had a duty to make arrangements for the welfare of residents and for the supervision of hygiene (under directions issued under Circular DHSS 13/74, now reissued with LAC(93)10). The parents complained that, for example, the care and staffing provided was poor; that their son shared a room with a man who needed attention several times a night, with the result that their son's sleep was continually interrupted; that his personal belongings were stolen or destroyed by other residents; that lavatory seats were missing for months on end and laundry was often lost; and that staff failed to notice that their son was in pain and requiring emergency dental treatment. The ombudsman found 'serious failures' and maladministration, with the consequence that the son's quality of life was significantly lowered.

Providing for developmental needs. Under s.29 of the National Assistance Act 1948 and directions made under it (now in Circular LAC(93)10), the council had a duty to make arrangements for disabled people, including for the provision of social rehabilitation and adjustment to disability. A support worker was provided for 30 hours a week; this seemed to the ombudsman to be a reasonable, but there was a lack of precision in setting, working towards and recording the meeting of targets; this was maladministration.

Failure to administer medication. The council had a duty to ensure that residents received medical attention and any necessary NHS services (under s.21 of the 1948 Act and directions now in LAC(93)10). The council conceded that it had failed to provide the required medication – for instance, failing on several occasions to give medication prescribed for the control of epilepsy. This was maladministration.

Handling of the complaint. The parents wrote letters, met and corresponded with the director of social services over a period of over two years, during which time problems persisted at the hostel and the responses from the council failed to deal with all the issues raised by the parents. The director pointed to the need to view 'provision within a context which includes financial restrictions and service reductions'. The ombudsman concluded that some of the complaints were neither properly investigated nor replied to; had they been, there would have been earlier recognition of the need to deal with the difficulties.

Recommendations. The ombudsman found that the parents had suffered significant injustice in seeing their son suffer unnecessarily; although they were not seeking financial compensation, she was satisfied that 'the legitimate stress, anxiety and concerns that have been caused to caring parents for their vulnerable child is injustice' and warranted a payment of £1,000 in compensation (which took account also of the time and trouble in making the complaint).

Manchester City Council 1994 (92/C/2376). *Home adaptations: necessity, desirability and self-assessment; Chronically Sick and Disabled Persons Act 1970,s.2; disabled facilities grants*
This case concerned the wish of a woman, with a long-standing chronic and disabling illness, to have an extra bedroom in her one-bedroom council flat – so that a carer could be accommodated.

Overall, the ombudsman did not conclude that the council was under a duty to provide the extension. Although 'at times different messages have emerged from the Council its present view is that any duty can be met by providing suitable alternative accommodation. Whilst I can well understand Ms Ash's reluctance to move, there must be limits on what it is practical and reasonable to provide and at some point an alternative to providing adaptations may be a fair response'. Furthermore, it was 'obviously not unreasonable for the Council to argue that an extra room is not strictly necessary' and it therefore did not translate into a legal obligation; nor did the ombudsman fault the council's view that a disabled facilities grant for such an extension was not mandatory and that a discretionary disabled facilities grant should not be awarded.

Self-assessment and going back on its word. However, the waters had become muddied because at the relevant time, the council had operated a demand-led system, within which disabled people could specify their own needs. Under this system, the council at one time had agreed to the extension, only to go back on its word – on the basis that its 'willingness to provide an extension at this time did not indicate an acceptance of a duty to make that provision'. The extension might have been 'desirable' but not 'necessary and appropriate'. The ombudsman did not regard the undertaking as binding on the council but accepted that it had led to acute disappointment, frustration – and to the complainant carrying out other works (re-tiling, carpets, redecoration) which she might not have undertaken, had she realised the extension was not to be. This was maladministration and injustice warranting compensation of £1,000.

Manchester City Council 1995 (93/C/2893). *Policy on complaints procedures*
The case concerned a complaint by foster parents. The ombudsman accepted that it might not always be easy to identify the appropriate complaints channel, but that the council should have had 'a policy to guide officers in deciding whether a complainant has a sufficient interest to make a complaint' – in this case under the Children Act 1989. In addition, the council failed to consider in this case whether either of the statutory complaints pro-

cedures (ie, under the 1989 Act and under for adults under the Local Authority Social Services Act 1970) were applicable. This was maladministration.

Manchester City Council 1996a (93/C/2330). *Adult foster placement; visiting arrangements; complaints procedure*
The sister of an adult woman with severe learning disabilities who had been placed in the care of a foster family complained that the council changed the arrangements for the sister to visit home without consulting her and her family.

Change of arrangements without consultation. After the placement had been made, the council arranged that the woman should visit her mother every second Saturday. These visits were subsequently being cancelled at short or no notice. The mother complained and the council undertook to investigate, but further disruption occurred; the mother complained again. An MP intervened, the council admitted there had been problems and decided to deal with the matter as a formal complaint. It produced a report, sent it to the mother and proposed to change the visits from Saturdays to Wednesdays. The mother told the council she did not agree to these changes; in response, the council nevertheless wrote confirming the changes but that her complaints would be dealt with at a review panel hearing. The review panel recommended that the visits be changed to the satisfaction of all concerned; the council acted on these recommendations and the ombudsman found that it took reasonable steps in this respect.

Maladministration. However, the ombudsman decided that maladministration had occurred in relation to a) the delay of five months in responding to the complaint, and b) changing the visiting arrangements without a promised discussion with, and confirming them against the wishes of, the family. The ombudsman recommended a full apology and payment of £100.

Further report (May 1996). The council acknowledged unacceptable delay but maintained that in such cases it was difficult to reconcile the needs of service users and carers with the wishes of families. Therefore, it had agreed to apologise for the delay but refused to pay compensation. The ombudsman now looked to the council to make the apology and pay the £100 'without delay'.

Manchester City Council 1996b (94/C/1571). *Handling of complaint; adequacy of respite care facilities*
The complainants had an adult daughter with cerebral palsy and severe mental and physical disabilities. They complained to the ombudsman about a) the way in which the council had investigated their complaint about injuries suffered by their daughter in respite care, and b) the adequacy of the respite care facilities.

Flawed handling of complaint. The ombudsman found that the council's investigation of the complaint was flawed in a number of respects amounting to maladministration. The council did not respond to, or even acknowledge, the formal complaint within the statutory target time of 28 days; nor were the parents told about their right to request a review panel – indeed 'a conscious decision was made not to offer this facility'. The initial investigation seemed thorough, but the subsequent one less so – for example, in respect of the injuries, the investigating officer failed to seek the views of those who had seen the injuries: ie, the parents.

Furthermore, a question arose about the independence of the investigator: 'The question of the independence of the investigator may be one of perception. It may be evident to officers of the council that Officer E, an officer involved in the purchasing of services, is separate and independent from the providers of such services. However, I can certainly understand that this officer was not seen by Mr and Mrs Marsh as being independent. She worked within the same Directorate in the broad area of residential services for those with learning disabilities and Mr and Mrs Marsh had, in fact, had previous contact with her regarding the provision of services for their daughter. Additionally the officer in question had known and had some contact with a key person involved in the complaint and was the line manager of another at the time of the investigation. Whilst I have no reason to doubt the integrity and professionalism of the investigating officer I believe that she may not have been sufficiently independent and certainly did not appear to be so to the complainants'.

Respite care. The council had only one short-stay respite house available for women in the north of the city. It had no bathing facilities on the ground floor, and a range of adaptations were still in progress 21 months after the property had come into use. Of further concern was that staff recruitment difficulties led not only to re-liance on agency staff, but on relief staff from an agency about which council officers had 'expressed concern'. Despite the efforts being made by the council to improve matters, the facilities offered at the time were 'unsat-isfactory'; this was maladministration.

Recommendations. The council apologised and offered a review panel hearing and had 'taken steps to rectify the situation which gave rise to these complaints'. In addition, the ombudsman recommended the making of a small payment in respect of the injustice suffered by the parents and their daughter.

Further report (February 1997). The council disagreed with the ombudsman's findings and refused to pay any compensation; it apologised for its failure to respond within 28 days, but the parents never accepted this apology as covering the whole complaint. The ombudsman stated that the council's response to her report was inadequate since the complainants and their daughter undoubtedly suffered injustice – which was 'such that it would not be matched by a further, belated apology'. She now looked to the council to pay £100 to the parents 'without further delay'.

Manchester City Council 1998 (97/C/1814). *Delay in processing renovation grant*

The complainant claimed that the council had failed to process her application for a mandatory renovation grant under the Local Government and Housing Act 1989. As a consequence, her application was dealt with according to successor legislation, the Housing Grants, Construction and Regeneration Act 1996, under which mandatory renovation grants were no longer available. Consequently, she was awarded a discretionary grant substantially smaller than she would have received under the previous legislation. The council argued that the reason for the delay was that the woman's application had been incomplete, because she had not sub-mitted a certificate of owner occupation (which it had not supplied to her).

Deliberate delay. The ombudsman accepted that though technically correct, this was 'entirely as a conse-quence of the Council's own administrative procedures'; she was satisfied 'that the Council did not intend to provide … an owner occupation certificate any earlier than the Council was ready to complete the application process by undertaking a visit to … carry out a final check of her resources'. This 'allowed it to delay indefi-nitely treating [the woman's] application as complete despite her acceptance of the Council's offer of its service to grant applicants which included 'assistance with completing the application' … The Council's failure prop-erly to provide [her] with all the necessary documents to complete her application and its deliberate action to delay the completion of the application process is maladministration'.

Conclusion. The maladministration caused a refusal of her application under the 1989 Act. The council had taken steps to reassess the application, and so long as it paid to the applicant a sum equivalent to that she would have been entitled to by way of mandatory grant, the ombudsman would accept that the injustice caused had been remedied. She also commended the council for reviewing its system for grant applications – and sug-gested it review other particular applications which had suffered a similar fate to that of this complainant.

Merthyr Tydvil 1994 (93/218. In: *Local Government Review Reports*, 26 August 1995,pp.673–683). *Delay in pro-cessing renovation grant*

This was a complaint about delay in processing an application for a renovation grant. The local ombudsman for Wales set out the following steps in relation to formulating policies about such grants:

'(a) to review and clarify its priority system; the review should be the subject of a formal and comprehensive report to the appropriate committee containing the recommendations of professional officers on objective and clear criteria for determining priorities between applicants for grants;

(b) any revised policy should be the subject of a formal resolution adopted by the council, and details of that priority system should be made known to inquirers and applicants in a consistent and uniform way – by publication of an explanatory leaflet or information sheet for example;

(c)   in revising its procedures, the council should ensure that queries and requests for information
      from inquirers and applicants are met with a helpful and meaningful response particularly with
      regard to progress in dealing with the inquiry'.

Middlesbrough Borough Council 1996 (and *Cleveland County Council*: 94/C/0964 and 94/C/0965). *Delay in assessment and in approval of grant for home adaptations*
The complainant claimed that the county council had delayed in assessing and meeting her needs, and that the borough council had not dealt properly with her application for a disabled facilities grant. Consequently, she could not use a shower or toilet for a considerable length of time. She was an elderly woman confined to a wheelchair.

Assessment by social services. The woman had requested an assessment from the social services department of the county council but waited seven months; this was maladministration, since she had 'a right to expect that help will be given within a reasonable length of time'. The council stated that the wait was due to a shortage of occupational therapists; in response, the ombudsman pointed out that if 'such expertise is not available councils need to find an alternative way of meeting their statutory responsibilities'.

The assessing occupational therapist had made various recommendations in relation to modified doorways to allow easier access to shower and toilet, enlarging of the bathroom by moving a wall, a different shower tray and higher toilet, widened front doorway and ramps at the front and rear of the flat. (The occupational therapy team leader subsequently said that the 'general bathing needs' the woman had might be included in a reassessment of what it would be reasonable to recommend: transport to use nearby bathing facilities could be provided instead).

The delay in assessment meant that a recommendation to the borough council for a disabled facilities grant was delayed by five months; this warranted a payment of £300 in compensation (including time and trouble in making the complaint).

Processing of grant application. The borough council failed to process the application for a disabled facilities grant within the statutory timescale of six months; this was maladministration. However, the ombudsman recognised that the borough council was experiencing financial difficulties caused by the increased demand for grants, which in turn arose from the increased activities of the county council's occupational therapists. Its failure to anticipate this was not unreasonable. Further, the ombudsman felt that it was not improper for the council to approve discretionary grants, even though it was not fulfilling its statutory duty in respect of mandatory grants. The complainant had not been treated differently than other comparable applicants and so did not suffer any injustice 'above and beyond' others waiting for grants. By the time of the ombudsman's report, the adaptations were complete.

Newham London Borough Council 1993a (91/A/3602). *Delay in processing application for disabled facilities grant*
The case concerned a 97-year-old, registered blind, woman who had lived in the same street for 46 years, and a) the calculation of her housing benefit; b) her application for a disabled facilities grant; and c) delays in repairs.

On the issue of her application for a disabled facilities grant, the ombudsman found that it was not determined within the statutory six-month time period; that misfiling of the application had caused a delay of four months; and that the council had not responded to a letter from the woman's grandson. The ombudsman found that the delay was unreasonable and amounted to maladministration, but that since it was decided ultimately that she was ineligible for a disabled facilities grant, this did not affect obtaining of the grant itself. However, it did cause injustice because it meant that there was delay in fitting two additional grab rails, and it also led to the employment of a private occupational therapist to speed up assessment of the grandmother. Had the council assessed more quickly, this might not have been seen as necessary – though the ombudsman recognised that the private occupational therapist might still have been employed to challenge any assessment the council made.

Newham London Borough Council 1993b (91/A/3911) *Delay in assessment and provision of home adaptations; inconsistent treatment; disabled facilities grants*

The complainant first applied to social services for help with adaptations in October 1989 but was not visited by an occupational therapist until September 1992; she also submitted an initial enquiry form for a grant in July 1990, but the application was not approved until September 1993.

The ombudsman acknowledged that there were various reasons for the delays in dealing with the grant application, but that guidance from central government stated that the initial enquiry should not involve an unreasonably long wait. Furthermore, he was concerned that the council had not addressed the serious resourcing problems it faced; and though staffing had been inadequate for many years, the issue had only been first considered by members of the council in October 1991: it should have been looked at years before. It could not be 'fair or reasonable that an applicant for a renovation grant in one part of the Borough has an application dealt with in a matter of weeks, whilst others ... wait for years'. Even a disruption of several months by industrial action did not remove the statutory duties of councils; senior officers should have considered ways around it.

Ultimately, the woman was not eligible for a disabled facilities grant, although a handrail had now been supplied; but had an assessment taken place in a reasonable time, she would have had it three years earlier. In addition, the delays meant that it took an extra 19 months for her renovation grant application to be determined; the ombudsman recommended compensation of £500 for the 'inconvenience' of waiting for the grant and managing without the handrail on the stairs, and that the council should review its procedures.

Newham London Borough Council 1995 (92/A/4120). *Disabled facilities grants' Chronically Sick and Disabled Persons Act 1970,s.2; assessment; responsibility of applicant*

The complainants alleged that the council were at fault in dealing with their application for home adaptations for their 16-year-old disabled daughter – who had cerebral palsy and epilepsy, used a wheelchair, was incontinent, had minimal comprehension and needed full care in all activities of daily living.

Assessment. The original assessment had been carried out within about six weeks of referral by a qualified occupational therapist, who made recommendations for various equipment. Initially she would not agree either to an ordinary stairlift because of safety issues (there were three winding steps at the top of the stairs) or a platform stairlift to take the wheelchair (the stairs were to narrow). Instead she recommended a vertical lift, which the parents did not want (it would have meant moving a fitted wardrobe). The mother complained about the fact that the therapist had come to this decision in a short time and without consulting the doctor, social worker and physiotherapist – and that the occupational therapist had insisted that her view take precedence.

Eventually, six months later, the occupational therapist observed changes in the daughter's weight-bearing ability for transfers and that her epilepsy was now well controlled; consequently, she now stated that a stairlift would be acceptable. Adaptations were agreed: to widen and straighten the staircase and to add on a small first floor extension. Planning permission and approval took some time – but, overall, the ombudsman found not maladministration in relation to the assessment process.

Approval of unsatisfactory work. The parents complained that the council had approved unsatisfactory work. However, the ombudsman explained that they had misunderstood the council's role, which was simply to ensure that public money was spent wisely and that statutory building regulations were satisfied in the public interest. Thus, the inspections carried out by the council were to protect the public revenue and not the recipients of the grant. It was up to the latter to ensure that works were carried out to a high standard – hence the Department of Environment's guidance that suggested an architect or surveyor be employed. Therefore, despite the alleged defective work, the ombudsman could not conclude that the council was responsible for it.

Collusion with the builder. It was also claimed that the council had colluded with the builder. The ombudsman found that a) though there had been misconduct in other cases, there was not conclusive evidence in this case; b) the builder might have said he was 'well-connected' but there was no evidence that he received favours from the council; c) it was not improper for the council to base the grant on the lowest estimate; d) it was not the council's responsibility to take up the builder's references, since the contract was between the builder and the complainants; and e) 'moonlighting' by council workers had been alleged (eg, in respect of an electrician who did some of the work), and in one case, the council was holding a disciplinary hearing which was outside the jurisdiction of the ombudsman. Thus, there was not maladministration.

Incorrect VAT. The ombudsman did find maladministration in respect of incorrect addition of VAT to a payment and a lack of a 'properly documented grants procedure'; but neither of these matters caused injustice to the complainants.

Newham London Borough Council 1996 (94/A/3185). *Rumours; complaints procedure*

The case concerned the handling of a complaint made by a woman with a personality disorder who claimed that malicious rumours had been allowed to circulate about her allegedly violent behaviour in a local housing office.

Defects in handling of complaint. The ombudsman expressed 'serious concerns' about the operation of the complaints procedure. There was confusion about which stage of the procedure was being followed. The complainant believed a formal investigation was taking place and did not agree to informal handling of the complaint. The complaint was not thoroughly investigated, but instead the 'presenting problems' (assistance with managing her anger and housing) were focused on. Relevant case records were not examined and key people not interviewed. Timescales were not adhered to. The complainant was not informed of the progress of the investigation. A letter sent at the conclusion of the investigation did not advise what the complainant could do if she was still dissatisfied, and did not enclose a copy of the investigation report.

Furthermore, although the passage of time made it difficult to establish the facts of what had allegedly occurred at the housing office, had proper enquiries been made promptly, this might have been possible. There was further misunderstanding when an account of the alleged incident was passed between three different teams and details were not checked with the original referrer and any other witnesses.

Recommendations. All this maladministration caused the injustice of frustration and anxiety of not having the complaint investigated properly and not being told how to take it further. The ombudsman recommended payment of £250 and asked that the council send him its end-of-year report on the performance of its complaints procedure.

Newham London Borough 1997a (94/A/2213). *Renovation grants; system of payments to builder*

The ombudsman found maladministration in the use of public money – in relation to how the council made payments to the builder for renovation grant works under the Local Government and Housing Act 1989. Problems included the fact that a) payments were made to the builder without the grant recipient's authority; b) the signature on the forms confirming that the work was satisfactory a) did not authorise payments direct to the builder, and b) was not the applicant's signature anyway; c) there was not relationship between the work done and the sums authorised; d) the grant calculation was based on inadequate detailed estimates; e) approval was given for work to start before the grant had been approved – without any reasons as required by the legislation (then the Local Government and Housing Act 1989, now the Housing Grants, Construction and Regeneration Act 1996); f) progress of work on site visits was not properly recorded; g) one particular payment made before the foundations were layed should have only been made when the extension was nearly completed; h) additional amounts were approved for works when there was no evidence that such works were required; i) additional works which were approved and paid for duplicated works already in the original specification.

Newham London Borough 1997b (94/A/0503 and others). *Renovation grants; system of handling applications; demand outstripping supply*

A number of similar complaints were received about renovation grants under provisions (now superseded) of the Local Government and Housing Act 1989; the ombudsman investigated them together and made the following points.

Insufficient resources. Quite properly, the council had assessed the likely demand for grants and made the proper request for funding. However, it simply did not receive sufficient funds; this was not the council's fault. It was also reasonable to adopt a queuing system; the council did not fetter its discretion by giving priority to disabled people or to houses with dangerous structures – because exceptional circumstances could be considered by the director of housing or by the fortnightly meeting of a sub-committee.

Uneven waiting times, inadequate records, inconsistent application of criteria. However, there was maladministration on three counts. First, waiting times in the north of the borough were much longer than in the south. Second, the council did not have adequate records of what information it gave to enquiries. Third, it did not explain clearly a) the grounds for priority; b) the difference between initial enquiry and formal application; c) that a council survey was not a necessary condition of making an application; and d) that works should not be started before a grant had been approved. Third, priority criteria were applied inconsistently. Lastly, the enquiry form asked for too little information about structural danger to decide whether priority was appropriate.

Nevertheless, although such maladministration was the cause of delay in some cases, though not in others, the: 'fundamental cause was the mismatch between supply and demand. This affected thousands of people. Even if there had been no maladministration, there would have been long waits. While I sympathise with the frustration, anxiety and difficulties of the complainants, I do not consider that it would be equitable to single them out by recommending compensation for them (unless there is some exceptional fault peculiar to the complainant); that would be unfair to all the other people who waited and did not complain to me. And it would be unfair to the taxpayer because the overwhelming reason for delay was beyond the council's control'.

North Tyneside Metropolitan Borough Council 1994 (92/C/1381). *Delay in dealing with renovation grant application; applicant completes work before approval given*

In this case the applicant applied for a renovation grant in May 1991; by March 1993 his application had still not been considered. At that point, he decided that, given how unpleasant his kitchen was, he would proceed with the work by borrowing money and doing whatever he could himself. (However, local authorities are not legally permitted to approve renovation (or disabled facilities) grants for work which has already been completed before the application has been approved).

The ombudsman recommended that the council now assess which works would have been eligible for a mandatory renovation grant and pay a sum (plus interest) to the complainant equivalent to what he would have received by way of grant. In addition, it should pay compensation of £250 for the uncertainty, delay and poorer standard of living suffered by himself and his family.

North Yorkshire County Council 1993 (and *Harrogate Borough Council 1993*: 91/C/0565 and 92/C/1400). *Assessment and provision of equipment and home adaptations; Chronically Sick and Disabled Persons Act 1970, ss.1 and 2; disabled facilities grants*

The complainant was severely disabled from birth, had limited use of his arms and legs, used a non-electric wheelchair throughout the day, and lived in council accommodation with a full-time carer.

In June 1990 he wrote to the county council requesting a written assessment of his need for aids and adaptations. The council replied in August, saying that an occupational therapist would soon visit; the visit took place in February 1991, the delay being caused by work pressure on the occupational therapy service. When the assessment took place, various potential needs were discussed: bathroom adaptations (layout change, bidet-type toilet and electric overhead hoist), second ramped access at rear, work processor, video tape selector, mobile telephone, electric wheelchair, lowering of reading table, intercom to the bedroom, emergency care cover.

Bathroom. The county council made a recommendation to the borough council; the borough council put the work on hold in May 1991 because its budget for that financial year had already been spent. The adaptations were not ready for use until the beginning of 1993. The ombudsman found maladministration both in respect of the delay in assessment (above) and the borough council's delay; the ombudsman felt the assessment should have been carried out within five months, and the works within six. The borough council had also failed to notify formally the complainant of the delay; this, too, was maladministration.

Second ramped access. The complainant had previously had a request for a second ramped access from his dining room turned down; the borough council's suggestion of an alternative ramp from the kitchen door had not been taken up. In response to this new request, the county council first said that he did need the dining room ramp, but then changed its mind (after the occupational therapist and housing officer had consulted). The ombudsman found that the council 'was entitled to change its view of the situation but it should have notified its client formally of any change. I consider its failure to do so is maladministration'.

Word processor. The county council occupational therapist had agreed that the complainant needed a word processor to be attached to his 'POSSUM' (an environmental control system) in order to study; she gave him information about grants available from the education department of the county council. He was provided with the hardware by a private firm and the software by the council. There was no maladministration here.

Mobile telephone. The occupational therapist considered that this was not necessary because the already had access to a telephone through the POSSUM. No maladministration.

Electric wheelchair. The occupational therapist carried out an assessment for such a wheelchair; the council explained that wheelchair provision was primarily an NHS function. However, it would assess for electric wheelchairs; the client would then either use mobility allowance or the council would attempt to find charitable funding. In this case, although the complainant had a trial with a manufacturer, he felt the cost was prohibitive; not charitable funding was sought. The council's 'failure to follow up the issue' was maladministration.

More generally, the ombudsman stated that there appeared to be 'some confusion as to whose responsibility it is to provide electric wheelchairs for indoor and outdoor use. I am reluctant to view the county council as having no responsibility for this under the Chronically Sick and Disabled Persons Act'.

Holiday. The council did not respond adequately to a request for assistance with transport before the man went on holiday, and was then slow to sort matters out after he had returned. However, the council did pay £93 petrol money plus interest retrospectively. Thus, the maladministration and any injustice had been remedied by the council.

Information under Chronically Sick and Disabled Persons Act 1970, s.1. In September 1990, the complainant requested information about other services; the council provided a range of information leaflets in respect of its duty under s.1 of the Chronically Sick and Disabled Persons Act 1970. After the man's complaint had reached the ombudsman, a council officer visited in March 1992 specifically to go through the relevant legislation and left copies of the relevant legislation. There was no maladministration, since the man now had the information he wanted and access to further information through his care manager.

Recommendations. The social services committee of the county council had already agreed to pay £500 in compensation; the ombudsman recommended that the borough council pay £800 in respect of the bathroom and ramp.

Northumberland County Council 1989 (88/C/0814). *Assessment; delay; applicant carries out home adaptations; retrospective payment sought; Chronically Sick and Disabled Persons Act 1970,s.2; Disabled Persons (Services, Consultation and Representation) Act 1986*

The husband of a woman with multiple sclerosis complained that the council had delayed in assessing his wife and would not pay for provision of a downstairs WC. She had been diagnosed with multiple sclerosis in October 1987, but no assessment 'of any substance' was undertaken until October 1988. An interim visit had been made solely to inspect the work undertaken by the husband – who had claimed a retrospective payment for it. He had gone ahead and installed the downstairs WC because he had wanted to help his wife but, having initially looked to the council, had been told that an assessment would not take place for some considerable time.

Confused policy on retrospective payments. The council regarded the WC as being in the wrong place and at a floor level which could prove difficult for the wife. However, since the council delayed giving advice, the ombudsman understood why the husband had got on with the work. The ombudsman found confusion within the council about the issue of retrospective payments; members of the social services sub-committee believed there was a policy of not making them; but two of the officers concerned thought that where the work coincided with what would have been recommended (had there not been such a long delay in assessment), then payment would be made.

The ombudsman found maladministration and injustice in that the council had failed to deal with the request for assistance within a reasonable time; it had not even attempted a partial assessment. The council should now compensate the husband for expenditure on the WC, and such a payment 'should not prejudice any application ... for assistance with the relocation of this WC in the future should that be necessary: the extra cost to public funds which might be involved in that would be a consequence of the council's maladministration'.

Nottinghamshire County Council 1998 (97/C/2126). *Level of support; professional decision; break in management and supervision of case; Children Act 1989*
A child care case in which the ombudsman did not criticise the professional decision to allocate a particular level of support, which later proved to be inadequate given the emergence later of child protection issues, because it was so 'unreasonably deficient as to amount to maladministration'. However, a break in management and supervision of the case when it was between a specialist team and an area office was maladministration.

Pendle Borough Council 1994 (92/C/0579). *Disabled facilities grant; amount; extra works; lack of clear information*
The complainant claimed that he was misled by a council officer about the amount of disabled facilities grant he would receive; as a result he was £425 in debt.

Mismatch between estimate and grant. His wife had Huntingdon's Chorea. In November 1988, county council officers visited and advised that a downstairs and toilet be installed. A grant application was not made until 1990; in January 1991, by which time the national grants system had changed, an officer from the borough council visited. The man claimed that the officer said that 100 per cent funding would be available; the officer said he had explained that the man might have to make a contribution. The council's grant came to less than the builder's estimate, because it felt the overall estimated cost was excessive, although it could not pinpoint any particular proposed item as excessive.

Lack of clarity. When the council had drawn up a revised schedule of works, a non-slip floor had been included, not mentioned in the previous schedule. The complainant believed that the council had not that the complainant might have to pay something, but he could understand why the complainant believed the floor had not been taken into account – the council did not make clear which works it had considered when arriving at the final amount.

Responsibility of council to make clear financial implications. A social worker involved had doubted that the husband would knowingly get into debt; the ombudsman accepted that this would have been 'a degree of recklessness ... out of character'. The ombudsman realised that the grants system and legislation was complex but the council had a responsibility to ensure that the applicant, who was 'in a vulnerable position, understood fully the financial implications of the application he was making'. The failure to provide clear information was maladministration causing injustice in the form of the debt the complainant owed; the council should pay compensation of £800.

Powys County Council 1990 (88/484). *Duty to assess a disabled person; Chronically Sick and Disabled Persons Act 1970,s.2; Disabled Persons (Services, Consultation and Representation) Act 1986,s.4*

The complainant had worsening arthritis which had now gone beyond her wrists and hands to affect her knees and legs, and was fearful of a fall while bathing or going up and down the steep stairs in a remote rural cottage (her husband was away on work for part of the week). She telephoned the social services department in July 1988, specifically asking for a home assessment and advice about equipment. Failing any response, she and her husband visited the department in October, where she was interviewed by a duty social worker. The council did not employ occupational therapists to assess disabled people; social workers did this. In November she was visited by an officer who provided a bath seat but explained that she could not do a full assessment because of her own inexperience: somebody else would have to. However, on returning to the office, it was decided that pressure of work did not justify a further visit and assessment.

In January 1989, the woman fell downstairs, suffered a lacerated skull and severe concussion, and was taken to hospital. Consequent on a home visit made by a hospital occupational therapist, the council supplied further equipment including bath aids and a curved handrail for the top of the stairs. The hospital occupational therapist had also recommended rails right down the stairs but the council said that it did not stock these; the husband therefore bought and fitted them himself. The ombudsman concluded that the woman had experienced 'unnecessary difficulty in receiving the assessment' which it had a duty to do, 'reasonably promptly' (under s.4 of the Disabled Persons (Services, Consultation and Representation) Act 1986. This was maladministration and the ombudsman recommended a gracious apology and compensation for the cost of the rails.

Redbridge London Borough Council 1993a (92/A/4108). *Request for help with the bath; long wait for assessment; Chronically Sick and Disabled Persons Act 1970,s.2; Disabled Persons (Services, Consultation and Representation) Act 1986; Local Authority Social Services Act 1970,s.6*

The complainant was 86 years old with arthritis, asthma and sciatica which made it difficult to get in and out of her high-sided bath. Since falling and breaking a hip, she had been unable to use the bath at all.

Bathing help; three-year wait for assessment. In November 1990, the woman's general practitioner wrote to the council requesting a handrail for the bath; in January 1991, her daughter wrote requesting kitchen adaptations to accommodate a washing machine (the council told her this work was discretionary and that it was not approving such requests at that time). In October 1991, following her fall and hip operations, the woman wrote to the council from hospital enquiring about progress on 'her bathing problems'. The council replied that she was not on the waiting list for a shower because she had not requested it; instead she was on the OTA3 (ie, occupational therapy assistant) waiting list for a bath rail. In February, she wrote again; in March she received bath aids; in July she and her brother visited the council's disability advice centre to discuss the bathing difficulties.

Complaint. In September, she wrote to the council making a complaint. In October, the council replied that there was enormous demand for occupational therapy assessments and enclosed details of the priority guidelines. The woman remained unhappy and requested that her complaint be considered by a review panel. It was accepted at the hearing that bath aids would not help, a major adaptation was required, and she should be 'reprioritised' to the OT3 (ie, occupational therapist) waiting list. The panel found that she had been dealt with consistent with the guidelines and policies, but that these gave rise to concern – since category 3 or 4 assessments could take two or three years to take place. It recommended strongly that the council review its priorities, and encouraged the woman to take the case further to the ombudsman. At the time of the ombudsman's report, an assessment was due to take place in November 1993.

Conclusion: serious shortcomings. The ombudsman said there were 'serious shortcomings', a three year delay was 'totally unacceptable' and there was 'a wider failure of the occupational therapy service'. In 1987, the occupational therapy manager realised that there were serious problems; this was reported to the social services committee in January 1988. However, the situation was not properly monitored, adequate records of the number of people waiting and average waiting times were not kept, backlogs increased because of decentralisation of the service and staff reductions – and only in February 1992 when the service was recentralised was there proper monitoring, investigation and action to improve the situation. (Earlier in the report the ombudsman had referred to s.6 of the Local Authority Services Act 1970, and the authority's duty to provide adequate staff for the director of social services).

Recommendations. All this was maladministration; the three year wait caused injustice. It would have been 'reasonable in the circumstances to expect the assessment of her needs to have been begun within six months of the first approach'. The council's delay therefore retarded provision by 30 months, during which time the woman could not have a bath or shower. The ombudsman recommended a payment of £900, plus £30 for every month of further delay in the assessment; in addition, £250 should be paid for the time and trouble of bringing the complaint. The council should continue to monitor the service closely, and ensure that applicants were assessed in a reasonable time.

Redbridge London Borough Council 1993b (92/A/1173). *Delay in assessment; 20 months; second highest priority category; Chronically Sick and Disabled Persons Act 1970,s.2; Disabled Persons (Services, Consultation and Representation) Act 1986; Local Authority Social Services Act 1970,s.6*
The complainant acted on behalf of his grandmother, who was 88 years old, and suffered from arthritis, dizzy spells, obesity and had cataracts in both eyes. She could not walk up or down the stairs, but had to crawl up and come down on her bottom. She lived in a house with two of her grandsons, the wife of one of whom did virtually everything for her. The family wanted to apply for a downstairs extension and completed a disability referral form in September 1991.

Considerable delay followed and the ombudsman found that a wait of 20 months for assessment – for a person who was initially in the second-highest priority category and then in the highest – was 'totally unacceptable'. It would have been reasonable 'in the circumstances to expect the assessment of her needs to have been begun within a month or two of the first approach to the Council'. There was additional fault because the council failed to inform the family of the priority awarded, to explain about priority categories, to state how long the wait for an assessment might be, and to advise about the council's complaints procedure. The ombudsman also repeated his concern about the 'wider failure' of the occupational therapy service (see the *Redbridge CC 1993a* investigation immediately above).

The delay caused the woman to remain in unsuitable accommodation about 18 months longer than was necessary. A remedy for this injustice was compensation of £900 for the woman, and £250 for her grandson for his time and trouble.

Redbridge London Borough Council 1998 (95/C/1472 and 95/C/2543). *Residential/nursing home care or living at home; cost of care package; disputed ordinary residence; lifting and handling law; Secretary of State directions; fulfilling of contract care home; unauthorised undertakings by staff leading to unfulfilled expectations of person; National Assistance Act 1948,ss.21,26,29; Manual Handling Operations Regulations 1992; Chronically Sick and Disabled Persons Act 1970,s.2*
A particularly detailed and long (running to over 90 pages) ombudsman report examining a dispute about whether a disabled person should live in the community in his own home (as he wished) or in a residential or nursing home (against his wishes). It illustrates a number of key issues in community care including:

(a) *wishes and resources:* the extent to which a disabled person's wish to live in his own accommodation was consonant with the resources of the two local authorities concerned (an annual care package at various amounts, of up to £70,000 was at times being considered);

(b) *choosing carers:* the wish and ability of the person to choose his own carers;

(c) *lifting and handling:* the conflict between the man's wish to be handled, moved and lifted manually rather than by means of a hoist, the related health and safety factors in issue including the adequacy of risk assessments and the training of carers, the person's wish to choose his own carers, and a dispute as to why the person wished to be handled only by women (see p.178 of this book);

(d) *contracted duty of care home to provide specified services*: the contractual obligation of the care home to provide the 24-hour care it was being paid by the council to provide, despite a breakdown in relationship between some of the staff and the disabled person (see p.453 of this book);

(e) *dispute about funding and the ordinary residence of the person*: a protracted dispute between two local authorities as to the ordinary residence of the person – first if he stayed in the care home (where he had been placed by Redbridge in another authority's area. The Secretary of State was applied to for resolution of the dispute (for ordinary residence issues, see p.169 of this book);

(f) *Secretary of State's directions*: refusal of the Secretary of State to issue specific directions as to what care should be provided by which authority (see p.437 of this book);

(g) *false expectations*: the misleading raising of the disabled person's hopes as a result of unauthorised and ultimately unfulfilled undertakings by particular staff (see p.50 of this book).

Care package: maladministration. In conclusion, the ombudsman found that there was maladministration on the following grounds. First, a decision had been made by an officer not authorised to do so; this led to a misleading offer of a community care package. Second, this offer was not rescinded in writing for a considerable time and then only in a letter less than frank about the failures that had occurred and without an apology. Third, there was delay in making clear that in any case the council was not empowered fully to support the home care package because, it was argued, s.2 of the Chronically Sick and Disabled Persons Act 1970 which contained a duty to provide such support applied only to people ordinarily resident in the area of the authority, and not to people who had become ordinarily resident in another area. For these latter people, only limited services could be provided under a power (rather than a duty) contained in 2.29 of the National Assistance Act 1948. Fourth, misleading advice from the council's own legal department on this issue contributed to the maladministration.

All this resulted in a) the person's expectations being 'unreasonably raised, somewhat dashed but then not clearly extinguished for a long time' and to great disappointment and stress; b) the man's move from the care home being delayed unnecessarily for over two-and-a-half years; c) enormous time, trouble and expense on the part of himself and his relatives; and d) and a 'huge waste' of the council's own resources, particularly the time of its own officers.

Lifting and handling: maladministration. There was further maladministration on the following grounds. First, the council was aware of the complications surrounding lifting and handling from a previous placement but did not plan what to do if they recurred in the new placement; this was maladministration, although it was balanced by the fact that the man moved to the care home initially without the council's approval.

Second, for a substantial period of time the person did not receive an 'appropriate level of care' and so 'suffered considerably as a result'. His elderly parents, who undertook the caring tasks (instead of the care home staff), were put to a 'huge amount of stress, time and trouble that should not have been necessary'. However, the man contributed to the problem by behaving antagonistically to some of the care home staff; although this behaviour in turn might have been in part due to the frustration caused by his expectations (see above) which had been raised misleadingly by the council.

Third, although it was 'very difficult' for Redbridge's officers to deal with these 'complex problems' at a distance (ie, in the area of the other authority), this was no excuse, since the owners of the care home were acting on behalf of the council which had to 'take full responsibility for the ultimate failure to make appropriate provision'.

Lastly, there was a predominant medical view that use of a hoist could harm the man (in his thirties with a rare genetic disease which was progressively immobilising him) by further damaging his muscles. And despite the conflicting conclusions of expert lifting and handling assessments, there was a predominant view also that manual handling could be carried out safely if the right method was employed. However, the council did not deal with this issue effectively, particularly when a senior officer wrote to the man telling him that he would have to stay in bed for the time being. This was 'unacceptable', 'insensitive' – and 'inappropriate', since the officer was not medically qualified and the man's general practitioner had stated that remaining in bed would be detrimental to the man's condition.

Ordinary residence dispute. The council delayed in attempting to resolve the dispute as to the area of ordinary residence of the person both in relation to negotiating with the other council involved (12 months delay) and then in relation to seeking a resolution by the Secretary of State (8 months delay). This was maladministration, which 'significantly extended' the period of uncertainty for the person and caused him great frustration.

Remedy. The ombudsman recommended £5,500 in compensation.

Rochdale Metropolitan Borough Council 1995 (93/C/3660). *Waiting times for equipment; over-simplistic priorities; Chronically Sick and Disabled Persons Act 1970, s.2*
A children's case in which a disabled child had to wait 15 months for new seating, including a 12-month wait for assessment. The assessment had been prioritised as complex, which meant that it was on a longer waiting list than existed for cases categorised as emergency or simple. The council did not disagree with the view of the College of Occupational Therapists – consulted by the ombudsman – that such a child's needs should have been treated as urgent. The ombudsman concluded that the system of priorities was 'over-simple', because within the category of complex cases, there was 'no provision for relatively simple solutions to tide people over until a full assessment' could be made. Furthermore, there was no provision of treating some cases more urgently within the 'complex' category, even though they were not emergency in nature. This over-simple system meant that the child's needs were not met promptly and was maladministration.

The ombudsman did not criticise the council for wanting to use paediatric occupational therapists for such assessments. However, in that case, it should have attempted to free them from other work, so as to give them more time for assessment work. In addition, in the light of a recruitment problem, the council had failed to use one obvious avenue: the College of Occupational Therapist's directory of occupational therapists in private practice. This, too, was maladministration.

Rotherham Metropolitan Borough Council 1995 (94/C/2287). *Lift installation; delay; disabled facilities grants*
The complaint was about delay in installing a lift in a woman's council home to help her care for her severely disabled son. The property had originally been allocated to her so that adaptations (including an adapted upstairs bathroom) could be carried out. She subsequently requested a through-floor lift in March 1993 by means of an application for a disabled facilities grant under the Local Government and Housing Act 1989; it was finally installed in February 1995.

The ombudsman considered the causes of the delay. In part it had been due to the complainant in so far as she at one time during the process requested that the possibility of a stairlift be investigated. She had insisted that, if possible, chimney breasts be removed. This was to maximise space: in fact her neighbour, concerned about noise nuisance caused by a hydraulic lift against the common wall, refused permission. In turn the council's officers had to seek legal advice about the matter of nuisance, and to carry out survey work.

Lack of explanation, breakdown in communication, delay in processing application. However, at three points, the council was at fault for the delay. First, for a period of six months the woman did not pursue her application for the lift because she thought her application for rehousing was being actively considered. In fact, she had been awarded no priority on grounds of medical transfer, but this was not explained to her. Second, after she had decided to take up the option of the lift again, communication failures within the council meant that a message from her social worker to the relevant officer was never received. This resulted in a further delay of two months. Third, another five months passed because the relevant officer did not process the application owing to work pressures.

Conclusion and recommendations. All this had led to one year's delay, requiring the woman to carry her growing child up and down the stairs for longer than would otherwise have been necessary; this was injustice. In addition, it meant additional time and trouble in pursuing the disabled facilities grant application. The ombudsman recommended £500 compensation.

Salford City Council 1993 (91/C/1972). *Poor coordination; duty of social services department to assist with adaptations; disabled facilities grants; Chronically Sick and Disabled Persons Act 1970,s.2*
The complainants were the parents of three children, one with severe learning disabilities, poor physical skills, epilepsy and double incontinence. They applied for a ground-floor extension in November 1988. Their original application (under the old improvement grant system) was unacceptable and had to be resubmitted, because of failure on the part of the council to coordinate the activities of different departments. For instance, the assessment of needs, drawing up of plans, obtaining grant aid, and getting planning permission involved three different council departments (and two separate sections within one of the departments). This was maladministration.

The new application (now under the new grants system) for the disabled facilities grant was handled properly, but after the complainants told the council they could not afford their assessed contribution, the social services department did nothing for 20 months, having appeared 'to ignore the fact that their statutory responsibility to provide assistance did not come to an end with the offer of a grant'. This was also maladministration.

The consequence was that the extension could only be proceeded with at the end of 1992 instead of what the ombudsman concluded to be a reasonable date: the beginning of 1991. The ombudsman recommended compensation of a total of £2,000.

Salford City Council 1996 (94/C/0399). *Adequacy of assessment; eligibility; handling of complaint; equipment and adaptations; NHS and Community Care Act 1990,s.47; Chronically Sick and Disabled Persons Act 1970,s.2; Disabled Persons (Services, Consultation and Representation) Act 1986,s.4; NHS Act 1977,schedule 8*
The complaint was made by an advice centre, on behalf of the next-of-kin of a man, an AIDS sufferer, who had died. It focused on the alleged failure of the council to respond to a request for help and information and to make adequate provision for the man's needs, and on the delay over investigating his complaints. The man lived alone; he was reported to be easily distressed, subject to extreme noise sensitivity because of a brain disorder – and to night sweats, a chronic skin condition, acute diarrhoea and weight loss.

Request for information; no action taken. In June 1992, he received an 'Orange Badge' from the council in recognition of his restricted mobility. In September he asked for information about services for people with AIDS. He was referred to the disability services team by a social worker who recorded that there might be a three or four month wait for an assessment. A senior social worker explained in retrospect that is was up to the man to make clear what his needs were to the duty officer, that at the time he was not substantially disabled, and that he was well able to articulate his needs and wishes. In the event, no further action was taken and the case was closed. Subsequently in the same month, the Independent Living Fund (ILF) wrote to the council requesting information about the man – since it was considering what help it could provide. The council did not reply; the senior social worker said that since there had been no plans to provide social services for the man, there was no need to respond to the ILF's request.

Inaction of social services. An occupational therapist then visited with no prior notice but found the man out; she left a postcard. He made no contact, and the case was now closed as well by the occupational therapists in mid-October. It was normal practice not to follow up cases because of the long waiting list for assessments, and because clients had good reasons for not wanting an occupational therapist to visit. In November, the ILF approved a request to increase its contribution towards the man's nursing care; in February it wrote again to the social services department, pointing out that the man was severely disabled and in need of substantial support.

Home help approved but no telephone; influence of resources. A social worker then visited the man in March. As a consequence, home help was put in place, but a request for a telephone was refused because he did not meet the criteria: although he lived alone, a carer was always present. In addition, she considered he could use the caretaker's telephone – but the man would not have felt able to, because of a past breach of confidence. She subsequently accepted that she had referred to the lack of resources as a significant reason for the refusal and to the 'freeze' until the next financial year. The council also later confirmed that its telephone budget had been spent. In the interim, the man's carer installed a telephone at his own expense.

Special fund for HIV/AIDS; fragmented assessment. By April, the social worker was going to visit again, but following what was perceived to be a critical letter sent to the council by a voluntary organisation on behalf of the man, she was advised to have no further contact – which meant she could not arrange for further services. She was unaware of the special fund which the social services department had for people with AIDS. In May, the carer said the council finally installed a telephone despite the fact that he had already done so – although the council had no record of this.

In March, an occupational therapist visited; she recorded his serious condition and recommended various items including walking sticks, height adjusters and a sheepskin. These were delivered within days; a shower were later installed, paid for by the special AIDS fund, since the housing department said it had no resources. Between March and April, the man was assessed on three separate occasions by three different parts of the social services department – a fragmented approach which, the carer claimed, added to the stress the man was under in trying to obtain appropriate services.

Failure to assess and provide essential facilities. The ombudsman found maladministration. First, the council had breached various statutory obligations: it had failed 'properly to assess and make provision for [the man's] needs at the earliest possible date ... which denied him appropriate and essential services and facilities at a critical time of his life'. The ombudsman had earlier set out the relevant legislation: ss.1. (information provision) and 2 of the Chronically Sick and Disabled Persons Act 1970, s.4 of the Disabled Persons (Services, Consultation and Representation) Act 1986, schedule 8 of the NHS Act 1977 (home help and laundry facilities), and s.47 of the NHS and Community Care Act 1990.

Eligibility for telephone. The council had also failed properly to determine the man's eligibility for a telephone and had confused the issues of funding and need; this caused distress and extra expense.

Dealing with the complaint, In addition, the council failed to deal with the man's complaint within the statutory time limit, despite his request that it be dealt with quickly. It ignored his request to keep the advice centre informed and instead communicated with another party (albeit with the best of intentions) without the man's knowledge. The man died in July 1993 without knowing the outcome of his complaint. The council also did not investigate fully what had occurred in September 1992 (the investigating officer had at the time received little guidance or support and had not fully understood her role). All this was maladministration causing injustice.

The ombudsman commended the council for making a positive response to the complaint – but did not feel that an apology and an undertaking to amend practices and procedures was sufficient. She recommended that £500 compensation be paid to the man's estate.

Sandwell Metropolitan Borough Council 1995 (93/B/3956). *Home lift; home adaptations; handling of complaint; Chronically Sick and Disabled Persons Act 1970,s.2*
The complaint concerned the council's refusal to fund extra adaptation work in connection with the installation of a vertical lift, allegedly on the basis of inaccurate and incomplete information – and also the delay in installing a ramp.

Effect of delay and inefficiency on a disabled person. The ombudsman noted that as a wheelchair user, the complainant was 'especially dependent on the Council's services for his social and physical well-being – far more dependent than an able-bodied citizen would be. Under these circumstances it is vital that the Council assesses his needs and responds to them as quickly and effectively as its finances and competing statutory demands allow. Delay and inefficiency are not mere irritants ... they afflict and blight his quality of life'.

Report to committee flawed in content and timing. The report submitted to a council committee for the decision about extra funding was written only two days after the receipt of an increased quotation; in the rush, it was not surprising that it was badly flawed. Given the high quotation, the officer concerned should have demanded sufficiently detailed costings to enable a comparison to be made with other alternative suppliers. The report did not explain why the extra works were necessary, contained factual errors, did not explain why the complainant refused to accept the lift being sited in the lounge. Alternative sites had never been properly evaluated or costed. To refuse the works on such 'uncertain evidence' was maladministration.

Delay; no system of checking completion of works. The ramp was ordered nine months after its provision had been agreed, and not installed for a further six months; and there was no system for checking that works which had been ordered were in fact completed. This was maladministration. The man's informal complaint was not properly investigated and he was not informed of the findings; this too was maladministration.

Difference between complaint and appeal. The man also complained that he was not allowed to make a formal complaint about the way in which the committee had reached its decision; the council viewed his request as an appeal against the committee's decision and felt the complaints procedure would be inappropriate. But the ombudsman felt that the complaint should have been investigated – it was not an appeal, but a complaint that 'his situation had been misrepresented and officers had not passed relevant information to Members' of the committee. It was maladministration not to consider this as a further complaint in its own right.

Conclusion and recommendations. The injustice arising was that the man had been forced a) to wait 16 months for the ramp and thus for safe and convenient access to the front of the property; b) to continue to use an unsatisfactory electric hoist which did not comply with current safety standards for some 15 months longer than necessary; and c) to defer adaptation of his kitchen. He had not also not been afforded the opportunity to have his complaint investigated properly. The ombudsman recommended an apology, £1,250 compensation for the delay and £250 for time and trouble in pursuing the complaint.

Sandwell Metropolitan Borough Council 1997 (94/B/4662 and 94/B/4686). *Renovation grants; lack of communication*

A case concerning delay in the award of mandatory renovation grants (as they were then under the Local Government and Housing Act 1989). The delays were three years and three-and-a-half years for the two complainants respectively – and an inspection had still not been carried out.

The ombudsman accepted that the council was faced with a 'huge demand for a statutory entitlement it cannot afford to meet', due to central government's financial restrictions. There was no priority system; but an application for urgent inspection could be make in case of danger. Nevertheless, the three-year wait in the first case was too long and maladministration; as was a lack of communication from the council about what was going on, thus depriving the person of knowledge about her entitlement or alternative options. In the second case, despite being informed of an electrical fire and the potential danger, the council still did not visit – until the ombudsman intervened, when it concluded that the house was not fit for human habitation. This was maladministration.

The ombudsman recommended £250 compensation in the first case and £1,500 in the second.

Sheffield City Council 1989 (88/C/1048). *Delay in assessment; shortage of professionals; Chronically Sick and Disabled Persons Act 1970,s.2; Disabled Persons (Services, Consultation and Representation) Act 1986,s.4*

A case involving an application in February 1998 by an elderly couple for an 'intermediate grant' under the Housing Act 1985 (before the advent of the disabled facilities grant system) for a WC in a house which did not have one internally. The wife had previously obtained an 'Orange Badge' from the council – a condition of receiving this badge was permanent and substantial disability. There were placed in the lowest priority group where they would have to wait some time for an assessment by social services; and they were told that it might be 12 months before any work was carried out. In September 1998, they had a WC fitted at their own expense.

The ombudsman accepted that in order to determine whether the WC was necessary, the council wished to take 'suitable advice' and that there 'may be many fields of activity where the Council – or one of its citizens – would prefer in an ideal world to act only on the advice of a professional person. That ideal is not always achievable either because of cost or because of a shortage of suitable professionals. Postponing action for a year or more may be one option but is certainly not the only alternative. If the action required is to fulfil a statutory duty then postponement for a year should not even be an option'.

Furthermore, the Orange Badge should have enabled the council to establish quickly that the existing WC was not readily accessible and to make available the grant. The ombudsman recommended that a payment be made equivalent to the amount of grant which would have been awarded.

Sheffield City Council 1994 (93/C/0005). *Delay in assessment; Chronically Sick and Disabled Persons Act 1970,s.2; Disabled Persons (Services, Consultation and Representation) Act 1986,s.4*
The complaint was made by the sister of a woman who was ill with Asperger's Syndrome, a form of autism. By 1992, the woman's condition had deteriorated to such an extent that she was eating and drinking little and her physical health was endangered. Several requests for assessment were made to the council to which it did not respond over a period of four months. Given the seriousness of the woman's condition, this was maladministration.

The case had been allocated to a particular officer, even though she was about to take leave; the ombudsman was unimpressed that the case supposedly required that particular officer's expertise, given that she had no direct experience of autism. More delay then occurred because when the officer did not return to work for a further period, the case was not reallocated. The delay in assessing the woman's needs and funding appropriate care meant that her condition did not improve and may even have deteriorated; and her family was subjected to more stress and anxiety than necessary. The ombudsman recommended £800 compensation in total.

Sheffield City Council 1995 (93/C/1609). *Failure to assess; disabled person; housing for wheelchair; Chronically Sick and Disabled Persons Act 1970,s.2; Disabled Persons (Services, Consultation and Representation) Act 1986*
The complainant claimed that the council had failed to consider properly her request for assistance in housing her electric vehicle. She lived in a council house and received income support and mobility allowance. She was in poor health, had difficultly in walking and was entirely reliant on a neighbour to go shopping or to other facilities as the local library.

Private purchase of electric wheelchair. In order to alleviate these problems, she had brought an electric wheelchair but now required a shelter for it for protection against the whether and vandals. She had identified a pre-fabricated store costing £1,000, and a charity had given her £600 towards the cost. She hoped to enter into an agreement with the supplier to pay the rest by instalment but was concerned that this financial commitment was beyond her means.

Danger, eligibility and Chronically Sick and Disabled Persons Act 1970. The council had some years ago provided a hardstanding and pavement crossing for the woman when she still had a car (since given up). However, now it claimed that it had 'no budgetary provision' for storage facilities for wheelchairs. It further argued that no legal duty arose under s.2 of the Chronically Sick and Disabled Persons Act 1970 'in the absence of any suggestion of personal danger or serious inconvenience'. The council's files held no record of any assessment of the woman's need. The council wrote to the woman, stating that 'a request had been made for her needs to be assessed, but that from the information received she did not appear to meet the Council's criteria for a service and would not therefore receive a visit'. Enclosed with the letter was a copy of the council's criteria of eligibility; the letter did state that the woman should contact the council if she felt that she had missed out important details from her application.

Taking account of financial means of the applicant. By now, the ombudsman was involved and the council did agree to assess her needs. It noted that she could walk only a short distance, required oxygen, received mobility allowance and attendance allowance, had an indoor wheelchair from the NHS, had no family to help, and was using the attendance allowance to buy private care. The council sent a copy of its assessment report to the ombudsman, together with the claim that since the woman appeared to have the money to buy the storage, it had no duty to provide the facility. However, the report made no mention of an assessment of the woman's means – furthermore, the logic of the council's position was undermined because it had in the past provided a ramp and shower for her. The council also stated a) that because the storage facility was not needed for her immediate well-being, she did not come within the department's priorities for assistance; and b) that its policy was that outdoor mobility needs should be met by mobility allowance where that was being received.

Failure to assess; flawed reference to person's means. The ombudsman found maladministration. First, the council had made no assessment at the outset, and had then on reconsideration decided that she did not merit a visit (an assessment) because she did not meet the criteria it had sent her. Furthermore it had set out its criteria in an 'exhaustive list'. All this meant that the council was in breach of its duty to decide – on a request made under s.4 of the Disabled Persons (Services, Consultation and Representation) Act 1986 – whether services under s.2 of the Chronically Sick and Disabled Persons Act 1970 were needed.

In respect of the assessment that the council eventually carried out, the ombudsman accepted that 'an individual's private means may be relevant as to whether or not the Council itself needs to make any provision'. Nevertheless the council had raised this argument only 'very late in the day' – and had in any case apparently made no effort to establish what the mobility allowance was already being spent on in reality.

Recommendations. The ombudsman recommended that the council now carry out a proper assessment and make such provision as was necessary to meet its legal obligations; it should anyway pay £250 compensation for the time and trouble expended on the complaint.

Sheffield City Council 1996 (94/C/1563). *Stairlift, differing recommendations, user preference; blanket policy; disabled facilities grants; Chronically Sick and Disabled Persons Act 1970,s.2*
The complainant had chronic, progressive multiple sclerosis. She had limited mobility and got around the house by walking on her knees. After initial diagnosis she funded a number of adaptations herself, believing that her income was too high for her to receive help from the council.

Vertical lift recommended; stairlift policy. Subsequently, she requested an assessment. An occupational therapist did this, recommending and providing a number of aids, and discussing how the woman could get up and down the stairs. The woman wanted a curved stairlift, but claimed that the therapist had told her that the council never gave stairlifts to people with multiple sclerosis – and that she might be offered a vertical, through-floor lift which would allow, as and when necessary, wheelchair use upstairs. The woman was unhappy at the loss of living space this would entail, and questioned the logic of the decision in relation to wheelchair use – since the restricted space upstairs would preclude wheelchair use. She then made a formal complaint.

Disputed assessment; straight stairlift recommended. A second assessment by an occupational therapist took place, although the woman claimed that it had been cursory and she had not been able to demonstrate her abilities and needs. Conflicting views were expressed to the ombudsman. The therapist concluded that if the woman became wheelchair-bound, then the house would not be suitable – there was indeed no point providing a vertical lift. Instead she recommended that the woman should move house, and in the short-term use a straight stairlift to reduce fatigue. However, this would terminate at a small landing short of the top of the stairs, leaving the woman to manage three steps by herself. The woman felt this was dangerous; the therapist denied that there would be a safety problem in the short term.

Complaints review panel. The woman complained again, so that the complaint now progressed to the third and final stage of the complaints procedure – a review panel. The panel recommended the vertical lift, and the director of social services supported this decision.

Reassessment; curved stairlift recommended. The woman continued to protest. This time a senior officer visited her, stating that she would not normally reassess a professional decision, but that she had an 'uncomfortable feel' about this particular case. After close checking of the woman's abilities, a look around the house, and a long talk to the woman and her husband, this officer recommended the curved stairlift. She explained that although the 'previous decisions had been professionally and technically correct she did not consider that they sufficiently reflected [the woman's] personal feelings and circumstances'.

No blanket policy; assessments not flawed. The ombudsman found no maladministration, because a) she did not accept that the council had a blanket policy to deny stairlifts to people with multiple sclerosis, since two different types of stairlift were recommended; b) the original decision to offer a vertical lift followed a proper assessment and was not 'perverse or arbitrary'; c) she was satisfied that the therapist who recommended the straight stairlift had 'in her possession adequate information to form a view'; d) the review panel's decision to recommend again the vertical lift was not maladministration for the same reasons the original recommendations was not.

Sheffield City Council 1996 (95/C/2483). *Hospital discharge, delay in social services*

The complainant claimed that the council failed to respond to his request for assistance following discharge from hospital after a major operation. He had been told in hospital that help would be provided when he got home. Normally, a council officer would have visited the day after discharge. In this case, no visit was made for 10 days; when it was made the man was angry and 'gave them the rough edge of his tongue'. He had survived on mostly tinned food and managed to get to the shops with considerable difficulty. The ombudsman stated that the man had been deprived of a service which would have alleviated some of his discomfort. However, he was not entirely alone nor completely immobile and could have contacted the council during those 10 days. He chose not to.

The ombudsman concluded that £300 compensation was warranted – rather than the £1,000 the man had been seeking.

Sheffield City Council 1997a (95/C/3741). *Delay in assessment and provision; stairlift; disabled facilities grants; Chronically Sick and Disabled Persons Act 1970,s.1; Disabled Persons (Services, Consultation and Representation) Act 1986,s.4*

The complaint concerned an application for a stairlift by a 90-year old widow living in council property. After a period in hospital, she returned home in 1993 and her daughter came to live with her. She could not get up the stairs and so her bed was moved downstairs and she used a commode. In December 1993 her daughter applied for an assessment to consider stairlift provision. The mother died in December 1995, nine weeks before estimated delivery.

The ombudsman considered the same general issues as in her investigation immediately below (*Sheffield CC 1997b*) and set out the same limits to reasonable delay. In this case, the mother had undergone at least nine months of 'unreasonable delay' over and beyond these limits; this was maladministration. The recommended remedy was also the same as below.

Sheffield City Council 1997b (95/C/4413). *Delay in assessment and provision; shower; disabled facilities grants; Chronically Sick and Disabled Persons Act 1979,s.2; Disabled Persons (Services, Consultation and Representation) Act 1986,s.4*

The complaint concerned delay in providing bathing facilities for a man who had suffered a stroke in early 1993 – which had left him physically disabled and unable to speak. When he returned home from hospital, the council arranged a transfer to more suitable accommodation; however, his wife had to strip him because he could not use the bath.

Assessment. The wife wrote in June 1994 to the council asking for a shower to be installed. An assessment was made by an occupational therapist in June 1995; this wait was caused by a reduction in the social services budget of £4 million and the consequent reduction in occupational therapy posts from ten to six. The council then sent a letter explaining that criteria for provision had been met and a technical officer would visit – but that there would be a wait of about two years for the adaptation.

Policy on adaptations for public sector tenants. It was also alleged that the council unfairly prejudiced its public sector tenants who had to wait two years after assessment – whereas private sector tenants who applied for disabled facilities grants would only wait six months. The council defended its policy by pointing out that public sector tenants did not have to go through a means-test and potentially contribute financially to the adaptation. It also stated that were public sector tenants to apply for a disabled facilities grant, they would still have to wait for two years – because the council would delay sending an adaptations officer to draw up the schedule of works, without which a fully completed application could not be submitted.

Duty to provide shower; unreasonable delay. The ombudsman stated that the council was clearly under a duty to provide the shower; the question to be decided was whether a two year delay was reasonable. This might 'well vary with circumstances but I believe that in any case there is an upper limit … Given the level of priority initially afforded … I would see a need for an assessment within four months. I would also see in the circumstances a further delay of 12 months as not wholly unreasonable'. However, the husband had already waited 15 months longer than that timescale and probably had to wait a further five months still.

Conclusion and recommendations. This was unreasonable delay and maladministration. Whilst the ombudsman accepted that 'there are no easy answers to what is essentially a problem of resources', she could not avoid criticism: the man continued 'to live without the benefit of the shower that the law clearly intended him to have'. This was injustice. The ombudsman did not seek financial redress 'for one applicant when the problem is general and where that problem arises from a lack of money'. Instead the remedy was for the council to satisfy her that it was doing all it could to eliminate such delays and ensure that provision was made for the particular complainants by the summer, 1997. The council should also make a small payment for the time and trouble involved in pursuing the complaint.

The ombudsman faulted neither the quicker procedure for private sector tenants, nor the fact that the council did not encourage (but did not prevent) council tenants applying for disabled facilities grants.

Stockton-on-Tees Borough Council 1997 (Unitary Authority) (and the former *Stockton-on-Tees Borough Council* and the former *Cleveland County Council 1997*; 96/C/1523 and others). *Welfare benefits; advice and support from social services; National Assistance Act 1948,s.29*
A case in which various complaints were made – one of them being that inadequate advice about welfare benefits ('advice and support' under s.29 of the National Assistance Act 1948) was given. The ombudsman found that the social workers who had dealt with the complainant 'did not have sufficient training or relevant experience to understand the complex benefit implications of her case'. She did not criticise them for being unfamiliar with the detailed rules about living alone, and the premiums for severe disability and carers. However, their reluctance to refer to the welfare rights service meant that the latter became involved only belatedly. This had happened because of confusion amongst both social workers and welfare rights officers about exactly what the latter could offer – only specialist checks or general benefit checks as well.

The failure 'to provide or ensure the provision of accurate and reliable advice required' was maladministration. This led to injustice, since for about three months the complainants lived in poor housing conditions which could have been alleviated by receipt of the additional benefits to which they were entitled.

Tower Hamlets London Borough Council 1992 (91/A/0726). *Delay in processing application for home adaptations; Chronically Sick and Disabled Persons Act 1970,s.2*
The complainants, man and wife, complained about delay in carrying out adaptations to their council property – beginning in March 1989 through to August 1992 when the works were finally completed. The husband had multiple sclerosis, the wife a deteriorating respiratory condition. As a result of the delay the husband was confined to the ground floor of the house, was unable to bath or shower properly, and could not leave the house in his wheelchair by either the front or back door. The property had been offered to them in March 1989 (they moved in October 1989) on the 'clear understanding' that the necessary adaptations would be in place beforehand.

The ombudsman found maladministration; between March 1989 and October 1989, the property was empty and finance was available, but no major work was undertaken. Between October 1989 and December 1990 no progress was made despite pressure from the hospital (where the wife was treated) and an MP. Consequently, by the time the list of adaptations had been submitted, the budget for next year 1990/91 had been committed elsewhere. Between December 1990 and March 1991 nothing happened; in March a request for priority was not progressed; the request was not updated to include additional works; the availability of funding for 1991/92 was not checked. From June 1991 to October 1991, misunderstanding persisted between the occupational therapist and surveyors. The ombudsman also pointed out that the decentralisation of the occupational therapy service had occurred so quickly, that it had outstripped new procedures for budgets, surveys etc; but given the vulnerability of the client group, decentralisation should have been prepared more carefully.

The ombudsman recommended £1,500 compensation for the delays, and time and trouble in pursuing the complaint.

Tower Hamlets London Borough Council 1993 (92/A/1374). *Support for person with mental health problems; Chronically Sick and Disabled Persons Act 1970,s.2; NHS and Community Care Act 1990,s.47*
The complaint was about allegedly inadequate support for a man with mental health problems (a history of depression, attempted suicide and alcoholism) following his discharge from hospital back to his council home.

Lack of proper care plan. The ombudsman accepted that the man was not easy to deal with, but nevertheless the council was at fault in a number of ways. Although a social services officer gave practical support, this would have been more effective if set in the context of a 'properly thought out care plan'.

Hospital discharge plan flawed. This discharge from hospital was not properly planned, since the man was without any kind of support for over a month.

Failure to balance needs with resources and to assess in structured manner. The ombudsman did not believe that the views of the hospital social worker and charge nurse – to the effect that the man should receive social worker support – were 'fully considered and balanced against the Council's financial resources'. There was also no evidence that the man's needs were 'assessed in any structured way or that information was sought from his general practitioner about his physical and mental health'.

Lack of action. The council did not help the man sort out his disputed gas bill, nor did it investigate his complaints that his heating was not working.

Refusal to advocate. The ombudsman found a team manager's letter 'unhelpful'; it expressed a refusal to advocate on behalf of the man with either the housing department or the Department of Social Security. Such responsibility could not be 'evaded by stating that Social Services have no managerial responsibility for Housing or the DSS. Instead the decision whether or not to advocate should have been based on objective criteria of the client's need and the Council's resources'.

Conclusion. This was all maladministration causing injustice in the form of worry and stress. The man had received no support when most vulnerable having (been discharged from hospital) and his needs had not been properly assessed (although the ombudsman felt that even had he been, his circumstances would probably not have been considered so pressing as to attract allocation of a social worker).

Recommendations. By way of remedy, the ombudsman recommended that the council reassess the man's needs under s.47 of the NHS and Community Care Act 1990 in the light of his most recent admission to hospital and the views of the consultant concerned. It should also, if the man wished, arrange for debt counselling and help arrange his budget; in addition, it should pay him compensation of £300 for the delays and £350 for his time and trouble.

The ombudsman did not find fault in the hospital social worker's attempt to obtain extra help for the man by applying to charitable funds: he had done what he could.

Further report (November 1993). The ombudsman issued a further report after the council did not agree to make the recommended payments, and asked the ombudsman to take into account the relevant officer's comments and the facts of the case. However, the ombudsman had already carried out 'the investigation and had taken account of all relevant facts so revealed' when coming to his conclusions. He could not therefore accept the suggestion of the council, which was 'in essence to reinvestigate the matter' simply because it disagreed with his findings. He asked the council to make the payments originally recommended, since a vulnerable member of the public had suffered injustice through poor administration – and 'good administration and a sense of justice require that the Council should promptly provide the remedy recommended by the impartial umpire established by Parliament'.

Tower Hamlets London Borough Council 1994 (93/A/2071). *Home help services and equipment; Chronically Sick and Disabled Persons Act 1970,s.2; NHS Act 1977,schedule 8; NHS and Community Care Act 1990,s.47*
The complainant, who had symptomatic HIV positive infection, claimed that the council did not deal properly with the assessment of his community care needs and with the provision of home help services and equipment.

Community care procedures not in place. The ombudsman did not criticise the fact that not all the procedures relating to the implementation of s.47 of the NHS and Community Care Act 1990 (duty to assess) were in place until six months after that date – given that it was a 'major piece of new legislation'.

Speed of assessment and provision. The council's procedures referred to a timescale of two to three weeks from referral to assessment. The man's home help service commenced five weeks after he had moved to London and been given a high priority by the council; given the nature of his needs and the fact that the had informal help at the time, the ombudsman did not consider this to be significant delay. The senior occupational therapist had sought specialist help – because of the degenerative nature of the man's infection – before fully assessing and recommending equipment. She visited some seven weeks after he had moved in; and the equipment she ordered was delivered two weeks later; this, too, was not unreasonable delay.

Confidentiality. The man had alleged breach of confidentiality. However, a) in line with his wishes, individual officers sought specialist help from others in a general way, without mentioning the man's name; and b) when an internal memorandum was sent in relation to the man's complaint to the ombudsman, it was sent in a sealed envelope marked 'confidential' to a named officer. The ombudsman found no fault.

Delay in providing bathpole. A floor-to-ceiling bathpole was not installed for five months, which meant that the man could not use the bath seat and rest which had already been provided. The ombudsman was not satisfied by the council's explanation that there were problems with the contractor, since the work had been marked non-urgent form the outset. This was maladministration.

Copy of assessment and care plan. For no apparent good reason, the man did not receive a copy of his assessment of care plan for five months; this was maladministration.

Limits on home help available. Although staff had been instructed (in the light of the implementation of the NHS and Community Care Act 1990,s.47) not to apply limits on the amount of home help available per week, the home care manager was still applying a limit of two hours for housework. This 'limit inhibited the proper assessment of each individual's needs' and was maladministration.

Conclusion and recommendations. The injustice caused was the man's difficulty in using the bath, his inability to check the care plan, and the fact that difficulties cannot have helped his condition (even if there were other factors at work in the deterioration which occurred over the relevant period). The ombudsman was pleased that the council's procedures and administration practices were now in place, and recommended that a) it ensure that its assessments for home help related to individual needs, and b) it pay £300 for the injustice, and for the time and trouble in bringing the complaint.

Tower Hamlets London Borough Council 1997 (96/A/1219). *Delay in assessment and resolving conflicting views within council; failure to make interim provisions; disabled facilities grants; Chronically Sick and Disabled Persons Act 1970,s.2*
The complainant, an AIDS sufferer, claimed that the council delayed either in providing him with suitable accommodation or in adapting his home.

Assessment of options. In November 1994 he first requested central heating. His needs were assessed. The occupational therapy manager, having received information about the man's condition from a hospital registrar, recommend central heating (although the council surveyor had queried whether this would set a precedent, and whether storage heaters would be preferable) – although she said that he would at some point need rehousing once he became dependent on a wheelchair. By now the man had also applied for rehousing on medical grounds.

Objections to central heating and setting a precedent. The council's building manager objected to the central heating because it would be structurally difficult and he was concerned about 'repercussions from the neighbours'. The occupational therapist agreed to recommend instead an electric radiator in the bedroom, heated towel rail, and 650 watt electric tubular heater in the lavatory. The towel rail could not be installed, so a fan heater was recommended instead. The man objected on grounds of running costs. The occupational therapists decided now to 'push for central heating' – because, despite the urgent priority for rehousing, it appeared that a move was unlikely in the near future due to the number of people needing rehousing to allow repairs to take place. The building manager still refused, referring to the setting of a precedent and the demands from the 'many aged tenants' who would then claim that central heating would improve their health. Storage heaters were again suggested but rejected on grounds of cost and efficiency.

Alternative accommodation. A centrally heated flat on a large estate was then offered; it would need adapting, was remote from public transport and noisy. The man refused the offer.

Central heating reconsidered. The housing manager now finally got sight of a letter (it had previously gone astray) from the hospital registrar which stated that central heating was essential for the man's comfort and that 'his life might be at risk in its absence'. The building manager agreed to reconsider central heating. Subsequently, a surveyor and mechanical engineer visited; the latter then wrote to the occupational therapist stating that the nature of the distribution pipework would cause heat starvation in the flat, and possibly in other flats as well, were extra radiators to be installed. (The man's flat already had radiators in the living room, hall and kitchen but nowhere else. These existing radiators were fed by a district heating system which served several blocks, was about 40 years old – of which the boiler and pumps, but not the distribution network (ie, the 'riser' pipes), had been renewed over this period. The engineer recommended alternative heating. Having come off the rehousing list, the man now went back on it, and in October 1996 he was offered a suitable flat – ground-floor, centrally heated and already adapted for wheelchair use.

Delay in identifying technical problems and resolving conflicts of opinion. However, the ombudsman identified faults in the way in which the request for heating was dealt with. First, it took far too long to identify the technical problems, the main objection previously being the setting of an unwanted precedent. Second, the divergence of opinion between the occupational therapists and the housing department 'was allowed to drag on unresolved for well over a year. There can be legitimate differences of opinion on such a matter but the issue was crucial to the health of a man who, the Council had been told, was very ill and probably had only a short time to live. There can be no excuse for the Council's failure to put both opinions to a person with the knowledge and authority to resolve the matter promptly and decisively'.

Third, during the wait for the eventual transfer, the council under its welfare functions 'was under an obligation to consider other ways to meet' the needs in the interim. There was no evidence that it did so.

Recommendations. The consequent frustration and distress experienced amounted to significant and serious injustice for a person in his situation; the ombudsman recommended £1,000 compensation and that the council review liaison arrangements between its housing and social services departments.

Trafford Metropolitan Borough Council 1996 (94/C/3690). *Assessments; provision of adequate day care services; Chronically Sick and Disabled Persons Act 1970,s.2; Disabled Persons (Services, Consultation and Representation) Act 1986,s.4; NHS and Community Care Act 1990,s.47.*
The complainants claimed that the council had failed to assess, and to make adequate day care provision for, the needs of their physically disabled, 25-year-old son.

The ombudsman concluded that a proper assessment had been carried out – and whether an assessment carried out in May 1993 was intended to be under the NHS and Community Care Act 1990, s.47 was 'immaterial', since there was no evidence that it failed to meet the requirements of that Act. However, she found that the council had 'failed properly to investigate and put in place adequate day provision'. It had not seriously explored the possibility of day services outside the district – indeed it had no policy on the funding of such services, despite recognition that provision for young disabled people was very limited within its own area. Eventually, it was the parents who arranged attendance for their son at a suitable centre.

This was maladministration causing injustice, by way of denying the son access to appropriate facilities at the earliest possible time, and causing stress for him and his parents. The ombudsman recommended £300 compensation to the son for this delay, and £250 to the parents for their distress, time and trouble.

Trafford Metropolitan Borough Council 1997 (94/C/4968). *Residential care; investigation of incident; handling of complaint; non-statutory complaints*
This case concerned the handling of a complaint, made to the council, by the owners of a residential home about the way in which an incident involving a resident had been investigated by the council.

Information about complaints procedure. The ombudsman found that the council had treated the complaint formally, having acknowledged, investigated and formally responded to it. However, along the way it had not given the complainants any 'substantive information about the procedure to be followed' despite being asked. This was maladministration. Also, the social services department had no written information available to the public about complaints procedures; the ombudsman found that such procedures must be 'transparent if they are to be perceived as fair and such an attitude is not in keeping with current best practice in customer service'.

Appropriate complaints procedure. Even worse, there was no evidence a) that there was in place a formal complaints procedure to cover complaints not coming within the statutory procedure (ie, under s.7 of the Local Authority Social Services Act 1970); or b) that the Chief Executive's complaints procedure was routinely used when there was no other satisfactory alternative.

Unreasonable delay in handling the complaint. The ombudsman also found that the complaint had been handled with unreasonable delay. No time targets set out in the Chief Executive's complaints procedure were met; and the main cause of the delay was that the council had regarded the complaint as inextricably connected to legal action (a notice issued under the Residential Care Home Regulations 1984) being taken by the council against the home. However, this was to confuse council's 'regulatory functions with its responsibility to address a reasonable complaint'; one action in question concerned a regulatory matter, but a second did not.

Conclusion and recommendations. The delay was unreasonable and maladministration. Overall, the complaint could have been dealt with in three months rather than eight. This caused frustration. However, the council's offer to reimburse the costs of services provided for the complaints by their adviser was a fair way to settle the dispute; in addition, a sum of £100 should be paid for the time and trouble of pursuing the complaint.

Wakefield Metropolitan District Council 1992 (90/C/2203). *Policy under s.2 of the Chronically Sick and Disabled Persons Act 1970; eligibility for telephone aids*
This was a discontinued investigation concerning a complaint by the British Deaf Association about the provision of minicoms (equipment which is attached to telephones to enable written inputs or outputs).

The council's initial policy – in the light of a restricted budget was to provide minicoms only for people who already had a telephone. The Association's view was that prior possession of a telephone was an irrelevant consideration in deciding whether a deaf person needed a minicom under s.2 of the Chronically Sick and Disabled Person Act 1970, and that if a duty in law arose, then the council could not argue lack of resources. The ombudsman agreed with this view. The council then changed its policy to one which allowed the provision of minicoms to deaf people irrespective of whether they already had a telephone. It argued that although it might have a duty to provide, there was not an obligation to do so immediately; some delay was acceptable. The ombudsman commented that whether delay was excessive would 'depend on the facts of the individual case'.

The ombudsman saw no benefit in pursuing the investigation, though he noted that the council's 'initial position was flawed and probably in breach of their statutory duty'.

Wakefield Metropolitan District Council 1993 (91/C/1246). *Advice and support; social security benefits; National Assistance Act 1948,s.29*
This case concerned the provision of advice and support under s.29 of the National Assistance Act 1948. The complainant claimed, on behalf of her brother (aged 70 with partial brain damage and Parkinsons Disease), that the council failed to tell them about an allowance for which her brother might have been eligible, and also advised them that he was not so eligible. He had lived for nearly 30 years in a home provided by the NHS and received an allowance (not attendance allowance) for days spent away from the home with his mother. In 1981 he moved to a home run by a council; his income decreased because there was no longer any form of allowance for days away; the sister was told that the brother was in fact eligible, but the Department of Social Security refused to pay any arrears (ie, before the date of the eventual claim) for what amounted to, over a period of nine years (up to 1990), 259 days in the council's view and 408 days in the sister's view.

Giving advice or pointing the way. The ombudsman found maladministration, stating that the council 'cannot be expected to offer expert advice on an allowance which is not the Council's responsibility but can be expected to point the way to getting sound advice. The Council certainly should not offer advice unless justifiably confident as to the extent of its knowledge. The Council did, however, give a very firm view that because [the man] was resident in a local authority home, he was not entitled to Attendance Allowance. That view overlooked the possibility that in particular situations such an allowance could be paid to cover the kind of visits from the home which [he] made'. Thus the inadequate advice was maladministration causing injustice.

Recommendations. However, the ombudsman was not prepared to go along with the sister's compensation claim for over £1,700 based on 408 lost days. This was because a) the exact number of days could not be certainly established since the relevant records prior to 1990 had been destroyed; and b) the sister had to bear some responsibility since during this period she had persistently questioned the council and had also known that advice was available from the Department of Social Security but not availed herself of it. The ombudsman recommended that the council pay £750 in total (including an element for time and trouble).

Wakefield Metropolitan District Council 1997 (95/C/3422). *Incidents at adult training centre; handling of complaint*
This case concerned the investigation carried out by the council in response to a complaint by parents that their son, who had severe learning disabilities, was being physically abused at an adult training centre run by the local authority. The ombudsman was satisfied that the injuries could probably be broken down into three categories: those caused by the son himself, those by staff restraining him with the best of intentions, and those which were non-accidental.

The ombudsman criticised the council for limiting its information-gathering during the investigation to council officers – and for not seeking medical evidence and the views of other people who knew the son. This was maladministration; however, she did not believe that a wider investigation would have come to a different conclusion than the one reached – thus there was no injustice suffered.

Walsall Metropolitan Borough Council 1996 (94/B/3584). *Renovation grant; delay*
A renovation grant case (when such grants were still mandatory if certain conditions were met under the Local Government and Housing Act 1989).

Huge demand, queuing system, fettering of discretion. The ombudsman accepted that the council was subject to a 'huge demand for a statutory entitlement it could not afford to meet'; he further accepted that policy decisions on the allocation of resources belonged in the 'democratic arena' and were not for him to criticise. Furthermore, a queuing system was 'administratively unavoidable and proper' – for example, when priority was given to the most unfit properties. However, the criterion of eligibility based on the means-test, and entailing that a prospective applicant's contribution be assessed at 'zero', was rigidly applied and took no account of individual circumstances; this was a fettering of discretion and maladministration.

Three-year delay for preliminary survey. In addition, a three year wait for a preliminary survey was maladministration; as was a) the council's refusal to give the complainant an application form, since preventing formal application was not an acceptable method of rationing demand, and b) its failure to inform her of her right to make a formal application.

Recommendations. The ombudsman recommended that the council assess the woman's formal application. If she were to satisfy the criteria under the 1989 Act, she should be paid the appropriate grant – even if this were now determined after the 1989 Act ceased to apply, and renovation grants were no longer mandatory under the successor legislation (the Housing Grants, Construction and Regeneration Act 1996). Also, the council should anyway make a £500 payment in compensation for the woman's time and trouble in pursuing the complaint – and review its mechanism for reviewing special cases.

Further report (April 1997). The council agreed to invite the woman to submit a formal application and to review its mechanism for special cases – but did not agree to the other recommendations, commenting that the ombudsman was encouraging queue-jumping by the complainant. The ombudsman issued a further report calling on the council to implement his recommendations in the original report – since it was 'only fair' that the complainant 'should now be given the opportunity of obtaining something to which, in the absence of the Council's maladministration, she may have been entitled'. Indeed, it was now almost seven years since her most recent enquiry about grant assistance.

Walsall Metropolitan Borough Council 1997 (95/B/2950). *Residential home; registration; erroneous advice; Registered Homes Act 1984*

This case concerned advice given by the council to the complainant, who alleged that it had failed to explain that his application for registration of a residential home was bound to be refused on grounds relating to room-partitions (curtains as suitable dividers) and to part-time management arrangements. The complainant wanted compensation of £4,300 for solicitor's fees, which he claimed would not have been incurred but for the council's misleading advice. The ombudsman upheld the complaint and recommended that amount of compensation, together with £250 for the time and trouble in pursuing the complaint.

Further report (January 1998). The council refused to make the level of payment recommended, maintaining that its offer of £1,070 was reasonable. The ombudsman published a further report stating that he had seen no arguments invalidating his initial recommendation, and that the council should make the payment originally recommended.

Waltham Forest London Borough Council 1993 (92/A/0543). *Complaints; threat of litigation; independent advocacy; Chronically Sick and Disabled Persons Act 1970,s.2*

A case concerning a dispute over a disabled person's need for bathing equipment and adaptations; following a hospital discharge in February 1990, it took over 30 months for a shower unit to be installed.

At issue was the extent to which the council was to blame for this delay. At one point, it had suspended the works because of threatened legal action by the person in relation to the installation of stair rails. However, the council a) did not explain this suspension to the man; and b) should anyway not have allowed the threatened legal action over the rails to affect the work on the shower. On the other hand, the man himself had begun to make unreasonable demands on the council, had 'personalised' the dispute by threatening legal action against a particular manager and had not pursued the council's suggestion of an independent advocate to act as mediator. All this resulted in delay for which the man was himself 'largely responsible'.

The maladministration identified did not cause significant injustice because, given the overall difficulties of the situation which could not be blamed on the council, it was unlikely that the shower would have been installed any sooner.

Waltham Forest London Borough Council 1994 (93/A/2536). *Home adaptations; waiting times; Chronically Sick and Disabled Persons Act 1970,s.2; disabled facilities grants*
The complainant lived with her adult daughter who was mentally and physically handicapped, with poor motor-coordination and increasing locomotion difficulties. The daughter had increasing difficultly getting up the stairs (she had to crawl, and over the last three years (to which the complaint related) her condition had deteriorated: her balance was poor and she could not stand unaided.

Assessment. When the mother first contacted the social services department in December 1991, the main problems were that her daughter kept falling over on the slope up to the house, and the increasing difficulty she had in getting to her bedroom, bathroom and WC upstairs. The council acknowledged the letter in January 1992 but warned that they could not respond immediately and that there was a waiting list. In July 1992, an occupational therapist visited to assess. A ramp was ordered, a visit with a contractor made in September and the work completed in November. As to the bathroom and WC (there was an outside WC), the mother was advised in September to apply for a disabled facilities grant; in the meanwhile a commode was supplied for downstairs use. However, she was also told that there was a twelve-month wait for a disabled facilities grant inspection. On October 20th, the case was closed.

Referral back to social services. The mother completed the disabled facilities grant enquiry form in September 1992; at the beginning of October she received a letter from the grants section, saying that the form had been referred back to the social services department for a disabled facilities grant assessment for which there might be considerable delay. In fact, the application was then placed by social services in the third priority category, although the mother was not told this. The reason for not awarding a higher priority was that the daughter was mobile within the home and did not have a rapidly deteriorating condition such as multiple sclerosis or motor neurone disease. By October 1993, nothing had happened, and a complaint was made to the ombudsman.

Second assessment visit. In November 1993, an occupational therapist visited and recommended a vertical lift, despite the mother's wish for an extension; the mother claimed the options were discussed without proper reference to the daughter's needs or condition. For instance, there was a question about what would happen when her daughter further deteriorated, and would have difficulty getting in and out of her wheelchair and into the bathroom and WC – or is she were to have an epileptic fit in the lift. In response to a letter written by a voluntary organisation on behalf of the mother, the council replied that the lift was the preferred option because the house was large enough to accommodate it and it was cheaper than an extension. The woman still wanted the extension; the voluntary organisation pointed out that the lift would cost £7,000 plus the cost of associated works to the bathroom and WC – surely the council should at least cost the alternative option of an extension.

'Double' waiting time: maladministration. The ombudsman found as follows. The initial wait from December 1991 did not involve maladministration; the first visit in July 1992 did not amount to unreasonable delay. In addition, the allocation (in October 1993) of the daughter's needs to the third category of priority had taken place according to the council's scheme (although this was not particularly clear from the written terms available). At the time, no target time had been set up for seeing people in the third category; the council had since set a 12-month target and the ombudsman commended this. However, it was maladministration when the waiting time for assessment for the disabled facilities grant application was now taken to run from September 1992 – and not from December 1991, the date of the original request for assistance. The ombudsman expressed no option about the options of a lift or an extension, since this was a professional matter.

Recommendations. The ombudsman recommended a) that £400 compensation be paid (about £10 per week for the nine months of added delay, including an element for time and trouble in bringing the complaint); b) that the assessment of the options of lift and extension be completed quickly and the mother be informed of the outcome with reasons; c) that any disabled facilities grant application from the mother be handled as a matter of priority; and d) that the voluntary organisation which had assisted the mother be paid £100.

Warwickshire County Council 1997 (96/B/2562). *Care arrangements; handling of complaint; NHS and Community Care Act 1990,s.47*

The complainant claimed that there were shortcomings in the council's involvement with her parents, and in dealing with her complaints – of which there were a number. Her mother had been suffering short-term memory loss and confusion and her father had been struggling to cope.

Both the investigating officer and the review panel upheld a number of the claims: there was delay in arranging day care, her parents received inadequate information, her father was not assessed for services, there were no care plans, appropriate support and expertise were lacking, 'everything possible' was not done to ensure that the mother was admitted to hospital appropriately, a support system for complainants and information about the review panel was lacking, record-keeping was generally poor, and supervision and post-complaint resources were 'insufficiently responsive and informative'. For example, although the council had offered to send the daughter details of changes to its procedures in the light of the original complaint, it failed to send sufficient information (this last failure which prompted the complaint to the ombudsman).

All this was maladministration – as with the failure of the council and the review panel properly to evaluate the daughter's claim for compensation and to make recommendations back to the council, something a panel 'is ideally placed' to do.

Recommendations. The ombudsman recommended that the council ensure that its review panel properly evaluate injustice and recommended steps by way of remedy, clearly inform the complainant about the changes it had implemented as a result of her complaint, and pay £1,500 compensation (as opposed to the £50 the council had hitherto offered) for anxiety, effort, time and trouble. He did not recommend that it compensate the daughter for the residential home costs she incurred when her parents went into a residential care home – because the council had stated clearly at the time that it would not pay (the home was being de-registered at the time).

Westminster City Council 1996 (93/A/4250). *Home help policy; not formally approved; consideration of individual circumstances; Chronically Sick and Disabled Persons Act 1970,s.2; Disabled Persons (Services, Consultation and Representation) Act 1986,s.4; NHS Act 1977,schedule 8; NHS and Community Care Act 1990,s.47*

The complainant concerned the provision of home help for a 66-year-old man who was an amputee, a wheelchair user, diabetic and double incontinent.

Comprehensive assessment and home help policy. Even after April 1993 (when community care was implemented via s.47 of the NHS and Community Care Act 1990) – and although Department of Health guidance (SSI/SWSG 1991a) stated that comprehensive assessments should be offered to disabled people irrespective of presenting need – the council did not automatically offer such assessments. Its domiciliary care service included shopping, pension collection and payment of bills, laundry and cleaning. However, whenever demand exceeded supply, shopping, medication-taking and hospital discharge cases would take precedence over cleaning (which did not pertain to 'life and limb').

Single-service assessments. The man was assessed in February 1991 for home help (ie, a 'single-service' assessment) three times a week (one each for pension, cleaning and laundry); he was not offered an assessment of his potential need for any other service. Another narrow assessment was carried out in December 1991 of his need for a special chair. The man subsequently complained about various aspects of the home help service, including different personnel from visit to visit, cancellations and the lower priority given to cleaning. In March 1994, an assistance care manager considered the case and decided that the council's policy did not indicate the need for a comprehensive assessment. In November 1995, he was reassessed by the domiciliary care manager, and in January 1996 by a care manager (although it was still not clear whether this was a comprehensive assessment).

Failure to assess comprehensively. The ombudsman found maladministration in the failure to carry out a comprehensive assessment, doubting that the council's policy was consistent with its legal obligations. The injustice caused could not be gauged, but the man possibly might have benefited from other services.

Home help policy: informally and application. The policy of prioritising shopping over cleaning had not been expressly put to members of the social services committee, nor were there guidelines. The man had consistently complained about this policy, since he was concerned that 'his health and indeed his life' had been placed at risk. There was no evidence that the council had considered the man's medical circumstances and whether they justified a cleaning service to be maintained. This was maladministration; the injustice was that the man had been fearful for four years about his survival.

Irregular and erratic service. Over particular periods of time 1993 and 1994, the man had often received less than the three visits each week agreed; the council provided no 'sufficient reason' for this failure (in addition, there was no system to tell users about cancelled or delayed visits). This was maladministration; the injustice was that the man had received an irregular and erratic service for a total thirteen months – not even knowing whether or not to expect the service.

Handling of complaints. The man's complaints were not handled adequately. At the first stage, they were not recorded properly and little investigation took place. At the second (formal) stage, there was only 'cursory' investigation – and standard, rather than, specific responses were given. The director of social services sent one memo, similar to a reply already sent to a councillor by the complaints officer, expressing 'confidence that the incidence of cancellations is no greater than those experienced by other users'; yet no figures had been compiled about the particular experience of the complaint. A second memo he sent was a standard letter alluding to staff leave and other factors causing disruption of services. Ultimately, the man had accepted a reduced number of visits each week – not as a reflection of his needs, but because of his dissatisfaction with the council.

Recommendations. The ombudsman recommended that the council a) carry out a comprehensive assessment with specific consideration to be given to the issue of the cleaning service; b) pay, following the assessment, 'an appropriate amount of compensation to reflect any services he should have received since 1991' – the amount to be agreed with the ombudsman; c) pay £250 for the man's time, trouble and frustration in bringing the compliant; d) review urgently its policy on assessing disabled people; e) review the policy on prioritising shopping over cleaning and – if the policy survived – issue guidelines for resource allocation; f) review its complaints procedures.

Wirral Metropolitan Borough Council 1992a (89/C/1114 and five other cases). *Extent of duty in relation to home adaptations; delay in assessment and handling of applications; Chronically Sick and Disabled Persons Act 1970, s.2*
A legal advice centre complained on behalf of a number of people about the way in which their requests for home adaptations were handled. The ombudsman found that in every case the council failed to identify needs and to meet those needs within a reasonable time. The council had argued that it could discharge its duty by assistance and advice rather than direct provision (under s.2 of the Chronically Sick and Disabled Persons Act 1970); the ombudsman found that even if this was right, the council had in fact undertaken to identify and then meet needs, and so had a responsibility to see that the needs were met without 'undue delay'.

There was no single explanation; one person waited five months for assessment, another five years. The ombudsman accepted that they was a shortage of occupational therapists and that it was necessary to operate a priority system. However, if there were insufficient occupational therapists, then the council should have found another way of assessing people's needs. In another case, a six-month delay was caused by inadequate coordination between council departments. In two other cases, there were long delays in preparing and arranging for works to be carried out. Two of the complainants had to wait six and twelve months respectively for approval of an improvement grant (predecessor to the disabled facilities grant) from the housing department; but this absence of funding did not remove the council's 'obligation to make provision' in a reasonable time (ie, under s.2 of the Chronically Sick and Disabled Persons Act 1970) in its social services capacity.

Thus, one complainant waited 22 months longer than necessary for installation of a shower; a couple waited 14 months longer than necessary for a shower (for their son) to work properly; another person waited eight months longer than necessary for her shower; yet another person had waited two years for an assessment (for heating) which might never take place (one of the council's officers explained that the 'tail-end' of the low priority waiting list might never be reached); another, one year for a shower installation, and another six months longer than necessary for replacement of a shower.

The ombudsman recommended that the council should apologise to all the complainants and make compensation payments in line with the extent of need and length of delay in each case.

Wirral Metropolitan Borough Council 1992b (90/C/2413). *Delay in dealing with application for home adaptations and inadequate supervision; Chronically Sick and Disabled Persons Act 1970, s.2*
The complainant alleged long delays and inadequate supervision in relation to adaptations to her home. She had rheumatoid arthritis and used a wheelchair for mobility in the home; a few years before, the council had installed a stairlift and flat-access shower. She suffered also from a condition which caused frequent vomiting and now requested a ground-floor shower and WC. After medical advice had been sought these were approved.

Delays. The ombudsman did not criticise the council for initial delays caused by the seeking of medical advice and then the obtaining of planning permission. However, once the medical advice had been received, the occupational therapist delayed three months in visiting again to discuss the extension; an additional three-month delay occurred between the woman's approval of a revised plan and the submission of a planning application. This overall delay of six months was maladministration, amounting to 'a significant injustice to a disabled person awaiting for necessary adaptations to her home'.

Monitoring of work. The work carried out by the contractor was faulty – although the council claimed that is had adequately monitored the work. However, the ombudsman concluded otherwise since there were no records available to support this claim, and the necessary shower levels and surface were not achieved. This was maladministration and injustice; as was the fact that, although the council had ordered the works to be done again, some of them had to be redone three or four times. The council had clearly failed to ensure that the faults were rectified properly and promptly.

Recommendations. The ombudsman recommended compensation of £1,000.

Wirral Metropolitan Borough Council 1992c (91/C/2038). *Delay in assessment and provision; home adaptations; Chronically Sick and Disabled Persons Act 1970, s.2*
This case concerned the council's delay in assisting with the provision of adaptations. The complainant had a number of medical problems including arthritis and angina (he had suffered three heart attacks). In 1989 he applied for assistance with a shower and also getting up the stairs. He then had to wait 21 months for an assessment of his needs. This was maladministration; if the council 'were unable to provide assessments by qualified occupational therapists during this time, they should have sought other means to ensure that disabled people did not wait an unacceptable length of time for an assessment of their needs'.

Even after the assessment, it took another nine months for the shower to be installed and 12 months for a hard-standing for the car. This meant a total of at least 33 months from the time of first approach to the council to the meeting of needs. This was maladministration and had meant that the man had been dependent on his wife for bathing all that time, and his mobility had been restricted. This was significant injustice which warranted a compensation payment of £650 (inclusive of the time and trouble in making the complaint).

Wirral Metropolitan Borough Council 1992d (91/C/0729). *Delay in handling request for home adaptations; Chronically Sick and Disabled Persons Act 1970, s.2*
The complainant alleged delay in the assessment and provision of home adaptations. She was in her thirties, had two teenage children and had severe psoriasis and chronic arthritis which severely limited her ability to

move. The woman was not placed in the first priority group, because she was judged not to be at risk (her priority was subsequently raised when a social worker later reported to the occupational therapists that the woman was virtually immobile and quite desperate). This meant a possible two-year wait for assessment.

The ombudsman accepted that there was a shortage of occupational therapists but that it could not be 'acceptable for a client in need to face a two year wait before their needs are even quantified. If qualified staff are not available to make assessments within a reasonable period of time, then the Council should look at other means of providing assessment'. This was maladministration, as was further delay in the processing of grant aid. The ombudsman recommended compensation of £30 per month for every month of delay.

Wirral Metropolitan Borough Council 1993a (91/C/0831). *Assessment; information gathering; substantial permanent handicap; home adaptations; Chronically Sick and Disabled Persons Act 1970,s.2*
The complainant alleged that the council had delayed unreasonably in assessing his needs for adaptations. In his sixties, he lived with his elderly mother-in-law, his wife and his disabled cousin. Having suffered a heart attack, he had been told to avoid exertion. In September 1990, he approached the social services department for help with repairs; although this request in itself was inappropriate in relation to social services, he was put on a waiting list for an occupational therapy assessment because of his disability.

Priority and substantial and permanent handicap. In June 1990, the man's doctor provided a medical note relating to the difficulty in climbing stairs; however, an occupational therapist explained that this did not give him priority. Council officers explained to the ombudsman that they had first to assess whether the man was substantially and permanently handicapped before deciding about services; to do otherwise might mean resources spent on people without a substantial handicap, rather than those with a more serious disability. The council solicitor suggested that this could give rise to a breach of legal duty. However, another officer did concede that the council could not say whether the complainant was substantially and permanently handicapped – precisely because he had not yet been assessed.

No proper assessment. The ombudsman stated in April 1993 – at which time the man had still not been fully assessed – that a wait of up to two years for assessment was too long. This was maladministration, resulting in anxiety and uncertainty for the man about whether of how his needs might be met. Although the council still had to carry out a full assessment in order to establish the qualifying disability, the man's doctor was in no doubt about his disability.

Recommendations. The ombudsman recommended that an assessment be carried out and appropriate facilities provided – as well as £500 be paid in compensation for the delay. However, she did commend the council for 'moving towards a system of gathering at an early stage the information which will decide whether they can assist a client or not'.

Wirral Metropolitan Borough Council 1993b (91/C/1258). *Home adaptations; poor record-keeping; remedial work*
The complainant was a woman who attended hospital for treatment of a heart condition (any sudden movement could cause a blackout), had arthritis and was being treated for cancer. She lived by herself in a flat; bathing was a great strain, and it was difficult to use the bath seat which had been provided for her.

Assessment for shower. She was assessed by an occupational therapist and a shower was recommended. However, the council installed a different type of flooring to the shower than had originally been agreed and did not seek the woman's approval; this was maladministration, though it did not cause any substantial injustice.

No record of payment of grant. The council had no record of payment of the improvement grant paid (under the Housing Act 1985, before disabled facilities grants had been introduced). This was maladministration, causing injustice because of the extra confusion it caused when the woman was pursuing her complaint.

Remedial work delayed and treated as new application. When the woman first complained, her complaints were not followed up properly; for ten months the council made no attempt to test the drainage of the shower, to replace a curtain or to fill certain holes. This was maladministration and led to the injustice of the woman being unable to use the shower. Once it was finally decided that remedial work was required, the ombudsman stated that it should have been done quickly; instead, the work was treated as a new application for grant which meant it was then held up for a further 15 months when it was caught up in the delays caused by the change in the grant system in 1990. The woman now had a useable and safe shower, but the ombudsman recommended that the council should pay her £500 for the injustice, and for her time and trouble in complaining.

Wirral Metropolitan Borough Council 1993c (91/C/1852). *Delay in assessment (two years); bathing need; disabled facilities grant; Chronically Sick and Disabled Persons Act 1970, s.2; Disabled Persons (Services, Consultation and Representation) Act 1986, s.4*

The complainant alleged unreasonable delay in respect of the provision of adaptations. He and his wife lived in sheltered accommodation; he had arthritis in his hips, she had suffered several strokes seriously affecting her mobility and she frequently used a wheelchair. He used the bath with difficulty, she could not use it at all; the shower was over the bath. In February 1991, the warden of the accommodation applied to the social services department for a bath hoist. By April 1993 no full assessment had been carried out, although an NHS occupational therapist had now ordered a bath lift through the NHS.

The ombudsman regarded it as unacceptable that a person might wait two years for an assessment; this was maladministration causing the injustice of the wife being unable to use the bath for 23 months. The council's claim that it did not have sufficient information in order to allocate a priority was no excuse; it should now make a payment in compensation of £300. However, the ombudsman did commend the council for 'moving towards a system of gathering at an early stage the information which will decide whether they can assist a client or not'.

Wirral Metropolitan Borough Council 1993d (91/C/3108). *Delay in assessment; disabled facilities grants; Chronically Sick and Disabled Persons Act 1970, s.2*

The complainants were man and wife who lived in a large Victorian house. She suffered from emphysema and had suffered a stroke. They complained about the long delay in processing their application for adaptations.

The ombudsman found no evidence that the council had ever received an application form submitted originally in 1988; the availability generally of records of correspondence relating to grants persuaded her that 'on the balance of probabilities' it had never been received – consequently there was no maladministration.

In June 1990, following the wife's stroke, they contacted the council again – but had to wait a year for assessment by an occupational therapist. This was maladministration, since if councils 'are unable to provide an assessment by an occupational therapist within a reasonable period of time, then they should look at other ways of providing the assessment. [The wife] could have expected to have been seen within four or five months of her request'. The delay meant that the calculation of the couple's contribution to the works was in turn set back – which meant that it was assessed at double what the council had originally predicted (although the council subsequently revised the figure downwards).

The ombudsman recommended compensation of £250 in relation to the delay in assessment by the occupational therapist (and including time and trouble in making the complaint), and recommended that the council keep its procedures under review so as to avoid unreasonable delay.

Wirral Metropolitan Borough Council 1993e (91/C/3811). *Delay in assessment; breakdown in communication; delay in processing recommendation; stairlift; Chronically Sick and Disabled Persons Act 1970, s.2*

The complainant was a victim of thalidomide in his early thirties; in the past he had been able to use artificial limbs but his mobility was now reduced following surgery for an arthritic hip. He complained about long delays in the provision of adaptations; he had approached the council for substantial assistance in May 1987, but some of it was not provided until June 1992.

Delay in assessment. First there was a delay of eight months between the first approach and an assessment visit; this was because although the man's referral had been marked as urgent, a newly appointed occupational therapist was clearing the backlog of non-urgent cases. The ombudsman found it 'unacceptable' and maladministration that the backlog should be cleared in such a way as to adversely affect people with urgent needs. Second, a delay of 11 months then followed before the works were ordered. The council maintained that such delay was not unusual; the ombudsman was concerned that the council should 'regard delay in provision of services with such apparent equanimity'. The delays, 'usual or not' were maladministration.

Breakdown in communication between departments. Progress was then made; garage doors were in place within four months, and a ground-floor WC within eight, although some of the work had to be redone. Nevertheless, the bathroom adaptation was subject to a 'complete breakdown of communications between departments'. Once the confusion became evident, it should have been 'a matter of days' to rectify the situation; instead sixteen months went by before a new order was raised. This considerable delay was maladministration.

Request for stairlift lying dormant to control budget. During the course of all this it had become apparent that the man required a stairlift, and although progress was affected by some of his own doubts, by October 1991 the occupational therapist had requested urgent provision of the lift. The request lay 'dormant' for three months until, hearing that the man was now in great pain, the occupational therapist followed it up. The delay, employed 'as an administrative mechanism to control a budget cannot be acceptable' in relation to an urgent need; this was more maladministration.

Conclusion and recommendations. The long delays amounted to 'considerable injustice' warranting both £2,000 in compensation and completion of the works remaining.

Wirral Metropolitan Borough Council 1993f (92/C/1254). *Delay in assessment and provision; disabled facilities grants; Chronically Sick and Disabled Persons Act 1970,s.2*

The complainant alleged delays in assessment of her needs and arranging works of adaptation. She had restricted mobility and sometimes used a wheelchair, and had moved with her husband in December 1990 to a property which they knew would have to be adapted. They informed the social services department that they would require adaptations a month before they moved in (but had not originally consulted the council prior to purchase). The referral was placed on the low priority list. This was not maladministration.

Priority and assessment. In January 1991, after the wife had informed social services of her difficulty with the stairs, she was upgraded first to middle, then to top, priority – and visited in March. The feasibility of a downstairs extension was explored, then the possibility of an internal lift. The wife suggested it might be better to close in the staircase – disagreeing with the occupational therapist who favoured the lift. The occupational therapist sought further advice from the woman's general practitioner; the ombudsman did not criticise this. A further month's delay then occurred when the woman said she wanted no further help, suggesting she was dissatisfied with the council; however, the ombudsman found nothing to criticise the council about. The council pursued a full survey of the property, after an initial report had identified structural instability. By March 1992, the wife had sold her share in the house and left, blaming delays by the council for contributing to the breakdown of her marriage.

Conclusion: no maladministration. The ombudsman concluded that although there appeared to have been lengthy delay, this was not due to maladministration since the council could not be held responsible for the couple's buying of a house in need of modification, but the condition of which made such modification difficult.

Wirral Metropolitan Borough Council 1994a (91/C/2376). *Home adaptations; delay; disabled facilities grants; Chronically Sick and Disabled Persons Act 1979,s.2*

A solicitor complained on behalf of a woman who had requested the provision of adaptations for her disabled adult daughter who used a wheelchair on a permanent basis as a result of an undiagnosed illness. In early 1990, an occupational therapist visited and assessed that a grant might be available for a ramp, downstairs toilet and purpose-built show in the bedroom.

Eligibility for grant. In relation to eligibility for a grant, three different assessments were carried out and this was confusing; however, the second and final ones were accurate, the mistake in the first one having been corrected. Significant injustice did not flow from the mistake; in the event the woman and her husband were not eligible for grant.

Continuing duty to assist under s.2 of the Chronically Sick and Disabled Persons Act 1970. At first, with the housing grant denied, the council maintained that in general and as a matter of policy, it had no further duty under its social services function (s.2 of the Chronically Sick and Disabled Persons Act 1970), once the housing department test of resources had established that applicants could afford to do the work themselves. However, the council altered its policy by first asking applicants to see if they could raise a private loan (although the woman in this case was not asked to do this), before it would consider offering assistance. Furthermore, the woman's solicitor had challenged the council that the ability to raise a private loan was a suitable yardstick in such circumstances. Subsequently, the council devised its own hardship test to apply in such situations. In this particular case, the council's unwillingness to consider its social services duty had not in fact caused any injustice.

Design of ramp, conflict of view. The ombudsman did not criticise the council for its reservations about the design of ramp which the woman favoured; there were possible problems relating to a gutter, gradient and turning platform. The woman had complained of the delay and had had the ramp installed herself – against advice and at her own risk.

Delay in reaching decision. However, overall, the council had taken 19 months to reach a decision, instead of about six months. There were many visits made involving two different occupational therapists and three different surveyors; there was poor record-keeping and the council may have lost some papers sent to them. This meant that the woman was left uncertain for 19 months about what was going on. By the time the (adverse) decision was made; it was too late for her too carry out the adaptations herself because the daughter had now moved away; and the daughter had been without the benefit of the adaptations for more than a year.

Conclusion and recommendations. This was maladministration and injustice, warranting £400 compensation and £250 for time and trouble. In addition, the council should amend its procedures to prevent such delays, and ensure that proper records were kept of all visits made in relation to grant applications.

Wirral Metropolitan Borough Council 1994b (92/C/0298). *Delay; home adaptations; disabled facilities grants; Chronically Sick and Disabled Persons Act 1970,s.2*
A woman complained on behalf of her husband about the way in which a request for adaptations was handled. The couple lived by themselves in a two-storey house; the council had already installed a vertical lift for the husband who used a wheelchair all the time. The upstairs bathroom had a bath but no shower; the wife had great difficulty bathing her husband.

Delay in sending application form. An occupational therapist from the social services department visited in August 1990 and recommended a shower. It took the housing department seven-and-a-half months to send a preliminary form for a disabled facilities grant: this was maladministration.

Disappointed expectations. Another six months then went by before the couple were informed that they were ineligible for grant. This dashed their expectations because they had believed that an earlier informal assessment had indicated that they would be eligible; however, this was not maladministration, since the ombudsman found no evidence that they had been substantially misled and their mistaken expectations were dispelled sooner rather than later.

Continuing duty under the Chronically Sick and Disabled Persons Act 1970. The council finally accepted that where hardship would otherwise be caused, in relation to people's inability to pay assessed contributions to disabled facilities grants under housing legislation, it had a continuing duty through its social services department (under the Chronically Sick and Disabled Persons Act 1970,s.2) to assist. After the couple (neither of whom was employed) had applied unsuccessfully to a building society, the council finally agreed in February 1993 to provide an interest-free loan of £3,260 (for the shower and ramp), repayable at a rate of £12 per month. The first instalment of the loan was paid in October 1993. However, the two years it took to agree and arrange the loan was maladministration causing uncertainty and distress.

Such was the delay caused by the maladministration, that the cost of the shower had now risen from £1,423 at the end of 1991 to £2,790. Thus, the ombudsman recommended that the council pay the difference of £1,367, and should amend its procedures so as to eliminate such unacceptable delays.

Wirral Metropolitan Borough Council 1994c (92/C/1403). *Delay in assessment; failure to keep person informed; home adaptations; Chronically Sick and Disabled Persons Act 1970,s.2; Disabled Persons (Services, Consultation and Representation) Act 1986,s.4*
The complainant alleged in particular that the council had taken too long in assessing her needs for adaptations. She had arthritis and an ileostomy, and could not step in and out of her bath (over which was a shower). An occupational therapist requested an assessment for a walk-in shower to be installed. The woman was allocated to the waiting list as a low priority. Two years later, no assessment had been carried out.

The council explained that it faced great demands and was forced to work to a priority system which favoured those with the greatest needs. The ombudsman sympathised with the complainant but, given the restriction on staff and resources, did not criticise the council for the two-year wait, even though the woman had still not been assessed. However, the complainant had 'received no clear indication about how long she would have to wait. Indeed she was told well over a year ago that she would be visited as soon as possible ... it is maladministration for the Council not to give her clearer information and to leave her in such uncertainty for so long. That uncertainty and her inability to plan is injustice...'.

The ombudsman recommended a payment of £250 in compensation for the woman's time and trouble in making the complaint, and that the council should review its procedures to ensure that people are given proper, if approximate and provisional (given changing circumstances), indications of how long they will have to wait.

Wolverhampton Metropolitan Borough Council 1997 (94/B/3524). *Sheltered housing; failure of alarm system; investigation*
This case concerned the death of a tenant in purpose-built council housing (with warden) for older people – he was found dead the morning after the alarm system had malfunctioned. His daughter believed that he might not have died had the alarm been functional. The ombudsman considered carefully the possible causes of the failure and the adequacy of the council's investigation.

He found maladministration on a number of counts. First, the emergency call system should have had a malfunction alarm, or at least have been tested regularly (eg, by a test call every hour). Second, there was no procedural guidance on what to do in c
ase of malfunction (eg, in relation to resetting and checking the computer following apparent malfunction). Third, the council could have done more in its investigation to ensure that valuable information was recorded – in order to identify the likely cause of the malfunction. Fourth, the council did not give the complainant a 'full explanation of the possibilities' that might have caused the failure. Lastly, the council was not sufficiently forthcoming in providing information for the ombudsman when asked to do so.

The ombudsman recommended that the council pay for the memorial seat the daughter wanted, pay her £1,000 compensation for her concern, anxiety and efforts in pursuing the complaint, and satisfy itself about the operation of the alarm system and associated procedures.

CHAPTER 19

LEGAL JUDGMENTS: DIGEST OF CASES

Various areas of law have been outlined already in the previous chapter, namely judicial review, breach of statutory duty, negligence and contract. The following selected and summarised cases illustrate all of these, although judicial review is predominant. All are referred to at some point in the main text of the book. In judicial review, the law courts principles of administrative law across public bodies as a whole, not just local authority social services departments or health authorities. Therefore, some of the cases included are drawn from beyond the social or health care context in order to illustrate particular points of relevance.

(N.B.. Homelessness and housing allocation, previously covered by the Housing Act 1985, are now covered by the Housing Act 1996. Likewise, provisions for special education covered in the Education Act 1981 were superseded by those first in the Education Act 1993 and then the Education Act 1996. And general educational provisions covered in the Education Act 1944 have been superseded by those in the Education Act 1996).

Law report abbreviations are as follows: AC (Appeal Cases), All ER (All England Law Reports), ALR (Administrative Law Reports), BMLR (Butterworths Medical Law Reports), CCLR (Community Care Law Reports), Ch (Chancery), CL (Current Law), COD (Crown Office Digest), EHHR (European Human Rights Reports), ELR (Education Law Reports), FCR (Family Court Reporter), FLR (Family Law Reports), HLR (Housing Law Reports), IRLR (Industrial Relations Law Reports), JPL (Journal of Planning Law), LGR (Local Government Reports), LGRR (Local Government Review Reports), Lloyds Rep (Lloyds Reports), MLR (Medical Law Reports), PIQR (Personal Injury Quantum Reports), PLR (Planning Law Reports), RepLR (Reparational Law Reports), SC (Session Cases), SCLR (Scottish Civil Law Reports), SLT (Scottish Law Times), TLR (Times Law Reports), VATTR (VAT Tribunal Reports), WLR (Weekly Law Reports), SJLB (Solicitor's Journal).

In addition, the status of a case is indicated by QBD (High Court), CA (Court of Appeal) and HL (House of Lords).

Anderson v Lothian Health Board [1996] SCLR 1068 (Scotland, Outer House, Court of Session). *Lifting and handling: Manual Handling Operations Regulations 1992*
A hospital laundry worker was injured lifting 44lb load of laundry. Before the accident, the occupational health doctor had recommended a system involving the lifting of no more than 40lb loads. Information about this was passed to operators by word of mouth.

The court found a contravention of r.4(1)(a) of the Manual Handling Operations Regulations (duty to avoid, so far as reasonably practicable, the need for manual handling operations involving risk of physical injury), reasoning as follows. First, the risk of injury need not be probable, but merely a foreseeable possibility. In the present case there clearly had been both a manual handling operation, and one that involved a risk of injury. It was for the employers to show that it was an operation that was not reasonably practicably avoidable. In fact, a) the employer had not invoked such a defence; and b), if it had done so, it would still have failed, since the judge was not satisfied on the evidence that it was not reasonably practicable to avoid the handling of the laundry. Liability was therefore established.

Liability being thus established, the case brought under r.4(1)(b) (risk assessment and taking of reasonable steps to reduce risk of injury) did not arise. However, had it done so – in circumstances in which it was decided that it was not reasonably practicable to avoid the manual handling – then liability would also have been established. This was because measures taken under r.4(1)(b) had to reduce the risk of injury to the lowest level reasonably practicable. The employer had in fact passed down instructions by word of mouth that loads were not to exceed 40lbs, but not posted up written notices – until after the accident. Yet clearly if it was reasonably practicable to place such notices after the accident, it would clearly have been reasonably practicable beforehand.

Associated Provincial Picture Houses v Wednesbury Corporation [1947] 2 All ER 680 (CA). *Reasonableness and relevant factors; cinema licensing*
A case frequently referred to as setting out classic principles of unlawfulness on the part of public bodies, in particular the taking account of relevant (and the exclusion of irrelevant) factors and unreasonableness. It was about whether a local authority had rightly taken into account, when imposing licensing conditions on a cinema (a 'cinematograph theatre') opening on a Sunday, considerations relating to the physical and moral health of children.

The court ruled that: it was 'entitled to investigate the action of the local authority with a view to seeing whether it has taken into account matters which it ought not take into account or, conversely, has refused to take into account or neglected to take into account matters which it ought to take into account. Once that question is answered in favour of the local authority, it may still be possible to say that the local authority, nevertheless, have come to a conclusion so unreasonable that no reasonable authority could have ever have come to it. In such a case, again, I think the court is entitled to interfere. The power of the court to interfere in each case is not that of an appellate authority to override a decision of the local authority, but is that of a judicial authority which is concerned, and concerned only, to see whether the local authority has contravened the law by acting in excess of the powers which Parliament has confided in it'.

Attorney General ex rel Tilley v London Borough of Wandsworth [1981] 1 All ER 1162 (CA). *Individual and general duties; children; Children and Young Persons Act 1963*
A case pre-dating the Children Act 1989, but indicating nonetheless a) that local authorities should beware of fettering their discretion by failing to consider provision of accommodation for children in need; and b) that even in the case of a generally expressed duty, authorities might need to consider the individual needs of children.

Policies, fettering of discretion and individual needs. The case concerned the generally expressed duty under s.1 of the Children and Young Persons Act 1963 to make available advice, guidance and assistance etc to promote the welfare of children by diminishing their need for care. The Court of Appeal held that a resolution (mandatory in appearance) of the authority – not to provide accommodation under this section of the Act was unlawful – since such provision could be covered by the word 'assistance'.

The court also stated that even if the resolution had allowed of exceptions and had been a general policy and not a mandatory order, nevertheless this 'would not get rid of the vice that a local authority, dealing with individual children, should not make a policy or an order that points towards fettering its discretion in such a way that the facilities offered to the child do not depend on the particular circumstances of that child or of its family, but follow some policy which is expressed to apply in general ... Dealing with children, the discretion and powers of any authority must depend entirely on the different circumstances of each child before them for consideration'.

Avon County Council v Hooper and Another [1997] 1 All ER 532 (CA). *Community care; charges for non-residential services; Health and Social Services and Social Security Adjudications Act 1983, s. 17*

The local authority had been providing services for a person who had been seriously brain-damaged at his birth in 1978 due to foetal anoxia; he was consequently severely disabled, both physically and mentally, and died in 1991. The services provided from 1981 to 1989 were residential accommodation under schedule 8 of the NHS Act 1977 (the relevant part of this schedule is now obsolete), and welfare services under s.29 of the National Assistance Act 1948. In 1989, a negligence award was made, under which the health authority paid £289,000 to the person.

Local authority's attempt to recover cost of services. In 1991, the local authority brought a case to recover the cost (£232,000) of some of the care which it had been providing. The claim was subject to a six year limitation period imposed by s.9 of the Limitation Act 1980, and so could cover the period of care from June 1985.

The case was brought against both the disabled person's estate and the health authority, which – when the negligence claim was settled – had originally agreed to indemnify the disabled person against any liability for care provided prior to the date of the settlement. This would be both in respect of the Leonard Cheshire home involved, and any financial liability of the person to the county council. Thus, the county council hoped to recover the cost of the care not from the person's estate but from the health authority.

Retrospective charges. The local authority was attempting to make charges retrospectively; the question was whether this was a lawful exercise of its power, under s.17 of the Health and Social Services and Social Security Adjudications Act 1983, a) to make reasonable charges, which b) it was satisfied was reasonably practicable for the person to pay.

Reasonableness in exercising power to charge. The court found in favour of the local authority, emphasising the all-embracing effect of the term 'reasonable'.

It observed that s.17 of the 1983 Act was the starting point, under which the local authority had a power, but not a duty, to charge. It 'was implicit both in the language of the section and in the general law governing the activities of local authorities that the power must be exercised reasonably, that is to say, that the local authority must have relevant and reasonable grounds for choosing to exercise the power ... Thus, there is an overriding criterion of reasonableness'.

In assessing whether an authority is acting reasonably in imposing charges the court stated that the following should be considered: 'If the right to charge has been waived, clearly no charge can be recovered. If the service was provided in circumstances under which it would be unreasonable for the authority subsequently to charge for it, then the authority is not entitled later to seek to recover a charge. Similarly, if having provided a service, the local authority seeks to recover a charge, it must be prepared to justify the reasonableness of doing so. The reasonableness of any conduct falls to be assessed at the time of the relevant conduct and having regard to all the relevant circumstances then existing. If the claim is first made some time after the provision of the services, the local authority must be prepared to justify the reasonableness of making the claim notwithstanding the delay'.

Making charges after services have been provided. The court further considered the argument that charges had to be made at the time of providing services, not afterwards. It rejected the argument that the power to charge under s.17 of the 1983 Act was phrased in the present tense and should be exercised only when the services were provided, not later: 'like a shopkeeper asks a purchaser for the price at the time of sale or a hotel-keeper tells the visitor the room charge on arrival'.

This was not 'a reasonable interpretation of the section. The primary duty of the local authority is to provide the services to those in need of them. The power to charge is consequential upon the provision of the service. Whether it is reasonable to charge has to be considered at an appropriate time which will not necessarily be before the time the services are rendered and will most probably be later when the local authority has put itself in possession of the relevant information. Similarly, the question of means and the practicability of paying will very often have to be the subject of later enquiry and consideration'.

Imposing a charge which it is reasonably practicable for a person to pay. The court stated that first an authority has to decide to make a charge and has to be 'acting reasonably in doing so' – but then the person has to persuade the authority about whether it is reasonably practicable for him or her to pay the charges: 'the person availing himself of the service has, in those circumstances, to satisfy the authority under [s. 17 of the 1983 Act] that his means are insufficient for it to be reasonably practicable for him to pay the amount which he would otherwise be obliged to pay. It is for the recipient of the service to discharge his burden of persuasion. He must show that he has insufficient means. The time at which he has to do this is the time when the local authority is seeking to charge him for the service. If his means have been reduced, as might be the case with a business man whose business had run into difficulties after his being injured, the reduction in his means is something upon which he would be entitled to rely as making it impracticable for him to pay, even though at an earlier date he might have been better off'.

Assessing the resources of a person. The court stated that the word 'means' in s. 17 of the 1983 Act referred to more than just cash, since as a: 'matter of the ordinary use of English, the word 'means' refers to the financial resources of a person: his assets, his sources of income, his liabilities and expenses. If he has a realisable asset, that is part of his means; he has the means to pay ... If he has an asset which he can reasonably be expected to realise and which will (after taking into account any other relevant factor) enable him to pay, his means make it practicable for him to pay'.

Baker v Baker and Another [1993] 2 FLR 247 (CA). *Purchasing of house for son and daughter-in-law; in return rent-free accommodation to be provided; breakdown of arrangements*
This case illustrates the dangers of gifts and transfers of property or money. A man provided the money (£33,950) towards purchase of a house for his son and daughter-in-law. He would then live there rent-free for the rest of his life. The arrangement broke down when the son accused the father of sexually molesting the latter's young granddaughter; it was subsequently clear that the accusation was unfounded and made without reasonable grounds. The High Court ruled that the full sum was recoverable on the basis of a doctrine known as proprietary estoppel (basically about a persons's expectation); however, the Court of Appeal ruled that the expectation lost was not the full sum, but the value of the father's expectation to live in the house rent-free for the rest of his life. This would be a smaller amount than the original sum he had contributed.

Barrett v Enfield Borough Council [1997] 3 WLR 628 (CA). *Negligence; social services; child care*
Concerning child care, the case involved a claim that a local authority acted negligently towards a child who was in its care from the age of ten months until he was eighteen years old. Amongst the complaints were failure to arrange for adoption, inappropriate foster placements, lack of proper monitoring and supervision whilst at different placements. The appeal was against a county court decision to strike out the action for damages against the local authority.

Statutory role excludes common law duty of care. The court ruled that the plaintiff had no prospect of succeeding, and that the local authority and its staff would not be liable for negligent exercise of discretion in caring for the plaintiff. This was in accord with the House of Lords decision *X v Bedfordshire CC.* Lord Woolf pointed out that, unless they were performed unreasonably, functions performed in the exercise of an authority's statutory role cannot give rise to a common law duty of care. Indeed: 'The decision whether or not to place the child for adoption; the decision as to whether to place a child with particular foster parents; the decision whether to remove a child from a foster parent; the decisions as to the child's relationship with his mother and sister; all involve the exercise of discretion in the performance of the differing statutory responsibilities of the local authority'.

Just and reasonable to impose a duty of care? Even if such unreasonableness were to be established in relation to such functions, the court would have to decide whether the harm suffered was reasonably foreseeable, and whether the relationship between the plaintiff and defendant was 'sufficiently proximate'. In this case, both of these principles were established. However, then the court would still have to assess whether it was 'just and reasonable to impose a duty of care'.

The court thought not, because it would be contrary to the public interest: the 'very fact that the defendant is stated to have been in the position of a parent to the plaintiff at the material time brings home the public policy aspects ... In the situation disclosed by the present appeal there would be decisions which were of an inter-disciplinary nature. Sometimes the decisions will involve seeking to determine which of two imperfect solutions is preferable. It would be unfortunate if the possibility of litigation years afterwards could cause a more defensive and cautious approach to taking positive decisions as to a child's future than would otherwise be the case. Social workers are all too often open to criticism for intervening but intervening is often what is necessary and when it is they should not be discouraged from doing so by the possibility of litigation ... I also bear in mind that if complaint is made, then an investigation by an ombudsman is more likely to result in a satisfactory conclusion than the investigation by the courts'.

Proving how the harm was caused. It was also added by one of the other judges (Lord Justice Evans) that, logically, the first question is not about whether there was a duty of care', but rather "what damage or injury has the plaintiff suffered, is it actionable at law and was it caused or contributed to by the defendant or by the acts of omissions of any person for whom the defendant is vicariously liable?". He went on to suggest that the case would fall on the causation question, since there was: 'no prospect of the evidence establishing that there were individual acts of negligence which singly or taken together could be said to have caused or even made any substantial, ie, non-negligible, contribution to the injury from which he alleges that unhappily he now suffers'.

Blanket immunity and negligence in an operational manner? Nevertheless, the court was not conferring a general immunity on local authorities, but simply 'an immunity in relation to the making of those decisions as to the future of a child which are normally made by a parent'. Thus, 'social workers and other members of staff could however be negligent in an operational manner. They could, for example, be careless in looking after property belonging to the child or in reporting what they had observed for the purposes of an interdisciplinary assessment of what action should be taken in relation to a child. They could also be negligent in failing to carry out instructions properly...'.

Beasley v Buckinghamshire County Council [1997] PIQR P473 (QBD). *Lifting and handling*

The plaintiff was a paid foster parent to a handicapped teenage boy, placed by the local authority. She claimed to have suffered a back injury when trying to catch, lift, save or restrain him. She argued that she should have been provided with a hoist or other lifting equipment earlier than she was; that the defendant failed properly to assess the placemement; and that had it done so, it would not have placed such a heavy and disabled child with her, in the light of her complete lack of experience in caring for a child with such a disability; and that she should have been trained in lifting techniques and should have been warned of the risks to her which the work involved.

The local authority attempted to have the case struck out on grounds of public policy, based on the child care judgment by the House of Lords in X v Bedfordshire CC. The court found that the case should not automatically be struck out. First, it concerned the practical manner in which the local authority was proceeding, not policy; and the judge could not see why the imposition of a duty of care was inconsistent with, or would discourage, the due performance of the authority in carrying out its statutory duty. Furthermore, on the public policy question, it would surely be 'poor public policy' to impose a heavy burden on charitable, lowly paid volunteer foster parents, but for those parents to have no recourse if the authority behaved carelessly. The judge referred to the foster parent as a 'quasi-employee' of the authority and pointed out that it would be odd if a nurse could sue a health authority but a foster parent could not sue a local authority. He also was not prepared to rule out the existence of a contract, because whilst the foster agreement stated that it was not a legally binding document, the courts are prepared to look at the substance of agreements.

Blankley and Others v Lyon [1998] 20 January 1998, Nottingham County Court (summarised in Casserley,C.(1998)). *Disability Discrimination Act 1995; provision of goods and services*
A group of ten residents with learning disabilities from a residential home were asked to leave a public house by the landlady on account of their disabilities. The court awarded £800 to each person, totalling £8,000. An application to appeal the judgment was refused.

British Oxygen Co Ltd v Board of Trade [1971] AC 610 (HL). *Rigid policies and fettering of discretion; items costing under £25; industrial grants*
This case shows that even in respect of a power – not just a duty – to do something, authorities should beware of fettering their discretion through rigid policies.

Under the Industrial Development Act 1966, the Board of Trade had the power to give grants towards approved capital expenditure for particular purposes. British Oxygen applied for grants for various items, including metal cylinders for pressurised gases costing just under £20 each, and on which it had spent a total of over £4 million – hence its interest in obtaining grants. The Board of Trade denied that the various items were eligible for grants, and that in the case of the cylinders – even if they were potentially eligible – it had a policy not to give grants for items costing under £25.

In respect of the cylinders, the House of Lords ruled that the Board was entitled to have a policy, but should not shut its ears to applications, since a 'large authority may have had to deal already with a multitude of similar applications and then they will almost certainly have evolved a policy so precise that it could well be called a rule. There can be no objection to that, provided the authority is always willing to listen to anyone with something new to say'.

Bromley London Borough Council v Greater London Council and Another [1983] AC 768 (HL). *Fiduciary duty; spending of public money*
This case illustrated how the courts might intervene with policy-making in local government and underlined the general duty on local authorities to spend public money carefully. It involved a scheme of the Greater London Council scheme to cut substantially London Transport fares. The scheme had been a plank of the GLC's election manifesto, although its implementation necessitated the raising of an unforeseen extra precept from rate-payers; the House of Lords ruled that this would place the GLC in breach of its 'fiduciary duty' to be thrifty and to avoid placing an inordinate burden on rate-payers.

Cheese v Thomas [1994] 1 All ER 35 (CA). *Contribution to purchasing house for great-nephew; in return rent-free accommodation to be provided; breakdown of arrangements*
This case illustrates the dangers of gifts and transfers of property or money. An elderly man contributed (£43,000) towards the purchase (for £83,000) of a house by his great-nephew (and in the latter's sole name) in return for living in it for the rest of his life. The nephew defaulted on the mortgage repayments, and the man tried to retrieve his money. This was not without complications; eventually the Court of Appeal ruled there had been undue influence exercised, and that he could recover a proportion, but not the whole, of the original amount. This was because the house was sold for only £55,000. The man could not recover his original £43,000, but only an amount (£28,700) corresponding to the proportion (ie, 43:40) he had contributed to the original purchase price.

Chief Adjudication Officer v Palfrey and Another [1995] SJLB 65 (CA). *Income support; valuation of claimant's capital and property interests; actual market, rather than theoretical, value*
The claimant had a joint beneficial interest with his daughter in the family home. His claim for income support had originally been rejected by a social security appeal tribunal on the grounds that his capital exceeded the prescribed limit (£8,000). A tribunal of social security commissioners allowed his appeal on the grounds that his interest in the home was to be taken by reference to the current market value, and not to his share of the whole beneficial interest. The Court of Appeal confirmed the commissioners' decision.

Chief Adjudication Officer and Another v Quinn and Gibbon [1996] 1 WLR 1184 (HL). *Residential accommodation; dispute about rules for payment of income support*

This case was essentially a dispute between local and central government as to which would provide support out of public funds for people in residential accommodation. The particular residential homes involved had originally been managed by the local authorities (Dorset County Council and Cumbria County Council) under Part 3 of the National Assistance Act 1948 – but had since been transferred by the authorities to voluntary organisations.

The court held that since the transfer arrangements did not contain a provision satisfying s.26 of the 1948 Act – under which local authorities must pay the independent provider of residential accommodation at an agreed rate – the authority could not have been making arrangements under s.26. Therefore, higher rates of income support were payable to the relevant residents from central government (ie, the Department of Social Security).

As a consequence of this decision, the law was changed from November 1996, so as to overturn the effect of the House of Lords ruling in relation to homes transferred since August 1991: see SI 1996/2614).

Clunis v Camden and Islington Health Authority [1998] 3 All ER 180 (CA). *Community care; negligence; breach of statutory duty; adequacy of after-care services for person with a mental disorder; Mental Health Act 1983, s.117*

A negligence case in which the plaintiff, who had stabbed to death Jonathan Zito at Finsbury Park underground station in London, had since been detained at Rampton Special Hospital, following his plea of guilty to manslaughter on grounds of diminished responsibility had been accepted.

He now brought a case against the health authority for breach of its common law duty of care to treat him with reasonable professional skill and care – and in particular one doctor's responsibility for monitoring, liaison and coordination in relation to the plaintiff's care plan. Breach of statutory duty was also alleged under s.117 of the Mental Health Act 1983. The High Court had resisted the health authority's attempt to have the action struck out; the authority had now appealed against this decision.

Not rewarding unlawfulness. The court held to the principle that it would not help a person who was relying on his own criminal or immoral act. Although this principle did not apply if the person did not know that he was behaving unlawfully, in the present case diminished responsibility only partially removed liability for the criminal act, and therefore the principle was relevant and the court would allow the appeal of the health authority on this ground.

Breach of statutory duty. The court held also that, following the case of *X v Bedfordshire CC*, there would need to be very clear language in the legislation sanctioning private law rights to damages for breach of the duty to provide after-care services under s.117 of the 1983 Act. But there was no such clear wording.

Duty of care in negligence. The court stated that after-care services (undefined in the Act) normally included social work, helping with employment, accommodation, family relationships, domiciliary services, day centres, and residential facilities. Thus, the health authority actions, through the particular doctor responsible, were 'essentially in the sphere of administrative activities in pursuance of a scheme of social welfare in the community'. But whether or not a common law duty of care existed parallel with statutory obligations was 'profoundly influenced by the surrounding statutory framework' – which in this case was a 'major consideration in deciding whether it is fair and reasonable for the local health authority to be held responsible for errors and omissions of the kind alleged. The duties of care are, it seems to us, different in nature from those owed by a doctor to a patient whom he is treating and for whose lack of care in the course of such treatment the local health authority may be liable'.

Coad v Cornwall and Isles of Scilly Health Authority [1997] 8 Med LR 154 (CA). *Lifting and handling; negligence; limitation period for bringing an action*
A state enrolled nurse was injured, lifting a quadriplegic patient, in August 1983. She did not issue a writ until nearly 10 years later. She had acquired knowledge for the purpose of s.14 of the Limitation Act 1980 (which imposes a limit of three years on bringing a negligence action), on the date of the accident. But the court chose to exercise its discretion under s.33, to disapply the limitation period because she did not know and and did not realise that she could bring an action against the defendants (because she had been able to return to work). The Court of Appeal held that s.33 should be interpreted subjectively rather than objectively when looking at all the circumstances of the case, and in particular to the length of the delay and the reasons for it on the part of the plaintiff'. One factor supporting the exercise of this discretion was the availability of good documentation to support the case. Some of the evidence referred to the fact that there was no lifting equipment in that part of the hospital on the evening of the accident – and that there was never a hoist in the bathroom of the ward and slings were never seen in the hospital.

Cocks v Thanet District Council [1983] 2 AC (HL). *Breach of statutory duty by a local authority; private law actions for damages; homelessness legislation*
A key case in the string of generally unsuccessful attempts to win damages in private law from local authorities for breach of statutory duty – in relation to housing and social welfare obligations.

The House of Lords stated that claims for damages for breach of statutory duty (under the Housing (Homeless Persons) Act 1977, now superseded) were possible in the homelessness context, so long as private law rights and obligations had arisen after a public law decision had been made first and separately. Basically, this meant that the existence of executive, as opposed to decision-making functions, might give rise to a duty enforceable in private law: 'On the other hand, the housing authority are charged with executive functions. Once a decision has been reached by the housing authority which gives rise to the temporary, the limited or the full housing duty, rights and obligations are immediately created in the field of private law. Each of the duties referred to, once established, is capable of being enforced by injunction and the breach of it will give rise to a liability in damages. But it is inherent in the scheme of the Act that an appropriate public law decision of the housing authority is a condition precedent to the establishment of the private law duty'.

(The *Cocks* case must now be read in the light of *O'Rourke v Camden London Borough Council* (June 1997), in which the House of Lords has restricted further still the possibility of successful private law actions for breach of social welfare duties).

Colclough v Staffordshire County Council (1994 (liability) and 1997 (damages) reported in Zindani 1998) (QBD). *Social worker; lifting and handling; negligence*
In 1989, a social worker visited a client at home who weighed 15 stone. She found him lying half out of bed, with a neighbour there (a nurse). The nurse guided the social worker in moving him. She felt something go in her lower back. She had received no training in lifting techniques. Judgment was given on liability in June 1994; the present case dealt with damages.

Very detailed evidence was given relating to the woman's prior medical history and events subsequent to this injury. She was eventually awarded over £200,000 in relation to claims for both past and future loss of earnings, the cost of past and future domestic and gardening assistance, loss of pension rights and some minor expenses. She had claimed the injury led to pain, suffering, disability, stress, anxiety, breakdown of marriage, loss of employment.

(The council had accepted that an injury had occurrred but argued that the discs in her back were already vulnerable to injury through degeneration, that the injury itself gave rise to short-term symptoms only; that longer term effects were due to pre-existing degeneration and complicated by emotional and psychological problems, difficulty in coping with work and with her family situation).

Council of Civil Service Unions v Minister for the Civil Service [1985] AC 374. *Irrationality of public bodies; trade union membership*

This House of Lords case concerned the Prime Minister's (as Minister for the Civil Service) successful attempt to deny trade union membership to staff at Government Communications Headquarters (GCHQ). Lord Diplock formulated the legal meaning of irrationality: 'a decision so outrageous in its defiance of logic or of accepted moral standards that no sensible person who had applied his mind to the question to be decided could have arrived at it'.

Cross v Kirklees Metropolitan Borough Council [1998] 1 All ER 564 (CA). *Performance of an absolute duty; highways (icy pavements)*

The case concerned an action for damages for breach of statutory duty in respect of the local authority's obligation, under s.41 of the Highways Act 1980, to maintain the highway. The plaintiff had slipped on an icy pavement and been injured. Though not a community care case, it dwelt on the nature of what appeared to be an 'absolute duty' under the Act (compare s.2 of the Chronically Sick and Disabled Persons Act as explored in the *Gloucestershire* case) and how quickly it must be complied with.

Performing an absolute duty in a reasonable time. The court decided that though there was an absolute duty to achieve a particular result, a) reasonable standards applied in establishing what that result should be, and b) sufficient measures should be taken within a reasonable time. Thus, the correct question in this case was whether the evidence established that sufficient time had elapsed to make it prima facie unreasonable for the authority to have failed to take remedial measures – before the plaintiff had her accident. The answer was no (but see the later case of *Goodes v East Sussex CC*).

Cullen v North Lanarkshire Council [1998] SC 451 (Scotland, Inner House (2nd Division), Court of Session). *Lifting and handling; civil case; Manual Handling Operations Regulations 1992*

A worker was employed to repair and replace fencing. He was injured when unloading fencing from a truck; whilst holding a section of fencing above his head, he caught his heel on some of the other fencing material and fell backwards out of the truck, striking his shoulder on the ground. The court at first instance gave judgment against the pursuer, stating that the general mischief addressed by the regulations was strain injury through the handling of loads. It was agreed that the load he had been holding above his head was not of excessive weight either of itself or when considered in the light of other ergonomic factors.

However, the Court of Session overturned this, finding that no such restriction was to be implied. It considered the wording of the original European directive on which the United Kingdom regulations are based – and concluded that the relevant risk was not limited to the risk of back injury or strain injury, or to risks arising from excessively heavy loads. Thus the definition of injury was largely unrestricted. The directive defined the manual handling of loads as a number of activities with a load 'which by reason of its characteristics or of unfavourable ergonomic conditions, involves a risk particularly of back injury to workers'. It appears to us to be natural to interpret the involvement of risk as referring to those activities rather than to the load itself'. Liability was established by the pursuer; damages had already been agreed at £36,553.

Cumbria Professional Care Limited v Cumbria County Council. *Community care; residential accommodation; purchasing care from the independent sector*

The case concerned an association of proprietors of private sector residential homes, who made a wide-ranging attack on the decisions of the local authority in respect of arrangements for the provision of residential accommodation – including the way in which the authority performed its statutory duties, and its failure to comply with guidance, directions and a European Community directive on public contracts. The judge found in favour of the local authority, the Court of Appeal subsequently refusing the association leave to appeal.

(High Court) *Cumbria Professional Care Limited v Cumbria County Council* (1996) CL 5527 (otherwise unreported). The court found that the authority's decision not to contract with the applicants for planned respite care was not unlawful. The argument that the local authority had erred, in relation to the 85 per cent of the special transitional grant (STG) which should have been spent on private sector provision, failed. This was in part because it was: 'fallacious to pick out one particular of the budget with a view to showing that that particular area may have been treated unevenly, or even favourably towards the public sector, as the basis of an argument that the local authority is to that extent in breach of its public law duty'.

Public services contracts: European directive. The judge rejected the claim in relation to the directive on public service contracts (EEC Directive 92/50), on the basis that an administrative decision by a public body that a service be delivered by an in-house service provider, could not amount to a contract: 'a body cannot make a contract with itself'. Therefore, the directive could not apply.

Allocation of resources to the local authority's homes. The judge rejected the assertion that the authority had acted unfairly by allocating capital resources to its own residential homes.

Waiting lists. Lastly, the judge dismissed the claim that the local authority had been operating unlawful waiting lists and denying potential residents a choice of home. He referred to the *Rixon* case in which the judge had stated that 'even an unequivocal set of statutory duties cannot produce money where there is none or by itself repair gaps in the availability of finance'. He went on to state that it was: 'manifest that the duty to assess and to provide accommodation is one that is owed by the respondents to the potential resident and not to any providers of private sector homes. There is no direct evidence that the respondents ever had, let alone operated, an unlawful policy in regard to waiting lists ... It was never submitted ... nor could it properly have been, that the [authority] operated a system which cynically disregarded its own declared policy'.

(Court of Appeal) **Cumbria Professional Care Limited v Cumbria County Council** (1996) (transcript) (CA) (unreported). At a subsequent hearing, the Court of Appeal denied the Association leave to appeal from the High Court judgment, pointing out that for judicial review to succeed, unreasonableness would have to be demonstrated: yet there was no prospect of this. The court also agreed that where the authority had made arrangements with one of its own Departments, there was no public service contract to which the European directive could apply.

Edwards v National Coal Board [1949] 1 All ER 743 (CA). *Health and safety at work; meaning of 'reasonably practicable'*
A health and safety at work case in which the meaning of the term 'reasonably practicable' was discussed (a term prevalent in health and safety legislation, including the Manual Handling Operations Regulations 1992: see p.178 of this book).

The court stated that: "Reasonably practicable is a narrower term than 'physically possible', and seems ... to imply that a computation must be made by the owner in which the quantum of risk is placed on one scale and the sacrifice involved in the measures necessary for averting the risk (whether in money, time or trouble) is placed in the other, and that, if it can be shown that there is a gross disproportion between them – the risk being insignificant in relation to the sacrifice – the defendants discharge the onus on them'.

Dickson v Lothian Health Board [1994] SLT 525 (Scotland, Outer House, Court of Session). *Lifting and handling; negligence*
A 38-year-old nurse had been one of two nursing staff who were lifting a patient from the floor of the hospital ward. She suffered an episode of acute back pain during the course of the lift. The health board was found to be at fault because it had failed to institute an effective system of tuition in lifting techniques.

Fraser v Glasgow Health Board [1996] Rep LR 58. *Lifting and handling; negligence; Manual Handling Operations Regulations 1992*

A nursing auxiliary sustained a back injury when she was assisting another nurse in moving an elderly patient up the bed. The accident arose from an emergency situation, when the patient collapsed onto her bed and had to be returned to an upright position as soon as possible (in case she drowned in her own chest fluid). The nurse in charge had asked the pursuer to help her lift the patient (weighing 14 stone) back up, by employing the 'Australian lift'; the pursuer injured her back when using this lift.

The court held that the employers owed a duty of care to provide adequate and proper training for nurses – for the safe lifting and moving of patients. This duty had not been performed satisfactorily; the evidence established that the instructions given 'were so inadequate and insufficiently clear' that nurses such as the pursuer 'reasonably formed the view' that their free hand should be placed round the back or at the base of the scapula of the patient, instead of used like a strut on the bed or bed head. The court also found that the nurse in charge had failed to check where the pursuer's free hand was. Liability in negligence was thus established.

The court then considered the Manual Handling Operations Regulations 1992. It concluded that a) the nature of the emergency situation meant that the operation, though involving a risk of injury, could not reasonably practicably be avoided (r.4(1)(a)). Second, it was difficult to see how r.4(1)(b) – which imposed a duty to carry out a risk assessment and to take appropriate steps to reduce the risk of injury to the lowest level reasonably practicable – applied in the circumstances. This was because the regulation was 'applicable to manual handling operations regulations which are regularly undertaken as a matter of course in the furtherance of the employer's business, and that it does not apply where a manual handling operation is undertaken as an emergency on the initiative of an employee. Besides, the defenders supplied mechanical assistance to avoid the need for a manual handling operation. It just was not sufficiently to hand to be used on the particular occasion'.

G v Wakefield City Metropolitan District Council (1998) 96 LGR 69 (QBD). *Joint working; education and social services; respite care; division of statutory responsibilities; Education Act 1996, s.322*

A special education case in which a special educational needs tribunal had stated that the education authority should make a request to the local authority social services department for the provision of respite care. The request would be made under s.322 of the Education Act 1996 which states that education authorities may request help from a local authority (eg, social services) in exercise of any of its (ie, the education authority's) functions.

Local authority quixotically asking itself for help. The judge made a point of stating that this request could apply as between the education and social services departments of the same authority – because although 'it would be quixotic for a body to make a request of itself', nevertheless if this were not the case then 'the local education authority could seek assistance from non-educational departments of any local authority except its own. Parliament cannot have intended so bizarre a conclusion'.

Respite care not part of special education. The court stated that this constituted a recommendation for action which would be outside the sphere of special educational provision and therefore not permissible under s.322; any provision lay under social welfare legislation. Conditions in the home would, as a matter of common sense and ordinary human experience, always have some effect on a child's learning and education – but some more direct relation had to be shown for domestic problems to come within the remit of the tribunal.

Gaskin v United Kingdom (1989) 12 EHRR 36 (Series A, no.160). *Access to personal information; European Convention on Human Rights*

A case concerning rights to personal information held by a social services department, in which the United Kingdom was held to be in breach of article 8 of the Convention (right to respect for private and family life): see p.188 in this book.

General Medical Council v Goba [1988] IRLR 424 (EAT). *Race Relations Act 1976; relationship to other legislation*
A Race Relations Act case brought against the General Medical Council. It involved an Employment Appeal Tribunal considering the implications of an exclusion in the Act which states 'nothing in Parts II to IV shall render unlawful any act of discrimination done ... in pursuance of any enactment or Order in Council'. (A similar exclusion is to be found in the Disability Discrimination Act 1995).

At an extreme, the Council was maintaining that this meant that any act carried out by a statutory body (ie, created and functioning by virtue of legislation) would be immune from the Race Relations Act. The Tribunal could not accept this, since this would mean that 'complete protection is given even for acts which are grossly and inexcusably discriminatory'. Instead the Tribunal felt that it meant the 'act complained of must have been one which was reasonably necessary in order to comply with any condition or requirement of the statute or Order. This would include carrying out the duties or other necessary functions'.

Goodes v East Sussex County Council (1999) TLR 7 January 1999 (CA). *Local authority; breach of statutory duty; ice on the roads*
This was a private law breach of statutory case, involving a claim for damages. Having received a weather warning at 11.45 pm the previous evening, the local authority began to pre-salt the roads at 5.30am the following morning. At 7.10am that morning the plaintiff suffered injuries of the utmost severity when he skidded on a stretch of untreated road; the salting lorry would have reached that stretch about fifteen minutes later. In a 2-1 split decision, the court held, referring to *Cross v Kirklees MBC*, that the authority was in breach of its statutory duty to take reasonable remedial measures in time.

H v Norfolk County Council [1997] 2 FCR 334 (CA). *Negligence; social services; child care*
A case in which the plaintiff, now 22 years old, was appealing against the striking out of his claim for damages in common law negligence – in relation to alleged physical and sexual abuse by his foster father with whom he had been placed by the local authority between ages of 5 and 14 years.

Foster care a special case. The case was argued on the basis that because it concerned foster care, it could be distinguished from *X v Bedfordshire CC* – in which the House of Lords severely restricted the possibility of establishing liability against local authorities for negligence in relation to child care. However, the Court of Appeal found that the Bedfordshire ruling applied to the present case in terms of the type of legislation and policy considerations.

Foster care compared to school care. It was also claimed that this case should be compared with the care of children by schools – in which context the *Bedfordshire* case accepted that liability in negligence might be established in certain circumstances. The court rejected this too, noting that: 'The school analogy is unhelpful, because the liability there will generally be based on vicarious liability for the actions of the school's employees. Furthermore, the degree of control exercisable over activities taking place within the confines of a school is likely to be substantially greater than that which can practically be exercised by a local authority over foster parents'.

Hampson v Department of Education and Science [1990] IRLR 302 (HL). *Race Relations Act 1976; effect on other legislation*
A Race Relations Act case brought against the Department of Education and Science. It involved, amongst other things, consideration of the implications of the exclusion in the Act that 'nothing in Parts II to IV shall render unlawful any act of discrimination done ... in pursuance of any instrument made under any enactment by a Minister of the Crown'. (A similar exclusion is to be found in the Disability Discrimination Act 1995).

The House of Lords concluded (agreeing with a dissenting judgment given in the Court of Appeal by Sir John Balcombe) that to adopt a wide interpretation of this provision would give any body or authority which is a 'creature of statute' so much immunity that the object of the Act would be defeated. This would happen if protection against the Act were to be given not only to acts done in performance of an express obligation, but also those done in exercise of a power or discretion created by the instrument.

Thus, in this particular case, requirements imposed by the Secretary of State in relation to granting teacher status to a Hong Kong Chinese-trained teacher were not automatically protected from being discriminatory. This was because the requirements imposed were based on administrative practice and discretion, and not prescribed by legislation.

Harrison v Cornwall County Council (1991) 156 LGRevR 703 (CA). *Community care; registered Homes Act 1984; meaning of personal care*
A case involving registration under the Registered Homes Act 1984 which found its way to the Court of Appeal via cancellation of registration by the local authority, a Registered Homes Tribunal and the High Court.

It hinged on the number of residents being cared for and, in particular, whether two of them were receiving 'personal care' as defined in the 1984 Act. If they were, they would be counted as relevant residents and the home owner would be in breach of the registration conditions. The Court of Appeal, ruling in favour of the local authority, decided that the definition of personal care contained in s.20 of the 1984 Act meant that personal care did not *necessarily* include assistance with bodily functions; thus, even when such assistance was not being given, a person could still be receiving personal care for the purposes of the Act.

Hawkes (Dorrell Grant) v Southwark London Borough Council (1998, unreported, CCRTF 97/0501 CMS2). *Lifting and handling; Manual Handling Regulations 1992; reasonably practicable measures*
A carpenter was hanging heavy doors in a block of flats. The doors weighted 72lbs. There were no lifts. He lost his balance on a landing and fell down the stairs injuring his back. The judge at first instance dismissed the case, because although there had been no risk assessment under r.4(1)(b) of the Manual Handling Regulations 1992, even if there had been one, the evidence suggested that the supervisor would still not have sanctioned assistance.

The Court of Appeal overturned this, finding that a proper assessment would have concluded that the task of moving the doors was a two-man job and assistance would have been provided. However, the court referred to the assessment duty as an exhortation with no sanction attached, though it was 'a very wise precaution'. The court accepted that reasonably practicable in the Regulations bore the meaning generally accepted by the courts since 1938 (involving a form of cost-benefit analysis: see eg, *Edwards v National Coal Board*). Thus although the risk of injury was relatively slight, so too would have been the cost of providing an assistant to help with the hanging of the doors – which should therefore have been provided, in order to reduce the risk of injury to the lowest level reasonably practicable.

Hughes v Department of Health and Social Security [1985] AC 776 (HL). *Change in policy; legitimate expectation; civil servants; retirement age*
Civil servants had been led to believe by a departmental circular that they would retire at 65 years of age; a subsequent circular reduced this to 60. They claimed that their reasonable expectations had been unlawfully destroyed; the court ruled that: 'Administrative policies may change with changing circumstances, including changes in the political complexions of governments. The liberty to make such changes is something that is inherent in our constitutional form of government'.

Inland Revenue Commissioners v National Federation of Self-Employed and Small Businesses [1982] AC 617 (HL). *Maladministration and unlawfulness; ombudsmen and law courts; tax evasion; casual Fleet Street workers*
A case in which the court pointed out that not all maladministration, as investigated and established by ombudsmen, is necessarily unlawful in the eyes of the courts.

Kent v Griffiths and Others [1998] TLR 23 December 1998 (CA). *Ambulance service; potential negligence; slow response to a 999 call*
The plaintiff was a 26-year-old woman, asthmatic and pregnant for the second time. On the day in question she was very wheezy and phoned her general practitioner (Dr. Griffiths, the first defendant). The doctor telephoned the ambulance service; the person who answered said somebody would be down right away; the dis-

tance was seven miles, and the national standard was 14 minutes between telephone call and ambulance arrival. After two more telephone calls, one from the plaintiff's husband and one from the general practitioner, the ambulance finally arrived 38 minutes after the original call. During the journey, the woman suffered a respiratory arrest.

The consequences were tragic, including serious impairment of memory, change of personality and a miscarriage. After initially conceding that it had a duty to provide a service as soon as reasonably practicable, the ambulance service was now arguing that the case should be struck because, as a matter of law, it did not owe any duty of care to the plaintiff, whether the call was an emergency one or not.

In a 2-1 split decision, the court distinguished this case from a recent, partially comparable fire brigade case (*Capital and Counties plc v Hampshire County Council* [1997] QB 1004) – stating that once an individual call had been accepted, it was at least arguable that the ambulance service had entered a relationship of sufficient proximity with the individual, and that it might be just, fair and unreasonable to impose a duty of care. Therefore, matters should be argued at trial, not under cover of an application simply to strike the case out.

L v Clarke and Somerset County Council [1998] ELR 129 (QBD). *Specificity of provision; statement of special educational needs*

A dispute about the specificity of provision agreed in a statement of special educational needs, about the number of hours of help a child would receive for literacy, study and numeracy skills, and for keyboard training. The court decided that although there was some room for flexibility in certain circumstances, the real question was whether a statement was 'so specific and clear as to leave no room for doubt as to what has been decided is necessary in the individual case'. The statement in the present case did not pass this test – for instance, in relation to close monitoring (not further specified) or to 'regular, preferably daily, individual or small group work' (which could, the judge pointed out, 'as a matter of language' be met with various form of provision).

Lambert v West Devon Borough Council [1997] 96 LGR 45 (QBD). *Negligent statement; duty of care; planning permission*

A building control officer had made a negligent statement to the plaintiff in relation to planning permission, stating that he had the power to grant such permission in respect of alterations to a proposed scheme of building works. The plaintiff sued for damages when he was obliged to stop work after planning permission was ultimately refused. The court held that the council had a duty of care which it had breached, since it was reasonable in the special circumstances of the case for the plaintiff to have relied on the officer's unequivocal statement. The officer should have realised that the plaintiff was relying on him, and had represented himself as having the power to give such permission.

McCaffery v Datta [1997] CL 3678 (CA). *Lifting and handling; negligence*

A nurse was injured when her assistant, who had not been sufficiently trained, failed to take the full weight of her share of the patient. The employer was therefore liable in negligence; however, a finding of one third contributory negligence was also found on the part of the nurse. This was based on the fact that she had suffered a previous back injury and been given medical advice not to undertake heavy lifting – and that she had not arranged the patient's bed so as optimise the effectiveness of the lifting method.

McCarthy and Stone (Developments) Ltd v Richmond upon Thames London Borough Council [1991] 4 All ER 897 (HL). *Charges made by local authorities; Local Government Act 1972, s.111; planning advice*

This case established that charges cannot be made by local authorities under s.111 of the Local Government Act 1972 (which enables authorities to do things to facilitate, or which are conducive or incidental to, the discharge of any of their functions).

It involved the giving of pre-application planning advice by the authority. This was in itself permissible since such advice facilitated, or was conducive or incidental to, the authority's statutory planning functions. What was not permissible was the making of charges for this advice, since such charges were at best 'incidental to the incidental and not incidental to the discharge of the [statutory] functions'. More generally, it was long-established law that if a charge is imposed by a local authority then it must be shown that Parliament had authorised the charge. Yet if charging for a service was regarded as incidental to a function under s.111 of the 1972 Act, then authorities would be permitted to charge for the performance of every function, obligatory or discretionary. The court could not possibly justify such an interpretation of s.111.

Norweb PLC v Dixon [1995] 1 WLR 636 (QBD). *Statutory arrangements; whether a contract is precluded; supply of electricity*

A dispute between a customer and an electricity company. One of the points in issue was whether a contract existed for the supply of electricity. The court thought not: 'the legal compulsion as to both the creation of the relationship and the fixing of its terms is inconsistent with the existence of a contract. As regards the creation of the relationship, the supplier is obliged by section 16(1) of the Act of 1989 to supply if requested to do so'. Whilst there was explicit provision in s.22 of the Act for negotiated, special agreements to meet the particular requirements of customers, this did not cover the more general supply to 'tariff customers' – on whom terms were imposed by the supplier and who did not have scope to bargain (as would be expected in a contractual arrangement).

O'Rourke v Camden London Borough Council [1997] 3 All ER 23 (HL). *Breach of statutory duty; social welfare; housing; private law; damages; homelessness legislation*

A homelessness case under the Housing Act 1985 (the relevant parts now superseded by the Housing Act 1996). It involved a claim for damages for breach of statutory duty in private law (rather than a public law action via judicial review). The case illustrates the extreme reluctance of the courts to consider awarding damages for breaches of health and welfare duties imposed by legislation.

Schemes of social welfare. Lord Hoffman compellingly explained that the legislation was 'a scheme of social welfare, intended to confer benefits at the public expense on grounds of public policy. Public money is spent on housing the homeless not merely for the private benefit of people who find themselves homeless but on grounds of general public interest: because, for example, proper housing means that people will be less likely to suffer illness, turn to crime or require the attention of other social services. The expenditure interacts with expenditure on other public services such as education, the National Health Service and even the police. It is not simply a private matter between the claimant and the housing authority. Accordingly, the fact that Parliament has provided for the expenditure of public money on benefits in kind such as housing the homeless does not necessarily mean that it intended cash payments to be made by way of damages to persons who, in breach of the housing authority's statutory duty, have unfortunately not received the benefits which they should have done'.

Test for claims in damages for breach of statutory duty. The test laid down in *X v Bedfordshire CC* was approved. This was whether legislation shows an intention to afford a remedy in damages, and 'appears intended for the protection of a limited class of people but provides no other remedy for breach'.

In the present case, judicial review was an obvious remedy; furthermore, there were other contra-indications to the existence of a private law remedy. First, the legislation involved social welfare (see immediately above). Second, the duty to provide the accommodation was dependent 'a good deal' on the judgement of the housing authority. For instance, it had to 'have reason to believe', and it was 'necessary to satisfy' itself. Such discretion 'makes it unlikely that Parliament intended errors of judgement to give rise to an obligation to make financial reparation'.

In addition, some of the reasoning in the *Cocks* case was attacked. In that case it had been stated that if a housing authority is 'charged with executive functions' (ie, involving the implementation or execution, rather than the taking of a decision), then a private law duty automatically arises. But in fact the House of Lords now found that such executive functions were not enough to establish the duty: a 'careful examination of the statutory intent' is still required. The case of *Wyatt v Hillingdon LBC* was also quoted from approvingly.

Parkes v Smethwick Corporation [1957] 121 JP 415 (CA). *Lifting and handling; ambulance worker; negligence*
An ambulance worker suffered a hernia injury. He argued that a more suitable stretcher should have been supplied. The court dismissed the case on the grounds that the corporation was not under a duty a) to examine the plaintiff's capacity to undertake the work (he already suffered from a hernia); b) to fit all ambulances with retractable stretcher gear; c) to lay down an exact system of working for ambulance men.

Patchett v Leathem (1949) TLR 4 February 1949 (KBD). *Guidance from central government; cursed and confusing; post-war requisition of buildings*
A case about government Circulars and their potential shortcomings. It concerned the delegation, through a Circular, by the Minister of Health of his powers to requisition buildings to town clerks.

The judge stated, voicing obvious frustration, that whereas: 'ordinary legislation, by passing through both Houses of Parliament ... is thus twice blessed, this type of so-called legislation is at least four times cursed. First, it has seen neither House of Parliament; secondly, it is unpublished and is inaccessible even to those whose valuable rights of property may be affected; thirdly, it is a jumble of provisions, legislative, administrative or directive in character, and sometimes difficult to disentangle one from the other; and, fourthly, it is expressed not in the precise language of an Act of Parliament or an Order of Council but in the more colloquial language of correspondence, which is not always susceptible to the ordinary cannons of construction'.

Pepper v Hart [1993] AC 593 (HL). *Law courts and referral to Parliamentary proceedings; tax*
A tax case in which the House of Lords changed the rule that prevented the courts from referring to Parliamentary proceedings in certain circumstances. These are a) that the legislation is 'ambiguous, obscure or lead to an absurdity'; b) the Parliamentary materials being referred to should be 'one or more statements by a minister or other promoter of the Bill together if necessary with such other Parliamentary material as is necessary to understand such statements and their effect'; c) such statements should be 'clear'; d) such reference should not infringe any 'defined privilege'.

Pfizer Corporation v Ministry of Health [1965] AC 512 (HL). *Provision of statutory services; lack of legally binding contract; NHS prescription*
In a case concerning the legal status of the NHS prescription process, the House of Lords stated that: 'Sale is a consensual contract requiring agreement, express or implied. In the present case there appears to me to be no need for any agreement. The patient has a statutory right to demand the drug on payment of 2s. The hospital has a statutory obligation to supply it on such payment. And if the prescription is presented to a chemist he appears to be bound by his contract with the appropriate authority to supply the drug on receipt of such payment. There is no need for any agreement between the patient and either the hospital or the chemist, and there is certainly no room for bargaining. Moreover the 2s. is not in any sense the price; the drug may cost much more and the chemist has a right under his contract with the authority to receive the balance from them. It appears to me that any resemblance between this transaction and a true sale is only superficial'.

Phelps v Hillingdon London Borough Council [1998] ELR 587 (CA). *Negligence; education; dyslexia*
The case concerned a claim that an education authority was vicariously liable for the negligence of its employee, an educational psychologist, in failing to identify that a child had a special learning difficulty or dyslexia – and instead ascribing to emotional difficulties a) the great discrepancy between both the chronological and predicted reading ages of the child (as she was at the time), and b) her unusual difficulty in writing. The High Court (*Phelps v Hillingdon LBC* [1998] ELR 38), citing *X v Bedfordshire CC* (which had contemplated the potential liability of educational psychologists in some circumstances), had found liability and awarded damages of over £45,000.

Duty of care to whom? The Court of Appeal now overturned this judgment, stating that the educational psychologist could not be liable unless she had assumed personal responsibility to the plaintiff. In fact she had only a duty of care towards her employer, the education authority, to enable it to perform its statutory functions. The court would guard against vicarious liability (ie, on behalf of the employee's negligence) being imposed on the local authority by the backdoor – unless such an assumption of responsibility could be shown, so as to give rise to an additional common law duty. In the absence of such extra responsibility being assumed, there were strong policy reasons not to impose vicarious liability.

Policy reasons for non-liability of educational psychologist and of local authority vicariously. The reasons for not imposing vicarious liability included the following. First, there was a danger of vexatious claims being brought against educational psychologists and teachers. Second, parents should instead use judicial review, rather than negligence, proceedings by way of challenge. A judicial review application must be brought near to the relevant time, when memories are fresh and immediate remedial action can be taken, rather than many years later (which the law of negligence allows in some circumstances). Indeed, the relevant decisions in this case had been made over 10 years previously. Third, such decisions are likely to be the summation of the views of many professionals. It would be invidious to single one out and make him or her a scapegoat; and to sue many would circumvent the immunity (from direct, as opposed to vicarious, liability) of the local authority. Fourth, causation – ie, showing whether, or what, harm was caused by the negligence – might present enormous difficulties. Lastly, the defensive practices adopted because of fears of negligence might result in excessive and time-consuming testing of children, which would be wasteful of resources.

Princess Louise Scottish Hospital v The Commissioners [1983] VATTR 191 (VAT Appeal Tribunal). *Hospital overbed tables; defining equipment designed for disabled people; VAT zero-rating*
A case about whether VAT zero-rating should apply to overbed tables supplied to a hospital on the basis that they were 'designed solely' for use by chronically sick or disabled people. The tribunal ruled that they were not eligible, because although that type of table was of particular value to that group of people, nevertheless it was 'eminently practicable and convenient for all sorts of hospital patients and was not designed with a particular class in mind'.

R v Avon County Council, ex parte M [1994] 2 FCR 259 (QBD). *Community care; residential care; needs and preferences; psychological needs; complaints review panel*
The case involved a 22-year old man with Down's Syndrome, for whom the local authority was under a duty to make arrangements for residential accommodation under s.21 of the National Assistance Act 1948. The man had an 'entrenched' wish to go to a particular home, whilst the Council had decided to place him in a cheaper one which would still, it claimed, meet his needs. The dispute went to the complaints procedure review panel which recommended that the Council make arrangements for provision at the man's choice of home. The panel found, having consulted expert opinion, that the assessment should be based on current need including psychological, educational, social and medical needs. The entrenched position of the man formed part of his psychological need. The social services committee of the Council, worried about setting costly precedents, rejected the panel's findings.

Psychological need. The judge stated that needs 'may properly include psychological needs' – and that the authority was not therefore being forced to pay more than it otherwise would have normally (something it was not required to do under the Choice of Accommodation Directions in LAC(92)27): it would 'simply be paying what the law required'. He also referred to guidance (LAC(92)15) on adults with learning disabilities, which states that services should be arranged on an individual basis (and which goes on: 'taking account of age, needs, degree of disability, the personal preferences of the individual and his or her parents or carers, culture, race and gender').

Local authority not following the complaints review panel decision. It was unlawful for the council to have disregarded the recommendation of the review panel without a good reason, given the weight and the 'one way' nature of the evidence informing the panel's findings. Neglecting to do this did not impugn 'the credibility of the review panel, but instead ignores the weight to which it [the panel] is *prima facie* entitled because of its place in the statutory procedure, and further, pays no attention to the scope of its [the panel's] hearing and clear reasons that it had given'.

R v Berkshire County Council, ex parte Parker [1996] 95 LGR 449 (QBD). *Community care; duty to assess even if services not provided; ordinary residence*

This case confirmed that local authorities should assess people for community care services which could be provided *in principle* (ie, because there was at least a power to provide them), even if *in practice* the authority happened not to be providing them: ie, the services were not 'physically' available and no duty arose to provide them.

It concerned a seriously disabled man suffering from viral brain damage and epilepsy, who was resident at the British Home and Hospital for Incurables, but whose mother felt that he required different types and levels of care not available at the hospital. She had solicitors write to a social services department requesting a community care assessment. Before the court, the authority produced a document purporting to record the results of the assessment. However, the mother claimed that it was not a lawful assessment, since it merely described the services her son was receiving – and did not identify his needs. This particular issue was not decided in court, although the authority did appear to admit that the document had not been drawn up in accordance with good practice.

The hub of the case was whether the authority had a duty to make an assessment at all, because – it claimed – the man was not ordinarily resident within its area. The authority argued that the effect of s.29 of the National Assistance Act 1948 (together with Directions and Approvals contained in LAC(93)10) was that authorities had a *general* power to make arrangements to provide for those not ordinarily resident – but did not have a power in relation to any *specific* services. Therefore, it maintained, there was nothing for its duty of assessment under s.47 the NHS and Community Care Act 1990 to bite on. The authority had argued that if no relevant services (which there was only a general power to provide) were physically available, then the duty to assess would not arise at all in the case of somebody not ordinarily resident. As the judge put it, this argument rested the duty of assessment on a factual capacity to provide services rather than a legal capacity. This could not be right.

The judge rejected this argument and confirmed that the duty of assessment did not depend on the physical availability of services. He also expressed 'a degree of judicial unease' at reliance on the Department of Health's guidance to ascertain the meaning of legislation – even if it did contain directions and approvals.

R v Bexley London Borough, ex parte B [1995] CL 3225 (QBD). *Support for a family; Chronically Sick and Disabled Persons Act, s.2; Children Act 1989, s.17*

A case involving the inter-relationship between s.17 of the Children Act 1989 and s.2 of the Chronically Sick and Disabled Persons Act – and exposing the apparent tendency of some authorities to ignore the 1970 Act in respect of children. It was common ground that the specific duty under the 1970 Act in relation to practical assistance in the home was stronger than the general duty to provide services for children in need under s.17 of the Children Act 1989. However, the authority argued that since no request had been made (under s.4 of the Disabled Persons, Services, Consultation and Representation Act 1986), it had no duty to make an assessment for services under the 1970 Act.

The judge said in effect that the authority should not put its head in the sand by ignoring the 1970 Act, since provision under it was the 'only conclusion which a reasonable authority could reach'. Furthermore, the circumstances were such that the authority had, in reality, been 'satisfied that it was necessary to provide practical assistance for him in the house'. The authority had therefore failed to 'apply their minds to the true position' and to 'take into account a material consideration'. Indeed, although no formal request under the 1986 Act had been made, the conditions governing the obligation to arrange services under s.2 of the CSDPA did not include the condition that a request be made. In reaching his conclusion, the judge did concede that the relationship between the Children Act 1989 and the 1970 Act was 'an uneasy one'.

The judge also considered whether financial damages might be available if an authority breaches its specific duty under s.2 of the 1970 Act. Cautiously, he suggested that the duty might be capable of giving rise to a claim for damages for the tort of breach of statutory duty. (But this is to be doubted: see eg, *O'Rourke v Camden LBC* and *X v Bedfordshire CC*).

R v Birmingham City Council, ex parte A (minor) [1997] 2 FCR 357 (QBD, Family Division). *Child care; delay in placement; attitude of courts*
A child care case illustrating the reluctance of the courts to deal with cases which are solely about delay, without points of law. It concerned a child who had entered a psychiatric unit for assessment, where her doctor decided that a special foster placement was required as soon as possible (the accommodation and care to be provided under s.20 of the Children Act 1989). This had proved difficult and the child was still, nearly a year later, in the unit.

The judge held that it was not appropriate for the court to make a declaration to the effect 'that the authority erred in law, in not acting with reasonable diligence and expedition to make arrangements to ensure that the applicant be placed in appropriate accommodation'. Such a declaration would not be appropriate in the context of judicial review, because the precise circumstances of the situation could not be properly investigated by the court. Instead, it was more appropriate that the complaints procedure under s.26 of the Children Act 1989 be used – which provided 'for a wide ranging complaints procedure to investigate cases where there is an allegation of culpable conduct on the part of a local authority'.

Even so, the judge added: 'it must not be considered that the making of the application itself was, in fact, unwarranted ... [since it] brought the matter to a head and ... concentrated the minds of the local authority upon the position, and to that extent it has had an effect'.

R v Birmingham City Council, ex parte Darshan Kaur [1991] 155 LGRevR 587 (QBD). *Public meeting; consultation; interpreters; Race Relations Act 1976*
An education case involving consultation procedures in relation to closure of a school in Ladywood, Birmingham. The school's ethnic composition was 44 per cent Indian, 27 per cent Pakistani, 11 per cent Bangladeshi, 8 per cent Afro-Caribbean, 8 per cent indigenous, 2 per cent Vietnamese. The main complaint was that the consultation had been conducted in English and inadequately translated; only one interpreter had been provided, and it was alleged that the local authority was in breach of the Race Relations Act 1976. The court stated that whilst it would be sensible to arrange for interpreters to be present, this was not a necessary obligation. It also referred to *R v Governors of Small Health School, ex parte Birmingham City Council*, in which the Court of Appeal stated, in relation to a similar consultation exercise, that when a statute demands that information be provided, it need only be provided in English.

R v Birmingham City Council, ex parte Taj Mohammed [1998] 1 CCLR 441 (QBD). *Disabled facilities grants; necessity and appropriateness; resources not relevant*
The case concerned the approval of a disabled facilities grant (DFG) under the Housing Grants, Construction and Regeneration Act 1996 and, in particular, whether in deciding whether works were 'necessary and appropriate' under s.24, resources could be taken into account. The court concluded emphatically that they could not.

Resources and the 1996 Act. The judge found that the 1996 Act bore all the marks of the draftsman's full awareness of the issue of resources. For instance, the Act had reduced the provision of other grants to powers only (with the inevitable resource implications), but had maintained a duty in relation to DFGs. Second, the other test applied to applications for DFGs was whether proposed works were 'reasonable and practicable', a test which implied the relevance of resources. This was because of 'an appreciation of the fact that it was not a sensible use of resources to make a DFG to improve an old dilapidated building, or a dwelling which was not fit for human habitation'.

Therefore, had the draftsman wanted resources to be taken into account in respect of necessity and appropriateness, he would have said so. Furthermore, the housing authority had a duty to consult a social services authority about necessity and appropriateness – yet one 'would not expect' a social services authority to advise a housing authority about the latter's finances..

Other cases compared. The judge considered the House of Lords decision in *R v Gloucestershire CC, ex p Barry*, in which it was decided that resources could be taken account of in determining 'necessity' under s.2 of the Chronically Sick and Disabled Persons Act 1970. The judge chose not to follow this case. Having referred to the danger identified in another House of Lords case (*R v East Sussex, ex p Tandy*) of downgrading duties to powers, he pointed out firstly that the needs of disabled people for access to and use of their dwellings as set out in s.23 of the 1996 Act were 'real needs' and not comparable with the some of the services in s.2 of the 1970 Act, which were deemed in the *Tandy* case as not giving rise to needs in a stringent sense of the word. Second, he referred to the legislative background surrounding the 1996 Act, clearly indicating that the draftsman was 'alive to the issue of financial resources'; whereas such 'clues as to the intention of Parliament' were not present in the case of the 1970 Act.

Conclusion. The judge finally referred to the fact that the 1996 Act had deliberately reduced from a duty to a power the provision of four types of grant, but not DFGs. As pointed out in the *Tandy* case, the court 'should be slow to downgrade' a duty to a mere discretion; if 'Parliament wishes to redirect public expenditure on meeting the needs of disabled occupants of buildings, then it is for Parliament so to provide'. In the 1996 Act it was clearer even than in the *Tandy* case (which had identified an absolute duty in education legislation) that resources were not relevant – in this situation to the necessity and appropriateness of works of adaptation.

R v Bournewood Community and Mental Health NHS Trust, ex parte L [1998] 1 CCLR 390 (HL). *Informal admission of patient under s.131 of the Mental Health Act 1983; mental capacity; best interests of a patient; common law doctrine of necessity*

The House of Lords held that it was permissible to admit informally to hospital, under s.131 of the Mental Health Act 1983, patients who lacked the capacity to consent but who did not positively object. The argument that, in the absence of capacity, s.131 could not be used and formal sectioning under ss.2–5 of the 1983 Act was instead required, was overcome by the court stating that the removal, care and treatment of the person had been in his best interests and was justified by the common law doctrine of necessity, which was not excluded by the provisions of the 1983 Act. However, it was pointed out by Lord Steyn that this doctrine had attached to it no formal safeguards such as those contained in the Act for the protection of vulnerable individuals – and that it was a 'comfort' that the Secretary of State had stated reform of the law was under active consideration.

R v Bradford Metropolitan District Council, ex parte Parkinson, R v Further Education Funding Council, ex parte Parkinson [1997] 2 FCR 67 (QBD). *Community care; division of responsibilities for education and social services; Chronically Sick and Disabled Persons Act, s.2; National Assistance Act 1948, s.29*

An education case concerning further education for a 20-year old man with severe mental and physical disabilities. Part of the case considered the extent of duties of the local authority under its social services functions – s.2 of the Chronically Sick and Disabled Persons Act 1970, and s.29 of the National Assistance Act 1948 – to fund an education course at a college.

As to the potential duty under s.2(1)(b) of the 1970 Act, the judge had to interpret the possible scope of the words 'provision for that person of lectures, games … or assistance to that person in taking advantage of educational facilities available to him'. He concluded that the reference to such facilities was 'not to providing such facilities but providing assistance to take advantage of them if they are available'. Thus, the duty did not extend to funding the course.

Under s.29 of the 1948 Act, approvals (see p.193) confirmed that there was a power to make arrangements for disabled people for the 'instruction in their own homes or elsewhere in methods of overcoming the effects of their disabilities'. The judge noted a) that this amounted only to a power (ie, not a duty), which could not be 'read into' s.2(1)(b) of the 1970 Act; and b) in any case, the wording could not 'refer to that which is purely educational'.

The provision and funding of further education was provided for under education, not social services, legislation.

R v Bradford Metropolitan Borough Council, ex parte Sikander Ali [1994] ELR 299 (QBD). *Publishing information; local education authority; Education Act 1980*

An education case illustrating the difficulty likely to be encountered in enforcing a general duty to publish information about services. The education authority was under a duty in s.8 of the Education Act 1980 to publish information about its admissions policy. The adequacy of the information was challenged.

The court stated that: 'The statutory requirement is to publish information about the policy to be followed in deciding submissions. That does not require that every nut and bolt of what is to be done has to be spelt out in the information to be provided. [It was claimed] that the applicant did not know whether he was in a traditional catchment area or not and that the failure to inform him of that meant that it was really an unexpressed policy. I am afraid I do not agree. It seems to me that the policy was quite adequately set out in the booklet when one adds to it the information which the booklet said was available at various places. It was open to the applicant to ask questions about the admissions and catchment areas in relation to traditional areas. It does not seem to me that the applicant was under informed or misled'.

R v Brent London Borough Council, ex parte Connery [1990] 2 All ER 353 (QBD). *Taking account of resources; housing benefit rules*

A housing benefit case about the ability of a local authority to take account of resources when making decisions – and foreshadowing some of the arguments about resources explored more fully in the *R Gloucestershire CC, ex p Barry*.

It was common ground that when deciding whether the rent paid by an applicant for housing benefit is unreasonably high – compared to that payable for suitable alternative accommodation – the authority could not take account of its own resources. However, the court ruled that in then deciding by how much to reduce the 'eligible rent' figure, the authority could take account of its own financial situation (though not so as to reduce the eligible rent below that allowed by the legislation – ie, not below the cost of suitable alternative accommodation). The judge stated: 'Authorities, generally, in the carrying out of their functions are bound to have regard to the financial implications of any action or inaction on their part save in those cases … where there is an absolute duty to something…'.

R v Brent London Borough Council, ex parte D [1998] 1 CCLR 235 (QBD). *Community care; residential accommodation; illegal immigrant / overstayer; fundamental right to life and minimum standard of health; National Assistance Act 1948, s.21*

The person involved was a Brazilian with advanced HIV/AIDS who had illegally overstayed in the United Kingdom, following expiration of his six-month visitor's visa. In breach of immigration rules he worked until he became too ill to do so. He had been admitted to hospital suffering from pancreatitis and bilateral pneumonia. On discharge from hospital he was unable to afford the rent at the hostel in which he had been staying, although the owner allowed him to sleep in the garage. An application for exceptional leave to remain was made to the Home Office by the Immunity Legal Centre, on the grounds that he was too unfit to travel. In the meantime, a Camden Citizen's Advice Bureau wrote to the local authority seeking residential accommodation under s.21 of the National Assistance Act 1948.

Residence condition implying lawfulness? The local authority replied that it was under no obligation to provide assistance to illegal immigrants. The judge noted that had assistance under s.21 depended on a residence qualification (which it did not because provision would be governed by the direction concerning urgent need: see p.253), then 'it might have been possible to imply a qualification that the residence must be lawful. Whether a qualification of residence implies that the residence must be lawful will depend on the statutory context'.

Right to assistance precluded by wrongdoing. The court went on to accept the local authority's argument that a person could not acquire a right to assistance by virtue of a criminal offence or wrongdoing.

Overriding principle of right to life and health. However, there was another overriding principle at play: 'namely the duty of all civilised nations to safeguard life and health'. The court referred to the old case of *R v Inhabitants of Eastbourne* (1803) 4 East 103, which had identified 'the law of humanity, which is anterior to all positive laws', and to articles two and three of the European Convention on Human Rights. But there was no need to rely on the Convention in order 'to uphold so fundamental a right'.

Fitness to travel. Thus, the local authority had to consider whether to provide assistance under s.21 of the 1948 Act; however, a duty to assist would only arise if the man was unfit to travel, since if he could, care and attention would be otherwise available to him (ie, in Brazil).

Adequacy of assessment. Nevertheless, the council had previously agreed to conduct an assessment of his needs, even when though it had denied that any duty would arise. The conclusion of this assessment, conducted whilst he had been in hospital, had been that he was not too ill to travel; thus, in any case, no duty of assistance of arose even aside from the illegality argument. It was claimed that the assessment was flawed because the assessors should have made more enquiries than they actually did of the relevant doctors about the man's fitness for travel. The judge did not accept that the assessment under s.47 of the NHS and Community Care Act 1990 was faulty, but noted that the council would now have the 'opportunity to consider the effect of the absence of shelter and accommodation on his illness, whilst he is not fit to travel'.

R v Brent London Borough Council, ex parte Macwan [1994] 2 FCR 604 (CA). *Carrying out a duty through interim provision; delay in performance of final duty; local housing authority; homelessness legislation*

The case concerned a delay on the part of a housing authority in carrying out its acknowledged duty to find permanent accommodation for a person under homelessness legislation (Housing Act 1985, the relevant provisions now in the Housing Act 1996). The authority had decided to perform the duty in stages, the first of which was to provide temporary accommodation for three years. The relevant code of guidance for local authorities on homelessness stated that once the duty arose to provide permanent accommodation, the authority should set about providing it immediately. However, the court held that the code was not law, that the authority had to have regard to it but not necessarily follow it, and that its decision – in all the circumstances – was not unreasonable.

R v Brent and Harrow Health Authority, ex parte Harrow London Borough Council [1997] 3 FCR 765 (QBD). *Division of responsibilities between education authorities and the NHS; provision of various therapy*

Under s.166 of the Education Act 1993 (now s.322 of the Education Act 1996), a health authority was obliged to assist with provision for children with special educational needs, unless, in the light of resources, it was not reasonable for it to comply with the obligation. On this basis, the court decided that the health authority was entitled to refuse the education authority's request that the health authority provide speech and language therapy (one hour a week), occupational therapy (one hour a week) and physiotherapy (at least 45 minutes a week) for a six-year old child with cerebral palsy. The case was heard parallel with *R v Harrow London Borough Council, ex parte M.*

Under s.166 of the 1993 Act, it appeared that each case should be dealt with on its individual merits. However, it was clear that under the NHS Act 1977, which governed its functions, a health authority could not be expected to consider its resources on a daily basis as each individual case arose. Instead it developed priority categories and then genuinely considered under which each individual came. In this case, the child came under the highest category, but the health authority had informed the education authority that there were nevertheless insufficient resources available to meet all the needs; it would therefore meet only one half of the assessed needs for the speech and language therapy and the occupational therapy. The judge found this to be an impeccable approach.

R v Bristol City Council, ex parte Bailey and Bailey [1995] 27 HLR 307 (QBD). *Fettering discretion; letter-writing; renovation grants under housing legislation*

A case about discretionary home renovation grants (ie, grants which the authority had a power but not a duty to provide), illustrating that the courts are prepared to consider whether an authority is fettering its discretion – even in the case of a *power*, rather than a duty, to do something. The legislation was the Local Government and Housing Act 1989, the relevant provisions of which have been superseded by the Housing Grants, Construction and Regeneration Act 1996.

The judge held that a letter which stated, in effect, that no discretionary grants were available, would have amounted to an unlawful fettering of discretion had it truly represented the Council's policy. In fact, the policy did *in practice* allow for the giving of discretionary grants on individual merits – as well as for other discretionary assistance in the form of minor works assistance and other assistance. At the same time, the authority had been justified in adopting its restrictive policy, given the lack of resources.

(The judge's additional ruling that the council had no duty to give reasons either under the legislation or under the general banner of fairness has now been overtaken by legislative change in s.34 of the Housing Grants, Construction Act 1996 which imposes a duty to give reasons in this particular context).

R v Bristol City Council, ex parte Penfold [1998] 1 CCLR 315 (QBD). *Community care assessment; assessment a benefit in it own right; resources not relevant*

The applicant was a 52-year-old woman suffering from anxiety and depression who lived with her dependant daughter. She had returned to Bristol to live with her two sons, and then subsequently in temporary accommodation provided by a housing association. She relied on care and support from members of her family living in the centre of Bristol.

Homelessness legislation. The local authority had accepted that she was unintentionally homeless and in priority need – but she had rejected an offer of accommodation (under housing legislation) on grounds of claustrophobia. The authority treated its homelessness duty as discharged, but said she could remain on the ordinary housing list; she subsequently rejected another offer on various grounds.

Community care assessment. The woman's solicitors wrote to the council asking for an assessment under s.47 of the NHS and Community Care Act 1990, the Children Act 1989 and the Carers (Recognition and Services) Act 1995. The local authority apparently refused to carry out an assessment and maintained that the applicant had failed to get what she wanted under housing legislation – and was now seeking preferential treatment through community care legislation. Furthermore, it stated that if she were to succeed in such a blatant attempt to circumvent homelessness legislation, it would lead to a flood of requests from dissatisfied and unsuccessful housing applicants.

Refusal to assess. The authority had been unable to make up its mind whether legally it should say that it had refused to carry out an assessment – or that it had carried out an assessment, albeit a simple, informal one. In the event, a letter written by the assessor, that it would have been preferable to have maintained that an assessment had been carried out, gave the game away; the judge concluded that it had in fact not been carried out. He added that, if he was wrong in this conclusion, then the authority had still acted unlawfully since any assessment it claimed to have carried out would have been in breach of policy guidance which talks of a comprehensive and flexible procedure able to determine appropriate responses to requests for assessment. The implications of this were that an assessment is directed at a particular person, and should fully explore need in relation to services which the authority has the power to supply.

Futility of assessments. The authority argued that it was futile for local authorities to spend large sums of money on assessments when it was clear in advance that there was no hope of meeting any needs. Thus, authorities could and should take account of resources when deciding whether people 'may' be in need of community care services and whether they qualify for an assessment.

However, the judge rejected the idea that resources can play a part at this initial stage of deciding whether to carry out an assessment; he felt that s.47 of the 1990 Act provided a very low threshold test for assessment. Furthermore, he did not accept that it was pointless to carry out assessments even when it was clear that needs would not be met – since assessment could serve a useful purpose all the same. In reaching this decision the judge managed to circumvent *R v Gloucestershire CC, ex p Barry* which had allowed resources into the picture at the later stages of assessment of need and decision about services.

'Normal housing' as community care service. The judge further ruled that housing could in principle be provided for the primary purpose of meeting a social welfare need (and thus under community care legislation), rather than a housing need (under housing legislation). The authority claimed that 'normal housing' could not be provided under s.21 of the National Assistance Act 1948; whereas the judge accepted the view that it could be provided as part of community care if it met a person's care needs – for instance, when a person needs to live next door to a drug rehabilitation centre. In reaching this conclusion, the judge looked to the Court of Appeal judgment in *R v Westminster CC, ex p A* involving asylum seekers – in which the scope and flexibility of s.21 of the 1948 Act had been demonstrated.

Propositions. By way of summary, the judge accepted the following propositions: a) an authority had to carry out an assessment when there was apparent need for a service which it had the power to provide; b) this duty remained even if there was no sensible prospect of services being provided; c) the discharge by a housing authority of its functions under homelessness legislation did not preclude the need for a community care assessment; d) a local authority could provide 'normal accommodation' under s.21 of the National Assistance Act 1948, so long as it was providing for a need which would otherwise be met by other community care services; e) it was unlawful for the authority not to assess.

R v Bristol Corporation, ex parte Hendy [1974] 1 WLR 498 (CA). *Local authorities; delay in carrying out duty; response of law courts; compulsory purchase; provision of accommodation*
A case illustrating circumstances in which the courts a) will tolerate delay; and b) will in some cases not intervene even if an authority is breaching its statutory duty.

It concerned the provision of accommodation for a person under the Land Compensation Act 1973. In fulfilling its duty to provide longer term accommodation, the housing authority was first of all offering temporary accommodation. The applicant claimed that there was a breach of duty and asked for an order from the court forcing the authority to remedy this. On the issue of delay in providing the longer term accommodation, the court stated that in carrying out its duty, the authority was acting reasonably, since it was not required 'to give the applicant as a displaced person any priority other than, on his displacement, immediate accommodation, albeit temporary'.

Furthermore, even if there were to be a clear breach of duty, but 'in a situation such as this, there is evidence that a local authority is doing all that it honestly and honourably can to meet the statutory obligation, and that its failure, if there be failure, to meet that obligation arises really out of circumstances over which it has no control, then ... it would be improper for the court to make an order ... compelling it to do that which either it cannot do or which it can only do at the expense of other persons not before the court who may have equal rights with the applicant and some of whom would certainly have equal moral claims'.

R v Buckinghamshire County Council, ex parte Sharma; R v Wiltshire County Council, ex parte Lakhbir Kaur [1998] COD 182 (QBD). *Rigid policies; fettering of discretion; defining exceptional circumstances; educational grants*
Two education cases concerning the power to award grants under s.2 of the Education Act 1962 and whether the authorities were fettering their discretion. The applicants failed because the court decided a) that there were statistics showing that some other applicants had succeeded as exceptions to the policy of not making awards, under an 'exceptional circumstances' proviso to the policy; and b) it was precisely because this proviso was directed towards unforeseen circumstances, that the 'exceptional circumstances' covered did not have to be defined within the policy.

R v Cambridge Health Authority, ex parte B (A Minor). *NHS treatment; rationing*
The case concerned the refusal by a health authority to provide possibly lifesaving treatment for a 10-year-old child suffering from leukaemia. One of the grounds for the refusal was that the proposed treatment would not be an effective use of resources. The High Court judgment was overruled on the same day by the Court of Appeal.

(High Court) *R v Cambridge Health Authority, ex parte B* (A Minor) [1995] 1 FLR 1055. The judge ruled against the authority on various grounds. In particular, he attempted to lay open its policy and reasoning to scrutiny: 'But merely to point to the fact that resources are finite tells one nothing about the wisdom or, what is relevant for my purposes, the legality of a decision to withhold funding in a particular case ... I have no idea where in the order of things the [authority] place a modest chance of saving the life of a 10-year old girl. I have no evidence about the [authority's] budget either generally or in relation to 'extra-contractual referrals'. Dr Zimmern's evidence about money consists only in grave and well-rounded generalities. I quite accept, as Re J enjoins me, that the court should not make orders with consequences for the use of health service funds in ignorance of the knock-on effect on other patients. But where the question is whether the life of a 10-year old child might be saved, by however slim a chance, the responsible authority must in my judgment do more than toll the bell of tight resources. They must explain the priorities that have led them to decline to fund the treatment. They have not adequately done so here'.

(Court of Appeal) *R v Cambridge Health Authority, ex parte B* (A Minor) [1995] 6 MLR 250. The Court of Appeal, on the same day, overturned the High Court's decision. On the question of resources, it stated that it was not for the law courts to take decisions about the optimum – ie, utilitarian – allocation of resources. It was: 'common knowledge that health authorities cannot make ends meet. They cannot pay their nurses as much as they would like; they cannot provide all the treatments they would like; they cannot purchase all the extremely expensive equipment they would like ... Difficult and agonising judgements have to be made as to how a limited budget is best allocated to the maximum advantage of the maximum number of patients. That is not a judgement which the court can make...'

In addition, the court dismissed the argument that if the health authority had money in the bank which it had not been spent, 'then they would be acting in plain breach of their statutory duty if they did not procure this treatment'. Indeed, 'it would be totally unrealistic to require the Authority to come to the court with its accounts and seek to demonstrate that if this treatment were provided for B then there would be a patient, C, who would have to go without treatment. No major Authority could run its financial affairs in a way which would permit such a demonstration'.

R v Central Birmingham Health Authority, ex parte Collier [1988] (unreported) (CA). *NHS treatment; rationing*
This case was about the failure of the health authority to carry out a heart operation on a child (likewise *R v Central Birmingham Health Authority, ex parte Walker*). Leave for permission to bring a judicial review case was sought but denied by both High Court and Court of Appeal.

The Court of Appeal agreed with the High Court in declining to intervene: 'this is a hearing before a court. This is not the forum in which a court can properly express opinions upon the way in which national resources are allocated or distributed. There may be very good reasons why the resources in this case do not allow the beds in the hospital to be used at this particular time ... From the legal point of view, in the absence of any evidence which could begin to show that there was a failure to allocate resources in this instance in circumstances which would make it unreasonable in the Wednesbury sense to make those resources available, there can be no arguable case ... whilst I have for my part every sympathy with [the family] ... and can understand their pressing anxiety in the case of their little boy, it does seem to me unfortunate that this procedure has been adopted. It is wholly misconceived ... The courts of this country cannot arrange the lists in the hospital'.

R v Central Birmingham Health Authority, ex parte Walker. NHS treatment; rationing
The case concerned a baby with a heart condition and the postponement of an operation; the health authority accepted that the baby required the operation but stated that it was unable to conduct it. Leave for permission to bring a full judicial review case was sought but denied by both High Court and Court of Appeal.

(High Court) *R v Central Birmingham Health Authority, ex parte Walker* [1987] 3 BMLR 32 (QBD) The court could find no illegality, procedural defect or unreasonableness: 'The fact that the decision is unfortunate, disturbing and in human terms distressing, simply cannot lead to a conclusion that the court should interfere in a case of this kind ... I detect a general criticism of the decisions as to staffing and financing of the National Health Service and of those who provide its funds and facilities. It has been said before, and I say it again, that this court can no more investigate that on the facts of this case than it could do so in any other case where the balance of available money and its distribution and use are concerned. Those, of course, are questions which are of enormous public interest and concern – but they are questions to be raised, answered and dealt with outside the court'.

Court of Appeal: *R v Central Birmingham Health Authority, ex parte Walker* [1987] 3 BMLR 32 The Court of Appeal upheld the decision (made the day before) of the High Court: 'It is not for this court, nor indeed any court, to substitute its own judgment for the judgment of those who are responsible for the allocation of resources' unless the failure in allocation was legally unreasonable. 'Even then, of course, the court has to exercise a judicial discretion. It has to take account of all the circumstances of the particular case'.

If the court were to intervene 'in all or even most cases where patients are, from their points of view, very reasonably disturbed at what is going on, we should ourselves be using up National Health Service resources by requiring the authority to stop doing the work for which they were appointed and to meet the complaints of the patients. It is a very delicate balance ... the jurisdiction does exist. But it has to be used extremely sparingly'.

R v Cleveland County Council, ex parte Cleveland Care Homes Association and Others [1993] 158 LGRevR 641 (QBD). *Community care; residential care; contractual terms between local authority and care homes; unreasonableness*
This case illustrates use of the concept of unreasonableness to strike down a local authority's decision as unlawful.

An association of residential home owners (and others) challenged the contractual terms on which the local authority was prepared to enter contracts with the homes, in fulfilling its community care obligations to make arrangements to provide residential accommodation for people in need of it under s.21 of the National Assistance Act 1948.

The challenge rested on a number of grounds: a) that the authority had failed to consult with the association as required by community care legislation, or – alternatively – that the association had a freestanding legitimate expectation to be consulted; b) that contractual terms going beyond the statutory requirements imposed by the Registered Homes Act 1984 were unlawful; and c) that the contract terms were unlawful on grounds of unreasonableness.

The judge found in favour of the association, on ground c), unreasonableness, because he was satisfied that the effect of the contract terms would have been to frustrate the purpose of the NHS and Community Care Act 1990 – by threatening the very existence of the private homes, and thus the choice of potential residents. Although the duty to consult under s.46 of the NHS and Community Care Act 1990 – about community care plans and the local authority's strategy for the provision of community care services – did not cover consultation about contractual arrangements, nevertheless, 'the [common law] duty to act reasonably required the [authority] to consult, and if necessary negotiate, with homeowners on those terms and conditions which imposed more onerous standards than had hitherto been insisted on'.

R v Cleveland County Council, ex parte Ward [1994] COD 222 (QBD). *Community care; local authority contracting for nursing home care; full accounts of home required; whether beyond its powers or unreasonable*
The owner of a registered nursing home tendered for a contract with the local authority for providing nursing home services. The owner of the home submitted abbreviated accounts; the local authority insisted that full audit accounts be provided. This was to try to ensure that frail elderly people should receive the best possible service – by checking that potential homes were financially viable and able to provide long-term care and accommodation. The applicant for judicial review was in fact a resident of the nursing home.

The court held that the local authority was acting neither beyond its powers nor unreasonably. Having regard to the local authority's reasoning, the court could not make a finding of unreasonableness or perversity.

R v Cornwall County Council, ex parte Goldsack [1996] (unreported) (QBD). *Community care; assessment of needs and decision about services; assistance with mobility at a day centre; health and safety*
A case which looked, amongst other things, at a) the provision of walking assistance under s.29 of the National Assistance Act 1948; b) the strength of the duty under the 1948 Act compared with that under s.2 of the Chronically Sick and Disabled Persons Act; c) the distinction between needs and arrangements to meet those needs; and d) the relevance of health and safety matters.

Walking assistance at day centre. The case concerned a 21-year-old woman who had suffered brain damage at the age of two, and later (at the age of 15) developed a viral illness which caused serious disability and loss of walking ability. By 1992 she could walk again, though only with assistance. She had cerebral palsy, a right hemiplegia, and was partially sighted and epileptic. She had been attending a day centre, until her parents removed her, feeling that her needs were being grossly neglected. They were particularly disturbed that she was being pushed around the centre in a wheelchair, rather than walking. Their formal complaints had been rejected by the local authority.

When she first attended the centre, the woman had received assistance with walking; but latterly a wheelchair and a rollator (a walking frame with wheels) was being used because, the council claimed, staff had complained of back pain when they walked with her. At one stage, the council offered to allow the woman to walk alone with protective headgear – so long as the parents would absolve the council of liability in case of accident and injury. However, no agreement about this was reached.

Distinguishing the need from the means to meet it. The judge had to consider the following: within the 15 hours of one-to-one assistance with mobility which the Council had decided that the woman needed each week, how much – if any – of the assistance was to involve walking? Was the 'term' mobility to be taken in a narrow sense of walking, or in a wider sense which might or might not include walking? And was assistance with walking a need, or simply an arrangement to meet the need?

The judge had some difficulty in ascertaining exactly what the assessment of need had been, as opposed to the decision about what services were to be provided to meet the need. The decision had not been formally recorded, and it was not clear even when the assessment had been completed. Nevertheless, he decided that the assessment of need was at the general level: ie, 15 hours of one-to-one mobility assistance. The particular content of this assistance – eg, assistance with walking – was not part of the assessment of need. If it had been, it would have represented a level of excessive detail. The judge pointed out that, in general, if assessments of need are too detailed, then this would in turn mean that whenever provision needed to be varied – even slightly – to take account of changing circumstances, a formal reassessment would be required. This would be cumbersome and would also mean that until reassessment was complete the authority would be in breach of its statutory duty – something Parliament could not have intended.

General duty under the 1948 Act. Therefore, withdrawal of the walking element of the assistance did not involve a breach of statutory duty in failing to meet agreed needs. Furthermore, given that the assistance was being provided under the general duty contained in s.29 of the National Assistance 1948, it was also quite clear that resources could be a relevant factor in deciding both whether or how to meet needs.

Health and safety. The judge also stated that health and safety – ie, potential back injury to staff – was also a material consideration in deciding what should be provided.

R v Coventry City Council, ex p Coventry Heads of Independent Care Establishments (CHOICE) and Peggs

[1998] 1 CCLR 379 (QBD). *Community care; contract terms between local authority and independent care homes; whether public law or private law contractual dispute; National Assistance Act 1948,s.26*

The local authority decided not to increase its rates of payment for residential or nursing home care purchased from the independent sector under s.26 of the National Assistance Act 1948. The care homes, through their representative organisation, sought judicial review.

The court decided that although s.26 of the 1948 Act governed the making of arrangements for residential or nursing home care over all, it did not cover the actual making of payments. This was because 'once the agreement has been made the ordinary law of contract comes into play and a failure to pay in accordance with the terms of the contract amounts to a breach of contract giving the service provider the right to sue for breach of contract'. Therefore, it was a private law, contractual matter, and did not concern 'a public law right at all'.

However, it was also claimed that the care homes had a legitimate expectation that payments would continue to increase in line with a previously used formula, unless they were notified in good time. This would require consultation. The judge found no such duty in the contract, and also accepted the local authority's argument that consultation in the circumstances would be wholly impractical. This was because the local authority's decision was on resource considerations affecting all of its social services functions – and so consultation would have to involve all service providers across a whole range of services. This would have been 'a quite unreasonable exercise' which would anyway have probably not benefited the care homes, because 'on any view' tough decisions had to be made.

The judge also dismissed the argument that relevant factors had not been taken into account, namely a) the terms of the contractual agreement; and b) the impact on the care homes, on the availability of residential care places, and on the recipients of community care services. On the second point, the judge accepted what the affidavit of the director of social services had to say – that the members of the relevant committee would have been very aware of all these factors when they made their decision.

R v Cumbria County Council, ex parte 'NAB' (1994) 159 LGRR 729 (QBD). *Fettering of discretion; writing letters; special education*

A special education case illustrating, amongst other things, the importance of the content of letters written by local authority officers. It was about whether the local authority's policy on developmental quotients and the making of statements of special educational needs (under the Education Act 1981, now superseded by the Education Act 1996) was irrational and rigid. On the second point, the judge decided that the policy did not fetter the authority's discretion and that it had not shut its ears to exceptions. He referred to the final paragraph of a letter written to the child's mother – which had explicitly offered further consideration of the authority's decision if requested by the mother.

R v Cumbria County Council, ex parte P [1995] ELR 337 (QBD). *Assessment of need; specificity of need; speech therapy; special education*

A special education case concerning in part the detail in which provision of speech therapy should be set out in part 3 of a statement of special educational needs (under the Education Act 1981, now superseded by the Education Act 1996). (Compare the assessment of needs and making of care plans in community care).

Whilst the vagueness of what had been expressed was not helpful to the parents, the judge decided against making a general declaration that the statutory provisions required that the 'number and length of weekly speech therapy sessions' be specified, so that the parents could choose to appeal on firm grounds (eg, that agreed provision had not been made). Instead, such matters were best dealt with case by case and with the help of the appeal process.

However, in this particular case, the judge concluded that the statement was unsatisfactory in several respects (including the absence of detail about the number of speech therapy sessions and what was to happen in them); the authority should therefore produce a new one, making it clear to the parents 'what the authority consider their son ought to receive by way of special educational provision and non-educational provision for his profound communication difficulties. Then the parents will be in a position to appeal if they wish to'. However, this was simply a point made by the judge at the conclusion of his judgment; the formal application for judicial review failed.

R v Department of Health and Social Security, ex parte Bruce [1986] TLR 8 February 1986 (QBD). *Community care; practical assistance; Chronically Sick and Disabled Persons Act 1970, s.2; high threshold of unreasonableness*
This case illustrates how the courts sometimes apply strictly the concept of unreasonableness in judicial review, thus making it difficult to show that an authority has behaved unreasonably or irrationally.

A challenge was made against West Sussex County Council for breach of its duty in providing practical assistance in the home under s.2 of the Chronically Sick and Disabled Persons Act – and against the Secretary of State for failing to exercise his default powers against the Council. The judge found against the applicant, and set out with some emphasis the hurdles to be surmounted. The judge stated that the Secretary of State's power to intervene would only arise in the same situation in which the court's power to do so arose. For this to occur, the applicant would first have to establish a) the specific need, b) the specific arrangements required to meet it, c) that an express request had been made to the local authority to meet the need, and d) that the authority had clearly failed to satisfy the request. Second, the applicant would have then to show – 'and no doubt it would be yet more difficult' – that 'the refusal to meet the identified need or contended for need was irrational ... that no local authority, properly discharging their duty and having regard to the facts before them, would have declined that request'.

R v Devon County Council, ex parte Baker and Johns; R v Durham County Council, ex parte Curtis and Broxson [1992] 158 LGRevR 241 (CA). *Community care; closure of residential care homes; duty to consult; legitimate expectation*
These two cases, heard together in the Court of Appeal, highlighted the common law duty which local authorities have in certain circumstances to consult service users before withdrawing or changing services. They concerned the closure of local authority residential homes.

Scrupulously fair consultation. The appeal of the residents was dismissed in the *Devon* case, the court finding that the residents knew about the proposed closure of the homes long before the final decision was made; that they had ample time to make representations; and that the council's officers were 'scrupulously fair' in putting before councillors representations and objections.

Unfairness in consultation. However in the *Durham* case, the court found that the residents had been informed only at the eleventh hour about the closure of the home. The duty of the authority to act fairly to the residents would have been satisfied if the residents a) had known well in advance of the final decision about closure; b) had been given a reasonable amount of time to object; and c) had had their objections considered by the authority. This did not happen and so the decision was unlawful. However, the court did add that the residents did not necessarily have an individual right to be consulted face to face, but that consultation could be achieved by meetings held with residents generally.

Legitimate expectation. The court also went on to outline the nature of legitimate expectation. One point made was that where the concept is used to refer to a claimant's interest in a benefit, 'the demands of fairness are likely to be somewhat higher when an authority contemplates depriving someone of an existing benefit or advantage than when the claimant is a bare applicant for a future benefit. That is not to say that a bare applicant will himself be without any entitlement to fair play...'.

Using the default powers of the Secretary of State instead of judicial review. It was held that it was appropriate for the dispute to come before the law courts, rather than be channelled toward the Secretary of State's power to declare an authority in default of its duty. This was because a) it was not clear that the duty to consult residents was a statutory social services function (if it was not, the Secretary of State had no power to intervene); and b) the matter was one of law in a developing field and thus for the courts and not the Secretary of State to deal with. Further, although convenience, efficacy and expedition were relevant in deciding on the appropriate means of redress, judicial review should be preferred for authoritative resolution of a legal issue.

R v Ealing District Health Authority, ex parte Fox [1993] 1 WLR 373 (QBD). *Community care; individual duty to provide after-care services under s.117 of the Mental Health Act 1983*
A case contrasting, amongst other things, specific and general duties. It concerned a hospital discharge decision and after-care arrangements to be made under s.117 of the Mental Health Act 1983. The judge found that the duty to provide after-care services under that section was 'not only a general duty but also a specific duty owed to the applicant to provide him with aftercare services'.

This contrasted with the more general duty imposed on the health authority under s.3 of the NHS Act 1977 to provide after-care. He stated that 'the duty is not only a general duty but a specific duty owed to the applicant to provide him with aftercare services until such time as the district health authority and local social services authority are satisfied that he is no longer in need of such services … I consider a proper interpretation of this section to be that it is a continuing duty in respect of any patient who may be discharged and falls within section 117, although the duty to any particular patient is only triggered at the moment of discharge.'

However, even if he was wrong and s.117 did not in fact apply in the circumstances of the particular case (involving a mental health review tribunal decision that the person be conditionally discharged) – the duty to provide after-care services could still be spelt out from the 'general statutory framework' requiring comprehensive hospital and health services to be provided under the NHS Act 1977.

Finally, the judge had prefaced this judgment by stating that the question raised by the case concerned a health authority's inability or unwillingness 'to make available care in the community for *reasons other than lack of resources*' (italics added).

R v Ealing London Borough Council, ex parte Jennifer Lewis [1992] 24 HLR 484 (CA). *Welfare services in sheltered housing; acting outside the legislation*
A council tenant, unhappy about recent rent increases, complained that the Council was paying out of the housing revenue account for certain welfare services provided by wardens in its sheltered housing. The court held that the legislation (which was however later changed) was not capable of supporting this arrangement and the authority was therefore behaving unlawfully.

R v Ealing London Borough Council, ex parte Leaman [1984] TLR, 10 February 1984 (QBD). *Holidays; Chronically Sick and Disabled Persons Act,s.2; unlawful policy*
The case concerned an application by a disabled person under s.2 of the Chronically Sick and Disabled Persons Act 1970 for assistance with a privately arranged holiday. The authority responded to the request with the following statement: '"Due to financial cut-backs, Ealing [does] not currently provide grants, but will sponsor applicants for council-organised holidays for handicapped persons"'.

The applicant's lawyers claimed that this response amounted to breach of statutory duty, fettering of discretion, taking into account an irrelevant consideration and making a decision so unreasonable that no local authority could have taken it. The judge put it more simply: the authority was 'quite wrong': not because it ultimately failed to provide the assistance, but because it did not even consider the application in the first place. The authority had deprived itself of the 'opportunity of asking' the question of whether the person's needs were such that it was necessary for the authority to meet them by means of assistance with a privately arranged holiday – something the wording of the Act clearly envisages when it refers to holidays 'otherwise arranged'.

R v East Hertfordshire District Council, ex parte Beckman [1998] JPL 55 (QBD). *Consistency of local authority planning decisions; clear reasons; irrelevant factors*
A land planning case in which, following the rejection of two identical planning applications, a third – involving no relevant change of circumstances from the first two applications – was approved. The council claimed

that in the third instance, it had taken account of a letter which was a new factor. However, the letter had in fact been considered on one of the earlier applications. Therefore the council had taken account of an irrelevant consideration and its decision was quashed. The judge went on to point out that where a council's decision seriously affects a citizen, the decision should be prepared with care and approved only after careful consideration. Furthermore, when 'a decision of the council is to reverse a position taken twice in so recent a period, fairness and good administration require that the reasoning advanced by the council should be clear and unambiguous; it should not be contradictory, unsatisfactory or pregnant with possibilities of error'.

R v East Sussex County Council, ex parte Tandy. Resources; suitable education; community care; social services and Chronically Sick and Disabled Persons Act,s.2; Education Act 1993
This education case concerned the reduction in the amount of home tuition received by a girl suffering from myalgic encephalomyelitis. The High Court, Court of Appeal and House of Lords judgments made ample reference to the community care *R v Gloucestershire CC ex parte Barry*, since the question was at heart the same in both cases: the degree to which a lack of resources could offset a duty to meet people's needs.

The question was whether a local education authority could take into account its own resources when deciding what was 'suitable' education, under s.298 of the Education Act 1993 (now s.19 of the Education Act 1996), for a child who could not attend school as a result of ill health. The High Court ruled that resources could not be a relevant factor in deciding this question; the Court of Appeal, in a split 2-1 decision, overruled the High Court. However, five judges in the House of Lords then unanimously overruled the Court of Appeal and restored the original High Court decision.

At particular issue was first s.298(1) and the duty 'to make arrangements for the provision of ... education at school or otherwise for those children of compulsory school age who, by reason of illness, exclusion from school or otherwise, may not for any period receive suitable education unless such arrangements are made for them'. Second, s.298(7) goes on to state that "suitable education', in relation to the child or young person, means efficient education suitable to his age, ability and aptitude and to any special educational needs he may have'.

(High Court): *R v East Sussex County Council, ex parte Tandy* [1997] ELR 311 (QBD). The judge pointed out that whilst the words 'necessary' and 'needs' were not defined in s.2 of the Chronically Sick and Disabled Persons Act, Parliament had by contrast ensured that the term 'suitable education' was explained in s.298 of the 1993 Act. This stated that suitable education for a child or young person meant 'efficient education suitable to his age, ability and aptitude and to any special educational needs he may have'. Nowhere was there mention of resources.

However the judge also pointed out that this did not mean that resources were altogether irrelevant: having decided on what suitable education was, there might be different options – some cheaper than others – for providing it. At this stage, the authority could take into account its resources in deciding how to provide the suitable education.

(Court of Appeal) *R v East Sussex County Council, ex parte Tandy* [1997] 3 FCR 525. In overturning the High Court decision, the following points were amongst those made.
Inevitability of taking account of resources and meeting the needs of other sick children. Whilst the legislation defined 'suitable education' in relation to each individual child, the duty actually to make arrangements for suitable education was for sick children (in the plural). The contrast between provision for 'children' in s.298, as opposed to 'each child' elsewhere in education legislation, was dwelt on by the court. This meant that such arrangements had 'to be made with an eye to meeting the needs of all the sick children to whom the LEA are beholden' – and that inevitably the cost of making such arrangements had to be taken into account.

Furthermore, it was pointed out that even the 'lode-star' of five hours of tuition, the original provision, involved cost since the child's 'true need, considered from her best interest alone, would be for a home-tutor to be available to her during those days when she is fit and well enough to concentrate and make best use of the service. It may be more than five hours on a good week, less on a bad. But that degree of personal service cannot be provided. It is simply too expensive. The decision to afford 5 hours home tuition is itself a decision taken with an eye to the management of the available budget. In reduced times, all have to suffer. That may not be a satisfactory position from [the child's] point of view but the remedy is a political one, not a legal one. Consequently it is not for us'.

The dissenting judge, like Lord Lloyd (dissenting) in the *Gloucestershire* case, pointed the finger at central government, by saying that once a local authority had made what savings on non-mandatory items it could – by, for example, cancelling a proposed leisure centre or, a football ground – then its inability to carry out its statutory duty could only be remedied by Parliament.

Balancing exercise: weighing different factors. It was suggested that the education authority had treated budgetary considerations as paramount and that the decision was tainted by an improper purpose or that only lip service had been paid to the needs of the particular child. The court rejected this, stating that it was quite clear that the individual child had been considered, and that, so long as the authority had regard to all material considerations, it was not for the court to say what weight should have been given to each consideration.

Shortcomings in decision but no irrationality. The authority's decision was also attacked as irrational on a number of counts including a) that it had misunderstood a doctor's report; b) it had ignored the fact that the doctor had not seen the child for some time; c) it should have recognised a conflict between the advice of two doctors involved; d) that from a general policy of reintegration it did not follow that this particular child should be reintegrated at school; e) it had obtained no contemporary advice from an educational psychologist; f) it had made a mistake about how much of the home tuition previously provided, the child had taken up; g) it had suggested the alternative of a 'nurture unit' in school, yet there was no evidence that such a suitable unit was available; h) it had made incorrect assumptions that the child's brother was receiving home tuition.

Consequently, both majority judges acknowledged shortcomings in the decision which had been made. One suggested that it 'may seem hard to justify when there was so little evidence to show any diminution in … need for five hours home-tuition a week'. The other conceded that his concerns were stirred about the detail of the decision-making. But neither were prepared to strike the decision down as irrational, since if they were to examine decision-making over-critically, 'there is a danger that a legitimate exercise in review of legality becomes an impermissible appeal on the merits and that imperfections in the process are equated with irrationality in the result'.

(House of Lords): *R v East Sussex County Council, ex parte Tandy* [1998] 2 All ER 769 (HL). The House of Lords, as did the courts beneath it, recognised the 'unenviable position' of the local authority. It could obtain the 'financial resources necessary to discharge its functions as it would like to do' neither from central government nor from local taxation. Although central government 'of whatever political colour' aimed to reduce public spending, local authorities had not been correspondingly relieved of statutory duties imposed 'in times past when different attitudes prevailed'.

Individual or general duty? However, unlike the Court of Appeal, the House of Lords decided that s.298(7) was decisive in meaning that the council owed a duty to 'each sick child individually, and not to sick children as a class'. Furthermore, there was nothing in s.298 (compared to some other sections in the same Act on other matters) that suggested that 'suitable education' could be determined in the light of resources; both the term itself and its definition 'connote a standard to be determined purely by educational standards'. As a matter of 'pure construction' there was no reason to treat resources as a relevant consideration.

Preference for using money in certain ways. In addition, while the local authority might not want 'to bleed its other functions of resources so as to enable it to perform the statutory duty', nevertheless it could divert money from other discretionary functions. Thus, the 'argument is not one of insufficient resources to discharge the duty but of a preference for using the money for other purposes. To permit a local authority to avoid performing a statutory duty on the grounds that it prefers to spend the money in other ways is to downgrade a statutory duty to a discretionary power'. Indeed, if 'Parliament wishes to reduce public expenditure on meeting the needs of sick children then it is up to Parliament so to provide. It is not for the courts to adjust the order or priorities as between statutory duties and statutory discretions'.

Gloucestershire case: necessities under s.2 of the Chronically Sick and Disabled Persons Act 1970. In reaching its decision, the House of Lords had to explain away its apparently contradictory decision in *R v Gloucestershire CC, ex parte Barry*. Under s.2 of the CSDPA, the 'statutory duty was to arrange to arrange certain benefits to meet the 'needs' of the disabled persons but the lack of certain benefits enumerated in the section could not possibly give rise to 'need' in any stringent sense of the word. Thus it is difficult to talk about the lack of a radio or a holiday or a recreational activity as giving rise to a need: they may be desirable but they are not in any ordinary sense necessities. Yet, according to the section the disabled person's needs were to be capable of being met by the provision of such benefits. The statute provided no guidance as to what were the criteria by which a need of that unusual kind was to be assessed. There was no definition of need beyond the instances of possible benefits. In those circumstances, it is perhaps not surprising that the majority of your Lordships looked for some other more stringent criteria enabling the local authority to determine what was to be treated as a need by reference to the resources available to it'.

Gloucestershire case: safeguard of unreasonableness. The House of Lords in the *Gloucestershire* case had suggested that applicants could demonstrate a breach of statutory duty under s.2 of the Chronically Sick and Disabled Persons Act by showing that the local authority had behaved legally unreasonably. However, the House of Lords now thought that 'with respect [to the previous decision] this is a very doubtful form of protection. Once the reasonableness of the actions of a local authority depends upon its decision how to apply scarce financial resources, the local authority's decision becomes extremely difficult to review. The court cannot second-guess the local authority in the way in which it spends its limited resources'.

R v Essex County Council, ex parte Bucke [1997] COD 66 (QBD) *Community care; reassessment; change of service; exercise of balancing needs and resources; Chronically Sick and Disabled Persons Act, s.2*
The case was essentially about how, by performing a balancing exercise, a local authority can take resources into account when assessing and reassessing people's needs, and when deciding how to meet those needs, under s.2 of the Chronically Sick and Disabled Persons Act.

Review of care providers by cost. The applicant was a fifty-year old man with learning disabilities, poor eyesight and requiring assistance in looking after himself. In order to save money, the local authority was conducting a review of its care arrangements – and transferring the provision of care for some people to cheaper providers. The social worker 'was supposed to go down the list, starting with the cheapest, until he or she found a provider who was able to provide the care that was needed'. This entailed a change of provider for the applicant – from the male support worker to a female carer – a change he did not want. The authority was accused of fettering its discretion in only making exceptions when the change in provision would be 'significantly detrimental' – and of making resources the prevailing or predominant consideration.

Fettering of discretion and correct balancing exercise? The judge did not find a fettering of discretion, and stated that the authority could take account of resources 'provided that it never forgets that the needs of the user are to be regarded as of greater importance than the need to save money'. The judge accepted that the changes were resource-led in that they would not have been made unless there was a need to cut costs – but they were not on that account unlawful, so long as the 'correct balancing exercise' had been carried out in reassessing individual needs. The reassessment exercise had in fact resulted in seven out of 13 users remaining with the more expensive care agency. Consequently there was nothing 'to indicate that resources were regarded as paramount or that the Council manifestly got the balance wrong'.

R v Gateshead Metropolitan Borough Council, ex parte Lauder [1996] 29 HLR 360 (QBD). *Fettering of discretion; rigid policy; housing allocation; housing legislation*
A housing allocation case about the rigidity of a policy, the fettering of an authority's discretion, and the role of letters of decision.

It concerned the rule that allocation points would be withheld if somebody had moved into an overcrowded property. However, the particular applicant had done so because of violent treatment received at the hands of her husband. The judge held that the policy fettered the authority's discretion by imposing an inflexible approach; yet 'the vice ... could easily be cured by the insertion of the word "usually" or ... "in exceptional cases" at some appropriate point'. Any doubts the judge may have had were removed by the decision letter sent to the applicant – which indicated that the authority had decided 'without more' (ie, without proper investigation) to withhold the points. The decision was therefore unlawful.

R v Gloucestershire County Council, ex parte Barry (originally, in the High Court, *ex parte Mahfood*). *Community care; needs; resources; eligibility criteria; reassessment; Chronically Sick and Disabled Persons Act, s.2*
A major community care case which culminated in a House of Lords decision in March 1997 – supporting the High Court's decision nearly two years before – to allow local authorities to take account of resources both when assessing people's needs and when deciding whether it is necessary to meet them, under s.2 of the Chronically Sick and Disabled Persons Act. All the decisions – High Court, Court of Appeal and House of Lords – are summarised below.

Background. The case arose when the council informed about 1,500 people that their home help services would be reduced or withdrawn, owing to an unexpected shortfall of about £3 million in grant money from central government.

Applicants. The original four people making the challenge were as follows. The first was 71 years old, lived alone, suffered from decreased mobility, pain and stiffness, had suffered a stroke, and received income support and attendance allowance. He was receiving assistance with bed making, ironing and cleaning: the council now informed him that he would no longer be provided with housework assistance.

The second was 79 years old, had suffered several heart attacks, had previously fractured his femur, had a hip replacement, could only walk short distances aided by a stick, was partially sighted, and receiving income support. He had been provided with cleaning, laundry, shopping and community meals; now the cleaning services were withdrawn and the laundry provision reduced.

The third was 76 years old, and his wife 71. He was a double amputee, wheelchair-bound and had prostate cancer. His wife had arthritis, high blood pressure and a heart condition. He had been assessed as needing respite care for a period of two weeks in every six – to give his wife short-term breaks. Both had been assessed as requiring assistance in the home; now the respite care was cancelled and the assistance drastically reduced.

The fourth person was 79 years old, and suffering from severe rheumatoid arthritis, unable to walk. She had been assessed as needing a hoist: now the council 'rescinded' the decision to provide it. As a consequence, she had been unable to leave hospital and return to her own home.

(High Court): ***R v Gloucestershire County Council, ex parte Mahfood and Others*** [1995] 160 LGRevR 321 (QBD). The following decision of the High Court was overturned by the Court of Appeal before being reinstated by the House of Lords (see below). The judge acknowledged, but did not succumb, to the force of the argument that resources were totally irrelevant to the assessment of people's community care needs, and went on to find the following.

Balancing exercise. The assessment (or reassessment) of a person's needs had to involve a balancing exercise, involving the needs of the individual, the needs of others, and the resources available.

Individual focus of assessment and role of resources. The balancing exercise had to be conducted in respect of each individual – the council could not simply make blanket decisions as it had done in this case. So, in order even to contemplate reducing or withdrawing services, the council would have to reassess each individual, and even then resources could not be the sole factor taken into account (because of the nature of the balancing exercise).

Triggering an absolute duty. Once the authority was satisfied that it was necessary to make arrangements to meet the needs, then – subject only to a reassessment – there was an absolute duty to make them, since at that stage 'resources do not come into it'. The judge also acknowledged the 'impossible task faced by councils, unless they could 'have regard to the size of the cake so that in turn they know how fairest and best to cut it'.

Taking account of resources for both need and necessity to meet the need. The local authority 'was right to take account of resources both when assessing needs and when deciding whether it is necessary to make arrangements to meet those needs'.

High Court (no. 2): *R v Gloucestershire County Council, ex parte Royal Association for Disability and Rehabilitation* [1996] COD 253 (QBD). In the first High Court case (see immediately above), the court had ordered that, although the authority could take resources into account when reassessing people's needs and reducing or withdrawing services, it must nevertheless reassess people individually before doing so. Following this decision, but still pending the appeal to be heard in the Court of Appeal, the council began the process of reassessment gradually, since the cost was estimated at £200,000. The Royal Association for Disability and Rehabilitation (RADAR) claimed that the Council had not complied with the original High Court judgment.

The judge found that the practicalities of the situation meant that it was reasonable for the Council not to restore services (which had been withdrawn or reduced) in advance of reassessment. However, he also ruled that the duty to reassess people individually was not satisfied by the authority's writing to them, and offering a reassessment only if they replied in the affirmative to the offer.

This was because in: 'some areas of the law that might be an adequate response, where those affected can be assumed to be capable of looking after their own interests, and where silence in response to an offer can be treated as acceptance or acquiescence. However, that approach is not valid in the present context. The obligation to make an assessment for community care services does not depend on a request but on an 'appearance' of need. Indeed under section 47(2) of the 1990 Act, where it appears that a person is disabled, the authority is specifically required to make a decision as to the service he requires without waiting for a request. Of course, the authority cannot carry out an effective reassessment without some degree of cooperation from the service user or his helpers. However, that is a very different thing from saying that they can simply rest on having sent a letter of the type to which I have referred'.

The judge also concluded that RADAR did have the standing to bring the case, and that the local authority's complaints procedure would not have been a 'suitable or alternative remedy' because the case was about 'a general issue of principle as to the authority's obligations in law'.

(Court of Appeal): *R v Gloucestershire County Council, ex parte Barry* [1996] 4 All ER 422. The Court of Appeal – by a majority of 2 to 1 – overruled the High Court (see above) but was, in turn, overruled by the House of Lords (see below). The reasoning of the majority was attractively, though deceptively, simple and as follows.

Judgement about need. Ascertaining a person's needs involved assessment and judgement, not an exercise of public law discretion by the authority which might allow resources to be taken into account.

Absurdity of measuring need in terms of resources. It was 'difficult to see how a third party's resources or the needs of others can be relevant' to assessment of a person's needs. Indeed, were such factors to be taken into account, 'then the logical consequence would be that if the local authority had no resources, then no disabled person in its area could have any needs'.

Necessity of meeting needs. Resources could not be relevant to a judgement about whether it was necessary to meet the assessed needs. Otherwise it would be 'inescapable that if a local authority has no money in the relevant budget, then it would be open to the local authority to make an assessment or judgement that a disabled person has a need which it is necessary to meet applying objective criteria, but they are not required to meet it because of shortage of funds, resulting in an unmet need'. But this would seem to 'fly in the face of the plain language' of the 1970 Act.

Distinction between need and desirability. 'The need for cleaning services may be met by a person cleaning his house once a week, even though it may be desirable that his house be cleaned every day'.

Taking account of resources when deciding how to meet needs. However, resources could be taken into account, insofar as 'the manner in which the need was met, for example, by someone doing his laundry at home in a washing machine or by it being taken away, was within the discretion of the authority and costs would be a relevant consideration'.

(House of Lords): *R v Gloucestershire County Council, ex parte Barry* [1997] 2 All ER 1

Majority decision. In a split decision (3–2), the House of Lords finally ruled in this long-drawn out case, that local authorities could take account of resources when determining, under s.2 of the Chronically Sick and Disabled Persons Act, both the needs of disabled people and then whether it is necessary to meet them. The original High Court decision of 1995 was restored (see above).

Resources and needs. It was stated that 'needs for services cannot sensibly be assessed without having some regard to the cost of providing them', and that 'when assessing needs under section 2(1) a local authority may take its resources into account'. This was because a) the need for a service could not be decided 'in a vacuum from which all considerations of cost have been expelled'; b) a more precise yardstick than 'individual notions of current standards of living' was required – namely, resources. General standards of living alone were too imprecise to measure a person's need, not least because they vary, as do people's expectations about them. In addition, the words 'necessary' and 'needs' were relative terms – and in the context of the Act, their role is not explained by reference either to a dictionary or to the 'values of a civilised society'.

Resources and necessity. The court held as well, that resources could be taken into account when determining whether it was necessary to meet needs: in 'deciding whether there is a necessity to meet the needs of the individual some criteria have to be provided ... The determination of eligibility ... requires guidance not only on the assessment of the severity of the condition or the seriousness of the need but also on the level at which there is to be satisfaction of the necessity to make arrangements. In the framing of the criteria to be applied ... the severity of a condition may have to be matched against the availability of resources ... It may also be observed that the range of the facilities which are listed as being the subject of possible arrangements, 'the service list', is so extensive as to make it unlikely that Parliament intended that they might all be provided regardless of the cost involved. It is not necessary to hold that cost and resources are always an element in determining the necessity. It is enough for the purposes of the present case to recognise that they may be a proper consideration'.

Balancing exercise. Like the High Court, the House of Lords referred also to a balancing exercise: 'the relative cost will be balanced against the relative benefit and the relative need for the benefit'. Thus, in setting eligibility criteria the authority (social services committee) had to 'take into account the nature and extent of disability', the improvement in quality of life which a service at a particular level (eg, home help once a week or more frequently) would achieve, the cost of providing a service (eg, cost of daily home care, installing a ground-floor lavatory, widening a doorway for wheelchair use).

Stringency of eligibility criteria. Depending on the financial position of the authority, its eligibility criteria 'may properly be more or less stringent'. However, a safeguard against the 'collapse' and emasculation of the duty contained in s.2 of the 1970 Act was that authorities had to carry out their duty reasonably – ie, by not lapsing into 'unreasonableness'. The duty anyway still retained its force because once it arose (ie, the authority had accepted it was necessary for it to meet a person's needs), it had to be performed and lack of resources was no defence for non-performance.

Parliament's intention. There was no basis for supposing that Parliament had intended that resources be ignored when assessing disabled people's needs. Furthermore, although views and guidance from central government 'were not proper material for the construction of the critical provision', nevertheless they chimed with the conclusion of the court.

Saving local authorities. The court also found it satisfactory that its conclusion meant that it avoided 'the considerable practical difficulties which the council would otherwise face in the provision of a coherent scheme of community care in its area'.

<u>*Minority decision.*</u> In a strong dissenting judgement, Lord Lloyd (with Lord Steyn agreeing) made various points, including the following.

Civilised standards. The yardstick for measuring a person's needs, be they simple or complex, was 'the standards of civilised society as we know them in the United Kingdom, or, in the more homely phraseology of the law, the man on the Clapham omnibus'.

Parliament's intention. It could not have been Parliament's intention in 1970 a) that the threshold of need should be artificially manipulated because of lack of resources – and b) that 'the standards and expectations for measuring the needs of the disabled in Bermondsey should differ from those in Belgrave Square'.

Professional judgement. The measurement of needs was for the 'professional judgement of the social worker concerned, just as the need for a by-pass operation is left to the professional judgement of the heart specialist'.

Irrelevance of resources. Any imprecision associated with the attempt of an authority to identify such standards could not be alleviated by taking account of resources, which might impose cash limits on what was provided but could not 'help to measure need'. It was clearly possible to set eligibility criteria without reference to resources, and there was 'no necessity on grounds of logic, and no advantage on grounds of practical convenience, in bringing resources into account as a relevant factor when assessing needs'. Thus, if a child needed a new pair of shoes, its need was 'not the less because his parents cannot afford them'.

Collapse of duty. The arbitrary reduction in assessed need by raising the threshold of need artificially, because of lack of resources, would collapse the duty under s.2 of Chronically Sick and Disabled Persons Act into a power.

Central government. The local authority was in an 'impossible position; truly impossible, because even if the Council wished to raise the money themselves to meet the need by increasing council tax, they would be unable to do so by reason of the government-imposed rate capping'. Furthermore, it was the government's departure from its 'fine words' in the community care White Paper that had brought about the situation. The 'passing of the 1970 Act was a noble aspiration. Having willed the end, Parliament must be asked to provide the means'.

R v Gloucestershire County Council, ex parte Mahfood: see *R v Gloucestershire County Council, ex parte Barry*

R v Gloucestershire County Council, ex parte P [1994] ELR 334 (QBD). *Delay; whether reasonable; special education*

A special education case involving an appeal against a statement of special educational needs, and what appeared, on the face of it, to be unreasonable delay on the part of the local authority – in the form of six months of inaction. However, although the delay might appear unreasonable, the judge, considering the circumstances, found it not be 'reprehensible' – and so even if he had been minded to make a finding against the authority, he would not have exercised his discretion because (referring to the words of Rules of the Supreme Court Order 53, r.1(2)) it was not 'just and convenient in all the circumstances of the case' to make a declaration.

R v Haringey Council, ex parte Norton [1998] 1 CCLR 168 (QBD). *Community care; reassessment; reduction of services; social, recreational and leisure needs; Chronically Sick and Disabled Persons Act 1970,s.2*

Since being assessed in 1994, a man suffering from multiple sclerosis had received a 24-hour-a-day package of care from the local authority, via a voluntary organisation. In early 1997, a reassessment of his needs led to a reduction of care to about three hours a day. This was subsequently increased to five hours a day to cover assistance with personal care (getting in and out of bed, washing, dressing, cleaning teeth, washing hair and using toilet), meal preparation etc, shopping, laundry, cleaning, laundry, ironing.

Exclusion of social, recreational and leisure needs. Details of this assistance was set out in a letter outlining the care plan which would only cater for the man's personal needs; the letter explained that in relation to the man's social, recreational and leisure needs, he could approach a local resource centre himself. The authority was unable to meet these needs because it was not in a position 'to meet or address all the demands made [and so was] forced to make decisions upon prioritising need and working within existing resources'.

Rewriting of history. The local authority argued that the 1994 assessment and care plan had been generous, did not reflect the person's real needs (which would have been less than 24-hour care each day) and so should not be taken at face value.

The judge indicated the reluctance of the courts to allow such retrospective explanation since 'there is a need for very considerable caution before the admission of affidavit evidence which purports to supplement, amend or impugn a document enshrining a decision which on its face bears no mark of invalidity'. However, in this particular case, he was prepared to admit the evidence – in order for the court to be able to assess the lawfulness of the local authority's evaluation of the 1994 care plan, when coming to its 1997 reassessment decision.

Irrational or unreasonable decision? The judge, avoiding a ruling on the merits of the local authority's decision, decided that the reassessment and revised care plan did not constitute unreasonableness or irrationality, since on the evidence available, the authority had not 'taken leave of its senses'. Nevertheless, he did say that he had 'grave misgivings as to whether 5 hours per day of care plus meals on wheels and domiciliary nursing can meet the applicant's needs consistent with the [authority's] resources'. He went on to give an example of an authority taking leave of its senses and the high threshold necessary to warrant judicial intervention. Under its housing allocation system, an authority had awarded 0 points, on a scale from 0 to 250, to a woman 'with possibly recurrent cancer and gross breathing difficulty, of whom two consultants at London teaching hospitals said in categorical terms that were she to have climb stairs this would endanger her life. In such circumstances a Court can properly but most exceptionally conclude that the authority must have taken leave of its senses'.

Ambit of expert opinion from an occupational therapist. The judge also sharply criticised the attempt to use the report of an expert, an occupational therapist, to 'adduce evidence' that the authority had behaved unreasonably in the legal sense of the word. Such questions were: 'for the Court, and the Court alone ... it can never be permissible for an expert either to express an opinion that a local authority's decision was or was not reasonable ... The opinion is all the more objectionable in this case because an occupational therapist cannot claim to know as much as the [authority] about its available resources and competing needs, nor perhaps about Haringey's local standards'.

Unlawful decision in relation to breadth of a person's 'needs'. However, the judge did find the decision unlawful on the basis that the authority had misdirected itself in law, under s.2 of the Chronically Sick and Disabled Persons Act, because it was 'impermissible to carry out the reassessment by putting social, recreation and leisure needs on one side and saying that 'I would be happy to provide you with details of the Winkfield Road Resource Centre'. The care package which should have been assessed ... had to be a multi-faceted package. This

Applicant has been able to overcome or at least live with some of the most awful characteristics of his illness by the social intercourse achieved in recreational facilities such as the playing of bridge, swimming etc. A reassessed care package should have comprehended such matters and should not have discriminated in the manner that it did'.

The judge went on to quote the Department of Health guidance (SSI/SWSG 1991a,p.12) which refers to need as a 'multi-faceted concept' covering personal/social care, health care, accommodation, finance, education/employment/leisure, transport/access.

R v Haringey Council, ex parte Norton (no.2) [1998] (unreported) (QBD). *Community care; care package; financial limit; Chronically Sick and Disabled Persons Act 1970*
Following the first case (immediately above), the council carried out a reassessment and proposed a care package amounting to 39 hours a week and costing £240 per week. This was challenged on the basis that the ceiling of £240 represented resource-led provision irrespective of the applicant's needs. By the time the case was heard, this had been increased to 45 hours per week at a cost of £280. Having regard to these latest arrangements, the judge found that this was reasonable provision and that the local authority had acted neither perversely or irrationally.

R v Harrow London Borough Council, ex parte Carter [1992] 158 LGRevR 601 (QBD). *Homelessness; fettering of discretion; shuttlecocks; Housing Act 1985*
A homelessness case concerning the policy of the local authority in relation to homelessness and people's 'local connection'. Two of the children had previously experienced serious reading difficulties at school in Camden; but since attending school in Harrow, they had made good progress. However, Harrow now stated that the family could not be housed in its area and referred the family back to Camden.

Residence test: fettering of discretion. The court found that although the policy itself (involving a five year residence test applied to relatives of the applicant) might have been lawful if it had allowed for the exercise of discretion in exceptional cases – it did not in fact do so. For instance, letters written to the applicant by the local authority 'were evidence of the application of a strict policy from which officers were not allowed to depart' – and the judge was 'far from satisfied that the policy of the respondents recognised that in all cases there must be room for exceptions and that there must be consideration of the circumstances of the [other] local housing authority to which a reference might be made'. (The legislation made reference to consideration of 'special circumstances', and these should have been interpreted to have included the residence of a sister in Harrow for just under five years, the mother's need for support and the schooling issues).

Batted to and fro like a shuttlecock between authorities. The local authority also maintained that the court should not give relief to the applicant, because a) if its original decision was overruled, the authority could legitimately come to the same decision again, and b) the case had been brought by the applicant after undue delay. The judge did not agree that the evidence was so compelling as to mean the authority necessarily would come to the same decision; indeed, given the prolonged delay, for which the applicant was not responsible, the judge suggested that the family should be allowed to remain in Harrow. Second, as to delay, the applicant was 'a shuttlecock being batted to and fro between [Harrow] and the London Borough of Camden'; it was not her fault, and the court would extend the time for the judicial review application.

R v Harrow London Borough Council, ex parte M [1997] 1 ELR 62 (QBD). *Joint working; special education; therapy; dispute between NHS and education authority; Education Act 1993*
The disputed provision in this case related to speech and language therapy (one hour a week), occupational therapy (one hour a week) and physiotherapy (at least 45 minutes a week) for a six-year old child with cerebral palsy. The case was heard parallel with *R v Brent and Harrow Health Authority, ex parte Harrow London Borough Council.*

The court found that underlying the dispute and an 'unhappy state of affairs' was 'the problem of chronic under-funding of public bodies who have a statutory duty to fulfil but only a limited budget out of which to meet their statutory obligations'. Under s.168 of the Education Act 1993, it held that the education authority had a non-delegable duty to arrange the special educational provision set out in the child's statement of special educational needs. It was no defence for the education authority to argue that it was not required to make the provision, on grounds of the health authority's failure to provide the necessary resources. In other words, though assistance was indeed not forthcoming from the health authority, s.168 of the 1993 Act did not give the education authority a let-out from its obligations; otherwise the Act would 'manifestly fail to serve the child for whose benefit' it exists.

R v Havering LBC, ex parte K [1998] 1 FCR 641 (QBD). *Special education; going back on a statement of need and provision*

A special education case, in which the court ruled that a local education authority, having specified a particular school in a child's statement of special educational needs, could not – because of transport problems – simply disregard this, informally review the statement and decide that the child should go to one of three other local mainstream schools. If it were permissible to do this, there would be little point having a statement because it would be possible for members or officers, without the necessary powers, to review and amend statements 'by sidewinds'. (The statement had explicitly made the mother responsible for transport to the named school, but eventually she had found it impossible to comply with requirement and asked the local authority to arrange the transport).

(Compare, in community care, the making of a detailed care plan to reflect the discharge of a statutory duty to arrange services in the meeting of a need: see p.152).

R v Hereford and Worcester Local Education Authority, ex parte Jones [1981] 1 WLR 768 (QBD). *Education; distinction between charging for a service and not providing it; Education Act 1944*

The local education authority notified parents that it would charge fees for music lessons. The court ruled that so long as the music remained part of the curriculum, this would be unlawful under what was then s.61 of the Education Act 1944 which precluded fees being charged. However, had the authority instead said "much as we regret it we have got to cut something" from the curriculum, the court would not interfere unless there was legal unreasonableness involved.

R v Hertfordshire County Council, ex parte Three Rivers District Council [1992] 157 LGR 526 (QBD). *Public transport for elderly and disabled people; taking account of resources; Transport Act 1985*

A case about the provision of public transport in relation to elderly and disabled people, a general lack of resources and the split responsibilities of a county council and district council.

The county council's duty was 'to secure the provision of such public transport services as the council consider it appropriate to secure to meet any public transport requirements within the county which would not in their view be met apart from any action taken by them for the purpose' (Transport Act 1985, s.63). The judge stated that a) it was entitled to take into consideration available funds; b) it could not simply make cuts for the sake of saving money but had genuinely to consider the public transport requirements, including those of elderly and disabled people (however, the council had done this); c) had a district been left without any public transport at all, the decision might have been legally flawed.

R v Hertsmere Borough Council, ex parte Woolgar [1995] 160 LGRevR 261 (QBD). *Keeping control of decision-making under statutory responsibility*

A homelesssness case illustrating that local authorities must retain control of decision-making which is imposed on them by legislation. It concerned the delegation of a housing authority's duty, under the Housing Act 1985, to investigate (ie, make an assessment of) a person's homelessness status and eligibility for accommodation. The court ruled that it was lawful for the authority to transfer the 'active and dominant' part of the investigations to a housing association, so long as 'all decision-making ... is kept exclusively within the local authority'. (The legislation has since been altered to allow transfer of such decision-making: see SI 1996/3205).

R v Hillingdon London Borough Council, ex parte Governing Body of Queensmead School [1997] ELR 331 (QBD). *Special education; resources; ultimate duty on education authority; Education Act 1993*
An education case which illustrates how the courts seize on a precedent established in one field (community care) and apply it to another related one (education). The case was decided with reference to the Court of Appeal judgment in *R v Gloucestershire CC, ex p Barry* (before the latter was overturned by the House of Lords in March 1997).

Resources and children's special educational needs. The case concerned a funding formula used by the education authority, which effectively reduced the amount it was making available to the school for meeting the requirements of pupils with special educational needs. The judge ruled that a lack of resources could play no part in the assessment of a child's special educational needs – and that financial constraints could be considered only in deciding how to meet those needs (so long as, one way or another, the needs were still actually met). This followed from *R v Gloucestershire, ex p Barry* (at the Court of Appeal stage – the House of Lords hearing had not yet taken place).

The duty of the education authority to provide for children's needs specified in statements of special educational needs was non-delegable, and thus it could not force the school to make up the shortfall with the school's own funds (although a school could do so if it wished by agreement with the authority). In which case, ultimate responsibility for provision remained with the education authority.

R v Inner London Education Authority, ex parte Ali and Another [1990] 2 ALR 822 (QBD). *Target duties; elasticity; education; Education Act 1944*
An education case concerning the adequacy of provision of schools for children within Stepney and Tower Hamlets, under the duty in s.8 of the Education Act 1944 to provide 'sufficient schools' – which meant 'sufficient in number, character and equipment to afford for all pupils opportunities for education offering such variety of instruction and training as may be desirable in view of their different ages, abilities and aptitudes and of the different periods for which they may be expected to remain at school...'

The court typified such statutory obligation as constituting a 'target duty', and not an 'absolute duty'; it was couched in 'broad and general terms', possessed a 'degree of elasticity' and was a 'common feature of legislation which is designed to benefit the community' – for example, s.1 of the NHS Act 1977.

The court explained its reluctance to intervene when such duties were breached. First, even if an education authority had not complied with a more precise (than the above general duty) statutory standard which had been set under the legislation, it would not automatically be in breach of the legislation – for example, in the case of 'changing situations which could not be anticipated' (but not resources or priorities). Second, even if there was a breach of legislation, the court had the discretion to do nothing, 'if by the time the matter comes before the Court the local education authority is doing all it reasonably can to remedy the situation' – which was 'best left in the hands of the bodies to whom Parliament has entrusted performance of the statutory duty if they are seeking to fulfil that duty'.

On the question of damages, the court pointed out that the section of the legislation in question was for the benefit of the public in general and not intended to give individuals a cause of legal action. This was fatal to a claim for damages, since only in very exceptional and well-recognised circumstances could damages be claimed for breach of statutory duty.

R v Islington London Borough Council, ex parte Aldabbagh [1994] 27 HLR 271 (QBD). *Decisions made outside of a policy and without authority; housing; rent arrears*
A housing case concerning arrears of rent and unlawful delegation of decision-making. One aspect of the case focused on the housing authority's policy which stated that decisions in relation to rent arrears of over £50 should be delegated to, and be decided by, a neighbourhood manager. In fact, the arrears were above £250 but the decision was taken by an officer at a lower level. This meant that the decision had been taken 'without au-

thority' and so was unlawful, especially since the decision might have been different if the manager had taken it.

R v Islington London Borough Council, ex parte Bibi [1996] 29 HLR 498 (QBD). *Supplying reasons retrospectively; rewriting history; homelessness; Housing Act 1985*

A homelessness case illustrating (amongst other things) the reluctance of the courts to allow local authorities to supplement their decisions at a later date.

The local authority attempted to remedy a defect (an omission to take account of the applicant's financial circumstances) in its original letter of decision, by submitting an affidavit to the court which did refer to the financial situation. It claimed that this was not a fundamental alteration of the reasons given in its original decision, but mere 'elucidation and confirmation'. The court did not agree, finding a) that the affidavit added materially to the reasons and b) that it did so 'on a basis that … [was] difficult to reconcile with the evidence the council had before it'. It held that the original decision was accordingly unlawful.

R v Islington London Borough Council, ex parte McMillan [1995] 160 LGRevR 321 (QBD). *Community care; balancing exercise; discontinuity in service; Chronically Sick and Disabled Persons Act, s.2*

This case (heard with *R v Gloucestershire CC, ex p Mahfood*) illustrates the court's consideration of a balancing exercise carried out by a local authority, when weighing up the needs of disabled people against available resources. It focused on obligations arising under s.2 of the Chronically Sick and Disabled Persons Act.

Following meetings, conversations and visits from local authority staff, the applicant had been informed that his home care service might suffer from discontinuity in certain circumstances (eg, when home carers were ill or on leave). The applicant complained about the discontinuity that duly followed.

The judge found that the council had a) performed a proper balancing exercise 'taking into account resources and the comparative needs of the disabled in their area'; b) given clear notice about the possible interruptions to the service; c) provided what they had undertaken to provide and what had been assessed as needed; d) at no time withdrawn the service; and e) not interrupted a service to a person for whom any interruption of the service would have been intolerable. For instance, missing a day's meal would not have been acceptable, but missing a day's cleaning would have been.

R v Islington London Borough Council, ex parte Rixon [1997] 1 ELR 477 (QBD). *Community care; resources; care plans; Chronically Sick and Disabled Persons Act, s.2*

The case concerned a 25-year-old man who suffered from Seckels syndrome and who was blind, microcephalic, virtually immobile, doubly incontinent and mostly unable to communicate. He also suffered from severe deformities of the chest and spine, a hiatus hernia and a permanent digestive disorder. His weight and size were those of a small child, his dependency that of a baby. The dispute concerned the provision for his social, recreational and educational needs; having left a special needs school, the applicant had requirements which the local authority could not meet because, it pleaded, it was short of resources.

Provision of recreational facilities despite lack of resources. The judge found that the local authority had failed to provide for the person's recreational needs under s.2 of the Chronically Sick and Disabled Persons Act. The duty under the Act was 'owed to the applicant personally' to provide 'recreational facilities outside the home to an extent which Islington accepts is greater than the care plan provides for. But the authority has, it appears, simply taken the existing unavailability of further facilities as an insuperable obstacle to any further attempt to make provision. The lack of a day centre has been treated, however reluctantly, as a complete answer to the question of provision'.

The judge accepted that although the exercise of assessment should be needs-led, resources could not be ignored, commenting that 'even an unequivocal set of statutory duties cannot produce money where there is none or by itself repair gaps in the availability of finance'. But nevertheless, resources should be a 'balancing and not a blocking' factor, and there was no indication that the authority had in practice undertaken anything like the balancing exercise described in the Gloucestershire case (High Court) 'of adjusting provision to need'.

Care plans and guidance. The judge also stated that although legislation does not refer to care plans, nevertheless – given the status afforded them in community care guidance – 'a care plan is the means by which the local authority assembles the relevant information and applies it to the statutory ends, and hence affords good evidence to any inquirer of the due discharge of its statutory duties'.

He analysed the content of the care plan in question and found that it conformed to neither policy guidance nor practice guidance. The policy guidance (DH 1990, para 3.24) referred to the recording of the objectives of social services intervention as well as of the services to be provided. The care plan failed to do this, and thus was in breach of the guidance. This, in turn, amounted to a breach of duty, in the absence of a considered decision for departure from the guidance: such departure would have to be with 'good reason, articulated in the course of some identifiable decision-making process even if not in the care plan itself'.

In addition, the care plan breached practice guidance (SSI/SWSG 1991a, p.67) in respect of its contents, specification of objectives, agreement on implementation, leeway for contingencies and the identification and feedback of unmet needs. Practice guidance did not, the judge explained, carry the force of the policy guidance, but even so, the authority should have had regard to it: 'Whilst the occasional lacuna would not furnish evidence of such disregard, the series of lacunae ... does, in my view, suggest that the statutory guidance has been overlooked'.

Individual and general duties. The court also dismissed the attempt to convert the general, target duties under s.29 of the National Assistance Act 1948 into a more specific, stronger duty. This had been attempted by referring to the specificity of the directions given under the 1948 Act, and to the gateway of individual assessment (ie, of 'any person') under s.47 of the NHS and Community Care Act 1990.

Education legislation. On behalf of the applicant, it was argued that the local authority had a duty under (what was then) s.41 of the Education Act 1944, which stated that it 'shall be the duty of every education authority to secure the provision for their area of adequate facilities for further education', and that in 'exercising their functions under this section a local education authority shall also have regard to the requirements of persons over compulsory school age who have learning difficulties'.

Although the judge accepted that the duty was of the 'target' type and he was not prepared to 'bring the duty home [to the applicant] personally', nevertheless there was force 'in the contention that the s.41 target duty involves giving appropriate consideration to the admittedly small group' to which the applicant belonged. The local authority had retreated from its position that responsibility lay only with the Further Education Funding Council, but had still been maintaining – in opposition to the applicant's mother and professionals involved – that the applicant's educational needs could be met under s.2 of the Chronically Sick and Disabled Persons Act. The judge stated that though it was not for the court to adjudicate on this, it was 'something which the local authority must take very seriously and assess with care and sensitivity'. In addition, guidance issued by the Department for Education – about provision for students with learning difficulties over the age of 19 years – 'must be conscientiously taken into account ... in coming to its decision'.

The judge also concluded that in the event of a breach of s.41, the proper recourse was to the Secretary of State (under ss.69 and 99 of the 1994 Act, empowering intervention in the case of unreasonableness or failure to discharge a duty. rather than to court.

Limitations on the court. The complexity of the case, as the judge pointed out, presented the court 'with problems some of which are beyond the competence of the law courts'. He was also tempted to exercise the discretion courts have in judicial review not to grant any relief (eg, an injunction or declaration) because of 'the present fluid situation, and given the genuine endeavours being made on both sides to do the right thing'. However, two declarations were eventually granted.

R v Kensington and Chelsea Royal London Borough Council, ex parte Kihara [1996] 29 HLR 147 (CA). *Housing; asylum seekers; eligibility*

This homelessness case involved asylum seekers, and was heard before restrictive regulations were struck down as invalid by the Court of Appeal (only to be replaced by provisions in the Asylum and Immigration Act 1996) and foreshadowing some of the arguments in the community care case of *R v Westminster CC, ex p A* about asylum seekers.

Essentially, in this case, the court decided that the term 'other special reason' in housing legislation, governing whether a person is vulnerable (under the test for priority need and homelessness), could cover asylum seekers. This was because of their 'total resourcelessness' and their inability to obtain food, nourishment, blankets to keep warm etc.

R v Kingston and Richmond Health Authority, ex parte Paxman [1995] COD 410 (QBD). *Consultation; registration of nursing homes; health authority*

A case in which the court held that a health authority, as registration authority for nursing homes, had consulted inadequately with proprietors of local nursing homes over its new policy that multi-bed rooms should be phased out.

Although there was no statutory duty to consult, the court found that the terms of the consultation were ill-defined, and did not emphasise that they were about the merits as well as the practicality of the proposals. Furthermore, the consultation method was flawed. Discussing the matter at the end of inspections was 'inappropriate and unsatisfactory', precluding the giving of sufficient reasons which would in turn allow for intelligent consideration and response by the home owner. An issue of such importance warranted a special or separate appointment with home owners. The procedure was unfair and unreasonable and the local authority's decision to implement the new policy was quashed.

R v Kingston upon Thames Royal Borough, ex parte T [1994] 1 FLR 799 (QBD). *Children; social services; judicial review; complaints review panels; resources; unreasonableness*

A child care case (revolving around s.20 of the Children Act 1989), relevant to this book because of the consideration given to a) the appropriateness of judicial review when there is an alternative remedy in the form of a statutory complaints procedure available instead; b) the failure of a local authority to heed a complaints review panel's recommendation; c) the unreasonableness of a local authority decision; and d) the relevance of resources.

Complaints procedure instead of judicial review. The judge stated that judicial review should not be used if there is another effective and convenient remedy to be exhausted first – in this case the complaints procedure set out in s.26 of the Children Act 1989. He found that in this case, the complaints procedure was the appropriate remedy. First, the panel could 'get to the heart of the complaint and face head on and directly whether the decision was appropriate or not'; the panel was not – as a court would be – confined to whether the decision was legally unreasonable or plainly wrong. Instead it could 'consider the matter de novo [afresh] exercising its own independent judgement on the merits of the facts including any new facts placed before it'.

Second, the complaints procedure is 'infinitely quicker' than judicial review. Third, the judge did not agree that 'because the complaints review panel can be dominated by two members of the local authority, there is an inbuilt unfairness in the representation'. He disagreed because he could not believe 'it correct to proceed on the basis that professional people who sit in judgment on the panel would do so from bias'. Fourth, there was little difference – in terms of effectiveness – between a panel's recommendations compared to a court order. Not only could the independent person on the panel persuade the authority to follow the panel's decision, but if an authority does not do so then judicial review could still be invoked at that stage. Lastly, the judge stated that Parliament had 'quite clearly assigned certain functions in controlling the lives of children to the local authorities. Parliament has most definitely denied the court power to intervene...'

Unreasonable decision? The judge referred to well-worn definitions of unreasonableness (absurdity, defiance of logic or moral standards, taking leave of senses etc). He then pointed out that the relevant decision (that one of two sisters did not require accommodation but could still be looked after by her mother) taken by the local authority might have been 'right or wrong' – but that it was 'certainly a tenable view to hold and one which I could not, by any stretch of the imagination, hold to be perverse'.

Resources. The judge was satisfied 'that the financial restrictions which confronted this local authority, as they confront local authorities up and down the length and breadth of the land as I know from sitting in this court week in and week out … were legitimate and proper factors to take into account'.

R v Kirklees Metropolitan Borough Council, ex parte Daykin [1996] 3 CL 565 (QBD). *Community care; specificity of assessed need; assessment decisions*

This case illustrates a) the confusion which can arise in the absence of formal procedures for assessment, especially if recommendations are made by staff not authorised – according to the authority's policy of delegation – to take decisions about providing services; b) the significance of differentiating clearly between needs, and the options to meet those needs; and c) that, in the absence of statutory timescales, local authorities should perform their duties as soon as is reasonably practicable.

Background. The case concerned a couple in their 60s, both disabled, she suffering from rheumatoid arthritis, he with chronic obstructive airways disease and a short time to live. There was a fear – shared by both GP and hospital specialist – that a move of accommodation could be fatal to the husband.

A health authority occupational therapist recommended that they should have installed either a vertical lift or a stairlift to give them ingress and egress from their first floor council flat. The recommendation was also backed by an 'advocacy officer' of the council. The recommended home adaptations were eventually refused by the housing department of the council on grounds of cost. The applicants claimed that having assessed the need, the council was obliged to meet it.

Failure to carry out an assessment. The judge decided that, in fact, the council had failed to carry out an assessment under s.47 of the NHS and Community Care Act 1990 and s.2 of the Chronically Sick and Disabled Persons Act. Confusingly for the service users, the statements of the advocacy officer, the care plan she had drawn up and the recommendation of the occupational therapist did not carry sufficient weight, since the provision of services was 'the concern of the council itself or of any committee or officer to whom a specific power is delegated'. Thus, under the policy of delegation, these staff were not authorised to carry out assessment and to decide about service provision.

Differentiating need from the means to meet it. The judge stated that need should be differentiated from the means to meet it, and that the requirement of the stairlift fell into the latter, but not the former, category – so it was 'impossible to regard the provision of stair lift at home as 'the need''. Instead the need was 'for the applicants to get in and out of the premises' – for which the authority could review various options and take account of cost. Indeed, the authority was 'perfectly entitled to look to see what is the *cheapest* way for them to meet the needs which are specified' (italics added).

Thus, the judge found not that the authority was in breach of its statutory duty to provide the stairlift, but that it had been profiting from its failure to carry out the assessment. He stated that generally, if a decision about need were to be properly made, then 'it is the duty of the authority to meet the needs and that means to meet them as soon as is reasonably practicable … Once they have identified after discussion the manner in which those needs are to be met, then the Act requires that they get on with it and meet those needs'.

Therefore, the sooner the authority carried out a formal assessment, drew up a care plan and so complied with its statutory duty, the better. However, in this particular case, the judge was not prepared to strike down the authority's proposals for a move (rather than adaptations). Although the authority had originally not appreciated the need for adaptations and for staying in the same area, it did so now. Furthermore, the judge was not prepared to strike down the authority's proposals on grounds of irrationality; it had balanced the medical evidence, the costs and the effect on neighbours.

R v Kirklees Metropolitan Borough Council, ex parte Good [1996] 11 CL 288 (transcript) (QBD). *Community care; home adaptations; Chronically Sick and Disabled Persons Act 1970; Carers (Recognition and Services) Act 1995*

An elderly, disabled couple (Mr and Mrs Good senior) lived on the ground floor – and Mr and Mrs Good junior with four children lived on the floor above. The dispute was about whether in addition housing improvement work downstairs for the Goods senior, the Goods junior upstairs should also receive a grant so as to alleviate their own situation and thus enable them to provide improved care for the Goods seniors. The Carers (Recognition and Services) Act 1995 was argued in support of this.

Relevance of legislation. The judge pointed out, however, that simply making an assessment under the 1995 Act 'does not get anyone anywhere'. It was actual provision of assistance that was in question – and the Act did not require the authority to provide a grant for the carers in respect of the upstairs premises. Indeed, the 1995 Act was simply not relevant to an application for a grant under housing legislation (then, the Local Government and Housing Act 1989). He also went on to consider whether the authority came under a duty towards the family upstairs under s.2 of the Chronically Sick and Disabled Persons Act, which refers to adaptations to the home – and found that no duty arose (though it did for the elderly couple downstairs).

Nature of assessment. Commenting on the nature of assessment, the judge seemed summed up the import of policy guidance: 'It may be complicated, in which case a full scale enquiry will need to be put in hand and a written document provided and so on. There may be other cases where it is so simple that a decision can be made with the conclusion being reached that nothing needs to be done. In effect that [sic] is a matter for the local authority to determine the extent of the assessment'.

R v Lambeth London Borough Council, ex parte A [1997] 10 ALR 209 (CA). *Disabled child; social services; assessment; provision of alternative accommodation*

A child care case in which the Court of Appeal considered duties to rehouse a family with a disabled child under housing legislation, and to carry out assessments under the Chronically Sick and Disabled Persons Act, the Children Act 1989 and the Carers (Recognition and Services) Act 1995. The court adopted a down-to-earth approach, taking into account the difficulties facing the local authority, and its own discretion in judicial review not to interfere – and not being over-concerned with the formalities of assessment.

Suitable accommodation and facilities for severely disabled child. The child involved was fifteen years old with severe disabilities including cerebral palsy, incontinence, learning disabilities – and inability to dress, feed or toilet himself, or to walk or lift himself. His mother cracked the base of her spine four years before from lifting him, and was now unable to lift him and not permitted to drive a car. The husband gave up his job to care for his son.

The flat the family lived in had become unsuitable. For example, the son was heavy and – immobile and incontinent as he was – items such as overhead hoists and special shower were needed; but the flat was not large enough nor its fabric sufficiently strong. Similarly, the wheelchair he used was larger than normal with stabilisers – because of the epilepsy attacks he suffered – and could not easily be manoeuvred around the flat.

Duty to rehouse: balancing exercise. By 1994, Lambeth had accepted that the family required urgent rehousing, and offers had been made and withdrawn as unsuitable. One offer remained on the table, its suitability in dispute in relation to size, access and location. The Court of Appeal agreed with the High Court that the duty on the housing authority under housing legislation (whether in respect of general allocation of its housing, or of homelessness) involved a balancing exercise, weighing the 'claims of one needful applicant against those of another. No claimant, however strong his needs, has an absolute right to be rehoused immediately'. The court suggested that *R v Gloucestershire CC, ex p Barry* would support this approach to the housing duty.

Prose of government departments. In respect of cooperation between different arms of the local authority (ie, housing and social services), the court acknowledged the aims expressed in guidance (DoE 10/92) that there should be a 'seamless service'. Nevertheless, it pointed out: 'That is, with respect, the sort of prose which comes easily to ministerial advisers at departmental headquarters. It seems to me that it is an aspiration and not an operating manual that can be relied on invariably to produce those results. Neither ministerial circulars, nor declaration or exhortation from this court, can automatically raise the standards of day to day administration in a hard pressed local authority providing services for some of the least affluent parts of London'.

Importance of assessment. It also dismissed the argument that — irrespective of the housing legislation — proper assessments should be carried out under the Chronically Sick and Disabled Persons Act 1970, the Children Act 1989 and the Carers (Recognition and Services) Act 1995. It 'did not accept that at all. There have been numerous assessments in this case ... It may be that some are better than others. It may be that some do not explicitly state under what statute or statutes they have been made ... The judge exercised his discretion properly ... with eminent good sense, when he said that 'What this lad needs and what his parents need is a new home' ... any correction of a lack of formal assessment in the past would simply be a bit of tidy minded putting the files in order and would not assist resolution of the real problem'.

Complaints procedure more suitable than judicial review? In relation to the failure to assess for or provide services under s.2 of the CSPDA 1970, the court also stated that in the absence of a question of law, the statutory complaints procedure 'may provide a more suitable means of redress'.

Specialist equipment. As to the provision in particular of specialist equipment – hoists, frames, special bathing and toilet equipment, special beds and commodes – they would have to 'for the most part await successful completion of rehousing'. Indeed the family had found it necessary either to store or return some of these because there was not room enough in which to use them. The court did say that Lambeth should bear in mind the particular problems relating to the supply of bed linen and padding to prevent accidental injury to the son.

R v Lambeth London Borough Council, ex parte Ashley [1996] 29 HLR 385 (QBD). *Rigid policy; fettering of discretion; housing allocation; Housing Act 1985*

The local authority would only give points in relation to the condition of the existing accommodation if the authority's medical officer made specific recommendations or if a room in the property was deemed uninhabitable. A maximum of 20 points could also be awarded if there was opposite-sex (other than partners) sharing of a room. However, points could be awarded only per household; thus the policy could take no account of how many people were affected within one household. This was illogical, rigid and inflexible and gave no consideration to individuals.

R v Lambeth London Borough Council, ex parte Caddell [1998] 2 FCR 6 (QBD). *Children; social services; continuing duty; residence dispute; Children Act 1989, s.24*

This case concerned a dispute between two local authorities about which of them was responsible for continuing to provide advice, assistance and support for a child who had reached the age of 18 years. The child had been placed by Lambeth with a foster mother in Kent, before, at the age of 18, moving into independent accommodation. Referring to s.24 of the Children Act 1989, the court ruled that the authority, within whose area the child was living at the time, bore the responsibility: ie, Kent.

R v Lambeth London Borough Council, ex parte Carroll [1987] 20 HLR 142 (QBD). *Decision-making responsibility; relevant factors; homelessness*

In deciding about a person's vulnerability in relation to priority need for accommodation under the Housing Act 1985 (the relevant provisions have since been superseded in the Housing Act 1996), the housing authority had relied on the medical opinion of a doctor. The court found the decision unlawful because it had not enquired into housing or social welfare matters which were also relevant to the decision. The: 'authority should always bear in mind that it is its function and no one else's to decide whether an applicant is vulnerable or not and that it is their duty, in order to enable it [sic] to satisfy themselves whether a homeless person has priority need to make all necessary enquiries'.

R v Lambeth LBC, ex parte Sarhangi [1998] TLR 9 December 1998 (QBD). *Asylum seeker from Iran via Sweden; prison sentence in United Kingdom; eligibility for assistance under s.21 of the National Assistance Act 1948*

The applicant had originally been granted political asylum from Iran in Sweden. He came to the United Kingdom where he was convicted of drug offences and imprisoned. A deportation order and directions for his removal to Sweden were made, but the Swedish authorities would not permit his re-entry. The man was cooperating fully with the United Kingdom authorities; indeed he did not want to remain in the UK. The applicant was not permitted to work and, on his release from prison, requested assistance under s.21 of the National Assistance Act 1948.

The council refused on the grounds that he was not lawfully present in the United Kingdom. He had not sought asylum in the UK and was fit to travel. Furthermore, in the case of R v Brent LBC, ex p D, it was held that, as a matter of public policy, an illegal entrant or overstayer would be precluded from receiving assistance – if he could travel without serious risk to his health or life – on the basis that he should not benefit from his own wrongdoing.

However, the court held that such a public policy principle did not apply in the present case, since the applicant was in fact lawfully in the United Kingdom; he had served a lawful prison sentence and was unable to leave – through factors entirely beyond his control. He was not exercising a choice to remain illegally.

R v Lancashire County Council, ex parte M [1989] 2 FLR 279 (CA). *Joint working; speech therapy; dispute between the NHS and an education authority*

A case about the provision of speech therapy, illustrating the buck-passing which sometimes takes place between different local authorities and the NHS.

An education authority, having classed a child's need for speech therapy as an educational need, claimed that it had made a mistake – and that, as a matter of law, speech therapy could not be special educational provision (and so should be provided by the NHS). Thus, it was not empowered to provide the therapy, even if it wanted to. The court ruled against the education authority, agreeing with a previous decision R v Oxfordshire CC, ex p W) that speech therapy could be either educational or non-educational – ie, depending on the circumstances.

R v Lancashire County Council, ex parte Royal Association for Disability and Rehabilitation and Another [1996] 4 All ER 422 (CA). *Community care; resources; different options to meet need; residential placement; care in person's own home*

This case confirmed limits to the notion of choice within community care, and the importance of distinguishing between a need and the 'service options' to meet it.

It concerned a local authority's decision – taking resources into account – to cease to support an elderly woman in her own home, and instead to meet them in a nursing home. The High Court had found in favour of the council. The Court of Appeal upheld this decision, stating that an assessed need for '24 hour care' gave the authority the option of providing home support services or a residential placement – and in making that choice of how to meet the need, the authority could take account of resources (ie, choose the cheapest option still consonant with meeting the need).

R v Leeds City Council, ex parte Hendry [1993] 158 LGRevR 621 (QBD). *Adhering to local authority policies; taxi-licensing*

A taxi-licensing case in which the court stated that a local authority officer could not simply depart from the authority's policy – unless that policy had been formally (ie, by the licensing committee) amended.

R v Mid-Glamorgan County Council, ex parte B [1995] ELR 168 (QBD). *Committee hearing; allegation of bias; special education*

A special educational needs case concerning allegations of bias in relation to an appeal committee hearing. The judge accepted that it was unfortunate that the three council members on the committee had referred to 'our authority' and 'our officers', and that one member had reacted with overt hostility (a 'nasty flare-up') when it was suggested that the local authority had been influenced by financial considerations.

However, on the first point, he found that although such terminology gave the 'impression' of bias, nevertheless it was the normal kind of terminology used by council members, there was nothing 'sinister' about its use, and there was consequently no 'real danger of bias'. On the second, it was clearly a 'regrettable incident that should not have happened', but was short in duration (no more than 10–15 seconds), was followed by an apology from the councillor concerned and came late in the proceedings. Again it was impossible to say that the incident gave rise to a real danger of bias.

R v Ministry of Agriculture, Fisheries and Food, ex parte Hamble (Offshore) Fisheries Ltd [1995] 2 All ER 714 (QBD). *Rigid policies; fettering of discretion; building exceptions into a policy; consistency and individual consideration; fishing licences*

A case involving a change in licensing policy for fishing (trawling) which meant that the applicant's expectation of obtaining the appropriate license entitlement – which he had worked towards – were disappointed. The case centred mainly on the limits of the legal concept of 'legitimate expectation', and the extent to which it was not only procedural (eg, entitling the applicant to consultation before being denied or losing a benefit) but also substantive (ie, entitling the applicant to the expected benefit).

However, the judge also considered whether the Ministry had fettered its discretion by adopting a policy on licences (with certain prescribed exceptions in-built), such that it appeared not to be giving separate consideration to the applicant's peculiar position. The problem for the Ministry was that if it made an exception in the case of the applicant it 'would have had to have regard to the risk of justified accusations of partiality or arbitrariness' – and that any general relaxation of the policy for people in a similar position would have seriously weakened the Ministry's ability to control the fleet and fish stocks.

The judge accepted this pointing out a) that the 'line between individual consideration and inconsistency, slender enough in theory, can be imperceptible in practice'; and b) that whilst 'the framer of a policy for the exercise of a governmental discretion must be prepared to consider making exceptions where these are merited, the inclusion of thought-out exceptions in the policy itself may well be exhaustive of the obligation'.

R v Ministry of Defence, ex parte Murray [1998] COD 134 (QBD). *Giving reasons for decisions; court martial*

A court martial case concerning a violent offence by a soldier with an exemplary record, associated with an anti-malarial drug he had been taking and whether reasons should have been given for the decision.

It was decided that, in the circumstances, fairness required that reasons be given for the decision of the court martial. Before reaching this decision, the court considered the law generally in relation to the giving of reasons by distilling the principles emerging from *R v Civil Services Appeal Board, ex parte Cunningham; R v Secretary of State for the Home Department, ex parte Doody*; and *R v Higher Education Funding Council, ex parte Institute of Dental Surgery*.

In summary, the points made included the following: a) the law did not recognise a general duty to give reasons; b) the courts would ensure that statutory decisions affecting individuals followed prescribed procedure and would supply additional procedural standards to ensure that fairness is attained; c) where reasons were not given, a challenge had to show that the procedure was unfair; d) there was a perceptible trend towards greater openness in decision-making; e) in deciding whether fairness required that a tribunal give reasons, the availability and nature of any appeal remedy or remedy via judicial review would be considered; f) the carrying out of a judicial function by a tribunal additionally favoured the requirement of reasons, particularly where personal liberty was involved; and g) if justice could not be achieved in the absence of reasons, then they should be given.

Advantages in the giving of reasons were that it a) concentrated the mind of the decision-maker and demonstrated that this had occurred; b) showed how issues had been conscientiously considered and the result achieved; and c) alerted the recipient of the decision to a justiciable flaw. Disadvantages were that it a) placed a burden on decision-makers; b) demanded an appearance of unanimity where there was in fact diversity; c) called for the articulation of sometimes inexpressible value judgements; and d) invited the 'captious' to scrutinise reasons for previously unsuspected grounds of challenge.

R v Newcastle-upon-Tyne Council, ex parte Dixon [1993] 158 LGRevR 441 (QBD). Community care; residential and nursing home care; contracts with the local authority

A case illustrating conflict between local authorities and the private sector over contracts for residential and nursing home care. It was brought by the Newcastle Association of Care Homes in protest at the local authority's standard form of agreement. The objection was that the contract terms went beyond the statutory requirements laid down in the Registered Homes Act 1984, with which home owners must comply. The court held that the authority had not behaved unreasonably by imposing such a stricter contractual regime, when fulfilling its duty under the National Assistance Act 1948.

Indeed, the authority's 'insistence upon high contractual standards coupled with firm and economical means of enforcing them is an essential means of achieving ... a balance' – between providing statutory services and adhering to the fiduciary duty not to waste the money of local council tax payers.

R v Newham London Borough Council, ex parte Gorenkin [1997] 30 HLR 278 (QBD). Community care; residential accommodation; food vouchers; asylum seekers

The applicant was one of a number of asylum seekers. He had found a room in Forest Gate and some assistance with the rent which was £20 per week. However, he sought assistance from Newham Council with his food needs, and was accordingly provided with food vouchers under s.21 of the National Assistance Act 1948. This assistance was stopped when the council received legal advice that there was no legal power to make such provision – ie, it could not provide food, without providing accommodation as well under s.21 of the 1948 Act. The local authority was unhappy at this situation, since it foresaw that the withdrawal of the food vouchers would result in some people losing the support they had been receiving, and re-approaching the council for both accommodation and food.

The court held, somewhat reluctantly, that s.21 of the 1948 Act meant that local authorities could provide food (or food vouchers) and accommodation, but not food vouchers alone – because the 'care and attention', which was a condition for provision, had to be seen in the context of residential accommodation. It was on this basis that the authority had already, for the most part lawfully, reassessed individual applicants, offering assistance only to those who were 'either without accommodation or are likely to become so imminently'.

However, the judge stated that the authority's policy was flawed to the extent that it was not prepared to look ahead to some extent: 'where someone has accommodation of some sort, but is otherwise wholly destitute, it is certainly possible that he may reach a stage where he is in need of care and attention as defined in the section. A person who is starving in a garret may certainly need such attention, and it would be very odd if the authority could not review his position while he remains there. What the authority have to consider is whether, looking at the person's position overall, it has arrived at a position where they ought to take responsibility for him by securing residential accommodation and the food that goes with it, and that position may, as I say, be arrived at while he still has a roof over his head'.

R v Newham London Borough Council, ex parte Medical Foundation for the Care of Victims of Torture [1998] 1 CCLR 227 (QBD). Community care; residential accommodation; asylum seekers

The case involved asylum seekers and interpretation of s.21 of the National Assistance Act 1948. The council claimed that the only accommodation it could offer under s.21 was accommodation which included a package of services such as food, laundry, and facilities to maintain personal hygiene. It further claimed that because it could not find any such accommodation in Newham, it was compelled to offer accommodation in Eastbourne.

However, the applicants wished to remain in Newham where they had received support from community groups and had been able 'to find comfort from both strangers and those in a like situation'. They maintained that there was nothing to stop the council from providing small flats and bed and breakfast accommodation –

for example, by obtaining leases from private individuals in the form of what was termed 'bare' or 'ordinary' accommodation.

Different types of accommodation and board. In construing the meaning of residential accommodation in s.21 of the National Assistance Act 1948, the judge considered various options. He rejected the idea that the term 'residential' connoted 'permanence' or an 'institutional quality'. Furthermore, he felt that the wording of s.21(5) and s.26(1A) of the Act clearly indicated that residential accommodation without board and personal care might be provided. In other words, a 'wide variety of accommodation must be contemplated' – and board and other services could, as s.21(5) states, be provided 'in connection' with the accommodation, not necessarily in it as part of a package.

Policy guidance, directions etc. Having reached this conclusion on the legislation, the judge then pointed out that he was fortified by a) policy guidance (DH 1990) which referred to provision preserving or restoring normal living (para 3.24) and securing cost-effective services meeting the care needs of users and taking account of their preferences (para 3.25); b) the *Asylum Seekers Accommodation Special Grant Report no.24* (February 1997) which stated that reasonably incurred expenditure could include accommodation with meals or food provided separately; and c) the *National Assistance Act 1948 Choice of Accommodation Directions 1992* (see p.264) which stated that the wishes of the person to be accommodated must be followed subject to certain conditions including expense.

R v Newham London Borough Council, ex parte Plastin [1997] 30 HLR 261 (QBD). *Community care; residential accommodation; asylum seekers*

The applicant was a 51-year-old British citizen, holder of a British passport with right of abode in the United Kingdom. He was ineligible for social security benefits because he was not classed as habitually resident in the UK and did not speak English. The manager of a night shelter – where the man had been staying, but which was now closing – wrote on his behalf, seeking for residential accommodation to be provided by the local authority under s.21 of the National Assistance Act 1948.

An assessment was carried out, with the conclusion that though without benefits and homeless, the man was able-bodied and had worked previously as a ship's captain and cook, was not physically disabled except for dental problems for which he could receive NHS treatment, and was aware of his situation. On this basis his application was refused.

Decision not perverse. The judge found that it was not 'perverse' of the local authority to have refused assistance. For instance, the present applicant was not ineligible from seeking accommodation under homelessness legislation, was not 'under any physical or mental disability', was able-bodied and of working age. He also referred to the Court of Appeal's judgment in *R v Westminster CC, ex p A*, which emphasised that s.21 of the 1948 was not a safety net for anybody short of money or accommodation. Nor could the judge fault the local authority's assessment, finding that it was 'not arguable that they left out of that consideration any material matter'.

True to the principles of judicial review, the judge also emphasised that he was exercising a 'supervisory', as opposed to an appeal, jurisdiction. Thus, he was deciding not that the man 'truly is a person in need', but that the local authority had not acted perversely. There 'was a choice available to the local authority here on the facts which they could properly exercise ... In my judgment the Authority was clearly entitled to reach the conclusion which they did, namely that he was not in urgent need of care and attention, given the facts to which I have referred'.

R v Norfolk County Council, ex parte Thorpe [1998] COD 208 (QBD). *Duties; resources; public footpaths*

A case brought by a person with a visual disability in relation to the local authority's duty to provide 'a proper and sufficient footway as part of the highway in any case where they consider the provision of a footway is necessary or desirable for the safety or accommodation of pedestrians' (s.66(1), Highways Act 1980). Drawing on the House of Lords decision in *R v Gloucestershire CC, ex p Barry*, the judge held that the authority 'was entitled to have regard to its financial resources in considering whether a footway is necessary or desirable'.

R v North and East Devon Health Authority, ex parte Coughlan [1998] TLR 29 December 1998 (QBD: appeal awaited at the time of writing). *Closure of NHS unit for disabled people; adequate consultation; unlawful continuing care criteria; unlawful lack of multi-disciplinary assessment; promise for life broken; general and nursing care sole responsiblity of the NHS; European Convention on Human Rights*

In 1993 a group of severely disabled people, receiving long-term care from the NHS moved into Mardon House (NHS premises), having been given an oral assurance by the health authority that it would be a home for life for them. The authority now proposed to close the unit and to transfer the group elsewhere – although it would in any event continue to fund their care. The applicant, one of the disabled people, had been injured in a road traffic accident in 1971. She was tetraplegic and doubly incontinent, had a partially paralysed respiratory tract, experienced great difficulty in breathing, wore a corset to keep her abdominal organs in place and had a potentially fatal neurological condition that caused recurrent pounding headaches. This proposed action was successfully challenged on a number of grounds. The judge ruled as follows.

Breaking the promise: overriding public interest? The promise was one which could only be broken if there was an overriding public interest in doing so; the burden of showing such an interest fell to the health authority. But the authority could not establish such an interest, given that it had conceded that there were finely balanced arguments for and against closure.

Adequate consultation? The authority had not followed an adequate and lawful process of consultation – for example, some of the arguments eventually cited by the authority as justifying closure had not been seen by the applicant and she had therefore been unable to comment on or refute them. Overall, the consultation process should have been undertaken at a formative stage in the decision-making process, and have included the giving of sufficient reasons and adequate time to allow intelligent and conscientious consideration of the matter. This did not happen.

Multi-disciplinary assessment and risk assessment. The guidance on continuing care, HSG(95)8 called for multi-disciplinary assessment of people being discharged from hospital. The 'doctor and nurse' assessment, carried out without an input from social services (which had separately assessed that Mardon House was suitable for the applicant), did not amount to such multi-disciplinary activity. Nor had there been a risk assessment as referred to in other guidance on the transfer of frail older people from hospital (HSC 1998/048).

Alternative placements. The argument for the plaintiff had been that under both continuing care guidance (HSC(95)8) and the guidance of transfer of frail older people from hospital (HSC 1998/048) – the latter of which would apply also to other vulnerable people – alternative placements should have been identified. The fact that they were not, nor even an attempt made, meant that the authority had failed in its obligations.

Eligibility criteria for continuing care, and responsibility for nursing care, general and specialist. The health authority's policy and criteria were based on the misconception that it was no longer empowered to provide long-term general nursing care, but could only provide specialist nursing. This approach was wholly misconceived, took account of irrelevant matters and was outwith the continuing care guidance (HSC(95)8). Indeed, the court found that this guidance did not change NHS responsibilities for health and nursing care services; both 'general and specialist nursing care remain the sole responsibility of the health authorities'; and thus 'health care' could never be 'social care'.

European Convention on Human Rights. Although the Human Rights Act 1998 was not yet in force, nevertheless the European Convention was persuasive authority as to the content of the common law – and there was a breach in this case of article 8 (right to respect for private and family life and home). None of the exceptions, that could have justified interference with that right, applied (namely interests of national security, public safety, economic well-being of the country, prevention of disorder or crime, protection of health or morals, protection of the rights and freedoms of others).

R v North and East Devon Health Authority and North Devon Healthcare NHS Trust, ex parte Lorna Beatrice Pow, Mary Beatrice Geall, Edith Mary Prid and Metcalfe [1998] 1 CCLR 280 (QBD). *Health authority; closure of hospitals; consultation*

A case concerning closure of Lynton and Winsford hospitals in Devon and the duties on health authorities a) to balance their books, and b) to consult the local community health council about proposals which will have a substantial effect on local health services.

Whilst acknowledging the duty under s.97A of the NHS Act 1977 not to overspend, the judge found that under r.18 of the *Community Health Council Regulations 1996* (SI 1996/640), the health authority had gone wrong in relation to consultation. The authority had been under the impression that it was not under a duty to consult until a proposal had been finalised – but the court pointed out that this suggested that the authority would be consulting about a decision, not a proposal.

Furthermore, although in case of urgency, a health authority was relieved of the duty to consult under the regulations, the judge stated that if an authority were permitted deliberately to allow time to pass to the point where matters were urgent – it would be undermining the purpose of the legislation. Similarly, an authority which believed that consultation was pointless or anxiety-making might delay announcement of a decision until it was simply too late to consult.

All this meant that the authority had 'erred in law in failing to appreciate the proposal temporarily to close Lynton and Winsford Hospitals was a proposal within the meaning of Regulation 18(1) such as to trigger the duty to consult'.

R v North Derbyshire Health Authority, ex parte Fisher [1998] 8 MLR 327 (QBD). *Health authority; failing to take account of guidance; treatment for people with multiple sclerosis*

A case notable for a) unusual success for the applicant in a case about rationing by a health authority, b) the 'back-door' way, via guidance, in which this was achieved, and c) consideration of the effect of guidance. It concerned a person with multiple sclerosis who was being denied treatment with the drug, Beta Interferon, by the health authority. The NHS Executive, part of the Department of Health, had issued a Circular (EL(95)97) in connection with the prescription of such drugs for multiple sclerosis.

Direction or guidance from the Secretary of State? The judge considered the effect of the Circular and the obligations it placed on the authority. First, he decided that the Circular did not amount to directions which would create an 'absolute duty' of compliance since, although it carried words such as 'asks', 'suggested' and 'taking into account', it did not include the word 'shall' or any of the other 'badges of mandatory requirement'. Nevertheless, he found that the Circular constituted 'strong guidance' and that the health authority, contrary to it, had in effect operated a blanket ban on treating patients in Derbyshire.

Having regard to guidance. The judge stated that the health authority 'had to have regard to that national policy [in the Circular]. They were not obliged to follow the policy, but if they decided to depart from it, they had to give clear reasons for so doing, and those reasons would have been susceptible to a Wednesbury [ie, on grounds of unreasonableness] challenge ... Moreover, if the [health authority] failed properly to understand the Circular, then their policy would be as defective as if no regard had been paid to the policy at all ... [The health authority] did not take the Circular into account and decide[d] exceptionally not to follow it. They decided to disregard it altogether throughout 1996, because they were opposed to it ... and did not properly take it into consideration'.

Resources and clinical decisions. The health authority argued that under s.97 of the NHS Act 1977, it had a duty not to overspend; and that clinical decisions had to be taken with due regard to available resources. The judge: 'unreservedly accept[ed] both propositions as correct. But on the facts of this case, they do not assist the [health authority, which] had funds available, but chose not to allocate them. As for clinical decisions, they were not for the [health authority] to take'.

Fettering of discretion and legitimate expectation. The applicant also maintained that the health authority had fettered its discretion by operating a blanket ban, and also created – through a letter written to the applicant about the possibility of treatment – either a substantive or procedural legitimate expectation. The judge did not go on to rule on these issues, having already found the authority's policy unlawful on the grounds explained above.

R v North West Lancashire Health Authority, ex parte G, A and D [1998], The Times, 22 December 1998 (QBD). *Health authority policy not to fund sex-change operations for trans-sexuals*
The High Court held that the health authority had behaved unlawfully and irrationally – apparently (at time of writing the case is unreported) by not considering what was proper treatment of a recognised illness. The health authority argued that it could take account of its scarce resources, but the judge stated that the policy it operated interfered with its duty under s.3 of the NHS Act 1977 to prevent illness and care for people who were ill.

R v North West Thames Regional Health Authority, ex parte Daniels [1993] 4 MLR 364 (QBD). *Health authority; closure of bone marrow unit; consultation; irrationality*
The case concerned the closure of a bone marrow transplant unit in an NHS hospital; the court ruled that the health authority had failed to consult the local community health council as it was obliged to under regulations. Such a failure was 'material' because the CHC might have been able to intervene effectively, before staff had been dispersed and the unit closed. As to whether the closure decision was irrational, the court identified defects – such as a failure to balance the cost of maintaining the unit with the benefit to the public – but ultimately declined to make a decision because of the limited amount of information before the court.

R v North Yorkshire County Council, ex parte Hargreaves [1994] 26 BMLR 121 (QBD). *Community care; respite for a disabled woman; taking account of people's preferences; acting on recommendations of complaints review panels; NHS and Community Care Act 1990,s.47*
The case illustrates how the law courts might find fault with local authorities which follow neither guidance nor the recommendations of a complaints review panel.

A 55-year-old woman with serious intellectual impairment was heavily dependent on daily support from her brother. The dispute centred on the amount and type of respite care which the council would provide for them each year – in particular whether it should be at an establishment such as the Winged Fellowship or simply provided through domiciliary support at home. The council accepted that both brother and sister needed respite care.

Preferences of the user. The judge granted an order against the council on the grounds that when it had carried out its assessment, it had failed to obtain the preferences of the woman herself – and could not assume that they were necessarily the same as her brother's. The judge accepted that it was not necessarily easy to obtain the woman's preferences, since the brother was protective of his sister, and the social worker might well have thought that he was being obstructive. Nevertheless, such difficulties did not absolve the council of its duty. It is notable that the judge based this breach of statutory duty on the failure of the authority to follow policy guidance (DH 1990,paras 3.16 and 3.25), since the legislation does not itself explicitly refer to people's preferences.

Review panel recommendations. The judge also found that it was not unlawful for the council to have failed to follow the recommendations of its complaints review panel, about the transitional arrangements to be made during the course of the dispute. He made it plain that, despite the case of *R Avon CC, ex p M*, there was no general rule that the recommendations of a review panel must be followed – though in particular circumstances the failure to do so without a rational reason might be unlawful.

R v North Yorkshire County Council, ex parte Hargreaves (no. 2) [1997] 96 LGR 39 (QBD). *Community care; holidays for disabled people; unlawfulness of policy; reassessment; Chronically Sick and Disabled Persons Act 1970, s. 2*
Under s. 2 of the Chronically Sick and Disabled Persons Act 1970, the authority had a duty – if it was satisfied that it was necessary for it to meet the needs of a disabled person – to make arrangements for facilitating the taking of a holiday. The authority was prepared to pay the holiday costs of the woman's brother (as carer), but not her own basic costs. Its reasoning was at least twofold. First, it argued that the section did not envisage direct provision of a holiday since the word 'facilitate' was used. Second, the holiday was an ordinary cost incurred by everybody, not just by disabled people; and the authority's obligations under the Act did not amount to basic relief of poverty, but only to relieving the extra expense of disability. Therefore it would meet additional costs such as special transport or accommodation expenses, but not basic costs unrelated to disability.

Facilitating holidays. The judge ruled that the authority's reasoning was awry. First, the authority did have a discretion, under the word 'facilitate', to provide holidays directly, because the section envisaged that one means of facilitating was in fact to provide council-arranged holidays. Therefore, depending on whether it was reasonably practicable for the applicant to contribute to the costs (under the Health and Social Services and Social Security Adjudications Act 1983, s. 17), the authority might in some circumstances end up having to foot the whole bill.

Fettering of discretion. Therefore, the judge concluded, the authority had fettered its discretion by adopting a policy which denied the possibility of making such provision: it had misunderstood the scope of the legislation. The question the authority should have been asking was whether the need for the holiday arose from the disability. If it did, 'then the cost of the holiday to the disabled person must be capable of being an additional cost which is the result of the disability, although the question may well arise as to whether in the particular case it is necessary, in order to facilitate the holiday, to assist with that cost'.

However, the judge also indicated that reassessment remained open to the local authority: 'It follows that the policy adopted by the Council unlawfully fetters its discretion, and the decision based upon that policy is flawed and must be quashed. However, this will not inevitably result in any different decision in relation [to the applicant]. The Council may well wish to reassess her needs, both because of the passage of time, and the decision of the House of Lords' (ie, in *R v Gloucestershire CC, ex p Barry*).

R v Northamptonshire County Council, ex parte W [1998] ELR 291 (QBD). *Retrospective reasons; education; exclusion from school; education; Education Act 1996*
The court emphasised that even if it were confident that reasons supplied retrospectively by a local authority nevertheless genuinely represented the original reasons given at the time of the decision in question – even so the court would not automatically agree to receive the material submitted at the later date. However, in this case it would receive the affidavit in question.

R v Northavon District Council, ex parte Palmer [1995] 27 HLR 576 (CA). *Breach of statutory duty; homelessness*
A homelessness case reiterating what had been established in Cocks v Thanet DC, that a damages claim in private law for breach of statutory duty (ie, for failure to provide accommodation) could only be brought once the local authority's public law decision-making (ie, as to her entitlement) had been concluded. The decision-making, in effect a condition precedent, could only be challenged by judicial review.

R v Northavon District Council, ex parte Smith [1994] 2 FCR 859 (HL). *Joint working between authorities; housing and social services; limits to judicial intervention; children*
A housing authority decided that it had no duty to secure permanent accommodation for a homeless family (because it judged that the homelessness was intentional). The social services authority then declined to exercise its power to give assistance in cash to the family – as part of its duty to safeguard and promote the welfare of the children – under s. 17(6) of the Children Act 1989. Instead it tried to rely on s. 27 of the 1989 Act which stated that it had the power to request the assistance of other authorities, who 'shall comply with the request if it is compatible with their own statutory or other duties and obligations and does not unduly prejudice the dis-

charge of any of their functions'. The housing authority, unsurprisingly, having already assessed the application in the negative, now refused to offer long-term accommodation.

On the issue of cooperation between authorities, the House of Lords stated that the: 'two authorities must cooperate. Judicial review is not the way to obtain cooperation. The court cannot decide what form cooperation should take. Both forms of authority have difficult tasks which are of great importance and for which they may feel their resources are not wholly adequate. The authorities must together do the best they can ... In this case the housing authority were entitled to respond to the social services authority as they did'.

R v Oxfordshire County Council, ex parte W [1987] 2 FLR 193 (QBD). *Joint working; speech therapy; NHS or educational provision; Education Act 1981*

This case illustrates the buck-passing which sometimes takes place between different statutory authorities when, short of resources, they argue over statutory responsibilities.

The court held that an education authority was entitled to class speech therapy as a non-educational service which it did not have to provide (but which the NHS might), as opposed to a special educational service which it would itself have been under a duty to arrange. Speech therapy could be classed either way, depending on the circumstances, and therefore the authority's decision was certainly neither irrational nor unreasonable.

R v Powys County Council, ex parte Hambidge [1998] 1 CCLR 458 (CA). *Community care; charging disabled people for services*

This case concerned a challenge to the legality of charging disabled people under s.2 of the Chronically Sick and Disabled Persons Act 1970.

Essentially, the question hinged on the following; s.17 of the Health and Social Services and Social Security Adjudications Act 1983 expressly gave local authorities the power to charge under various Acts including s.29 of the National Assistance Act 1948 – but did not mention s.2 of the 1970 Act. Thus, if s.2 of the 1970 Act were regarded as part of s.29 of the 1948 Act, it would be legal to make charges; if it were regarded as freestanding, then any charges for services under it would be unlawful. The High Court (*R v Powys CC, ex p Hambidge* [1997] 1 CCLR 182) concluded that charges under s.2 of the 1970 Act were lawful; the Court of Appeal now confirmed this.

Self-authorisation of the 1970 Act. In *R v Islington LBC, ex p Mcmillan*, the High Court had stated, to cut through a circuitous argument relating to the anti-duplication measure which affects s.29 of the 1948 Act and schedule 8 of the NHS Act 1977 (see p.325), that what authorised the local authority to make arrangements under s.2 of the 1970 Act was precisely s.2 of the 1970 Act – not s.29 of the 1948 Act. The Court of Appeal now chose not to explore this argument.

Special provision for the 1970 Act in community care. The duty of assessment in s.47 of the NHS and Community Care Act 1990 carries special reference in s.47(2) to a decision about services under the 1970 Act. The court accepted this but did not see its relevance to the question in hand.

Children Act 1989. The Children Act 1989, when passed, had taken children out of the ambit of s.29 of the 1948 Act, but s.28A had been inserted into the 1970 Act to ensure that children were still covered by the 1970 Act. Again the court could not see the relevance of this submission.

Social services functions. Under the Local Authority Social Services Act 1970, schedule 1, a list of social services functions are given. Section 2 of the Chronically Sick and Disabled Persons Act is listed separately from the 1948 Act. It was argued that this signified that s.2 of the 1970 Act must be freestanding, otherwise its inclusion here in addition to s.29 would not be necessary. The court rejected this, accepting that the draftsman was simply demonstrating an abundance of caution to spell out to social services committees that s.2 of the Chronically Sick and Disabled Persons Act 1970 constituted a social services function.

Mental Health Act 1983. The Mental Health Act 1983 was not listed in the Health and Social Services and Social Security Adjudications Act 1983, which confers the power to make charges, and it was argued that therefore local authorities were not permitted to not make charges for services provided under it, however wealthy the person concerned. In the same way, the absence of reference to the 1970 Act in the Health and Social Services and Social Security Adjudications Act 1983 meant that disabled people should also not be charged, no matter how wealthy. The court was not prepared to go along with this argument, pointing out that there had in fact been 'a long history of express powers to make charges' in relation to disabled people.

Wyatt v Hillingdon LBC. The court did not examine *Wyatt v Hillingdon LBC,* in which the Court of Appeal had assumed that s.2 of the Chronically Sick and Disabled Persons Act 1970 was part and parcel of s.29 of the 1948 Act, but was 'content to observe that the decision is consonant with the view' reached independently in the present case.

R v Redbridge London Borough, ex parte East Sussex County Council [1993] COD 256 (QBD). *Community care; residential accommodation; ordinary residence*

This was a dispute between two local authorities about ordinary residence and about which authority had statutory responsibility for making arrangements for two autistic twins with learning disabilities. Their parental home had been in Redbridge but they had attended a residential Rudolf Steiner school in East Sussex. The parents then sold the house in Redbridge and returned to Nigeria. The imminent closure of the school subsequently sparked the dispute between the two councils about which would be responsible for making arrangements for the provision of residential accommodation under s.21 of the National Assistance Act 1948.

The judge, referring to the case of *Shah v Barnet LBC* found that the parents' departure and sale of the family home meant that the twins had ceased to be ordinarily resident in Redbridge, and that the duty to make provision fell to East Sussex.

R v Secretary of State for Education, ex parte C [1996] 1 ELR 93 (QBD). *Consistency of decisions; education*

An education case involving a gifted child with certain difficulties and illustrating the scope the courts allow public bodies to arrive at inconsistent decisions, before ruling that they have behaved unreasonably. The Secretary of State had become involved and reached two separate decisions about the same child on the basis of 'substantially the same material'. The court decided that 'there is nothing on the face of it irrational even in the same person [let alone two different people] reaching a different conclusion when he re-examines the same facts'.

R v Secretary of State for Education and Science, ex parte E [1992] 1 FLR 377 (CA). *Assessment of need; provision to meet needs; special education; Education Act 1981*

An education case in which the Court of Appeal stated that local education authorities were under a clear duty to set out in a statement of educational needs all the special educational needs of the child, to specify all the special educational provision required to meet those needs, and to arrange that special educational provision (whether to be made by itself directly or through a school).

R v Secretary of State for the Environment, ex parte Kingston upon Hull City Council; R v Secretary of State for the Environment, ex parte Bristol City Council and Woodspring District Council [1996] COD 289 (QBD). *Resources; defining estuaries; sewage treatment*

Under a European Community directive, countries are obliged to give two types of sewage treatment to waste water: primary or secondary. The latter is more stringent and expensive and applies to sewage discharged into estuaries; the former, cheaper and less extensive, applies to discharge into coastal waters.

In order to save money, the Secretary of State for the Environment decided to limit the purported extent of certain estuaries, and thereby extend coastal waters. The court pointed out that there were various relevant considerations in relation to establishing estuarine limits. For example, the directive did not state that salinity or topography were the criteria which had to be used; thus there was a discretion. However, that discretion could not extend so far as to include the cost of sewage treatment as a factor, since such a consideration was irrelevant to a genuine and rational assessment of what an estuary is. The Secretary of State's decision was therefore quashed.

R v Secretary of State for Health, ex parte Alcohol Recovery Project [1993] COD 344 (QBD). *Community care; consultation; specific grant for people dependent on drugs or alcohol*
In relation to the power of the Secretary of State to make special grant payments to voluntary organisations providing care to people dependent on drugs or alcohol – under s.7E of the Local Authority Social Services Act 1970. Having initially been consulted on policy in relation to this power, the Project was not subsequently consulted when the Department of Health changed its mind and announced that there would be no such specific grants.

The Project claimed that it had a legitimate expectation of being consulted at the later stage; the court disagreed. In addition, the court found that the Project had unduly delayed its application for judicial review (the announcement was made on October 12th, the application made 23rd December). The court dismissed the Project's contention that the delay was due to seeking other forms of redress first – ie, by immediately organising a Parliamentary lobby.

R v Secretary of State for Health, ex parte Hammersmith and Fulham London Borough Council and Others. *Community care; residential accommodation; power to make cash payments; asylum seekers*
The case concerned the making of cash payments to asylum seekers being provided with residential accommodation under s.21 of the National Assistance Act 1948. Short of appropriate accommodation – its own residential homes were for elderly people and people with mental health problems, whilst independent homes in the borough were residential homes for elderly people or nursing homes – the council had placed the asylum seekers in bed and breakfast accommodation. For meals other than breakfast and for other 'necessary incidents of everyday life such as toiletries', the council had made cash payments to the asylum seekers. To have made provision in kind would, according to the council, have entailed inconvenience, inefficiency and expense.

However, the making of such payments was inconsistent with guidance issued by the Department of Health (LAC(97)6), which set out the type of expenditure which would be reimbursed by central government to local authorities by central government in the form of Asylum Seekers Accommodation Special Grant (ASAG). The guidance indicated that there was no power to make cash payments under s.21 of the 1948 Act, although provision in kind would be possible (eg, through arrangements with a supermarket chain).

(High Court): ***R v Secretary of State for Health, ex parte Hammersmith and Fulham London Borough Council and Others*** [1997] 30 HLR 525. The local authorities challenged the correctness of the guidance, arguing that the phrase 'make arrangements for providing' (under s.21 and applying to s.26 of the National Assistance Act 1948) could cover cash payments. The judge did not agree, stating: 'the expression ... means in its context that the outcome of any arrangements is that their beneficiaries should, in consequence of them, directly receive in kind the forms of provision contemplated by the statute, and nothing else. This construction marches, I think, with the ordinary sense of the words. Payment of money for persons to buy their own necessities leaves them to make the arrangements to get what they need'.

The judge also dismissed a) the argument that payments could be made under s.111 of the Local Government Act 1972 (which allows authorities do a thing which is 'calculated to facilitate, or is conducive or incidental to, the discharge of any of their functions'); and b) the point that there was no express prohibition of cash payments under s.21 (compared eg, to the prohibition under s.29: provision of welfare services).

(Court of Appeal): ***R v Secretary of State for Health, ex parte Hammersmith and Fulham London Borough Council and Others*** [1998] TLR, 9 September 1998. The Court of Appeal upheld the decision of the High Court on with the following reasoning.

Arrangements for provision. First, under ss.21 and 26 of the National Assistance Act 1948, a local authority had a duty to make arrangements for providing accommodation. There was 'no hint or suggestion' that such arrangements might include giving people cash for them to choose what accommodation or other commodity to spend it on. Under s.21(5), the provision of board and other services, amenities and requisites (subsidiary to the accommodation), there was even less suggestion that cash payments were permitted to give people the option or opportunity of spending money – since such benefits were restricted to what the authority managing the premises considered necessary.

Old Acts, new mischiefs. Second, whilst it was true that Acts of Parliament are 'always speaking' (as pointed out in *R v Westminster CC, ex p A*), nevertheless this was not authority for the proposition that Parliament intended an Act to be interpreted 'to cure whatever mischief may arise in the future, however unforeseen and unforeseeable'. Furthermore, the particular mischief and difficulty surrounding asylum seekers had been of Parliament's own making when it passed the Asylum and Immigration Act 1996, limiting their rights to other services and so putting strain on the National Assistance Act 1948. Had Parliament wished to rewrite the 1948 Act, 'it had only to say so' but had not in fact done so.

Absurdity or inconvenience. Third, it was good law that the wording of legislation should be given its ordinary meaning, unless the consequences were that it produced inconsistency, absurdity or inconvenience. In this case, both the asylum seekers and the local authorities claimed on a number of grounds that it was absurd and inconvenient that cash payments could not be made. However, the court felt that authorities simply had to make new administrative arrangements for dealing with asylum seekers – just as they already had for old, disabled and mentally ill people, as well as for children. This did not entail 'such a degree of inconvenience as to justify straining the language of the statute', especially since the Department of Health was prepared to accept as lawful the issuing and use of vouchers by way of prior arrangement with a supermarket.

Comparison with other statutory provisions. It was claimed that because s.21 of the 1948 Act did not carry an explicit prohibition relating to cash payments – unlike s.29 of the 1948 Act (welfare services etc) – this meant that cash payments were permitted under s.21. The court came to exactly the opposite conclusion, stating that without the prohibition in s.29, cash payments would have been possible because of the broad wording 'make arrangements for promoting the welfare of persons'. This was in comparison with wording of s.21 (discussed above) which was simply not capable of supporting cash payments, and so required no express prohibition on cash payments.

Attempting to evade this conclusion, it was then argued that the directions made under s.21 actually carried wording nearer to that contained in s.29. At one point they refer to the making of arrangements for the 'welfare of all persons for whom accommodation is provided' (see p.253). It was also claimed that the reference in policy guidance (DH 1990,para 3.25) to cost-effective packages of care would also support the making of cash payments. However, the court did not accept that either the directions or the guidance could in effect increase the powers conferred by Parliament in s.29 of the 1948 Act itself.

R v Secretary of State for Health, ex parte Manchester Local Committee [1995] 2 CL 3621 (otherwise unreported) (QBD). *Health service; legal effect of guidance*

The case illustrates the confusion sometimes surrounding the status, legal effect and nomenclature of guidance, and how peremptory language in guidance might amount to a direction and associated duty. It concerned a dispute between the Manchester Local Medical Committee and the Secretary of State about the reimbursement of funds to general practitioners in accordance with the relevant guidance. There was some uncertainty about the effect of the 'Red Book' and related guidance notes and whether in fact they contained a binding direction, which the Secretary of State had the power to issue under s.97 of the NHS Act 1977.

The judge stated that there was 'no magic form of words that is required and I do not think that the use of the word 'direct' is necessary in order to constitute a 'direction'. Nevertheless, it was obviously desirable that, if the Secretary of State was intending to direct, she should have made clear that she was indeed directing. Normally, the way to make that clear is to use the word 'direct' and it would have saved a lot of time and money in this case if only the Secretary of State had done just that … The language used in the guidance notes … is, in passages, peremptory'.

R v Secretary of State for the Home Department, ex parte Hargreaves [1997] 1 All ER 397 (CA). *Legitimate expectation; changing policies*

A case concerning the expectations of three prisoners of home leave, which were disappointed by a change of policy. Considering the issue of legitimate expectation and changing policies in general, the court confirmed that public bodies must be free to change policies and that this might involve the destruction of reasonable expectations and their replacement by new ones – whether, for instance, in relation to parole for prisoners or to retirement age for civil servants (see *Hughes v Department of Health and Social Security*).

R v Secretary of State for the Home Department, ex parte Brind and Others [1991] 2 WLR 588 (HL). *European Convention on Human Rights; Northern Ireland; terrorist organisations*

A case about the broadcasting ban imposed in relation to interviews, discussions etc with Sinn Fein, Provisional Sinn Fein, the Ulster Defence Association or any proscribed terrorist organisation. Part of the challenge to the ban referred to article 10 of the European Convention on Human Rights (freedom of expression). The court stated that because there was no ambiguity in the legislation, the Convention could not be used to interpret its meaning. Furthermore, on a slightly different ground of challenge, if the Secretary of State had been obliged, in drawing up the legislation, to have regard to article 10 to the extent of conforming with it, then this would have incorporated the Convention into domestic law by the back door.

R v Secretary of State for the Home Department, ex parte Khan [1984] 1 WLR 1337 (CA). *Legitimate expectation; immigration*

This immigration case illustrates how the courts might – at least in some contexts – state that people have a legitimate expectation not only to consultation, but also to the substantive benefit or service they had expected. The Court of Appeal ruled that the Secretary of State could only depart from criteria of eligibility set out in guidance if a) the person affected was given a hearing; and b) in any event only if overriding public interest demanded the departure.

R v Secretary of State for the Home Office, ex parte Zakrocki [1998] 1 CCLR 374 (QBD). *Community care; unreasonableness; immigration*

A community care case in which the rights of a British citizen to community care (provided by his family) 'trumped' the immigration aspect of the case.

A Polish couple in their sixties came to the United Kingdom to care for their ageing mother. Their leave to remain was extended so that they could care for the wife's brother, a British Citizen who suffered from epilepsy, had learning difficulties and spoke no English. They again applied for leave to remain, with the support of Hackney Council which pointed out that the alternative of residential care was very costly, not acceptable to the brother and in its view not an appropriate solution. The Secretary of State refused the application.

Balancing exercise, satisfaction and unreasonableness. The judge stated that the critical issue was that the brother was a British citizen who was entitled to remain in the United Kingdom and to be cared for in accordance with the policies and duties (ie, in relation to community care) applying to citizens in general. First, he drew a parallel with another immigration case in which the Secretary of State had not performed the appropriate balancing exercise in comparing immigration issues with the rights of British citizens. Second, there was no evidence supporting the Secretary of state's assertion that he was satisfied that alternative arrangements could be made for the brother. In fact, the government's community care policy, to enable people to remain in their own homes, was consistent in this case with domiciliary care provided by the family rather than residential care. He concluded that the Secretary of State's decision was unreasonable and should be overturned.

R v Secretary of State for Social Security, ex parte Joint Council for the Welfare of Immigrants [1996] 4 All ER 385 (CA). *Unlawful regulations; asylum seekers; housing benefit; social security*

An asylum seekers' case in which the Court of Appeal struck down as invalid regulations which removed rights to social security and housing benefit (and therefore, in effect, housing) – thus making it impossible for asylum seekers to remain in the country whilst having their claims to asylum considered.

The regulations rendered the rights conferred by the primary legislation (Asylum and Immigration Appeals Act 1993) 'nugatory'. They also contemplated 'for some a life so destitute that to my mind no civilised nation can tolerate it. So basic are the human rights here at issue, that it cannot be necessary to resort to the Convention for the Protection of Human Rights and Fundamental Freedoms'. The court referred to an 1803 case, *R v Eastbourne (Inhabitants)* and to the reference in it to the 'the law of humanity, which is anterior to all positive laws' and which obliged that relief be given to prevent poor foreigners from starving.

(However, the government subsequently overturned the effect of this decision by passing the Asylum and Immigration Act 1996 and associated regulations, thus triggering a number of community care cases involving asylum seekers).

R v Secretary of State for Social Services, ex parte Association of Metropolitan Authorities [1986] 1 All ER 164 (QBD). *Consultation; housing benefit regulations*
The Secretary of State had failed in his statutory duty to consult local authorities about housing benefit regulations, notwithstanding the fact that the regulations had been passed as a matter of urgency. Nevertheless, as a matter of the court's discretion, the regulations would not be quashed because they were already in force and being administered by local authorities. However, the judge did grant a declaration that the Secretary of State had failed to comply with the duty.

In any context, 'the essence of consultation is the communication of a genuine invitation to give advice and a genuine consideration of that advice ... it must go without saying that to achieve consultation sufficient information must be supplied by the consulting to the consulted party to enable it to tender helpful advice. Sufficient time must be given by the consulting to the consulted party to enable it to do that, and sufficient time must be available for such advice to be considered by the consulting party. Sufficient, in that context, does not mean ample, but at least enough to enable the relevant purpose to be fulfilled'.

R v Secretary of State for Social Services, West Midlands Regional Health Authority and Birmingham Area Health Authority, ex parte Hincks [1980] 1 BMLR 93 (CA). *Health service; rationing; resources; waiting for orthopaedic treatment*
The case concerned people in Staffordshire who had been on a waiting list for NHS orthopaedic treatment for some years and who sought a declaration that the Secretary of State was not providing a comprehensive health service. The applicants had waited for periods longer than 'medically advisable'; the delay occurred because of a shortage of treatment facilities which was due partly to a decision not to build a new block on the grounds of cost. They claimed that the Secretary of State, regional health authority and area health authority had all breached their statutory duties under both s.1 and s.3 of the NHS Act 1977.

Provision of NHS services within the resources available. One of the judges (Lord Denning) stated that s.3 of the NHS Act 1977 did not impose an absolute duty, since it was inevitably governed by resources. Indeed, the only way it could be read was to supply extra words which did not actually appear in the Act at all. These were as follows (italics added): 'duty to provide throughout England and Wales, to such extent as he considers necessary to meet all reasonable requirements *such as can be provided within the resources available*'. He went on to point out that it 'cannot be supposed that the Secretary of State has to provide all the latest equipment [or] to provide everything that is asked for ... That includes the numerous pills that people take nowadays: it cannot be said that he has to provide all these free for everybody'.

Illusion that the courts will run the NHS. Another of the judges, sounding a cautionary note, added that he felt 'extremely sorry for the particular applicants in this case who have to wait a long time, not being emergency cases, for necessary surgery. They share that misfortune with thousands up and down the country. I only hope that they have not been encouraged to think that these proceedings offered any real prospects that this court could enhance the standards of the National Health Service, because any such encouragement would be based upon manifest illusion'.

R v Sefton Metropolitan Borough Council, ex parte Help the Aged. *Community care; residential accommodation; assessment of means; triggering of duty of provision*

The case was brought, with the assistance of the charity, Help the Aged, on behalf of two people in residential care. The High Court found in favour of the local authority, only to be overturned by the Court of Appeal.

Under challenge was a twofold policy adopted by the Council in relation to the provision of residential accommodation under ss.21 and 26 of the National Assistance Act 1948. The Council accepted that once it had arranged for accommodation under the 1948 Act then the regulations governing the assessment of people's resources applied. These dictated that capital of up to £10,000 was disregarded, capital of between £10,000 and £16,000 triggered a partial contribution by the resident, and capital over £16,000 meant that the resident had to pay the full cost of the accommodation until the capital had reduced to the £16,000 figure.

Sefton found itself in a difficult situation, given that one area within its boundaries, Southport, attracts a large number of elderly, retired people – whilst another area was considerably disadvantaged.

First limb of the policy. The Council maintained that if a person had already arranged, or needed to enter for the first time, residential accommodation – and thus in either case the Council had not so far made any arrangements – then it was under no obligation to make those arrangements simply because the person's capital had fallen below £16,000. Its policy of considering intervention only when the person's capital had fallen below £1,500 was in fact based both on the lack of its own resources and those of the applicant. This was because, in the council's opinion, such a person had enough money to make their own arrangements, and this in turn meant that accommodation was, under s.21 of the 1948 Act, 'otherwise available' to him or her – and therefore the council did not have to make arrangements until the lower figure of £1,500 was reached.

Second limb of the policy. If the Council had originally made arrangements for accommodation for a resident, but the resident's capital subsequently rose above £16,000, then the council would regard itself as having ceased to make arrangements – even though the resident still remained in the same accommodation. This would mean that when the resident's capital sank below £16,000 again, the regulations would not apply, and the council could apply the first limb of its policy to the resident – as it could to a person for whom it had never previously made arrangements.

(High Court): ***R v Sefton Metropolitan Borough Council, ex parte Help the Aged*** [1997] 3 FCR 392. The judge concluded that the first limb of the policy was lawful, though he added one or two qualifications. He decided – on the authority of *R v Gloucestershire CC, ex p Barry* (House of Lords) case – that the authority was permitted to take into account its own resources when 'considering the need of an applicant who seeks to be provided with Part III accommodation under section 21(1)(a) and when deciding whether the need which triggers the duty to provide such accommodation has been established'.

Physical, mental and financial resources. He accepted also that, generally, people possessing resources of their own are able to make their own arrangements – and that therefore the duty of the local authority to make arrangements under s.21 of the National Assistance Act 1948 will not necessarily arise.

However, he did point out that there will be various circumstances in which, even if a person does have adequate financial resources, he might be unable to make his own arrangements: 'Resources should be understood in a broad sense to include not only financial resources but non-financial resources including the applicant's own physical and mental resources, if he lacks the ability to make sensible decisions for himself, whether he is able to call on others for disinterested and prudent advice and timely action. In many cases a sufficiency of means to make private arrangements to receive the needed care and attention is likely to be decisive of whether a duty is owed … However, there will obviously be cases in which, despite the adequacy of his means, someone is unable to call on the kind of advice and assistance of which he stands in need. Circumstances can vary so much from person to person that it would be unprofitable to attempt to define them or to enumerate all the factors which an LA may or should in appropriate cases take into account'.

The judge also stated that, just like under s.2 of the Chronically Sick and Disabled Persons Act 1970, once the authority had identified a need which triggered a duty in a particular case under s.21 of the 1948 Act, it could not 'pray in aid' a lack of resources for failing to perform the duty and provide the accommodation.

The second limb of the policy – at least in respect of the particular applicant – was deemed unlawful, since nothing had been said or done to indicate that at any point the resident had ceased to be provided with accommodation arranged by the authority.

(Court of Appeal): *R v Sefton Metropolitan Borough Council, ex parte Help the Aged* [1997] 3 FCR 573. In overturning the High Court decision and stating that the authority's policy (ie, the first limb) was unlawful, the Court of Appeal emphasised the following points.

Deferring payment for care. The court stated that Sefton was not denying that the applicant needed care and attention, but simply deferring consideration and payment because of a shortage of resources. Indeed, it was clear that the applicant concerned had at no time gone without the care she needed – but this had been provided at her own expense until her capital of £17,500 had fallen to £1,500.

The court ruled that the authority had behaved unlawfully because, under s.21 of the 1948 Act, 'once the authority has come to the conclusion that the person is in need of care and attention, which is not otherwise available to them, then the residential accommodation is to be provided'. The court observed that this departed from the two-stage test applying to s.2 of the Chronically Sick and Disabled Persons Act 1970, which had been identified by the House of Lords in *R Gloucestershire CC, ex p Barry*: ie, first establishing need, and then deciding whether it is 'necessary' to meet it. By contrast, the word 'necessary' was not to be found in s.21 of the 1948 Act. The court further made the point that 'many of the matters dealt with by Section 2(1) [of the Chronically Sick and Disabled Persons Act 1970], while very important to the recipient, are not of the same significance as accommodation itself which is dealt with in Section 21 [of the 1948 Act]'.

Nevertheless, the court was clearly in some difficulty in reconciling its decision in this case, with the *Gloucestershire* decision: 'While I fully accept in accordance with the decision in [*Gloucestershire*], that it is possible to perform a cost-benefit analysis in relation to a person's needs for services listed in s.2(1) [of the Chronically Sick and Disabled Persons Act 1970] and then decide if they are necessary, taking into account the resources of the authority, I find it very much more difficult to perform the same exercise when deciding whether a person in is in need of care and attention. However ... I am compelled to conclude that there is a limited subjective element in making the assessment of whether the ailments of the person concerned do or do not collectively establish a need for care and attention'.

Need for care and attention not otherwise available. The court also needed to deal not just with the implications of whether somebody was in need of 'care and attention', but also whether it was 'otherwise available' to him or her. The local authority, and the High Court in this case, clearly thought that if people had the physical, mental and financial ability to arrange residential accommodation, then care and attention was otherwise available to them (even if their capital was below £16,000). Nevertheless, and without detailed explanation, the Court of Appeal now dismissed the local authority's policy: 'The statutory scheme rests upon the assumption that care and attention is not to be regarded as 'otherwise available' if the person concerned is unable to pay for it according to the means test regime provided for in section 22' (of the 1948 Act) – a statutory scheme which Sefton was totally defeating.

R v Sheffield Health Authority, ex parte Seale [1994] 25 BMLR 1 (QBD). *Health service; rationing; infertility treatment*

A 37-year-old woman attempted to challenge a health authority's decision to deny her infertility treatment because of her age. She claimed that the authority had acted illegally, improperly and irrationally.

The judge ruled that the authority was entitled legally to employ the criterion of age when faced with budgetary restrictions; and was not obliged to provide the service on demand 'regardless of the financial and other concerns of the authority'. The authority had acted on medical advice that in-vitro fertility treatment was generally less effective for women over the age of 35; the judge said that it was not for the courts to impose the appropriate cut-off point.

Furthermore it was not irrational in the sense that individual circumstances were not taken account of: 'Clinically speaking, there is no doubt good sense in such a submission [ie, individual consideration]. And a clinical decision on a case by case basis is clearly desirable and, in cases of critical illness, a necessary approach. However, it is reasonable, or it is at least not ... unreasonable ... of an authority to look at the matter in the context of the financial resources available to it to provide this and the many other services for which it is responsible under the National Health Service legislation. I cannot say that it is absurd for this authority, acting on advice that the efficacy of this treatment decreases with age and that it is generally less effective after the age of 35, to take that as an appropriate criterion when balancing the need for such a provision against its ability to provide it and all the other services imposed upon it by the legislation'.

R v Social Fund Inspector, ex parte Connick [1994] COD 75 (QBD). *Social Fund; health service; rationing; incontinence pads; cost-shunting*
On the basis that incontinence pads were medical items provided by the NHS, a Social Fund officer had denied a 26-week supply of pads to a woman who was incontinent, arthritic and had asthma. The relevant health authority did provide free incontinence pads in principle, but in practice its criteria were so stringent – regular double incontinence or terminal illness – that the woman did not qualify.

The judge found that the decision of the Social Fund officer, that the pads were medical items and thus excluded by the Social Fund rules, was wrong. She had asked whether the pads were needed for a medical problem and were thus necessarily a medical item. However, it was 'quite clear that a handkerchief might not be needed, but for a severe attack of a runny nose in a heavy cold. It is quite clear that a bowl might not be needed unless there was a medical problem of a severe bout of vomiting but nobody would think of those articles, the handkerchief or the bowl, as medical items'.

R v Social Fund Inspector, ex parte Taylor [1998] COD 152 (QBD). *Social Fund; assessment of need preceding decision about assistance*
A case in which the court ruled that assessment of a person's need for assistance from the Social Fund was separate – a distinct aspect of the overall exercise – from consideration of the impact on the budget of meeting the need. The circumstances were distinguished from those considered in *R v Gloucestershire CC, ex p Barry* in relation to the Chronically Sick and Disabled Persons Act 1970. In that Act, resources were not mentioned at all; whereas the Social Fund legislation expressly did refer to resources, but not in relation to assessing need, only in respect of meeting it.

R v Somerset County Council, ex parte Harcombe [1997] 96 LGR 444 (QBD) (and see article in: *The Times*, 29 April 1997). *Community care; residential accommodation; charging rules; taking account of a person's home*
This case was about the application of the charging rules for residential accommodation, and in particular about the power of the local authority to disregard the value of the home of a person who had gone into residential care.

Looking after a parent. The son of the woman in question gave up his job in Australia to return to England to look after her; she was suffering from Parkinson's disease and had been forced to go into residential care. On his arrival, she returned to her own home, but suffered a series of strokes and had to return to residential care.

Under the regulations governing the assessment of people's means in relation to payment for residential accommodation, the local authority had a power to disregard the value of the woman's home (see p.305). The authority did not do this and, though it did not force the son to sell the house, it created a charge of £500 a month on it. In April 1997, the mother died with a bill of £25,000 outstanding – and interest began to accrue from date of death.

Reasonable decision in all the circumstances. The judge decided that 'in all the circumstances of the case it was not reasonable to disregard the value of the house'. One factor – though not the only one – in the overall decision was that the son had returned to Australia after his mother had gone into residential care for the second time, in order to attempt to resume his career. This meant that on his second return to England, occupation of the house had become attributable not to the need to look after his mother, but to the decision to give up the job and accommodation in Australia. Overall, the judge was satisfied that the decision had been taken by the local authority's officer within the ambit of the regulations, was 'properly based on conclusions of fact to which he was entitled to come on the material which he had to consider', and 'was based on full and proper assessment of all the facts and circumstances of the case'.

R v Southwark London Borough Council, ex parte Melak [1996] 29 HLR 223 (QBD). *Rigid policies; fettering of discretion; built-in exceptions to a policy; housing allocation*
A housing allocation case illustrating a fettering of the authority's discretion by a rigid policy about rent arrears and the inadequacy of 'built-in' exceptions to a policy.

The court found that by operating the policy inflexibly, the authority was unable to take account of all relevant considerations in the individual case before coming to a decision. The authority argued that it was not acting inflexibly because part of its policy provided that 'some people in a priority category' would be an exception to the arrears rule. However, this argument was flawed because this exception was 'part of the rule' and did not indicate whether the non-priority category who were in rent arrears would have their applications dealt with on their merits.

The court was further unimpressed by a letter written to the applicant offering to reconsider the application – because it had been written only after the service of judicial review proceedings. Up to that point, its response to the original judicial review application had been a 'deafening silence'. The letter could not save the policy; it had been rigidly applied and the decision was therefore unlawful.

R v Staffordshire County Council, ex parte Farley [1997] 7 CL 572 (QBD). *Community care; reassessment; night sitter services; irrationality; Chronically Sick and Disabled Persons Act 1970,s.2*
The case concerned an 86-year old woman who had a reassessment which resulted in an altered care plan and the loss of the night-sitting service which had previously been provided. Pending a full hearing of the judicial review case, an interim injunction was sought restoring the original care package. The local authority argued also that if such an order were made, it should be on condition that the applicant reimburse the costs of such interim provision were she were eventually to lose the case.

Function of the service. The woman suffered from severe arthritis and had poor mobility and a very weak bladder, which meant that she needed assistance from chair or bed to commode or toilet throughout the day and night. The night-sitting service under the original care plan involved a person in attendance between 10pm and 7am to help with undressing, ensure that she was properly provided for and able to visit the toilet frequently during the night. The revised care plan involved only a person in attendance between 10pm and 10.30 pm, to undress the woman, make her a drink and see that she was comfortable for the night.

Irrational decision? The judge noted that nothing in the new care plan suggested a change either in the woman's needs or in any other relevant circumstances. Thus, 'there is a very strong case here in support of the applicant's submission that the respondent's apparent decision, that she no longer has an identified need for night care services appears to have been based on no evidence whatsoever and is, therefore, irrational or unreasonable … In those circumstances, I have no hesitation in coming to the conclusion that an interim injunction would … be appropriate in these proceedings for judicial review'.

Undertaking to pay costs? The judge decided that the woman should not have to give an undertaking to pay the cost of the interim care should she eventually lose the case at the full hearing. This was for the following reasons. First she was 'indisputably very infirm' and attempts by her to go to the toilet would result in physical problems, danger and possible extreme physical discomfort: to 'expose her to that sort of indignity and risk would be, in my judgment, inhumane to say the very least'. Second, the woman had no means to pay. Third, her family had done all it could but could no longer meet further costs. Fourth, if the injunction were not granted, the woman would undoubtedly lose her night sitting service. Finally, the amount of money involved, over the four weeks before the full hearing, would amount to about £800 – a 'trivial' amount of money, compared to the degree of risk the woman would be exposed to.

R v Sunderland City Council, ex parte Redezeus [1994] 27 HLR 477 (QBD). *Taking account of irrelevant factors; housing renovation grants*
The case concerned the award of renovation grants under the Local Government Housing Act 1989. The relevant parts (now superseded by the Housing Grants, Construction and Regeneration Act 1996) of the Act clearly listed the specific and exclusive factors authorities should take into account when deciding how much grant to give. Nevertheless, the authority had added its own rule that effectively limited the maximum grant payable to 20 per cent of the total cost of the works. The judge found nothing in the Act which gave the Council a discretion 'to impose some arbitrary limit on the amount payable or to take account of financial resources or their absence.' Express language in the legislation would have been required to sanction such a policy.

Rose v Bouchet (100/98, Sheriff's Court, Edinburgh, August 1998). *Disability Discrimination Act 1995; provision of goods and services*
A blind person with a guide dog was refused, by the landlord, the let of a week's accommodation during the Edinburgh festival. The reason given was the absence of a rail on steps up to the flat. The court held that the less favourable treatment fell into one of the prescribed categories of justification – ie, health and safety – and that it was reasonable in all the circumstances for the landlord to hold that opinion. (The case is due to be appealed some time in 1999).

R v Sutton London Borough Council, ex parte Tucker [1998] CCLR 251 (QBD). *Community care; delay in deciding about services; breach of statutory duty; care plans; suitability of judicial review; NHS and Community Care Act 1990, s.47*
A case illustrating the failure of an authority a) to perform the duty of deciding what services were called for under s.47 of the NHS and Community Care Act 1990; and b) to formulate a lawful care plan. It is also an example of a dispute, held by the court, to be suitable for resolution via judicial review, rather than by means of an alternative remedy such as the local authority complaints procedure or the Secretary of State's default powers.

Background. It concerned a 32-year old woman with learning disabilities, sensory impairments, consequent social and communication difficulties and various physical and mental health needs. She had profound bilateral deafness and congenital nystagmus and myopia.

In November 1993 she was placed in NHS premises for assessment; by 13th April 1994 she had received an assessment and was ready for discharge by July 1994. At the time of the hearing in 1996 she was still resident at the NHS premises, even though they had only ever been intended as an interim measure and had since become an emergency respite centre, making them even more unsuitable. Some disagreement had arisen between the woman's mother and the local authority: she favoured the recommendation of a consultant from SENSE (National Deaf, Blind and Rubella Association), which recommended a specialist, local placement. The authority had decided that this placement – which would mean setting up a two-person residential unit – was not viable.

Alleged lack of a care plan. It was argued not only that the authority had failed to come to a decision about service provision, but had also not produced an adequate care plan as envisaged by community care guidance. For example, there was no stated overall objective in terms of long-term obligations, no criteria for measurement of any objectives, no costings, no considerations of long-term options for residential care, no recorded points of difference between the parties, no reference to a date for review.

Breach of guidance and statutory duty. The judge accepted the argument that the authority had no lawful care plan and that the situation was similar to that which occurred in *R v Islington LBC, ex p Rixon*. He found a clear breach of two paragraphs of the policy guidance in particular: 3.24 (care plans and their objectives) and 3.41 (hospital discharge, and the undesirability of a person remaining in hospital when care could be provided more appropriately elsewhere). He also found the authority to be in breach of its statutory duty under s.47(1)(b) of the 1990 Act, since it had 'still not made the decision which is called for by that section'. The authority had 'used its undoubted discretion to make short term and interim decisions in relation to the care of the applicant', but such discretion could not 'replace the duty to make a service provision decision as to the long term future of the applicant'. It had failed both to make a decision about the services she needed or to provide them.

Suitability of judicial review. Rejecting the authority's argument that even if it had breached its duty, judicial review was not the appropriate remedy, the judge explained that the case involved consideration of a 'discrete point of law', for which neither the Secretary of State's default powers, nor the local authority complaints procedure were adequate remedies. For example, the latter would have involved the woman's mother arguing points of law before a non-qualified body: that would not have been 'convenient, expeditious or effective'. Judicial review was therefore appropriate.

R v Swansea City and County Council, ex parte Littler, R v St Edmundsbury Borough Council, ex parte Sandys [1998], TLR 9 September 1998 (CA). *Welfare services; housing benefit*

The Court of Appeal confirmed a decision of the High Court that housing benefit was not payable for service charges which did not relate closely to the provision of physically suitable and therefore adequate accommodation. The service charges thus excluded from eligibility for payment, in the two particular cases before the court, were a) counselling by the landlady for her tenant with a high level of learning disability; and b) supervision in relation to food handling and behaviour.

R v Tower Hamlets London Borough Council, ex p B [1993] 2 FLR 605 (QBD). *Local authority asking itself for help; homelessness and social services; Children Act 1989, s.27*

One of the issues in this case was the refusal, by the local authority housing department following a request from the social services department of the same authority, to rehouse a family – on the grounds that the single parent involved was intentionally homeless. The request had been made under s.27 of the Children Act 1989 which empowers a social services authority to ask 'any authority or other person' [ie, another social services, education, housing or health authority] for help, and places a duty on the requested authority to comply with the request if it is compatible with its statutory or other duties. The parent challenged the decision to turn down the request.

The court found that s.27 could not be interpreted as applying to a request from one department to another department *within the same local authority*. It could only apply as between different authorities; any other interpretation would 'offend the plain and natural meaning of the words used in the section'.

R v Tower Hamlets London Borough Council, ex parte Mohib Ali [1993] 25 HLR 218 (QBD). *Consistency of policy within a local authority; housing allocation*

A housing authority operated 'standard lettings criteria' for rehousing and homelessness applications. It then introduced 'amended lettings criteria' which, in order to avoid delays, allowed the allocation to families of smaller properties than would have been permitted under the standard criteria.

Following concern expressed about the policy by the Commission for Racial Equality, a number of safeguards were introduced, including monitoring by panel members, a right of appeal, and automatic entry on the transfer list for people who were obliged to accept accommodation that did not conform to the standard criteria. However, these safeguards were subsequently abandoned. In addition, the responsibility for allocation of housing was devolved to seven neighbourhoods, within which the operation of the amended criteria was not mandatory; this led to inconsistency and to a significantly higher proportion of homeless Asian families than white families being housed under the amended criteria.

The court found no breach of the Race Relations Act 1976, but concluded that 'the removal of those safeguards, together with the apparently arbitrary and random way in which the ALC [amended lettings criteria] operate in different neighbourhoods, without any proffered justification, demonstrates unfairness and irrationality requiring intervention by the court'.

R v Tower Hamlets London Borough Council, ex parte Bradford [1997] 29 HLR 756 (QBD). *Children in need; scope of assessment; community care; NHS and Community Care Act 1990, s.47; Carers (Recognition and Services) Act 1995; Chronically Sick and Disabled Persons Act 1970, s.2; Children Act 1989, s.17*
A child care and housing case illustrating that even when there is only a somewhat vague and general duty to provide for people's needs, local authorities should beware of limiting the scope of assessment.

Disabled parent, child in need, harassment. It concerned a family with various problems. The mother was severely disabled, suffering from epilepsy (leading to double incontinence) and arthritis. The family was subject to very considerable harassment in the area. This included bullying of the 11-year old son, abusive telephone calls, attempted arson and the daubing of phlegm and faeces over the front door and car.

Request for rehousing, community care and child care assessment. The family applied for rehousing and also requested comprehensive assessment under the NHS and Community Care Act 1990, the Chronically Sick and Disabled Persons Act 1970, and the Children Act 1989. The request for rehousing was turned down on the grounds that the family had been assessed as having no points for medical priority. However, it was clear that the child was a child in need under the Children Act 1989, since he was experiencing a number of problems including the bullying, and non-attendance at school.

Unlawful limitation of scope of assessment under the Children Act 1989. The essential point before the court was whether, in addition to considering rehousing under housing legislation (then the Housing Act 1985), the local authority should have assessed also the possibility of rehousing the family under s.17 of the Children Act 1989 – which placed a general duty on the authority to safeguard and promote the welfare of children in need. The local authority believed that it could not lawfully provide accommodation under s.17 – since s.20 of the Act (which did not apply in this situation) explicitly referred to the provision of accommodation, whilst s.17 did not.

The judge found that 'those responsible for the assessment approached it with a fundamental misunderstanding of their powers in relation to rehousing under the Children Act 1989 ... the assessment that was made was fundamentally flawed and that whilst ... it was done without any deliberate or improper intent, the undertaking given [previously] to the Court to assess [the child's] needs under section 17 has not been fully and properly complied with'.

R v Tower Hamlets London Borough Council, ex parte Khatun [1994] 27 HLR 465 (CA). *Assessment; interview; resources; homelessness; Housing Act 1985*
A homelessness case, in which, at first instance, the court had agreed that an interview to determine the applicant's eligibility was inherently flawed because the interviewer was a council officer aware of the housing shortage and the finite resources of the council. Therefore, the council should have arranged for an advisor or counsellor to be present at the interview.

The Court of Appeal disagreed, stating that it was for 'the local authority and not the courts to determine how the necessary inquiries are made'. The court could only intervene if there was reason to believe that the style of questioning inhibited the applicant from putting forward his or her case together with relevant facts – for instance, if there was a bullying interviewer.

R v Tower Hamlets London Borough Council, ex parte Spencer [1995] 29 HLR 64 (QBD). *Assessment; taking account of relevant evidence; irrationality; housing allocation*
The local authority was held by the court to have acted procedurally unfairly by relying on an original medical assessment, but not taking into account subsequent evidence from an occupational therapist and a hospital consultant. In addition, having told the applicant that it would obtain an updated medical assessment, the au-

thority failed to do so. Given that the applicant's condition had improved (as borne out by the occupational therapist and consultant), the court held that it was irrational for the authority to conclude that premises, adapted for a much higher level of disability than that of the applicant, were suitable for her.

Trustees of the Dennis Rye Pension Fund v Sheffield City Council [1997] 30 HLR 645 (CA). *Duty to pay repair grant; grant not paid; private law action; whether abuse of process*
The local authority served the plaintiffs with repair notices, requiring them to carry out works to a number of houses. The plaintiffs applied for mandatory grants. The applications were approved. The local authority refused to pay because of a dispute about whether the grant conditions had been fulfilled in the carrying out of the works. The plaintiffs issued private law proceedings in the county court for the amount of the unpaid grant. The local authority, relying heavily on *O'Rourke v Camden LBC*, argued that the action should be struck out as an abuse of process – since any legal proceedings should have been by way of public law (ie, judicial review).

The Court of Appeal ruled that there was no reason why the plaintiffs could not bring such an action to recover the amount of grant as an ordinary debt. It was true that normally, when dealing with grant applications, a local authority would be performing a public law function which precludes the existence of private law rights – for example, the refusal to approve a grant. However, following the case of *Roy v Kensington and Chelsea Family Practitioner Committee* [1992] 1 AC 624 (HL), the court held that the present case was one, 'where the plaintiff's relationship with a public body whether statutory or contractual would confer on him conditional rights to payment so that the bringing of ordinary actions to enforce those rights was not in itself an abuse of process'. The authority could not withold payment of the grant if the works were carried out to a good and workmanlike in accordance with a specified standard. It was for the authority to specify a reasonable standard (which would be challengeable only in judicial review); but a dispute about its refusal to express satisfaction with the work would require an examination of factual issues, which would be more appropriately dealt with in ordinary, private law proceedings than in judicial review.

R v Waltham Forest, ex parte Vale [1985] TLR 25 February 1985 (QBD). *Community care; residential accommodation; ordinary residence*
An ordinary residence case about which local authority had responsibility for providing residential accommodation under s.21 of the National Assistance Act 1948.

The person concerned was 28 years old and mentally handicapped from birth. In 1961 she had moved to Ireland with her parents where she lived in residential homes. Her parents returned to England in 1978 to live in Waltham Forest; she returned in 1984 and lived for one month with her parents before being placed in a home in Buckinghamshire. Waltham Forest now denied financial responsibility for the placement on the grounds that she had been ordinarily resident in Ireland and that the stay with her parents had been merely temporary.

The judge disagreed. First, the woman concerned was so mentally handicapped that she was totally dependent on her parents and was in the same position as a small child. Concepts such as 'voluntarily adopted residence' or 'settled purpose' – used in *Shah v Barnet LBC* – were irrelevant to the case. Therefore, the woman's ordinary residence was that of her parents – which was not her 'real home' (a concept rejected in the *Shah v Barnet LBC* case) but her 'base'. Should he have been mistaken in this view, the judge went on to state that in any case the one month stay with her parents was sufficient to constitute ordinary residence – since the *Shah* case made clear that ordinary residence could be of short duration. Thus, responsibility lay with Waltham Forest and not Buckinghamshire.

R v Wandsworth London Borough Council, ex parte Beckwith [1996] 1 FCR 504 (HL). *Community care; transfer or closure of residential homes*
This case concerned the provision of residential care by a local authority, and the legal correctness of Department of Health guidance. At issue was whether certain wording in s.26 of the National Assistance Act 1948 meant that a local authority was not obliged itself to make any direct provision of residential accommodation

under s.21 of the Act. In other words, could it make arrangements for provision entirely with the independent sector and so transfer or close all its own residential homes? The court ruled that it could, and that Department of Health guidance on the matter, advising the opposite (in LAC(93)10), was 'entitled to respect' but was 'simply wrong'.

R v Wandsworth London Borough Council, ex parte Beckwith (no.2) [1995] 159 LGRevR 929 (QBD) *Community care; residential homes; closure; consultation*

An issue in the main *Beckwith* case (see immediately above), but dealt with separately in the law courts, was whether consultation about the closure of the authority's residential homes had been adequate (see immediately above). The court's ruling that it had not been, reinforced an earlier judgment *R v Devon CC, ex P Baker*) about the need for proper consultation with residents. It also went a little further, because the judge held that in the circumstances, 'proper consultation' should have been extended not only to the residents of the particular home in issue (George Potter House) – but also to those 'properly interested at the Council's other homes'.

R v Wandsworth Borough Council, ex parte M [1998] ELR 424 (QBD). *Competence of local authority staff; providing agreed services; special education*

The statement of special educational needs of an autistic child had been amended according to an order from the Special Educational Needs Tribunal – and now specified that he should receive provision from teachers who were experienced in teaching pupils with significant learning difficulties and autism/communication disorders. A supply teacher was taken on through an agency; the question for the court was whether any reasonable education authority could have regarded her as experienced.

The court expressed its reluctance to intervene except when a decision appeared irrational. However, in this case, the judge found that the local authority could not reasonably have characterised the teacher as 'experienced'; since although she undoubtedly had 'some experience' of teaching autistic children, nevertheless "experienced' signifies having a real and significant fund of experience and not merely having encountered in practice a particular subject or topic. In relation to the teaching of children with autistic and communication disorders it must mean having a substantial track record of teaching and working with such children'.

Thus the authority was in breach of its duty to arrange the special educational provision specified in the statement of need.

R v Warwickshire Council, ex parte Collymore [1995] ELR 217 (QBD). *Rigid policies; fettering discretion; appeals procedure; educational grants*

The case concerned discretionary grants which the education authority had a power, but not a duty, to award. The authority operated a policy of refusing all awards, but then of inviting appeals when exceptional circumstances were being claimed. On the face of it this saved the policy from being rigid and fettering the discretion of the authority. However, in practice, of 300 appeals made over a period of 3 years, all had been rejected. The judge could only conclude that the policy had been implemented 'far too rigidly', albeit in good faith. In addition, he also doubted, though did not strike down, the aspect of the authority's policy which stated that only in the 'most extraordinary circumstances' would an exception be made. This came very close to being a blanket policy, which would have been unlawful.

R v Westminster City Council and Others, ex parte A and Others. *Community care; residential accommodation; asylum seekers; need of care and attention*

Four asylum seekers – from Iraq, Rumania, Algeria and China – sought judicial review of the refusal of three London Boroughs (Westminster, Hammersmith & Fulham, Lambeth) to provide assistance in the form of residential accommodation under s.21 of the National Assistance Act 1948. The applicants had turned to the social services departments of the local authorities because, under the Asylum and Immigration Act 1996, they were ineligible for social security benefits or housing, although they were still permitted (under the Asylum and Immigration Appeals Act 1993) to remain in the United Kingdom, pending a decision on their claim to asylum.

The applicants were not allowed to work during the first six months of their stay whilst their applications were being considered. They had no money of their own, no friends to approach for assistance and had been sleeping rough in the areas of the councils concerned. The councils denied that they could lawfully provide residential accommodation under s.21 of the 1948 Act, since the need of the applicants was not 'care and attention', but money – something not covered by the section.

(High Court): *R v Westminster City Council and Others, ex parte A and Others* [1997] 1 CCLR 69 (QBD). The judge sympathised with the justification by the councils of their narrow interpretation of s.21(1) given financial restraints, and 'on the basis that they will be quite unable to cope with those who clearly fell within its terms if they also have a duty to those who are in difficulties because of lack of money but are otherwise healthy and not in need of care and attention. I have great sympathy with them, but financial constraints and the problems which will be created if the duty is wider than was believed are irrelevant to the proper construction of the section'.

After analysis of the history of the National Assistance Act 1948, the judge concluded that s.21 – referring to people who were in need of care and attention through age, illness, disability or any other circumstances – 'should be available as a safety net for those unable to fend for themselves and who are therefore in need of care and attention'.

Any other circumstances and care and attention. The term 'any other circumstances' did not necessarily have to be of a kind with age or infirmity (the original wording of s.21 before being amended to age, illness or disability): it was freestanding. But, the judge had reasoned, even if it did have to be of a kind, the term 'an inability to fend for himself' was surely the broad genus, being consequent not only on the situation of the asylum seekers, but also somebody who was aged or ill – 'physical conditions beyond the control of the individual', producing the need for care and attention.

Furthermore, 'in ordinary English usage someone who is unable to provide for himself the basic necessities of life can properly be said to be in need of care and attention. He needs at least shelter, warmth and food. It is said that these applicants need only money, not care and attention. The point is that they cannot get money and without it they cannot fend for themselves. If they have access to money, they do not need care and attention. Without such access, they do'. The provision was 'of last resort'. Local authorities were entitled to be sure that there was 'truly no other source of assistance available'.

Fundamental human rights. The judge accepted the argument that when Parliament passed the 1996 Act, it knew that it was passing a draconian measure, given the huge costs of asylum seekers, some 75 per cent of whom were thought not to be genuine (and to be mere economic migrants). However, he thought that had Parliament intended to deny all assistance to asylum seekers, it 'could have made clear beyond doubt that that was what it was doing'; whereas in fact the 1996 Act did not refer to s.21 of the 1948 Act. He referred to the 'law of humanity' identified in an 1803 case *(R v Inhabitants of Eastbourne* 4 East 103) by the Lord Chief Justice who said: 'As to there being no obligation for maintaining poor foreigners before the statutes ascertaining the different methods of acquiring settlements, the law of humanity, which is anterior to all positive laws, obliges us to afford them relief, to save them from starving'.

The judge equated this law of humanity with, in modern parlance, the fundamental right to human life. He could not accept that Parliament had really intended that an asylum seeker should be 'left destitute, starving and at risk of grave illness and even death because he could find no-one to provide him with the bare necessities of life'. If Parliament had intended this, then 'it would almost certainly put itself in breach of the European Convention on Human Rights and of the Geneva Convention and that is another reason why I find it unlikely that the safety net has been removed'.

(Court of Appeal): *R v Westminster City Council and Others, ex parte A and Others* [1997] 30 HLR 10 (reported as *R v Hammersmith and Fulham LBC, ex p M*). The Court of Appeal upheld the High Court's decision, though slightly narrowed the 'safety net' aspect of that court's judgment. The appeal court recognised that the 'plight of asylum seekers who are in the position of the respondents obviously can and should provoke deep sympathy. Their plight is indeed horrendous ... The 1948 Act brought to an end 350 years of the Poor Law ... We emphasise the significance of the Act because it is a prime example of an Act which is 'always speaking', and so should be construed on a construction which continuously updates its wording to allow for changes since the Act was initially framed' (for this last point, the court drew on a classic legal work, Bennion's *Statutory Interpretation*).

The court went on to find that, under s.21 of the 1948 Act, the applicants might be in need of care and attention, not through age, illness or disability, but owing to other circumstances. The meaning of this later term, 'other circumstances', was not necessarily limited by the words (age, illness, disability) preceding it. However, even if it did have such a limited meaning, it was clear that the circumstances of the asylum seekers could result in illness or disability, and thus trigger eligibility for assistance. The circumstances were a combination of 'lack of food and accommodation ... their inability to speak the language, their ignorance of Britain and the fact that they had been subject to the stress of coming to this country in circumstances which at least involved their contending to be refugees'.

The court stressed the combination of these circumstances, because the Act was not a 'safety net provision on which anyone who is short of money and/or short of accommodation can rely'. However, those circumstances meant that 'authorities can anticipate the deterioration which would otherwise take place in the asylum seekers' condition by providing assistance under the section. They do not need to wait until the health of the asylum seeker has been damaged'.

Temporary accommodation and the prevention of illness. The court concluded that the asylum seekers came within the Secretary of State's directions and approvals made under s.21 of the National Assistance Act 1948; in particular the direction 'to provide temporary accommodation for persons in urgent need thereof in circumstances where the need for that accommodation could not reasonably have been foreseen'; and the approval to arrange accommodation for the prevention of illness (see p.253 of this book).

R v Westminster City Council, ex parte Ermakov [1995] 28 HLR 819 (CA). *Retrospective reasoning; homelessness; Housing Act 1985*
A homelessness case in which the local authority attempted, retrospectively and by means of an affidavit in judicial proceedings, to supplement its reasons for an adverse decision. The court stated that the courts 'can and, in appropriate cases, should admit evidence to elucidate or, exceptionally, correct or add to reasons; but should ... be very cautious about doing so. I have in mind cases where, for example, an error has been made in transcription or expression, or a word or words inadvertently omitted, or where the language used may be in some way lacking in clarity ... Certainly there seems to me to be no warrant for receiving, and relying on as validating the decision, evidence – as in this case – which indicates that the real reasons were wholly different from the stated reasons...'.

R v Westminster City Council, ex parte P [1998], TLR 31 March 1998 (CA). *Community care; residential accommodation; choice of accommodation; asylum seekers; suitability of judicial review*
A case involving asylum seekers and ostensibly about a) whether they had a right to be informed about their entitlement to choose their preferred accommodation (subject to certain limitations set out in directions issued by the Secretary of State: see p.253) provided under s.21 of the National Assistance Act 1948; and b) whether local authorities were under a duty actively to find accommodation for asylum seekers in London. The local authority claimed that the dispute was simply a question of fact, namely whether there was alternative accommodation in London; it believed not, and so had decided to house 17 Albanian asylum seekers on the east coast.

The court ruled first that it would be convenient, expeditious and effective for an application to the Secretary of State to be made in respect of use of the default powers under s.7D of the Local Authority Social Services Act 1970 (see p.???). Second, at issue was the proper construction and application of the Secretary of State's directions and guidance. Third, a government review of the treatment of asylum seekers was pending –

and another asylum seeker case had been delayed so as to avoid the possibility of an adverse judgment, which would deprive asylum seekers of all assistance from social services departments before alternative arrangements were available.

The court also accepted that the real dispute was factual (rather than legal) as to whether or not there was accommodation available in London; such a question could not be solved by deciding whether or not the local authority was under a duty to do its best to find accommodation in London.

R v Wigan Metroplitan Borough Council, ex parte Tammadge [1998] 1 CCLR 581 (QBD). Community care need for accommodation; assessment of need; once decision taken duty must be performed; NHS and Community Care Act 1990, s.47; National Assistance Act 1948, s.21; Children Act 1989, s.17

The applicant was the mother of three teenage boys who were severely mentally handicapped and had behavioural problems – and of a 10-year-old daughter. By 1994, various health and social care professionals had expressed the opinion that larger accommodation was required. A planning meeting in 1995 of all the relevant departments and agencies agreed unanimously that assistance from the housing department was of prime importance. However, no such accommodation could be found; and social services refused to pay the cost of converting and adapting two smaller properties – although it accepted that, in principle, the provision of 'normal' or 'bare' accommodation could, in some circumstances, amount to a community care service under s.21 of the National Assistance Act 1948 (see: R v Bristol CC, ex p Penfold).

Complaints review panel: apparent acceptance of recommendations. A complaint was made, which progressed to the review panel stage. The panel concluded that the social services department had discharged its functions toward the applicant, but that nevertheless the applicant needed larger accommodation and that the director of social services should investigate the possibility of ascertaining and adapting a suitable property. Following this recommendation, the director wrote to the applicant stating that she would reconsider; a social services officer then visited the applicant on 22nd October 1996 and made it clear that the social services department had accepted the review panel's findings and recommendations.

Backtracking. Following another meeting of the relevant departments and agencies, a report was prepared; it concluded that there were considerable resource implications (about £7,000 plus professional fees, for converting two properties) warranting a further meeting of senior officers. This subsequent meeting decided not to commit the authority to the purchase or conversion of accommodation, but to provide continuing support for the family in the present accommodation.

Taking account of resources in assessing need. The court rejected the applicant's argument that resources could not be taken account of when assessing need under s.21 of the National Assistance Act 1948; the judge felt bound by R v Sefton MBC, ex p Help the Aged, in which the Court of Appeal had concluded that resources could, to a limited extent, be taken into account.

Unlawfulness of retracting statutory decision to meet need. However, the judge found against the authority on the following ground. The review panel's finding as to the need for larger accommodation was 'perfectly clear ... Moreover, that conclusion is entirely in keeping with views of Wigan's own professional qualified staff and advisers, as expressed both before and after the hearing ... I am therefore satisfied that, by a date no later than 22 October 1996 (when it was acknowledged that Wigan had accepted the ... [review panel finding]), Mrs Tammadge's need for larger accommodation was established ... As a result, from that date Wigan have been obliged to make provision of such accommodation ... Once the duty had arisen in this way, it was not lawful of Wigan to refuse to perform that duty because of a shortage of or limits upon its financial resources or for any of the other reasons expressed...'.

Specific court order to provide a service within a specified time. The court ordered that Wigan's decision be quashed and that it now provide the accommodation in line with the review panel's recommendations and a subsequent report produced by a social services manager. The court went into further detail by specifying not only a three-month period of consultation within which to identify a property and the relevant requirements, but also that the property should be made available within three months of being identified.

Re J (a Minor) (Wardship: medical treatment) [1992] 4 All ER 614 (CA). *Health service; non-intervention by the courts; clinical decisions*

An NHS case, illustrating the reluctance of the courts to interfere with clinical decisions made by doctors. It concerned the giving of artificial ventilation and intensive therapy to a profoundly disabled 16-month-old child. The High Court had made an order to the effect that the health authority must provide such treatment.

The Court of Appeal overturned the decision, stating that it would not order a doctor to treat a patient against the doctor's will. Further, the order had been made against the health authority, but the authority could scarcely comply with it, since it had 'no power, contractual or otherwise, to require doctors to act in a way which they do not regard as medically appropriate. If it could comply, it would be obliged to accord to this baby a priority over other patients to whom the health authority owes the same duties, but about whose interests the court is ignorant'.

Re Findlay [1985] 1 AC 318 (HL). *Changing policies; legitimate expectation; necessity of having a policy; prisoners; parole*

A change of policy meant that some prisoners had lost their expectation of parole. Amongst various matters considered, the House of Lords had 'difficulty in understanding how a Secretary of State could properly manage the complexities of his statutory duty without a policy' – and distanced itself, though did not overrule, the decision in the child care case of *Attorney General ex rel Tilley v Wandsworth LBC*. (In that case, the Court of Appeal had stated that the duty in question meant that every case had to be considered individually and precluded the application of a policy, even one hedged around with exceptions).

The court considered the lawfulness of a policy adopted by the Secretary of State which excluded consideration of prisoners in specified classes, except where there were exceptional circumstances or compelling reasons. The court found nothing wrong with such a policy – even though it meant there was an inevitable and intended presumption against parole being granted. As to the legitimate expectation of two of the prisoners, this was, at most, that their cases would be examined individually under whatever policy was in operation. Were it to be otherwise, it would so restrict the unfettered discretion of the Secretary of State as to hamper or even prevent changes in policy.

Re L [1994] ELR 16 (CA). *Matching provision of services with assessment of need; special education*

A case concerning the extent to which a statement of special educational needs and its implementation met the needs of a child. At one point the court considered the relationship between part 2 of a statement dealing with the identification of needs, with part 3 covering the provision to meet those needs. (Compare, in community care, the identification of needs which will be met by a local authority, with the care plan it draws up of services to be provided).

The court stated, referring to a previous case, that it was not a question of 'inviting a line by line examination of the parts in order to gauge the degree of correspondence between them. Inelegant or even imperfect matching, whether or not the product of poor draftsmanship, would not be enough. Only if there were a clear failure to make provision for a significant need would the court be likely to conclude that there was such a dereliction of duty by a local education authority' as to call for some form of intervention.

Re S [1995] 1 FLR 1075 (CA). *Mental capacity; best interests*

A dispute between the family of a man who had become unable to express his preference following a severe stroke, and the woman with whom he had set up home – as to where he was to be cared for and by whom. The court accepted that the issue as to where the patient's best interests lay was a matter it could deal with.

The family had tried to remove the man from a hospital in England and to take him back to Norway; the woman had obtained an interim injunction preventing this. The family claimed that in the absence of a legal relationship between the man and woman, the court had no jurisdiction to grant such relief. The Court of Appeal now found, in the light of the evidence relating to the relationship between the man and woman, that the court anyway did have jurisdiction; but that also, the woman could have demonstrated a legal right had it been necessary for her to do so, which it was not.

Re T (Accommodation of Child by Local Authority) [1995] 1 FCR 517 (QBD). *General duties; children; social services; Children Act 1989*
A child care case illustrating how the courts are apt to regard general duties as of somewhat doubtful force. It concerned a local authority's refusal to consider providing accommodation for a child under s.20 of the Children Act 1989 (specific duty to each individual child). One of the considerations in reaching this decision related to the services provided in the past under s.17 of the Act (containing the 'general duty' to safeguard and promote the welfare of children in need). However, the judge found this to be an error, because the 'director of social services could not, at the time when he made the decision, by any means be sure how his local authority would exercise their powers under s.17 in the future ... because those powers and duties are discretionary in nature, it does not seem to me that they can amount to factors to which much weight should be attributed for the purpose of s.20(3)'.

Richardson v Solihull [1998] ELR 319 (CA). *Specificity of assessment of need; special education*
An education case concerning, amongst other matters, the specificity to be contained in children's statements of special educational needs (compare questions of specificity of need and services to be provided in community care assessments and care plans). The Court of Appeal held that whilst a particular school could be named in the statement, it was not implicit in the Education Act 1996 (s.324) that the school be named in every case.

Shah v Barnet London Borough Council [1983] 2 AC 309 (HL). *Ordinary residence; education*
An education case about ordinary residence – an issue which regularly triggers disputes in the community care context. It concerned the application, under s.1 of the Education Act 1962, for educational awards by several students who had entered the United Kingdom at least three years previously. The education authorities involved claimed that the students had failed to establish that they were ordinarily resident within the areas of the authorities.

The House of Lords ruled in favour of the students. Lord Scarman stated that unless 'therefore, it can be shown that the statutory framework or the legal context in which the words are used requires a different meaning, I unhesitatingly subscribe to the view that 'ordinarily resident' refers to a man's abode in a particular place or country which he has adopted voluntarily and for settled purposes as part of the regular order of his life for the time being, whether of short or of long duration'. Thus, an intention to live in a place permanently or indefinitely was *not* a necessary component in establishing ordinary residence.

Southwark London Borough Council v Williams and Another [1971] 1 Ch 734 (CA). *Secretary of State's default powers; temporary accommodation; necessity*
This case suggested that the Secretary of State's default powers – rather than the law courts – should be used for enforcement of a duty under the National Assistance Act 1948.

Squatters. The case concerned two families, who – at a time of extreme housing shortage in London – sought assistance from a squatters' association and made an orderly entry into empty council property. When the local authority applied to the court for an order of immediate possession, the families relied on two defences: that the authority was under a duty to provide temporary accommodation under s.21(1)(b) – since repealed in the light of homelessness legislation – of the National Assistance Act 1948, and that there was also a defence of necessity.

Breach of duty, default powers, and necessity. The court doubted whether s.21(1)(b) applied, since it was relevant only when the circumstances could not reasonably have been foreseen – yet this was not so in this particular case. Furthermore, even if the council had been in breach of its duty, enforcement of that duty could only be achieved through exercise of the Secretary of State's default powers. The case fell within the principle that:

"'where an Act creates an obligation, and enforces the obligation in a specified manner, we take it to be a general rule that performance cannot be enforced in any other manner'".

(The defence of necessity was also rejected – on the grounds that only extreme need could justify it. An example, from an old case, was of shipwrecked sailors who, in order to save their own lives, killed the cabin boy and ate him: even these circumstances did not constitute necessity. Liberal use of the defence 'would open a way through which all kinds of disorder and lawlessness would pass', and 'open a door which no man could shut'. Thus, the courts had to deny 'the plea of necessity to the hungry and the homeless: and trust that their distress will be relieved by the charitable and the good').

Staffordshire County Council v J and J [1996] 4 ELR 418 (QBD). *Meeting needs; resources; considering the future and longer term issues; balancing exercise; special education*
An education case, appealed by the local authority from the Special Educational Needs Tribunal, about looking to the future, not just the present, when weighing up efficient use of resources against needs in a balancing exercise.

Conductive education. The case concerned a four-year-old child with quadriplegia, cerebral palsy and consequent mobility problems, and whether she could continue to attend the Birmingham Institute for Conductive Education. Although the authority claimed that an alternative, a nursery, would be cheaper and still meet the child's needs, the parents argued that continued attendance at the Institute would accelerate her entry into mainstream education – and therefore save the authority resources in the longer term.

Resources and longer term considerations. The Special Educational Needs Tribunal stated that she should remain at the Institute because this might expedite mainstream education for her (though it did not mention resources). The education authority challenged the Tribunal's decision. The court found that the Tribunal had been entitled to come to this decision by 'not accepting that the authority was necessarily right to say that simply because [the nursery] costs less now, therefore it is an efficient use of resources to send [the child] there, because one would clearly have to do a balancing exercise to decide whether the more expensive education now, which would be likely to lead to mainstream education earlier, would overall create a greater efficiency in the use of resources'.

Steane and Another v Chief Adjudication Officer and Another [1996] 1 WLR 1195 (HL). *Residential accommodation; attendance allowance*
Similar to *Chief Adjudication Officer v Quinn* (which was about income support rather than attendance allowance), this case exposed the cost-shunting to which public bodies – in this instance, a local authority and central government – are partial when resources are scarce.

It concerned a 79-year-old woman with diabetes and problems of mobility who went to live in a residential home run by the Isle of Wight County Council. A limited company, Islecare, was then set up to manage the home formerly run by the Council. The woman claimed attendance allowance, on the basis that she was no longer in residential accommodation arranged by the council under s.26 of the National Assistance 1948, and thus could claim the allowance (she could not have claimed it if arrangements were still being made under the 1948 Act). The House of Lords ruled that, because the local authority was not making payments to Islecare in conformity with s.26 of the 1948 Act, no accommodation was being provided under that Act and thus the attendance allowance could be claimed.

Stretch v West Dorset District Council [1998] 10 ALR 129 (CA). *Decisions taken beyond legal powers; land*
A land case, showing that if a local authority acts beyond its powers, the decision might be struck down by the law courts as invalid – even if an individual has relied on and suffered as a consequence. In this case, although the local authority was empowered to let land in its possession (under s.164 of the Local Government Act 1933), it was not empowered to grant an option to renew a lease. So its decision to grant such an option could not stand.

Tidman v Reading Borough Council [1994] 3 PLR 72 (QBD). *Negligent statement; planning permission*
The plaintiff claimed damages against the local authority after he had sought advice from the council about planning permission, which he subsequently applied for unsuccessfully. One of the questions in issue was the circumstances in which advice-giving might give rise to a duty of care. The judge pointed out that the approach for advice in this case was 'informal, over the telephone, and on the basis of very slight information given by the applicant. It cannot reasonably be thought that in such cases, if the planning officers respond to the inquiry to give such help as they are able, they are immediately placing the local authority under obligations springing from the law of negligence. Indeed, it would be seriously contrary to the public interest if such were held to be the law, since the likely outcome would be that local authorities would be forced to cease to give any guidance at all: indeed it was argued that that was an option that had been open to them, and reasonably open to them, in dealing with this case'.

T (A Minor) v Surrey County Council and Others [1994] 4 All ER 577 (QBD). *Breach of statutory duty; negligence; children; social services*
A case brought for breach of statutory duty and negligence concerning the failure of a local authority to deregister a childminder who was under suspicion and investigation. Subsequently, an infant was seriously injured whilst in the childminder's care.
    The court found that the Act did not indicate any intention on the part of Parliament that authorities should be liable for breach of statutory duty. As to straightforward negligence, the court too declined to impose liability, especially as the case concerned the authority's failure to prevent a third party from acting negligently and causing the damage complained of. However, liability was imposed on grounds of a negligent misstatement made to the mother by the local authority's nursery and child-minding adviser. He had said to her that he was quite happy that the child be placed with the childminder, even though there was by then a question-mark about an injury suffered by another child in the care of the childminder.

Secretary of State for Education and Science v Tameside Metropolitan Borough Council [1977] AC 1014 (HL). *Decision-making; subjective satisfaction; education*
A case illustrating how the courts – if they are minded to – interfere with the decisions of public bodies, even if the legislation apparently allows the decision-maker to come to a subjective view.
    A local council, which had recently changed political hands, decided to modify the previous local policy on comprehensive education. However, under s.68 of the Education Act 1944, the Secretary of State decided that he was satisfied that this was unreasonable and issued a direction to the authority, which he subsequently tried to enforce through a court order. The House of Lords ruled against the Secretary of State, finding that there were no grounds on which he could have been satisfied that the local authority had behaved unreasonably.

Vandyk v Oliver (Valuation Officer) [1976] AC 659 (HL). *Disabled person; adaptations to the home; whether exemption from rating; National Assistance Act 1948, s.29*
A rating case hinging on whether adaptations made to the home of a man who was now disabled, having contracted poliomyelitis, attracted rating exemption – either in respect of the whole dwelling or at least two rooms. Amongst the criteria for exemption in s.45 of the General Rate Act 1967 was one referring to any 'structure' belonging to a local authority within the meaning of s.29 of the National Assistance Act 1948 and supplied under s.29. During the course of a detailed judgment which attempted to make sense of this section of the 1967 Act – 'a labyrinth, a minefield of obscurity' – the House of Lords noted that s.29 of the 1948 Act could not authorise the provision of residential accommodation.

Vicar of Writtle and Others v Essex County Council [1979] 77 LGR 656 (QBD). *Negligence; children; social services*

The case concerned a child, with a record of fire-raising, in the care of the local authority who set fire to a local church. The vicar, churchwardens and other people interested in the church, brought an action alleging negligence.

The court found that in failing to warn his head office, a social worker was not exercising a statutory discretion (eg, there was no evidence that the decision not to pass on the information had been taken in the interests of the child), and that therefore the scope of the duty of care owed by the local authority was not limited (as it otherwise might have been). Damages amounting to £99,000 (including interest) were awarded.

W and Others v Essex County Council and Golden. *Negligence; social services; child care; fostering*

A negligence case involving child care, in which both the High Court and Court of Appeal held that the authority could potentially be liable in negligence, notwithstanding the House of Lords decision in *X v Bedfordshire CC* which had demonstrated the courts' reluctance to impose negligence liability on local authority social services departments.

It was alleged that the local authority and/or its social worker knew at the time that a child, who went to live with a foster family, was a sexual abuser. He subsequently sexually abused the family's two children. The local authority attempted to have the case struck out and prevent it proceeding to trial; it claimed that it owed no duty of care to the family, and would not have owed it even if the child had 'previously been convicted of rape, indecent assault, robbery or an offence of violence' – and even if the social worker had deliberately deceived the family.

(High Court): ***W and Others v Essex County Council and Golden*** [1998] 2 FCR 232. Having dealt with the various obstacles to imposing a duty of care listed in *X v Bedfordshire CC* case, the judge did not strike out the parts of the claim relating to a duty of care – finding essentially that the relationship between social worker and foster carer could, in principle, give rise to vicarious liability on the part of the local authority for the negligence and the negligent statement of the social worker. (This meant the case could go to trial, where the ordinary principles of negligence would be applied to attempt to establish actual liability). The judge also concluded that the agreement between local authority and foster carer was contractual. However, the code of practice which stated that the foster parents should be fully informed of a child's background specifically stated that it was not legally binding, and so did not form part of the contract. The code aside, the judge was not convinced of the existence of an implied term in the agreement to the effect that the authority would inform the family of any knowledge or suspicion it had of the child being a sexual abuser.

(Court of Appeal): ***W and Others v Essex County Council and Golden*** [1998] 3 All ER 111. The Court of Appeal ruled that although no claim for damages was possible in respect of a decision within the statutory discretion of the local authority, such a claim could lie if the decision was so unreasonable as to lie outside of that discretion. However, in that case, it would still not be just and reasonable for the court to impose a duty of care – because such a duty would cut across the whole statutory framework, the local authority and its staff had an extraordinarily difficult and delicate task, local authorities would begin to behave defensively, social workers would be put in an impossible position, and the injuries suffered by the children could anyway be compensated for through the Criminal Injuries Compensation Scheme.

However, the court stated that there was still room for liability because a) it was possible that the claim about the social worker's negligent statement did relate to a common law duty of care, standing apart from the statutory framework; b) the express assurances given by the local authority that a sexual abuser would not be placed in the home arguably qualified policy grounds for exclusion or undermined the public policy argument in favour of immunity; and c) any duty of care which was precluded in the case of children to whom the local authority bore a statutory duty (eg, to children it looked after), might not apply to children for whom it was not performing any statutory duty at all (ie, the abused children of the family).

In respect of the fostering agreement amounting to a contract, the decision of the judge in the High Court was reversed. The Court of Appeal decided that there was no contract. It was precluded because a contract 'is essentially an agreement that is freely entered into on terms that are freely negotiated. If there is a statutory obligation to enter into a form of agreement the terms of which are laid down, at any rate in their most important respects, there is no contract'.

Warren v Harlow District Council [1997] CL 2622 (Central London CC). *Lifting and handling; Manual Handling Operations Regulations 1992*
The plaintiff was a 60-year old woman, five foot five inches tall, with a pre-existing back problem. She suffered a further injury when lifting a bucket of water weighing 21 pounds out of a sink, the height of the lift being 52 inches. The injury occurred somewhere between removal of the bucket from the sink, resting it on the lip of the sink and then execution of a one-handed lift comprising a twisting and lowering motion. Liability was established, since the risk was more than merely minimal or theoretical and called for a risk assessment. Such an assessment would have shown that it was reasonably practicable to avoid the lifting operation by means of a hose which could have filled the bucket whilst it was resting on the floor. Since the employer took no steps to avoid the lifting operation it was in breach of regulation 4. A total of £7,920 damages was awarded.

Welton v North Cornwall District Council [1997] 1 WLR 570 (CA). *Advice; negligence; environmental health functions*
A case in which the Court of Appeal stated that a local authority could be liable in negligence for poor 'advice'; this consisted of a series of requirements set out by an environmental health officer in respect of a hotel kitchen, backed up by a threat to close the hotel. As a result of the advice, the owners made various alterations and incurred considerable unnecessary expense.

Nature of advisory service. The court accepted that so far as an advisory service is 'part and parcel' of a discharge of statutory responsibility, liability would not arise. But so far as it goes beyond this, an advisory service could give rise to a duty of care – and the fact that it 'is offered by reason of the statutory duty is immaterial'. In this case, the court decided that the advisory service was akin to the psychological advisory service in *X v Bedfordshire CC* case, which the House of Lords held could give rise to negligence liability. Indeed, the environmental health officer's actions did not accord with what he was empowered to do under the legislation; nor was he adhering to the authority's policy of differentiating (in writing) legal requirements from non-legally enforceable recommendations.

By upholding the liability imposed by the High Court, the Court of Appeal 'was not intruding upon the manner in which they [the local authority] exercise their powers. The burden of performing the advisory service carefully, which is the burden cast upon those in the private sector, is not so onerous or demanding upon a fair allocation of finite resources as to make it unreasonable to expect care to be taken'.

Public policy. As to public policy considerations which might preclude liability even given the existence of a duty of care, the court pointed out that 'policy demands that the plaintiffs should have a remedy to compensate them for damages caused by the instructions of an official vested with authority who not only directed them negligently as to what was required to achieve compliance with the statutory provisions, but also gave them inaccurate information about the true extent of his authority and omitted any reference to their own rights under the statutory provisions. It would be neither fair nor just nor reasonable to hold that a duty of care did not exist or that liability could not be established'. The award of damages was upheld though reduced to £34,000.

White v Chief Adjudication Officer [1993] TLR, 2 August 1993 (CA). *Nursing homes; NHS inpatients; income support; contractual agreements; topping up*
The health authority had transferred patients to a nursing home under a block grant agreement, where they would claim income support which would be payable to the nursing home except for a personal allowance. However, the court found that under s.128 of the NHS Act 1977, the nursing home was in fact a hospital because of the nurses amongst the permanent and resident staff. Thus the patients were still NHS patients, whom

the home was contractually bound to accept from the health authority and who were ineligible for the income support normally payable to people independently resident in nursing homes.

Williams v Gwent Health Authority [1983] CL 2551 (Cardiff CC). *Lifting and handling; unsafe system of work*

The plaintiff was a state enrolled nurse (SEN) employed at a small hospital housing 29 patients. She sustained a back injury when moving, together with another SEN, a patient from bed to chair. The patient was partially paralysed and weighed over 12 stone; the plaintiff nurse weighed less than 8 stone. She and the other nurse were performing a lift which involved placing one arm under each of her armpits and the other resting on the bed, and then lifting and turning the woman on to the chair near the bottom of the bed. The woman made an unexpected movement during this manoeuvre.

The health authority was found 100 per cent liable for an unsafe system of work. In the light of agreed statistics relating to lifting accidents in the hospital, within the area of the health authority and nationally, there was a foreseeable risk of injury to nurses involved in handling patients. Furthermore, the method of lifting used by the plaintiff and her colleague was, despite being approved at the hospital, in fact unsafe and negligent, imposing as it did extra strain on the spine.

Willmore and Willmore (Trading as Lissenden Poultry) v South Eastern Electricity Board [1957] 2 Lloyds Rep 375 (QBD). *Statutory services; whether or not a contract exists*

A case concerning a dispute over damage done to a poultry concern following an interruption to the electricity supply; the court however denied the existence of a legally binding contract, referring to the 'the supply of electricity by the Board not as the acceptance of an offer ... to take and pay for a supply, so as to create a contract, but as given in pursuance of the Board's statutory duty to give a supply to a consumer who, being entitled, demands it'.

Woolger v West Surrey and North East Hampshire Health Authority [1993] TLR 8 November 1993 (CA). *Lifting and handling; negligence*

The method by which a trained nurse lifted a patient was a matter for the nurse's individual judgement. The hospital was not in breach of its duty to exercise reasonable care by warning her against using a method which caused her back injury.

Wyatt v Hillindon London Borough Council [1978] 76 LGR 727 (CA). *Community care; home help etc; breach of statutory duty; negligence*

This case, concerning the Chronically Sick and Disabled Persons Act 1970, illustrates the reluctance of the law courts to entertain claims for damages for breach of statutory duty or in negligence, when there is a failure to provide welfare services. It concerned a woman who suffered from disseminated sclerosis and who, with her husband, claimed damages against the authority – in negligence and/or breach of statutory duty – in relation to provision of home help, practical assistance in the home, or an 'invalid bed' under s.2 of the 1970 Act.

Default powers more appropriate for dispute about 'comforts to the sick and disabled'. The court found that any remedy for breach of statutory duty lay through the Secretary of States's power to declare an authority in default of its functions under s.36 (now obsolete) of the National Assistance Act 1948 – which was relevant because of the interaction between the 1948 and the 1970 Acts.

The judge at first instance had held that 's.1 and 2 [of the 1970 Act] were incorporated into s.29 of the National Assistance Act 1948'. The Court of Appeal upheld this view, finding that 'the importance of [section 2], particularly the last words of it, is to indicate that in the end it is s.29 and the other relevant sections of the National Assistance Act 1948 which are the governing factors in this sort of situation'. Furthermore: 'It is upon s.29 therefore, that the activities of the local authority are based'.

Breach of statutory duty. The court stated (the following passage has recently been cited with approval by the House of Lords in *O'Rourke v Camden LBC*) that 'a statute such as this which is dealing with the distribution of benefits – or, to put it perhaps more accurately, comforts to the sick and disabled – does not in its very nature give rise to an action by the disappointed sick person. It seems to me quite extraordinary that if the local authority ... provided, for example, two hours less home help than the sick person considered herself entitled to that that can amount to a breach of statutory duty which will permit the sick person to claim a sum of monetary damages by way of breach of statutory duty'.

Negligence. The claim in negligence was also rejected, since the duty in issue arose from the Act of Parliament only (ie, it did not constitute a free-standing common law duty of care). However, the court noted that a claim in negligence might have been possible if, for example, a home help had dropped the woman and injured her, or the bed provided by the local authority had been defective, collapsed and caused injury.

X and others (minors v Bedfordshire County Council, M (a minor) and another v Newham London Borough Council and others, E (a minor) v Dorset County Council, and other appeals [1995] 3 All ER 353 (HL). *Negligence; breach of statutory duty; children; social services; education*

A case in which the House of Lords considered in detail the circumstances in which private law claims in damages might, in principle, succeed against local authorities, for negligence or breach of statutory duty – in both the social services (child care) and education fields. On public policy grounds, a decision was made that local authorities should be immune from liability. (At the time of writing, one of the social services cases has been referred to the European Court of Human Rights).

Background. Several cases were heard together, but those concerning social services and child care were as follows. In the first (*Bedfordshire*), five children were living in appalling circumstances. Despite reports being made over a period of years to the local authority – by relatives, neighbours, police, the general practitioner, a headteacher, the National Society for the Prevention of Cruelty to Children (NSPCC), a social worker and a health visitor – none of the children were placed on the child protection register, nor any court orders made. In the second case (*Newham*), a social worker and psychiatrist assumed that the name given by a child – who was suspected to be the subject of sexual abuse – was that of her mother's boyfriend. The child was removed and the mother barred her boyfriend from her home. It later transpired that the child had been referring not to the boyfriend but to a cousin with the same first-name.

Negligence (social services). As far as negligence in respect of social services (child care) went, the House of Lords basically ruled that the authorities would neither be directly, nor vicariously (ie, on behalf of its staff) liable. The authorities could not be directly liable because the decisions challenged might be 'non-justiciable' – ie, related to resources or general policy. Furthermore, even if the decision did not relate to policy or resources (and so was an 'operational' decision), whether a duty of care existed was 'profoundly influenced by the statutory framework', because 'a common law duty of care cannot be imposed on a statutory duty if the observance of such common law duty of care would be inconsistent with, or have a tendency to discourage, the due performance by the local authority of its statutory duties'.

If the decisions challenged fell into neither of these categories, the House of Lords stated that the authority would still not be liable because, applying the ordinary test for negligence, it would not be 'just and reasonable' to impose a duty of care, for a number of reasons. These included a) the complex statutory system for the protection of children at risk; b) the 'extraordinarily delicate' task facing local authorities in relation to children; c) the danger of legal liability provoking local authorities into defensive approaches to their duties; d) the danger of encouraging 'hopeless', 'vexatious and costly' litigation; and e) the fact that there were other remedies available, such as complaints procedures and the local ombudsman.

The local authority staff – and therefore the authority also vicariously – would not be liable because the staff owed a duty of care to the local authority and not to the plaintiffs. But, the House of Lords went on, even if they did owe a duty of care to the children, it would still not be just and reasonable to impose a duty of care – for the same reasons as applied in the case of direct liability of the authority (immediately above).

Breach of statutory duty (social services). As for breach of statutory duty, the House of Lords stated that a cause of action could only arise if it could be shown that the particular legislation in question both created a duty to protect a 'limited class of the public' and also conferred on members of that class private law rights – ie, a right to sue for damages. In order to decide this question, the legislation had to be examined for 'indicators'. One such was if the legislation provided another remedy for breach of duty (eg, appeal to the Secretary of State); this would normally indicate that private legal actions were not contemplated by Parliament. However, the existence of such alternative remedies would not *necessarily* deprive people of private law remedies: each case depended on the interpretation of the legislation in question.

However, the it was pointed out that 'it is significant that your Lordships were not referred to any case where it had been held that statutory provisions establishing a regulatory system or a scheme of social welfare for the benefit of the public at large had been held to give rise to a private right of action for damages for breach of statutory duty. Although regulatory or welfare legislation affecting a particular area of activity does in fact provide protection to those individuals particularly affected by that activity, the legislation is not to be treated as being passed for the benefit of those individuals but for the benefit of society in general'.

The conclusion was that although the relevant child care legislation was for the protection of a limited class – ie, children at risk – nevertheless the duties contained in it were 'dependent upon the subjective judgement of the local authority'. For instance, there were phrases such as 'where it appears to the local authority', 'such inquiries as they consider necessary', 'take reasonable steps'. Such duties could not give rise to private law rights. In addition, s.17 of the Children Act 1989 imported a general duty to safeguard children in need and, so far as is consistent with that, to promote their upbringing by their families. It was 'impossible to construe such a statutory provision as demonstrating an intention that even where there is no carelessness by the authority it should be liable in damages if a court subsequently decided with hindsight that the removal, or failure to remove, the child from the family either was or was not 'consistent with' the duty to safeguard the child'.

Negligence (education). Both cases (*Dorset* and *Hampshire*) involved assessment, advice and decisions in relation to the special educational needs of children with dyslexia. A third case (*Bromley*) was also considered.

As with the social services cases, the House of Lords ruled that the local authorities could owe no duty of care in negligence directly when carrying out their functions under legislation (the Education Act 1981, now replaced by the Education Act 1996). However, not only was there a duty of care for obvious operational matters such as the physical safety of pupils, but there might also be such a duty in relation to what was at issue here – the offering of a psychological advice service. Although in the absence of legislation, the authority could not offer it, nevertheless once it had opened its doors to the service, it was in a position analogous to a hospital and had a duty to exercise reasonable care. Therefore, in principle, the authority could owe a duty of care in respect of such a service, although this duty might be excluded or limited if it proved on further investigation that the service was 'part and parcel' of its statutory functions. Similarly, the allegation that a headmaster and an educational adviser had been negligent in failing to identify the needs of the child was a pure common law claim and did not arise from the statutory machinery of the 1981 Act. Again there was no reason to exclude a duty of care.

As to the vicarious liability of the authority in relation to its employees, there was similarly no reason to hold that a duty of care could not exist in respect of the educational psychologists who offered advice. They were in a different position from the social workers in the child care cases, insofar as there appeared to be no conflict between such a duty of care and the carrying out of statutory duties by the authority.

Yule v South Lanarkshire Council (1998) SLT 490 (Outer House of the Court of Session, Scotland). *Residential accommodation; charging rules; taking account of a person's home gifted to a third party*
This case involved the taking account of 'notional capital' when assessing a person's contribution to nursing home care being arranged by a local authority. The notional capital was represented by a gift of property for nil consideration, given by the (now) nursing home resident to her granddaughter, over six months before she entered the nursing home and while she was still in good health. The local authority claimed that it had been disposed of for the purpose of avoiding accommodation charges.

Although this was a Scottish case, it applies equally to England since the legislation relevant to the particular point at issue is to all intents and purposes the same. For the rules in issue, see p.303 of this book.

The petitioner (the woman's son) claimed that a) the local authority had no legal power to make the woman liable for payment in these circumstances, and b) its decision was unreasonable. The second of these claims was not considered before the court because of limitations on the time available. The petitioner argued that a local authority could impose financial liability a) under s.21 (applying to both England and Scotland) of the Health and Social and Security Adjudications Act 1983 where an asset had been disposed of not more than six months (see p.308 for the rule); or b) under s.23 of that Act (in Scotland: s.22 is the equivalent in England) where a person retained ownership of a property, in which case the authority could put a charge on it.

However, what the authority could not do, so it was claimed, was to impose liability where capital had been disposed of more than six months before – since r.25 of SI 1992/2977 (see p.303), apparently containing the power to do this, was in fact governed by the six-month limit contained in s.21 of the 1983 Act.

The judge rejected this claim under point a), stating that the local authority did have the power to take into account an asset disposed of more than six months before. However, point b), concerning whether it was reasonable for the authority to exercise the power (given, for example, that the woman had been in good health when making the gift) was not considered.

REFERENCES

GENERAL

Abberley, P. (1995). 'Disabling ideology in health and welfare: the case of occupational therapy'. *Disability and Society:* 1995; 10(2), pp.221–232.

ACC *et al.* (1996). Association of County Councils, Association of Directors of Social Services, Association of District Councils, Association of Metropolitan Authorities, Local Government Management Board. *Survey of disabled facilities grants 1995: housing departments and social services departments.* London: ACC etc.

ACC, AMA (1971). Association of County Councils; Association of Metropolitan Authorities (1971). *Chronically Sick and Disabled Persons Act 1970 provision of telephones as amended by ACC/AMA letter 20/4/72.* London: ACC; AMA.

ACC, AMA (1995). Association of County Councils; Association of Metropolitan Authorities. *Who gets community care? A survey of community care eligibility criteria.* London: AMA.

ACC, AMA (1996). Association of County Councils; Association of Metropolitan Authorities. *Discretionary charges: a good practice handbook.* London: ACC, AMA.

ACHCEW (1993). Association of Community Health Councils for England and Wales. *NHS complaints procedures: a submission to the Complaints Review Committee.* London: ACHCEW.

ACO (1996). Association of Charity Officers; Age Concern England. *Preserved rights to income support: results of an Age Concern/Association of Charity Officers survey.* London: ACO.

Adams, M. (1996). *Community care information: making it clear.* Cardiff: Welsh Consumer Council.

Age Concern Cheshire (1996). *Older people at the sharp end: the problems caused by underfunding of community care services in Cheshire.* Chester: Age Concern Cheshire.

Age Concern Cheshire (1997). *Rights and risks: the implications of Cheshire County Council's policy and procedures on financing long term care.* Chester: Age Concern Cheshire.

Age Concern England (1990). *Left behind? Continuing care for elderly people in NHS hospitals: a review of Health Advisory Service reports.* London: Age Concern England.

Age Concern England (1991). Meredith, B. *Issues in continuing care of older people relating to findings by the Health Service Commissioner: submission to the House of Commons Select Committee on the Parliamentary Commissioner for Administration.* London: Age Concern England.

Age Concern England (1992). *Home help and care: rights, charging and reality.* London: Age Concern England.

Age Concern England (1993). *No time to lose: first impressions of the community care reforms.* London: Age Concern England.

Age Concern England (1994a). *Preserved – and protected? A report and recommendations about the community care reforms and people with preserved rights to Income Support.* London: Age Concern England.

Age Concern England (1994b). *The next steps: lessons for the future of community care.* London: Age Concern England.

Age Concern England (1995). *Inquiry into long-term care: evidence to the Health Select Committee by Age Concern (the National Council on Ageing).* London: Age Concern England.

Age Concern England (1997). *Paying for residential and nursing home fees from income support and attendance allowance.* London: Age Concern England.

Age Concern England (1998a). *Age of individuals: factors in the receipt of social care, a note to the Royal Commission, May 1998.* London: Age Concern England.

Age Concern England (1998b). *Beyond bricks and mortar: dignity and security in the home: submission by Age Concern England to the Royal Commission on long term care for the elderly.* London: Age Concern England.

Age Concern England (1998c). *Disabled facilities grants and older people: agenda for action.* London: Age Concern England.

Age Concern England (1998d). *Meeting the needs of today's pensioners: Age Concern's second paper to the Royal Commission.* London: Age Concern England.

Age Concern England (1998e). *Raising income or capital from your home. Factsheet 12 (July 1998).* London: Age Concern England.

Age Concern England (1998f). *Paying for care in a residential or nursing home if you have a partner. Fact sheet 39.* London: Age Concern England.

Age Concern London (1995). *Hospital afterthought: support for older people discharged from hospital.* London: Age Concern London.

Aldersea, P. (1996). *National prosthetic and wheelchair services report.* London: College of Occupational Therapists.

Alzheimer's Disease Society (1993). *NHS psychogeriatric continuing care beds.* London: ADS.

AMA (1993). *DoH advice on assessment: AMA trawl on authorities' response to that advice*. London: Association of Metropolitan Authorities.

AMA, ACC, ADSS (1994). Association of County Councils; Association of Metropolitan Authorities; Association of Directors of Social Services. *Guidance on contracting for residential and nursing home care for adults*. London: AMA.

AMA, ACC, ADSS (1995). Association of County Councils; Association of Metropolitan Authorities; Association of Directors of Social Services. *Guidance on contracting for domiciliary and day care services*. London: AMA.

AMA, LGIU (1991). Association of Metropolitan Authorities; Local Government Information Unit. *Too high a price? Examining the cost of charging policies*. London: AMA; LGIU.

AMA, LGIU (1994). Association of Metropolitan Authorities; Local Government Information Unit. *Commentary on Social Services Inspectorate advice note on discretionary charges for adult social services*. London: AMA, LGIU.

Appleton, N. (1996). *Handyperson schemes: making them work*. York: York Publishing.

Appleton, N., Leather, P. (1997). *Review of the provision of equipment and adaptations for older people*. London: King's Fund.

Appleton, N., Leather, P. (1998). *Housing Corporation programme for the funding of adaptations*. London: Housing Corporation.

Arblaster, L., Conway, J., Foreman, A., Hawtin, M. (1998). *Achieving the impossible: interagency collaboration to address the housing, health and social care needs of people able to live in ordinary housing*. Bristol: Policy Press (for Joseph Rowntree Foundation).

Arnold, P., Bochel, H., Brodhurst, S., Page, D. (1993). *Community care: the housing dimension*. York: Joseph Rowntree Foundation; Community Care.

Ashton, G. (1995a). 'Elderly people and residential care (1)'. *Solicitors Journal*, 6 October 1995, pp.978–980.

Ashton, G. (1995b). 'Elderly people and residential care (2)'. *Solicitors Journal*, 13 October 1995, pp.1010–1012.

Ashton, G. (1995c). 'Elderly people and residential care (3)'. *Solicitors Journal*, 20 October 1995, pp.1036–1038.

Ashton, G. (1995d). 'Elderly people and residential care (4)'. *Solicitors Journal*, 27 October 1995, pp.1074–1075.

Audit Commission (1992). *Community revolution: personal social services and community care*. London: HMSO.

Audit Commission (1993). *Progress with care in the community*. Bulletin. London: Audit Commission, 1993.

Audit Commission (1994). *Finding a place: a review of mental health services for adults*. London: HMSO.

Audit Commission (1995a). *Setting the records straight: a study of hospital medical records*. London: HMSO.

Audit Commission (1995b). *United they stand: co-ordinating care for elderly patients with hip fracture*. London: HMSO.

Audit Commission (1997a). *Coming of age: improving care services for older people*. London: Audit Commission.

Audit Commission (1997b). *Take your choice: a commissioning framework for community care*. London: Audit Commission.

Audit Commission (1998). *Home alone: the role of housing in community care*. London: Audit Commission.

Audit Commission; Social Services Inspectorate (1997). *Reviewing social services: annual report 1997*. London: Audit Commission.

Audit Commission; Social Services Inspectorate (1998a). *Getting the best from social services: learning the lessons from joint reviews*. London: Audit Commission.

Audit Commission; Social Services Inspectorate (1998b). *Cornwall: a report of the review of social services in Cornwall County Council*. London: Audit Commission.

Baldock, J., Ungerson, C. (1994). *Becoming consumers of community care: households within the mixed economy of welfare*. York: Joseph Rowntree Foundation; Community Care.

Baldwin, M. (1995a). *The meaning of care management*. Norwich: Social Work Monographs.

Baldwin, R. (1995b). *Rules and government*. Oxford: Clarendon Press.

Baldwin, S., Lunt, N. (1996). *Charging ahead: the development of local authority charging policies for community care*. Bristol: Policy Press.

Balloch, S. (1993). *AMA/ACC survey of social services charging policies 1992–1994*. London: Association of Metropolitan Authorities. (Draft version).

Balloch, S. (1994). *A survey of social services charging policies 1992–1994*. London: AMA. (Published version).

Balloch, S., Robertson, G. (1995). *Charging for social care*. London: National Institute for Social Work and Local Government Anti Poverty Unit.

Barclay, P. (Chairman) (1996). *Meeting the costs of continuing care: report and recommendations*. York: Joseph Rowntree Foundation.

Barron, A., Scott, C. (1992). *Citizen's Charter Programme. Modern Law Review*: 1992; 55(4), 526–546.

Beardshaw, V. (1988). *Last on the list: community services for people with physical disabilities*. London: King's Fund Institute.

Beattie, A. (1995). *Home comforts: home support for disabled people*. London: Age Concern London.

Begum, N. (1995). *Beyond samosas and reggae: a guide to developing services for black disabled people*. London: King's Fund.

Begum, N., Fletcher, S. (1995). *Improving disability services: the way forward for health and social services*. London: King's Fund.

Bennett, F. (1996). *Highly charged: policy issues surrounding charging for non-residential care*. York: Joseph Rowntree Foundation.

Berry, L. (1990). *Information for users of social services departments*. London: National Consumer Council; National Institute for Social Work.

Bewley, C., Glendinning, C. (1994). *Involving disabled people in community care planning*. York: Joseph Rowntree Foundation.

Bhuttarcharji, S. (1992). 'Misleading statements: the art of "statementing" for children with special educational needs'. *Therapy Weekly*: 1992; 19(6), p.7.

Booth, W., Booth, T. (1998). *Advocacy for parents with learning difficulties: developing advocacy support*. Brighton: Pavilion Publishing (for Joseph Rowntree Foundation).

Bottomley, V. (1994). 'National health, local dynamic'. *The Independent*, 22nd August 1994, p.14.

Bradley, G., Manthorpe, J. (1997). *Dilemmas of financial assessment: a practitioner's guide*. Birmingham: Venture Press.

Brazier, M. (1992). *Medicine, patients and the law*. 2nd edition. London: Penguin.

Bridges, L., Cragg, S., Hyland, G., Lang, B., Mullen, T., Poynter, R. (for the Public Law Project) (1995a). *Applicant's guide to judicial review*. London: Sweet and Maxwell.

Bridges, L., Meszaros, G., Sunkin, M. (1995b). *Judicial review in perspective*. London: Cavendish.

British Medical Association (1968). *Aids for the disabled*. London: BMA.

Bruce, I., McKennell, A., Walker, E. (1991). *Blind and partially sighted adults in Britain: the RNIB survey*. Volume 1. London: HMSO.

BSRM (1993). British Society of Rehabilitation Medicine. *Multiple sclerosis: a working party report of the British Society of Rehabilitation Medicine*. London: BSRM.

Burgner, T. (1996). *The regulation and inspection of social services*. London: Department of Health; Welsh Office.

Butt, J., Mirza, K. (1996). *Social care and black communities*. London: HMSO.

Calabresi, G., Bobbit, P. (1978). *Tragic choices*. New York: Norton.

Care Weekly (1995). 'NHS could pick up the tab for private residents'. *Care Weekly*, 16 March 1995, p.2.

Carnwath, R. (1996). 'The reasonable limits of local authority powers'. *Public Law*: Summer 1996,pp.244–265.

Casserly,C. (1998). Disability Discrimination Act update: goods,facilities and services. *Legal Action*,December 1998,pp.18–20.

CCF (1995). *Framework contract between residential care provider and resident*. London: CCC.

Challis, D., Gill, J., Hughes, H., Stone, S. (1997). *Research briefing: eligibility criteria for older people in England*. Manchester: University of Manchester, Personal Social Services Research Unit.

Challis, L., Henwood, M. (1994). 'Equity in community care'. *British Medical Journal*:4 June 1994;308,pp.1496–1499.

Chetwynd, M., Ritchie, J. (1996). *Cost of care: the impact of charging policy on the lives of disabled people*. Bristol: Policy Press (in association with Joseph Rowntree Foundation and Community Care).

Child Poverty Action Group (1998). *National Welfare Benefits Handbook*. 28th edition. London: CPAG.

Childright (1998). 'Bedfordshire case held admissible'. *Childright*: 1998(148),pp.4–5.

CIPFA (1998). Chartered Institute of Public Finance and Accountancy. *Community Care (Direct Payments) Act 1996: accounting and financial management guidelines*. London: CIPFA.

CLAE (1993). *Good administrative practice*. London: Commission for Local Administration in England.

CLAE (1994). Commission for Local Administration in England. *The Local Government Ombudsmen 1993/1994: annual report*. London: CLAE.

CLAE (1992). Commissioner for Local Administration in England. *Devising a complaints system*. London: CLAE.

CLAE (1998). Commission for Local Administration in England. *The Local Government Ombudsman 1997/1998: annual report*. London: CLAE.

Clark, H., Dyer, S., Horwood, J. (1996). *Going home: older people leaving hospital*. Bristol: Policy Press (for Joseph Rowntree Foundation and Community Care).

Clark, H., Dyer, S., Horwood, J. (1998). *That bit of help: the high value of low level preventative services for older people*. Bristol: Policy Press (for Joseph Rowntree Foundation and Community Care).

Clark, J. (Chair) (1998). *Community health care for elderly people: report of a Clinical Standards Advisory Group Committee*. London: Stationery Office.

Clarkson, J. (1997). *Cutting the cloth, tightening the belt*. London: Royal Association for Disability and Rehabilitation.

Clements, L. (1992). 'Duties of social services departments'. *Legal Action Journal*, September 1992.

Clements, L. (1994a). 'Community care: definition of "need"'. *Legal Action Journal* 1994; January, p.21.

Clements, L. (1994b). 'Shifting sands'. *Community Care*, 29 September – 5 October 1994,pp.24–25.

Clements, L. (1996a). *Community care and the law*. London: Legal Action Group.

Clements, L. (1996b). 'Secret Weapon'. *Community Care*, 17–23 October 1996,pp.28–29.

Clements, L. (1996c). 'Legislating for change'. *Community Care*, 12–18 September 1996,pp.24–25.

Clements, L. (1997). 'The collapsing duty: a sideways look at community care and public law'. *Judicial review*: September 1997; 2(3), pp.162–165.

Clements, L. (1998). 'Act of weakness'. *Community Care*: 8–14 January 1998,pp.26–27.

Clements, L., Ruan, G. (1997). *Signposts through the maze: a guide to carers and the law*. London: Carers National Association.

CNA (Holzhausen, E.) (1997a). *In on the Act? Social services' experience of the first year of the Carers Act*. London: CNA.

CNA (Wood, J., Holzhausen, E.) (1997b). *Still battling? The Carers Act one year on*. London: Carers National Association.

Coles, D., Willetts, G., Winyard, S. (1997). *A question of risk: community care for older visually impaired people in England and Wales*. London: Royal National Institute for the Blind.

Collyer, M. (1992). *Swept under the carpet: a report on domestic services for older people in London*. London: Age Concern Greater London.

Collyer, M., Hanson-Kahn, C. (1989). *Feet first: a reappraisal of footcare services in London*. London: Age Concern London.

Collyer, M., Hanson-Kahn, C. (1990). *Old and clean: a report on bathing services for elderly people in London*. London: Age Concern Greater London.

Community Care (1996). 'Users pay for rights'. *Community Care*, 19 December 1996 – 8 January 1997, p.1.

Community Care (1998a). 'Cash woes force council to withdraw free home help'. *Community Care*, 13–19 August 1998, p.1.

Community Care (1998b). 'Drive by Hackney council staff'. *Community Care* 1998: 3–9 September 1998. (News in brief), p.4.

Community Care (1998c). 'Council faces second legal challenge'. *Community Care*: 23–29 April 1998, p.3.

Community Care (1998d). 'News'. *Community Care*: 5–11 November 1998, p.2.

Community Care (1999). Councils cheating elderly service users. *Community Care*, 4–10 February 1999, p.1.

Consumers' Association (1993). *NHS complaints procedures: the way forward.* London: CA, pp.17–18.

Continence Foundation (1998). 'Boateng commits NHS to "high quality, prompt" NHS continence service'. *Continence Foundation Newsletter*: September 1998, p.1.

Cook, J., Mitchell, P. (1982). *Putting teeth in the Act: a history of attempts to enforce section of the Chronically Sick and Disabled Persons Act.* RADAR: London.

Coombs, M. (with Sedgwick, A.) (1998). *Right to challenge: the Oxfordshire Community Care Rights Project.* Bristol: Policy Press (for Joseph Rowntree Foundation).

Cooper, J., Vernon, S. (1996). *Disability and the law.* London: Jessica Kingsley.

Coopers and Lybrand (1988). *Information needs of disabled people, their carers and service providers: final report.* London: Department of Health and Social Security.

Counsel and Care (1992). *From home to a home: a study of older people's hopes, expectations and experiences of residential care.* London: Counsel and Care.

Counsel and Care (1995). *Under inspection.* London: Counsel and Care.

Counsel and Care (1998). *Bringing health to homes.* London: Counsel and Care.

CPA (1984). 'Centre for Policy on Ageing'. *Home life.* London: CPA

CPA (1996). 'Centre for Policy on Ageing'. *A better home life.* London: CPA.

CRAG (1993). Department of Health. *Charging for residential accommodation guide.* London: DH (looseleaf, regularly updated).

CRE (1997). Commission for Racial Equality. *Race, culture and community care: an agenda for action.* London: CRE; Chartered Institute of Housing; NHS Confederation.

CSP (1993). Chartered Society of Physiotherapists. *Survey of physiotherapy services to older people resident in private nursing homes.* London: CSP.

Customs and Excise (1997). *Drugs, medicines and aids for the handicapped: liability with effect from 1 January 1998.* VAT Information Sheet 6/97. London: Customs and Excise.

CVS Consultants, Prince Evans Solicitors (1995). *Caring for citizens: review of the fixed points and realistic choices in the financial rules surrounding the implementation of community mental health services.* London: Centre for Mental Health Services Development (King's College).

Cystic Fibrosis Trust (1997). *Fair care, a time for reappraisal: the care of children and adults with cystic fibrosis within the National Health service.* London: CFT.

d'Aboville, E. (1995). *Commissioning independent living: a guide to developing personal assistance schemes and support services.* London: King's Fund.

Darnborough, A., Kinrade, D. (1995). *Be it enacted: 25 years of the Chronically Sick and Disabled Persons Act 1970.* London: Royal Association for Disability and Rehabilitation.

Data Protection Registrar (1998). *The Data Protection Act 1998: an introduction.* Version 1. Wilmslow: DPR.

Davis, A., Ellis, K., Rummery, K. (1997). *Access to assessment: perspectives of practitioners, disabled people and carers.* Bristol: Policy Press (for Joseph Rowntree Foundation).

Davis, M. (1998). *Putting vision into community care.* London: Royal National Institute for the Blind.

Day, P., Klein, R., Redmayne, S. (1996). *Why regulate? Regulating residential care for elderly people.* Bristol: Policy Press.

Dearden, C., Becker, S. (1998). *Young carers in the UK.* London: Carers National Association.

DETR (1998). Department of Environment, Transport and Regions (News Release 178/ENV). *Better access planned for new homes.* London: DETR.

DETR, WO (1998). Department of Environment, Transport and the Regions; Welsh Office. *Approved document M: access and facilities for disabled people.* London: Stationery Office.

Devon SSD (1989). *Disabled Persons (Services, Consultation and Representation) Act 1986: code of practice.* Devon County Council: Exeter.

DfEE (1996). Department for Education and Employment. *Guidance on matters to be taken into account in determining questions relating to the definition of disability.* London: HMSO.

DfEE (1998). Department for Education and Employment. *Promoting disabled people's rights: creating a Disability Rights Commission fit for the 21st century.* London: DfEE.

DH (1989a). *Discharge of patients from hospital.* London: Department of Health.

DH (1989b). *Income generation: a guide to local initiative.* London: Department of Health.

DH (1990). Department of Health. *Community care in the next decade and beyond: policy guidance.* London: HMSO.

DH (1991). Department of Health. *NHS charges to overseas visitors: manual for NHS staff.* London: DH.

DH (1992a). *Equipped for independence? Meeting the equipment needs of disabled people.* London: Department of Health.

DH (1992b). Department of Health. *Provision of equipment by the NHS: EL(92)20.* Correspondence with the College of Occupational Therapists, 9 June 1992. London: DH.

DH (1993). *Implementing community care: population needs assessment: good practice guidance.* London: Department of Health.

DH (1994a). Department of Health. *Framework for local community care charters in England.* London: DH.

DH (1994b). Department of Health. *A framework for local community care charters in England: consultation document.* London: DH.

DH (1994c). Department of Health. *Hospital discharge workbook: a manual on hospital discharge practice.* London: DH.

DH (1994d). Department of Health. *Housing and homelessness: report of the community care monitoring special study,* October 1993 – April 1994. London: DH.

DH (1994e). Department of Health. *Monitoring and development: first impressions April–September 1993.* London: DH.

DH (1995a). Department of Health. *Building bridges: a guide to arrangements for inter-agency working for the care and protection of severely mentally ill people.* London: DH.

DH (1995b). *Building partnerships for success: community care development programmes.* London: DH.

DH (1995c). Department of Health. *Patient's Charter and you.* London: DH.

DH (1995d). Department of Health. *Practice guidance on joint commissioning for project leaders.* London: DH.

DH (1996a). Department of Health. *Carers (Recognition and Services) Act 1996: policy guidance.* London: DH.

DH (1996b). Department of Health. *Task Force to Review Services for Drug Misusers: report of an independent review of drug treatment services in England.* London: DH.

DH (1996c). Department of Health. *Court of Appeal judgment in the Gloucestershire judicial review.* Letter to the Association of County Councils, 22nd July 1996.

DH (1997a). Department of Health. *Patient's Charter: mental health services.* London: DH.

DH (1997b). Department of Health. *Community Care (Direct Payments) Act 1996: policy and practice guidance.* London: DH.

DH (1997c). Department of Health. *Purchasing effective and treatment and care for drug misusers: guidance for health authorities and social services departments.* London: DH.

DH (1997d). Department of Health. *Summary of the report of the Joint Strategy Group on local authority occupational therapy services.* London: DH.

DH (1998a). Department of Health. *Modernising health and social services: national priorities guidance 1999/00 – 2001/02.* London: DH.

DH (1998b). Department of Health. *Partnership in action: new opportunities for joint working between health and social services.* London: DH.

DH (1998c). Department of Health (letter to Age Concern England). *Ordinary residence: local authority responsibilities.* 17th April 1998. London: DH.

DH (1998d). Department of Health. *Modernising mental health services: safe, sound and supportive.* London: DH.

DH, DoE (1997). Department of Environment, Department of Health. *Housing and community care: establishing a strategic framework.* London: DH (sent out with covering joint Circular: LASSL(97)2, HSG(97)2)).

DH, SHHD, WO (1989). Department of Health; Scottish Home and Health Department; Welsh Office. *National Health Service and Community Care Bill: notes on clauses: House of Commons.* London: DH.

DH, WO (1993). Department of Health; Welsh Office. *Code of practice, Mental Health Act 1983.* London: HMSO.

DH, WO (1996). Department of Health; Welsh Office. *Mental Health (Patients in the Community) Act 1995, guidance on supervised discharge (after-care under supervision) and related provisions: supplement to the Code of Practice.* London: DH.

DHSS (1986). Department of Health and Social Security. *Management of private practice in health services hospitals in England and Wales.* London: DHSS.

Dimond, B. (1994). 'How far can you go? Boundaries of NHS responsibilities to pay for long-term care'. *Health Service Journal,* 14th April 1994, pp.24–25.

Dimond, B. (1997). *Legal aspects of care in the community.* Basingstoke: Macmillan.

Dimond, B. (1998). *Physiotherapy in a changing legal context.* Founders' Lecture 1998. London: Chartered Society of Physiotherapy.

Disability Alliance (1998). *Disability rights handbook, April 1998–April 1999.* 23rd edition. London: DA.

Disability Alliance (1998). *Disability rights handbook, 1998–1999 edition.* London: DA.

Douglas, A., MacDonald, C., Taylor, M. (1998). *Living independently with support: service users' perspectives on 'floating' support.* Bristol: Policy Press.

DSS (1998). Department of Social Security. Letter (reply to Age Concern England, no title/heading), 12/1/1998.

Economist (1998). 'Bevan's baby hits middle age'. *The Economist,* 4th July 1998, pp.33–35.

Edwards, F., Warren, M. (1990). *Health services for adults with physical disabilities.* London: Royal College of Physicians.

Ellis, K. (1993). *Squaring the circle: user and carer participation in needs assessment.* York: Joseph Rowntree Foundation.

Elliston, S., Britton, A. (1994). 'Is infertility an illness?' *New Law Journal,* 11th November 1994, pp.1552–1553.

Entwhistle, V., Watt, I., Bradbury, R., Pehl, l. (1996). 'Media coverage of the Child B case'. *British Medical Journal:* 22/6/1996; 312, pp.1587–1591.

Fiedler, B. (1988). *Living options lottery: housing and support services for people with severe physical disabilities:* 1986/88. London: Prince of Wales' Advisory Group on Disability.

Fiedler, B. (for Social Services Inspectorate) (1996). *Young carers: making a start.* London: Department of Health.

Fitzgerald, J. (1998). *Time for freedom? Services for older people with learning difficulties.* London: Centre for Policy on Ageing; Values Into Action.

Fletcher, S. (1995). *Evaluating community care: a guide to evaluations led by disabled people*. London: King's Fund.

Fordham, M. (1997). *Judicial review handbook*. 2nd edition. London: Wiley.

Fordham, M. (1998). 'Reasons: the third dimension'. *Judicial Review*: September 1998; 3(3), pp.158–164.

French, S. (1994). 'Attitudes of health professionals towards disabled people: a discussion and review of the literature'. *Physiotherapy*: October 1994; 80(10), pp.687–693.

Ganz, G. (1987). *Quasi-legislation: recent developments in secondary legislation*. London: Sweet & Maxwell.

Garden, B. (1990). *Information on disability: final report of the Lothian Project*. Edinburgh: Disability Scotland.

George, M. (1996). 'Access to change'. *Community Care*: 5–11 December 1996, pp.32–33.

Godfrey, M., Moore, J. (1996). *Hospital discharge: user, carer and professional perspectives*. Leeds: Nuffield Institute for Health, Community Care Division.

Gordon, R. (1993). *Community care assessments*. London: Longman.

Gordon, R., Mackintosh, N. (1996). *Community care assessments: a practical legal framework*. 2nd edition. London: FT Law and Tax.

Gould, J. (1994). *Not just fine tuning: a review of shire county community care plans for rural areas*. London: National Council for Voluntary Organisations.

Grant, C. (1995). 'Lifting aids: the patient's opinion'. *British Journal of Therapy and Rehabilitation*: June 1995; 2(6), p.331.

Gregory, W. (1996). *Informability manual: making information more accessible in the light of the Disability Discrimination Act*. London: HMSO.

Griffiths, J. (1998). 'Meeting personal hygiene needs in the community: a district nursing perspective on the health and social care divide'. *Health and Social Care in the Community*: 1998; 6(4), pp.234–240.

Griffiths, R. (1988). *Community care, an agenda for action: a report to the Secretary of State for Social Services by Sir Roy Griffiths*. London: HMSO.

Grimley Evans, J. (1995). 'Long term care in later life'. *British Medical Journal*; 9 September 1995; 311,p.644.

Guthrie, T. (1997). 'The House of Lords and community care assessments'. *Scottish Law and Practice Quarterly*: 1997;2,225–229.

Hadley, R., Clough, R. (1996). *Care in chaos: frustration and challenge in community care*. London: Cassell.

Ham, C., Pickard, S. (1998). *Tragic choices in health care: the case of Child B*. London: King's Fund.

Harding, T. (1997). *A life worth living: the independence and inclusion of older people*. London: Help the Aged.

Hardy, B., Wistow, G., Leedham, I. (1994). (Community Care Division, Nuffield Institute for Health). *Analysis of a sample of English community care plans 1993/94*. London: Department of Health.

Harris, D.J., O'Boyle, M., Warbrick, C. (1995). *Law of the European Convention on Human Rights*. London: Butterworths.

Harvey, A., Robertson, G. (1995). *Survey of charges for social care 1993–95*. London: Local Government Anti Poverty Unit.

HaSC (1998). Health and Safety Commission. *Manual handling in the health services*. Sudbury: HSE Books.

Hasler, F., Zarb, G., Campbell, J. (1998). *Key issues for local authority implementation of direct payments (March 1998)*. London: Policy Studies Institute.

Health Advisory Service (1997). Health Advisory Service. *Services for people who are elderly*. London: Stationery Office.

Health Advisory Service (1998). *Not because they are old: an independent inquiry into the care of older people on acute wards in general hospitals*. London: HAS.

Health Service Commissioner (1990). *Annual report for 1989–1990*. HC 538. London: HMSO.

Health Service Commissioner (1991). *Annual report for 1990–91*. London: HMSO.

Health Service Commissioner (1994). *Annual report for 1993–94. Fourth report 1993–94*. HC 499. London: HMSO.

Health Service Commissioner (1996a). Health Service Commissioner. *Guide to the work of the health service ombudsman*. London: HSC.

Health Service Commissioner (1996b). Health Service Commissioner. *Investigations of complaints about long term NHS care*. Fifth report for session 1995–96. HC 504. London: HMSO.

Healy, J., Yarrow, S. (1997). *Parents living with children in old age*. Policy Press: Bristol.

Help the Aged (1998). *One year on: the 'Sefton' judgment and residential care funding, a report by the Help the Aged's National Advice Services*. London: Help the Aged.

Henwood, M. (1994). *Fit for change? Snapshots of the community care reforms one year on*. Leeds: Nuffield Institute for Health, University of Leeds; King's Fund Centre.

Henwood, M. (1995). *Making a difference? Implementation of the community care reforms two years on*. Leeds: Nuffield Institute for Health, University of Leeds; King's Fund Centre.

Henwood, M. (1996). *Continuing health care: analysis of a sample of final documents*. Leeds: Nuffield Institute for Health, University of Leeds.

Henwood, M. (1998a). *Ignored and invisible? Carers' experience of the NHS*. London: Carers National Association.

Henwood, M. (1998b). *Our turn next: a fresh look at home support services for older people*. Leeds: Nuffield Institute for Health, Community Care Division.

Heritage, J. (1996). *Residential care fees: don't let them grab the house*. Edinburgh: Spinning Acorn Press.

Heywood, F. (1994). *Adaptations: finding ways to say yes*. Bristol: SAUS Publications.

Heywood, F. (with Smart, G.) (1996). *Funding adaptations: the need to cooperate*. Bristol: Policy Press.

Hills, J. (1997). *Future of welfare: a guide to the debate*. Revised edition. York: Joseph Rowntree Foundation.

Hinton, C. (1997). *Using your home as capital 1997–98*. London: Age Concern England.

Hirst, J. (1998). 'Canny lad is haway to the Lords'. *Community Care*, 23–29 July 1998,p.14.

Home Office (1998). *Fairer, faster and firmer: a modern approach to immigration and asylum*. Cm 4018. London: Home Office.

House of Commons Health Committee (1993). *Community care: the way forward*. 6th report 1992–1993. 2 vols. London: HMSO.

House of Commons Health Committee (1995). *Long-term care: NHS responsibilities for meeting continuing health care needs*. Volume 1. HC 19–1. London: HMSO.

House of Commons Health Committee (1996). *Long-term care: future provision and funding*. Volume 1. HC 59–1. London: HMSO.

House of Commons Health Committee (1998). *Relationship between health and social services*. HC 74–1. London: Stationery Office.

House of Commons Public Accounts Committee (1993). *Health services for physically disabled people*. HC 538. London: HMSO.

House of Commons Select Committee on Public Administration (1997). *Further government response to the first report from the Select Committee on the Parliamentary Commissioner for Administration (session 1996–1997) on the report of the Health Service Ombudsman for 1995–96*. London: Stationery Office.

HSE (1998). Health and Safety Executive. *Manual handling: Manual Handling Operations Regulations 1992, guidance on regulations*. Sudbury: HSE Books.

Hunt, L. (1994). 'Pensioner in pain says age and cost influenced care'. *Independent*, 15th April 1994.

Hunter, M. (1998). 'Reaching out'. *Community Care*, 23–29 July 1998,pp.20–21.

ILF (1997). 'Independent Living Fund'. *Independent Living Funds: a report, July 1997*. Nottingham: ILF.

IRS (1995). 'Independent Review Service for the Social Fund (1995)'. *Social Fund Commissioner's report 1994/95*. London: HMSO.

Ivory, M. (1998). 'Thinking outside the checklist'. *Community Care*, 2–8 July 1998,p.16.

Jeffrey, J. (1994). 'Rise of the broker: care management is a new phenomenon for social workers: how are social services departments interpreting it?' *Care Weekly*:9 June 1994,pp.10–11.

Jones, R. (1993a). *Encyclopedia of social services and child care law*. London: Sweet and Maxwell (looseleaf, regularly updated).

Jones, R. (1993b). *Registered Homes Act manual*. 2nd edition. London: Sweet and Maxwell.

Joule, N. (1994). *London hospitals: discharging their responsibility?* London: Greater London Association of Community Health Councils.

Judge, K., Mays, N. (1994). 'Allocating resources for health and social care in England'. *British Medical Journal*; 21 May 1994, pp.1363–1366.

Keep, J., Clarkson, J. (1993). *Disabled people have rights: a two year project to enforce section 2 of the Chronically Sick and Disabled Persons Act 1970, interim report*. London: Royal Association for Disability and Rehabilitation.

Keep, J., Clarkson, J. (1994). *Disabled people have rights: final report of a two year project funded by the Nuffield Provincial Hospitals Trust*. London: Royal Association for Disability and Rehabilitation.

Kenny, D., Edwards, P., Stanton, R. (1994). *From social security to community care: the impact of the transfer of funding on local authorities*. Luton: Local Government Management Board.

Kent County Council SSD (1993). *Summary community care plan for Kent (adult and children's services) 1993/94–1995/96*. Maidstone: Kent County Council.

Kestenbaum, A. (1996). *Independent living: a review*. York: Joseph Rowntree Foundation.

Kestenbaum, A. (1997). *Disability-related costs and charges for community care*. London: Disablement Income Group.

Kestenbaum, A., Cava, H. (1998). *Work, rest and pay: the deal for personal assistance users*. York: York Publishing Services (for Joseph Rowntree Foundation).

Knaffler, S. (1998). 'Economic, social and cultural rights in an international context'. *Legal Action*: October 1998, pp.8–9.

KPMG Peat Marwick (1993). *Informing users and carers*. London: Department of Health.

Laing, W. (1993). *Financing long-term care: the crucial debate*. London: Age Concern England.

Laing, W. (1998). *A fair price for care? Disparities between market rates for nursing/residential care and what state funding agencies will pay*. York: Joseph Rowntree Foundation.

Lamb, B., Layzell, S. (1994). *Disabled in Britain: a world apart*. London: SCOPE.

Lamb, B., Layzell, S. (1995a). *Disabled in Britain: behind closed doors, the carers' experience*. London: SCOPE.

Lamb, B., Layzell, S. (1995b). *Disabled in Britain: behind closed doors, counting on community care*. London: SCOPE.

Langan, J., Means, R. (1995). *Personal finances, elderly people with dementia and the 'new' community care*. Oxford: Anchor Housing Association.

Law Commission (1993). *Mentally incapacitated and other vulnerable adults: public law protection*. London: HMSO.

Law Commission (1995). *Mental incapacity. Law Com no.231*. London: HMSO.

Law Commission (1996). *Privity of contract: contracts for the benefit of third parties*. Law Com no.242. Cm 3329. London: Stationery Office.

Law Society (1995). *Gifts of property: implications for future liability to pay for long term care: guidelines for solicitors*. London: Law Society, Mental Health and Disability Sub Committee.

Lee, S. (1988). *Judging judges*. London: Faber and Faber.

Leedham, I., Wistow, G. (1992). *Community care and general practitioners: the role of GPs in the assessment process with special reference to the perspectives of social services departments.* Leeds: Nuffield Institute for Health Care Studies, University of Leeds.

Leeds City Council (1995). *A guide to community care assessments.* Leeds: LCC (leaflet).

Letts, P. (1998). *Managing other people's money.* 2nd edition. London: Age Concern England.

LGA (1996). Local Government Association. *Bed blocking survey: preliminary results.* London: LGA.

LGMB (1997). Local Government Management Board. *Occupational therapy workload survey 1997.* London: LGMB.

Lord Chancellor (1997). *Who decides? Making decisions on behalf of mentally incapacitated adults.* London: Stationery Office.

Lord President of the Council and Leader of the House of the Commons *et al.* (1995). *Tackling drugs together: a strategy for England 1995/98.* London: HMSO.

Love, C. (1996). 'Economic considerations when choosing a hoist and slings'. *British Journal of Therapy and Rehabilitation:* April 1996; 3(4), pp.189–1988.

Loveland, I. (1994). *Irrelevant considerations? The role of administrative law in determining the local connection of homeless persons.* In: Richardson, G., Genn, H. (1994). *Administrative law and government action: the courts and alternative mechanisms of review.* Oxford: Clarendon Press.

Lovelock, R., Powell, J., Craggs, S. (1995). *Shared territory: assessing the social support needs of visually impaired people.* York: Joseph Rowntree Foundation.

Low, C. (1996). 'Disability models or muddles'. *Therapy Weekly:* February 1996; 22(29), p.7.

Lush, D. (1998). 'Taking liberties: enduring powers of attorney and financial abuse'. *Solicitors Journal:* 11 September 1998, 808–809.

Macfarlane, A., Laurie, L. (1996). *Demolishing special needs: fundamental principles of non-discriminatory housing.* Derby: British Council of Organisations of Disabled People.

Macintosh, S., Leather, P. (1993). *Minor works, a major step: minor works assistance in practice.* Nottingham: Care & Repair.

Macintosh, S., Leather, P., McCafferty, P. (1993). *Role of housing agency services in helping disabled people.* London: HMSO.

Mair, A. (1972). *Medical rehabilitation: the pattern for the future.* Edinburgh: HMSO.

Mandelstam, M. (1993). *How to get equipment for disability.* 3rd edition. London: Jessica Kingsley and Kogan Page (for the Disabled Living Foundation).

Mandelstam, M. (1997). *Equipment for older or disabled people and the law.* London: Jessica Kingsley.

Mandelstam, M. (1998). *An A to Z of community care law.* London: Jessica Kingsley.

Marks, L. (1994). *Seamless care or patchwork quilt? Discharging patients from acute hospital care.* London: King's Fund Institute.

Marks, O. (1998). *Equipped for equality.* London: SCOPE.

Martin, J. (1994). Elderly relatives, estoppel and undue influence. *New Law Journal,* 25 February 1994, pp.264–265.

Martin, J., Meltzer, H., Elliot, D. (1988). *OPCS surveys of disability in Great Britain, report 1: the prevalence of disability among adults.* London: HMSO.

McColl, I. (Chair). *Review of artificial limb and appliance centres.* London: Department of Health and Social Security.

McDonald, A. (1997). *Challenging local authority decisions.* Birmingham: Venture Press.

McKay, C., Patrick, H. (1997). *The care maze: the law and your rights to community care in Scotland.* 2nd edition. Glasgow: ENABLE.

McMurtrie, S. (1997). 'The waiting game: the Parliamentary Commissioner's response to delay in administrative procedures'. *Public Law:* Spring 1997, pp.159–173.

Means R., Brenton M., Harrison L., Heywood F. (1997). *Making partnerships work in community care: a guide for practitioners in housing, health and social services.* London: Department of Health, Department of the Environment, Transport and the Regions.

Means, J., Langan, R. (1995). *Personal finances, elderly people with dementia and the 'new' community care.* Oxford: Anchor Housing Association.

Medical Foundation for the Care of Victims of Torture (1997). *Past misery, present muddle: council by council survey of assistance to asylum seekers one year on.* London: MFCVT.

MENCAP (1999). *Fully charged: how local authority charging is harming people with a learning disability.* London: MENCAP.

Mental Health Foundation (1994). *Creating community care: report of the Mental Health Foundation into community care for people with severe mental illness.* London: MHF.

Meredith, B. (1993). *The community care handbook: the new system explained.* London: Age Concern England.

Meredith, B. (1994). *Next steps: lessons for the future of community care.* London: Department of Health.

Meredith, B. (1995). *The community care handbook: the reformed system explained.* 2nd edition. London: Age Concern England.

Middleton, L. (1997). *The art of assessment.* Birmingham: Venture Press.

Midgley, M., Munlo, I., Brown, M. (1997). *Sharing power: integrating user involvement and multi-agency working to improve housing for older people.* York: Joseph Rowntree Foundation; Community Care.

Ministry of Health; Department of Health for Scotland (1944). *A National Health Service.* London: HMSO.

Morris, A. (1997a). All the help Parliament prescribed. *The Times,* 26th May 1997.

Morris, J. (1995). *The power to change: commissioning health and social services with disabled people.* London: King's Fund Centre.

Morris, J. (1997b). *Community care: working in partnership with service users.* Birmingham: Venture Press.

Mullen, T., Pick, K., Prosser, T. (1996). *Judicial review in Scotland.* Chichester: Wiley.

NAHA (1984). National Association of Health Authorities and Trusts. *Registration and inspection of nursing home: a handbook for health authorities.* Birmingham: NAHAT.

NAHA (1988a). National Association of Health Authorities and Trusts. *Registration and inspection of nursing home: a handbook for health authorities: 1988 supplement.* Birmingham: NAHA.

NAHA (1988b). National Association of Health Authorities. *Health authority concerns for children with special needs: a report on a survey of health authorities on the implementation of the Education Act 1981.* Birmingham: NAHA.

NAHAT (1991a). National Association of Health Authorities and Trusts. *Care in the community: definitions of health and social care: developing an approach: a West Midlands study.* Birmingham: NAHAT.

NAHAT (1991b). National Association of Health Authorities and Trusts. *NHS Handbook.* London: Macmillan.

NAO (1992). National Audit Office. *Health services for physically disabled people aged 16–64.* London: HMSO.

National Council for Hospice and Specialist Palliative Care Services (1996). *Eligibility criteria for continuing health care: palliative care.* London: NCHSPCS.

NCC (1993). National Consumer Council. *Consumer concerns 1993: a consumer view of health services: the report of a MORI survey.* London: NCC, pp.29–37.

NCC (1994). National Consumer Council. *Meeting long-term health care needs: response to NHS Executive draft guidelines on NHS responsibilities.* London: NCC.

NCC (1995). National Consumer Council. *Charging consumers for social services: local authority policy and guidance.* London: NCC.

NCC (1997). National Consumer Council. *Finding out about NHS continuing care.* London: NCC.

NDC (1996). National Disability Council. *Code of practice, rights of access: goods, facilities, services and premises.* London: Stationery Office.

NDC (1998). National Disability Council. *Proposals for a code of practice, rights of access: goods, facilities, services and premises.* London: NDC.

Neate, P. (1994). 'Under pressure: care managers are on the front line between clients and service providers.' In *The next key tasks.* Sutton: Community Care.

Neill, J., Williams, J. (1992). *Leaving hospital: elderly people and their discharge to community care.* London: HMSO. (National Institute for Social for Department of Health).

NFHA (1993). National Federation of Housing Federations. *Community care hotline: housing and community care: the loose connection?* London: NFHA.

NHSE (1994). NHS Executive. *Feet first: report of the joint Department of Health and NHS Chiropody Task Force.* London: Department of Health.

NHSE (1996). NHS Executive. *Complaints, listening, acting, improving: guidance on implementation of the NHS complaints procedure.* London: Department of Health.

NHSE (1998). *Directory of developments in occupational therapy, physiotherapy and speech and language therapy services.* London: Department of Health.

NHSME (1993). NHS Management Executive. *Establishing district of residence.* Leeds: Department of Health.

Nocon, A., Baldwin, S., Jones, L., Stuart, O. (1995). *Social support needs of physically and sensorially disabled adults: a literature review.* Belfast: Department of Health and Social Services, Social Services Inspectorate; University of York, Social Policy Research Unit.

Nocon, A., Baldwin, S. (1998). *Trends in rehabilitation policy: a review of the literature.* London: King's Fund.

North, C., Ritchie, J., Ward, K. (1993). *Factors influencing the implementation of the Care Programme Approach.* London: HMSO.

NWTROTAG (1993). North West Thames Regional Occupational Therapy Advisory Group. *Statement on EL(92)20 [charging for equipment].* Stanmore: NWTROTAG.

O'Brien, C., Wurr, J. (1993). *Community care plans 1993/94: alcohol and drug use.* London: Standing Conference on Drug Abuse.

O'Leary, J. (1997). *Beyond help? Improving service provision for street homeless people with mental health and alcohol or drug dependency problems.* London: National Homeless Alliance.

O'Sullivan, D. (1998). The allocation of scarce resources and the right to life under the European Convention on Human Rights. *Public Law:* Autumn 1998, pp.389–395.

Office of Fair Trading (1998). *Older people as consumers in care homes: a report by the Office Fair Trading.* London: OFT.

Oliveck, M. (1998). 'New scheme: a slow start'. *Therapy Weekly,* 21 May 1998, p.6.

Oliver, M. (1990). *Politics of disability.* Basingstoke: Macmillan.

Oliver, M. (1996). *Understanding disability: from theory to practice.* Basingstoke: Macmillan.

Parker C., Gordon R. (1998). *Pathways to partnership: legal aspects of joint working in mental health.* London: Sainsbury Centre for Mental Health.

Parker, G. (1992). *Counting care: numbers and types of informal carers.* In: Twigg, D. (ed) (1992). *Carers: research and practice.* London: HMSO.

Parker, H. (1997). *Money to spend as they wish: the personal expenses allowance in care homes.* London: Age Concern England.

Pearson (Lord) (Chair) (1978). *Royal Commission on Civil Liability and Compensation for Personal Injury.* Cmnd 7054. London: HMSO.

Pearson, M., Richardson, S. (1994). *Hidden health and social care needs in Tranmere*. Liverpool: Health and Community Care Research Unit.

Pettit, G. (1997). *Non-residential services in London: older people and adults*. London: London Research Centre.

Pieda (for Department of Environment) (1996). *Evaluation of the disabled facilities grants system*. London: HMSO.

Pollock, D. (1998). *The politics of continence: standards of service and VAT on pads*. London: Continence Foundation.

Pook, H. (1998). 'The Local Government Ombudsman'. *Adviser* 1998; 70, pp.5–7.

Preston-Shoot, M. (1996). 'Contesting the contradictions: needs, resources and community care decisions'. *Journal of Social Welfare and Family Law*: 1996; 18(3), pp.307–325.

Preston-Shoot, M., Roberts, G., Vernon, S. (1998a). 'Social work: from interaction to integration'. *Journal of Social Work Law and Practice*: 1998; 20(1),pp.65–80.

Preston-Shoot, M., Roberts, G., Vernon, S. (1998b). 'Working together in social work law'. *Journal of Social Work Law and Practice*: 1998; 20(2),pp.65–80.

Price, D. (1996). *Continuing care for older people: the responses to Circular HSG(95)8*. Newcastle: Social Welfare Research Unit, University of Northumbria.

Prime Minister (1991). *The Citizen's Charter*. London: HMSO.

Prime Minister (1999). *Caring about carers: a national strategy for carers*. London: HM Government.

Public Law Project (1994). *Challenging community care decisions: a briefing by the Public Law Project*. London: PLP.

Public Law Project (Collins, B.)(1995). *Challenging community care decisions in Northern Ireland*. London: PLP.

RADAR (1997). Royal Association for Disability and Rehabilitation. *Cost of community care*. London: RADAR.

Randall, B. (1995). *Staying put: the best move I'll never make*. Oxford: Anchor Housing Association.

Raynes, N.V. (1997). *Inspection reports: building on experience*. London: Social Services Inspectorate (Department of Health).

RCN, Spastics Society (1992). *Day in, day out: a survey of views of respite care*. London: Royal College of Nursing; Spastics Society.

RCP (1986). Royal College of Physicians. *Physical disability and beyond*. London: RCP.

RCP (1994). Royal College of Physicians. *Ensuring equity and quality of care for elderly people: the interface between geriatric medicine and general (internal) medicine*. London: RCP.

RCP (1995). Royal College of Physicians. *Setting priorities in the NHS: a framework for decision-making*. London: RCP.

Redmayne, S. (1995). *Spotlight on homes for the elderly: an analysis of inspection reports on residential care homes*. Bath: University of Bath.

Richards, M. (1996). *Community care for older people: rights, remedies and finances*. Bristol: Jordans.

Richards, M. (1997). *Revenue funding for supported housing: legal background*. Leeds: Nuffield Institute for Health, Community Care Division.

Richardson, G., Sunkin, M. (1996). 'Judicial review: questions of impact'. *Public Law*; Spring 1996, pp.79–103.

Ridout, P. (1998). *Registered homes: a legal handbook*. Bristol: Jordans.

Richmond, H. (1997). *Legal and professional responsibilities*. In: National Back Pain Association. *Guide to the handling of patients*. 4th edition. London: NBPA.

Ritchie, J.H. (chair) (1994). *Report of the inquiry into the care and treatment of Christopher Clunis: presented to the Chairman of North East Thames and South East Thames Regional Health Authorities, February 1994*. London: HMSO.

Roberts, S., Steele, J., Moore, N. (1991). *Finding out about residential care: results of a survey of users*. London: Policy Studies Institute.

Ross, F., Campbell, F. (1992). *If it wasn't for this wheelchair ... I might as well be dead: a study of equipment and aids for daily living in the community: a district nurse and consumer perspective*. London: Department of Nursing Studies, King's College London.

Royal Commission on Long Term Care (1999). *With respect to old age: executive summary*. London: Stationary Office.

Salvage, A. (1995). *Attitudes and concerns of older people about long-term care funding: evidence for the Joseph Rowntree Foundation Inquiry into meeting the cost of long-term care*. London: Age Concern England.

Salvage, A. (1996). *Stuck on the waiting list: older people and equipment for independent living*. London: Age Concern England.

Salvage, A. (1998). *On your feet? Older people and NHS chiropody services*. London: Age Concern England.

Sanderson, J. (1991). *An agenda for action on incontinence services*. London: Department of Health.

Schwehr, B. (1995). 'Rational rationing of community care resources'. *Public Law*: 1995, pp.374–381.

Schwehr, B. (1997a). 'A study in fairness in the field of community care law (I)'. *Journal of Social Welfare and Family Law*: 1997; 19(2),pp.159–172.

Schwehr, B. (1997b). 'A study in fairness in the field of community care law (II)'. *Journal of Social Welfare and Family Law*: 1997; 19(3),pp.247–266.

SCODA (1997). Standing Conference on Drug Abuse. *Drug-related early intervention: developing services for young people and families*. London: SCODA.

Secretaries of State (1981). Secretary of State for Social Services, Secretary of State for Scotland, Secretary of State for Wales, Secretary of State for Northern Ireland. *Growing older*. London: HMSO.

Secretaries of State (1989). Secretaries of State for Health, Social Security, Wales and Scotland. *Caring for people: community care in the next decade and beyond*. London: HMSO.

Secretary of State for Health (1997a). *Developing partnerships in mental health*. London: Stationery Office.

Secretary of State for Health (1997b). *The new NHS: modern, dependable*. London: Stationery Office.

Secretary of State for Health (1998). *Modernising social services: promoting independence, improving protection, raising standards.* London: Stationery Office.

Simons, K. (1995). *I'm not complaining but ... Complaints procedures in social services departments.* York: Joseph Rowntree Foundation.

Simons, K., Ward, L. (1997). *A foot in the door: the early years of supported living for people with learning difficulties in the UK.* Manchester: National Development Team.

Singh, P. (1995). *Community care: Britain's other lottery.* London: MENCAP.

Smale, G., Tuson, G., Biehal, N., Marsh, P. (1993). (National Institute for Social Work). *Empowerment, assessment, care management and the skilled worker.* London: HMSO.

Smith, J. (1994). *Power, older people and being cared for.* In: Hobman D, Hollingberry R, Means R, Lart R, Smith J (1994). *More power to our elders.* London: Counsel and Care.

Snell, J. (1995). 'Raising awareness'. *Nursing Times:* 2 August 1995; 91(31), pp.20–21.

SSI (1988a). Social Services Inspectorate. *Services for people with a physical disability: a report on an information trawl undertaken in 17 social services departments in north western England.* Manchester: Department of Health.

SSI (1988b). Social Services Inspectorate. *Managing policy change in home help services.* London: Department of Health.

SSI (1988c). Social Services Inspectorate. *Doing it better together: a report of developments in four locations to establish local procedures for multi-disciplinary assessment of the needs of elderly people.* London: Department of Health.

SSI (1988d). Social Services Inspectorate. *Health in homes: a review of arrangements for health care in local authority homes for elderly people.* London: Department of Health.

SSI (1988e). Social Services Inspectorate. *A wider vision: report of an inspection of the management and organisation of services for people who are blind or partially sighted.* London: Department of Health.

SSI (1989a). Social Services Inspectorate. *Sign posts: leading to better social services for deaf-blind people.* London: Department of Health. London: Department of Health.

SSI (1989b). Social Services Inspectorate. *Homes are for living in.* London: HMSO.

SSI (1990). Social Services Inspectorate. *Developing services for disabled people: results of an inspection to monitor the operation of the Disabled Persons (Services, Consultation and Representation) Act 1986.* London: Department of Health.

SSI (1991a). Social Services Inspectorate. *Hear me: see me: an inspection of services from three agencies to disabled people in Gloucestershire.* Bristol: Department of Health.

SSI (1991b). Social Services Inspectorate. *Right to complain: practice guidance on complaints procedures in social services departments.* London: HMSO.

SSI (1991c). Social Services Inspectorate. *Managing aids to daily living.* Bristol: Department of Health.

SSI (1991d). Social Services Inspectorate. *Report of an inspection of occupational therapy services in Dudley.* Birmingham: Department of Health.

SSI (1991e). Social Services Inspectorate. *Inspection of the occupational therapy services in Devon.* Bristol: Department of Health.

SSI (1991f). Social Services Inspectorate. *Getting the message across: a guide to developing and communicating policies, principles and procedures on assessment.* London: HMSO.

SSI (1991g). Social Services Inspectorate. *Community based services for people who misuse drugs: a study in north western region.* Manchester: Department of Health.

SSI (1991h). Social Services Inspectorate. *Complaints about the social services department: ideas for a practice booklet for clerks, receptionists and telephonists.* London: HMSO.

SSI (1992a) Social Services Inspectorate (Sutton C). *Confronting elder abuse.* London: Department of Health.

SSI (1992b). Social Services Inspectorate. *Mental illness specific grants: monitoring of proposals for use 1991/92.* London: Department of Health.

SSI (1993a). Social Services Inspectorate. *Whose life it anyway? A report of an inspection of services for people with multiple impairments.* London: Department of Health.

SSI (1993b). Social Services Inspectorate. *Caring for people progress review: North of England region.* Leeds: Department of Health.

SSI (1993c). Social Services Inspectorate (Southern England Region, Policy and Business Division). *Caring for people: progress on implementation.* London: Department of Health.

SSI (1993d). Social Services Inspectorate. *Achieving the change in SSI Central Region: fifth report on the implementation of Caring for People.* Birmingham: Department of Health.

SSI (1993e). Social Services Inspectorate. *Inspection of assessment and care management arrangements in social services departments: interim overview report.* London: Department of Health.

SSI (1993f). Social Services Inspectorate. *Inspection of projects funded by the mental illness specific grant.* London: HMSO.

SSI (1993g). Social Services Inspectorate. *Inspection of complaints procedures in local authority social services departments.* London: HMSO.

SSI (1993h). Social Services Inspectorate. *Social services for hospital patients III: users and carers perspective.* London: Department of Health.

SSI (1993j). Social Services Inspectorate. *Community care implementation: monitoring report for London.* London: Department of Health.

SSI (1993k). Social Services Inspectorate. *Progress on the right to complain: monitoring social services complaints procedures 1992/3.* London: Department of Health.

SSI (1994a). Social Services Inspectorate. *Inspection of assessment and care management arrangements in social services departments: October 1993 – March 1994: second overview report.* London: Department of Health.

SSI (1994b). Social Services Inspectorate. *Occupational therapy services, the community contribution: report on local authority occupational therapy services.* London: Department of Health.

SSI (1994c). Social Services Inspectorate. *Report of an inspection of assessment and care management arrangements in social services departments: London Borough of Harrow, 1–10 December 1993.* London: Department of Health.

SSI (1994d). Social Services Inspectorate. *Inspection of assessment and care management arrangements in social services departments: London Borough of Tower Hamlets.* London: Department of Health.

SSI (1994e). Social Services Inspectorate, Department of Health. *Inspection of local authority services for people affected by HIV/AIDS: overview.* London: HMSO.

SSI (1994f). Social Services Inspectorate. *The F factor: reasons why some older people choose residential care.* London: Department of Health.

SSI (1994g). Social Services Inspectorate (Warburton, R.W). *Home and away: a review of recent research evidence to explain why some elderly people enter residential care homes while others stay at home.* London: Department of Health.

SSI (1994h). Social Services Inspectorate. *Inspection of social services department arrangements for the discharge of elderly people from hospital to residential and nursing home care: Northumberland.* Gateshead: Department of Health.

SSI (1994j). Social Services Inspectorate. *Inspection of social work services for mentally ill people in the community, Stockport social services department.* Manchester: Department of Health.

SSI (1994k). Social Services Inspectorate. *Inspection of social work services for mentally ill people in the community, Bexley.* London: Department of Health.

SSI (1994m). Social Services Inspectorate. *Advice note for use by Social Services Inspectorate: discretionary charges for adult social services (section 17 of Health and Social Services and Social Security Adjudications Act 1983).* London: Department of Health.

SSI (1994n). Social Services Inspectorate (Hickey, A., Campbell, A.). *Inspection of complaints procedures in the London Borough of Newham, June/July 1994.* London: Department of Health.

SSI (1994o). Social Services Inspectorate. *Inspection of the complaints procedure: North Yorkshire County Council.* Leeds: Department of Health, 1994.

SSI (1994p). Social Services Inspectorate. *Report of the inspection of complaints procedures in West Sussex Social Services Department, November 1993.* London: Department of Health.

SSI (1994q). Social Services Inspectorate. *Second overview report of the complaints procedures in local authority social services departments.* London: Department of Health.

SSI (1994r). Social Services Inspectorate (Strettle, T., Lowe, E.). *Inspection of complaints procedures in Surrey Social Services Department, May 1994.* London: Department of Health.

SSI (1994s). Social Services Inspectorate (Ormiston, H., Cope, C.). *Inspection of complaints procedure, Tameside MBC Social Services Department, June 1994.* Manchester: Department of Health.

SSI (1994t). Social Services Inspectorate (Balfe, R., Barnes, J.). *Norfolk social services: inspection of complaints procedures, May 1994.* Nottingham: Department of Health.

SSI (1995a). Social Services Inspectorate. *A way ahead for carers, priorities for managers and practitioners: a summary of two SSI reports.* London: Department of Health.

SSI (1995b). Social Services Inspectorate. *Caring for people at home: an overview of the national inspection of social services department arrangements for the assessment and delivery of home care services.* London: Department of Health.

SSI (1995c). Social Services Inspectorate. *Caring today: national inspection of local authority support to carers.* London: Department of Health.

SSI (1995e). Social Services Inspectorate). *Inspection of community services for physically disabled people in Wirral, 9–20 October 1995.* Manchester: Department of Health.

SSI (1995f). Social Services Inspectorate. *Inspection of social services for people who misuse alcohol or drugs: overview report.* London: DH.

SSI (1995g). Social Services Inspectorate. *Moving on: report of the national inspection of social services department arrangements for the discharge of older people from hospital to residential or nursing home care.* London: Department of Health.

SSI (1995h). Social Services Inspectorate. *Moving on a further year: inspection of social services department arrangements for the discharge of older people from hospital to residential or nursing home care.* London: Department of Health.

SSI (1995j). Social Services Inspectorate. *Opportunities or knocks: national inspection of recreation and leisure in day services for people with learning disabilities.* London: Department of Health.

SSI (1995k). Social Services Inspectorate. *Responding to residents: a report of inspections of local authority residential care home for older people.* London: DH.

SSI (1995m). Social Services Inspectorate. *What next for carers? Findings from an SSI project.* London: Department of Health.

SSI (1995n). Social Services Inspectorate. *Young carers: something to think about.* London: Department of Health.

SSI (1996a) Social Services Inspectorate (Griffiths, G.). *Almost half: social services department inspection units, fourth overview of SSI inspections for the period October 1994 – July 1995.* London: Department of Health.

SSI (1996b) Social Services Inspectorate. *Assessing older people with dementia living in the community: practice issues for social and health services.* London: Department of Health.

SSI (1996c) Social Services Inspectorate. *Carers (Recognition and Services) Act 1996: practice guide.* London: Department of Health.

SSI (1996d). Social Services Inspectorate. *Caring for people at home: part II: report of a second inspection of arrangements for assessment and delivery of home care services.* London: Department of Health.

SSI (1996e) Social Services Inspectorate. *Progressing services with physically disabled people: report on inspections of community services for physically disabled people.* London: Department of Health.

SSI (1996f). Social Services Inspectorate. *Standards used by the Social Services Inspectorate, volume 2: children's services.* London: Department of Health.

SSI (1996g). Social Services Inspectorate. *Standards used by the Social Services Inspectorate, volume 3: children's residential care, secure accommodation and juvenile justice.* London: Department of Health.

SSI (1996h). Social Services Inspectorate. *Standards used by the Social Services Inspectorate, volume 4: community care.* London: Department of Health.

SSI (1996j). Social Services Inspectorate (Cope, C., Lindsey, R.). *Inspection of complaints procedures in Lancashire Social Services Department, February 1996.* Manchester: Department of Health.

SSI (1996k). Social Services Inspectorate (Owens, C., Horner, C., Johns, C.). *Inspection of local authority social services departments complaints procedures, Dorset, April 1996.* Bristol: Department of Health.

SSI (1996m). Social Services Inspectorate. *SSI inspection of complaints procedures in local authority social services departments, third overview report, January 1996.* London: Department of Health.

SSI (1996n). Social Services Inspectorate (Rourke, M., Clark, P.). *Inspection of complaints procedures, London Borough of Bromley, July 1996.* London: Department of Health.

SSI (1996o). Social Services Inspectorate (Fruin, D., Fean, L.). *Inspection of complaints procedures, Cumbria Social Services Department, January 1996.* Gateshead: Department of Health.

SSI (1996p). Social Services Inspectorate (Watson, A., Cope, C.). *Inspection of complaints procedures in Cheshire Social Services Department.* Manchester: Department of Health.

SSI (1996q). Social Services Inspectorate (Barnes, J., Wilson, J.). *Inspection of complaints procedures in Derbyshire SSD, July 1996.* Nottingham: Department of Health.

SSI (1997a). Social Services Inspectorate. *A service on the edge: inspection of deaf and hard of hearing people.* London: Department of Health.

SSI (1997b). Social Services Inspectorate (Brown, D., Fean, L.). *At home with dementia: inspection of services for older people with dementia in the community.* London: Department of Health.

SSI (1997c). Social Services Inspectorate (Gazdar, C., Fean, L.). *Cornerstone of care: inspection of care for older people.* London: Department of Health.

SSI (1997d). Social Services Inspectorate. *Inspection of case records, Haringey Social Services Department, August 1997.* London: Department of Health.

SSI (1997e). Social Services Inspectorate. *Inspection of case recording, Somerset Social Services Department, October 1997.* Bristol: Department of Health.

SSI (1997f). Social Services Inspectorate. *Inspection of hospital discharge (care management) services in Gloucestershire, June 1997.* Bristol: Department of Health.

SSI (1997g). Social Services Inspectorate. *Inspection of hospital discharge (care management) services in Sutton, June 1997.* London: Department of Health.

SSI (1997h). Social Services Inspectorate (Lindsey, R. et al.). *Inspection of social services combined with other functions: Walsall Housing and Social Services, December 1997.* London: Department of Health.

SSI (1997j). Social Services Inspectorate (Barnes, D.). *Older people with mental health problems living alone: anybody's priority?* London: Department of Health.

SSI (1997k). Social Services Inspectorate (Fiedler, B., Ellis, D.). *Planning for life no. 3: good practice in the independent sector, developing community services for people with complex multiple disabilities.* London: Department of Health.

SSI (1997m). Social Services Inspectorate. *Services for older people with learning disabilities.* London: Department of Health.

SSI (1998a). Social Services Inspectorate. *A sharper focus: inspection of services for adults who are visually impaired or blind.* London: Department of Health.

SSI (1998b). Social Services Inspectorate (Horne, D.). *Getting better? Inspection of hospital discharge (care management) arrangements for older people.* London: Department of Health.

SSI (1998c). Social Services Inspectorate. *Inspection of hospital discharge (care management) services in Bristol, June 1997.* Bristol: Department of Health.

SSI (1998d). Social Services Inspectorate (Fruin, D.). *Moving into the mainstream: the report of a national inspection of services for adults with learning disabilities.* London: Department of Health.

SSI (1998e). Social Services Inspectorate. *Signposts to services: inspection of social services information to the public.* London: Department of Health.

SSI (1998f). Social Services Inspectorate (Murray, U., Brown, D.). *They look after their own, don't they. Inspection of community care services for black and ethnic minority older people.* London: Department of Health.

SSI (1998g). Social Services Inspectorate. *A matter of chance for carers? Inspection of local authority support for carers.* London: Department of Health.

SSI (1999). Social Services Inspectorate. *Recording with care: inspection of case recording in social services departments.* London: DH.

SSI, Arthritis Care (1996). *Disability and isolation: a joint SSI/Arthritis Care study of isolated people with arthritis.* London: Social Services Inspectorate, Department of Health.

SSI, DLF (1992). Social Services Inspectorate, Disabled Living Foundation (Brearley, P., Mandelstam, M.). *Review of literature 1986–1991 on day care services for adults.* London: HMSO.

SSI, NHSME (1993). Social Services Inspectorate; National Health Service Management Executive. *SSI/RHA community care monitoring, September 1993: national summary.* London: Department of Health.

SSI, NHSE (1994a). Social Services Inspectorate; NHS Executive. *Care management.* London: Department of Health.

SSI, NHSME (1994b). Social Services Inspectorate; NHS Management Executive. *Assessment special study: a joint SSI/NHSME study of assessment procedures in five local authority areas.* London: Department of Health.

SSI, NHSME (1994c). Social Services Inspectorate; NHS Management Executive. *Special study of purchasing and contracting.* London: Department of Health.

SSI, NHSE (1994d). Social Services Inspectorate; NHS Executive. *Community care for people with HIV and AIDS.* London: Department of Health.

SSI, NHSME (1994e). Social Services Inspectorate; NHS Management Executive. *Implementing community care for younger people with physical and sensory disabilities.* London: Department of Health.

SSI, NHSE (1994f). Social Services Inspectorate; NHS Executive. *It's our lives: community care for people with learning disabilities.* London: Department of Health.

SSI, NHSE (1994g). Social Services Inspectorate, NHS Executive. *Community care packages for older people.* London: Department of Health.

SSI, NHSME (1994h). Social Services Inspectorate; NHS Management Executive. *Community care monitoring: special study: mental health services.* London: Department of Health.

SSI, NHSE (1994j). Social Services Inspectorate; NHS Executive. *Role of the GP and primary healthcare team.* London: Department of Health.

SSI, NHSME (1994k). Social Services Inspectorate; NHS Management Executive. *31 December agreements: reviewing the implementation.* London: Department of Health.

SSI, SIS (1991). Social Services Inspectorate; Social Information Systems. *Assessment systems and community care.* London: Department of Health.

SSI, SWSG (1991a). Social Services Inspectorate; Social Work Services Group. *Care management and assessment: practitioners' guide.* London: HMSO.

SSI, SWSG (1991b). Social Services Inspectorate; Social Work Services Group. *Care management and assessment: managers' guide.* London: HMSO.

Statham, R., Korczak, J., Monaghan, P. (1988). *House adaptations for people with physical disabilities: a guidance manual for practitioners.* London: HMSO.

Steele, J., Hinkley, P., Rowlands, I., Moore, N. (1993). *Informing people about social services.* London: Policy Studies Institute.

Steele, L. (1998). 'Paving the way for the next Act'. *Community Care:* 19–25 November 1998, pp.8–9.

Steering Committee of the Confidential Inquiry into Homicides and Suicides by Mentally Ill People. *Report of the confidential inquiries into homicides and suicides by mentally ill people.* London: Royal College of Psychiatrists.

Steyn, K. (1997). 'Consistency: a principle of public law?' *Judicial review:* March 1997; 2(1), pp.22–26.

Stone, D. (1984). *The disabled state.* Basingstoke: Macmillan.

Stuart, O. (1996). *Yes, we mean black disabled people too.* In: Ahmad, W., Atkin, K. (editors) (1996). *Race and community care.* Buckingham: Open University Press.

Therapy Weekly (1992). 'Patients charged illegally'. *Therapy Weekly,* March 12 1992; 18(34), p.1.

Thomas, M. (1994). *Charging older people for care: 1993/94 update.* Edinburgh: Age Concern Scotland.

Thompson, P., Lavery, M., Curtice, J. (1990). *Short changed by disability.* London: Disablement Income Group.

Tinker, A., McCreadie, C., Salvage, A. (1993). *Information needs of elderly people – an exploratory study.* London: Age Concern Institute of Gerontology.

Tomkin, Z. (1991). 'Footing the bill: the orthopaedic service at Guy's Hospital is trying to cut costs by offering patients stock shoes where possible, or inviting them to go private'. *Therapy Weekly* 1991; 18(9), p.4.

Topliss, E., Gould, B. (1981). *A charter for the disabled.* Oxford: Blackwell.

Tracy, M., Ruszala, S. (1997). *Introducing a safer handling policy.* In: National Back Pain Association. *Guide to the handling of patients.* 4th edition. London: NBPA.

Treasury Solicitor's Department (undated). *Judge over your shoulder: balancing the scales.* London: Cabinet Office.

Tunbridge, R. (Chair) (1972). *Rehabilitation: report of a sub-committee of the Standing Medical Advisory Committee.* London: HMSO.

Valios, N. (1998). 'Council launches court move to recover unpaid service charges'. *Community Care,* 2–8 July 1998, p.1.

Vellenoweth, C. (1996). 'Tectonic plates of community care'. *Community Care Management and Practice*, August 1996;4(4),113–117.

Wadham J., Mountfield H. (1999). *Blackstone's guide to the Human Rights Act 1998*. London: Blackstone Press.

Wagner, G. (Chair) (1988). *Residential care, a positive choice: report of the independent review of residential care*. London: HMSO.

Walker, A. (1994). *Half a century of promises: the failure to realise 'community care' for older people*. London: Counsel and Care.

Walker, A. (1996). *Young carers and their families: a survey carried out by the Social Survey Division of the Office of National Statistics on behalf of the Department of Health*. London: Stationery Office.

Warner, N. (1994). *Community care: just a fairy tale?* London: National Carers' Association.

Watson, L. (1997). *High hopes: making housing and community care work*. York: Joseph Rowntree Foundation.

Webster, C. (1996). *Health services since the war, volume II: government and health care, the National Health Service 1958–1979*. London: Stationery Office.

Whelan, J. (1998). *Equal access to cardiac rehabilitation: age discrimination in the NHS, cardiac rehabilitation services*. London: Age Concern England.

Wiggin, C., Carpenter, G. (1994). 'Going it alone: user control over resources'. *Community Care*: 8–14th September 1994.

Wilkinson, H.W. (1997). 'The home as a productive asset'. *New Law Journal*, 31 October 1997,pp.1583–1584.

Williams, T., Goriely, T. (1994). 'Big idea – any effect: the Charter complaints system as an alternative to statutory rights'. *New Law Journal 1994*; 144(6661), pp.1164–1165.

Wilson, A. (Chairman) (1994). *Being heard: the report of a review committee on NHS complaints procedures*. London: Department of Health.

Winchcombe, M. (1998). *Community equipment services: why should we care? A guide to good practice in disability equipment services*. London: Disabled Living Centres Council.

Wistow, G., Leedham, I., Hardy, B. (1993). *Community care plans: a preliminary analysis of a sample of English community care plans*. (Undertaken by the Nuffield Institute (Health Service Studies) for the Social Services Inspectorate). London: Department of Health.

Woodman R. (1999). 'Community care does not increase homicide risk in UK.' *British Medical Journal*, 9 January 1999; 318, p.77.

Worth, A. (1994). 'Quicker and sicker: how much so social workers really know about the discharge of elderly patients from hospital.' *Care Weekly*, 28 July 1994.

Wright, D. (1997). *Are older people being denied care?* London: Help the Aged.

Wright, F. (1998). *The effect on carers of a frail older person's admission to a care home*. (Findings 478, April 1998). York: Joseph Rowntree Foundation.

Wyatt, J. (1992). 'U-turn by health authority after three-year battle'. *Caring Times* 1992; 4(8),p.1.

Zarb, G., Hasler, F., Campbell, J., Arthur, S. (1997). *Implementation and management of direct payment schemes, first findings: summary (October 1997)*. London: Policy Studies Institute.

Zindani, J. (1998). *Manual handling law and litigation*. Birmingham: CLT Professional Publishing.

ACTS OF PARLIAMENT

Access to Personal Files Act 1987
Carers (Recognition and Services) Act 1995
Children and Young Persons Act 1963
Children Act 1989
Chronically Sick and Disabled Persons Act 1970
Chronically Sick and Disabled Persons (Northern Ireland) Act 1978
Commissioner for Complaints Act (Northern Ireland) 1968
Community Care (Direct Payments) Act 1996
Community Care (Residential Accommodation) Act 1992
Community Care (Residential Accommodation) Act 1998
Data Protection Act 1984
Data Protection Act 1998
Deregulation and Contracting Out Act 1994
Disability Discrimination Act 1995
Disabled Persons (Services, Consultation and Representation) Act 1986
Education Act 1944
Education Act 1981
Education Act 1993
Education Act 1996
Environmental Protection Act 1990
Health and Medicines Act 1988
Health and Social Services and Social Security Adjudications Act 1983
Health Services and Public Health Act 1968

Health Service Commissioners Act 1993
Housing Act 1974
Housing Act 1985
Housing Grants, Construction and Regeneration Act 1996
Human Rights Act 1998
Insolvency Act 1986
Local Authority Social Services Act 1970
Local Government Act 1972
Local Government Act 1974
Local Government and Housing Act 1989
Leasehold Renewal and Urban Development Act 1993
Mental Health Act 1983
Mental Health (Patients in the Community) Act 1995
National Assistance Act 1948
National Health Service Act 1977
National Health Service and Community Care Act 1990
Public Health Act 1936
Registered Homes Act 1984

STATUTORY INSTRUMENTS

SI 1974/284. *NHS (Charges for Appliances) Regulations 1974.*

SI 1984/1345. *Residential Care Homes Regulations 1984.*

SI 1984/1578. *Nursing Home and Mental Nursing Homes Regulations 1984.*

SI 1987/1967. *Income Support (General) Regulations 1987.*

SI 1988/551. *National Health Service (Travelling Expenses and Remission of Charges) Regulations 1988.*

SI 1989/206. *Access to Personal Files (Social Services) Regulations 1989.*

SI 1989/306. *NHS (Charges to Overseas Visitors) Regulations 1989.*

SI 1989/394. *National Health Service (Dental Charges) Regulations 1989.*

SI 1989/396. *National Health Service (Optical Charges and Payments) Regulations 1989.*

SI 1989/419. *National Health Service (Charges for Drugs and Appliances) Regulations 1989.*

SI 1990/2244. *Local Authority Social Services (Complaints Procedure) Order 1990.*

SI 1991/554. *NHS Functions Regulations 1991.*

SI 1992/563. *National Assistance (Charges for Accommodation) Regulations.*

SI 1992/635. *National Health Service (General Medical Services) Regulations 1992.*

SI 1992/664. *NHS (Service Committees and Tribunal) Regulations 1992. London: HMSO, 1992.*

SI 1992/2793. *Manual Handling Operations Regulations 1992.*

SI 1992/2977. *National Assistance (Assessment of Resources) Regulations 1992* (includes SI 1993/964).

SI 1992/3182. *Residential Accommodation (Determination of District Health Authority) Regulations 1992.*

SI 1993/462. *National Assistance (Sums for Personal Requirements) Regulations 1991.*

SI 1992/3182. *Residential Accommodation (Determination of District Health Authority) Regulations 1992.*

SI 1993/477. *Residential Accommodation (Relevant Premises, Ordinary Residence and Exemptions) Regulations 1993.*

SI 1993/553. *Housing Renovation etc. Grants (Grant Limit) Order 1993. London: HMSO, 1993.*

SI 1993/2711. *Housing Renovation etc. Grants (Grant Limit) (Amendment) Order 1993.*

SI 1993/554. *Assistance for Minor Works to Dwellings (Amendment) Regulations 1993.*

SI 1993/567. *NHS (Fundholding Practices) Regulations 1993.*

SI 1993/582. *Residential Accommodation (Determination of District Health Authority) (Amendment) Regulations 1993.*

SI 1993/2711. *Housing Renovation etc. Grants (Grant Limit) (Amendment) Order 1993.*

SI 1994/42. *Housing (Welfare Services) Order 1994.*

SI 1994/648. *Housing Renovation etc. Grants (Reduction of Grant) Regulations 1994.*

SI 1994/690. *National Health Service (Charges for Drugs and Appliances) Amendment Regulations 1994.*

SI 1994/826. *National Assistance (Sums for Personal Requirements) Regulations 1994.*

SI 1996/30. *Social Security (Persons from Abroad) Miscellaneous (Amendment) Regulations 1996.*

SI 1996/708. *National Health Service (Functions of Health Authorities and Administration Arrangements) Regulations 1996.*

SI 1996/1455. *Disability Discrimination (Meaning of Disability) Regulations 1996.*

SI 1996/2614. *Income Support (General) Amendment (no.3) Regulations 1996.*

SI 1996/2887. *Home Repair Assistance Regulations 1996.*

SI 1996/2888. *Disabled Facilities Grants and Home Repair Assistance (Maximum Amounts) Order 1996.*

SI 1996/2889. *Housing Renewal Grants (Services and Charges) Order 1996.*

SI 1996/2890. *Housing Renewal Grants Regulations 1996.*

SI 1996/2891. *Housing Renewal Grants (Prescribed Forms and Particulars) Regulations.*

SI 1997/734. *Community Care (Direct Payments) Regulations 1997.*

SI 1997/2744. *Value Added Tax (Drugs, Medicines and Aids for the Handicapped) Order 1997.*

SSI 1998/498. *National Assistance (Sums for Personal Requirements) Regulations 1998.*

SI 1998/1730. *National Assistance (Assessment of Resources) (Amendment no.2) Regulations 1998.*

SI 1998/2998. *Home Repair Assistance (Extension) Regulations 1998.*

DIRECTIONS AND APPROVALS

Community Care Plans Directions 1991 (with LAC(91)6; made under s.46(2) of the NHS and Community Care Act 1990).

Community Care Plans (Consultation) Directions 1993 (with LAC(93)4); made under s.7A of the Local Authority Social Services Act 1970, and s.46(2) of the NHS and Community Care Act 1990).

Community Care Plans (Independent Sector Non-Residential Care) Direction 1994 (with LAC(94)12); made under s.7A of the Local Authority Social Services Act 1970).

Complaints Procedure Directions 1990 (in DH 1990, appendix C; made under s.7B of the Local Authority Social Services Act 1970).

Directions by the Secretary of State as to the Conditions Governing Payments by Health Authorities to Local Authorities and Other Bodies under Section 28A of the National Health Service Act 1977 (with LAC(92)17; made under s.28 of the NHS Act 1977).

Directions by the Secretary of State as to the Establishment of Primary Care Groups by Health Authorities.

Inspection Units Directions 1994 (with LAC(94)16; made under s.7A of the Local Authority Social Services Act 1970).

National Assistance Act 1948 (Choice of Accommodation) Directions 1992 (with LAC(92)27; made under s.7A of the Local Authority Social Services Act 1970).

Payments to Voluntary Organisations (Alcohol or Drugs Misusers) Directions 1990 (in DH 1990, appendix C and in LAC(98)17; made under s.7E of the Local Authority Social Services Act 1970).

Payments to Voluntary Organisations (Alcohol or Drugs) Misusers Directions 1990 (as amended)

Secretary of State's Approvals and Directions under s.21(1.) of the National Assistance Act 1948 (with LAC(93)10; made under s.21 of the Act).

Secretary of State's Approvals and Directions under s.29(1) of the National Assistance Act 1948 (with LAC(93)10; made under s.29 of the Act).

Secretary of State's Approvals and Directions under paragraphs 1 and 2 of Schedule 8 to the National Health Service Act 1977 (with LAC(93)10; made under schedule 8 of the Act).

CIRCULARS

(N.B. There is sometimes confusion about the currency of Circulars. Even when a Circular has formally been cancelled, it may remain a useful indication of government policy if neither the Circular nor the message it contains have been superseded. Where such cancellation is known to the author, the Circular is marked with an asterisk. However, there are some Circulars probably obsolete but which have never been formally cancelled.

The abbreviations used for different series of Circulars are as follows: CI (Chief Inspector), CNO (Chief Nursing Officer), DHSS (Department of Health and Social Security), DoE (Department of Environment), DETR (Department of Environment, Transport and the Regions), EL (Executive Letter), HC (Health Circular), HN (Health Notice), HSS (Health and Social Services) HRC (Health Reorganisation Circular), HSC (Health Service Circular), HSG (Health Service Guidelines), LAC (Local Authority Circular), LASSL (Local Authority Social Services Letter), SW (Social Work).

*CI(92)34. Social Services Inspectorate. *Implementing caring for people: assessment.* London: Department of Health, 1992 (cancelled 31st March 1994).

CI(95)12. Social Services Inspectorate. *Young carers.* London: Department of Health.

CI(96)23. Social Services Inspectorate. *Ensuring quality services: standards developed by the Social Services Inspectorate for use in the inspection of local authority social services.* London: Department of Health.

CI(98)20. Social Services Inspectorate. *Good practice in disability equipment services.* London: Department of Health.

CI(991)1. Social Services Inspectorate. *Recording with care: inspection of case recording in social services departments.* London: Department of Health.

CNO(SNC)(77)1. Department of Health and Social Security. *Standards of nursing care: promotion of continence and management of incontinence.* London: DHSS.

DHSS (12/70), DES 13/70, MHLG 65/70, ROADS 20/70. Department of Health and Social Security; Department of Education and Science; Ministry of Housing and Local Government; Ministry of Transport. *The Chronically Sick and Disabled Persons Act 1970.* London: DHSS.

DHSS (19/71). Department of Health and Social Security. *Welfare of the elderly: implementation of s.45 of the Health and Public Health Act 1968.* London: DHSS.

*DHSS (45/71). Department of Health and Social Security. *Services for handicapped people living in the community: the Chronically Sick and Disabled Persons Act 1970.* London: DHSS.

*DHSS (53/71). Department of Health and Social Security. *Help in the home: section 13 of the Health Services and Public Health Act 1968*. London: DHSS.

DoE 10/90; LAC(90)7. Department of Environment; Department of Health. *House adaptations for people with disabilities*. London: HMSO. (Obsolete and superseded by DoE 17/96 in relation to the Department of Environment, Transport and the Regions – but still regarded as extant by the Department of Health: see p.??? of this book).

DoE 10/92; LAC(92)12. Department of Environment; Department of Health. *Housing and community care*. London: HMSO.

DoE 17/96 Department of Environment. *Private sector renewal: a strategic approach*. London: HMSO.

DoE 4/97. Department of Environment. *Housing Grants, Construction and Regeneration Act 1996: Part 1, changes to the renovation grant test of resources*. London: Stationery Office.

DoE 4/98. Department of Environment. *Housing Grants, Construction and Regeneration Act 1996: Part 1, changes to the renovation grant system*. London: Stationery Office.

EL(91)28. NHS Management Executive. *Continence services and the supply of incontinence aids*. London: Department of Health.

EL(91)129. NHS Management Executive. *Charging NHS patients*. London: Department of Health.

EL(92)20. NHS Management Executive. *Provision of equipment by the NHS*. London: Department of Health.

EL(93)14. NHS Management Executive. *Hospice funding*. Leeds: Department of Health.

EL(93)18; CI(93)12. NHS Management Executive; Social Services Inspectorate. *Implementing caring for people*. London: Department of Health.

EL(93)22. NHS Management Executive. *Implementation of caring for people: communications*. Leeds: Department of Health.

EL(94)3. NHS Management Executive. *Pressure sores: a key quality indicator*. Leeds: Department of Health.

EL(94)8. NHS Management Executive. *Hospital admission and discharge procedures*. London: Department of Health.

EL(94)14. NHS Management Executive. *Contracting for specialist palliative care services*. Leeds: Department of Health.

EL(95)97. NHS Executive. *New drugs for multiple sclerosis*. Leeds: Department of Health.

EL(96)8, CI(96)5. NHS Executive, Social Services Inspectorate, Department of Health. *NHS responsibilities for meeting continuing health care needs: current progress and future priorities*. London: Department of Health.

EL(96)85. NHS Executive. *A policy framework for commissioning cancer services: palliative care services*. Leeds: Department of Health.

EL(96)89, CI(96)35. NHS Executive, Social Services Inspectorate. *Progress in practice: initial evaluation of the impact of the continuing care guidance*. London: Department of Health.

EL(96)109. NHS Executive. *Funding for priority services 1996/97 and 1997/98*. London: Department of Health.

EL(97)1. NHS Executive. *Patient's Charter and mental health services: implementation guidance*. Leeds: Department of Health.

EL(97)39. NHS Executive. *NHS priorities and planning guidance 1998/99*. Leeds: Department of Health.

EL(97)62, CI(97)24. Department of Health. *Better services for vulnerable people*. London: DH.

EL(97)65. NHS Executive. *Health action zones: invitation to bid*. Leeds: Department of Health.

HC(77)9. Department of Health and Social Security. *Organisation and management of NHS chiropody services*. London: DHSS.

HC(78)16. Department of Health and Social Security. *NHS chiropody services*. London: DHSS.

HC(81)1. Department of Health and Social Security. *Contractual arrangements with independent hospitals and nursing homes and other forms of co-operation between the NHS and the independent medical sector*. London: DHSS.

HC(84)21. Department of Health and Social Security. *Registration and inspection of private nursing homes and mental nursing homes (including private hospitals)*. London: DHSS.

*HC(89)5. Department of Health. *Discharge of patients from hospital*. London: DH.

HC(90)23, LASSL(90)11. Department of Health. *Care programme approach for people with a mental illness referred to the specialist psychiatric services*. London: DH.

HN(89)7, HN(FP)(89)9. Department of Health. *Health care in local authority residential care homes for elderly people*. London: DH.

HN(84)12. Department of Health and Social Security. *Communication aids centres (CACs): procedures for out of district referrals*. London: DHSS.

HN(88)26, HN(FP)(88)(25), LASSL(88)8. *Health service development: the development of services with people with physical or sensory disabilities*. London: DH.

HN(90)5, HN(FP)(90)1, LASSL(90)1. Department of Health. *Certification of blind and partially sighted people: revised form BD8 and procedures*. London: DH.

HRC(74)16. Department of Health and Social Security. *Statutory provisions: charges under section 2(2) of the National Health Service Reorganisation Act 1973*. London: DHSS.

HRC(74)33. Department of Health and Social Security. *Chiropody*. London: DHSS.

HSC 1998/004. Department of Health. *NHS wheelchair voucher scheme: funding in 1997–98 and 1998–99*. London: DH.

HSC 1998/048. NHS Executive. *Transfer of frail older NHS patients to other long stay settings*. London: Department of Health.

HSC 1998/115. Department of Health. *Palliative care*. London: DH.

HSC 1998/167. LAC(98)23. Department of Health. *Health improvement programmes*. Leeds: DH.

HSC 1998/200. Department of Health. *Good practice in disability equipment services*. London: DH.

HSC 1998/220. Department of Health. *Standards of NHS hospital care for older people*. London: DH.

HSC 1998/228. LAC(98)32. Department of Health. *Primary care groups: delivering the agenda*. Leeds: DH.

HSC 1998/230. LAC(98)31. Department of Health. Governing arrangements for primary care groups. Leeds: DH.

HSC 1999/019. NHS Executive. GP fundholding transitional issues. Leeds: DH.

HSC(98)159. LAC(98)22. Modernising health and social services: national priorities guidance 1999/00 – 2001/02. London: DH (enclosed guidance booklet of the same title).

HSG(92)10. Department of Health. Charges for drugs, appliances, oxygen concentrators and wigs and fabric supports. London: DH.

HSG(92)36. NHS Management Executive. Patient's Charter: monitoring and publishing information on performance. London: Department of Health.

HSG(92)42. NHS Management Executive. Health services for people with learning disabilities (mental handicap). London: Department of Health.

HSG(92)43. NHS Management Executive. Health authority payments in respect of social services functions. London: Department of Health.

HSG(92)50. NHS Management Executive. Local authority contracts for residential and nursing home care: NHS related aspects. London: Department of Health.

HSG(93)30. NHS Management Executive. Provision of haemophilia treatment and care. London: DH.

HSG(93)45. NHS Management Executive. Code of practice: section 118 of the Mental Health Act 1983. London: Department of Health.

HSG(93)48. NHS Management Executive. Home dialysis patients: costs of metered water used for home dialysis. London: DH.

HSG(94)5. NHS Management Executive. Introduction of supervision registers for mentally ill people from 1 April 1994. London: Department of Health.

HSG(94)27. NHS Management Executive. Guidance on the discharge of mentally disordered people and their continuing care in the community. London: Department of Health.

HSG(95)8. Department of Health. NHS responsibilities for meeting continuing health care needs. London: DH.

HSG(95)39. Department of Health. Discharge from NHS inpatient care of people with continuing health or social care needs: arrangements for reviewing decisions on eligibility for NHS continuing inpatient care. London: DH.

HSG(95)45. NHS Executive. Arrangements between health authorities and NHS Trusts and private and voluntary sector organisations for the provision of community care services. London: Department of Health.

HSG(96)34. Department of Health. Powered indoor/outdoor wheelchairs for severely disabled people. London: DH.

HSG(96)53. Wheelchair voucher scheme. London: DH.

HSG(97)14. NHS Executive. Purchasing effective treatment and care for drug misusers. London: Department of Health.

HSG(97)22. NHS Executive. GP fundholding: revised list of goods and services. Leeds: Department of Health.

HSS(OS5A)4/76. Department of Health and Social Services. British Wireless for the Blind Fund: batteries supplied by health and social services boards. Belfast: DHSS.

HSS(PH)5/79. Department of Health and Social Services. Help with television. Belfast: DHSS, 1979.

HSS(OS5 A)5/78. Department of Health and Social Services. Telephones for the handicapped and elderly. Belfast: DHSS, 1978.

LAC(86)6. Department of Health and Social Security. Registration of residential homes. London: DHSS.

LAC(87)6. Department of Health and Social Security. Disabled Persons (Services, Consultation and Representation) Act 1986: implementation of sections 4, 8(1), 9 and 10. London: DHSS.

LAC(88)2. Department of Health and Social Security. Disabled Persons (Services, Consultation and Representation) Act 1986: implementation of s.5 and s.6. London: DHSS.

LAC(88)17. Department of Health. Personal social services: confidentiality of personal information. London: DH.

LAC(89)2; HN(89)3; HN(FP)(89)3. Department of Health. I. Access to Personal Files Act 1987: Access to Personal Files (Social Services) Regulations; II. Local Authority Social Services Designation of Functions Order 1989. London: DH.

LAC(89)7. Department of Health. Discharge of patients from hospital. London: DH.

LAC(90)12. Department of Health. Community care: policy guidance. London: DH.

LAC(91)6. Department of Health. Secretary of State's Direction – s.46 of the NHS and Community Care Act 1990: community care plans. London: DH.

LAC(92)10. Department of Health. Registered Homes Act 1984: I. Small residential care homes. II. Inspection. London: DH.

LAC(92)15. Department of Health. Social care for adults with learning disabilities (mental handicap). London: DH, 1992.

LAC(92)17. Department of Health. Health authority payments in respect of social services functions. London: DH.

LAC(92)24. Department of Health. Local authority contracts for residential and nursing home care: NHS related aspects. London: DH.

LAC(92)27. Department of Health. National Assistance Act 1948 (Choice of Accommodation) Directions 1992. London: DH.

LAC(93)2. Department of Health. Alcohol and drug services within community care. London: DH.

LAC(93)4. Department of Health. Community care consultation directions. London: DH.

LAC(93)6. Department of Health. Local authorities' powers to make arrangements for people who are in independent sector residential care and nursing homes on 31 March 1993. London: DH.

LAC(93)7. Department of Health. Ordinary residence. London: DH.

LAC(93)8. Department of Health. National Assistance (Sums for Personal Requirements) Regulations 1993. London: DH.

LAC(93)10. Department of Health. Approvals and directions for arrangements from 1 April 1993 made under schedule 8 to the National Health Service Act 1977 and sections 21 and 29 of the National Assistance Act 1948. London: DH.

LAC(93)12. Department of Health. *Further and Higher Education Act 1992: implications for sections 5 and 6 of the Disabled Persons (Services, Consultation and Representation) Act 1986.* London: DH.

LAC(93)18. Department of Health. *National Assistance Act 1948 (Choice of Accommodation) (Amendment) Directions 1993: amendment to the statutory direction on 'choice'.* London: DH.

LAC(93)19. Department of Health. *Code of practice: section 118 of the Mental Health Act 1983.* London: DH.

LAC(94)1. Department of Health. *Charges for residential accommodation: CRAG amendment no. 2. Charges for non-residential adult services under section 17 of the Health and Social Services and Social Security Adjudication Act 1983.* London: DH.

LAC(94)12. Department of Health. *Community care plans (independent sector non-residential care) direction 1994.* London: DH.

LAC(94)16. Department of Health. *Inspecting social services.* London: DH.

*LAC(94)24. Department of Health. *Framework for local community care charters in England.* London: DH (cancelled 1st April 1997).

LAC(95)19. Department of Health. *Community care plans from 1996/97.* London: DH.

LAC (97)9. Department of Health. *Purchasing effective treatment and care for drug misusers.* London: DH.

LAC(98)3. Department of Health. *Persons from abroad children's grant (PFACG): special grant report no.28.* London: DH.

LAC(98)5. Department of Health. *Adult asylum seekers' accommodation special grant (ASAG) report no. 30.* London: DH.

LAC(98)6. Department of Health. *Specific grant for making payments to voluntary organisations providing services for drug and alcohol misusers: 1998/999.* London: DH.

LAC(98)7. Department of Health. *Specific grant for the development of social care services for people with a mental illness 1998/99.* London: DH.

LAC(98)8. Department of Health. I. *Charges for residential accommodation: CRAG amendment no. 9. II. National Assistance (Sums for Personal Requirements) and (Assessment of Resources) Regulations 1998.* London: DH.

LAC(98)9. Department of Health. *Support grant for social services for people with AIDS and related expenditure: financial year 1998/99.* London: DH.

LAC(98)10. Department of Health. *Supplementary credit approval for the development of social care services for people with a mental illness 1998/99.* London: DH.

LAC(98)16. Department of Health. *Specific grant for the development of social care services for people with a mental illness 1998/99: the Partnership Fund.* London: DH.

LAC(98)17. Department of Health. *Specific grant for making payments to voluntary organisations providing services for drug and alcohol misusers 1998/99: development programme for drug and alcohol misusers with mental illness (dual diagnosis/complex needs).* London: DH.

LAC(98)19. Department of Health. *Community Care (Residential Accommodation) Act 1998.* London: DH.

LAC(98)21. Department of Health. *Developing primary care groups.* London: DH.

LAC(98)21. *The new NHS, modern and dependable: developing primary care groups.* London: DH.

LASSL(96)10. Department of Health. *List of current circulars.* London: DH.

LASSL(97)13. Department of Health. *Responsibilities of local authority social services departments: implications of recent legal judgments.* London: DH.

LASSL(97)15. Department of Health. *List of current Local Authority Circulars (LACs) and Local Authority Social Services Letters (LASSLs).* London: DH.

LASSL(97)27. Department of Health. *Local authority occupational therapy services.* London: DH.

LASSL(98)2. Department of Health. *Joint finance and mental health.* London: DH.

LASSL(98)14. Department of Health. *List of current Local Authority Circulars (LACs) and Local Authority Social Services Letters (LASSLs).* London: DH.

LASSL(98)16. Department of Health. *Data Protection Act 1998.* London: DH.

LAC(99)3. Department of Health. *Specific grant for making payments to voluntary organisations providing services for drug and alcohol misusers: 1999/2000.* London: DH.

LAC(99)4. Department of Health. *Additional specific and special grants for the provision of services drug misusers: 1999/2000.* London: DH.

PL/CNO(89)3. Department of Health and Social Security. *Social Services Inspectorate report: 'Health care in local authority residential homes for elderly people'.* London: DHSS.

SW7/1972. Social Work Services Group. *Telephones for severely disabled persons living alone.* Edinburgh: Scottish Office.

SWSG 6/94. Social Work Services Group. *Choice of accommodation: cross border placements.* Edinburgh: Scottish Office.

INVESTIGATIONS OF THE HEALTH SERVICE OMBUDSMAN (AND PARLIAMENTARY OMBUDSMAN)

Avon Health Authority and Bristol Healthcare NHS Trust 1996 (E.615/94–95). *Discharge arrangements: advice to family about cost, responsibility for funding.* In: Health Service Commissioner (1996). *Investigations of complaints about long term NHS care.* Fifth report for session 1995–96. HC 504. London: HMSO.

Bromley Health Authority and Ravensbourne NHS Trust 1994. (W.256/92–93 and W.579/92–93). *Discharge to a nursing home where fees were payable.* In: Health Service Commissioner (1994). Third report 1993–94. HC 498. London: HMSO, 1994.

Buckinghamshire Health Authority 1996 (E.118/94–95). *Discharge arrangements: advice to family about cost, responsibility for funding.* In: Health Service Commissioner (1996). *Investigations of complaints about long term NHS care.* Fifth report for session 1995–96. HC 504. London: HMSO.

East Kent Health Authority 1996 (E.685/94–95). *Discharge arrangements: undue pressure to accept financial responsibility for private nursing care.* In: Health Service Commissioner (1996). *Investigations of complaints about long term NHS care.* Fifth report for session 1995–96. HC 504. London: HMSO.

East Norfolk Health Authority 1996 (E.213/94–95). *Failure to advise patient or relatives of financial consequences of transfer.* In: Health Service Commissioner (1996). *Third report for session 1995–96: selected investigations completed October 1995 to March 1996.* HC 464. London: Stationery Office.

East Norfolk Health Authority 1997 (E.1190/94–95). *Policy for funding incontinence supplies to residential care homes and complaint handling.* In: Health Service Commissioner (1997). *Second report session 1997–98: investigations completed October 1996 to March 1997.* HC40. London: Stationery Office.

Gwent Health Authority 1998 (W.61/96–97). *Health authority's handling of a request for payment of nursing home fees.* In: Health Service Commissioner (1998). *Fourth report session 1997–98: investigations completed October 1997 to March 1998.* HC 812. London: HMSO.

James Paget Hospital NHS Trust 1998 (E.1430/96–97). *Inadequate hospital care, discharge to care home and handling of complaint.* In: Health Service Commissioner (1998). *Fourth report session 1997–98: investigations completed October 1997 to March 1998.* HC 812. London: Stationery Office.

Leeds Health Authority 1994 (E.62/93–94). *Failure to provide long term NHS care for a brain damaged patient.* In: Health Service Commissioner (1994). *Second report for session 1993–94.* HC 197. London: Stationery Office.

North and Mid-Hampshire HA 1996 (E.639/94–95). *Inadequate discharge arrangements: consultant's consent to the discharge, response to the complaint.* In: Health Service Commissioner (1996). *Third report for session 1995–96: selected investigations completed October 1995 to March 1996.* HC 464. London: Stationery Office.

North Cheshire Health Authority 1996 (E.672/94–95). *Discharge arrangements: advice to family about cost, responsibility for funding.* In: Health Service Commissioner (1996). *Investigations of complaints about long term NHS care.* Fifth report for session 1995–96. HC 504. London: HMSO.

North Worcestershire Health Authority and Kidderminster Health Care NHS Trust 1996 (E.985/94–95). *Adequacy of communication with relatives: responsibility for cost of long term care and specialist feeding equipment.* In: Health Service Commissioner (1996). *Second report for session 1996–97: selected investigations completed April to September 1996.* HC 87. London: Stationery Office.

North Worcestershire Health Authority 1995 (E.264/94–95). *Discharge to private nursing home care.* In: Health Service Commissioner (1995). *First report for session 1995–96: selected investigations completed April to September 1995.* HC 11. London: Stationery Office.

Oxfordshire Health Authority 1996 (E.787/94/95). *Delay in deciding on provision of long-term health care.* In: Health Service Commissioner (1996). *Investigations of complaints about long term NHS care.* Fifth report for session 1995–96. HC 504. London: HMSO.

PCA (C.12/K). *Departmental advice to local authorities about the Chronically Sick and Disabled Persons Act 1970.* In: Parliamentary Commissioner for Administration (1976). Sixth report for session 1975–1976. London: HMSO.

PCA (5/325/77). *Provision of batteries for a hearing aid.* In: Parliamentary Commissioner for Administration (1978). *Third report for session 1977–1978.* London: HMSO.

PCA (5/915/78). *Failure to provide a suitable hearing aid.* Parliamentary Commissioner for Administration (1979). *Fourth report for session 1978–1979.* HC 302. London: HMSO.

PCA (C.799/81). *Assistance under Chronically Sick and Disabled Persons Act 1970.* In: Parliamentary Commissioner for Administration (1982). *Fifth report for session 1981–1982.* London: HMSO.

PCA (C656/87). *Delay in investigating a local authority's duty to provide a 'Vistel' telephone aid.* In: Parliamentary Commissioner for Administration (1988). 6th report 1987–1988. HC 672. London: HMSO.

Plymouth Hospitals NHS Trust 1997 (E.906/95–96). Summarised in: Health Service Commissioner (1997). *Annual report for 1996–97.* HC 41. London: Stationery Office.

Redbridge Health Care NHS Trust 1997 (E.58/94–95). Summarised in: Health Service Commissioner (1997). *Annual report for 1996–97.* HC41. London: Stationery Office.

Royal Cornwall Hospitals NHS Trust (W.524/92–93). *Unexpected costs after transfer to a nursing home.* In: Health Service Commissioner (1994). *Third report 1993–94.* HC 498. London: HMSO.

South Devon Healthcare NHS Trust and South and West Devon Health Authority 1997 (E.935/95–96). In: Health Service Commissioner (1997). *Annual report for 1996–97.* HC41. London: Stationery Office.

SW.28/84–85. *Care of an elderly patient.* In: Health Service Commissioner (1985). *1st report 1985–1986.* HC 27. London: HMSO.

SW.81/92–93. *Rights under the Patient's Charter.* In: Health Service Commissioner (1993). *First report 1993–1994.* HC 30. London: HMSO.

SW.82/86–87). *Unsatisfactory discharge arrangements.* In: Health Services Commissioner (1988). *4th report 1987–1988.* HC 511. London: HMSO.

W.24 and 56/84–85. *Failure in care and communication about discharged patient.* In: Health Service Commissioner (1985). *2nd report 1984–1985.* HC 418. London: HMSO.

W.40/84–85. *Proposals to discharge younger chronic sick patient.* In: Health Service Commissioner (1985). *2nd report 1984–1985.* HC 418. London: HMSO.

W.68/77–78. *Use of 'means test' by NHS.* In: Health service commissioner (1978). *2nd report 1977–1978.* HC 343. London: HMSO.

W.111/75–76. *NHS patient in private nursing home: refusal to refund charges.* In: Health Service Commissioner (1977). *3rd report for session 1976–1977.* HC 321. London: HMSO.

W.113/84–85. *Failures in care and communication.* In: Health Service Commissioner (1985). *2nd report 1984–1985.* HC 418. London: HMSO.

W.194/78–79. *Refusal of NHS treatment after private consultation.* In: Health Service Commissioner (1980). *1st report 1980–1981.* London: HMSO.

W.194/89–90. *Inability to provide NHS care for man in need of a hospital bed.* In: Health Services Commissioner (1991). *2nd report 1990–1991.* HC 482. London: HMSO.

W.224/78–79. *Waiting time for orthopaedic treatment.* In: Health Service Commissioner (1979). *1st report 1978–1979.* London: HMSO.

W.226/91–92. *Refusal to provide prescribed orthoses free of charge.* Health Service Commissioner (1992). *First report 1991–1992.* HC 32. London: HMSO.

W.254/88–89. *Discharge of patient and attitude to bereaved relatives.* In: Health Services Commissioner (1990). *1st report 1989–1990.* HC 199. London: HMSO.

W.263/83–84. *Reimbursement of cost of privately purchased medical equipment.* In: Health Service Commissioner (1985). *1st report 1984–1985.* HC 33. London: HMSO.

W.286/86–87. *Discharge arrangements made for domiciliary care.* In: Health Services Commissioner (1988). *4th report 1987–1988.* HC 511. London: HMSO.

W.340/80–81). *Care and treatment provided for a paralysed patient at home.* In: Health Service Commissioner (1982). *2nd report 1981–1982.* HC 372. London: HMSO.

W.360/77–78. Failure to provide a community nursing service. In: Health Service Commissioner (1979). *1st report 1979–1980.* London: HMSO, 1979.

W.371/83–84). *Delay in providing hearing aid.* In: Health Service Commissioner (1984). *4th report 1983–1984.* HC 476. London: HMSO.

W.420/83–84. *Discharge arrangements for an elderly, immobile patient.* In: Health Service Commissioner (1984). London: HMSO.

W.421/88–89. *Discharge of an elderly patient.* In: Health Services Commissioner (1990). *1st report 1989–1990.* HC 199. London: HMSO.

W.478/89–90. *Provision of long-term care.* In: Health Services Commissioner (1991). *2nd report 1990–1991.* HC 482. London: HMSO.

W.533/87–88). Referred to in: Health Service Commissioner (1990). *Annual report for 1989–1990.* HC 538. London: HMSO.

W.547/92–93. *Care of a patient at risk of developing pressure sores.* In: Health Services Commissioner (1993). *First report 1993–1994.* HC 30. London: HMSO.

W.599/89–90). *Provision within the NHS of long-term care.* In: Health Services Commissioner (1991). *2nd report 1990–1991.* HC 482. London: HMSO.

W.707/85–86. *Provision by hospital eye service (HES) of NHS contact lenses.* In: Health Service Commissioner (1988). *3rd report 1987–1988.* HC 232. London: HMSO.

W.783/85–86. *Failures in speech therapy service.* In: Health Services Commissioner (1988). *3rd report 1987–1988.* HC 232. London: HMSO.

WW.3/79–80). *Refusal to provide crutches.* In: Health Service Commissioner (1981). *1st report 1981–1982.* HC 9. London: HMSO.

Index